A HISTORY OF GREEK ART

A HISTORY OF GREEK ART

2

MARTIN ROBERTSON

The right of the University of Cambridge to print and sell all manner of books was granted by Henry VIII in 1534. The University has printed and published continuously since 1584.

CAMBRIDGE UNIVERSITY PRESS

Cambridge

New York Port Chester

Melbourne Sydney

Published by the Syndics of the Cambridge University Press
The Pitt Building, Trumpington Street, Cambridge CB2 1RP
40 West 20th Street, New York, NY 10011-4211, USA
10 Stamford Road, Oakleigh, Melbourne 3166, Australia

Library of Congress Catalogue Card Number: 73–79317

ISBN 0 521 20277 9

First published 1975
Reprinted 1991

Printed in Great Britain by
Antony Rowe Ltd, Chippenham, Wiltshire

CONTENTS

VOLUME TWO

NOTES

PROLOGUE: ART IN GREECE BEFORE THE IRON AGE

1. *Hesp.* 25 (1956) 175–7 and frontispiece (J. L. Caskey and M. Eliot).
2. *BMCat.Sc.* I i 3ff., A5–A34, figs. 3–12, pls. 1 and 2 (A34, fig. 12, a fragmentary group of two figures); Boardman *PC* fig. 2; Bossert *AAC* 404–24 (411, a figure of normal type with another smaller on its head; also Vermeule pl. 7D; Zervos *Cycl.* fig. 319); Demargne *OGA* figs. 64–78; Vermeule pl. 7; Zervos *Cycl.* figs. 244–55, 293–302, 316f., 319, 333f., *Grèce* figs. 7f., 21f. Examples from Crete: Demargne *OGA* fig. 61; Pendlebury pl. 12, 2; Zervos *Crète* figs. 106–17. A classification: C. Renfrew in *AJA* 73 (1969) 1–32, pls. 1–10.
3. Berlin: 8092 (said to be from the Troad) Neugebauer *MAGB* pl. 1. Others: Boardman *PC* fig. 5; Bossert *AAC* 310–22; Demargne *OGA* figs. 218, 220, 222–3; Lamb pls. 4–9; Matz *KMT* pl. 63; Neugebauer *ABS* pls. 7–11; Pendlebury pl. 39, 2; *PM* III 459–62; Zervos *Crète* figs. 452–8.
4. Early stone and bone: Bossert *AAC* 282; Pendlebury pl. 12, 1; Zervos *Crète* figs. 92–7, 104f., 188–91. Terracotta: Bossert *AAC* 285–8, 291–301; Matz *KMT* pl. 22; Pendlebury pl. 20, 1 and 2; Zervos *Crète* figs. 224–35, 246, 249, 253f. Faience: Bossert *AAC* 258–62, 289f.; Matz *KMT* pls. 60f.; Pendlebury pl. 28, 2; Zervos *Crète* figs. 410–17. Stucco; Bossert *AAC* 256f.; Pendlebury pl. 33, 1. Ivory; Bossert *AAC* 263–5, 302–5; Pendlebury pl. 39, 1. Steatite (on the designation see Boardman *IG* 15ff.): Bossert *AAC* 269–81, 308; Pendlebury pl. 37; an example here, pl. 1d (below, n. 10). A small stone figure from Phaistos in the style of the bronzes Zervos *Crète* fig. 459.
5. Stone vessels: Bossert *AAC* 370–4; Pendlebury pls. 11, 1–2 and 28; Zervos *Crète* figs. 139–77. A limestone vessel in the form of an animal's head: Bossert *AAC* 306; Zervos *Crète* fig. 520. Seals: Bossert *AAC* 388–401; Matz *KMT* pls. 20, 50–4; Zervos *Crète* figs. 207–20, 302–9, 628–85.
6. Bossert *AAC* 327–43; Demargne *OGA* 124 (fish) – 130; Matz *KMT* pls. 19, 68, 70; Pendlebury pls. 19, 22; M. Robertson 18 (fish); Zervos *Crète* figs. 323–78.
7. Boardman *PC* fig. 15; Bossert *AAC* 224–47; Demargne *OGA* figs. 190, 193, 198; Matz *KMT* pls. 34–7, 48f.; Pendlebury pls. 25 and 32, 2; *PM* I 524–41, II 431–67; Zervos *Crète* pl. iii.
8. Bossert *AAC* 130f.; Lamb pl. 6; Matz *KMT* pl. 51; *PM* III 207f. An accident seemingly shown on a steatite vase: Bossert *AAC* 271, 273; Demargne *OGA* figs. 230, 232; Pendlebury pl. 37, 1; *PM* III 224 fig. 157 (cf. figs. 158f.); see further, p. 7 with n. 19.
9. Miniature frescoes; Boardman *PC* fig. 10; Demargne *OGA* figs. 185–8; Matz *KMT* pls. 36f.; Pendlebury pl. 25, 3; *PM* III 81–106. Dancers on ring: Zervos *Crète* fig. 362. Mixed creatures and maskers: *KB* 94; *PM* IV 431–67; and see p. 10 with n. 28.
10. Herakleion, from Agia Triada: *Mon. Linc.* 13 (1903) 78–131, pls. 1–3 (Savignoni); Bossert *AAC* 276–81; Demargne *OGA* figs. 233–4; Zervos *Crète* figs. 552–5.
11. Faience plaques with houses: Pendlebury pl. 21, 1; *PM* I 301–14. Miniature fresco with crowd: Boardman *PC* fig. 10; Bossert *AAC* 261; Pendlebury pl. 25, 3; *PM* III 33; Zervos *Crète* fig. 301.
12. Boardman *PC* fig. 11; Bossert *AAC* 344; Pendlebury pls. 26, 1a and c, 27, 1 and 2; M. Robertson 22; Zervos *Crète* fig. 425.

13. Boardman *PC* fig. 12; Bossert *AAC* 255; Demargne *OGA* figs. 200, 202; Matz *KMT* pls. 71–3; Pendlebury pl. 34; M. Robertson 23; Zervos *Crète* figs. 426, 509ff., 556–77.
14. Bossert *AAC* 255; Demargne *OGA* figs. 250–1; Matz *KMT* pl. 49; M. Robertson 21. The succession of palaces at Phylakopi: Atkinson and others *Excavations at Phylakopi* (London 1904). See also p. 11.
15. Marinatos in *AAA* 1 (1968) 3–9, 13–16 figs. 3–13, 213–20 figs. 1–14; 2 (1969) 374f. and cover; 3 (1970) 1–5 figs. 1–7; 4 (1971) 407–12 figs. 1–3; Marinatos *Thera* 1; brief reports also in *AR 1967/8* 19, *1968/9* 28f., *1969/70* 25, *1970/1* 22f.; *BCH* 92 (1968) 961–6, 94 (1970) 1121–9.
16. A splendid account of mainland culture in the Bronze Age in Vermeule, with bibliography. Views on the political background are expressed in Evans (*PM*), Lorimer, Mylonas (*AM, GBM, MMA*), Pendlebury, Wace (*Mycenae*); see also H. Kantor in *AJA* 51 (1947) 1–103, 'The Aegean and the Orient in the Second Millennium B.C.'. Greek speech in the Bronze Age: Ventris and Chadwick; Palmer; see also p. 9 with n. 25.
17. Examples: Bossert *AAC* 120ff. (mainland finds), 355ff. (Cretan finds); *ILN* 27/4/57 (mainland); *KB* 85, 1–6 (mixed); Pendlebury pls. 33–5 and 40, 1–2 (Cretan); Vermeule pl. 18 (mainland). Technical distinctions: H. Catling in *Archaeometry* 4 (1961) 31; and, with E. Richards and A. Blin-Stoyle, in *BSA* 55 (1963) 94.
18. The material from the later but much longer known Grave Circle, that enclosed within the later walls of the citadel (Circle A), is well published by Karo; on that from Circle B, see now Addendum to Bibliography, p. 759 (Mylonas); some of it is illustrated and discussed by Mylonas (*AM, GBM, MMA*) and Vermeule. On *tholoi* see below, n. 32.
19. Vaphio cups (Athens, National Museum): Boardman *PC* fig. 16; Bossert *AAC* 70–5; Demargne *OGA* figs. 282–6; *KB* 88, 1–4; Matz *KMT* pls. 64f., Mylonas *MMA* fig. 120, Boxer vase from Knossos: above, n. 8.
20. Dagger-blades from Mycenae (Athens, National Museum): Boardman *PC* fig. 19; Bossert *AAC* 167–71 (cf. 165f. and 172); Demargne *OGA* figs. 263–6; *KB* 88, 7 and colour-plate opposite 84, 2 and 3; Lamb pls. 1 and 2; Matz *KMT* pl. 96; Vermeule pls. 12 and 13. From Myrsinochorion (Athens, National Museum): *ILN* 27/4/57; Vermeule pl. 13B. From Thera, with axes (Athens, National Museum): Vermeule pl. 13C. Engraved blade from Crete: Lamb pl. 7.
21. *BMCat.Sc.* 1 i 27ff. figs. 25f., A46 and 47; Bossert *AAC* 20f. They come from the Elgin collection which included other material from Mycenae but none from Crete.
22. Tombstones from Circle A: Karo pls. 5–10; Bossert *AAC* 66f.; Demargne *OGA* fig. 255; *KB* 86, 2; Lorimer pl. 24; Matz *KMT* pl. 95; Wace fig. 79; from Circle B: Mylonas *AM* fig. 45, *MMA* fig. 87; see Vermeule 90–4, figs. 17f. Gold masks: Karo pls. 47–52; Demargne *OGA* figs. 256–61; *KB* 86, 10; Matz *KMT* pls. 86–7; Mylonas *AM* fig. 50, *MMA* fig. 7d, 84, 97; Vermeule pl. 11A.
23. Mylonas *AM* fig. 8, *MMA* fig. 13, show the whole gate after restoration; Matz *KMT* pl. 79, Mylonas *MMA* fig. 11 and Wace *Mycenae* fig. 72 the gate in its setting.
24. *KB* 93, 1 (cf. 2–4, 8–10); Pendlebury 219 fig. 39e. Potnia Theron: p. 64 (Chapter 2 n. 66).
25. Decipherment: above, n. 16; the vast literature cannot and need not be cited here. It is not universally accepted; an attempt to discredit it: A. J. Beattie in *JHS* 76 (1956) 1–17. On the dating controversy see Boardman and Palmer (the extreme positions under one cover); again there is a huge literature. Sensible statement of the position and select bibliography in Vermeule. See also p. 14.
26. Knossos throne-room: *PM* IV 901ff.; Bossert *AAC* 225; Matz *KMT* pl. 31; Pendlebury 188f., pl. 30, 1. Pylos throne-room: Blegen in *AJA* 57 (1953) 27f.; 60 (1956) 95f.; and on the relation of the two in Grumach (ed.) *Minoica* 61–6. Frescoes: see following notes.
27. Knossos griffins: *PM* IV 910ff. with figs. and pl. Cup-bearer: *PM* II 704ff. with figs. and pl.; Bossert *AAC* 231; *KB* 91, 3; Matz *KMT* pl. 38; Pendlebury pl. 29, 2; Zervos *Crète* pl. iv.
28. Mainland frescoes: Bossert *AAC* 26–44; *KB* 94, 17; Lorimer pls. 12, 3; 27, 1 and 2; 28, 1 and 2; Matz *KMT* pls. 102–6; M. Robertson 31; Vermeule pls. 27–30. Full publication of the Pylos frescoes in Lang. Demons and maskers: above, p. 5 with n. 9. Seals: a corpus is

being compiled, edited by Matz; see also Kenna passim; Bossert *AAC* 388–401; *ILN* 27/4/57; *KB* 93; Vermeule pls. 19, 43.

29. H. Wace passim; Wace *Mycenae* 83ff. and pls. 101–3; Vermeule pl. 38 and p. 20, supposing it an heirloom.

30. *ML* 19 (1908) 6–86, pls. 1–3 (Paribeni); Bossert *AAC* 248–54; Demargne *OGA* figs. 191–7; *KB* 91, 12 and colour-plate; Matz *KMT* pls. 46f.; M. Robertson 26–9; Zervos *Crète* figs. 753ff.

31. Mycenae plaster head: Boardman *PC* cover; Bossert *AAC* 87; Demargne *OGA* fig. 343; Matz *KMT* pl. 107; Vermeule pl. 40C. Terracottas from Mycenae: *AR 1968/9* 11f. figs. 11–12; *1969/70* 12 figs. 18–19. Keos goddesses: Vermeule pl. 40A–B.

32. Mainland palace-architecture: Bossert *AAC* text-fig. 1 (contrast Cretan 9ff.); *KB* 73f. (contrast Cretan 75ff.); D. S. Robertson fig. 13 (contrast Cretan figs. 2, 3 and 5); Vermeule pls. 22–5 and chapter 6. Tholos-tombs: a full account in Wace with many pictures; Bossert *AAC* 14–19, 22–5; *KB* 81; D. S. Robertson 34 fig. 15 and pl. 1a.

33. See p. 6 with n. 14.

34. Mycenaean influence in East: see particularly Demargne *LCD* chap. 3 and *OGA* chap. 12; also Vermeule 271ff.; Bossert *AAC* 493–515. Contacts with Egypt: Pendlebury *Egyptiaca*; Vercoutter. Western contacts: Taylour.

35. Warrior vase; Bossert *AAC* 133ff.; Demargne *OGA* figs. 331, 336; Lorimer pl. 3, 1: Matz *KMT* pl. 109; Vermeule pl. 33D; Wace fig. 82; cf. a painted stone slab from Mycenae: Bossert *AAC* 45; Lorimer pl. 2, 1. Kraters from Cyprus: Bossert *AAC* 475–8, 483; Karageorghis *MAC* pls. 1–16; *KB* 96, 7–9 and 11; Vermeule pls. 32, 33A and p. 206 fig. 36. Other figured vases: *BMCat.Vas.* I ii 64–88 (C333–47) with figs.; Bossert *AAC* figs. 132, 136, 458, 502; Demargne *OGA* figs. 345, 347–9, 355; *KB* 96, 2; Lorimer pls. 12, 1 and 2; 16, 3 and 4.

36. Late Cretan pottery: e.g. Zervos *Crète* figs. 725–42. Cretan *larnakes* (clay chests): Bossert *AAC* 361ff.; Pendlebury pl. 43, 3 and 4; M. Robertson 32; Zervos *Crète* figs. 776–82. Mainland examples: Vermeule pls. 34–5 and p. 213 fig. 37.

37. On the dark age see particularly Desborough *GDA* and *LMS* and Snodgrass *DAG*; also remarks and a bibliography in Vermeule.

CHAPTER I: THE SEEDS OF GREEK ART: THE GEOMETRIC AND ORIENTALISING PERIODS

(*i*) *Submycenaean, Protogeometric, Geometric*

1. Submycenaean: the material from the Kerameikos (the principal cemetery of Athens) is collected in *Ker.* I pls. 5–27 (pl. 14 top shows the transition to Protogeometric). Other examples: *BMCat.Vas.* I i nos. A1091–1102, pl. 16 and figs. 292–6; Bossert *AAC* 210 no. 364; Matz *KMT* pl. 112, bottom 1.

2. E.g. Lacy 222ff. fig. 93.

3. Protogeometric: Desborough *PP* passim; good examples of early style, pl. 2, of late pls. 6 and 12–13. Cook *GPP* 5–13, pls. 1 and 2b. See also Snodgrass *DAG* chap. 2, esp. 43ff. with figs.

4. 'Light on dark' Cretan: above, p. 4 with Prologue n. 6. Neolithic from Thessaly *BMCat. Vas.* I i nos. A107 (pl. 3), 132–7 (fig. 36), 212, 2 and 3 (fig. 44). Early and Middle Helladic pottery produced on the mainland over the third and second millennia B.C. is often decorated with geometrical motives, painted or incised, e.g.: Neolithic–EH, Bossert *AAC* 59f. nos. 98–100; MH ibid. 64 nos. 117–19; Matz *KMT* pl. 110, top 1; Mylonas fig. 59; Wace figs. 80, 105.

5. Cyprus: Bossert *AS* figs. 238–49; Syria: ibid. figs. 1158, 1161–6; Phrygia: Bossert *AA* figs. 1059–78.

6. The Attic material is presented in *Ker.* I and IV, as well as in Desborough *PP*. Pictures in BDFH pls. 57–60 (41–4); Demargne *OGA* figs. 369–73.

7. On this development see Snodgrass *DAG*, esp. chap. 2 'The Regional Pottery Styles'. Crete: p. 29 with n. 36.

8. Horses on Attic Protogeometric: *Ker.* IV pl. 27; also pl. 6; I pls. 56, 58; Desborough *PP* pls. 5 and 6; BDFH pls. 60 (44) and 63 (47). Cf. goats on a Cretan Protogeometric vase: Desborough *PP* pl. 33; Brock pl. 4, 45;

Demargne *OGA* fig. 386; but see p. 29. Attic stag-vase: *Ker* IV pl. 26; BDFH pl. 59 (43) below. Lefkandi Centaur: Desborough, Nicholls and Popham in *BSA* 65 (1970) 21–30, pls. 7–11. Centaurs: pp. 20 with n. 17, 55 with Chapter 2 n. 48, 280 with Chapter 4 n. 222.

9. Kraiker in *Schweitzer Festschrift* pl. 2.
10. Kurtz and Boardman 57f.
11. Attic Geometric: Coldstream 8–90, pls. 1–15, with earlier literature; Cook *GPP* 17–22, pls. 3–6; *Ker.* V I passim; other pictures: BDFH pls. 61–9 (45–53); *CVA* Louvre 11 (Villard); Demargne *OGA* figs. 374–7; and often.
12. Rings for wheel-naves: Müller-Karpe in *JdI* 77 (1962) 66; see Snodgrass *DAG* 263 and 432; models, ibid.; also *AJA* 61 (1957) pl. 84, 9; *BCH* 90 (1966) 743 fig. 5.
13. See Benson *HBM*; and cf. p. 147 with Chapter 3 n. 154. Protocorinthian stirrup-vase: B.M. 1970. 9-10. 2 (unpublished).
14. Richter *AGSA* 9; and see p. 108 with Chapter 3 n. 79.
15. Hesiod *Works and Days* 654–9. On tripod-cauldrons see Willemsen *OF* III; also Benton in *BSA* 35 (1938) 56–68, 74–130; and next note.
16. Reliefs: Willemsen *OF* III pls. 46 and 63 (also, later, 92; see p. 108 n. 42); pictures also: BDFH 69 (53) r. and 123 fig. 97 (75, fig. 123); Kunze *NMO* figs. 3–5; Schefold *ML* pl. 4b. Attached figures: Willemsen *OF* III pls. 85–90; *BSA* 35 (1938) pls. 11–24; Kunze *NMO* figs. 6–7, 11–13; *Ol.Ber.* IV pl. 37, VII pl. 59.
17. BDFH pls. 68 (52) and 70 (54) r., 71 (55), l.; Beazley and Ashmole figs. 4–5; Demargne *OGA* figs. 400–6; Homann-Wedeking 24 figs. 10f.; Kunze *NMO* figs. 3–13; Lamb pls. 13–17; Neugebauer *ABS* figs. 12–16; *Ol.* IV pls. 10–16; *Ol.Ber.* IV pls. 32–6, VII pl. 58; Richter *H* figs. 250–1; Schefold *ML* pl. 4b. 'Zeus'-figures from Olympia (all latest Geometric or after): *Ol.Ber.* IV pls. 38–46, and see Kunze ibid. 123ff.; Kunze *NMO* figs. 12–17; see p. 48 with Chapter 2 n. 36.
18. A good collection of battle scenes on fragmentary grave-vases: *CVA* France 18 (Louvre 11) pls. 1–7; Schefold *ML* pl. 3.
19. Late Geometric figure-scenes: Attic: Hampe *FgS* pls. 22f., *Gl.* pls. 8–11; *Hesp.* 5 (1936) 26f. figs. 23f.; Pfuhl figs. 14f.; Schefold *ML* pl. 5; Argive: Courbin, *CGA* esp. pls. 7f., 11f., 28–37, 40–9, 100–3, 145–7; Corinthian: Johansen *VS* pl. 1, 3; Payne *PV* pls. 2 and 3; Western Greek: *RM* 60/1 (1953/4) pls. 14–17 and pp. 37–55 figs. 1–3 (Buchner).

(*ii*) *Orientalising*

20. On colonisation see Boardman GO, Dunbabin *WG*, Woodhead *GW*.
21. Oriental objects found in Greece: a general survey of material available at the beginning of the century; Poulsen *OFK*; shorter recent surveys: Amandry 'Objets orientaux en Grèce et en Italie aux viiie et viie siècles avant J-C' in *Syria* 35 (1958) 73–109; Barnett 'Oriental influences on archaic Greece' in *Goldman Studies* (1956): a useful selection in Demargne *OGA* figs. 418f., 422–4, 479, 495. Ivories (general): Barnett 'Early Greek and oriental ivories' in *JHS* 68 (1948) 1–25 (from Samos, Perachora, Athens, Crete; see also, for the background, his *Catalogue of the Nimrud ivories in the British Museum*, 1957); from Samos: *NDA* figs. 12f.; from Perachora: *Perachora* II pl. 193A. Bronzes: from Samos: Jantzen *AOB*; *NDA* 207f., figs. 9f.; from Olympia: Herrmann *OF* VI; *Ol.Ber.* II 115ff. fig. 72 and list (Kunze), V 81f. n. 11 (list, Herrmann), 83 figs. 37f.; from Crete: *Mus.It.* II pl. 6, 1 and 2; Demargne *LCD* 227 figs. 34f. Carved and engraved tridacna-shells: from Rhodes, Kos, Aegina and Perachora (Amandry 1.c.96–100 and pl. 8; *Perachora* II 527 and pl. 194, K1).
22. Urartu: below p. 31 with n. 40. Phrygia: see especially the preliminary reports of the American excavations at Gordion, in *AJA* from 1955.
23. See Jeffery 1–42.
24. Al Mina: Woolley in *AJ* 17 (1937) 1ff., *JHS* 58 (1938) 1–30, 133–70, and *AFK* 172–88; M. Robertson in *JHS* 60 (1940) 2–21; Boardman in *BSA* 52 (1957) 5–8, *Historia* 7 (1958) 250, *Anatolian Studies* 9 (1949) 163–9, *GO* 61–79; du Plat Taylor in *Iraq* 21 (1959) 62–92. Euboean pottery: Boardman in *BSA* 52 (1957) 1–29, pls. 1–7; Coldstream 164–95, pl. 41.
25. Preliminary reports by G. Buchner on his excavations in Ischia, in *Atti Magna Grecia* from

1954; also in *Atti VI Cong. Inst. Scienze Preist. Protost. 1962* 3 (1966) 7–11; *Expedition* VIII 4 (Summer 1966) 12; *AR 1955* 59f., *1957* 40f., *1966/7* 30f.

26. Greek contacts with the East: above, n. 21; also Akurgal, Boardman *GO*, Demargne *LCD* and *OGA*, Dunbabin *GEN*, Jeffery; Maxwell-Hyslop in *Iraq* 18 (1956) 155f.

27. Geometric and orientalising vase-painting in Corinth: Coldstream 91–111, pls. 16–21; Johansen *VS*; Payne *NC* and *PV*; also Benson *GKV*; Cook *GPP* 23ff., 43–52; Kraiker *Aig.* 35–77, pls. 6–40; *Perachora* (I) 53–66, 98–100, pls. 11–15, 23–33, II 4–132, pls. 1–57; Weinberg *Cor.* VII i and in *AJA* 45 (1941) 30ff.; other articles: Benton in *BSA* 48 (1953) 253ff.; Dunbabin and Robertson ibid. 172ff.; Robertson in *BSA* 43 (1948) 9ff. esp. 53–9; pictures in BDFH pl. 73 (57).

28. Attic orientalising: J. M. Cook in *BSA* 35 (1934/5, printed 1938); *CVA* Berlin 1 (Germany 2, 1938; Eilmann and Gebauer), Mainz 1 (Germany 15, 1959; Hampe and Simon); Hampe *FAG*; *Kerameikos* VII; Kraiker *Aig.* 84–92, pls. 41–7; Kübler *AAM*; Mylonas *PAE*; also Cook *GPP* 62–8; Beazley *Dev.* Chapter 1; pictures in Arias and Hirmer, pl. 10 and 11; BDFH pls. IV–V, 74–5 (58–9) and pp. 150ff., figs. 109–11 (86ff., figs. 135–7); Demargne *OGA* figs. 425–6, 430–3, 436. See further below, pp. 54f.

29. See Hampe *FGS* and Schefold *ML*.

30. East Greek vase-painting, Geometric and orientalising: Coldstream 262–301, pls. 58–64; Cook *GPP* 29–32, 116–30, 337f., 345f., and in *BSA* 34 (1936) 2 n. 1 and *Gnomon* 37 (1965) 506f.; also Blinkenberg *L*, Kardara *RA*, Kinch *V*, Price *EGP*, M. Robertson in *JHS* 60 (1940) 8ff., Rumpf in *JdI* 48 (1933) 55–83, Schiering *WOK*; pictures and grave-groups in *Cl.Rh.* passim; pictures also in Arias–Hirmer pls. 26f., 29; BDFH pl. 77 (61); Demargne *OGA* figs. 437, 445–7. On Chiot see p. 55 with Chapter 2 n. 50.

31. Cycladic vase-painting, Geometric and orientalising; Coldstream 164–95, pls. 32, 34–40; Cook *GPP* 28f., 104–16, 337, 344f.; also Boardman in *BSA* 47 (1952) 1–48, Bocci *RCC*, Buschor in *AM* 54 (1929) 142–63, Dragendorff *TG*, Dugas *CC* and *Delos* 10 and 15 passim, Karusos in *JdI* 52 (1937) 166–97; Kontoleon in *AM* 73 (1958) 117–39; Payne in *JHS* 46 (1926) 203–12; Pfuhl in *AM* 28 (1903) 1–290; pictures in Arias and Hirmer pls. 22–5 and V; BDFH pl. 76 (60); Demargne *OGA* figs. 382, 438, 440; Schefold *ML* pls. 9–10, 24b. See also p. 55 with Chapter 2 n. 50. Thasian: *BCH* 82 (1958) 810ff. fig. 11, 83 (1959) 776f. fig. 3; Bellerophon, ibid. 84 pls. 4–6.

32. Relief-pithoi: Schäfer passim. More recent refs.: Cretan: Boardman *CCO* 146f.; Laconian: Christou in *Delt.* 19 (1964) 164–265, pls. 78–103; Cycladic: Ervin in *Delt.* 18 (1963) i 37–75, pls. 17–30 (publication of the Iliupersis vase with important general discussion); pictures in BDFH pls. 82f. (66f.); Schefold *ML* 11b, 12f., 15b, 25, 30f., 34f., 36b.

33. Laconian vase-painting, Geometric and orientalising: *AO* 52–72 (Droop and Dawkins; on the dating see Boardman in *BSA* 58 (1963) 1–7); Lane in *BSA* 34 (1936) 99–121; Coldstream 212–19, pl. 46; Cook *GPP* 26f., 91ff., 337, 343. Boeotian vase-painting, Geometric and orientalising: Ure *BPGA*; Coldstream 196–211, pls. 42–5; Cook *GPP* 27f., 100, 337, 343; Desborough *PP* 195–8; Demargne *OGA* figs. 385, 366; Hampe *FGS* 20–31.

34. Argive vase-painting, Geometric and orientalising: Courbin *CGA* and in *BCH* 77 (1953) 258–67; 79 (1955) 1–32; Coldstream 112–47, pls. 22–31; Cook *GPP* 22, 91, 336, 343; J. M. Cook in *BSA* 48 (1953) 34–50; Shefton in *Perachora* II 368–71. See also p. 51 with Chapter 2 n. 41.

35. Ithacan vase-painting, Geometric and orientalising: M. Robertson in *BSA* 43 (1948) 60–95, 103–13; Benton in *BSA* 48 (1953) 265–337; Coldstream 220–32 (West Greek); Cook *GPP* 26, 61, 336, 340. Geometric and orientalising imitations of Greek vase-painting in Italy and Sicily: Cook *GPP* 62, 146–52, 338f.; Åkerstrom *GSI*; Buchner in *RM* 60/1 (1953/4) 37–55; Dohan *ITG*; Dunbabin *WG* 487–96; Payne *NC* 205–9, *PV* 21 (on pl. 4, 1); Schweitzer in *RM* 62 (1955) 78–106; Vallet and Villard *MH* 139–99, pls. 122–218, and in *Mél.d'arch.et d'hist.* 1956, 7–11.

36. Cretan vase-painting, Geometric and orientalising: Coldstream 233–61, pls. 51–7; Cook *GPP* 32ff., 142–6, 338, 347; Boardman *CCO* 130f.,

144ff.; Brock; Demargne *OGA* figs. 386, 441–4; Hartley in *BSA* 31 (1933) 56–114; Levi in *Ann.* 10/12 (1931) and *Hesp.* 14 (1945) 1–32; Payne in *BSA* 29 (1931) 224–98.

37. Kunze *KBR*: Benton in *BSA* 39 (1942) 52–64; Boardman *CCO* 79–84, 138f.; Demargne *OGA* figs. 460, 462, 465f., 469.

38. Boardman in *BSA* 62 (1967) 57–75, pls. 7–17. Bronzes: p. 39 with Chapter 2 n. 16. Stone reliefs: p. 57 with Chapter 2 n. 52.

39. Cut-out plaques: Boardman *CCO* 46–8, pl. 16; Demargne *OGA* fig. 461; Lamb 59f., pl. 19. Armour: *BCH* 7 (1883) pls. 1–3 (good photographs of a corselet); Boardman *CCO* 141–4; Demargne *OGA* fig. 460; *Ol.* IV pls. 58–9; Pfuhl fig. 135; Schefold *ML* pls. 11, 15a, 26. Mitrai from Olympia: Bartels in *Ol.Ber.* 8 (1967) 196–207, pls. 100–5, fig. 74. Very important recent finds: Mitten and Doering *MBCW*; Hoffmann and Raubitschek *ECA*; also the exhibition catalogue *DKK*.

40. Urartu: Piotrovskii (cauldrons and attachments), 36–43 with figs. 26–7, 29; 83 fig. 59; 87 fig. 62; pls. 13f. Oriental cauldrons from Olympia: Herrmann *OF* VI passim.

41. Oriental griffins and their relation to Greek: Barnett in *JHS* 68 (1948) 9f. with 11 fig. 9 (stone relief from Ankara), pl. 11d (stone head from Nimrud). Lefkandi griffins: *AR 1964/5*, 19, fig. 22; Boardman *PC* 47 fig. 24. Olympia mother-griffin: Kunze *NMO* 23f.; *Ol.Ber.* 1 (in *JdI* 52, 1937) pls. 34f.

42. Representations of griffin-cauldrons: Herrmann *OF* VI figs. 1–4; see also M. Robertson in *BSA* 43 (1948) 47ff. and *Perachora* II 536. The finest picture is the bronze-relief, which comes (rather touchingly) from the leg of a very late tripod-cauldron: Kunze *NMO* fig. 26; Willemsen *OF* III 157f. and pl. 92.

43. On technique see especially Jantzen GG with full discussion and references; also Herrmann *OF* 6, but most of the bowls, stands and attachments he publishes are oriental imports (above, n. 40), the Greek examples being reserved for another volume. The big head, a masterpiece: Kunze *NMO* figs. 34f.; *Ol.Ber.* 2 (in *JdI* 53, 1938) pls. 43–5; BDFH pl. 79 (63); Boardman *PC* fig. 62; Lullies and Hirmer pl. 4 (another pl. 5).

44. *Perachora* (I) pls. 39f., and a discussion by Payne pp. 130ff.

45. Small clay standed bowl from Athens with griffin-heads: *Ker.* VI 2 pl. 43; others which go with it (pls. 44f.) have cock's heads or flower-forms. Clay bowl from Afrati (Arkhades, in Crete): *Ann.* 10–12 (1931) 323ff. figs. 420a–d; Demargne *OGA* fig. 442; *Goldman Studies* pl. 20, fig. 2. Cycladic clay griffin-head not from bowl but a jug spout: B.M. *JHS* 46 (1926) pl. 8, 68 (1948) pl. 11e; Demargne *OGA* fig. 440. Gold griffin-heads from Rhodes: CMV fig. 26; from Melos: Boardman *PC* fig. 60; Higgins *GRJ* 107 fig. 17. Higgins has a good account of the revival of goldwork in Greece at this period under eastern influence.

46. Ivories from Athens: p. 44 with Chapter 2 n. 30; from Ephesus: p. 72 with Chapter 3 n. 5. Gem-engraving: pp. 147f. with Chapter 3 notes 154–7.

47. Greek and oriental ivories: refs. above, n. 21, especially Barnett in *JHS*. Ivory and bone from Sparta: *AO* 203–48, pls. 91–178 (Dawkins); Marangou *LEB*; from the Argive Heraion: *AH* II 351–3, pls. 138–40; Perachora: *Perachora* II 403–51, pls. 171–90 (J. Stubbings); Ithaca: M. Robertson in *BSA* 43 (1948) 115ff., pls. 47f. Ivory seals: Boardman *IG* 145–55, pls. 18–20; Richter *EGGE* 43f. nos. 70–80.

48. Imports: above, n. 21. The lion-tamer from Delphi: *BCH* 63 (1939) pl. 37; Demargne *OGA* fig. 521; *JHS* 68 (1948) 25 fig. 22 and pl. 12c and d: Richter *AGA* fig. 166. Kneeling youth from Samos: Buschor *ASS* 4 figs. 23–8 48; *AM* 74 (1959) 42–56, Beil. 87–97, figs. 1–8 (Ohly, with the reconstruction as a lyre); BDFH pl. 88 (72) and p. 157 fig. 113 (91 fig. 139); Boardman *PC* fig. 61; Demargne *OGA* fig. 61. Belted kouroi: pp. 40–3 with Chapter 2 notes 21–7).

49. Imported head: Perachora II pl. 173a–e; *JHS* 68 (1948) pl. 3c. Sphinx: *Perachora* II pl. 171; *JHS* l.c. pl. 5b; Demargne *OGA* fig. 468.

CHAPTER 2: THE BEGINNING OF MONUMENTAL GREEK ART: THE EARLY ARCHAIC PERIOD

(i) *The 'daedalic' style and the beginning of monumental sculpture*

1. 'Daedalic': see especially Jenkins. The dating is over-precise and the 'Dorian' character over-emphasised, but it is an essential work. A different approach (a valuable corrective) is found in Homann-Wedeking. On Daedalus see p. 59 with n. 55. Cycladic marble lamps: Beazley in *JHS* 60 (1940) 22–49, figs. 1–30 and pls. 5–7.
2. On terracotta production see especially Higgins *GT* 1ff.
3. All these are discussed in this and the following sections.
4. Possible surviving cult-statues: pp. 47–8 with n. 36, 100 with Chapter 3 n. 61, 202 with Chapter 4, n. 85, 355 with Chapter 5 n. 156, 410 with Chapter 6 n. 132.
5. Richter *Korai* 23f., 26 no. 1, with refs., figs. 25–8; *AGA* fig. 42; *H* 53, fig. 54; *Sc.* fig. 263; BDFH pl. 84 (68) left; Bruneau and Ducat pl. 1a–c; Lawrence *S* pl. 1a. Inscription: Homann-Wedeking 50 fig. 19; Jeffery 291, 303 no. 2, pl. 55.
6. Early sculptors' families: see pp. 59 with n. 55, 68f. with n. 74. For a quite different account of the origin of the Daedalic style, see R. M. Cook, below, n. 9.
7. Terracotta: Higgins *GT* pl. 10D–F. Bone: *AO* pl. 119. Bronze: Jenkins pl. 3, 1; BDFH pl. 80 (64) left. Gold: Higgins *GRJ* pls. 18–20; BDFH 156 fig. 112 (90 fig. 138); Boardman *PC* fig. 59; CMV figs. 27–8. Wood: BDFH pl. 85 (69) left; cf. pp. 38–9 with n. 15, and 71 with Chapter 3 n. 4.
8. Perirrhanteria collected with refs. in Richter *Korai* 27–30, nos. 5–11, figs. 35 and 37–56; a later example 52f. no. 74, fig. 235. Bronze gorgon: Louvre Br. 2570; de Ridder *Cat.* 98 pl. 92; *Enc.Phot.* 75c. See also p. 272 with Chapter 4 n. 203.
9. R. M. Cook in *JHS* 87 (1967) 24–32 'Origins of Greek Sculpture'; cf. n. 6, above.
10. Colour: Richter *Sc.* 148–58 (archaic, 149–51); the fullest and best treatment in Reuterswård (archaic, 35–47). See also pp. 85 and 100f. (archaic, Chapter 3 notes 31, 62 and 63), 393 (classical, Chapter 6 n. 89), 482 (Chapter 7 n. 91), and 569 (Chapter 8 n. 172).
11. Geneleos group: pp. 73–4 with Chapter 3 n. 8. Athena-figures on Acropolis: pp. 106–7 with Chapter 3 n. 74.
12. See Payne in Payne and Young 9f., n. 3; Richter *Kouroi* 1f., *Korai* 3f.
13. Richter *Korai* 32f. no. 18, with refs., figs. 76–9; *H* 53 fig. 55; *Sc.* fig. 262; *Mon.Piot* 20 (1913) pls. 1f.; BDFH pl. 84 (68) right; Beazley and Ashmole fig. 23; Demargne *OGA* figs. 463f.; *KB* 197, 7; Lawrence *S* pl. 2b; Lullies and Hirmer pl. 6; head only: Jenkins pls. 5, 2; 10, 1.
14. Pp. 57–8 with n. 53.
15. Wooden statuette from Samos: above, n. 7. Figure from Eleutherna, in Herakleion: Homann-Wedeking 109 fig. 56; Jenkins pls. 7, 1; 8, 1; 9, 1; 10, 2; Richter *AGA* fig. 60. Figure from Tegea (Hagigeorghitika), Athens, N.M. 57: *BCH* 14 (1890) 382–4 with pl.; Jenkins pl. 9, 2; *KB* 197, 3; Karouzou *Cat.* pl. 1; *RA* 11 (1908) 165 fig. 7. Figure from Tanagra (Skimatari) in Thebes: *AJA* 28 (1924) 267ff. figs. 3–5; Karouzos *M.Th.* 11 figs. 1–2, *RA* 11 (1908) 190ff. figs. 1f.; see Jenkins 71ff.
16. Dreros triad: *AA* 1936, 217ff. figs. 2f.; *BCH* 60 (1936) pl. 63; Demargne *OGA* figs. 552–5. The god alone: BDFH pl. 80 (64) right; Homann-Wedeking 102 fig. 52; Richter *AGA* fig. 55; *H* 175 fig. 253; *Kouroi* 26 figs. 12–13; *Sc.* fig. 14. Goddesses alone: Richter *Korai* 32 nos. 16–17, figs. 70–5. On the dating see Boardman in *BSA* 62 (1967) 61.
17. Dreros temple: Marinatos in *BCH* 60 (1936) 219–56, pls. 26, 31. Early temples: Dinsmoor 38–58; D. S. Robertson 53ff.; Lawrence *A* 88ff.; *Perachora* (I) 27–42 (Payne) and 42–50 (H. Bagenal). See further pp. 57f., 60f. with notes 53, 60.
18. Apollo of Amyclae: Pausanias III 19 1f. (O. 360). The word σφυρήλατος was applied by the Greeks themselves to images, apparently of this kind.
19. Olympia goddess: *AR* *1964/5* 14 fig. 15, *1965/6* 10 fig. 12. There are fragments of figures

in the same technique from other Cretan sites: Benton in *BSA* 40 (1939/40) 55 no. 33 (pl. 28, from Palaikastro), 57, nos. 31 (pl. 31)–33, from Praisos.

20. Karlsruhe head: *DKK* pl. 21, B10; Demargne *OGA* figs. 450–1; Jenkins pl. 4, 6. Olympia griffin-head: p. 32 with Chapter 1 n. 43.
21. Rolley *FdeD* v no. 172, pls. 28f.; BDFH pl. 85 (69) right; Beazley and Ashmole fig. 24; Jenkins pl. 6, 2 and 2a (Cretan); Homann-Wedeking 69 fig. 23 (stressing the connection with the Cycladic marbles).
22. 'Backboard': p. 60 with n. 58. Off-frontal setting: Jeffery in *BSA* 57 (1962) 153.
23. On the kouros-type in general see Richter *Kouroi* 1–6 (Egyptian influence, 2); Egyptian influence denied by R. M. Cook (above, n. 9); more moderate doubts in Homann-Wedeking 130ff.
24. Technique: see Adam, who largely supersedes earlier work on the subject (Blümel *GSW*, Casson *Technique*). Naxos colossus: Blümel *GSW* 14 fig. 23, 16 fig. 24; other unfinished works illustrated there and in Casson and Adam.
25. Delos A4085; Richter *Kouroi* 27, figs. 20f., its very early character noted. Delphi bronze: above, n. 21.
26. Delos A334; Richter *Kouroi* 27, figs. 22–4; Bruneau and Ducat pl. 2b; Homann-Wedeking 66, fig. 21.
27. Delos A333; Richter *Kouroi* 53 no. 17, figs. 87–90; Bruneau and Ducat pl. 3b; Homann-Wedeking 68 fig. 22 (he stresses the connection with the Delphi bronze).
28. Euthykartides's (or, as originally read, Iphikartides's) base, Delos A728; Richter *Kouroi* 53 no. 16 (not illustrated); Homann-Wedeking 54 fig. 20; Jeffery 291, 304 no. 3, pl. 55 (inscription). Bruneau and Ducat 40, discuss and reject a proposed association of the base with another fragment with buttocks and thighs (the front destroyed), A4052, pl. 3a, not in Richter *Kouroi*.

(*ii*) *The Attic tradition and the second generation of sculptors*

29. Examples: Demargne *OGA* figs. 428f., 492; Homann-Wedeking 77 figs. 33ff.; *Ker.* VI 2 pls. 32–40; Richter *Korai* pl. vi a–c and figs. 31–4, 36; Schefold *GP* pls. 8–10 (cf. the bronze, pl. 7; refs. on p. 68). See further below, p. 45.
30. Contents of grave: *BCH* 19 (1895) 273ff. (pottery figs. 1–7, lions figs. 13–16; Perrot). Good photographs of the ivories and related material, with important discussion: Kunze in *AM* 55 (1930) 141–62 with pls. 5–8, Beil. 38–47. The finest illustrated: BDFH pl. 70 (54) left; Beazley and Ashmole fig. 6; Richter *Korai* figs. 16–19; two others, figs. 20f.; the possible import, fig. 22; bronze from Acropolis, fig. 23. Imported ivory from the Acropolis: *JHS* 68 (1948) 5, fig. 3 (Barnett, with refs. and parallels, figs. 2 and 4).
31. Above, n. 29.
32. Kouros of Tenea: p. 113, with Chapter 3 n. 90; Phrasikleia: pp. 89, 100, with Chapter 3 notes 40, 62. Attic kouroi of Sunium Group: Richter *Kouroi* 30, 41–7 nos. 1–9, figs. 25–71 (face of principal figure from Sunium before restoration, figs. 36ff.); CMV figs. 18–22. Other pictures: Dipylon head (Athens N.M. 3372): BDFH pl. 96 (80) left; Karouzou *Cat.* pl. 3; Richter *AGA* fig. 12, *H* 50 fig. 50; and often; a hand found nearby (*Kouroi* figs. 65ff.) no doubt belongs; fragments of a body found in the Agora associated with it: Harrison in *Hesp.* 24 (1955) 290–34, pls. 81–4, with an illuminating reconsideration of the whole group; the association questioned by Richter: *Kouroi* 47 no. 7, figs. 54–9, 68. Principal Sunium figure (Athens N.M. 2720): BDFH pl. 96 (80) right; Beazley and Ashmole fig. 33; Homann-Wedeking 79 fig. 37; Karouzou *Cat.* pl. 4; Richter *H* 49 fig. 49; and often. Sunium torso (Athens N.M. 3645): Homann-Wedeking 80f. figs. 38f. New York statue (32.11.1): Richter in *MMS* v i (1934) 20ff. (detailed publication with full illustration and discussion), and *MM Cat.Sc.* 1f., no. 1, pls. 1–3; pictures also; BDFH pl. 95 (79); Beazley and Ashmole fig. 34; Homann-Wedeking 78 fig. 36; Lullies and Hirmer pls. 11ff.; Richter *AGA* figs. 10f., *H* 51 fig. 51. There is also another hand (*Kouroi* 47 no. 8, figs. 63f.); and an under life-size torso with faceless head, from the Kerameikos, so a grave-statue (*Kouroi* 47 no. 9, figs. 69ff.).

Down-dating of the group, and of archaic Attic sculpture in general: Harrison *Agora* II, 3–18.

33. The story in Herodotus I 31. The statues: Richter *Kouroi* 49f. nos. 12A and B, figs. 78–83; *AGA* fig. 32; *H* 52 figs. 52f.; BDFH pl. 99 (83); Beazley and Ashmole figs. 25f.; CMV fig. 23; *KB* 198, 1–2; Lullies and Hirmer² pls. 14f.; and often.

34. Colossus: Richter *Kouroi* 51f. no. 15, figs. 87–90; BDFH pl. 94 (78); Homann-Wedeking 76 figs. 30–2. Cult-statue: pp. 88–9 with n. 54; 182 with Chapter 4 n. 44; 294 with Chapter 5 n. 6.

35. Thasos ram-bearer: Richter *Kouroi* 51, no. 14, figs. 84ff., 106; Blümel *GSW* 16f. figs. 6–8; Homann-Wedeking 74, fig. 28. Other animal-bearers: pp. 94f. with Chapter 3 notes 51f.

36. The head (p. 35 with n. 3): *Ol.* III, 1–4, fig. 1 and pl. 1. Base and other fragment: ibid. figs. 2–4. Cult-statues in temple of Hera: Pausanias V 17 1 (cf. p. 21 with Chapter 1 n. 17). Other pictures of the head: BDFH pl. 98 (82); Beazley and Ashmole fig. 26; CMV fig. 25; *KB* 198, 3; Lullies and Hirmer pl. 10; Richter *AGA* fig. 85; *H* 54 fig. 56. Down-dating: see above, n. 32.

37. *Ol.* III 5–26, figs. 1–23 (architectural limestone); 26–9, figs. 24–9 and pl. 5, 3–5 (perirrhanteria); 29–34, figs. 30–3 and pl. 6 (late archaic marble warriors; cf. p. 184 with Chapter 4 n. 47); 34, fig. 34 (feet and hand, from small kouroi?).

38. Cf. p. 87 with Chapter 3 n. 37.

39. Acropolis gorgons: Dickins *CAM* I 269f. no. 701; Payne and Young 10f., pls. 1 and 13, 2–6; Schrader 319–24, nos. 441–7, figs. 368–74 and pl. 184. The head illustrated: Langlotz and Schuchardt pl. 1; Richter *AGA* fig. 13; *Sc.* fig. 180. Origin of the gorgoneion: most recently Boardman *AGG* 37f.; also Kunze *AS* (*OF* II) 65–72; Mylonas *PAE*; Payne *NC* 79–89.

(iii) The beginning of free painting

40. Texts on the beginning of Greek painting: Pliny XXXV 15–17 (O. 375f.; cf. 377–84).

41. Tiryns shields: Lorimer pls. 9f.; smaller and front of larger: *BSA* 42 (1947) pl. 18A; front of larger: BDFH 130 fig. 105 (82 fig. 131); Rumpf *MZ* pl. 5, 7; Schefold *ML* pl. 7b. Argive Polyphemus: Courbin in *BCH* 79 (1955) 1–49, figs. 1–4 and 12 bis, pl. 1; also pictured: *AM* 62 (1955) pl. 41, 1; M. Robertson 44; Schefold *ML* 45 fig. 15. Aristonothos krater: Schweitzer in *AM* 62 (1955) 78–106, pls. 34–5; 36, 3; 40, 1; also pictured: Buschor *GV* 47 fig. 43; Pfuhl *MuZ* figs. 64f.; Rumpf *MZ* 26, pl. 6, 1. Eleusis amphora: Mylonas *PAE* passim; other pictures: *AM* 62 (1955) pl. 41, 2; BDFH pl. 75 (59) and col. pl. V; Demargne *OGA* figs. 432f.; Richter *H* 286 figs. 404f.; M. Robertson 42 and 45; Schefold *ML* pl. 16 and col. pl. 1.

42. Praisos plate: Beazley and Ashmole fig. 13; Buschor *GV* 49, fig. 57; Pfuhl *MuZ* fig. 57; Rumpf *MZ* pl. 8, 8; Schefold *ML* 40, figs. 11–12; see Boardman *CCO* 146. Prinias frieze: p. 58 with n. 53. Delos fragment: p. 43 with n. 27.

43. Discussions of Protocorinthian polychrome style: Johansen *VS* 138–56 (Boston Bellerophon, pl. 30, 2; Berlin Centauromachy pl. 30, 1; and see following note); Payne *NC* 94–7, *PV* 13ff. (Bellerophon, pl. 20, 2–4; Centauromachy pl. 21; and see following notes); Matz *Gesch.* I 211–14, 232–6. Centauromachy also illustrated: BDFH pl. 73 (57) bottom; Beazley and Ashmole fig. 18; Schefold *ML* pl. 24a. Corinth alabastron: *JHS* 71 (1951) pl. 29a; see Dunbabin ibid. 65f.; Payne *NC* 94f., 269.

44. Macmillan battle-aryballos: Johansen *VS* pl. 31 (fullest illustration); Buschor *GV* fig. 35; Cook *GPP* pl. 9c; Demargne *OGA* fig. 439; Lane *GP* pl. 23D; Payne *NC* pl. 1, 7; *PV* pl. 22, 1, 2 and 5; Richter *H* 290 fig. 409. Berlin battle-aryballos: Johansen *VS* pl. 32 (fullest illustration); Payne *PV* pl. 23, 1 and 2; Pfuhl *MuZ* fig. 58. Chigi jug: *AD* II pls. 44f.; *CVA* Villa Giulia fasc. 1, pls. 1–4; *NC* figs. 17, 19b; Johansen *VS* pls. 39f.; Payne *PV* pls. 27–9; other pictures: BDFH pl. 92 (76), col. pl. VI; Beazley and Ashmole fig. 19; Buschor *GV* fig. 37; CMV figs. 30f.; Lane *GP* pl. 24B; Pfuhl *MuZ* fig. 59; M. Robertson 48f.; Rumpf *MZ* pl. 6, 7; Schefold *ML* pl. 29b.

45. Temple of Apollo at Thermon: Dinsmoor 51ff. fig. 18 and pl. 17, top; D. S. Robertson

65ff. and 52 fig. 20; Lawrence *A* 96f. fig. 51; see also p. 62 with n. 63. Metopes: *AD* II pls. 49–52; Dörig in *AM* 77 (1962) 72–91, Beil. 23; Koch in *AM* 39 (1914) 237–55, pls. 13–15; Payne in *BSA* 27 (1925/6) 124–32 and *NC* 96f., 125 figs. 23D, 33; other pictures: BDFH pl. 93 (77) col. pl. VII and p. 160 fig. 116 (94 fig. 142); CMV figs. 3, 33, 34; Pfuhl *MuZ* figs. 480–3; Rumpf *MZ* pl. 8, 1 and 2; Schefold *ML* 22 fig. 6 and pls. 18–21. Polychrome vases from Megara Hyblaea: Vallet and Villard *MH* II, pls. 182f., 190, 214–18; CMV fig. 32.

46. Eleusis amphora: pp. 50f. with n. 41. Ram-Jug Painter: J. M. Cook in *BSA* 35 (1938) 189ff. pl. 53; Beazley in *Dev.* 8ff. pls. 3f. Other pictures of his work: BDFH 150, figs. 109f. (86, figs. 135f.); *CVA* Berlin fasc. 1, pls. 5, 18–21; Demargne *OGA* fig. 430; Kraiker *Aig.* pl. 45, 566; Kübler *AAM* figs. 51f.; Schefold *ML* pls. 29a, 36a, 37.

47. Nettos vase (Athens, N.M. 1002): Beazley *ABV* 4, Nettos Painter no. 1; *Paral.* 2, Nettos Painter no. 6, with refs.; *Dev.* pl. 5, 1 (detail); pictures: BDFH pl. 104 (88); CMV fig. 50; Cook *GPP* pl. 17; Kübler *AAM* figs. 86f.; Schefold *ML* pl. 59; and often. Other vases of the same character by the painter (now compounded with the Chimaera Painter, *ABV* 3f.; see *Paral.*) and his circle: Karouzou *ATA* passim; also Beazley *Dev.* pls. 5f.; *CVA* Berlin 1 pls. 46–8; Kraiker *Aig.* pls. 45–7; Kübler *AAM* figs. 14–20.

48. Lefkandi Centaur: p. 18 with Chapter 1 n. 8; Geometric Centaurs: p. 21 with Chapter 1 n. 17. The Centaur as all-purpose monster: Buschor in *AJA* 38 (1934) 128ff.; Kunze *AS* (*OF* II) 82ff. Protocorinthian 'Zeus and Centaur': Boston: Johansen *VS* pl. 22, 2; Payne *PV* pl. 11, 1–5; also in BDFH 127 fig. 101 (79, fig. 127); Cook *GPP* pl. 9B; Schefold *ML* fig. 4. Zeus and Typhoeus on sixth-century vase: Rumpf *Ch.V* pl. 25; *CVA München* 6 pl. 281. Herakles using brands against the Centaurs: Apollodorus II 5 4; on Corinthian vase, early sixth century: Louvre L 173; Payne *NC* no. 941, pl. 31, 9–10 and p. 129; Schefold *ML* pl. 62; for this interpretation of the Boston vase, see Fittschen *UBS* pl. 3 no. SB5, 119–28. Relief-pithoi: pp. 28f. with Chapter 1 n. 32; the Medusa-relief: *Enc.Phot.* 22, 56f.; Hampe *FGS* 36 and 38; Richter *H* 296 fig. 415; Schefold *ML* pl. 15b; Minotaur: ibid. pl. 25a.

49. P. 60 with n. 58.

50. Orientalising vase-painting of eastern Greece and the Cyclades: p. 28 with Chapter 1 notes 30f. Polychrome figure-styles: East Greek ('Rhodian'): BDFH pl. 91 (75); CMV fig. 38; Lane *GP* pl. 20A; Rumpf *MZ* pl. 7, 4; Chiot: *JHS* 44 (1924) 217ff., figs. 54–8 and 63, pls. 5f. (Price); CMV figs. 39, 41; Pfuhl *MuZ* fig. 119; Rumpf *MZ* pl. 11, 11; Schefold *ML* pl. 75, see also p. 80 with Chapter 3 n. 19; Cycladic ('Naxian'): C. Karusos in *JdI* 52 (1937) 166 figs. 1–3; Buschor *GV* 55 fig. 65; Homann-Wedeking 138 fig. 65; Rumpf *MZ* pl. 6, 6; Schefold *ML* pl. 9; 'Melian': BDFH pl. 78 (62); CMV fig. 40; Pfuhl *MuZ* figs. 104–10; Richter *H* 301, figs. 420f.; Rumpf *MZ* pl. 6, 5; Schefold *ML* pl. 10 and fig. 45.

51. Late archaic picture on terracotta: p. 226 with Chapter 4 n. 121. Painting on marble: pp. 111 with Chapter 3 n. 85, 157 with Chapter 4 n. 7. Archaic wooden panels: p. 120 with Chapter 3 n. 104. Wall-painting on wood: pp. 244–5 with Chapter 4 notes 152ff.

(*iv*) *The beginning of relief and architectural sculpture*

52. Relief from Chania: Boardman *CCO* 137f., with refs. in n. 6, fig. 53; also in *BSA* 62 (1967) 60; Knossos fragment: ibid., and *BSA* 49 (1954) pl. 30.

53. Early temples: p. 39 with n. 17. Prinias temple: Dinsmoor 45–7; D. S. Robertson 56, fig. 21; Lawrence *A* 96, fig. 50. Sculptures: Pernier in *Ann.* 1 (1914) 19ff., and *AJA* 38 (1934) 175ff.; CMV figs. 11–13; Demargne *OGA* figs. 456f.; Jenkins pl. 10, 2; *KB* 197, 4–6; Lawrence *S* 102, fig. 17; Richter *AGA* figs. 53f.; *Sc.* fig. 347. Jenkins's idea (79ff.) that the goddesses are later than the horsemen is rejected, surely rightly, by Pernier and Richter; see also Boardman *CCO* 147. Praisos plate: p. 51 with n. 42.

54. Three-figure reliefs from Gortyn (Herakleion museum inv. 385 and 379): Levi in *Ann.* 17/18 (1955/6) 300, figs. 15ff. (terracottas showing naked goddesses, alone, a pair, a triad, ibid.

250 ff. figs. 39–42; clothed, fig. 44); the one with a male in the centre: Demargne *OGA* fig. 459; both, Rizza and Scrinari 156f. nos. 8 and 9, with refs., pl. 4 and p. 49 figs. 77–8. Cult-statue of Apollo at Delos; Pausanias II 32 5 and IX 35 3; Plutarch *De Mus.* 14 (O. 334–7); see also p. 47 with n. 34; p. 182 with Chapter 4 n. 44. Hellenistic Three Graces: p. 550 with Chapter 8 n. 120. Number of the Muses: see West in Hesiod *Theogony* 176, n. to line 60; also p. 127 with Chapter 3 n. 117, 395 with Chapter 6 n. 94. Kerameikos ivories, Acropolis bronze and oriental prototypes: p. 44 with n. 30.

55. Daidalos: O. 74–142; Dipoinos, Skyllis and their school: ibid. 321–37; cf. p. 36 with n. 6. Dipoinos and Skyllis sons of Daidalos by a woman of Gortyn: Pausanias II 15 1 (O. 323); Pliny XXXVI 9 (O. 321) says they were born in Crete but settled in Sicyon, and dates them 'in the time of the Medes' rule, before Cyrus began to reign over the Persians; that is about the fiftieth Olympiad' (579–576 B.C.); for a possible explanation of this dating, see Jex-Blake and Sellers, note ad loc.

56. Chiot family of sculptors: p. 69 with n. 74.

57. All the Mycenae fragments (Athens N.M. 2869ff.): Kourouniotis in *JdI* 16 (1901) 18–22, figs. 1–5; woman: Rodenwaldt in *Cor.Curt.* 63ff., pls. 7–10; BDFH pl. 86 (70); Karouzou *Cat.* pl. 2b; *KB* 199, 1; Lawrence *S.* pl. 2a; Lullies and Hirmer pl. 7. See also Wace in *JHS* 59 (1939) 210.

58. 'Backboard': p. 41 with n. 22. Dermys and Kittylos (Athens N.M. 56): Richter *Kouroi* 48 no. 11, figs. 76f., with refs.; *AGSA* 13 no. 9, figs. 31ff., 192–5; Karouzou *Cat.* pl. 2a. On the inscriptions see also Jeffery 92, 94 no. 8, 155; and p. 55 with n. 49. Monte Casale figure: Richter *Korai* 41f. no. 46, figs. 155–8; Langlotz and Hirmer pl. 28; see also p. 115 with Chapter 3 n. 95. East Greek reliefs of related character: p. 84, with Chapter 3 notes 31ff.

59. Early architecture east of the Aegean: pp. 70 and 82 with Chapter 3 notes 1 and 27.

60. Pre-Doric temples: pp. 39 and 57–8 with notes 17 and 53. Models: apsidal from Perachora: *Perachora* (I) 34–51, pls. 8–9; rectangular from Argive Heraion: D. S. Robertson 54 and pl. 1b–c; both: *Perachora* (I) 43, fig. 7; Lawrence *A* 90, fig. 47. Thermon temple: pp. 53f. with n. 45; p. 62 with n. 63.

61. The Doric order: Dinsmoor 69–122; D. S. Robertson 37–45, 48–51; Lawrence *A* 99–112. The Pindar ref. is *Ol.* 13, 71f.

62. Origins of Doric: Dinsmoor 50–8; D. S. Robertson 62–8; Lawrence *A* 113–20; Plommer 181ff.; also R. M. Cook in *BSA* 46 (1951) 50ff. and 65 (1970) 17ff.; von Gerkan in *JdI* 63/4 (1948/9) 1–13. Temple of Apollo at Thermon: pp. 53–4 with n. 45, with n. 60. Temple of Hera at Olympia: Dinsmoor 53–8, figs. 19, 44, pl. 17; D. S. Robertson 62ff., fig. 24; Lawrence *A* 115f., pls. 25, 26B, 29; see also pp. 38–9 with n. 17, 47 with n. 36.

63. Terracotta face-antefixes from Thermon: *AD* II pl. 49, 2 (Kawerau); *RM* 30 (1915) 63 fig. 27 (Koch): Payne *NC* pl. 47, 10; from Calydon: Poulsen and Rhomaios fig. 41; Payne *NC* pl. 47, 11. Architectural terracottas in general: Van Buren *GFR*, *AFR* and *FTR*; see also pp. 64–6 with notes 68 and 70 (Sicily), 117 with Chapter 3 n. 97 (S. Italy), 170 with Chapter 4 n. 24 (Corinth), 277 with Chapter 4 n. 215 (Olympia, perhaps Corinthian), 592 with Epilogue notes 4 and 5 (Corinth and Etruria).

64. Corfu temple: Dinsmoor 73ff., fig. 25; D. S. Robertson 69ff., fig. 26; Lawrence *A* 113f. figs. 161f. The sculptures: Rodenwaldt *Kork.* II passim and *ABK* pls. 12–36; BDFH pls. 100f. (84f.); CMV figs. 16f., 24; Lullies and Hirmer pls. 15ff.; Richter *AGA* figs. 20–3; *H* 55 fig. 59; *Sc.* figs. 61, 76, 96, 109, 141, 153, 374; Schefold *ML* figs. 42f.; and often; see further below, n. 69.

65. Continuous carved band on another early Doric building: p. 81 with Chapter 3 n. 25.

66. Potnia Theron: in the Aegean Bronze Age, see p. 9 with Prologue, n. 24; a Syrian example, under strong Aegean influence, in profile with goats on an ivory box-lid from Ugarit (Ras Shamra), dated to the 13th or 12th century: Demargne *OGA* fig. 356; on Idaean shield: ibid. fig. 462; Kunze *KBR* pl. 3; *KB* 101, 2; on Cretan vase: Demargne *OGA* fig. 44; Levi in *Ann.* 10–12 (1927–9) 330 fig. 431; on Rhodian gold: p. 37 with n. 7; in vase-painting (with profile head): e.g. Payne *NC* pl. 12, 3

and 7; Buschor *GV* 34, fig. 41; see also next note. Chest of Cypselus: Pausanias v 17 5–19 10 (O. 256; winged Artemis with beasts, 19.5); see also pp. 121 and 141f. with Chapter 3 notes 106 and 144, 383 with Chapter 6 n. 63.

67. The plate: London B.M. 60.4–4.2, from Kameiros; the bronze relief (attachment for the armband of a shield): *Ol.Ber.* 3, pl. 33.

68. Medusa's body with the children: e.g. Payne *NC* 132 fig. 46 with remarks p. 133; Woodward *Perseus* figs. 19, 21, 22. Syracuse plaque: *Mon.Ant.* 25 pl. 16; Demargne *OGA* fig. 525; Langlotz and Hirmer col. pl. 1; Payne *NC* 80, fig. 23E; Richter *AGA* fig. 81.

69. Titanomachy: Dörig in Dörig and Gigon, where the gable-remains are illustrated and discussed in other connections also. Kronos and Rhea's tower and throne: Pindar *Ol.* 2 68–77.

70. Terracotta pediment-gorgoneion from Selinus: Lawrence *A* 123f., fig. 68; see also Dinsmoor 81ff., D. S. Robertson 72; also p. 118 with Chapter 3 n. 102. Pediments from the Acropolis: Chapter 3 (iii), pp. 90–4 with notes 44–9. Fountain-building on vase with disk and snakes: Beazley *Dev.* pl. 38, 1 and 2; Pfuhl *MuZ* fig. 286; M. Robertson 87.

71. Pointed out by Payne, *NC* 242f.; denied by Hampe *AM* 60/1 (1935/6) who holds that the figure represents Perseus; but with Rodenwaldt and the majority of scholars I am unable to accept this.

72. Full publication of the metopes, and explanation of the building as a *monopteron*: de La Coste Messelière *AMD* 19–233, with plates 1–18. Pictures of all the near-complete slabs also: de La Coste Messelière *D* pls. 40–3; *KB* 198, 4–7; of some: CMV fig. 128; Lawrence *S* pl. 6; Richter *AGA* fig. 143; *Sc.* figs. 358, 404. Dinsmoor (116f. and *BCH* 36 (1912) 467–73) argues for these metopes belonging not to a Sicyonian building but to an old treasury of Syracuse. This is part of a theory that the sculptured metope was an invention of the western Greeks; but the existence of painted terracotta metopes from certainly older wooden buildings in old Greece makes this most improbable. Figures deemed to be partly concealed by vase-handles: see Beazley *Dev.* 29, on the François vase (pp. 124–8 with Chapter 3 notes 111ff.).

73. P. 48 with n. 39.

74. Nike from Delos (Athens N.M. 21): Karouzou *Cat.* pl. 6; *KB* 207, 1–2; Lawrence *S.* pl. 1b; Richter *Korai* pl. XIVA; *AGA* figs. 186, 190; *H* 62, fig. 71; *Sc.* figs. 77f. Inscriptions: Jeffery 305 no. 30; also 173 n. 1 and 294f. with n. 1, where she puts forward the theory about misunderstanding of the inscription leading to a false genealogy; Löwy *Inschr.* 3f. no. 1; Marcadé *R* II 21f. The Chiot family (p. 59): O. 314–19; 315, scholiast on Aristophanes *Birds* 573, Archermos and the winging of Victory; 314, Pliny XXXVI 11, Boupalis and Athenis contemporaries of the poet Hipponax in sixtieth Olympiad (539–536 B.C.) and this brings Melas, four generations back, to the first Olympiad (779–776 B.C.). For collations of this passage with the inscription, see Jex-Blake and Sellers ad loc., as well as Jeffery and Marcadé. Nike of Paionios: pp. 248 and 288 with Chapter 4 notes 227 and 234, 350 with Chapter 5 n. 139.

CHAPTER 3: RIPE ARCHAIC ART

(*i*) *The rise and influence of an East Greek style in sculpture*

1. Origins of Doric: pp. 39, 57, and 60ff. with Chapter 2 notes 17, 53 and 60ff. Early Ionic and related styles: Dinsmoor 58–64, 124–46; D. S. Robertson 57–61, 90–105; Lawrence *A* 130–42; also Boardman in *Ant.J.* 39 (1959) 170–218; Akurgal in *Anatolia* 5 (1960) 1–7.

2. Sites and architecture: Smyrna: *BSA* 53/4 (1958/9) 1–181; Miletus and Didyma: Wiegand *Milet*; Ephesus: Hogarth *Ephesus*; Samos: Reuther *HTS*; Rhodes: Blinkenberg; Kinch *Vroulia*; *Cl.Rh.* Sculpture: important collections in Berlin (*Kat.Sk.* II 1; Blümel *AGSB*); Istanbul (Mendel *Cat.Sc.*); and London (*BM Cat.Sc.* I i); much Samian material published in Buschor *ASS*; further refs. in following notes.

3. Scent-bottles ('Gorgoneion Group'): Maximova *VP* pl. 24, 95; Higgins *GT* pl. 12B and D (full-length figure) and pp. 28–32 (discussion of the group and its relation to the succeeding 'Aphrodite Group'); *BMCat.Terr.* II pl. 5f., 1608–17; Ducat *VPR*; see p. 146 with n. 152.
4. Samian wooden head: Homann-Wedeking 119 figs. 60f.; Only in *AM* 68 (1953) 84ff. Beil. 16f.; he also publishes other interesting wooden sculptures from the site; cf. pp. 37–9, with Chapter 2 notes 7 and 15; terracottas: ibid. Beil. 38f.
5. Ephesus ivories: Hogarth *Eph.* 155–85, pls. 21–7 (C. Smith); Jacobsthal in *JHS* 71 (1951) 90–3, pls. 34–6, with revised dating and parallels in other materials; other illustrations: Beazley and Ashmole figs. 10f. Richter *Korai* figs. 257–62 (the hawk-priestess, Istanbul, and another); *AGA* fig. 72; *H* 181 fig. 272; CMV fig. 164; Homann-Wedeking 30 fig. 14.
6. Louvre 686: Richter *Korai* 46 no. 55 fig. 133ff.; other pictures and discussions: BDFH 120 (104) left; Beazley and Ashmole fig. 30; Buschor *ASS* figs. 86–91; CMV fig. 163; *Enc.Phot.* 144; *KB* 201, 2; Lawrence *S.* pl. 1c; Lullies and Hirmer pls. 30f. (32f.); Richter *AGA* fig. 165; *H* 59 fig. 65.
7. Cheramyes's other dedications: Berlin: Blümel *AGSB* no. 34, figs. 94–8; Buschor *ASS* figs. 341–4; Richter *Korai* 46 no. 56 figs. 186–9; male leg in Samos: Buschor *ASS* fig. 262f. Girl with partridge from Miletus in Berlin: Blümel *AGSB* no. 47 figs. 129–32; Buschor *ASS* fig. 352; Richter *Korai* 47 no. 57 figs. 190–3, *AGA* fig. 166; Weickert *GP* 12 fig. 5.
8. Geneleos's group: Buschor *ASS* 26ff. figs. 90–101, 84ff. figs. 345–8 (Ornithe), 349f. (general views of base with four statues *in situ*); cf. BDFH 180 fig. 199 (105 fig. 155), *NDA* 222 fig. 27, Richter *Korai* (fig. on p. 50). Identification of reclining figure as the father: Himmelmann-Wildschütz in *MWP* 1963, 13–17; sixth figure a female child and the group not a family but an association of temple-women and girls: Gerhard Schmidt in *AA* 84 (1969) 507. Other pictures and discussions: Blümel *AGSB* no. 36 (Ornithe) figs. 102–5 and 123; Richter *Korai* 50 nos. 67 (Philippe) and 68 (Ornithe) figs. 217–24; also BDFH pls. 120 (104) right (Philippe), 121 (105; reclining figure, front and back); CMV figs. 165 (Ornithe, back) and 166 (recliner); Richter *AGA* figs. 167 (Philippe), 168 (Phileia), 169 (recliner, back). Inscription: Jeffery 319, 341 no. 6 (doubtfully suggesting a reading of the recliner's name as ... narche). Male recliners from Myus in Berlin: Blümel *AGSB* nos. 66–8 figs. 212–16.
9. Seated figures from Didyma: *BMCat.Sc.* I i 106ff., nos. B271–80, pls. 6–15; Tuchelt nos. 40–62, pls. 7–12; other pictures: CMV fig. 169; Lawrence *S* pl.14a; Richter *H* 60 fig. 67, *Sc.* fig. 264. Aiakes's dedication: Buschor *ASS* figs. 141–7, 363; Richter *AGA* 168 fig. 261. Similar but smaller seated figures from Miletus: Blümel *AGSB* nos. 50–6 figs. 139–55. Earlier seated figures from Crete and Peloponnese: p. 38 with Chapter 2 n. 15; later from Athens; p. 106 with n. 74.
10. East Greek heads: from Didyma: *BMCat.Sc.* I i 114ff. nos. B233f., figs. 174f.; Tuchelt pls. 10–12; from Miletus: Blümel *AGSB* no. 58 figs. 159–61; Richter *Korai* 59 no. 98 figs. 293ff.; also Eckstein in *AP* I figs. 13ff. (see next note); Richter *AGA* figs. 180f.; Rodenwaldt *KdA* pl. 6; from Rhodes: Richter *Kouroi* 110 nos. 125ff., figs. 373–6; from Samos: see next note, where others are also cited.
11. Cyzicus kouros: Akurgal in *AK* 8 (1965) 99–103 pls. 26–8. Larger Samian colossus: Richter *Kouroi* 56 nos. 24–5, figs. 96, 93, with earlier refs.; new fragments: Buschor *ASS* figs. 257ff. Smaller Samian colossus: Buschor *ASS* 68 figs. 270–4; the head: Richter *Kouroi* no. 127 figs. 369f.; head and body-fragments combined: *Kouroi* 3 figs. 632–4, after Eckstein in *AP* I (1962) 45–57, pls. 45–54; a good collection of East Greek heads, ibid. figs. 2–22; cf. Buschor *ASS* figs. 364–72, 393–9, 402f.; a small head from Xanthos (Metzger *Xanthos* II pl. 51, 1–3) resembles *ASS* figs. 364–70; also from Samos is a tiny rather crude version in Berlin of the masterpiece from Miletus in the same collection. Didyma kouros: Blümel *AGSB* no. 60 figs. 169–76 (a small head from Myus noted as very like it, ibid. no. 70, figs. 220–1); Tuchelt pls. 11, 2; 18; 19, 1. Other East Greek naked kouroi: Richter *Kouroi* 86 no. 77 figs. 358ff., 108 no. 120 figs. 359ff., 109

no. 124 figs. 367f., 125 nos. 153f. figs. 441, 447ff.; Tuchelt pls. 13–17, 20–2. Kneeling boy from Agora at Athens: *Hesp.* 6 (1937) 426–41 figs. 1–7, pl. 10; 7 (1938) 393 fig. 30; Higgins *GT* pl. 16.

12. Clothed kouros from Samos: Buschor *ASS* 46 figs. 160ff.; *KB* 202, 5; Richter *AGA* fig. 170; from Pitane: *NDA* 106f. figs. 34f.; from Myus: Blümel *AGSB* no. 69 figs. 217ff.; of Dionysermos, Louvre MA 3600/2: Devambez and Robert in *RA* 1966, 195–222; Bousquet in *RA* 1967 39; Richter *Kouroi*[3] 155 figs. 616–19; CMV fig. 290. It is possible that the Samian figure, which was found at Cape Phoneas, was brought there from the mainland opposite (Buschor l.c.).

13. Dress of the canonical kore type: Payne and Young 25f.; Richter *Korai* 6–10. Colouring most fully preserved on Acropolis 675: illustrated in colour in BDFH pl. XVIII, Lullies and Hirmer[1] pl. 66; in black and white ibid. pl. 67 (70); Payne and Young pl. 49, 4; Richter *Korai* fig. 397; Schrader pl. 60. Details of dress-patterns in colour: Schrader pls. I–IV; a good selection in black-and-white: Richter *Korai* 69–87, 100–2 (after colour plates in Lermann *AGP*).

14. The series from the Acropolis fully published by Langlotz in Schrader; also Payne and Young, and Richter *Korai*; and see pp. 102–5.

15. Signatures of Chiot sculptors on the Acropolis of Athens: Raubitschek 7f. no. 3, 14f. no. 9. Ionic lettering and name: see next note. Cycladic sculptors and sculpture in Attica: pp. 87 with n. 37, 89 with n. 40, 101 with n. 62.

16. East Greek korai from the Acropolis: Payne in Payne and Young, Note I (55–63); see also p. 103 with n. 66. 453: Payne and Young pl. 43, 3 and 4; Langlotz in Schrader 151 no. 162 pl. 110. 1360: Dickins *Cat.* 280f.; Payne and Young pl. 45; Langlotz in Schrader 71f. no. 29 pl. 41. 136: Payne and Young pl. 44; Langlotz in Schrader 176f. no. 271 pl. 111; Langlotz and Schuchardt pl. 25; Richter *Korai* 83 no. 132 figs. 429f. 594: Dickins *Cat.* 128f.; Payne and Young pls. 46–8; Langlotz in Schrader 102ff. no. 54 pls. 76f.; Langlotz and Schuchardt pl. 30; Richter *Korai* 80 no. 124 figs. 398–400; CMV fig. 282 (colour). Pythis: Raubitschek 15f. no. 10 (also 98f. no. 90); and see p. 106 with n. 74. Torso in Delos (4063): p. 89 with n. 41; connection with Acropolis 594: Payne in Payne and Young 29.

17. Genelean figure in Samos: Buschor *ASS* figs. 112–14; Richter *Korai* 50 no. 69 figs. 225–7; from Samos in Berlin: Blümel *AGSB* no. 37 figs. 106–9; Buschor *ASS* fig. 373; Richter *Korai* 90 no. 153 figs. 491–4. Partridge-carriers: Berlin from Miletus: Blümel *AGSB* no. 49 figs. 135–8; Buschor *ASS* fig. 125; Richter *Korai* 92 no. 161 figs. 512–15; *AGA* fig. 269; London from Theangela: *BMCat.Sc.* I i 149 no. B318 fig. 188; Richter *Korai* 93 no. 167 figs. 532–5; Samos: Buschor *ASS* figs. 357–9 and 361; also (one fragment before the discovery of the rest) 124: a fourth figure of the same type is from Thrace in Salonica (929: together with a damaged kouros, 930). Paris from Clazomenae: Richter *Korai* 92 no. 163 figs. 520–3, *AGA* fig. 194; Langlotz *FGBS* pl. 60, 2.

18. Chios torsos: Boardman in *AP* I (1962) 43ff., pls. 38–44 with refs. and a date of *c.* 580–570 B.C.; Richter *Korai* 38 nos. 37f. figs. 122f., *AGA* figs. 187f.

19. Archermos and the Nike from Delos: p. 68 and Chapter 2 n. 74. Chiot pottery (p. 55 with Chapter 2 n. 50): first found at Naucratis in the Nile Delta and called Naucratite; Chiot origin established through excavations on the island (Kourouniotis in *Delt.* 2 (1916) 193ff.; Lamb in *BSA* 35 (1934/5) 138–64); Boardman in *BSA* 51 (1956) 35–62 suggests some made by Chiots settled in Naucratis. Dedications painted before firing are found on vases in Naucratis and Aigina (R. M. Cook and Woodhead in *BSA* 47 (1952) 159–70).

20. Samos fragments: Buschor *ASS* figs. 136 and 384, 385–92. Cnidian Caryatid and ex-Cnidian head: Richter *Korai* 57 nos. 86ff., figs. 270–4, 282f.; *FdeD* IV ii 1ff. pl. 26; CMV figs. 174 and 231 (head); *KB* 209, 3; see also Payne in Payne and Young 58f. Separation of head and body: de La Coste Messelière in *BCH* 62 (1938) 285ff.; de La Coste Messelière and Marcadé in *BCH* 77 (1953) 346ff. Miss Richter, in *BCH* 82 (1958) 92ff., has shown that the head, although dissociated, must be of about the same early date.

21. Siphnian Caryatid: p. 89 with n. 41. Cyrene

korai: Richter *Korai* 93f. nos. 168f. figs. 563–9; Paribeni *Cat.Sc.Cir.* nos. 8 and 9 pls. 12–15; other pieces, nos. 1–7 pls. 1–11. Spartan sculpture and Bathycles at Amyclae: pp. 114–15 with notes 92f.

22. Blümel *AGSB* no. 39 figs. 112–15; CMV fig. 195. A greaved shin and another fragment in Samos (Buschor *ASS* figs. 172f.) probably come from the same statue.

23. See pp. 141–6 with notes 145–51 (small bronzes); 180ff. with Chapter 4 notes 41–6 (beginning and technique of large-scale bronze statuary).

24. Chariot-relief from Cyzicus in Istanbul: CMV fig. 197; Richter *AGA* fig. 184; Schede *Meist.* pl. 4a and b. Set from Myus in Berlin: Blümel *AGSB* figs. 193–211 (201 is a reconstruction based on fragments of several slabs). London dancers: *BMCat.Sc.* I i 116f. no. B285 pl. 17; Tuchelt pls. 79ff., K86, and pp. 111f. correcting earlier accounts; *KB* 203, 1. Europa in Berlin: Blümel *AGBS* no. 29 fig. 81.

25. Temple of Athena at Assos and its sculptures (in Istanbul and the Louvre): Clarke, Bacon and Koldewey *Assos*. The temple also: Dinsmoor 88 and 87 fig. 33 (dated probably not before 540 B.C.; D. S. Robertson 82, 84 fig. 36, 325 ('? *c.*560'); Lawrence *A* 119 and pl. 38A (probably quite late in the century). The sculptures also: CMV fig. 198; *Enc.Phot.* 142f.; *KB* 204, 4f.; Lawrence *S* pl. 9; Richter *AGA* fig. 185, *Sc.* fig. 407. Ionic parallels: pp. 83–5ff. with notes 28 (Ephesus) and 31 (Didyma); a carved architrave on a classical Ionic building in Lycia: p. 403 with Chapter 6 n. 116.

26. Xanthos, Lion Tomb: *BMCat.Sc.* I i 118f. no. B286 fig. 176 and pls. 18–20. The fragment with lioness and cubs has since been detached and attributed to a separate monument, on the grounds of difference of material; but see Demargne in *Xanthos* I 31 (with a date *c.*560 B.C.): other fragments ibid. pls. 4 and 13. See also Akurgal *Gr.Rel.* 1–51, pls. 1–5 (date of *c.*540). Reliefs from Isinda: Akurgal ibid. 52–97, pls. 6–13. Monumental sculpture inspired by small-scale work: pp. 114 with n. 93, 116f. with n. 96, 119f. with n. 102.

27. Origins of Ionic: above, n. 1. Samian Heraion: Dinsmoor 40, 45f., 48, 221ff.; D. S. Robertson 90, 95, 105 n.; Lawrence *A* 91ff. figs. 48f., 123–7 figs. 75, 77; Buschor in *AM* 55 (1920) 1–99, pl. 1, Beil. 1–27, figs. 1–45; Reuther *HTS*.

28. Assos: p. 82 n. 25; Corfu: p. 63 with Chapter 2 n. 64; Prinias: p. 58 with Chapter 2 n. 53.

29. Ephesus temple: Dinsmoor 127–32 pl. 30 and fig. 48; D. S. Robertson 90–4, figs. 39–42; Lawrence *A* 132–6, fig. 76; Hogarth *Ephesus*. The sculptures: *BMCat.Sc.* I i 47–99, nos. B86–268, pls. 4f., figs. 39–163 (drums, B86–138, pls. 4f., figs. 39–69; possible piers, B139, 141–4, figs. 70, 72–5; parapet, B145–268, figs. 77–163; architectural fragments, 35–46, B4–85, figs. 31–8); *KB* 203, 3–5; Richter *AGA* figs. 182ff.; 265; *Korai* figs. 263–9; *Sc.* figs. 265f. On the position of the carved drums see further p. 407, discussion of the fourth-century temple, with refs. in Chapter 6 n. 125. Wiegartz, l.c. there, thinks the archaic ones must have been set low (46f.).

30. Ex-Cnidian Caryatid: p. 80 with n. 20; Siphnian: p. 89 with n. 41. The Siphnian building with its other sculptures: pp. 152–9 with Chapter 4 notes 1–10.

31. Didyma drum-fragments (Berlin): Blümel *AGSB* no. 59 figs. 162–8; Richter *Korai* figs. 296–300; with other fragments: Tuchelt pls. 72–5; Gruben in *JdI* 78 (1963) 78–182, esp. 102–12 figs. 7–13 and reconstruction p. 158 fig. 39; carved architrave: ibid. and Tuchelt pls. 76–9. Other pictures of drum fragments: CMV fig. 168; Griefenhagen *AK* pl. 1; Lullies and Hirmer pl. 40 (42); Weickert *GP* 14ff.; of architrave: *KB* 2032. Intersection of worlds in Hellenistic sculpture: p. 538 with Chapter 8 n. 90. Miletus reliefs (Berlin): Blümel *AGSB* nos. 44f. figs. 126f.; Richter *Korai* figs. 228f. Olympia bronze: *Ol.* IV pl. 7, no. 74; CMV fig. 167; Lamb pl. 36c; see also pp. 104 and 142 with notes 70 and 146.

32. London: *BMCat.Sc.* I i 50 no. B89 pl. 4; Beazley and Ashmole fig. 32; Lullies and Hirmer pls. 38f.; Richter *AGA* fig. 265; *Korai* figs. 267f.; Rodenwaldt *KdA* 200f.

33. Cyzicus drum: Akurgal in *AK* 8 (1965) 99–103 pl. 28, 3. Ring-dance on early Attic vase: ibid. 100 fig. 1; on sixth-century East Greek vase (Clazomenian): Pfuhl *MuZ* fig. 143 (all girls); François vase: pp. 124–7 with notes 111–16.

34. Friezes of the Siphnian Treasury: pp. 152–7 with Chapter 4 notes 3–8.
35. Shrine from Sardis (Manisa museum): Richter *Korai* 92 no. 164 with refs., figs. 524–7. Korai from Samos, Miletus and Theangela: p. 79 with n. 17. Relief in Berlin: Blümel *AGSB* no. 46, fig. 128.
36. Lions from Didyma in London: *BMCat.Sc.* I i 112ff. nos. B281f. figs. 171ff. and pl. 16 (B281); B281 also Richter *AGA* fig. 69. This bears a dedicatory inscription to Apollo by the sons of Orion: Jeffery 332f. and 342 no. 22, pointing out that statues in the plural are mentioned. B282 is of different type; but Cabelmann in *MWP* publishes a fine fragment still at Didyma of a lion heraldically antithetical to 281, and identifies it as the pair. Lion from Miletus in Berlin: Blümel *AGSB* no. 62 figs. 179–83; CMV fig. 298; Richter *AGA* fig. 271. Head from Miletus: p. 75 with n. 10.

(ii) *Cycladic sculpture*

37. Acropolis fragments: Dickins *Cat.* 150 no. 619, 219, no. 677; Payne and Young 12f. pls. 18ff.; Langlotz in Schrader 63ff. nos. 22ff. pls. 33f.; Langlotz and Schuchardt fig. 7; *KB* 201, 3. These are often held to be Samian, but Dickins's and Payne's attribution to Naxos is surely right, though Dickins apparently held that Cheramyes's dedication in the Louvre was also Naxian. Delphi sphinx: *FdeD* IV 1, 41ff. pls. 5–6; de La Coste Messelière *D* pls. 47ff.; BDFH pl. 103; CMV fig. 138; Richter *AGA* fig. 46. Delos lions: Bruneau and Ducat 112ff. pl. 2, 1; Bethe in *Die Antike* 14 (1938) 93ff.; Richter *AGA* figs. 47f.
38. Delos sphinxes and capitals: Bruneau and Ducat 44f. pl. 6. Capitals from Delos, Paros and Athens: Kontoleon in *AAA* 1 (1968) 178–81 figs. 1–5.
39. Fragments from Thera: Richter *Kouroi* 54 nos. 18A and B, 19 figs. 97–105. Head from Naxos in Copenhagen (2821): Richter *Kouroi* 70 no. 50 figs. 172f.; Homann-Wedeking 88 fig. 47. Thera kouros (Athens N.M. 8): Richter *Kouroi* 69 no. 49 figs. 178–83; CMV fig. 140 (head). Kouros from New Phaleron (Athens, N.M. 3858): Richter *Kouroi* 63 no. 31 figs. 132f., 136f.; Homann-Wedeking 87 fig. 46; the suggestion that it is Cycladic: Chr. Karousos in *Eph.Arch.* 1953/4 19–29. Melos kouros (Athens N.M. 1558): Richter *Kouroi* 96 no. 86 figs. 273–9; *AM* 84 (1969) pl. 12, 2 (head); CMV fig. 150; Karouzou *Cat.* pl. 5; Lullies and Hirmer pls. 32f. (34f.). Head from Thasos in Copenhagen (2823): Richter *Kouroi* 105 no. 109 figs. 328f., 334; CMV fig. 149. Torsos: from Paros: Richter 107f. nos. 116 (Louvre, with head) figs. 365–8, 117 (Copenhagen 2030) figs. 347ff., 118 (Paros) figs. 350f.; in Andros: Richter *Kouroi* 108 no. 119 fig. 352; from Naxos in Berlin (1555): Richter *Kouroi* 106 no. 115 figs. 353ff.; in Delos: A3997: Richter *Kouroi* 69 no. 47 figs. 174f.; A4045: Richter *Kouroi* 69 no. 48 figs. 176f.; A4083: Richter *Kouroi* 105 no. 111 figs. 342, 345; A4048: Richter *Kouroi* 106 no. 112 figs. 343, 346; A1047: Richter *Kouroi* 124 no. 151 figs. 443f., Bruneau and Ducat pl. 4.
40. Kouros from Keos in Athens (N.M. 3686): Richter *Kouroi* 122 no. 144 figs. 419–24; CMV fig. 191; Karouzou *Cat.* pl. 10. Kouros from Epidaurus in Athens, N.M. 63, head and part of lower torso: Richter *Kouroi* 98 no. 91 figs. 293–6. Aristion of Paros and statue of Phrasikleia: p. 100 with n. 62. Friezes of Siphnian treasury: pp. 152–7 with Chapter 4 notes 3–8.
41. Siphnian Caryatid: Richter *Korai* 66 no. 104 figs. 317–20; *FdeD* IV pls. 18–20; de La Coste Messelière *D* pls. 63ff.; CMV fig. 201. Friezes: see last note. Kore from Paros in New York (07.306): Richter *CGS* 4 no. 5 pl. 8, *Korai* 89 no. 151 figs. 433–6. Acropolis torso (627): Payne and Young 61, pl. 121, 2 and 5; Langlotz in Schrader 100 no. 50 pl. 72 (thought very late, *c.*480 B.C.). Torso from Andros in Copenhagen (1196): Richter *Korai* 89 no. 152 figs. 487–90. Torsos from Delos: Richter *Korai* 88f. nos. 147 (A4064, Delos) figs. 468–71; 148 (Athens N.M. 22) figs. 472–5; 149 (A4067, Delos) figs. 479–82; 150 (A4063, Delos) figs. 476–8; on this last and Acropolis 594, see p. 79 with n. 16. Ex-Cnidian head: p. 80 with n. 20.
42. Bruneau and Ducat 45 (A4098–4102, without

illustration). Attic horseman: p. 97 with notes 57f.

43. Munich 241; Hausmann *GW* 20 fig. 9; Langlotz *FGBS* pl. 86 b. Frontal faces: p. 127 with n. 117.

(iii) Sculpture in Athens and Attica

44. Limestone animal-pediments: Dickins *Cat.* 67ff. nos. 3 and 74–8, with refs.; Heberdey *Porossk.* 77f., fig. 54; Schuchardt *AGK* figs. 2ff.; Buschor *AM* 47 (1922) 92ff.; other pictures: BDFH 164 figs. 19ff. (97 figs. 145ff.); *KB* 205, 2 and col. pl.; Richter *Sc.* fig. 376; Schefold *ML* figs. 1–3. See following notes and further refs. in Dickins.

45. Hydra-pediment: Dickins *Cat.* 57 no. 1; *KB* 205, 1; Richter *Sc.* fig. 376; Wiegand *Porosarch.* pl. 8, 4. Hydra-pictures on Corinthian vases: Payne *NC* 126ff. figs. 45A–C; Brommer *VL* 65 (Attic black-figure, 63f.).

46. Small Triton pediment: Dickins *Cat.* 60 no. 2; Wiegand *Porosarch.* 195 fig. 213. Large Triton pediment: p. 93 with n. 49.

47. Introduction pediment: Dickins *Cat.* 62ff.; Heberdey *Porossk.* pl. 1; Wiegand *Porosarch.* 208, 211 figs. 236, 238f.; also *AM* 84 (1969) pls. 17, 5; 20, 1–2 (details); CMV fig. 124; *KB* 205, 5f.; Richter *Sc.* fig. 380. The draped figure: Dickins *Cat.* 89f. no. 55 (cf. nos. 48, 50, 54); *AM* 84 (1969) pl. 19, 1–2 (head). The subject in vase-painting: Brommer *VL* 131f.

48. Olive-tree pediment: Dickins *Cat.* 69ff.; Heberdey *Porossk.* pl. 2; Buschor in *AM* 47 (1922) pl. 6 and pp. 81ff. with the interpretation as the ambush of Troilos; also *AM* 84 (1969) pl. 21, 1–2 (girl's head); *KB* 205, 4; Richter *AGA* fig. 104; *Korai* figs. 151–4. François vase: pp. 124–7 with notes 111–16. Troilos-scenes on vases: Brommer *VL* 264–7. The story: *BICS* 17 (1970) 11–15 pls. 1f.; the Three Spells: *GRBS* 11 (1970) 24ff.

49. Lions and bull: Dickins *Cat.* 67ff. no. 3. Corner-groups: Dickins *Cat.* 78ff. nos. 35f.; Heberdey *Porossk.* pls. 3f.; Wiegand *Porosarch.* pl. 4; see also Schuchardt in *AM* 60/1 (1935/6) 1ff.; other pictures: Beazley and Ashmole figs. 38f.; BDFH pls. VIII and 102 (86); CMV figs. 125ff.; *KB* 205, 3 and col. pl.; Lawrence *S* pl. 7b; Lullies and Hirmer pls. 24 and 25 (26); Richter *AGA* figs. 105f., *Sc.* figs. 377ff.; Schefold *GP* pl. 56. Head of Herakles: Broneer in *Hesp.* 8 (1939) 91ff. pl.

50. Erechtheum inscription: pp. 364–5 with Chapter 6 notes 4ff. Design and execution: see also p. 157 with Chapter 4 n. 8.

51. Moschophoros: Dickins *Cat.* 156ff. no. 624; Payne and Young 1ff. pls. 2–4; Schuchardt in Schrader 278–81 no. 409 figs. 342f. pls. 153f.; Langlotz and Schuchardt pls. 3f.; other pictures: Beazley and Ashmole fig. 35; BDFH pl. 87; CMV fig. 117; *KB* 206, 5; Lawrence *S* pl. 8; Lullies and Hirmer pls. 22f. (24f.); Richter *AGA* figs. 92f. The Moschophoros Master and the Triton pediment: Schefold *GP* 34–41; Dörig in BDFH 87.

52. Cretan kriophoros (Berlin 7477): *DKK* 46ff. no. B5 with refs., pls. 18f. and col. pl.; Lamb pl. 25b; Neugebauer *ABS* pl. 17. Thasos colossus: p. 47 with Chapter 2 n. 35.

53. Kouros from Volomandra in Athens (N.M. 1906): Richter *Kouroi* 79 and 80f. no. 63 figs. 208–16; *AM* 84 (1969) pl. 16, 2 (head); CMV figs. 144 (back), 145 (head). Aristion of Paros: p. 89 with n. 40, p. 100 with n. 62. Kouros-fragments in Louvre (MNC 548): Richter *Kouroi* 82 no. 66 figs. 221–5. Head from Acropolis (617): Payne and Young pl. 9, 3 (see Payne, p. 3). Boston kouros-torso (39.552, from Attica?): Richter *Kouroi* 83 no. 69 figs. 230–3. Later Attic kouroi: pp. 105–6 with notes 71f.

54. Rampin Master: Payne in Payne and Young 4–9, 18–21; Karouzos in *BSA* 39 (1942) 99ff.; Langlotz in Schrader 47; Schuchardt ibid. 225. Dubiously identified with Phaidimos (Schefold *GP* 41–6) or Endoios (Rumpf; see below n. 75). See also p. 109, particularly n. 81.

55. Acropolis head (654): Dickins *Cat.* 192; Payne in Payne and Young 3f., pl. 11 and fig. 1e; Langlotz in Schrader 127 no. 85 pl. 94; Langlotz and Schuchardt pl. 9a and b. 'Berlin goddess': p. 99 with n. 61; 'Aphrodite of Lyons': p. 102 with n. 64.

56. Frontal chariots: reliefs from Acropolis:

Dickins *Cat.* 114–17 nos. 575f., 578ff.; Payne and Young 51, pl. 16; Schuchardt in Schrader 293–8 no. 418 figs. 340–3, pls. 153f.; face, Acrop. 637: ibid. 297f. figs. 344f.; *AM* 84 (1969) pl. 21, 3f. and p. 5; horses also: Langlotz and Schuchardt pls. 49f. Sicilian metopes: pp. 119–20 with n. 102. Vase-paintings: pp. 128–9 with n. 122 (Nearchos), 131ff. with notes 126–33 (Exekias), 136, 138 with notes 135, 141 (frontal chariots).

57. Rampin horseman (head, Louvre 3104; body, Acrop. 590; other fragments of this and pair, collected and listed by Schuchardt in Schrader): Dickins 124f. (main body-fragment); Payne in Payne and Young 6ff. (associating head and body) pls. 11A–C; 124, 1; 133, 3–4; Schuchardt in Schrader 212–24 no. 312 figs. 210–48, pls. 134–7 (identifying more fragments and establishing existence of second figure); Langlotz and Schuchardt pls. 5f.; other pictures: Beazley and Ashmole fig. 37 (head); BDFH pl. 126 (110); CMV fig. 118; *KB* 206, 7 (head); Lawrence *S* pl. 10a; Lullies and Hirmer pls. 28f. (30f.); Richter *AGA* fig. 94, *H* fig. 70. Horseman from Themistoclean wall: Payne in *JHS* 53 (1933) 272 and 275 fig. 6. Delos horsemen: p. 89 with n. 42. Other horses and riders from Acropolis: Dickins *Cat.* 102f. no. 148, 114 no. 571, 131f. no. 597 (rider on a Hippalektryon – cock-horse – a creature almost confined to late archaic Attic art), 138–41 no. 606, 155f. and 283 nos. 623 and 4119, 267f. no. 700; Payne in Payne and Young 7 and 51f., pls. 101 and 134–40; Schuchardt in Schrader 225–40 nos. 313–21 figs. 249–79 pls. 134–41; Langlotz and Schuchardt pls. 51–7. Lion from Miletus: p. 86 with n. 36.

58. Rampin horseman and his fellow as Peisistratids (?): Schuchardt in Schrader 225; as possibly Dioscuri: Richter *AGA* 65. Exekias: pp. 131–5 with notes 126–33. Cheramyes statue: pp. 72–3 with n. 6.

59. Sabouroff head: Berlin 308; Blümel *Berlin Kat. Sk.* 6ff. A46 pls. 13ff.; *AGSB* 13–16 no. 6 figs. 16–19, with the suggestion about stucco (also in *AA* 52 (1937) 52, figs. 1–3); Langlotz and Schuchardt, frontispiece; CMV fig. 187; *KB* 206, 6; Lawrence *S* pl. 10b; Schefold *GP* 47 pl. 46 (connected with Endoios). Aristodikos: p. 175 with Chapter 4 n. 30. Head-fragment in Boston: p. 105 with n. 72. Stele of mother and child: p. 112 with n. 87.

60. Torsos from the Acropolis: Dickins *Cat.* 120–8 nos. 582ff., 589, 593; Payne in Payne and Young 9 pls. 12 and 14; Langlotz in Schrader 43ff. nos. 1–3 pls. 1 and 2; Langlotz and Schuchardt pls. 10–13; Richter *Korai* 40 no. 43 figs. 147–50.

61. Berlin 'goddess': Blümel *Berl.Kat.Sk.* 1ff. A1 pls. 1–8, *AGSB* 7–10 no. 1 figs. 1–8; Richter *Korai* 39 no. 42 figs. 139–46, *AGA* figs. 90f., *H* figs. 63f., *Sc.* figs. 139f.

62. Aghios Joannis Rendis statue: Lazaridis in *AAA* 1 (1968) 34f. fig. 3; *AR 1967/8* 6 fig. 7. Korai from Cyrene: *AJA* 75 (1971) 39ff. (Pedley), 47ff. (White), with pls. 6–8 (a kouros and a sphinx also illustrated); the later and finer kore also: Goodchild *Kyrene und Apollonia* fig. 4 (other archaic pieces from Cyrene, figs. 2f.). Phrasikleia: Mastrokostas in *AAA* 5 (1972) 298–324, col. pl. 3 and figs. 13f.; kouros, fig. 12; inscribed base, figs. 17f.; fig. 16 shows the lead found with the kore fitted into the depression in the surface of the base; other figs. show the statues in the ground, being lifted etc. Bronze from Ptoion (Athens N.M. 7389): Lamb pl. 34b; *BCH* 12 (1888) pl. 11. Artemis Daidala, from Mazi (Elis) in Boston: (98.658): *Cat.GREB* 20f. no. 19 with refs.; Lamb pl. 35d; Neugebauer *ABS* pls. 18f.; Langlotz *FGBS* pl. 44, 47; on this and the Vix krater, see pp. 142–5 with notes 146, 150. Inscription on Boston figure: Jeffery 191, 202 no. 67, pl. 39.

63. Acropolis 679 ('Peplos kore'): Dickins *Cat.* 223ff.; Payne in Payne and Young 18–22 pls. 29–33; Langlotz in Schrader 44–8, pls. 3–8, figs. 86ff.; Langlotz and Schuchardt pls. 10–13; Richter *Korai* 72 no. 113 figs. 349–54, *AGA* figs. 123f., *H* figs. 86ff.; BDFH pl. 127 (111); CMV figs. 119f.; Lawrence *S* pl. 14a; Lullies and Hirmer pls. 41ff. (43ff.); Ridgway *SS* fig. 24; and often.

64. 'Aphrodite of Lyons' and Acropolis fragments (269; Dickins *Cat.* 106): Payne in Payne and Young 14–19, pls. 22–6 with earlier refs.; Langlotz in Schrader 66f. no. 25 figs. 31f. pls. 21, 26f.; Richter *Korai* 57 no. 89 figs. 275–81, *AGA* fig. 112.

65. Sphinx from Spata (Athens N.M. 28): Richter *AGSA* 16 no. 12 figs. 40f.; *AM* 84 (1969) pl.

19, 3f. (head). Relation to Lyons figure: Payne in Payne and Young 15 n. 4.

66. East Greek korai from the Acropolis: p. 78 with n. 16. 669: Dickins *Cat.* 204; Payne in Payne and Young 23 pls. 27f.; Langlotz in Schrader 68ff. no. 28 pls. 38ff.; *AM* 84 (1969) pl. 12. 682: Dickins *Cat.* 232–5; Payne in Payne and Young 27ff. pls. 40f.; Langlotz in Schrader 86–90 no. 41 pls. 53–6; Richter *Korai* 73 no. 116 figs. 362–7; CMV fig. 272; Ridgway *SS* fig. 25.

67. Acropolis 681 and inscribed base: Dickins *Cat.* 228–32; Payne in Payne and Young 31–4, 63ff., pls. 51–3 and 124, 4; Langlotz in Schrader 81–5 no. 38 pls. 50ff., 109; Langlotz and Schuchardt figs. 14f.; Richter *Korai* 69f. no. 110 figs. 336–40, *AGA* fig. 234, *H* 72 fig. 89; *KB* 213, 5; Lawrence *S* pl. 18b; Raubitschek 232f. no. 197; *AM* 84 (1969) pls. 9 and 10, 1–2. On the association of statue and base, and other works associated with Antenor, see particularly Payne l.c., Richter l.c., Schefold *GP* 49–54, Rumpf in *Festschr.Mercklin* 139 n. 27; also Deyhle, *AM* l.c. 39–46; this important article, 'Meisterfragen der archaïschen Plastik Attikas' is the most comprehensive, and the most sensible, consideration of the interesting, difficult problem of the allotment of the considerable surviving bulk of archaic Attic sculpture among individual hands. On the problems of this kore and its base, see further pp. 130 with n. 124, 162 with Chapter 4 n. 15, 186 with Chapter 4 n. 49.

68. 674: Dickins *Cat.* 213f.; Payne in Payne and Young 34f. pls. 75–8; Langlotz in Schrader 93ff. no. 44 pls. 62–7; Langlotz and Schuchardt pls. 26–9; Richter *Korai* 81 no. 127 figs. 411–16, 434, *AGA* fig. 234, *H* 73 fig. 91; Beazley and Ashmole fig. 49; CMV figs. 313, 315; *KB* 217, 3; Lawrence *S* pl. 14b; Lullies and Hirmer pl. 75.

69. 678: Dickins *Cat.* 220–3; Payne in Payne and Young 21f. pls. 34 and 35, 3–4; Langlotz in Schrader 53f. no. 10 pls. 20f.; Richter *Korai* 71 no. 112 figs. 345–8; *AM* 84 (1969) pl. 1, 2 (head). 611: Dickins *Cat.* 143f.; Payne and Young pl. 60, 4–6; Langlotz in Schrader 54f. no. 11 pl. 22; possible association with base signed by Gorgias: Raubitschek 9ff. no. 5 and 502f. (this Gorgias doubtfully identified with one mentioned by Pliny XXXIV 49 among bronzeworkers and perhaps defined as Laconian; there are other bases signed by Gorgias on the Acropolis, Raubitschek l.c., some of which supported marble statues, some bronze). 685: Dickins *Cat.* 240f.; Payne in Payne and Young 35 pls. 79f.; Langlotz in Schrader 97f. no. 47 pls. 70f.; Langlotz and Schuchardt pls. 32f.; Richter *Korai* 100 no. 181 figs. 573–7 (dated later than La Delicata); *AM* 84 (1969) pl. 4, 2 (head).

70. Dickins *Cat.* 205ff.; Payne in Payne and Young 36 pls. 65ff. (with a harsh judgement); Langlotz in Schrader 50f. no. 8 pls. 14ff.; Langlotz and Schuchardt pl. 18; Richter *Korai* 76 no. 119, *AGA* fig. 223; CMV figs. 283f.; *KB* 214, 4; *AM* 84 (1969) pl. 7, 2 (head). Bronze statuette: pp. 84f. with n. 31; p. 142 with n. 146. 683: Dickins *Cat.* 235ff.; Payne in Payne and Young 34 pl. 59, 1–3; Langlotz in Schrader 51f. no. 9 pls. 17ff.; Richter *Korai* 77 no. 120 figs. 381–4 (with new fragment added by E. B. Harrison, *Hesp.* 24 (1955) 169ff. pl. 65); Raubitschek 313 no. 292 (associated with base inscribed with dedication to Athena by Lysias and Euarchis); *KB* 217, 4. Endoios: see pp. 106–8 with notes 74ff., 157 with Chapter 4 n. 9, 227 with Chapter 4 n. 122.

71. Acrop. 643 (another fr., 307, joins): Dickins *Cat.* 185f.; Payne in Payne and Young 37 pls. 70f.; Langlotz in Schrader 131f. no. 96 pls. 97f.; Langlotz and Schuchardt pl. 24; Richter *Korai* 82 no. 128 figs. 417ff.; *AM* 84 (1969) pl. 6, 1; Beazley and Ashmole fig. 50; CMV figs. 286f. Rayet head (Copenhagen 418; Poulsen 11): Richter *Kouroi* 120 no. 128 figs. 408f.; *AM* 53 (1928) Beil. 21, 2 and 22, 1; CMV fig. 188; Lullies and Hirmer² figs. 46f.; Schefold *GP* 48f. fig. 51. Associated fragments and the connection: *AM* 84 (1969) 12–20 (Deyhle), 65–75 (Schmidt), 76–86 (Knigge) with pls. 27–37 and refs. Endoios: see pp. 106ff. (refs. in last note).

72. Boston head (34.169, from Attica?): Richter *Kouroi* 122 no. 143 figs. 413f.; see also p. 98 with n. 59. Acropolis torso: Dickins *Cat.* 200ff.; Payne in Payne and Young 43 pls. 97f.; Schuchardt in Schrader 189f. no. 298 pls. 115f.; Richter *Kouroi* 120 no. 137 figs. 406ff.; *AM* 84 (1969) pl. 5, 2 (back); the well-preserved

feet exist with plinth, and part of base with sparse remains of inscription: Dickins *Cat.* 130f.; Payne and Young pl. 132, 3; Schuchardt in Schrader 190 fig. 177, 192 fig. 182; Richter *Kouroi* figs. 436 and 442; Raubitschek 65f. no. 62. 'Mask' from Ikaria (Athens N.M. 3072): Karouzou *Cat.* pl. 11a; Schefold *GP* 48 fig. 52; Wrede in *AM* 53 (1928) pl. 1, Beil. 21, 3 and 22, 2. Fragments of seated statue: Athens N.M. 3897, 3073–4. Seated Dionysus from Athens (N.M. 3711): *AP* 6 (1967) 7–20, pls. 1–6, figs. 1–5, text figs. 1–12, with refs.; *Delt.* 13 (1930/1; 1933) 119–35, figs. 1–9; *AM* 84 (1969) pl. 23, 3–4 (feet).

73. Volomandra kouros: p. 96 with n. 53. Kouros in Munich (169): Richter *Kouroi* 118 no. 135 figs. 391–4, 399. Kouros from Anavysos in Athens (N.M. 3851): Richter *Kouroi* 118ff. no. 136 figs. 395–8, 400; Lullies and Hirmer pls. 53–7 (57–61); *AP* 6 (1967) pls. 7, 8a; *AM* 84 (1969) pls. 5, 1 (back), 13, 3 (head); *BSA* 36 (1935/6; 1939) pls. 1–5. Kroisos inscription: Richter *Kouroi* 115f. fig. 401; Jeffery in *BSA* 57 (1962) 143f. no. 57. Relief from Anavysos: p. 112 with n. 87.

74. Pythis: p. 79 with n. 16. Athena-head from Acropolis (661): Dickins *Cat.* 197f.; Payne and Young pl. 58; Langlotz in Schrader 132 no. 98 pl. 96; Richter *Korai* 83 no. 131, figs. 426ff. Aiakes's dedication: p. 75 with n. 9. Seated Athena from Acropolis (625): Dickins *Cat.* 160; Payne in Payne and Young 46f. pl. 116; Langlotz in Schrader 109ff. no. 60 pl. 85; Richter *AGA* fig. 261. See also next note.

75. Korai 670, 683: p. 104 with n. 70. 602: Dickins *Cat.* 136; Payne in Payne and Young 36, pl. 60, 1–3; Langlotz in Schrader 30 no. 7 pl. 13; associated with inscribed base: Raubitschek 491ff. The second name is damaged and is there read Philermos, but another base has been found with the sculptor's signature Philergos, and that is no doubt the correct restoration here: *AM* 84 (1969) 60 and 83ff., pl. 36.

76. Texts on Endoios: O. 348–53 (348, Pausanias I 26 4 seated Athena on Acropolis; 351, VII 5 9, statues at Erythrae, on which see further p. 108. Platean oath and Peace of Kallias: pp. 172 with Chapter 4 n. 26, 292 with Chapter 5 n. 2.

77. Potter relief (Acropolis 1332): Dickins *Cat.* 272; Payne in Payne and Young 48 pls. 129–30; Schuchardt in Schrader 301f. no. 422 pl. 126, fig. 349; *AM* 84 (1969) pls. 23b, 28. Rayet head and associated body fragments: p. 105 with n. 71; association with relief and painted statue-bases: pp. 226–7 with Chapter 4 n. 122. Siphnian friezes: pp. 153–7 with Chapter 4 notes 3–9. Attempts to reconstitute Endoios's personality: Rumpf in *C.d'A* 14 (1938) 41–8, pls. 29–32; Schefold *GP* 46ff.; Deyhle in *AM* 84 (1969) 12–39 (see above, n. 67).

78. Low relief: p. 56; in East Greece: p. 81 with n. 24. Hydra pediment: p. 91 with n. 45. Architectural low relief: p. 160 with Chapter 4 n. 13.

79. Archaic Attic grave-stelai: fully discussed and referenced in Richter *AGSA* with an epigraphical Appendix by M. Guarducci; on the inscriptions see also Jeffery in *BSA* 57 (1962) 115–53, pls. 32–41, with important matter on the monuments as well. Plain slabs on Geometric graves: p. 20 with Chapter 1 n. 14; seventh-cent. slab; Richter *AGSA* 9 fig. 27. Early sphinxes: Richter *AGSA* nos. 1–4, figs. 1–20; one, fig. 139; cf. also p. 102 with n. 65 (Sphinx from Spata). Contemporary capitals and shafts with incised patterns and inscriptions: Richter *AGSA* nos. 5–8, figs. 21–30. The Boeotian stele of Dermys and Kittylos (p. 60 with Chapter 2 n. 58) included by Miss Richter as no. 9, is of a totally different type, and does not justify the fanciful reconstruction (ibid. 14) of an Attic stele of this phase with a figure in relief on the shaft; though of course we cannot be sure that there never were such. Sphinx as 'Dog of Hades' in a Thessalian epitaph: Richter *AGSA* 6; but the inscription is now dated well into the fifth century: Jeffery 97ff. no. 8. Sphinxes dedicated on the Acropolis: Dickins *Cat.* 168f. no. 630, 176f. no. 632; Payne in Payne and Young 10, pls. 5–9; Schuchardt in Schrader 258ff. nos. 371f. pls. 164f. (other fragments nos. 373–6); *AM* 84 (1969) pls. 2, 1 (630, head), 18, 2 (632, head); Ridgeway *SS* fig. 53 (632).

80. Gorgon predella (Athens N.M. 2687): Richter *AGSA* 22 no. 27 figs. 83f.; other predelle: ibid. fig. 126 (chariot), figs. 154, 159, 163f. (horsemen). Grave-statues of women: Phrasikleia (p. 100 with n. 62); an inscribed base bears

the sandalled feet of a kore, a statue set up to a dead daughter and signed by a sculptor Phaidimos: Richter *Korai* 58f. no. 91 figs. 284f.; and see next note. Grave-stones in classical Athens: Chapter 6 (i).

81. Women's stelai: lost stone of Lampito, the base surviving with Endoios's signature and cutting for a wide slab: Jeffery in *BSA* 57 (1962) 130 no. 24 (cf. 121 no. 12, 129 no. 22, and remarks 149f., broader format for women's stelai because shown seated?); fragment from Anavysos with seated woman holding child: p. 99 with n. 59, p. 112 with n. 87; see also p. 199 with Chapter 4 n. 76. Endoios: pp. 106–8 with notes 74–7; pp. 226–7 with Chapter 4 n. 122. Phaidimos signed the statue-base mentioned in the last note (Jeffery l.c. 137 no. 44); a stele-base (Jeffery l.c. 118, no. 2) set up by a father to his son; and a stele set up to a brother and sister (Jeffery l.c. 139f. no. 48; Richter *AGSA* 25 and 157f. no. 35, fig. 102) of which only the lower part survives with the inscription in the place of a predella; see also Dörig in *AA* 1967, 15–18 figs. 99ff., convincingly ascribing to Phaidimos a number of works including the defaced youth's stele with the Gorgon predella (above, n. 80) and defining him as related to the Rampin Master but older, perhaps his teacher; also Deyhle in *AM* 84 (1969) 46–57. Kallonides signed a kouros-base found in Athens (Jeffery l.c. 131 no. 28). Aristokles: p. 110 with n. 84. Aristion of Paros: pp. 89 and 100 with n. 62. On all these sculptors and the letterers who worked with them see Jeffery l.c. 152.

82. Diskobolos-stele (Athens N.M. 38): Richter *AGSA* 21 no. 25 figs. 77f.; Karouzou *Cat.* pl. 7; assigned to the Rampin Master by Karouzos (*BSA* 39, 1938/9, 99ff.). Brother-and-sister stele (New York 11.185; Berlin A7): Richter *AGSA* 27 no. 37 figs. 96–109, 190 (inscription, 159ff. fig. 204, Jeffery *BSA* 57 (1962) 146f. no. 63), *Korai* 85 no. 137, figs. 439f., *MMCat.Sc.* 15 no. 15 pls. 15ff.; Berlin fragments: Blümel *Berl.Kat.Sk.* 8 no. A7 pls. 16ff.; other pictures: *AM* 84 (1969) pl. 1a (girl in Berlin); CMV fig. 123; Lawrence *S* pl. 12b; Richter *AGA* figs. 119–22, *H* 63 fig. 73, *Sc.* fig. 243. Youth's head in New York (42.11.36): Richter *AGSA* 35 no. 52 fig. 132, *MMCat.Sc.* 16 no. 17 pl. 21. Boxer-stele (Athens, Kerameikos Museum): Richter *AGSA* 23 no. 31 fig. 92; CMV fig. 123. Horsemen-base (Athens, Kerameikos Museum): P1001: Holscher pl. 9, 1. Other bases: p. 108 n. 77; pp. 226–7 with Chapter 4 n. 122. Stele set up by a mother: Jeffery l.c. 119 no. 7; a sister dedicates a monument of a different form: ibid. 147 no. 64. Brother and sister were named and probably shown on the stele signed by Phaidimos (last note), where the inscription is in the predella-position.

83. Capital from Lamptrai (Athens N.M. 41): Richter *AGSA* 18f. no. 10 figs. 66–9. Acropolis 683: p. 104 with n. 70. Samian stele-capitals: Buschor in *AM* 58 (1933) 22ff. with figs. and plate; their relation to Attic: Richter l.c. 37f. E. B. Harrison in *Hesp.* 25 (1956) 36ff.

84. Aristokles: Aristion's stele (Athens N.M. 29): Richter *AGSA* 47 no. 67 figs. 155–8, 180 (inscription, 170 figs. 211f.; Jeffery *BSA* 57, 141 no. 52, with parallels for the simple genitive); Karouzou *Cat.* pl. 8; CMV fig. 300; see also next note; inscribed base for statue of Tymnes: Jeffery l.c. 126f. no. 18; fragments of a life-size kouros found with this and another base in the Themistoclean wall: Richter *Kouroi* 137f. no. 161 bis, figs. 483f. Stele also illustrated: Richter *H* fig. 102, *Sc.* fig. 424; *KB* 213, 2; and often. Sabouroff head: p. 98 with n. 59.

85. Stele of Lyseas (Athens N.M. 30): Richter *AGSA* 48 no. 70 figs. 159f. (inscription, 170 fig. 215; Jeffery *BSA* 57 (1962) 141 no. 53); CMV fig. 358; Pfuhl *MuZ* fig. 487; Rumpf *MZ* pl. 22, 5. This and the stele of Aristion (last note) were found in 1838/9 in a cemetery of east Attica. Other painted stelai, some with engraved outlines: Richter *AGSA* nos. 24, fig. 79; 54, fig. 137; 57, figs. 138f.; 58, fig. 146; 71 figs. 163f.; 72, fig. 170; 73, fig. 167; with refs.; nos. 24 and 73 (Berlin A2 and 8) also illustrated in Blümel *AGSB* figs. 9 and 20.

86. Engraved and cut-out sphinxes (?akroteria) from the Acropolis (232; 3709): not in Dickins or Schrader; Wiegand *Porosarch.* 179 and pl. 11; Payne in Payne and Young 13 n. 1 and 68, pl. 17, 4–6. Delian pieces: *AM* 17 (1892) 43 no. 40 and fig. on p. 37; *BCH* 45 (1921) 234 fig. 4.

87. Stele in Copenhagen (I.N. 2787, from near

Athens?): Richter *AGSA* 50 no. 77 fig. 172. Mother and child from Anavysos (Athens N.M. 4472): Richter *AGSA* 42 no. 59 figs. 151ff.; *AM* 84 (1969) pl. 3, 2. Broad format for women's stelai: above, n. 81. 'Dying warrior' relief (Athens N.M. 1959): Karouzou *Cat.* pl. 12 and pp. 22f., with the view that it is not a gravestone; shared by Johansen *Att.Gr.* 103 n. 1, and Richter *AGSA* 42 n. 11. Other pictures: *KB* 213, 4; Richter *H* 76 fig. 97, *Sc.* fig. 84; Schefold *GP* pl. 63, and pp. 53f., accepting it as a gravestone and ascribing it to the school of Antenor (p. 103 with n. 67; pp. 162 and 186 with Chapter 4 notes 15 and 49); this connection also made by Karouzos *Aristodikos* 49. H. Wiegartz in *MWP* 1965 46–64, pls. 12–16, argues that it is a votive relief for a victory in the Pyrrhic dance (in armour); he gives good parallels for the position of the arms in dance-pictures, but I cannot see this as a dance. On the broad stele-form, see further p. 199 with Chapter 4 n. 76.

(*iv*) *Other sculpture of mainland Greece*

88. Kouroi from the Ptoion sanctuary: Ducat *KP*, full publication with other finds from the site; Richter *Kouroi* 48 no. 10 figs. 72–5, 64f. nos. 34–8 figs. 141–3 and 147–9, 99ff. nos. 94–8 figs. 302–15, 102 nos. 100–1 figs. 319–23, 122ff. nos. 145–7 figs. 425–35 and 437, 134 no. 155 figs. 450–7; CMV fig. 192. Other kouroi probably from Boeotia: Richter l.c. 64 no. 33 figs. 138–40, 66 no. 39 figs. 151–3, 101f. no. 99 figs. 316–18, 134 no. 156 figs. 458–60. Boeotian gravestone imitating Attic type (Boston 08.288): Richter *AGSA* 22 no. 28 figs. 80–2, 199. Dermys and Kittylos: p. 60 with Chapter 2 n. 58.
89. Megara colossus (Athens N.M. 13): Richter *Kouroi* 99 no. 92 figs. 297–9. Small kouros from Megara (Eleusis museum): ibid. no. 93 figs. 300–1.
90. 'Apollo of Tenea' (Munich 168): Richter *Kouroi* 84f. no. 73 figs. 245–50, *AGA* figs. 140f., *H* 56 fig. 60, *Sc.* figs. 22, 147; BDFH pl. 124 (108); CMV figs. 147f.; *KB* 220, 1; Lawrence *S* pl. 41a; Lullies and Hirmer pls. 34ff. (36ff.). Attribution to Corinth: Payne *NC* 237f., followed by Richter *Kouroi* 75; to Cleonae: Langlotz *FGBS* 69 no. 18 and 74; to Ionia: Pfuhl in *AM* 48 (1923) 162; to Attica (surely wrong): De Luca in *Arch.Class.* 11 (1959) 1ff. Corfu head: *AAA* 1 (1968) 67f. fig. 2. Seated marble sphinx from Corinth (head turned, as Attic grave-sphinxes): *AAA* 6 (1973) 181–7, figs. 1–7 (E. Protonotariou-Deilaki).
91. Torsos from Actium (Louvre NMB 767 and 766): Richter *Kouroi* 66f. no. 40 figs. 154ff., 85f. no. 74 figs. 255ff.; CMV fig. 146. Fragments from Epidaurus: p. 89 with n. 40.
92. Laconian relief-pithoi: p. 28 with Chapter 1 n. 32; sixth-century vase-painting: pp. 136f. with n. 138. Stele from Chrysapha (Berlin 131): Blümel *Berl.Kat.Sk.* A22 pl. 22, *AGBS* no. 16 figs. 42ff.; CMV fig. 183; Hausmann *GW* 24; *KB* 204, 3; Lawrence *S* pl. 11. Others: Tod and Wace 102ff., 133ff.; Blümel *Berl.Kat. Sk.* A13 pl. 25, *AGSB* no. 17 fig. 45. Four-sided relief: Tod and Wace 132f. no. 1 figs. 26f.; Richter *Sc.* fig. 465. Sicyonian metopes: pp. 67f. with Chapter 2 n. 72.
93. Sculpture inspired by small-scale work: p. 82 with n. 26; p. 116 with n. 96. Limestone carvings from Artemis Orthia: *AO* 185–95 pls. 63–7. Bathycles at Amyclae; Pausanias III 18 9 (O. 360); remains of 'Throne': Fiechter in *JdI* 33 (1918) 166ff.; Buschor in *AM* 52 (1927) 1ff.; Delivorrias in *AAA* 1 (1968) 43 figs. 4–6; Dinsmoor 141ff.; D. S. Robertson 104ff. Slavochori relief: Schröder in *AM* 29 (1904) 32–42 figs. 3f., 30 (1905) 409ff.; Fiechter l.c. 209f. figs. 54f.; Langlotz *FGBS* 137 no. 12 pl. 86a; see also Tod and Wace no. 655.

(*v*) *Sculpture in the West*

94. Doric in the West: Dinsmoor 75–86; D. S. Robertson 69–80, 86f.; Lawrence *A* 119–29. On the differences between western and mainland Doric see particularly Shoe *PGM* and *PWGM*; also p. 118 with n. 100.

95. A good conspectus of western Greek art in Langlotz and Hirmer. Sombrotidas's kouros: Richter *Kouroi* 112 no. 134 figs. 288–90; Langlotz and Hirmer pl. 7. Head from Laganello: Richter *Korai* 39 no. 41 figs. 135–8; Langlotz and Hirmer pl. 3. Monte Casale kore: p. 60 with Chapter 2 n. 58. Caltagirone relief: Langlotz and Hirmer pl. 13; comparable vases, Payne *NC* pl. 34, 1 (sphinxes and palmettes), 34, 2 (dancers); the relief mentioned ibid. 124.

96. The buildings at Foce del Sele and their sculptures: Zancani I (later building: temple) and II (earlier building: 'treasury'); further metopes from the 'treasury' discovered later: *AR 1960/1* 41 and *1963/4* 39 fig. 6 (Sisyphus). Eighteen appear to illustrate adventures of Herakles, eleven stories from the Trojan cycle. Turtle-rider (Odysseus suggested): Zancani II no. 27 pls. 90f.; mourners, no. 21 pls. 82f.; pursuit (?Dioscuri and Leucippidae), nos. 30f. pls. 99f. Other pictures: CMV figs. 132, 134f., 137 (all 'treasury'); Langlotz and Hirmer pls. 9–11 ('treasury'), 30f. (temple); von Matt *Gr.gr.* figs. 31–8 ('treasury'), 39–42 (temple); Richter *AGA* figs. 204ff. ('treasury'), 291 (temple), *H* 66 fig. 80 ('treasury'), 82 fig. 108 (temple). Pictorial frontality: p. 127 with n. 117. Paros dancers: p. 90 with n. 43. Sculpture influenced by small-scale work: pp. 82 with n. 26, 114 with n. 93. Argive bronze-reliefs: pp. 141f. with n. 145. Corfu frieze: p. 63 with Chapter 2 n. 64.

97. Terracotta relief from Reggio (Mus. Naz. 786c): Langlotz and Hirmer pl. II (colour).

98. Locrian terracotta reliefs and related marbles: pp. 202–9 with Chapter 4 notes 86ff.

99. Paestan temples: Dinsmoor 92–9; D. S. Robertson 71–81; Lawrence *A* 127ff.; Krauss *Paestum* and *DTP* I. See also p. 305 with Chapter 5 n. 34.

100. Temples at Selinus: Dinsmoor 78–84, 98f.; D. S. Robertson 71–81; Lawrence *A* 119–24. Heavy western mouldings: Shoe *PWGM*.

101. Metopes from 'Temple Y': Langlotz and Hirmer pl. 8 (Europa); CMV fig. 131 (Europa); *KB* 199, 2–3 (Europa and sphinx); Richter *AGA* figs. 200ff. (all three), *H* 65 fig. 78 (Europa).

102. Metopes from 'Temple C': Langlotz and Hirmer pls. 14f. (Kerkopes and Perseus); *KB* 199, 4–8 (all three and two other heads); Richter *AGA* fig. 203 (Perseus), *H* 65 fig. 3 (Kerkopes), *Sc.* fig. 405 (Perseus); CMV figs. 133 (Perseus detail), 135 (Kerkopes). Recutting of Perseus metope: Ross Holloway in *AJA* 75 (1971) 435ff. pl. 96. Terracotta gorgoneia: p. 66 with Chapter 2 n. 70. Newly found metopes: Tusa in *Arch.Class.* 21 (1969) 153–71 pls. 36–42 (goddesses), 43–7 (chariot). Man between horses (unwinged) on Argive shield-relief (p. 114 with n. 145): Kunze *AS* 61f. pls. 42 (XVa, 25a), 48 and Beil. 5.1; heraldic winged horses: ibid. 59f. pl. 58 and Beil. 3, 3–4 (other heraldic animals 54f. with refs.). Man between winged horses on Laconian cup: B.M. B2, cf. n. 138. Frontal chariots: p. 97 with n. 56 and p. 136 with n. 135. Ivory from Samos: *AM* 60/1 (1935/6) pl. 99, 2; BDFH pl. 71; Richter *AGA* fig. 63; Schefold *ML* pl. 17. Kerkopes metope from Foce de Sele; Zancani II no. 13 pls. 69ff. Kerkopes on Argive shield-relief: Kunze *AS* pl. 56 (XXIXa); Schefold *ML* pl. 61a.

103. Metope from Demeter sanctuary: CMV fig. 307. Metopes from 'Temple F': Benndorf *MS* pls. 5f.; *KB* 221, 7; Richter *Sc.* fig. 181.

(*vi*) *Painting and vase-painting*

104. Panels from Pitsa: Orlandos in *EAA* VI 201–6 (s.v. Pitsa); sacrifice, col. pl. at p. 202 (after a water-colour copy); the two larger-scale fragments, 204 figs. 225f. (the second must be very late sixth or early fifth century); other finds from the cave (terracottas, early archaic to Hellenistic; a fifth-cent. vase), 201ff., 205f., figs. 220–4, 227–9; the cave itself, 201 fig. 19.

The sacrifice-scene also illustrated: Hausmann *GW* 14 fig. 4; CMV fig. 357. See also *AA* 1934, 194; 1935, 197; Rumpf *MZ* 66. 'Conversation-piece': Philippaki *Vases of the National Museum, Athens* 71f. fig. 29.

105. Clay-pit plaque from Pente Skouphia: *AD* I pl. 8, 7; CMV fig. 80; Pfuhl *MuZ* fig. 186; other plaques from the site, below n. 108. Battle on C Painter's lekanis-lid in Naples (*ABV* 58 no. 119): Beazley *Dev.* pl. 10 and in *MMS* 5 108; CMV fig. 62; *Mon.Linc.* 22 (1913) pl. 7; cf. the painter's tripod-kothon, Louvre CA616 (*ABV* 58 no. 122): Beazley *Dev.* pl. 8, 1 and in *MMS* 5, 109; Arias and Hirmer pl. 48.

106. Amphiaraos vase (Berlin 1655; destroyed in the war): FR III pl. 122; Buschor *GV* 70f. figs. 81f.; CMV fig. 76; Pfuhl *MuZ* fig. 179; Schefold *ML* pl. 67a; and see Payne *NC* 139ff. and cat. no. 1471. Chest of Cypselus: p. 64 with Chapter 2 n. 66; pp. 140–1 with n. 144, 383 with Chapter 6 n. 63.

107. Harmonia's necklace in the fourth century: Ephoros (or his son Demophilos) quoted in Athenaeus 6.232.Eff. (*Frr.Hist.Gr.* II A 70 F 96).

108. Plaques from Pente Skouphia (mainly in Berlin and Corinth): *AD* I pls. 7f. (Timonidas 8, 13), II pls. 23f., 29f., 39f.; Pfuhl *MuZ* figs. 180–9; (Timonidas 182); Rumpf *MZ* pls. 13.7–8 (Timonidas), 17.9; Timonidas also: *EAA* VII 862 fig. 968. Timonidas's bottle (Athens N.M., C.C. 620): Buschor *GV* 67 fig. 78; CMV fig. 48; Payne *NC* pl. 34, 5, and see p. 103 and cat. no. 1072; Pfuhl *MuZ* fig. 174. Story of Troilos: p. 92 with n. 48. 'Herakles' plaque: Corinth, Museum. Terracotta altars: Broneer in *Hesp.* 16 (1947) 214–23, pls. 50–3; also *BSA* 48 (1953) 345f. pl. 64; *CV Robinson* I pl. 48; *Perachora* II 273 no. 2775 pls. 133f.; M. Robertson 78f.

109. Lion jug (B.M. B33; *ABV* 9, Gorgon Painter no. 13): Payne *NC* 192 fig. 86. Larger work by the same artist: e.g. amphora, Louvre E817 (*ABV* no. 7); Gorgon dinos, Louvre E874 (*ABV* no. 1): Arias and Hirmer pls. 35–7; BDFH pls. 89f.; CMV figs. 53, 55; *Enc.Phot.* 278; Pfuhl *MuZ* fig. 272; Rumpf *MZ* pl. 10, 1. See also p. 127 with n. 118 (Sophilos).

110. Evidence for a Corinthian vase-painter settling in Athens at a slightly earlier date: Dunbabin *BSA* 45 (1950) 193–202 figs. 1–4 and pls. 17f.

111. Metal volute-kraters and the connection with Laconia: see pp. 144–5 with n. 150. François vase (Florence 4209; *ABV* 76 no. 1): FR I pls. 1–3 and 11–13; Arias and Hirmer pls. 40–6; BDFH pls. 107–12 (91–5): Beazley *Dev.* pl. 11, 1–2 and see pp. 26–37; CMV figs. 6, 64–9; Milani in *Atene e Roma* 5 705–20; these are only a few of the refs.; see also following notes.

112. Undeformed pygmy on one of the Corinthian altars mentioned above, n. 108 (M. Robertson 79); deformed on a fragmentary Attic cup of the second half of the century (band-cup; below, n. 129) in Berlin (unpublished); see also *BSA* 43 (1948) 38 n. 9.

113. On the interpretation of the dance-picture, see Johansen *Thesée*. Theseus in Athenian art: pp. 163–4 with Chapter 4 n. 18. Centaur-battle at wedding of Peirithous: pp. 280–3 with Chapter 4 n. 222.

114. Weddings of Peleus and Thetis, Cadmus and Harmonia and others on Attic and other vases: Haspels in *BCH* 54 (1930) 1–30, especially 10–23. Loutrophoros: p. 371 with Chapter 6 n. 26. Second-hand pottery exported to Etruria: p. 133 with n. 130.

115. Troilos scene and Amphiaraos vase: p. 121 with n. 106; Troilos's story: p. 92 with n. 48.

116. Padded dancers common on Corinthian and Attic vases of early sixth cent.: Payne *NC* 118–202; Greifenhagen *EASV*; Seeberg *CKV*; Beazley *Dev.* 19–21. Sicilian relief: p. 116 with n. 95. Satyr-mask antefixes: p. 62 with Chapter 2 n. 63. Early representations of Dionysus and satyrs: Beazley *Dev.* 32, with notes 15f.; Brommer *Satyroi* and *Satyrspiel*. Classical sculpture and drama: pp. 170, 283, 354.

117. Dancer relief (Acropolis 702): Dickins *Cat.* 270f.; Payne in Payne and Young 49f. pl. 128, 3; Schuchardt in Schrader 311ff. no. 430 pls. 178f. and col. pl. VI; Langlotz and Schuchardt pl. 20; Hausmann *GW* 11, fig. 1. Relief from Paros in Munich: p. 90 with n. 43. Relief-fragment from Piraeus in Berlin: Blümel *Berl.Kat.Sk.* no. A9 pl. 20, *AGSB* no. 9 figs. 25f. Cf. also the mourners on the metope from Foce del Sele, p. 117 with n. 96. Muses in Hesiod's *Theogony* (75–9) and elsewhere (varied numbers): see p. 58 with Chapter 2 n. 54, p. 395 with Chapter 6 n. 94.

118. Fragmentary dinos by Sophilos (Acropolis 557; *ABV* 39 no. 15): Graef pl. 26; Buschor *GV* 102 fig. 117; CMV figs. 59–60; Pfuhl *MuZ* fig. 202. Virtually complete replica with stand in London (1971. 11–1. 1): see *Paralipomena* 19 no. 16 bis; Shefton in Arias and Hirmer 285; a publication is being prepared by Dr Ann Birchall. See also p. 131 with note 125. Significance of 'potter-signatures': see R. M. Cook in *JHS* 91 (1971) 137f.; M. Robertson in *JHS* 92 (1972) 180ff.; Stähler in *ÖJh* 49 (1971) Hauptblatt 79–113. Early Cycladic painter-signature: Shefton in Arias and Hirmer 279.

119. Introduction pediment: pp. 91f. with n. 47. Statue on vase (B.M. B49; *ABV* 326, middle): *CV* pl. 35, 2; Gerhard *AV* pl. 241; *JdI* 52 (1937) 39 fig. 5.

120. Signatures of Kleitias and Ergotimos: *ABV* 76ff. nos. 1, 7, and 12–15; 79, bottom (Ergotimos alone); with refs. Cups: *JHS* 49 (1929) 265ff. pl. 17.11–19 and 21–2 (Beazley and Payne): 52 (1932) 185f. (Beazley); 71 (1951) 143–6, fig. 1 (M. Robertson). 'Stand' with gorgoneion (New York 31.11.4; *ABV* 78 no. 12): Beazley *Dev.* pl. 11, 3; *Bull.Met.* 26, 290f.; Richter *MMH* fig. 37c; Richter and Milne fig. 189.

121. Acropolis 606 (*ABV* 90 no. 1): Graef pls. 30ff. and pp. 68f.; *BCH* 71/2 (1947/8) 424a and b; Beazley *ABS* pl. 4; *Dev.* pls. 13, 1–2 and 14, 1–2; CMV fig. 70.

122. Nearchos: *ABV* 82f. Aryballos with potter-signature and miniature decoration (New York 26.49; *ABV* no. 4): *AJA* 36 (1932) 273 pls. 10f. Gigantomachy kantharos (Acrop. 612; *ABV* no. 3): Graef pl. 36. Achilles kantharos (Acrop. 611; *ABV* no. 1): Graef pl. 36; Beazley *Dev.* 40 pl. 14, 2; CMV fig. 72; Lane *GP* pl. 45B; Pfuhl *MuZ* figs. 236f.; M. Robertson 59. On the signature: M. Robertson in *JHS* 92 (1972) 181 n. 5.

123. Chariot-harnessing as genre scene: e.g. Beazley *Dev.* pl. 36, 2 (Psiax, p. 217 with Chapter 4 n. 109); Buschor *GV* 115 fig. 132 (Exekias, pp. 131–5 with notes 126ff.); see also p. 364 with Chapter 6 n. 5. Moschophoros: p. 94 with n. 51.

124. Inscribed base with Nearchos's dedication and Antenor's signature, associated with kore 681: p. 104 with n. 67; pp. 162 and 186 with Chapter 4 notes 15 and 49. Dedicator described as τέκτων: Raubitschek 231 no. 196. Euphronios: pp. 212, 228 and 261 with Chapter 4 notes 116, 124 and 179. Tleson: *ABV* 178–83; Beazley *ABS* 17 and pls. 1, 4 and 5, 1, *Dev.* 55 and pls. 21, 2 and 22, 3, and in *JHS* 52 (1932) 172f. with fig. 5, 176f. with figs. 9f., 180, 184, 186, 191, 193 and 195f. Ergoteles: *ABV* 162; Beazley in *JHS* 52 (1932) 180, 192 and 200. Eucheiros and his son: *ABV* 162f.; Beazley *ABS* 17 and pl. 5, 2, *Dev.* 53, and in *JHS* 52 (1932) 169, 175, 176, 178, 192 and 200. Little Masters in general: Beazley *ABV* 159–97, *Dev.* 50–7, pls. 21f., and in *JHS* 52 (1932) 167–204, pls. 5f. and figs. 1–20.

125. Sophilos: p. 127 with n. 118; his plaques (Athens, Vlastos Collection; *ABV* 42 nos. 38–40): *AM* 62 (1937) pls. 48ff. Lydos: *ABV* 106–13; Beazley *Dev.* 39–49 and pls. 15–19; Rumpf *Sakonides* passim, but see Beazley in *ABV* 106, 114–32, 170ff. Plaques (Athens, Vlastos Collection; *ABV* 113 no. 84): Beazley *Dev.* 48 and pl. 19; CMV fig. 71; Rumpf *Sakonides* pl. 14. Prothesis-cup (Athens, Kerameikos Museum; *ABV* 113 no. 81): *AM* 59 (1934) Beil. 1 and pls. 1–3. Return of Hephaestus (column-krater, New York 31.11.11; *ABV* 108 no. 5): Beazley *Dev.* 44f.; Buschor *GV* 114 fig. 31; Richter in *AJA* 36 (1932) 96f. figs. 4f. and *MMS* 4 pl. 1; Rumpf *Sakonides* pls. 21–3. Psykter-amphora (B.M. B148; *ABV* 109 no. 29): *Bull.Met.* 27, 76; *CV* pl. 25, 5; *JHS* 19 (1899) pl. 6; *MMS* 4, 174; Richter and Milne fig. 89. Sphinx from Spata: p. 102 with n. 65.

126. Exekias: *ABV* 143–7; Beazley *ABS* 17–21, 29–31 and pls. 6f., *Dev.* 63–72, pls. 27–31; Technau *Exekias*; Mary Moore in *AJA* 72 (1968) 357–68, pls. 119–22; see also following notes, and p. 221 with Chapter 4 n. 115. Plaques (Berlin 1811–26; Athens 2414–17; *ABV* 146, nos. 22f.): *AD* II 5f. pls. 9f.; Arias and Hirmer pls. 60f.; BDFH pls. 116, 117 top (100, 101 top); Beazley *Dev.* 71f. and pl. 32; CMV figs. 114f.; Pfuhl *MuZ* fig. 298; Rumpf *MZ* pl. 12, 1–4; Technau *Exekias* pls. 14–18 and 19a–b; see p. 22 on the possibility that there were two sets, but the woman's prothesis and the mourning women are certainly from the same. Tombstone of Ampharete and grandchild: p. 366 with Chapter 6 n. 12.

127. Death of Ajax (Boulogne 558; *ABV* 145 no. 18): Beazley *ABS* 20 and pl. 17; *Dev.* 69 and pl.

32, 1; Buschor *GV* 119; CMV fig. 12; Pfuhl *MuZ* fig. 234; Rumpf *MZ* pl. 12, 11; Technau *Exekias* pl. 24; the chariot-scene on the back: *AJA* 72 (1968) pl. 120 fig. 3.

128. Warrior's departure (Orvieto, Faina 77; *ABV* 144 no. 10): Technau *Exekias* pls. 7f. and pp. 11f. (the interpretation is his). Warriors and horses (Philadelphia 4873; *ABV* 145 no. 16): Beazley *Dev.* 69 and pl. 31.

129. Komast cups: *ABV* 32ff.; Payne *NC* 194–201 with pl. 51, 6; Greifenhagen *EASG* with pls. 1f. Siana cups: *ABV* 51–75; Beazley in *MMS* 5, 93–115, *JHS* 51, 275–85. Gordion cups: above, n. 120, cups with signatures of Ergotimos and Kleitias. Little Master cups: (lip-cups and band-cups): above, n. 124. Corinthian Gorgoneion-cups: Payne *NC* 311 nos. 986–93 and pp. 102f., with pl. 32. Exekias's Dionysus cup (Munich 2044; *ABV* 146 no. 21): on the shape see Bloesch *FAS* 2 with pl. 1, 1; pictures: Arias and Hirmer pls. XVI and 59; Beazley *Dev.* pl. 27, 2; Buschor *GV* figs. 144f.; CMV fig. 116; FR I 227 and pl. 42; Lane *GP* pl. 41; Pfuhl *MuZ* fig. 231; M. Robertson 71; Rumpf *MZ* pl. 12, 6; Technau *Exekias* pls. 5f. Intentional red glaze: Farnsworth and Wisely in *AJA* 62 (1958) 165–73, pl. 36 and col. pl.; Noble 64 and fig. 205; see also p. 228 with Chapter 4 n. 125.

130. Ship-dinos (Villa Giulia 50599, M.446; *ABV* 146 no. 20, with the explanation of the inscriptions given in the text): Hoppin *BF* 105; *JHS* 78 (1958) 128 and pl. 15c (R. T. Williams); Pfuhl *MuZ* fig. 233; *WV* 1888 pl. 5, 3. Second-hand market: cf. p. 126 with n. 114. See now Webster *Potter and Patron*.

131. Tyrrhenian neck-amphorae (the same workshop occasionally produced other shapes): *ABV* 94–106; Bothmer in *AJA* 48 (1944) 161–70 pls. 3–6. Polyxena vase (B.M. 97.7–27.2; *ABV* 97 no. 27): *JHS* 18 pl. 15 and p. 283; *BICS* 17 (1970) pl. 1b, and pp. 11–15 with the story (cf. p. 92 with n. 48).

132. Penthesilea neck-amphora (B.M. B210; *ABV* 144 no. 7): Arias and Hirmer pls. XVIII and 64f.; BDFH pl. 117 (101) bottom; Beazley *Dev.* pl. 27, 1; Bothmer *Am.* pl. 51, 1 and pp. 72f.; CMV fig. 113; *CV* pl. 49, 2; Jacobsthal O. pl. 37a; Technau *Exekias* pl. 25.

133. Dioscuri amphora (Vatican 344; *ABV* 145 no. 13): Arias and Hirmer pls. XVII and 62f.; BDFH pl. 102; Beazley *ABS* pl. 6, *Dev.* pls. 28f.; Beazley and Ashmole fig. 45; CMV figs. 110f.; Cook *GPP* pl. 22; FR III 65, 71ff. and pls. 131f.; Lane *GP* pls. 44 and 45, 2; Pfuhl *MuZ* figs. 229f.; Richter *AGA* fig. 127; M. Robertson 60ff.; Rumpf *MZ* pl. 12, 5. Peplos kore: pp. 101–2 with n. 63: Moschophoros: pp. 94–6 with n. 51. 'Dying warrior' stele: p. 112 with n. 87.

134. Amasis and the Amasis Painter: *ABV* 150–8; Beazley *ABS* 21f., 31–6 with pls. 9, 1; 10, 1; 11, 1, *Dev.* 56–62 with pls. 23–6 and in *JHS* 51 (1931) 256–75; Karouzou *Amasis*. Possible rivalry of Exekias and Amasis: Beazley *Dev.* 61, bottom; M. Robertson 67; see also p. 111. Neck-amphora (Cab.Méd. 222; *ABV* 152 no. 25): Arias and Hirmer pls. XV and 56f.; BDFH pl. 115 (99); Buschor *GV* 117 fig. 133; CMV fig. 97; Cook *GPP* pl. 23; *CV* pls. 36f.; Jacobsthal O. pl. 75a; Karouzou *Amasis* pl. 31; Lane *GP* pl. 42; Pfuhl *MuZ* fig. 220; M. Robertson 63, 65. Cups (*ABV* 156f. 81–9): Beazley *Dev.* 56 and 61f. with pl. 26; Karouzou *Amasis* pls. 12, 1; 14, 1–2; 39; two exceptional ones (not Little Masters): Boston 10.651, *ABV* 157 no. 86, *AK* 12 (1969) pl. 7 (E. Vermeule): King's Point, Schimmel, *Paralipomena* 67, Hoffmann *Schimmel* no. 24. Vintage-amphora (Würzburg 265; *ABV* 151 no. 22): Langlotz *GVW* pls. 73f.; Arias and Hirmer pl. 55; BDFH pl. 113 (97); Buschor *GV* pl. 122; Karouzou *Amasis* pls. 25, 1; 28, 2; 29.

135. Frontal chariots: pp. 97 and 119 with notes 56 and 102; p. 138 with n. 141. Amasis Painter's chariot-oenochoe (B.M. B524; *ABV* 154 no. 47): *ABS* pl. 11, 1; *Festschr. Bloesch* 81ff. pl. 29; also p. 217 with Chapter 4 n. 108. Framing figures: Beazley in *JHS* 51 (1931) 259 ('Rosincrantz and Guildenstern' – they are most often two youths). Group E: *ABV* 133–43; Beazley in *BSA* 32 (1931/2; 1934) 3–8, figs. 1f. pls. 1ff. Affecter: *ABV* 238–48; Beazley *ABS* 22, 37, pl. 9, 2; Buschor *GV* 118 fig. 134; Pfuhl *MuZ* figs. 223ff. Elbows Out: *ABV* 248–51; Beazley *ABS* 23, 38, pl. 11, 2, and in *PBSR* 11 (1929) 4f. no. 4 pls. 1, 2; 3, 1; 4, 1f.

136. Other Attic painters and workshops of this phase: *ABV* 296–316; and see Beazley in *BSA* 32 (1931/2; 1934) 1–22, pls. 1–11; also p. 137

with n. 139. Later black-figure: pp. 214–21 with Chapter 4 notes 103, 107ff., 113.

137. Sixth-century Boeotian pottery: Cook *GPP* 101ff., pl. 28a; Ure *Sixth* passim; *CV* Reading pls 15–20; Richter *AGA* fig. 157. Eretrian: Cook *GPP* 103f.; Boardman in *BSA* 47 (1952) 1–48 pls. 1–14, 52 (1957) 22, pls. 1–27.

138. Laconian black-figure: Cook *GPP* 91–100, pls. 26f.; Lane in *BSA* 34 (1933/4; 1936) 128–85, pls. 28–48; Shefton in *BSA* 49 (1954) 299–310, and in *Perachora* II 378–85 pls. 158ff.; Pelagatti in *EAA* IV 445–50 figs. 516–24, and in *Ann.* 33/4 (1957) 11–44 figs. 3–12. Boread cup (Villa Giulia): M. Robertson 70. Arkesilas cup (Cab.Méd. 4899): Arias and Hirmer pls. XXIV and 74; Buschor *GV* 74f. figs. 84f.; *CV* pls. 20ff.; *EAA* IV fig. 521; Pfuhl *MuZ* fig. 193; Rumpf *MZ* pl. 14. Warrior-cup (Berlin 3404): Buschor *GV* 76 fig. 86; CMV fig. 81 (others figs. 42, 82–5, including Arkesilas); *EAA* IV fig. 522; *JHS* 59 (1939) pl. 10a; Pfuhl *MuZ* fig. 199.

139. Fikellura: Cook *GPP* 136ff. pl. 32b, and in *BSA* 34 (1933/4; 1936) 1–98 pls. 1–17, and B.M. *CV* fasc. 8, II D l pls. 1–14. Orchard cup (Louvre F68): Arias and Hirmer pl. 51; BDFH pl. 112 (96); Buschor *GV* 90 fig. 104; CMV fig. 104; Cook *GPP* pl. 33; *CV* fasc. 8 pl. 510, 3, 5 and 6; Lane *GP* fig. 21A; Richter *AGA* fig. 109; M. Robertson 69. Attic mourner (Vatican 350; *ABV* 140 no. 1): Albizzati *VV* pl. 44; Beazley *ABS* 21 and pl. 8, *Dev.* 74 and pl. 33; CMV fig. 109; Pfuhl *MuZ* fig. 290; Rumpf *MZ* pl. 12, 12; Technau *Exekias* pl. 29.

140. Clazomenian and related: Cook *GPP* 136ff. pl. 32B, B.M. *CV* fasc. 8 II D n pls. 1–13 (Clazomenian), 14 and some fragments on 7–10 (related), and in *BSA* 47 (1952) 124–52 pls. 29–33, with refs. Clazomenian sarcophagi: Cook *GPP* 138f., B.M. fasc. 8 II D q pls. 1–6 and p. 45, and in *JHS* 56 (1936) 58–63 and 128; Johansen in *Act.Arch.* 13 1–64, and *From the Coll.* 3 (1942) 123–43. Ionian Little Masters: Cook *GPP* 130f.; Kunze in *AM* 59 (1934) 81–122; see also Beazley *ARV*² 1967, Addendum to 1529.

141. Chalcidian: Cook *GPP* 157–60 pl. 36; Rumpf *Ch.V.*; H. R. W. Smith *Origin*; Walters-Karydi in *CV* Munich fasc. 6 pp. 23f., to pls. 280–8, with the remarkable theory that this is the continuation of the Cycladic 'Melian' group (pp. 28 with Chapter 1 n. 31, 55 with Chapter 2 n. 50) localised, like that according to Kontoleon (*AM* 73 (1958) 133ff.) in Paros; pictures: Buschor *GV* 79–86 figs. 89–98; Lane *GP* figs. 54B, 55B, 56f. Battle over Achilles's body (lost neck-amphora): Buschor *GV* fig. 92; Pfuhl *MuZ* fig. 163; Rumpf *Ch.V.* no. 5 pl. 12. Psykter-amphora, battle (Melbourne): Trendall *Felton* 5–8 pls. 1–4; CMV fig. 90; on the shape see below. Geryon neck-amphora (Cab.Méd. 202): Beazley and Ashmole fig. 41; CMV figs. 86f.; Lane *GP* pl. 56; Rumpf *Ch.V.* pls. 6–9; the frontal helmeted charioteer is on the back of this vase; similar heads in both battle-pieces cited and others, e.g. Rumpf *Ch.V.* pls. 139, 142. Phineus cup (Würzburg 354): Buschor *GV* 85 fig. 97; Langlotz *GVW* pls. 26f.; Pfuhl *MuZ* fig. 164; Rumpf *Ch.V.* no. 20 pls. 40–3. Psykter-neck-amphora with satyr and dancing nymph (Villa Giulia, Castellani 47): Rumpf *Ch.V.* no. 111 pls. 119, 118a. These *psykters* (wine-coolers) are in appearance amphora or neck-amphora but double-walled, the interior reached by the mouth, the outer compartment through a spout on the shoulder; a regular usage in Chalcidian, rare in Attic (an example p. 131 with n. 125, small psykter-amphora by Lydos); the psykter as an independent shape is a later invention: p. 221 with Chapter 4 n. 115. East Greek eye-bowls: Cook *GPP* 118; faces on other East Greek vases: M. Robertson in *JHS* 60 (1940) 10f. fig. 5g.

142. Caeretan hydriai: Cook *GPP* 160f.; Callipolitis in *Ant.Class.* 24 (1925) 348–411; Devambez in *Mon.Piot* 41, 29–62; Hemelrijk *De Caer.Hydr.*; Johansen in *Op.Rom.* 4 (1962) 61–81; Santangelo in *Mon.Piot* 44, 1–43; Webster in *JHS* 48 (1928) 196–205. Hydra (London, Count Seilern): *Mon.Piot* 44 8 fig. 6. Busiris (Vienna 3576): *Ant.Class* 24 (1955) pl. 4; Beazley and Ashmole fig. 46; Buschor *GV* 96 fig. 112; CMV fig. 107 (others 105f.); FR pl. 51; Masner no. 217 pl. 2; M. Robertson 76. Arimasp and griffin (B.M. 1923. 4–19.1): *JHS* 38 (1928) pls. 11, 1 and 12. Chiot pottery: pp. 28 with Chapter 1 n. 30, 55 with Chapter 2 n. 50. 'Situlae' from Daphne (Tell Defenneh): Cook *GPP* 139f., and in B.M. *CV* fasc. 8 II D m pls. 1–10. On the pottery from Naucratis and Daphne see especially Cook in B.M. fasc. 8, Appendices, with refs. to earlier discussions.

(*vii*) *Other and minor arts*

143. Vix Krater: p. 144 with n. 150. Beginnings of bronze statuary: Chapter 4 (iii); Rhoikos and Theodoros, pp. 148 with n. 156, 181 with Chapter 4 n. 41; Peiraeus kouros, p. 183 with Chapter 4 n. 43. Samian Heraion: also pp. 70 and 82 with notes 1 and 27.

144. Ephesus ivories: pp. 71–2 with n. 5. Figure with lion from Delphi: p. 23 with Chapter 1 n. 48; early classical bronze: p. 192 with Chapter 4 n. 61. Ivory and gold from Delphi *cache*: Amandry in *BCH* 63 (1939) 86ff. pls. 19–42, 64 (1950) 271f. pls. 18–20; de La Coste Messelière *D* 53 fig. 42 (ivory face), 54f. figs. 43f. (gold and ivory reliefs); Richter *AGA* figs. 197ff. (ivory reliefs); Schefold *ML* pl. 64b (ivory reliefs, Boreads pursuing Harpies and another). Chest of Cypselus: pp. 64 with Chapter 2 n. 66 and 121 with n. 106; 383 with Chapter 6 n. 63. Ivory Daughters of Proitos (New York 17.190.73): Dörig in *AM* 77 (1962) 72ff. Beil. 11, 1 (Thermon metope, Beil. 23, 2), and in BDFH p. 160 (94) and pl. 81 (65); Thermon metope, p. 160 fig. 116 (94, fig. 142); on the metopes, see p. 53 with Chapter 2 n. 45. Samos ivory and Selinus metope: p. 119 with n. 102. Figured designs on clothes: e.g. François vase (p. 124 with n. 111); Richter *H* 371, figs. 496f.

145. Shield-strips: Kunze *AS* passim (full account, with earlier refs.); inscriptions ibid. 212 (Argive); Corinthian inscription, Kunze in *Delt.* 17 (2) 120 and pl. 137c. Strip from Noicattaro: Gervasio *Bronzi arcaici* 109ff., pls. 15–18; see Kunze *AS* 231f. Figured shield-strip in Nearchos's vase-painting: Graef pl. 36, 612b (carried by goddess in Gigantomachy, p. 129 with n. 122); another on a fragment by the Kleophrades Painter (on whom see pp. 233ff. with Chapter 4 notes 135–41): *Hesp.* 35 (1966) pl. 10 no. 4 (see Ashmead, ibid. 27 n. 31, with refs. to comparable representations). Foce del Sele metopes: p. 116 with n. 96.

146. Delphi kouros: p. 40 with Chapter 2 n. 21. Olympia kore: pp. 84f. and 104 with notes 31 and 70. Chimaridas's Artemis: p. 101 with n. 62; Vix kore: ibid. and p. 144 with n. 150. Acropolis kouros (Athens N.M. 6443): Richter *Kouroi* 138 no. 162 figs. 474–7; attribution to Rayet master: Schefold *GP* 48 with pl. 89; Rayet master and Endoios: Deyhle in *AM* 84 (1969) 12ff. (see p. 105 with notes 70f.; pp. 187 and 226f. with Chapter 4 notes 9 and 122). Rayet head and Acrop. 643: p. 105 with n. 71.

147. Samos rider: Buschor *ASS* figs. 190ff., 198f.; Richter *AGA* figs. 257f. Grumentum rider (B.M. 1904. 7–3.1): Lamb pl. 39b. Mirror-handles: e.g. Langlotz *FGBS* pls. 15ff., 44, 46f., 54, 73; *Perachora* (1) pl. 34, 3–5. Mirror supported by naked girl (New York 38.11.3): Richter in *AJA* 42 (1938) 337–44, figs. 1–7; *MMH* pl. 22a (others, b–f).

148. Running girl (B.M. 208; from Albania?): *BMCat.Br.* pl. 3; Langlotz *FGBS* 88 no. 41 pls. 48a, 53 (Laconian). Banqueter (B.M. 1954. 10–18.1; from north Greece?): Haynes in *BMQ* 20 (1955) 36ff. pl. 12 (Peloponnesian – Laconian or Corinthian; late sixth century). Distinction of schools: see especially Langlotz *FGBS*; Attic: Niemeyer in *AP* 3 (1964) 7–31, pls. 1–33; South Italian and Sicilian: Jantzen *BWS*.

149. Tripod from Metapontum (Berlin Fr. 768): Lamb pl. 45a. Bronze vessels from Sala Consilina and Paestum: Vallet and Villard in *BCH* 79 (1955) 50–73, pl. 2. On the underground shrine at Paestum and its contents see Sestieri in *BdA* 40 (1955) 53–64 and *Archaeology* 9 (1956) 22f.; Neutsch *TNEH*; other pictures: *AJA* 59 (1955) pls. 85f. figs. 2–8; *AR 1954/5* (1956) 55f. figs. 8f.; black-figure vase: *Paralipomena* 170, Chiusi Painter no. 6 (belonging to the Leagros Group, p. 220 with Chapter 4 n. 113).

150. Bronze vessels from Trebenischte: Filow *Trebenischte* passim (suggesting a Corinthian origin); Payne *NC* 216ff. (supporting Filow's view), and in *Perachora* (1) 105 (withdrawing from Corinthian hypothesis in favour of Laconian). Vix krater (at Châtillon-sur-Seine): Joffroy *Vix* 6–30 pls. 4–18 (Tarentum?), and *Sépultures* 70ff. (Cumae?); *EAA* VII 1193ff. figs. 1335ff. Italian origin also claimed by Vallet and Villard in *BCH* 79 (1955) 50–73 (see last note) and Charbonneaux *Bronzes*. Attribution to Laconia: Rumpf in *B.Ant.Besch.* 29 (1954) 8ff. and *Charites* 127–35 (with the

suggestion that 'Laconian krater' means volute-krater); Jeffery 190f. and 375; to Argos: Delepierre *Sujet*; to Corinth: Gjødesen in *AJA* 67 (1963) 336–50 pls. 69–80 (mainly comparative material; he demonstrates the early dating). Graffiti describing fifth-century Attic column-kraters as 'Corinthian': Rumpf *Ch.V.* 123; Beazley in *AJA* 31 (1927) 350f. Bronze krater sent by Spartans to Croesus: Herodotus I 70. Attic black-figure 'Droop cup' from Vix tomb: Joffroy *Vix* pl. 26, 1; *ABV* 201, Wraith Painter no. 14.

151. Gitiadas: Pausanias III 17 2 (O. 357, Chalkioikos), 18.7 (O. 358, Amyclae; cf. IV 14 2 O. 359). Excavations in Chalkioikos sanctuary: Dickins in *BSA* 13 (1906/7) 137–54. Bronze-workshops at Samos: Jantzen *Gr.Gr.* 57ff.; at Olympia: *Ol.Ber.* I, 28ff., *JdI* 84 (1969) 1–28 figs. 1–30. On the question of workshops in sanctuaries see also Dunbabin in *Perachora* II Appendix I, 528ff.

152. Terracottas: see especially Higgins *GT* (East Greek girls pls. 13f.), and *BMCat.Terr.* I pls. 10, 12f. Plastic vases: see also p. 71 with n. 3; kneeling boy from Agora: p. 76 with n. 11.

153. Architectural terracottas: Van Buren *GFR* passim (the Thebes head, p. 133; fig. 120; fragments from Athens, pls. 13ff.). The Attic series: Buschor *Tondächer*; the Corinthian: Payne *NC* 248–62, figs. 106–12 (Calydon and Thebes heads, pl. 47, pp. 238ff.). Head from Olympia: *Ol.Ber.* I 95ff. pls. 26f.; Richter *AGA* figs. 289f. (other examples, figs. 244f.). See also *AJA* 52 (1948) 331–5, pls. 32f. (Richter), and 53 (1949) 262–6 (Weinberg, maintaining against Richter the idea that most large-scale terracotta sculpture in Greece is Corinthian). Plaques from Phrygia: BDFH 24 fig. 22 (26 fig. 28); see also Demangel *Frise* 130–56. See also pp. 62 with Chapter 2 n. 63, 117 with n. 97; pp. 170 and 277 with Chapter 4 notes 24 and 215, 592 with Epilogue n. 5.

154. Bronze-age seals: p. 10 with Prologue n. 28. 'Island Gems' and other early Greek seals: Furtwängler *AG* III 68ff. pl. 5 (and cf. pl. 4); and now especially Boardman *IG* passim; also Richter *EGGE* 27–44, nos. 1–69; *H* 237 fig. 343. Ivory seals: see also p. 22 with Chapter I n. 47. Bronze-age survivals: see also p. 20 with Chapter I n. 13.

155. On 'faience' scarabs, and the industry in general, see James in *Perachora* II 461ff. pls. 192f. with refs. Onesimos and Syries: Boardman *IG* 78ff. with refs.

156. Theodoros: O. 273–93 (considered as two artists of the same name, but probably wrongly: see Lippold in *RE* V A, s.v. Theodoros 195). See also p. 140 with n. 143; p. 181 with Chapter 4 n. 41. The lyre: Clement of Alexandria *Paid.* 3 59 (O. 310). Mnesarchos: O. 307f. (Diogenes Laertius and Apuleius); Herodotus (IV 95) names Pythagoras's father so but does not give his profession (see *RE* 2270ff. s.v. Mnesarchos 3 and 6); see also p. 211 with Chapter 4 n. 97. Caeretan hydriai: p. 139 with n. 142.

157. Archaic gems: Furtwängler *AG* III 69ff. with pl. 8 (and cf. pl. 7); and now especially Boardman *AGG* passim; also Richter *EGGE* 45–73 nos. 81–217. Youth with jug and cup: Boardman *AG* pl. 7, 97, and *Ionides* no. 1; Beazley and Ashmole fig. 216 (good late archaic pieces, figs. 217–21). Satyr: Boardman *AG* pl. 6, 93. Herakles: *Perachora* II 454 no. B24, pl. 191. Other pieces: Beazley *AGLH* nos. 14–35bis pl. 2 (comparative material, pl. A); *BMCat. Gems* pls. 8f.; Richter *Cat.Eng.Gems MMA* pls. 5–10.

158. Splendid pictures of coins and an admirable brief account of origins and history: Kraay and Hirmer (origin and purpose, 11f., 353ff., pls. 177f.). The late dating given there and accepted in the text is now generally received, but the old earlier dates are defended in Seltman *GC*[2]. Phanes: Kraay and Hirmer pl. 177 no. 585; Seltman *GC* pl. 1, 19. Deer's head on coin of Miletus: Kraay and Hirmer pl. 178 no. 591. Stag on fourth- and third-century coins of Ephesus: Kraay and Hirmer, pl. 179 nos. 600f. Apollo with deer on coins of Caulonia: Kraay and Hirmer pls. 90f. nos. 259–63. Stag on hand of Apollo at Didyma: Pliny XXXIV 75 (O. 406); and see p. 182 with Chapter 4 n. 44. Two good plates of archaic coins: BDFH pls. 137/8 (121/2).

159. Sixth-century East Greek coins: Kraay and Hirmer pls. 178f., nos. 589–98; 182, nos. 611f.; 196, nos. 686f.; 198f. nos. 702–6, 708–10. Aegina turtles: Kraay and Hirmer pl. 113, 335f. Boeotian shield: Kraay and Hirmer pl.

144 nos. 449, 453. Corinthian Pegasus and Athena-head: Kraay and Hirmer pls. 152f. Koppa in Corinthian: see Jeffery 32f., 116.

160. Athenian '*Wappenmünzen*': Kraay and Hirmer pls. 114f. (oil-jar, 114 no. 379); Seltman *GC* pls. 3, 8–11 (oil-jar), 12–15, 18–20 and 4, 8–12. Panathenaic festival: pp. 227–8 with Chapter 4 n. 144, 306, 346 and 359 with Chapter 5 notes 36, 131 and 168.

161. Athena-head and owl coins: Kraay and Hirmer pls. 116–19 (cf. 120). An owl in profile on a red-figure cup by Douris of the early fifth century (Vatican *ARV*² 437 no. 116); a profile Gorgon-head attached to a hairy monster led by Herakles on a black-figure skyphos of the same period from the Acropolis: Graef pl. 75, 1306.

162. Dating: Seltman *GC*² 43–53 (amphora Solonian; other *Wappenmünzen* between Solon and Peisistratus; first Athena/owl types Peisistratus, 566 B.C.; further *Wappenmünzen* during Peisistratus's exile in mid-century and during earliest phase of the Democracy after 510); Kraay in Kraay and Hirmer (*Wappenmünzen* Peisistratan; first Athena/owl Peisistratid); early dating defended by Cahn in *Mus.Helv.* 3 (1946) 133–43 fig. 1, and *Gr.Münze arch.Zeit* figs. 22ff.; Schefold in *Mus.Helv.* 22 (1965); see also Raven in *Essays ... Stanley Robinson* 58, n. 2. Laurion silver-mines: p. 172 with Chapter 4 n. 26.

163. 'International' coinages of northern Greece: Kraay in Kraay and Hirmer 328, 334f.; Macedonian pre-regal coins: pls. 123–6 (nymphs with jar pl. 123 no. 374); Thasian coins: pl. 140 no. 435.

164. Western Greek coinages: see pp. 210–11 with Chapter 4 notes 97f.

CHAPTER 4: THE GREAT CHANGE: LATE ARCHAIC AND EARLY CLASSICAL

(*i*) *Ripe and Late Archaic architectural marbles*

1. Herodotus III 57f. (Siphnian prosperity and the treasury; attack by Samian exiles linked to Spartan attack on Polycrates); III 39 (Spartan attack on Polycrates contemporary with Cambyses's invasion of Egypt).
2. Siphnian treasury: *FdeD* IV 2, 57–171. The building: Dinsmoor 138f.; D. S. Robertson 100 pl. 3a; Lawrence *A* 138 pl. 32. Sculpture: de La Coste Messelière *AMD* 237–476 pls. 20–49 (partly comparative), and *D* figs. 60–93; F. Poulsen *Delphi* 101–42 figs. 31–57. Pictures also: BDFH pls. 134f. (118f.); CMV figs. 199–207; *KB* 209f.; Lawrence *S* pl. 13; Lullies and Hirmer pls. 44–51 (48–55); Richter *AGA* figs. 162ff., *H* 79 fig. 104, *Sc.* figs. 93, 123, 382, 418f., 487. Caryatids: see pp. 84 (drum) and 89 with Chapter 3 notes 30 and 41. Frieze and pediment: see following notes.
3. On the continuous frieze, see Demangel *Frise*. Ephesus: pp. 83–4 with Chapter 3 n. 29; Corfu: p. 63 with Chapter 2 n. 64. Assos: p. 82 with Chapter 3 n. 25. Didyma: p. 85 with Chapter 3 n. 31. Prinias: p. 57 with Chapter 2 n. 53.
4. Inscriptions and subjects of eastern and northern friezes: de La Coste Messelière in *BCH* 68/9 (1944/5) 5–35, figs. 1–3; Mastrokostas in *Neon Athenaion* 1 (1955) 100f., and in *AM* 71 (1956) 74–82.
5. Interpretation of southern frieze: Poulsen *Delphi* 112ff. (rape of Leukippos's daughters, following Homolle); de La Coste Messelière *AMD* 360–88 (Pelops and Hippodameia; on that subject, see pp. 277–8 with n. 215). Cattle-raid on Sicyonian metope: p. 67 with Chapter 2 n. 72.
6. Subject of the west frieze: de La Coste Messelière *AMD* 392–412 (Judgement of Paris).
7. Three-quarter chariots in vase-painting and on the Siphnian frieze: White *Perspective* 11–22, pls. 1–2; see also p. 224 with n. 119. Foreshortened sails: White *Perspective* 20f. pl. 3a; shields, 21 pl. 3b; discus, 20 n. 2, 23 n. 2.
8. For a possible parallel, nearly contemporary, see p. 164 with n. 19.
9. Endoios and the Siphnian Treasury: p. 108 with Chapter 3 n. 77; see further p. 227 with n. 122. Aristion of Paros: pp. 89 and 106–7 with Chapter 3 notes 40 and 62.
10. Siphnian pediment: Ridgway in *AJA* 69 (1965) 1–5 pls. 1 and 2 (central figure identified as Zeus), and *SS* fig. 19. Struggle for tripod on

eighth-century tripod-leg: Kunze *NMO* figs. 4f.; Willemsen *OF* III pl. 63 (B1730). List of vases with the subject: Brommer *VL* 30–8.

11. Building: Dinsmoor 90; he thinks (71f.) that the limestone figures (p. 93 with Chapter 3 n. 49) adorned a building on the site of the Parthenon; D. S. Robertson 88 (with 81 fig. 34); Lawrence *A* 117. A recent discussion with refs. of the unsolved, perhaps insoluble, problem of the temples on the archaic Acropolis: Plommer in *JHS* 80 (1960) 127–49.

12. Gigantomachy fragments: Dickins *Cat.* 169–76 nos. 631, 4097f., 4100, 3074; Payne in Payne and Young 52ff. pls. 1–2 and 36–8; Schrader 245–77, figs. 405–68, pls. 185–97; Langlotz and Schuchardt figs. 61f.; other pictures: *AM* 84 (1969) pls. 24; 25, 1; CMV figs. 276f.; *KB* 214, 1; Lullies and Hirmer pl. 65 (69); Lawrence *S* pl. 17a; Richter *H* 80 fig. 105, *Sc.* figs. 112, 285.

13. Lion-head spouts: Payne in Payne and Young 50f. pl. 132; Schuchardt in Schrader 317 no. 439 pls. 180f.; Langlotz and Schuchardt figs. 59f. 'Frieze': Dickins *Cat.* 275–9 nos. 1342f.; Payne in Payne and Young 47f. pl. 27, 1–4; Schrader 387–99 nos. 474–9, pls. 198–200; CMV fig. 299; *KB* 214 fig. 2. Akroterion: Dickins *Cat.* 257 no. 694; Payne and Young pl. 119, 3–4; Langlotz in Schrader 116f. no. 67 pl. 90. Lions and bull: Payne in Payne and Young 54, pl. 17, 3; Schrader 377–87 figs. 469–96. Small animal-pediment (New York 42.11.35 and Athens N.M. 1673): Richter *MMCat.Sc.* 5f. no. 7 pl. 10; Karouzou *Cat.* pl. 11b.

14. The building: Herodotus v 62; Dinsmoor 91f.; D. S. Robertson 89. Sculpture: *FdeD* IV 3 and *D* figs. 140–9; Poulsen *Delphi* 143–57 figs. 58–73; other pictures: *AM* 84 (1969) pl. 11; CMV figs. 278f.; *KB* 215 figs. 1f.; Lawrence *S* pl. 17b; Richter *AGA* fig. 237, *Sc.* figs. 381, 384, 386f.; Ridgway *SS* fig. 27.

15. 'Kore of Antenor' and its relation to the Delphi sculptures etc.: p. 103 with Chapter 3 n. 67; Payne in Payne and Young 63ff. Note 2 questions the relation between the kore and the temple-sculptures; see however Harrison in *Agora* 11, 7ff.; Deyhle in *AM* 84 (1969) 39 (pls. 9f.); Tyrannicides: pp. 185–6 with n. 49. Acropolis Theseus group: Dickins *Cat.* 99ff. nos. 145, 370; Payne in Payne and Young 43f. pls. 105f., 107, 4; Schuchardt in Schrader, 281ff. pls. 155ff.; Langlotz and Schuchardt fig. 23; CMV fig. 280.

16. Megarian Treasury: the building: Dinsmoor 105ff.; D. S. Robertson 45, n. 2; Lawrence *A* 118 n. 5. Sculpture: *Ol.* III 5–15 pls. 2–4; *KB* 221, 8; Richter *AGA* fig. 237, *H* fig. 283.

17. Cyrene: *Ol.* III 19–23 figs. 18ff. pl. 4h. Massalia: *FdeD* IV 2, 25–55, figs. 10–28, pl. 3. Cyrene and the lion on Laconian cup: FR III 212 fig. 102; Pelagatti in *Ann.* 33/4 (1955/6) 42ff. fig. 42.

18. The building: Dinsmoor 91; D. S. Robertson 72; and see p. 305 with Chapter 5 n. 34. Sculpture: *AD* III pls. 277ff.; Furtwängler *Aigina* 321–6, with important discussion; Konstantinu in *AM* 69/70 (1954/5) 41–4, publishing two fragments in Chalcis (Beil. 22f.) as well as attributing the Amazon-figure in Rome (pls. 3–6); this independently ascribed to the gable by Bothmer *Am.* 124 no. 2 pl. 67, 2, with an interesting discussion of the remains, pointing out that Antiope was standing in the chariot; his chapter VIII (124–30 with pls. 67f.) deals comprehensively with representations of the story (cf. p. 168 with n. 23). Other pictures of Eretria gable-fragments: Beazley and Ashmole fig. 52; *KB* 215, 7; Lullies and Hirmer pls. 62ff. (66ff.); Richter *AGA* fig. 250, *Sc.* figs. 281, 284, 442. See also next note.

19. Inscribed fragment of chariot-rail: Furtwängler *Aigina* 325. Signature on Siphnian frieze: p. 157 with n. 8. Names inscribed below metopes of fourth-century Temple of Athena Alea at Tegea: p. 453 with Chapter 7 n. 18; above and below Pergamene Gigantomachy: p. 540 with Chapter 8 n. 94.

20. Temple of Aphaia on Aegina: Furtwängler *Aigina*. The building: Dinsmoor 105ff.; D. S. Robertson 112; Lawrence *A* 144f. Other pictures of the sculpture: BDFH pls. 162–7 (146–51): Beazley and Ashmole fig. 54; CMV figs. 232–7; Karouzou *Cat.* pl. 13; *KB* 222ff.; Lullies and Hirmer pls. 73–83 (82–7); Richter *AGA* figs. 249–51, *H* 82f., figs. 109f., *Sc.* figs. 103, 113f., 186, 388f., 525. Theory of 'bronze-clad' pediment: Ridgway *SS* 14 (pictures, figs. 1, 3–10, 12). Preliminary report on removal of restorations: Ohly in *AA* 81 (1966) 515–18, figs. 1–12.

21. Aphaia: Pausanias II 30 3. Unspecified heroic

battles at Aigina: Beckel *Gött.* 80f. A beardless (whiskered) Herakles in the struggle for the tripod on a late-sixth-century Attic vase (*ARV* 23, Phintias no. 2; Arias and Hirmer pl. 93); see also pp. 237 with n. 143, 273 with n. 207.

22. Bronze head from Acropolis: p. 184 with n. 46. Dying warrior from Aegina: Furtwängler *Aigina* pl. 97, bottom; Richter *Sc.* fig. 186; Ridgway *SS* fig. 10. Selinus head: CMV fig. 308; Richter *Sc.* fig. 181; and see p. 120 with Chapter 3 n. 103.

23. Athenian Treasury: Pausanias x 11 5; *FdeD* iv 4 (1957, de La Coste Messelière). The building: Dinsmoor 117; Lawrence *A* 143f. Sculpture: de la Coste Messelière *D* figs. 123–7; Bothmer *Am.* 117ff. with discussion and refs.; Harrison in *Agora* 11 9ff., suggesting the intermediate date. Other pictures: CMV figs. 328–31; Lullies and Hirmer, pl. 79; Richter *AGA* fig. 232, *Sc.* figs. 124, 406–9; Ridgway *SS* fig. 2.

24. Pediment at Thebes: Curtius in *AM* 30 (1905) 375ff. pl. 13; Furtwängler *Aigina* 501 fig. 408; Bothmer *Am.* 117. Terracotta pediment at Corinth: Stillwell in *Class. Studies ... Capps* 318–22 figs. 1–4; Bothmer *Am.* 116 pl. 66, 1; see also p. 146 with Chapter 3 n. 153; pp. 277 with n. 215, 592 with Epilogue n. 5.

25. See p. 113 with n. 17.

(ii) Sculpture at Athens in the time of the Persian wars

26. Laurion mines: cf. p. 150 with Chapter 3 n. 163. Plataean oath: Lycurgus *c. Leochratem*; cf. Diodorus xi 29, Pausanias x 35 2; see Meiggs 'The political implications of the Parthenon' in *Parthenos and Parthenon* (Suppl. to *Greece and Rome* 10 (1963) 36–45; see also p. 107 with Chapter 3 n. 76. Peace of Kallias: ibid.; and for fuller refs. see p. 292 with Chapter 5 n. 2 (cf. n. 5; also Chapter 6 n. 64). Walling and terracing on the Acropolis: Hill *Athens* 147–51; but see also p. 294 with Chapter 5 n. 5. Dedications on Acropolis between Persian sack and Periclean rebuilding: e.g. relief with 'Mourning Athena', p. 178 with n. 35; Pheidias's colossal bronze Athena Promachos appears to have been dedicated in the sixties (pp. 285 with n. 229 and 320 with Chapter 5 n. 67).

27. Kore of Euthydikos (Acrop. 686 and 609): Dickins *Cat.* 241–4; Payne in Payne and Young 40ff. pls. 84–8; Langlotz in Schrader 77–80 pls. 45–9 (the design of chariots p. 79 fig. 44); Langlotz and Schuchardt figs. 36ff.; Richter *Korai* 99f. no. 180 figs. 565–72; other pictures: BDFH pl. 181 (165); Beazley and Ashmole fig. 48; CMV fig. 317; *KB* 219 figs. 3–5; Lawrence *Sc.* pl. 23a. Acropolis 643: p. 105 with Chapter 3 n. 71.

28. 'Fair-haired boy' (Acrop. 689): Dickins *Cat.* 248ff.; Payne in Payne and Young 45f. pls. 113–15; Schuchardt in Schrader 197f. no. 302 fig. 187 pls. 125f.; the body-fragment (no Acrop. number; brilliantly identified by Bieber in *AM* 37 (1912) 151ff. with pls. 9f.), ibid. pl. 127 below; fragment of a right foot (Acrop. 424a) associated, ibid. 198f. fig. 188; the relevance of the body-fragment is doubted by some who thinks it belongs to a figure on a larger scale. The head also illustrated; Langlotz and Schuchardt figs. 45f.; Richter *Kouroi* 149 no. 191 figs. 570f. (body fragment, figs. 572ff.); BDFH pl. 180 (164); Beazley and Ashmole fig. 68; CMV fig. 318; *KB* 218, 5f.; Lawrence *S* pl. 23b. See also pp. 180 with n. 40, 290 with n. 239.

29. 'Kritian boy' (Acrop. 698): Dickins *Cat.* 264ff.; Payne in Payne and Young 44f. pls. 109–12; Schuchardt in Schrader 191–5 no. 299 figs. 183–6 pls. 120–3; Langlotz and Schuchardt pls. 42ff. (see also pl. 41); Richter *Kouroi* 149 no. 190 figs. 564–9; other pictures: BDFH pl. 178 (162); Beazley and Ashmole fig. 68; *KB* 219, 1; Lullies and Hirmer pls. 85ff. (89ff.); Richter *H* fig. 84, *Korai* pl. xx, e–f; Ridgway *SS* figs. 41, 43f.

30. Aristodikos (Athens N.M. 3938): Karusos *Aristodikos*; Richter *Kouroi* 139 no. 165 figs. 489, 492f.; *AM* 84 (1969) pl. 5, 3; Karouzou *Cat.* pl. 15; Ridgway *SS* fig. 40. 'Strangford Apollo' (B.M. B475): *BMCat.Sc.* 1 i 204f. pl. 43; Richter *Kouroi* 136 no. 159 figs. 461ff.; Beazley and Ashmole fig. 47; Lullies and Hirmer² 88.

31. Tyrannicides: pp. 185–7 with n. 49.

32. 'Marathon Nike' (Acrop. 690): Dickins *Cat.*

250–3; Payne and Young pl. 120, 1–2; Langlotz in Schrader 122f. no. 77 figs. 80–3 pls. 91f.; Raubitschek 18ff. no. 13 (dedicatory inscription and its connection with the statue), and in *AJA* 44 (1940) 55 (ascribing it to same hand as kore of Euthydikos); the inscription (*IG* I^2 609) also, Shefton in *BSA* 45 (1950) 140–64; Harrison in *GRBS* 12 (1971) 5–24; Meiggs and Lewis *Selection* no. 18 Bronze *kerykeion*-fragment: Hampe in *Die Antike* 15 (1939) 168–74 figs. 1–4. The statue also illustrated: Richter *H* 76, fig. 98. Upper and lower parts do not join and are set too far apart in the reconstruction and pictures. Assimilation of Victory to other deities: pp. 212 with n. 99, 348 with Chapter 5 n. 137. Running girl in Eleusis: Willemsen in *AM* 69/70 (1954/5) 33–40 Beil. 19 and 20r (cf. Beil. 20, l and 21, pls. 1f.); Himmelmann-Wildschütz in *MWP* 1957 9ff. figs. 20ff.; Ridgway *SS* figs. 36f., 156.

33. Marathon mask (Berlin 100): Blümel *Berl.Kat.-Sc.* III K 2, *AGSB* no. 12 figs. 29f., 32f. (cf. 31); Weickert *GP* 37 fig. 19; Wrede in *AM* 53 (1928 pls. 2f., Beil. 23, 2); ascribed to same hand as kore of Euthydikos and fair-haired boy: Ashmole in *JHS* 56 (1936) 249. Pan on Attic vases: Brommer in *Marb.Jb. für K.* 15 (1949/50) 5–42, figs. 14–38; other representations, ibid. figs. 1–13 (3f., *kerykeion*-fragment, last note) and 39–52; Boardman and Pope pl. 2. Cave of Pan at Marathon: *AR 1957* 4, and especially *AR 1958* 6; *BCH* 82 (1958) 681–6 figs. 27f., 83 (1959) 587ff. figs. 10–15. See also p. 376 with Chapter 6 n. 41 (Acheloos, ibid. n. 40).

34. Archaic Attic grave-reliefs: pp. 108–12 with Chapter 3 notes 79–87; continuation of tradition outside Attica; p. 197 with notes 73f.; classical tombstones in Attica and law putting an end to them: pp. 363–82, Chapter 6 (i) with notes, especially 8. Sunium relief (Athens N.M. 3344): BDFH pl. 179 (163); Buschor and Hamann fig. 28; *Die Antike* I pl. 34; Karouzou *Cat.* pl. 18; Langlotz *FGBS* 155f. no. 20 pl. 11; Lullies and Hirmer pl. 92 (96); Ridgway *SS* fig. 70, and pp. 49f., interpreted as a grave-relief and considered post-Persian; head from south slope (Athens, N.M. 1949): Karouzou *Cat.* pl. 21b; Langlotz *FGBS* pl. 87r.

35. Relief-fragment from Acropolis: (Acrop. 1350): Dickins *Cat.* 281; Payne in Payne and Young 50, pl. 125, 4; Schuchardt in Schrader 315 no. 433 fig. 358. See also pp. 202–3 and 210 with notes 87, 96. 'Mourning Athena' (Acrop. 695): Dickins *Cat.* 258ff.; BDFH pl. 186 (170); Br.Br. pl. 783; Carpenter *Gr.Sc.* 144 (interpreted as a boundary-stone); Lullies and Hirmer pl. 137 (134); Richter *Sc.* fig. 206; Ridgway *SS* fig. 69; Schrader *Phidias* 92 fig. 75.

36. Herakles's head from Agora: Harrison *Agora* II pp. 12 and 37 no. 97A pl. 18.

37. Euenor's Athena (Acrop. 140): Dickins *Cat.* 93; Langlotz in Schrader 48f. no. 5 pls. 9ff.; Raubitschek 26ff. no. 22 and in *BSA* 40 (1943) 31–6; Ridgway *SS* fig. 39. Euenor's kore (Acrop. 318 and 344, 497): Raubitschek 28f. and in *BSA* l.c 30f. figs. 33, 33A; Langlotz in Schrader 149 no. 156 (no illustration), 172f. no. 254 fig. 160. Euenor, Parrhasios, Pheidias etc.; Raubitschek 496ff. and in *BSA* l.c.

38. Propylaea kore (Acrop. 688): Dickins *Cat.* 246; Payne in Payne and Young 40 with n. 2 pl. 89 (early classical); Langlotz in Schrader 62f. no. 21 pls. 30ff. (just before or just after 480); Beazley and Ashmole 34 fig. 69 (post-Persian); Ridgway *SS* fig. 46 and p. 31 (probably post-Persian).

39. Samos torso: Richter *Kouroi* 143 no. 176 figs. 518ff. with refs.; placed in Ptoon 20 Group (the last group of true kouroi) but as noted by its earlier publishers, Wiegand (in *AM* 25 (1900) 153f. no. 6 with fig.), Bieber in *AM* 37 (1912) 157 fig. 2 and Buschor (in *ASS* I 54 figs. 204ff.), the kouros-structure is abandoned, and it properly belongs with the figures treated in Richter's Epilogue. Bronze Poseidon from near Plataea: p. 183 with n. 45.

40. Schools of Argos and Sicyon: see further remarks p. 197 with n. 72. Bronze head of youth from Acropolis (Athens N.M. 6590): BDFH pl. 182 (166); Ridgway *SS* fig. 178; Langlotz *FGBS* 81f. no. 17, pl. 43r; Langlotz attributes the fair-haired boy (ibid. 69 no. 25 and 73ff. with pl. 39) to his School of Cleonae, to which he also gives the earlier bronze kouros-statuette from the Acropolis (ibid. pl. 35b; p. 142 with Chapter 3 n. 146).

(iii) Bronze statuary and Roman copies

41. Texts on the very confused subject of Rhoikos and Theodoros (p. 148 with Chapter 3 n. 156) collected by O., nos. 262, 273–93, 311. Rhoikos is generally called the son of Phileas and Theodoros of Telekles, but Diodorus I 98 (O. 279) speaks of Telekles and Theodoros sons of Rhoikos, statuaries who learned from Egypt; he seems to have in mind the kouros-type rather than any technical skill. Diogenes Laertius II 103 (O. 282) likewise calls Theodoros son of Rhoikos; and O. distinguishes an older and a younger Theodoros, but the separation is not easily made. A Theodoros is named as an architectural colleague of Rhoikos in another connection (Pliny XXXVI 90, O. 283; cf. XXXIV 82, O. 292), and as author of a book on the Heraion (Vitruvius VII praef. 12, O. 274) which probably implies his collaboration in that (cf. p. 328 with Chapter 5 n. 86). Temple of Hera at Samos: p. 82 with Chapter 3 n. 27. Two Polycrates: Barron in *CQ* 14 (1964) 210–29; cf. *BICS* 16 (1969) 119ff. (Barron) and 17 (1970) 11ff. (M. Robertson).

42. Technique of bronze-casting: Kluge and Lehmann-Hartleben I; Haynes in *AA* 1962, 803ff. (most important as establishing the practice of piece-moulding in Greece in the first half of the fifth century) and in *RA* 1968, 101–12 (including observations on the distinction between fine detail put in on the model and that added at the end on the cold bronze).

43. Piraeus kouros (Athens N.M.): Richter *Kouroi* 136 no. 159bis, figs. 478ff., with refs.; classed as transitional between Anavysos-Ptoon Group and Ptoon 20 Group, whose dividing line is set about 520 B.C. See further below, n. 45.

44. Cult-statue of Apollo at Delos: p. 47 and 58–9 with Chapter 2 notes 34 and 54. Kanachos: O. 329, 403–10, 418. There is no direct statement about his date, but his Apollo was at Didyma (on the temple see p. 85 with Chapter 3 n. 31) by 494 B.C. and was certainly purely archaic in scheme. He seems to have been thought of as younger than Rhoikos and Theodoros and older than Kalamis (p. 184 with n. 48) who can be placed in the early classical period. Antenor: pp. 103–4 and 130 with Chapter 3 notes 67 and 124; pp. 162–85 and 227 with notes 15, 49 and 123.

45. Piraeus *cache*: Orlandos in *Ergon* 1959/60 161ff.; another figure from it, pp. 386 and 410 with Chapter 6 notes 72 and 132. Sullan sack: pp. 413 with Chapter 6 n. 141, 560 with Chapter 8 n. 113. Piraeus kouros not archaic: P. E. Corbett tells me he and others have doubts. Piombino Apollo: p. 560 with Chapter 8 n. 148. Herculaneum head (Naples): Br.Br. 506; Langlotz *FGBS* 33 no. 41 pls. 22f. Zeus-head from Olympia (Athens N.M. 6440): *Ol.* IV pl. 1. Youthful head from Acropolis: p. 180 with n. 40. Poseidon from Kreusis-Livadhostro, near Plataea (p. 180 with n. 39; Athens, N.M. 11761): *Eph.Arch.* 1899, 57–74 pls. 5f.; Lippold pl. 37, 1; Bulle *SM* pl. 39; Buschor and Hamann pl. 35; as illustrated the figure is heavily restored, but recent cleaning shows torsion and movement as part of original design. Artemision figure: p. 196 with n. 69. Zeus from Dodona (Berlin 10.501): Lamb pl. 54a; Neugebauer *AB* fig. 28; *JHS* 54 (1934) 166 fig. 3; others collected by Schwabacher (see below, n. 70). Herakles from Perachora (Athens N.M.): Payne in *Perachora* (I) 140f. pl. 45, and in *JHS* l.c. 164 fig. 2. Herakles (Athens, Benaki Museum): Payne in *JHS* l.c. pl. 7 and 163 fig. 1.

46. Mould from Agora: *Hesp.* 6 (1937) 82f. fig. 43 and 343f. fig. 8 (later bronze-foundry in the same neighbourhood, 341f. fig. 7). Foundry-cup (Berlin 2294; ARV^2 400 no. 1 with refs.): *CV* 2 pls. 72f., 76, 4; H. Thompson in *Essays ... Lehmann* 323–8 figs. 1–3 (cf. figs. 4, 5), interpreting the statues as Achilles the warrior and the runner, in harmony with the interior tondo. Aegina sculptures: pp. 165–7 with notes 20ff.; Aeginetan bronze-school: pp. 184 and 197 with notes 48 and 72. Bronze head from Acropolis (p. 167 with n. 22; Athens N.M. 6446): BDFH pl. 152; *KB* 221, 5; Lawrence *S* pl. 22a.

47. 'Leonidas' (Sparta, Museum): Richter *Sc.* fig. 104. Olympia warriors: *Ol.* III 30 (cf. p. 48 with Chapter 2 n. 37). Relief from Amyclae: *AM* 51 (1926) 41ff. fig. 1 and pl. 1; see also p. 197 with n. 73.

48. Pythagoras: O. 489–507 (refs. to the Samian, 499 and 507); spoken of by Diogenes Laertius (VIII 46; O. 507) as not far removed in time from his namesake the philosopher; by Pliny (XXXIV 59; O. 499) as a successful rival of Myron (pp. 339–45 with Chapter 5 notes 112ff.; his dates also uncertain, but he perhaps worked across the mid-century); by Pausanias as making a statue of a victor in the Olympic games in the seventy-third, -fourth and -fifth Olympiads, which fell in the eighties and seventies of the fifth century; a passage of Pliny which brackets him with a motley crew in the ninetieth Olympiad (419–416 B.C.) is incapable of rationalisation; see also p. 591 with Epilogue n. 1. Kalamis: O. 508–32; one of his commissions (Pausanias VI 12 1; O. 524) was a group to celebrate a victory of Hieron of Syracuse in 464; another, a statue dedicated by Pindar (518–438 B.C.); see also p. 190 with n. 56. Aeginetan school: O. 416–42; Kallon and Kanachos are spoken of as near-contemporaries (Pausanias VII 18 10; O. 418); and both are referred to as stiffer or harder (more archaic) than Kalamis, with whom Onatas worked on Hieron's dedication (Cicero *Brut.* 18 70; O. 529; and Quintilian XII 10 7; O. 530).
49. Tyrannicides: literary refs.; O. 443–7 (Antenor), 457–62 (Kritios and Nesiotes). Inscriptions of Kritios and Nesiotes and of Antenor: Raubitschek nos. 120–3, 160 and 197, and pp. 481–3, 513–17. Monograph with refs.: Brunnsåker; chest to chest arrangement: Shefton in *AJA* 64 (1960) 173–9 pls. 49–52. Late dating of Antenor's group: Raubitschek in *AJA* 44 (1940) 53; convincingly against this, Rumpf in *Festschr. . . . Mercklin* 131–51. 'Webb head' (B.M. 2728; perhaps after Antenor's Harmodios): *BCH* 17 (1893) pl. 12, 3; Langlotz *FGBS* pl. 62B; recently, with bibliography, Dörig in *AK* 12 (1969) 41–50 pls. 25, 1–2 and 26, 1–2, with a discussion of Roman copies after lost archaic works; cf. Langlotz in *AM* 71 (1956) 49–52 (attempt to identify a copy of the head of Antenor's Aristogeiton). The Naples group also illustrated: BDFH pl. 177 (161); Richter *Sc.* figs. 565ff.; Ridgway *SS* figs. 115ff.; and constantly.
50. Ostia Themistocles: Richter *GP* I 99ff. figs. 413–25, with refs.; also illustrated *H* 91 fig. 120; Ridgway *SS* fig. 137; and see further below, notes 51f. Heads from Aegina and Selinus: p. 167 with n. 22; similar heads in vase-painting: pp. 223, 263 and 265 with notes 117, 184, 187.
51. Picture of Themistocles in the Parthenon: Pausanias I 1 2; his sons also dedicated on the Acropolis a bronze statue of Artemis Leukophryene, the name by which she was known at Magnesia (Pausanias I 26 4; O. 928). Shield of Parthenos: pp. 314–16 with Chapter 5 notes 52–5. Marathon picture: pp. 244 with n. 151, 323 with Chapter 5 n. 74.
52. 'Greco-Persian' portraits: pp. 506–7 with Chapter 8 n. 8; cf. also p. 111 with Chapter 3: n. 84. Themistocles's monument at Magnesia. Thucydides I 138; see Rhousopoulos in *AM* 21 (1896) 18–26, with coin (fig. on p. 22). The figure seems bearded like the head from Ostia, but wreathed which the head is not: he stands at a circular altar, the forepart of a sacrificial beast at his feet; but if the figure is based, as it looks, on a statue, these could be additions of the coin-designer.
53. 'Pausanias' type: Richter *GP* I 99ff. figs. 413–25; L'Orange in *Mélanges Picard* 668ff. figs. 1ff.; the 'naturalistic' version (Oslo 2) also, Bielefeld in *AA* 1962, 70–89 figs. 1–6. The bronze statues at Sparta: Thucydides I 134, Pausanias III 17 7 and 9. Epicurus: pp. 524–5 with Chapter 8 n. 57. Armed satyrs: neck-amphora attributed to the Kleophrades Painter (p. 233 with notes 135–41); Harrow School Museum 55; *ARV*[2] 183 no. 11 with refs.; Beazley *Kl.* pl. 9, 1–2.
54. Charioteer: Chamoux *FdeD* IV 5 (1955) with full illustration, discussion and refs. Dating: ibid. 26–31; Wade-Gery in *JHS* 53 (1933) 101ff. The figure is constantly illustrated, e.g.: BDFH pls. XXVII and 172 (156); Beazley and Ashmole fig. 66; de La Coste Messelière *D* pls. 151–61; *KB* 237, 3 and 4; Lawrence *S* pl. 26; Lullies and Hirmer pls. 98–101 (102–4); Richter *H* 85 fig. 113, *Sc.* figs. 162, 285; Ridgway *SS* figs. 47f. See also notes 55, 57.
55. Fragments of the Delphi group: *FdeD* IV 5 pls. 3–6; de La Coste Messelière *D* pl. 158 (horse's legs) and p. 35 fig. 25 (small arm). Olympia horse: *Ol.Ber.* I pls. 60ff.; Lullies and Hirmer pl. 104 (106); Richter *AGA* fig. 299.

Horse in New York: Br.Br. 726 *Bull.Met.* (1923) 39ff.; Richter *Animals* figs. 62f., *MMH* pl. 46. Acropolis horses: p. 98 with Chapter 3 n. 57. Olympia horses: p. 291.

56. Kalamis's horses: O. 525–8; see also p. 184 with n. 48. Bronze horse from the Artemision wreck: p. 558 with Chapter 8 n. 145.

57. Pythagoras: p. 184 with n. 48. Sotadas: Hampe in Br.Br. pls. 786–90, pp. 22f.; the connection dismissed by Chamoux *FdeD* IV 5 34–8; he himself ascribes the work to Kritios, ibid. 77–82.

58. Hestia: Beazley and Ashmole 35 and fig. 30; Br.Br. 491; *KB* 231, 4; Richter *Sc.* fig. 257; Ridgway *SS* fig. 103; (copy in conservatori) and see V. Poulsen *St.St.* 123; also below, n. 60. Herms: p. 285 with n. 230.

59. Madonna del Parto (Monterchi, cemetery): e.g. Clark *Piero della Francesca* pls. 99f.; Risen Christ (Borgo San Sepolcro): ibid. pls. 11–14. Olympia sculptures: section vii. Hermes (Acropolis Museum 1346): Casson *Cat.* 250ff.; Bieber in *AM* (1912) 174–7, pl. 13; copies: Florence, Contini: Arndt–Amelung 318 (with false head): Leningrad: *AM* ibid. 174 fig. 4, Reinach *Rep.* III 32, 1; see also p. 473 with Chapter 7 n. 69.

60. Amelung in *RM* 15 (1900) 181ff.; Orlandini *Calamide* 92ff. with refs. Pictures of Amelung's reconstruction: e.g. Beazley and Ashmole fig. 71; *KB* 236, 5 and 6. Statuette from Hama: Ingholt *Rapp.Prél.* 25 pl. 7, and see below, n. 63. Statue from Baiae: Napoli in *Boll.d'Arte* 39 (1954) 1–10 figs. 1–8 and 12; also BDFH pl. 170 (154); V. Poulsen in *Berytus* 6 (1959/60) 1ff.; Ridgway *SS* figs. 106–8 (105, another copy of the head). Orlandini, Napoli and others identify the figure with a famous work by Kalamis, the 'Sosandra', which Lucian describes as on the way up to the Acropolis at Athens, and which is probably identical with a statue of Aphrodite by that master which Pausanias saw in the same area; but see p. 193 with n. 63. Hestia's feet: see V. Poulsen *St.St.* 123 Copies of Greek ideal statues with portrait-heads: pp. 598 and 605 with Epilogue notes 23 and 39.

61. Mirror-supports and other early classical small bronzes with fluted skirt: e.g. Lamb pls. 55b, 57a–c; Langlotz *AMG* pls. 88, 92; *FGBS* pls. 8, 24ff., 73; Neugebauer *ABS* fig. 36; Richter *H* 208 figs. 211f. Nearest parallel to Amelung's goddess (from Italian Locri): Charbonneaux *Bronzes* 86 pl. 21, 2; Langlotz *AMG* pl. 91; Matt *Gr.* figs. 134f.; Ridgway *SS* fig. 110. Delphi figure: Rolley in *FdeD* v no. 199 pls. 44–7; Will in *Mon.Piot* 40 (1944) 53–68 figs. 1–4 pls. 5f.; also illustrated *BCH* 64/5 (1940/1) pl. 20; Richter *H* 185 fig. 280.

62. L. Forti *Danzatrici*; Ridgway *SS* 134, 144f. no. 9, figs. 170f.; *KB* 235, 5–7; Richter *Sc.* figs. 260, 497.

63. See M. Robertson in *JWCI* 20 (1957) 1ff. pl. 1a (the figure from the vase), b and c (the inscribed statuette) and d (the Hama statuette). The vase (Adolphseck, Landgraf Philipp von Hessen, *ARV*² 1346, Kekrops Painter no. 1): *CV Cassel, Schloss Fasanerie* 1 pls. 46ff.; see also p. 420 with Chapter 6 n. 161. Inscribed statuette (New York 24.97.31): Richter *MMCat.Sc.* 25f. no. 30. The sarcophagus (Cliveden): *JHS* 20 (1900) pl. 8b–d; the appearance of this figure on it and its significance noted by Prof. Evelyn Harrison. Aeschylus's *Carians*: see Lloyd-Jones in *Aeschylus*, Loeb² vol. 2 (1957) 599ff.

64. See pp. 338–9, 388 and 465–6.

65. Choiseul-Gouffier: *BMCat.Sc.* no. 209 (head from Cyrene, ibid. no. 210; another replica no. 211). Omphalos (Athens N.M. 45): Karouzou *Cat.* pl. 24. Both often pictured: e.g. BDFH pl. 176 (160; both); Beazley and Ashmole fig. 65 (Choiseul-Gouffier); *KB* 233, 9 (Choiseul-Gouffier); Richter *H* 87 figs. 115f. (Omphalos), *Kouroi* 151 no. 97 figs. 589–91 (Omphalos); Ridgway *SS* figs. 96 (Choiseul-Gouffier), 94f., 97 (Omphalos). There are many replicas: see V. Poulsen *St.St.* 136–9; Ridgway *SS* 61–70.

66. Conservatori 'charioteer': recent discussion in Ridgway *SS* 134f. and 147 with figs. 172f. (perhaps a pastiche) following Homann-Wedeking (*RM* 55 (1940) 214ff.) and Steuben and Zanker (*AA* 1966, 68–75, with refs.); Hafner *Gesch.gr.K.* 148ff. figs. 133, 134, 136, suggests Theseus and the bull of Marathon; Guerrini (*Arte Classica* 11 (1959) 171–8 pl. 41) Theseus and Antiope; Paribeni, more convincingly, that the figure should be tilted forward and is Theseus lifting the rock (*Bull. Comm.*

Arch.Rom. 74 (1951/2) 13–18; against this Sourvinou-Inwood in *JHS* 91 (1971) 108 n. 60).

67. Bronze torso (Florence, from Leghorn): Richter *Kouroi* 150 no. 195 figs. 585–8. Bronze torso (New York 20. 194): *Bull.Met.* (1923) 32f.; *AM* (1935/6) 201ff., 212, pls. 77ff. Miletus colossus (Louvre MND 2792): Richter *Kouroi* 149f. no. 192 figs. 579–81; *Enc.Phot.* 150. Oxford torso: Richter *Kouroi* 150 no. 194 figs. 577f. Gortyn fragment (Herakleion 37): Richter *Kouroi* 143 no. 177, figs. 525f. Roman date for Miletus torso?: Ridgway *SS* 40 no. 9. Acropolis fragment: p. 175 with n. 28. Originality in Roman Asia Minor: pp. 541–3 with Chapter 8 notes 97f., 608 with Epilogue notes 48–51.

68. Chatsworth head (B.M. 1958.4–18.1): *JHS* 58 (1938) 90–5 pls. 2–9 (Wace); ibid. 255 (M. Robertson); *AJA* 66 (1962) 317f. (Schuchardt, with the suggestion that it is Hadrianic; see also p. 202 with n. 85); *RA* (1968) 101–12 (Haynes, with full technical description and discussion).

69. Artemision god (Athens, N.M. 15161): Karusos in *Delt.* 13 (1930/1) 41–104 pls. 1–5. Beyen *Artemision*; other pictures: BDFH pls. XXVIII and 173–4 (158–9); Beazley and Ashmole figs. 67, 67bis; Karouzou *Cat.* pl. 23; Lullies and Hirmer pls. 132f.; Ridgway *SS* figs. 98f.; and often. See also next note.

70. Pre-Pheidian cult-statue at Olympia: Schwabacher in *Archaeology* 14, 104–9 figs. 1–8, *AK* 5 (1962) 9–17 pls. 4–8, and *RM* 72 (1965) 209ff., replying to Gross, ibid. 70 (1963) 13. 'Myron's Erechtheus': V. Poulsen in *Act.Arch.* 11 (1940) 41f. (also 10f. fig. 17 and pls. 1f.). Myron: pp. 339–45 with Chapter 5 notes 112–22. Pheidian Zeus: pp. 316–22 with Chapter 5 notes 59–66.

71. See pp. 209–10 with n. 96.

72. Sources for the Argive school: O. 388–402 (Ageladas, 389–99); for the Sicyonian: see also pp. 180, 182 and 184 with notes 40, 44, 48 (Pythagoras, Kalamis and the Aeginetan school). Hegias (Hegesias): O. 420, 422, 452–6, 530. Modern attempts to reconstruct schools: Langlotz *FGBS*; V. Poulsen *St.St.*; Beyen and Vollgraf *Argos et Sicyone*; sensible criticism of the methods in Ridgway *SS*.

(*iv*) *Sculpture in North, East and West*

73. Archaic tombstones: pp. 108–12 with Chapter 3 notes 79–87, 178 with n. 34. Cessation in Attica and spread elsewhere in the early fifth century: Richter *AGSA* 53ff.; Johansen *AGR* 120–45. Later Attic series: pp. 363–82 with Chapter 6 notes 2 and 9ff.; cessation: p. 365 with Chapter 6 n. 8. Fragment from Amyclae: p. 184 with n. 47. Stele from Nisyros (Istanbul, 1142): Mendel *Cat.Sc.* 1 no. 11; BDFH pl. 185 (169) left; Johansen *AGR* 127 fig. 62; *RA* 39 (1901) 158ff. pl. 15; Ridgway *SS* fig. 61; Schede *Meist.* pl. 6.

74. Alxenor (Athens, N.M. 39): Johansen *AGR* 123 fig. 59; *KB* 212, 5; Lawrence *S* pl. 27b; Richter *AGA* fig. 255, *H* 78 fig. 103, *Sc.* fig. 425. Naples stele: Br.Br. 416; *KB* 212, 4. Stele of Anaxandros from Apollonia Pontica (Sofia): *AM* 1896, 136f.; *JdI* 17 (1902) pl. 1; *KB* 212, 3. Stele of Agasinos from Korseia: *AM* 4 (1879) 271 pl. 14, 2 (cf. *AM* 3 (1878) 313 no. 7).

75. Thasian reliefs: *Enc.Phot.* 25, 148ff.; *Ét.Thasiennes* I *Les Murailles* pls. 3, 13, 16, 26ff., 34–7, 42 and pp. 47 fig. 15, 50 fig. 16, 87 fig. 34, 89 fig. 35, 114 fig. 47; see also p. 377 with Chapter 6 n. 45.

76. Thessalian stelai: Biesantz *TG* (excellent full account and discussion, with all the other sculpture from the area collected and related). Stele from Pharsalos (Louvre 701): Biesantz *TG* 22 no. 36 pl. 17; Br.Br. 58; *Enc.Phot.* 147; Johansen *AGR* 141f. fig. 73; Langlotz *FGBS* pl. 10; Ridgway *SS* fig. 68; Hampe in *BWP.* 107 (1951) argues that the flowers are really a form of knuckle-bone, and that both figures are standing; against the knuckle-bones, Besque in *Rev. des Arts* 1953 57; the standing restoration is widely accepted (Biesantz l.c.; Richter *AGA* 157 n. 135) but rejected by Schefold *Meist.* 222 no. viii 249 (fig. on p. 219) and pp. 59f. Relief from Phalanna with two standing girls: Biesantz *TG* 7 no. 4 pl. 18. Stele of Kineas and Phrasimeda: Biesantz *TG* 18f. no. 30 pls. 19f. (fragment of another similar, 23 no. 38 pl. 20). Attic fragment (Athens N.M.

36): *BCH* 4 (1880) pl. 6; Conze 20 pl. 12; Johansen *AGR* 139f. fig. 72; Richter *AGSA* fig. 174, *Korai* fig. 445 (no. 141); Svoronos 87f. no. 36 pl. 31, 2. Acropolis relief (581): Dickins *Cat.* 118ff.; Payne in Payne and Young 48f. pl. 126, 1; Schuchardt in Schrader 304f. no. 424 pl. 175. Laconian reliefs: p. 114 with Chapter 3 n. 92.

77. Oxford metrological relief: *JHS* 4 (1883) pl. 4 and pp. 335–50; *Hesp.* Suppl. 8, 338 n. 10; Langlotz *FGBS* 183 no. 16. Melos disk (Athens, N.M. 3990): Karusos in *JHS* 71 (1951) 96ff. pl. 37; BDFH pl. 184 (168) top and p. 130 (identification as the Moon); Karouzou *Cat.* pl. 17; Lullies and Hirmer pl. 136 (138).

78. Seated statue from Paros: Ashmole *GSSSI* fig. 82; Rösch *Alt.Marm.* pl. 1. 'Tubular' folds: p. 78 with Chapter 3 n. 16; p. 203 with n. 87. Nike: BDFH pl. 183 (167) left; Lippold *GP* pl. 39, 2; Ridgway *SS* figs. 56, 58.

79. Nisyros stele: p. 197 with n. 73; Kos orgy: Laurenzi in *Cl.Rh.* 9, 73–80 figs. 46–8 and pl. 6; Lippold pl. 66; *AM* 77 (1964) Beil. 35 and pp. 124ff. (Karusos, arguing for funereal use).

80. Miletus torso: p. 195 with n. 67. Lion Tomb at Xanthos: p. 82 with Chapter 3 n. 26.

81. Metzger *Xanthos* II 77–84.

82. Harpy Tomb (B.M. 94): *BMCat.Sc.* I i 122ff., B287, pls. 21–4; Demargne *Xanthos* I 37–47; *KB* 208, 4–6; Lawrence *S* pl. 29, 1; Richter *AGA* fig. 272; Ridgway *SS* figs. 127f.

83. 'Building F', cock-and-hen frieze (B.M. 82): *BMCat.Sc.* I i 137ff. B299–306, fig. 183; Metzger *Xanthos* II 74f. pl. 48, 1; gable (B.M. 93): *BMCat.Sc.* I i 130f. B289 pl. 25; Metzger *Xanthos* II 70–5 pl. 48, 2. 'Building H', sphinx-gables (B.M. 89–92): *BMCat.Sc.* I i 132ff. B290–1, figs. 180ff.; Metzger *Xanthos* II 66 pl. 47; Ridgway *SS* fig. 38. 'Building G' or 'temple': Metzger *Xanthos* II 49–61, pls. 30–41; internal frieze (B.M. 86f.): *BMCat.Sc.* I i 142ff. B309f. fig. 186 and pl. 29; Metzger *Xanthos* II 57ff. pl. 41, 2–3; Ridgway *SS* fig. 33; external frieze (B.M. 86): *BMCat.Sc.* I i 144ff. B311–14 pl. 31; Metzger *Xanthos* II 52ff. pls. 38f.; Ridgway *SS* fig. 34; plinth frieze (B.M. 81): *BMCat.Sc.* 134–7 B92–8 pl. 38; Metzger *Xanthos* II 50 pl. 33, 1; statues (B.M. 96ff.): *BMCat.Sc.* I i 147f. B316ff. pls. 32f. (torsos); M. Robertson in *BMQ* 13 (1938/9) 39f. pl. 18 (head-fragment); Metzger *Xanthos* II 51 pls. 35f. (torsos and new head-fragment; this has been shown to join, as Marcadé suggested, the head-fragment in the B.M.).

84. Greek work and influence in Achaemenian Persia: Richter in *AJA* 50 (1946) 15–30, figs. 1–28 (sketches on shoe, fig. 26), *AGA* 178ff. fig. 273; Boardman *GO* 118–22 fig. 33 and pl. 7c (shoe).

85. Seated goddess (Berlin 1761): Blümel *Berl.Kat. Sk.* 16ff. no. A17 pls. 33–8, *AGBS* 29–33 no. 21 figs. 55–61 and 65; BDFH pl. 171 (155); Langlotz and Hirmer pls. 50f.; Lawrence *S* pl. 24; Lullies and Hirmer pls. 93–7 (97–101); Richter *AGA* fig. 286, *H* 75 fig. 96, *Sc.* figs. 65, 161; Ridgway *SS* fig. 125. Ludovisi colossus (Rome M.N.): Paribeni *Cat.* II no. 1 fig. 1a and b; Ashmole *GSSSI* 26 figs. 66, 74; Langlotz and Hirmer pls. 62f.; Ridgway *SS* fig. 157. Apollo of Crimisa (Cirò; at Reggio): Orsi *TAA* 135–70 pls. 16–20; Ashmole *GSSSI* 25 figs. 60f., 63; Langlotz and Hirmer pls. 118f.; Matt *Gr.Gr.* figs. 160ff.; Ridgway *SS* fig. 158; Schuchardt in *AJA* 66 (1962) 317 pl. 85 (making it Hadrianic; but see Ridgway l.c. 122f.; and cf. p. 196 with n. 68).

86. Locrian reliefs: Zancani-Montuoro in *AMSMG* n.s. 1 (1954) 71–106 pls. 13–20, and *ASCL* 24 (1955) 283ff.; Ashmole *GSSSI* 15–18, figs. 24–8; Langlotz and Hirmer pls. IX and 71–5; Matt *Gr.Gr.* figs. 137, 140ff., 144–9 and pl. at p. 11; Richter *H* 226 fig. 333 and 367 fig. 489; Ridgway *SS* fig. 129f.; Prückner *Die lokrische Tonreliefs*; Ridgway and Scott in *Archaeology* 26 (1973) 43–7. Painted votive plaques from Corinth: pp. 121 and 123 with Chapter 3 notes 105, 108; from Athens: p. 131 with Chapter 3 notes 125f.; p. 226 with n. 121. Relief-plaques from Athenian Acropolis: Casson *Cat.* 414–25, nos. 1320ff.; Melian reliefs: p. 209 with n. 95.

87. Esquiline stele (Rome, Conservatori): *Cons.Cat.* 212f., Arc. 5 pl. 80; Lawrence *S* pl. 27, 1; Richter *AGA* fig. 285, *H* 97 fig. 128. Villa Albani relief: Br.Br. 228; Johansen *Att.Gr.* 141 fig. 74; *KB* 208, 3; Lawrence *S* pl. 28; Ridgway *SS* fig. 126. Laconian reliefs: p. 114 with Chapter 2 n. 92. 'Tubular' folds: pp. 78–9

with Chapter 3 n. 16, 199–200 with n. 78 (statue from Paros). Pediment-figures from Selinus: Ashmole *GSSSI* 29 and figs. 80f.; *Mon.Linc.* 32 (1927) pls. 25f. Acropolis fragment: p. 178 with n. 35; p. 210 with n. 96.

88. The literature of the 'thrones' is vast. These are some readily available pictures; for some of the more important discussions, see n. 90. Ashmole *GSSSI* figs. 29 (Boston, main face) and 84 (Ludovisi, detail of goddess's head); *KB* 238, 1–6 (all faces of both); Lawrence *S* pls. 30ff. (Ludovisi; Boston, main face and detail of old woman's head); Paribeni *MNCat.Sc.* 12f. no. 3, fig. 3a–c (Ludovisi with refs.); Richter *Sc.* figs. 474–9 (all faces of both; details also figs. 183ff., 189, 289); Simon *Geburt* figs. 1–4 and 9 (Ludovisi), 34–7, 41–3 and p. 92 (Boston).

89. Relief from Gortyn: p. 58 with Chapter 2 n. 54. Ivories: p. 54 with Chapter 2 n. 30. Bronzes: p. 143 with Chapter 3 n. 147. Female nudes in vase-painting: p. 234 with n. 138; in narrative sculpture: pp. 319 and 358 with Chapter 5 notes 64 and 164; in substantive statuary: pp. 390–3 with Chapter 6 notes 82–6.

90. Interpretations of Ludovisi (Rome M.N. 8670): Aphrodite: Petersen in *RM* 7 (1892) 32ff., and very many since, including Simon *Geburt* with the interpretation of Boston discussed in the text, and a valuable collection of parallel material (vases with Aphrodite received by Eros, figs. 23–5, 28 with cloth, 29; Persephone rising, figs. 9 and 30; analogous scenes, figs. 6, Erichthonios delivered by Earth and received by Athena in her aegis, 7 and 31; silver gilt medallion from Galaxidi in Louvre, Aphrodite received by Eros with cloth, 26; on this see also p. 318 with Chapter 5 n. 63). Persephone: Ashmole in *JHS* 42 (1922) 243–53; Paribeni in *MNCat.* 12ff. no. 3. Ritual bath: Casson in *JHS* 40 (1920) 137ff.; Langlotz *Lud.Rel.*; Kardara in *AM* 76 (1961) 81ff. with useful refs. to earlier literature. Birth-scene: Wolters in *Eph.Arch.* 1892, 227ff. (goddess or heroine); Klein *Gesch.gr.Kunst* I (Leto); and other variations, including Carpenter in *MAAR* 16 (1951) 41ff. (Eileithyia).

91. Psychostasia: Homer *Iliad* 208–13; no relevant fragment of the *Aethiopis* survives, and no certain fragment of Aeschylus's play. Vases with Psychostasia: Simon *Geburt* (cf. last note) figs. 45–50.

92. Simon *Geburt* passim (cf. last two notes).

93. Authenticity of Boston attacked: von Gerkan in *ÖJh* 25 (1929) 125–72, and 39 (1952) 51; Quarles van Ufford in *B.Ant.Besch.* 2 (1936) 1–16; Picard *Manuel* II 142. Circumstances of finding of Boston: Nash in *RM* 66 (1959) 104–37. Deposit under the base of Boston: Ashmole in *Bull.MFA* 63 (1965) 59ff. with figs. Boston a Roman work: van Essen in *Med.Ned. Hist.Rom.* 17 (1937) ascribing it to Pasiteles; Colin in *RA* 25 (1946) 23–42, 139–72 (Tiberian); Johnson in *AJA* 60 (1955) 57 and 61. The Ludovisi also ascribed to Pasiteles: Zadoks-Jitta in *RA* 36 (1950) 152f. Boston by a local sculptor of Italy, Ludovisi imported or by a sculptor from Greece: Ashmole in *JHS* 42 (1922) 243–53, *GSSSI* 18; so also Buschor, Pfuhl, Rumpf, Carpenter, Demangel, Langlotz and Rodenwaldt, cited by Möbius in *Charites* 47–58, a full argument with refs. of this position, though not ruling out the possibility that Boston might be false. Piombino Apollo: p. 183 with n. 45; p. 560 with Chapter 8 n. 148. Head from the south slope: p. 178 with n. 34.

94. 'Metopes of Modena': e.g. Venturi *Storia* III (1903) 147; *Trésors d'art* (Petit Palais, 1952) no. 84, pls. 22f. Venus-statue in 12th- or 13th-cent. Rome: Magister Gregorius *Narracio* 20f.; possible identification with Capitoline Venus (p. 549 with Chapter 8 n. 116): Rushforth in *JRS* 9 (1919) 25f.

95. Type used for Penelope on vases and gems: see Ohly in *Boehringer* 433–48 figs. 15–18 (Melian relief ibid. fig. 23). Melian reliefs: Jacobsthal *MR* (Penelope, nos. 87–93, pls. 48–52; Electra, nos. 1, 2, 94, pls. 1 and 53). Locrian relief with decorated chest: Langlotz and Hirmer pl. 75; Richter *H* 367 fig. 489. *Ajouré* bronze decorations: p. 30 with Chapter 1 n. 39 (cf. p. 144 with Chapter 3 n. 150); ivories: p. 141 with Chapter 3 n. 144. Selinus metopes: pp. 212–14 with n. 102.

96. 'Penelope' from Persepolis: Olmstead in *AJA* 54 (1950) 10–18 pls. 8–10, Roman copies pls. 11f., with refs.; Ohly in *Boehringer* 433–8, figs. 1–7 and 11 (figs. 10 and 13f.; Vatican statue; fig. 12, relief-version in Vatican; fig.

24, adaptation on Roman terracotta relief; see also last note); Langlotz in *Mus.Helv.* 8 (1951) 157–70, 'Die Larisa des Telephanes', figs. 1–4 (Persepolis and Vatican statues), 5–12 (parallel material). Richter *AI* 48 fig. 161 (158–60, Roman versions: 162, Melian relief; 163, mourner from Boston throne; 164–7, related types); full discussion in Ridgway *SS* 101–5, with figs. 104 (Copenhagen head) and 139f. (Persepolis and Vatican statues). Hestia and Apollo: pp. 191 and 194 with notes 58, 65. Myron: pp. 339–45 with Chapter 5 notes 112–22. Acropolis relief: pp. 178 and 203 with notes 35, 87.

97. 'Incuse' coins of South Italy: the practical explanation: Kraay in Kraay and Hirmer 302, with pls. viii, 75, 77–9, 81, 90, 92, 102; the Pythagorean: Seltman *GC* 76ff. with pl. 10. Tarentine coins of this period: Kraay and Hirmer pls. 102–4; Seltman *GC* pl. 19, 9–12.

98. Syracusan coins of this period: Kraay and Hirmer pls. 23–9 ('Demareteion', pls. 26–7; doubts as to its identification, p. 228); Seltman *GC* pls. 8, 13f.; 9, 1–6; 14, 8–11 ('Demareteion', 14, 9). Apollo-heads of Leontini: Kraay and Hirmer pls. 6f.; Seltman *GC* pl. 14, 12. River-god of Selinus: Kraay and Hirmer pls. 66f.; Seltman *GC* pl. 24, 8f. Eagle and crab of Akragas: Kraay and Hirmer pl. 59; Seltman *GC* pl. 26, 8f. Dionysus-head and silen of Naxos: Kraay and Hirmer, pl. 2; Seltman *GC* pls. 25, 9 and 64, 3. Silen's head and Zeus of Aetna: Kraay and Hirmer pls. II and 11; Seltman *GC* pl. 25, 7.

99. Hermes heads of Aenus: Kraay and Hirmer pls. 136f.; Seltman *GC* pls. 29, 6–9 and 64, 2. Nymph's head of Troezen: Seltman *GC* pls. 16, 8 and 64, 4. Coins of Elis in this period: Kraay and Hirmer pls. 154f., and see p. 342 on the 'medallic' character; Seltman *GC* pls. 13, 9–12 and 15, 4–10; Victory in Penelope-pose: *Mus.Helv.* 8 (1951) 162 fig. 8; Regling *Münze als Kunstwerk* pl. 21, 459; *Nomisma* 8 (1913) pl. 6 (Seltman *TCO* pl. 4), 19 and 21; there are two examples, struck from a single die. Nike identified with other goddesses: p. 177 with n. 32; p. 348 with Chapter 5 n. 137. Coins and medals of Elis: also p. 359 with Chapter 5 n. 170. Nike on vase: see p. 262 with n. 182.

100. Youth from Adrano (under Aetna; in Syracuse): Langlotz and Hirmer pls. x and 84f.; Ashmole *GSSSI* 25f., fig. 70 (resemblance to Selinus coin-type noted); Lamb pl. 56a; Langlotz *FGBS* pl. 93, 4; Neugebauer *ABS* 37. Dancing boy (Copenhagen, Thorwaldsens Museum 17): *AA* 1962, 89f. figs. 10–11; Langlotz and Hirmer pl. 128, top. Child in late archaic vase-painting: Beazley *VA* 90, fig. 58 and remarks: differentiation of age in bodies of Olympia sculptures: pp. 278–82. Other small bronzes from the West: Jantzen *BWS*; Langlotz and Hirmer pls. 64, 82f., 88–93. Bronze youth from Selinus (Castelvetrano; stolen in 1962 but now returned): Marconi *Efebo* 3; Richter *Kouroi*[3] figs. 651–6; Langlotz and Hirmer pl. 81; Ridgway *SS* fig. 93. Kouros from Agrigento: Richter *Kouroi* no. 182 figs. 574–9; Langlotz and Hirmer pl. 81; Ridgway *SS* fig. 92. Other kouroi from Sicily: Richter *Kouroi* nos. 183–9, figs. 544–6, 550–9. Miniature marble head from Selinus: Ashmole *GSSSI* 28 figs. 76f.

101. Temple of Zeus at Akragas: Dinsmoor 101–6, figs. 140f.; D. S. Robertson 122 fig. 52; Lawrence *A* 146f. figs. 85f. Atlantes: Griffo *Breve Guida* figs. 12–14.

102. Temple E (or R; of Hera) at Selinus: Dinsmoor 109 fig. 28, pl. 20. The metopes: Langlotz and Hirmer 100–8 (four existing metopes), 109–13 (heads from lost metopes); Fuchs in *RM* 63 (1956) 102–21, pls. 49–56 (with attempt to reconstruct two of the lost metopes); Duca di Serradifalco *Antichità di Sicilia*; Benndorf *MS*; Ashmole *GSSSI*, 27f. figs. 71–3 and 83; *KB* 245, 1–5 (a metope from another temple, 6); Lawrence *S* pl. 34b; Richter *Sc.* figs. 410–13, 187; Ridgway *SS* figs. 32, 35. Locrian plaque: p. 202 with n. 86. Death of Actaeon: see also pp. 253 and 269 with n. 168, 383 with Chapter 6 n. 63. clad in skin: cf. vase from Acropolis (Langlotz 760 pl. 65 *ARV*[2] Pan Painter no. 20)

(*v*) *The revolution in painting, 1: red-figure vase-painting and the pioneers of the new style*

103. Later black-figure and its relation to red-figure: Beazley *Dev.* Chaps. 7 and 8, and lists in *ABV* (most of Part I from Section xiii (p. 198) on, and Part II). Red-figure: far the best general account remains Beazley's *VA*; the basis for all detailed study in *ARV*² (with *Paralipomena*); Richter *ARVS* is also useful. Change of decorative principle: see especially pp. 223 and 236–7.

104. Technique: Richter *Craft* (an unfinished vase, fig. 47); on certain questions, especially the composition of the 'glaze', this is out of date: see Richter *ARVS* 23ff.; Lane *GP* 1–7; Noble in *AJA* 64 (1960) 207–18, where the theory is advanced that the relief-line was produced by a syringe; and especially Noble *Technique* (unfinished vase, figs. 196f. and cf. fig. 247; relief-line, figs. 206, 217). Preliminary sketch: ibid. figs. 191ff., and especially Corbett in *JHS* 85 (1965) 16–28, pls. 1–15. Wrong limbs: e.g. two left hands, Beazley *Berl.M.* pl. 27, 4, *Panm.* pl. 9; two right feet, FR pl. 75f. (second figure from left and fifth from right); all these on fine, careful work; see M. Robertson in *JHS* 74 (1954) 229f. and cf. the similar error, Beazley *Berl.M.* pl. 18, 2 and Beazley's remarks ibid. 11.

105. See especially Bothmer in *Bull.Met.* 24 (1965/6) 210f. figs. 12ff.

106. Cretan 'red-figure': *Ann.* x–xii 338–41, fig. 443a–d (animals on the shoulder drawn in outline, the background blacked in but stopping short of the outline; the figures on the neck are simply in outline, the background not blacked), 359f. fig. 472a–b (background absorbing outline and thinning figures); see Boardman *PC* 114f., *CCO* 145 with n. 2; and p. 217 with n. 108. A good example of the thinning effect in very early Attic red-figure: Graef and Langlotz pl. 54, 602 (*ARV*² 5 no. 2).

107. Lysippides/Andokides Painter question: Beazley *VA* (1918) 3–5 with fig. 1 (implied that they are the same); *AV* (1925) 7 (some of the black-figure certainly not by the same hand as the red-figure; following Langlotz *ZB* (1920) 23–31); *ABS* (1928) 40 with pl. 10, 2 (might be the same); *ARV* (1942) 1 (the same); *Dev.* (1951) 75–8 with pls. 34ff. (the same); *ABV* (1956) 254 (different; this opinion maintained thereafter, e.g. CB III (1963) 3–8 with pls. 65ff., suppl. pl. 17; *ARV*² 1963, 2). See also Rumpf *MZ* (1953) 60f. with pl. 16, 1 and 2 (the same); E. Paribeni in *EEA* 1 (1958) 357f. (different); Schauenburg in *JdI* 76 (1961) 48–71 with much illustration (the same); Marwitz in *ÖJh* 46 (1961/3) Hauptbl. 73–104, figs. 39–69 (the same; the fullest statement of the case); M. Robertson in *AJA* 66 (1962) 312 and *JHS* 85 (1965) 92 (the same); Bothmer in *Bull.Met.* 24 (1955/6) 201–12 with figs. 1–5, 9–11, 14 (different). Other pictures: Arias and Hirmer pls. XXIf. and figs. 82–9; BDFH pls. XX and 128f. (112f.); Cook *GPP* pl. 38; Lane *GP* fig. 63b; Pfuhl *MuZ* figs. 262f., 265f., 313–16; Richter *ARVS* fig. 34.

108. Amasis Painter: pp. 135–6 with Chapter 3 notes 134f.; outline against black: e.g. Beazley *Dev.* pls. 23, 1 and 26, 1, Karouzou *Amasis* pls. 25, 2; 28, 1; 30; 31, 1; 32, 1; Bruckner in *AK* 1 (1958) pls. 17; 19, 3; panther-mask (at root of handle of chariot-oenochoe, p. 136 with Chapter 3 n. 135): M. Robertson in *Zur griechischen Kunst: Hansjörg Bloesch zum 60. Geburtstag* (*AK* Beiheft 9, 1973) 81–4, pl. 29.

109. Antimenes Painter: *ABV* 266–75 with refs. (particularly Beazley in *JHS* 47 (1927) 63–92 figs. 1–23, pls. 11–14, *ABS* 41 pl. 12, *Dev.* 79ff. pl. 38; another picture: M. Robertson 87f.); his circle: *ABV* 276–91, with refs.; see also pp. 220–1 with notes 114f., 364 with Chapter 6 n. 5. Psiax: *ABV* 292ff. and *ARV*² 6–9 with refs. (especially Smith *Menon*; Richter in *AJA* 38 (1934) 547–54; Beazley *Dev.* 78f., all with pictures); other pictures Arias and Hirmer pls. 66ff.; Pfuhl *MuZ* figs. 264, 317f. See also below, notes 111, 114. Hilinos: see below, n. 115.

110. Eye-cups: see pp. 133 and 139 with Chapter 3 notes 129 and 141; the red-figure examples listed and classified: *ARV*² 37–52. On cup-development over this period see Bloesch *FAS*.

111. Oltos: *ARV*² 53–69 with refs. (especially Beazley *VA* 7–12 with figs. 2–4 and in CB III 9f. no. 117 with pl. 69, 3; Bruhn *Oltos*; Johnson in *Art Bull.* 19 (1937) 537–60 with figs. 1 and 4–9; Kenner in *CV* Vienna 1 pls. 7f. and in *ÖJh* 28 (1933) Hauptbl. 41–51 with figs. 23f.;

M. Robertson in *ÖJh* 47 (1964/5) Hauptbl. 107–19 with figs. 65–8); other pictures: Arias and Hirmer figs. 99–104; Lane *GP* figs. 62, 64; Pfuhl *MuZ* figs. 358–60; Richter *ARVS* fig. 35; Rumpf *MZ* pl. 16, 5. On the psykter-shape, see p. 221 with n. 115. Epiktetos: *ARV*² 70–9 with refs. (especially Beazley *VA* 14–18 figs. 7–10); other pictures Arias and Hirmer figs. 96ff.; Lane *GP* figs. 70A, 71; Pfuhl *MuZ* figs. 322–9; Richter *ARVS* fig. 37; Rumpf *MZ* pl. 17, 1 and 2. Black-figure plates by Psiax: *ABV* 294 nos. 17–20 (B.M. B589–91 and Berlin 2099; pictures, *JHS* 29 (1909) pls. 10f.; Smith *Menon* pl. 4; Richter *Furn.* fig. 115, *Furn.*² fig. 239, *H* 325 fig. 428; Lane *GP* pl. 52B); the plate *ABV* no. 21 (Meggen, Käppeli), Richter *ARVS* fig. 36, is different.

112. Plate signed by Epiktetos both as potter and painter (Athens N.M., Acrop. 6): *ARV*² 72 no. 102; Graef and Langlotz pl. 2. Calyx-krater with names of Andokides and Epiktetos (Rome, Villa Giulia): *ARV*² 77 no. 90; *Mon. Linc.* 42 (1955) 889f.; both inscriptions are incised. Hischylos: *ARV*² 161f.; Bloesch *FAS* 31–5. Python: pp. 231f. with notes 131f.; Pistoxenos: p. 261 with n. 178. Chelis: *ARV*² 109; Bloesch *FAS* 35f. and 50. Tleson: p. 130 with Chapter 3 n. 124; Oltos-Tleson cup (Naples 2627): *ARV*² 66 no. 127; Bloesch *FAS* 39. Kachrylion: *ARV*² 13, 55 and 107ff.; Bloesch *FAS* 45ff.; also p. 228 with n. 125. Euxitheos: *ARV*² 13f., 32, 52f. and 60; Bloesch *FAS* 43f.; and p. 222, with n. 116. On potters and painters see Beazley *PPAA*; R. M. Cook in *JHS* 91 (1971) 137f.; M. Robertson in *JHS* 92 (1972) 180ff. Euphronios: pp. 221f. with notes 115f., 228 with n. 124, 229f., 261.

113. Leagros Group: *ABV* 354–98 with refs. (especially Beazley *ABS* 26ff. and 43–6, pls. 13–16, *Dev.* 81–7, pls. 39–43). Pioneer Group: *ARV*² 13–36 with refs.; and see following notes.

114. Antimenean fountain-scenes: *ABV* 266 nos. 1–3, 276, ii no. 1, 280 nos. 1–2; Leagran fountain-scenes: *ABV* 365f. nos. 70–4; of similar character 334 nos. 1–4; and see M. Robertson 85–90. Early cup by Phintias showing influence of Psiax: Munich 2590, *ARV*² 24 no. 12 with refs.; Lullies and Hirmer *GVRZ* pl. 9; see Smith *Menon*. Minor painters using both techniques: Dikaios Painter (*ABV* 400; *ARV*² 30f.); Nikoxenos Painter (*ABV* 392f.; *ARV*² 220ff.). Fifth-century black-figure: pp. 237f. with n. 144.

115. Swallow-vase (Leningrad 615): *ARV*² 1594, Leagros Kalos no. 48 with refs.; pictures: *AA* 1927 Beil. 1 and 2; Peredolskaya 22f. no. 16 pls. 1; 17, 1; 165, 4–7 and 166, 1 (inscriptions); perhaps the earliest surviving example of the shape. Black-figure pelikai (all of 'red-figure period'): Bothmer in *JHS* 71 (1951) 40–7, pls. 20ff. Alabastron and its origins: Payne *NC* 267f.; Dunbabin in *Perachora* II 25; Richter and Milne 17 figs. 109ff.; the vases signed by Psiax and Hilinos (p. 217; *ARV*² 7 nos. 4f.) are of this form. Chiot 'chalice': p. 55 with Chapter 2 n. 50. Exekias: pp. 131–5 with Chapter 3 notes 126–33; his calyx-krater: Athens, Agora Museum (North Slope); *ABV* 145 no. 19; *Hesp.* 6 (1937) 468–86 figs. 1–10; Exekian calyx-krater (Volos): *ABV* 148 no. 9 (further refs. in *Paralipomena* 518). Antimenean calyx-kraters and psykters: *ABV* 275 nos. 134ff., 280 nos. 56–9, 281 nos. 17ff., 282 no. 22, 289 nos. 27f. Oltos's psykter (New York 10.210.18): *ARV*² 54 no. 7; Richter and Hall pl. 4. Phintias's psykter (Boston 01.8019): *ARV*² 24 no. 11; *JHS* 27 (1907) 259; CB II pls. 31 above and 32; psykter signed by Euthymides (Turin 4123) *ARV*² 28 no. 11; *JHS* 35 (1915) pls. 5f. and pp. 190f.; on these two see further p. 226 with n. 121. Psykter signed by Euphronios (Leningrad 644): *ARV*² 16 no. 15; FR pl. 63; Pfuhl *MuZ* fig. 394; Buschor *GV* 141; Peredolskaya 24f. no. 17 pls. 14f.; 166, 2–7 (inscriptions).

116. Euphronios: *ARV*² 13–17 with refs.; Beazley *VA* 26f., 30f. fig. 14; Rumpf *MZ* 74, pl. 20, 2f.; Johnson in *Art Bull.* 19 (1937) 537f., 557ff., figs. 2f.; E. Vermeule in *AK* 8 (1965) 34–9 pls. 1ff. (a new calyx-krater, Munich 8935, *Paralipomena* 322 no. 3bis). On Euphronios as cup-painter and as potter see pp. 228–30 with notes 124f., 261 with n. 179. Antaios krater (Louvre G103): *ARV*² 14 no. 2; Arias and Hirmer figs. 108–11 (other works, figs. 112f.); Pfuhl *MuZ* figs. 392f. (other works figs. 391, 394f.); and often. Fragment with Herakles and the lion (Louvre G110): *ARV*² 14 no. 3; *Mon. Piot* 45 pl. 1, 1. Andokides Painter's Herakles and lion (red-figure picture on bilingual

amphora, B.M. B193): *ARV*² 4 no. 8; *CV* pl. 1; CB III suppl. pl. 17. Euxitheos–Euphronios Sarpedon-krater (New York 1972.11.10): Bothmer in *Bull.Met.* 31 (1972/3) no. 15, with illustrations on cover, frontispiece, and middle pages.

117. Euthymides: *ARV*² 26–9 with refs.; Beazley *VA* 27f., 32f. figs. 15–18, *VP* 13ff. pls. 4–6; Rumpf *MZ* 73f. Pictures: *CV München* 4 pls. 161–71 (the three amphorae); Arias and Hirmer figs. 116f.; BDFH pls. 132 (116), 140 (124); Pfuhl *MuZ* figs. 364–9; M. Robertson 91f.; see also p. 228 with n. 125. Phayllos: see Beazley in CB II 4f., and further, p. 226 with n 121. Priam's stage-mask: Webster and Trendall 56f. III i 20f.; see further p. 234 with n. 136

118. Phintias: *ARV*² 22–5 with refs.; Beazley *VA* 27ff. fig. 13 and in CB II 3ff. no. 67, pls. 31 above and 32 (above, n. 115); Rumpf *MZ* 73, pl. 20, 1. Pictures: Arias and Hirmer figs. 90–5; BDFH pl. 130 (114); Pfuhl *MuZ* figs. 381ff.; Richter *ARVS* fig. 46. On the relevance of Euthymides's boast over Euphronios to the particular figures it is written by, see Richter l.c. 55 (with fig. 44); Phintias sometimes greets Euthymides by name on his vases.

119. Early three-quarterings: p. 157 with n. 7; advanced rendering of chariot on vase: White pl. 2a. Three-quarter faces: pp. 239 with n. 146, 360 with Chapter 5 n. 175. Full-face in Pioneer Group: e.g. Pfuhl *MuZ* fig. 394 (drinking girl on psykter by Euphronios, above n. 115); Beazley *RG* pl. 25 (piping boy on hydria by Euthymides, *ARV*² 28 no. 14); Arias and Hirmer fig. 95 (satyr on amphora by Phintias, *ARV*² 23 no. 2). Three-quarter chariots in late fifth century: pp. 360 with Chapter 5 n. 173, 416 with Chapter 6 n. 150.

120. See p. 234 with n. 137.

121. Warrior-plaque (Acropolis Museum 1037): *ARV*² 1598 no. 5 ('related to Euthymides') with refs.; Graef and Langlotz pl. 80; M. Robertson pl. 94; and see below. 'Black-figure' Athena plaque (part, Athens Acrop. 2590; part, Oxford 1927.4602): *ARV*² ibid. with refs.; Graef pl. 109; *JHS* 76 (1956) pls. 1f. The warrior was attributed to Euthymides by Stuart-Jones; the Athena by Boardman (*JHS* l.c. 20ff.) who argues the identity of the dedicator with Euthymides's father and with the sculptor. Pollias's signatures: Raubitschek 522ff. The suggestion that artists name their fathers only when the fathers were artists too: Robert in *RE* s.v. Euthymides: also p. 227 with n. 123. Single letters for double: pp. 55 and 60 with Chapter 2 notes 47 and 58. Phayllos: p. 223 with n. 117; Beazley in CB II 4f. gives two lamdas in his transcriptions of Euthymides's renderings of the name, but this is a mistake: see *CV München* 4 p. 69 (the amphora) and *JHS* 35 (1915) pl. 6 (the Turin psykter, above n. 115). Phintias on his psykter (ibid.) also uses one only; the artist of the amphora B.M. E256 (*ARV*² 168, middle) two; in a possible fifth occurrence, on a fragmentary stamnos by Euphronios Leipzig T523 (*ARV*² 15 no. 8) not enough is left of the name to tell. Sons of Nearchos and Ergotimos: p. 130 with Chapter 3 n. 124. Another artist's patronymic: p. 227 with n. 123. Sculptural dedications by potters: pp. 103–4 with Chapter 3 n. 67 (not certain), 107 with Chapter 3 n. 77; there is also a base from the Acropolis for a bronze statue dedicated by Mnesiades, who describes himself as a potter, and Andokides (*IG* I² 627; Raubitschek 213ff. no. 178; *Bull.Met.* 24 (1955/6) fig. 7); and another by Euphronios (*IG* I² 516; Raubitschek 255ff. no. 225); also one from the Agora with the name of a potter Peikon (*Hesp.* 4 (1935) 150 no. 2); and other uncertain cases (see Beazley *PPAA* 21ff., 23 n. 1).

122. Endoios and the Siphnian Treasury: pp. 106–8 with Chapter 3 notes 74–7, 157 with n. 9. The three bases from the Themistoclean wall (Athens N.M. 3476–8): *BCH* 46 (1922) 2–35 figs. 2–3, 6–8, pls. 1–7; discussed by Jeffery in *BSA* 57 (1962) 127f., with refs. and suggestion that all three are from one monument, the lost statues by Endoios; also Deyhle in *AM* 84 (1969) 16ff. with pl. 2, 1; and see p. 108 with Chapter 3 n. 77 on these, the Rayet kouros and the potter relief. Other pictures of the carved bases: Karouzou *Cat.* pl. 16; Lawrence *S* pl. 16; Lullies and Hirmer figs. 62–5; Richter *AGA* fig. 231, *H* 81 fig. 107, *Sc.* fig. 283; Zervos *Grèce* figs. 229–34. New base (Ker. Mus. P1002): Hölscher pl. 8, 1 and 2 (beasts and horsemen); *AR 1962/3* 7 fig. 5 (athletes); Travlos *PDAA* 404f. (beasts and athletes).

123. Antenor: p. 103 with Chapter 3 n. 67; signature with father's name (cf. above, n. 121): Raubitschek 232 no. 197 and pp. 481–3 (where the divergence Eumares/Eumaros is ignored). Eumaros: O. 377 (Pliny xxxv 53); Rumpf *MZ* 32. Kimon of Kleonai: O. 377ff.; Rumpf l.c. 71f. Kritios/Kritias (Critias): O. 542–3, 457, 459–63.

124. Euphronios as potter: *ARV*^{2} 13, 313f., 859f.; Bloesch *FAS* 70–80 and see pp. 230 and 261 with notes 128 (Onesimos) and 179. A potter-signature of Euthymides has recently come to light, incised on the foot of a fragmentary oenochoe, but the painting, though by another hand, cannot be much later than Euthymides's own. On the significance of potter-signatures, see p. 128 with Chapter 3 n. 118.

125. Kachrylion-Euphronios cup (Munich 2620): *ARV*^{2} 16 no. 17; Bloesch *FAS* 45 no. 13, pl. 13, 1; pictures: FR pl. 22; Lullies and Hirmer *GVRZ* figs. 12–16; Pfuhl *MuZ* fig. 391; on the subject see M. Robertson in CQ 19 (1969) 214–21. Cup signed by Euthymides (seven scattered fragments: apparent remains of a potter-signature also; coral-red within): *ARV*^{2} 29 no. 19; see Beazley in CB III 13ff. no. 121, Suppl. pl. 19, 1.

126. Sosias, potter: *ARV*^{2} 21; Bloesch *FAS* 55f. Sosias cup (Berlin 2278): *ARV*^{2} 21 no. 1; pictures: BDFH pl. 139 (123); FR pl. 123; Greifenhagen *AKW*^{1} 56f. (*AKW*^{2} 66f.); Pfuhl *MuZ* fig. 418; Rumpf *MZ* pl. 20, 5; and often. Melos disk: p. 199 with n. 77.

127. Boy with hare (B.M. E46): *ARV*^{2} 315, Protopanaetian Group no. 1; picture: Pfuhl *MuZ* fig. 413; Rumpf *MZ* pl. 25, 1; and often. Girl with cauldron (Brussels A889): *ARV*^{2} 329, Onesimos no. 130; pictures: Langlotz *GV* pl. 20, 30; M. Robertson 105; Rumpf *MZ* pl. 25, 3. Onesimos: see next note. Theseus and Sinis (Munich): M. Dumm-Ohly in *Münch.Jb.* 22 (1971) 7–22, figs. 1–5, with attribution to the Elpinikos Painter (*ARV*^{2} 119). Protoattic goblins (Berlin): *CV* 1 pls. 19ff.; on the subject see Metzger in *RA* 1972, 31–4 figs. 1f. (Protoattic vase), 3f. (Corinthian vases). 'Strife-motive': see pp. 276 with n. 213; 297, 299 and 357 with Chapter 5 notes 14, 18 and 162; 539 with Chapter 8 n. 92.

128. Onesimos: *ARV*^{2} 318–30; Beazley *VA* 82–9, figs. 50bis–56, *VP* 22f. pls. 8, 1 and 9, 1–4; also in CB II 21–36, pls. 37–43 and suppl. pls. 7–9; see also last and next notes. Theseus cup (Louvre G104): *ARV*^{2} 318 no. 1; pictures: BDFH pl. 149 (131); FR pls. 5 and 41; Pfuhl *MuZ* fig. 318; Richter *H* 329 fig. 443; and often. Ariadne's Crown: see Hampe *FgS* 78; Kunze *AS* 131f.; Schefold *ML* 70f. Brygos and the Brygos Painter: see next note and pp. 232f. with notes 133f.

129. Onesimos's revel (Boston 95.27): *ARV*^{2} no. 76; Beazley in CB II 31ff. no. 79 pls. 41f.; Pfuhl *MuZ* figs. 409ff. Brygos Painter's revel (Würzburg 479): *ARV*^{2} 372 no. 32; pictures: Langlotz *GVW* pls. 145–9; Arias and Hirmer pl. XXII and fig. 138; BDFH pl. XXIV (interior); Cook *GPP* pl. 47 (one side of exterior); Lane *GP* pl. 75A (same); M. Robertson 104 (interior).

130. Hieron: *ARV*^{2} 481f.; Bloesch *FAS* 91–6. Makron: *ARV*^{2} 458–81; Beazley *VA* 101–6, fig. 65; and in *AJA* 25 (1921) 325–36 figs. 1–6 (cf. fig. 7), and *BSA* 29 (1927/8) 187–215, pls. 3f., figs. 1f., and CB III 32–9 no. 140. Possible fragmentary signature (pyxis, Acrop. 560): *ARV*^{2} 479 no. 336; Graef and Langlotz pl. 43. Hieron-Makron skyphos (Boston 13.186): *ARV*^{2} 458 no. 1; pictures: Beazley in CB III pls. 76f.; FR pl. 85; Pfuhl *MuZ* figs. 435f.; and often. Paris cup (Berlin 2291): *ARV*^{2} 459 no. 4; pictures: *CV* 2 pls. 84ff., 127, 4 and 8 and 134, 9. Maenad cup (Berlin 2290): *ARV*^{2} 462 no. 48; pictures: *CV* 2 pls. 87ff., 128 1 and 5.

131. Brygos Painter's Louvre cup: below, n. 134. Python: *ARV*^{2} 70 and 426f.; Bloesch *FAS* 26f. and 98–101. Douris: *ARV*^{2} 425–48; Beazley *VA* 97–100 and in CB III 17–27, nos. 125–32, pls. 70–4. Herakles and Athena (Munich 2648): *ARV*^{2} 441 no. 185 ('school-piece'?); pictures: FR pl. 24; Lullies and Hirmer *GVRZ* pl. 80, below (exterior, pls. 88f.). Eos and Memnon (Louvre G115): *ARV*^{2} 434 no. 74; pictures: *Enc.Phot.* 15 (exterior, 14); Pfuhl *MuZ* fig. 458. Jason (Vatican): *ARV*^{2} 437 no. 116. Revellers (London E54): *ARV*^{2} 436 no. 96. Signature-practice: M. Robertson in *JHS* 82 (1972) 182ff. Kleophrades and the Kleophrades Painter: pp. 233–6 with notes 135–41. Potter-signatures of Douris: kantharos, Brussels A718, *ARV*^{2} 445 no. 256 with

refs. (painter-signature also); aryballos, Athens N.M. 274, *ARV*² 447 no. 254, with refs.

132. Python and Epiktetos (p. 219 with n. 112): cup, B.M. E38, *ARV*² 72 no. 16, with refs. Douris symposium-cups, B.M. E49 and E54, *ARV*² 432 no. 52, and 436 no. 96 with refs. Epiktetos and Pistoxenos: p. 261 with n. 178.

133. Douris's Arms of Achilles (Vienna 3690): *ARV*² 429 no. 26; pictures: *CV* I pls. 11f. and 13, 1–2; Pfuhl *MuZ* figs. 459f. Brygos: *ARV*² 398f., with additions in Addenda (p. 1649f.) and *Paralipomena* (369, 371f.); Bloesch *FAS* 81–6. Brygos Painter: *ARV*² 368–85; Beazley *VA* 89–93, figs. 57–61, *VP* 24f. pls. 10 and 11, 2 and in CB I 13ff. 17–23, pls. 6–9; Cambitoglou *Br.P.* Arms cups: Greenwich (Conn.), Bareiss; *ARV*² 367 no. 1bis; an incomplete picture of tondo, *Bull.Met.* (1969) 434 fig. 11 (there and in *ARV*² called Clytemnestra with the body of Agamemnon); B.M. E69; *ARV*² 369 no. 2; pictures, *Archaeologia* 32 (1847) pls. 8f. and 11; Ghali-Kahil *H* pl. 86, 1 (interior); Hofkes-Brukker pl. 10 (exterior).

134. Brygos's Iliupersis (Louvre G152): *ARV*² 369 no. 1; pictures: Arias and Hirmer figs. 139ff.; BDFH pls. 145 (129), 155 (139); *Enc.Phot.* 18f.; Pfuhl *MuZ* figs. 419f., 428 and often. Polyxena: p. 92 with Chapter 3 n. 48.

135. Kleophrades: *ARV*² 191 (Cab.Méd. 535 and other frr., Kleophrades Painter no. 103), 429 (Berlin 2283, Douris no. 21; 2284, Douris no. 22, a fragmentary replica, is signed by the painter) and 1555; Bloesch *FAS* 58 and 161; on the Cab.Méd. cup the potter names Amasis (p. 135 with Chapter 3 notes 134f.), apparently as his father. Kleophrades Painter (Epiktetos II; painter-signatures on both sides of pelike, Berlin 2170, *ARV*² 185 no. 28): *ARV*² 181–95; Beazley *VA* 40–4, figs. 23ff., *Kl.* passim, and in *JHS* 30 (1910) 38–68, pls. 1–9, figs. 1–4; Richter in *AJA* 40 (1936) 100–15, figs. 1–17, with a discussion of the name. Amazonomachy cup (Cab.Méd. 535 etc.): *ARV*² 191 no. 103; pictures: Beazley *Kl.* pls. 8; 10, 1; 11–12; 15, 1–6 and 30, 5. Theseus cup (Cab.Méd. 536 etc.): *ARV*² 191 no. 104; pictures: Beazley *Kl.* pls. 9; 10, 2; 13–14 and 15, 8–12. 'Continuous style': pp. 544 with Chapter 8 n. 107, 607 with Epilogue n. 45.

136. See p. 223 with n. 117.

137. 'Archaic' statues in classical scenes: see pp. 358 with Chapter 5 n. 164, 397 with Chapter 6 n. 101. 'Space' in Leagran black figure: p. 225 with n. 120.

138. Iliupersis hydria (Naples 2422): *ARV*² 189 no. 74; pictures: Arias and Hirmer fig. 125; BDFH pl. 144 (128); Beazley *Kl.* pl. 27; FR pl. 34; Pfuhl *MuZ* fig. 378, and often.

139. Calyx-kraters: *ARV*² 185f. nos. 31–49; some pictures: Beazley *Kl.* pls. 16–19 (calyx-composition), 26 (many-figured); Richter in *AJA* 40 (1936) 101 fig. 1 (many-figured). Early amphorae: *ARV*² 186f. nos. 1–4; some pictures: Beazley in *JHS* 30 (1910) pl. 4; FR pls. 52 and 103; Pfuhl *MuZ* figs. 374, 376f. Pointed amphora (Munich 2344): *ARV*² 187 no. 6; often illustrated, e.g.: Arias and Hirmer pls. XXXf., figs. 122ff.; BDFH pls. XXIf.; Beazley *Kl.* pls. 3–6; FR pls. 44f.; Pfuhl *MuZ* figs. 379f.; M. Robertson 100ff. Wine-amphorae: Grace and Frantz passim; the nearest to the fine-ware versions, fig. 35; cf. Sparkes, Talcott and Frantz figs. 12f. Black-figure examples with stands: *ABV* 382, Acheloos Painter no. 1, and *Paralipomena* ad loc. Late fifth-century miniatures: cf. p. 418 with Chapter 6 n. 156.

140. Wing-dance in Kleophrades Painter's work: Beazley *Kl.* pl. 26, and in *AK* 1 (1958) pls. 2–5; in Brygos Painter's work: Cambitoglou *Br.P.* pl. 7; Pfuhl *MuZ* fig. 47.

141. Late amphora (Würzburg 508): *ARV*² 187 no. 5; Langlotz *GVW* pl. 176; other pictures Beazley *Kl.* pl. 20, 2; Buschor *GV* 168; FR pl. 104.

142. Berlin Painter: *ARV*² 196–214 with important additions in Addenda and *Paralipomena*; Beazley *VA* 35–40, *Berl.M.*, *Berl.P.*, and in *JHS* 31 (1911) 276–95, pls. 8–17, figs. 1–9, and 42 (1922) 70–98 pls. 2–5, figs. 1–8, *AK* 4 (1961) 49–67, pls. 20–6 (Basle amphora with Athena and Herakles; also in *Berl.P.* pls. 9f.; and see Cahn in *CIBA Journal* 17 (1961) 22–7; Bloesch in *AK* 5, 1962, pls. 9 and 10, 2, figs. 1–10). The lotus and palmette band is normally a rim-pattern, on calyx-kraters (e.g. *ARV*² 205 no. 117, *Berl.M.* pl. 32); or doubled on the upper register of volute-krater necks (as pl. 99a, below n. 145). Athena with wine between Zeus and Hera, on a stamnos in Castle Ashby (*ARV*² 207 no. 141; *Berl.M.* pls. 24, 2 and 27,

1–3. Athena pouring for a standing Zeus, on a big column-krater: Leningrad 17 1899.75; *ARV*² 247, Diogenes Painter no. 1; Beazley *VA* 53 fig. 33bis; M. Robertson in *AK* 13 (1970) pls. 7–9 (photographs and Beazley's drawings).

143. Amphora with Hermes and satyrs (Berlin 2160): *ARV*² 196 no. 1; constantly illustrated, e.g. Arias and Hirmer figs. 140–3; BDFH pl. 154 (138); Beazley *Berl.M.* pls. 1–5, *Berl.P.* pls. 1f.; FR pl. 159, 2 and III 255; Pfuhl *MuZ* fig. 473. Black-figure hydria with Hephaestus (B.M. B302); *ABV* 261 no. 40; Arias and Hirmer pls. XXI and 69; Beazley *Dev.* pl. 36, 1; Richter *Furn.* fig. 315; on the subject see Beazley *Dev.* 77f. and M. Robertson in *JHS* 70 (1950) 25 n. 7. Beardless Herakles: see p. 166 with n. 21; p. 273 with n. 207.

144. Panathenaic prize-vases: p. 150 with Chapter 3 n. 160; *ABV* 403–17; Beazley in *AJA* 47 (1943) 441–65; Corbett in *JHS* 80 (1960) 52–8; Peters *SP*; see also Davison in *JHS* 78 (1958) 23–42, especially 26–9. The traditions about the origin and development of the Panathenaic festival in its various forms are deeply confused and obscure, but the beginning of the series of inscribed vases is consistent with indications of some change introduced by Peisistratos and given a date corresponding to 566 B.C. See further p. 306 with Chapter 5 n. 36. Eucharides Painter: *ABV* 395–7; *ARV*² 226–32; Beazley *VA* 45ff. figs. 26–8 and in *BSA* 18 (1911–12) 217–33, pls. 10–15, figs. 1–6. Achilles Painter: pp. 324–5 with Chapter 5 notes 79f.

145. Panathenaic amphora with Apollo and Herakles (Würzburg 300): *ARV*² 197 no. 8; pictures, Langlotz *GVW* pls. 165f. and 183; Beazley *Berl.M.* pls. 8, 2 and 9, 2; FR pl. 134, 2; Pfuhl *MuZ* fig. 472. Volute-krater with Achilles (B.M. E458): *ARV*² 206 no. 132; pictures, Beazley *Berl.M.* pls. 29–31. François vase: p. 124 with Chapter 3 n. 111; Vix krater: pp. 144f. with Chapter 3 n. 150.

146. Three-quarter shields shown very occasionally by the Berlin Painter: see M. Robertson in *JHS* 70 (1950) 33f. and *AJA* 62 (1958) 59. Three-quartering and shading of shields by the Brygos Painter: battle of gods and giants on exterior of cup, Berlin 2293, *ARV*² 370 no. 10, *CV* pls. 67f., FR pl. 160 (shading visible on original and in Reichold's drawing but not in photographs; on the beautiful interior tondo with Selene see M. Robertson 111). Three-quarter face in Kleophrades Painter's work: see Beazley in *JHS* 30 (1910) 58 with n. 69 and pl. 11 (other early examples also cited). Centauromachy-psykter (Rome, Villa Giulia): not in *ARV*, but in Beazley *AV*, end of addenda, said to be related to the Harrow Painter; FR pl. 15; Pfuhl *MuZ* fig. 491; see also below, n. 148.

(vi) *The revolution in painting, 2: wall-painting and vase-painting after the Persian wars*

147. A useful collection of Egyptian and Near Eastern spatial experiments: Groenewegen-Frankfort *Arrest and Movement*; stele of Naram-sin, ibid. pl. 62. Tomba della Caccia e Pesca: *MPASI* 1, *Tarquinia* 2; Rumpf *MZ* pl. 19, 7 and p. 70 n. 5 with refs. Paestan tomb: M. Napoli *TT*.

148. Odysseus and the sirens on a red-figure Attic stamnos (B.M. E440): *ARV*² 289, Siren Painter no. 1; FR pl. 124; Pfuhl *MuZ* fig. 479. Spatial effects in Kleophrades Painter's Iliupersis: p. 234 with n. 137. Centauromachy psykter: p. 239 n. 146; the earliest back-view of a helmeted head is surprisingly on a cup by Psiax (p. 217 with n. 109), evidently painted at the end of the sixth century under the influence of the Pioneers (New York 14.146): *ARV*² 8 no. 9; Smith *Menon* pl. 2 and p. 12 fig. C; Richter and Milne pl. 1.

149. Polygnotos: O. 1042–79 (also 1083, 1091); Aristophon, his brother: O. 1127–9 (also 1046); Aglaophon, their father and teacher: O. 614f. (also 1042f., 1046–90). On the younger Aglaophon see pp. 415–17 with Chapter 6 notes 148f. Mikon son of Phanochos: O. 1080–97 (also 1054, 1058, 1070f.). The modern literature is vast, especially on Polygnotos: see Rumpf *MZ* 91ff. (refs. to earlier literature in notes); Löwy *Polygnot*; Weickert *Pol.*: further refs. in following notes. Simonides's epigram: Pausanias X 27 4; *Anth.Pal.* IX 700; Plutarch *de Def.Or.* 47, without a poet's name. The Lesche of the

Cnidians at Delphi and its pictures: pp. 247–52 and 266–70 with notes 157–66, 188–200. Stoa Poikile at Athens: pp. 243–4 with notes 150f., 323 with Chapter 5 notes 74f.

150. Mikon's horses: Aelian *Nat.Animal.* IV 50; Tzetzes *Chil.* XII 559ff.; Pollux *Onom.* II 69 (quoting Simon; see p. 505 with Chapter 8 n. 5; O. 1090–2). Theseion and its paintings: Wycherley *Agora* 3, 113–19 nos. 339–62, especially 116 no. 351 (Pausanias I 17 2f.; O. 1086); and see p. 247 with n. 155; for the possibility that Polygnotos as well as Mikon may have worked in this building see Wycherley 37 no. 68 (Harpocration) and 41f. no. 86 (Plutarch *Cimon* 4 5f. with the quotation from Melanthios; O. 1044); late fifth-century vase-painting with Theseus at the bottom of the sea: p. 420 with Chapter 6 n. 160; Theseus's end: pp. 253–8 with n. 170. Amazonomachies on vases: pp. 258 f., 263 with notes 174, 184; Centauromachy at Olympia and on vases: pp. 256 f., 259 with notes 170, 174, 280–3 with n. 222. Anakeion and its paintings: Wycherley *Agora* 3 61–5 nos. 133–51, especially 63 no. 140 (Pausanias I 18 1; O. 1058 and 1085). Stoa Poikile and its paintings: Wycherley *Agora* 3 31–45 nos. 47–98, especially 39ff. no. 80 (Pausanias I 15 1–16 1; O. 1054) but many of the others are very important for the paintings (cf. O. 1081–4, 1091, 1099–1108); see also following notes and p. 323 with Chapter 5 notes 74f.

151. Elpinice and Laodice: Plutarch *Cimon* 4 5f. (O. 1044). Fragments perhaps from the Stoa: see next note. Battle of Oenoe: see Jeffery in *BSA* 60 (1965) 41–57, with refs. and a very interesting discussion and interpretation. Panainos and the Battle of Marathon: pp. 323–4 with Chapter 5 n. 74.

152. Wall-painting on plaster in Bronze-age Greece: pp. 5 f., 9 f. with Prologue notes 13ff., 26ff., in Hellenistic and Roman times: Chapter 8 (iv) passim and pp. 598–600, 606 with Epilogue notes 22–9 and 42; in Etruscan tombs: see p. 242 with n. 147, pp. 592–5 with Epilogue notes 9f., 12, 15f.; in archaic Phrygia: *AJA* 60 (1956) 255ff. pls. 85f., figs. 18–21. A full account of the technique of the early fifth-century tomb at Paestum (p. 240 with n. 147): Napoli *TT* 95–108. Treatment of Hephaisteion walls: Dinsmoor 179. Coloured plaster from Lesche: Pouilloux *FdeD* II 126f., 136f.; block with pin-hole; ibid. 130, 137; and see p. 247 with n. 157. Fragments probably from Poikile: Thompson in *Hesp.* 19 (1960) 327ff. pl. 103; panelling removed from Poikile: Synesius *Epist.* 54 and 135 (Wycherley *Agora* 3, 43f., 93 and 94 with note: O. 1057). Stoa of Attalos at Delphi prepared for painted panelling: Roux in *BCH* 76 (1950) 166–85, especially 182ff.; see also pp. 489–90 with Chapter 7 n. 113. Lucian on Polygnotos's materials: *Imagg.* 483. Isthmia: Broneer (Bibl. addenda) 33ff.

153. The whole ingenious theory outlined in the text is Dinsmoor's: see Dinsmoor 198 and ap. Swindler *AP* 424 n. 14a. Paintings by Polygnotos in the Propylaea: Pausanias I 22 6 (O. 1060; cf. 1061). Mnesikles's Periclean Propylaea: pp. 347 with Chapter 5 n. 133 and 368 with Chapter 6 n. 18.

154. Picture in Rome: Pliny XXXV 59 (O. 1063). Cup (Boston 95.28): *ARV*[2] 816, Telephos Painter no. 1; pictures: CB III pl. 89 (on the subject see Beazley ibid. 57ff.); Pfuhl *MuZ* fig. 449. Painting in the temple of Athena Areia at Plataea (also p. 255 with n. 170): Pausanias IX 4 1 (O. 1059); Plutarch *Aristides* 20 (O. 636); Pheidias's cult-statue, p. 294 with Chapter 5 n. 7. Polygnotos's wall-paintings at Thespiae restored by Pausias (pp. 489–90 with Chapter 7 n. 113. Polygnotos's Salmoneus: *Anth.Gr.* II 255 3 (O. 1064); Salmoneus on vase (Chicago 89.16): *ARV*[2] 585 no. 29; pictures: *AJA* 15 (1899) pl. 4; *EAA* VI 1076 fig. 1185; see M. Robertson in *GRBS* 13 (1972) 44. Nausicaa on vase (neck-amphora, Munich 2322): *ARV*[2] 1107; pictures FR pl. 138, 1; Pfuhl *MuZ* fig. 514. Polygnotos's Sophocles playing the lyre: Wycherley *Agora* 3, 42 no. 90 (*Vit.Soph.*, *Biogr. Graec.* ed. Westermann 127). Polygonotos's hare: Wycherley *Agora* 3, 63 no. 141 (Photius; in the Anakeion); O. 1065 (*Mantiss.Prov.* II 66). Late fifth-century vase with Thamyras and hare (volute-krater, Ferrara T127): *ARV*[2] 1171. Polion no. 1; pictures: Aurigemma *Sc.di Spina* pls. 1–16; Alfieri and Arias pls. 108–11; see *BSA* 60 (1965) 43 n. 12. Thamyras in the Lesche, and other vase-paintings: p. 270 with n. 199.

155. H. Thompson in *Mycenaean Seminar* 17 Feb. 1965; Professor Thompson, however, now re-

jects the identification. Heroon at Gjölbaschi-Trysa: pp. 405–6 with Chapter 6 n. 119. Hero-shrines at Olympia: Dörpfeld *Ol.* II 165; Gardiner *Olympia* 204; Hege and Rodenwaldt 17 and 28f. Picture of Themistocles in Parthenon: p. 187 with n. 51.

156. Pausanias x 26 4; see Pouilloux *FdeD* II 138 with n. 4.

157. The Lesche: Pouilloux *FdeD* II 120–39, with full illustration and refs., superseding all previous discussions; architectural terracottas: 132, pl. 71, 1 (a set from an earlier building found mixed with them, pl. 72, 2); the date of *c.* 480 there quoted from Le Roy for the later set seems unnecessarily early, and Pouilloux (ibid. 137f.) assumes that the Lesche was built after the Eurymedon (cf. p. 242 with n. 149). Lighting: 133f. (favouring openings in the south-east wall); see also above, n. 152. The paintings: Pausanias x 25–31 (O. 1050; other ancient refs. 1045, 1051–3; also Plutarch *de Def.Or.* 412D with 436B); modern discussions and reconstructions: Robert *Nekyia*, with earlier refs., 133f., and *Iliupersis*, by far the most important; also Löwy *Polygnot* 7–10 and passim; Weickert *Pol.* 9–23; see also the commentaries on Pausanias by Hitzig and Blümner in their edition and by Frazer to his translation.

158. On the epigram, see p. 242 with n. 149.

159. Robert in his commentaries (above, n. 157) and in the graphic reconstructions which accompany them (reproduced by Frazer, vol. 5 at pp. 360 and 372) makes the pictures looking-glass to my view, as though Pausanias described each from the outer edge to the point of junction in the centre (since the Troy was on the right to one entering). The one shield-device Pausanias describes (Menelaus's in the Troy; x 26 3) belongs to a figure certainly facing in the direction from which Pausanias approaches him; on my scheme such a figure would naturally present his left side.

160. On the question of couch or fountain (κλίνη or κρήνη) and on Epeios's action, see M. Robertson in *BSA* 62 (1967) 1–12; see also p. 250 with n. 163.

161. Pp. 243–4 with n. 151.

162. Jebb and Pearson, fr. 620.

163. See M. Robertson in *BSA* (1967) 10ff. If purification were a special feature of Delphic religion, as is often said, this would be particularly appropriate: but see Dyer in *JHS* 89 (1969) 38–56.

164. Laomedon's tomb and the three spells: M. Robertson in *GRBS* 11 (1970) 23–6. Antenor's relations with the Greeks: Beazley 'Ελένης 'Απαίτησις (*Helenes Apaitesis*).

165. For an attempt to show that Polygnotos intended no temporal implications at all, see Weickert *Pol.*

166. Further discussion of these points with refs.: M. Robertson in *BSA* 62 (1967) 8f. with notes. Fra Angelico's picture: e.g. Pope-Hennessy *Angelico* pl. 105.

167. Berlin Painter's followers: pp. 324–7 with Chapter 5 notes 77–83. Birth of Erichthonios (Munich 2413; a stamnos, see above, n. 142): *ARV*² 495 no. 1; pictures: Buschor *GV* 182; FR pl. 137 and III 95; Rumpf *MZ* pl. 30, 5; Simon *Geburt* 73; see further, p. 327 with Chapter 5 n. 83. Ludovisi throne: pp. 201–9 with notes 88–93.

168. Pan Painter: *ARV*² 550–60; Beazley *VA* 113–18, figs. 70–4, *Panm.* passim, and in *JHS* 32 (1912) 354–69, pls. 6–9, figs. 1–8, CB II 45–55, nos. 93–8, pls. 47–51, suppl. pl. 11, 4; Follmann passim. Pan/Actaeon vase: *ARV*² 550 no. 1; pictures in all Beazley's works just cited (fullest publication in CB II); also Beazley and Ashmole fig. 81; FR pl. 115; Pfuhl *MuZ* figs. 475f.; M. Robertson 118f.; and often. Berlin Painter's bell-kraters: *ARV*² 205f., nos. 123–6; pictures: e.g. Arias and Hirmer pls. XXXVI and 154–7; Beazley *Berl.M.* pl. 20; M. Robertson 98. Metope from Selinus (and the story): pp. 212–14 with n. 102; Pharsalos stele: pp. 198–9 with n. 76.

169. Niobid Painter: *ARV*² 598–608; Beazley *VA* 145–50, figs. 88ff. and in CB II 72–82 nos. 107f. pls. 47, 2 and 57–60; Webster *Niobidenm.*; Simon in *AJA* 67 (1963) 43–62, 'Polygnotan painting and the Niobid Painter'. Calyx-krater (Louvre G341): *ARV*² 601 no. 22; illustrated in all the works just cited; other pictures: Arias and Hirmer pls. 173–5; BDFH pls. 158f. (142f.); Beazley and Ashmole fig. 82; FR pls. 108 and 165 and II 244 and 251; Löwy *Polygnot* pls. 1f.; Pfuhl *MuZ* fig. 492; M. Robertson 124; see also next note and p. 319 with Chapter 5 n. 65.

170. Subject of obverse of Louvre krater: earlier interpretations listed by Simon in *AJA* 67 (1963) 43–62; her own is Theseus in the Underworld, but derived not from the picture in the Theseion but from an unrecorded one (there must have been many) in the Temple of Poseidon Hippios at Colonus. Seven against Thebes: Jeppesen Ἐτεοκλέους σύμβασις (*Acta Jutlandica* 40, 1968); suggested derivation from picture by Onasias at Plataea; cf. p. 245 with n. 154. Anatomical observation and identification of original as the Theseion picture: Barron in *JHS* 92 (1972) 20–45, pls. 1–7. Painter of the Woolly Satyrs: *ARV*² 613f.; Beazley in *JHS* 79 (1959) 16ff.; his Centauromachy on neck of volute-krater with Amazonomachy on body (New York 07.286, 84): *ARV*² 613 no. 1; pictures: FR pls. 116f.; Pfuhl *MuZ* fig. 506; Richter and Hall no. 98, pls. 97f. and 171; Richter and Milne figs. 51f.; M. Robertson 123; and often; detail of neck: Ashmole, Yalouris and Frantz fig. 20; and see further pp. 259 and 280 with notes 174 and 222.

171. Irrational relation of spear to cornice in Pompeian painting (Naples, from villa at Boscoreale): M. Robertson in *JRS* 45 (1955) 59 pl. 12; see pp. 571–4 with Chapter 8 n. 183; cf. also pp. 584–5 with Chapter 8 n. 225, 599 with Epilogue n. 25. Spatial contradictions in Renaissance painting: the relative positions of the sleeping soldiers in Piero della Francesca's Resurrection at Borgo San Sepolcro (above, n. 59; there is nowhere for the legs of the one with the shield); the relation of the foreground figures to the architecture in Raphael's Mass of Bolsena in the Vatican Stanze (e.g. Venturi *Short History* 282). See also p. 584 with Chapter 8 n. 225.

172. Earlier back-views of heads: p. 241 with n. 148. Early classical cup with back view and hint of *profil perdu*: see p. 263 with n. 184; later examples of *profil perdu*: p. 324 with Chapter 5 n. 77.

173. Butes: Zenobius IV 28 (Wycherley *Agora* 3 44 no. 96 with refs. also to Hesychius, Photius and the Suda; see also O., note to 1085). Zenobius and the Suda mention the stoa; Photius Nikon (a common mistake for Mikon, who also appears as Kimon); and Zenobius that the name was written beside the exiguous figure.

174. Amazonomachy calyx-krater (New York 07.286.86): *ARV*² 616, Painter of the Berlin Hydria no. 3; pictures: Bothmer *Am.* pl. 74, 2; FR pls. 118f. and II 326f. Pfuhl *MuZ* figs. 506f.; Richter and Hall no. 99, pls. 99 and 170. Volute-krater: above, n. 170; wounded Amazon: see also p. 335 with Chapter 5 n. 104. On both see Beazley *VA* 152; on these and other vases with 'big battles' see Bothmer *Am.* 161–74. Niobid Painter's Centauromachy-fragment (Berlin 2403: *ARV*² 599 no. 9; pictures: Ashmole, Yalouris and Frantz fig. 21; Webster *Niobidenm.* pl. 24, 6.

175. 'White-figure' amphora by the Andokides Painter and inscribed with the name of the potter Andokides (Louvre F203): *ARV*² 4 no. 3; pictures: *AJA* 11 (1896) 2f.; Pottier pl. 78. Bothmer *Am.* 153f., suggests that the bathing women are Amazons too. Triton-fragment (Eleusis 618): *ARV*² 314, Eleusis Painter no. 3; pictures: *Delt.* 9, fig. on p. 24, 2; Boardman *PC* fig. 66; Philippart *CAB* pl. 13a; M. Robertson 97. White cup with maenad (Munich 2645): *ARV*² 371, Brygos Painter no. 15; pictures: BDFH pl. xxv; FR pl. 49c and I 250; Lane *GP* pl. 87; M. Robertson 107.

176. Polygnotos a 'four-colour' painter: Cicero *Brutus* 18 70 (O. 1067); Dionysius Hal. *de Isaeo* 4 (O. 1069) seems to have a better understanding of the situation, saying that ancient painters used simple not mixed colours. Four-colour painting later: p. 500 with Chapter 7 n. 143. Blue and green on late fifth-century vases: e.g. M. Robertson 154f.; see also p. 424 with Chapter 6 n. 169. Possible blue on early classical cup: below, n. 179.

177. Aeschylus *Septem* 432ff., 465ff. Polygnotos's warrior: p. 246 with n. 154. Ambrogio Lorenzetti's figures: e.g. Venturi *Short History* 137 (Pax; see further, p. 577 with Chapter 8 n. 202); Van Eyck annunciation: e.g. Baldass *Van Eyck* pls. 85ff., 92f.

178. Pistoxenos: *ARV*² 1554; Pistoxenos Painter: see next note. Syriskos: *ARV*² 259. Double signature: *Paralipomena* 353. Epiktetos and Pistoxenos: pp. 217 with n. 112, 232 with n. 132.

179. Pistoxenos Painter: *ARV*² 859–63; Diepolder *Pist.* Aphrodite cup (B.M. D2): *ARV*² no. 23; pictures: Buschor *GV* fig. 176; Diepolder

Penth. pl. 6; Lane *GP* pl. D; Pfuhl *MuZ* fig. 498; M. Robertson 113. Orpheus cup (Acrop. 439): *ARV²* 860 no. 2; pictures: Graef and Langlotz pl. 36 and 35, 2; Diepolder *Penth.* pls. 5 and 17, 2–3, *Pist.* 18; Pfuhl *MuZ* fig. 406. Maenad cup (Taranto): *ARV²* 860 no. 3; pictures: *Arch.Class* 3 (1951) pls. A, B, 1f. and 3, 1: *EAA* VI pl. at p. 30; M. Robertson title-page.

180. Covered cup with Apollo and Muse (Boston 00.356): *ARV²* 741; pictures: CB I pl. 15; *EAA* V 298 fig. 398; Langlotz *GV* pl. 35; M. Robertson 132. Covered cups: Beazley *SAVCM* 44 (a list) with pl. 6, 1 (Pistoxenos Painter). Eriphyle and Salmoneus's daughter (Tyro, but Pausanias does not name her): Pausanias X 29 7. Similarly composed metope from Olympia: p. 275 with n. 212.

181. Athena and woman on small neck-amphora ('Nolan amphora'; B.M. E316): *ARV²* 857, Trophy Painter no. 6; pictures: *BMCat.Vas.* 3 pl. 12; *CV* pl. 58, 1; Pfuhl *MuZ* fig. 513; see M. Robertson in *JRS* 45 (1955) 65 n. 46; Hauser in *ÖJh* 8 (1905) 28 fig. 3, suggests an extract from a picture of Nausicaa; Jeppesen in *Act.Arch.* 34 (1963) Athena and Pandora.

182. White bobbins: e.g. *ARV²* 890 nos. 175 (Diepolder *Penth.* pl. 19; Richter and Hall pl. 76) and 176 (*AA* 1940, 335); another M. Robertson 110f. White pyxides: e.g. *ARV²* 774 no. 1 (CB I pl. 15); 890 no. 173 (*VA* 128 with remarks); 899 nos. 144 (*AA* 1941, 451–4), 145, 146 (*AM* 32, 80–3); 1213 no. 1 (Richter *ARVS* fig. 104). White oenochoai: e.g. *ARV²* 403 no. 38 (Bieber *GK* 2 fig. 4); 1213 no. 2 (Murray *WAV* pl. 21, 6). White calyx-kraters: Hermes and Dionysus (Vatican) *ARV²* 1017, Phiale Painter no. 54; pictures: FR pl. 169 and III 202; Perseus and Andromeda (Agrigento): *ARV²* 1017 no. 53; pictures: *Breve Guida* 29; *Fast.Arch.* 12 pl. 4; Griffo *Mus.Civ.Agr.* 29 fig. 9 and *Guide* fig. 160; Matt and Griffo *Das ant.Siz.* 120. Fragments of others: *ARV²* 619, Villa Giulia Painter nos. 11bis and 12; 634 no. 6 (perhaps Methyse Painter); *AJA* 54 (1950) pl. 21 and p. 120. White squat lekythos with Nike (Brussels A1021): *ARV²* 1213 top no. 3 (recalls the Shuvalov Painter; p. 418 with Chapter 6 n. 156); see also p. 212 with n. 99.

183. Niobid Painter's early Iliupersis (Bologna 268): *ARV²* 598 no. 1; pictures: *Mon.* 11 pls. 14f.; Webster *Niobidenm.* pl. 6; more attractive early work, e.g. ibid. pl. 9.

184. Penthesilea Painter: *ARV²* 879–90; Beazley *VA* 129–32, figs. 80–2; Furtwängler in FR I 281–5; Swindler in *AJA* 12 (1909) 143–50, 18 (1915) 398–417. Penthesilea cup (Munich 2688): *ARV²* 879 no. 1; pictures: Diepolder *Penth.* pl. 13–15; FR pls. 6 and 36, 1–3, and I 31; M. Robertson 115f.; and often. Calyx-krater (Bologna 289): *ARV²* middle; pictures: Beazley and Ashmole fig. 83; Bothmer *Am.* pl. 74, 1 (and see pp. 164f.); FR pls. 75f. Spina cup (Ferrara T. 18C VP): *ARV²* 882 no. 35; picture: Alfieri and Arias pls. 28–33; back view of head: p. 257 with n. 172. Themistocles's portrait: pp. 187–8 with n. 50; Euthymides's Priam: p. 223 with n. 117; Aigina and Selinus heads: p. 167 with n. 22; Kimon of Kleonai: p. 327 with n. 123.

185. Sotades and the Sotades Painter: *ARV²* 763–73; Beazley *VP* 27–9, pls. 15f.; Buschor *Krokadil*; Hauser in FR III 92–4. Knucklebone (B.M. E804): *ARV²* 765 no. 10; pictures: *CV* pls. 26f.; Curtius *Astragal* pl. 1, with the suggestion of the Clouds; FR pl. 136, 2; Lane *GP* pl. 76B; Rumpf *MZ* pl. 29, 1. Makron's skyphos: p. 231 with n. 130.

186. Aeschylus *Septem* 491–6. On this cup and the one with the apple-pickers see next note.

187. Sotadean white cups (B.M. D5, 6 and 7): *ARV²* nos. 1–3; pictures: Murray *WAV* pls. 16ff.; Pfuhl *MuZ* figs. 526ff.; M. Robertson 129ff.; Rumpf *MZ* pl. 29, 6.

188. Niobid Painter's masterpiece: pp. 253–8 with notes 169f. Thamyras vase: p. 246 with n. 154. Apollo cup: p. 261 with n. 180. Andromeda krater: p. 262 with n. 182. Athena and woman: p. 262 with n. 181. On gestures and their significance, see Neumann *Gesten.* See also p. 278 with n. 217.

189. Black-figure neck-amphorae with Sisyphus (p. 269; cf. p. 116 with chapter 3 n. 96): Munich 1494, *ABV* 308, Swing Painter no. 81 (with figures doubtfully identified as Persephone and Ajax), *CV* pls. 360ff.; Munich 1493, *ABV* 316 Bucci Painter no. 7 (with the Leaky Jar, and on the other side Herakles and Cerberus; on the Leaky Jar see p. 267 with n. 191), *CV* pls. 355f.; Leyden XV.1.59 (PC 49), *ABV*

371, Leagros Group no. 153, Roulez pl. 15; Naples 2490, *ABV* 383, Acheloos Painter no. 11; Munich 1549, ibid. no. 12, Pfuhl *MuZ* fig. 283; Orvieto, Faina 124, *ABV* 392, Nikoxenos Painter no. 1 (with Persephone and Cerberus); Berlin 1844, ibid. no. 2 (with Persephone); St Louis, Mylonas, *ABV* 405 and *Paralipomena* 176, Kleophrades Painter no. 19 *Vente xi Bâle* pl. 18, 327, *AJA* 60 (1956) pl. 12 and pl. 13, 59–60; no doubt already fifth century (cf. p. 238 with n. 144).

190. Charon is frequently shown on Attic white lekythoi of the second half of the century (p. 326 with Chapter 5 n. 81) but always standing in the boat and holding a pole, perhaps following some painting at Athens. Boatmen at the oars on Attic red-figure vases of the same period: e.g. *ARV* 1056 no. 86 (Phaon; Pfuhl *MuZ* fig. 557); 1064 no. 2 (*AJA* 39 (1935) 484).

191. Kleoboia: see further p. 370 with Chapter 6 n. 25. The ship metaphor: Aeschylus *Septem* 855–60. The Leaky Jar: this punishment is later associated with the Danaids, the fifty daughters of Danaus who (except Hypermnestra) had killed their bridegrooms, the fifty sons of their father's brother Aegyptus, on their wedding night. In the black-figure vase-painting of the sixth century (above, n. 189) small winged figures, seemingly male, pour from hydriai into a huge pithos. The neighbouring groups of Sisyphos and Herakles with Cerberus show that it is a scene from the Underworld, but what the painter understood by it we do not know. Oknos: see also p. 490 with Chapter 7 n. 115.

192. Red-figure pelike with Odysseus and Elpenor (Boston 34.79): *ARV²* 1045, Lykaon Painter no. 2; Beazley in CB II 86ff. no. 111, pl. 63 and suppl. pl. 16; see also p. 327 with Chapter 5 n. 84; and cf. 426–7 with Chapter 6 n. 175. Parthenon squatter: p. 300 with Chapter 5 n. 21.

193. Protesilaus: see pp. 338 and 343f. with Chapter 5 notes 109 and 121. Exekias's Memnon (B.M. B209): *ABV* 144 no. 8; Technau *Exekias* pl. 26; M. Robertson 64. Animal-support for helmet-crest: p. 429 with Chapter 6 n. 180.

194. Theseus and the two swords: M. Robertson in *JWCI* 15 (1952) 99f. and 28 (1965) 316f.

195. Girl in swing on Attic vases: sixth-century black-figure neck-amphora (Boston 98.918): *ABV* 306, Swing Painter no. 41, *BSA* 32 pl. 6; another in the Louvre, *Ars Antiqua V* (7.xi.64) pl. 29 no. 121; not certain that these are connected with the ritual; red-figure skyphos of mid fifth-century (Berlin 2589): *ARV²* 1301, Penelope Painter no. 7, Pfuhl *MuZ* fig. 567 (the swing pushed by a satyr; a satyr carries a parasol over a girl walking on the other side of the vase); small hydria of the later fifth century (Berlin 2394): *ARV²* 1131, Washing Painter no. 172; Greifenhagen *AKW¹* pl. 42, 2, *AKW²* pl. 48, 2 (the swing, which is a legged stool, is pushed by a woman; wool-basket, pithos and a cloth on the wall show that it is an indoor scene); these two are surely connected with the Anthesteria, and so are two late fifth-century *choes* (see p. 371 with Chapter 6 n. 27) which show swings: Athens, Vlasto, *ARV²* 1949, Eretria Painter no. 14, van Hoorn *Choes* fig. 10, man putting little boy on swing; and New York 75.2.11, *ARV²* 1313, Meidias Painter no. 11, van Hoorn *Choes* fig. 12, Richter and Hall pl. 158, women perfuming clothes on swing. See also M. Robertson in *JWCI* 15 (1952) 99f. and 28 (1965) 316f. 'Fates' of Parthenon East pediment (Aphrodite and Dione): see pp. 303–4 with Chapter 5 n. 26.

196. Actaeon: see p. 213 with n. 102. Athena on a rock: p. 262 with n. 181.

197. Orpheus singing: e.g. column-krater of mid or later fifth century (Berlin inv. 3172): *ARV²* 1103, Orpheus Painter no. 1; Greifenhagen *AKW²* 51; Pfuhl *Muz* fig. 554. Orpheus's death among trees: hydria (Boston 90.156): *ARV²* 605, Niobid Painter no. 62; Beazley in CB II 72ff. no. 107 pls. 57 and 47, 2.

198. B.M. 1960.2–1.1; *AK* 4 (1961) pl. 15; *BMQ* 23 (1961) pls. 31–4. Sanctuary of Apollo Smintheus on Chryse: p. 456 with Chapter 7 n. 25.

199. Contest of Thamyras and Apollo: p. 246 with n. 154. Picture of Thamyras punished (hydria, Oxford 530): *ARV²* 1061, Group of Polygnotos, undetermined, no. 152; Pfuhl *MuZ* fig. 512. Thamyras playing, Muses and his mother present, is shown on two fine vases by the Phiale Painter (pp. 262–3 with n. 182; p. 326 with Chapter 5 n. 82): hydria in

the Vatican, *ARV²* 1020 no. 92, Pfuhl *MuZ* fig. 511, *ÖJh* 8 (1905) 38; and hydria in Naples (3143), *ARV²* 1020 no. 93, *Mon.* 8 (1864/8) pl. 43, 2, *ÖJh* 8 (1905) 39 fig. 7.

200. On the story of Marsyas, see pp. 341–3 with Chapter 5 notes 116–19; 395 and 435 with Chapter 6 notes 94f., 200; 536 and 584 with Chapter 8 notes 87, 221. There is a conspectus of the Underworld on an Attic red-figure vase of the third quarter of the fifth century, but it is exceedingly poor, dull work and does not appear to have any significant relation to Polygnotos: calyx-krater (New York 08.258.21): *ARV²* 1086, Nekyia Painter no. 1; see Jacobsthal in *MMS* 5, 117–45 with figs. 6–10.

(vii) *The Temple of Zeus at Olympia; Paionios and Alkamenes*

201. Temple of Hera and its images: pp. 21 with Chapter 1 n. 17, 47–8 with Chapter 2 n. 36; see also p. 386 with Chapter 6 n. 73.

202. Monuments around the temple: Becatti *Maestro* 28ff.; Onatas: p. 184 with n. 48. The war between Elis and Pisa (below, n. 204) is often asserted to have taken place 'about 470' and so to give a *terminus post quem* for the beginning of the project, but there is virtually no information in ancient sources about this shadowy conflict.

203. Tripod and snake-column of Plataea: Herodotus IX 81; Pausanias X 13 9; see Poulsen *Delphi* 200–3, figs. 95f. Phocians at Delphi: p. 122 with Chapter 3 n. 107; p. 446 with Chapter 7 n. 3. Vix krater and vessel sent by Spartans to Croesus: p. 145 with Chapter 3 n. 150. Gorgon from sea: p. 37 with Chapter 2 n. 8. Apollo of Naxians on Delos: p. 47 with Chapter 2 n. 34; knocked down by Nikias's palm-tree: Plutarch *Nikias* 3. Antiochus's gorgoneion: Pausanias I 21 3; V 12 4; p. 532 with Chapter 8 n. 76. Palm: p. 407 with Chapter 6 n. 123.

204. Temple built out of booty from war between Elis and Pisa: Pausanias V 10 2. Spartan dedication for Tanagra: ibid. 4. The inscribed block: *Ol.* V 369–74 no. 257; later refs. in Becatti *Maestro* 31f. See also next note.

205. A suggestion for the character of a conjectured pre-Pheidian cult-image rejected: p. 196 with n. 70. Hephaisteion and cult-statues: pp. 285 with n. 228, 344–5 and 354 with Chapter 5 notes 124f., 153. Akroteria: Pausanias V 10 4; cuttings for the Nike in inscribed block above the east gable: *Ol.* V 373f.; see last note, and p. 284 with n. 227. Rarity of marble at Olympia: p. 48 with Chapter 2 notes 36f. On this question see especially Ashmole *ASCG* 12–22.

206. The temple: Pausanias V 10 2; *Ol.* II 4–27; Dinsmoor 151–3; D. S. Robertson 40f. fig. 17, 112f., 327; Lawrence *A* 149f., 154 figs. 89f., pl. 44; Rodenwaldt and Hege 30ff. pl. 18. The sculpture: *Ol.* III (Treu) 44–181, figs. 51–209, pls. 9–45; Buschor and Hamann passim; Becatti *Maestro* (documentation: inscriptions, texts; find-spots; bibliography to 1943 with survey of views on authorship, reconstruction etc.); Ashmole, Yalouris and Frantz (best pictures, fine text, and notes on recent additions and reconstructions); Ashmole *ASCG* 1–89 (sculpture illustrated figs. 26–103; particularly important on the practical problems of the work). The sculptures are constantly illustrated (e.g. Lullies and Hirmer, pls. 107–25; BDFH pls. 188–96 (172–80)). See following notes.

207. Beardless Herakles: pp. 166 and 237 with notes 21 and 143.

208. Find-spots (metopes and pediment-figures): *Ol.* III 148 fig. 172; Becatti *Maestro* 35f., to figs. 2 and 3; *JdI* 4 (1889) 266.

209. The twelve labours and the position of these metopes in the development of the theme: Brommer *Herakles* 5, 53, 57f.; and each metope treated under its subject. Augean stables: Pindar *O.* 10, 27f., quoted by Brommer 28. The metopes: Pausanias V 10 9; *Ol.* III 138–81 figs. 170–89; Buschor and Hamann pls. 79–101; Becatti *Maestro* 44–7; Ashmole, Yalouris and Frantz figs. 143–211, pp. 22–9 (Ashmole), 181–4 (Yalouris; additional fragments); Ashmole *ASCG* 60–89, figs. 79–103 (some comparative material). Suggested rearrangement: Stucchi in *Ann.* 30–2 (1955) 117–26 (part of an important article, 75–130, cited further p. 283 with n. 226).

210. Both versions were current at this time. Herakles in the garden on a black-figure lekythos, *ABV* 499 no. 34, *JdI* 57 (1942) 110f., a later

fifth-century relief, p. 374 with Chapter 6 n. 35 (citing early classical rf. vase.)

211. Interpretation of the motive in the metope of the stables: Brommer *Herakles* 27f.; Beckel *Gött.* 62f.; Ashmole in Ashmole, Yalouris and Frantz 29, *ASCG* 78ff. with figs. 90ff.

212. Apollo and Muse, Athena and woman: pp. 261f. with notes 180f. Selinus metope: p. 214 with n. 102; Parthenon metope: p. 298 with Chapter 5 n. 16.

213. Cup with Theseus and Sinis: p. 229 with n. 127; motive on Parthenon: pp. 298f. with Chapter 5 n. 18 (cf. 342 and 357 with Chapter 5 notes 119 and 162, 298 with Chapter 8 n. 92).

214. Herakles and the lion: see p. 222 with n. 116; the lion in the metope, p. 291 with n. 242.

215. Story of Pelops: Apollodorus *Ep.* II 2–9; Pindar *O.* I, 36–96. Terracotta group: Kunze in *Hundertes Winck.* (1940) 25–50, pls. 1–10, figs. 1–8; with head of Ganymede (found later) Kunze *NMO* 63–9; Lullies and Hirmer pl. V; Richter *H* 84 fig. 111. Large-scale terracotta and Corinth: pp. 146–7 with Chapter 3 n. 153, 170 with n. 24; p. 592, with Epilogue notes 4f.

216. Various proposed arrangements for these and other figures in the gable: see list of opinions, with refs., in Becatti *Maestro* 36 to figs. 5–8; Ashmole in Ashmole, Yalouris and Frantz 12–17 with fig. 14, *ASCG* 24f. figs. 26ff. 27–42, figs. 29–47; Yalouris in Ashmole, Yalouris and Frantz 172–7 with fig. 15. Find-spots: above, n. 208. An attempt to show that Zeus's head was turned to his proper left and that Pelops stood there: Kardara in *AJA* 74 (1970) 325–9 pls. 7f.

217. See Ashmole in Ashmole, Yalouris and Frantz 13f., *ASCG* 29; also Squarciapino in *Ann.* 30–2 (1955) 131–40; Kardara in *Eph.Arch.* 1965, 168ff.

218. Amphiaraos vase: pp. 121f. with Chapter 3 n. 106. Iamidai: also p. 517 with Chapter 8 n. 34.

219. Woman's shoe fastened or unfastened by a kneeling figure: e.g. on a late fifth-century vase (Attic red-figure hydria, New York 19.192.86): *ARV*[2] 1130 Washing Painter no. 152; Richter and Hall no. 146 pls. 148, 172; the woman (seated) is Helen, the servant Eros.

220. Ashmole's solution: Ashmole, Yalouris and Frantz 16 with fig. 14.

221. Seated boy: see especially Ashmole *ASCG* 30ff. figs. 29–32 (31, photograph of girl diver). Identification as Arkas: Yalouris in Ashmole, Yalouris and Frantz 176 with fig. 11 (fourth-century Arcadian coin). Geometric helmet-maker: p. 21 with Chapter 1 n. 17. Scamander in Homer: *Iliad* 21 211ff. On the Kladeos see especially Ashmole *ASCG* 35ff.

222. Early Centaurs: pp. 18, 20 with Chapter 1 n. 8, 55 with Chapter 2 n. 49. Herakles and the Centaurs of Arcadia: p. 52 with Chapter 2 n. 43. François vase: pp. 124ff. with Chapter 3 notes 111ff. Red-figure vase-paintings and Theseion picture: p. 259 with n. 174. Later Centauromachies: pp. 297, 344 and 358 with Chapter 5 notes 14f., 124 and 164.

223. Peirithoos in the Underworld: p. 268 with n. 194. Zeus Areios: Kardara in *Delt.* 25 (1970) 12–19 pl. 5.

224. Find-spots: p. 274 with n. 208.

225. P. 259 with n. 174.

226. Stucchi in *Ann.* 30–2 (1955) 112ff.; Ashmole in Ashmole, Yalouris and Frantz 22; Yalouris ibid. 179.

227. Paionios: O. 851f. The victory and its pillar: Pausanias V 26 1 (O. 852) *Ol.* V 377–84 no. 259 (the inscription; also Becatti *Maestro* 26) *Ol.* III 182–94, pls. 46–8 (the statue; also Becatti *Maestro* 47 to pl. 27, figs. 79f.). The statue is often illustrated: e.g. BDFH pl. 236 (220); Hege and Rodenwaldt pls. 82ff.; Lullies and Hirmer[2] pl. 178; Richter *H* 114 fig. 158, *Sc.* figs. 637, 642; Ridgway *SS* fig. 57; copies of the head (Rome, Palazzo Venezia and Vatican): *Ol.* III 188f. fig. 222; Richter *Sc.* figs. 639–41. See further pp. 287–8 with n. 234, 350 with Chapter 5 n. 139.

228. Settlement of Lemnos: see Lamer in *PW* XII s.v. Lemnia, 1904f. (cf. p. 320 with Chapter 5 n. 68). Alkamenes: O. 808–28 (Aphrodite in the Gardens, 812–15; competition with Agorakritos (pp. 350–1 with Chapter 5 notes 142ff.), 808, n., 834; Hera, 834; Thebes relief, 823 (cf. p. 309 with Chapter 5 n. 43); Hephaestus, 821f.) Hephaisteion statues: *IG*[2] 370f.; see Dinsmoor *Hesp.Suppl.* 5 (1941) 110 n. 243; Morgan in *Hesp.* 32 (1963) 96 and 98; cf. p. 345 with Chapter 5 n. 125. Hephaestus's head: Vatican; Helbig *Führer* 293; Br.Br. 244. Vase-painting showing Hephaestus in workman's

cap: e.g. Nolan amphora, Boston 13.188, *ARV*² 306, Dutuit Painter no. 2; Beazley in CB II pl. 44 above, and in *JHS* 33 (1913) pl. 11 and p. 110. On Alkamenes see further pp. 284–7 with notes 230ff., 345 with Chapter 5 notes 125ff.

229. Date of Promachos: Raubitschek 200, with full earlier refs.; of Zeus: pp. 320 with Chapter 5 n. 67, 411f. with Chapter 6 n. 137.

230. Herms: Crome in *AM* 60/1 (1935/6) 300–17, pls. 101–8 (Siphnos Herm) and 62 (1937) 149 pl. 67 (sixth-century Attic marble Herm); Harrison *Agora* 11 108–76 (important discussion of Athenian herms; Hermes Propylaios, 122ff.). Epiktetos: pp. 218–20 with notes 111f.; Hermoglyph cup (Copenhagen 119): *ARV*² 75 no. 59; *AM* 60/1 (1935/6) pl. 108, 2; *CV* pl. 139, 2; Beazley *VA* 17 fig. 9bis. Herms on vases: Metzger *Imagerie* 77–91. Pan Painter: p. 253 with n. 168.

231. Hermes Propylaios: Pausanias I 22 8; on the most natural punctuation of the passage, Pausanias ascribes this work to Socrates, along with a Three Graces (see Harrison *Agora* 11 122ff., and p. 314 with Chapter 5 n. 51). Herm from Pergamon, in Istanbul: Winter in *Perg.* VII 48ff. Beibl. 5 fig. 6; Picard *Manuel* II 554f. n. 3 with refs., fig. 227; Lippold pl. 71, 2; Richter *H* 112 fig. 156. Herm from Ephesus, in Smyrna (of better quality but ruined): *ÖJh* 29 (1935) 23–31 figs. 20–4; Picard l.c. n. 4. Hecate Epipyrgidia of Alkamenes: Pausanias II 30 2. Hekataia: see Harrison *Agora* II 82–107, pls. 32–9; Lippold pl. 67, 1; Picard l.c. 553 fig. 226 and 558 notes 4f.

232. Procne and Itys: Pausanias I 24 3: Πρόκνην δὲ τὰ ἐς τὸν παῖδα βεβουλευμένην αὐτήν τε καὶ τὸν Ἴτυν ἀνέθηκεν Ἀλκαμένης. The statue: Praschniker in *ÖJh* 16 (1913) 121–40; Casson *Cat.* II 257ff., nos. 1358, 2789; Dohrn *Att.Pl.* 69ff. (Roman copy); and especially Adam 89–91 with a fine appreciation. See further pp. 345–6 with Chapter 5 n. 127. *Tereus* of Sophocles and that of Philocles dated 427 and 426 B.C. respectively: Radke in *RE* XXIII.1 251ff. s.v. Prokne; Sophocles's version put shortly before 414 in Jebb–Pearson II 221–38, because parodied in Aristophanes's *Birds* of that year; but Philocles's play evidently came between; Willige and Bayer *Sophocles* 1012 say before 431. Picture of Medea preparing to kill her children: pp. 589–90 with Chapter 8 n. 240.

233. Earlier Alkamenes: J. P. Barron, in a lecture at Cambridge, summer 1971, to be published. Sculptors called Kephisodotos and Praxiteles: pp. 383–4 with Chapter 6 notes 65f. Alkamenes and archaism: p. 346 with Chapter 5 notes 130f.

234. Nike of Paionios: refs. above in n. 227. Nike from Paros: p. 200 with n. 78.

235. On the question of models, see Ashmole in Ashmole, Yalouris and Frantz 20; cf. Blümel *GSW* 51ff.

236. On this see especially Ashmole's discussion, *ASCG* 40ff. with figs. 45–7.

237. On this point see Ashmole's important remarks in *Ideal.*

238. See pp. 258–9 with n. 174.

239. Fair-haired boy: p. 175 with n. 28. Miletus head: p. 75 with Chapter 3 n. 10. Nisyros stele: p. 197 with n. 73.

240. Drapery-ends: e.g. Ashmole, Yalouris and Frantz figs. 41–3 (east ped.); 135f. and 142f. (west ped.); cf. 155 (west metope). Pubes e.g. ibid. figs. 7, 18f. 49 (e. ped.); 71f., 92 (and 95), 101 (and 103–5), 133 (and 139, 141f. w. ped.); 153, 162 (and 167; w. metopes); 188 (twice, e. metopes). On work in the quarry, transport and construction, see particularly Ashmole *ASCG* 12–23.

241. On problems of design and execution see Ashmole in Ashmole, Yalouris and Frantz 8–10. Bronze diskobolos (New York 78): Richter *Sc.* 55 and figs. 31f.; Ridgway *SS* fig. 118.

242. Lion-head spouts: Willemsen *Ol.Forsch.* IV, distinguishing the phases of replacement and with a very full study of comparative material, including a discussion of the treatment of the mouth. One of the original set: Hege and Rodenwaldt 30 fig. 17; Ashmole *ASCG* 67 fig. 76 (metope-lion fig. 75); a selection from different periods: Ashmole, Yalouris and Frantz figs. 7–10.

CHAPTER 5: THE CLASSICAL MOMENT

(i) *The Parthenon and Pheidias*

1. Accounts for Parthenon and Parthenos: *IG* I^2 339–53; summary and discussion by Burford 'The builders of the Parthenon' in *P. and P.* 23–35, esp. 23f., 29–32. Dating of Hephaisteion: Dinsmoor 180 and in *Hesp. Suppl. V* (1941) 128–64; see also p. 306 with n. 35.
2. Plataean Oath and Peace of Kallias: pp. 106–7 with Chapter 3 n. 76, 172 with Chapter 4 n. 26; p. 383 with Chapter 6 n. 64. The Peace, like the Oath, has been considered a forgery by some ancient as well as some modern authorities, surely wrongly: see most recently S. K. Eddy in *CP* 65 (1970) 8–14 with refs. to earlier literature; believers include Wade-Gery, Meiggs, Andrewes, Oliver, Eddy; unbelievers Stockton, Sealey; the ancient doubters were Callisthenes (ap. Plutarch who himself believed in it, *Cimon* XIII 4) and Theopompos (ap. Harpocrates s.v. Attikois grammasin; *Frr.Hist.Gr.* 115 F 154).
3. Possible early temple on site of Parthenon: Dinsmoor 71f.; D. S. Robertson 113f.; Plommer in *JHS* 80 (1960) 140–6; and see p. 159 with Chapter 4 n. 11. Earlier and later Parthenon: Dinsmoor 149ff. with n. and 159–65; D. S. Robertson l.c. and 327; Lawrence *A* 159–61; Plommer l.c. 134–40; and see p. 294 with n. 5.
4. παρθενών is a formation of exactly the same kind as γυναικών 'women's quarters' and ἀνδρών 'men's quarters' (hence, dining-room).
5. Carpenter *Arch.Parth.*
6. Gold and ivory figures from Delphi: pp. 140–1 with Chapter 3 n. 144. Apollo of Amyclae: pp. 39 with Chapter 2 n. 18, 114–15 with Chapter 3 n. 93. Promachos: p. 285 with Chapter 4 n. 229; p. 320 with n. 67.
7. Temple and statue of Athena Areia at Plataea: Pausanias IX 4 1 (O. 635; cf. 636, Plutarch *Aristides* 20); see also p. 245 with Chapter 4 n. 154. Acroliths: p. 202 with Chapter 4 n. 85. Pheidias on marble and ivory: O. 654 (Parid. epit. Valer. Max. I I ext. 7; Nepotian ibid.).
8. Relative dating of Parthenos and Zeus: p. 322 with n. 71. Pheidias overseer of Pericles's works: Plutarch *Pericles* 13 (O. 625).
9. Only a small selection can be given from the most important works on the sculptures of the Parthenon. Fuller bibliographies will be found in Brommer's works and in *P. and P.* 58–60; see also following notes. The only attempt at a full publication is Smith *Parth.*, where Carrey's drawings are illustrated: these are also now separately published in Bowie and Thimme. For pediments and metopes Smith is now supplemented and corrected by Brommer *Giebel* and *Metopen*; a study of the frieze by Brommer, which will complete this series, is in preparation. Other general studies are Praschniker *Parthenonstudien* (particularly important for the metopes); and Collignon *Parthénon.* The best short account is Corbett *Sc.Parth.*; see also *B.M. Hist.Guide*, and M. Robertson in *P. and P.* Selections are illustrated in all hand-books, histories and picture-books: e.g. Lullies and Hirmer pls. 140–69 (142–71); BDFH pls. 203–15 (187–99).
10. See pp. 363–5 with Chapter 6 n. 4.
11. See p. 309 with n. 42.
12. See p. 318 with n. 62.
13. On the metopes in general, besides Brommer and Praschniker (above, n. 9) see Picard in *REA* 47 (1945) 177–213 (developing Praschniker's theory of the north metopes); Bothmer *Am.* 298f. (on the west metopes); Brommer in *JdI* 75 (1960) 37–83. See also following notes.
14. South metopes: Brommer *Metopen* 71–129, pls. 145–244. Metope on building (S.1): Smith *Parth.* pl. 16, 1; Brommer *Metopen* pls. 154–63. Greek attacking Centaur from behind (S.27): Smith l.c. pl. 22, 1 and fig. 63; Brommer l.c. pls. 216–20; Corbett *Sc.Parth.* pl. 2; *P. and P.* pl. 25a: 'strife-motive': pp. 229 and 276 with Chapter 4 notes 127 and 213; pp. 299 and 357 with notes 18 and 162, 539 with Chapter 8 n. 92. Centaur and dead Lapith (S.28): Smith l.c. pl. 22, 2; Brommer l.c. pls. 221–3. On colouring see also p. 569 with Chapter 8 n. 172. 'Cimonian Parthenon': Rhys Carpenter, above, n. 5. Warriors from Aigina: pp. 165–7 with Chapter 4 n. 20. Hephaisteion: p. 344 with n. 124. Myron, pp. 339ff. with notes 112ff.

15. Subject-matter of south metopes: Brommer *Metopen* 230–40. Women at image (S.21): Smith *Parth.* fig. 59; Brommer *Metopen* pls. 151, 209; example in later Centauromachy: p. 358 with n. 164. Combat (S.16): Smith l.c. fig. 54; Brommer l.c. pls. 151, 202–5.
16. Subject-matter of east metopes: Brommer *Metopen* 198–209 with refs.; of west: ibid. 191–5, with refs.; Bothmer *Am.* 298f.; of north: Brommer l.c. 212–21 with refs. Menelaus and Helen (N.24–5): Smith *Parth.* figs. 80–2; Brommer *Metopen* pls. 99–110. Helios and Selene (N.1 and 29): Smith *Parth.* figs. 75 and 84; Brommer *Metopen* pls. 85–90, 93, 99, 123–6. Goddesses (N.32): Smith *Parth.* pl. 21, figs. 85f.; Brommer *Metopen* pls. 99, 132–8; *P. and P.* pl. 5b.
17. Stymphalian birds: p. 275 with Chapter 4 n. 212. Selinus metope: p. 214 with Chapter 4 n. 102. Victory of Paionios: pp. 284 and 288 with Chapter 4 notes 227, 234; p. 350 with n. 139.
18. Pediment-composition: p. 162 with Chapter 4 n. 16. 'Strife-motive': above, n. 14. West pediment: Smith *Parth.* 15–21, pls. 4, 1 and 7–12: Brommer *Giebel* 30–61, 158–70, pls. 63–131, 152; Harrison in *Essays . . . Wittkower* 1–9, figs. 1–19. Carrey's drawing: Smith *Parth.* fig. 27; Brommer *Giebel* pl. 64. Vase (Leningrad KAB 6A): Schefold *UKV* no. 161 pl. 28; Pfuhl *MuZ* fig. 604; Roscher s.v. Poseidon fig. 4. See also following notes.
19. See Harrison in *AJA* 71 (1967).
20. Athena and Poseidon (L and M): Smith *Parth.* pl. 10 and figs. 31–3; Brommer *Giebel* pls. 97–101, 103–6; see also p. 304 with n. 31. Remains of chariot-horses: Brommer *Giebel* pls. 94–6. Amphitrite (O): Smith *Parth.* pl. 11, 1 and fig. 34; Brommer *Giebel* pls. 115f. Hermes (H): Smith *Parth.* pl. 9, 1 and fig. 30; Brommer *Giebel* pls. 91–3. Iris (N): Smith *Parth.* pl. 4 and fig. 20; Brommer *Giebel* pls. 111–13; *P. and P.* pl. 7a; and constantly. Paionios: see refs. in n. 17 above.
21. 'Ilissos' (A): Smith *Parth.* pl. 7 and fig. 28; Brommer *Giebel* pls. 81–4; *P. and P.* pl. 6c; and constantly. Squatter (V): Smith *Parth.* pl. 10 and fig. 36; Brommer *Giebel* pls. 81–4; *P. and P.* pl. 7b; Polygnotos's Odysseus: see p. 268 with Chapter 4 n. 192. 'Kallirrhoe' (W): Smith *Parth.* pl. 12 and figs. 37–9; Brommer *Giebel* pls. 129–31; see also p. 371 with Chapter 6 n. 26. Copies from Eleusis and Agora: Brommer *Giebel* pls. 143–7; Harrison in *Essays . . . Wittkower* figs. 3, 8–15, 18f. Kekrops and his daughter (B and C): Smith *Parth.* pl. 8 and fig. 29; Brommer *Giebel* pls. 85–9. Pelops's seer and river-gods at Olympia: pp. 278ff. with Chapter 4 notes 218, 221.
22. Athena and Hermes on vases: e.g. amphorae of Panathenaic shape (Vatican): *ARV*² 197 Berlin Painter no. 5, Beazley *Berl.M.* pl. 11; (Würzburg): *ARV*² 249 Syleus Painter no. 7, Langlotz *GVW* pls. 167f.; cup (Athens Acrop. 322): *ARV*² 477 Makron no. 292, Graef and Langlotz pl. 21; Nolan amphora (B.M. 1928.1-17.57): *ARV*¹ 529 Alkimachos Painter no. 12, *BSA* 40, pl. 12, 42. Tree-fragments: Brommer *Giebel* pl. 102 and p. 41; vase: p. 299 with n. 18.
23. Birth of Athena in Attic black-figure, e.g. cup (B.M. B424): *ABV* 168f. Phrynos Painter no. 3, Beazley *ABS* pl. 1, *Dev.* pl. 21; in red-figure, e.g. pelike (B.M. E410): *ARV*² 494, Painter of the Birth of Athena no. 1, Smith *Parth.* fig. 10; on the subject in general, see Brommer, in *Jb. des röm-germ. Zentralmuseums Mainz* 1961, 66–83.
24. East pediment: Smith *Parth.* 6–14 pls. 1–6; Brommer *Giebel* 3–29, 141–57, pls. 1–62; Harrison in *AJA* 71 (1967) 27–58 pls. 13–28. Madrid relief: Smith *Parth.* fig. 11. Brommer does not accept its derivation from the pediment: see article cited in last note and especially excursus in 'Studien zu den Parthenongiebeln IV', *AM* 73 (1958) 103–16; i–iii of this important series of articles appeared in *AM* 69/70 (1955) 47–66, 71 (1956) 29–50 and 232–44.
25. Running girl (G, Artemis? – see p. 303 with n. 28): Smith *Parth.* pl. 3 and fig. 19; Brommer *Giebel* pls. 38–42. 'Demeter and Persephone' (E and F): Smith *Parth.* pl. 3 and figs. 13–18; Brommer *Giebel* pls. 32–8. 'Theseus' (D, Dionysus?, Herakles?): Smith *Parth.* pl. 2 and fig. 16; Brommer *Giebel* pls. 26–32; *P. and P.* pl. 6a; and constantly. Identification as Herakles: Harrison in *AJA* 71 (1967) 41–5; Lloyd-Jones in *AJA* 74 (1970) 181, with reference to Herakles's initiation at Eleusis, discussed by him in *Maia* 19 (1967) 152. Helios (A–C): Smith *Parth.* pl. 1 and figs. 12–16; Brommer *Giebel*

pls. 21–5. Figure from Monument of Lysicrates (p. 482 with Chapter 7 n. 88): Br.Br. 488; *KB* 316, 1; Elgin's cast: *Mus.Marb.* IX pl. 24.

26. Selene (N–O): Smith *Parth.* pl. 6 and figs. 24–6; Brommer *Giebel* pls. 52–62; the well-preserved horse's head constantly; Selene or Nyx: see Harrison in *AJA* 71 (1967) 45. 'Aphrodite and Dione' (L and M) and 'Hestia' (K): Smith *Parth.* pl. 5 and figs. 21ff.; Brommer *Giebel* pls. 45–51; *P. and P.* pl. 6b (the pair); and constantly.

27. Siphnian pediment: p. 158 with Chapter 4 n. 10. The most convincing of many reconstructions of the east pediment of the Parthenon seems to me that of E. Harrison in *AJA* 71 (1967) 27–58, pls. 13–22, but some questions certainly remain open; other attempts are by Berger in *AM* 71 (1956) 152–72, pls. 6–12; Carpenter in *Hesp.* 2 (1933) 1–88, pls. 1–2.

28. Fragments identified as Hera: Wegner in *AM* 57 (1932) 92–101; given by Carpenter to one of the Fates; accepted as Hera by Brommer (*Giebel* pls. 136f.) and Harrison; see also below, n. 30. God's torso (H): called Hephaestus by Brommer (*Giebel* pls. 43f.; he uses it as an argument against the Madrid relief) following Sauer in *AM* 16 (1891) 89; called Poseidon by Harrison, following Carpenter and Berger. Running girl called Artemis by Buschor in *Eph.Arch.* 1937 (ii) 454; this accepted by Brommer and Harrison. Acropolis fr. 6713: identified as belonging to Parthenon by Wegner in *Festschr.Schweitzer* 185–91, and thought female; accepted by Brommer (*Giebel* pl. 138) and by Harrison, but she identifies it as seated Apollo (*AJA* 71 (1967) 27f., pl. 20 figs. 24ff.).

29. On the 'Dionysus' and 'Ilissus' in a wider context, see Clark *The Nude* especially Chapter 9. See also p. 548 with Chapter 8 n. 114.

30. Laborde head (Louvre): Smith *Parth.* pl. 14a no. 18; Brommer *Giebel* pl. 132; Harrison in *AJA* 71 (1967) pl. 19 fig. 20; *Enc.Phot.* 161; and often. Veiled head-fr. (Acropolis 2181): assigned to one of the pediments of the Parthenon by Sauer in *Festschr.Overbeck* 74–8, who recognised it as female; associated with Helios by Marcadé in *Mon.Piot.* 50, 11–47 (a valuable article) and elsewhere; association disproved (pace Marcadé in *BCH* 88 (1964) 623f.) by Brommer in *MWP* 1957, 7f. and elsewhere, and by Harrison in *AJA* 71 (1967) 34f. n. 62; associated with 'Hera' by Berger, Brommer and Harrison. Demeter of Cherchel and Berlin 83: Kekule von Stradonitz in *BWP* 57 (1897) pls. 1–6; Cherchel also: BDFH pl. 216 (200) Beazley and Ashmole fig. 94; Lippold pl. 63, 4. Metope with goddesses: p. 298 with n. 16. Hestia: p. 191 with Chapter 4 n. 58.

31. Tritons and Giants from Agora: Thompson in *Hesp.* 19 (1950) 31–141, especially 101–23, pls. 61–76. Monte Cavallo horse-tamers: ibid. pl. 77; Furtwängler *MP* 98 (one head); Carpenter *Gr.Sc.* pl. 47B.

32. Brommer *Giebel* pls. 7 (E) and 79 (W); and see his pp. 56, 144, 162, 164, and in *AM* 68/70 (1944/5) 58–60; 71 (1956) 237; 73 (1958) 106. Ashmole *ASCG* 107ff. with n. 64 and figs. 120f., suggests that they are for bollards to hoist the sculptures, a convincing solution.

33. P. 269 with Chapter 4 n. 195.

34. Continuous figured bands on archaic buildings: pp. 57–8 with Chapter 2 n. 53 (Prinias), 63 with Chapter 2 n. 64 (Corfu), 82 with Chapter 3 n. 25 (Assos), 83ff. with Chapter 3 notes 29 (Ephesus) and 31 (Didyma), 153ff. with Chapter 4 notes 2–8 (Siphnian Treasury and canonical Ionic), 160 with Chapter 4 n. 13 (supposed frieze of Athena-temple on Acropolis). 'Temple of Ceres' at Paestum: p. 117 with Chapter 3 n. 99. Eretria temple: *Archaeology* 21, 4 (Oct. 1968) 276f. (cf. p. 163 with Chapter 4 n. 18). Ionic fountain-houses on late sixth-century Attic vases: see Dunkley in *BSA* 36 (1935/6) 161 with notes 5 and 7, 162 with notes 1–3, pl. 22b, figs. 4 and 5; B.M. *CV* 6 pls. 88, 4 and 90, 2. Athenian stoa at Delphi: Dinsmoor 142; D. S. Robertson 127, 335; Amandry in *FdeD* II (1953) 33–121. Temple of Olympian Zeus at Athens (original form): Dinsmoor 71; D. S. Robertson 102f., 331 (classed as probably Ionic, but Dinsmoor has demonstrated that it was Doric); Lawrence *A* 117; and see pp. 532 with Chapter 8 n. 76, 604 and 609 with Epilogue notes 37 and 52. 'Poikile' fragments: p. 245 with Chapter 4 n. 152. On Doric and Ionic at Athens, see further p. 347 with notes 132ff.

35. Ionic columns in Parthenon: Dinsmoor 164; D. S. Robertson 115. Temples by 'Hephais-

teion architect' and their Ionic friezes: Dinsmoor 179–82, especially 181f.; Plommer in *BSA* 45 (1950) 66–112 and 55 (1960) 218–33; also D. S. Robertson 115 with n. 3, 118 and 328; Demangel *Frise* 318–24 with fig. 68. Carpenter, *Arch.Parth.* 170ff., identifies the 'Hephaisteion architect' with Kallikrates, designer of his 'Cimonian Parthenon'; he attributes to the same architect, as well as the Ionic Temple by the Ilissos and Nike Temple (pp. 348–9 with notes 136f.) the Doric Temple of the Athenians on Delos (p. 356 with n. 159). Hephaisteion sculpture: p. 344 with n. 124. On the Temple at Rhamnus, see further pp. 352 and 354 with notes 148, 155.

36. Panathenaia and Panathenaic vases: pp. 150 with Chapter 3 n. 160, 237–8 with Chapter 4 n. 144; 346 with n. 131, 359 with n. 168. Nike Temple site (p. 349 with n. 137) claimed as original home of image: Kardara in *Eph. Arch.* 1961, 64–114. On Athena, see especially Herington *APAP*, and in *P. and P.* 61–73.

37. Panathenaic ship: Smith *Parth.* 50f. with fig. 97. Ship-cart of Dionysus: Attic black-figure skyphos, early fifth century, Athens Acrop. 1281, Graef pl. 74, Haspels *ABFL* 250, Theseus Painter no. 29. On the nature of the procession shown in the frieze, see p. 309 with n. 42; and cf. Corbett *Sc.Parth.* 22f. On the frieze see also: Buschor *Parthenonfr.*; Haynes *Parth. Frieze*; Schuchardt in *JdI* 45 (1930) 218–80; Schweitzer in *JdI* 53 (1938) 1–89, 54 (1939) 1–96, 55 (1940) 170–241, and in *Festgabe zur Winckelmannsfeier . . . Leipzig* (1936); now also Robertson and Frantz (Bibliography, addenda).

38. The most elaborated interpretation of the frieze as showing the whole movement of the procession from the Outer Kerameikos (the west end) to the top of the Acropolis (the east end): Fehl in *JWCI* 24 (1961) 1–44 'The rocks on the Parthenon frieze'.

39. Kardara in *Charisterion* II 22f. pls. 1 and 2, points out the resemblance of this figure to a boy (?) on a red-figure cup (Acrop. 396): *ARV*¹ 628, top, no. 1 (akin to Penthesilean); omitted from *ARV*²: Graef and Langlotz pl. 29; Diepolder *Penth.* pl. 27, 1. This child, long-haired and olive-wreathed, drinks from a phiale in the presence of Athena. Kardara identifies both this and the child on the frieze as Erechtheus/Erichthonios; see also n. 42 below. Stele from Paros: p. 363 with Chapter 6 n. 3.

40. The twelve Olympians are shown on a sub-archaic relief of the first half of the fifth century, said to be from Tarentum and certainly of South Italian Greek style: Br.Br. 660; Roscher 6, 791 fig. 2 (in article 'Zwölfgötter', which see). Hestia at home: Plato *Phaedrus* 247A.

41. The statues of the ten Eponymous Heroes were a feature of the Agora: see Wycherley *Agora* 3 85–90 nos. 229–45, especially note on last.

42. Mythological interpretation: Kardara in *Eph. Arch.* 1961, 115–58; see also n. 39 above. Two stools for two robes: M. Robertson in *P. and P.* 56; see also p. 346 with n. 130.

43. Sunium relief and 'Mourning Athena': pp. 177–8 with Chapter 4 notes 34 and 35. Eleusis relief (Athens N.M. 126): Svoronos I 106–20, pls. 24f.; Karouzou *Cat.* pl. 20; Lullies and Hirmer pls. 172f.; Richter *Sc.* fig. 481; Schrader *Phidias* 89 fig. 73. Persephone's gesture is obscure; Svoronos suggests the implanting of a magic lock, comparing the story of Nisos; see also p. 314 with n. 51. Alkamenes: pp. 284–6 with Chapter 4 notes 228–31; pp. 345–6 with notes 126–30 (Caryatids).

44. See pp. 602–4 with Epilogue n. 36.

45. Parthenos, texts: O. 645–90 (649, Pausanias I 20 5; 661, Pliny XXXVI 18). Among modern studies one may mention: Becatti *PF* 109–24, pls. 62 (Varvakeion) and 63; Brommer *AP*, pls. 1 (Pergamon), 2 (Lenormant), 3 (Varvakeion), 7 (Copenhagen); Leipen *APR*, illustrating most of the material; Lippold 145ff.; Schrader *Phidias* 34–44, figs. 4–12; the Varvakeion (Athens N.M. 129) also: BDFH pl. 201 (185); Karouzou *Cat.* pl. 31. On the subsidiary adornments, see following notes.

46. Gigantomachy on shield-interior: Pliny XXXVI 18 (relief); remains of painting on interior of Strangford, and related vases: von Salis in *JdI* 55 (1940) 90–169, with full and fascinating discussion and much illustration; see also Leipen *APR* 46–50 with refs. and figs. 84–7; and see further pp. 324 with n. 77, 420 with Chapter 6 n. 161. There are traces of paint also on the interior of the shield in the Patras copy. Decorations of the Promachos shield: p. 411

with Chapter 6 n. 137. Panainos at Olympia and Elis: pp. 317 and 323 with notes 60 and 74. Pheidias as painter: Pliny XXXV 54 (O. 623); and see Rumpf *MZ* 103, 111.

47. Parthenos base and Drago relief: Becatti *PF* 52–70, pls. 8–11; and see pp. 318 and 354 with notes 62 and 152. Pergamon base, also: *Perg.* VII 1 no. 24 pl. 7; *KB* 246, 4; and see p. 546 with Chapter 8 n. 111.

48. Medici Athena: p. 320 with n. 67. Aegis so worn in vase-painting: e.g. Attic red-figure cup of the later fifth century (Bologna PU273): *ARV*² 1268, Kodros Painter no. 1; *CV* pls. 19–22.

49. Medusa Rondanini and Pheidias: Buschor *MR* with illustrations and refs.; also below, n. 108.

50. Theory of burning and reconstruction: Dinsmoor in *AJA* 38 (1934) 93–106; the fire dated to the Roman period: Stevens in *Hesp.* 24 (1955) 239–76 (a most important article on the construction of the statue). Removal of the gold: p. 322 with n. 72.

51. Three Graces on Acropolis 'by Socrates': O. 907–15 (and see above, p. 286 with Chapter 4 n. 231). A Theban sculptor Socrates, contemporary of Pindar: Pausanias IX 25 3 (O. 478). Copies of relief: Ridgway *SS* figs. 153ff.; (from Acropolis) Casson *Cat.* 243f. nos. 1341–1341γ. On the name and the relief, see Poulsen *St.St.* 134 (before the finding of the Peiraeus copies, which are unpublished). Eleusis relief: above, n. 43; Roman copy (fragments) in New York: Richter *MMCat.Sc.* 27f. no. 34 pl. 32; possible adaptation: ibid. no. 35; *Sc.* fig. 510. Three Graces: pp. 58–9 with Chapter 2 n. 54; pp. 318–19 with n. 63, 494 with Chapter 7 n. 126, 550 with Chapter 8 n. 120. Copying practice: Richter *AI* chapter 3, app. 1 (pointing-boss on Varvarkeion, pp. 109f. fig. 297), *TCP* chapter 3.

52. Reconstruction of the shield: see Leipen *APR* 41–50 with refs. and figs. 23–36, 50 and 81–7; the most important earlier attempts are by Stavropoulos *Aspis* (publication of the Piraeus reliefs); Ras in *BCH* 68/9 (1944/5) 163ff.; Brommer in *MWP* 1948, 10ff.; Schlörb in *AM* 78 (1963) 156ff.; Harrison in *Hesp.* 35 (1966) 107–33 pls. 36–41, with very interesting discussion and interpretation; Strocka *Pir. u. Parth.*; see also Becatti *PF* 111ff., 244ff., pls. 64–8, 103–12; Bothmer *Am.* 209–14, pl. 87.

53. Penthesilea cup: p. 263 with Chapter 4 n. 184.

54. 'Heroic diagonal': Clark *The Nude* 173.

55. Portrait-head in Copenhagen thought to be based on 'Pheidias' on shield: V. Poulsen *Portraits* 54–5 no. 26 pl. 18; Richter *POG* 1 figs. 850f. (849, the figure on the Strangford shield; she does not accept the identification of the Copenhagen head). See also Frel in *Ant.Gr.-Rom.ac Temp.Nostra* frontispiece; and for another type identified as portrait of Pheidias: Metzler in *AK* 7 (1964) 51f. (approved but not illustrated, Richter *POG* 151). Centaur-head: Becatti *PF* pl. 31, figs. 107f. 'Capaneus' thought original of a time between Olympia pediments and Parthenon metopes: Lawrence *S* 183, pl. 140.

56. Marble vase in Madrid with Centauromachy-groups: Becatti *PF* pl. 69; Leipen *APR* 30, with refs. and figs. 73–5. Related relief in Lateran: Langlotz *Phidiaspr.* pl. 12, above.

57. Pheidias's workshop: pp. 321–2 with n. 71.

58. Boardman in *Gymnasium* 74 (1967) 508f.; Stevens in *Hesp.* 24 (1955) 239–76 (cf. above n. 50, and p. 322 with n. 73).

59. Texts on Zeus: O. 692–754 (698, Strabo VIII 353; 696, Pausanias V 11 1; 721, Quintilian XII 10 9). Modern studies: (among many): Becatti *PF* 125–40, pls. 71–3 (coins and Cyrene head); Liegle *Zeus* pls. 1 and 15ff. (coins); Schrader *Phidias* 44ff. figs. 13f. (coins). Cyrene head: Paribeni *Cat.* 77 no. 182, pls. 104f., with refs. Three Graces: refs. in n. 51 above. On other points, see following notes.

60. Panainos and his work pp. 322–4 with notes 74ff. Figures holding *aphlasta* (stern-ornaments) on Athenian vases, all a little earlier than this but post-Persian: column-krater (Bari 4402), *ARV*² 550, Pan Painter no. 4; votive shields from Acropolis of Athens (1071f.), Graef and Langlotz pl. 83, *ARV*² 535 no. 6 (near the Alkimachos Painter) and 537, Boreas Painter no. 48; skyphos (Acrop. 516), Graef and Langlotz pl. 40 (not in Beazley's lists). Statue at Delphi: Herodotus VIII 121; Pausanias X 14 5; see Poulsen *Delphi* 200.

61. Bothmer *Am.* 142.

62. Parthenos's base: p. 312 with n. 47. Base of Nemesis: p. 353 with n. 152.

63. The Graces: refs. in n. 51, above; a single Charis: p. 494 with Chapter 7 n. 126. Silver-

gilt disk from Galaxidi (Louvre): *Gaz.Arch.* 5 (1879) 171–4, pl. 19, 2; and often since, e.g. from old drawing: *RM* 7 (1892) 49 fig. 9; *AM* 69/70 (1954/5) Beil. 35, above; Jacobsthal *MR* 167 fig. 47; Langlotz *Phidiaspr.* pl. 15a (and pp. 48f.); from a photograph: Simon *Geburt* 43 fig. 26 (cf. p. 205 with Chapter 4 n. 90). Clay disk from Vourvoura: Sparkes in *AK* 11 (1968) 14f. fig. 7 and pl. 8, 6.

64. Niobe and her children: Homer *Il.* XXIV 602–9 (six of each); Sappho, Lobel and Page frr. 142 and 205 (nine of each). Representations in art listed by R. M. Cook *Niobe* 42–53, with bibliography (41) and discussion, especially of the pediment statues (30–9, with suggested restorations of composition). These statues (Rome Mus.Naz. 72274 and Copenhagen 520, *Cat.* 398, and 472, *Cat.* 399): Br.Br. pls. 706–14; Lippold pl. 65, 1–3; Richter *Sc.* figs. 4, 92, 118; *KB* 250, 3 (Rome); and elsewhere. The only archaic pictures are on two Attic black-figure neck-amphorae of the second quarter of the sixth century ('Tyrrhenian'; p. 134 with Chapter 3 n. 131; Cook nos. 1 and 2, with refs.). See also following notes.

65. Louvre calyx-krater (Cook no. 3): pp. 253 with Chapter 4 nn. 169, 258. Melian relief (Cook no. 7): Berlin Terr. inv. 6286 and Oxford 1938.911; Jacobsthal *MR* 62f. pl. 42, and in *JHS* 59 (1939) 68ff. pl. 8.

66. Niobid reliefs in Leningrad, Rome (Villa Albani), Florence (Coll. Milani) and Bologna (Palazzo Bevilacqua), and disk in London (B.M. 2200, Cat. III pl. 26): Becatti *PF* 135–8 with refs. and pls. 74–6; Langlotz *Phidiaspr.* 45ff. pls. 13–15. Vase in Leningrad: observation of Brian Shefton, who will publish it. Evidence for the decoration of the throne is collected by Fink *Der Thron des Zeus in Olympia.*

67. Demeter of Cherchel: p. 304 with n. 30. Dresden Zeus: Schrader *Phidias* 55–60 figs. 35–7; Becatti *PF* 157f. pl. 83; *KB* 247, 3; most recently Despinis 133–45, pls. 106f. (108, replica in Olympia), with attribution to Agorakritos. Berlin Nike: Becatti *PF* pl. 72. Philadelphia Nike: *Eph.Arch.* 1953/4 ii 41–54 pls. 1–2; *Expedition* 2 (1959) 34ff. Aphrodite in Berlin: Schrader *Phidias* 71–6, figs. 57f.; Becatti *PF* pl. 100; Langlotz *Phidiaspr.* 83–96, pl. 36; *KB* 283, 1. Aphrodite Ourania at Elis: Pausanias VI 25 1 (O. 755; cf. 756); in Athens: Pausanias I 14 7 (O. 691). Medici Athena (Louvre): *Enc. Phot.* 179; *KB* 283, 6; Schrader *Phidias* 76–9, figs. 63f.; Langlotz *Phidiaspr.* 69–72 pls. 19, 21; Furtwängler *Meist.* 46f. fig. 2, *Mast.* 28 fig. 6 (Promachos); used by Becatti *PF* pl. 87 for reconstruction of Promachos. Promachos: pp. 285 with Chapter 4 n. 229, 411–12; O 637–44.

68. Sources for Lemnia: O. 758–64 (758, Pausanias I 28 2). Dresden/Bologna statue: Furtwängler *Meist.* 4–16, pls. I–III, *Mast.* 4–26, pls. 1–3; Becatti *PF* 169–74, pls. 84f.; *KB* 249, 1 and 286, 4; Richter *Sc.* figs. 614ff.; and often.

69. Pheidias as marble-sculptor: Pliny XXXVI 15 (O. 767; cf. 774); and see p. 294 with n. 7; the Aphrodite in Athens ascribed to Pheidias by Pausanias (last note) was also in marble. Bronze Amazon at Ephesus by Pheidias: pp. 334–5 with n. 103. Theokosmos of Megara: Pausanias I 40 4 (O. 855, the Zeus at Megara), X 9 8 (O. 979, the dedication at Delphi; cf. below, p. 475 with Chapter 7 n. 75), VI 7 1 (O. 1035; his son Kallikles active at Olympia).

70. Lucian *Gall.* 24 and *Jup.Tr.* 8; see Blümner in *RE* V 2363ff. Socket for 'mast' of Parthenos: Stevens in *Hesp.* 24 (1955) 239–76 (cf. n. 50 above).

71. Text on Pheidias's workshop: Pausanias V 11. Remains: Mallwitz and Schiering *Werkstatt* I (*OF* V; the architecture and the finds not directly connected with the construction of the statue, which will be treated in part 2). Pheidias's mug: ibid. pl. 64, with discussion of shape pp. 169–82, figs. 45–57; red-figure: pls. 80–91 (82f., calyx-krater fragments, *ARV*² 1144, Kleophon Painter no. 7). Some of these and of the other finds published by Kunze in *NDA* 278–95, figs. 12ff. (building), 15–22 (drapery-moulds), 23 (glass palmette-leaves), 24–7 (moulds for palmette-leaves etc.), 28 (ivory fragments), 29 (obsidian fragments), 30 (bits of sheet-bronze), 31 (lead templates), 32 (bone tools), 33 (bronze hammer-head), 34 (principal fragment of Kleophon Painter's vase). Collocation of historical and archaeological evidence: H. Bloch, reviewing Jacoby, in *Gnomon* 31 (1959) 494–9.

72. Agora head and 'Golden Nikai': H. Thompson in *Harvard Studies* Suppl. 1 (1940) 183–210;

D. B. Thompson in *Hesp.* 13 (1944) 173–239, figs. 1–14, with refs. Stripping of the gold by Lachares: Pausanias I 25 6 (O. 685; cf. 686f.).

73. 'Phaidruntai': Pausanias V 14 4 (O. 744). Statue at Epidaurus: p. 399 with Chapter 6 n. 107; on the tradition of the 'well' see Roux *Argolide* 119. Basins in front of Parthenos and Zeus: p. 317 with n. 58.

(ii) Panainos; vase-painting in Periclean Athens

74. Panainos (pp. 244–5 with Chapter 4 notes 151f., and 317 with n. 60): O. 1094–1108 (1094, Strabo, Panainos Pheidias's nephew; 1095, Pausanias, Panainos Pheidias's brother and author of Marathon; 1096f., Pliny, Panainos Pheidias's brother, collaborating with Kolotes, O. 844–50, at Elis, and plastering walls in the temple there; see p. 245 with Chapter 4 n. 152); see also next note. Battle of Marathon (p. 244 with Chapter 4 n. 151): Pausanias I 15 3 (O. 1054D; cf. 1099–1108); modern studies: e.g. Robert *Marathon*; and most recently Harrison in *AJA* 76 (1972) 353–78, pls. 73–8 (cf. p. 348 with n. 137). Pleistainetos: Plutarch *de Glor.Ath.* 2 (O. 1109). Praxiteles and Nikias: p. 393 with Chapter 6 n. 89.

75. Echetlos: Pausanias I 15 3; I 32 5, where he is called Echetlaios, but the same person is certainly meant; cf. p. 416 with Chapter 6 n. 150.

76. Panainos's advances in colour and portraiture: Pliny XXXV 57 (O. 1099). Four-colour painting: p. 260 with Chapter 4 n. 176; p. 500 with Chapter 7 n. 143. Parrhasios, Apollodoros and Agatharchos: Chapter 6 (iv) with notes 135, 137–40, 144ff.

77. Back view of head with hint of *profil perdu*: pp. 258 and 263 with Chapter 4 notes 172, 184. Vases with Gigantomachy derived from Parthenos's shield: p. 312 with n. 46. Achilles Painter: see notes 79f. Shading: refs. below, n. 84.

78. White lekythoi: *ARV*² esp. 1226–46, 1371–90; Beazley *AWL*; Buschor *ALP* and *Grab*; pictures in Riezler and Fairbanks; see also following notes. Roman copies of fifth-century panels: Cook *GA* fig. 30; Rumpf *MZ* pl. 37, 1; Maiuri *RP* 29; Rizzo *PER* pl. 90A; Curtius *WP* 95ff., figs. 66f.; Pfuhl *MuZ* figs. 719f.; all in Rome Mus.Naz. from 'Farnesina House' or 'house by the Tiber'; see further p. 606 with Epilogue n. 42.

79. Achilles Painter: *ARV*² 986–1001, *ABV* 408f.; Beazley *VA* 163ff. with figs. 99ff., *AWL* 13–16, and in *JHS* 34 (1914) 179–266, figs. 1–31 and pls. 13–16. Achilles amphora (Vatican; *ARV*² 987 no. 1): Arias and Hirmer pls. xl and 188; Buschor *GV* 201; FR pl. 167, 2 and III 293; Lane *GP* pl. 85; Rumpf *MZ* pl. 32, 6; and often. Pointed amphora (Cab.Méd. 357; *ARV*² 987 no. 2; Dionysiac, one maenad in *profil perdu*): *Mon.Piot* 7 pls. 2f.; Shefton in *WZUR* 16 (1967) pls. 89–92. White lekythoi: *ARV*² 995–1001 nos. 118–45 (with added white), 146–206 (glaze outlines), 207–12 (matt outlines). Panathenaic: Rumpf *MZ* pl. 32, 8.

80. Against the interpretation of dead and living at tomb together: Kurtz and Boardman 104f. Two youths (B.M. D54; *ARV*² 1000 Achilles Painter no. 193): M. Robertson 143. Woman and girl (Athens N.M. 12792; *ARV*² 1229, Thanatos Painter no. 28): Pfuhl *MuZ* fig. 541. Youth and woman at tomb (Athens N.M. 1935; *ARV*² 1227, Bosanquet Painter no. 1): Pfuhl *MuZ* fig. 534. Woman and maid (Boston 13.187; *ARV*² 998, Achilles Painter no. 157): Pfuhl *MuZ* fig. 537. Seated woman and warrior (Athens N.M. 1818; *ARV*² 998, Achilles Painter no. 161): Pfuhl *MuZ* fig. 543; M. Robertson 144–5. Mistress and maid with clothes (B.M. D48; *ARV*² 997, Achilles Painter no. 148): Buschor *Grab*² 43. Youths and hare (B.M. D60; *ARV*² 1230, Thanatos Painter no. 37): Rumpf *MZ* pl. 29, 4. Muses (Munich; *ARV*² 997, Achilles Painter no. 155); M. Robertson 136–9; Arias and Hirmer pls. 3, xxxviii–xxxix.

81. Sleep and Death lifting Sarpedon's body on red-figure cup signed by potter Pamphaios (B.M. E12; *ARV*² 126, Nikosthenes Painter no. 24): FR pl. 156; Lane *GP* pl. 70B; Pfuhl *MuZ* fig. 345. A splendid calyx-krater with the same subject, signed by the painter Euphronios and the potter Euxitheos (p. 222 with Chapter 4 n. 116) has recently been acquired by New York; Hypnos and Thanatos (named)

are both bearded, but the hair of Thanatos is drawn in outline, not solidly blacked like that of Hypnos. Fourth-century relief with Thanatos p. 408 with Chapter 6 n. 127. Lekythos with Sleep and Death (B.M. D58; *ARV*² 1228, Thanatos Painter no. 12): Pfuhl *MuZ* fig. 535; Beazley lists eight other examples. Charon (relatively frequent), e.g. Berlin inv. 3160, *ARV*² 1229, Thanatos Painter no. 29; Buschor *Grab* 11; with child and woman (New York 09.221.44): *ARV*² 1168, Painter of Munich 8335 no. 128; Beazley *AWL* pl. 7, 3. On Charon, see also p. 266 with Chapter 4 n. 190. Carved tombstones: Chapter 6 (i).

82. Phiale Painter: *ARV*² 1014–24; 167–70, figs. 103–5, *VP* 50–3, pls. 19, 4 and 23 and in *BSA* 30, 109–12, figs. 1–2, pls. 17–18. White calyx-kraters: p. 262 with Chapter 4 n. 182. Phiale Painter's white lekythoi (Munich 2797 and 2798): *ARV*² 1022 nos. 138f. (others 139bis, 140f.); Buschor *ALP* pls. 1–3, *Grab* 12f. and 54f. (*Grab*², 66f.); Beazley *AWL* pls. 5 and 1, 2; Arias and Hirmer pls. xlif. and 189; M. Robertson 152. Red-figure stamnos (Warsaw 142465): *ARV*² 1019 no. 82; Beazley *VP* pl. 23; *CV* 26; Pfuhl *MuZ* fig. 571. Other such mergings of the worlds: p. 418 with Chapter 6 n. 156.

83. Persephone bell-krater (New York 28.57.23): *ARV*² 1012, Persephone Painter no. 1; Pfuhl *MuZ* fig. 556; Richter *ARVS* fig. 92, *MMH* pl. 80c; Richter and Hall pl. 124; Simon *Geburt* 18. Munich stamnos: p. 253 with Chapter 4 n. 167.

84. Vase-painter Polygnotos: *ARV*² 1027–33; his group, 1033–64; Lykaon Painter, 1044–6; Odysseus pelike: pp. 267–8 with Chapter 4 n. 192. Polygnotos as vase-painter's name: *ARV*² 1027; Rumpf *MZ* 64f. Earlier use of shading: pp. 238–9 with Chapter 4 n. 146, 324 with n. 77.

(iii) Polykleitos, Kresilas, Amazons

85. Literary sources on Polykleitos: O. 929–77 (929, Pliny XXXIV 55, Sicyonian; 941, Plato *Protagoras* 311C, Argive): Pausanias qualifies the name as Argive several times, but not in his account of the Hera of Argos (II 17 4; O. 932), and he once (VI 6 2; O. 939) distinguishes an Argive Polykleitos from the man who made the Hera. The Polykleitos who made the Hera is described as Argive by Parmenio in *Anth.Gr.* II 185 5 (O. 939). Sources also collected in Bianchi Bandinelli *Pol.* nos. 1–29 (inscriptions, 11, 13, 15, 17). Pliny's dating-passage: see p. 339 with n. 111. Burning of Argive Heraeum: Thucydides IV 133; date of rebuilt temple: Dinsmoor 183; D. S. Robertson 145, 328; Shoe *PGM* (1936) 69, 159; Roux *Argolide* 57–64, especially 58, and 404; see also Waldstein *AH* I 117–27, figs. 56–64 and pls. 14–19. Temple-sculptures: Picard *Manuel* 816–24; and see pp. 396f. with Chapter 6, notes 100f. Suggestion that the Hera was the work of a younger Polykleitos: Amandry in *Charites* 79–87. See also following notes.

86. Polykleitos and Pheidias: Quintilian XII 10 7–9 (O. 968 and 721; Bianchi Bandinelli *Pol.* no. 23). The Canon (book and statue): Galen *de plac. Hipp. et Plat.* 5 (O. 959; Bianchi Bandinelli *Pol.* no. 21; other texts on Doryphoros, O. 935–61). Agatharchos: pp. 414–15 with Chapter 6 notes 144ff. Iktinos and Karpion on the Parthenon: Vitruvius VII Praef. 12. Rhoikos and Theodoros on the Samian Heraion: p. 181 with Chapter 4 n. 41. 'When the clay is at the nail': Plutarch *de proc. in virt.* 17 and *Quaest. Conviv.* II 3 2 (O. 970f.; Bianchi Bandinelli *Pol.* no. 24).

87. Vitruvius III 1(60) (Bianchi Bandinelli *Pol.* no. 27; partly quoted by O. in n. on 959).

88. Doryphoros: Bianchi Bandinelli *Pol.* figs. 32–4 (34, 36, Naples 6011, marble statue from Pompeii; 32, 38, 42f., Naples 4885, bronze head from Herculaneum; 33, Florence Uffizi 307, basalt torso); Arias *P* pls. 30–3 (Naples 6011), 34 and vii–viii (Naples 4885), 42 and ix (Florence Uffizi 307); 6011 also BDFH pl. 226 (210); Br.Br. 273; Lawrence *S* pl. 61; Lippold pl. 59, 1; Richter *H* fig. 153, *Sc.* fig. 645; and constantly; 4885 also Br.Br. 336; Lawrence *S* pl. 62; Richter *Sc.* fig. 648. Relief from Argos (Athens N.M. 3153): *AM* 3 (1878) pl. 13; Bianchi Bandinelli *Pol.* fig. 31; Arias *P* pl. 48; Richter *Sc.* fig. 649.

89. Kritian boy: p. 175 with Chapter 4 n. 29. Choiseul-Gouffier (Omphalos) Apollo: p. 194

with Chapter 4 n. 65. Apollo from the Tiber (Rome, M.N. 108): Paribeni *Cat.* no. 13 with refs. and list of replicas; Furtwängler *Meist.* 77ff., *Mast.* 49ff., figs. 8f.; Br.Br. 462. An analogous figure, the Cassel Apollo: p. 337 with n. 108.

90. Artemision god: p. 196 with Chapter 4 n. 69.

91. See p. 41 with Chapter 2 n. 23.

92. Pliny XXXIV 56 (O. 967; Bianchi Bandinelli *Pol.* no. 3).

93. Texts on Diadoumenos: Pliny XXXIV 35 (O. 952; Bianchi Bandinelli *Pol.* no. 3); Lucian *Philops.* 18 (O.900). Copies: Bianchi Bandinelli *Pol.* figs. 57–67 (66, Athens N.M. 1826, from Delos); Arias *P* pls. 66–82 and xviif.; BDFH pl. 227 (211); Lawrence *S* pl. 63; Lippold pl. 59, 2; Richter *H* 154, *Sc.* 650; and often, generally the Delos copy.

94. Victor-statues at Olympia by 'Polykleitos': O. 947–51 (Pausanias's texts); Bianchi Bandinelli *Pol.* nos. 9–17 (texts and inscriptions). Younger Polykleitos: O. 1004f. On the dating of victor-statues and the number of sculptors called Polykleitos: Amandry in *Charites* 63–79 (cf. p. 328 with n. 85). Kyniskos: Pausanias VI 4 11 (O. 948; Bianchi Bandinelli *Pol.* no. 10; the inscribed base ibid. 11 and fig. 1; *Ol.* V no. 149; *IG* 99; see also Amandry in *Charites* 75. Westmacott athlete (B.M. 1754): identified with Kyniskos by Collignon *Hist.Sculpt.* I 499; Petersen in *RM* 8 (1893) 101ff.; Furtwängler *Meist.* 453–61 figs. 72–5, *Mast.* 249–55 figs. 102–5; rejected by Hafner *Eph.West.* Pictures: Bianchi Bandinelli *Pol.* figs. 23 reconstruction of type, 24 (Westmacott copy), 25–30 (heads); Arias *P* pls. 6ff. and v (Westmacott), 19–28 (other copies), 29 (reconstruction); Lippold pl. 60, 1; Richter *Sc.* fig. 658; a fine head in Cambridge (Fitzwilliam GR.3.1948), Budde and Nicholls *Cat.* no. 42 pls. 12–13.

95. Idolino (Florence; found at Pesaro in 1530): Bianchi Bandinelli *Pol.* fig. 82; Arias *P* pls. 91 and XIXff.; Br.Br. 274–7; Lawrence *S* pl. 79; and constantly; identified as lamp-holder: Rumpf in *Crit.d'Arte* 4 (1939) 17ff.; see also Dohrn in *Festschr.Rumpf.* 59–75 pls. 12–16 (with parallel material; cf. Ridgway *SS* figs. 180–4); also p. 601 with Epilogue n. 33. Bronze statuette in Louvre: de Ridder *Cat.* no. 232; Bianchi Bandinelli *Pol.* fig. 13; Arias *P* pls. 10 and I–II; Lamb pl. 61, b; Furtwängler *Meist.* 492, pl. 28, *Mast.* pl. 13 and p. 280 fig. 119; Lullies and Hirmer pl. 183; and see n. 97. Xenokles: Pausanias VI 9 2 (O. 950); Bianchi Bandinelli *Pol.* no. 14; the inscribed base ibid. 15 and fig. 10; *Ol.* V no. 164; Furtwängler *Meist.* 491 fig. 85, *Mast.* 279 fig. 118.

96. Louvre head: Charbonneaux *SGL* pl. 22; *Enc.Phot.* 84f.; Furtwängler *Mast.* pl. 14; its origin: *RA* 27 (1895.II) 276ff. fig. 1 (M. Tyskiewicz, the collector who bought it at Naples from J. Sambon who had bought it at Benevento). Oxford head: Arias *P* pl. 79; *JHS* 39 (1919) 69–78, figs. 1f. and pl. 1.

97. Herakles: Bianchi Bandinelli *Pol.* figs. 45–56; Furtwängler *Meist.* 428–34, *Mast.* 234–7. Hermes in Boboli Gardens: Bianchi Bandinelli *Pol.* fig. 19; 'Hermes' head in Berlin (1833): Bianchi Bandinelli *Pol.* fig. 11; Arias *P* pl. 1; Blümel *Kat.* 4 K146, pls. 28f. (K147, pl. 30, another copy, wingless); Copenhagen head: Bianchi Bandinelli *Pol.* fig. 12; see Blümel in *BWP* 90, identifying the original as a diskobolos and associating the bronze statuette in the Louvre (above, n. 95).

98. Hera: p. 328 with n. 85. Apollo, Artemis and Leto on Mt Lycone: Pausanias II 24 5 (O. 934; Bianchi Bandinelli *Pol.* no. 29). Aphrodite in Amyclae: Pausanias III 18 7 (O. 942; Bianchi Bandinelli *Pol.* no. 19). Kanephoroi: Cicero *Verr.* IV 3 5 (O. 964; Bianchi Bandinelli *Pol.* no. 18).

99. Amazons at Ephesus: Pliny XXXIV 53 (O. 946); Bianchi Bandinelli *Pol.* no. 8; Lucian's ref. to Pheidias: *Imagines* 4 (and 6; O. 768). See further in following notes (texts on Kresilas and 'Ktesilaos' n. 105).

100. Five types listed, illustrated and argued to be independent: Richter in *Archaeology* 12 (1950) 111–15. A selection of copies of various types: Arias *P* pls. 50–65 and xiii–xv. A discussion of the problem in Bothmer *Am.* 216–22 with pl. 89. On the three main types and their designations see following notes. Ephesus pillars: Eichler in *ÖJh* 43 (1956–8) Hauptbl. 1–14 (head-fr. of Capitoline type, fig. 3; torso-fr. apparently of Lansdowne type, fig. 4; frr. of variant types related to Capitoline, figs. 1–2; a fourth pillar with satyr of Hellenistic style, figs. 5–6). 'Artemis' in Villa Doria-Pamphili

(variant of Lansdowne type, the dress fastened on both shoulders and covering the breasts): Richter in *Archaeology* 12 (1950) 112 right. Revolutionary approach to story, now Ridgway *AJA* 78 (1974) 1–14, pls. 1–4.

101. Lansdowne–Berlin–Sciarra–Copenhagen type, ex-Lansdowne copy (New York 32.11.4): Richter *MMCat.Sc.* no. 37 pls. 34ff., *H* fig. 160, *Sc.* figs. 655f., and in *Archaeology* 12 (1950) 112 left; Bothmer *Am.* pl. 89, 3 (a torso of the same type, Oxford 24, pl. 89, 6): Furtwängler *Mast.* 135 fig. 55 and pl. 8; Berlin copy: Blümel *Kat.* IV K176 pls. 67–70; Becatti *PF* pl. 95, 291; Lippold *GS* pl. 61, 3: ex-Sciarra copy (Copenhagen 54): BDFH pl. 223 (297); V. Poulsen *Am.Kres.* pls. 1f. and 7. 'Narcissus': Beazley and Ashmole fig. 91 (B.M.); Bianchi Bandinelli *Pol.* fig. 84 (Munich); *Enc.Phot.* 177f. (Louvre); Furtwängler *Meist.* 483ff. fig. 84, *Mast.* 272–5 fig. 115 (Berlin); see also p. 387 with Chapter 6 n. 75.

102. Capitoline-Sosikles type: the only nearly complete copy is in the Capitoline Museum, Rome (no. 33) and bears the signature of a copyist Sosikles; there are many copies of the head; pictures: Bianchi Bandinelli *Pol.* fig. 77; Furtwängler *Meist.* 291–8 fig. 39 and pl. 11, *Mast.* 132f. figs. 53f.; V. Poulsen *Am.Kres.* pl. 4; Richter *H* fig. 161, *Sc.* figs. 626f. and p. 236 fig. 632 (type shown on engraved gem), and in *Archaeology* 12 (1950) 114.

103. Mattei type: the Mattei copy is in the Vatican; other fairly complete copies, except for the head, in the Capitoline (restored, for greater confusion, with a head of the Capitoline type) and from Hadrian's Villa at Tivoli (with the wound, discussed in the text). A figure of this type from Loukou, in Athens, adapted to a Caryatid, has the head, but the work is so miserable as to tell us little but that it was of the same general type as the others: Becatti *PF* pl. 81, 280; Bothmer *Am.* pl. 89, 4; Langlotz *Phidiaspr.* pl. 16a; Richter *Sc.* fig. 618). On the sculptures from Loukou in the Thyreatis, see S. Karouzou in *RM* 76 (1969) 253–65, pls. 81 (the Amazon-Caryatid) – 87. Pictures of the Mattei type: Becatti *PF* pl. 89, 281 (basalt torso), 282 (gem), 279 (bronze head from Herculaneum, Naples 4889), and pls. 92f. (marble head, Rome M.N. 124666, Paribeni *Cat.* no. 98) and 94 (reconstruction, using cast of bronze head: also in V. Poulsen *Am.Kres.* pl. 3); Furtwängler *Meist.* 300 fig. 40, *Mast.* 139 fig. 57 (bronze head).

104. Wounded Amazon on volute-krater, New York 07.286.64 (p. 259 with Chapter 4 n. 174): Richter and Hall pl. 97, top right; Bothmer *Am.* pl. 75b (resemblance to Capitoline type noted ibid. 220). Anticipation of sculptural developments in painting: cf. pp. 556–7 and 584 with Chapter 8 notes 139f., 223; cf. also p. 550 with Chapter 8 n. 120.

105. Texts on Kresilas: O. 870–6 (870, Amazons at Ephesus, see above, n. 99; 871 and 873, Pliny XXXIV 74, wounded man dying – pp. 338 and 344 with notes 109, 121 – and Pericles; 872 and 874, Pliny XXXIV 75, 'Ctesilaus' (Ktesilaos), wounded Amazon and Doryphoros). See also following notes.

106. Heads of Pericles: Richter *POG* I 102–4, figs. 429–31 (B.M. 549; also Br.Br. 411f.; Furtwängler *Meist.* pl. 9, *Mast.* pl. 7 and fig. 46; and often), 432f. and 435 (Vatican 269), 437–9 (Rome, Barracco), 440f. (Berlin K127, Blümel *Kat.* 4 pls. 8f.; V. Poulsen *Am.Kres.* pls. 5f.), 442f. (Princeton). Strategos-statuette (Hartford, Conn., Wadsworth Athenaeum): Bielefeld in *AP* I 39ff., pls. 30–7.

107. Diomed: Furtwängler *Meist.* pls. 12ff., *Mast.* 146–56 figs. 60–2 (fragmentary statue in Munich; lost head); Schuchardt in *AP* I 33–8, pls. 28f.; Thalwill statuette, ibid, pls. 22–7.

108. Cassel Apollo: Bieber *Kat.* no. 1, pls. 1–8; BDFH pl. 199 (183); Ridgway *SS* fig. 176; and often; other copies: Furtwängler *Meist.* 373ff. figs. 51–2, *Mast.* 192ff., figs. 80f. (statue in Louvre), 82 (head in Rome, Barracco): Richter *Sc.* fig. 194 (head of copy in Florence, Palazzo Vecchio.) Furtwängler ascribed to Kresilas the original of the Medusa Rondanini (p. 313 with n. 49).

109. Bronze statuette, St Germain-en-Laye: BDFH pl. 224 (208); Richter *Sc.* figs. 127, 625. Alternative 'wounded man': p. 344 with n. 121. Diitrephes: Pausanias I 23 3 (O. 871, quoting the inscription).

(iv) Other names and works in sculpture

110. Pliny XXXIV 10 (with Polykleitos), 49 (list).
111. Skopas: Chapter 7 (ii) with notes 11 and 17–27. Kritios and Nesiotes: pp. 184–6 with Chapter 4 n. 49. Ageladas and Pythagoras: pp. 184 and 197 with Chapter 4 notes 48 and 72.
112. Texts on Myron: O. 533–610 (533, Pliny XXXIV 57, list of works and discussion; 534, Pliny XXXIV 49 – above, n. 110; 535, Pausanias II 30 2, Hekate; 546–9, Pausanias VI 2 2, 8 4f. and 13 2. Olympic victors; on the dating see *Ox.Pap.* II pp. 89–95, col. 2 lines 4 and 34; see also following notes. Lykios: O. 861–7 (867, Pliny XXXIV 79, statue commemorating victory of 422 B.C.); Acropolis base: *Delt.* 1889, 179. The drunken old woman, identified in a copy, is thought by some to have been this artist's work (recently Carpenter *GS* 134), but see pp. 561f. with Chapter 8 n. 153.
113. Perseus: Pausanias I 23 I (O. 541). Ladas: *Anth.Gr.* IV 185 318; Catullus 55 25 (O. 542f.). Diskobolos: Lucian *Philopseudes* 18 and Quintilian II 13 8 (O. 544f.); see next note.
114. Best copy (Lancellotti) in Rome, Museo Nazionale: Paribeni *Cat.* no. 20 (other copies, ibid. 21ff.); BDFH pl. 218 (202); Richter *H* 100; and often; with other copies: *KB* 252; Richter *Sc.* figs. 578 (reconstruction) – 582 and 31f.; reconstruction also, Ridgway *SS* fig. 122.
115. Many of the moments are shown in vase-paintings and statuettes: e.g. Norman Gardiner *Athletics* 154–63 figs. 11–35; Beazley *Berl.M.* pl. 7.
116. Texts on Athena and Marsyas: Pliny XXXIV 57 (O. 533, with note f, Pausanias I 24 I on Acropolis group).
117. Copies and versions: *KB* 253; Richter *Sc.* figs. 584–92 (593, reconstruction; also BDFH pl. 219 (203)); both figures: Lawrence *S* pl. 46; Athena: Ridgway *SS* figs. 123f.; Marsyas: Richter *H* 101 fig. 134. Red-figure jug (Berlin F2418): not in Beazley's lists; *CV* fasc. 2, pls. 147, 1 and 3; 150, 2, with refs. Against the identification of the statues with Myron's work: Carpenter in *MAAR* 18 (1941) 5–18, pls. 2f., 5f. (6c, torso of Marsyas in Castel Gandolfo).
118. Apollo and Marsyas in vase-painting, Melanippides's dithyramb, and the convincing suggestion that the group on the Acropolis may have been the poet's dedication for his victory: Boardman in *JHS* 76 (1956) 18ff. Possible sculptural dedications for literary victories: pp. 193 and 287 with Chapter 4 notes 63 and 232. Marsyas's story: see further pp. 395 and 435 with Chapter 6 notes 96 and 200, 536 with Chapter 8 n. 87; and cf. p. 270 with Chapter 4 n. 200, p. 584 with Chapter 8 n. 221; see also Clairmont in *YCS* 15 (1957) 161–78.
119. *BMCat.Br.* no. 269; Richter *Sc.* figs. 190, 592; cf. also p. 395 with Chapter 6 n. 96.
120. Theseus and the Minotaur on Acropolis: Pausanias I 24 2. Minotaur in Rome Mus.Naz.: Paribeni *Cat.* no. 33; Minotaur in Athens: N.M. 704: see Paribeni l.c.; Picard in *Mel. d'Arch. et d'Hist.* 55 (1938) 28–41 with pls. 1 (Athens 'group'), 2 (Rome 'Theseus'), figs. 1f. (coin-representations), 3 and 5 (Rome Minotaur), 4 (Athens Minotaur).
121. 'Protesilaus': Richter in *MMS* 1 (1929) 187–200, figs. 1–7, 15–18 (New York), 8–9, 10–11 (B.M. torso and base): N.Y. copy also: Richter *Cat.* 22 no. 27 pls. 25f.; *MAAR* 18 (1941) pl. 4; B.M. fragments also: *BMCat.Sc.* III no. 1538; Schröder in *JdI* 29 (1914) pl. 10, fig. 26. Identification as Kresilas's *volneratus deficiens*: Frel in *Bull.Met.* 1970, 170–7, figs. 1–14 (N.Y. statue, B.M. torso and plinth, Lansdowne Amazon, Vatican Pericles); but see p. 338 with n. 109.
122. Myron's cow: O. 550–91. Animals on classical gems: pp. 361–2 with notes 178–82.
123. Youth's head from Acropolis: Dickins *Cat.* 266 no. 699; Lawrence *S* pl. 44a.
124. Hephaisteion (p. 306 with n. 35): the building: Dinsmoor 179–82, figs. 53, 67, and in *Hesp.* Suppl. v (1941): D. S. Robertson 118, 328; Lawrence *A* 176f., pl. 76f. Sculptures: Morgan in *Hesp.* 31 (1962) 210–35 pls. 71–84 and 32 (1963) 91–108 pls. 33–5; Picard *Manuel* II 2, 714–32, figs. 290–8. Metopes: Morgan in *Hesp.* 31 (1962) 211–19, pls. 71–6; *KB* 279, 3–6; Richter *Sc.* fig. 417. Friezes: Morgan in *Hesp.* 31 (1962) 221–5, pls. 77–84; *KB* 278 and 279, 1–2; Richter *Sc.* fig. 293. Pediments: H. Thompson in *Hesp.* 18 (1949) 230–68 (fragments, pls. 49–52); Morgan in *Hesp.* 32

(1963) 91–4, 96f. pls. 33a, 34, 35a. Akroteria: Thompson in *Hesp.* 18 (1949) pls. 53f. and 55, 1–2; Morgan in *Hesp.* 32 (1963) 95 and 97f., pl. 35c.

125. Cult-statues and Alkamenes: p. 285 with Chapter 4 n. 228. Statue-base: Dinsmoor *Hesp.* Suppl. v (1941) 105–10; cf. p. 354 with n. 153.

126. Erechtheum: the building: Stevens *Erechtheum*; Dinsmoor 187–95, figs. 70–2, 74, pls. 1, 45–9, 51–2; D. S. Robertson 127–35 and 332, figs. 16, 54–7, pls. 3b–5a; Lawrence *A* 164ff. figs. 96f., pls. 67–75. Friezes (Acropolis Museum): Casson *Cat.* 174–218 with figs.; Stevens *Erechtheum* 239–76, figs. 150–77, pls. 40–6; *KB* 288, 8f.; Richter *Sc.* figs. 296, 728; Picard *Manuel* II 2, 742–60, figs. 301–3; Patricia Boulter in *AP* 10 (1970) 7–25, pls. 1–50.

127. Caryatids: below, n. 130. Euenor's Athena: p. 179 with Chapter 4 n. 37. Sterope and Hippodameia at Olympia: p. 278 with Chapter 4 n. 217. Parthenos: pp. 311–12 with n. 45. Lemnia: pp. 320f. with n. 68. Demeter of Cherchel: p. 304 with n. 30. Procne: p. 287 with Chapter 4 n. 232.

128. Casson *Cat.* 178f. no. 1073; Stevens *Erechtheum* pl. 43, 66; *KB* 283, 8.

129. Erechtheum inscriptions: pp. 364–5 with Chapter 6 notes 4–6.

130. Caryatids: Stevens *Erechtheum* 232–8, figs. 145–9, pls. 38f.; *KB* 283, 2; Lawrence *S* pl. 66; Picard *Manuel* II 2, 735–42, figs. 299f.; Richter *Sc.* fig. 502. The 'porch': Stevens *Erechtheum* 110–19, figs. 68f., especially 111, n. 1. Relation to the frieze of the Parthenon: M. Robertson in *P. and P.* 57. Hadrianic copies: *Bull.Met.* 21 (1963) 1160f. figs. 12f.; see also p. 352 with n. 146.

131. 'Panathenaic Oinochoai' from Agora: Green in *Hesp.* 31 (1962) 82–94, figs. 1–3, pls. 28–32; p. 420 with Chapter 6 n. 161.

132. E.g. in Euripides's *Ion*.

133. The Parthenon almost certainly had four Ionic columns in the back room: Dinsmoor 164. Propylaea (p. 245 with Chapter 4 n. 153; pp. 368 and 415 with Chapter 6 notes 18 and 148): Dinsmoor 198–205, figs. 75f., pls. 1; 48, 2; 49, 2; 50f.; D. S. Robertson 118–22, figs. 50f., pl. 4b and p. 375; Lawrence *A* 161–4, fig. 94, pls. 55–63; Bundgaard *Mnesicles*; it has an Ionic interior. Ionic temples in Athens and Attica: pp. 348f. with notes 135–7. Doric temples in the Peloponnese: of Apollo at Bassae (pp. 356–8 with notes 160–6), Ionic interior, the date or dates between the middle and end of the fifth century uncertain; of Hera at Argos (p. 328 with n. 85; pp. 396f. with Chapter 6 notes 100f.), end of fifth century; of Asklepios at Epidaurus (pp. 397–401 with Chapter 6 notes 103–12), earlyish fourth century; of Athena at Tegea (pp. 452f. with Chapter 7 notes 17f.), mid fourth century, Corinthian interior; of Zeus at Nemea, third quarter of the fourth century, Corinthian interior; of Artemis at Epidaurus, same period, Ionic interior.

134. 'Doric' and 'Ionic' applied to architectural elements: *IG* II² 1666 (356/5–353/2 B.C.) A55, B9; 1665 (ante med. s.iv) 19ff.; 1685 (init.s.iii) B2 2, B3 2, B4 3. On 1666 (=IG II² 1054 b/c) γεῖσα Δωρικά, γεῖσα Ἰωνικά, see D. S. Robertson 382, s.v. cornice, interpreting as horizontal and raking cornice in a Doric building, the raking cornice being plain like the cornice of an Ionic building, without the mutules of a Doric horizontal cornice; cf. Tomlinson in *JHS* 83 (1963) 144; also Plommer in *BSA* 65 (1970) 186 n. 9, with the suggestion that Doric was perhaps first given that name in Ionia.

135. Temple of Athena at Sunium: Dinsmoor 184; D. S. Robertson 332; it had colonnades only on the east front and south side, and is mentioned by Vitruvius in a list of irregular temples (IV 8 4). A new study, based on further excavation, is being prepared by H. Thompson.

136. Temple by the Ilissus: the building: Stuart and Revett *Ant.Ath.* I ch. 2; Dinsmoor 185, pl. 44; D. S. Robertson 125f., 332; Lawrence *A* 141f., fig. 82, pl. 36; Möbius in *AM* 60/1 (1935/6) 234–68; Carpenter *Arch.Parth.* 83–97, figs. 30, 32, 34f., 40. Sculptures: Studniczka in *Leipziger Winckelmannsblatt* 1910; *AD* 3 pl. 36; *JdI* 21 (1916) 169ff.; Blümel *KGSB* 88 no. 107 (all the frieze-slabs and fragments in Berlin, Vienna and Athens collected and illustrated with refs.); Picard *Manuel* II 2, 709–14, figs. 287–9; *KB* 277, 1–4; Stuart and Revett *Ant.Ath.* pl. 6.

137. Nike identified with other deities: pp. 177 and 212 with Chapter 4 notes 32 and 99. Nike Temple: building: Dinsmoor 185–8, figs. 67–9,

pls. 44, 51; D. S. Robertson 125f., fig. 53, and p. 332; Lawrence *A* 162ff., fig. 95, pls. 57, 64ff. Friezes: Blümel *FAN* pls. 1–7; *KB* 277, 5–8; Lawrence *S* pl. 55a; Picard *Manuel* II 2, 760–72, figs. 304–8; Richter *Sc.* figs. 295, 297; and see Harrison in *AJA* 76 (1972) 353–78 (south frieze; see p. 323 with n. 74), and Pemberton, ibid. 303–10 (west and east friezes, interpreting battle on west as Tolmides's victory over the Corinthians at Megara soon after 460).

138. Nike parapet: Carpenter *SNTP*, with division by 'masters', figs. 1–11, 13–15 (12, Roman version), pls. 1–10, 1 and 11–34 (pls. 5–6, one slab with work by two 'masters'); BDFH pl. 237 (221); Blümel *FAN* pl. 8; *KB* 286, 1–3 (4–5, Roman versions); Lullies and Hirmer pls. 189–91; Picard *Manuel* II 2, 772–84, figs. 309–15; Richter *Sc.* figs. 504, 506 (505, 507, Roman versions).

139. Nike of Paionios: pp. 284 and 288 with Chapter 4 notes 227 and 234. Palatine 'Aura' (Rome, Mus.Naz.): Paribeni *Cat.* no. 5 with refs.; Br.Br. 766; *AJA* 43 (1939) 33ff.; Picard *Manuel* II 2, 815 fig. 325; Richter *Sc.* fig. 305. Agora Nike (S 312): *Agora Guide* (1962) 136 pl. 12; *Hesp.* 4 (1935) 374–9, figs. 4f. and 7 (wing-fragments: 6, a related head), and pl. 4.

140. Carpenter *SNTP* pl. 27; Lullies and Hirmer pl. 191; BDFH pl. 237 (221); *KB* 286, 2; Lawrence *S* pl. 72a; Picard *Manuel* II 2, 781, fig. 312; Richter *Sc.* fig. 504.

141. 'Genetrix': *Enc.Phot.* 176; *KB* 267, 4; Picard *Manuel* II 2, 617–20, figs. 247–9; Rizzo *Thiasos* 38–41, fig. 25, refs. in n. 38. 'Palatine Charis': Br.Br. 474; Picard *Manuel* II 2 622 fig. 250; Lawrence *S* pl. 72b ('torso of Genetrix type'). Other cases of looking-glass copies: pp. 465 with Chapter 7 n. 45, 607 with Epilogue n. 47. Find-spot of the Louvre statue: Picard *Manuel* II 2, 621 n. 1 (not Fréjus in the 17th cent., as used to be said, but more probably the neighbourhood of Naples in the 16th). See also p. 601 with Epilogue n. 32.

142. Alkamenes's 'Aphrodite in the Gardens': p. 285 with Chapter 4 n. 228. Kallimachos: pp. 358–9 with n. 166, 405–7 with Chapter 6 notes 120–3.

143. Agorakritos: see following notes, especially 144f. and 156. The motive of the lifted cloak occurs on the Drago relief, which certainly includes figures derived from Pheidias's Parthenos-base, but see p. 312 with n. 47, p. 354 with n. 153.

144. Texts on Agorakritos: O. 829–43 (829, Pliny XXXVI 17, Pheidias's love-gifts; 831, Pliny ibid., Mother of the Gods at Athens by Agorakritos; 832f., Pausanias I 3 5 and Arrian *Peripl. pont. Eux.* 9, the same statue ascribed to Pheidias): on the Nemesis, see next note.

145. Texts on Nemesis: O. 834–43 (834, Pliny XXXVI 17, and 835, Strabo IX 396, statue by Agorakritos; 836–9, Zenobius V 82 (quoting Antigonos), the Suda and Tzetzes, statue by Pheidias but given to Agorakritos and bearing his signature; 840, Pausanias I 33 2, statue by Pheidias; so also 841–3, Hesychius, Pomponius Mela and Solinus. Remains of the statue and its base: see following notes.

146. In the Hellenistic gold treasure of Panagurishte: Simon in *AK* 3 (1960) 3–29 pls. 1–4, with earlier refs.; the phiale, ibid. pls. 1, 1 and 3, 1–2; on this see Bothmer in *Bull.Met.* 21 (1962/3) 161ff. figs. 14ff., with analogous material, including a terracotta phiale from Locri with negro heads, 164 fig. 17. The phialai carried by the Roman copies of the Erechtheum Caryatids (above, n. 130) were of similar design but embossed with acorns instead of heads: ibid. figs. 12–13; actual gold examples, figs. 2–8.

147. The story: *Cypria* fr. 7 (Athenaeus 334B); Apollodorus 3 127. Vase-paintings: see Beazley *EVP* 39–42, 115f., with earlier refs. and lists.

148. Temples at Rhamnus: Gandy in *Un.Ant.Att.* 41ff.; Orlandos in *BCH* 48 (1924) 305–20, pls. 9f.; Zschietzschmann in *AA* 44 (1929) 441ff.; Dinsmoor 88, fig. 34 (smaller), 181ff. (larger); D. S. Robertson 115 and 328 (larger); Plommer in *BSA* 45 (1950) 66–112, especially 95–109 (larger). There are dedications to Themis from the site (cf. p. 459 with Chapter 7 n. 32), and the smaller temple is sometimes thought to have been dedicated to her; it is sometimes thought archaic (*c.* 487, Dinsmoor), sometimes later than the larger and archaistic (Zschietzschmann).

149. Cratinus *Nemesis*: Kock *FCA* I, 47–51, frr. 107–20. It was produced before Pericles's death (429); but the evidence for the assertion, sometimes made, that it was after the outbreak of war (432) is not compelling (see Kock l.c.).

Vase-paintings: above, n. 147. Idea of Nemesis: pp. 312 and 319 with n. 64.

150. Helen's wooers: 'Hesiod' *Cat.Mul.*, Merkelbach and West fr. 204 (absence of Achilles, lines 87–92). Achilles and Helen on Leuke (White Island) in the Black Sea: Pausanias III 19 3; Philostratus *Her.* 746.

151. Fifth head (Athens N.M. 204): Ashmole in *Netherlands Year-book for the History of Art* 1959, 1–3, figs. 1–3, and *AJA* 66 (1962) 233f., pl. 59, 2. It belongs as Ashmole has shown, to a relief of more than a century later; see p. 378 with Chapter 6 n. 48.

152. Fragments of Nemesis base (Athens N.M. 203 and 205–14; on 204, see last note): *Eph.Arch.* 1891, 63–70, pls. 8 and 9 (8, 2 is N.M. 204); Svoronos 167–79, pls. 41–2 (41, 1 is N.M. 204); Kjellberg *Studien* 103–16, figs. 1–17, 19–22 and 23; Pallat in *JdI* 9 (1894) 1–22, pls. 1–7 (pl. 3 no. 9a is N.M. 204); also Br.Br. 464; Karouzou *Cat.* pl. 29a; Richter *Sc.* figs. 635, 727. Copy (Stockholm, N.M. 150): Kjellberg *Studien* fig. 24; Picard *Manuel* II 2, 539, fig. 223.

153. Parthenos base and Drago relief: p. 312 with n. 47. Hephaisteion base: p. 345 with n. 125. 'Altar of Ares': *Hesp.* 21 (1952) 94ff. pls. 22f.; *Agora Guide*[2] 68 and 129f. Temple of Ares: Dinsmoor in *Hesp.* 9 (1940) 1–52. Cult-statue by Alkamenes: Pausanias I 8 4 (O. 818). Ares Borghese (Louvre 886): BDFH pl. 229 (213)r.; *Enc.Phot.* 179. Frieze of Nike temple: p. 348 with n. 137. A later base: p. 395 with Chapter 6 notes 94ff.

154. Classical frontality: Beazley in *JHS* 59 (1939) 38 and 69 (1949) 12, pointing the connection with Byzantine. Frontality at Doura-Europos: e.g. Rostovtzeff *Dura-Europos and its Art* pls. 1, 1 and 2; 11, 1; 12f.; 14, 1; 15, 1 and 2; 17f.; 21–4; and throughout the excavation reports. See further pp. 435–6 with Chapter 6 n. 200, 577 with Chapter 8 n. 199, 610 with Epilogue n. 56.

155. Metope (Rome, Villa Albani): Langlotz in *Scritti . . . Nogara* 224–30, pl. 21, suggesting that it came from the temple at Rhamnus; Dinsmoor in *Hesp.* 29 (1960) 304 n. 1, and 30 (1961) 199–203, pl. 32d, demonstrating that the measurements do not fit; but his calculations are perhaps too fine.

156. Fragment of Nemesis head (B.M. no. 460): Richter *Sc.* fig. 633. Fragments of head and body, copies and reconstruction: Despinis *SMEA*; see also Despinis in *AAA* 3 (1970) 409–13, figs. 1–11; and Schefold in *AK* 14 (1971) 130ff. fig. 1. 'Aphrodite and Dione': p. 303 with n. 26. Niobids: p. 319 with n. 66. Aphrodite in Berlin: p. 320 with n. 67. Victories with bull on Nike balustrade: p. 350 with n. 138. 'Genetrix': pp. 350f. with n. 139.

157. Alkamenes's bronze athlete: Pliny XXXIV 72 (O. 826); his chryselephantine Dionysus: Pausanias I 20 3 (O. 819). On the temple in which the Dionysus was, see p. 483 with Chapter 7 n. 94.

158. Sunium temple: p. 306 with n. 35. Frieze: *AM* 60 (1941) 89–115, pls. 42–53 (a fragment of the pediment-sculpture, ibid. 115–23, pls. 54–7).

159. Athenian temple of Apollo on Delos: Dinsmoor 183f.; D. S. Robertson 328 and 125 n. 2; Lawrence *A* 180. Akroteria: Marcadé in *BCH* 75 (1951) 82–7, correcting Furtwängler's reconstruction (*AZ* 40 (1882/3) 335–64 with figs.); Corby in *Délos* XII 237–41 with figs. 270–8 and pls. 14ff.; Bruneau and Ducat 46 and 84; Boreas and Oreithyia also *BCH* 3 (1879) pl. 11.

160. Temple of Apollo at Bassae-Phigaleia: Pausanias VIII 41 7f.; Dinsmoor 154–9 with fig. 56 and pls. 35a and 36f.; D. S. Robertson 328 and 136–41 with figs. 58, 59a; Lawrence *A* 177f. with fig. 99 and pls. 79–81a; Roux *Argolide* 21–56 with figs. 1–21 (dating, 55f. and 404); Corinthian capital or capitals: below, n. 166.

161. Bassae frieze: *BMCat.Sc.* I 277–88 nos. 520–44; Kenner (slab with gods in chariot, pl. 4); Dinsmoor in *MMS* 4 (1931/2) 204–27, figs. 1–22, pls. 1–2. The frieze is now exhibited in a new arrangement by Corbett, but the justification is not yet published. Other pictures: *KB* 280f.; Lawrence *S* pl. 67; Picard *Manuel* II 2, 803–17 with figs. 321–4 and 326; Richter *Sc.* figs. 106, 197ff., 201–4, 298f.; and see following notes.

162. Principal slab of Amazonomachy: Kenner pl. 21; in position in reconstruction, Dinsmoor pl. 37, right. Parthenon pediments: centre of west, p. 299 with n. 18; 'Ilissos' from west, p. 300 with n. 21; 'Dione' from east, p. 319 with n. 26. Tightened skirt on Phigaleia frieze: e.g. Kenner pls. 14ff.

163. Composition of Mausoleum Amazonomachy: pp. 450–2 with Chapter 7 notes 8–14. Throne of Zeus at Olympia: pp. 317–20 with notes 64ff. Parthenos shield: pp. 314–16 with notes 52ff. Groups with wounded at Bassae: Kenner pls. 12, 22f.; similar groups on Parthenos shield; Leipen *APR* fig. 81 and p. 47 nos. 5–6 (pp. 45f. with refs. in n. 160).

164. Slab with dead Centaur: Kenner pl. 8; with woman at image: Kenner pl. 5. Kleophrades Painter's Cassandra: p. 230 with Chapter 4 n. 137. Peplos kore: p. 101 with Chapter 3 n. 63. Archaising images: see further pp. 397 and 401 with Chapter 6 notes 101, 112.

165. Bassae metopes: *BMCat.Sc.* I 274–7, nos. 510–19; Richter *Sc.* figs. 300–1; Roux *Argolide* 32.

166. Corinthian capital from Bassae: Dinsmoor 156ff. and pl. 37b; D. S. Robertson 139ff. with fig. 59a; postulated also for two half-columns: Dinsmoor 157 with n. 4; this rejected by F. A. Cooper in *AJA* 76 (1972) 202f. Corinthian order: Dinsmoor 279–84; D. S. Robertson 141–5. Kallimachos and the invention: Vitruvius IV 1 (86f.); and see pp. 397 and 406 with Chapter 6 notes 102 and 121ff. 'Corinthian' capital of Varvakeion statuette (p. 311 with n. 45): Lehmann in *JdI* 47 (1932) 34f.; Weickert *EP* 17f. figs. 9f.; see Roux *Argolide* 406.

167. Heraion at Argos and Asklepieion at Epidaurus: see pp. 396–401 with Chapter 6 notes 100–112.

(*v*) *Coins and gems*

168. Panathenaics: pp. 150 with Chapter 3 n. 160, 237–8 with Chapter 4 n. 144; Athena-head and owl coins: p. 150 with Chapter 3 n. 161; see also p. 347 with n. 131.

169. Coins of Thurii (Thurium): Seltman *GC* pl. 18, 5–8; Kraay and Hirmer 308 nos. 250–4, pls. 86ff.

170. Coins of Olympia (Elis; see also p. 212 with Chapter 4 n. 99): Seltman *GC* pls. 35, 1–7; 36, 1–4; 64, 6 (the eagle's head enlarged); Kraay and Hirmer 342f. nos. 489–508, pls. 154–8 (pl. 157, no. 500, the eagle's head) and XVII (no. 503, Zeus-head).

171. Syracusan tetradrachms through the fifth century: Seltman *GC* pl. 22; Kraay and Hirmer pls. 28–33. Tetradrachm signed by Euainetos (reverse): Seltman *GC* pl. 23, 4; Kraay and Hirmer pl. 34, 104.

172. Decadrachms: Seltman *GC* 127, pl. 22, 12 (Euainetos), 23, 6 and 24, 1 (Kimon); Kraay and Hirmer 288 (doubting connection with the Athenian defeat and associating Kimon's dies with Dionysius's defeat of the Carthaginians), nos. 104–6, pls. 34–6 (Euainetos), 116–21, pls. 40–3 and V (Kimon).

173. Three-quarter chariots on earlier Syracusan tetradrachms: Seltman *GC* pl. 22, 10–12; Kraay and Hirmer pls. 32f. The motive in archaic art: pp. 156f. and 224 with Chapter 4 notes 7 and 119. Concern with space in the later fifth century: pp. 414–17 with Chapter 6 notes 144–51 (chariots, n. 150).

174. Eukleidas: Seltman pl. 23, 1; Kraay and Hirmer pls. IV, no. 111, and 39, no. 122. On die-signatures in general see also Seltman *Masterpieces*, especially pp. 14–22.

175. Earliest three-quarter faces: see Beazley in *JHS* 30 (1910) 58f. with notes 68ff. Late archaic and early classical examples: ibid. pl. 2; Arias and Hirmer figs. 173–5, 177, 179; Pfuhl *MuZ* figs. 374, 403, 490ff., 504, 506, 508a, 509, 572; see also Corbett in *JHS* 85 (1965) 18f. fig. 1.

176. Amphipolis: Seltman *GC* pl. 17, 15ff.; Kraay and Hirmer pls. 134f., nos. 414ff. Catana: Seltman *GC* pl. 26, 3; Kraay and Hirmer pls. III no. 44 and 15, no. 43. Rhodes: Seltman *GC* pl. 30, 13ff.; Kraay and Hirmer pls. 189 nos. 345ff. Larisa and Pherae in Thessaly: Seltman *GC* pl. 34, 10ff. and 15; Kraay and Hirmer pls. 148f. nos. 468, 470f. Tarsos: Seltman *GC* pl. 42, 13f. Mausolus of Caria: Seltman *GC* pl. 43, 2; Kraay and Hirmer pl. 187 no. 638. Lycia: Kraay and Hirmer pl. 191 no. 660. Clazomenae: Seltman *GC* pl. 41, 12f.; Kraay and Hirmer pl. 181 no. 608. Panticapaeum: Seltman *GC* pls. 39, 11 and 64, 11; Kraay and Hirmer pl. XV no. 442. Croton: Kraay and Hirmer pl. 94 no. 270.

177. Akragas: Seltman *GC* pls. 26, 8–11 and 27, 2 (decadrachm); Kraay and Hirmer pls. 59–63 (62f., decadrachm).

178. Myron's cow: p. 344 with n. 122. Kalamis: p. 184 with Chapter 4 n. 48. Beasts of the

Parthenon frieze: p. 307. Polygnotos's donkeys and hare: pp. 250, 267 and 246 with Chapter 4 n. 154.

179. Bronze-age gems in archaic times: p. 147 with Chapter 3 n. 154.

180. Phrygillos, die-sinker: Seltman *GC* 126, pl. 22, 11; Kraay and Hirmer 291 no. 107, pl. 37; ibid. no. 108 (Phry). Phrygillos, gem-engraver: Furtwängler *AG* pl. 14, 6. On the identification of the die-sinkers Phrygillos, Phry and Ph and the gem-engraver Phrygillos, see Seltman *Masterpieces* 16f. and 66–81; *EAA* VI 139 s.v. Phrygillos, with refs. The further supposition (Seltman and *EAA*) that a bird shown on some of these and some other coins is a finch (φρυγίλος) and so a punning signature is very doubtful; see Thimme in *Jb.d.Staatl.Kunstsammlungen in Baden-Württemberg* 6 (1967) 14 n. 8.

181. Dexamenos: Furtwängler *AG* III 137–9; Beazley *AGLH* 48f.; Vollenweider in *Conn. des Arts* Feb. 1959 48f.; Borelli in *EAA* III 81f., s.v., fig. 108; Diehl in *Berl.Mus.Ber.* 17 (1967) 41ff.; most recently Boardman in *Burl.Mag.* 1969, 591–5, figs. 21–31 (21, signed head; 29f., signed bird; 31, signed group); Richter *EGGE* no. 277 (signed group), 326 (signed head), 467f. (signed birds; unsigned heron, 466). Portrait-coins: see p. 506 with Chapter 8 notes 7 and 8.

182. Gems mainly of this period illustrated: Richter *EGGE* nos. 219–480 (music-makers, 264, 378; animals, 373–479).

CHAPTER 6: DEVELOPMENTS INTO THE FOURTH CENTURY

(*i*) *Grave-reliefs, votive reliefs and others*

1. Archaic Attic tombstones: above, pp. 108–12 with Chapter 3 notes 79–87; their end: p. 197 with Chapter 4 n. 73. White lekythoi: pp. 324–6 with Chapter 5 notes 78–82; also pp. 421–4 with notes 163f., 169.

2. Classical Attic tombstones in general: Conze; Diepolder *AG*; Johansen *Att.Gr.*; their ornament: Möbius *OGG*; their setting: Brückner *Friedhof*. Tall palmette-stelai without figure-decoration: Möbius *OGG* pls. 11a, 13a, 22a, 23a; with a figured panel: pls. 10a, 16a and others; Brückner *Friedhof* 110 fig. 171; with a single big figure: Möbius *OGG* pl. 15b; Diepolder *AG* pl. 38, 1. Grave-plots reconstructed: Brückner *Friedhof* 57–64, figs. 29–35 (Dexileos; p. 369 with n. 21), and 82 fig. 47, 91 fig. 58, 105 fig. 66. Marble vases: pp. 371–2 with notes 26–9.

3. Early classical stones from various areas: pp. 197–9 with Chapter 4 notes 73–6. Delphi stele: de La Coste Messelière *Delphes* pl. 236; Langlotz *FGBS* 133 no. 15, pl. 81. Vatican stele: Johansen *Att.Gr.* 129 fig. 63. 'Giustiniani' stele (Berlin K19): Blümel *Berl.Kat.Sk.* III pls. 27f., *KGSB* 12f. no. 2, figs. 2, 4, 6, 9; Johansen *Att.Gr.* 132 fig. 66; Lullies and Hirmer pls. 138f.; Ridgway *SS* fig. 67. Girl with doves (New York 73): Richter *MMCat.Sc.* pl. 60; Ridgway *SS* fig. 66; and see p. 308 with Chapter 5 n. 39.

4. Erechtheum inscriptions: Stevens *Erechtheum* 277–422; the passage cited here (XVII col. 1): ibid. 389, 406 and 415; see further below, n. 6; also p. 346 with Chapter 5 n. 129; p. 397 with n. 103 (inscriptions from Epidaurus).

5. Antimenes Painter's hydria (B.M. B304): *ABV* 267 no. 4; Beazley *Dev.* pl. 28, 3 and in *JHS* 47 (1927) pl. 13. On the painter see also p. 217 with Chapter 4 n. 109.

6. See Randall in *AJA* 57 (1953) 199–210, especially 207; cf. also pp. 397–401 with notes 103–12 (Epidaurus).

7. Praxiteles: pp. 386–96 with notes 73–99; memorials by him: Pliny XXXVI 20 (O. 1282) 'works in the Ceramicus at Athens'; Pausanias I 2 3 (O. 1281) 'there is a tomb not far from the gate, and on it a soldier standing by his horse. Who he is I do not know, but Praxiteles made both the horse and the soldier'. Nikias and painted tombstones: pp. 436–7 with n. 204.

8. Demetrius of Phalerum controlled Athens from 317 till 307; that his legislative programme belongs to the beginning of this period is demonstrated by Dow and Travis in *Hesp.* 12 (1943) 144–65, especially 154, 159, 165. On Demetrius see also pp. 437 with n. 205, 487 and 489 with Chapter 7 notes 106, 111.

9. Sosinos's stele (Louvre): Conze 618 pl. 119;

Enc.Phot. 170. Xanthippos's (B.M. 628): Diepolder *AG* pl. 4.

10. Tynnias son of Xynnon of Trikorystia (Athens N.M. 902): Conze 617 pl. 118; Diepolder *AG* pl. 29; Johansen *Att.Gr.* 15 fig. 1; very like Sosinos and Xanthippos. Doubtful significance of the name unqualified: p. 369 especially the stone of Chairedemos and Lykeas (n. 22). Citizens, metics and slaves among the Erechtheum workmen: see Randall in *AJA* 57 (1953) 199–210.

11. Mynno (Berlin K23): Blümel *Berl.Kat.Sk.* III pl. 23, *KGSB* 24 no. 16, fig. 24; Conze 38 pl. 13; Johansen *Att.Gr.* 14, and 16 fig. 2; *KB* 285, 2. Woman with lekythos (New York 08.258.42): Richter *MMCat.Sc.* 50 no. 75 pl. 61; Diepolder *AG* pl. 7; Johansen *Att.Gr.* 153, fig. 77.

12. Ampharete's stone (Athens, Kerameikos Museum): Johansen *Att.Gr.* 17, fig. 4; *AA* 1933, 279ff. fig. 17; AM 59 (1934) 25ff. pl. v, Beil. 3. Similarly posed figure on lekythos by the Achilles Painter (Athens N.M. 1818): p. 325 with Chapter 5 n. 80. Seated statue: Becatti *PF* 201–6, pls. 96ff. (Pheidias); Langlotz *Aphrodite* (Alkamenes).

13. Exekias's plaque: p. 131 with Chapter 3 n. 126.

14. Hegeso's stele (Athens N.M. 3624): Conze 68 pl. 30; Diepolder *AG* pl. 20; Johansen *Att.Gr.* 17f., fig. 5; BDFH pl. 238 (222); Karouzou *Cat.* pl. 22; *KB* 284, 4; Lawrence *S* pl. 75; Lullies and Hirmer pl. 185 (187); Richter *Sc.* fig. 429; and often. See also p. 370 with n. 24.

15. Athens N.M. 715: Conze 1032 pl. 204; Diepolder *AG* pl. 6; Karouzou *Cat.* pl. 25; *KB* 285, 1; Lullies and Hirmer pl. 180 (182). This was in a collection on Aegina in the eighteen-thirties; Attic tombstones are not otherwise known from the island, but there are many from Salamis, some of the highest quality (e.g. that of Chairedemos and Lykeas, p. 369 with n. 22).

16. Stele from near the Ilissos: p. 382 with n. 61. The dead (?) seated on tomb-steps on lekythoi: p. 326 with Chapter 5 n. 82; p. 422 with n. 164.

17. Timarete and baby (B.M. 1947.7–14.1, ex-Cook): Conze 888 pl. 173; Diepolder *AG* pl. 39, 2; Johansen *Att.Gr.* 25ff. fig. 10. Mnesagora and Nikochares (Athens N.M. 3845): Conze 887 pl. 172; Diepolder *AG* pl. 5; Johansen *Att.Gr.* 25ff. fig. 12; see also p. 370 with n. 24.

18. Propylaea: pp. 245 with Chapter 4 n. 153, 347 with Chapter 5 n. 133, pp. 415–16 with n. 148. Aristomache's stone (Athens N.M. 1680): Conze 1226 pl. 262; Diepolder *AG* pl. 8, 2.

19. Public monument in Rome (Villa Albani): Conze 1153 pl. 247; Diepolder *AG* pl. 9; Br.Br. 437; Helbig *Führer* 3257; *KB* 285, 5; Lullies and Hirmer pls. 177–9 (179–81); Richter *H* 118 fig. 167; Schrader *Phidias* fig. 260; see also next note.

20. Dating of Villa Albani relief: Schrader *Phidias* 286, Parthenonian; Diepolder *AG* 16f., later than the Parthenon; Richter *H* 118, *c.* 430–420; Bieber *H* 10, already fourth century; Clairmont *Gr.Ep.* 73, 431 (commemorating the dead in the first year of the Peloponnesian War, also honoured in Pericles's funeral speech: Thucydides II 35–56). Battle of 408: Diodorus XIII 72; the association with Sophocles *O.C.* 1044–95 made in a lecture by Professor Page.

21. Public monument of 394 B.C. (Athens N.M. 2744): Conze 1157 pl. 24 and 1529 pl. 317; *AM* 35 (1910) pl. 11. Dexileos (Athens, Kerameikos Museum): Conze 1158 pl. 248; BDFH pl. 241 (225); *KB* 285, 7; Lullies and Hirmer pl. 191 (192); Richter *Sc.* fig. 215; and often. On Dexileos's grave-plot see also above n. 2 and pp. 420–1 with n. 161.

22. Stele of Chairedemos and Lykeas (Piraeus Museum, from Salamis): Diepolder *AG* pl. 16; Johansen *Att.Gr.* 20ff. fig. 15; BDFH pl. 228 (212); Lullies and Hirmer pl. 182 (184); *AA* 1916, 142; *Eph.Arch.* 1916 4ff. pl. 2. Significance of unqualified names: pp. 365f. with n. 10. Dating: p. 370 with n. 24. Dermys and Kittylos: p. 60 with Chapter 2 n. 58.

23. Samos relief: p. 414 with n. 145. Stele of Krito and Timarista (Rhodes Museum): *Cl.Rh.* IV 37–42, figs. 10f. pl. 1; V 31–5, fig. 17 pls. 4–7; Lullies and Hirmer pl. 183 (185); see also next note. Other stone with curved top (New York 11.141, said to be from Liatani in Boeotia; Pentelic marble): Richter *MMCat.Sc.* no. 74, with refs., pl. 60b.

24. Reworking of Krito's hair: Frel in *AAA* 5 (1972) 75 no. 4, 77 fig. 5 (cf. his observations in *AAA* 3 (1970) 369). Fourth-century date suggested for lettering on this stone: Hiller von Gaertringen ap. Segre 'Tituli Camirenses' in *Ann.* 27/9 (1952) 266 no. 162; I owe this refer-

ence to P. M. Fraser, who would date the letter-forms to the mid fourth century. The stele of Mnesagora and Nikokles (p. 368 with n. 17) is described by Karouzou, *Cat.* 49, as 'one of the earliest Attic stelai of the fifth century ... About 440 B.C.'. Late dating of other stones: Dohrn *Att.Pl.* 96–114 (Hegeso) and 164–7 (Chairedemos and Lykeas).

25. Demokleides's stele (Athens N.M. 752): Conze 623 pl. 122. Kleoboia: pp. 266–7 with Chapter 4 n. 191.

26. Lekythoi: pp. 324–6 with Chapter 5 notes 78–82; pp. 421–4 with notes 163f., 169. Loutrophoroi: Richter and Milne 5f., figs. 40ff. Early seventh-century hydria: e.g. Kübler *AAM* 9 fig. 4; later seventh-century grave-vase, ibid. 61, fig. 53; early sixth-century loutrophoros: *Delt.* 19 pl. 37 (*Paralipomena* 15, KX Painter). White loutrophoros (Louvre; not in Beazley's lists): L. Ghali-Kahil in *Gestalt und Geschichte* 146–51 pls. 51ff.; *MM Aukt* XXVII 81f. no. 153 pl. 55. Battle-loutrophoroi: Beazley in *Mus.J.* (Philadelphia) 23, 4–22, figs. 1–17. Sanctuary of the Nymph; *Prakt.* 1955, 51f.; 1957, 25f. fig. 1 and pls. 1–4; *BCH* 80 (1956) 234, 82 (1958) 660–6, figs. 8–14; *Arch. Rep. 1955* (1956) 7, *1957* (1958) 5; see also Beazley in *ARV*² Preface viii and Instructions for Use xlv. Kallirrhoe: p. 300 with Chapter 5 n. 21. Lebes gamikos: Richter and Milne 10 with fig. 11 and figs. 72–5.

27. Choes: van Hoorn *Choes* (marble example, fig. 34); see also p. 420 with n. 161.

28. Potter and sculptor in Kerameikos: pp. 20 with Chapter 1 n. 14, 108 and 131 with Chapter 3 notes 79 and 125f.; p. 424 with n. 169 (Group of the Huge Lekythoi). Aristophanes *Ecclesiazusae* 995f. (lekythos-painter; see further p. 426 with n. 173), 1110f. (lekythos as tomb-monument), 1030ff. (lekythoi placed beside the corpse).

29. Examples of marble vases: lekythoi: Stais 122 no. 835, 145 no. 1824, 152f. nos. 1095 and 1055; loutrophoroi: 87 no. 808, 121 no. 844, 141 no. 953. Slabs showing vases in relief: Stais 125 no. 884 (loutrophoros between two lekythoi), 127 no. 931 (man and loutrophoros), 128 no. 1863 (Hagnostrate with her loutrophoros; p. 381 with n. 57), 132 no. 896 (siren above loutrophoros on which are shown girls with loutrophoros), 133 no. 899 (standing and seated men clasping hands in presence of slave-girl; below loutrophoros on which are shown soldier and slave), 159 no. 873 (loutrophoros on which are shown athlete and slave); many examples in Conze and elsewhere (e.g. *KB* 285, 4).

30. 'Record reliefs': see especially Süsserott 27–68 and 216ff., with earlier refs., and pls. 1–5, 9, 11.1; see also n. 32 below for particular refs.

31. Siphnian friezes: pp. 153–7 with Chapter 4 notes 4–9. 'Hestia' and 'Amelung's goddess': pp. 191–2 with Chapter 4 notes 58 and 60. Procne: p. 286 with Chapter 4 n. 232; and Erechtheum Caryatids: p. 345 with Chapter 5 notes 126f. and 130. Paionios's Nike: pp. 284 with Chapter 4 n. 227, 350 with Chapter 5 n. 139.

32. Record reliefs: of 422/1 (Eleusis Museum): *RM* 47 (1932) 37f. pls. 8 and 9, 1; Hausmann *GW* 42, fig. 20;
of 409/8 (Louvre) *RM* 47 (1932) pl. 10, 3; Süsserott pl. 1, 1;
of 406/5 (Athens, Epigraphical Museum): Süsserott pl. 1, 2;
of 403/2 (Athens, Acropolis Museum): *RM* 47 (1932) pl. 13, 2; Casson *Cat.* 234ff. no. 1334;
of 400/399 (Athens N.M.): *RM* 47 (1932) pl. 12, 2; Svoronos 663 no. II 643, pl. 203;
of 398/7 (Athens, N.M.): Svoronos 601–5 no. 1479, pl. 107; Süsserott pl. 1, 4;
of 394/3 (Athens, Epigraphical Museum): Süsserott pl. 2, 1;
of 375/4 (Athens, N.M.): Svoronos 588 no. 1467; Süsserott pl. 3, 2;
of 362/1 (Athens, N.M.): Svoronos 598f. no. 1481, pl. 106; Süsserott pl. 4, 1.
See also Süsserott pl. 5, 1–4, reliefs with dates in the thirties; and cf. p. 378 with n. 49.

33. Relief with two goddesses (Athens, Acropolis Museum): Casson *Cat.* 253ff. no. 1348. Relief with goddesses and athlete (Athens, Acropolis Museum): Casson *Cat.* 229f. no. 1339.

34. 'Three-figure reliefs' and Altar of Pity: Thompson in *Hesp.* 21 (1952) 47–82, pls. 14–18 (earlier refs. for the reliefs, ibid. 60 n. 35; most importantly *RM* 53 (1938) 189–280, where Götze collects the earlier literature). G. Carattoni in *BdA* 52 (1967) 148–51 figs. 31–5, publishes fragments of another relief, found with fragments of an Orpheus and Eurydice,

which he believes to give a fifth type; this would of course be incompatible with the location on the Altar of Pity.

35. Love of a Hesperid for Herakles: Götze in *JdI* 63/4 (1948/9) 91–9; Möbius *Portlandvase* 10ff.; Thompson in *Hesp.* 21 (1952) 69; the Pompeian painting (House I.7.7): Maiuri *Mon.d.Pitt.* 3 ii, 2; Möbius *Portlandvase* 17 n. 70a; Rizzo *PER* pl. 95; and see Schefold *Pomp.Mal.* 109, *WP* 30f.; Attic red-figure hydria (unknown to Beazley; attributed by Cahn surely rightly to the Syracuse Painter; not later than the mid fifth century): *AK* 15 (1972) i, adv. pages vi 'Lekythos'; known to me also in a photograph kindly supplied by Dr Cahn.
36. Votive relief (Athens N.M. 1388, from the Asklepieion at Athens): Svoronos, 333f. no. 1388 pl. 53, with refs.; Hausmann *GW* 67ff. fig. 37, noting dependence on 'three-figure reliefs'; it shows Asklepios seated on a rock between a male and Hygieia. On the Athenian shrine, see next note and p. 376 with n. 42.
37. Shrines below the Acropolis: Pan and Nymphs on the north slope: Hill *ACA* 100 with refs.; Asklepios and Hygieia on south slope: Judeich[2] 320 n. 3; Hill *ACA* 125ff. with plans and refs. Asklepieion at Epidaurus: pp. 397–401 with notes 103–15. There were other sanctuaries of Pan and Nymphs in Attica; by the Ilissos (Plato *Phaedrus* 229B, 279B; Pausanias I 19 5; see Judeich[2] 416, with refs. to reliefs found there); and at Marathon (p. 177 with Chapter 4 n. 33).
38. Athens N.M. 1329, from the south slope of the Acropolis: Svoronos 243 no. 26 pl. 44; Arndt–Amelung v no. 1242; Br.Br. 429A; Stais 181.
39. See pp. 545 6 with Chapter 8 n. 110.
40. Cave-reliefs: e.g. Karouzou *Cat.* pl. 48 (Athens N.M. 1445); Stais 205f.; Svoronos 442–52, nos. 1443–9 pls. 72ff., 1859 pl. 97, 2007–10 pls. 99f.; pls. 96–100 show examples of the tenon, which also appears on pls. 72 no. 1442, 89 no. 1518, 90 no. 1326; set on pillars pl. 182; for one so shown in another relief, see p. 377 with n. 43. Two-faced reliefs: pp. 416 and 437 with notes 150 and 204.
41. P. 177 with Chapter 4 n. 33.
42. Asklepios, his story and his family: see s.v. in *RE* and Roscher. Asklepieion at Athens: above, n. 37; at Epidaurus: pp. 397–401 with notes 103–15. Account of incubation: Aristophanes *Plutus* 410–12, 620f. and especially 659–747.
43. Asklepios relief (Piraeus Museum 405): Hausmann *GW* 59 fig. 28. Oropos sanctuary: Androutsopoulos; Karidas. Archinos relief (Athens N.M. 3369): Karouzou *Cat.* pl. 47a; *Eph.Arch.* 1916, 119 fig. 2; Karidas 50–64 with fig. and refs.
44. Thyrea relief (Athens N.M. 1402): Svoronos 351f. no. 1402, pl. 35; Karouzou *Cat.* pl. 45b; Stais 199. 'Topographical' relief from Acropolis (Athens N.M. 1377): Svoronos 294 no. 74, pl. 48; Stais 190.
45. Hero-reliefs: e.g. Svoronos pls. 82–7; Hausmann *GW* 25–31 figs. 12–15; early classical example in Istanbul from Thasos: Hausmann *GW* fig. 17; Lawrence *S* pl. 29b; Ridgway *SS* figs. 62–5. Red-figure plaque-fragment (Athens N.M. 1244): *RM* 42 (1927) Beil. 14; *JHS* 76 (1956) pl. 3, 3 (see Boardman ibid. 24f.); Schefold *UKV* 119.
46. Snakes: e.g. Athens N.M., Svoronos pl. 231 no. II 1445; Berlin, Blümel *KGSB* figs. 111, 119, 122 (the last two dedicated to Zeus Meilichios); and cf. Archinos's relief, above, with n. 43. Parts of body: e.g. Athens N.M. 3526, Svoronos 673 no. 467 pl. 237, Karouzou *Cat.* pl. 47b. The Hero on the Sandal: Athens N.M. 2565; Svoronos 484–93 no. 167 pl. 60, with literary refs.
47. *BMCat.Sc.* no. 2155 pl. 24.
48. Rhamnus relief (B.M. 1953. 5–30.1): the pertinence of Nike's head demonstrated by Ashmole in *Netherlands Year-Book for the History of Art* 1954, 91–100, figs. 1–6; 1959, 1–3 figs. 1f.; *AJA* 66 (1962) 233f. pl. 59; and see p. 353 with Chapter 5 n. 151.
49. Record relief of 340/39: Süsserott pl. 5, 1; panathenaic of same date, pls. 4, 4 and 6, 1–2; of 336/5 (Pythodelos) pl. 7, 1–2. New proportions on Mausoleum: p. 451 with Chapter 7 n. 13; in Lysippos, p. 464 with Chapter 7 n. 43.
50. Panathenaic prize-vases: pp. 150 with Chapter 3 n. 160, 237–8 with Chapter 4 n. 144, 346 and 359 with Chapter 5 notes 131 and 168; archaism also pp. 285–7 with Chapter 4 notes 230f.; and see Beazley *Dev.* 88–100 (archons' names, 96–100; archaism, 98) with pls. 44–9. New proportions in grave-reliefs: p. 382 with notes 60ff.

51. Family stele (Athens N.M. 717): Conze 322 pl. 82; Diepolder *AG* pl. 42, 1. Examples of clasped hands in Diepolder pls. 1–3, 12, 15, 23–5, 32, 34, 39, 42–6; and see Johansen *Att.Gr.* 53–64 with figs. 13, 16–20, 23–5.

52. Cf. Johansen *Att.Gr.* 152ff. Heroisation of Brasidas: Thucydides v 11; of Timoleon: Plutarch *Timoleon* 39; Diodorus xvi 90 1.

53. New York 11.100.2: Richter *MMCat.Sc.* 82f. no. 83, pl. 67, with an account of the inscribed gables (one, ibid. no. 84 pl. 68e); Diepolder *AG* pl. 30, 1; Johansen *Att.Gr.* 41f. fig. 22; Beazley and Ashmole fig. 135.

54. Stele of Thraseas and Euandria (Berlin K43): Blümel *KGSB* 34f. no. 28, figs. 39, 41, 54f.; Diepolder *AG* pl. 44.

55. 'Visitation' stele (Athens N.M. 870): Conze 320 pl. 78; Diepolder *AG* pl. 47; Beazley and Ashmole fig. 136; Karouzou *Cat.* pl. 40a.

56. Record-relief of 347/6 B.C. (Athens N.M.): Süsserott pl. 43, 3; Diepolder *AG* 46, fig. 11. Aristonautes's stone (Athens N.M. 738): Conze 1151 pl. 738; Diepolder *AG* pl. 50.

57. Hagnostrate's stele (Athens N.M. 1863): Diepolder *AG* pl. 52, 1; Stais 157; on the significance of the loutrophoros, see pp. 371–2 with notes 26, 29. Silenis's stele (Berlin K40): Blümel *KGSB* 35 no. 29, fig. 47; Diepolder *AG* pl. 47. Record relief of 355/4 (Palermo Museum): Süsserott pl. 4, 2; Diepolder AG 41, fig. 10. Aristion's stele (Athens, Kerameikos Museum): Conze 35 pl. 207; Diepolder pl. 36, 2 (36, 1 in text); Johansen *Att.Gr.* fig. 8.

58. Sphinx (Aigina Museum): Furtwängler in *Münchener Jb.d.bildenden Kunst* 1906; Picard *Manuel* II 80; Ridgway *SS* figs. 51f.; Roscher s.v. Sphinx (iv, 181f.); Welter *Aigina* 53, fig. 40. On the Greeks and mixed creatures, see Carpenter *Greek Art* 20, and remarks in *JHS* 87 (1967) 186.

59. Palmette-finial (Berlin K55): Blümel *Kat.* 3 pl. 58, *KGSB* 46f. no. 46, fig. 72. Mourning women (Berlin K13a and b): Blümel *Kat.* 3 pls. 18–21, *KGSB* 45 no. 45, figs. 62–9.

60. Late woman's stele (Athens N.M. 1005): *AM* 84 (1969) pl. 74; and see Karouzou *Cat.* 126. New drapery-style: see pp. 471f. and 479f. with Chapter 7 notes 61ff. and 84. Old man's stele (Athens N.M. 2574): Diepolder *AG* pl. 53; Lullies and Hirmer pls. 226f.; Papaspyridi pl. 11.

61. Ilissos stele (Athens N.M. 869): Diepolder *AG* 48; BDFH pl. 264 (248); Beazley and Ashmole fig. 138; Karouzou *Cat.* pl. 39; Lullies and Hirmer pl. 218 (226). Stele in New York: p. 380 with n. 53. Stele from Aegina or Salamis: p. 367 with n. 15. Children in Hellenistic art: pp. 553–61 with Chapter 8 notes 129, 137, 142ff.

62. Stele with couple (Athens, N.M. 833): Conze 1084 pl. 221; Diepolder *AG* pl. 54; BDFH pl. 265 (249); Lullies and Hirmer pl. 219 (227).

(ii) *Kephisodotos and Praxiteles*

63. Hygieia: pp. 376–7 with notes 42ff. Dike and Adikia on Chest of Cypselus (pp. 64 with Chapter 2 n. 66, 121 and 141 with Chapter 3 notes 106 and 144): Pausanias v 18 2 (Night, Sleep and Death, ibid. 1); on Attic red-figure neck-amphora (with black-figure neck; Vienna 3722, ex Oest. Mus. 319): *ABV* 320 no. 11, *ARV*² 11 no. 3; *CV* pl. 51. Lyssa on Attic red-figure bell-krater (Boston 00.346): *ARV*² 1045, Lykaon Painter no. 7; Beazley in CB II 83, pl. 62. Athanasia on Attic red-figure bell-krater fragment (New York 12.229.14): Richter and Hall 171f. no. 136, pl. 138; the same subject on a lost vase: *JHS* 67 (1947) 1 fig. 1 (Beazley, discussion of the subject 1–7, New York fragment 3, fig. 2). Story of Actaeon: pp. 214, 253 and 269 with Chapter 4 notes 102, 168 and 196.

64. Aristophanes's *Plutus*: p. 376 with n. 42. Altar to Peace in Athens in mid fifth century: Plutarch *Cimon* 13 4. Mid-fifth-century Peace of Kallias: pp. 106–7 with Chapter 3 n. 76, 172 with Chapter 4 n. 26, 292 with Chapter 5 n. 2. Altars to Peace in Athens after 371: Isocrates xv (*Antid.*) 109f.; Cornelius Nepos *Timotheus* 2.

65. Statue of Eirene and Ploutos at Athens: Pausanias I 8 2 (O. 1143) and IX 16 1 (O. 1142). Two sculptors named Kephisodotos: Pliny XXXIV 87 (O. 1137 and 1331); younger: O. 1331–41; elder, O. 1137–43. Xenophon: O. 1140, 1142, 1144. Group at Megalopolis: Pausanias VIII 30 10 (O. 1140). Tyche and Ploutos at Thebes by Xenophon and Kallistonikos: Pausanias IX 16 1 (O. 1142). Two

groups of Muses on Mt Helikon, by a Kephisodotos alone and by Kephisodotos, Strongylion and Olympiosthenes: Pausanias IX 30 1 (O. 878, under Strongylion; see also p. 480 with Chapter 7 n. 85). Strongylion: O. 877–92 (884, Pausanias I 23 8, and 885, Aristophanes *Birds* 1128, Wooden Horse; see also p. 475). Praxitelean Muse base: p. 395 with n. 94.

66. Kephisodotos's Hermes and infant Dionysus: Pliny XXXIV 87 (O. 1137): engraving of a lost statue sometimes thought to be copied from it: Richter *H* 132 fig. 190; Rizzo *Prassitele* pl. 12, left. Praxitelean Hermes and Dionysus: pp. 386–8 with notes 73f. Phokion's first wife: Plutarch *Phokion* 19. Elder Praxiteles: Furtwängler *Meist.* 52ff., 133ff., 514, 670, *Mast.* 32ff., 99ff., 296, 417; see also p. 287 with Chapter 4 n. 233.

67. Munich statue (first connected with Kephisodotos by Overbeck, in a note to 1143): BDFH pl. 247 (231); Beazley and Ashmole fig. 114; *KB* 293, 3; Lawrence *S* pl. 78a; Richter *H* 128 fig. 184, *Sc.* fig. 659; Ridgway *SS* fig. 177; Rizzo *Prassitele* pls. 1–3; and constantly. Other copy of Eirene (New York 06.311): Richter *Cat.* 65 no. 98, pl. 70, *Sc.* fig. 660; Rizzo *Prassitele* pl. 9. Other copies of Ploutos (Dresden): Richter *Sc.* figs. 662f. (coin, fig. 661) (Athens N.M.); Rizzo *Prassitele* pl. 5, 1; cf. also Rizzo *Prassitele* pls. 4–8. Panathenaic: *AAA* 2 (1969) 409–16, figs. 4f. (P. G. Themelis).

68. Later dating: Rumpf *Archäologie* II 88–95 with pl. 10; see further p. 409 with n. 129. 'Diotima' relief from Mantinea (Athens N.M. 226): Karouzou *Cat.* 58 and pl. 30.

69. Acrolithic statues: p. 202 with Chapter 4 n. 85. Early classical metopes from Selinus: pp. 212–14 with Chapter 4 n. 102. Apollo of Olympia: p. 291. Example of a late fourth-century marble with the head carved in a separate piece: p. 462 with Chapter 7 n. 39. Supposed models kept in Praxiteles's workshop for production of statues in various materials: Wace *Approach* 49f.; cf. pp. 389–90 with n. 80. Elder Kephisodotos in Pliny: above, n. 65. Praxiteles: pp. 386ff., with notes 73–96. Younger Kephisodotos: pp. 396 with n. 99, 480 with Chapter 7 n. 84, 518 with Chapter 8 n. 37.

70. Erechtheum Caryatids: pp. 345–6 with Chapter 5 notes 127, 130: Procne: ibid. and p. 286 with Chapter 4 n. 232. Myron's Diskobolos: p. 340 with Chapter 5 n. 114.

71. Capitoline Amazon: pp. 333–4 with Chapter 5 n. 102. 'Venus Genetrix': p. 350 with Chapter 5 n. 141. Polykleitan Hermes with child: p. 333 with Chapter 5 n. 97. Works of Alkamenes and Praxiteles in a double temple at Mantinea: Pausanias VIII 9 1 (O. 824, 1192, 1201); and see p. 392 with n. 94.

72. *Cache* of bronzes in Piraeus: p. 182 with Chapter 4 n. 43. Association of Piraeus Athena and Athena Mattei with Kephisodotos, reached independently by Schefold: *AK* 14 (1971) 37–42 pls. 15f. and 133; and Waywell: *BSA* 66 (1971) 373–82, pls. 66–72; both with earlier refs. Association with Euphranor: Palagia in *AAA*; p. 410 with n. 132. Pergamene Parthenos: p. 312 with Chapter 5 notes 45, 47; p. 546 with Chapter 8 n. 111.

73. Text on Hermes of Olympia: Pausanias V 17 7. Main publication of the statue: *Ol.* III 194–206 pls. 49–53, with refs. before 1897. The conclusions in my text are based mainly on the recent discussion by Adam, 124–8, with refs. to most of the more important contributions to the vast literature; others in Blümel *HEP* (with the hypothesis that it is the work of a Hellenistic sculptor with the name Praxiteles). Other pictures: BDFH pl. 249 (233); Beazley and Ashmole fig. 116; Lawrence *S* pls. 80b, 81; Lullies and Hirmer pls. 220–3 (228–31); Richter (who regards it as an original) *H* 133f. figs. 191f., *Sc.* figs. 170, 444, 664f., 667; and constantly. The treatment of the garment: Adam l.c. Copy of a Praxitelean statue replacing original removed to Rome: p. 390 with n. 81. Texts on Praxiteles: O. 1190–1300: and see following notes.

74. Pompeian painting: Richter in *Bull.Met.* 1913, 178f. and *Sc.* fig. 666; Rizzo *Prassitele* pl. 97.

75. Amazons: pp. 333–9 with Chapter 5 notes 99–105. 'Narcissus': p. 334 with Chapter 5 n. 101. Aphrodite in Naples: pp. 391 and 410 with notes 84 and 133 (with 'Paris').

76. Texts on Sauroktonos: Pliny XXXIV 30 (O. 1217); Martial XIV 172 (O. 1218). Copies of statue: *KB* 294, 3; (Vatican); Lawrence *S* pl. 82a and b (head in Dresden); Richter *H* 129 fig. 185 (Vatican), *Sc.* figs. 673 (coin), 675 (Albani), 676 (Vatican); Rizzo *Prassitele* pls.

59–61 and 62, 1–4. The principal marble is in the Vatican; another in the Louvre (*Enc.Phot.* 190); a fine torso in Cambridge (Budde and Nicholls *Cat.* no. 51, pl. 15); a bronze statuette in Rome, Villa Albani.

77. Apollo and mouse at Chryse: p. 456 with Chapter 7 n. 25. An interesting theory that the lizard is caught in a noose dependent from the god's left hand: Maxmin in *Greece and Rome*, 20 (1973) 36f.; *AAA* 6 (1973) 296ff. figs. 1–2).

78. Hermaphrodite: pp. 551–2 with Chapter 8 notes 122f.

79. Cf. Clark *The Nude* 343f.

80. Texts on Erotes: O. 1249–61 (Thespiai), 1263f. (Parion); also 1262 and 1265ff. Eros on coins of Parion: Rizzo *Prassitele* pl. 93; on other Roman coins, ibid. pls. 62, 6–9, and 65f.; possible Roman copies of Praxitelean Erotes: ibid. pls. 27–33; see also Furtwängler *Meist.* 538–41, figs. 99ff.; *Mast.* 313ff., figs. 133ff. Leaning satyr: *KB* 295, 2; Richter *Sc.* fig. 54; Rizzo *Prassitele* pls. 48–55; the best-known copy is in Rome, Capitoline; another, Museo Torlonia; and there are many torsos, e.g. Louvre (*Enc. Phot.* 191). Texts on satyrs: O. 1224–5 (the artist's favourite, seen by Pausanias, I 20 1, in the Street of the Tripods at Athens), 1226 (Pausanias I 43 5, in the Temple of Dionysus at Megara). A satyr offering a cup in the Temple of Dionysus by the theatre in Athens seems also to be ascribed to Praxiteles by Pausanias (I 20 1, O. 1224); see next note. Models: see p. 385 with n. 69; p. 394 with n. 92.

81. Copies associated with 'satyr offering a cup' (last note): Furtwängler *Meist.* 334f., figs. 97f., *Mast.* 310, fig. 131; *KB* 297, 7; Richter *Sc.* figs. 682ff.; Rizzo *Prassitele* pls. 19–26. Marathon boy (Athens N.M. 15118): BDFH pls. 251 (235) and xxxiv; Beazley and Ashmole fig. 126; Lullies and Hirmer pls. 210–12 (221–3); Richter *Sc.* figs. 172f.; Rizzo *Prassitele* pl. 69. Eros at Thespiai: see last note. Copy of a painting made to replace an original taken to Rome: p. 413 with n. 141.

82. 'Cycladic idols': pp. 2–3 with Prologue n. 2 (cf. n. 1). Minoan and Mycenaean goddesses: pp. 3 and 10 with Prologue notes 3 and 29. Ivories from Athens: p. 44 with Chapter 2 notes 29f. Reliefs from Gortyn, and other naked goddesses in archaic art: p. 58 with Chapter 2 n. 54. Naked girls in bronze as mirror-handles: p. 143 with Chapter 3 n. 147.

83. Naked women in vase-painting: e.g. Pfuhl *MuZ* figs. 295, 319, 377f., 469, 564f.; and cf. pp. 234–5. Naked or near-naked Niobids: p. 319 with Chapter 5 notes 64ff.; naked woman on Bassae frieze: p. 358 with Chapter 5 n. 164. Ludovisi Throne: p. 205 with Chapter 4 n. 89. 'Venus Genetrix': p. 350 with Chapter 5 n. 141. Amazons: pp. 333–9 with Chapter 5 notes 99–103.

84. Esquiline Venus and replica: see p. 601 with Epilogue n. 33. Bronze statuette (Munich, from Beroea in Macedonia): *MJb* 5 (1910) 1; Bulle *SM* 150; Lamb pl. 62b and c; Lullies and Hirmer pl. 194 (199); Rodenwaldt *KdA* pl. 24; and see p. 549 with Chapter 8 n. 118. Marble torso (Naples 294): Bulle *SM* 151; *KB* 379, 3; see also p. 387 with n. 75; p. 410 with n. 133.

85. Texts on Cnidia: O. 1227–45. Copies (most complete in Vatican) collected and discussed by Blinkenberg *Knidia*; other pictures: BDFH pl. 248 (232) right; Lawrence *S* pls. 79b, 80a; Lippold pl. 83, 3; Richter *H* 130 fig. 187, *Sc.* figs. 668–72; and often. See also following notes.

86. Hellenistic Aphrodites and related figures: pp. 548–57 with Chapter 8 notes 116ff.

87. See Gombrich 'Raphael's *Madonna della sedia*' in *Norm and Form* 64–80.

88. Classical bronze hydriai: see especially Diehl *Die Hydria* pls. 8–28 (pl. 19, the hydriai from two copies of the Cnidia in the Vatican); other comparable pieces: Lamb pl. 61; Richter *H* 204 fig. 305.

89. Pliny XXXV 133 (O. 1294 and 1824). On sculptural polychromy in Greece see Reutersward (4th-cent., especially 83ff.; archaic, 35–45, 74–80); see also pp. 481–2 with Chapter 7 n. 87 (Alexander sarcophagus), 569 with Chapter 8 n. 172. Nikias: pp. 396 and 436–9 with notes 99, 204f. Sluter and Malouel: see David *Claus Sluter* chapter 5, especially 91ff.

90. Leconfield head: Furtwängler *Meist.* 640ff. pl. 31, *Mast.* 344 fig. 148 and pl. 17; Lawrence *S* pl. 83; Rizzo *Prassitele* pls. 108f., pl. 110, right. Aberdeen head (B.M. 1600): *BMCat.Sc.* pl. 3; Furtwängler *Mast.* pl. 18; Rizzo *Prassitele* pl. 111.

91. Texts on portraits of Phryne: O. 1246, 1251, 1274 (Thespiai), 1269–77 (Delphi; 1270, Athenaeus XIII 591b, situation and Krates's comment; cf. 1272 and 1274f., Plutarch). Portraiture: pp. 504–27 (Chapter 8 (i) with notes). Head from sanctuary of Demeter at Knidos: B.M. 1314.

92. Aphrodite of Kos: Pliny XXXVI 20 (O. 1217; cf. 807, Cicero *Orat.* 2 5). Half-draped Aphrodite of Arles: p. 553 with Chapter 8 n. 132. Statues in the studio: Pausanias I 20 I.

93. Statuette of Artemis from Cyprus (Vienna): Beazley and Ashmole fig. 125; *KB* 296, 6; Furtwängler *Mast.* 327, fig. 141; Rizzo *Prassitele* pl. 15. Head from Chios (Boston): Caskey *Cat.* 29; BDFH pl. 273 (257); Beazley and Ashmole fig. 119; *KB* 297, 3; Lawrence *LGS* pl. 6; Richter *H* 137, fig. 195, *Sc.* figs. 174, 446. Head from Athens (Boston): Caskey *Cat.* 28; Beazley and Ashmole fig. 121; Richter *Sc.* fig. 175.

94. Praxiteles's Mantinea group and base: Pausanias VIII 9 I (O. 1201; cf. p. 386 with n. 71). Slabs from Mantinea (Athens N.M.): *KB* 296, 1–3; Richter *Sc.* figs. 679–81; Rizzo *Prassitele* pls. 180ff. Number of Muses: see p. 58 with Chapter 2 n. 54.

95. Nemesis base and Pheidian bases: pp. 352–4 with Chapter 5 notes 149–53.

96. Myron's Marsyas: pp. 341–3 with Chapter 5 notes 116–19; Apollo and Marsyas, ibid. n. 118.

97. Late grave relief: p. 382 with n. 60. Mausoleum figures: below pp. 457–9 with Chapter 7 notes 29ff.

98. Statue of Hygieia: the material collected and illustrated by Ashmole in 'Hygieia on Acropolis and Palatine' in *PBSR* 10 (1927) 1–11, figs. 16–38 and pls. 1–5; the Hope statue also illustrated: Lawrence *S* pl. 77. Dionysus ('Sardanapalus'): *KB* 293, 4; Rizzo *Prassitele* pls. 144–7. Bronze Athena from Arezzo (Florence): Rizzo *Prassitele* pls. 139–41. Record relief of 336 (Athens, Agora Museum I 6524): *Agora Guide* pl. 8; *Archaeology* 5 (1952) 150; *EAA* II 75, fig. 101; *Hesp.* 21 (1952) pl. 90; Lang *Ath.Cit.* fig. 29; and see p. 436 with n. 201. Tanagras and their Attic origin: D. Thompson in *AJA* 70 (1966) 51–63, pls. 17–20; Higgins *GT* 97–103, pls. 41–5; and see pp. 480 with Chapter 7 n. 84, 546 with Chapter 8 n. 110. Children at Agrai: Bulle *SM* pl. 187a; Karouzou *Cat.* pl. 43; *Eph.Arch.* 1917, 87 pls. 1a and 2 (Svoronos); *BMQ* 15 (1941–50) 64ff., pl. 29 (M. Robertson); at Brauron: Karouzou in *Eph.-Arch.* 1957, 68–83; *Ergon* 1958, 36f., figs. 38f., 1959, 16f., figs. 15ff.; *Prakt.* 1959 pl. 12b–d; *BCH* 83 (1959) fig. 27; Frel in *Bull.Mus.Hong.* 24 (1964) 3–8 figs. 1–4.

99. Dates: Pliny XXXIV 50 (O. 1191, Praxiteles), 51 (O. 1331, Timarchos and the younger Kephisodotos; p. 518 with Chapter 8 n. 37). Praxiteles on the Mausoleum: Vitruvius *Praef.* 12 (O. 1178). Statue of Artemis Brauronia on Acropolis: Pausanias I 23 7 (O. 1215); inscription: *IG* II 75ff.; see Studniczka *Verm.z.gr.K.* 20f.; Robert *Arch.Märchen* 151f.; Rizzo *Prassitele* 65. Artemis of Gabii (Louvre): *Enc.Phot.* 187; *KB* 297, 6; Lippold pl. 83, 4; Richter *Sc.* fig. 686; Rizzo *Prassitele* 94–8. Dedication of clothes: Linders *Studies*. Nikias's *floruit*: Pliny XXXV 133 (O. 1824).

(iii) *Other works and names in sculpture*

100. Temple of Hera at Argos and authorship of cult-statue: p. 328 with Chapter 5 n. 85. Dexileos: p. 369 with n. 21. Eupolemos: Pausanias II 17 3. Younger Polykleitos (Chapter 5 n. 85): O. 995 and 1004f.

101. Subject-matter of temple-sculptures: Pausanias II 17 3. Remains (Athens N.M. 1561–82 and others): Waldstein *AH* I 139–94, figs. 70–90, pls. 30–41. Other pictures (head, N.M. 1571): Karouzou *Cat.* pl. 28a; Lawrence *S* pl. 71b; Lippold pl. 74, 3; Richter *Sc.* fig. 165; (floral with birds, Waldstein *AH* 124 fig. 61): Karouzou *Cat.* pl. 28b; see also Roux *Argolide* 61. Archaising image: p. 358 with Chapter 5 n. 164; p. 401 with n. 112.

102. Bassae: pp. 356–8 with Chapter 5 notes 160–6. Corinthian as interior order: ibid.; also Chapter 5 n. 133 and pp. 406–7 with notes 121ff. Tholos at Delphi: Dinsmoor 234ff., pls. 57, 59; D. S. Robertson 141, 328, pl. 15b; Roux *Argolide* 60f., 329, 404; Charbonneaux *FdeD* II 4; metopes: de La Coste Messelière *Delphes* pls. 230f.

103. Temple of Asklepios at Epidaurus: Pausanias II 27 1f. (slight; mainly on the image). The architecture: Dinsmoor 218; D. S. Robertson 146, 329; Lawrence *A* 191; Roux *Argolide* 83–138 (date, 129f.). Accounts inscriptions: *IG* IV² 1, 102; Roux *Argolide* 84ff., a translation 424–32; Burford *Epidaurus*, especially appendix 1, translation 212–20. Date from Plato's *Ion*: Keil in *AM* 20 (1895) 75–9; accepted by Crome *SAE* 11. Sculptures: see following notes.

104. Texts on Timotheos: O. 1177f. (Pliny XXXVI 30, Vitruvius VII praef. 12; both on the Mausoleum), 1307 (Vitruvius II 8 11; Ares at Halicarnassus, disputed between Timotheos and Leochares, on whom see pp. 460–2 with Chapter 7 notes 35, 39), and 1328ff. (1329, Pausanias II 32 4, statue at Troezen).

105. Another possible case: p. 490 with Chapter 7 n. 113; cf. also pp. 347f. with Chapter 5 n. 134.

106. Roux *Argolide* 114f., with n. 2, referring to an article of his in *BCH* 80 (1956) 519–21, and one of S. Kayser in *Musée Belge* 6 (1902) 157f.

107. Reliefs of seated gods (Athens N.M. 173, 174): Richter *Sc.* figs. 714f., *H* 126 fig. 181 (173); *KB* 309, 4 (174, finer but more damaged; the face is largely lost and may not have had a beard, so this might be Apollo). Thrasymedes: Pausanias II 27 2 (O. 853; see also p. 322 with Chapter 5 n. 73).

108. Remains of temple-sculpture (Athens N.M. 136ff. and others): Crome *SAE* passim. I owe my knowledge of Yalouris's work to conversations with him in Princeton early in 1969 and to a lecture he gave there. Other pictures: BDFH pl. 244 (228) above; *KB* 298, 1–2 and 4–7; Lawrence *S* pl. 76b; Lippold pl. 79, 1–2; Richter *H* 127 figs. 182f., *Sc.* figs. 710–13, 716–19. Detailed refs. in following notes.

109. Western akroteria: centre (N.M. 155): Crome *SAE* pls. 1–3; *KB* 298, 7; Richter *Sc.* fig. 713; side-figures (N.M. 156, 157): Crome *SAE* pls. 6–8; *KB* 298, 1–2; Richter *H* figs. 182f., *Sc.* figs. 710f.; head associated with central figure: Crome *SAE* pls. 4–5; *KB* 298, 5.

110. Eastern akroterion (N.M. 162): Crome *SAE* pl. 11; BDFH pl. 244 (228) above; *KB* 298, 6; Richter *Sc.* fig. 712. Eros on bronze hydria (New York 44.11.9): Richter *MMH* fig. 305, and in *AJA* 50 (1946) pl. 22. 'Revealing' drapery: pp. 550 and 556 with Chapter 8 notes 121, 137.

111. West pediment: mounted Amazon (N.M. 136): Crome *SAE* pls. 13–15; Richter *Sc.* figs. 716–17. Head-fragment (N.M. 141): Crome *SAE* pl. 36, above. Warrior-torso (then Epidaurus Museum 16): Crome *SAE* pls. 28f. On Yalouris's work see above, n. 108.

112. East pediment: Athena and hand (then Epidaurus Museum 17): Crome *SAE* pl. 39; head of Priam (N.M. 144): Crome *SAE* pls. 40f.; *KB* 298, 4; woman and child (N.M. 146): Crome *SAE* pl. 44; Richter *Sc.* fig. 719; woman and dying man (N.M. 147): Crome *SAE* pls. 32f.; Ajax (then Epidaurus Museum 5): Crome *SAE* pls. 32f. Dead youth from corner (then Epidaurus Museum 42): Crome *SAE* pl. 26.

113. Hygieia from Epidaurus (Athens N.M. 299): Karouzou *Cat.* pl. 38; Adam pls. 40f. and pp. 92ff.; BDFH pl. 245 (229). Original in same style from Athens (Agora Museum S182): *Hesp.* 2 (1933) 526f.; another (original or copy) in London, Burlington House.

114. Leda (completest copy in Rome, Capitoline): BDFH pl. 246 (230); *KB* 298, 8; Lippold pl. 79, 3. Athena (Florence, Uffizi, ex Rospigliosi): Beazley and Ashmole fig. 115. Brussels A1140: perhaps Hygieia; see Cumont *Cat.*

115. 'Armed Aphrodite' from Epidaurus: Lippold pl. 68, 3. Copy with skin (Munich 236): *Einz. Auf.* 1361; a third, without attribute: *Einz.Auf.* 822. 'Barberini Suppliant' (Louvre 3433): BDFH pl. 217 (201); Richter *Sc.* fig. 501 (detail); Karouzou in *BCH* 64/5 (1940/1) 251f. and 70 (1946) 436ff.; identified as Danae); Dörig in *JdI* 80 (1965) 138–66, figs. 1 and 4–7 (2–3, other copies), 174ff. figs. 19, 21, 23 (head; identified as Alkmene).

116. The Nereid monument has recently been reconstructed in the British Museum, after new discoveries on the site by the French Institute in Istanbul: see Coupel and Demargne *Xanthos* III, with refs. to earlier accounts. Architecture also: Dinsmoor 256f., fig. 95; D. S. Robertson 135, 335; Lawrence *A* 190f. Sculpture: *BMCat. Sc.* II 1–45, nos. 850–939, pls. 1–4; *KB* 264f., 266, 1–2; Lawrence *S* pl. 76a; Lippold pls. 71ff.; Richter *Sc.* figs. 302–4, 397, 467, 490, 492. Pictorial reliefs: p. 431 with notes 188f.

Carved architraves at Assos and Didyma: pp. 81f. and 85 with Chapter 3 notes 25 and 31.

117. Sidon sarcophagi (Istanbul): Hamdy Bey and Reinach *Nécropole*; Kleemann *Satrap.* (monograph on Satrap sarcophagus, with full illustration and reference). Other pictures: *KB* 260, 1–5 (Satrap), 261, 1–6 and colour-plate (Lycian), 313, 5–6 (Mourning Women), colour-plate at 320, 335, 4 and 336f. (Alexander); also, Satrap: Lawrence *S* pls. 42f.; Ridgway *SS* fig. 135; Lycian: Akurgal *Turkey* pl. 21; Lawrence *S* pls. 73f.; Lullies and Hirmer² pls. 193–7; Richter *H* 119 fig. 170; Ridgway *SS* fig. 54; Mourning women: Akurgal *Turkey* pl. 22a; Lawrence *S* pl. 84; Lullies and Hirmer² pls. 207–9; Richter *Sc.* figs. 316, 398; the hunting frieze: Hiller in *MWP* 1960, 1–12, pl. 1. Alexander Sarcophagus: pp. 481–2 with Chapter 7 n. 87. Three-quarter chariots: pp. 156 and 224 with Chapter 4 notes 7 and 119; 360 with Chapter 5 n. 173; p. 416 with notes 150f.

118. Lycian tombs: Bossert *AA* 41–55, figs. 228–62; Akurgal *Turkey* pls. 5f.; *BMCat.Sc.* 46–59 nos. 950–5, pls. 5–12. City views: p. 431 with n. 188.

119. Heroon of Gjölbaschi-Trysa (the sculptures in Vienna): Benndorf and Niemann *Heroon* (full illustration in engravings); Eichler *Reliefs* (full photographic illustration with discussion and refs.). Other pictures: *KB* 262f.; Lawrence *S* pl. 65b; Richter *H* 125 fig. 180, *Sc.* figs. 326, 421f., 516; see also next note, and p. 431 with notes 188f. Theseum at Athens: p. 247 with Chapter 4 n. 155.

120. Dancing girls at Gjölbaschi-Trysa: Benndorf and Niemann *Heroon* pl. 6; Eichler *Reliefs* pl. 1. Reliefs in Berlin (K184, 185): Blümel *Kat.* IV 45f., pl. 77, with refs.; Eichler *Reliefs* 11 fig. 4; Schrader *Phidias* 346ff. figs. 313f.; in Athens: Schrader *Phidias* 346ff. figs. 315f. Texts on Kallimachos: O. 893–6 (Pliny, Pausanias and Vitruvius, all alleging his over-elaboration), 531 and 795 (Dionysius of Halicarnassus on his lightness and grace); see also next note. Maenad-reliefs: *KB* 267, 5; Lawrence *S* pl. 133b, *LGS* pls. 83ff.; Richter *AI* figs. 137–41, *MMCat.Sc.* 58–61 nos. 58ff., pls. 50–2, with further refs., *Sc.* figs. 514–15, *TCP* figs. 137–41.

121. Kallimachos and the Corinthian capital: Vitruvius IV 1 8–10; see also pp. 359 with Chapter 5 n. 166, 397 with n. 102. Vase with Caryatids (Naples): Spinazzola pl. 203; White *Perspective* pl. 6b; *BCH* 32 (1908) 218 fig. 28; Poulsen *Delphi* 263 fig. 128. See also next note, and p. 440 with n. 211.

122. Acanthus-column at Delphi: Homolle in *BCH* 32 (1908) 205–35, with illustration; Poulsen *Delphi* 246–64, figs. 113 and 121–5 (connecting it with Praxiteles); de La Coste Messelière *Delphes* pls. 165–71; Richter *Sc.* fig. 312; divorced from earthquake of 373 and connected with base of later fourth century: Pouilloux and Roux *Énigmes* 123–49, pls. 23–8.

123. Acanthus-column on Athenian vase of Kallimachos's time (volute-krater fragment, Leningrad 33a): *ARV²* 1408, Painter of New York Centauromachy no. 1, with refs.; Hahland pl. 17a; a later vase: *BCH* 40 (1916) 219 fig. 9; Poulsen *Delphi* 252 fig. 119; also on a panathenaic prize-vase from Eleusis with the name of the archon Charikleides (362/3 B.C.): *ABV* 414 Charikleides Group no. 1, with refs.; Schmidt *Archaistische Kunst* pl. 7, 1; *Rend.Pont.* (3 ser.) 17, 89. Palm-tree at Delos: p. 272 with Chapter 4 n. 203. Kallimachos's lamp in Erechtheum: Pausanias I 26 6 (O. 894).

124. Delphi column perhaps fallen by 109 B.C.: Pouilloux and Roux *Énigmes* 144. Roman acanthus-columns in S. Prassede: *BCH* 32 (1908) 216 fig. 6; Poulsen *Delphi* 253, fig. 120; others in the door of a palace in Piazza S. Caterina della Rota, Rome; those in Corinth mentioned by Dinsmoor, 253. On those in Philibert de l'Orme's chapel at Villers-Cotterêts, and on the whole question, see Blunt *Philibert de l'Orme* 118–22, figs. 32–3 (a new 'French Order') and pl. 65a (Delphi column), b (S. Prassede), c and d (columns in Roman wall-painting), e (Villers-Cotterêts). Mannerism in late fifth-century vase-painting: see Becatti *Meidias: un manierista antico.*

125. Skopas: pp. 339 with Chapter 5 n. 111; pp. 452ff. with Chapter 7 notes 11 and 17–27. Temples at Ephesus: archaic, p. 83 with Chapter 3 n. 29; fourth-century: architecture, Dinsmoor 223–5, 227 fig. 81; D. S. Robertson 147f. fig. 63, 332; Lawrence *A* 196–9 fig. 109. Position of carved column-drums: Bammer *AJAE* 21ff., reconstruction p. 10 fig. 6, and in *ÖJh* 48 (1964/5)

Hauptblatt 131–7, figs. 77–9; Wiegartz in *MWP* 1968, 41–73 with fig. 1 on p. 51. Sculptures: *BMCat.Sc.* II 165–84, nos. 1200–17 with pl. 23 (drum 1206 set on pier 1204); see also next note and p. 409 with n. 131.

126. Drum 1206: last note; also pictured: *KB* 308, 5; Lawrence *S* pl. 93; Lullies and Hirmer pls. 214f. (pl. 223); Richter *Sc.* figs. 328 (below, n. 129), 703, 705.

127. Sleep and Death on vases: pp. 222 with Chapter 4 n. 116, 326 with Chapter 5 n. 81. Three-figure reliefs: p. 374 with notes 34ff.

128. Hecate on vase with Persephone's return: p. 327 with Chapter 5 n. 83. Interpretations of Ephesus drum: Picard *Manuel* IV 119–33, with pl. 3 and figs. 57f. giving list of earlier interpretations and proposing Iphigenia in Aulis.

129. Figure resembling Eirene: Richter *Sc.* fig. 308; see p. 384 with n. 68 and refs. there.

130. Antikythera shipwreck: Bol *SSA* with full earlier refs.; bronze youth (Athens N.M. 13396): ibid. 18–24 (probably Greek original), pls. 6–9; other pictures: BDFH pl. 250 (234); Karouzou *Cat.* pl. 52; *KB* 310, 4; Lullies and Hirmer pls. 208f. (218ff.).

131. Fight (B.M. 1204): *BMCat.Sc.* II pl. 23. Corner (B.M. 1200): BDFH pl. 272 (256). Mausoleum sculptures: pp. 447–63 with notes (Chapter 7, ii). Silanion: p. 508 with Chapter 8 notes 11f. Lysippos: pp. 463–75 with notes (Chapter 7, iii).

132. Euphranor's date: Pliny XXXV 128 (O. 1786); see further, pp. 433–6 with notes 192–201 (on his painting). Texts on his sculpture: O. 1798–1806 (1708, Pliny XXXIV 77, list of his works in bronze, including statues of Philip and Alexander). Text on statue of Apollo: Pausanias I 3 3 (O. 1799). Temple of Apollo and statue: H. Thompson in *Eph.Arch.* 1953/4 pls. 1f., figs. 1f. Statue also: Adam 94–7, pls. 42f.; Richter *H* 144 fig. 208. Roman copy in Vatican: *Eph.Arch.* 1953/4 32 fig. 3a–b. Bronze Athena associated with Apollo: Palagia in *AAA* (p. 386 with n. 72, with further refs. for Athena). 'Timothean' style: pp. 401–2 with notes 112ff.

133. Text on Paris: Pliny XXXIV 77 (O. 1798). Statue (p. 387 with notes 75 and 84): Furtwängler *Mast.* 357ff., noting the connection with the Aphrodite in Naples (pp. 387 and 391), and illustrating the two in figs. 154f. on p. 358; the 'Paris' also: *Sotheby Cat. 4 Dec. 1972* no. 126, pl. 24. A related figure identified as Euphranor's Paris: Dörig in *JdI* 79 (1964) 241–56, figs. 1–18.

(*iv*) *The painters of transition and echoes of their work*

134. Aglaophon, Cephisodorus, Erillus, Evenor: Pliny XXXV 60 (O. 1130 and 1641). Aglaophon: pp. 415–16 with notes 148f. Euenor is mentioned as Parrhasios's father also by Pausanias (I 28 2; O. 637), Harpocration s.v. Parrhasios (O. 1694) and Athenaeus (XII 543; O. 1700), who quotes a verse used by Parrhasios as a signature in which his father's name occurs; improbable identification of this Ephesian painter with a sculptor active in Athens in the early fifth century: p. 179 with Chapter 4 n. 37; accepted by Rumpf in *AJA* 55 (1951) 2. Zeuxis and 'the brush': see further p. 485 with Chapter 7 n. 99.

135. Texts on Apollodoros: O. 1641 (see last note)–1646 (1645, Plutarch *de glor. Athen.* 2). Quintilian on Zeuxis: see next note.

136. Texts on Zeuxis: O. 1647–91 (1647, Pliny XXXV 61f., date and Apollodoros's epigram; 1651ff., near-contemporary references: 1651, Plato *Protagoras* 318D, where the manuscripts give the name as Zeuxippos; 1652, id. *Gorgias* 453C; 1653, Xenophon *Symposium* IV 63; two other refs. in Xenophon: *Oecon.* X 1, O. 1684, and *Mem.* I 4 3, O. 972; 1654, Aelian *Var.Hist.* XIV 17, sojourn with Archelaos to adorn his palace; a Pan painted for Archelaos, Pliny XXXV 61, O. 1661; 1660, Schol. Aristophanes *Acharn.* 991; 1680, Quintilian XII 10 4).

137. Texts on Parrhasios: O. 1680 (Quintilian, see last note), 1696–1730 (1703, Seneca *Controv.* X 5, prisoner tortured for Prometheus; Toronaean prisoners, Thucydides V 3, but see Rumpf in *AJA* 55 (1951) 2 for the view that Seneca's story is wholly apocryphal; 1720, Pausanias I 28 2, collaboration with Mys on shield of Promachos; date of Promachos, p. 285 with Chapter 4 n. 229; Panainos and Pleistainetos:

pp. 240 with Chapter 4 notes 151f., 322–4 with Chapter 5 notes 74, 76; Iliupersis engraved by Mys: Athenaeus XI 782B, O. 1721.) On Parrhasios see also following notes.

138. Quintilian XII 10 4 (O. 1680 and 1725); Pliny XXXV 67 (O. 1724). On the parallel with the Quattrocento see Bianchi Bandinelli *Storicità* 45–61, pls. 32–5; Rumpf *AJA* 55 (1951) 1–12, figs. 1–7, especially 5ff. Grapes and curtain: Pliny XXXV 64 (O. 1649). Illusion of nature in Parrhasios: Xenophon *Mem.* III 10 1 (O. 1701). Shading on women's skin: pp. 424f. and 436 with notes 169f., 204. Parrhasios's Theseus: Plutarch *Theseus* 4f. (O. 1352) and *de glor. Athen.* 2 (O. 1704); Pliny XXXV 69 (O. 1705); and see p. 434 with n. 195, on this picture and Euphranor's.

139. Zeuxis and Polygnotos contrasted: Aristotle *Poet.* 6 (O. 1077). Parrhasios's Philoctetes: p. 422 with n. 165; his Ajax: Pliny XXXV 71 (O. 1699); Athenaeus XII 543E (O. 1700). Timanthes: p. 414 with n. 143. Archaic cups: p. 202 with Chapter 4 n. 133. Exekias's Ajax and its 'classical' character: p. 132 with Chapter 3 n. 127. Parrhasios's erotics: Pliny XXXV 72; Suetonius *Tiberius* 44 (O. 1718f.); cf. also p. 418 with n. 156. Rape of Cassandra: p. 234 with Chapter 4 n. 138.

140. Parrhasios's sketches: Pliny XXXV 68 (O. 1722). Arrogance and display: Pliny XXXV 71 (O. 1699, Parrhasios), 61 (O. 1647, Zeuxis).

141. Zeuxis's Herakles and the snakes: Pliny XXXV 62f. (O. 1665f.); his Centaur-family: Lucian *Zeuxis* 3 (O. 1663). Female Centaurs: pp. 488 with Chapter 7 n. 108, 545 with Chapter 8 n. 108. Copies made to replace works of sculpture removed to Rome: Praxiteles's Eros at Thespiai, p. 390 with n. 80; also perhaps the Hermes at Olympia, p. 387 with n. 73. A copy of a famous fourth-century painting made in the second century A.D. for a different reason: p. 435 with n. 199; see also p. 574 with Chapter 8 n. 189. The Sullan sack: p. 182 with Chapter 4 n. 45; p. 548 with Chapter 8 n. 115.

142. Zeuxis's Helen: O. 1667–75 (1667, Pliny XXXV 64, painted for Akragas; 1674, ibid. 66, at Rome; 1668f., Cicero *de invent.* II 1 1, and Dionysius of Halicarnassus *de prisc.script.cens.* 1, painted at Croton). All these repeat the anecdote of the parade.

143. Texts on Timanthes: O. 1649, 1699, 1734–44. Iphigeneia: O. 1734, Pliny XXXV 73; 1735, Quintilian II 13 12 (with reference to defeat of Kolotes); 1736, Cicero *Orat.* XXII 74. Cyclops: O. 1742, Pliny XXXV 74. Ajax: above, n. 139. Relief with Iphigeneia (Florence, Uffizi): Picard *Manuel* IV 125ff., figs. 60, 62f.; Pfuhl *MuZ* fig. 638; Rumpf *MZ* 121 fig. 10; *RM* 20 (1905) 307 fig. 2. Three-figure reliefs: p. 374 with notes 34ff. Krito and Timarista: p. 369 with n. 23. A painting of the sacrifice from Pompeii, with Agamemnon's face veiled: Curtius *WP* pl. V.

144. Texts on Agatharchos: O. 1118–25: Aeschylus's set and commentary: Vitruvius VII praef. 11 (O. 1120; the part about Democritus and Anaxagoras omitted by O.); explanation given in the text: Rumpf in *JHS* 67 (1947) 13 and *MZ* 121. Sophocles and scene-painting: Aristotle *Poet.* 14 16 (1449a). See further, pp. 586–8 with Chapter 8 notes 228–234.

145. Samos relief: *AM* 71 (1956) 83–9, Beil. 48f. (Holm, mythological interpretation); *BCH* 86 (1962) 265, fig. 14; Schuchardt in *Essays ... Lehmann* 293–9, fig. 1, with earlier refs. (votive); *AK* 9 (1966) 16–20, pls. 5, 1 and 4 (Zanker, gravestone).

146. (Andokides) IV *c. Alcibiad.* 17; Plutarch *Alcibiades* 16; Demosthenes *c. Midian* 147 (O. 1123–5); see Burn in *CQ* 4 (1954) 138–42.

147. Zeuxis and Archelaos: p. 411 with n. 136; p. 488 with Chapter 7 n. 108. Wall-decoration at Olynthus: *Olynthus* VIII, chapter 9, 291–301, with fig. 30 and pl. 86. Pebble-mosaics: pp. 486–9 with Chapter 7 notes 104–9 (Olynthus, Motya and Gordion n. 104).

148. Athenaeus XII 534D (O. 1132); Plutarch *Alcibiades* 16 (O. 1134); Pausanias I 22 6 (O. 1133, the picture in the Propylaea; on the building and its picture-gallery, see pp. 245 with Chapter 4 n. 153, 347 with Chapter 5 n. 133). Aristophon: O. 1127–9 and 1134: Aglaophon the younger: O. 1130 (Pliny XXXV 60, date) – 1135 (Aelian *Nat.anim.epit.*, the horse); see also p. 242 with Chapter 4 n. 149. The motives in vase-painting: p. 418 with n. 156. Olympias: p. 212 with Chapter 4 n. 99; p. 434 with n. 196. See further, next note.

149. Relief-base with horses (Athens N.M. 1464): Svoronos 465–70, no. 161, figs. 219–21 and

pl. 67, with the suggestion repeated here. Paintings on marble: p. 422 with n. 166. Nikias's painted tombstone: p. 437 with n. 204.

150. Two-faced relief with Echelos and Basile (or Iasile; Athens, N.M. 1783): Svoronos 120–36, pls. 28 and 182; Karouzou *Cat.* pl. 27; Lullies and Hirmer pl. 186 (188); Walter in *Eph.Arch.* 1937, 97–119, figs. 2 and 3. Echetlos or Echetlaios in the Marathon: p. 323 with Chapter 5 n. 75. Three-quarter chariots: above pp. 156 and 224 with Chapter 4 notes 7 and 119, 360 with Chapter 5 n. 173; in 5th- and 4th-cent. relief-sculpture: Waywell in *BSA* 62 (1967) 19–26, pls. 1–3; in vase-painting of this period: White 36f.; pictures: e.g. Pfuhl *MuZ* figs. 583f., 593; Arias and Hirmer figs. 212f., 215, 221, 229 (Etruscan).

151. Apobates bases (Athens, Agora Museum S399): *Agora Guide* p. 134 (not illustrated); (Acropolis Museum 1326): Casson *Cat.* 227; cf. also reliefs, Athens N.M. 1391, from Oropos, Stais 197; Berlin K80, Blumel *Kat.* III pl. 69. 'Valerian' or 'Herulian' wall: H. Thompson in *JRS* 49 (1959) 64f.; cf. *Hesp.* 28 (1959) 95f.

152. Parrhasios's Demos: Pliny XXXV 69 (O. 1710); and see p. 434 with n. 195; other representations of the subject, ibid. and pp. 436–7 with n. 201, 490 with Chapter 7 n. 114. Two-expressioned masks: Webster in *AJA* 66 (1962) 333, pl. 88, 1–2; associated with Parrhasios's Demos: Rumpf *MZ* 116f.

153. Texts on Pauson: O. 1078f. (Aristotle *Poet.* 2 and *Polit.* VIII 5 7); 1110–51 (Aristophanes *Acharnians* 354, *Thesmophoriazusae* 948, and *Plutus* 602; and three refs. in late writers).

154. Apotheosis of Herakles: e.g. *ARV*² 1419f., Painter of London F64 nos. 1–5 (one illustrated FR II 257 fig. 90); 1424, Group of Ferrara T. 376B nos. 1–3 (unpublished); 1437, Uppsala Painter nos. 4 and 13 (with Apollo, unpublished); several are illustrated in Metzger *Rép.*, pls. 22, 28. Parody: *ARV*² 1335, Nikias Painter no. 34 (oinochoe, Louvre N3408); Pfuhl *MuZ* fig. 572; *AJA* 55 (1951) 9 and 11; *Hesp.* 24 (1955) pl. 34b. Perseus parody (Athens, Vlastos): *ARV*² 1215. Group of the Perseus Dancer no. 1; *JHS* 65 (1945) pl. 1; Brommer *Satyrspiele* 26f. figs. 17ff. (ibid.², 29ff.).

155. Kleophon Painter: *ARV*² 1143ff.; Beazley *VA* 181ff. with figs. 113ff. and in 'Spina e la ceramica greca' in *Spina e l'Etruria padana* (suppl. to *St.Etr.* 25), 54f. figs. 3–6 (the volute-krater Ferrara T. 57C VP, *ARV*² no. 1; also illustrated Alfieri and Arias *Spina* pls. 82–7; *EAA* IV 371). Dinos Painter: *ARV*² 1151ff.; no. 2 (stamnos, Naples 2419): Arias and Hirmer pls. 206–11; FR pls. 36f.; Pfuhl *MuZ* fig. 582. I cannot remember where I learnt about Lola Montez's copy, but have seen classicising copies which keep the red-figure appearance. Polion: *ARV* 1171ff.; Beazley in 'Spina', cited above, 53f., figs. 1f. (no. 1, volute-krater Ferrara T.127, on which see also p. 246 with Chapter 4 n. 154).

156. Eretria Painter: *ARV*² 1247ff.; Beazley *VA* 179f., figs. 110bis and 111, *VP* 61–4, pls. 29, 2 and 30, *SAVCM* 46–9, pl. 7, 1, CB III, 168f. no. 162, pl. 98, 1–3. No. 34 (onos, Athens N.M. 1629): *Eph.Arch.* 1897, pls. 9f.; Arias and Hirmer pl. 23; Beazley and Ashmole fig. 108; Pfuhl *MuZ* fig. 561; Richter *ARVS* fig. 101, *H* 338, fig. 455. Meidias Painter: *ARV*² 1312ff.; Beazley *VA* 185–9, figs. 117f. No. 34 (hydria B.M. E224, signed by potter Meidias): Beazley and Ashmole, fig. 111; Becatti *Meidias* pls. 1f., 16, 3 and 18, 2; Buschor *GV* 230f.; FR pls. 8f.; Pfuhl *MuZ* fig. 593; Richter *H* 339, fig. 455. Washing Painter: *ARV*² 1126f.; Beazley *VA* 196, note to 183; *VP* 64f. No. 196 (pyxis, Würzburg 541): Langlotz *GVW* pls. 200f.; Greifenhagen *Eroten* 42–5. Shuvalov Painter: *ARV*² 1206ff.; no. 41 (oinochoe Berlin 2414): *CV* II pls. 146, 1f., 145, 2; Greifenhagen *AKW*² 57. Lebes gamikos with bride on Aphrodite's knees and Eros crowning both (Athens 1454): *ARV*² 1178, Painter of Athens 1454 no. 1; *AM* 32 (1907) pl. 5, 2; Hahland pl. 3. Pointed amphoriskos (Berlin inv. 30036): *ARV*² 1173, Heimarmene Painter no. 1; *EAA* III 1133; FR pl. 170, 2; *RM* 47 (1932) pl. 7, 4. Pointed amphorae: p. 235 with Chapter 4 n. 139. Pheidias's mug: p. 321 with Chapter 5 n. 71. Stamped black ware: Sparkes and Talcott *Agora* XII, 21–31; Corbett in *Hesp.* 18 (1949) 290–341, and 24 (1955) 172–86; Talcott in *Hesp.* 4 (1935) 481–92; A. D. Ure in *JHS* 64 (1944) 67–77. Stamped figure-scenes: Sparkes in *AK* 11 (1968) 3–16, pls. 1–8.

157. Stemless cup (Berlin 2728): *ARV*² 1275 no. 4;

pictures of inside: Blümel *Sport und Spiel* pl. 19, *SH* 33; Gardiner *Athletics* fig. 214, *GAS* 355, and in *JHS* 27 (1907) 268. Phiale Painter, p. 326 with Chapter 5 n. 82; no. 33, small neck-amphora with athlete resting (Naples, 3083): *BSA* 30 (1932) 112, fig. 2.

158. Chous with drunk (New York 37.11.19): not in Beazley: Richter *MMH* pl. 82f. (p. 102, n. 92, with refs.).

159. Iliupersis fragments (not in Beazley): see Bulle in *Eph.Arch.* 1937, 473–82; the inferior (Heidelberg, from Athens), ibid. fig. 2; the better (Würzburg from Taranto), fig. 1; the Würzburg fragment also Walter in *AM* 87 (1962) 193–6 (with the true interpretation) Beil. 54, 2; *Hesp.* 9 (1940) 48, fig. 18.

160. Theseus krater (Bologna 303): *ARV*² 1184f., Kadmos Painter no. 6; *JHS* 18 (1898) 279 and 39 (1919) 133; Pfuhl *MuZ* fig. 570. Mikon's picture: p. 243 with Chapter 4 n. 150.

161. Europa on vase: p. 193 with Chapter 4 n. 63. Gigantomachy vases: pp. 312 and 324 with Chapter 5 n. 46; see also *ARV*² 1345f., Suessula Painter. Jug with Athena and Marsyas: p. 341 with Chapter 5 n. 117. Jugs with Tyrannicides (not in Beazley): Boston 98.936, from Dexileos's burial-plot (p. 369 with n. 21); Villa Giulia; both, Brunnsåker *Tyrant-slayers* pl. 24; Boston also, Hahland pl. 6a, and see end of note; Villa Giulia also, *ÖJh* 33 (1941) fig. 13. Panathenaics with Tyrannicides as shield-device (London B605; Hildesheim 1253 and 1254): *ABV* 411, Kuban Group no. 4, and 412, Hildesheim Group nos. 1 and 2; *AA* 1919, 79 figs. 1 and 2 , nos. 86a and b; Beazley and Ashmole fig. 64; Brunnsåker *Tyrant-slayers* pl. 23; see Beazley in *AJA* 47 (1943) 453ff., *Dev.* 96. Red-figure jugs with archaising Athena: p. 347 with Chapter 5 n. 131. Vases from Dexileos's plot: E. Vermeule in *JdI* 85 (1970) 94–111 (Tyrant-slayers, 96 fig. 2, 105 fig. 7), arguing that both plot and vases were bought for Dexileos's burial.

162. Fragment with Dionysus (calyx-krater, Jena inv. 382): not in Beazley: Hahland pl. 16a. White for women's skin in black-figure: p. 214 with Chapter 4 n. 108. Shading used for men, not women: p. 412 with n. 138; pp. 424–5 with notes 169ff., 436 with notes 203f.

163. Achilles and Phiale Painters: pp. 324–6 with Chapter 5 notes 79–82. Parrhasios's drawings or sketches: p. 413 with n. 140.

164. Reed Painter: *ARV* 1376–82; Group R: *ARV*² 1383f.; on both and the relation see Beazley *AWL* 24f., pl. 8 (Group R); other pictures, e.g.: Arias and Hirmer pls. xiv and 200; BDFH pl. at p. 378 (157); Pfuhl *MuZ* fig. 552; M. Robertson 154f.; Rumpf *MZ* pl. 37, 3. See also next note. Picture of 'Theseus's End': pp. 253–7 with Chapter 4 notes 169–71.

165. Silver cup (Copenhagen): Johansen *Hoby-Fundet* pl. 9. Parrhasios's Philoctetes: Glaukos in *Anth.Gr.* II 348 5 (O. 1709). On the connections between Parrhasios, the Hoby cup, and the lekythoi of Group R, see especially (besides Johansen 132–6, French summary 160), Rumpf in *AJA* 55 (1941) 1–12, figs. 1–7; Bianchi-Bandinelli *Storicità* 47–61, pls. 31–5 (cf. p. 412 with n. 138). Euphronios and Euthymides: pp. 221–6 with Chapter 4 notes 115–21.

166. Painted stele with clasped hands (Athens N.M. 17751): S. Karouzou in *AM* 71 (1956) 124–39, pl. A, Beil. 69f., fig. 1. Painted stele with dog (Athens, Kerameikos Museum): M. Robertson 157. 'Maltese' dogs: J. Busuttil in *Greece and Rome* 16 (1969) 205–8; examples in early fifth-century vase-painting, e.g.: Beazley *Berl.M.* pl. 8, 1; Philippaki pl. 22, 1. Foreshortened vase-mouths in vase-painting, e.g. Richter and Hall pl. 122 (Phiale Painter), 126. Carved fillet on tomb-relief: Beazley in *AJA* 55 (1941) 334 and pl. 32A. Vase-pictures of tombstones with fillets tied round them, e.g. the vases of Group R, cited in n. 164, and constantly.

167. Theban tombstones: *AAA* 1 (1968) 92–6, figs. 1f. (Kalogeropoulou, with refs.); *Eph.Arch.* 1963, 13–15 (Chronika); Karouzos *M.Th.* nos. 54ff. figs. 24ff.; Pfuhl *MuZ* figs. 633f.; Rumpf *MZ* pl. 37, 4 and 5. Stones from Chios, in like technique but less fine, with various subjects: Kontoleon in *BCH* 71/2 (1947/8) 273–301, pls. 47f.; and 73 (1949) 384–97, pl. 20; Lawrence *LGS* pl. 42.

168. Plate-fragment with eagle: Athens, Agora Museum. Lion-rider (Boston 10.187): *ARV*² 1337 no. 10, Hahland pl. 17b; Metzger *Rép.* pl. 19, 2; M. Robertson in *JHS* 85 (1965) pl. 22, 2; relation to Delos mosaic (pl. 22, 1) p. 88; mosaic also: *Délos* 14 pls. 1–3 and pp. 13–22, figs. 4f. Pictures in Temple of Dionysus at

Athens: Pausanias I 20 2; their possible date and influence: M. Robertson in *GRBS* 13 (1972) 44–8; see also pp. 441 with n. 213, 483 with Chapter 7 n. 94, 579 with Chapter 8 notes 209f.

169. Group of the Huge Lekythoi: *ARV*² 1390, 1–5 and *Paralipomena* 522, addenda to 487; see especially Brommer in *Mad.Mitt.* 10 (1969) 155–71, pls. 18–24 and col. pls. 1 and 2; the old drawings, reproduced in Pfuhl *MuZ* fig. 535 and Rumpf *MZ* pl. 39, 1, are not satisfactory. Marble lekythoi: pp. 371f. with n. 29.

170. Pliny XXXV 64 (O. 1648): *pinxit et monochromata ex albo*. Jex-Blake and Sellers translate 'in white', and comment 'i.e., on a dark ground'; the same view is taken in the Loeb, but it does not seem certain.

171. Pausanias X 30 2 (Polygnotus's Underworld, pp. 266–70 with Chapter 4 notes 189–200).

172. Knucklebone players (Naples 9562). Elia 40, no. 49, fig. 13; Curtius *WP* 3 fig. 1; Pfuhl *MuZ* fig. 629; Rumpf *MZ* pl. 39, 6. Sappho: Lobel and Page no. 142; see Page ad loc. Nessos (Naples 9560): Elia 41 no. 50, fig. 14; Pfuhl *MuZ* fig. 630; Rumpf *MZ* pl. 41, 1. Chariot (Naples 9564): Elia 41f. no. 51, fig. 15; Pfuhl *MuZ* fig. 631; Rumpf *MZ* pl. 41, 4. Charon and Thanatos on white lekythoi: p. 326 with Chapter 5 n. 81. Zeuxis's Triton and Boreas: Lucian *Timon.* 54 (O. 1664); his Pan for Archelaos: Pliny XXXV 62 (O. 1662); his bound Marsyas, 66 (O. 1661).

173. P. 371 with n. 28.

174. Beginning of South Italian vase-painting: N. Moon in *PBSR* 11 (1929) 30–49, pls. 12–16; Trendall *FV*, *SIV* and *RLCS*; Cambitoglou and Trendall *AVPS*. Texts on Zeuxis: above, n. 136.

175. Teiresias krater (Paris, Cab.Méd. 422): Trendall *RLCS* 102 no. 532 with refs.; FR pls. 60 and 147; Pfuhl *MuZ* fig. 479 (Odysseus); Trendall *FV* pl. 16 (Odysseus). Shading on rocks, e.g. Trendall *FV* pls. 11b, 12a; on foreshortened vase-mouths: pl. 10a (= 11a); on pillars: pls. 8a, 9; on rounded vessel: pl. 5. Reflections: pp. 443 with n. 217, 501 with Chapter 7 n. 145.

176. Birth of Dionysus (Taranto): Trendall *FV* pl. 31a, and in *JHS* 54 (1934) 175–9 pls. 8f.; Rumpf *MZ* pl. 38, 5.

177. Berlin Painter: pp. 236–9 with Chapter 4 notes 142ff.; bell-krater: p. 253 with Chapter 4 n. 168.

178. Dolon vase (B.M. F157): Trendall *RLCS* 102 no. 533 with refs. and pl. 52; FR pl. 110; Pfuhl *MuZ* fig. 800; M. Robertson 159; Rumpf *MZ* pl. 38, 2.

179. Homer *Iliad* X; Euripides (?) *Rhesus*.

180. Exekias' Memnon: p. 268 with Chapter 4 n. 193. Apollodorus and Odysseus's *pilos*: Schol. *Il.* X 265 (O. 1643).

181. Trendall *RLCS* 54f. no. 280, Karneia Painter, with refs. and pl. 24 (back), *FV* pls. 24ff.; Arias and Hirmer pls. 230–5.

182. Heidelberg 26.87: Trendall *FV* pl. 29 and pp. 27, 41 no. 35, Sarpedon Painter.

183. Pliny XXXV 29; see Rumpf in *JHS* 67 (1947) 14, *MZ* 137.

184. Birth of Dionysus: p. 427 with n. 176. Calyx-krater fragments (Amsterdam 2579): Trendall *FV* pl. 32 and pp. 28, 42 no. 97.

185. Volute-krater with Talos (Ruvo, Jatta 1501): *ARV*² 1338, Talos Painter no. 1; FR pls. 38f.; Pfuhl *MuZ* fig. 574; Sichtermann *GVU* pls. 1 and 24–34. A calyx-krater fragment from Spina (Ferrara 'Erratico presso T.312', has a replica of the Talos, the other figures different: *ARV*² 1340, middle; Aurigemma *Sc.di Spina* I pl. 138; see M. Robertson in *Gnomon* 39 (1967) 821.

186. Calyx-krater fragment from Taranto (Würzburg): Bulle *Skenographie* 3ff. and pls. 1–2; Rumpf *MZ* pl. 44, 1 and p. 136, denying stage connection.

187. Calyx-krater fragment with actor (Würzburg 832): Langlotz *GVW* pl. 240; Bulle in *Festschr. Loeb* 5–43, pl. 2 (top) and figs. 1, 1a and 6; Rumpf *MZ* 136 and pl. 44, 4. Bell-krater fragment with Konnakis (Taranto): *AA* 1950, 534; Rumpf in *JHS* 67 (1947) 14, fig. 2 and *MZ* pl. 45, 1 and p. 136.

188. Buildings shown on Nereid Monument (pp. 403f. with n. 116): second frieze, *BMCat.Sc.* II nos. 869–72 and 876ff.; Brunn *Denkm.* 216ff.; *Mon.* 10 pls. 15f.; see also next note. Buildings on friezes at Gjölbaschi-Trysa (p. 405 n. 119): Eichler *Reliefs* and see next note. Tombs at Tlos and Pinara (p. 405): Tlos, Benndorf *Reisen* 144 fig. 186d (a cast in B.M. *Cat.* no. 955); Pinara, Benndorf *Reisen* 54 figs. 36f.

189. Siege at Gjölbaschi-Trysa: Eichler *Reliefs* pls. 18–21 (another building pl. 25). Rank on Nereid monument: *BMCat.Sc.* II no. 868 and pl. 2. Chigi vase: p. 53 with Chapter 2 n. 44. Gigantomachy vases: p. 312 with Chapter 5 n. 46.

190. Sicyonian School: pp. 484–91 Chapter 7 (iv).

191. See pp. 586–8 with Chapter 8 notes 230–4.

(*v*) *Euphranor, Nikias and other painters; fourth-century vase-painting and Roman wall-painting*

192. Euxeinidas and Aristides: Pliny XXXV 75 (O. 1778); Aristides of Thebes, contemporary of Apelles: ibid. 98 (O. 1779); Aristides, son and pupil of Nikomachos: ibid. 110 (O. 1775); Aristides of Thebes, master of Euphranor: ibid. 111 (O. 1785); see Jex-Blake and Sellers, notes ad loc. Nikomachos and Philoxenos: pp. 501–2 with Chapter 7 n. 147. Euphranor as sculptor: p. 410 with notes 132f.; texts on his painting: O. 1785–1810, and see following notes.

193. Texts on Stoa Basileios: Wycherley 21–5, nos. 4–23; on Stoa of Zeus: 23–30, nos. 24–46; suggested identity of two: 30f., and H. Thompson in *Hesp.* 6 (1937) 64ff. and 225; Stoa of Zeus published ibid. 5–77, pls. 1f. and 9 (reconstruction, p. 54, fig. 34). Independent Stoa Basileios discovered: *Arch.Rep.1969/70* 3f. fig. 1.

194. Akroterion of Stoa of Zeus: p. 350 with Chapter 5 n. 139. Altar of Pity: p. 374 with n. 34.

195. Euphranor's pictures in Stoa: Pausanias I 3 3f. (O. 1791; Wycherley *Agora* 3 no. 30); all three also mentioned by Pliny at the beginning of his list of the painter's works (XXXV 129; O. 1790); cf. also O. 1793–5 and 1704 (Plutarch *de glor.Athen.* 2, reporting the anecdote about the Theseus). Parrhasios's Theseus and Demos: pp. 412 and 417 with notes 138 and 152. See also p. 490 with Chapter 7 n. 114.

196. New proportions: p. 378 with notes 48–50; pp. 464 and 466 with Chapter 7 notes 44ff. Olympias on panathenaic (Harvard 1925, 30–124): *ABV* 414, Nikomachos Series no. 2; Beazley *Dev.* 98f. and pl. 48; see also pp. 212 with Chapter 4 n. 99, 415–16 with n. 148 (Aglaophon).

197. Lysippos and the Doryphoros: pp. 462f. with Chapter 7 n. 42.

198. Gryllos: Pausanias IX 15 5; Ephoros ap. Diog. Laert. 54.

199. Hadrianic room at Mantinea with copy of Euphranor's picture: Pausanias VIII 9 8 (O. 1796). Copies of paintings: p. 413 with n. 141; p. 574 with Chapter 8 notes 189ff. Antinous: p. 609 with Epilogue, n. 51.

200. Kerch vases: *ARV*² 1456–83, especially 1474ff.; Schefold *UKV* and *KV*; Pelike with Peleus and Thetis (B.M. E424): *ARV*² 1475 no. 4; Schefold *KV* pls. 16f.; Arias and Hirmer pl. xlvii; Buschor *GV* 250; Cook *GPP* pl. 51; Rumpf *MZ* pl. 43, 3. Eleusinian scenes: the finest, a lost pelike: Metzger *RIA* pl. 14, 1 and p. 34 no. 2; others *ARV*² 1476, Eleusinian Painter nos. 1 and 2 (pelikai, Leningrad St. 1792, 1793): Metzger *Rép.* pls. 8, 3; 15, 1; 34, 2; 36, 1; FR pls. 69f. and II 47 and 52; Pfuhl *MuZ* fig. 597; Schefold *UKV* pls. 32, 1 and 2 and 35; E. Simon in *AK* 9 (1966) 72–91, pls. 17ff. Lebes gamikos (Leningrad inv. 15592): *ARV*² 1475 no. 1; Schefold *UKV* pls. 33f., *KV* pls. 19f.; Arias and Hirmer pls. 225–8; Kraiker *MG* pl. 59; Rumpf *MZ* pl. 43, 2; and see further p. 436. Marsyas (calyx-krater, Oxford 1939.599, from Al Mina): not in Beazley's lists; see Beazley in *JHS* 59 (1939) 35–44, pls. 2–6. Judgement of Paris (hydria, Munich 2439): not in Beazley's lists; FR pl. 140; Pfuhl *MuZ* fig. 598. Etruscan mirrors: see Beazley in *JHS* 69 (1949) 1–17, figs. 1–22 and pls. 1–11; cf. also his remarks on the Marsyas vase, l.c. 38; and see below, pp. 576–7 with Chapter 8 n. 198, 610 with Epilogue n. 56.

201. Relief on inscription of anti-tyranny law (Athens, Agora Museum): *Hesp.* 21 (1952) 355ff., pls. 89f.; Lang *Ath.Cit.* fig. 29. Korinthos and Leukas, on bronze mirror, the figures silvered, from Corinth (Louvre 609): de Ridder *Cat.* II no. 1699, pl. 81; Pfuhl *MuZ* fig. 264; Züchner *Gr.Kl.* 98, no. KS163 with refs. and 185 fig. 99. 'Frontality': p. 354 with Chapter 5 n. 154; pp. 576–7 with Chapter 8 n. 198, 610 with Epilogue n. 56.

202. Eretria panathenaics (above, n. 67): Themelis in *AAA* 2 (1969) 409–16, figs. 1–5; best pictures of reverses: Commercial Bank of Greece Calendar, 1972, February and June.

203. Antidotos: Pliny xxxv 130 (O. 1810). Texts on Nikias: O. 1810–26, and see next note.

204. Pliny xxxv 130 (O. 1823): Nikias painter of women; light and shade; 38 (O. 1822): burnt matter and shadows. Praxiteles and Nikias: p. 393 with n. 89 Praxiteles's tomb-monument: p. 365 with n. 7. Tombstone at Triteia painted by Nikias: Pausanias vii 22 6 (O. 1821); Megabyzos's tomb: Pliny xxxv 131 (O. 1816).

205. [Demetrius Phalereus] *de Eloc.* 76 (O. 1825). On the treatise, see Solmsen in *Hermes* 66 (1931) 241–67; Grube *A Greek Critic*; Wehrli *Demetrios von Phaleron*, 88f.

206. Pausias of Sikyon: pp. 485–90 with Chapter 7 notes 102–113. Texts on Androkydes of Cyzicus: O. 1649, 1731ff. (1731, Plutarch *Pelopidas* 25 7, the battle). Fish-plates and mosaics: p. 580 with Chapter 8 n. 212. Alexander Mosaic and Philoxenos of Eretria: pp. 497–503 with Chapter 7 notes 136–51.

207. Io, Andromeda, Calypso: Pliny xxxv 132. The Roman pictures associated with these: Rumpf *MZ* 143ff. with refs. and pl. 47, 1 (Perseus and Andromeda, Naples 8998) and 2 (Io and Argus, Macellum); these also Pfuhl *MuZ* figs. 646f.; the Palatine Io: Pfuhl *MuZ* fig. 708; Curtius *WP* 258, figs. 154f. and 89 fig. 62; Rumpf *MZ* pl. 59, 2f. Macellum Calypso (often called Penelope): Naples 9107; *ÖJh* 32 (1940) 54 fig. 34; *RM* 42 (1927) Beil. 6, 2. The sketchy version of the Andromeda (Naples, Helbig 1187): Maiuri *RP* 79; Curtius *WP* 256, fig. 153 (the big version, pl. 3 and 255 figs. 151f.; the Macellum Io, fig. 157).

208. Etruscan sarcophagus: *JHS* 1 (1880) pl. 36; Ducati *St.Art.Etr.* pls. 190, 192; Giglioli pls. 429f.; Pallottino *EP* 93ff.; Rumpf *MZ* pl. 47, 3.

209. Phillips in *AJA* 72 (1968) 1–23, pls. 1–20. See further p. 589 with Chapter 8 n. 237.

210. Blanckenhagen in *RM* 70 (1963) 100ff., on the *Odyssey* paintings (pp. 588f. with Chapter 8 notes 235, 237), and 75 (1968) 106–43, pls. 27–47, 'Daedalus and Icarus on Pompeian Walls', especially pp. 134–43.

211. Florals on vase-necks, and related: p. 486 with Chapter 7 n. 103. 'Gnathia': pp. 430f. with notes 186f. Hades and Persephone in palace with Caryatids: p. 406 with n. 121 (acanthus-column, n. 122). Achilles and Phoenix (Boston 03.804): White pl. 6c; *AJA* 12 (1908) pl. 19 and p. 407, fig. 1; Fairbanks and Chase *Greek Gods* fig. 74.

212. Assteas's Herakles (calyx-krater, Madrid 11094): Trendall *PP* 31f., 115 no. 33 with refs., pl. 7; on the painter see further, p. 491 with Chapter 7 notes 117f. 'Admetus and Alcestis' (Naples 9025 and two unnumbered): Elia 53f. nos. 82f. and 90; Helbig 1157–9; one, less like the vase-composition: Ducati *Pitt.* pl. 68; Herrmann pl. 84; Napoli *PAI* pl. 42. Hellenistic developments: pp. 582–6 with Chapter 8 notes 219ff. Sicilian calyx-krater (Syracuse): Libertini in *B.d'A* 53 (1950) 97–107, figs. 1–10; sketch of composition in Langlotz and Hirmer 29 fig. 10; Trendall *RLCS* 602, no. 102, pl. 236, 1–2; *EUA* vi pl. 380, 3; *EWA* vii pl. 76.

213. Theseus and Ariadne (stamnos, Boston 00.349): Trendall *FV* 24 and 40 no. B52, with refs., pl. 23a; FR iii 105 fig. 5; Pfuhl *MuZ* fig. 632. Paintings of the subject (Naples 9052, 115396 and others): Elia 79f. nos. 170, 172; Helbig 1217–20; Helbig 1218, Pfuhl *MuZ* fig. 632. Paintings in temple: p. 424 with n. 168; pp. 483 with Chapter 7 n. 94, 579 with Chapter 8 notes 209f.

214. Iphigeneia calyx-krater (Ferrara T.1145; *ARV*[2] 1440, Iphigeneia Painter no. 1; *AA* 1932, 458; Aurigemma[1] 221–3 (= Aurigemma[2] 251–3); Aurigemma *Sc. di Spina* ii pls. 24ff.; Aurigemma and Alfieri pl. 28; Arias and Alfieri pl. 41; Alfieri and Arias *SG* pl. 46; Metzger *Rep.* pl. 37, 3. Painting (Naples, from Pompeii, Casa del Citarista): Helbig 1333; Pfuhl *MuZ* fig. 663; Curtius *WP* 244f. figs. 142f. See also following notes.

215. Timomachos: pp. 589–90 with Chapter 8 n. 240; on the date of the Tauris picture, Pliny xxxv 136 (O. 2119).

216. Second Iphigeneia painting (Naples So.585, from Pompeii, House of Caecilius Jucundus): Curtius *WP* 246f., figs. 144f.

217. Athena showing Perseus the reflection (calyx-krater, Gotha): Trendall *FV* 25 and 41, no. B74 with refs., pl. 28a; (bell-krater, Boston 1970.237): Museum *Year 1969/70*, 38 (reflection in shield). Paintings of Perseus showing it to Andromeda (Naples 8996–8 and others):

Elia 66ff., nos. 115, 120, 122; Helbig 1192–1202; Curtius 253 fig. 150.

218. Herculaneum Theseus (Naples 9049); Elia 19f. no. 20; Helbig 1214; Curtius *WP* 10f. figs. 7f.; Maiuri *RP* 67 (detail); Pfuhl *MuZ* fig. 656; M. Robertson 178. Arcadia: p. 577 with Chapter 8 n. 201; see also 584 with Chapter 8 n. 221.

219. Ficoroni cista (Rome, Villa Giulia): see now Dohrn *Ficoronische Cista* for full illustration and discussion of the vessel and its decoration, and the relation of the main design to a painting, as well as refs. to earlier literature: other pictures: Giglioli pls. 286–9, 290, 2; Pfuhl *MuZ* fig. 628; Riis *EA* figs. 70 and 84; *WV* 1889 pl. 12, 1; on the original see also Beazley *EVP* 58ff. See also p. 595 with Epilogue n. 15.

220. Man on gang-plank in Polygnotos's Troy: p. 248. Talos vase: p. 530 with n. 185.

CHAPTER 7. THE SECOND CHANGE: CLASSICAL TO HELLENISTIC

(*i*) *The historical background*

1. Archelaos and Zeuxis: p. 411 with Chapter 6 n. 136.
2. Olynthus: p. 415 with Chapter 6 n. 147; and especially p. 486 with n. 104. Red-figure from Olynthus: *Olynthus*, especially v and xiii.
3. Snake-pillar: pp. 271f. with Chapter 4 n. 203.

(*ii*) *The Mausoleum and its sculptors*

4. Greek workmen in Persia: p. 201 with Chapter 4 n. 84. Sidon sarcophagi: p. 404 with Chapter 6 n. 117; pp. 481–2 with notes 87–92 (Alexander sarcophagus). Lycian tombs: p. 405 with Chapter 6 n. 118. Nereid Monument: p. 403 with Chapter 6 n. 116.
5. Effect of Mausoleum: Martial *Spect.* I 5. Deir-el-Bahari: e.g. Edwards *Pyramids* 172 fig. 45. Texts on Mausoleum: Pliny xxxvi 30f. (O. 1177); Vitruvius vii praef. 12 (O. 1178); also Lucian *Dial.Mort.* 24.1 (O. 1179) and others. Mausoleum, architecture: Dinsmoor 257–61, pls. 55, 63; D. S. Robertson 150f. fig. 63 and n. 1; Lawrence *A* 195f.; all with some reference to the vast literature: see also next note. Mausoleum sculpture: *BMCat. Sc.* ii 65–135, nos. 980–1099, with earlier refs.; most recently Ashmole *ASCG* 147–220, figs. 168–220; other pictures, e.g. BDFH pls. 254, 256 (238, 240); *KB* 302–5; Lawrence *S* pls. 87ff.; Lullies and Hirmer pls. 201–7 (211–17); Richter *Sc.* figs. 209, 228, 314, 352, 697–702; and see following notes. Position of friezes: most recently, Ashmole *ASCG* 159, 162f., 165f.
6. 'Pytheos', his temple at Priene and his book: Vitruvius I 8 5 (where MSS give Pythios, Pithios or Pithius) and vii praef. 4 (where they give Phyleos or Phileos; but the two passages must certainly refer to the same man). A papyrus-fragment ascribed to the second century B.C., has lists of men celebrated in different fields, and that of architects includes an entry read and restored as Π̣ύ̣θ̣ε̣[ος τὸ ἐν Ἁλι]καρνάσσῳ̣ [Μαυσσωλεῖον] (Diels in *Abh. Akad.Berl.* 1904 ii 7f.; Riemann in *RE* xxiv 371, s.v. Pytheos). The temple at Priene: Dinsmoor 221–3, pl. 55; D. S. Robertson 44f. figs. 18f., 147f. fig. 64, 162 n., 332, 371; Lawrence *A* 192–5, figs. 105ff. Apelles's father: the Suda, s.v. Apelles: Ἀπελλῆς... υἱὸς Πυθέου; the name in this context is normally cited as Pytheas, but the genitive could equally be of Pytheos.
7. Two stages in the Mausoleum sculptures: Buschor *MuA*. 'Mausolus and Artemisia' works of the second century: Carpenter *Gr.Sc.* 214ff.; followed by Havelock *HA* 35f., pl. 18; see further pp. 457–9 with notes 29ff.; and cf. p. 462 with n. 39.
8. 'Heroic diagonal': p. 316 with Chapter 5 n. 54.
9. Slabs 1013–15; *BMCat.Sc.* pl. 18 (1014–15); Arias *Sk.* pls. 3–5, figs. 9–15; Ashmole *ASCG* 178f., figs. 206–8 (1013–15); BDFH pl. 254 (238, 1013–14); Bieber *H* fig. 61 (1014); Buschor *MuA* figs. 7, 11, 14, 16; *KB* 304–5, bottom row; Lippold, pl. 90, 1–2; Lullies and

Hirmer pls. 202–3 (214–15) top; Picard *Manuel* IV 28–33, figs. 13–16. 1016: Buschor *MuA* fig. 7.

10. Strong and Jeppesen in *Act.Arch.* 35 (1964) 195–9, figs. 2–4 (other new fragments 197–203, figs. 5–9); the main fragment also illustrated *ILN* 22 Aug. 1964, 261; *Arch.Rep.1964/5* 56, fig. 24.

11. Against this view, Ashmole in *JHS* 71 (1951) 16ff. with pl. 13, attributing 1013–15 (but probably not 1016) to Leochares (pp. 460–2 with notes 35–9); see also Ashmole *ASCG* 162, 177, 182.

12. Joining of 1008 and 1010: Ashmole in *JHS* 89 (1969) 22f., pl. 1; joined slabs illustrated: Ashmole *ASCG* 175 fig. 202; 1007: ibid. figs. 201, 203; 1007–8: Buschor *MuA* figs. 29, 31f.; *KB* 304, top; Picard *Manuel* IV 55ff. figs. 22f.; 1010–12: Buschor *MuA* figs. 24–6, 33.

13. 1009: Buschor *MuA* figs. 44f., 50; *KB* 305, second row, left. 1022: Ashmole *ASCG* 168f., figs. 191ff.; Buschor *MuA* figs. 35, 38, 40f., 43; *KB* 304, middle; Picard *Manuel* IV 37, fig. 17. 1018 and 1020–1: Ashmole *ASCG* 170f. figs. 194ff. (1020–1); Buschor *MuA* figs. 60 (1021, part), 62 (1018, part), 65 (1020, part); *KB* 304, second row (1020–1); Lullies and Hirmer pl. 204 (217; 1020–1).

14. 1006: Ashmole *ASCG* 177 fig. 205; Buschor *MuA* fig. 8; *KB* 305, middle; Lullies and Hirmer pl. 203 (215) below; Picard *Manuel* IV 45 fig. 18. 1019: Ashmole *ASCG* 174, fig. 200; Buschor *MuA* figs. 56f.; *KB* 305, second row right; Lullies and Hirmer pl. 201 (216) above. 1017: Buschor *MuA* fig. 6; Picard *Manuel* IV 53, fig. 21. 1023–31: Buschor *MuA* figs. 2f. (1030), 20f. (1026, 1027).

15. Ashmole *ASCG* 190 fig. 220. A full publication of the friezes and fragments is being prepared by Ashmole, Strong and B. F. Cook.

16. Centauromachy frieze (1032–5): Ashmole *ASCG* 164 fig. 188 (1032); Picard *Manuel* IV 63, fig. 26. Charioteer frieze (1037): *BMCat.Sc.* pl. 18 (reconstructed slab); Ashmole *ASCG* 160–3, figs. 182 (reconstructed slab), 185–7; Bieber *H* fig. 64; Buschor *MuA* figs. 28, 30; Picard *Manuel* IV 63–7 figs. 27ff. and pl. 1; see Ashmole in *JHS* 71 (1951) 18, pl. 14b (cf. n. 11 above), where this too is ascribed to Leochares; and see his remarks in *ASCG* 162.

17. Maenad: see p. 455 with n. 23. Temple of Athena Alea at Tegea: Pausanias VIII 45 5f. (O. 1150). The architecture: Dinsmoor 217–20, fig. 79, pl. 58; D. S. Robertson 142ff. with figs. 61f., 329, 377; Lawrence *A* 191f., fig. 104, pl. 95; Roux *Argolide* 365ff.; Dugas and others *SAAT*. Tholos at Delphi: p. 397 with Chapter 6 n. 102; at Epidaurus: Dinsmoor 235f., fig. 85, pl. 58; D. S. Robertson 144, 329, pl. 5c; Lawrence *A* 185f., fig. 102, pls. 88f.; Roux *Argolide* 131–200; Burford *Epidaurus* 63–8, 222f., pls. 88f. See also p. 486 with n. 102.

18. Tegea sculptures: Pausanias VIII 45 6f. (pediments), 47 1 (statues within the temple); Dugas *SAAT* 77–116, pls. 96–111 (only the scraps p. 100 nos. 90–6, partly illustrated pl. 111, are thought to belong to the metopes). Inscribed architrave-blocks: Dugas *SAAT* 35f., 103f., pls. 58E, 88A. Pictures of heads from pediments, e.g.: Arias *Sk.* pl. 8f., figs. 28–31 (fig. 27 torso of 'Atalanta'; see p. 454, with n. 20); Bieber *H* fig. 55 ('Atalanta' torso, fig. 58); *KB* 300, 2–4 (6, 'Atalanta' torso); Lawrence *S* pl. 25; Lippold pl. 90, 3–4; Picard *Manuel* IV 167 fig. 77 (fragment of head ascribed to Atalanta), 169 fig. 78 (boar), 181–3 figs. 81f., 189, fig. 86, and pls. 4f.; Richter *Sc.* figs. 690–4 ('Atalanta' torso, fig. 696); see also p. 454 with n. 22.

19. Aigina temple: pp. 165–7 with Chapter 4 n. 20. Stamnos by the Berlin Painter (pp. 236–9 with Chapter 4 notes 142–6): Munich 2406; *ARV*² 207, no. 137, with refs.; Lullies and Hirmer *GVRZ* pls. 62f.

20. The identification of this torso (above, n. 18; below, n. 22) and its pair as akroteria is due to A. F. Stewart, the publication of whose important work on the sculptures of this temple is eagerly awaited.

21. François vase: pp. 124–8 with Chapter 3 n. 111. Apulian vases: Berlin (one, 3258; Gerhard *Ap.V.* pls. 8ff.); the figure occurs also on an Etruscan terracotta ash-urn of the second century B.C. and on two Roman sarcophagi, as noted by Kleiner, who uses it in his very interesting reconstruction of an early classical wall-painting with this subject (*AK* 15 (1972) 7–19,

figs. 1–6 and pls. 2–4). Literary references: Euripides fr. 530; Apollonius Rhodius I 161–71.

22. 'Hygieia' head: *KB* 300, 5, Lippold pl. 92, 3; Lullies and Hirmer pl. 199 (205); Picard *Manuel* IV 193–204, figs. 89f. and pl. 6, assigns this head and the 'Atalanta' torso (figs. 87f.) to Nymphs or Muses from the altar (Pausanias VIII 47 2).

23. Skopas's maenad: Kallistratos *Stat.* 2 (O. 1164), and several epigrams (O. 1162f.). Dresden statuette: Arias *Sk.* figs. 34ff.; BDFH pl. 255 (239); Beazley and Ashmole fig. 128; Bieber *H* figs. 59f.; Lawrence *LGS* pl. 9b; Richter *Sc.* fig. 709.

24. Ostia tritoness: BDFH 442, fig. 171 (178, fig. 197). Skopas's sea-group: Pliny XXXVI 26 (O. 1175).

25. Asklepios and Hygieia at Tegea: Pausanias VIII 7 1 (O. 1151; see p. 454 with n. 22); at Gortys: ibid. 28 1 (O. 1152); Hecate: ibid. II 27 2 (O. 1153); Aphrodite at Elis: ibid. VI 25 1 (O. 755); Athena: ibid. IX 10 2 (O. 766); Artemis ibid. 17 1 (O. 1166); Apollo at Rhamnus: Pliny XXXVI 25 (O. 1159); at Chryse: Strabo XIII 64 and Eustathius *ad.iliad.* p. 30, 16 (O. 1168f.; cf. 1170, Menand.Rhet.); it is Eustathius who appears to ascribe the mouse only to Skopas (see Grace in *JHS* 2 (1932) 228ff.; Richter *Sc.*[2] 274), but he seems to be quoting Strabo incompletely, and Strabo's sentence could mean that both god and emblem were Skopas's work. Furies: O. 1155–8 (Clement Alex. *Protrept.* 473; Schol. *Aischin. c.Tim.* 747; Schol. Sophocles *OC* 39; Pausanias I 28 6, where the sculptor is not named).

26. Naked Aphrodite and seated Ares in Rome: Pliny XXXVI 26 (O. 1173f.). Ares Ludovisi: p. 474 with n. 73. Pliny's muddled note: p. 339 with Chapter 5 n. 111. Skopadic Herakles: Arias *Sk.* pl. 1, figs. 1–4; *KB* 301, 1; Lippold pl. 91, 1; Richter *Sc.* fig. 707; Pausanias II 10 1 (O. 1154), saw a Herakles in Marble by Skopas at Sicyon. Meleager: Arias *Sk.* pls. 10–12, figs. 39f.; Bieber *H* figs. 54, 46f.; *KB* 301, 3; Richter *Sc.* fig. 708.

27. Ephesus drum: pp. 407–9 with Chapter 6 notes 125f. Skopas and Praxiteles at Megara: Pausanias I 43 6 (O. 1165). Aphrodite and Pothos (?) on Samothrace: Pliny XXXVI 25 (O. 1167). Skopadic 'Pothos': Arias *Sk.* pls. 13f., figs. 44–7; Bieber *H* fig. 62; Lippold pl. 91, 3; alternative 'Pothos': Galli in *Rass.d'Arte* 9 (1922). Cross-legged statues doubtfully associated with Euphranor: pp. 391 and 410 with Chapter 6 notes 84 and 133.

28. Apolline head from Mausoleum (1028): *BMCat.Sc.* pl. 20, 2; Buschor *MuA* fig. 58; *KB* 303, 3; Picard *Manuel* IV 96, fig. 46. Trousered horseman (1045): *BMCat.Sc.* pl. 19; Buschor *MuA* figs. 51, 55; *KB* 303, 1; Picard *Manuel* IV 98 fig. 47. Old man (1055): Buschor *MuA* fig. 1; Picard *Manuel* 104, fig. 51; *JHS* 68 (1948) 35 fig. 10 (Jongkees). Cross-legged torso (1048): Buschor *MuA* fig. 61.

29. 'Mausolus' and 'Artemisia' with remains of chariot-horses and wheel: *BMCat.Sc.* pl. 16. Horse (1002): Buschor *MuA* fig. 34; *KB* 302, 6; Picard *Manuel* IV 73 fig. 31, pl. 16. On the figures see also above n. 7 and following notes.

30. 'Mausolus' (1000): Ashmole *ASCG* 157f., figs. 179ff.; BDFH pl. 256 (240); Bieber *H* figs. 245f., 249; Buschor *MuA* figs. 17, 22f.; *KB* 302, 2–3; Lawrence *S* pl. 86; Lippold pl. 93, 2; Lullies and Hirmer pls. 205ff. (211ff.); Picard *Manuel* IV 85ff. figs. 37ff., pl. 2; see also last note and p. 507 with Chapter 8 n. 8.

31. 'Artemisia' (1001): Bieber *H* fig. 249; Buschor *MuA* fig. 17; *KB* 303, 2; Lawrence *S* pl. 86; Picard *Manuel* IV 93 figs. 41f.; Richter *Sc.* fig. 313; see also n. 29. *Adorans*: Jongkees in *JHS* 68 (1948) 29–39, nos. 1–13, figs. 1 (Berlin, marble), 2 (Paris, porphyry and marble), 3 (Rome, basalt), 4 (Cherchel, marble). Relief from Tegea (B.M. 1914.7–14.1): *JHS* 36 (1916) 65–70, fig. 1; 68 (1948) 31ff., fig. 6 (Jongkees); *Mon.Piot* 18, 145–75, fig. 1; Picard *Manuel* IV 76, fig. 72. Standing Sarapis: bronze statuette (Florence): *JHS* 68 (1948) 35 fig. 9 (an example of the seated type, ibid. fig. 8); a head: Bieber *H* figs. 296f. On the origins of the Alexandrian Sarapis (more correct than Serapis) see Fraser in *Op.Ath.* VII (1967) 23–45 (the attribution of the statue to Bryaxis discussed pp. 28 and 36 n. 55). Roman priestess, from Atrapalda near Avellino (Campania): B.M. *Cat.* 1988.

32. Delphi base: *BCH* 33 (1899) 383f. (Homolle); *JdI* 69 (1954) 1–31 (Drerup): Bieber in *Anthemon* (*Scritti in onore di C. Anti*, Florence 1955); *Mnemosyne* iv.xi (1958) 136f. (Jongkees). Chairestratos's Themis (Athens, N.M. 231):

Karouzou *Cat.* pl. 56; Beazley and Ashmole fig. 146; Lippold pl. 108, 1.

33. Texts on Bryaxis: O. 1316–27 (1316 Pliny xxxiv 42, bronze colossi on Rhodes; 1317, Pliny xxxvi 22, Zeus and Apollo at Patara; 1318, Pliny xxxvi 22, marble Dionysus at Knidos; 1319, Pausanias i 40 6, Asklepios and Hygieia at Megara; 1320, Pliny xxxiv 73, Asklepios; 1321–4, various late authors on Apollo at Daphne; 1325, Clement of Alexandria *Protrept.*, Sarapis; 1327, bronze Seleucus). Tripod-base (Athens N.M. 1733): *KB* 300, 10; Lippold pl. 94, 1; Richter *Sc.* figs. 723f.

34. Timotheos: pp. 397–402 with Chapter 6 notes 103–14. Praxiteles: pp. 386–96 with Chapter 6 notes 73–99.

35. Texts on Leochares: O. 1301–15 (1301, Pliny xxxiv 50, *floruit*; 1308, Pliny xxxiv 79, and 1309, Tatian *c.Graecos* 56, Ganymede; 1312, Pausanias v 20 9, Philip's family at Olympia; 1313, Plutarch *Vit. X orat.*, *Isocr.* portrait of Isocrates). Tholos at Olympia (Philippeion): Pausanias v 20 9; Dinsmoor 236ff. fig. 86 (old reconstruction); D. S. Robertson 333, 45, fig. 62 (Corinthian capital); Lawrence *A* 186f.; full publication, discussion and new restoration, Schleif and Zschietzschmann in *Ol.Forsch.* i (1944) 1–52, figs. 1–4, pls. 1–21 and Atlas pls. 1 (improved reconstruction)–10; new reconstruction also illustrated by Kunze in *NDA* 296, fig. 55. Tholoi at Delphi and Epidaurus: pp. 397 with Chapter 6 n. 102, 453 with n. 17.

36. Vatican Ganymede: *KB* 299, 1; Lippold, pl. 98, 1; Richter *Sc.* fig. 737; Phillips in *Art.Bull.* 42 (1960) fig. 23 to p. 260, with a discussion of the subject (cf. p. 578 with Chapter 8 n. 206). Gold ear-rings (New York 37.11.9–10): Hoffmann and Davidson *Greek Gold* 83, fig. 12g; Richter *MMH* 156f. pl. 129c. Apollo Belvedere (Vatican): BDFH pl. 253 (237); *KB* 299, 2 (3 and 4, head in Basle); Lippold pl. 98, 3; Richter *Sc.* fig. 736; and often. Artemis of Versailles (Louvre): *Enc.Phot.* 198f.; *KB* 312, 3; Lippold pl. 98, 2.

37. Text on Niobids: Pliny xxxvi 28 (O. 1180). Florence group (Uffizi 289ff.): Mansuelli *Gall. Uff.* i, 101f., with refs., pls. 70–81; Arias *Sk.* pls. 52f.; Bieber *H* figs. 253–65 (255 and 265, Vatican; 261, Herakleion; 262f., reconstructions); *KB* 307 and 306, 5; see also Cook *Niobe* 47. Leda: p. 402 with Chapter 6 n. 114. 'Ariadne' from Acropolis (Athens N.M. 142): Beazley and Ashmole fig. 143; Br.Br. 174a; Karouzou *Cat.* pl. 53; Lawrence *LGS* pl. 10c; Richter *Sc.* fig. 508 (509, Roman copy in Berlin).

38. Hypnos and Thanatos on Attic vases: p. 326 with Chapter 5 n. 81; Thanatos on Ephesus drum: p. 408 with Chapter 6 notes 126f. Statue of Hypnos (marble copy in Madrid): Beazley and Ashmole fig. 123; Lawrence *S* pl. 79a; (bronze head, B.M. 267): Murray *Gr.Br.* pl. 2; *Sel.Br.* pl. 15; (statuettes): a list in Winnefeld *Hypnos* 8, illustrating one in Vienna; further refs. in Furtwängler *Mast.* 395 n. 8. Aristonautes's stele: p. 381 with Chapter 6 n. 56.

39. Alexander-head (Acropolis 1331) and Demeter of Knidos (B.M. 1300): Ashmole in *JHS* 71 (1951) 13–28, figs. 1f. and pls. 1–7a–c and e, 9a–c, 11c, 12b and d, 15a, 16a (Demeter), 11a–b, 12a and c, 16c (Alexander) with refs. in notes 3 (Demeter) and 19 (Alexander); the hypothetical kore-statue: ibid. 25–8 with pl. 10 (marble head, coin, terracottas). Alexander also: Casson *Cat.* 232 no. 1331 with earlier refs.; Lawrence *LGS* pl. 10b; Richter *POG* iii fig. 1727 (1726, copy in Berlin, Blümel *Kat.* 5 K203); copy in Erbach: Stark *ZA* 12. Demeter also: Beazley and Ashmole fig. 124; BDFH pl. 252 (236); Bieber *H* figs. 70f.; Lawrence *S* pl. 91; Lullies and Hirmer pls. 216f.; Richter *Sc.* fig. 315.

(iii) Lysippos and his pupils

40. Both Richter (*Sc.* 287) and Bieber (*H* 31) make this curious deduction. At an exhibition at Burlington House, *Italian Art in Britain* (1960), no. 138 in the catalogue was a portrait (belonging to Mrs Colin Davy) of a young boy, inscribed on the frame 'Cardinal York'. The sitter was Prince Henry Benedict Maria Clement Stewart ('Henry IX'), 1725–1807. The picture, by Louis-Gabriel Blanchet, 1705–72, is signed and dated 1738. Prince Henry was created

Cardinal in 1747. See also p. 502 with n. 147.

41. Texts on Lysippos: O. 1443–1512 (1443, Pliny XXXIV 51, *floruit*; 1449, Athenaeus XI 784, anecdote connecting Lysippos with foundation of Cassandreia in 316 B.C.; note to 1449, inscription from portrait of Seleucus, Löwy *Inschr.* no. 487, Richter *Sc.* 287, but see last note; 1478, Pliny XXXIV 63, portraits of Alexander from boyhood; on Lysippic Alexander-portraits, see p. 514 with Chapter 8 n. 26; 1497, Pausanias VI 5 1, Poulydamas victorious in 409 B.C.; see further p. 469 with n. 58; 1498, Pausanias V 5 4, Troilos victorious in 372; the surviving dedicatory inscription, Löwy *Inschr.* no. 94, Furtwängler in *AZ* 37 (1879) 145). Inscription from Thebes for statue of Koraidas, victorious in the boys' *pancration*: Löwy *Inschr.* no. 93; *IG* VII 2533; Johnson *Lysippos* 62ff.; Richter *Sc.* 287; the victory is argued to date from 342. Further texts in following notes.

42. Pliny XXXIV 61 (O. 1444), quoting Duris of Samos as saying that Lysippos had no master but while working as a coppersmith was inspired by Eupompos's remark; Cicero *Brutus* 86 296 (O. 954), Lysippos and the Doryphoros. Texts on Lysistratos: O. 1513–15; and see p. 513 with Chapter 8 n. 23. Eupompos: p. 484 with n. 96.

43. Pliny XXXIV 65 (O. 1508).

44. Number of statues: Pliny XXXIV 37 (O. 1445). Zeus at Tarentum: O. 1451–3 (Lucilius ap. Norius s.v. *cubitus*; Strabo VI 278; Pliny XXXIV 40); Chares's Colossus of Rhodes, pp. 476–7 with notes 79ff. Statues of Herakles by Lysippos: O. 1468–77; and see pp. 467 and 473f. with notes 50 and 71. Portraits of Alexander and his circle: O. 1478–92; and see above, n. 41, p. 514 with Chapter 8 n. 26. Athletic victor-statues: O. 1497–1501; see also above, n. 41 pp. 468–9 with notes 56ff. Apoxyomenos: Pliny XXXIV 62 (O. 1502); see also next note; Perixyomenos of Daippos: p. 478 with n. 82. Lysippos's pupils: pp. 470ff. and 476ff. with notes 61–8, 79–83. A Poseidon at Corinth by Lysippos: p. 516 with Chapter 8 n. 32.

45. Vatican statue: BDFH pl. 258 (242); Beazley and Ashmole, fig. 130; Bieber *H* figs. 74f.; Johnson *Lysippos* pl. 12; *KB* 331, 1 and 2; Lawrence *S* pls. 96, 97a; Lippold 279f.; Richter *Sc.* figs. 739, 742f. Statuette (Fiesole): *AP* 2 (1963) 78f. pls. 60–2. Copy in reverse (Rome, M.N.): *Bonn.Jb.* 167 (1967) 119–28; V. Rodio in *Annali della Facoltà di Lettere e Filosofia dell'Università di Bari* 13 (1968) 217–46, argues that this represents the original direction. Another case of a 'looking-glass' version: p. 351 with Chapter 5 n. 141; and cf. p. 607 with Epilogue n. 47.

46. Polykleitos's Doryphoros: pp. 328–30 with Chapter 5 n. 88. Myron's Diskobolos: p. 340 with Chapter 5 n. 114.

47. Acropolis relief: Walter *Beschr.* 195ff., figs. A–C; Bieber *H* fig. 77; Süsserott pl. 23, 1. Figure from Parthenon frieze (pp. 305–11 with Chapter 5 notes 34–45); west, slab xvi.30; Smith *Parth.* pl. 71; Corbett *Sc.Parth.* pl. 25. Delphi stele: p. 363 with Chapter 6 n. 3; on the relation: Langlotz *Phidiaspr.* 29. Praxitelean base from Mantinea: p. 395 with Chapter 6 n. 94.

48. Cf. p. 419 with Chapter 6 n. 157.

49. Texts on Eros: Pausanias IX 27 3 (O. 1461). Possible copies: Bieber *H* fig. 87 (B.M. 1673) and 88f. (heads in Baltimore and B.M. 1680); *Enc.Phot.* 197 (Louvre); Johnson *Lysippos* pl. 17 (B.M. 1679), 18 (head in Copenhagen), 19 (torso in Smith College); *KB* 332, 2 (Rome, Capitoline).

50. Farnese Herakles (Naples): Bieber *H* fig. 84; *KB* 333, 4; Johnson *Lysippos* pl. 37 (cf. 38); Lippold pl. 101, 1; Richter *Sc.* fig. 749; a finer fragment (Basle): BDFH pl. 258 (242) left; inscribed copy (Florence): Amelung *Führer . . . Florenz* no. 186; Br.Br. 284; Löwy *Inschr.* no. 506; inscription false: Richter in *AJA* 76 (1972) 102; capital from Baths of Caracalla with the figure: Rodenwaldt *KdA* 634; other sculpture from the Baths: p. 608 with Epilogue n. 48. 'Narcissus': p. 334 with Chapter 5 n. 101.

51. Old satyr and child (copies in Louvre, Munich and Vatican): Bieber *H* fig. 85 (Vatican); Br.Br. 64; *Enc.Phot.* 232f. (Louvre); Johnson *Lysippos* pls. 33 (Louvre), 34 (head in Rome, M.N.); Lawrence *LGS* pl. 19 (Munich); Lippold pl. 101, 2 (Louvre).

52. Text on satyr at Athens: Pliny XXXIV 64 (O. 1462). Statue of young satyr piping (Louvre): Bieber *H* fig. 86; *Enc.Phot.* 205.

53. Text on drunken flute-girl: Pliny xxxv 63 (O. 1460). Probable copies, all fragmentary and lacking the head (Berlin; Frankfurt; Paris, Cab.Méd., a statuette; Rome, M.N.): Bieber *H* figs. 90f. (Rome) and 92 (Paris); Johnson *Lysippos* pl. 61 (Frankfurt); *KB* 343, 2 (Berlin); Lippold pl. 101, 4 (Rome).
54. Texts on Kairos: O. 1463–6 (*Anth.Gr.* II 49 13; Kallistratos *Stat.* 6; Himerius *Ecl.* XIV 1; Tzetzes *Chil.* VIII 428. Relief (Turin 317): BDFH pl. 261 (245) above.
55. Pp. 198f. with Chapter 4 n. 76.
56. Dedication of Daochos: the monument: Pouilloux *FdeD* II 67–80 with illustration and earlier refs.; the statues: Picard and de La Coste Messelière pls. 63–7; Will in *Delt.* 62 (1938) 289–304 pls. 30–2; see also next note and n. 60 below.
57. The inscriptions (Delphi): *IG* IX 2 no. 49; *Sylloge*[3] 244; (Pharsalos): *IG* IX 2 no. 249; Johnson *Lysippos* 123. Statue of Agias at Delphi: above, n. 56; also *KB* 333, 1; de La Coste Messelière *Delphes* pls. 184–7; Lawrence *S* pl. 94a; Lippold pl. 102, 3; Richter *Sc.* figs. 738, 740f.
58. Statue of Poulydamas: p. 463 with n. 41; the base: *Ol.* III 209ff. pl. 55, 1–3; Lippold pl. 94, 2; Richter *Sc.* fig. 752. Statues of Promachos: Pausanias VII 27 2.
59. Bronze from Antikythera: p. 409 with Chapter 6 n. 130.
60. Other figures from dedication: above, n. 56; also de La Coste Messelière *Delphes* pls. 183 (Sisyphos II, leaning), 188–91 (Agelaos); and see Johnson *Lysippos* 115–33.
61. Texts on Eutychides: O. 1516 (Pliny XXXIV 51, date), 1530–4 (1530, Pausanias VI 2 6, and 1531, Malalas *Chron.* XI 276, Tyche); see also below, notes 63, 66. Copies of Tyche: see following notes. Xenophon and Kallistonikos's Tyche and Ploutos: p. 383 with Chapter 6 n. 65. Alexander of Pherae and his dagger Tychon: Plutarch *Pelopidas* 29 4; see M. Robertson in *JWCI* 15 (1952) 99 n. 4; Tychon, Attic fertility god: Strabo XIII 487 8; Diodorus IV 6 4; see Metzger *RIA* 79 with n. 8; M. Robertson in *JHS* 88 (1969) 235.
62. Representations of the Tyche of Antioch: coins: Richter *Sc.* fig. 755 (Tigranes); Head *Hist.Num.* 779 fig. 343 (Augustan Antioch). Statue and statuettes: Beazley and Ashmole figs. 153 (Florence, bronze statuette), 154 (Paris, de Clercq, bronze statuette), 155 (Budapest, marble statuette); Bieber *H* fig. 102 (Vatican marble); *KB* 340, 1 (Vatican); Lawrence *S* pl. 103a (Vatican); Lippold pl. 106, 2 (Paris, de Clercq); Richter *Sc.* figs. 753 (Vatican), 754 (New York, bronze statuette). See also p. 610 with Epilogue n. 56.
63. Malalas *Chron.* VIII 200f.
64. Parthenos: pp. 311–17 with Chapter 5 notes 45–58.
65. Apollo on Delos: p. 47 with Chapter 2 n. 34; of Amyclae: p. 39 with Chapter 2 n. 18. Athena Promachos: pp. 285 with Chapter 4 n. 229, 320 with Chapter 5 n. 67, 411 with Chapter 6 n. 137; Lysippos's Zeus at Tarentum: p. 464 with n. 44.
66. Eurotas: Pliny XXXIV 78 (O. 1532).
67. Seated girl (Rome, Conservatori): Beazley and Ashmole fig. 156; Bieber *H* fig. 103; Lawrence *LGS* pl. 23a.
68. 'Penelope': p. 210 with Chapter 4 n. 96.
69. Early classical seated Hermes: p. 191 with Chapter 4 n. 59.
70. Seated figure sometimes identified as Alkamenes's 'Aphrodite in the Gardens': p. 366 with Chapter 6 n. 12. Seated philosopher-portraits: pp. 509 and 524ff. with Chapter 8 notes 13–16, 56–60.
71. Colossal seated Herakles at Tarentum (later in Rome, then Constantinople): Pliny XXXIV 40 (O. 1453, transfer to Rome; also 1468f., Strabo VI 278 and Plutarch *Fabius Maximus* 22); O. 1470–2 (the Suda s.v. βασιλική; Nicetas Choniates *de Alexio* III 687 and *de signis Constantinopol.* 5 (899); the statue in Constantinople and its destruction). Texts on Herakles Epitrapezios: Martial IX 44 (O. 1475), Statius *Silvae* IV 6 (O. 1476): small copies of figure: Bieber *H* figs. 80 (B.M. 1726) and 81 (Naples); Johnson *Lysippos* pl. 16 (cast in Dresden from lost original); Richter *Sc.* figs. 751 (B.M. 1725); fig. 750 is an imperial coin of Amastris in Paphlagonia which shows the type; fragments of colossal copy from Alba Fucens: de Visscher *Herakles Epitrapezios*.
72. Seated Hermes from Herculaneum (Naples): Beazley and Ashmole fig. 161; Bieber *H* figs. 106–8 (related statuettes, figs. 109–11); Johnson

Lysippos pl. 35; *KB* 333, 1; Lawrence *S* pl. 120; Richter *Sc.* fig. 72.

73. Ares Ludovisi (p. 456 with n. 26; Rome, M.N.): Paribeni *Cat.* no. 72; Bieber *H* fig. 103; Johnson *Lysippos* pl. 28 (head); Picard *Manuel* III. Replicas of the torso: Bieber *H* figs. 104 (Pergamon), 105 (Naples); Johnson *Lysippos* pl. 29 (Naples). Stele from Ilissos: p. 382 with Chapter 6 n. 61.

74. Tyrannicides: pp. 184–6 with Chapter 4 n. 49. Athena and Marsyas: pp. 341ff. with Chapter 5 n. 116. Strongylion's horse: p. 383 with Chapter 6 n. 65.

75. Monuments at Delphi: Pausanias X 10 (3–4, O. 1571, Argive; 1–3, O. 638, Pheidias's Marathon memorial; 7–10, O. 979, Lysander's dedication for Aeguspotami). Athenodoros and Dameas (Demeas) of Kleitor: Pliny XXXIV 50 (O. 979); Theokosmos of Megara: p. 321 with Chapter 5 n. 69.

76. Granicus monument: O. 1485–9 (1485, Pliny XXXIV 64, brought from Macedonia to Rome; 1486, Arrian *Anab.* I 16 7, dedicated at Dion; 1487, Plutarch *Alex.* 16 and 1488, Velleius Paterculus I 11 3, in Rome, brought from Macedonia). Lion-hunt: Pliny XXXIV 64 (O. 1490; only Lysippos named); Plutarch *Alexander* (O. 1491; Lysippos and Leochares); see further p. 460 with n. 35, p. 482 with n. 90. Niobids: p. 461 with n. 37.

77. Text on Lysippos's Herakles and hind: *Anth.Pal.* XVI; *App.Planud.* 96 (see Bieber *H* 36). A series of the labours at Alyzia in Acarnania: Strabo X 459 (O. 1477). Bronze group (Palermo): Bieber *H* fig. 78; *KB* 357, 4.

78. Artemis and Iphigeneia (Copenhagen I.N. 481–2): Bieber *H* figs. 268f.; Lawrence *S* pl. 98a; Studniczka in *Abh.Sachs.Akad.* 37 (1926); and see Rodenwaldt in *RM* 24 (1919) 65.

79. Texts on Chares: O. 1539–56 (1539–54, Pliny XXXIV 41, Strabo XIV 652, and others, on the Colossus of Rhodes; see also next note). Coins of Rhodes with rayed head (beginning early third century): Kraay and Hirmer pl. 189 nos. 647f. (earlier heads, unrayed, pls. 188f. nos. 344ff.); Seltman *GC* pl. 61, 14f. (earlier, pls. 30, 13ff. and 61, 13; and see his remarks p. 253). Relief (Rhodes): *Cl.Rh.* V 2 (1932) 24ff. pl. 2 and fig. 15, *JHS* 76 (1956) 71, fig. 1 (rayed coin-head, fig. 4). 'Hellenistic Ruler': p. 520 with Chapter 8 n. 39. Cnidia: pp. 390–4 with Chapter 6 n. 85.

80. 'Philo Byzantius' *de Septem Miraculis*, Mirac. iv, Orelli p. 14 (O. 1547; see Maryon in *JHS* 76 (1956) 68–86, corrected by Haynes in *JHS* 77 (1957), 311f.); Pliny XXXIV 41 (O. 1539); Constantine Porphyrogenitus *de Admin.Imp.* 20f. (O. 1554, with note, the ultimate disposal of the bronze).

81. 'Dancing Faun' from Pompeii (Naples): Beazley and Ashmole fig. 201; Bieber *H* figs. 95f.; *KB* 368.1. Marble dancing satyr (Rome, Borghese): Bieber *H* fig. 94; *KB* 343, 1; Lippold pl. 104, 3.

82. Bronze adorans (Berlin): Beazley and Ashmole fig. 162; Bieber *H* fig. 93; Br.Br. 283; *KB* 340, 3; Lawrence *S* pl. 102a; Lippold pl. 105, 2; Richter *Sc.* fig. 54. Texts on Boedas: Pliny XXXIV 66 (O. 1516) and 73 (O. 1521); on Euthykrates: Pliny XXXIV 66 (O. 1516 and 1522); Tatian *c.Graecos* 52f. (O. 1523f., naming four statues of *hetairai* by this artist); on Daippos: Pliny XXXIV 66 (O. 1516), 51 (O. 1517, date) and 87 (O. 1520, Perixyomenos; also p. 464 with notes 44, 47); Pausanias IV 12 6 and 16 5 (O. 1518f., statues of Olympic victors); on Tisikrates: Pliny XXXIV 67 and 89 (O. 1525f.); on Xenokrates: Pliny XXXIV 83 (O. 1527); Diogenes Laertius IV 15 (O. 1528).

83. Girl from Anzio (Antium; Rome, M.N.): Carpenter in *MAAR* 18 (1941) 70ff. pl. 23, argues for the identification (originally suggested by Furtwängler in *MJb* 2 (1907) 9) of this figure as a copy of Phanis's statue; Bieber, *H* 30 with figs. 97–100, makes it the original; Br.Br. 583f.; *KB* 358, 3–5; Lullies and Hirmer pls. 232f. (247f.). Text on Phanis: Pliny XXXIV 80 (O. 1516, 1529).

84. Matron and Maiden of Herculaneum: (Dresden 140, 141): Br.Br. 310, 348; *KB* 394, 1 (Matron); Rizzo *Prassitele* pls. 135f. Better copy of Maiden (Athens, N.M. 1827, from Delos): Karouzou *Cat.* pl. 33b, and in *AM* 84 (1969) 148–57 and pls. 75f. (Dresden Matron pl. 71; other copies, pls. 69f., 72f.). Bronze statue from sea (Smyrna): Ridgway in *AJA* 71 (1967) 329–34, with refs., pls. 97ff. Later bronze head (University of North Carolina, Chapel Hill, Ackland Museum 6724.1): S. Immerwahr in *Hesp.* 38 (1969) 150–6, pls. 42ff.; *Ancient Portraits* (Ackland Art

Center, 1970), 2. Ephesus athlete and relation to Lady from the Sea: S. Lattimore in *AJA* 76 (1972) 13–16 with refs. and pls. 7f. Mantinea base, bronze Athena from Arezzo, and Tanagra figurines: pp. 395–6 with Chapter 6 notes 94, 97. Latest Attic grave-reliefs: pp. 381–2 with Chapter 6 notes 60ff.

85. Muses in Vatican: Amelung and Lippold III 1 pls. 4–9, Sala delle Muse 499, 503, 505, 508, 511, 517; Bieber *H* figs. 44 (Thalia), 45f. (Polyhymnia); *KB* 362, 4 (Melpomene) and 5 (Thalia); Lawrence *S* pl. 105b (Thalia), *LGS* pl. 23b (Melpomene); Lippold pl. 107, 4 (Thalia). Muses on Mt Helikon: p. 383 with Chapter 6 n. 65. Texts on sons of Praxiteles: O. 1331–41 (1331, Pliny XXXIV 51, date; 1332, Pliny XXXIV 87, portraits of philosophers by Kephisodotos; 1333, Plutarch *Vit.x Orat.*, *Lycurgus* 38, portraits of Lycurgus and his sons; 1337f., inscription and Pausanias I 21 1, portrait of Menander, on which see pp. 518–19 with Chapter 8 notes 37f.; 1339, Pliny XXXVI 24, Kephisodotos's marble symplegma; other marbles, ibid., O. 1340). Later group of Muses: pp. 562–4 with Chapter 8 notes 155–8.

86. Monument of Thrasyllos: Dinsmoor 339 with fig. 87 (reconstruction of original form, without Thrasykles's additions). Dionysus of Thrasykles (B.M. 432): Bieber *H* fig. 213; Br.Br. 119; *KB* 344, 2.

87. Alexander sarcophagus (Istanbul 68): full publication with illustration and earlier refs. in von Graeve *Alexandersarkophag*; see also Schefold *Alexander-Sarkophag*; other pictures: BDFH pls. XXVI and 271 (155); *KB* 335, 4; 336–7; col. pl. at p. 320; Lawrence *S* pl. 91; Lullies and Hirmer² pls. 232–7; Richter *Sc.* figs. 176, 399, 400, 748. The other Sidon sarcophagi: pp. 404–5 with Chapter 6 n. 117. Alexander mosaic: pp. 497–503 with notes 136–51.

88. Monument of Lysicrates: Dinsmoor 237f., pls. 59f.; D. S. Robertson 144f., 335. Frieze: *BMCat.Sc.* I 248–57, nos. 430f. (casts taken by Elgin; see also p. 302 with Chapter 5 n. 25). Corinthian order: pp. 358–9 with Chapter 5 n. 166, 397 and 406 with Chapter 6 notes 102, 121, 460 with n. 35.

89. Pp. 497–503 with notes 136–51.

90. Bronze lion-hunt at Delphi: pp. 460 and 475 with notes 35, 76. Louvre relief: *KB* 334, 8. Mosaics: p. 488 with notes 108f.

91. Reutersward 60ff.

92. Amazon sarcophagus (Vienna): *KB* 306, 1.

93. Bronze krater from Derveni (Salonica): *Arch.Rep. 1961/2* 15ff. figs. 15 (krater unrestored), 16 (head of satyr-statuette); *BCH* 86 (1962) 793 fig. 1 (vessel in ground); 87 (1963) pls. 16–20 (views and details after cleaning and restoration). To be fully published by E. Yuri.

94. One-booted Lycurgus: *Anth.Pal.* XVI 127; see Bruneau in *BCH* 90 (1966) 406, 407 n. 1. Half-shod characters in Greek legend in general: Deonna in *RHR* 112 (1935) 61ff., and in *Rev.Arch. de l'Est et du Centre-Est* 7 (1956) 156. Maenad and child on Attic rf. pyxis (B.M. E775): *ARV²* 1328, manner of Meidias Painter no. 92; *BMCat.V* III pl. 20; Curtius *Penth.* pl. 12. 'Lycurgus' on lost red-figure pyxis: Curtius *Penth.* figs. 2–6. Neo-Attic relief with maenad (Venice): Curtius *Penth.* fig. 16. Relief with Dionysus and Ariadne: in private hands, unpublished; I owe my knowledge of it to Bernard Ashmole, who showed me a photograph. On all these and their relation to paintings seen by Pausanias: M. Robertson in *GRBS* 13 (1972) 39–48.

95. Barberini Faun and Sleeping Ariadne: pp. 534f. with Chapter 8 notes 83f.

(iv) Painting: the school of Sicyon; mosaic and vase-painting

96. Texts on Eupompos: Pliny XXXIV 61 (O. 1444, imitation of nature: p. 463 with n. 42); XXXV 64 (O. 1649, associated with Timanthes, Androkydes and Parrhasios); XXXV 75 (O. 1745, taught Pamphilos, master of Apelles, in time of Parrhasios and Timanthes when Euxeinidas was teaching Aristides; picture of an athlete by him; founder of Sicyonian school). Parrhasios: pp. 411–13 with Chapter 6 notes 137–40; Timanthes: p. 414 with Chapter 6 n. 143. Euxeinidas and the Aristides problem: p. 433 with Chapter 6 n. 192. Androkydes: p. 437 with Chapter 6 n. 206; p. 580 with Chapter 8 n. 212.

97. Texts on Pamphilos: O. 1745–53 (1745, 1748, Pliny xxxv 75f., pupil of Eupompos, necessity of arithmetic and geometry, painting part of liberal education; 1746f., the Suda s.v. Apelles, Pamphilos, Amphipolitan or Sicyonian, master of Apelles; 1749, Plutarch *Aratus* 12, his works among Old Masters taken to Egypt by Aratus, p. 490 with n. 116; 1750, Quintilian xii 10 6, golden age of painting from Philip to Alexander's successors, he and Melanthios outstanding for intellect; 1751, Pliny xxxv 123, he painted in encaustic and taught Pausias, see following notes; 1753, Pliny xxxv 76, battle-piece and Odysseus on raft). O. 1752 gives Aristophanes's *Plutus* 302–5 and the scholium on it, but this is a confusion of the scholiast; the Pamphilos referred to is an Athenian general, not the painter: see M. Robertson ap. Jeffery in *BSA* 60 (1965) 47. Aristotle on painting in education: *Politics* viii 2f., quoted by O. on 1748.

98. Texts on Melanthios: O. 1748, 1750 (see last note) and 1754–9 (Pliny, Diogenes Laertius, Plutarch); as writer: O. 1756 (Pliny i ind. auct. lib. xxxv) and 1757 (Vitruvius vii praef. 4, where MSS give 'Melampus').

99. Encaustic: Pliny xxxiv 122 (O. 1072), mentioning Polygnotos, and 149 (note by Jex-Blake and Sellers); Vitruvius vii 9 (cf. Pliny xxi 83); Nikias's signature: Pliny xxxv 27 (O. 1817; *Nicias scripsit se inussisse, tali enim usus est verbo*). Nikias: pp. 436–9 with Chapter 6 notes 204–7. Encaustic taught by Pamphilos to Pausias: Pliny xxxv 123 (O. 1740). Zeuxis and the brush: Pliny xxxv 60f. (O. 1641 and 1647; p. 411 with Chapter 6 n. 136). See also following notes.

100. Hektoridas's design: p. 398 (refs. to the inscriptions, Chapter 6 n. 103; this item, Col.B iii 307, Burford *Epidaurus* 220, Roux *Argolide* 432), there are other references to encaustic in the accounts; see also below, n. 106.

101. Column-krater (New York 50.11.4): Bothmer in *Bull.Metr.* 9 (1950/1) 156–61, figs. 157f. and 163; Richter *MMH* pl. 96e. Calyx-krater fragment in Amsterdam with Apollo and his statue: p. 430 with Chapter 6 n. 184; *Bull.Metr.* l.c. fig. 159; coin and statues, l.c. figs. 160ff. Youth from Antikythera and Polykleitan tradition: pp. 409 with Chapter 6 n. 130, 470 with n. 59. Parrhasios: pp. 411–13 with Chapter 6 notes 137–40; his Herakles at Lindos: Pliny xxxv 69 (O. 1706); the claim ibid. 71.

102. Texts on Pausias: O. 1760–5; the main text (1760) is Pliny xxxv 123–7 (taught encaustic by Pamphilos, speed, small pictures mostly of boys, Glycera – on this see also xxi 4); 1761, Pausanias ii 27 2, pictures at Epidaurus; see further pp. 489–90 with notes 111–13. Pompeian still lives: p. 580 with Chapter 8 n. 213. Tholos at Epidaurus: p. 453 with n. 17; theatre: Dinsmoor 244ff., fig. 90, pl. 62; D. S. Robertson 165 with fig. 71, 334; Lawrence *A* 283f., fig. 166, pls. 147f., 151f.; Burford *Epidaurus* 75f., 83, 134. Eros with lyre on early fifth-century Attic vases, e.g.: Beazley *Berl.M.* pls. 10 and 12, 4, *Panm.* pl. 6, 1; Greifenhagen *Eroten* 16–19 figs. 9–12, 23 fig. 18, 27 fig. 20, 29f., figs. 22f.; Jacobsthal *O.* pl. 100.

103. 'Pausian' florals on South Italian vases (p. 440 with Chapter 6 n. 211): Jucker *Bildnis in Blätterkelch* figs. 126–8; in mosaic, see following notes; and see M. Robertson in *JHS* 85 (1965) 90–103, especially 82f. and pl. 20, 2 and in 87 (1967) 133–6, pls. 23f.

104. Pebble-mosaic: p. 415 with Chapter 6 n. 147; p. 578 with Chapter 8 notes 204ff.; M. Robertson in *JHS* (last note; hereinafter 'Robertson 1965' and 'Robertson 1967'). Motya floor: Whitaker *Motya* 194–202, fig. 24A–D; Robertson 1965, 76 and 84, pls. 19, 1–2 and 22, 3. Corinth fragment: *AJA* 41 (1937) 546f., fig. 1; *Anc.Cor., Mus.Guide* pl. 2; Robertson 1965, 84 with n. 62; 1967, pl. 23, 5. Early floor from Gordion: *ILN* 17/11/56, 859 fig. 11; *AJA* 61 (1957) 322 pl. 89, fig. 7; and especially Young in *Expedition* 7 (1965), 3, 4–13 with figs. and cover-picture; see also Robertson 1965, 72f., 83. Olynthus mosaics: Robinson *Olynthus* viii *The Hellenic House* and v *Mosaics* passim; Robertson 1965, 73–6 and 83f., pl. 18. Archelaos's palace and Zeuxis: pp. 411 and 415 with Chapter 6 notes 136 and 147. A recently found floor at Eretria with a circular emblema showing Scylla and a lozengy threshold like that of the Pella stag-hunt (below, n. 109): *Arch.Rep.* 1971/2, 7, fig. 11.

105. Lead and terracotta strips: Robertson 1967, 135 ii (correcting his own earlier mis-statements), and iii 4. 'Relief-contour' in red-figure: p. 214. 'Pausian' floor from Sicyon: Robertson 1967,

133f. pl. 24; see also Orlandos in *Prakt.* 1941, 59 fig. 6 (this floor) and 60 fig. 7 (another); this one also in *BCH* 64/5 (1940/1) 241 fig. 7; others *Prakt.* 1935, 82f. figs. 15–17; *JHS* 59 (1939) pl. 13c; *EAA* v 209 fig. 294; and see Robertson 1965, 83. Other Peloponnesian floors: ibid. 85f. with refs.; 1967, 135f., III 3 and 5. On the pebble floor in the entrance of the Temple of Zeus at Olympia (Robertson 1965, 85f. with n. 69), see p. 580 with Chapter 8 n. 212.

106. Aristratos, tyrant of Sicyon, and the Macedonians: Demosthenes *De Corona* XVIII 48 and 296; see Cauer in *RE* and Robertson 1965, 85 with n. 66; also pp. 493 with n. 122, 589 with Chapter 8 n. 239. Pausias as painter of ceilings: Pliny XXXV 124 (O. 1760). On painted Hellenistic tombs and their relation to palace-architecture, see pp. 568–9. Athens mosaic: Robertson 1967, 134 I, 3, pl. 23, 1–4; also p. 489 with n. 111. Painted coffers in Epidaurus accounts (pp. 397–8 with Chapter 6 n. 103, 485 with n. 100): Roux *Argolide* 429 (Col. A I 65f.). Painted coffer from Nereid monument (p. 404 with Chapter 6 n. 116): *JdI* 20 (1905) 157 fig. 3; Rumpf *MZ* pl. 39, 2, and in *JHS* 67 (1947) 12.

107. Mosaic from Epidamnus (Dyrrhacchium, Durazzo, Durrës): *ÖJh* 21/2 (1922/4) Beiblatt 203–14, figs. 142f.; Rumpf *MZ* 109 fig. 16; see Robertson 1965, 82; it was uncovered by a bomb in 1918 and before being covered in was photographed and drawn, and has recently been rediscovered: *Konferenca e Pare e Studimeve Albanologjike* 460f. with fig. 1; I owe my knowledge of this to Miss Jean Allen; *Shqiperia Arkeologjike* 99. Floor at Vergina-Palatitsa: *SMA 13, Vergina* fig. 14 (room E on plan fig. 10); *AJA* 61 (1959) pl. 80, figs. 14–16; *Arch.Rep. 1956* 19, fig. 16; see also Robertson 1965, 84f. Floors at Pella: Petsas in *ILN* 2/8/1958, 197ff.; *Archaeology* 11 (1958) 146–54, and 17 (1964) 74–81 (plan on p. 76); *Balkan Studies* 1 (1960) 113–28, and 4 (1963) 155–70; *SMA 14, Pella*; *Mos.G-R.* 41–51; Makaronas in *Scientific American* Dec. 1966, 98–105; Robertson 1965, especially 75–82, pl. 20; 1967, 135 II and III 1–2. Further discoveries: Laourdas and Makaronas *Arkhaia Makedonia* (1970) pl. 18; see p. 568 with Chapter 8 n. 168. See also following notes.

108. Plan of buildings at Pella: *Archaeology* 17 (1964) 76. Dionysus on leopard: *Archaeology* 11 (1958) figs. on pp. 252f., 17 (1964) 78 fig. 7 (detail of underside); *SMA 14, Pella* fig. 3; *BCH* 82 (1958) 763, figs. 14f., pl. 52 above; *Delt.* 1960, pls. 40a–d, and 41f.; Robertson 1965, 76f. and pl. 20, 1; *Scientific American* Dec. 1966, pl. at p. 99 above; *Mos.G-R.* figs. 2 and 18. Lion-hunt (p. 482 with n. 90): *Archaeology* 11 (1958) fig. on p. 253 below (*in situ* showing border), 17 (1964) 78 fig. 4; *SMA 14, Pella* fig. 2; *BCH* 82 (1958) 764 fig. 16, 83 (1959) 705 fig. 23; *Scientific American* Dec. 1966, pl. at p. 99 below, and cover (detail); *Balkan Studies* 1 (1960) pls. 7 and 8; *EAA* v 209 fig. 295 and col. pl.; *Mos.G-R.* figs. 3–4 and 12–17; M. Robertson 166 and 169; and see Robertson 1965, 80f. Centaur-threshold: *Archaeology* 17 (1964) 78 fig. 6; *Delt.* 1960 pl. 47; *Mos.G-R.* fig. 5. Female Centaurs: see Robertson 1965, 77f.; Strong in *BMQ* 30 (1965) 36–40 with pl. 6; and p. 545 with Chapter 8 n. 108. Zeuxis: pp. 411 and 415 (work for Archelaus), 413 (Centaur-family), with Chapter 6 notes 136, 141, 147.

109. Stag-hunt (p. 482 with n. 90): *Archaeology* 17 (1964) 80 fig. 8; *SMA 14, Pella* fig. 5; *Balkan Studies* 4 (1963) pl. 13; *Delt.* 1960 pls. 244–7; *BCH* 86 (1962) 810 fig. 24, pls. 27f.; *Mos.G-R.* figs. 8–11 and a–b; see Robertson 1965, 81f., pl. 20, 2.

110. Theseus and Helen: *Archaeology* 17 (1964) 80 fig. 8; *SMA 14, Pella* fig. 4; *Delt.* 1961/2 pls. 241–3 (top); *Balkan Studies* 4 (1963) pl. 14; *BCH* 86 (1962) pls. 25–6; *Mos.G-R.* fig. 6; see Robertson 1965, 78ff.

111. Duris passage: Athenaeus XII 542D (O. 2161); see Robertson 1965, 84f. Demetrius of Phalerum: p. 365 with Chapter 6 n. 8 (anti-luxury laws). Athens floor: p. 487 with n. 106.

112. Nikias's alleged remarks: p. 437 with Chapter 6 n. 205. Pausias's Sacrifice: Pliny XXXV 126f. (O. 1760). Cast shadows: pp. 501–3 with notes 145, 151.

113. Pausias at Thespiai: Pliny XXXV 123 (O. 1760). Sanctuary of Eros: pp. 389 and 394 with Chapter 6 notes 80 and 91, 466 with n. 49. Polygnotos: pp. 241–70 with Chapter 4 notes 149ff. Restoration of Lesche at Delphi: p. 245 with Chapter 4, n. 152. Copying or restoration

of paintings at Delphi in second century B.C.: Roux in *BCH* 63 (1939) 170, and in 76 (1952) 184f.; Daux *Delphes au IIe et au Ier siècle* 509 and n. 1; M. Robertson in *BSA* 62 (1967) 8 with n. 26. Panelled stoa of Attalos I at Delphi: p. 245 with Chapter 4 n. 152. Difference between literary and epigraphic practice: p. 399 with Chapter 6 n. 105; cf. also pp. 347 f. with Chapter 5 n. 134.

114. Text on Aristolaos: Pliny XXXV 137 (O. 1764). Apoxyomenos and Perixyomenos: pp. 464 and 478 with notes 44 and 82. Euphranor's and Parrhasios's Theseus: p. 434 with Chapter 6 n. 195.

115. Texts on Nikophanes: Pliny XXXV 137 (O. 1763), 111 (O. 1766); also Athenaeus XIII 567B (O. 1762) and perhaps Plutarch *de audiend. poet.* 3 (O. 1767). Socrates is mentioned only in the first passage of Pliny and ibid. XXXVI 32 (O. 915). Polygnotus's Oknos: p. 267 with Chapter 4 n. 191.

116. Text on Eutychides as painter: Pliny XXXV 141 (O. 1535); as sculptor: pp. 470–2 with notes 61ff. Texts on Arkesilaos: Pliny XXXV 146 (O. 1768); Pausanias I I 3 (O. 1769). Ptolemy II's pageant: Athenaeus V 196 A 25–35 (quoting Kallixenos of Rhodes (O. 1990)); the pavilion: ibid. 25f.; the Sicyonian pictures, 26. Aratus and Ptolemy III: Plutarch *Aratus* 12–13 (O. 1749). Later Sicyonian painting: p. 589 with Chapter 8 n. 239.

117. Assteas's Herakles: p. 440 with Chapter 6 n. 212. His Cassandra and Ajax (Rome, Villa Giulia): Trendall *PP* 28–31 with refs. pl. 26 and fig. 13; Pfuhl *MuZ* fig. 803. Mythological burlesques in Middle Comedy: see recently Arnott in *Greece and Rome* 19 (1972) 65–80, especially 71–5.

118. Phlyax vases: Trendall *Phl.* passim, *PP* pl. 22; Arias and Hirmer pl. 240; Beazley and Ashmole fig. 140; Pfuhl *MuZ* figs. 804f. Fine fragment (Würzburg 823): Langlotz *GVW* pl. 239; *Die Antike* 7 (1931) 94 fig. 14.

119. 'Phlyax'-fragment of a bell-krater from Corinth (Corinth CP534): Luce in *AJA* 34 (1930) 342, fig. 6; see Trendall *Phl.* 21 no. 15 (a similar Corinthian bell-krater, Athens CC1927, ibid. no. 14, and see Trendall's remarks on Corinthian red-figure, on which also Corbett in *Perachora* II 286ff., pl. 116). Red-figure made at Olympia: *Arch.Rep. 1963/4* 12f. fig. 13; also perhaps *Ol.Ber.* II (1938) 39 fig. 25, there described as Corinthian; at Vourvoura (Laconia): *Ergon* 1956, 83ff. and 1957, 66ff.; *Prakt.* 1956, 185f., 1957, 110f. and 1961, 167f.; in Boeotia: Lullies in *AM* 65 (1940) 1–27, pls. 1–28; A. D. Ure, *CV* Reading I, pl. 28, 9, and in *AJA* 57 (1953) 245–9, pls. 66–72 and 62 (1958) 381–95, pls. 102–7; Pfuhl *MuZ* 714ff. with earlier refs., figs. 607–10. Cabiric vases: Wolters and Bruns *Kabirenheiligtum* 95–128, pls. 5–17, 26–33, 36–7, 44–61; other pictures: *JHS* 84 (1964) 154f. pls. 5f.; Pfuhl *MuZ* figs. 613–18 (Odysseus and Circe, figs. 615f.); Odysseus vase (Oxford G249) Gardner pl. 26, 1. Pamphilos's Odysseus: p. 484 with n. 97. Hellenistic caricature: pp. 497 with n. 135, 557–8 with Chapter 8 n. 142.

(*v*) *Apelles, Protogenes and other painters; the Alexander mosaic*

120. Quintilian XII 10 6.

121. Texts on Apelles: O. 1827–1906. Date, and origin in Kos: Pliny XXXV 79 (O. 1827); from Kolophon, Ephoros his first master: the Suda s.v. Apelles (O. 1828); taught by Pamphilos: ibid., also Pliny XXXV 76 and 123 (O. 1745, 1748), and Plutarch *Aratus* 13 (O. 1832); pictures of Philip: Pliny XXXV 93 (O. 1833); Calumny for Ptolemy: Pliny XXXV 89 (O. 1837), Tzetzes *Chil.* VIII 394 (O. 1838), Lucian *Cal.* 2ff. (O. 1839); and see p. 496 with n. 133. Antiphilos: p. 497 with n. 135. Procession of Megabyzos: Pliny XXXV 93 (O. 1887; Nikias and Megabyzos: p. 437 with Chapter 6 n. 204). Apelles and Alexander: O. 1833–6, 1875–80. The three portraitists: Pliny VII 125 (O. 1446; Lysippos and Alexander, p. 463 with n. 41; Pyrgoteles, p. 514 with Chapter 8 n. 27). Pancaspe: Pliny XXXV 86 (O. 1836; cf. 1885, Lucian *Imagines* 7). Alexander in the studio: Pliny XXXV 85 (O. 1834; ibid. note, Megabyzos, Plutarch *de ad. et am.* 15).

122. Portraits of Alexander: on horseback, Aelian *Var.Hist.* II 3 (O. 1835); with thunderbolt, Pliny XXXV 92, Plutarch *de Alex.M.s.virt.s.fort.* 2 and *Alexander* 4 (O. 1875–7; 1878, Cicero

Verr. IV 60 5, might refer to either of the pictures in Ephesus); two in Rome: Pliny XXXV 27 and 93 (O. 1979f.). Medallion with Alexander: p. 507 with Chapter 8 n. 9; and cf. p. 514 with Chapter 8 n. 26. Aristratos with his chariot: Plutarch *Aratus* 13 (O. 1759; see also p. 589 with Chapter 8 n. 239, and on Aristratos p. 487 with n. 106. Bound Marsyas: p. 435 with Chapter 6 n. 200.

123. Apelles's self-portrait: *Anth.Gr.* IV 185, 314 (O. 1886). Pheidias on the shield: p. 316 with Chapter 5 n. 55. Portrait of Antigonos: Pliny XXXV 90, Quintilian II 13 12, Strabo XIV 657 (O. 1883f., and 1827); other portraits of Antigonos: p. 495 with n. 130.

124. Battle of Marathon: p. 323 with Chapter 5 n. 74. Euphranor's Mantinea: pp. 433–5 with Chapter 6 notes 195, 199. Alcibiades's portraits: pp. 415–16 with Chapter 6 n. 148. Portraits in Roman wall-paintings, e.g.: Maiuri *RP* 98–102; Pfuhl *MuZ* figs. 716f.; mummy-portraits: Pfuhl *MuZ* figs. 677–83; Coche de la Ferté *Les Portraits Romano-Égyptiens du Louvre*; Shore *Portrait-painting from Roman Egypt*. Three-quarter heads on coins: p. 360 with Chapter 5 notes 174–6; Hellenistic coin-portraiture: pp. 520–3 with Chapter 8 notes 30–2, 41–4, 47–50. Portraits of Federigo da Montefeltro: e.g. Clark *Piero della Francesca* pls. 104, 106, 140f., figs. 58 and 60 (by Piero), fig. 61 (by another painter), fig. 59 (medal); other profile portraits, ibid. pls. 23ff., 103. Renaissance portrait-medals; e.g., Goldscheider *Unknown Renaissance Portraits* passim.

125. Praxiteles's Cnidia rejected by Koans: p. 394 with Chapter 6 n. 92. Apelles's Aphrodite Anadyomene: O. 1847–63; Cicero *Verr.* IV 60 135 (O. 1863; in Kos; other passages, O. 1860–2 and 806); Strabo XIV 657 (O. 1847; Antigonos in Kos, Anadyomene taken to Rome); Pliny XXXV 91 (O. 1848; in Rome, lower part damaged, copy by Dorotheos); Pliny XXXV 86 (O. 1836; Pancaspe the model); Athenaeus XIII 590F (O. 1846; Phryne the model); Phryne: p. 394 with Chapter 6 n. 91; various Greek and Roman poems describing the action (O. 1849–59). Unfinished picture in Kos of Aphrodite: Pliny XXXV 92 and 145 (O. 1864 and 1772); Cicero *Ep.ad fam.* I 9 15 and *de Off.* III 2 10 (O. 1865f.). Sculptural type perhaps related to Apelles's Anadyomene: p. 557 with Chapter 8 n. 140.

126. Charis: Pausanias IX 35 6 (O. 1867). Representations of the Three Graces: pp. 58–9 with Chapter 2 n. 54, 314 with Chapter 5 n. 51; p. 550 with Chapter 8 n. 120. A single Charis as Hephaestus's wife: p. 318 with Chapter 5 n. 63. Artemis: Pliny XXXV 96 (O. 1870). Calumny: Lucian *Cal.* 4 (O. 1874) and 2 (O. 1870); and see next note.

127. Botticelli's version, e.g. L. Venturi *Botticelli* pl. 92; Mantegna's: e.g. Popham and Pouncey *BMCat.Italian Drawings* pl. 146. Early classical space: Chapter 4 (vi) with notes. Apollodoros, Zeuxis and Agatharchos and their inventions: Chapter 5 (iv) with notes; Euphranor and Nikias: Chapter 5 (v) with notes. Apelles's claim: Pliny XXXV 80 (O. 1775 and 1895), 107 (O. 1896) and 79 (O. 1897). Asklepiodoros: also O. 1954ff., Pliny ind.auct. XXXV (as writer), XXXIV 86 (as statuary).

128. Apelles's technical inventions: Pliny XXXV 42 (O. 1892) and 97 (O. 1893); easel-pictures only: 118 (O. 1890).

129. Wall-painting on wood: p. 244 with Chapter 4 n. 152; on plaster: ibid. and Chapter 8 (iv) with notes. Third-century stoa at Delphi: pp. 244–5 with Chapter 4 n. 152, 490 with n. 113.

130. Texts on Protogenes: O. 1907–36. Protogenes and Apelles: Pliny XXXV 81f. (O. 1841; and see below, n. 132), 87f. (O. 1840, Apelles's appreciation and help). Protogenes a Kaunian: Pliny XXXV 101 (O. 1907), Pausanias I 3 5 (O. 1908 and 1932), Plutarch *Demetrius* 22 (O. 1909, 1915, 1921); a Xanthian: the Suda s.v. Protogenes (O. 1910, 1917), Constantine Porphyrogenitus *de Themat.* I 14 (O. 1911; also decoration of Temple of Dionysus at Rhodes). Ialysos: Pliny XXXV 102–5 (O. 1907, in Rome; the story of the siege, also in Plutarch *Demetrius* 22, O. 1915, with reference to portraits of Antigonos; Aulus Gellius XV 31, O. 1916; and the Suda, O. 1917); Strabo XIV 652 (O. 1918, in Rhodes; works of art in Temple of Dionysus and Gymnasium); Plutarch *Demetrius* 22 (O. 1921, effect on Apelles; also in Aelian *VH* XII 41, O. 1922); other comments in Cicero (O. 1861, and 1919f.), and Fronto (O. 1923). The satyr: Pliny XXXV 105f. (O. 1907, painted under

the sword); Strabo XIV 652 (O. 1924; and see below, n. 132). Praxiteles's satyr: p. 389 with Chapter 6 n. 80; Lysippos's p. 468 with n. 52. Protogenes as sculptor: Pliny XXXV 106 and XXXIV 91 (O. 1930f.). See also following notes.

131. Portraits of Antigonos, Philiskos and Aristotle's mother; Aristotle's advice and the Pan and Alexander: Pliny XXXV 106 (O. 1930–1).

132. Anecdote of the lines: Pliny XXXV 81–3 (O. 1841); 'Giotto's O': Vasari *Lives of the Painters, Giotto*. Protogenes's writings: the Suda s.v. Protogenes (O. 1936). 'Four layers of colour' on Ialysos: Pliny XXXV 102 (O. 1907). The partridge: Strabo XIV 652 (O. 1924; cf. 1925f.). *Parerga* in Athens picture: Pliny XXXV 101 (O. 1907; cf. O. 1908, Cicero *Verr.* IV 60 135). Ialysos's dog: Pliny XXXV 102–3 (O. 1907; and cf. pp. 589 with Chapter 8 n. 239, 595 with Epilogue n. 16).

133. Apelles's Calumny: p. 494 with notes 126f. Texts on Aetion (or Eetion): O. 1937–41. Wedding of Alexander and Roxane: Lucian *Herod.s.Aetion* 4 (O. 1938) and *Imagines* 7 (O. 1939); see also p. 573 with Chapter 8 n. 185; a list of the painter's works in Pliny XXXV 78 (O. 1937; also for the date) includes a bridal picture, but it does not seem to be this one; the painter is also mentioned by Cicero (O. 1067 and 1940). Mars and Venus with Erotes (Naples 9248): Helbig 320 (cf. 319); Elia no. 121, with refs. and fig. 21; Pfuhl *MuZ* fig. 668. Herakles and Omphale: Helbig 1137–9 (1140, see pp. 575–7 with Chapter 8 n. 194). Botticelli's Mars and Venus, e.g.: Davies *National Gallery: the Earlier Schools* I pl. 69. Sodoma's Alexander and Roxane (fresco in Rome, Palazzo Farnesina): e.g. Berenson *Italian Painters of the Renaissance* pl. 372.

134. Texts on Theon: O. 1946–9 (1948, Aelian *VH* II 44, the soldier; 1946, Pliny XXXV 138, and 1947, Plutarch *de audiend.poet.* 3, Orestes; 1949, Quintilian XII 10 6, *phantasiai*).

135. Texts on Antiphilos: O. 1942–4; also 1512, 1839 (quarrel with Apelles, p. 492 with n. 121) and 1904. Pliny XXXV 114 (O. 1943, list of works, including Gryllos) and 138 (O. 1942, other works); Quintilian XII 10 6 (O. 1944, indication of date). Hellenistic caricature: p. 558 with Chapter 8 n. 142.

136. Alexander mosaic (Naples 10020): Elia 134–7 no. 396, with some refs. to the vast literature and fig. 49. Pictures: e.g. Beazley and Ashmole fig. 142; Curtius *WP* 325–31, figs. 182ff.; Maiuri *RP* 69; Pfuhl *MuZ* fig. 648; Rumpf *MZ* pl. 49. Further refs. below, in notes 141f., 147.

137. Pebble-mosaics: pp. 486–9 with notes 104, 107–11; early tessera-mosaics and the transition: pp. 578–81 with Chapter 8 notes 205–16.

138. Dancing faun: p. 478 with n. 81; the house also pp. 502 with n. 148, 580 with Chapter 8 n. 212.

139. Battle of Marathon: pp. 244 and 323 with Chapter 5 n. 74; of Mantinea: pp. 433–5 with Chapter 6 notes 195, 199.

140. Alexander sarcophagus: pp. 481–2 with n. 87. Ephesus Amazons: pp. 333–9 with Chapter 5 notes 99–105.

141. This account owes most to Rumpf 'Das Alexander Mosaik' in *AM* 77 (1962) 229–41, who demonstrated that the cloth on the spear (part of which is lost in damage) cannot, as is often said, be the Persian banner. See also following notes.

142. Supposed shortening of the picture: Andreae *Alexandermosaik* 8 and pl. 1; against this: Rumpf in *AM* 77 (1962) 238 (see last note).

143. Four-colour painters: Cicero *Brutus* 18 70 (O. 1067); Pliny XXXV 50 (O. 1756); and see Rumpf in *AM* 77 (1962) 240f.; Beazley and Ashmole 40 and 65; and p. 260 with Chapter 4 n. 176.

144. Pp. 437–9 with Chapter 6 n. 207.

145. Pausias's ox: p. 489 with n. 112. Reflected faces in red-figure: pp. 427 and 443 with Chapter 6 notes 175, 217.

146. Amazonomachy on calyx-krater in New York: p. 258 with Chapter 4 n. 174. Battle of Marathon: pp. 244 and 323 with Chapter 5 n. 74. Pheidian Gigantomachies: pp. 312 and 324 with Chapter 5 notes 46 and 77.

147. Texts on Nikomachos and Philoxenos: Pliny XXXV 108–10 (O. 1771, 1775, 1777) and 145f. (O. 1772, 1776); Vitruvius III praef. 2 (O. 1773); Plutarch *de mul.virt.* praef. (O. 1774). The problem of the two Aristides: p. 433 with Chapter 6 n. 192; battle 'with Persians of a hundred men', Pliny XXXV 99 (O. 1779). 'King Seleucus': p. 463 with n. 40. Philoxenos and the Alexander mosaic: Fuhrmann *Philo-*

xenos. Echoes of the picture in Apulian vase-painting: Heydemann *Winckelmanns-programm Halle* 8 (1883); Robert ibid. 18 (1895; against Heydemann's interpretation); Metzger in *REG* 80 (1967) 308–13, figs. 1f.

148. Text on Helen: Ptolemaeus Hephaestion, ap. Photium *Bibl.* p. 482 (O. 1976). The Nile-scene from the House of the Faun: Elia 138, fig. 151. Alexandrian elements in Hellenistic painting and mosaic: pp. 579 and 589 with Chapter 8 notes 211 and 236.

149. Anaxandre, daughter of Nealkes (on whom see p. 589 with Chapter 8 n. 239): Clement of Alexandria *Strom.* IV 124 (O. 2104); Timarete, daughter of a painter Mikon (distinguished from Polygnotos's colleague as 'the younger'): Pliny XXXV 59; Eirene, daughter and pupil of a painter Kratinos; Kalypso; Aristarete, daughter and pupil of Nearchos (Pliny XXXV 141, O. 2154); Olympias who had a pupil Aristoboulos: all these except Anaxandre, Pliny XXXV 147f. (O. 2153). Woman painters in Pompeian wall-painting: Naples 9018, Elia 97 no. 251, Helbig 1443; another 1444.

150. Lysippos and Eupompos: p. 463 with n. 42. Hellenistic observation: pp. 527 and 556–9 with Chapter 8 notes 64 and 142–6.

151. Surrender of Breda (Madrid, Prado): e.g. Lafuente *Velazquez* pl. 73, comparison in Beazley and Ashmole 65. Piero's Constantine and Maxentius (Arezzo, S. Francesco): e.g. Clark *Piero della Francesca* pls. 57–62; Heraclius and Chosroes, pls. 77–86. Reliefs of Monument of Julii, St Rémy: *KB* 404, 1; Becatti *AAGR* 314 fig. 287; Bianchi Bandinelli *RCP* 248 fig. 277, *Storicità* pls. 117ff. and p. 219 on the Hellenistic pictorial tradition in them. Reliefs on the attic of the arch at Orange: Espérandieu *Rec.gén.des bas-reliefs de la Gaule Romaine* I 1, 188–205, especially 191–5; Bianchi Bandinelli *RCE* 146ff. figs. 134, 136ff.; their Hellenistic character, Lawrence *S* 336. Uccello's Rout of San Romano (London, National Gallery 583; Florence, Uffizi, 52; Louvre 1273): e.g. Pope-Hennessy *Uccello*, frontispiece, pls. 45–63, and folding pl. at p. 52; spears in perspective construction: ibid. p. 21 (also 10f., 28).

CHAPTER 8: HELLENISTIC ART

(*i*) *Portraiture: coins and sculpture*

1. Vase-painting: pp. 223 and 263; narrative sculpture: p. 167 with Chapter 4 n. 22. Battle of Marathon: pp. 244 and 323 with Chapter 5 n. 74. Picture of Themistocles in the Parthenon: p. 187 with Chapter 4 n. 51. Polygnotos's Elpinike: pp. 243–4 with Chapter 4 n. 151, and 249. Pheidias on the shield: p. 316 with Chapter 5 n. 55. Ostia Themistocles: p. 187 with Chapter 4 notes 50, 51.

2. Mausolus: p. 457–9 with Chapter 7 n. 30; p. 517. The character of naturalism in Egyptian portraiture: see Richter in *JRS* 45 (1955) 40–4, pls. 1–5, and *POG* I 29f. Portraiture in Greek-oriental ambience: pp. 110–11 with Chapter 3 n. 84, 187 and 201 with Chapter 4 notes 51 (Themistocles) and 84; pp. 506f. with n. 8.

3. Texts on Demetrios of Alopeke: O. 897–903 (900–902, Lucian *Philops.* 18–20, the 'man-maker', Pellichos; 903, Quintilian XII 10 9, loving truth more than beauty); and see following notes.

4. Lysimache: Pliny XXXIV 76 (O. 898). Acropolis base: *IG* II² 3453 (II 3.1376); *ÖJh* 19/20, 307 n. 10, fig. 192; Lewis in *BSA* 50 (1955) 1–12, fig. 2 (see also next two notes). Heads (B.M. 2001; the better preserved); *ÖJh* 19/20 fig. 195; Richter *POG* 155, figs. 877ff.; (Rome, M.N.): Richter *POG* I 156, figs. 880f. Torso (Basle, inv. B.S. 202): *AK* 11 (1968) pls. 31, 1 and 33, 4f. (33, 1–3, restored with a cast of the B.M. head). On all three and their association with the base and with Lysimache, see Berger in *AK* 11 (1968) 67–70. Character of Bassae frieze: p. 358.

5. Lysimache and Lysistrata: see Lewis in *BSA* 50 (1955) 1–12 (cf. last note). Simon: Pliny XXXIV 76; Xenophon *Hippic.* I 1; Aristophanes *Knights* 292 and schol. (all, O. 898 with note). Mikon's mistake: p. 243 with Chapter 4 n. 150.

6. Syeris base: *IG* II² 3464 (II 3.1378); *ÖJh* 19/20 299–301 with fig.; Lewis in *BSA* 50 (1955) 8. Bronze statuette in Vienna: *ÖJh* 19/20, 296–8

(Banko) and 299–316 (Reisch), with figs. 191, 194 and pl. 6. Another base with signature of Nikomachos as sculptor, likewise from the Acropolis: *IG* II² 3038 (II 3.1249; O. 1385); *ÖJh* 19/20, 306–11 with n. 18 and fig. 193; see Lewis in *BSA* l.c.; and cf. last two notes.

7. Pythagores on coins of Abdera: Seltman *GC*² pl. 28, 11 and p. 144 (arguing for identification with the philosopher); Richter *GP* IV 18f. with fig. 16, and *POG* I 79 with fig. 205 (against identification); Schwabacher in *Op. C.Kerenyi ded.* 59–63, figs. 1 and 2, with refs. (reaffirming identification with new evidence). Daric: Seltman *GC* pl. 6, 5–7 and p. 62 (the King); Seyrig in *Syria* 36 (1959) 54f., n. 5 (casting doubt); Kraay and Hirmer 358 nos. 618–20, pl. 183.
8. Satrap coins: Kraay and Hirmer pl. 184, 621f. (Tissaphernes), 623 (Pharnabazus, uninscribed); Hill *PCG*² pls. 8, 15 (Pharnabazus, inscribed), 19, 41 (Tissaphernes, lyre), 51, 4 (Tissaphernes, owl); see Robinson in *NC* 8 (1948) 48–56, pl. 5, 8 and 8a. Orontas: Babelon *Traité* pl. 88, 11. Mausolus: pp. 457–9 with Chapter 7 notes 29, 30.
9. Alexander's Alexandrian coins: Seltman *GC* 212 with pl. 49, 8 (asserting their portrait-character); Kraay and Hirmer 349f. with pl. 172 no. 569 (cf. 570–2; doubting it). Hydaspes decadrachm (p. 492 with Chapter 7 n. 122; cf. p. 514 with n. 26): Seltman *GC* pl. 49, 6–7; the king's headgear: Plutarch *Alexander* XVI 4. Alexander sarcophagus: pp. 481–2 with Chapter 7 n. 87; Alexander mosaic: pp. 479–503 with Chapter 7 notes 137–51.
10. Alexander-portraits on Ptolemy's coins: Seltman *GC* 240 with pl. 58, 1; Kraay and Hirmer 381f. with pl. 217 nos. 796–8; on other Successors' coinages: p. 514 with n. 27.
11. Texts on Silanion: O. 1350–63. Date: Pliny XXXIV 51 (O. 1350 and 1443); p. 463 with Chapter 7 n. 41; p. 513 with n. 23; Jocasta: Plutarch *de audiend. poet.* 3 30 (O. 1350 and 1128), and *Quaest.Conv.* V 12 (O. 1354); statue of Apollodoros: Pliny XXXIV 81 (O. 1359). Apollodoros as statuary: Pliny XXXIV 86 (O. 1364). Aristides: pp. 432–3 with Chapter 6 n. 192, 502 with Chapter 7 n. 147. Silanion's Sappho: Cicero *Verr.* IV 57 125; Tatian *c. Graecos* 52 p. 114 (O. 1355ff.); his Corinna: Tatian l.c. (O. 1357). Corinna's Hellenistic date: Page *Corinna* (Tatian's evidence dismissed, 73f. n. 6). The statuette (Compiègne, Musée Vivenel): Richter *POG* I 144 with refs. and figs. 780f.; Bieber *H* 44 with figs. 120ff.; life-size torsos (Argos): *BCH* 87 (1963) 43ff. no. 49, figs. 10ff.; (Salamis): Karageorghis and Vermeule I 22f. no. 13, pl. 20; heads: Schmidt in *JdI* 47 (1932) 281ff., figs. 32, 34; Richter *POG* I 144 with fig. 782. See also following notes.
12. Silanion's Satyros at Olympia: p. 517 with n. 34; his Plato: Diogenes Laertius III 25 (O. 1358); and see next note.
13. Portrait-heads of Plato: Richter *POG* II 164–70, figs. 903–75; inscribed Herm (Berlin, K192): no. 10, figs. 903ff., 908 (another at Tivoli, no. 8, fig. 906; a forged copy of that inscription, fig. 907); statuette: p. 167 fig. 690 (reconstructed cast with head). See also p. 510 with n. 17.
14. Descriptions of Socrates: Plato *Symposium* 215a ff.; Xenophon *Symposium* V 5–7.
15. Lysippos's Socrates: Diogenes Laertius II 43 (O. 1493).
16. Portraits of Socrates: Richter *POG* I 109–19, figs. 456–573; differentiation of types, 110; inscribed Herms: (Naples inv. 6415), no. 12, figs. 483, 500f., 503; (Berlin 371), no. 20, figs. 528–31. Lysippic dancing satyr: p. 478 with Chapter 7 n. 81. Seated figure (Copenhagen I.N. 2812): Richter *POG* I 116, figs. 556ff.; engraving with head, fig. on p. 110; reconstruction, fig. 559; heads of this type, figs. 483–51; Villa Albani head, no. 3, figs. 458, 460; heads of similar character from the high Hellenistic age, pp. 526–7 with notes 60–4; heads of the other type: Richter l.c. figs. 456f., 459, 461–82; statuette in British Museum, 116, figs. 560–2.
17. Standing Plato from Memphis: Richter *POG* II 168, fig. 961. Statue of Plato in Cicero's villa: Cicero *Brutus* VI 24 (see Richter 164).
18. Lycurgan decree: Plutarch *Vit. x orat. Lycurgus*, p. 841.
19. The statues: Pausanias I 21 1–2 (O. 1409); cf. O. 1410, 1412f., and see Richter *POG* I 21. Portraits of Aeschylus: Richter 121–4, figs. 577–610; of Sophocles: 124–33, figs. 611–716; of Euripides: 133–40, figs. 717–79. Inscribed

heads of Sophocles: 125 with text fig. and no. 1, figs. 611–13; 128f. no. 1, figs. 678f. Sophocles–Euripides Herms: 128 no. 27 and 136 no. 24, figs. 670, 672 and 749f.; 128 no. 28 and 136 no. 25, figs. 667f. and 755f.; 136 no. 28 with text-fig. Small bronze heads from the sea (Florence): Amelung *Führer ... Florenz* 276f. nos. 271–4; Homer (1646); p. 526 with n. 62; Aeschylus: Richter 122, left, no. 2, figs. 583ff.; Sophocles (1645): Richter 129 no. 9, figs. 686ff.; the fourth is unidentified; see also Arndt in Arndt-Bruckmann 405f.; McDowall in *JHS* 24 (1904) 81f. Sophocles–Aeschylus Herm (Rome, Colonna): Richter 122 no. 1 and 127 no. 15, figs. 577ff., 586, 635ff., 644. Lateran Sophocles (Vatican): Richter 129 no. 2, figs. 675–7 (cast of head before restoration), 680. Later head: p. 526 with n. 63.

20. Statue of Aeschines (Naples, inv. 6018, from Herculaneum): Lippold pl. 108, 3; Ridgway *SS* fig. 111; Richter *POG* II 213 no. 6, figs. 1369–71; inscribed Herms: (Vatican 297), Richter 213 no. 1, figs. 1372ff.; (B.M. 1839), 214 no. 7, figs. 1375, 1378f.; other heads: 214 nos. 8–10, figs. 1376, 1389f.

21. Texts on Polyeuktos's statue of Demosthenes: O. 1365–8; Plutarch *Vit. x orat., Demosthenes* 44 (O. 1365; near Altar of Twelve Gods), *Demosthenes* 30 (O. 1366, anecdote of clasped hands); Pausanias I 8 2 (O. 1367, near statues of the Eponymous Heroes). Only pseudo-Plutarch mentions the sculptor. Portraits of Demosthenes: Richter *POG* II 215–23, figs. 1397–1513; Herculaneum bust (Naples inv. 5467), 217f. no. 12, figs. 1438–40; statues: (Vatican inv. 2255), 216 no. 1, figs. 1397, 1404ff.; (Copenhagen I.N. 2782), 219 no. 32, figs. 1398–1402; clasped hands (Vatican inv. 15060), 222, figs. 1511f.; best head (Oxford 1923.882), 219 no. 27, figs. 1424–7; bronze statuette, 222, figs. 1511f. Other pictures: Beazley and Ashmole fig. 148 (Vatican); *KB* 319, 2 (Vatican); Lawrence *S* pls. 104 (Vatican), 105a (Oxford), *LGS* pl. 20b (Oxford); Lippold pl. 97, 1 (Vatican); Richter *Sc.* fig. 747 (Copenhagen).

22. Text on statue of Hypereides: *Ox.Pap.* XV (1922) no. 1800, fr. 8, lines 30–3; Richter (*POG* 210) interprets the phrasing as giving a date of 307 B.C., but it suits 280 B.C. better, and the same words are used in the same papyrus (fr. 3, lines 29–32) of the statue of Demosthenes, which we know to belong to 280; see M. Robertson in *Burl.Mag.* March 1966, 150. Possible heads of Hypereides: Richter *POG* 210f. figs. 1350–64, 1368; double Herm, 211 no. 3, figs. 1355–7. Phryne: pp. 394 with Chapter 6 n. 91, 493–4 with Chapter 7 n. 125. Statue-base with name of Hypereides and signature of Zeuxiades: Richter 210 with refs.; text on Zeuxiades pupil of Silanion: Pliny XXXIV 51 (O. 1350).

23. Texts on Lysistratos: O. 1513–15. Date: Pliny XXXIV 51 (O. 1513; also 1343, 1350, 1443, 1601; above, pp. 463 with Chapter 7 n. 41, 493–4 with n. 11). Innovation: Pliny XXXV 153 (O. 1514); the passage is corrupt, but this seems certainly the sense (see Jex-Blake and Sellers ad loc.). Faces at Olympia: p. 283; Polykleitos: pp. 328–33 with Chapter 5 notes 85ff. Demetrios of Alopeke: pp. 504f. with notes 3ff. Mausolus: pp. 457–8 with Chapter 7 n. 29, 507 with n. 8. Plato and Socrates: pp. 508–10 with notes 12–16. Demosthenes: p. 512 with notes 21f.

24. Portraits of Alexander: Bernoulli *Darst.Alexanders*; Bieber *Alexander*, with refs. to earlier work; a selection, Richter *POG* 255f., figs. 1716–40; see also following notes. Acropolis head, Leochares and the chryselephantine group: p. 462 with Chapter 7 n. 39.

25. Headless Herm inscribed with designation as Praxiteles's Eubuleus: Vatican, Helbig 51. Eleusis 'Eubuleus' (Athens N.M.): *KB* 297, 1; Lawrence *S* pl. 100a (another copy, pl. 100b); and pp. 261ff., rejecting the identification and the attribution to Praxiteles; Richter *Sc.* fig. 512 (another copy, fig. 511) and pp. 181, 264. The unfinished Agora copy: Harrison in *Hesp.* 29 (1960) 382–9, pl. 85c and d, with list of ten replicas, identifying as Alexander; identification accepted by Bieber *Alexander* 26, with pls. 4 fig. 9 (Eleusis) and 5 fig. 10 (Agora), but not apparently by Richter, who illustrates the unfinished copy, *POG* fig. IV, for its technical character, not as a portrait. 'Leocharean' type (Alexander Rondanini): p. 516 with n. 32.

26. Texts on 'Alexander pose', its rendering by sculptors, and its imitation by the Successors: Plutarch *de Alex.M.s.f.s.v.* II 2 (O. 1479), *Alexander* 4 (O. 1480). Lysippos and Apelles:

Plutarch *de Is. et Os.* 24 (O. 1481). Apelles's portraits: pp. 492f. with Chapter 7 n. 122. Hydaspes medallion: p. 507 with n. 9 (cf. p. 492 with Chapter 7 n. 122). Bronze statuette (Louvre 370): BDFH pl. 263 (247) right; Bieber *Alexander* pl. 10, fig. 18; *KB* 334, 3; Richter *Sc.* fig. 52. Azara Herm (Louvre, Ma 436, from Tivoli; called after a former owner): Bieber *Alexander* pls. 8–9, figs. 13–17; *Enc.Phot.* 194A (other portraits, 194B, 195); *KB* 334, 1 and 2; Richter *POG* figs. 1733–5, *Sc.* fig. 74. Apoxyomenos: p. 464 with Chapter 7 n. 45. Apollo Belvedere: p. 460 with Chapter 7 n. 36.

27. Coins of Lysimachos: Seltman *GC* pl. 49, 9; Kraay and Hirmer 352, nos. 580f., pl. 176; Bieber *Alexander* pls. 7 fig. 44, 22 fig. 43; BDFH pl. 320 (304), 1. Pyrgoteles, Apelles and Lysippos: p. 492 with Chapter 7 n. 121. Priene statuette: Bieber *Alexander* pl. 23 figs. 47–9, *H* figs. 412ff.

28. Guimet head (Louvre): Bieber *Alexander* pl. 6 fig. 22; Richter *Sc.* fig. 746. Pergamon head (Istanbul): *Pergamon* VII 1 no. 131, pl. 33, Beibl. 21; BDFH pl. 305 (289); Bieber *Alexander* pls. 36–8 figs. 71f.; Buschor *Hell.Bild.* fig. 27; *KB* 334, 6 Lawrence *LGS* pl. 46a; Lippold pl. 97, 2; Lullies and Hirmer[2] pls. 260f.

29. Statue from Magnesia (Istanbul): Bieber *Alexander* pl. 40, figs. 78f.; *KB* 335, 6; *Mon.Piot* 3 (1896) 155–65, pls. 16–18. Venus of Milo and Poseidon: pp. 533–4 with notes 132f. Zeus of Olympia pediment: p. 278. Head from Alexandria (B.M. 1857): Bieber *Alexander* pl. 25, fig. 53; Richter *Sc.* fig. 745.

30. Coin-portraits of Ptolemy I: Seltman *GC* pl. 58, 4f.; Kraay and Hirmer 381f. nos. 799f. pls. 218 and xix; BDFH pl. 320 (304), 5; Bieber *H* fig. 304; Richter *POG* III fig. 1775. Marble face (Copenhagen I.N. 2300): Bieber *H* figs. 203f.; Richter *POG* 260 no. 1, figs. 1773f. Stucco profiles of Ptolemy and Berenice (Alexandria, inv. 24345): Bieber *H* fig. 307 (306, double coin-portrait); Richter *POG* III 260 no. 3, fig. 1778 (1779, double coin-portrait).

31. Coin-portraits of Seleucus: Seltman *GC* pls. 52, 3 (Syria) and 57, 5 (Pergamon); Kraay and Hirmer figs. 740 (Syria) and 736 (Pergamon); BDFH pl. 320 (304), 3 (Pergamon): Bieber *H* fig. 140 (Pergamon); Richter *POG* III fig. 1866 (Pergamon). Herculaneum bust (Naples inv. 5590): Bieber *H* figs. 141–3; *KB* 338, 7; Lippold pl. 109, 1; Richter *POG* figs. 1867f. Statues of Seleucus recorded: by Lysippos, p. 463 with Chapter 7 n. 41; by Bryaxis: Pliny XXXIV 73 (O. 1327); Aristodemos, Pliny XXXIV 86(O. 1605). Basalt: cf. p. 329.

32. Coins of Demetrius Poliorcetes with portrait and Poseidon: Seltman *GC* pl. 50, 5; Kraay and Hirmer fig. 753; Bieber *H* figs. 147f.; Richter *POG* III fig. 1744. Herculaneum statuette (Naples inv. 5026): Bieber *H* fig. 149; Lippold pl. 105, 1; Richter *POG* III fig. 1743. Herm (Naples inv. 6149): Bieber *H* figs. 145f.; Richter *POG* III figs. 1741f. Text on Lysippos's Poseidon for Corinth: Lucian *Jup.Trag.* 9 (O. 1457). Poseidon on coins of Roman Corinth: Imhoof-Blumer and Gardner *Num.Com.* pl. D fig. 43. Lateran statue (Vatican): Br.Br. 243; *KB* 332, 4; Johnson *Lysippos* pl. 24. Alexander Rondanini (Munich): Bieber *Alexander* pls. 6, figs. 6f. and 7 fig. 8. Louvre statuette: p. 514 with n. 26. Lysippos and Leochares at Delphi: p. 482 with Chapter 7 n. 90.

33. 'Jason' (copies in Copenhagen, Munich, Louvre, Athens Acropolis, the last unfinished): Arndt–Amelung 733 (Athens, Acrop., Casson *Cat.* 226 no. 1325) *Enc.Phot.* 196 (Louvre); *JHS* 11 (1891), 141 fig. 6 (Athens); Johnson *Lysippos* pls. 36f. (Copenhagen, ex-Lansdowne), 32A (Athens, head), B (head in B.M.); *KB* 332, 1 (Copenhagen); Lawrence *LGS* pl. 11a (Louvre); Lippold pl. 100, 2 (Copenhagen).

34. Silanion's Satyros (p. 508 with n. 12): Pausanias VI 4 5 (O. 1360). Iamidai: p. 279 with Chapter 4 n. 218. Bronze head from Olympia (Athens N.M. 6349): *Ol.* IV 10f. no. 2 pl. 2; BDFH pl. xl; *KB* 317, 7; Lawrence *LGS* pl. 16b; Lullies and Hirmer pls. 244f. (260f.); Rodenwaldt and Hege pls. 92f.

35. Bronze head from Cyrene (B.M. 268): Br.Br. *Portr.* 41f.; Lawrence *LGS* pl. 27; Lullies and Hirmer[1] pl. 198; Richter *POG* I fig. xxxviii.

36. Marble portrait-head (Delphi): *FdeD* IV Album p. 40, pl. 73 (4th cent.); de La Coste Messelière *Delphes* pls. 195ff. (2nd cent.); Laurenzi *Ritr.* no. 103 (1st cent.); Bieber *H* 163 (with further refs.) and figs. 692f. (1st cent.); Richter *POG* I 38 with fig. XLIV (1st cent.); Chamoux in *BCH* 89 (1965) 211–24 with figs. 2f., 6ff.

(portrait of Flaminius, who 'liberated' Greece in 197 B.C.; cf. pp. 522 and 537; coin-portraits of Flaminius, ibid. figs. 4f.; Richter *POG* III fig. 1761; Bieber *H* fig. 323; Seltman *GC* pl. 50, 12; Kraay and Hirmer fig. 579). See also M. Robertson in *Burl.Mag.* March 1966, 150. The treatment of the teeth in this marble and the bronze head (last note) pointed out to me by Denys Haynes.

37. Text on statue of Menander: Pausanias I 12 I (O. 1409). Statue-base: *Eph.Arch.* I (1862) cols. 158f., 178f. 183; Löwy *Inschr.* no. 108; O. 1337; Richter *POG* II 225, figs. 1518ff. Texts on Kephisodotos the younger and Timarchos: p. 480 with Chapter 7 n. 85 (cf. 383 and 396 with Chapter 6 notes 65 and 99). The type and the problem: see Richter *POG* II 224–36, figs. 1514–1643. Medallions: ibid. 227f. no. 1 (lost), old drawings figured 228; 2 (ex Marbury Hall, Cheshire), figs. 1528ff.; 3 (ex Smyrna), figs. 1522f. and on p. 228. Tickets: ibid. nos. 4 and 5, figs. 1531f. Painting: ibid. no. 7, fig. 1515. Mytilene mosaic: 10f., fig. 1517 (other mosaics, 6, 8 and 9, figs. 1514, 1516); cf. especially the marble heads figs. 1561, 1634, 1636f.; the Mytilene floors now published in Charitonidis, Kahil and Ginouvès, the portrait 27–31, pls. 2, 1 and 15, 1; see further p. 581 with n. 216. Reliefs: Richter *POG* II 228 nos. 11–12, figs. 1526f. The head: ibid. 229–34, nos. 1–54, figs. 1533–1636; with wreath, no. 26 (Oxford), figs. 1592–5; with drapery, no. 15 (Venice, among the best), figs. 1573–6 (and on p. 231); double Herm with Homer, no. 7 (Rome, M.N.), figs. 1548f. (the Homer, p. 48 no. 3, figs. 31–4); with probable Hesiod, no. 8 (Rome, Albani), figs. 1551–2 (the 'Hesiod', p. 59 no. 6, figs. 140f.; see p. 527 with n. 64); with another (Richter suggests Aristophanes), nos. 18 (Bonn), figs. 1580–2, and 30 (Wilton), fig. 1591. Epigram on Homer and Menander: see Richter *POG* II 226 no. 4, with fig. Double Herm of Herodotus and Thucydides: ibid. 146 no. 2, figs. 810ff.; 148 no. 1, figs. 825ff. Identification of the type as Menander: Studniczka in *Neue Jahrbücher* 21 (1918) 1–31, followed by a majority of scholars; as Virgil: Carpenter in *MAAR* 18 (1941) 96–100, pls. 29–34 (Villa Medici relief, pls. 31f.), following Lippold in *RM* 33 (1918) 1–18, and Crome *Bildnis Vergils*; as Theocritus: Möbius in *B.Ant.Besch.* 29–31 (1951) 57ff.; as Callimachus: V. Poulsen *Portraits* 74; I am sure I have seen an identification as Apollonius Rhodius, but cannot trace it; Jongkees, in *Mnemosyne* 18 (1965) 145–9, suggests Aristotle. Inscribed bronze bust (Malibu, J. Paul Getty Museum): Ashmole *AJA* 77 (1973) 61, pls. 11f. Similar inscribed bronze busts of Sophocles, p. 510 with n. 19; of Demosthenes, p. 511 with n. 21; of Epicurus, Hermarchos and Zeno, p. 525 with notes 57ff.

38. Among the best of these heads, besides that in Venice cited in the last note, are Richter *POG* II 231ff., nos. 17 (Verona), figs. 1564f.; 35 (Copenhagen I.N. 577), figs. 1589f.; 38 (Boston inv. 97.288), figs. 1621ff.; 45 (Rhodes), figs. 1627ff. The Boston head is also illustrated in Beazley and Ashmole fig. 144 (as Menander); one in Philadelphia (Richter no. 40, figs. 1608ff.) in Lawrence *LGS* pl. 18, 1 (as Menander). Augustan classicism: pp. 602–5 with Epilogue notes 34–40.

39. 'Hellenistic Ruler' (Rome, M.N.): *KB* 339, 6–7; Lippold pl. 105, 4 placed in the period 310–280 B.C.); Laurenzi *Ritr.* pls. 38f. and p. 129 no. 4 (150–140 B.C.); Lullies and Hirmer pls. 250f. (264f.; mid 2nd cent.); Bieber *H* 161f. with refs. and figs. 682f. and 685 (accepting date in mid 2nd cent. and identification as Demetrius I of Syria before his accession in 162 B.C.; Lawrence *LGS* pl. 51 (the same); Richter *POG* III 271, figs. 1886, 1889 (the same; 1887f., coin-portraits of Demetrius); BDFH pl. 312 (296; end of 2nd cent.). See also next note.

40. Identification as Lucullus or Sulla: Carpenter in *MAAR* 18 (1941) 81–93 (as Lucullus) and in *AJA* 49 (1945) 353–7 (as Sulla); part of an allegorical group of the Dioscuri and Amykos, as argued by P. Williams (Lehmann), ibid. 330–47. Bronze boxer (Rome, M.N.): Beazley and Ashmole fig. 202; *KB* 339, 1; Lawrence *LGS* pl. 28; Lippold pl. 134, 2; Lullies and Hirmer pls. 259–61 (275–7); the signature: Carpenter in *MAAR* 6 (1927) 133–6, pls. 49–51; against its existence, Guarducci in *Ann.* 37/8 (N.S. 21/2), 1959/60, 361–5, figs. 1–5. Belvedere torso: p. 543 with n. 104. Ficoroni cista: p. 444 with Chapter 6 n. 219; p. 595 with Epilogue n. 15. Head from Olympia: p. 517 with n. 34.

41. Seleucid coins: Seltman *GC* pls. 52ff. (Antiochus III, 53, 1; Demetrius I, 54, 1); Kraay and Hirmer figs. 740–62 (Antiochus III, 746f.; Demetrius I, 750); Richter *POG* III figs. 1865–77 (Antiochus III, 1865ff.), 1880f., 1884f., 1887f. (Demetrius I), 1892–1909; see also next note. Marble head of Antiochus III (Louvre 1204): Richter *POG* III 271, figs. 1878f.; Arndt-Bruckmann 103f.; Bieber *H* 87, figs. 319f. (coin-portrait, fig. 321); Buschor *Hell. Bild.* fig. 25; *Enc.Phot.* 242f. Head from Cyprus (B.M. 1879): Hinks *G. and R.Port.Sc.* 16 and fig. 186 (mid 1st cent.).

42. Coin-portrait of Antiochus IV: Seltman *GC* pl. 53, 4 and 5; Kraay and Hirmer fig. 749; Richter *POG* III fig. 1884 (1882f., bronze head from Herculaneum, Naples inv. 5596, doubtfully identified). On Antiochus IV see further p. 532. Coin-portraits of Macedonian kings: p. 522 with n. 48.

43. Parthian coins: Seltman *GC* 236, pl. 56; Kraay and Hirmer 379 nos. 781f., pl. 212; Richter *POG* III 277f. figs. 1951–69.

44. Bactrian coins: Seltman *GC* 234f., pl. 55 (2, Euthydemus I; 1, Demetrius I; 4f., Eucratides I; 3, Antimachus I); Kraay and Hirmer 378f., pl. 212 nos. 777 (Demetrius I), 778 (Antimachus I), 779 (Heliocles I), 780 (Archebios); Richter *POG* III figs. 1973 (Diodotus, the Satrap who first revolted from Syria), 1974f. (Euthydemus I), 1976f. (Demetrius I); 1978 (Demetrius II), 1982 (Euthydemus II; 1979–81 show a marble head doubtfully identified with him), 1983 (Agathocles), 1984 (Antimachus I), 1985f. (Eucratides I), 1987 (Plato), 1988 (Heliocles I); 1989–99, Bactrian kings who ruled various parts of India after the collapse of the kingdom; Bieber *H* 86, figs. 310 (Euthydemus I), 316 (Antimachus I).

45. Head in topee (Rome, Albani, ex Torlonia): Richter *POG* III figs. 1970f.; Bieber *H* figs. 311ff.; *KB* 339, 4 (5, coin of Euthydemus I); Lawrence *LGS* pl. 37a. Sacrifice relief (Munich 206): Richter in *Mél.Michalowski*, 625ff., identifying figure as Euthydemus I, figs. 1 (relief), 3 (detail), 2 (coin), and *POG* 278, fig. 1975a (detail); see also p. 545 with n. 110, giving further refs. for the relief. Diademed head (Copenhagen 455): Laurenzi *Ritr.* no. 95, pl. 38; Bieber *H* 87 figs. 317f. (identified as Antimachus I of Bactria); Richter *POG* III figs. 1918f. (identified as Attalos III of Pergamon; on the Pergamene dynasty, see pp. 527–9, 537–8, 546–7).

46. Ay Khanoum: Bernard in *CRAI* 1966, 127–33, figs. 1–3; 1967, 306–23, figs. 1–11 (inscription, 317f.); 1968, 263–79, figs. 1–12; 1969, 313–55, figs. 1–27; also a brief note by Frye in *AJA* 70 (1966) 286.

47. Pontic coin-portraiture: Seltman *GC* 237f., pls. 56, 8 (Mithradates III), 9 (Pharnaces I), 10 (Mithradates IV), 57, 1 (Mithradates IV and his sister-wife Laodice), 2f. (Mithradates VI); Kraay and Hirmer 376f., pls. 200f., nos. 769 (Mithradates III), 770 (Pharnaces I), 771 (Mithradates IV), 772 (Mithradates IV and Laodice), 773–5 (Mithradates VI); Richter *POG* III 275, figs. 1925 (Mithradates III), 1926 (Pharnaces I), 1927 (Mithradates IV), 1928f. (Mithradates VI); Bieber *H* figs. 314 (Mithradates III), 325 (Mithradates IV), 480f. and 484 (Mithradates VI). Marble head (Louvre 2321): Richter *POG* III figs. 1930, 1933; Bieber *H* figs. 482f. See also below pp. 547f. with n. 113.

48. Macedonian coin-portraits: Seltman *GC* pls. 50f. (51, 1 and 2, Philip V; 51, 3, Perseus); Kraay and Hirmer 350ff. pl. 175 nos. 577 (Philip V) and 578 (Perseus); Richter *POG* III 257, figs. 1746 (Philip V; 1747, gem-portrait doubtfully identified); 1748 (Philip V or Perseus); 1749 (Perseus). Flaminius and Aemilius Paulus: p. 518 with n. 36; p. 547 with n. 112.

49. Ptolemaic coin-portraits: Seltman *GC* pls. 58f.; Kraay and Hirmer 381ff., pls. 218–20 and xix–xx, nos. 800–9; Richter *POG* III figs. 1775f., 1779, 1781, 1801f., 1807, 1813f., 1820f., 1827f., 1832, 1835–9; Bieber *H* figs. 306, 308, 340, 344, 356, 360, 364f. See also following notes.

50. Coin-portraits of Berenice II: Seltman *GC* pl. 58, 8f.; Kraay and Hirmer nos. 804 (pl. xx), 805 (pl. 219); Richter *POG* III figs. 1820f.; Bieber *H* fig. 344. Marble head from Cyrene (Benghazi): Richter *POG* figs. 1822f.; Bieber *H* 92, with refs. and figs. 346f.; Laurenzi *Ritr.* no. 71, pls. 25f. Bieber *H* fig. 345 shows a faience jug with a relief-figure of the queen, figs. 357ff., another with Arsinoe III; this class is now studied with full illustration, reference and discussion, by D. Thompson *POPF*. Coin-por-

traits of Ptolemy III: Seltman *GC* pl. 58, 10; Kraay and Hirmer pl. 219 no. 803; Richter *POG* III figs. 1807, 1813f.; Bieber *H* fig. 340. Herm from Herculaneum (Naples): Richter *POG* figs. 1782f. (as Ptolemy II); Bieber *H* figs. 342f. (as Ptolemy III); Laurenzi *Ritr.* no. 56, pl. 21.

51. Marble heads of Ptolemy IV and Arsinoe III (Boston 57–8): Richter *POG* III figs. 1829f. and 1833f. (coin-portraits, figs. 1827f.); Bieber *H* figs. 336–9. Head of Ptolemy VI (Alexandria): Bieber *H* figs. 361–3 (coin-portrait fig. 360); Richter *POG* III figs. 1844–6 (coin-portrait fig. 1838); the head in Providence (54.002; ibid. figs. 1847ff.) is surely a forgery: see *Bulletin of Rhode Island School of Design* 56, 2 (Winter 1969), 'Ptolemy VI: a Prince or a Forgery'; 6–19, Ridgway condemning it; 20–35, Conticello defending it; figs. 1, 3, 5, 7, 10–11, 13, 15, Providence head; 2, 4, 6, 8, 12, 14, Alexandria head; 9, coin-portrait.

52. Coin-portraits of Cleopatra VII: Seltman *GC* pl. 59, 7f.; Kraay and Hirmer pl. 220 no. 809; Richter *POG* III figs. 1790f.; 1805f.; Bieber *H* figs. 364f. Marble head (Vatican): Richter *POG* 1863f.; Bieber *H* figs. 366f. Limestone head (B.M. 1873): Richter *POG* fig. 1862; Bieber *H* figs. 368f.; Hinks *G. and R.Port.Sc.* pl. 18a. Plutarch on the basis of Cleopatra's appeal: *Antony* XXVII 2–4.

53. Examples of Egyptian Ptolemy-portraits: Richter *POG* figs. 1790f., 1805f.; Bieber *H* figs. 350ff., 370f. Egyptianising Greek portraiture: Richter *POG* figs. 1842f.; Bieber *H* figs. 328–34, 348. Portraits of the Ptolemaic age in the Egyptian realistic tradition: Drerup *Äg.Bildnisköpfe gr.u.röm.Z.*, especially pls. 1 and 4–5.

54. Youth in turban (Athens): Lawrence *LGS* pl. 64.

55. Boy from Tralles (Istanbul): Sichtermann in *AP* 4 (1965) 71–85, pls. 39–52 (full publication with earlier refs.; dated to earlier 1st cent. B.C.); Fuchs in BDFH 205, pl. 282 (266; early imperial classicising); Lullies in Lullies and Hirmer[2] pls. 280f. (copy of work dated *c.* 275–50); Ridgway *SS* 69, 75, 126, fig. 114 (early imperial grave-monument); Lawrence *LGS* pls. 74f. Cross-legged pose: pp. 410 with Chapter 6 n. 133, 457 with Chapter 7 n. 27. Ilissos relief: p. 382 with Chapter 6 n. 61.

56. Plato and Socrates: pp. 508–10 with notes 13–17.

57. Portraits of Epicurus: Richter *POG* II 194–200, figs. 1149–1225; the head, 195ff. nos. 1–29, figs. 1149–1210; inscribed: no. 1 (Rome, Capitoline, Sala dei Filosofi 52), double Herm with Metrodorus (next note), figs. 1149f., 1153; no. 8 (Naples inv. 5465, from Herculaneum), small bronze bust with inscription (cf. next two notes), figs. 1175ff.; statue: 198f. nos. 1–5, figs. 1212–19 and on p. 198. Bieber *H* figs. 158 (gem-portrait; cf. Richter *POG* figs. 1221f.), 159 (Herculaneum bronze), 160 (Capitoline Herm), 161f. (head in New York 11.90, Richter *POG* no. 28, figs. 1200–3; also Richter *Cat.* pl. 130 no. 186, and often), 163–6 (statue) and 171.

58. Portraits of Metrodorus: Richter *POG* 200ff., figs. 1226–67; the head, 201f. nos. 1–16, figs. 1226–58; no. 1 (inscribed Herm in Capitoline; see last note), figs. 1230–2; statue: 202, nos. 1–3, figs. 1259–67. Bieber *H* figs. 172 (Capitoline Herm), 173 (statue). Portraits of Hermarchus: Richter *POG* 203–6, figs. 1268–1315; no. 10 (Naples inv. 5466, from Herculaneum), small bronze bust (same set as those in last and next notes, and that of Demosthenes, p. 509 with n. 21), figs. 1291–3; statue: 205, nos. 1f., figs. 1319–24. Bieber *H* figs. 175 (Herculaneum bronze), 176 (statue), 177.

59. Portraits of Zeno: Richter *POG* 186–90, figs. 1054–1105; no. 1 (Naples inv. 6128), inscribed Herm, figs. 1084f., 1089 and on p. 187; no. 2 (Naples inv. 5468, from Herculaneum), small bronze bust with inscription (see last two notes), figs. 1086ff.; no. 4 (Louvre 3242), small double Herm with Plato, figs. 1090f. (Plato, 1666 no. 13, figs. 936f.; cf. p. 509 with n. 13). Seated philosopher, doubtfully identified as Kleanthes, Zeno's successor as head of the Stoa and teacher of Chrysippus (next note); Richter *POG* 189f., figs. 1106–10 (1106, bronze, B.M. 348, *BMCat. Br.* pl. 65). Standing bronze philosopher (New York 10.231.1; *Bronze Cat.* no. 20): Richter *MMH* 124f., pl. 103a (perhaps Hermarchus), *GP* IV 40ff., pl. 21 and *POG* 199, fig. 1220 (perhaps Epicurus).

60. Portraits of Chrysippus: Richter *POG* 190–4, figs. 1111–48; coin of Soli: 191, 193 with fig., and fig. 1147; inscribed bust: 192f., no. 16

(Athens N.M. 3469, ex Epigraphic Museum 3496), fig. 1146; heads: 191f., nos. 1–15, figs. 1111–41; statue: 193, no. 17f., figs. 1142f., and 1144 (restored with cast of head): Bieber *H* figs. 234–7 (heads), 241 (statue), 238–40 and 242 (restored statue). Gem showing similar figure (Cambridge, Corpus Christi College): 191, fig. 1148. Texts on Euboulides: O. 2235–44 (2235, Pliny XXXIV 88, man counting on his fingers). Formula for Chrysippos-statues: Sidonius Apollinaris *Epist.* IX 4 (Richter, 190). On Euboulides see further p. 555 with n. 135.

61. Portrait of Attalus I (?): p. 536 with n. 88. Pergamene Alexander: p. 514 with n. 28. Albani Socrates: p. 509 with n. 16.
62. Portrait of Homer ('Hellenistic blind type'): Richter *POG* I 50, IV nos. 1–22, figs. 58–104; no. 8 (Florence inv. 1646), bronze, figs. 76ff.; no. 11 (Louvre 440), marble, figs. 79f.; Bieber *H* figs. 598 (Florence), 599 (Louvre); Louvre also *Enc.Phot.* 247 and often. Bronze busts in Florence from same set: p. 510 with n. 19. Other Homer types: Richter *POG* 47–50, figs. 1–57.
63. Hellenistic Sophocles (B.M. 847): Richter *POG* 13, IV no. 1, figs. 708–10 (no connection seen with earlier types, p. 510 with n. 19). Other pictures: Arndt-Bruckmann 998f.; *Selected Bronzes* pl. 64.
64. Portrait of 'Hesiod' (pseudo-Seneca): Richter *POG* 58–66, nos. 1–38, with some refs. to the enormous literature and discussion, and figs. 131–212; no. 12 (Naples inv. 5616), bronze from Herculaneum, figs. 165ff.; Bieber *H* figs. 596 (bronze) and 587, doubtfully identifying as Aristophanes. The identification as Hesiod was proposed by Crome in *Bildnis Vergils*; followed by Buschor, *Bildnisstufen* 183f.; Seeberg in *Symb.Osl.* 35 (1959) 110 (publishing two marbles in Oslo, figs. 1–2 and 3–5); and Richter *GP* IV 42f. and *POG* 65f. The bronze head is constantly reproduced: e.g. Beazley and Ashmole fig. 205; *KB* 345, 4; Lawrence *LGS* pl. 48b (a marble, 48a). Statues of Hesiod at Thespiai and in the Muses' sanctuary: Pausanias IX 27 5 and 30 2.
65. Portrait of Poseidonius (Naples inv. 6412): Richter *POG* III 282, fig. 2020; Bieber *H* figs. 696f.

(*ii*) *Sculpture in Pergamon and 'Hellenistic baroque'*

66. Aetolian dedication: Pausanias X 18 7. Coins: Seltman *GC* pl. 62, 3–4; Hill *PCG* 36, 13ff.
67. Coins of Pergamon with Philetaerus's portrait: Seltman *GC* pl. 57, 6; Kraay and Hirmer pl. 203, nos. 736ff.; Hill *PCG* pl. 32, 4; Richter *POG* III figs. 1913f.; Bieber *H* fig. 416; *KB* 339, 1. Herm from Herculaneum (Naples inv. 6418): Richter *POG* figs. 1910ff.; Bieber *H* figs. 418f.
68. Portraits of Antiochus III: p. 521 with n. 41; see further, pp. 537–8.
69. 'Battles of Eumenes and Attalus against the Gauls': Pliny XXXIV 84 (see p. 531 with n. 75). Dedication of Attalus in Athens: Pausanias I 25 2; Plutarch *Antony* LX (944).
70. Marbles presumed copied from Pergamene dedication at Athens (Aix, Louvre, Naples, Vatican, Venice): *KB* 350, 2–6 and 351, 1–9 (351, 6, restored drawing of Persian down on right knee, in Aix, is reversed); other pictures: Beazley and Ashmole fig. 168; Bieber *H* figs. 430–7 (437 shows Aix Persian correctly); *Enc.Phot.* 248A; Lawrence *S* pl. 107b, *LGS* pl. 37b; Lippold pl. 127, 1–4; Richter *Sc.* figs. 120, *H* fig. 232; Ridgway *SS* fig. 9. On the dying Gaul in Naples (*KB* 361, 1; Lippold pl. 127, 2; Richter *H* fig. 232) see further p. 531, with next note; on the dead Amazon in Naples (*KB* 351, 8–9; Lippold pl. 127, 4) see further p. 533 with n. 80. Maderno's St Cecilia (Rome, S. Cecilia): e.g. Venturi *Short History* 331; see also p. 552 with n. 125. Flemish Malchus (Munich, Alte Pinakothek): *Kat.* (1936) 27 no. 990 pl. 64 (ascribed there to Dirk Bouts; elsewhere to Ouwater or his following); see Curtius in *Schweitzer Festschrift* 378ff., pls. 85f.
71. Dying Gaul (Rome, Capitoline): BDFH pl. 288 (272); Bieber *H* figs. 426f.; *KB* 349, 1 (head, 348, 4); Lawrence *S* pl. 107a (head), *LGS* pl. 32; Richter *H* fig. 31; and often. Dying Gaul from small dedication: see last note.
72. Gaul and wife (Rome, M.N.): BDFH pl. 289 (273); Beazley and Ashmole, fig. 170; Bieber

H fig. 424 (man's head); *KB* 348, 1–3; Lawrence *S* pl. 106b; Richter *Sc.* figs. 108, 178 (man's head).

73. Dead Persian's head (Rome, M.N.): Beazley and Ashmole fig. 167; Bieber *H* fig. 425; Br.Br. 515; *KB* 349, 6; Lawrence *LGS* pl. 20; Richter *Sc.* fig. 424; Ridgway *SS* fig. 11.

74. Bases at Pergamon and relation to copies: Schober in *RM* 51 (1936) 104ff., figs. 4f.

75. Pliny XXXIV 84 (O. 1994); and see p. 529 with n. 69, pp. 532–4 with notes 77ff.

76. Acropolis Medusa-head: Pausanias I 21 4. Temple of Olympian Zeus: p. 305 with Chapter 5 n. 34; pp. 604 and 609 with Epilogue notes 37 and 52. Stoa of Eumenes: Hill *ACA* 111 with n. 171; of Attalus ibid. 65 with n. 7; Wycherley *Agora* 3, 46f.; Gymnasium of Ptolemy: Hill *ACA* 92 with n. 1; Wycherley *Agora* 3 142ff.

77. List of artists: p. 531 with n. 75. Isigonos: see p. 533 with n. 80. Pyromachos: see next note. Stratonikos: Pliny XXXIII 156 (O. 2167), XXXIV 85 (O. 2003) and 90 (O. 2002); Athenaeus XI p. 782B (O. 2168). Antigonos: Pliny I ind.auct.lib. XXXIII–XXXIV (O. 2004).

78. Pliny's further refs. to Pyromachos: XXXIV 51 (date; note to O. 2001); XXXIV 80 (chariot with Alcibiades, O. 921); XXXV 146 (master of painter or painters, O. 2001). Phyromachos's or Phylomachos's Asklepios at Pergamon: Diodorus Siculus *Exc.* I XXXI fr. 46 (Phyromachos, O. 1999); Polybius XXXII 25 (Phylomachos, O. 1928). Nikeratos's Asklepios and Hygieia: Pliny XXXIV 80 (O. 919); his Alcibiades and Demarete: ibid. 88 (O. 920); other refs. to the name, O. 917f. Signed base of Nikeratos and Phyromachos at Delos: Löwy *Inschr.* 92, no. 118. Phyromachos of Kephisia: p. 364 with Chapter 6 notes 4f.

79. Base from Delos signed by Nikeratos alone: Löwy *Inschr.* 109f. no. 147. Warrior from Delos (Athens N.M. 247): *BCH* 34 (1910) 478ff.; Beazley and Ashmole fig. 473; Bieber *H* fig. 422; Br.Br. 9; *KB* 351, 1. Gallic head from Delos: Bieber *H* figs. 420f.; another, *KB* 349, 3. Gallic head from Gizeh (Cairo): Bieber *H* figs. 372f.; *KB* 349, 4.

80. Signatures of Epigonos from Pergamon: Löwy *Inschr.* 126 no. 157; 389f. nos. 157a and b; *Perg.* VIII 1 nos. 12, 22b (?), 29 (?), 31 and 32. Text on Epigonos: Pliny XXXIV 88 (O. 2095). Drawing of Amazon and child: *JdI* 8 (1893) 119ff., figs. 2–4. Aristides's picture: Pliny XXXV 98 (O. 1779); Attalus's offer: ibid., and 24 (O. 1782) and VII 126 (O. 1783); cf. Strabo VIII 381, quoting Polybius who was himself present (see Jex-Blake and Sellers on Pliny XXXV 24); also p. 547 with n. 112. Woman's head (Rome M.N.): Bieber *H* figs. 452f.; *KB* 347, 3; Lawrence *LGS* pl. 35. Delacroix's *Massacres de Scio* e.g. Cassou *Delacroix* 5.

81. Menelaus and Patroclus: Bieber *H* fig. 272 and 276 (Florence), 273 (Pasquino), 274–5 (reconstruction), 277 (head of Menelaus in Vatican); *KB* 306, 2 (Pasquino) and 3 (Florence); Lawrence *S* pl. 106a (Florence), *LGS* pl. 112 (Vatican); and often. Iphigeneia group: p. 476 with Chapter 7 n. 78. Achilles and Penthesilea: Lugli in *B.d'A.* II 6 (1925–7) 133ff., figs. 9–12, and 9 (1929–30) 207ff., figs. 1–17; Bieber *H* figs. 278–80; a new reconstruction by Berger in *Gestalt und Geschichte* 61–75, with figs. 1 and 2 and pls. 16–29.

82. Myron's Marsyas: p. 341 with Chapter 5 notes 116f. Praxiteles's satyrs: pp. 389–90 with Chapter 6 notes 80f. Lysippos's satyrs: p. 467 with Chapter 7 notes 51f.; Lysippic dancers: p. 478 with Chapter 7 n. 81. Hellenistic satyrs: e.g. Bieber *H* figs. 559–76, 633–5; *KB* 368; and see pp. 553 and 560f. with notes 131, 149ff.

83. Barberini Faun (Munich): BDFH pls. 300–1 (284–5); Bieber *H* figs. 450f.; *KB* 346, 1; Lawrence *LGS* pl. 34b; Lippold pl. 118, 2; Lullies and Hirmer pls. 234f. (248f.). Bronze satyrs from Herculaneum (Naples): Lippold pl. 118, 3 (bearded); *KB* 346, 2 (beardless); *JdI* 16 (1901) 14, fig. 6 (the same), 1–18, figs. 1–5 and 7f., various restorations of Barberini Faun; removal of restorations: see *Burl.Mag.* June 1972, 435, with figs. 97 and 99 (before and after).

84. Sleeping Ariadne (Vatican): Amelung and Lippold II, Gall.delle statue no. 414, pl. 57; *KB* 364, 5; (Florence): Bieber *H* fig. 624; Milani *Mus. di Firenze* 313 nos. 40f., pl. 152; (both): Br.Br. 167f.; (reconstructed cast Rome, Museo delle Gessi): Richter *H* 157 fig. 326.

85. Victory of Samothrace (Louvre): BDFH pl. 297 (281); Beazley and Ashmole fig. 163;

Bieber *H* figs. 493–6; Br.Br. 85, 85a; *Enc.Phot.* 219–22; *KB* 342, 1 and 2; Lawrence *S* pl. 101; Lippold pl. 126, 4; Lullies and Hirmer pl. 248 (262); Richter *H* 158, fig. 227, *Sc.* fig. 95; and constantly. Dating by excavation, and new fragment of hand: *Hesperia* 21 (1952) 20 (Lehmann) and 44–6 (Charbonneaux), with pls. 12f. See also next note.

86. Victory of Samothrace Rhodian: Thiersch in *Nach.Ges.Gött.* (1931) 338ff. Pythokritos's inscriptions: O. 2009f.; and see Blinkenberg *L* II 53f., 395ff., nos. 147f., 150, 155, 159, 199, 203. The name occurs in a list of bronzeworkers: Pliny XXXIV 91 (O. 2011) qualified as 'makers of atheletes, armed men, hunters and sacrificers'; cf. below p. 555 with n. 135. 'Tragoedia' from Pergamon: *Perg.* VII 1, no. 47 pls. 14f.; Bieber *H* fig. 473; *KB* 359, 3.

87. Marsyas group: *KB* 347, 1 (Dresden disk), 2 (head of Marsyas in red copy, Rome Conservatori), 3 (torso of Marsyas, Berlin), 4 (Scythian, Florence), also 376, 8 (torso of Apollo, Berlin from Pergamon); Bieber *H* 110 with refs., figs. 438–40 (Marsyas, Istanbul, Louvre, Florence), 441–4 (Scythian), 445 (Apollo-torso); the disk in Dresden also: Amelung *Führer ... Florenz* 63f., fig. 16. Other pictures of the statues: BDFH pl. 299 (283; Scythian and Istanbul Marsyas combined in montage); Beazley and Ashmole figs. 171 (Marsyas, Istanbul) and 172 (Scythian); *Enc.Phot.* 232A (Marsyas, Louvre); Lawrence *LGS* pls. 29 (Marsyas, Istanbul), 30a (Scythian), 39 (red Marsyas, Rome, Conservatori). Figures of small Pergamene dedication: p. 530 with n. 70. Zeuxis: pp. 411–13 with Chapter 5 notes 138ff. Marsyas in literature and art: refs. pp. 341–3 with Chapter 5 n. 118 (Myron's group), 395 and 435 with Chapter 6 notes 94ff. (Praxitelean base from Mantinea) and 200 (fourth-century Athenian vase).

88. Chrysippus: p. 526 with n. 60. The wigged head (Berlin): *Perg.* VII 1 no. 130, pls. 31f. and pp. 147–50 figs. 130a–c; Bieber *H* 113 and figs. 452 (without wig), 455f. (with), *KB* 348, 5 (without); Richter *POG* III fig. 1915 (with). Coin-portrait of Eumenes II; *Perg.* VII 1 146, fig. 130d; Bieber *H* fig. 417; Richter *POG* fig. 1917.

89. The Great Altar (mainly Berlin), a selection of the literature: *Perg.* III 1 and 2 (Schrammen *Der große Altar*); von Salis *Altar v.P.*; Schuchardt *Meister*; Kähler *Fries* and *Pergamon*; Rohde *Pergamon*; E. Schmidt *Great Altar*; a good deal illustrated in *KB* 352ff.; and see following notes. Two fragments have recently been discovered in England by Denys Haynes: *Jb.Berl. Mus.* 5 (1963) 1–13, figs. 1–9. Altars of analogous form, of Athena at Priene: Wiegand and others *Priene*, 120ff., figs. 91, 95f.; von Gerkan in *Bonn.Jb.* 129 (1924) 15–35, figs. 1f., pls. 1–3; of Artemis at Magnesia: von Gerkan *Altar*; see also *AA* 38/9 (1923/4) 343–8, fig. 1; and p. 545 with n. 108.

90. Views showing relation of carving to steps, e.g.: *Perg.* III 2 pl. 22; Rohde *Pergamon* figs. 55f.; Schmidt *Great Altar* pls. 4f., 28f.; Bieber *H* fig. 470; Lullies and Hirmer pls. 238f. (251). Archaic temples at Ephesus and Didyma: pp. 83–5 with Chapter 3 notes 29 and 31; pier of later Ephesus temple: p. 409 with Chapter 6 n. 131. Temple of Nike on Acropolis: pp. 348–50 with Chapter 5 notes 137–40; the Victory on the balustrade who steps up: Carpenter *SNTP* fig. 15 and pl. 1.

91. Restoration of the Barberini Faun: p. 534 with n. 83. Transfer of terms: pp. 503, 548.

92. Slabs with Athena and Zeus: *Perg.* III 2, pls. 11f. and 24; Kähler *Fries* pls. 2f., *Pergamon* pls. 8f.; Schmidt *Great Altar* pls. 7, 8, 10 and 11; Beazley and Ashmole fig. 190 (Athena); Bieber *H* figs. 459f.; *KB* 352, 6 and 350, 3; Lullies and Hirmer pls. 240f. (252f.). Parthenon pediments: pp. 299–305 with Chapter 5 notes 18 and 24. Theseus at Marathon: p. 327 with Chapter 5 n. 83. Vase with Erichthonios: p. 253 with Chapter 4 n. 167. Apollo slab: *Perg.* III 2, pl. 9; Kähler *Fries* pl. 5, *Pergamon* pl. 20; Schmidt *Great Altar* pl. 13. Parthenon metopes: pp. 296–9 with Chapter 5 notes 9–17 (refs. on S27, p. 297 with n. 14). Villa Albani relief: p. 368 with Chapter 6 n. 19. Deity driving down on giant: *Perg.* III 2, pls. 4 and 25, 3. Marshal and chariot on Parthenon frieze (pp. 304–11 with Chapter 5 notes 34–43): N17 and 18; Corbett *Sc.Parth.* pl. 16A left. Poseidon from west pediment of Parthenon: pp. 299 and 304 with Chapter 5 n. 31.

93. Lysippic musculature: p. 467 with Chapter 7 n. 50. Piers of Ephesus temple: p. 409 with

Chapter 6 n. 131. Distortions of form on Pergamon frieze: e.g. *Perg.* III 2, pls. 26, 4 and 28, 2; Kähler *Fries* pls. 52ff., esp. 59, 61, 63 right, *Pergamon* pls. 31ff.; Schmidt *Great Altar* pls. 11 (Ge), 43, 46f., 50, 52; Richter *Sc.* fig. 177.

94. Slab with Nyx: *Perg.* III 2, pls. 17 and 25; Kähler *Fries* pl. 15, 26, *Pergamon* pls. 22, 28; Schmidt *Great Altar* pl. 36; Bieber *H* fig. 466; Lullies and Hirmer pl. 245 (257); Richter *Sc.* fig. 334. 'Beautiful head' associated with frieze by Luschey *Funde* 12–19 with figs. 9–14, comparison with Nyx; pictures of head: *Perg.* VII 1, no. 90 pl. 25, Beibl. 15; Beazley and Ashmole fig. 197; Bieber *H* fig. 475; *KB* 359, 1; Lawrence *Sc.* pl. 110b, *LGS* pl. 44; Lippold pl. 124, 4. Names inscribed on frame: cf. p. 453 with Chapter 7 n. 18 (metopes of temple at Tegea).

95. Akroteria: *Perg.* VII 2, 173f. nos. 166f., Beibl. 24; Schmidt *Great Altar* pls. 4–6; Bieber *H* fig. 469 (cf. 458, 470). Arch and vault in Greek architecture: D. S. Robertson 231ff. Michelangelo's Medici tombs in their setting (Florence, S. Lorenzo, New Sacristy): e.g. Touring Club Italiano *Toscana* 1, figs. 120–5.

96. See below, n. 101.

97. Blanckenhagen in *AA* 1969, 264 with n. 19; Magi in *Mem.Pont.Accad.* 3 Ser. 9 (1960), 20; Blinkenberg in *RM* 42 (1927) 180, fig. 1; see below, n. 101.

98. Sperlonga groups: Jacopi *L'Antro* and *L'Antro ed il Museo*; Andreae in *RM* 71 (1964) 238–44 and *Gnomon* 39 (1967) 82, and 41 (1969) 811–15; Säflund *Fynden* (citing further works, p. 110). Blanckenhagen (see last note and n. 101). The relevance of the ship of the Scylla group has been doubted (e.g. Blanckenhagen 268, n. 27) but seems now established.

99. Lysippic sandal-binder: p. 516 with n. 33. Farnese Bull: p. 608 with Epilogue, n. 48.

100. Lessing *Laocoon* Chapters 5 and 26; see Blanckenhagen (next note) 262f. with n. 17. Scarab (B.M. 98.7–15.6): *RM* 42 (1947) fig. 2; Richter *EGGE* no. 851.

101. Blanckenhagen 'Laokoon, Sperlonga und Vergil' in *AA* 1969, 256–75 with figs. 1–16. The literature of the Laocoon is vast; most important the full publication of the group, restored to its original form from the restorations of the Renaissance with much earlier reference: Magi in *Mem.Pont.Acad.* 3 Ser. 9 (1960). Text: Pliny XXXVI 37f. (O. 2031; 2032, Pliny XXXIV 86, a bronzeworker Athenodoros). Inscriptions (some, O. 2033–7) of 1st cent. B.C.: Blinkenberg in *RM* 42 (1927) 177f.; and in Blinkenberg *L* II (*Inscriptions*) i 29–32; their connection with the artist of the group accepted by e.g. Bieber *Laocoon* and *H* 134f., with figs. 530f. (cf. 532f.; the group dated *c.* 50 B.C.); rejected by e.g. Richter *TCP* 67–70, with figs. 66–8 and comparative material 69f. (heads from Pergamon altar) 71 (Centaur, p. 608 with Epilogue n. 50), 72 (Marsyas in Conservatori, above, n. 87; the group dated about 150 B.C.); and Magi l.c., dating it earlier than the altar. There is an interesting article by Ettlinger in *Panofsky* 121–6, figs. 96f. Pictures of the group: e.g. Beazley and Ashmole, figs. 169, 169bis; *KB* 383, 1–2 (3, head of Giant from altar); Lippold pl. 135, 2; Lullies and Hirmer pls. 262f. (278f.); Lawrence *S* pl. 121, *LGS* pl. 67; Richter *H* 163 fig. 265, *Sc.* 225, 708, 769; and constantly.

102. One-view group, or relief: p. 547 with n. 113. Three Graces: p. 550 with n. 120. Portraits of Homer and Hesiod: pp. 526f. with notes 62, 64.

103. Relief found at Catania in 1733: Säflund *Fynden*, 34 fig. 18. Michelangelo's Drunkenness of Noah: e.g. Carli *Tutta la Pittura di Michelangelo* pl. 29.

104. Belvedere torso (Vatican): Helbig *Führer* 3 no. 124; Br.Br. 240; Lippold pl. 134, 1; Richter *Sc.* fig. 771, *TCP* fig. 102. Interpretation as Marsyas: Carpenter in *MAAR* 18 (1941) 84–91, pl. 26; the Apollo torso (Rome, M.N.) 88ff. pls. 27f. Bronze boxer: p. 520 with n. 40.

105. Borghese warrior (Louvre): *KB* 382, 3; Lawrence *S* pl. 114; Richter *Sc.* fig. 107, *TCP* fig. 100. Heroic diagonal: p. 316 with Chapter 5 n. 54. Wrestlers (Florence, Uffizi): Bieber *H* fig. 267; Br.Br. 431; *KB* 340, 4.

106. Relief from Pergamon: *KB* 364, 3. Comparable early classical compositions: pp. 261 and 275 with Chapter 4 notes 180, 212. Wall-paintings from Boscoreale: pp. 571–3 with notes 181ff.

107. Telephos frieze: *Perg.* III 2; Kähler *Pergamon* pls. 36–41; *KB* 354, 5–10 and 355, 5–7 (355, 7, Herakles finding Telephos); Beazley and Ashmole fig. 199; Bieber *H* figs. 477f.; Lawrence *LGS* pl. 49; Lippold pl. 124, 1–2. Telephos at

Tegea: p. 453 with Chapter 7 n. 18; picture from Herculaneum: p. 577 with n. 201. Anticipation of 'continuous style': p. 233 with Chapter 4 n. 135; its development: p. 607 with Epilogue n. 45.

108. Altars at Magnesia and Priene: p. 538 with n. 89; figures from Magnesia altar: *KB* 356, 2; Lippold pl. 132, 2; from Priene altar: Lippold pl. 131, 1. Frieze from Magnesia (Louvre, Berlin, Istanbul): Humann and others *Magnesia* pls. 5 and 12–14; Herkenrath, passim; Bieber *H* fig. 702f. (Berlin); *Enc.Phot.* 250f. and *KB* 356, 1 (Louvre); Mendel *Cat.* nos. 148–87 (Istanbul). Hermogenes and his temples: Dinsmoor 273ff.; D. S. Robertson 153–7; Lawrence *A* 216f. Metopes from Troy: Goethert and Schleif, pls. 34–49 (Augustan); Bieber *H* fig. 488; Br.Br. 102a; *KB* 341, 1; Lippold pl. 110, 1; the temple: Dinsmoor 267; but see Goethert and Schleif. Slabs from Kos and Knidos (where?): Benndorf and Niemann *Reisen* I, pls. 2–4; *KB* 356, 6. Frieze from Teos (Smyrna?, and B.M.): *BMCat.Sc.* III 2570 (no picture); *KB* 356, 7; Arndt–Amelung 1345–8; *AZ* 1875, pl. 5; Pullan *Ant.Ionia* IV pl. 25. Mosaic from Pella: p. 488 with Chapter 7 n. 108 (refs. for Centauresses). Temple at Priene: p. 448 with Chapter 7 n. 6; the frieze (Berlin and B.M.): *BMCat.Sc.* 1165–76 (no picture); *KB* 356, 3–5. Temple of Hecate at Lagina: Dinsmoor 282; D. S. Robertson 338; the frieze (Louvre and Istanbul): Schober *Lagina*; Bieber *H* figs. 704–7; Lippold pl. 132, 3.

109. Copies in B.M., Louvre, Naples and Kephisia; Bieber *H* figs. 656 (B.M.; the woman on the couch has been removed in a restoration) and 657 (Kephisia; an abbreviated version; 655 shows a related relief in the Louvre without the background); *Enc.Phot.* 257 (Louvre); *KB* 366, 1 and Ruesch *Guida* no. 272 (Naples); Schreiber pls. 37–9 (B.M., Louvre and Naples). Praxitelean Dionysus: p. 396 with Chapter 6 n. 98. Lycian reliefs: p. 431 with Chapter 6 n. 188.

110. Sacrifice relief (Munich 206): identification of donor, p. 521 with n. 45; the supposed Rhodian connection, Laurenzi in *Cl.Rh.* V 2 (1932) 9ff., figs. 1–8 and pl. 1, and in *RM* 54 (1939) pl. 11 (cf. figs. 3 and 4); other pictures: Beazley and Ashmole fig. 200; Hausmann *GW* figs. 55f.; *KB* 356, 6; Lawrence *LGS* pl. 41a; Lippold pl. 125, 1. Tanagra figurines and the Herculaneum types: pp. 396 with Chapter 6 n. 98, 497–8 with Chapter 7 n. 84. Variety of scale: p. 375.

111. Pergamene Parthenos: *Perg.* VII 1 no. 24, pl. 8, Beil. 2f., figs. on pp. 34, 39; Kähler *Pergamon* pl. 4; *KB* 273, 1; and see p. 312 with Chapter 5 notes 45, 47. Boy from Tralles: p. 524 with n. 55. Girl from Priene (B.M. 1154): Pullan *Ant.Ionia* IV 31, fig. 16; Reinach *Rep.* II 673, 5. Myron's Athena: pp. 341–3 with Chapter 5 notes 116f.

112. Stoas and Propylon of Athena at Pergamon: *KB* 146, 1–4; Lawrence *A* 209, fig. 115 (stoa); Weickert *Ant.Arch.* fig. 9; Lippold pl. 129, 3–4 (details of sculptured balustrade). The Gaulish revolt: p. 531. Monument of Aemilius Paulus at Delphi: Richter *H* 170, fig. 247. Attalus's offer for Aristides's picture: p. 533 with n. 80.

113. Pergamene monument of Mithradates: *Perg.* VII 2 no. 168, pl. 37, Beil. 25, figs. on pp. 177, 179; Bieber *H* figs. 485–7; *KB* 364, 1 and 2; and see pp. 542–3 with n. 102 (one-view groups), 522 with n. 47 (portraits of Mithradates), 182 with Chapter 4 n. 44 and 413 with Chapter 6 n. 141 (the Sullan sack of Athens).

114. Nile (Vatican): Bieber *H* figs. 407–9 (405, a simpler but related statuette from Alexandria; also Lippold, pl. 117, 3); *KB* 375, 4; Lawrence *S* pl. 131. Tiber (Louvre): *Enc.Phot.* 295B. Parthenon figures: pp. 300–3 with Chapter 5 n. 29. Botticelli's Mars: p. 496 with n. 133; Michelangelo's Adam: e.g. Carli *Tutta la Pittura di Michelangelo* pls. 13 and 15; Venturi *Short History* 274, above; and constantly.

115. Roman Delos: see pp. 564 and 579 with notes 160 and 208, 598 with Epilogue n. 22.

(iii) *Other trends in sculpture*

116. Cnidian: pp. 390–4 with Chapter 6 notes 85ff. Medici (Florence, Uffizi): Br.Br. 734; *KB* 300, 4; (New York): *Bull.Met.* 11 (1953) 241–51 with full illustration. Capitoline (Rome, Capitoline): Bieber *H* figs. 34f.; *KB* 380, 5 and 381, 8; Lawrence *LGS* pl. 7a (cf. g); Richter *H* figs. 112f.; and see p. 209 with Chapter 4 n. 94. Botticelli's Venus: (Florence,

Uffizi): e.g. L. Venturi *Botticelli* pl. 68, and constantly.

117. Aphrodite (Syracuse): *KB* 380; Lawrence *S* pl. 145.

118. Aphrodite from Cyrene (Rome, M.N.): Bieber *H* figs. 386f.; *KB* 380, 6; Lawrence *LGS* pl. 76. 'Genetrix': p. 350 with Chapter 5 n. 141; p. 601 with Epilogue n. 32. Bronze girl (Munich): p. 391 with Chapter 6 n. 84; Esquiline Venus: ibid. and p. 601 with Epilogue n. 32.

119. Praxiteles's *Pseliumene*: Pliny xxxiv 69 (O. 1279). Bronze statuette with arms raised to neck (B.M. 1084): *BMCat.Br.* pl. 5; Bieber *H* fig. 36; Lamb pl. 62d; Richter *Sc.* fig. 49. Aphrodite adjusting sandal: bronze (B.M.): Lippold pl. 116, 3; (Louvre): *Enc.Phot.* 90f. D; marble (New York): Richter *Cat.* no. 156, pl. 112d and f; Bieber *H* fig. 394; terracotta (New York): Bieber *H* fig. 396; (Istanbul, from Priene): *KB* 381, 3.

120. The Three Graces in the round: list of copies, Becatti in *Bull.Comm.Arch.Rom.* 65 (1937) 41ff. figs. 1–12, pls. 1–4; (Siena, Piccolomini Library; found in Rome in mid 15th cent.): *KB* 380, 1; Richter *TCP* fig. 243; (Cyrene): *Not.Arch.* 2 (1916) 41ff. figs. 29f.; two other copies have been found there; (Vatican): Kaschnitz-Weinberg *Mag.del Vat.* pl. 59; (ex Ferroni coll.): *Mitt.d.Inst.* 1 (1949) pl. 7 (pl. 6, Siena). Relief-versions: (Louvre): Clark *The Nude* 88, fig. 72; (Vatican, sarcophagus): Amelung *Sk.Vat.Mus.* 1 2, no. 12, pl. 48. Paintings (Naples): Elia nos. 135, 137; Curtius *WP* 16–19, figs. 12–14; Richter *TCP* fig. 244. It is also a type on the coins of many Greek cities in the imperial period: e.g. Argos, Naxos, Paros, Magnesia on the Maeander, Aphrodisias and Tarsus; pictures: Macdonald *Hunterian* II pl. 60, 20; Grose *McClean* III pl. 329, 11 (both Tarsus).

121. Aphrodite arranging her hair, without drapery, e.g.: Bieber *H* figs. 604 (Rome Colonna), 605 (Baltimore), 390 (faience statuette, Brooklyn); with 'concealing' drapery, e.g.: *KB* 379, 6 (Rome, Capitoline); with 'revealing' drapery, e.g.: Bieber *H* fig. 610. Apollo of Cyrene (B.M. 1380): *KB* 375, 2–3 (ibid. 6, variation in Istanbul, from Tralles); Bieber *H* figs. 678f. (680, marble version in Rome, 681; basalt in Naples). Eros so shown: p. 400 with Chapter 6 n. 110; Hermaphrodite so shown: next note.

122. Cypro-Oriental bearded Aphrodite in Greece (7th-cent. Corinth): Jenkins in *Perachora* I 231f. no. 183, pl. 102, with refs. Carian breasted Zeus: p. 458 with Chapter 7 n. 31. Development towards the Hermaphrodite: p. 389. Types of Hermaphrodite: e.g. Lippold pl. 126, 1; *KB* 377, 3–5 (4, Istanbul, from Pergamon, leaning with 'revealing' drapery, like the Apollo of Cyrene, last note); Bieber *H* fig. 492 (statuette from Rhodes of same type as last); Richter *Sc.* fig. 53 (Istanbul). Hermaphrodites, satyrs, and nymphs: p. 552 with n. 126. See also next note. Story of Hermaphroditos: Roscher, s.v., 2314ff.; Salmacis (ibid. 2317f.): Ovid *Met.* 4 285–388.

123. Texts on sculptors called Polykles: Pliny xxxiv 50 (O. 1138, 102nd Olympiad, with Kephisodotos), 51 (O. 2206, 156th Olympiad), 80 (O. 1146, noble Hermaphrodite); also 34 (O. 2207) and refs. in Cicero (O. 2209), Dio Chrysostom (O. 1145) and Pausanias VI 4 5 and 12 8 and X 34 7 (O. 2208, 2210, 2212). Sleeping Hermaphrodite: Beazley and Ashmole figs. 178, 182 (Rome, M.N.); Bieber *H* figs. 623 (Louvre; mattress by Bernini); *Enc.Phot.* 230f. B and C (Louvre): *KB* 381, 1 (Rome).

124. Pergamene dedications: pp. 529–34 with notes 70ff. Barberini Faun and Sleeping Ariadne: pp. 534–5 with notes 83f.

125. Rokeby Venus: e.g. Lafuente *Velazquez* pl. 146; La Petite Morfi: e.g Bell *French Painting*, pl. 20; Maderno's St Cecilia: p. 530 with n. 70.

126. Hermaphrodites or nymphs romping with satyrs, e.g.: Lippold pl. 113, 1; Bieber *H* figs. 626 (Hermaphrodite; Dresden; a group known in many copies) and 627 (nymph; Rome, Museo Nuovo).

127. Colette *L'Étoile Vesper* (Paris, 1946) 84.

128. Michelangelo's use of male models for female figures, e.g.: Goldscheider *Michelangelo, Drawings* nos. 30 and 60.

129. Sleeping Eros (New York), bronze: Bieber *H* figs. 616–18 (620, marble version in Rome, Conservatori); Richter *Sc.* fig. 121, and in *AJA* 47 (1943) 365ff., figs. 1–7 (8–9, marble in Rome; this also in Beazley and Ashmole, figs. 183f., the original given to the same sculptor – Polykles? – as the Hermaphrodite, and in

Lawrence *LGS* pl. 41b; see also Ashmole in *JHS* 42 (1922) 244f., pl. 10).

130. Text on Aphrodite Kallipygos: Athenaeus XII 554c–e. Naples statue: *KB* 381, 6–7; Säflund *Kallipygos* argues that the figure originally looked forward, as in the tiny bronze statuette-finial of a spatula-handle (22f., figs. 9–11) and is a fourth-century creation; the figure with restorations removed, fig. 19; limestone relief in Kos, fig. 21 (also *Cl.Rh.* 10 (1938) 113–20, figs. 77, 79 (78, Naples statue)). See also M. Robertson in *JHS* 86 (1966) 289f.

131. Satyr-boy looking at his tail: Beazley and Ashmole fig. 165 (marble statuette in Rome, M.N., restored with cast of head in Florence); other copies in Vatican (Helbig *Führer* no. 336) and New York (207; Richter *Cat.* pl. 147a–b). Relief-versions in Vatican (Amelung *Sc.Vat. Mus.* I no. 706, pl. 86) and in reverse in New York (208; Richter *Cat.* pl. 147c; said to be from Hadrian's Villa at Tivoli); perhaps reversed as a pair to the Vatican relief or one like it; cf. pp. 350–1 with Chapter 5 n. 141, 465 with Chapter 7 n. 45; p. 607 with Epilogue n. 47.

132. Venus of Arles (Louvre): *Enc.Phot.* 186; Furtwängler *Meist.* 548, fig. 102, *Mast.* 320, fig. 136; *KB* 312, 2; Lippold pl. 82, 3; Richter *Sc.* fig. 685. Towneley Venus (B.M. 1574): Furtwängler *Meist.* 550, fig. 103, *Mast.* 320, fig. 137. Venus of Capua (Naples): Br.Br. 297; *KB* 312, 1; Furtwängler *Meist.* 629, fig. 127, *Mast.* 385f., figs. 170f. (and cf. p. 607 with Epilogue n. 45). Venus of Milo (Aphrodite of Melos; Louvre): see Furtwängler's account, *Meist.* 601–55, figs. 116–20, *Mast.* 367–401, figs. 158–63; pictures: BDFH pl. 307 (291); Beazley and Ashmole figs. 171–3; Bieber *H* figs. 673–7; Br.Br. 298; *Enc.Phot.* 200–3; *KB* 378; Lawrence *S* pl. 112a; Lippold pl. 130, 3; Lullies and Hirmer pls. 254f. (270f.); Richter *H* 159, fig. 229, *Sc.* fig. 535; and constantly. Bronze head from Satala near Erzincan (B.M.): *KB* 379, 7 (mistakenly as in Istanbul); Lullies and Hirmer pl. 264 (281); a rapturous early account: Newton *Essays on Art and Archaeology* 400ff., reprinted from *The Times* of 10 April 1873.

133. Poseidon from Melos (Athens, N.M. 225): Bieber *H* fig. 684; Karouzou *Cat.Sc.* pl. 66; *KB* 374, 8; Richter *H* 159, fig. 228, *Sc.* fig. 55. Poseidon from Pergamon (Berlin): *Perg.* VII 2 no. 149, p. 36 and fig. on p. 166; *KB* 374, 7. Zeus from Pergamon (Berlin): *Perg.* VII 1 no. 112, pl. 27; *KB* 374, 6. Bactrian coin: Seltman *GC* pl. 55, 3; Kraay and Hirmer pl. 212 no. 778. 'Hellenistic Ruler': p. 520 with notes 39f. Alexander from Magnesia: p. 514 with n. 29. Other figures so constructed: a second Zeus from Pergamon: *Perg.* VII 2 no. 185, Beil. 27; an Asklepios from Munychia (Athens, N.M. 253): Karouzou *Cat.Sc.* pl. 44.

134. Texts on Damophon: Pausanias IV 31 6 (O. 745 and 1757; repair of Pheidias's Zeus, and marble statue of Mother of the Gods at Messene), IV 31 7–10 (O. 1558f.; other marble statues at Messene; VII 20 5 and 7 (O. 1560f.; statues at Aigion in Achaia, one an acrolith); VIII 31 1–5 (O. 1562f.; marble reliefs and acrolithic statues at Megalopolis in Arcadia), VIII 37 1 (O. 1564; monument near Akakesion in Arcadia, in the territory of Lykosoura, the name generally used in modern times for the sanctuary). Excavations at Lykosoura: Cavvadias *Lycosoura*; but see below, n. 136. Reconstruction of monument: Dickins in *BSA* 12 (1903/4), 109ff. and especially 13 (1906/7) 356ff., figs. 1–25, pls. 12–14. Pictures of remains (Athens, N.M.): Bieber *H* figs. 665–7 (Anytos), 668 (coin), 670 (Despoina); *KB* 373, 1–4 (three heads and drapery fragment); Lawrence *LGS* pls. 54f. (two heads); Lippold pl. 124, 1 (Anytos) and 2 (Despoina); Richter *H* 169, fig. 244 (Anytos); *Sc.* figs. 758–61 (three heads).

135. Texts on Euboulides and Eucheir: Pliny XXXIV 88 (O. 2235; Euboulides's man counting on his fingers; p. 526 with n. 60), 91 (O. 2236, Eucheir in same list of bronze-workers as Pythokritos, p. 536 n. 86); Pausanias VIII 14 10 (O. 2237; marble statue in Athens by Eucheir son of Euboulides), I 2 5 (O. 2238; a sanctuary in a stoa in Athens with statues of gods). It is to this that the head of Athena and torso of Nike appear to belong; they were found in association with a base for a group and an inscription apparently belonging to it which can be restored as a signature of Euboulides son of Eucheir of the deme Kropia, O. 2240; Pausanias names Euboulides, but his phrasing suggests that he thought only one statue, an Apollo,

was this artist's. O. 2251: an inscription from Piraeus mentioning a Euboulides son of Eucheir of Kropia; O. 2242: signatures of Eucheir and Euboulides of Kropia, together in that order. Athena-head and Nike-torso: Julius in *AM* 7 (1882) 81ff.; Br.Br. 48f.; *KB* 373, 5f.; Athena-head: Bieber *H* fig. 669; Richter *H* 169 fig. 245, *Sc.* fig. 705. Texts on Eukleides: Pausanias VII 25 9 (O. 1147; marble statues at Boura in Achaia), 26 4 (O. 1148; marble statue of Zeus enthroned at Aigeira in Achaia). Head of Zeus (Athens, N.M.): Bieber *H* figs. 671f.; *KB* 370, 7.

136. Late dating of Lykosoura base: P. W. Lehmann in *Essays ... Lehmann* 190ff.

137. Apuleius *Met.* IV 28–VI 24. A figure of a girl with butterfly-wings appears in an Underworld scene on a lost tomb-relief from Teos, signed by a Rhodian sculptor Damatrios (Demetrios), of perhaps the third or second century B.C.: Bieber *H* fig. 490; Br.Br. 579; *KB* 363, 5: Lippold pl. 125, 3. Eros and Psyche, with bird and butterfly wings respectively, on bronze reliefs at the junction of hydria-handles: *AJA* 50 (1946) 364, figs. 5–9, pls. 24f. (Richter, dating them to the late fourth century; but see Bieber *H* 150 n. 109, who puts them later, surely rightly; cf. pp. 400 with Chapter 6 n. 110, 550 with n. 121). Winged version of the group in terracotta, from Alexandria: *Exp.v.Sieglin* II 2, 121 no. 1. The marble group (Rome, Capitoline): Bieber *H* fig. 638; *KB* 371, 1. There are many other copies, some early Christian.

138. Delos group (Athens, N.M. 3335): *BCH* 30 (1906) 610ff., pls. 13–15 (Bulard); Bieber *H* figs. 629f.; Karouzou *Cat.Sc.* pl. 68; Lawrence *LGS* pl. 63; Lippold pl. 155, 3. The interpretation in the text is Ashmole's (in a lecture, unpublished); message on sandal-sole: see *BM Guide to G. and R. Life* 134. Pan and Daphnis: Beazley and Ashmole fig. 189 (Rome, M.N., part); Bieber *H* fig. 628 (Naples); Br.Br. 731 (Rome); Lippold, pl. 113, 2 (Rome); there are other copies; see also p. 584 with n. 221.

139. Crouching Aphrodite washing: BDFH pl. 285 (269; Rome, M.N.); 757, Bieber *H* figs. 290f. (Louvre from Vienne), 292 (bronze statuette, private, from Beirut), 293 (Louvre ex Borghese); *Enc.Phot.* 228f.; *KB* 346, 3 (both Louvre from Vienne); Lawrence *LGS* pl. 25a (bronze statuette in Louvre); Lippold pl. 112, 1 (Rome); Richter *H* 156 fig. 224 (Rome), *TCP* figs. 150 (Rome), 151 (Vatican), 152f (coins). Dating in fourth century and parallels in minor arts: Lullies *Kauernde Aphrodite*. Doidalsas demolished: Linfert in *AM* 84 (1969) 158–64. Fighting Persians: p. 530 with n. 70; Scythian knifegrinder; p. 536 with n. 87. Painting and sculpture: pp. 335 with Chapter 5 n. 104, 550 with n. 120; p. 584 with n. 223.

140. Crouching Aphrodite wringing out her hair (Rhodes): BDFH pl. 315 (299): Bieber *H* figs. 294f.; Lullies and Hirmer pl. 257 (273); Richter *TCP* fig. 154 (155f. other copies). Standing figures busy with their hair: e.g. Bieber *H* figs. 37, 390, 604. Apelles's Anadyomene: pp. 494f. with Chapter 7 n. 125.

141. Statue in Rhodes (13635): *Cl.Rh.* V 1 (1931) 16–22, pl. 2 and figs. 9–12. Muses: pp. 562–4 with n. 155.

142. Negro musician (Cabinet des Médailles): BDFH pl. 302 (286); Bieber *H* fig. 381; *KB* 369, 3; Lamb pl. 74a; Richter *H* 187 fig. 285, *Sc.* figs. 588ff.; cf. p. 564 with n. 160. Head-jug (B.M. 1955.10–8.1): D. Haynes in *BMQ* 21 (1959) 19f., pl. 4. Similar piece from Egypt: Perdrizet *Coll.Fouquet* no. 94, pl. 25; *KB* 369, 4. Alexandrian terracottas and bronzes: e.g. Bieber *H* figs. 374–92, but similar pieces are found elsewhere: e.g. *KB* 369, 2, 5, 7–10, from various places in Asia Minor.

143. Wasted youth (Dumbarton Oaks 37.31): Richter *Cat.G. and R. Dumbarton Oaks* 32ff., no. 17 pl. 14, with refs. and discussion. Perdikkas and Perdix: see Richter for refs. Erysichthon: Callimachus's Hymn to Demeter, Pfeiffer II 36ff.; a fifth-century vase-painting perhaps of Erysichthon cutting the grove (Bonn): *ARV*[2] 1661, foot, *Paralipomena* 448; *MMAukt.* XIV pl. 20, 80. Discussion of the subject: M. Robertson in *GRBS* 13 (1972) 39–48, especially 42f. Other pictures of the bronze: Lamb pl. 77a; Richter *H* 192, fig. 291, *TCP* fig. 57.

144. Marble children from Agrai: Svoronos in *Eph.Arch.* 1917 87ff. pls. 1a and 2; Bieber *H* fig. 542; cf. M. Robertson in *BMQ* 15 (1952) 64ff. pl. 29. Brauron Bears: Karouzou in *Eph.Arch.* 1957 (1961) 68–83, figs. 1 and 7 and

pls. 18f. (Agrai children, fig. 8 and pl. 20); *BCH* 83 (1959) 595 fig. 25, 84 (1960) 606ff. figs. 6f., 85 (1961) 639f. figs. 2, 4f.; *Ergon* 1958, 56f. figs. 38f., 1959, 17 figs. 16f., 1960, 22ff. figs. 30, 32f.; *Prakt.* 1959, pl. 12b–d. Hellenistic statues of children; e.g. Bieber *H* figs. 534, 536, 538f., 540–50. A pretty head in the Louvre, said to be from Piraeus, *Enc.Phot.* 236B; another in Bonn, said to be from Delphi, B1, *Ant.aus d.Ak.Kunstmuseum, Bonn.* no. 10 pl. 7.

145. Sleeping Eros: p. 553 with n. 129. God from Artemision: p. 196 with Chapter 4 n. 69. Horse (Athens, N.M.): Buschor *GP* 74; Jockey: ibid. 105; Richter *H* 166 fig. 239.

146. Biter (B.M. 1756, from Rome): Br.Br. 54.

147. Marble boy with thorn (B.M. 1755, from Rome): *BMCat.Sc.* III pl. 8; Bieber *H* fig. 550; Br.Br. 322; Richter *AI* fig. 173, *Sc.* fig. 75. Terracotta from Priene: *KB* 369, 2. Bronze Spinario (Rome, Capitoline): Richter *AI* fig. 172 and p. 50, arguing the early date; Carpenter in *MAAR* 18 (1941) 35–41, pls. 15f.; *KB* 235, 3; Lawrence *S* pl. 119a; Ridgway *SS* fig. 164 (head); both dating late; and constantly. Marble bodies of Spinario type in Florence and Berlin, and two heads in Rome, Museo Nuovo (one illustrated, Mustilli *Mus.Muss.* and Carpenter l.c.); see also Richter l.c. 50f. notes 96, 97. Acropolis Hermes: pp. 191 with Chapter 4 n. 59, 473 with Chapter 7 n. 69. Crouching and seated figures from e. pediment at Olympia: p. 279 with Chapter 4 n. 220.

148. Piombino Apollo (p. 183; Louvre): arguments for late dating fully set out with refs. to earlier work by Ridgway in *AP* 7 (1967) 43–75, figs. 1–33, pls. 24–34. Pictures: Richter *AGA* figs. 287f., *Kouroi* no. 181 figs. 533–40; an appendix to the third edition (1970) 152f. with a note on the inscription by Guarducci, argues against Ridgway that the date is fifth century, though perhaps rather sub-archaic than truly archaic; Lippold pl. 37, 2; Lullies and Hirmer pls.88–91 (92–5); see also p. 605. 'Apollo-posture': p. 182.

149. Groups of Pan and satyr: 'all-round' group (Louvre): Bieber *H* fig. 634; 'two-view' group (Ostia): fig. 633; (Vatican): fig. 635. Three Graces: p. 550 with n. 120.

150. 'Invitation to the Dance': reconstruction by Klein in *Zeit.f.bild.Kunst* 20 (1909) 101ff. figs. 1–10; Bieber *H* figs. 562 (satyr, Florence), 563 (nymph, Florence, with false head), 564 (reconstruction), 565 (coin), 566 (nymph, Brussels, with false head), 567 (nymph's head, Venice); *KB* 368, 5–7; Lawrence *LGS* pls. 30b, 31. Tyche of Antioch and Conservatori girl: pp. 470–3 with Chapter 7 notes 61ff. Myron's Athena and Marsyas: pp. 340–3 with Chapter 5 notes 116f.

151. Boy embracing goose: Bieber *H* fig. 285 (Munich); Br.Br. 453 (Capitoline); *Enc.Phot.* 234f. (Louvre); *KB* 370, 1 and 2 (Munich); Lippold pl. 117, 2 (Munich); Richter *Sc.* fig. 762 (Munich); another copy in Vatican (Bieber *H* 81 n. 35). Baby squashing bird (Vienna, from Ephesus): Bieber *H* fig. 634; *KB* 370, 3; Lippold pl. 117, 1. See also next note.

152. 'Boethos': Pliny XXXIV 84 (O. 1597, boy and goose); Pausanias V 17 4 (O. 1596; gilded boy at Olympia by Boethos of Carthage); *Anth.Gr.* III 92, 9 and 10 (O. 1598f.; child dedicated to Asklepios); also Pliny XXXIII 155 (O. 2167) and Cicero *Verr.* IV 14 32 (O. 2184), both on decorative metal-work by 'Boethos'; inscription of Boethos son of Apollodoros of Carthage (Karchedonios) from Ephesus: see Lawrence *S* 301; signature on Herm from wreck at Mahdia of Boethos son of Athanieus of Chalcedon (Chalkedonios): ibid. and *Mon.Piot.* 17 (1909) 45; see further Rumpf 'Boethoi' in *ÖJh* 39 (1952) 86ff. Herm and Agon from Mahdia wreck (Tunis): *Mon.Piot.* l.c. 29–37, pls. 1f. and figs. 1f. (figs. 3f. also from wreck); Bieber *H* figs. 286–9; Richter *Sc.* figs. 763, 766. Most recently and fully: Fuchs *Schiffsfund von Mahdia* 12ff. no. 1 ('Agon' or Eros Enagonios of Boethos of Chalcedon – figure and Herm together – pls. 1–8 and fig. on p. 12).

153. Drunken old woman (Munich): BDFH pl. 282 (298); Beazley and Ashmole fig. 186; Bieber *H* fig. 284; Br.Br. 394; *KB* 345, 8; Lawrence *S* pl. 138b; Lippold pl. 112, 2; Richter *Sc.* fig. 72. Signature of Myron of Thebes from Pergamon *Perg.* VIII no. 136. Lagynos: see Leroux *Lagynos*: Cook *GPP* 207f. fig. 37; Buschor *GV* 260 fig. 276. A very good discussion of the statue and its problems, with refs. to earlier literature: Ridgway *SS* 131 and 146. 'Hesiod': p. 527 with n. 64.

154. Old and poor in Hellenistic sculpture: e.g. Bieber *H* figs. 585–95; *KB* 345, 6 and 7, 369, 6–10; Lawrence *LGS* pl. 68.

155. Early Hellenistic Muses: p. 480 with Chapter 7 n. 85. Circular relief-base from Halicarnassus with nine Muses (B.M. 1106): *KB* 303, 6. Archelaos relief (B.M. 2191, from Bovillae): *BMCat.Sc.* 244–54 with fig. 30; full discussion and refs. to earlier literature in Pinkwart, *AP* 4 (1965) 55–65 figs. 1–3, pls. 28–35, and *Relief des Archaelaos*; see also review by D. Thompson in *AJA* 73 (1969) 384f.; pictures: Bieber *H* fig. 497 (also 404, the portraits); Br.Br. 519; *KB* 363, 6; Lawrence *S* pl. 115; Richter *H* 171 fig. 249. See also notes 157f. below.

156. *Aphlaston*: p. 317 with Chapter 5 n. 60.

157. The Muses: pp. 58–9 with Chapter 2 n. 54, 395 with Chapter 6 n. 94, 480 with Chapter 7 n. 85. Mnemosyne: cf. p. 588 with n. 234.

158. Muses in the round related to those on reliefs: Pinkwart *Relief des Archelaos* pls. 2, 1; 4, 1–2; 7, 3 (leaner; torso in Berlin); 2, 2; 3, 2; 4, 2–4 (Muse with scroll in cave on Archelaos relief; torsos in Venice and Lindos); 3, 1 (Muse with small kithara on Archelaos's relief; torso in Izmir); 9, 1 (figure of similar character in Basle); 5, 2 (Terpsichore; torso from Miletus in Istanbul); 5, 3; 6, 1–2 (seated Muse looking back on Archelaos's relief; torsos in B.M. and Palestrina); 7, 1–2; 8, 1–2 (Urania; torso in Istanbul); 9, 1 (figure of similar character in Basle); 9, 2 (head of leaner, Dresden). Other pictures: Bieber *H* figs. 498 (Terpsichore, Istanbul); 499–500 (Muse in cave, torsos in Istanbul and Kos); 501 (figure of similar character in Istanbul from Miletus); 502 (leaner, torso in Berlin, with modern head of wrong style wrongly set); Lippold, pl. 120, 1 (leaner, Berlin torso restored with Dresden head); 120, 2 (Muse in cave, torso in Istanbul); 120, 3 and 4 (Terpsichore, torso in Istanbul; *KB* 361, 6 (Muse in cave, torso in Venice), 2–5 (figures in related style in Berlin, from Magnesia, Thera and Samos), 7 (leaner in Berlin restored with Dresden head); Beazley and Ashmole figs. 164 (the same) and 152 (Dresden head).

159. Text on Philiskos of Rhodes: Pliny XXXVI 34–5 (O. 2207). Statue from Thasos, probably belonging to base signed by Philiskos son of Polycharmos of Rhodes (Istanbul): Bieber *H* fig. 507; *KB* 361, 7. Seated Muse, perhaps related (Rome, M.N.): Bieber *H* fig. 504. Artemisia, Ada and Themis of Chairestratos: pp. 457–9 with Chapter 7 notes 29–32.

160. Bronze statuette of dancer (New York, ex Baker): D. Thompson in *AJA* 54 (1950) 371–85, figs. 1–3, 11 and 14; related terracottas figs. 4–10, 15, 16; Bieber *H* figs. 378f.; Richter *H* 189 fig. 288; Ridgway *SS* fig. 109. Negro musician: p. 557 with n. 142. Cleopatra and Dioscurides (Delos): *Délos* VIII 1, 218ff., fig. 95; BDFH pl. 311 (295); Bieber *H* fig. 511 (Cleopatra); Buschor *GP* 103 (Cleopatra).

161. Sculpture from Roman Delos: pp. 597–8 with Epilogue notes 22ff.; paintings and mosaics: ibid. and p. 579 with notes 209ff. Mithradates at Pergamon: p. 547 with n. 113. Monument at Nemrud Dagh (above Arsameia, the ancient capital of Commagene): Goell in *Archaeology* 5 (1952) 136–44 with pictures, and in *Mitt.d. deutsch-türkischen Gesellschaft* 30 (1939) 1–5; Akurgal *Turkey* pls. 109–12; Bossert *AA* figs. 1017–19; *ILN* 18 June 1955, 1095.

162. Sullan sack of Athens: pp. 182 with Chapter 4 n. 44, 413 with Chapter 6 n. 141, 548 with n. 115. Lakreitides's relief (Eleusis Museum): Lawrence *LGS* pl. 79. Caryatids of Appius Pulcher (Eleusis and Cambridge): ibid. pl. 65b (Eleusis); Budde and Nicholls *Cat.* pls. 24f. (Cambridge); discussion and refs. ibid. 44ff. no. 81; Hörmann *Inneren Propyläen* pls. 50ff.

163. 'Tower of the Winds' (Horologium of Andronicus Cyrrhestes): Vitruvius I 6 4; Varro *RR* III 5 17; Dinsmoor 289f.; D. S. Robertson 338 with n. 1; Lawrence *A* 237 with pls. 132b–135; the reliefs: Br.Br. 30; *KB* 375, 5–6. Relief with horse and groom (Athens, N.M. 4464): Karouzou *Cat.Sc.* pl. 49 (horse's head).

(*iv*) *Painting and mosaic*

164. Kazanlak tomb: Micoff and Vassiliev; both have fairly full illustration in black-and-white and colour, Vassiliev's in the main perhaps slightly better; some pictures also: *Antiquity* 27 (1953) 96f. pl. 102.

165. 'Pausian' florals: pp. 486–9 with Chapter 7

notes 103–111; pp. 568 with n. 170, 581 with n. 215.

166. Youth with horses: Micoff pl. 21; Vassiliev pls. 24f., 41f.; see also p. 570. Woman with tray: Micoff pls. 17 and 29; Vassiliev pls. 13 and 36. Soldier leaning on spear: Micoff pls. 16–18 and 31; Vassiliev pls. 27–8 and 43. Girl from Anzio: p. 479 with Chapter 7 n. 83; 'Hellenistic Ruler': pp. 519–20 with n. 39, and 554.

167. Interpretation as wedding: D. Thompson in *AJA* 60 (1956) 295f. Attic loutrophoroi: pp. 371–2 and 381 with Chapter 6 notes 26, 29 and 57.

168. Pausias's vaults and Athens mosaic: p. 487 with Chapter 7 n. 106. Palace at Vergina-Palatitsa: p. 487 with Chapter 7 n. 107. Circular floor at Pella: Laourdas and Makaronas *Arkhaia Makedonia* pl. 18.

169. Leucadia tomb: Petsas, with full and excellent illustration in black-and-white and colour. The façade restored in colour: pl. A′ (small reproduction in black-and-white, Kurtz and Boardman pl. 75; plan and section ibid. 275 fig. 61). See following notes.

170. Petsas pls. A′, B′, E′, I′, 30b, 32–3.

171. Frieze: Petsas pls. A′, 27–30; pediment: Petsas 171 fig. 36. 'Doors': Petsas pls. A′, 35f.

172. Metopes: Petsas pls. A′, Γ′, Δ′, I′, 28b, 29a, 31. Parthenon Centaur-metopes: p. 297 with Chapter 5 n. 14. Zeuxis's *monochromata ex albo* and Herculaneum paintings: p. 425 with Chapter 6 n. 170.

173. Painting from tomb of Mustafa Pasha at Alexandria: *Ann.du Musée gréco-romain à Alexandrie 1933–5* (1936) pl. 27; *Criticà d'Arte* 6 (1941) pl. 10, 21; Brown *Pt.P.* pl. 24, 1. Pergamene stoas: p. 546 with n. 112. Vergina palace: p. 487 with Chapter 7 n. 107.

174. Paintings between columns: Petsas pls. A′, Ϛ′, Z′, H′, Θ′, I′, 5–10; the Hermes also, in outline sketch: *AM* 76 (1961) 99 fig. 2 (Karouzou).

175. Petsas pls. Ϛ′, Z′, 5, 6.

176. Petsas pls. H′, 7, 9.

177. Petsas pls. Θ′, I′, 8, 10.

178. Pausanias x 30 8; on the picture, see pp. 266–70 with Chapter 4 notes 189ff.

179. Fight in 'Tomb at Niaousta': Kinch *Tombeau de Niausta* pl. 3; Pfuhl *MuZ* fig. 750; Rumpf *MZ* pl. 50, 5; Brown *Pt.P.* pl. 18, 2. Motive on the Bassae frieze: p. 358 with Chapter 5 n. 164. Stucco relief-frieze at Leucadia: above, n. 171; painted frieze at Kazanlak: p. 566. Alexander mosaic: pp. 497–503 with Chapter 7 notes 136ff. Alexander sarcophagus: pp. 481–2 with Chapter 7 n. 87.

180. *AAA* 6 (1973) 87–92 with colour-plate 1 (C. Rhomiopoulou).

181. Barnabei; the paintings of the great hall (H on plan, pl. 2): pls. 5–8 and pp. 47–62 with figs. 11 and 12. The other principal publication: P. W. Lehmann, a reliable and fully illustrated account, not only of the pieces in New York; the paintings of the great hall, pls. 1–9 and pp. 23–81. Other pictures in Sambon (catalogue of the sale); the paintings from the great hall pls. 1–3 and figs. on pp. 14f.; the 'reconstruction' on p. 12 (reproduced by Kraiker *MG* 134, and Curtius *WP* 110, fig. 77) is false (see Lehmann, 63); Beazley and Ashmole fig. 208; Curtius *WP* 86 and 119; Kraiker *MG* pls. 70–6; Maiuri *RP* 64; Pfuhl *MuZ* figs. 716–18 (see II 879); Rumpf *MZ* pl. 52, 1. The most important discussions are by Barnabei, Lehmann, Pfuhl and Rumpf; and Studniczka in *JdI* 38/9 (1923) 64ff., Bieber in *AJA* 57 (1953) 237ff. and 60 (1956) 171f. (with a note by Bothmer identifying some rediscovered fragments), M. Robertson in *JRS* 45 (1955) 58ff., and E. Simon *Fürstenbilder*; all with illustration. See also following notes.

182. The fragments are divided between Naples (the ruined Venus from the end wall and the figures from the left-hand wall) and New York (the figures from the right-hand wall and the little pictures shown as standing on the cornice of the end wall; on these see p. 574 with n. 190). Interpretations fall into three classes: mythological-religious (Barnabei, Lehmann); historical (Studniczka, Rumpf, Robertson, Simon); and portraiture contemporary with the house (Pfuhl, Bieber). I am convinced of the rightness of the historical approach, but not necessarily of my own interpretation (*JRS* l.c. last note) except for the identification of the figure in the *kausia* as a personification of Macedonia.

183. Spear and cornice: p. 257 with Chapter 4 n. 171; cf. pp. 584–5 with n. 225, 599 with Epilogue n. 25. Arcadia: p. 577 with notes 201f., Aetolia: p. 529 with n. 66.

184. *JRS* l.c. note 181.
185. Aetion's picture: p. 496 with Chapter 7 n. 133.
186. Tyche of Antioch: pp. 470–2 with Chapter 7 notes 61–3. Dying Gaul: p. 531 with n. 71. Barberini Faun: p. 534 with n. 83. Pictorial relief: p. 543 with n. 106.
187. Arcadia: p. 577 with notes 201f. Polygnotos: pp. 242–70 (Chapter 4, vi). Constantine's Dream: e.g. Clark *Piero della Francesca* pl. 52. Lunettes and spandrels on the Sistine ceiling: e.g. Carli *Tutta la Pittura di Michelangelo* pls. 78–83.
188. Architectural setting: pp. 578 with n. 203, 598 with Epilogue notes 24ff. Exploration of space: pp. 586–8 with notes 227ff. Centuripe vases: Libertini *Centuripe*; Richter in *MMS* 2 (1929/30) 187–205, figs. 1–15 and col. pl., and 4 (1932/3) 45–54, figs. 1–8 and col. pl. Rumpf *MZ* pl. 52, 2–3; M. Robertson 173f. Lipari vases: Trendall *RLCS* 579 and 652–64, pls. 235–6 (also a slightly earlier vase from Falcone on the mainland, 625 and frontispiece).
189. See p. 413 with Chapter 6 n. 141 (copy of Zeuxis's Centaur-family left in Athens when original was taken to Rome after the Sullan sack in 88 B.C.; presumably made then); and 435 with Chapter 6 n. 199 (copy of Euphranor's Battle of Mantinea (in the Stoa of Zeus at Athens) seen by Pausanias at Mantinea in a room otherwise devoted to Antinous, so probably painted soon after A.D. 130; on Antinous, see pp. 608f. with Epilogue n. 51).
190. Little pictures on the cornice above the big figures on the end wall in the great hall at Boscoreale: Barnabei 53, fig. 11 (sketch showing position of central one); P. W. Lehmann pl. 8A and B, pp. 29f., figs. 24, 26, pp. 63ff., 144ff.; and see M. Robertson in *JRS* 45 (1955) 65. Other such pictures are very frequent: e.g. Pfuhl *MuZ* figs. 689f. and 708; Rumpf *MZ* pls. 52, 5 and 59, 2; Ducati *Pittura* pl. 40, all these from houses in Rome ('House of Livia' and 'House by the Tiber'). The beautiful little pictures from the 'Imperial Villa' at Pompeii (Maiuri *RP* 106–9) are of the same kind, though the doors are not shown in the illustrations; they are very like those from the House by the Tiber.
191. Stabiae decorations, 9243 (Helbig 239, 'Diana'), 8978 (Helbig 1265, 'Medea'), 9546 (Helbig 150, 'Leda'), 8834 (Helbig 1886, 'Persephone'): Elia nos. 254–7, fig. 52 (flower-gatherer); Maiuri *RP* 82f. ('Diana' and flower-gatherer); flower-gatherer also: Curtius *WP* pl. 6; Pfuhl *MuZ* fig. 688; Rumpf *MZ* pl. 61, 6; and often. Girl from Anzio: p. 479 with Chapter 7 n. 83; Sotades Painter's apple-gatherer: p. 264 with Chapter 4 n. 187.
192. Inserted stuccoes from Herculaneum pp. 582–3 with n. 219.
193. Book illustration in antiquity: see Weitzmann *Roll and Codex* and *Illumination*.
194. Herakles and Omphale, from the House of Marcus Lucretius, Pompeii (Naples 8992): Helbig 1140, Elia no. 46; Beazley and Ashmole fig. 209; *Corolla Curtius* pl. 67; Herrmann pls. 59f.; Pfuhl *MuZ* fig. 664; Rumpf *MZ* pl. 63, 6.
195. Herakles and Omphale in landscape: Helbig 1137–9; *Mem.dell'Inst.* 2 pl. 7; *ÖJh* 13 (1910) 129; Raoul-Rochette *Choix* pl. 19. See also p. 496 with Chapter 7 n. 133.
196. Petronius *Sat.* 28 5.
197. Lysippic tired Herakles: p. 467 with Chapter 7 n. 50. Dionysus leaning on satyr: e.g. late fifth-century Attic red-figure oinochoai, Athens 1218 and 1219, ARV^2 1212 middle nos. 2 and 1; Pfuhl *MuZ* fig. 568; leaning on Ariadne: early fourth-century Attic red-figure cup, B.M. E129, ARV^2 1414, Meleager Painter no. 89; *JHS* 80 (1960) pl. 5. Cf. also the Hellenistic pictorial relief, p. 545 with n. 109. 'Revealing' drapery: p. 550 with n. 121.
198. Io in Egypt (Naples 9555, from Pompeii): Helbig 139; Elia no. 102; Curtius *WP* 216ff. figs. 127f.; Pfuhl *MuZ* fig. 21. Aphrodite and Ares (Naples 9248, from Pompeii): Helbig 320; Elia no. 121, fig. 21; Curtius *WP* pl. 1 and p. 252 fig. 149. Paris: Hermann pl. 219. Orpheus: Pompeii, House of Orpheus, garden, Hermann pl. 240. Tableaux: Theocritus XV (lines 110–29, O. 1989); Athenaeus, e.g. V 196A 33 (floats at great pageant of Ptolemy II, described by Kallixenos of Rhodes; O. 1990).
199. Classical and Late Antique frontality: pp. 353–4 with Chapter 5 n. 154, 435 with Chapter 6 n. 200; p. 610 with Epilogue n. 56.
200. Other pictures from House of Marcus Lucretius: child Dionysus on cart (Naples): Helbig 379; Curtius *WP* 299 fig. 172; Herrmann pl. 61 (cf. a small picture in the House of Lucretius

Fronto, Curtius *WP* 55 fig. 35 and 297 fig. 171); Trophy (still *in situ*) Helbig 565; Herrmann pls. 62f.

201. Herakles and Telephos from Basilica at Herculaneum (Naples 9008): Helbig 1143; Elia no. 19; Beazley and Ashmole fig. 210; Curtius *WP* 2–9, figs. 2–6; Pfuhl *MuZ* fig. 659; and see next note. Theseus: p. 443 with Chapter 6 n. 218. Other pictures from building: see p. 584 with n. 221. Small frieze of Great Altar of Pergamon: p. 544 with n. 107; Temple at Tegea: p. 453 with Chapter 7 n. 17.

202. Ingres's Madame Moitessier (London, National Gallery, 4821): e.g. *Burl.Mag.* 68 (1936) pl. 4c. Ambrogio Lorenzetti's Peace (Siena, Palazzo Pubblico; also above, Chapter 4 n. 177): e.g. Venturi *Short History* 137.

203. Paintings in Alexandrian tombs: Brown *Pt.P.* 52ff. pls. 22–31; Rumpf *MZ* pl. 57, 2; and see p. 569 with n. 173; in houses at Delos: *Délos* VIII passim; *Mon.Piot.* 14 (1908) pls. 6, 6A; D. S. Robertson pl. 22; Lawrence *A* pls. 38–42; Curtius *WP* 57 fig. 36, 67 fig. 43. 'First Pompeian Style' in Italy: Mau *Wandmalerei* 11–123; Curtius *WP* 61 fig. 41, 64 fig. 43; Maiuri *Pompeii* pl. 39. Architectural painting: pp. 598–9 with Epilogue notes 25ff.

204. See however p. 598 with Epilogue n. 22.

205. Pebble-mosaic: pp. 486–9 with Chapter 7 notes 104–10. Early mosaics from Alexandria: Brown *Pt.P.* 68f. nos. 50, pl. 44, 1 (hunting Erotes) and 51, pl. 44, 2 (fight); M. Robertson in *JHS* 85 (1965) 86f., pl. 21, 1 (fight) and 3 (Erotes).

206. Ganymede from Morgantina: Phillips in *Art Bull.* 42 (1960) 244–62 with illustration; see also p. 460 with Chapter 7 n. 36. Mosaics in Hieron's galley: Athenaeus V 206D 41 (O. 1985). Miniature mosaics: p. 581 with n. 216. The case for Sicilian priority is argued by Phillips. I owe my knowledge of the Euhesperides floor to Michael Vickers.

207. Brown *Pt.P.* 67f. no. 48, pls. 38–40.

208. Circle in square at Olynthus: Robinson *Olynthus* V pls. i, iii, 12, 13A; and in *AJA* 36 (1932) pls. 1–3; Richter *H* 276 fig. 396; at Corinth: *AJA* 23 (1929) 526ff. fig. 10; at Athens and Vergina: p. 487 with Chapter 7 notes 106f. Asklepiades's floor: *Délos* VIII pl. 53; *Mon.Piot* 14 (1908) pls. 12 and 13; details, Lawrence *A* pl. 141b; *JHS* 85 (1965) pl. 21, 2.

209. Delos pard-rider: *Délos* XIV pl. 3 and p. 15 fig. 4; *Mon.Piot* 14 (1908) pl. 15; Rumpf *MZ* pl. 56, 3; *JHS* 85 (1965) pl. 22, 1. Dionysus on panther from Pella: p. 487 with Chapter 7 n. 108.

210. Masks in mosaic-borders: from Pergamon: *Perg.* V 1, pl. 12; Rumpf *MZ* pl. 56, 4; from Pompeii: Rumpf *MZ* pl. 53, 3 and pl. 56, 1 (see also below, n. 214); Ducati *Pitt.* pl. 111 (in surround of a picture of Eros riding a lion). Attic red-figure plate-fragment (Boston 10.187): *ARV*² 1337 no. 10; Hahland pl. 17b; Metzger *Rép.* pl. 19, 2; *JHS* 85 (1965) pl. 22, 2; see refs. on the Derveni krater, pp. 482–5 with Chapter 7 notes 93f.

211. Nilotic mosaics: e.g. Elia figs. 50f.; Pfuhl *MuZ* fig. 698; Rumpf *MZ* pl. 69, 1; Ducati *Pitt.* pl. 105; also p. 502 with Chapter 7 n. 148; p. 589 with notes 236f.

212. Pompeian fish-mosaics: e.g. Naples 9997 (from the House of the Faun); Elia 139f. no. 400, fig. 52; Rumpf *MZ* pl. 56, 6; another, Pfuhl *MuZ* fig. 697. Pebble-mosaic from Temple of Zeus at Olympia: see now Yalouris in *AAA* 1 (1968) 78–82, figs. 1–4; earlier refs.: Blouet *Exp.de Morée* I pl. 64; Dörpfeld in *Ol.* II 10 pl. 105; Rumpf *MZ* 123f.; M. Robertson in *JHS* 85 (1965) 259. Fish-plates: Lacroix passim; Cook *GPP* 240 (but see Shefton in *JHS* 85 (1965) 259); Trendall in *JHS* 57 (1937) 268f.; Rumpf *MZ* 124f. (also on Androkydes). Fish in border: Apulian 'loutrophoros', Naples H3225; *AJA* 71 (1968) pl. 10 fig. 24. Texts on Androkydes of Cyzicus: O. 1649 (Pliny XXXV 64, in a list with Zeuxis, Timanthes, Eupompos and Parrhasios) and 1731–5 (1731, Plutarch *Pelopidas* 25 7, Androkydes working in Thebes at the time of the battle of Leuctra, 371 B.C.; 1732f., Athenaeus VIII 341 and Plutarch *Symposium* IV 2 3 8, Androkydes taking special pains with the fish in a picture of Scylla because he was fond of sea-food).

213. Cat-mosaic from the House of the Faun (Naples 9993): Pfuhl *MuZ* fig. 702; Rumpf *MZ* 57, 3; Ducati *Pitt.* pl. 116; Bianchi Bandinelli *Storicità* pl. 95, 1 (2 and 3, later versions from Rome). Pompeian still-life paintings on two levels: ibid. pls. 91f.; Elia fig. 43 (a different

composition, fig. 42; cf. nos. 315–36 and Rumpf *MZ* pl. 62, 6); with glass vessel: Beazley and Ashmole fig. 214; Pfuhl *MuZ* fig. 703. Pausias's flowers and glass: p. 486 with Chapter 7 n. 102. *Xenia*: Vitruvius 6 10.

214. Signatures on pebble-floors: (... on in Athens, Gnosis in Pella); pp. 487–9 with Chapter 7 notes 106, 108, 111. Sophilos and Asklepiades: p. 579 with notes 207f. Text on Sosos: Pliny XXXVI 184 (O. 2158; cf. 2159f.). Roman mosaics with versions of doves and vase: e.g. Pfuhl *MuZ* fig. 700 (from Hadrian's Villa at Tivoli; also Ducati *Pitt.* pl. 115, 1); Rumpf *MZ* pl. 56, 1 (Pompeii; in garland-border with masks; cf. above, n. 210); Unswept Floor: Nogara pls. 5–7; Swindler *AP* fig. 488.

215. Hephaistion's floor (from 'Palace V' at Pergamon, dated to reign of Eumenes II, 197–159 B.C.): *Perg.* V 1 Textb. pls. 27–8; Tafelb. pls. 16ff.; Brown *Pt.P.* pl. 39, 1; Rohde *Pergamon* figs. 11–13 (cartellino and details of scroll). 'Peopled scrolls': Toynbee and Ward-Perkins in *PBSR* 18 (1950) 1–43, pls. 1–26 (pl. 3, 2, detail of Hephaistion's; 3, 3, detail from border of Pompeian fish-mosaic); see also p. 608 with Epilogue n. 49.

216. Dioskourides's mosaics (Naples 9985 and 9987): Elia 141 nos. 401 (9985, musicians) and 402 (9987, women); Beazley and Ashmole fig. 213 (women); Curtius *WP* pls. 9f.; Pfuhl *MuZ* figs. 684f.; Rumpf *MZ* pl. 51, 5 and 8; Maiuri *RP* 96 (detail of musicians); and often. On the connection with Menander's *Synaristosai*, see Webster *GTP* 23f. Mosaic from Mytilene: Charitonidis, Kahil and Ginouvés pls. 5, 1 and 19, 2 (part of series with portrait of Menander, p. 518 with n. 37).

217. Stele of Helixo (Alexandria): Brown *Pt.P.* pl. 16, 1 (other Alexandrian stelai, on pls. 1–23); Rumpf *MZ* pl. 51, 7 (another, 6); and see Adriani in *BSRAA* 32 (1938) 113–31 pls. 13f. (others, figs. 1–4). Stele from Amathus (B.M. 6): Rumpf *MZ* pl. 51, 2; M. Robertson 171. Stelai from Pagasai (Volos Museum): Arvanitopoulos (Hediste pl. 2 and figs. 170–3); Rumpf *MZ* pl. 53, 1 (Hediste) and 2; Brown *Pt.P.* pls. 16, 2; 19, 3.

218. Niobe picture (Naples 109370, from Pompeii): Elia no. 52; *JdI* 42 (1927) 89 fig. 9; Pfuhl *MuZ* fig. 652; Rumpf *MZ* pl. 51, 3.

219. Inserted stuccoes (p. 575 with n. 192; Naples 9019–22): Elia nos. 245 (9019, actor), 246 (9022, women), 248 (9020, throned youth), 249 (9021, musicians); Pfuhl *MuZ* figs. 653 (actor) and 654 (musicians); Rumpf *MZ* pls. 51, 1 (actor) and 54, 1 (women); Curtius *WP* 269–75 figs. 160–3 (omitting musicians); Ducati *Pitt.* pls. 86 (actor) and 87 (musicians); Maiuri *RP* 82 (detail of actor); Bulle in *Festschrift Loeb* 10–12, figs. 2–4 (actor; cf. fig. 5). Fourth-century compositional scheme: p. 440 with Chapter 6 n. 212.

220. Achilles on Skyros (Naples 9110, fragment, and 116085, both from Pompeii): Elia nos. 21 (fragment, fig. 2) and 22; Pfuhl *MuZ* figs. 650f.; Bianchi Bandinelli *Storicità* pls. 86 (fragment) and 88 fig. 174; Curtius *WP* 207–9 figs. 124f. (fragment) and pl. 2; the fragment also, Beazley and Ashmole fig. 207; Ducati *Pitt.* pls. 62f.; Maiuri *RP* 73.

221. Painting of Cheiron and Achilles from Basilica at Herculaneum (Naples 9019): Elia no. 25, fig. 5; *HBr.* pl. 82; Curtius *WP* 13 fig. 9; Ducati *Pitt.* pl. 89; Napoli *Pittura* pl. 41; cf. also pp. 443 with Chapter 6 n. 218, 577 with n. 201. Marsyas and Olympos (Naples, no number): Elia no. 6; *HBr.* pl. 87 and fig. 29. Painting showing the two sculptural groups: Aphrodite and Adonis, *in situ* in Pompeii VI 7 18 (Casa di Adonide Ferito): Pfuhl *MuZ* fig. 669. Text on marble groups: Pliny XXXVI 29; see Bieber *H* 147. Head of Cheiron (Rome, Conservatori): Beazley and Ashmole figs. 187f.; Lawrence *LGS* pl. 46b. Group of Pan and Daphnis: p. 556 with n. 138. Polygnotos's Marsyas and Olympos: p. 270 with Chapter 4 n. 200.

222. Text on Athenion: Pliny XXXV 134 (O. 1975, with Pausanias I 26 3, which seems to link a painting of Athenion's with events of the end of the fourth century. Pliny's sentence about the painter's early death is omitted by O.).

223. Painting anticipating sculpture: pp. 335 with Chapter 5 n. 104, 556–7 with notes 139f.; but see also p. 550 with n. 120.

224. Thetis in Hephaestus's shop (Naples 9528, from Pompeii): Elia no. 128, pl. 4 (nos. 129f., inferior versions); Curtius *WP* 227 fig. 134 (figs. 130–3, inferior versions).

225. For instance in Raphael's Mass of Bolsena (p.

257 with Chapter 4 n. 171); see also p. 572 with n. 183; p. 599 with Epilogue n. 25.

226. Reflection in shield on Alexander Mosaic: p. 501 with Chapter 7 n. 145. Catoptromancy (distinguished from lecanomancy): Delatte *Catoptromancie*; Dunbabin in *BSA* 46 (1951) 67.

227. Architectural decorative schemes: p. 599 with Epilogue notes 25ff.

228. Cubiculum at Boscoreale: Barnabei 71–81 with figs. 17ff. and pls. 9f.; these show the room as it was found; the painted walls were detached, and have been reconstructed as a room in New York (see p. 599 with Epilogue n. 25); full and admirable publication (though I disagree with her interpretations) by P. W. Lehmann. Other pictures: Curtius *WP* 103–9 figs. 20–3; Pfuhl *MuZ* fig. 707; Rumpf *MZ* pls. 54, 3–5; 57, 11; Sambon pls. 8–10, figs. on pp. 22–5; Webster *GTP* pl. 23.

229. Barnabei 72; the vaulted ceiling visible in pl. 9, the mosaic floor in pl. 10.

230. Vitruvius v 6 9 (definition of tragic, satyric and comic sets), vii 5 2 (their use by wall-painters); see Rumpf in *JHS* 67 (1947) 18; Webster *GTP* 26.

231. Barnabei 64f., figs. 13 (Naples) and 14 (Mariemont); the Naples wall also Lehmann 20, Curtius *WP* 84f. figs. 58f.; M. Robertson 177; White pl. 7b; the Mariemont: Lehmann 21; Curtius *WP* 82f. figs. 56f. (fig. 55 appears to be a lost fragment from a third wall); Sambon pl. 7 and fig. on p. 18.

232. Corinthian oecus of the House of the Labyrinth, Pompeii: Beyen 25f., fig. 94; White pl. 7a. Room of the Masks in the House of Augustus on the Palatine, Rome: Carettoni in *BdA* 40 (1961) 191–9 figs. 4–12; Little *RPPAS* 8f. frontispiece, above; pls. 3, 1 and 3, and 9. Vitruvius on perspective: i 2 2 and vii praef. 11; see White 43–69, with full discussion of the texts and evidence from Roman wall-painting; also Little *RPPAS* passim. Agatharchos: pp. 414–15 with Chapter 6 notes 144ff.; also p. 588 with n. 234.

233. Evidence from Oropos, Priene and Ephesus, connected with Boscoreale paintings: Rumpf in *JHS* 67 (1947) 18f.; Webster *GTP* especially 140. Reconstruction of Priene theatre in this form: D. S. Robertson 107 fig. 73; *KB* 155, 5. Good example of permanent stone stage at Aspendus (2nd. cent. A.D., but the principle goes back to Republican times): D. S. Robertson 278 fig. 117; *KB* 176, 8.

234. Text on Apaturius of Alabanda: Vitruvius vii 5 4 (O. 2117). Texts on Eudoros and Simonides: Pliny xxxv 141 and 143 (O. 2154). Mnemosyne: p. 563 with n. 155.

235. Odyssey landscapes: see especially Blanckenhagen in *RM* 70 (1963) 100–46, pls. 44–53, with earlier refs. and advancing the theory here outlined; see also n. 237. Pictures: e.g. Beazley and Ashmole fig. 215; Pfuhl *MuZ* figs. 721f.; Rumpf *MZ* pl. 55, 1–2. Landscape in Hellenistic reliefs: pp. 544–6 with notes 107, 109f.

236. Texts on Demetrios: Diodorus Siculus *Exc.* i xxxi p. 534 ('Demetrios son of Seleukos'), and *Exc. Vat.* iii p. 96 ('Demetrios topographos'); Valerius Maximus v i i ('Alexandrinus pictor'); all in reference to the same anecdote (O. 2141f.). Dawson 51f. followed by Brown *Pt.P.* 88, questions whether *topographos* means painter, and whether Demetrios necessarily came from Alexandria, but this is to ignore the evidence of Valerius Maximus (M. Robertson in *JHS* 83 (1963) 219). Nilotic scenes: pp. 502 with Chapter 7 n. 148, 579–80 with n. 211.

237. Vitruvius vii 5 2. The analysis in the text is taken from Blanckenhagen in *RM* 70 (1963) 100ff. See also p. 439 with Chapter 6 n. 210.

238. Text on Euanthes: Achilles Tatius iii 6 (O. 2144). The iconography of Andromeda in east and west: Phillips in *AJA* 72 (1968) 1–23, pls. 1–20 (pl. 1, figs. 2 and 3, and pl. 3, romantic Pompeian paintings). See also p. 439 with Chapter 6 n. 209.

239. Texts on Nealkes: Plutarch *Aratus* 13 (O. 1759; picture of Aristratos; see also pp. 487 and 493 with Chapter 7 notes 106, 122); Pliny xxxv 104 (O. 1907; anecdote of sponge told of Protogenes (Ialysos's dog) and Nealkes; of Apelles, Dio Chrysostom *Orat.* 67, 4; O. 1889).

240. Texts on Timomachos: Pliny xxxv 136 (O. 2119; date and list of pictures); also 26 (O. 2121), 145 (O. 1772) and vii 126 (O. 2120). Iphigeneia picture: pp. 441–3 with Chapter 6 notes 214–16. Medea from Herculaneum (Naples 8976): Elia no. 77; Curtius *WP* 305 fig. 175 and pl. 8; Pfuhl *MuZ* fig. 660; Rumpf *MZ* pl. 58, 2. Gems: Furtwängler *AG* pl. 37, 42–4; Pfuhl *MuZ* fig. 661. Pompeian pictures:

Naples 11140, Elia no. 36 (described as fragment with figure of Medea); 114321, Elia no. 37 (described as showing Medea seated, but she is standing in the picture illustrated fig. 9); standing Medea: Curtius *WP* 304 fig. 124 and pl. 7; Herrmann *Denkm.* 130; seated Medea: Curtius *WP* fig. 239; Herrmann *Denkm.* pls. 73f. Procne: pp. 286–7 with Chapter 4, n. 232, 345 with Chapter 5 n. 127. New York stele: p. 380 with Chapter 6 n. 53.

EPILOGUE: GREEK ART AND ROME

(*i*) *Magna Graecia, Etruria and the Roman Republic*

1. Foce del Sele: pp. 116–17 with Chapter 3 n. 96. Selinus, archaic: pp. 117–20 with Chapter 3 notes 100–3, 167 and 187 with Chapter 4 n. 22; classical: pp. 212–14 with Chapter 4 n. 102. Ludovisi throne: p. 203 with Chapter 4 notes 88f. Texts on Pythagoras of Rhegium: pp. 184 with Chapter 4 n. 48, 197 with Chapter 4 n. 72; the passage in Pausanias: VI 4 4 (O. 333 and 490). Klearchos: Pausanias III 17 6 (O. 332). Zeuxis: pp. 411–13 with Chapter 6 notes 136ff. Western coins: pp. 210–11 with Chapter 4 notes 97f., 359ff. with Chapter 5 notes 171–7.
2. Tarentine reliefs: Klumbach *Tarentiner Grabkunst*; Langlotz *AMG* pls. 136f., 153; *Arch.Rep. 1969/70* 42, fig. 21; Lawrence *LGS* pls. 90b, 92a.
3. Aristratos: pp. 487 and 498 with Chapter 7 notes 106, 122; 589 with Chapter 8 n. 239.
4. Damaratos and his artists: Pliny XXXV 15 (Ekphantos; O. 375) and 152 (Eucheir, Diopos, Eugrammos; O. 262).
5. Large-scale clay modelling in Corinth: pp. 146–7 with Chapter 3 n. 153, 170 and 277 with Chapter 4 notes 24 and 215.
6. Greek pottery perhaps made in Etruria: pp. 138f. with Chapter 3 notes 141f. Etruscan painted pottery on the Greek model: Dohrn *SEV*; Beazley *EVP*.
7. Etruscan temple-architecture: see e.g. D. S. Robertson 195–206 with figs. 87ff. Apollo of Veii and associated figures: e.g. Giglioli pls. 189–96 (cf. 160–88); Riis 65f. and fig. 53. Figures on sarcophagus-lids: e.g. Giglioli pls. 116–20; Riis fig. 45; later examples, p. 597 with n. 20.
8. Capitoline wolf (Rome, Conservatori): e.g. Giglioli pl. 197; Riis fig. 54. Arezzo Chimaera (Florence): e.g. Giglioli pls. 228f.; Br.Br. 319; Llewellyn-Brown *Etruscan Lion* pl. 57, 5 and p. 155, important discussion leading to a date in the early fourth century.
9. Phrygian paintings: p. 244 with Chapter 4 n. 152; Lycian paintings: *AJA* 75 (1971) pls. 50–2, 54–6. Greek sculptors in Lycia: pp. 82 with Chapter 3 n. 26, 200 with Chapter 4 notes 81–3, 403–5 with Chapter 6 notes 116–19. Tomb of the Bulls at Tarquinia: e.g. Giglioli pl. 107; Pallottino *EP* 29–32; Riis fig. 75. Tomb of the lionesses: e.g. Giglioli pls. 111f.; Pallottino *EP* 43–8; Ducati *MPASI* I 1. Tomb of the Triclinium: e.g. Giglioli pls. 109f.; Pallottino *EP* 73–80. Tomb of the Augurs: e.g. Pallottino *EP* 37–42; Riis fig. 76; Becatti and Magi *MPASI* I 3.
10. Tomb of Hunting and Fishing at Tarquinia and Tomba del Tuffatore at Paestum: p. 240 with Chapter 4 n. 147.
11. Attempt to down-date the expulsion of the Tarquins: Gjerstad *Early Rome.*
12. Tomb of Orcus: e.g. Giglioli pls. 246 (earlier) and 248, 1 and 3 (later); Pallottino *EP* 99–101 (earlier) and 111–13 (later); Riis fig. 82 (later). Bronze mirrors: Gerhard, Klugmann and Körte; Beazley in *JHS* 69 (1949) 1–17, figs. 1–22, pls. 1–11; Mansuelli in *St.Etr.* 19 (1946/7) 9–137, and 20 (1948); Giglioli pls. 286–90.
13. Pliny XXXIV 26; Plutarch *Numa* VIII 10; see Vessberg *Studien* 22, 936. Pythagoras and Magna Graecia: p. 211 with Chapter 4 n. 97.
14. Boscoreale figure-paintings: pp. 571–4 with Chapter 8 notes 181–3.
15. Ficoroni cista: refs. pp. 443–4 with Chapter 6 n. 219. François Tomb (most of the paintings, Rome, Villa Albani, Torlonia Collection): Pallottino *EP* 115–24; Riis figs. 85f., and see pp. 86f. on these and the cista.
16. Campanian tomb-paintings: e.g. Trendall *PP* pl. 31c; *Arch.Rep. 1969/70* 34 figs. 2f., 37 fig. 8. Etruscan red-figure: Beazley *EVP* 3–10, 25–180, pls. 4–28 (Faliscan, pp. 6ff., 70–112, pls. 15–26). Campanian and Etruscan Gnathia:

ibid. 208–16, pl. 39, 1 (Elephant plate, Rome, Villa Giulia), and 2–3 (Etruscan cup, Berlin). Etruscan cup illustrated: B.M. F542. Protogenes's Ialysos and dog: p. 496 with Chapter 7 n. 132.

17. Etruscan temple: p. 593 with n. 7. Italic temples: e.g. D. S. Robertson 199–212, figs. 90–3 and pl. 10b (Paestum, 'Corinthian-Doric' temple, 202ff. figs. 90f.).

18. Terracottas from Cività Alba: e.g. Riis figs. 102 (pediment), 103 (frieze) and pp. 106ff.; Giglioli pls. 380f. (pediment), 382 (frieze); Lawrence *LGS* pl. 94b (frieze); Pallottino *Art.Etr.* fig. 109 (detail of pediment; 108, 110, terracottas from other pediments). Pergamene Telephos frieze: p. 544 with Chapter 8 n. 107.

19. Tomb of the Typhon: Giglioli pls. 388f.; Pallottino *EP* 125ff.; Riis figs. 109f. Tomb of the Cardinal: Riis fig. 111. Tomb at Kazanlak: p. 566 with Chapter 8 notes 164–6. Giants of Pergamon altar: pp. 539f. with Chapter 8 notes 89–94.

20. Late 'Hellenistic' Etruscan sarcophagi and ash-urns and their lids: e.g. Giglioli pls. 346–60, 391–418; Pallottino *Art Etr.* figs. 111–16; Riis figs. 105f., 108; Herbig *Steinsark.*; Lawrence *LGS*, on pls. 93–101. Heads: e.g. Giglioli pls. 366 (bronze); 419, 1; 420 (terracotta); Pallottino *Art. Etr.* pls. 117 (stone), 119 and 122 (bronze), 120 and 121 (terracotta); Riis fig. 104 (terracotta). Roman with busts (Rome, Conservatori ex Barberini): Hekler pl. 127a.

21. Arringatore (Florence): Giglioli pls. 369f.; Riis fig. 107; Hekler pl. 131. Idrieus and Sarapis: p. 458 with Chapter 7 n. 31. 'Brutus' (Rome, Conservatori): Giglioli pls. 254–5; Riis fig. 120 (and pp. 126f., with the suggestions that it might be Greek or Renaissance); Hekler pl. 128a (set in modern marble bust).

22. Hellenistic Delos: pp. 533, 556 and 564, with Chapter 8 notes 79, 138 and 160 (sculpture), 579–80 with Chapter 8 notes 208–10 (mosaics). Mithradatic sack: p. 548 with Chapter 8 n. 115. Figured wall-paintings (mostly shrines and altars) from Delian houses: *Mon.Piot* 14 (1908) pls. 1–9c, figs. 4–10, 15–17, 22–4, 49–51; Pfuhl *MuZ* figs. 741f.; Rumpf *MZ* pl. 54, 10. Early Hellenistic Thracian tomb: pp. 566–8 with Chapter 8 notes 164–6; Hellenistic tombstones: pp. 581f. with Chapter 8 n. 217; late Hellenistic Etruscan tombs: p. 597 with n. 19.

23. Roman from Delos (Athens, N.M. 320): Hekler pl. 127b; Lawrence *LGS* pls. 57, 58a. Portrait-heads on ideal statues: p. 192 with Chapter 4 n. 60; p. 605 with n. 39. Poseidon of Melos and 'Hellenistic Ruler': pp. 554, 520 with Chapter 8 notes 133 and 39. Statue of C. Ofellius on Delos: Richter *TCP* fig. 111; the artists' signatures: Löwy *Inschr.* no. 242; texts on Dionysius and Timarchides: Pliny XXXVI 35 (O. 2207; Apollo by Timarchides; Hera by Dionysius; another by Polykles; Zeus by Polykles and Donysius son of Timarchides; all in a gallery in Rome with Philiskos's Muses, p. 564 with Chapter 8 n. 159, and statues by Pasiteles, p. 600 with n. 31; from the context they should all be marbles); Timarchides also occurs in the list of bronzeworkers who made athletes etc., Pliny XXXIV 91 (O. 2213), which we noticed as including Pythokritos (p. 536 with Chapter 8 n. 86) and Eucheir (p. 555 with Chapter 8 n. 135), as well as the painter Protogenes (p. 498 with Chapter 7 n. 130). Attic sculptors Timokles and Timarchides are named by Pausanias, X 34 6, as makers of an Asklepios at Elatea in Phocis. From these references and from the occurrence of some of the names in inscriptions, Jex-Blake and Sellers compiled a family tree (A, opposite p. 208). Demetrios of Alexandria: p. 589 with Chapter 8 n. 236. 'Private' portraiture in Athens: e.g. Lawrence *LGS* pls. 59f.; in Rhodes: e.g. Hinks *GRPS* pl. 17.

24. Delian houses stuccoed in imitation of marble: *Délos* VIII; *Mon.Piot* 14 (1908) pls. 6–8, figs. 27f.; Dinsmoor 322ff., fig. 118, pl. 70; D. S. Robertson 297f. pl. 22; Lawrence *A* 247f., fig. 140, pls. 138–42. Cf. also p. 598 with n. 22.

25. Boscoreale Villa: pp. 571ff. and 586ff. with Chapter 8 notes 181–3 (figured hall), 227–30 (bedroom). Assertion of surface against illusion of space: pp. 256–7 with Chapter 4 n. 171, 572 and 585 with Chapter 8 notes 183 and 225.

26. Villa of the Mysteries, Pompeii: Maiuri *Pompeii* 83–7, figs. 16, 17, 93–5 and *VM* passim; bedroom pl. 16 and pp. 174–82, figs. 64–9; Curtius *WP* 368, fig. 260, 373ff. figs. 204f. Great hall: below, n. 28.

27. Tomb and shrine-paintings: pp. 597–8 with notes 19–22. Odyssey landscapes: p. 588 with Chapter 8 n. 235. *Columbarium* paintings: Bendinelli *MPASI* III 2 (Colombario di Villa Pamphili); a fine piece removed from this tomb is in the B.M., ibid. fig. 13; Hinks *BMCat.PM* no. 24, pl. 8. 'Popular painting' at Pompeii: Maiuri *Pompeii* figs. 50, 71, 79, *RP* 139–47; Pfuhl *MuZ* figs. 744f.

28. Hall of the Mysteries (cf. above, n. 26): Maiuri *VM* pls. 1–15 and pp. 121–73, figs. 43–62, *RP* 50–63; Curtius *WP* 344–59, figs. 186–97; Ducati *Pitt.* pls. 57–60; Napoli *Pittura* 69–73; Pfuhl *MuZ* figs. 711–15; Rumpf *MZ* pl. 58, 1 and 3; Schefold *PM* pls. 2–7; and constantly. Interpretation as a wedding-initiation: Toynbee in *JRS* 19 (1929) 67ff.; Bieber in *Review of Religion* 2 (1937) 10ff.

29. Usurpation of space: see White 71, with refs. to Byzantine parallels (Demus *BMD* 23ff.). Pergamon altar-steps: p. 538 with Chapter 8 n. 90. Girl from Anzio: p. 479 with Chapter 7 n. 83. Apollo of Cyrene: p. 550 with Chapter 8 n. 121. Fourth-century Niobids: p. 461 with Chapter 7 n. 37.

30. 'Base of Cn. Domitius Ahenobarbus' (Munich, three sides with procession of marine deities; Louvre, side with sacrifice): Becatti *AR* figs. 21–3, *AAGR* 304 figs. 279–80; *EAA* III 169ff. figs. 207–8; *Enc.Phot.* 272f. D–E (sacrifice); *KB* 384, 4 (sacrifice) and 5; Lawrence *S* pl. 123b and *LGS* pl. 66 (marine deities). Frieze from Basilica Aemilia: Bartoli in *BdA* 25 (1950) 289–94, figs. 1–9; Toynbee in *PBA* 39 (1953) pls. 10f.; Becatti *AR* figs. 28, 30, *AAGR* 206 fig. 282. Telephos frieze from Pergamon and frieze from Hecataion at Lagina: pp. 544–5 with Chapter 8 notes 107, 108.

31. Texts on Pasiteles: Pliny XXXIII 156 (O. 2167; 'around the time of Pompey'); XXXVI 39 (O. 2262; 'born on the Greek shore of Italy and granted Roman citizenship', ivory-carver and writer); XXXV 156 (O. 2263; models); Cicero *de Div.* I 36 79 (O. 2202; silver-chaser). Texts on Arkesilaos: Pliny XXXV 155f. (O. 2268; Genetrix, models); XXXVI 33 and 44 (O. 2269f.; marbles); on Genetrix, see also next note. Texts on Stephanos: Pliny XXXVI 38 (O. 2266; marble); inscription, O. 2265. Menelaus's inscription: O. 2267.

32. Stephanos's athlete (Rome, Albani): Br.Br. 103; *KB* 394, 3; *Festschr. Rumpf* pl. 13, 3; Richter *AI* fig. 302; Ridgway *SS* fig. 174. Menelaos's group (Rome, M.N.): *KB* 394, 4; Richter *AI* fig. 303. Orestes and Pylades (Louvre): Richter *AI* fig. 305; Orestes and Electra (Naples): Richter *AI* fig. 304; Ridgway *SS* fig. 175; various Orestes groups: Br.Br. 30–68. 'Venus Genetrix' ('Aphrodite of Fréjus'): p. 350 w th Chapter 5 n. 141; Hadrianic coins: Mattingly *BMCat.* nos. 944–9; Arkesilaos's statue: Pliny XXXV 156 (O. 2268).

33. Idolino and Pompeian lamp-holders: p. 332 with Chapter 5 n. 95. Esquiline Venus (p. 391 with Chapter 6 n. 84): Carpenter in *MAAR* 18 (1941) 30–5, with pls. 13f., explaining it as a pastiche; Richter *AI* 49f. with figs. 168f. (Esquiline statue) and 170f. (Louvre torso), maintaining its fifth-century character; Ridgway *SS* figs. 165f., and an interesting discussion on p. 133, rejecting the fifth-century claim. Spinario: p. 559 with Chapter 8 n. 147.

(ii) *Greek tradition and the Roman Empire*

34. A particularly illuminating account of the Imperial approach to propaganda through coin-types: Grant 'Pax Romana' (Inaugural lecture at Edinburgh, 1958, printed in *University of Edinburgh Journal*, Spring 1949, 229–40).

35. Ara Pacis: Moretti *APA*, the main publication, and *L'Ara*; discussion and interpretation: Toynbee in *PBA* 39 (1953) 67–95, pls. 5–32 (the monument itself, its sculptures, reconstruction of prototype, coin-pictures, and parallel material). Other pictures: *KB* 397–8; Lawrence *S* pls. 128f., *LGS* pl. 82; Bianchi Bandinelli *RCP* 186ff., figs. 200–4; and constantly.

36. Hellenistic landscape-reliefs: pp. 544ff. and 562 with Chapter 8 notes 107–10 and 155. Later derivatives of this manner: e.g. *Enc.Phot.* 254A, 255C; *KB* 399, 1–3; Lawrence *S* pl. 133b. Coins of Camarina: Kraay and Hirmer pl. 54, nos. 150f. Relief from Carthage (Louvre): *Enc.Phot.* 255B; Moretti *APA* 233 fig. 174; Richter *TCP* fig. 141; Toynbee in *PBA* 39

(1953) pl. 14. Ara Pacis and Parthenon frieze: p. 310 with Chapter 5 n. 44.

37. 'Carpet': Toynbee in *PBA* 59 (1953) 77; Pergamene and Attic parallels: ibid. 90f., pls. 24, 27. Temple of Olympian Zeus at Athens: pp. 305–6 with Chapter 5 n. 34, 532 with Chapter 8 n. 76; p. 609 with n. 52. Altar of Pity: p. 374 with Chapter 6 n. 34.

38. Toynbee in *PBA* 39 (1953) 92, quoting Rodenwaldt *KdA* 52.

39. See pp. 192 with Chapter 4 n. 60, 598 with n. 23.

40. Augustus from Prima Porta (Vatican): Becatti *AAGR* fig. 286; Bianchi Bandinelli *RCP* 185 fig. 197; Hekler 170f.; *KB* 395, 1; Lawrence *S* pl. 124; and constantly. Polykleitos's Doryphoros: p. 329 with Chapter 5 n. 88. 'Minatia Polla' (Rome, M.N.): Hekler 211; *KB* 395, 5; Rodenwaldt *KdA* pl. 38.

41. Portraits in the Republican tradition: e.g. Hekler 188–202; *KB* 402, 5. 'Neo-Attic' reliefs (p. 329 with Chapter 6 n. 120): e.g. *KB* 393, 5–6 and 394, 6; Lawrence *S* pl. 133b; Richter *AI* figs. 137–41, *TCP* figs. 104f., 107. Silver-work: Richter *AI* figs. 190–6 (193, Arretine reproduction); Rodenwaldt *KdA* 582–7; Corbett and Strong in *BMQ* 23 (1962) 68–86, pls. 31–7; S. Haynes in *AK* 4 (1961) 30–6, pls. 15–17; C. Vermeule in *AK* 6 (1963) 33–40, pls. 10–15. Arretine: Oxé and Comfort; Brown, A. C.

42. 'Third Style': e.g. Rumpf *MZ* pls. 59, 4–5, 60, 61. Copies of fifth-century paintings, p. 324 with Chapter 5 n. 78.

43. Flavian portraits: e.g. Hekler 218–29; *KB* 402, 4 and 403, 1–2; Lawrence *S* pls. 135b, 136; Rodenwaldt *KdA* 608–11 and pl. 41. Boy (Berlin): Hekler 217; *Arch.Class.* 20 (1963) pl. 116. 'Fourth Style': e.g. Rumpf *MZ* pl. 63, 1–2. Tomb of the Haterii (Vatican, ex Lateran): Bianchi Bandinelli *RCP* fig. 242; *KB* 171, 3–5 and 403, 4–5; Lawrence *S* pl. 139.

44. Arch of Titus: Becatti *AAGR* fig. 298; Bianchi Bandinelli *RCP* figs. 237–40; *KB* 171, 6; 172, 3; 402, 1–2; Rodenwaldt *KdA* 614f.; E. Strong pl. 20, figs. 71–4. Cancelleria friezes: Magi *Cancelleria*; Becatti *AAGR* figs. 299f.; Bianchi Bandinelli *RCP* fig. 325. Beneventum arch: Pietrangeli *L'Arc de Trajan*; Bianchi Bandinelli *RCP* 234f. figs. 261f.; *KB* 182, 1 and 409, 4–5; Lawrence *S* pl. 143a; Rodenwaldt *KdA* 618.

45. Spiral columns: Becatti *Colonna Cochlide*. Trajan's column: Lehmann-Hartleben *Trajanssäule*; Romanelli *Colonna Traiana*; Becatti *AAGR* figs. 301–9; Bianchi Bandinelli *RCP* 227f., figs. 235f., *Storicità* figs. 193–210, 212, 214, 216, 220; *KB* 182, 5 and 407f.; Lawrence *S* pl. 141; Rodenwaldt *KdA* 619–22. 'Continuous style': pp. 233 with Chapter 4 n. 135, 544 with Chapter 8 n. 107 (Telephos frieze). Big battle-frieze from Trajan's Forum (in Constantine's arch, p. 611 with n. 57): Pallottino *Grande Fregio*; Becatti *AAGR* fig. 310; Berenson *AC* pls. 6f.; Bianchi Bandinelli *RCP* 231, figs. 253f., 258f., *Storicità* figs. 211, 213, 215; *KB* 406, 4–5; Rodenwaldt *KdA* 616f. Aphrodite of Capua: p. 553 with Chapter 8 n. 132. Victory of Brescia: E. Strong pl. 28.

46. Arch at Orange: Bianchi Bandinelli *RLE* 146ff. figs. 134, 136–8; Couissin in *RA* 19 (1924) 29; *KB* 404, 1; D. S. Robertson pl. 21a; Schoppa *KRZ* pls. 4f. Monument of the Julii at St Rémy: Bianchi Bandinelli *RCP* 248, fig. 277, *Storicità* pls. 117–19; Garger in *RM* 52 (1933) 1ff.; Schoppa *KRZ* pls. 7f. On the reliefs of both these monuments see also p. 503 with Chapter 7 n. 151. Gallo-Roman reliefs: theory on origins and influence of their style: Bianchi Bandinelli *Storicità* 209–44, pls. 98–137. Aurelian column: Romanelli *Colonna antonia*; Becatti *AAGR* figs. 336–43; Bianchi Bandinelli *RCP* 320ff., figs. 360–7; *KB* 415. Arch of Septimius Severus at Rome: Brilliant in *MAAR* 29 (1967); Becatti *AAGR* figs. 348–51; Bianchi Bandinelli *RLE* 64–9 figs. 57–9, 62–3; *KB* 417, 5; E. Strong pls. 60f. This emperor's arch at Lepcis: p. 610 with n. 56.

47. Pantheon and Hadrian's Villa at Tivoli: D. S. Robertson 246–51, figs. 104f. and pls. 16a, 17 (Pantheon), 252ff., figs. 107, 134 (Villa). The Villa and its adornments: Aurigemma *Villa Adriana*. Reliefs of satyr-boy: p. 553 with Chapter 8 n. 131.

48. Laocoon and groups from Sperlonga: pp. 541–3 with Chapter 8 notes 96–103. Farnese Hercules: p. 467 with Chapter 7 n. 50. Farnese Bull (Naples): Bieber *H* fig. 529; *KB* 357, 1; Lawrence *S* pl. 152b. Torso from Rhodes: Bieber *H* 133f. and fig. 528. Text on Apollonios and Tauriskos of Rhodes: Pliny XXXVI 33 (O. 2038).

49. School of Aphrodisias: Squarciapino *Scuola di*

Afrodisia. Origins and spread of 'peopled scroll' (p. 581 with Chapter 8 n. 215): Toynbee and Ward Perkins in *PBSR* 18 (1950) 1–43, pls. 1–26 (in decorative sculpture from Aphrodisias, pls. 23; 24, 2; 26, 4; from Africa, pls. 24, 1; 25f.; from Rome, pls. 10–18; pls. 13 and 16, 1–2 are from the tomb of the Haterii, p. 606 with n. 43). Signatures of Aphrodisian sculptors: see following notes.

50. Centaurs by Aristeas and Papias of Aphrodisias (Rome, Capitoline): Stuart Jones *Mus.Cap.* 274ff., pl. 64; Squarciapino *Scuola di Afrodisia* pls. 6f.; Bieber *H* fig. 584 (young); *KB* 382, 2 and 411, 4–5; Lawrence *S* pl. 108a (old); old with Eros (in white marble; Louvre): Bieber *H* fig. 583; *KB* 382, 1; Squarciapino *Scuola di Afrodisia* pl. E; young with Eros (in white marble; Vatican): Amelung and Lippold 346 pl. 35; young with Eros (in red marble; Rome, Palazzo Doria): Arndt–Amelung 2271–2.

51. Antinous: Clairmont *Bildnisse*; Hekler 250–6 (250, Delphi statue); *KB* 411, 2 and 3 (Sylvanus relief, signed by Antonianos of Aphrodisias; and another); Lawrence *S* pl. 44a and b (a, detail of Delphi statue). Sylvanus relief also: *Ausonia* 3 (1908) pl. 1; Clairmont *Bildnisse* no. 5, pls. 7f.; Squarciapino *Scuola di Afrodisia*, frontispiece. Delphi statue also: de La Coste Messelière *Delphes* pls. 204f.; Clairmont *Bildnisse* no. 1, pls. 2 and 4. See also p. 435 with Chapter 6 n. 199.

52. Temple of Olympian Zeus at Athens: pp. 305–6 with Chapter 5 n. 34, 532 with Chapter 8 n. 76, 604 with n. 37; Pausanias I 18 6. Porphyry head of Hadrian: B.M. 1950. 11–4.1. Roman porphyry: Delbrück *Porphyrwerke*; and see p. 611 with n. 57.

53. Constantine's arch: p. 611 with n. 57. Hadrianic roundels: Berenson *AC* pl. 8–11; Bianchi Bandinelli *RCP* figs. 291–3; Br.Br. 565; *KB* 410, 1–2; Lawrence *S* pl. 159; E. Strong figs. 153–60. Antonine panels incorporated in arch: Berenson *AC* pls. 12f.; Lawrence *S* pl. 147b; others in Conservatori: Bianchi Bandinelli *RCP* 314ff., figs. 353–9; *KB* 410, 6–7 and 414, 2–3; E. Strong figs. 161–3. Columns of Trajan and Marcus Aurelius: p. 607 with notes 45f.

54. Sarcophagi: Robert *Sarkophagreliefs* (a corpus in many volumes); *KB* 411, 6; 412; 418f.; Rodenwaldt *KdA* 650–67; a collection of Hadrianic examples: Toynbee *Hadrianic School* pls. 27–43, 45–9, 51–6. Ludovisi sarcophagus (Rome, M.N.): Becatti *AAGR* fig. 360; *KB* 419, 4; Rodenwaldt *KdA* 660–5; E. Strong fig. 200.

55. Bust of Commodus as Herakles (Rome, Conservatori): Becatti *AAGR* fig. 345; Berenson *AC* pl. 73; Hekler 270A; *KB* 417, 2; Lawrence *S* pl. 159a; Rodenwaldt *KdA* 641. Bronze equestrian statue of Marcus Aurelius on the Capitol: Bianchi Bandinelli *RCP* 308f., figs. 349f.; Hekler 266; *KB* 414, 1; Rodenwaldt *KdA* 640. Bearded bust (B.M. 1649; from the Strangford collection, which was formed in Greece): Hinks *GRPS* pl. 40. Demosthenes: p. 512 with Chapter 8 n. 21. Head from Olympia (Athens, N.M.): Hekler 261; E. Strong fig. 234.

56. Classical and Hellenistic frontality: pp. 354 with Chapter 5 n. 154, 435 with Chapter 6 n. 200, 576f. with Chapter 8 n. 198; see also M. Robertson in *Proc.London Class. Soc.* 1 (1947–52) 11f. Tyche of Antioch: pp. 470–2 with Chapter 7 notes 61–3. Tychai from Dura: Cumont *Fouilles* pls. 49–51; Rostovtzeff *Dura-Europos* (from a water-colour, showing the design more clearly than the photographs in Cumont). Sacrifice-painting from Dura: Cumont pls. 31–5. Gateway of the Argentarii in Rome: Haynes and Hirst *Porta Argentariorum* (the sacrifice-relief, pl. 6; also pl. 4 and figs. 11f., and see the discussion pp. 17–27). Arch of Septimius Severus at Lepcis Magna: Becatti *AAGR* figs. 347–8; Berenson *AC* pls. 25 and 48–50 (chariot-relief, 48); Haynes *Tripolitania* pls. 2–4 (chariot-relief, pl. 3). Aurelian relief from Ephesus (Vienna): *KB* 416, 2 (1 and 3–6, reliefs from the same monument).

57. Porphyry groups: Delbrück *Ant.Porph.* pls. 31f.; Berenson *AC* pls. 48 (St Mark's) and 50–1 (Vatican). A joining fragment of the foot of one of the Venice figures has now been found in Istanbul. On the Vatican pair see also M. Robertson *BAAH* 5f., with reference also to the Arch of Constantine. Constantine's arch (also p. 609 with n. 53): Becatti *AAGR* fig. 379; Berenson *AC* pls. 1–3 (general), 6–13 (earlier insets), 14–24, 27–34, 36, 38, 40, 44f., 63–71 (Constantinian carvings); Bianchi Bandinelli

RLE figs. 66–71; Lawrence *S* pl. 159; Rodenwaldt *KdA* 698f.

58. Greek and Italian sculptors: see Richter in *PAPS* 95 (1951) 184–91, figs. 1–64, *AI* 34–104, and *TCP* 37–65. Ludius or Studius: Pliny xxxv 116 (O. 2384); see Rumpf *MZ* 176.

ABBREVIATIONS AND BIBLIOGRAPHY

Abbreviations are listed in with the Bibliography, and where an abbreviation would come alphabetically next to the full title and is obvious from it, it is omitted. The Bibliography is intended to include any work referred to in the book, but has no other claim to completeness. An author's works appear in chronological order.

AA. See *Archäologischer Anzeiger.*

AAA. See *Athens Annals of Archaeology.*

Abhandlungen der philologisch-historischen Klasse der Sächsischen Akademie der Wissenschaften. Leipzig, from 1888.

ABV. Attic Black-figure Vase-painters. See Beazley.

Acta Archaeologica. Copenhagen, from 1930.

Acta Jutlandica. See Jeppesen.

AD. See *Antike Denkmäler.*

Adam, S. *The Technique of Greek Sculpture in the archaic and classical periods* (*BSA Supplementary Paper* 5) London, 1966.

Agora. *The Athenian Agora. Results of excavations conducted by the American School of Classical Studies at Athens.* Princeton, from 1958. See Harrison, Sparkes and Talcott, Thompson (H.), Wycherley.

Agora Guide.[2] See *Athenian Agora.*

AH. The Argive Heraeum. See Waldstein.

AJA. See *American Journal of Archaeology.*

AK. See *Antike Kunst.*

Åkerstrom, A. *Der geometrische Stil in Italien.* Lund, 1943.

Akurgal, E. *Griechische Reliefs des VI. Jahrhunderts aus Lykien.* Berlin 1941. (*Gr.Rel.*)

The Birth of Greek Art: the Mediterranean and the Near East. London, 1963. (Akurgal)

Ancient Civilization and Ruins of Turkey. Istanbul, 1969 (2nd ed. 1970). (*Turkey*)

Albizzati, C. *Vasi antichi dipinti del Vaticano.* Rome, 1925–39.

Alfieri, N. and Arias, P. *Spina: die neuentdeckte Etruskerstadt und die Vasen ihrer Graben.* Munich, 1952 (also Florence, 1958). (*SG*)

See also Arias, Aurigemma.

AM. Athenische Mitteilungen. See *Mitteilungen.*

Amelung, W. *Führer durch die Antiken in Florenz.* Munich, 1897.

and Lippold, G. *Die Skulpturen des Vatikanischen Museums.* Berlin, 1903–56.

American Journal of Archaeology. Princeton, Norwood, Concorde, from 1885. (*AJA*)

AMSMG. See *Atti e Memorie della Società Magna Grecia.*

Anatolia: revue annuelle d'archéologie. Ankara, from 1958.

Anatolian Studies: Journal of the British Institute in Ankara. London, from 1951.

Ancient Corinth: a guide to the excavations. Athens, 1947 (4th ed.).

Ancient Portraits. (Exhibition catalogue: Ackland Art Center, University of North Carolina at Chapel Hill, 5 April–17 May 1970).

Andreae, B. *Das Alexandermosaik* (*Opus Nobile,* 14). Bremen, 1956.

Andronikos, M. and Makaronas, C. *To Anaktoron tis Verginas* (τὸ ἀνάκτορον τῆς Βεργίνας). Athens, 1961.

Vergina (Studies in Mediterranean Archaeology, 14) Lund, 1964.

Androutsopoulos, G. *To hierotherapeuterion tou Amphiaraou en Oropoi* (τὸ ἱεροθεραπευτήριον τοῦ Ἀμφιαράου ἐν Ὠρώπῳ). Athens, 1960.

Ann. See *Annuario della Scuola archeologica di Atene.*

Annali della Facoltà di Lettere e Filosofia dell'Università di Bari.

Annuaire du Musée gréco-romain à Alexandrie. Alexandria.

Annual of the British School at Athens. London, from 1894. (*BSA*)

ABBREVIATIONS AND BIBLIOGRAPHY

Annuario della Scuola Archeologica di Atene. Bergamo, from 1914. (*Ann.*)

Annuario del museo greco-romano di Alessandria. Alexandria, from 1934.

Die Antike. Berlin, 1925–44.

Antike Denkmäler. Berlin, 1887–1931. (*AD*)

Antike Kunst. Basle, from 1958. (*AK*)

Antiken aus dem akademischen Kunstmuseum, Bonn. Düsseldorf, 1969.

Antike Plastik, ed. W.-H. Schuchardt. Berlin, from 1962. (*AP*)

Ant. Ionia iv. See Pullan.

Antiquaries' Journal. London, from 1921.

Antiquitas graeca-romana ac tempora nostra. Prague, 1968.

L'Antiquité classique. Louvain, Wetteren, Brussels, from 1932.

AO. Artemis Orthia. See Dawkins.

AP. See *Antike Plastik.*

AR. See *Archaeological Reports.*

Archeologia classica. Rome, from 1949.

Archaeological Reports. London, from 1955. (*AR*)

Archäologischer Anzeiger. Berlin, from 1889; part of *JdI* until 1963. (*AA*)

Archaeology. Cambridge, Mass., from 1948.

Archivio storico per la Calabria e la Lucania. (*ASCL*)

Arias, P. E. *Mirone.* Florence, 1940.

and Alfieri, N. *Il museo archeologico di Ferrara.* Ferrara, 1955.

Skopas. Rome, 1956.

Hirmer, M. and Shefton, S. *A History of Greek Vase-painting.* London, 1962 (translated and revised from Arias and Hirmer *Tausend Jahre griechischer Vasenkunst,* Munich, 1960).

Policleto. Florence, 1964.

See also Alfieri.

Arkhaiologikon Deltion ('Αρχαιολογικὸν Δελτίον). Athens, from 1915. (*Delt.*)

Arndt–Amelung. Arndt, P. and Amelung, W. *Photographische Einzelaufnahmen antiken Skulpturen.* Munich, from 1893.

Arndt–Bruckmann. Arndt, P. and Bruckmann, F. *Denkmäler griechischer und römischer Skulptur.* Munich, 1890–5.

Ars Antiqua. (Auction catalogues). Lucerne, from 1959.

Art Bulletin. Providence etc., from 1913.

ARV and *ARV²*. *Attic Red-figure Vase-painters.* See Beazley.

ASCL. Archivio storico per la Calabria e la Lucania. See *Archivio.*

Ashmole, B. *Late Archaic and Early Classical Greek Sculpture in Sicily and South Italy* (from *Proceedings of the British Academy* 20). London, 1934. (*GSSSI*)

The Classical Ideal in Greek Sculpture (Lectures in memory of Louise Taft Semple). Cincinnati, 1964. (*Ideal*)

Yalouris, N. and Frantz, A. *Olympia, the Sculpture of the Temple of Zeus.* London, 1967.

Architect and Sculptor in Classical Greece (Wrightsman Lectures). London, 1972. (*ASCG*)

See also Beazley.

Atene e Roma. Florence, from 1898.

The Athenian Agora: a guide to the excavations and museum. Athens, 1962 (2nd ed.).

Athens, Acropolis Museum. See Casson, Dickins, Payne and Young, Schrader, Walter.

Athens Annals of Archaeology ('Αρχαιολογικὰ 'Ανάλεκτα 'Αθηνῶν). Athens, from 1968. (*AAA*)

Atti e Memorie della Società Magna Grecia. Rome, N.S. from 1954. (*AMSMG.*)

Atti della Pontificia Accademia Romana di Archeologia. Ser. iii. *Memorie* and *Rendiconti.* Rome, from 1923.

Aurigemma, S. *Il Reale Museo di Spina.* Ferrara, 1935 (Aurigemma[1]) and 1936 (Aurigemma[2]).

and Alfieri, N. *Il Museo Nazionale Archeologico in Ferrara* (*Itinerari,* 95). Rome, 1957.

La Necropoli di Spina in Valle Trebba. Scavi di Spina 1 and 2. Rome, 1960 and 1965. (*Sc.di Spina*)

La Villa Adriana. Rome, 1962.

Die Ausgrabungen zu Olympia. See Olympia.

Babelon, E. *Traité des monnaies grecques et romaines.* Paris, 1901–19.

Baldass, L. *Van Eyck.* London, 1952.

Balkan Studies. Salonica, from 1960.

Bammer, A. *Die Architektur des jüngeren Artemision von Ephesos.* Wiesbaden, 1972.

B.Ant.Besch. See *Bulletin van de Vereeniging.*

Barnabei, F. *La Villa Pompeiana di P. Fannio Sinistore.* Rome, 1901.

BCH. See *Bulletin de Correspondance Hellénique.*

BdA. See *Bollettino d'Arte.*

BDFH. See Boardman, Dörig, Fuchs and Hirmer.

Beazley, J. D. *Attic Red-figured Vases in American Museums.* Cambridge, Mass., 1918. (*VA*)

The Lewes House Collection of Ancient Gems. Oxford 1920. (*AGLH*)

Beazley, J.D. *Attische Vasenmaler des rotfigurigen Stils.* Tübingen, 1925. (*AV*)
Attic Black-figure, a sketch (from *Proceedings of the British Academy* 14). London, 1928. (*ABS*)
Greek Vases in Poland. Oxford, 1928. (*VP*)
Der Berliner Maler (*Bilder griechischer Vasen,* 2). Leipzig, 1930. (*Berl.M.*)
Der Panmaler (*Bilder griechischer Vasen,* 4). Berlin, 1931. (*Panm.*)
and Ashmole, B. *Greek Sculpture and Painting.* Cambridge, 1932.
Der Kleophradesmaler (*Bilder griechischer Vasen,* 6). Berlin, 1933. (*Kl.*)
Attic White Lekythoi. Oxford, 1938. (*AWL*)
La Raccolta B. Guglielmi nel Museo Gregoriano Etrusco. I. *Ceramica.* Vatican, 1939.
Attic Red-figure Vase-painters. Oxford, 1942 (*ARV*) and 1963 (*ARV²*).
Potter and Painter in Ancient Athens (from *Proceedings of the British Academy* 30). London, 1946. (*PPAA*)
Etruscan Vase-painting. Oxford, 1947. (*EVP*)
Some Attic Vases in the Cyprus Museum (from *Proceedings of the British Academy* 33). London, 1948. (*SAVCM*)
The Development of Attic Black-figure (Sather Classical Lectures). Berkeley and Los Angeles, 1951. (*Dev.*)
Attic Black-figure Vase-painters. Oxford, 1956. (*ABV*)
Helenes Apaitesis (Ἑλένης Ἀπαίτησις, from *Proceedings of the British Academy* 43). London, 1957.
The Berlin Painter. Melbourne, 1964. (*Berl.P.*)
Paralipomena. Oxford, 1971.
See also Caskey.
Becatti, G. *Il Maestro d'Olimpia.* Florence, 1943.
Meidias: un manierista antico. Florence, 1947.
Problemi fidiaci. Milan, 1951.
La colonna di M. Aurelio. Milan, 1957.
La colonna cochlide istoriata. Florence, 1960.
L'arte romana. Milan, 1962.
The Art of Ancient Greece and Rome. London, 1968 (translation of *L'età classica,* Florence, 1965).
and Magi, F. *Monumenti della pittura antica scoperti nell'Italia.* I, 3–4. *Tarquinii, le pitture delle Tombe degli Auguri e del Pulcinella.* Rome, 1945.
Beckel, G. *Götterbeistand.* Waldsassen, 1961.
Bell, C. *An Account of French Painting,* London, 1931.
Bendinelli, G. *Monumenti della pittura antica scoperti nell'Italia,* 3, 5. *Le pitture del Colombario di Villa Pamphili.* Rome, 1941.
Benndorf, O. *Die Metopen von Selinunt.* Berlin, 1873.
and Niemann, G. *Reisen in Lykien und Karien.* Vienna, 1884.
Das Heroon von Gjölbaschi-Trysa. Vienna, 1889.
Benson, J. L. *Die Geschichte der korinthischen Vasen.* Basle, 1953.
Horse, Bird and Man: the origins of Greek painting. Amherst, 1970.
Berenson, B. *Italian Painters of the Renaissance.* London, 1952.
The Arch of Constantine or the Decline of Form. London, 1954.
Berichte. See *Olympia-Berichte.*
Berlin *Kat.Sk.* See Blümel.
Berliner Winckelmannsprogramm. See Curtius, Diepolder.
Bernoulli, J. J. *Griechische Ikonographie.* Munich, 1901.
Die erhaltenen Darstellungen Alexanders des großen. Munich, 1905.
Berytus. Beirut, from 1934.
Beyen, H. G. *La Statue d'Artémision.* The Hague, 1930.
Die Pompeianische Wanddekoration vom 2. bis zum 4. Stil. The Hague, 1938–60.
and Vollgraf, W. *Argos et Sicyone: études à la sculpture grecque de style sévère.* The Hague, 1947.
Bianchi Bandinelli, R. *Policleto.* Florence, 1938.
Storicità dell'arte classica. Florence, 1940.
Rome, the Centre of Power. London, 1970.
Rome, the Late Empire. London, 1971.
BICS. See *Bulletin of the Institute of Classical Studies.*
Bieber, M. *Die antiken Skulpturen und Bronzen des K. mus. Fridericianum in Cassel.* Marburg, 1915.
Griechische Kleidung. Berlin, 1928. (*GK*)
The Sculpture of the Hellenistic Age. New York, 1955; 2nd ed. 1961. (*H*)
Alexander the Great in Greek and Roman Art. Chicago, 1964.
Laocoon. Detroit, 1967.
Biesantz, H. *Die Thessalischen Grabreliefs.* Mainz, 1965.
See also Matz.
Blinkenberg, C. and Kinch, K.-F. *Lindos* I. Berlin, 1931. (Blinkenberg *L*)
Knidia. Copenhagen, 1933.

Bloesch, H. *Formen attischer Schalen, von Exekias bis zum Ende des strengen Stils*. Bern, 1940.

Blouet, A. *Expédition scientifique de Morée*. Paris, 1831.

Blümel, K. *Der Fries des Tempels der Athena Nike*. Berlin, 1923. (*FAN*)

Sport und Spiel bei Griechen und Römern. Berlin, 1934.

Der Sport der Hellenen. Berlin, 1936.

Staatliche Museen zu Berlin. Katalog der Sammlung antiker Skulpturen.

2. *Katalog der griechischen Skulpturen des 6. und 5. Jahrhunderts v. Chr.* Berlin and Leipzig, 1940.

3. *Katalog der griechischen Skulpturen des 5. und 4. Jahrhunderts v. Chr.* Berlin, 1931.

4. *Römischer Kopien griechischer Skulpturen des 5. Jahrhunderts v. Chr.* Berlin, 1931.

5. *Römischer Kopien griechischer Skulpturen des 4. Jahrhunderts v. Chr.* Berlin, 1938.

Staatliche Museen zu Berlin. Römische Bildnisse. Berlin, 1933.

Der Hermes eines Praxiteles. Baden-Baden, 1944.

Greek Sculptors at Work. London, 1955 (translation of *Griechischer Bildhauer an der Arbeit*, Berlin, 1933). (*GSW*)

Die archaisch griechischen Skulpturen der staatlichen Museen zu Berlin. Berlin, 1963. (*AGSB*)

Die klassisch griechischen Skulpturen der staatlichen Museen zu Berlin. Berlin, 1966. (*KGSB*)

Blunt, A. *Philibert de l'Orme*. London, 1958.

BMCat.Br. See Walters.

BMCat.Gems. See Walters.

BMCat.Sc. See Pryce, Smith (A. H.).

BMCat.Terr. See Higgins.

BMCat.Vas. See Forsdyke, Pryce, Smith (C. H.), Walters.

BMGuide to G. and R. Life. See *Guide*.

BMQ. See *British Museum Quarterly*.

Boardman, J. *The Cretan Collection in Oxford: the Dictaean Cave and Iron Age Crete*. Oxford, 1961. (*CCO*)

and Pope, M. *Greek Vases in Cape Town*. Cape Town, 1961.

Island Gems (*Society for the Promotion of Hellenic Studies, Supplementary Paper* no. 10). London, 1963. (*IG*)

The Greeks Overseas. London, 1964; 2nd ed., 1973. (*GO*)

Dörig, J., Fuchs, W., and Hirmer, M. *The Art and Architecture of Ancient Greece*. London, 1966 (*Die griechische Kunst*. Munich 1966). Refs. are to the English edition, followed in brackets by those to the German. (BDFH)

Pre-Classical: from Crete to Archaic Greece. London, 1967. (*PC*)

Archaic Greek Gems. London, 1968. (*AGG*)

Engraved Gems: the Ionides Collection. London, 1968 (*Ionides*)

Greek Gems and Finger-rings, early Bronze Age to Late Classical. London, 1970. (*GG*)

See also Kurz, Palmer.

Bocci, P. *Ricerche sulla ceramica cicladica*. Rome, 1962.

Boehringer, E. and Hoffmann, W. (editors). *Robert Boehringer: eine Freundesgabe*. Tübingen, 1957. (*Boehringer*)

See also *Neue deutsche Ausgrabungen*.

Bol, P. C. *Die Skulpturen des Schiffsfundes von Antikythera* (*Athenische Mitteilungen*, Beiheft 4). Berlin, 1972.

Bollettino d'Arte. Milan and Rome, from 1907.

Bonner Jahrbücher. Bonn, from 1842.

Bossert, H. *The Art of Ancient Crete*. London, 1937 (based on *Altkreta*, Berlin, 1923). (*AAC*)

Altanatolien. Berlin, 1942. (*AA*)

Altsyrien. Berlin, 1951. (*AS*)

Boston, *Cat.GERB*. *Catalogue of Greek, Etruscan and Roman Bronzes*. See Comstock and Vermeule.

Boston Museum of Fine Arts, *Museum Year*. Boston, from 1965.

Bothmer, D. von. *Amazons in Greek Art*. Oxford, 1957.

Bowie, T. and Thimme, D. *The Carrey Drawings of the Parthenon Sculptures*. Indiana University Press, Bloomington and London, 1971.

Br.Br. See Brunn, Bruckmann and Arndt.

Br.Br.*Portr*. See Brunn, Arndt, Bruckmann and Lippold.

British Museum Quarterly. London, from 1926. (*BMQ*)

Brock, J. K. *Fortetsa: early Greek tombs near Knossos* (*BSA Supplementary Paper* 2). Cambridge, 1957.

Brommer, F. *Satyroi*. Würzburg, 1957.

Satyrspiele. Bonn, 1944 (2nd ed., 1959).

Herakles: die zwölf Taten. Münster and Köln, 1953.

Athena Parthenos (*Opus nobile*, 2). Bremen, 1957.

Vasenlisten zur griechischer Heldensage. 2nd ed., Marburg a.d. Lahn, 1960. (*VL*)

Brommer, F. *Die Skulpturen der Parthenon-Giebel. Katalog und Untersuchungen.* Mainz, 1963. (*Giebel*)
Die Metopen der Parthenon: Katalog und Untersuchungen. Mainz, 1967. (*Metopen*)
Brooke, D. See Casson.
Brown, A. C. *Catalogue of Italian terra-sigillata in the Ashmolean Museum.* Oxford 1968.
Brown, B. *Ptolemaic Paintings and Mosaics and the Alexandrian Style.* Cambridge, Mass., 1957.
Brückner, A. *Der Friedhof am Eridanos bei der Hagia Triada zu Athen.* Berlin, 1909.
Bruhn, A. *Oltos.* Copenhagen, 1943.
Bruneau, P. and Ducat, J. *Guide de Délos.* Paris, 1965.
Brunn, H., Arndt, P., Bruckmann, F. and Lippold, G. *Griechischer und römischer Porträts.* Munich, 1891–1942.
Bruckmann, F. and Arndt, P. *Denkmäler griechischer und römische Skulptur in historischer Anordnung.* Munich, 1888–95, and from 1895.
Brunnsåker, S. *The Tyrant-slayers of Kritios and Nesiotes: a critical study of the sources and restorations.* 2nd ed., Stockholm, 1971.
BSA. See *Annual of the British School at Athens.*
Budde, L. and Nicholls, R. *A Catalogue of the Greek and Roman Sculpture in the Fitzwilliam Museum, Cambridge.* Cambridge, 1964.
Bull.Com.Arch.Rom. See *Bullettino della Commissione Archeologica Comunale di Roma.*
Bulle, H. *Der schöne Mensch.* 2nd ed., Munich, 1912. (*SM*)
Eine Skenographie (*94. Winckelmannsprogramm*). Berlin, 1932.
Bulletin de correspondance hellénique. Paris, from 1877. (*BCH*)
Bulletin du Musée Hongrois des beaux-arts. Budapest.
Bulletin of the Institute of Classical Studies (University of London). London, from 1954. (*BICS*)
Bulletin of the Metropolitan Museum of Art. New York, from 1905 (*Bull.Met.*)
Bulletin of the Rhode Island School of Design. Providence, from 1913.
Bulletin van de Vereeniging tot Bevordering der Kennis van de antike Beschaving te's Gravenhage. Leiden, from 1926. (*B.Ant.Besch.*)
Bullettino della Commissione Archeologica di Roma. Rome, from 1872.
Bundgaard, J. A. *Mnesicles: a Greek architect at work.* Copenhagen, 1957.
Burford, A. *The Greek Temple-builders at Epidauros.* Liverpool, 1969.
Craftsmen in Greek and Roman Society. London, 1972.
The Burlington Magazine. London, from 1903.
Buschor, E. *Das Krokodil des Sotades.* Munich, 1919.
Die Tondächer der Akropolis. Berlin, 1924.
and Hamann, R. *Die Skulpturen des Zeustempels zu Olympia.* Marburg, 1924.
Attische Lekythen der Parthenonzeit. Munich, 1925. (*ALP*)
Altsamische Standbilder. Berlin, 1934–61. (*ASS*)
Die Plastik der Griechen. Berlin, 1936.
Grab eines attischen Mädchens. Munich, 1939 (2nd ed., 1941).
Griechische Vasen. Munich, 1940.
Bildnisstufen. Munich, 1947.
Das Hellenistische Bildnis. Munich, 1949 (2nd ed., 1971).
Maussollos und Alexander. Munich, 1950.
Medusa Rondanini. Stuttgart, 1958.
Der Parthenonfries. Munich, 1961.
BWP. Berliner Winckelmannsprogramm. See Curtius, Diepolder.
Cahn, H. A. *Griechische Münze archaischer Zeit* (*Les monnaies grecques archaiques*). Basle, 1947.
Cambitoglou, A. and Trendall, A. D. *Apulian red-figured vases of the plain style.* Rutland (Vermont) and Tokyo, 1961.
The Brygos Painter. Sydney, 1968.
Cambridge, Fitzwilliam Museum. See Budde and Nicholls.
Carli, E. *Tutta la pittura di Michelangelo.* Milan, 1951.
Carpenter, R. *The Sculpture of the Nike Temple Parapet.* Cambridge, Mass., 1929.
Greek Sculpture. Chicago, 1960.
Greek Art. Philadelphia, 1962.
The Architects of the Parthenon. London, 1970.
Caskey, L. D. and Beazley, J. D. *Attic Vase-paintings in the Museum of Fine Arts, Boston.* Oxford, 1931–63.
Casson, S. *Catalogue of the Acropolis Museum, 2. Sculpture and Architectural Fragments; with a section upon the Terracottas by Dorothy Brooke.* Cambridge, 1921. (Vol. 1, see Dickins).
The Technique of Early Greek Sculpture. Oxford, 1933. (Casson)
Cassou, J. *Delacroix.* Paris, 1947.

Cat.GREB. See Comstock and Vermeule.
CB. Caskey–Beazley; see Caskey.
Cavvadias, P. *Fouilles de Lycosoura.* Athens, 1893.
C.d'A. See *Critica d'Arte.*
Chamoux, F. *Fouilles de Delphes* IV. *Monuments figurés.* 5, *L'Aurige.* Paris, 1955.
Charbonneaux, J. *Les bronzes grecs.* Paris, 1958.
Fouilles de Delphes II, *Topographie et architecture*, 4, *Le sanctuaire d'Athéna Pronaia: le Tholos.* Paris, 1925.
La sculpture grecque au Musée du Louvre. Paris, 1936. (*SGL*)
Martin, R. and Villard, F. *Archaic Greek Art, 620–480 B.C.* London, 1971 (translated from *La Grèce archaïque* 3, Paris, 1968). (CMV)
Charisterion. See Orlandos.
Charites. Studien zur Altertumswissenschaft. (*Festschrift Ernst Langlotz*). Bonn, 1957.
Charitonidis, S., Kahil, L., and Ginouvés, R. *Les mosaïques de la Maison de Ménandre a Mitylène* (*Antike Kunst* Beiheft 6). Basle, 1970.
Chase, G. H. *Boston Museum of Fine Arts: Catalogue of Arretine Pottery.* Boston, 1916.
CIBA Journal. Basle, from 1957.
Clairmont, G. W. *Die Bildnisse des Antinous.* Neuchatel, 1966.
Gravestone and Epigram: Greek memorials of the archaic and classical period. Mainz, 1970. (Clairmont)
Clara Rhodos. Rhodes, 1928–38. (*Cl.Rh.*)
Clark, K. *Piero della Francesca.* London, 1951.
The Nude, London, 1956.
Clarke, J. T., Bacon, F. H. and Koldewey, R. *Investigations at Assos.* Boston, 1902–21.
Classical Philology. Chicago, from 1908. (*CP*)
Classical Quarterly. London, from 1907. (*CQ*)
Classical Review. London, from 1887. (*CR*)
Classical Studies presented to Edward Capps. Princeton, 1936.
Cl.Rh. See *Clara Rhodos.*
CMV. See Charbonneaux, Martin and Villard.
Coche de la Ferté, É. *Les portraits romano-égyptiens du Louvre.* Paris, 1932.
Coldstream, J. N. *Greek Geometric Pottery: a survey of ten local styles and their chronology.* London, 1968.
Collignon, M. *Histoire de la sculpture grecque.* Paris, 1892–7. *Le Parthénon.* Paris, 1912.
Comptes-rendus de l'Académie des inscriptions et belles-lettres. Paris, from 1882. (*CRAI*)
Comstock, A. and Vermeule, C. C. *Greek, Etruscan and Roman Bronzes in the Museum of Fine Arts, Boston.* Boston, 1971. (*Cat. GREB*)
Connaissance des Arts. Paris, 1952–8.
Cons.Cat. The Sculptures of the Museo Conservatori; see Stuart Jones.
Conze, A. *Die attischen Grabreliefs.* Berlin, 1903–22.
Cook, R. M. *Greek Painted Pottery.* London, 1960 (2nd ed., 1972).
Niobe and her Children. Cambridge, 1964.
Greek Art: its development, character and influence. London, 1972.
Corbett, P. E. *The Sculpture of the Parthenon.* London, 1959.
Corinth. See Weinberg; also *Ancient Corinth.*
Corolla Curtius. Stuttgart, 1937.
Corpus Vasorum Antiquorum. Paris and elsewhere, from 1922. (*CVA*)
Coupel, P. and Demargne, P. *Fouilles de Xanthos* 3. *Le monument des Néréides: l'architecture.* Paris, 1969.
Courbin, P. *La céramique géometrique de l'Argolide.* Paris, 1966.
CP. See *Classical Philology.*
CQ. See *Classical Quarterly.*
CR. See *Classical Review.*
CRAI. See *Comptes-rendus.*
Criticà d'Arte. Florence, from 1935. (*C.d'A*)
Crome, J. F. *Das Bildnis Vergils.* Mantua, 1935.
Die Skulpturen des Asklepiostempels zu Epidauros. Berlin, 1961. (*SAE*)
Cumont, F. *Fouilles de Doura-Europos.* Paris, 1926.
Curtius, L. *Der Astragal des Sotades* (from *Sitzungsberichte der Heidelberger Akademie*). Heidelberg, 1923.
Pentheus (*88, Berliner, Winckelmannsprogramm*). Berlin, 1929.
Die Wandmalerei Pompeiis. Leipzig, 1929.
See also *Corolla Curtius.*
CVA. See *Corpus Vasorum Antiquorum.*
Dädalische Kunst auf Kreta (exhibition catalogue). Hamburg, 1970. (*DKK*)
Daux, G. *Delphes au IIe at au Ier siècle.* Paris, 1936.
David, H. *Claus Sluter.* Paris, 1951.
Davies, M. *National Galley: Earlier Italian Schools* (Plates). London, 1953.
Dawkins, R. M., ed. *Artemis Orthia* (*Society for the Promotion of Hellenic Studies, Supplementary Paper* 5). London, 1929.
Dawson, C. M. *Romano-Campanian Mythological Landscape-painting* (*Yale Classical Studies* 9). New Haven, 1944.

Delatte, A. *La catoptromancie grecque*. Liège, 1932.

Delbrück, R. *Antike Porphyrwerke*. Berlin, 1932.

Delepierre, J. *Le sujet de la frise du cratère de Vix*. Paris, 1954.

Délos. See Dugas, Dugas and Rhomaios.

Delt. See *Arkhaiologikon Deltion*.

Demangel, R. *La frise ionique*. Paris, 1932.

Demargne, P. *La Crète dédalique*. Paris, 1947. (*LCD*)

Aegean Art: the Origins of Greek Art. London, 1964 (translated from *La naissance de l'art grec*, Paris, 1964). (*OGA*)

Fouilles de Xanthos I. *Les piliers funéraires*. Paris, 1958.

See also Coupel.

Demus, O. *Byzantine Mosaic Decoration*. London, 1957.

Desborough, V. R. d'A. *Protogeometric Pottery*. Oxford, 1952.

The Last Mycenaeans and their Successors. London, 1964.

The Greek Dark Ages. London, 1972.

Despinis, G. I. *Symvoli stin meletin tou ergou tou Agorakritou* (Συμβολή στὴν μελέτην τοῦ ἔργου τοῦ 'Αγορακρίτου). Athens, 1971.

Dickins, G. *Catalogue of the Acropolis Museum*, I. *The Archaic Sculpture*. Cambridge, 1912. (Vol. 2, see Casson).

Diehl, E. *Die Hydria: Formgeschichte und Verwendung im Kult des Altertums*. Mainz, 1964.

Diepolder, H. *Die attischen Grabreliefs des 5. und 4. Jahrhunderts v. Chr*. Berlin, 1931.

Der Penthesilea-Maler (*Bilder griechischer Vasen*, 10). Leipzig, 1936.

Der Pistoxenos-Maler (110. *Berliner Winckelmannsprogramm*). Berlin, 1954.

Dinsmoor, W. B. *The Architecture of Ancient Greece*. London and New York, 1950.

DKK. See *Dädalische Kunst auf Kreta*.

Dörig, J. and Gigon, O. *Der Kampf der Götter und Titanen*. Olten, 1961.

See also Boardman, Dörig, Fuchs and Hirmer.

Dohan, E. H. *Italic Tomb-groups in the University Museum*. Philadelphia, 1942.

Dohrn, T. *Die schwartzfigurigen etruskischen Vasen aus der zweiten Hälfte des 6. Jahrhunderts*. Berlin, 1937. (*SEV*)

Attische Plastik vom Tode des Phidias bis zum Wirken der großen Meister des 4. Jahrhunderts v. Chr. Krefeld, 1957.

Die Tyche von Antiocheia. Berlin, 1960.

Der Arringatore. Berlin, 1968.

Die Ficoronische Cista. Berlin, 1972.

Dragendorff, H. *Theräische Gräber* (*Thera* II). Berlin, 1903.

Drerup, H. *Ägyptische Bildnisköpfe griechischer und römischer Zeit*. Munster, 1957.

Duca di Serradifalco. See Serradifalco.

Ducat, J. *Les vases plastiques rhodiens archaïques en terre cuite*. Paris, 1966.

Les Kouroi du Ptoion. Paris, 1971.

See also Bruneau.

Ducati, P. *Storia dell'arte etrusca*. Florence, 1927.

Pittura etrusca, italo-greca e romana. Novara, 1952.

Monumenti della pittura antica scoperti in Italia, I.I.

Tarquinii, le pitture della Tomba dei Tori. Rome, 1937.

Dugas, C., with others. *Le sanctuaire d'Athéna Aléa à Tégée au IVe siècle*. Paris, 1924.

La céramique des Cyclades. Paris, 1925.

Délos 10. *Les vases de l'Héraion*. Paris, 1928.

and Rhomaios, C. *Délos* 15. *Les vases préhelléniques et géométriques*. Paris, 1934.

Dumbarton Oaks. See Richter.

Dunbabin, T. J. *The Western Greeks*. Oxford, 1948.

The Greeks and their Eastern Neighbours (*Society for the Promotion of Hellenic Studies, Supplementary Paper* 8; ed. J. Boardman). London, 1957.

See also *Perachora*.

EAA. See *Enciclopedia dell'Arte Antica*.

Edwards, I. E. S. *The Pyramids of Egypt*. London, 1947.

Eichler, F. *Die Reliefs des Heroon von Gjölbaschi-Trysa*. Vienna, 1950.

Einz.Auf. *Einzel-Aufnahmen*. See Arndt and Amelung.

Elia, O. *Pitture murali e mosaici nel Museo Nazionale di Napoli*. Rome, 1932.

Enciclopedia dell'Arte Antica. Rome, 1958–66. (*EAA*)

Encyclopedia of World Art (*Enciclopedia Universale dell'Arte*). New York and Florence, 1959–68. (*EWA*, *EUA*)

Encylopédie Photographique de l'Art. Le Musée du Louvre, 2–3. Paris, 1937–8.

Ephemeris Arkhaiologike ('Εφημερὶς 'Αρχαιολογική). Athens, from 1883. (*Eph*.)

To ergon tes Arkhaiologikes Etairias (τὸ ἔργον τῆς 'Αρχαιολογικῆς 'Εταιρίας). Athens, from 1956. (*Ergon*)

Espérandieu, E. *Recueil général des bas-reliefs de la Gaule romaine*. Paris, 1907.

Essays . . . Lehmann. See Lehmann, K.
Essays . . . Panofsky. See Panofsky.
Essays . . . Robinson. See Robinson, E. S. G.
Essays . . . Wittkower. See Wittkower.
Études Thasiennes. Paris, from 1944.
EUA. *Enciclopedia Universale dell'Arte.* See *Encyclopedia of World Art.*
Evans, A. J. *The Palace of Minos at Knossos.* London, 1921–36.
EWA. See *Encyclopedia of World Art.*
Excavations at Olynthus. See Robinson, D. M.
Expedition. Bulletin of the University Museum of the University of Pennsylvania. Philadelphia, from 1958.
Exp.v.Sieglin. See Sieglin.
Fairbanks, A. *Athenian White Lekythoi.* New York, 1907–14.
and Chase, G. H. *Greek Gods and Heroes.* Boston, 1948.
FdeD. *Fouilles de Delphes.* See Chamoux, Charbonneaux, Pouilloux, Rolley.
Festgabe zur Winckelmannsfeier des Archäologischen Seminars der Universität Leipzig am 12 Dezember, 1936. Leipzig, 1936.
Festschr. . . . Bloesch. See Addenda.
Festschr. . . . Loeb. See Loeb.
Festschr. . . . Mercklin. See Mercklin.
Festschr. . . . Overbeck. See Overbeck.
Festschr. . . . Rumpf. See Rumpf.
Filow, B. D. *Die archaische Nekropole von Trebenischte am Ochrida-See.* Berlin, 1927.
Fink, J. *Der Thron des Zeus in Olympia: Bildwelt und Weltbild.* Munich, 1967.
Fittschen, K. *Untersuchungen zur Beginn der Sagendarstellungen bei den Griechen.* Berlin, 1969.
Follman, A.-B. *Der Panmaler,* Bonn, 1968.
Forsdyke, E. J. *Catalogue of the Greek and Etruscan Vases in the British Museum* I, I. *Prehistoric Aegean Pottery.* London, 1925.
Forti, L. *Le danzatrici di Ercolano.* Naples, 1959.
Fouquet Coll. See Perdrizet.
FR. See Furtwängler and Reichold.
Frazer, J. G. *Pausanias's Description of Greece translated with a commentary.* London, 1898.
From the Collections of the Ny-Carlsberg Glyptothek. Copenhagen, from 1931.
Frr.gr.Hist. See Jacoby.
Fuchs, W. *Der Dornauszieher* (*Opus Nobile,* 8). Bremen, 1948.
Die Vorbilder der Neuattischen Reliefs. Berlin, 1959.
Der Schiffsfund von Mahdia. Tübingen, 1963.
See also Boardman, Dörig, Fuchs and Hirmer.
Fuhrmann, H. *Philoxenos von Eretria.* Göttingen, 1931.
Furtwängler, A. *Meisterwerke der griechischen Plastik.* Leipzig, 1893 (*Meist.*). Revised and translated as *Masterpieces of Greek Sculpture,* London, 1895 (*Mast.*).
Die antiken Gemmen. Leipzig, 1900. (*AG*)
and Reichold, K. (with F. Hauser, E. Buschor, C. Watzinger and R. Zahn) *Griechische Vasenmalerei.* Munich, 1904–32. (FR)
Aigina. Munich, 1906. (*A*)
See also *Olympia.*
Gardner, P. *Catalogue of the Greek Vases in the Ashmolean Museum.* Oxford, 1893.
Gardiner, E. N. *Greek Athletic Sports and Festivals.* London, 1910. (*GAS*)
Olympia, its history and remains. Oxford, 1925.
Athletics of the Ancient World. Oxford, 1930.
Gerhard, E. *Auserlesene Vasenbilder.* Berlin, 1840–58.
and Klugmann, A. and Körte, G. *Etruskische Spiegel.* Berlin, 1840–97.
Apulische Vasenbilder der K.Mus. zu Berlin. Berlin, 1845.
von Gerkan, A. *Der Altar des Artemistempels in Magnesia am Mäander.* Berlin, 1929.
Gervasio, M. *Bronzi arcaici e ceramica geometrica nel museo di Bari.* Bari, 1921.
Gestalt und Geschichte. Festschrift Schefold (*Antike Kunst,* Beiheft 4). Bern, 1967.
Ghali-Kahil, L. *Les enlèvements et le retour d'Hélène.* Paris, 1955.
Giglioli, C. Q. *L'arte etrusca.* Milan, 1935.
Gigon, O. See Dörig.
Gjerstadt, E. *Early Rome.* Lund, 1953–66.
Gnomon. Berlin, from 1925.
Goethert, F. W. and Schleif, H. *Der Athenatempel von Ilion.* Berlin, 1962.
Goldman Studies. See Weinberg.
Goldscheider, L. *Michelangelo Drawings.* London, 1951.
Unknown Renaissance Porrtaits. London, 1952.
Gombrich, E. *Norm and Form.* London, 1966.
Goodchild, R. G. *Kyrene und Apollonia.* Zürich, 1971.
Grace, V. R. and Frantz, A. *Amphoras and the Ancient Wine Trade* (*Excavations of the Athenian Agora, Picture Book* no. 6). Princeton, 1961.

Graef, B., with others. *Die antiken vasen von der Akropolis zu Athen* I. Berlin, 1901–25. (Graef)
and Langlotz, E. *Die antiken Vasen von der Akropolis zu Athen* II. Berlin, 1925–33.
von Graeve, V. *Der Alexandersarkophag*. Berlin, 1970.
Greece and Rome. Oxford, from 1932. See also *Parthenos and Parthenon*.
Greek, Roman and Byzantine Studies. San Antonio etc., from 1958. (*GRBS*)
Greifenhagen, A. *Eine attische schwartzfigurige Vasengattung und die Darstellung der Komos im VI. Jahrundert*. Königsberg, 1929. (*EASV*)
Griechische Eroten. Berlin, 1957.
Antike Kunstwerke. Berlin, 1960 (2nd ed., 1965). (*AKW*[1] and *AKW*[2])
Neue Fragmente des Kleophradesmalers (*Sitzungsberichte der Heidelberger Akademie der Wissenschaften*). Heidelberg, 1972.
Griffo, P. *Il Museo Civico di Agrigento*. Agrigento, 1952.
Breve Guida del Museo Civico di Agrigento. Agrigento, 1954.
Up-to-date guide for the visitor to the ruins of Agrigento (translated by J. Ward Perkins). Agrigento, 1962.
See also von Matt.
Groenewegen-Frankfort, H. A. *Arrest and Movement, an essay on space and time in the representational art of the ancient Near East*. London, 1951.
Grose, S. W. *Catalogue of the McClean Collection of Greek Coins, Fitzwilliam Museum*. Cambridge, 1923–9.
Grube, G. M. R. *A Greek Critic: Demetrios on Style*. Toronto, 1961.
Grumach, E. See *Minoica*.
A Guide to the Exhibition illustrating Greek and Roman Life, British Museum, 3rd ed., London, 1929
Gymnasium. Heidelberg, from 1894.
Hafner, G. *Viergespanne in Vorderansicht*. Berlin, 1938.
Zum Epheben Westmacott. Heidelberg, 1955.
Geschichte der griechischen Kunst. Zürich, 1961.
Hahland, W. *Vasen um Meidias* (*Bilder griechischer Vasen*, I). Berlin, 1930.
Hamdy, O., Bey and Reinach, S. *Une nécropole royale à Sidon*. Paris, 1892.
Hampe, R. *Frühe griechische Sagenbilder in Böotien*. Athens, 1936. (*FGS*)
Die Stele aus Pharsalos im Louvre. Berlin, 1951.
Die Gleichnisse Homers und die Bildkunst seiner Zeit. Tübingen, 1952.
Ein frühattischer Grabfund. Mainz, 1960. (*FAG*)
Harrison, E. B. *The Athenian Agora*, II. *Archaic and archaistic sculpture*. Princeton, 1965.
Harvard Studies in Classical Philology. Boston, from 1890.
Haspels, C. H. E. *Attic Black-figured Lekythoi*. Paris, 1936.
Hausmann, U. *Griechische Weihreliefs*. Berlin, 1960.
Havelock, C. M. *Hellenistic Art*. London, 1971.
Haynes, D. E. L. and Hirst, P. E. D. *Porta Argentariorum* (*British School at Rome, Supplementary Paper*). London, 1939.
The Antiquities of Tripolitania. London, 1955 (revised from *Ancient Tripolitania*, Tripoli, 1947).
Head, B. V. *Historia Numorum*. 2nd ed., Oxford, 1911.
Heberdey, R. *Altattische Porosskulptur*. Vienna, 1919.
Hege, W. and Rodenwaldt, G. *Olympia*. Berlin, 1936.
Hekler, A. *Greek and Roman Portraits*. London, 1912 (translated from *Die Bildniskunst der Griechen und Römer*).
Helbig, W. *Wandgemälde der vom Vesuv verschütterten Städte Campaniens*. Leipzig, 1868. (Helbig)
Führer durch die offentliche Sammlungen klassischer Altertümer in Rom. 4th ed., ed. H. Speier. Tübingen, 1963–9.
Hemelrijk, J. M. *De Caeretaanse Hydriae*. Rotterdam, 1956.
Herbig, R. *Die jüngeretruskischen Steinsarkophage* (*Die antiken Sarkophagreliefs*, 7). Berlin, 1952.
See also Herrmann, P.
Herkenrath, R. *Der Fries des Artemision von Magnesia*. Berlin, 1902.
Herrmann, H.-V. *Die Kessel der orientalisierende Zeit*, I. *Kesselattasche und Reliefuntersätze* (*Olympische Forschungen* VI). Berlin, 1966.
Herrmann, P. (continued by R. Herbig). *Denkmäler der Malerei des Altertums*. Munich, 1904–60. (Herrmann)
Hesperia. Athens, from 1932.
Heydemann, H. *Alexander der große und Dareios Kodomannos auf unteritalischen Vasenbildern* (*8. Hallisches Winckelmannsprogramm*). Halle, 1883.

Higgins, R. A. *Catalogue of Terracottas in the Department of Greek and Roman Antiquities, British Museum*. London, 1954–9. (*BMCat.Terr.*)

Greek and Roman Jewellery. London, 1961.

Greek Terracottas. London, 1967.

Hill, G. F. *A Guide to the Principal Coins of the Greeks*. London, 1932. (*PCG*)

Hill, I. T. *The Ancient City of Athens, its topography and monuments*. London, 1953.

Hinks, R. P. *Catalogue of the Greek, Etruscan and Roman Paintings and Mosaics in the British Museum*. London, 1933.

Greek and Roman Portrait-sculpture. London, 1935.

Historia. Milan, 1927–35.

Hölscher, F. *Die Bedeutung archaischer Tierkampfbilder*. Würzburg, 1972.

Hörman, H. *Die inneren Propyläen von Eleusis* (*Denkmäler antiker Architektur*, 1). Berlin, 1932.

Hoffman, H. *Norbert Schimmel Collection*. Mainz 1964.

and Davidson, P. F. *Greek Gold: jewelry in the age of Alexander*. Brooklyn, New York, 1965.

and Raubitschek, A. E. *Early Cretan Armourers*. Mainz, 1972.

Hofkes-Brukker, C. *Frühgriechische Gruppenbildung*. Leiden and Würzburg, 1935.

Hogarth, D. G. *Excavations at Ephesos: the archaic Artemisia*. London, 1908.

Homann-Wedeking, E. *Die Anfänge der griechischen Großplastik*. Berlin, 1950.

van Hoorn, G. *Choes and Anthesteria*. Leiden, 1951.

Hoppin, J. C. *A Handbook of Greek Black-figured Vases*. Paris, 1924.

Humann, C. and others. *Magnesia am Mäander*. Berlin, 1904.

Hundertes Winckelmannsprogramm. Berlin, 1940.

IG. See *Inscriptiones Graecae*.

The Illustrated London News, London. (*ILN*)

Imhoof-Blumer, F. and Gardner, P. *A numismatic commentary on Pausanias*. London, 1887.

Ingholt, H. *Rapport préliminaire sur sept campagnes de fouilles à Hama en Syrie*. Copenhagen, 1940.

Inscriptiones Graecae. Berlin, from 1873. (*IG*)

Iraq. London, from 1934.

Istanbul *Cat.Sc.* See Mendel.

Italian Art in Britain (Burlington House exhibition catalogue). London, 1960.

Jacobsthal, P. *Ornamente griechischer Vasen*. Berlin, 1927. (*O*)

Die melischen Reliefs. Berlin, 1931. (*MR*)

Greek Pins. Oxford, 1956.

Jacoby, F. *Die fragmente der griechischer Historiker*. Berlin, 1923–58.

Jacopi, G. *L'Antro di Tiberio a Sperlonga*. Rome, 1963.

L'Antro di Tiberio ed il Museo Nazionale di Sperlonga. Rome, 1965.

Jahrbuch der Berliner Museen. Berlin, from 1959.

Jahrbuch des Deutschen Archäologischen Instituts. Berlin, from 1886. (*JdI*)

Jahrbuch des Römisch-Germanisch Zentralmuseums Mainz. Mainz, from 1954.

Jahrbuch der staatlichen Kunstsammlungen in Baden-Württemberg. Baden-Württemberg.

Jahreshefte des Österreichischen Archäologischen Instituts. Vienna, from 1898. (*ÖJh*)

Jantzen, U. *Bronzewerkstätten in Großgriechenland*. Berlin, 1937. (*BWS*)

Griechische Greifenkessel. Berlin, 1955.

Ägyptische und orientalische Bronzen aus dem Heraion von Samos. Berlin, 1972.

Jb . . . Baden-Württemberg. See *Jahrbuch der staatlichen Kunstsammlungen*.

Jb.Berl.Mus. See *Jahrbuch der Berliner Museen*.

JdI. See *Jahrbuch des Deutschen Archäologischen Instituts*.

Jebb, R. C. and Pearson, A. C. *Sophocles, the Plays and Fragments*. Cambridge, 1883–1917.

Jeffery, L. H. *The Local Scripts of Archaic Greece*. Oxford, 1961.

Jeppesen, K. *Eteokleous Symbasis* ('Ετεοκλέους σύμβασις. *Acta Jutlandica*: Publications of the University of Aarhus, Humanities Series 49). Copenhagen, 1968.

Jenkins, R. J. H. *Dedalica*. Cambridge, 1936.

Jex-Blake, K. and Sellers, E. *The Elder Pliny's Chapters on the History of Art*. London, 1896.

JHS. See *Journal of Hellenic Studies*.

Joffroy, R. *Le Trésor de Vix (Côte-d'Or)* (*Monuments Piot*, 48, 1). Paris, 1954. (*Vix*)

Les Sépultures à Char du premier Âge du Fer en France. Paris, 1958.

Le Trésor de Vix: histoire et portée d'une grande découverte. Paris, 1962. (*Trésor*)

Johansen, K. F. *Hoby-fundet* (*Nordiske Fortidsminder* II 3; summary in French). Copenhagen, 1923.

Les Vases Sicyoniens. Paris and Copenhagen, 1923.

The Attic Grave-reliefs of the Classical Period. Copenhagen, 1951.

Johns, C. *Arretine and Samian Pottery*. London, 1971.

Johnson, F. P. *Lysippos*. Durham, N.C., 1927.

Journal of Hellenic Studies. London, from 1881. (*JHS*)

Journal of the Warburg and Courtauld Institutes. London, from 1937. (*JWCI*)

Jucker, H. *Das Bildnis im Blätterkelch*. Olten, 1961.

Judeich, W. *Topographie von Athen*. Munich, 1905; 2nd ed. 1931.

JWCI. See *Journal of the Warburg and Courtauld Institutes*.

Kähler, H. *Der große Fries von Pergamon*. Berlin, 1948. (*Fries*)

Pergamon. Berlin, 1961.

Karageorghis, V., with Vermeule, C. C. *Sculptures from Salamis*. Nicosia, 1964–6.

Mycenaean Art from Cyprus. Nicosia, 1968.

Kardara, C. *Rhodiaki Angeiographia* (Ῥοδιακὴ ἀγγειογραφία). Athens, 1963.

Karidas, P. *Das Amphiareion von Oropos*. Erlangen, 1968.

Karo, G. *Die Schachtgräber von Mykenai*. Munich, 1930.

Karouzos, C. See Karusos.

Karouzou, S. *The Amasis Painter*. Oxford, 1956. (*AP*)

Angeia tou Anagyrountos (Ἀγγεῖα τοῦ Ἀναγυροῦντος). Athens, 1963. (*ATA*)

National Archaeological Museum, Collection of Sculpture. A Catalogue. Athens, 1968. (*Cat.*)

See also Papaspyridi.

Karusos, C. *To Mouseion tis Thivas* (τὸ μουσεῖον τῆς Θήβας). Athens, 1934. (*M.Th.*)

Aristodikos: zur Geschichte der spätarchaisch-attischen Plastik und der Grabstatue. Stuttgart, 1961.

Karusu, S. See Karouzou.

Kaschnitz-Weinberg, G. *Le sculture del magazzino del Museo Vaticano*. Vatican, 1937.

KB. *Kunstgeschichte in Bildern*. See Winter.

Kenna, V. E. G. *Cretan Seals, with a catalogue of the Minoan gems in the Ashmolean Museum*. Oxford, 1960.

Kenner, H. *Der Fries des Tempels von Bassae-Phigaleia*. Vienna, 1946.

Kerameikos: Ergebnisse der Ausgrabungen (K. Kübler and others). Berlin, from 1939.

Kerenyi. See *Opuscula Carlo Kerenyi dedicata*.

Kinch, K. F. *Vroulia*. Berlin, 1914.

Le tombeau de Niausta, tombeau Macédonien. Copenhagen, 1927.

Kjellberg, E. *Studien zu den attischen Reliefs des V. Jahrhunderts v. Chr.* Uppsala, 1926.

Kleemann, I. *Der Satrapen-Sarkophag aus Sidon*. (*Istanbuler Forschungen* 20). Berlin, 1958.

Klein, W. *Geschichte der griechischen Kunst*. Leipzig, 1904.

Kluge, K. and Lehmann-Hartleben, K. *Die antike Großbronzen*. Berlin, 1927.

Klumbach, H. *Tarentiner Grabkunst*. Reutlingen, 1937.

Kock, T. *Comicorum Atticorum Fragmenta*. Leipzig, 1880–8.

Konferenca e Pare e Studimeve Albanologjike. Tirane, 1965.

Kraay, C. H. and Hirmer, M. *Greek Coins*, London, 1966 (same pictures as P. R. Franke and M. Hirmer *Die griechische Münze*, Munich, 1966).

Kraiker, W. *Aigina. Die Vasen des 10. bis 7. Jahrhunderts*. Berlin, 1951.

Die Malerei der Griechen. Stuttgart, 1958.

Krause, F. *Paestum: die griechische Tempel*. Berlin, 1943.

Die Tempel von Paestum. Berlin, 1959.

Kübler, K. *Altattische Malerei*. Tübingen, 1950.

See also *Kerameikos*.

Kunze, E. *Kretische Bronzereliefs*. Suttgart, 1931. (*KBR*)

Neue Meisterwerke griechischer Kunst aus Olympia. Munich, 1948. (*NMO*)

Archaische Schildbänder (*Olympische Forschungen* 2). Berlin, 1950. (*AS*)

Kurtz, D. C. and Boardman, J. *Greek Burial Customs*. London, 1971.

Lacy, A. D. *Greek Pottery in the Bronze Age*. London, 1967.

de La Coste Messelière, P. *Au musée de Delphes*. Paris, 1936.

Delphes. Paris, 1943.

See also Picard.

Lafuente, E. *Velazquez*. London, 1943.

Lamb, W. *Greek and Roman Bronzes*. London, 1929.

Lane, A. *Greek Pottery*. London, 1948.

Lang, M. L. *The Athenian Citizen* (*Excavations of the Athenian Agora, Picture Book* No. 4). Princeton, 1960.

The Palace of Nestor at Pylos II. *The Frescoes*. Princeton, 1969. (Lang)

Langlotz, E. *Zur Zeitbestimmung der strengrotfigurigen Vasenmalerei und der gleichzeitigen Plastik*. Leipzig, 1920. (*ZB*)

Langlotz, E. *Frühgriechische Bildhauerschulen*. Nuremberg, 1927. (*FGBS*)
Griechische Vasen in Würzburg. Munich, 1932. (*GVW*)
and Schuchardt, W. H. *Archaische Plastik auf der Akropolis*. Frankfurt, 1943.
Phidiasprobleme. Frankfurt, 1947.
Das Ludovisische Relief. Mainz, 1951.
Aphrodite in den Gärten. Heidelberg, 1954.
and Hirmer, M. *The Art of Magna Graecia*. London, 1967 (translation of *Die Kunst der Westgriechen in Sizilien und Unteritalien*. Munich, 1967).
See also *Charites*, Graef, Schrader.
Laourdas, V. and Makaronas, C. *Arkhaia Makedonia* (Ἀρχαῖα Μακεδονία). Salonica, 1971.
Laurenzi, L. *Ritratti Greci*. Florence, 1942.
Lawrence, A. W. *Later Greek Sculpture and its influence on East and West*. London, 1927. (*LGS*)
Classical Sculpture. London, 1929 (2nd ed., 1972). (*S*)
Greek Architecture. London, 1957. (*A*)
Lehmann, K. *Essays in memory of Karl Lehmann* (ed. L. F. Sandler). New York, 1964.
Lehmann, P. W. *Roman Wall-paintings from Boscoreale*. Cambridge, Mass., 1953.
Lehmann-Hartleben, K. *Die Trajanssäule*. Berlin, 1926.
Leipen, N. *Athena Parthenos: a reconstruction*. Ontario, 1971.
Lermann, W. *Altgriechische Plastik*. Munich, 1907 (2nd ed., 1961).
Leroux, G. *Lagynos*. Paris, 1913.
Libertini, G. *Centuripe*. Catania, 1926.
Liegle, J. *Der Zeus des Phidias*. Berlin, 1922.
Linders, T. *Studies in the treasure records of Artemis Brauronia at Athens*. Stockholm, 1972.
Lippold, G. *Die griechische Plastik* (*Handbuch der Archäologie*, 5). Berlin, 1950.
Little, A. M. G. *Roman Perspective Painting and the Ancient Stage*. Kennebunk, Maine, 1971.
Llewellyn-Brown, W. *The Etruscan Lion*. Oxford, 1960.
Lloyd-Jones, H. *Aeschylus*, Loeb² vol. 2. Cambridge, Mass. and London, 1957.
Lobel, E. and Page, D. *Poetarum Lesbiorum Fragmenta*. Oxford, 1955.
Loeb, J. *Festschrift für James Loeb*. Munich, 1930.
Löwy, E. *Inschriften griechischer Bildhauer, mit Facsimilen*. Leipzig, 1885.
Polygnot: ein Buch von griechischer Malerei. Vienna, 1929.
Lorimer, H. *Homer and the Monuments*. London, 1950.
Lullies, R. and Hirmer, M. *Griechische Vasen der reifarchaischen Zeit*. Munich, 1953. (*GVRZ*)
Greek Sculpture. London, 1957 (2nd ed., 1960), (translated from *Die griechische Plastik*, Munich, 1957).
Luschey, H. *Funde zu den großen Fries von Pergamon*. Berlin, 1962.
MAAR. See *Memoirs of the American Academy at Rome*.
Macdonald, G. *Catalogue of the Greek Coins in the Hunterian Collection, University of Glasgow*. Glasgow, 1899–1907.
Madrider Mitteilungen (*Deutsches Archäologisches Institut. Madrider Abteilung*). Heidelberg, from 1960.
Magi, F. *I rilievi flavi del Palazzo della Cancelleria*. Rome, 1945.
See also Becatti.
Magister Gregorius *Narracio de mirabilibus urbis Romae*. ed R. B. C. Huygens (*Textus Minores* 42). Leiden, 1970.
Maia: Rivista di letterature classiche. N.S., Bologna, from 1972.
Maiuri, A. *La Villa dei misteri*. Rome, 1931.
Monumenti della pittura scoperti in Italia 3, 1. *Pompeii: le case di 'M. Fabius Amandio', del 'Sacerdos Amandus', e di 'P. Cornelius Teges'*. Rome, 1940.
Roman Painting. Geneva, 1953.
Pompeii (*Itinerari*, 3). Rome, 1953.
Makaronas, A. See Andronikos, Laourdas.
Mallwitz, A. and Schiering, W. *Die Werkstatt des Pheidias in Olympia*, 1 (*Olympische Forschungen* 5). Berlin, 1964.
Mansuelli, G. A. *Galleria degli Uffizi. Le Sculture*. Rome, 1958–61.
Marangou, E.-L. *Lakonische Elfenbein- und Beinschnitzerei*. Tübingen, 1969.
Marburger Jahrbuch für Kunstwissenschaft. Marburg, from 1924.
Marburger Winckelmann-Programm. Marburg, from 1947.
Marcadé, J. *Recueil des signatures de sculpteurs grecs*. Paris, from 1953.
Marconi, P. *L'Efebo di Selinunte*. Rome, 1929.
Marinatos, S. N. *Excavations at Thera: preliminary reports*. Athens, from 1968.

Masner, K. *Die Sammlung antiker Vasen und Terrakotten im K.K. Österreichischen Museum.* Vienna, 1892.

von Matt, L. *Großgriechenland.* Würzburg, 1961.

and Griffo, P. *Das antike Sizilien.* Würzburg, 1959.

Mattingley, H. and Carson, R. R. C. *Coins of the Roman Empire in the British Museum.* London, 1923–62. (*Mattingley, BMCat.*)

Matz, F. *Geschichte der griechischer Kunst.* Frankfurt, from 1949.

Kreta, Mykene, Troja: die minoische und die Homerische Welt. Stuttgart, 1956.

and Biesantz, H. *Corpus der minoischen und mykenischen Siegel.* Berlin, from 1964.

Mau, A. *Geschichte der dekorativen Wandmalerei in Pompeii.* Berlin, 1882.

Maximova, M. I. *Les vases plastiques dans l'antiquité (époque archaïque).* Paris, 1927.

MBCW. Master Bronzes from the Classical World. See Mitten and Doeringer.

Mededeelingen van het Nederlandsch Historisch Instituut te Rome. The Hague, from 1921.

Meiggs, R. and Lewis, D. M. *A Selection of Greek Historical Inscriptions to the End of the Fourth Century B.C.* Oxford, 1969.

Mélanges d'archéologie et d'histoire. Paris, from 1881.

Mélanges d'archéologie et d'histoire offerts à C. Picard. Paris, 1949.

Mélanges ... Michalowski. See Michalowski.

Memoirs of the American Academy at Rome. Bergamo, from 1917. (*MAAR*)

Memorie dell'Instituto di Corrispondenza Archeologica. Rome, 1832–65.

Memorie della Pontificia Accademia. See *Atti.*

Mendel, G. *Musées impériaux Ottomans. Catalogue des sculptures grecques, romaines et byzantines.* Constantinople, 1912–14. (*Cat.*)

von Mercklin, E. *Festschrift Eugen von Mercklin,* ed. E. Homann-Wedeking and B. Segall. Waldsassen, 1964.

Merkelbach, R. and West, M. L. *Fragmenta Hesiodea.* Oxford, 1967.

Metropolitan Museum Studies. New York, 1928–34.

Metzger, H. *Les réprésentations dans la céramique attique due IVe siècle.* Paris, 1951. (*Rép.*)

Fouilles de Xanthos II. *L'acropole Lycienne.* Paris, 1963.

Recherches sur l'imagerie athénienne. Paris, 1965. (*RIA*)

Michalowski, K. *Mélanges offerts à Kasimierz Michalowski.* Warsaw, 1965.

Micoff, V. *Le tombeau antique près de Kazanlak.* Sofia, 1954.

Milani, L. A. *Il Reale Museo Archeologico di Firenze.* Florence, 1923.

Minoica. Festschrift zum 80. Geburtstag von J. Sundwall, ed. E. Grumach. Berlin, 1958.

Mitteilungen des Deutschen Archäologischen Instituts. Berlin, 1948–52.

Mitteilungen des Deutschen Archäologischen Instituts: Athenische Abteilunge. Athens, from 1876. (*AM*)

Mitteilungen des Deutschen Archäologischen Instituts: Römische Abteilung. Rome, from 1886. (*RM*)

Mitteilungen der deutsch-türkischen Gesellschaft.

Mitteilungen. See also *Madrider Mitteilungen.*

Mitten, D. G. and Doeringer, S. F. *Master Bronzes from the Classical World.* Mainz, 1968.

MJb. See *Münchner Jahrbuch.*

MMAukt. Münzen und Medaillen A.G. Basel, Auktion ... (Monnaies et Médailles S.A. Bâle, Vente ...). Auction catalognes.

MMS. See *Metropolitan Museum Studies.*

Möbius, H. *Die Ornamente griechischen Grabstelen klassischer Zeit.* Berlin, 1929.

Die Reliefs der Portlandvase. Munich, 1965.

Mon. See *Monumenti inediti.*

Mon.Piot. See *Monuments et Mémoires.*

Monumenti antichi pubblicati per cura della Reale Accademia dei Lincei. Milan and Rome, from 1889. (*Mon.Linc.*)

Monumenti inediti pubblicati dall'Instituto di Corrispondenza Archeologica. Rome, 1829–91. (Mon.)

Monuments et Mémoires publiés par l'Académie des Inscriptions et Belles-Lettres. Paris, from 1894. (*Mon.Piot*)

Moretti, M. *L'Ara Pacis Augustae (Itinerari, 67).* Rome, 1938. (*L'Ara*)

Ara Pacis Augustae. Rome, 1948. (*APA*)

La mosaïque gréco-romaine (Actes du Colloque Internationale organisé à Paris, 29 août – 3 septembre, 1963, par G. Picard et H. Stern). Paris, 1965. (*Mos. G-R*)

MPASI. Monumenti della pittura antica scoperti in Italia. See Becatti and Magi, Bendinelli, Ducati, Maiuri, Romanelli.

Münchner Jahrbuch der bildenden Kunst. Munich, from 1906. (*MJb*)

Munich, Alte Pinakothek. *Katalog der alte Pinakothek zu München. Amtliche Ausgabe.* Munich, 1936.

Murray, A. S. and Smith, A. H. *White Athenian Vases in the British Museum*. London, 1896. (Murray *WAV*)
Greek Bronzes. London, 1898.
Museo Italiano di antichità classica. Florence, 1884–90.
Museum Helveticum. Basle, from 1944.
The Museum Journal. Philadelphia, 1910–33. (*Mus.J.*)
Museum Year. See Boston.
Mus.J. See *The Museum Journal*.
Mus.Marb. *A description of the collection of ancient marbles in the British Museum*. London, 1812–61.
Mustilli, D. *Il Museo Mussolini*. Rome, 1939.
MWP. See *Marburger Winckelmann-Programm*.
Mycenaean Seminar (Institute of Classical Studies, University of London), minutes. London, from 1958.
Mylonas, G. E. *O protoattikos amphoreus tis Eleusinos* (ὁ πρωτοαττικὸς ἀμφορεὺς τῆς Ἐλευσῖνος). Athens, 1957. (*PAE*)
Ancient Mycenae, the capital city of Agamemnon. London, 1957. (*AM*)
Grave-circle B at Mycenae (*Studies in Mediterranean Archaeology*, 7). Lund, 1964. (*GBM*)
Mycenae and the Mycenaean Age. Princeton, 1966. (*MMA*)
Nachrichten von der Gesellschaft der Wissenschaften zu Göttingen. Göttingen, from 1751. (*Nach.Ges. Gött.*)
Napoli, M. *Pittura antica in Italia*. Bergamo, 1960.
La Tomba del Tuffatore. Bari, 1970.
NDA. See *Neue Deutsche Ausgrabungen*.
Nederlands Kunsthistorisch Jaarboek. Bussum, from 1947.
Neon Athenaion. Athens.
Neue Beiträge. See *Schweitzer Festschrift*.
Neue deutsche Ausgrabungen im Mittelmeergebiet und im vorderen Orient, ed. E. Boehringer. Berlin, 1959. (*NDA*)
Neue Jahrbücher für das klassische Altertum. Leipzig, from 1898.
Neugebauer, K. A. *Antike Bronzestatuetten*. Berlin, 1921. (*ABS*)
Die minoischen und archaischen griechischen Bronzen (*Staatlichen Museen zu Berlin. Katalog der statuarischen Bronzen im Antiquarium*, 1). Berlin, 1931.
Neumann, G. *Gesten und Gebärden in der griechischen Kunst*. Berlin, 1965.
Neutsch, B. *Tas nymphas emi hiaron* (ΤΑΣ ΝΥΜΦΑΣ ΕΜΙ ΗΙΑΡΟΝ): *zum unterirdischen Heiligtum von Paestum*. Heidelberg, 1957.
Noble, J. V. *The Techniques of Painted Attic Pottery*. London, 1966.
Nogara, B. *Scritti in onore di Bartolomeo Nogara*. Vatican, 1937.
Nomisma. Berlin, 1927–33.
Notiziario archeologico. Rome, 1915–27.
O. See Overbeck.
ÖJh. See *Jahreshefte*.
OF. See *Olympische Forschungen*.
Ol. *Olympia*. Berlin, 1890–7. I. Adler, F. and others *Topographie und Geschichte*. 1897.
II. Adler, F. and others *Die Baudenkmäler*. 1892.
III. Treu, G. *Die Bildwerke in Stein und Thon*. 1897.
IV. Furtwängler, A. *Die Bronzen*. 1890.
V. Dittenberger, W. and Purgold, K. *Die Inschriften*. 1896.
Olympia-Berichte. *Berichte über die Ausgrabungen zu Olympia*. 1–3 in *AM* 52 (1937), 53 (1938) and 56 (1941); 4 onwards, Berlin, from 1944.
Olympische Forschungen (*OF*). See Herrman, Kunze, Mallwitz and Schiering, Schleif and Zschietschmann, Willemsen.
Olynthus. See Robinson, D. M.
Opuscula Atheniensia. Lund, from 1953.
Opuscula Carolo Kerenyi dedicata (*Stockholm Studies in Classical Archaeology* 5). Stockholm, 1968.
Opuscula Romana. Lund, from 1954.
Orlandini, P. *Calamide*. Bologna, 1950.
Orlandos, A. K. *Charistirion is Anastasion K. Orlandon* (Χαριστήριον εἰς Ἀναστάσιον Κ. Ὀρλάνδον). Athens, 1965–8.
Orsi, P. *Templum Apollonis Alaei ad Crimisa*. Rome, 1933.
Overbeck, J. *Die antiken Schriftquellen zur Geschichte der bildenden Künste bei den Griechen*. Leipzig, 1868. (O.)
Festschrift für Johannes Overbeck. Leipzig, 1893.
Oxé, A. and Comfort, H. *Corpus Vasorum Arretinorum*. Bonn, 1968.
Oxyrrhynchus Papyri, ed. B. P. Grenfell, A. S. Hunt and others. London, from 1898.
P. and P. See *Parthenos and Parthenon*.
Page, D. L. *Corinna* (*Society for the Promotion of Hellenic Studies, Supplementary Paper* 6). London, 1953.
Poetae Melici Graeci. Oxford, 1962.
See also Lobel.

Pallottino, M. *Il grande fregio di Traiano*. Rome, 1938.
Etruscan Painting. Geneva, 1952.
Arte e civiltà degli Etruschi. Turin, 1967.
Palmer, L. R. *Mycenaeans and Minoans*. London, 1961 (2nd ed., 1965).
and Boardman, J. *On the Knossos Tablets* (L.R.P., *The Finding-places of the Knossos Tablets*; J.B., *The Date of the Knossos Tablets*). Oxford, 1963.
Panofsky, O. *Essays in Honour of Erwin Panofsky* (*De artibus opuscula* 40). New York, 1961.
Papaspyridi, S. (Mrs Karouzou). *Guide du Musée National*. Athens, 1927.
Papers of the British School at Rome. London, from 1902. (*PBSR*)
PAPS. See *Proceedings of the American Philosophical Society*.
Paralipomena. See Beazley.
Paribeni, E. *Museo Nazionale Romano. Sculture greche del V. secolo, originali e repliche*. Rome, 1953. (*MNCat.Sc.*)
Catalogo della scultura di Cirene. Statue e rilievi di carattere religioso. Rome, 1959.
Parthenos and Parthenon (*Greece and Rome*, Supplement to vol. 10). Oxford, 1963.
Payne, H. *Necrocorinthia: a study of Corinthian art in the archaic period*. Oxford, 1931.
Protokorinthische Vasenmalerei. Berlin, 1933.
and Young, G. M. *Archaic Marble Sculpture from the Acropolis*. London, n.d. (1936).
See also *Perachora*.
PBA. See *Proceedings of the British Academy*.
PBSR. See *Papers of the British School at Rome*.
Pendlebury, J. D. S. *Aegyptiaca: a catalogue of Egyptian objects found in the Aegean area*. Cambridge, 1930.
The Archaeology of Crete. London, 1939. (Pendlebury)
Perachora [I]. Payne, H. and others, Oxford, 1940.
II. Dunbabin, T. J. and others, Oxford, 1962.
Perdrizet, P. *Bronzes grecs d'Égypte de la Collection Fouquet*. Paris, 1911.
Peredolskaya, A. A. *Krasnofigurnye atticheskie vazy* (Краснофигурные аттические вазы). Leningrad, 1967.
Perg. *Altertümer von Pergamon*. Berlin, from 1885. iii, 1, Schrammen, J. *Der große Altar* (1906). iii, 2, Winnefeld, H. *Die Friese des großen Altars* (1910). vii. 1 and 2, Winter, F. *Die Skulpturen mit Ausnahmen der Altarreliefs* (1908). v. 1, Kawerau, G. and Wiegand, T. *Die Paläste vom Hochburg* (1930).
Peters, K. *Studien zu den panathenäischen Preisamphoren*. Würzburg, 1941.
Petsas, Ph. M. *Pella* (*Studies in Mediterranean Archaeology*, 14). Lund, 1964.
O taphos ton Lefkadion (ὁ τάφος τῶν Λευκαδίων). Athens, 1966.
Pfuhl, E. *Malerei und Zeichnung der Griechen*. Munich, 1923.
Philadelphia. See *Museum Journal*.
Philippaki, B. *The Attic Stamnos*. Oxford, 1967.
Vases of the National Museum, Athens. Athens, n.d. (*c*. 1972).
Philippart, H. *Les coupes attiques à fond blanc*. Brussels, 1936.
Picard, C. *La sculpture antique de Phidias à l'époque byzantine*. (*Manuels d'histoire de l'art*). Paris from 1926. (*Manuel*)
and de La Coste Messelière, P. *Fouilles de Delphes* IV. *Monuments figurés: sculpture, 2. Art archaïque: les trésors ioniques*. Paris, 1928.
Pietrangeli, C. *L'arc de Trajan à Benevento*. Paris, 1943.
Pinkwart, D. *Die Relief des Archelaos*. Kallmünz, 1965.
Piotrovskii, B. B. *Urartu: the kingdom of Van and its art*. London, 1967.
Plommer, H. *Ancient and Classical Architecture* (*Simpson's History of Architectural Development*, 1). London, 1956.
PM. See Evans, A. *The Palace of Minos at Knossos*.
Pollitt, J. J. *The Art of Greece, 1400–31 B.C., sources and documents*. Englewood Cliffs, N.J., 1965.
Art and Experience in Classical Greece. Cambridge, 1972.
Pope-Hennessy, J. *Paolo Uccello*. London, 1950 (2nd ed., 1969).
Fra Angelico. London, 1952.
Popham, A. E. and Pouncey, P. *Italian Drawings in the Department of Prints and Drawings in the British Museum. The fourteenth and fifteenth centuries*. London, 1950.
Pottier, E. *Les vases antiques du Louvre*. Paris, 1897–1922.
Pouilloux, J. *Fouilles de Delphes* II. *Topographie et architecture, La région nord du sanctuaire, de l'époque archaïque à la fin du sanctuaire*. Paris, 1960.
and Roux, G. *Énigmes à Delphes*. Paris, 1963.

Poulsen, F. *Das Orient und die frühgriechische Kunst.* Leipzig, 1912.
Delphi. London, 1920.
and Rhomaios, K. *Erster vorläufiger Bericht über die dänisch-griechischen Ausgrabungen von Kalydon.* Copenhagen, 1927.
Poulsen, V. H. *Der strenge Stil.* Copenhagen, 1937.
Les portraits grecs. Copenhagen, 1954.
Die Amazone des Kresilas (*Opus Nobile*, 1). Bremen, 1957.
Praktika (Πρακτικά). Athens, from 1871.
Praschniker, C. *Parthenonstudien.* Augsburg, 1928.
Price, E. R. *East Greek Pottery: the orientalizing style, 7th-6th cent.* (*Classification des céramiques antiques*, 13). n.pl., n.d. (Macon?, 1928).
Priene. See Wiegand.
Proceedings of the American Philosophical Society. Philadelphia. (*PAPS*)
Proceedings of the British Academy. London, from 1902. (*PBA*)
Prückner, H. *Die Lokrischen Tonreliefs: Beitrag zur Kultgeschichte von Lokroi Epizephyrioi.* Mainz, 1968.
Pryce, F. N. *Catalogue of Sculpture in the Department of Greek and Roman Antiquities*, I, 1, *Prehellenic and early Greek.* London, 1928.
2. *Cypriote and Etruscan*, London, 1930.
Pullan, A. P. *Antiquities of Ionia*, iv. London, 1881.
RA. See *Revue Archéologique.*
Rassegna d'arte. Milan, from 1901.
Raoul-Rochette, D. *Choix de peintures de Pompeii.* Paris, 1867.
Raubitschek, A. E. with L. H. Jeffery. *Dedications from the Athenian Acropolis.* Cambridge, Mass., 1949.
See also Hoffmann.
RE. Paulys Real-Encyclopedie der klassischen Altertumswissenschaft. Neue Bearb. herausg. von G. Wissowa. Stuttgart, 1894–1972.
REA. See *Revue des études anciennes.*
Regling, K. *Die antike Münze als Kunstwerk.* Berlin, 1924.
Reinach, S. *Répertoire de la statuaire grecque et romaine.* Paris, 1897–1930.
Rendiconti della Pontificia Accademia Romana. See *Atti.*
Reutersward, P. *Studien zur Polychromie der Plastik: Griechenland und Rom.* Stockholm, 1960.
Reuther, O. *Der Heratempel von Samos: der Bau seit der Zeit des Polykrates.* Berlin, 1957.
Revue Archéologique, Paris, from 1844.
Revue archéologique de l'Est et du Centre-Est. Dijon, from 1950.
Revue des arts. Paris, 1951–60 (succeeded by Revue du Louvre).
Revue des études anciennes. Bordeaux, from 1898.
Richter, G. M. A. *The Craft of Athenian Pottery.* New Haven, Conn., 1923.
The Sculpture and Sculptors of the Greeks. New Haven, Conn. 1929 (2nd ed., 1930; 3rd, 1949; 4th, 1970). (*Sc.*)
Animals in Greek Sculpture. Oxford, 1930.
and Hall, L. F. *Red-Figured Athenian vases in the Metropolitan Museum of Art.* New York, 1935.
and Milne, M. M. *Shapes and Names of Athenian Vases.* New York, 1935.
Kouroi. New York, 1942 (2nd ed., London, 1960; 3rd ed., 1970).
Attic Red-figured Vases: a survey. New York, 1946 (2nd ed., 1958).
Archaic Greek Art. New York, 1949. (*AGA*)
Three Critical Periods in Greek Sculpture. Oxford, 1951. (*TCP*)
Metropolitan Museum of Art, New York. Handbook of the Greek Collection. Cambridge, Mass., 1953. (*MMH*)
Metropolitan Museum of Art, New York. Catalogue of Greek Sculptures. Oxford, 1954. (*CGS*)
Ancient Italy. Ann Arbor, 1955. (*AI*)
Greek Portraits, i–iv. Brussels, 1955–62. (*GP*)
Catalogue of the Greek and Roman Antiquities in the Dumbarton Oaks Collection. Harvard, 1956.
Catalogue of the Engraved Gems, Greek, Etruscan and Roman, Metropolitan Museum. Rome, 1956.
A Handbook of Greek Art. London, 1959 (2nd ed., 1960). (*H*)
The Archaic Gravestones of Attica. London, 1961. (*AGSA*)
The Portraits of the Greeks. London, 1965. (*POG*)
The Furniture of the Greeks, Etruscans and Romans. London, 1966. (*Furn.*)
Engraved Gems of the Greeks, Etruscans and Romans. London, 1968. (*EGGE*)
Korai. London, 1968.
de Ridder, A. *Catalogue des vases peints de la Bibliothèque Nationale.* Paris, 1902.
Ridgway, B. S. *The Severe Style in Greek Sculpture.* Princeton, 1970.
Riezler, W. *Weißgrundige attische Lekythen.* Munich, 1914.

Riis, P. J. *An Introduction to Etruscan Art.* Copenhagen, 1953.
Rizza, G. and Scrinari, V. Santa Maria. *Il Santuario sull'Acropoli di Gortina* I (Monografie della Scuola Archeologica di Atene II). Rome, 1968.
Rizzo, G. E. *La pittura ellenistico-romana.* Milan, 1926.
Prassitele. Milan, 1932.
Thiasos. Rome, 1934.
RM. *Römische Mitteilungen.* See *Mitteilungen.*
Robert, C. *Archäologische Märchen.* Berlin, 1886.
Die antiken Sarkophagreliefs. Berlin, 1890–1966.
Die Nekyia des Polygnot (*16. Hallisches Winckelmannsprogramm*). Halle, 1892.
Die Iliupersis des Polygnot (*17. Hallisches Winckelmannsprogramm*). Halle, 1893.
Die Marathonenschlacht in der Poikile, und weiteres über Polygnot (*18. Hallisches Winckelmannsprogramm*). Halle, 1895.
Robertson, D. S. *A Handbook of Greek and Roman Architecture.* Cambridge, 1929 (2nd ed., 1943; reprinted in paperback as *Greek and Roman Architecture*, 1969). (D. S. Robertson)
Robertson, M. *Greek Painting.* Geneva, 1959. (M. Robertson)
Between Archaeology and Art History. Oxford, 1963.
Robinson, D. M. and others. *Excavations at Olynthus.* Baltimore, 1929–52.
Robinson, E. S. G. *Essays in Greek Coinage presented to Stanley Robinson*, ed. G. K. Jenkins and C. M. Kraay. Oxford, 1968.
Rodenwaldt, G. *Die Kunst der Antike. Hellas und Rom.* Berlin, 1927. (KdA)
Altdorische Bildwerke in Korfu. Berlin, 1938.
Korkyra: archaische Bauten und Bildwerke II. *Die Bildwerke des Artemistempels von Korkyra.* Berlin, 1939. (I. *Der Artemistempel: Architektur, Dachterrakotten, Inschriften*, by H. Schleif, K. A. Rhomaios and G. Klaffenbach, 1940).
See also Hege.
Rösch, G. *Altertümliche Marmorwerke von Paros.* Kiel, 1914.
Rohde, E. *Pergamon.* Berlin, 1961.
Rolley, G. *Fouilles de Delphes* V. *Monuments figurés. Les statuettes de bronze.* Paris, 1969.
Romanelli, P. *Monumenti della pittura antica scoperti in Italia* I, 2. *Le pitture della Tomba delle 'caccia e pesce'.* Rome, 1940.
La colonna antonina. Rome, 1942.
La colonna traiana. Rome, 1942.
Roscher, W. H. and others. *Ausführliche Lexikon der griechischen und römischen Mythologie.* Leipzig, 1884–1937.
Rostovtzeff, M. I. *Dura-Europos and its art.* Oxford, 1938.
Roulez, J. *Choix de vases peints du Musée d'Antiquités de Leyde.* Ghent, 1954.
Roux, G. *L'architecture de l'Argolide aux IVe. et IIIe. siècles avant J.C.* Paris, 1961.
See also Pouilloux.
Ruesch, A. *Guida illustrata del Museo Nazionale di Napoli.* Naples, 1911.
Rumpf, A. *Chalkidische Vasen.* Berlin, 1927.
Sakonides (*Bilder griechischer Vasen*, 11). Leipzig, 1937.
Festschrift Andreas Rumpf, ed. T. Dohrn. Krefeld, 1952.
Malerei und Zeichnung (*Handbuch der Archäologie* 4, 1). Munich, 1953.
Archäologie I and II. Berlin, 1953, 1956.
Säflund, G. *Aphrodite Kallipygos.* Stockholm, 1963.
Fynden i Tiberiusgrottan. Stockholm, 1966.
von Salis, A. *Der Altar von Pergamon.* Berlin, 1912.
Die Kunst der Griechen. Leipzig, 1919.
Sambon, A. *Les fresques de Boscoreale* (sale catalogue). Paris, 1903.
Samos. See Buschor, Jantzen, Reuther.
Schäfer, J. *Studien zu den griechischen Reliefpithoi des 8. bis 6. Jahrhunderts v. Chr. aus Kreta, Rhodos, Tenos und Boiotien.* Kallmünz, 1957.
Schede, M. *Griechische und römische Skulptur des Antikenmuseums* (*Meisterwerke der Türkischen Museen zu Konstantinopel*). Berlin, 1928.
Schefold, K. *Kertscher Vasen* (*Bilder griechischer Vasen*, 3). Berlin, 1930. (*KV*)
Untersuchungen zu den Kertscher Vasen. Berlin, 1934. (*UKV*)
Griechische Plastik I. *Die großen Bildhauer des archaischen Athen.* Basle, 1949.
Pompeianische Malerei. Basle, 1952.
Die Wände Pompeiis. Berlin, 1957.
Meisterwerke griechischer Kunst. Basle and Stuttgart, 1960.
Myth and Legend in Early Greek Art. London, 1968 (translated from *Frühgriechische Sagenbilder*, Munich, 1964). (*ML*)
and Seidel, M. *Der Alexander-Sarkophag.* Berlin, 1968.
See also *Gestalt und Geschichte.*
Schiering, W. *Werkstätten orientalisierender Keramik auf Rhodos.* Berlin, 1957.

Schleif, E. and Zschietzschmann, W. 'Das Philippeion' in *Olympische Forschungen* 1. Berlin, 1944.

Schmidt, E. *Archaistische Kunst in Griechenland und Rom.* Munich, 1922.

Schmidt, E. M. *The Great Altar of Pergamon.* London, 1965 (translated from *Der große Altar von Pergamon*, Leipzig, 1961).

Schober, A. *Die Fries des Hekataions von Lagina.* Vienna, 1933.

Schoppa, H. *Die Kunst der Römerzeit in Gallien, Germanien und Britannien.* Berlin, 1957.

Schrader, H. *Phidias.* Frankfurt, 1924.

with Langlotz, E. and Schuchardt, W. *Die archaischen Marmorbildwerke der Akropolis.* Frankfort, 1939. (Schrader)

Schrammen, J. *Der große Altar.* See *Perg.*

Schreiber, T. *Die hellenistische Reliefbilder.* Leipzig, 1889–94.

Schuchardt, W. H. *Archaische Giebelkomposition.* 1940.

Die Meister der großen Fries von Pergamon. Berlin, 1925.

See also *Antike Plastik*, Langlotz, Schrader.

Schweitzer Festschrift. Zur Kunst der Antike: ausgewählte Schriften; zum 70. Gerburtstag von B. Schweitzer, ed. U. Hausmann. Tübingen, 1963.

Scientific American. New York.

Scritti . . . Nogara. See Nogara.

Seeberg, A. *Corinthian komos vases.* London, 1971.

Selected Bronzes, Greek, Roman and Etruscan, in the British Museum. London, 1915.

Seltman, C. T. *The Temple-coins of Olympia.* Cambridge, 1921.

Greek Coins. London, 1933 (2nd ed., 1954).

Masterpieces of Greek Coinage. Oxford, 1949.

Serradifalco, Duca di. *Antichità di Sicilia.* 1834.

Shqiperia Arkeologjike. Tirane, 1971.

Shefton, B. See Arias.

Shoe, L. T. *Profiles of Greek Mouldings.* Cambridge, Mass., 1936.

Profiles of Western Greek Mouldings. Rome, 1952.

Shore, A. F. *Portrait-painting from Roman Egypt.* London, 1972.

Sichtermann, H. *Griechische Vasen in Unteritalien aus der Sammlung Jatta in Ruvo.* Tübingen, 1960.

von Sieglin, E. *Expedition Ernst Sieglin. Ausgrabungen in Alexandria unter Leitung von Theodor Schreiber.* Leipzig, 1908–27.

Siewert, P. *Der Eid von Plataiai* (*Vestigia. Beiträge zur alten Geschichte*, 16). Munich, 1972.

Simon, E. *Die Fürstenbilder von Boscoreale.* Baden-Baden, 1958.

Die Geburt der Aphrodite. Berlin, 1959.

SMA. Studies in Mediterranean Archaeology. Lund, from 1962. See Andronikos, Mylonas, Petsas.

Smith, A. H. *A Catalogue of Sculpture in the Department of Greek and Roman Antiquities, British Museum.* London, 1892–1904.

The Sculptures of the Parthenon. London, 1910.

Smith, C. H. *Catalogue of the Greek and Etruscan Vases in the British Museum* 3. *Vases of the Finest Period.* London, 1896.

Smith, H. R. W. *New Aspects of the Menon Painter.* Berkeley, 1929.

The Origin of Chalcidian Ware. Berkeley, 1932.

Snodgrass, A. M. *The Dark Age of Greece.* Edinburgh, 1971.

Sparkes, B. A., with Talcott, L. and Frantz, A. *Pots and Pans of Classical Athens* (*Excavations of the Athenian Agora, Picture Book no. 1*). Princeton, 1958.

and Talcott, L. *The Athenian Agora* 12. *Black and Plain Pottery of the 6th, 5th and 4th Centuries B.C.* Princeton, 1970.

Spina e l'Etruria padana (Supplement to *Studi Etruschi* 25). Florence, 1959.

Squarciapino, M. F. *La scuola di Afrodisia.* Rome, 1943.

Stais, V. *Marbres et bronzes du Musée National.* Athens, 1907.

Stark, K. B. *Zwei Alexanderköpfe.* Leipzig, 1879.

Stavropoulos, P. D. *I aspis tis Athinas Parthenou tou Pheidiou* (ἡ ἀσπὶς τῆς Ἀθηνᾶς Παρθένου τοῦ Φειδίου). Athens, 1950.

St.Etr. See *Studi Etruschi.*

Stevens, G. P. and Paton, M. *The Erechtheum.* Cambridge, Mass., 1927.

Stibbe, C. M. *Lakonische Vasenmaler des sechsten Jahrhunderts v. Chr.* Amsterdam, 1972.

Strocka, V. M. *Piräusreliefs und Parthenosschild.* Bochum, 1967.

Strong, D. E. *Roman Imperial Sculpture.* London, 1961.

Strong, E. *La scultura romana da Augusto a Constantino.* Florence, 1923–6.

Stuart, J., Revett, N. and others. *The Antiquities of Athens.* London, 1762–1830.

Stuart Jones, H. *Passages from ancient writers illustrative of the history of Greek Sculpture.* London, 1895.

Stuart Jones, H. *The Sculptures of the Museo Capitolino*. Oxford, 1912.
The Sculptures of the Museo Conservatori. Oxford, 1926. (*Cons. Cat.*)
Studi Etruschi. Florence from 1927.
Studnizcka, F. *Vermutungen zur griechischen Kunstgeschichte*. Vienna, 1884.
Süsserott, H. K. *Griechische Plastik des IV. Jahrhunderts v. Chr. Untersuchungen zur Zeitbestimmung*. Frankfurt, 1938.
Svoronos, J. N. *Das Athener Nationalmuseum. Phototypische Wiedergabe seiner Schätze mit erleuterndern Text*. Athens, 1908–37.
Swindler, M. *Ancient Painting*. New Haven, Conn., 1929.
Symbolae Osloenses. Oslo, from 1922.
Syria. Paris, from 1920.
Taylour, Lord William. *Mycenaean Pottery in Italy and Adjacent Areas*. Cambridge, 1958.
Technau, W. *Exekias* (*Bilder griechischer Vasen*, 9). Leipzig, 1936.
Thompson, D. B. *Ptolemaic Oinochoai and Portraits in Faience. Aspects of the Ruler-Cult*. Oxford, 1973.
Thompson, H. A. and Wycherley, R. E. *The Athenian Agora* 14. *The Agora of Athens: the history, shape and uses of an ancient city center*. Princeton, 1972.
Tod, M. N. and Wace, A. J. B. *A catalogue of the Sparta Museum*. Oxford, 1946.
Touring Club Italiano. *Toscana* I. Milan, 1934.
Toynbee, J. M. C. *The Hadrianic School*. Cambridge, 1934.
Travlos, J. *A Pictorial Dictionary of Ancient Athens*. London, 1970.
Trendall, A. D. *Paestan Pottery*. London, 1936.
Frühitaliotische Vasen (*Bilder griechischer Vasen*, 12). Leipzig, 1938. (*FV*)
The Felton Greek Vases in the National Gallery of Victoria. Canberra, 1958.
Phlyax Vases (*Bulletin of the Institute of Classical Studies, Supplement* 8). London, 1959.
South Italian Vase-painting. London, 1966.
The Red-figured Vases of Lucania, Campania and Sicily. Oxford, 1967. (*RLCS*)
See also Cambitoglou.
Trésors d'art du Moyen Âge en Italie (exhibition catalogue). Paris, 1952.
Treu, G. See *Olympia*.
Tuchelt, K. *Die archaischen Skulpturen aus Didyma*. Berlin, 1970.
Unedited Antiquities of Attica (Society of Dilettanti). London, 1817.
Ure, P. N. *Boeotian Pottery of the Geometric and Archaic Styles* (*Classification des céramiques antiques*, 12). Macon, 1927.
Sixth and Fifth Century Pottery from Rhitsona. London, 1927.
Vallet, G. and Villard, F. *Mégara Hyblaea* II. *La céramique archaïque*. Paris, 1964.
Van Buren, E. D. *Figurative Terracotta Revetments in Etruria and Latium in the VI and V Centuries B.C.* London, 1921.
Archaic Fictile Revetments in Sicily and Magna Graecia. London, 1923.
Greek Fictile Revetments in the Archaic Period. London, 1926.
Vassiliev, A. *Das antike Grabmal bei Kasanlak*. Sofia, 1959.
Vente xi Bâle. See *Münzen und Medaillen*.
Ventris, M. G. F. and Chadwick, J. *Documents in Mycenaean Greek*. Cambridge, 1956.
Venturi, A. *Storia dell'arte italiana*. Milan, 1901–40.
A Short History of Italian Art. London, 1926.
Venturi, L. *Botticelli*. London, 1949.
Vercoutter, J. *Égyptiens et Préhellènes*. Paris, 1954.
Vermeule, C. C. See Comstock, Karageorghis.
Vermeule, E. T. *Greece in the Bronze Age*. Chicago, 1964. (Vermeule)
Vessberg, O. *Studien zur Kunstgeschichte der römischen Republik*. Lund, 1951.
de Visscher, F. *Herakles Epitrapezios*. Paris, 1962.
Wace, A. J. B. *An Approach to Greek Sculpture*. Cambridge, 1935.
Mycenae: an archaeological history and guide. Princeton, 1949.
Wace, H. *Ivories from Mycenae* I. *The Ivory Triad*. Meriden, Conn., 1939.
Waldstein, C. and others. *The Argive Heraeum*. Boston and New York, 1902.
Walter, O. *Beschreibung der Reliefs im kleinen Akropolismuseum in Athen*. Vienna, 1923.
Walters, H. B. *Catalogue of the Bronzes, Greek, Roman and Etruscan, in the Department of Greek and Roman Antiquities in the British Museum*. London, 1899. (*BMCat.Br.*).
Catalogue of the Engraved Gems and Cameos, Greek, Etruscan and Roman, in the British Museum. London, 1926. (*BMCat.Gems*)

Walters, H. B. *Catalogue of the Greek and Etruscan Vases in the British Museum* 4. *Vases of the Latest Period*. London, 1896. (*BMCat.Vas.*4)

Webster, T. B. L. *Der Niobidenmaler* (*Bilder griechischer Vasen*, 8). Leipzig, 1935.

Greek Theatre Production. London, 1956.

and Trendall, A. D. *Illustrations of Greek Drama*. London, 1971.

Potter and Patron in Classical Athens. London, 1972.

Wehrli, F. *Demetrios von Phaleron*. Basle, Stuttgart, Schwabe, 1968.

Weickert, C. *Griechische Plastik*. Berlin, 1941.

Antike Architektur. Berlin, 1949.

Studien zur Kunstgeschichte des V. Jahrhunderts v. Chr. 1. *Polygnot*. Berlin, 1950. 2. *Erga Perikleous* (Ἔργα Περικλέους). Berlin, 1950.

Weinberg, S. *Corinth* vii 1. *The Geometric and Orientalizing Pottery*. Cambridge, Mass., 1947.

(editor) *The Aegean and the Near East: studies presented to Hetty Goldman on her 85th birthday*. New York, 1951. (*Goldman Studies*)

Weitzmann, K. *Illustration in Roll and Codex. A study in the origin and method of text illustration*. Princeton, 1947.

Ancient Book Illumination (*Martin Classical Lectures*, 16). Cambridge, Mass., 1959.

Welter, G. *Aigina*. Berlin, 1938.

West, M. L. Hesiod *Theogony*, Oxford, 1966.

See also Merkelbach, R.

Whitaker, J. I. S. *Motya, a Phoenician Colony in Sicily*. London, 1921.

White, J. *Perspective in Ancient Drawing and Painting* (*Society for the Promotion of Hellenic Studies, Supplementary Paper* 7). London, 1956.

Wiegand, T. and others. *Die archaische Poros-Architektur der Akropolis zu Athen*. Cassel and Leipzig, 1904. (Wiegand *Porosarch.*)

Priene. Berlin, 1904.

Milet. Die Ergebnisse der Ausgrabungen und Untersuchungen. Berlin, from 1906.

Wiener Vorlegeblätter. Vienna, 1869–91. (*WV*)

Willemsen, F. *Dreifußkessel von Olympia: alte und neue Funde* (*Olympische Forschungen*, III). Berlin, 1957.

Die Löwenkopf-Wasserspeier vom Dach des Zeustempels (*Olympische Forschungen*, IV). Berlin, 1959.

Winnefeld, H. *Hypnos*. Berlin and Stuttgart, 1886.

See also *Perg.*

Winter, F. *Kunstgeschichte in Bildern. Das Altertum*. Leipzig, 1900. (*KB*)

See also *Perg.*

Wissenschaftliche Zeitschrift der Universität Rostock. Rostock, from 1952. (*WZUR*)

Wittkower, R. *Essays in the History of Art presented to Rudolf Wittkower*. London, 1967.

Wolters, P. and Bruns, G. *Das Kabirenheiligtum bei Theben*. Berlin, 1940.

Woodhead, A. G. *The Greeks in the West*. London, 1962.

Woodward, J. M. *Perseus. A study in Greek art and legend*. Cambridge, 1937.

Woolley, L. *A Forgotten Kingdom*. London, 1953.

WV. See *Wiener Vorlegeblätter*.

Wycherley, R. E. *How the Greeks Built Cities*. London, 1949.

The Athenian Agora, 3. *Literary and Epigraphical Testimonia*. Princeton, 1957.

See also Thompson, H. A.

WZUR. See *Wissenschaftliche Zeitschrift der Universität Rostock*.

Xanthos. See Coupel, Demargne, Metzger.

Yale Classical Studies. New Haven, from 1928. (*YCS*)

Zancani Montuoro, P. and Zanotti Bianco, U., with Kraus, F. *Heraion alla Foce del Sele* I. *Il santuario. Il tempio della Dea. Rilievi figurati varii*. Rome, 1951. II. '*Il primo thesauros*'. Rome, 1954.

Zeitschrift für bildende Kunst. Leipzig, 1866–1932.

Zervos, C. *L'art en Grèce*. Paris, 1934.

L'art de la Crète, néolithique et minoenne. Paris, 1956.

L'art des Cyclades, du début à la fin de l'âge du bronze, 2500–1100, avant notre ère. Paris, 1957.

Züchner, W. *Griechische Klappspiegel*. Berlin, 1942.

ADDENDA

Broneer, O. *Isthmia* I. Princeton, 1971.

Mylonas, G. *O taphikos kyklos B ton Mykenon* (Ὁ ταφικὸς κύκλος Β τῶν Μυκηνῶν). Athens, 1973. See p. 614, Prologue n. 18.

Robertson, M. and Frantz, A. *The Parthenon Frieze*. London, 1975.

Zur griechischen Kunst: Hansjörg Bloesch zum 60. Geburtstag (*AK* Beiheft 9). Bern, 1973. (*Festschr. Bloesch*).

LIST OF ILLUSTRATIONS

FIGURES

(*pp.* 778–83)

PLATES

All photographs are reproduced by courtesy of the Museum, collector, scholar or photographer named. Further details of the objects, and references to the pages on which they are discussed, are given in the captions.

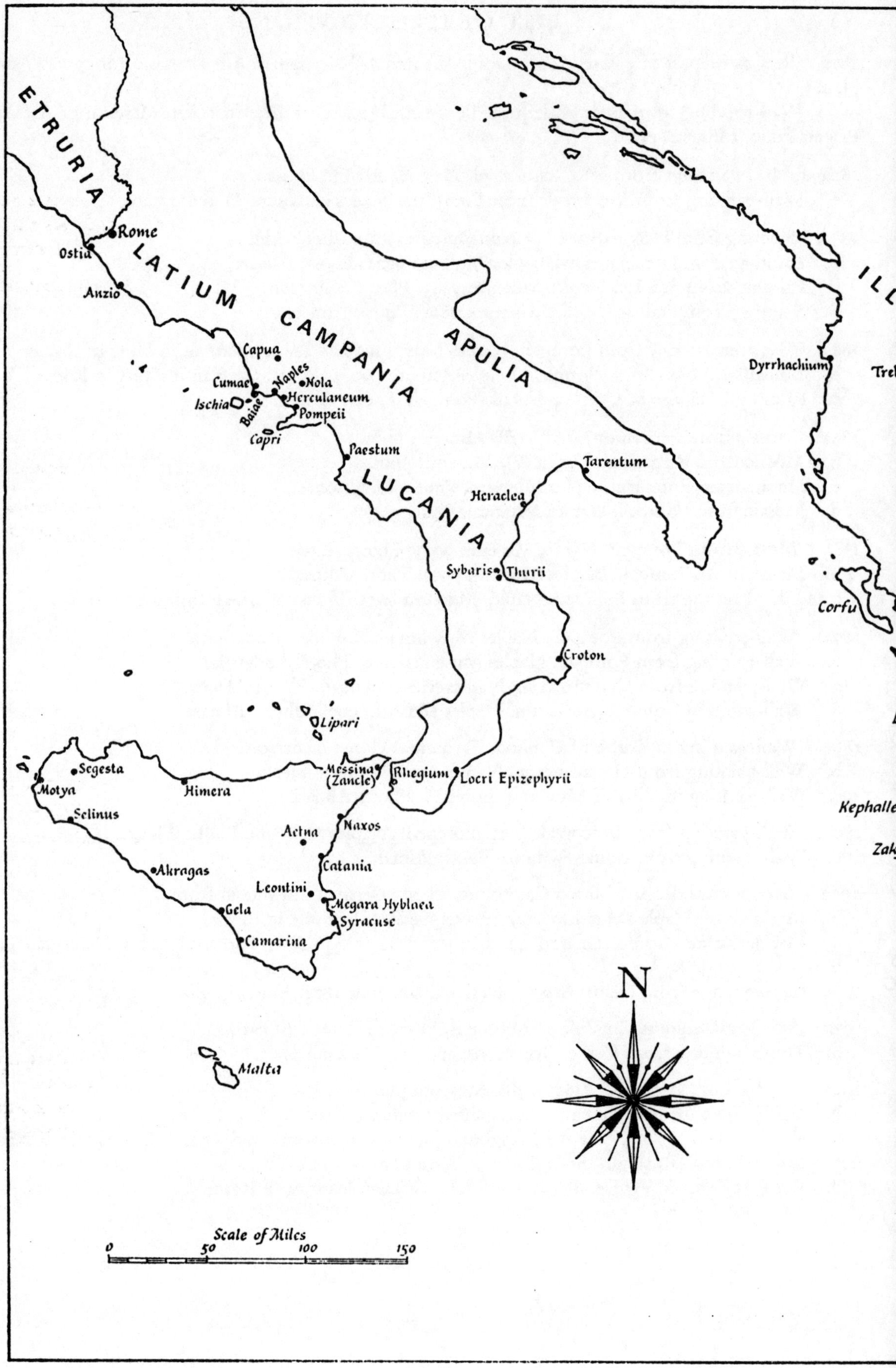
ETRURIA
LATIUM
CAMPANIA
APULIA
LUCANIA
ILL
Rome
Ostia
Anzio
Capua
Naples
Nola
Cumae
Ischia
Baiae
Herculaneum
Pompeii
Capri
Paestum
Tarentum
Heraclea
Sybaris
Thurii
Croton
Lipari
Messina
(Zancle)
Rhegium
Locri Epizephyrii
Segesta
Motya
Himera
Selinus
Aetna
Naxos
Catania
Akragas
Leontini
Megara Hyblaea
Syracuse
Gela
Camarina
Malta
Dyrrhachium
Corfu
Kephalle
N
Scale of Miles
0
50
100
150

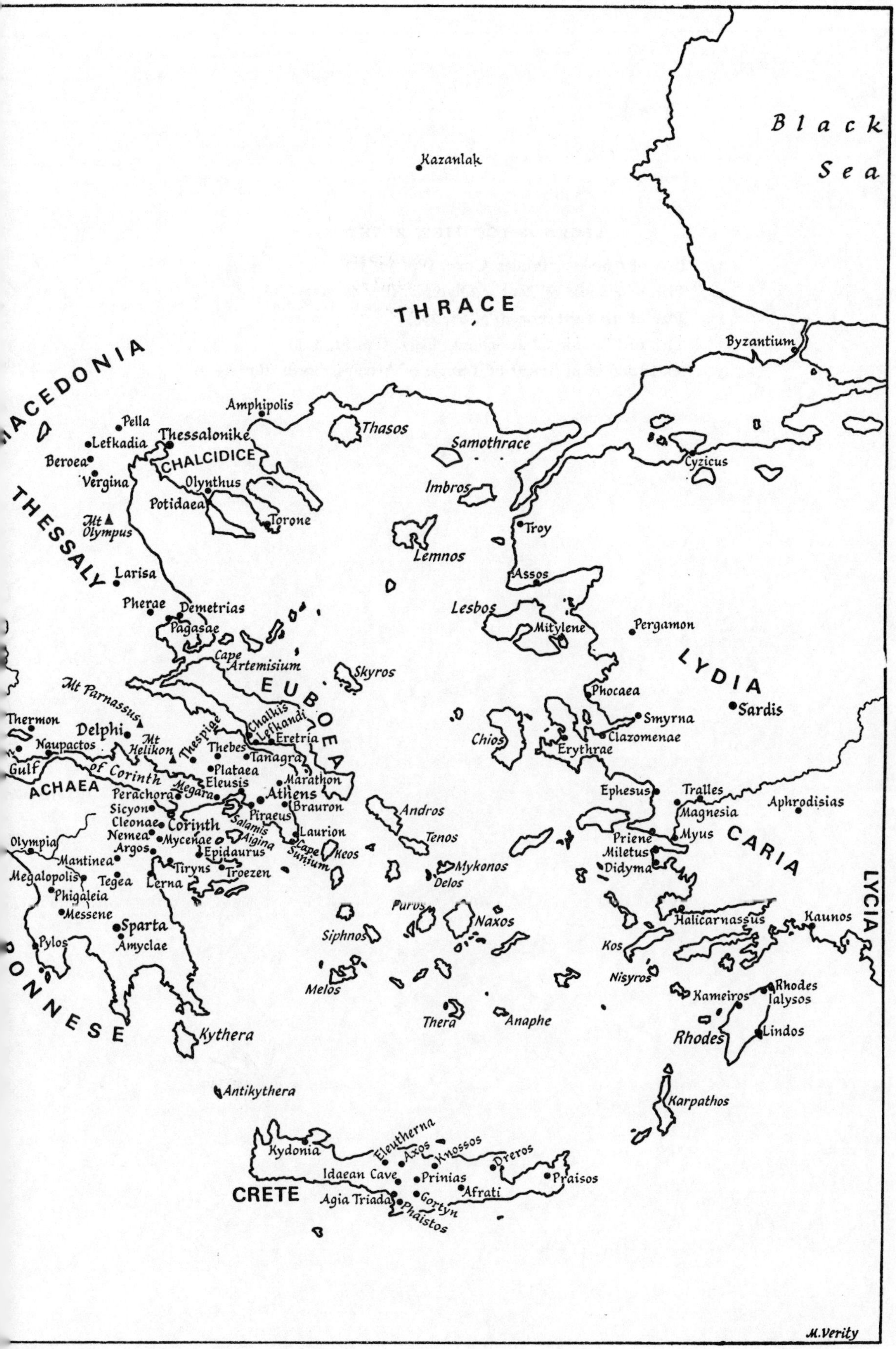
Black
Sea
Kazanlak
THRACE
Byzantium
MACEDONIA
Amphipolis
Pella
Lefkadia
Thessalonike
Beroea
Vergina
CHALCIDICE
Olynthus
Potidaea
Torone
Thasos
Samothrace
Imbros
Cyzicus
THESSALY
Mt Olympus
Lemnos
Troy
Larisa
Assos
Pherae
Demetrias
Pagasae
Lesbos
Mitylene
Pergamon
Cape Artemisium
Skyros
LYDIA
Mt Parnassus
EUBOEA
Phocaea
Thermon
Delphi
Chalkis
Lefkandi
Eretria
Smyrna
Sardis
Naupactos
Mt Helikon
Thespiae
Thebes
Tanagra
Chios
Clazomenae
Erythrae
Gulf of Corinth
Plataea
Eleusis
Marathon
ACHAEA
Perachora
Megara
Athens
Ephesus
Tralles
Sicyon
Piraeus
Brauron
Andros
Magnesia
Aphrodisias
Cleonae
Corinth
Salamis
Laurion
Nemea
Mycenae
Aigina
Tenos
Priene
Myus
Olympia
Argos
Epidaurus
Cape Sunium
Keos
Miletus
CARIA
Mantinea
Tiryns
Troezen
Mykonos
Didyma
Megalopolis
Tegea
Lerna
Delos
Phigaleia
Messene
Paros
Naxos
Halicarnassus
Kaunos
LYCIA
Sparta
Siphnos
Pylos
Amyclae
Kos
PELOPONNESE
Melos
Nisyros
Rhodes
Kameiros
Ialysos
Thera
Anaphe
Kythera
Rhodes
Lindos
Antikythera
Karpathos
Eleutherna
Kydonia
Axos
Knossos
Dreros
Idaean Cave
Prinias
Praisos
CRETE
Agia Triada
Gortyn
Afrati
Phaistos
M.Verity

LEGENDS FOR FIGS. 2 AND 3

2a. Plan of temple at Prinias, Crete. (Pp. 39, 37)

2b. Plan of Temple of Zeus at Olympia. (Pp. 61, 272)

2c. Plan of the Parthenon. (Pp. 61, 293)

2d. Plan of 'Temple C' at Selinus, Sicily. (Pp. 61, 118)

3. Restoration of pediment of Temple of Artemis, Corfu. (Pp. 63–7)

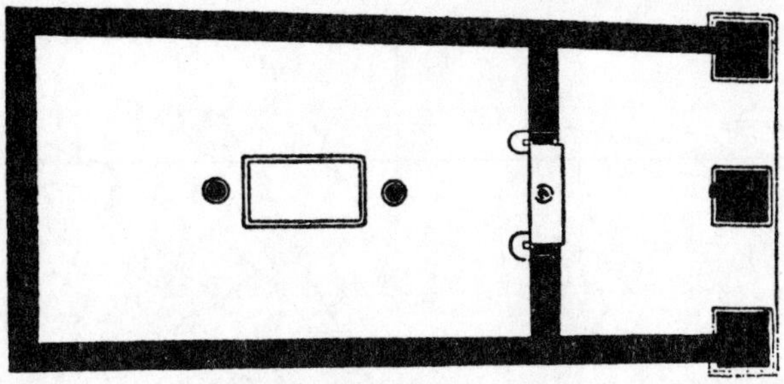

2a

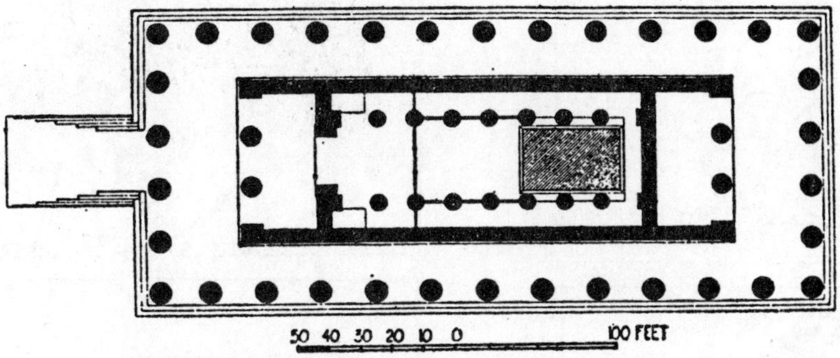

2b

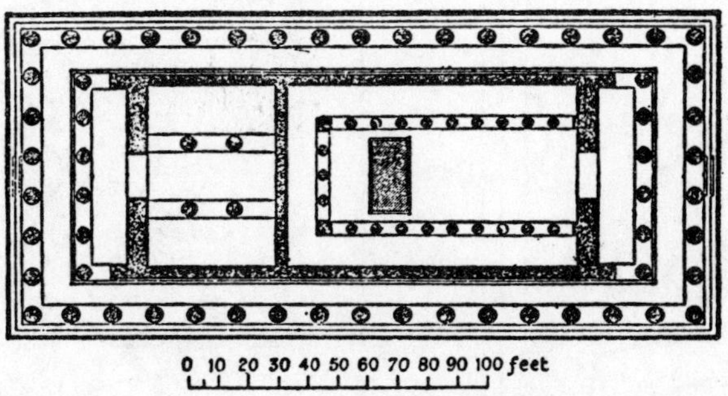

2c

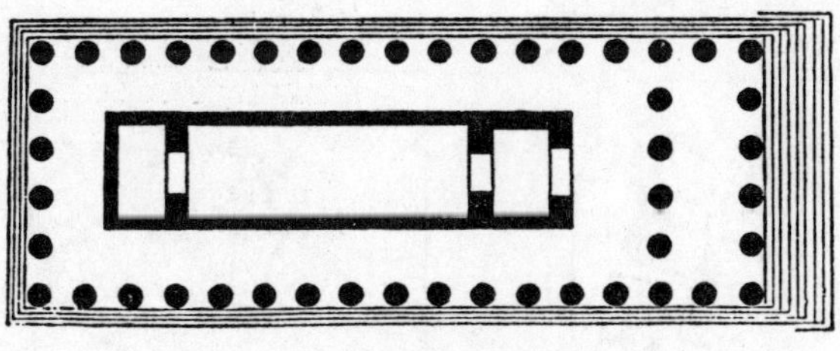

2d

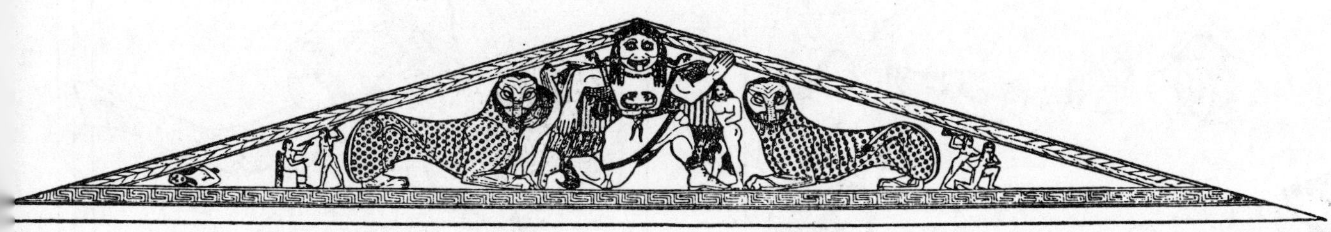

3

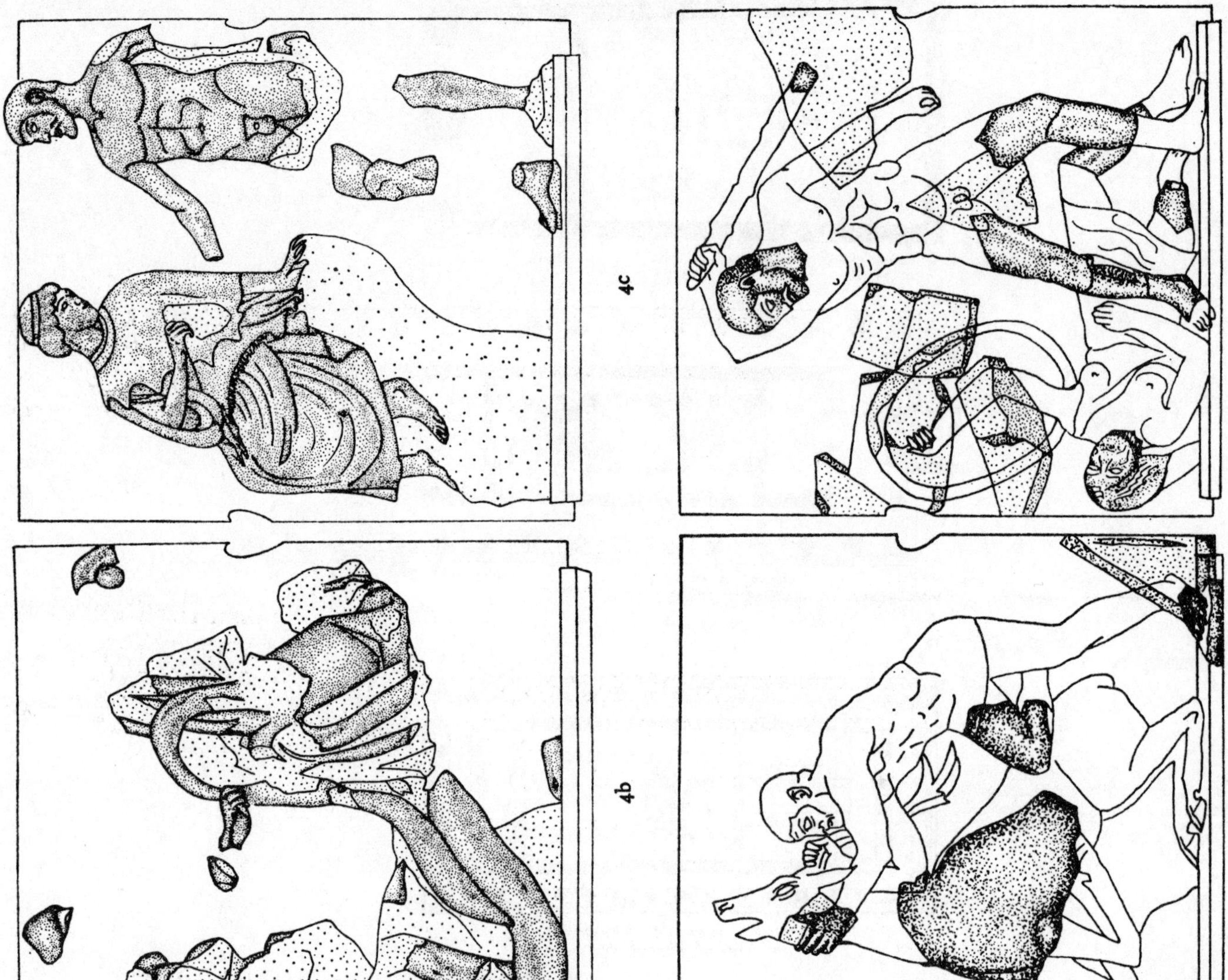
4a
4b
4c
4d
4e
4f

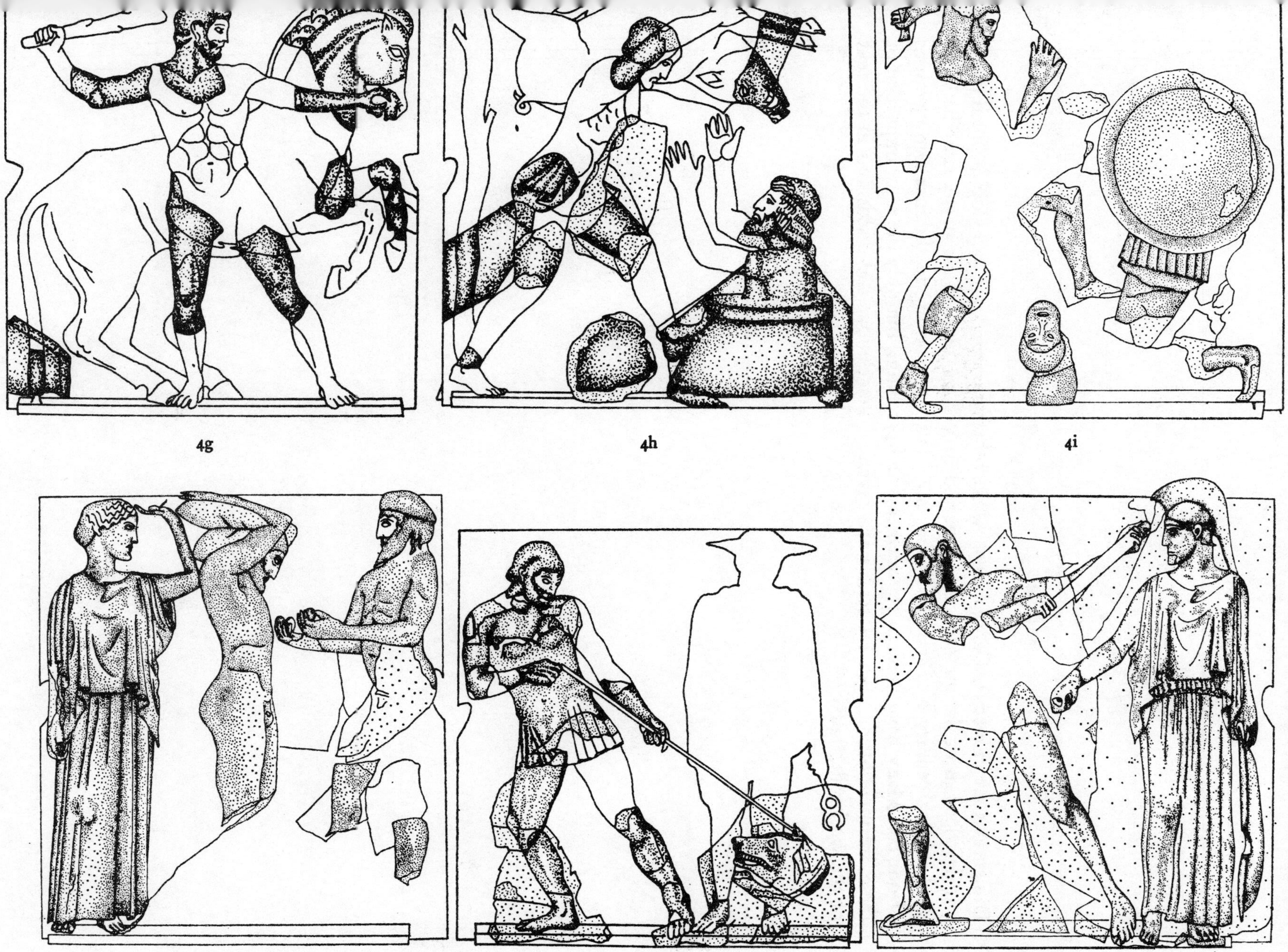

4g 4h 4i

4j 4k 4l

4g–l. East metopes of Temple of Zeus at Olympia. (Pp. 273–6)

NOTE

Dimensions are in metres. Dates, except where otherwise stated, are B.C. Copies (from pl. 61 on) described as of the imperial age or period may have been made at any time between the later first century B.C. and the fourth A.D., but most belong to the first two centuries of our era. Many have modern replacements and patchings, but only the most important of these are mentioned. Page references are given to descriptions and discussions in the text of the works illustrated.

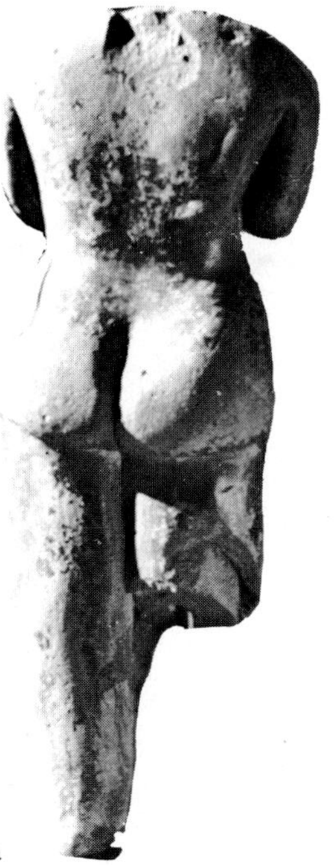

1a

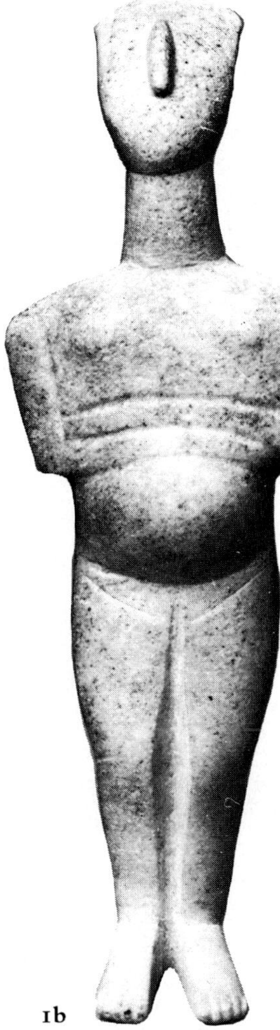

1b

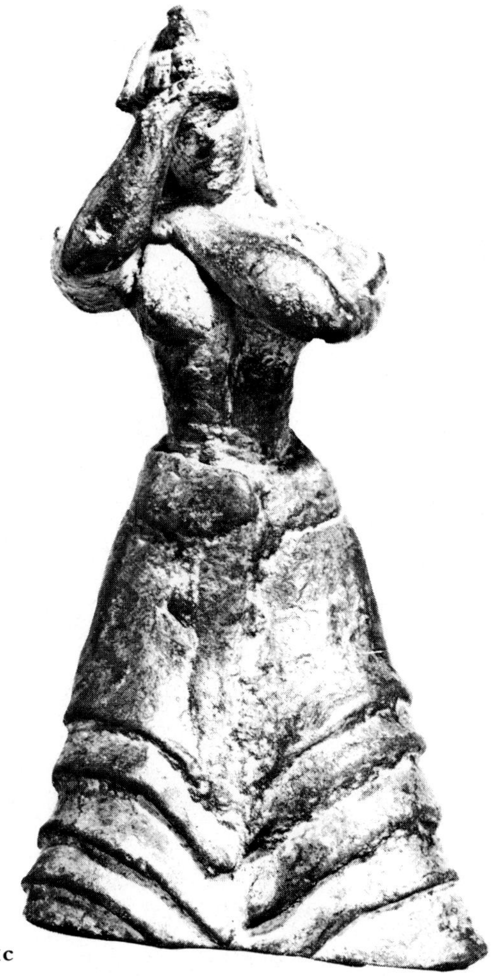

1c

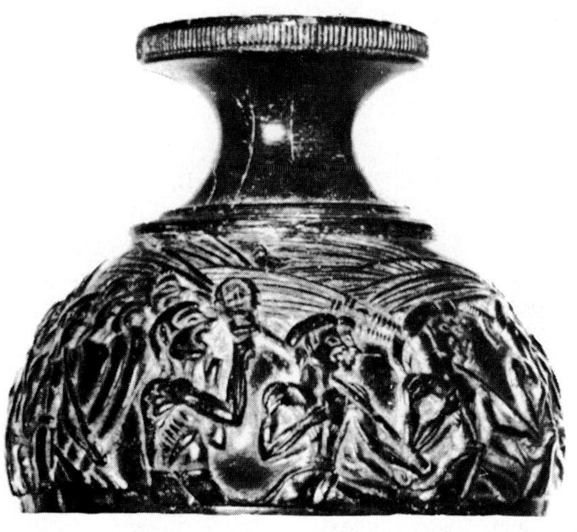

1d

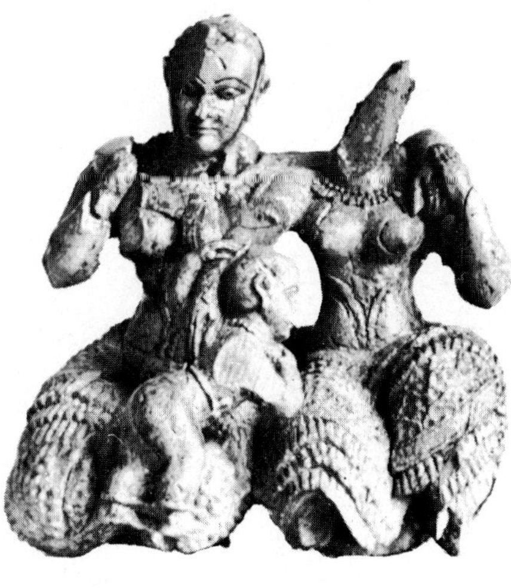

1e

1 **a** Terracotta figurine from Lerna (Argolid). Athens, National Museum. Early third millennium B.C. H. 0.13. (P. 2) **b** Cycladic marble figurine. British Museum 1932.10–18.1. Late third millenium B.C. H. 0.20. (Pp. 2, 390) **c** Bronze figurine, said to be from the Troad. Berlin (Charlottenburg) 8092. Sixteenth century B.C. H. 0.19. (Pp. 3, 9, 390) **d** Stone ('steatite') vessel, lower part missing, from Agia Triada (S. Crete). Herakleion Museum. Sixteenth century B.C. Preserved height 0.09. (Pp. 3, 5) **e** Ivory group from Mycenae. Athens, National Museum. Fourteenth century B.C.? H. 0.07. (P. 10).

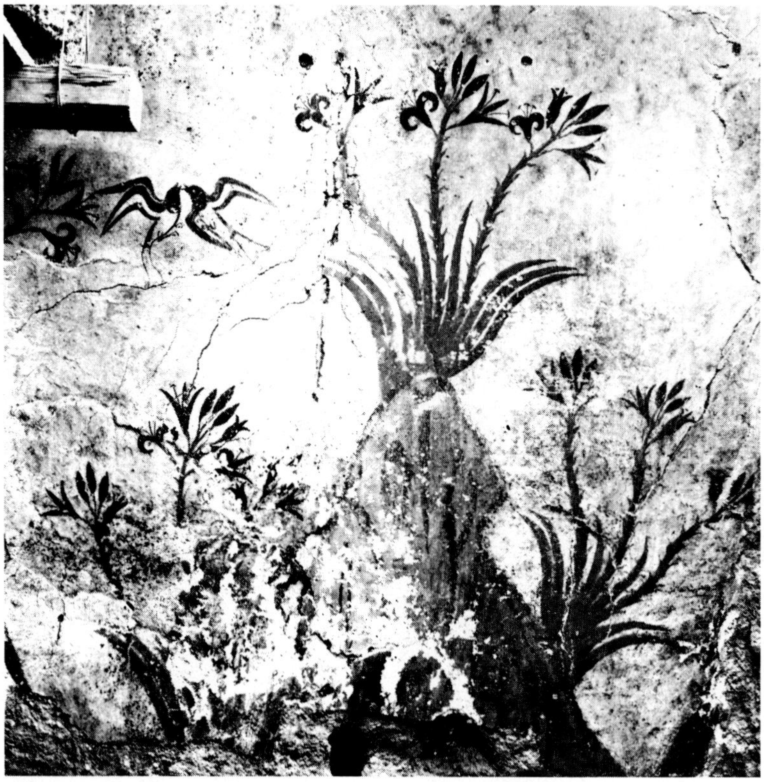

2a

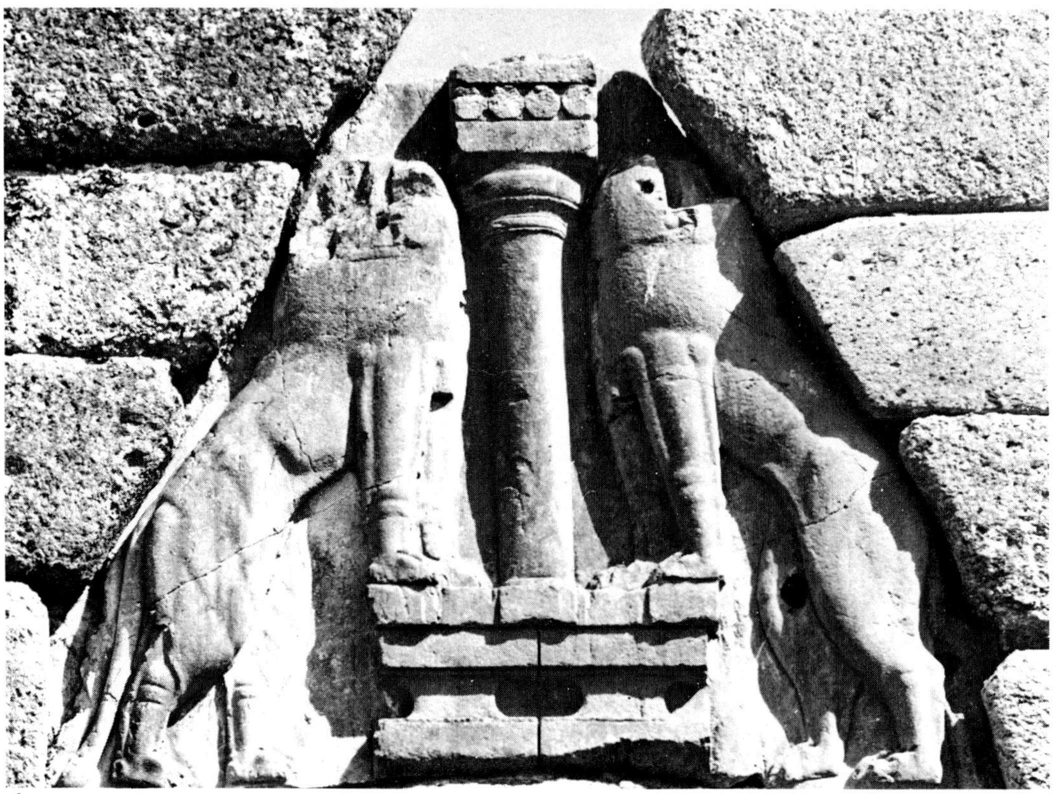

2b

2 **a** Wall-painting at Akrotiri (Thera, Santorin). Sixteenth century B.C. H. *c.* 1.50(?). (P.6) **b** Limestone relief over gate at Mycenae. Thirteenth century B.C. H. 3.00. (P. 8).

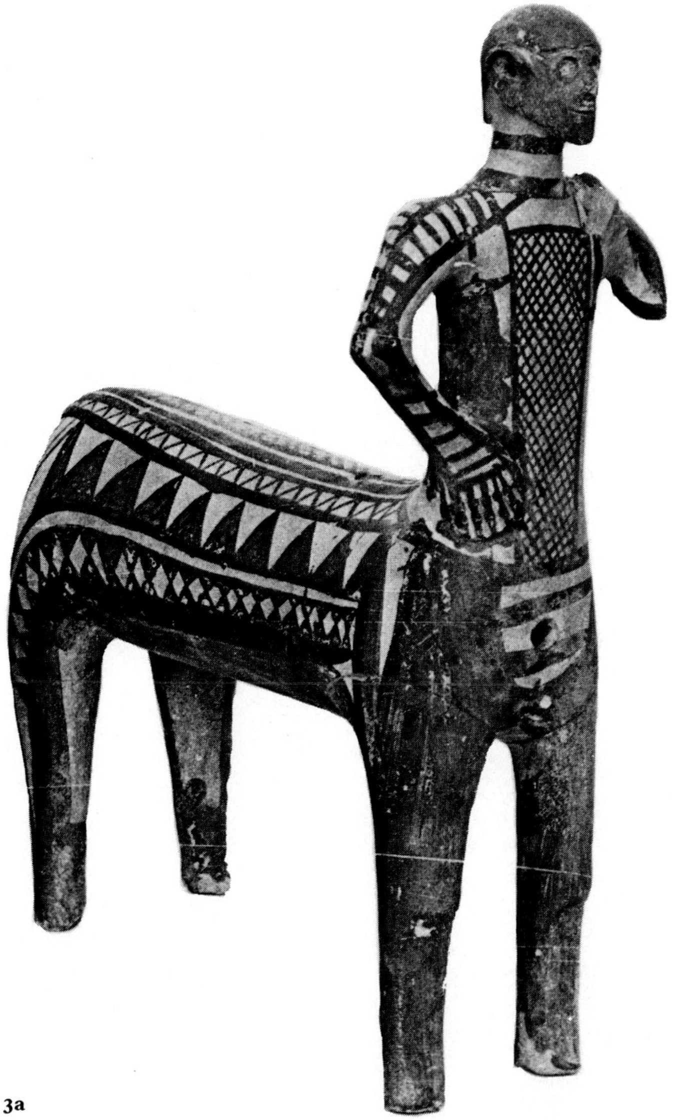

3a

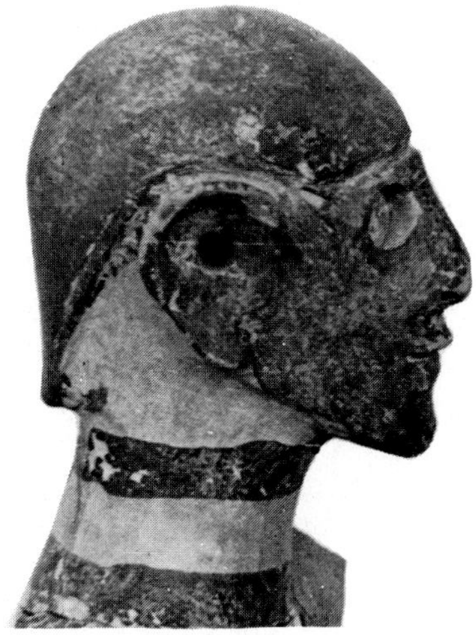

3b

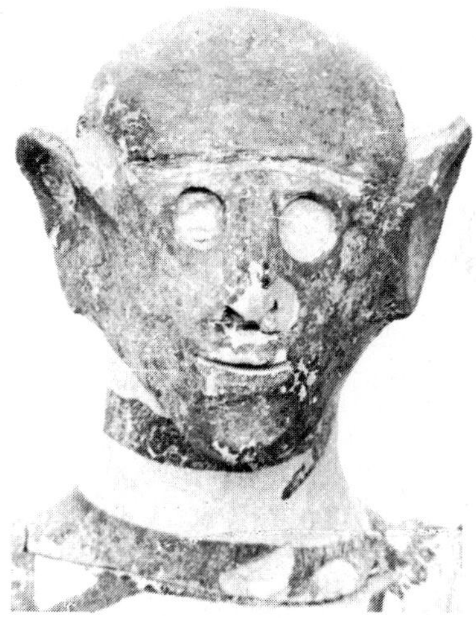

3c

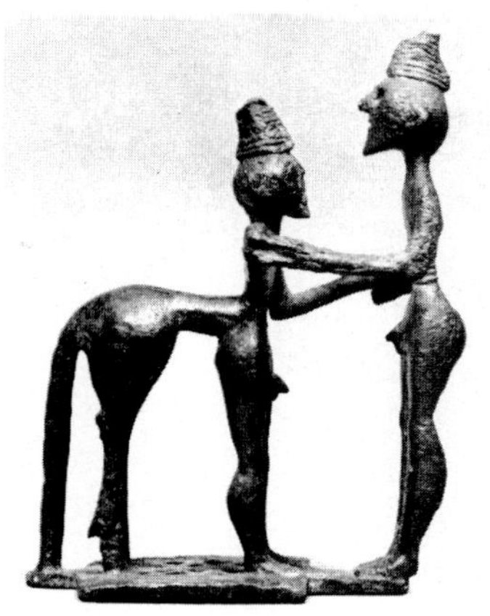

3d

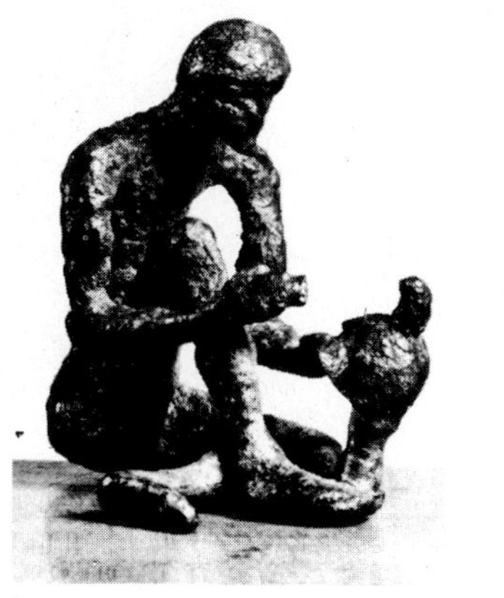

3e

3 **a–c** Terracotta figurine from Lefkandi (Euboea). Chalkis Museum. Tenth to ninth century B.C. H. 0.36. (Pp. 18, 55) **d** Bronze group. New York, Metropolitan Museum of Art, 17.190.2072, Gift of J. Pierpont Morgan. Eighth century B.C. H. 0.11. (Pp. 20, 55) **e** Bronze figurine. New York, Metropolitan Museum of Art 42.11.42, Fletcher Fund. Eighth century B.C. H. 0.05. (Pp. 21, 279).

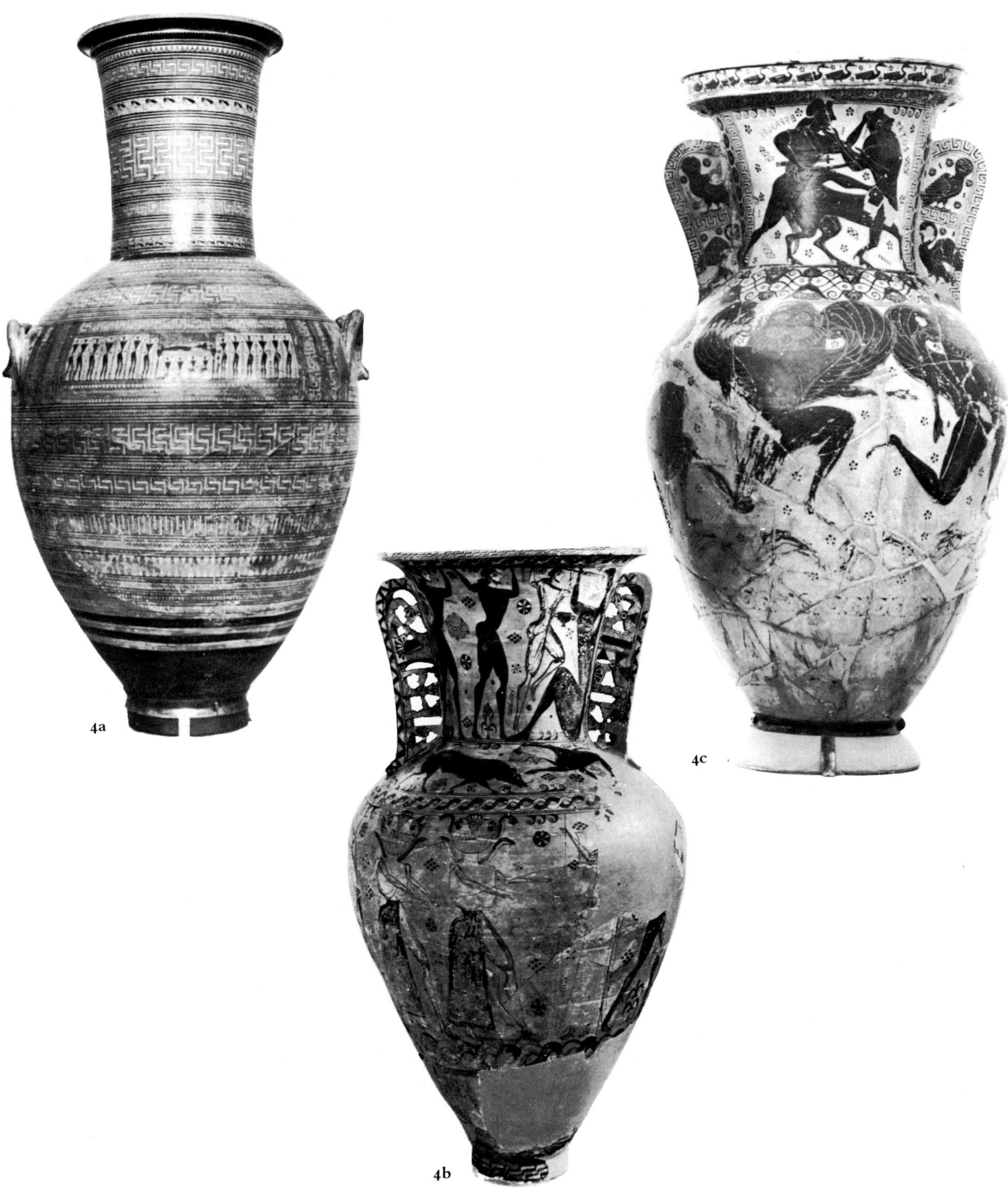

4 **a** Geometric grave-vase from Athens. Athens, National Museum 804. Mid eighth century B.C. H. 1.55. (P. 19) **b** Protoattic grave-vase from Eleusis. Eleusis Museum. Mid seventh century B.C. H. 1.42. (Pp. 27–8, 50, 54) **c** Protoattic black-figure grave-vase from Athens. Athens, National Museum 1002. Late seventh century B.C. H. 1.23. (Pp. 28, 54).

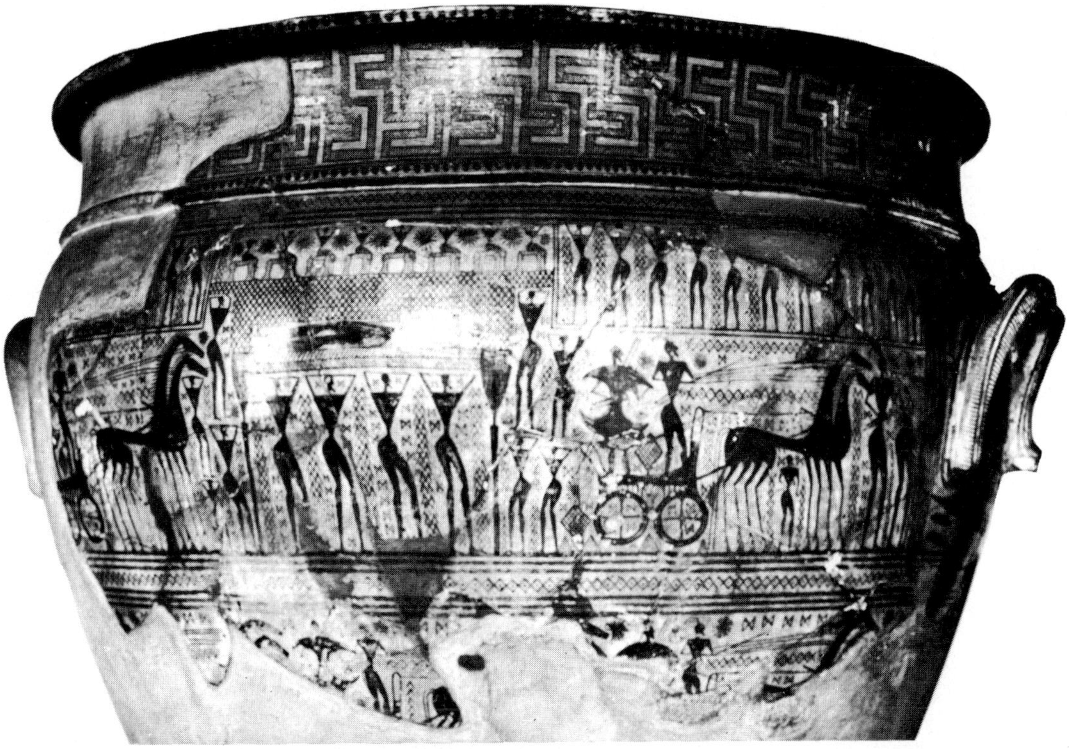

5a

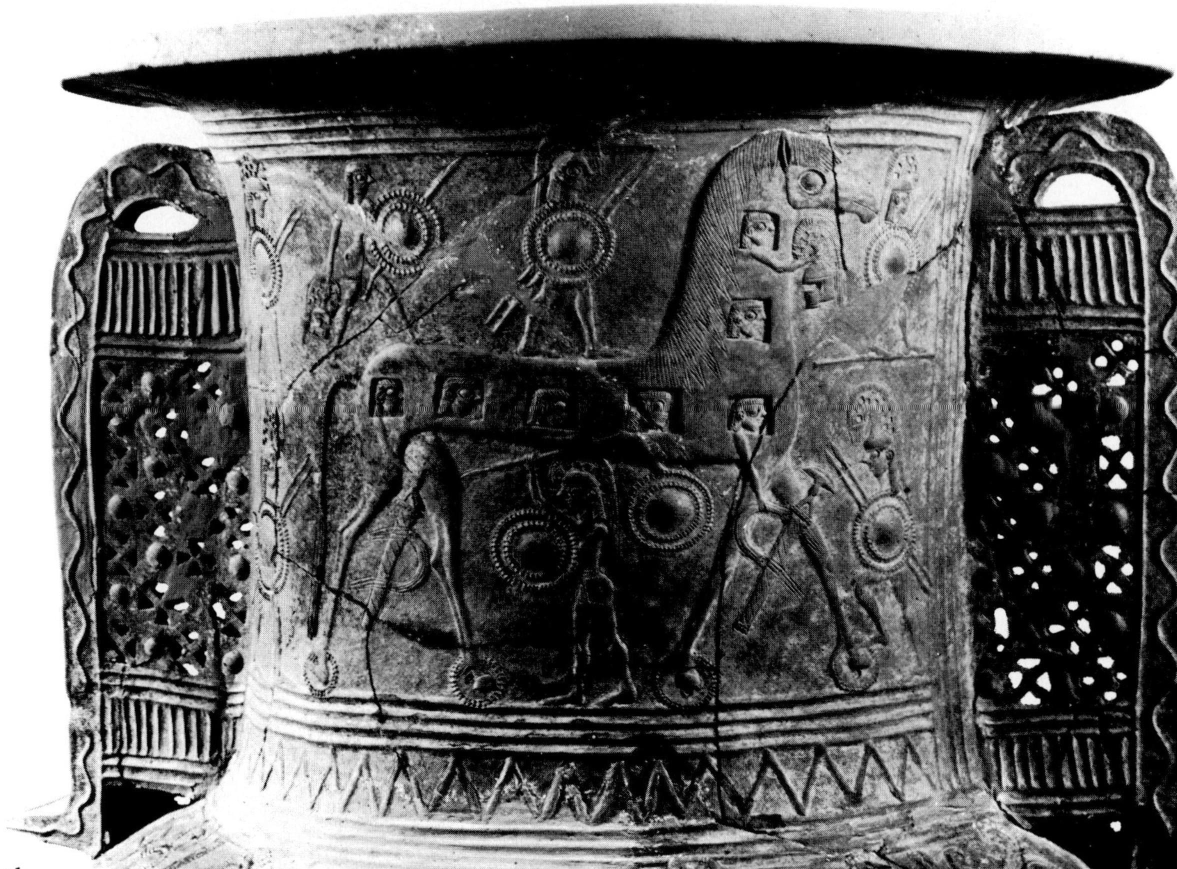

5b

5 **a** Picture from Geometric grave-vase from Athens. Louvre A 517. Mid eighth century B.C. H. of part shown *c.* 0.40. (Pp. 19–20) **b** Neck of relief-pithos from Mykonos. Mykonos Museum. Mid seventh century B.C. H. of part shown *c.* 0.45. (P. 29).

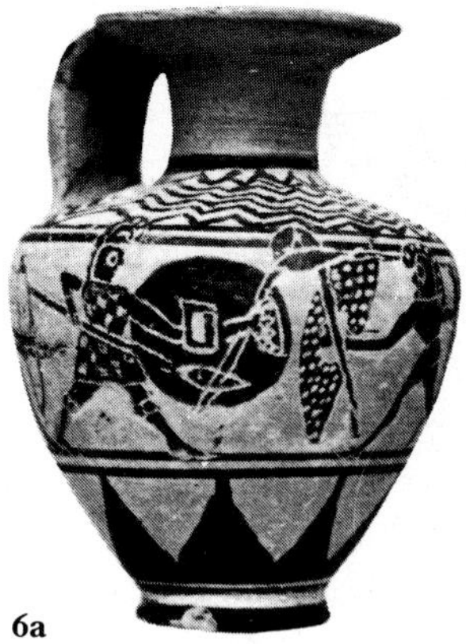

6a

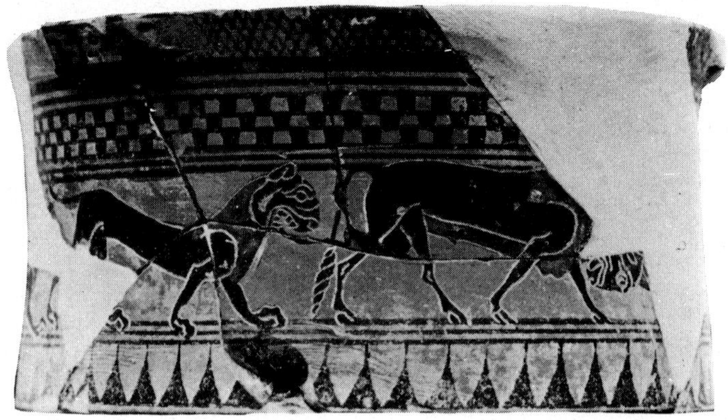

6b

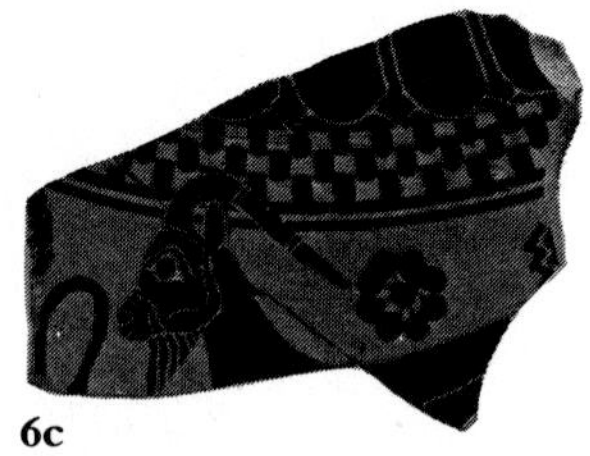

6c

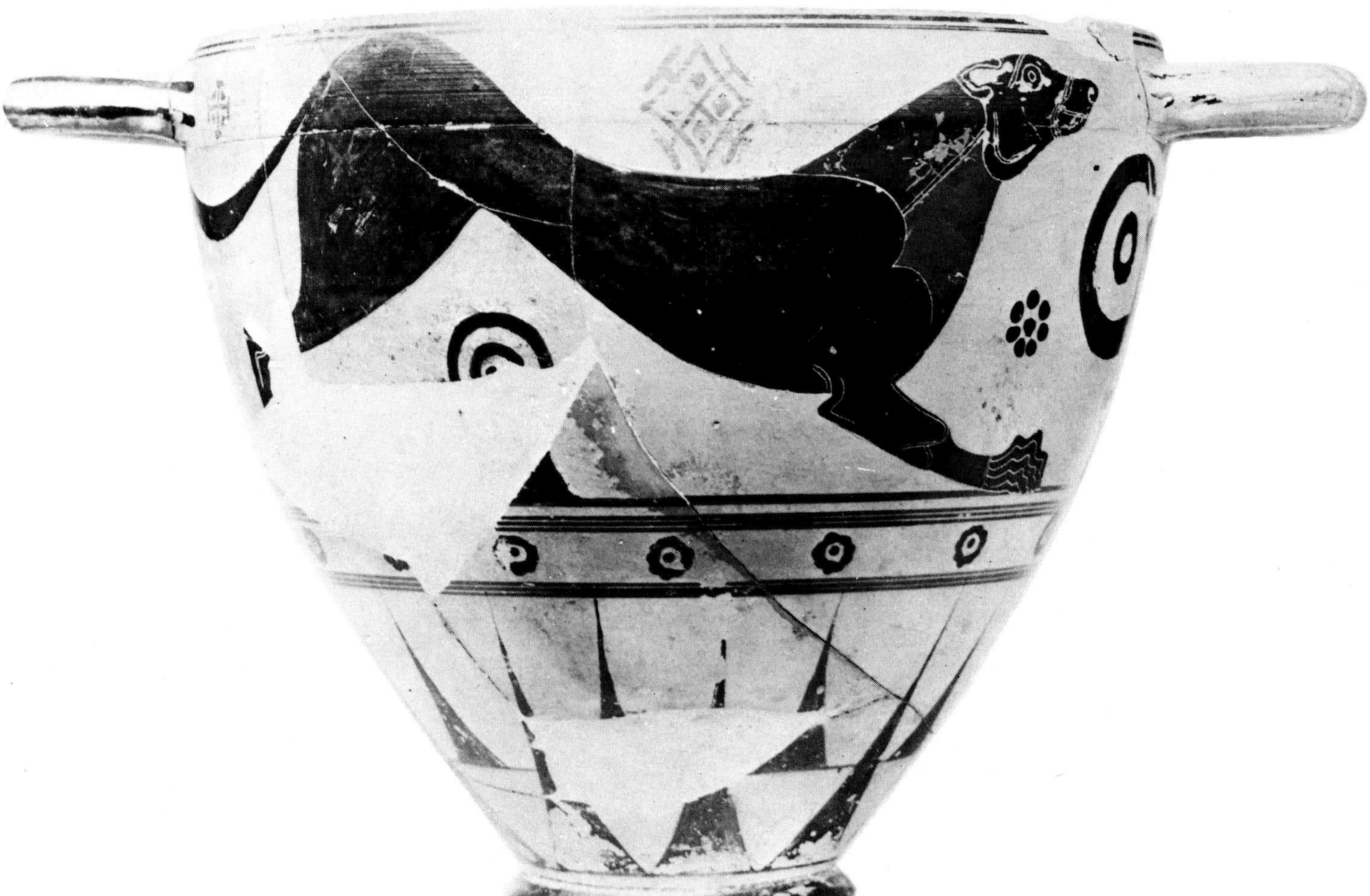

6d

6 **a** Protocorinthian aryballos from Lechaion (Corinth). Corinth Museum. Early seventh century B.C. H. 0.05. (Pp. 25–6) **b** Protocorinthian pyxis from Perachora. Athens, National Museum. Mid seventh century B.C. H. 0.05. (P. 26) **c** Protocorinthian oenochoe-fragment from Perachora. Athens, National Museum. Preserved height *c.* 0.025. (P. 26) **d** Protocorinthian kotyle from Rhodes, probably Kameiros. British Museum 64.4–4.18. Second quarter of seventh century B.C. H. 0.19. (Pp. 25–6).

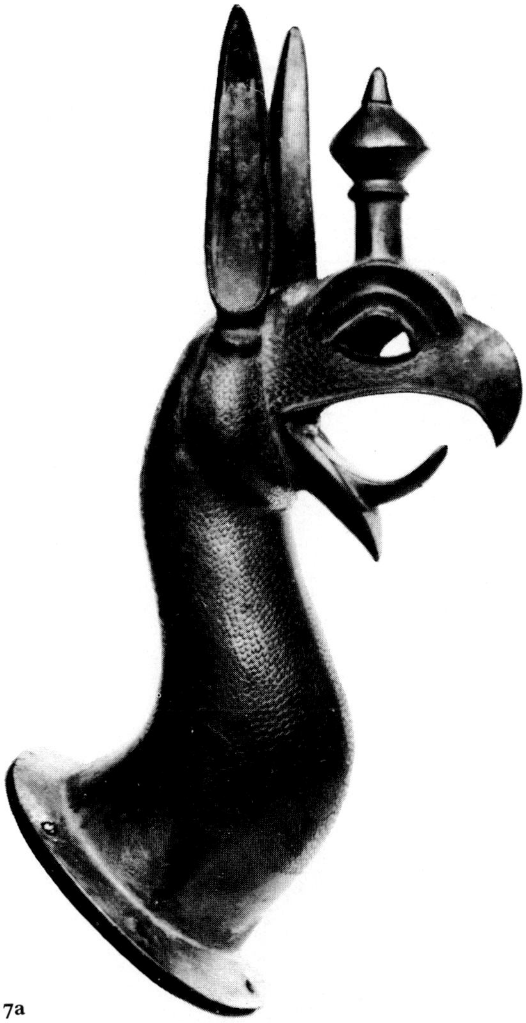

7a

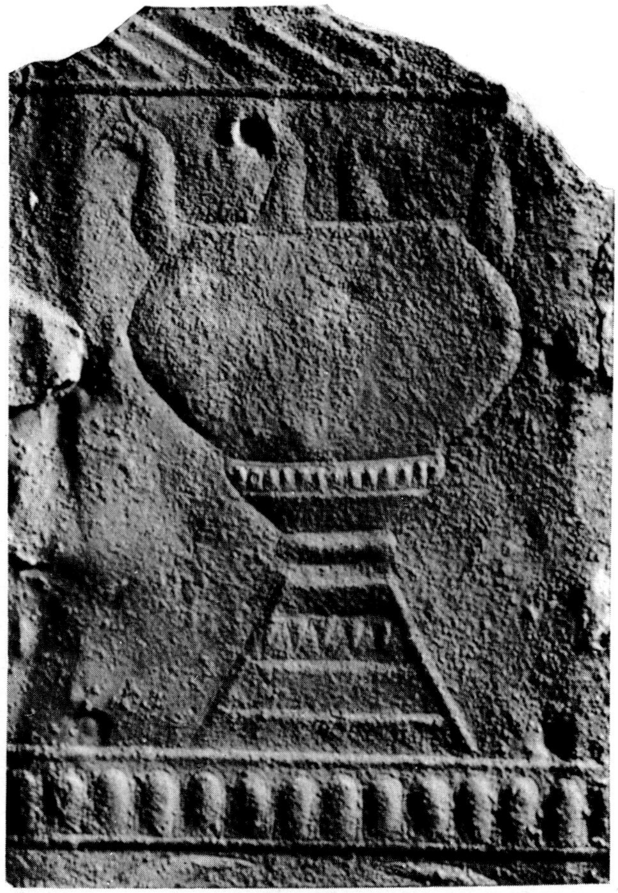

7b

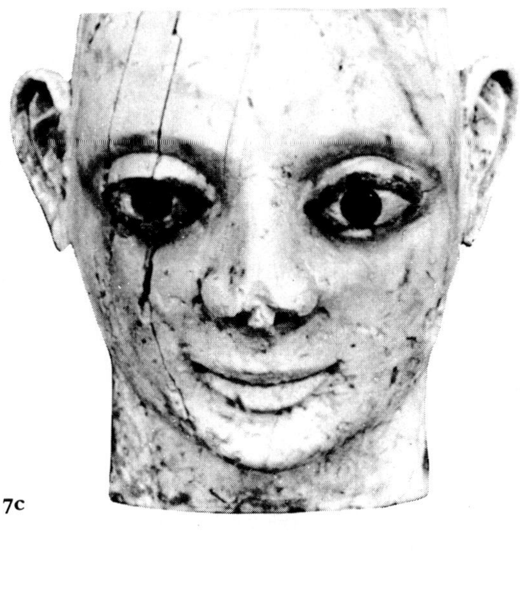

7c

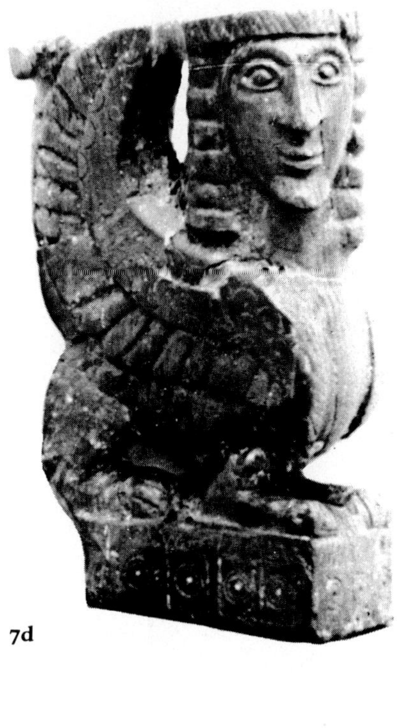

7d

7 **a** Bronze griffin-protome (cauldron-attachment) from Rhodes. British Museum 70.3–15.16. Seventh century B.C. H. 0.32. (P. 31) **b** Detail of bronze tripod-leg from Olympia. Early seventh century B.C. H. of part shown *c.* 0.20. (P. 31) **c** Ivory head from Perachora. Athens, National Museum 16520. 'Syro-Phoenician', probably seventh century B.C. H. 0.038. (P. 33) **d** Ivory sphinx from Perachora. Athens, National Museum 16519. Mid seventh century B.C. H. 0.077. (Pp. 33–4).

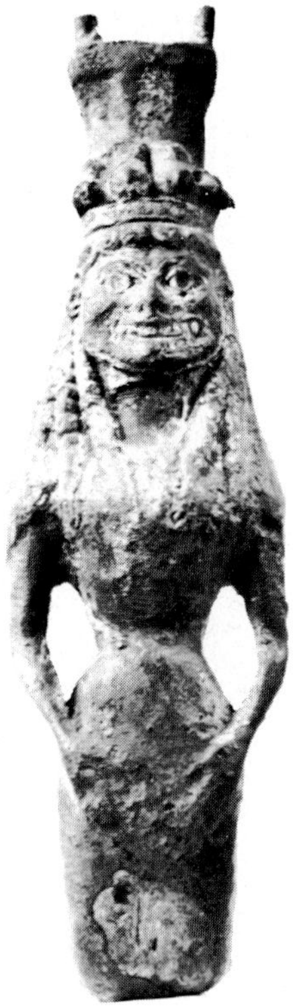

8a

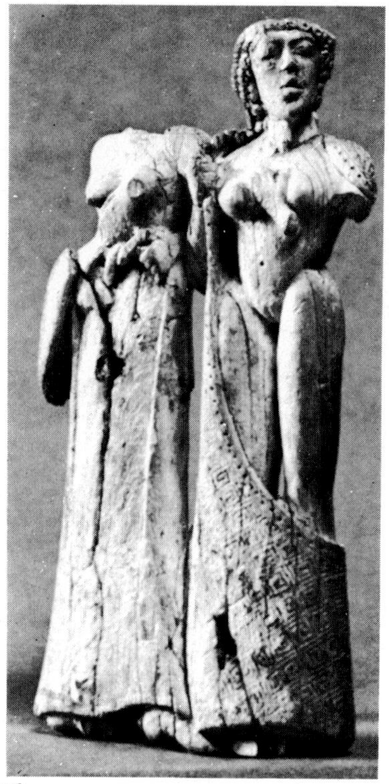

8b

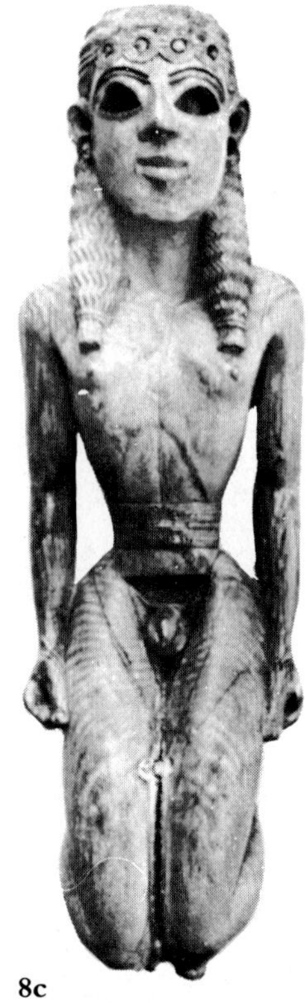

8c

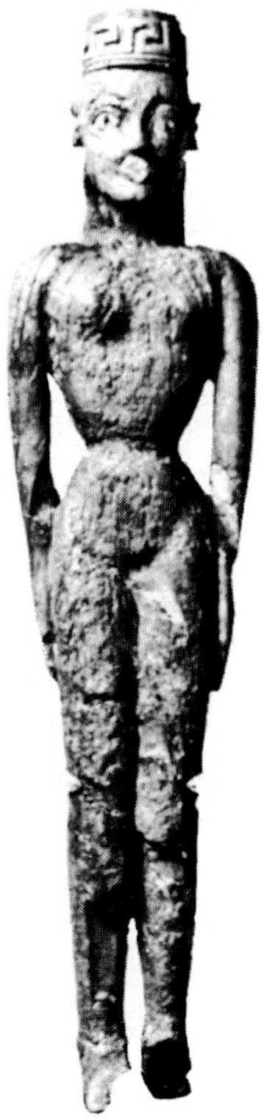

8d

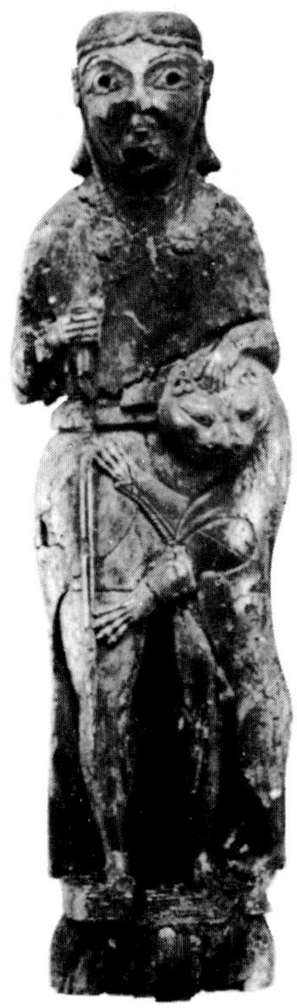

8e

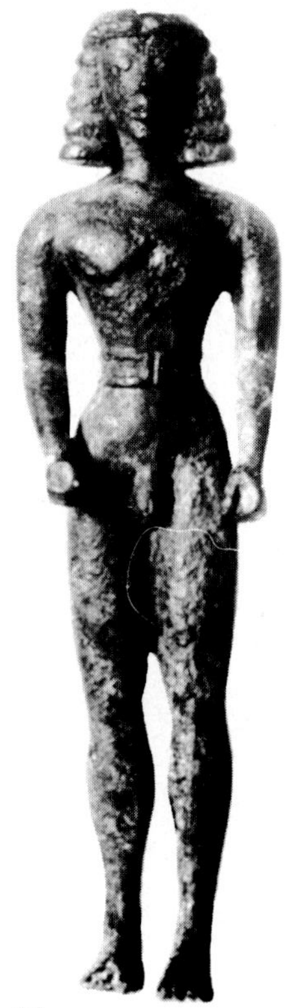

8f

8 **a** Bronze figurine (tripod-support) from sea off Rhodes. Louvre 2570. Second half of seventh century B.C. H. 0.55. (P. 37) **b** Ivory group. New York, Metropolitan Museum of Art 17.190.73, Gift of J. Pierpont Morgan. Mid seventh century B.C. H. 0.14. (P. 141) **c** Ivory figurine (part of lyre) from Samos. Samos Museum. Mid seventh century B.C. H. 0.14. (P. 33) **d** Ivory figurine from Athens. Athens, National Museum 776. H. 0.24. (Pp. 32, 44–5, 390) **e** Ivory group from Delphi. Delphi Museum. Early seventh century B.C. H. 0.18. (Pp. 33, 140) **f** Bronze figurine from Delphi. Delphi Museum 172. Middle or later seventh century B.C. H. 0.20. (Pp. 40, 42–3, 142).

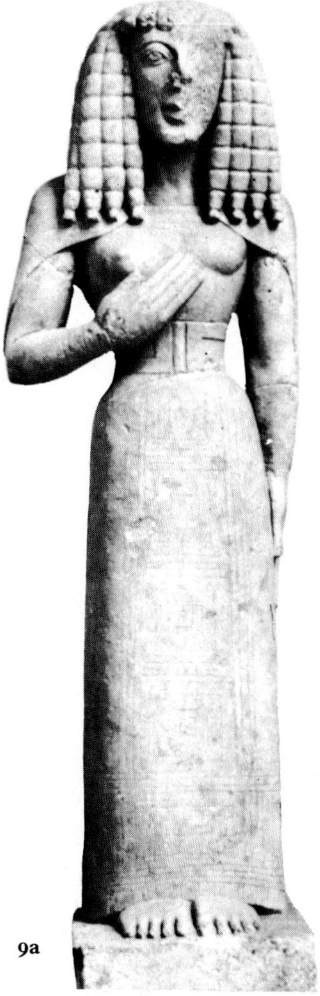

9a

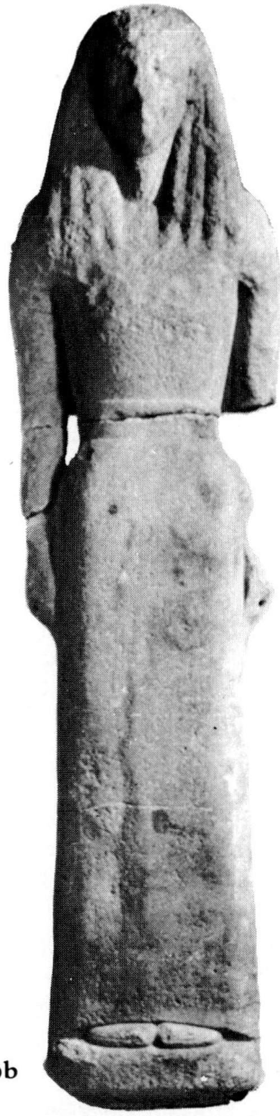

9b

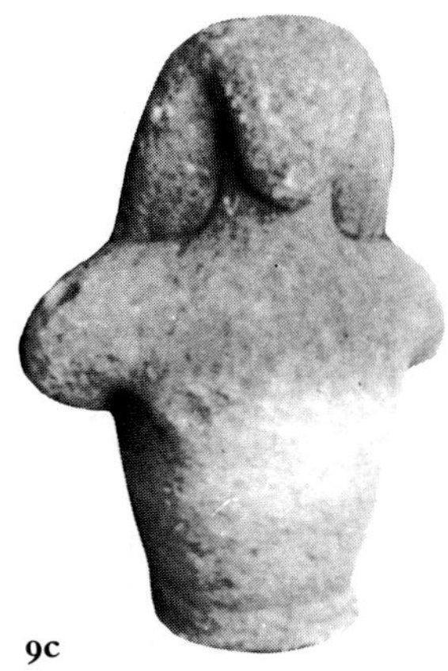

9c

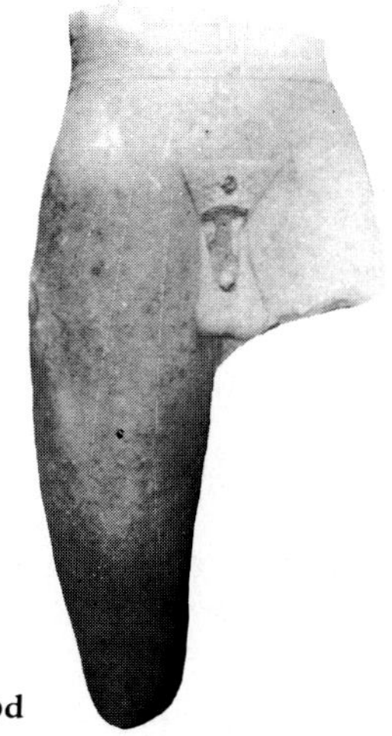

9d

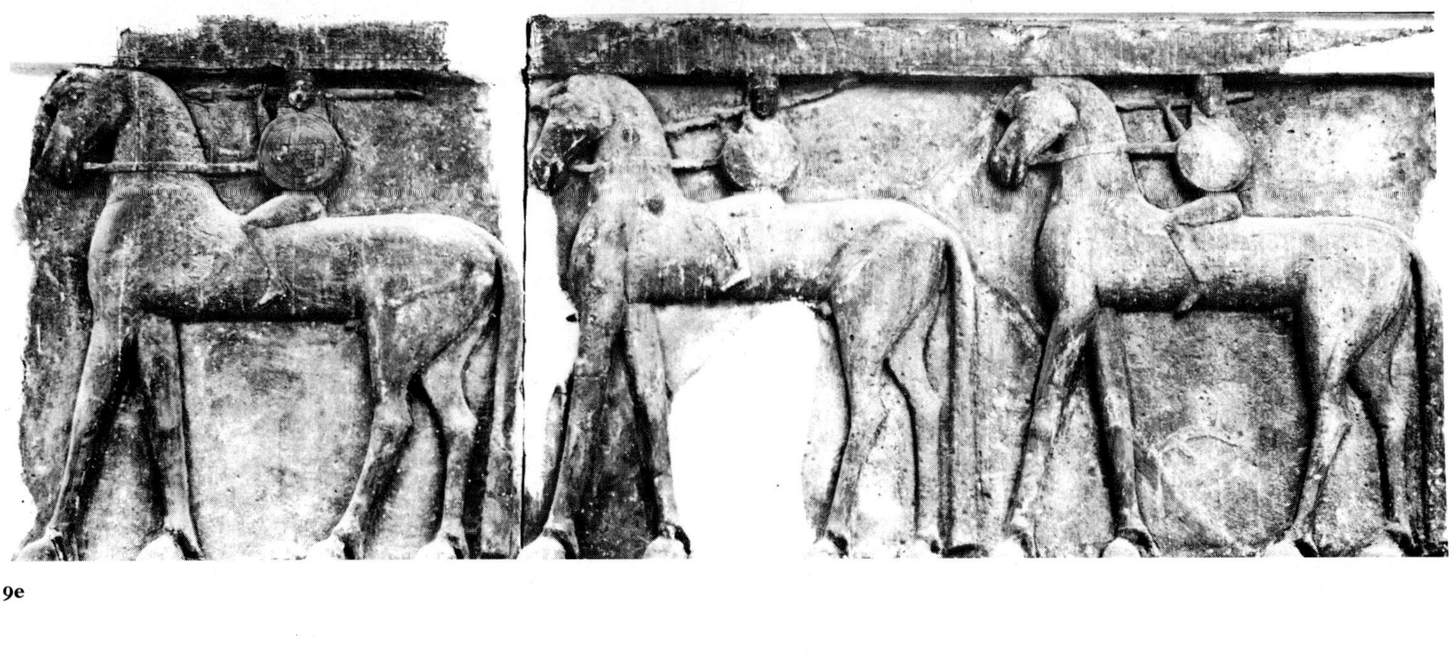

9e

9 **a** Limestone statuette. Louvre 3098. Mid seventh century or later. H. 0.65. (Pp. 38–9) **b** Marble statue from Delos. Athens, National Museum 1. Mid seventh century or later. H. 1.75. (Pp. 36–7) **c** Upper part of marble statue from Delos. Delos Museum A 334. Mid seventh century or later. H. 0.70. (Pp. 42–3) **d** Fragment of marble statue from Delos. Delos Museum A 333. Mid seventh century or later. H. 0.85. (Pp. 42ff.) **e** Limestone relief-frieze from Prinias (Crete). Herakleion Museum. Middle or later seventh century. H. 1.00. (Pp. 57–8, 97, 153).

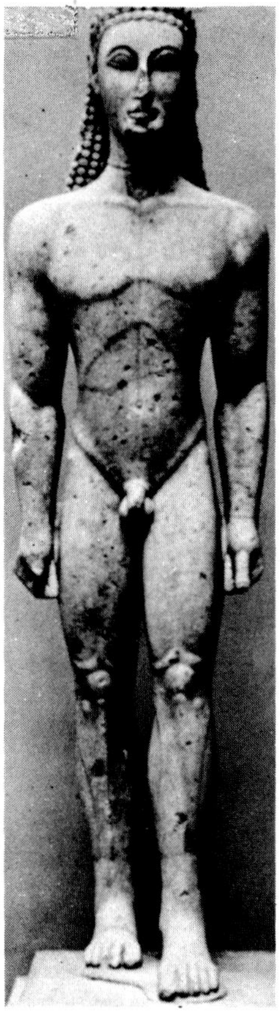

10a

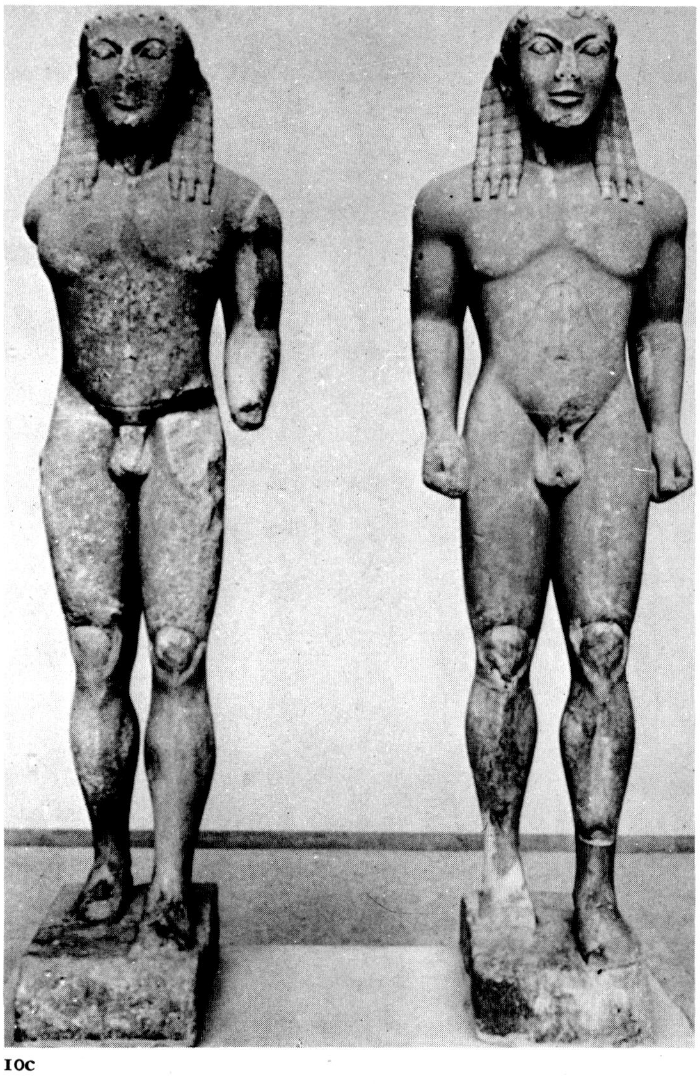

10c

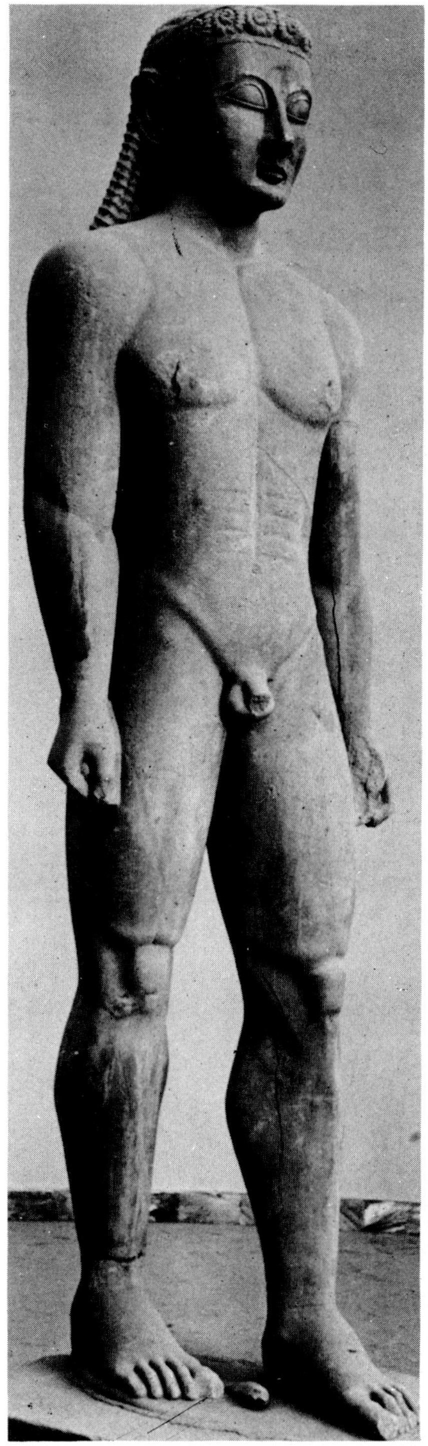

10b

10 **a** Marble statue. New York, Metropolitan Museum of Art 32.11.1, Fletcher Fund. Late seventh or early sixth century. H. 1.84. (Pp. 45–6) **b** Marble statue from Sunium. Athens, National Museum 2720. Late seventh or early sixth century. H. as restored 3.05. Modern: nose and chin with most of left half of face; l. arm and hand; part of r. arm; most of l. leg and foot; part of r. leg. (Pp. 45–6) **c** Pair of marble statues from Delphi. Delphi Museum 467 and 1524. Early sixth century. H. as restored with plinths 2.16–18. Modern, in l. hand figure, ankles and most of feet; in r. hand figure, most of legs and feet. (Pp. 46, 113, 186).

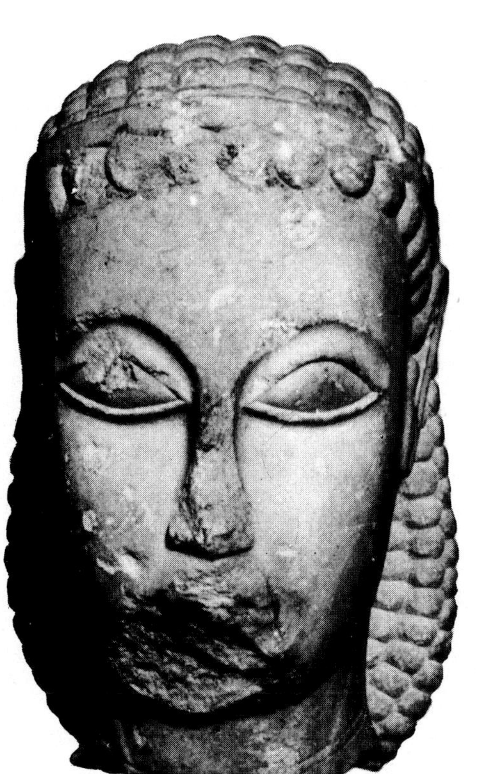

11a

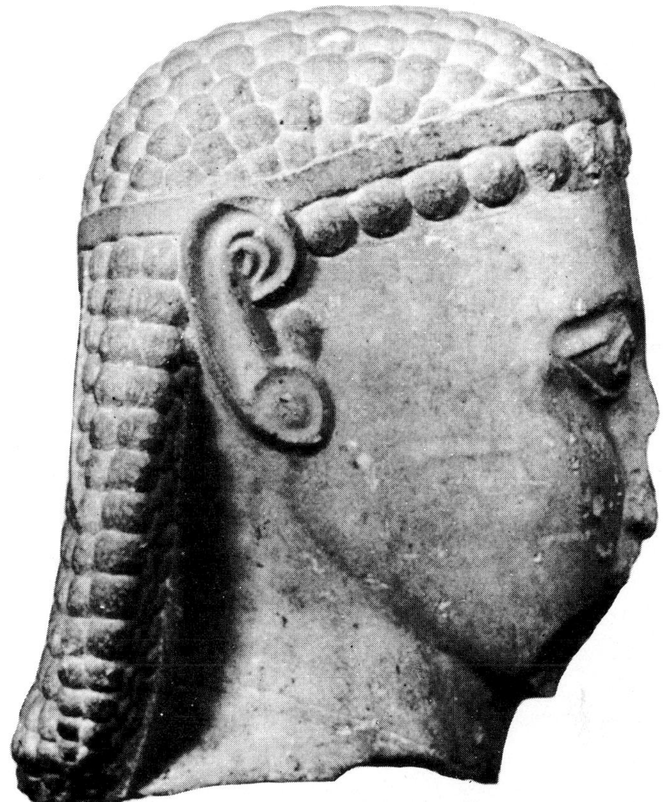

11b

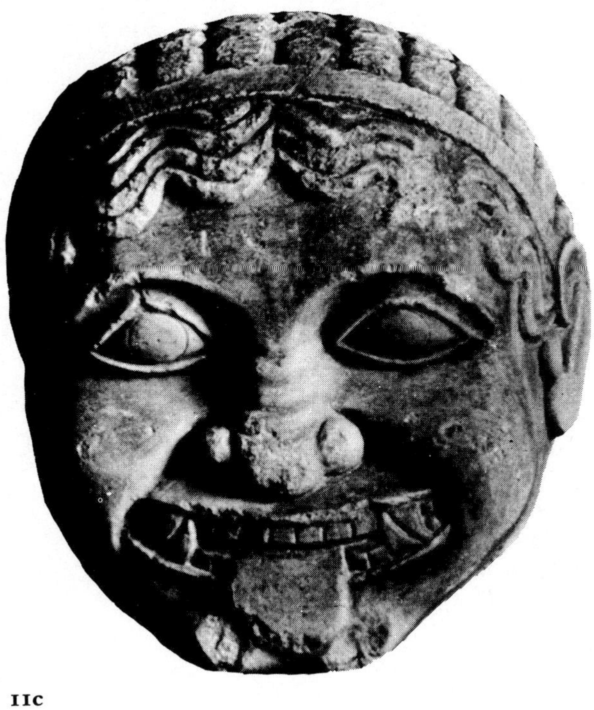

11c

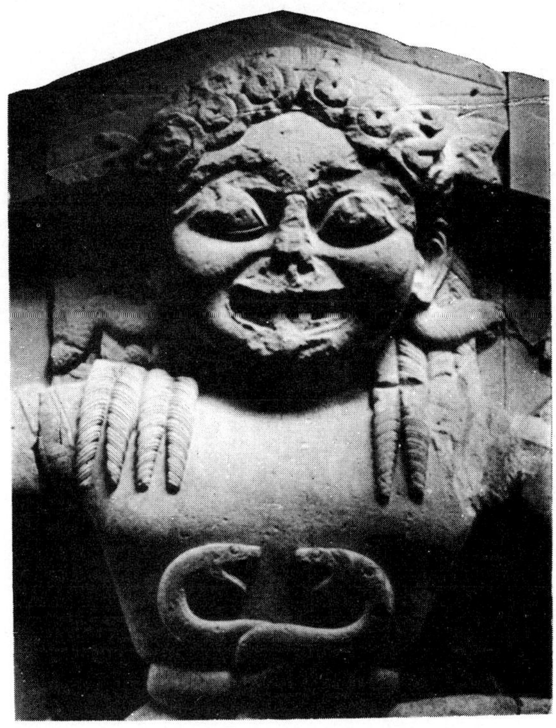

11d

11 **a** and **b** Marble head of grave-statue, from Athens. Athens, National Museum 3372. Late seventh or early sixth century. H. 0.44. (Pp. 45–6, 95) **c** Marble Gorgon-head from the Acropolis. Athens, Acropolis Museum 701. Early sixth century. H. 0.25. (Pp. 48–9) **d** Limestone Gorgon in relief from pediment of Temple of Artemis, Corfu (cf. pl. 13a and fig. 3). Corfu Museum. Fairly early sixth century. H. of head 0.75. (Pp. 63ff.).

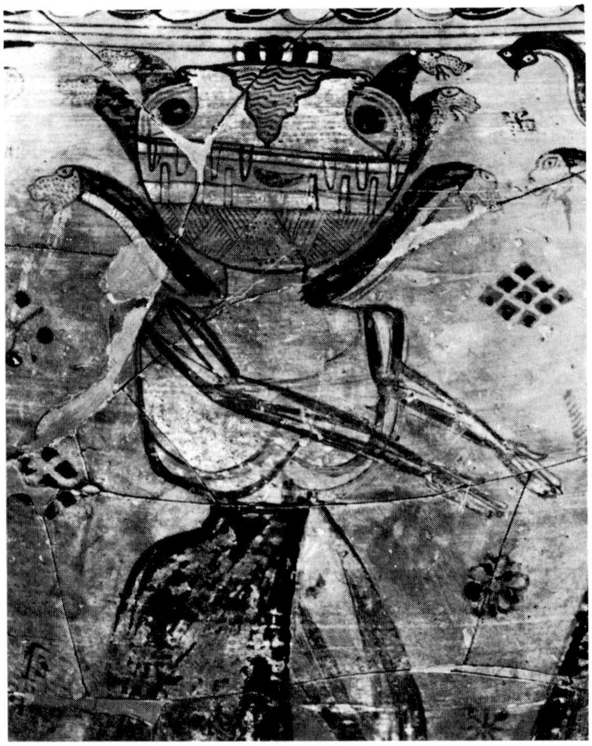

12a

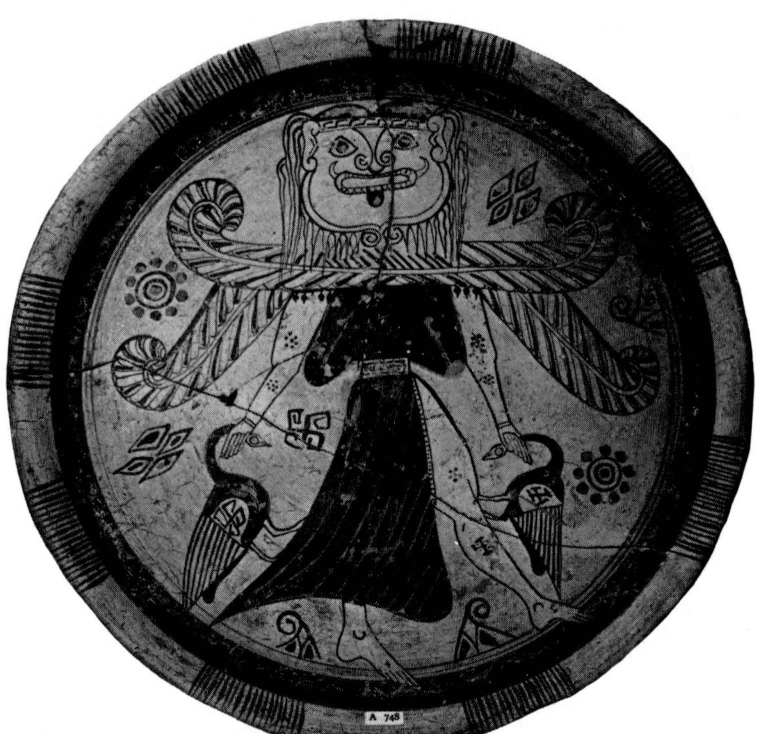

12b

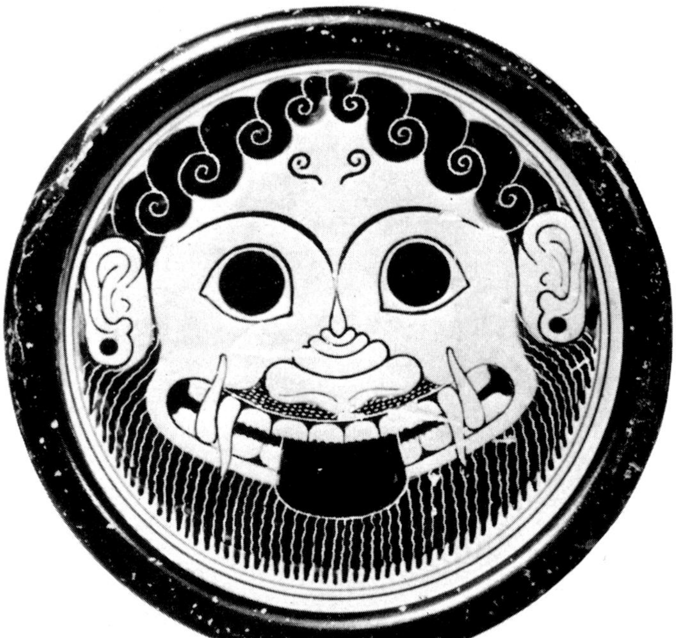

12c

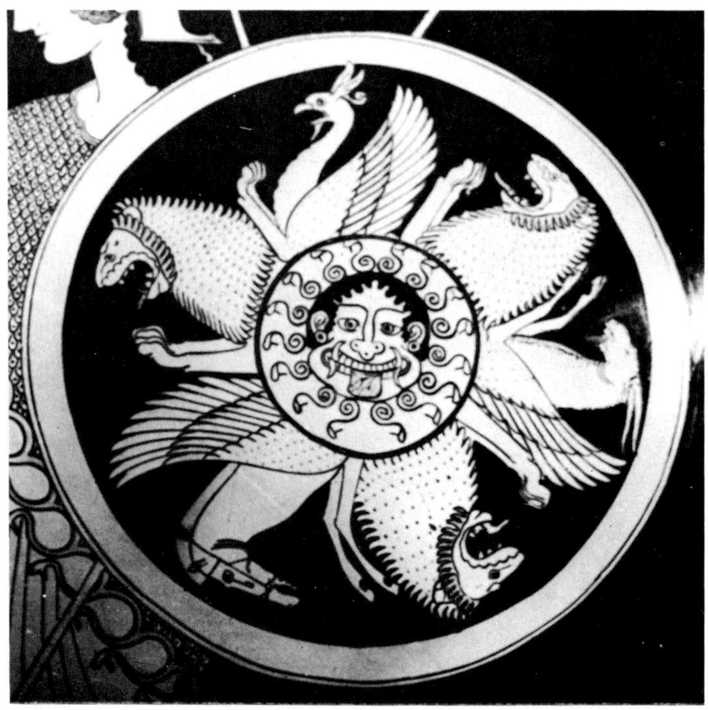

12d

12 **a** Gorgon from vase in pl. 4b. (Pp. 27, 49, 51) **b** Plate from Rhodes. British Museum 64.4–4.2. Late seventh or early sixth century B.C. D. 0.38. (Pp. 49, 64) **c** Gorgon-face on Attic black-figure 'standlet' from Vari (Attica). New York, Metropolitan Museum of Art 31.11.4. Second quarter of the sixth century. D. 0.09. (Pp. 49, 128) **d** Shield of Athena from vase in pl. 83b. (Pp. 49, 236, 267).

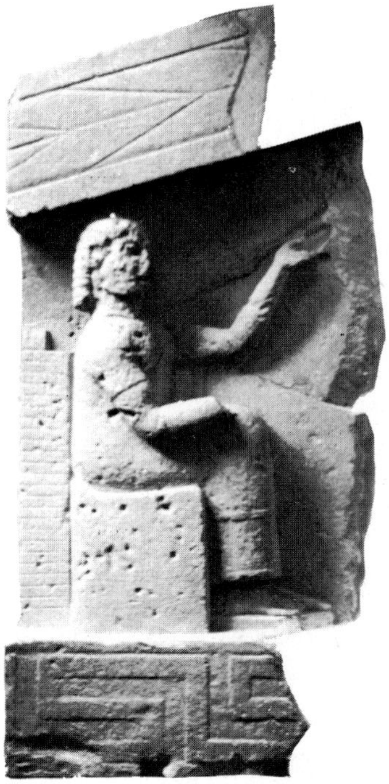

13a

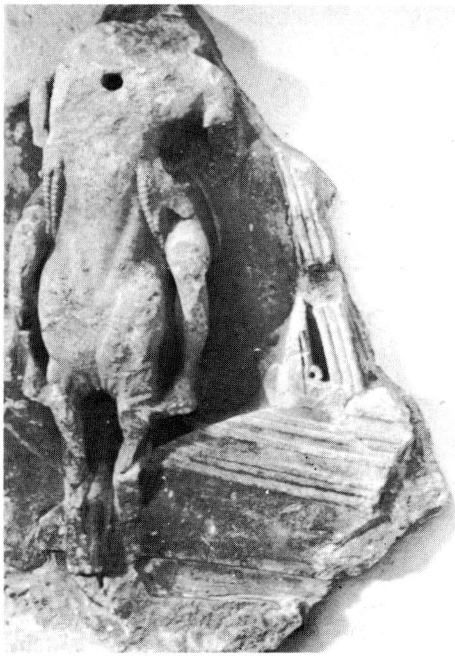

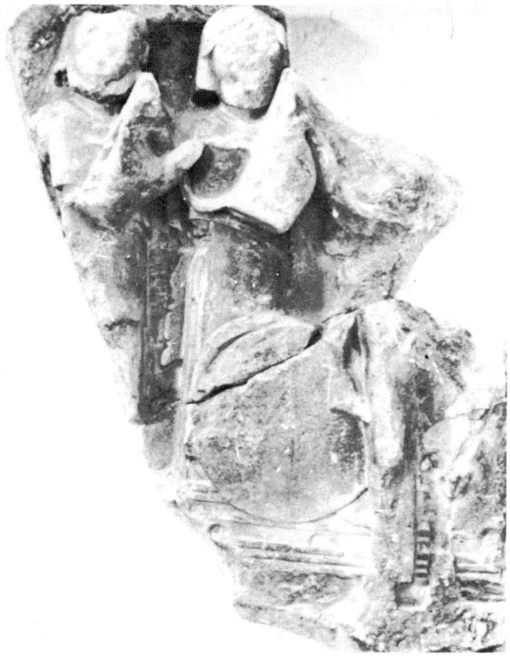

13b

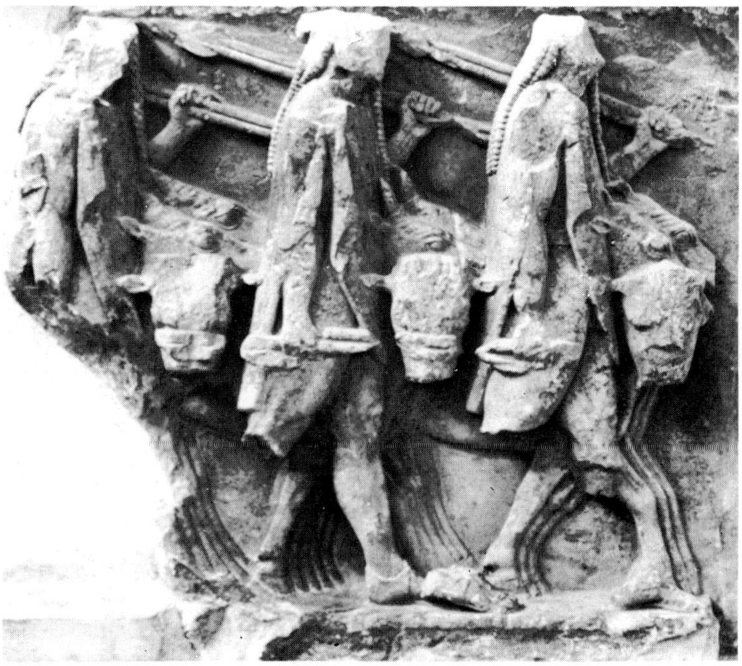

13c

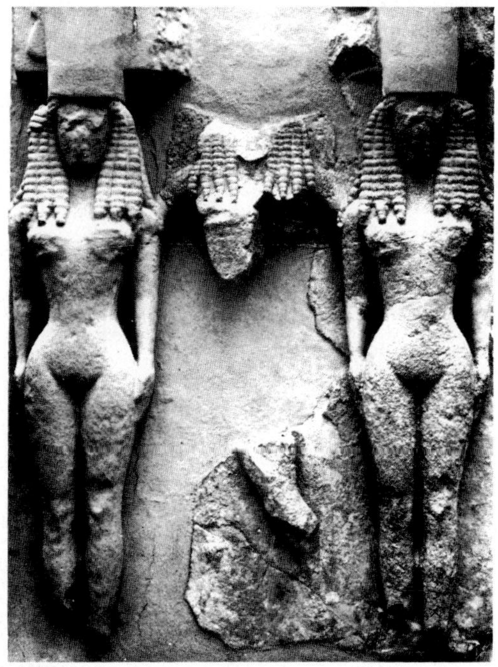

13d

13 **a** Limestone relief-figure from pediment of Temple of Artemis, Corfu (cf. pl. 11d). Corfu Museum. Fairly early sixth century. H. *c.* 0.62. (Pp. 63, 65ff.) **b** and **c** Limestone metopes from Sicyonian *monopteros*, Delphi. Delphi Museum. Second quarter of sixth century. H. 0.58. (Pp. 67–8, 97) **d** Limestone relief from temple at Gortyn (Crete). Herakleion Museum 379. Mid seventh century. H. 1.50. (Pp. 58, 391).

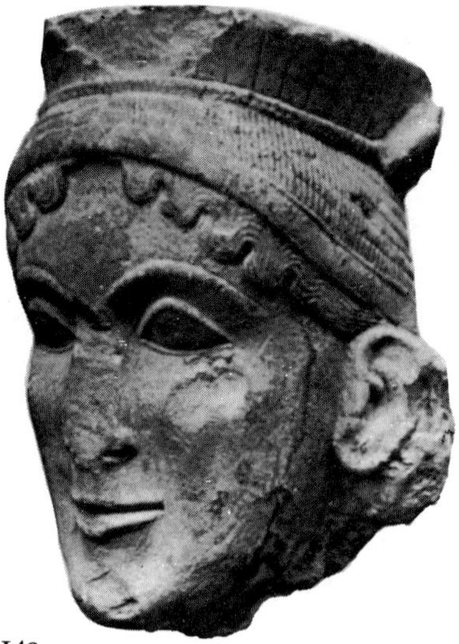

14a

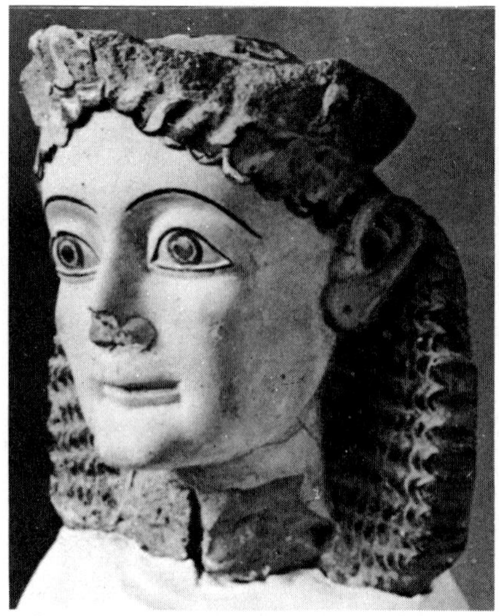

14b

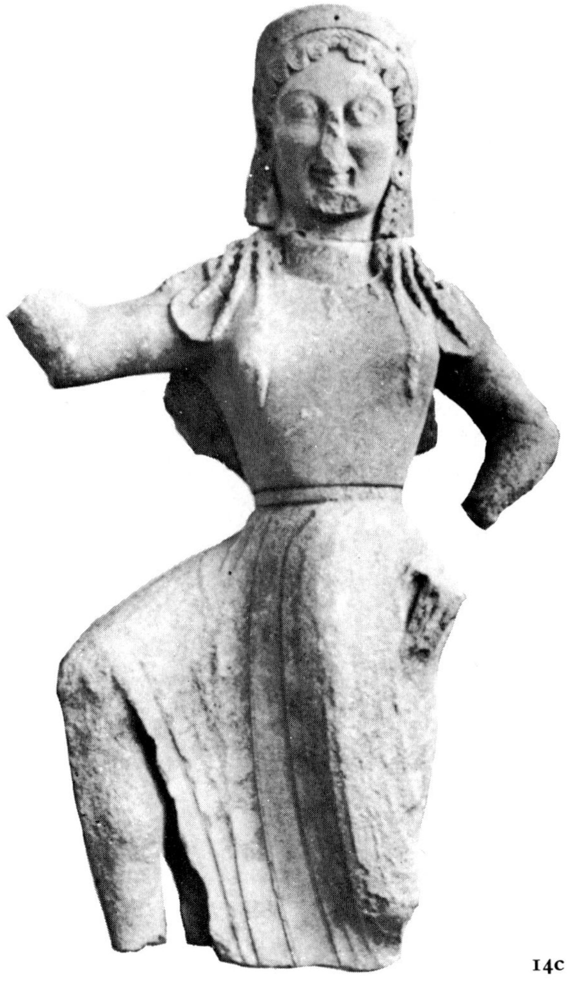

14c

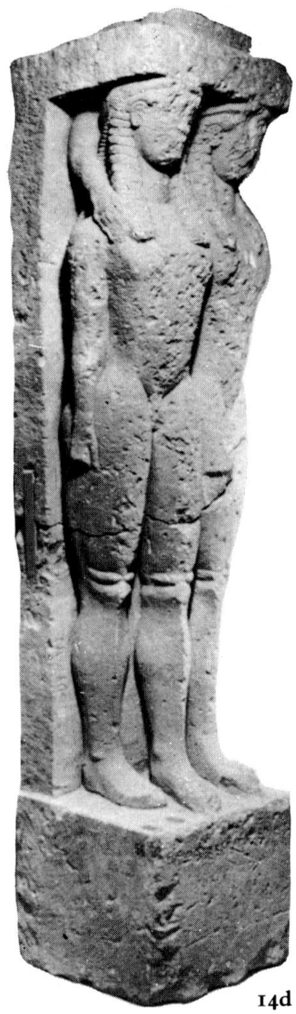

14d

14 **a** Limestone head of statue (probably Hera) from Temple of Hera, Olympia. Olympia Museum. Early sixth century. H. 0.52. (Pp. 47–8, 87) **b** Terracotta head of sphinx from akroterion of temple at Calydon (Aetolia). Athens, National Museum. Late seventh or early sixth century. H. 0.23. (Pp. 62, 146) **c** Marble statue from Delos, probably by Archermos of Chios. Athens, National Museum 21. Mid sixth century. H. 0.90. (Pp. 68–9, 79–80) **d** Limestone grave-relief of Kittylos and Dermys, from Tanagra. Athens, National Museum 56. Late seventh or early sixth century. H. *c.* 2.00. (Pp. 60, 369).

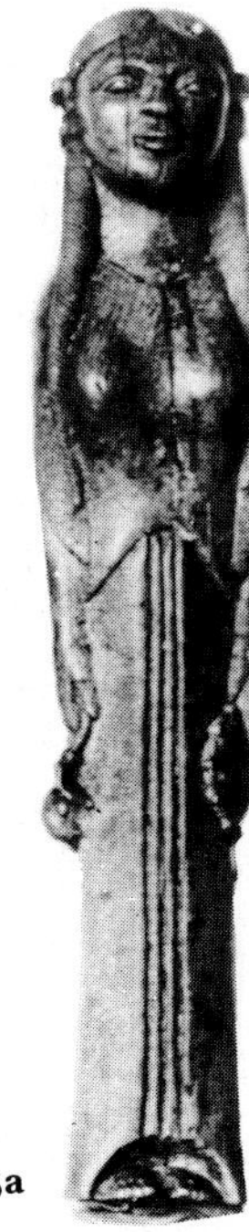
15a

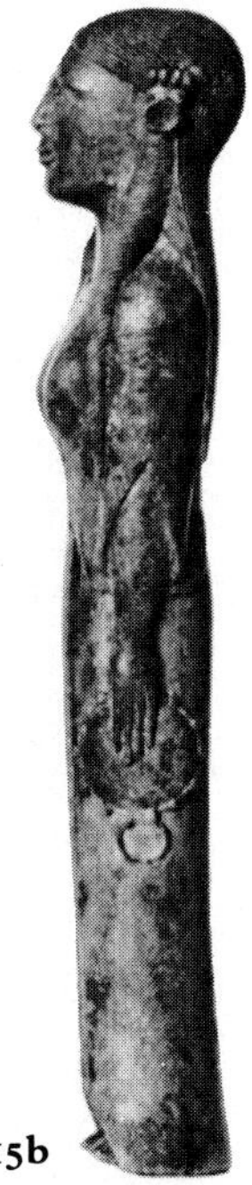
15b

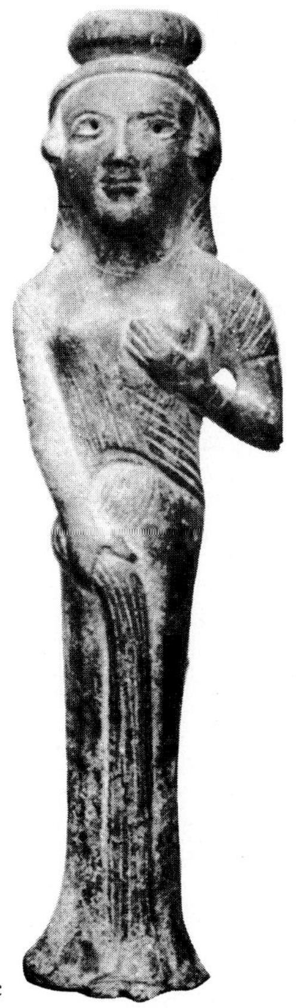
15c

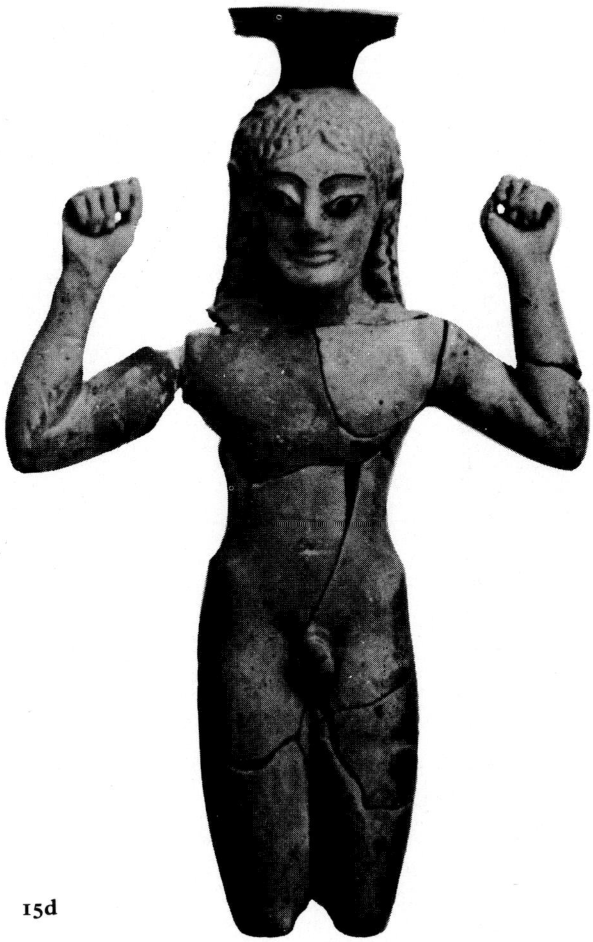
15d

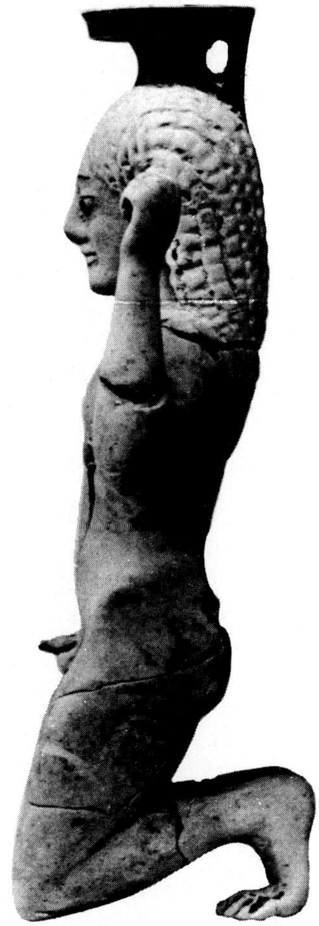
15e

15 **a** and **b** Ivory figurine (handle of wand) from Temple of Artemis at Ephesus. Istanbul, Archaeological Museum. Early sixth century. H. 0.11. (P. 72) **c** Bronze figurine from Olympia. Athens, National Museum 6149. Early sixth century. H. 0.22. (Pp. 84–5, 104, 142) **d** and **e** Terracotta vase-figure from Athens, Agora. Athens, Agora Museum P 1231. H. 0.25. (Pp. 76, 146).

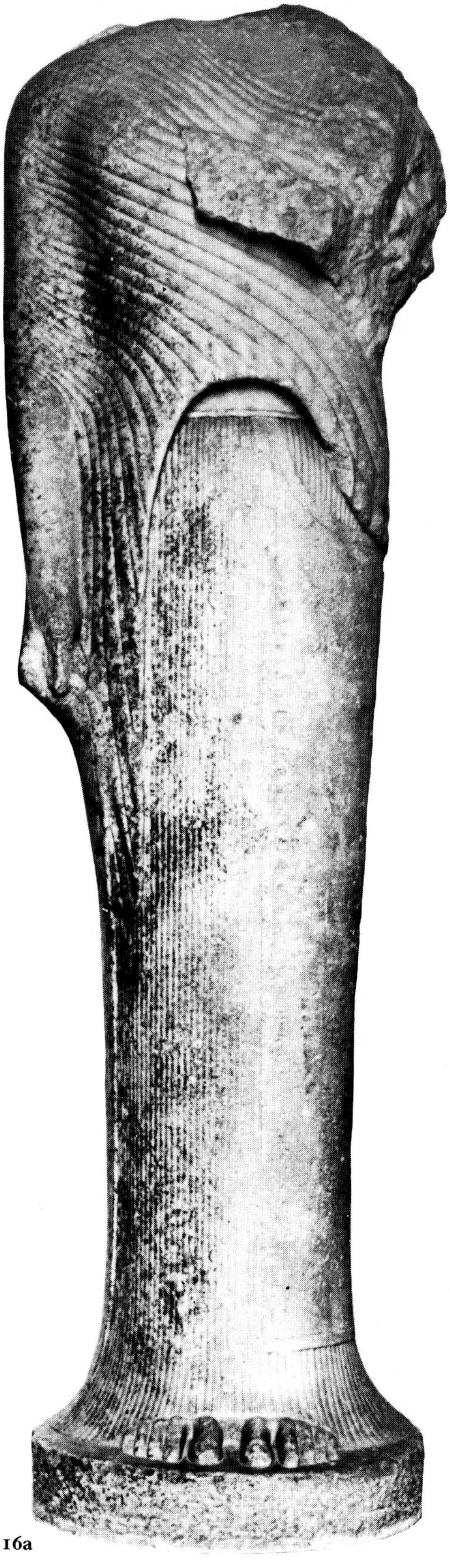

16a

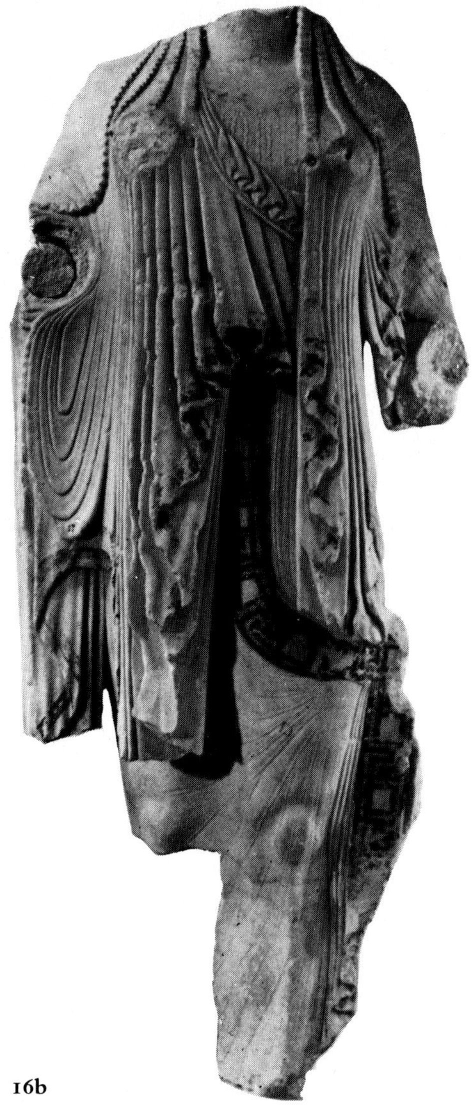

16b

16 a Marble statue from Samos, dedicated by Cheramyes to Hera. Louvre 686. Second quarter of sixth century. H. 1.92. (Pp. 72–3) **b** Marble statue from the Acropolis. Athens, Acropolis Museum 594. Third quarter of sixth century. H. 1.23. (Pp. 78–9, 89, 102).

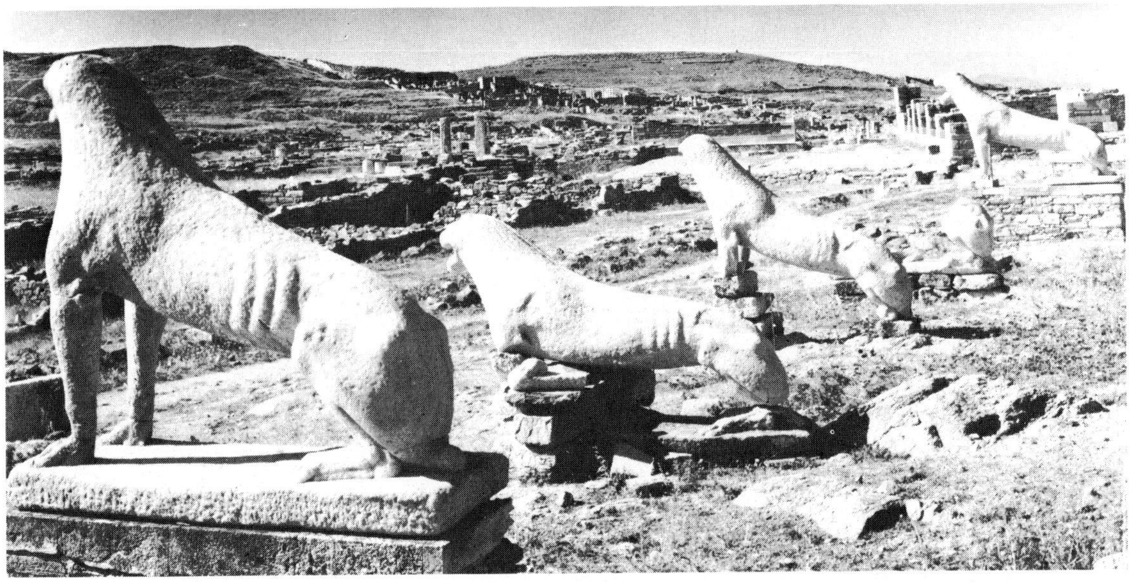

17a

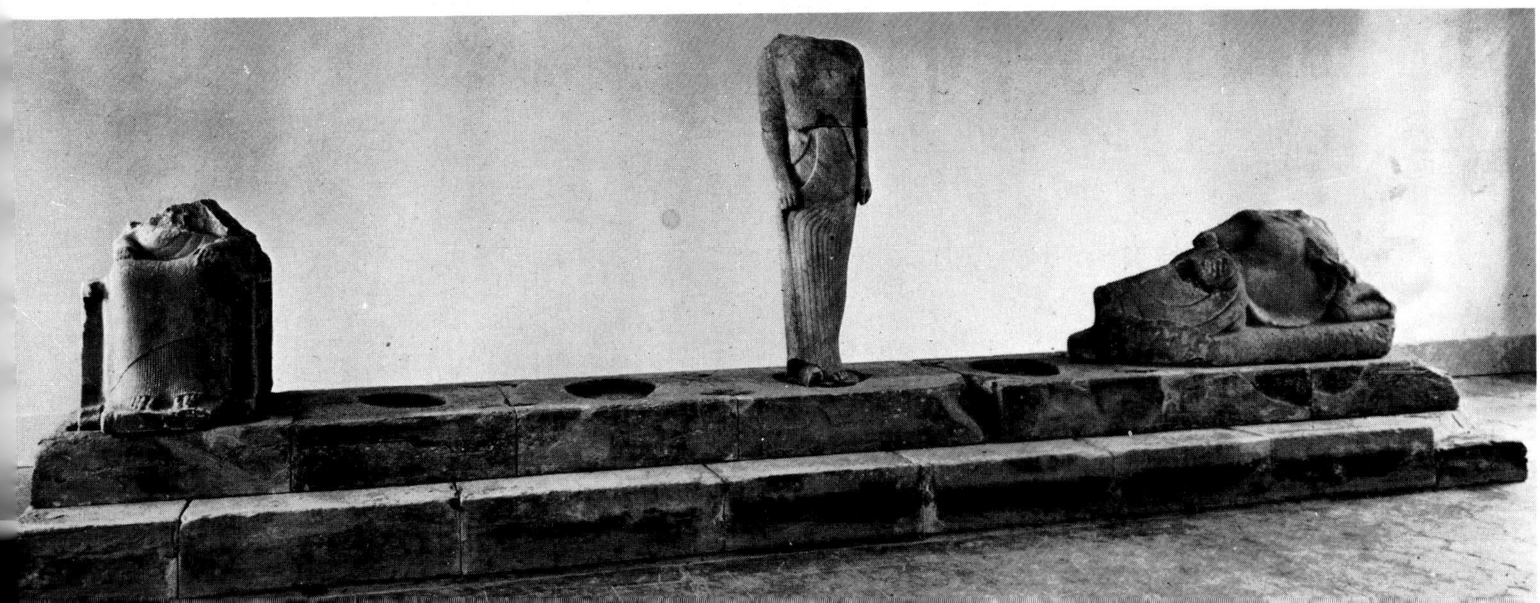

7b

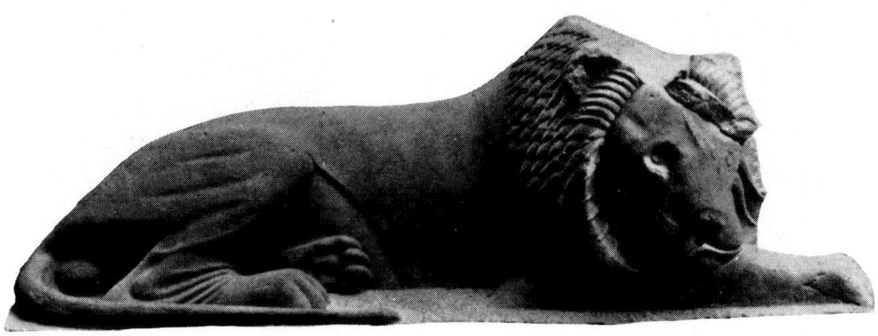

17c

17 **a** Marble lions in sanctuary of Apollo on Delos. Late seventh or early sixth century. H. of complete lions *c.* 1.20–1.40. (P. 87) **b** Reconstruction of base with marble statues by Geneleos from sanctuary of Hera on Samos. Towards middle of sixth century. H. of standing figure 1.61. (Pp. 73ff.) **c** Marble lion from Miletus. Berlin (E) 1790. Second half of sixth century. L. 1.71. (Pp. 86, 98).

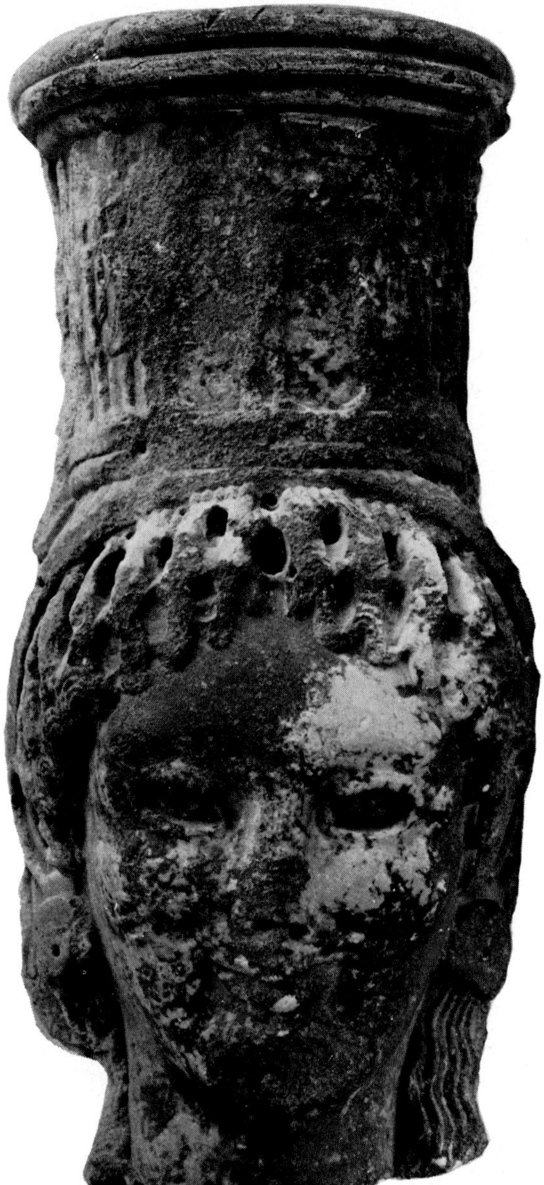

18a

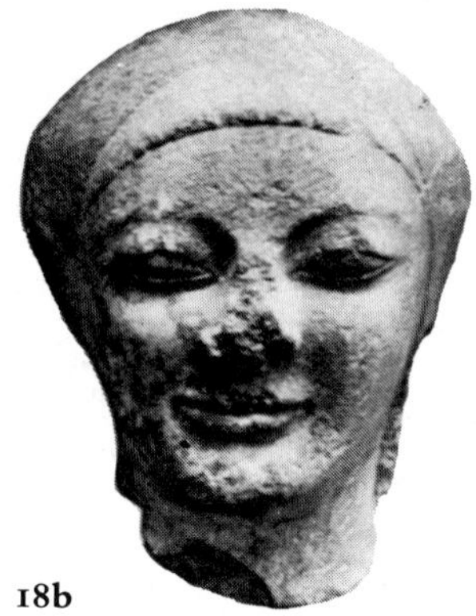

18b

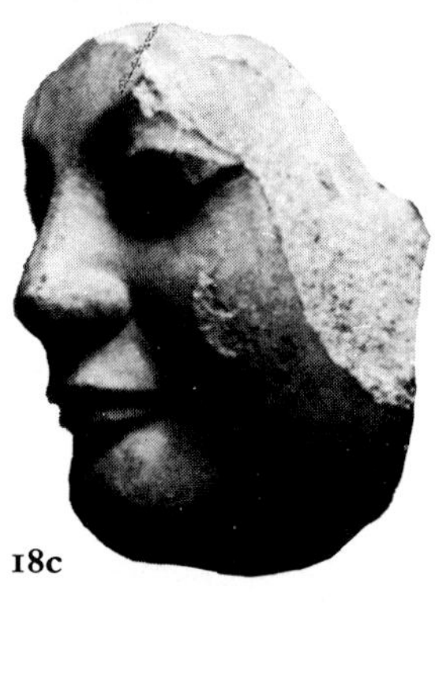

18c

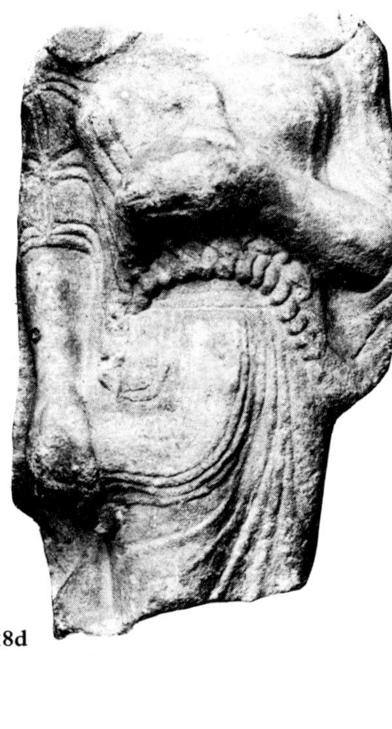

18d

18 **a** Marble head of Caryatid from unidentified treasury at Delphi. Delphi Museum. Mid sixth century. H. with *polos* 0.66. (Pp. 80, 84) **b** Marble head of statue from Miletus. Berlin (E) 1631. Second half of sixth century. H. 0.21. (Pp. 75–6, 290) **c** Marble face from relief on column-drum of Temple of Artemis at Ephesus. British Museum B 89. Second half of sixth century. H. 0.19. (P. 85) **d** Marble torso from Theangela (Caria). British Museum B 319. Third quarter of sixth century. H. 0.39. (P. 79).

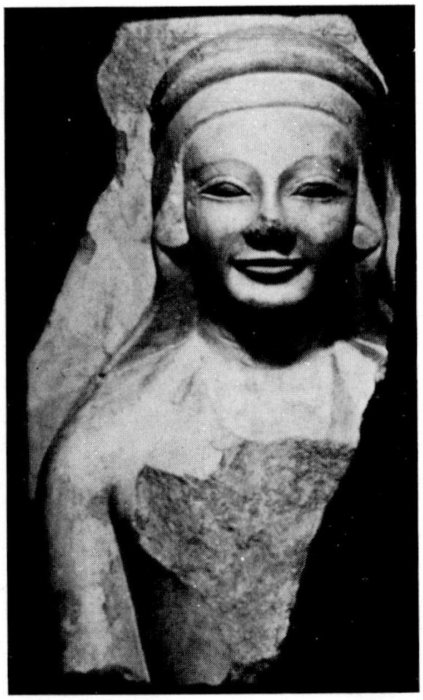

19a

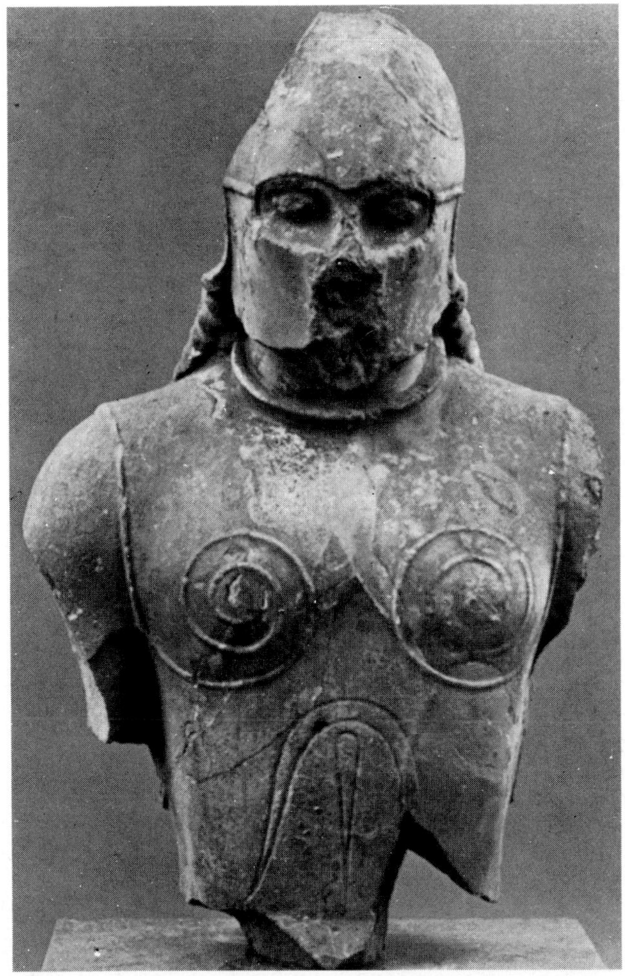

19b

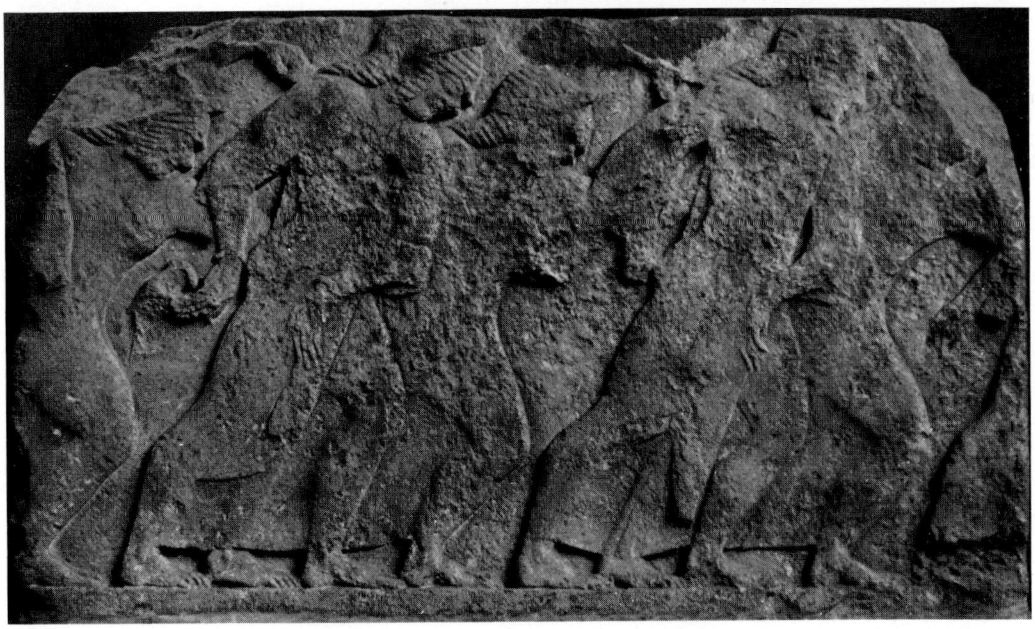

19c

19 **a** Fragment of marble relief-figure from column-drum in Temple of Apollo at Didyma. Berlin (Charlottenburg) F 724. Second half of sixth century. H. 0.55. (Pp. 84–5) **b** Upper part of marble statue from sanctuary of Hera on Samos. Berlin (E) 1752. Mid sixth century. H. 0.86. (Pp. 80–1) **c** Relief from Temple of Apollo at Didyma. British Museum B 285. Second half of sixth century. H. 0.53. (P. 81).

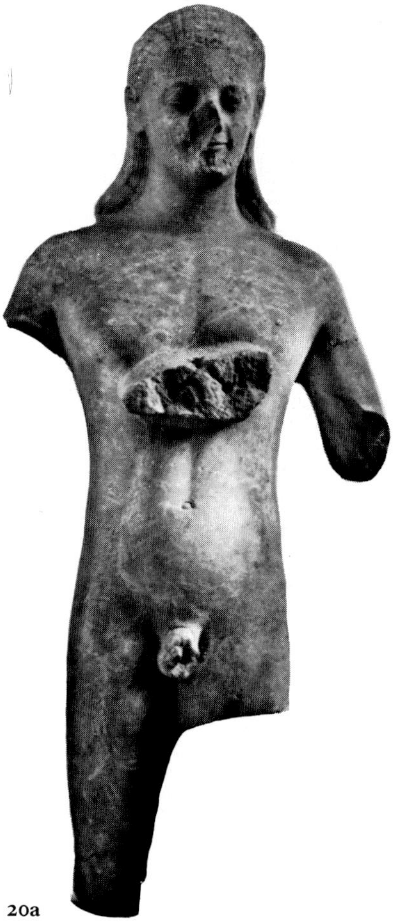

20a

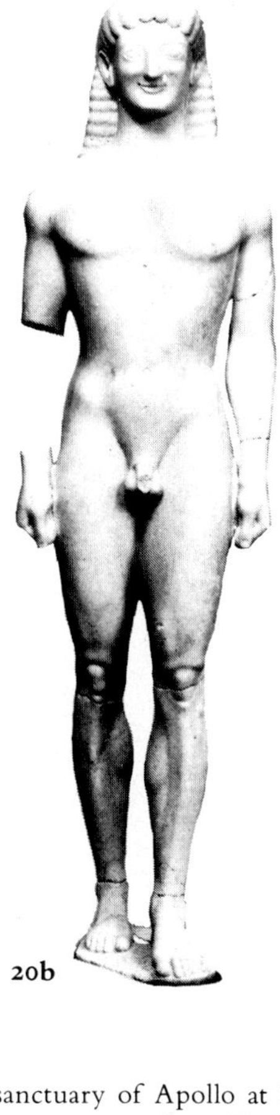

20b

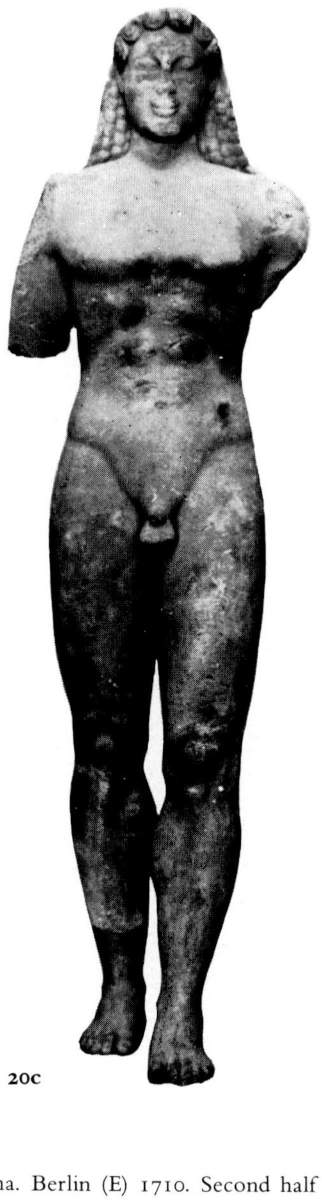

20c

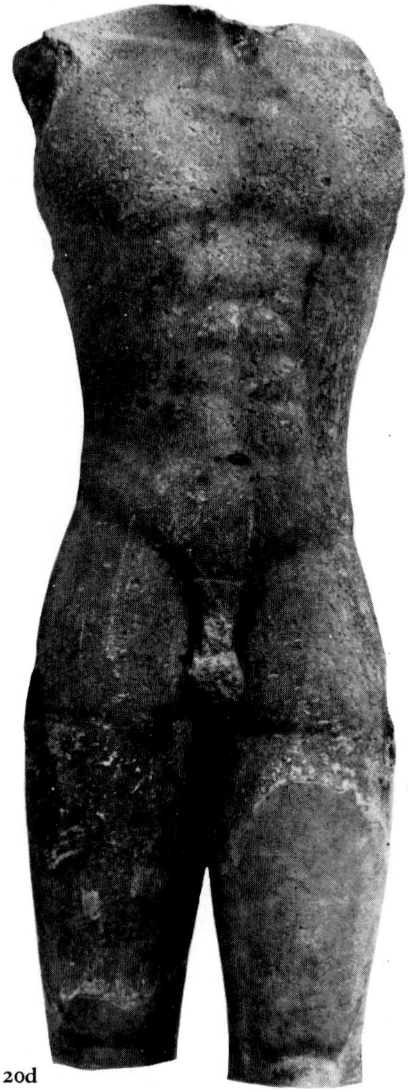

20d

20 **a** Marble statue from sanctuary of Apollo at Didyma. Berlin (E) 1710. Second half of sixth century. H. 1.66. (Pp. 76, 84) **b** Marble grave-statue from Tenea. Munich 168. Second quarter of sixth century. H. 1.53. (P. 113) **c** Marble grave-statue from Keos. Athens, National Museum 3686. Third quarter of sixth century. Over life-size. (Pp. 88–9, 114, 182) **d** Marble torso from Megara. Athens, National Museum 13. Mid sixth century. H. 2.00. (P. 113).

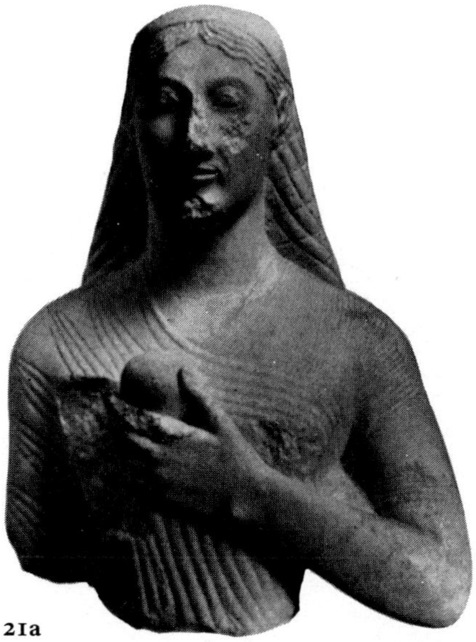

21a

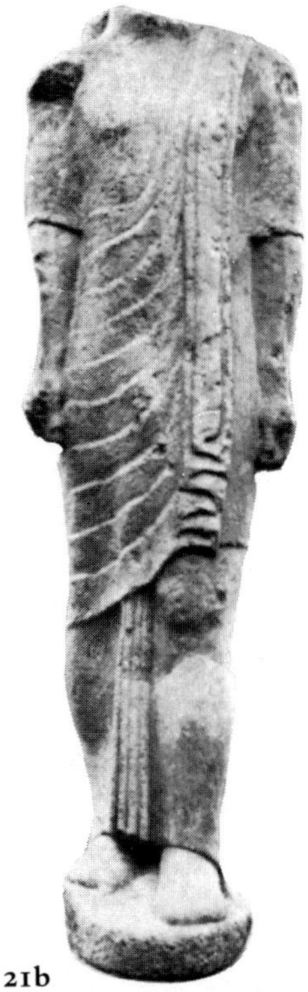

21b

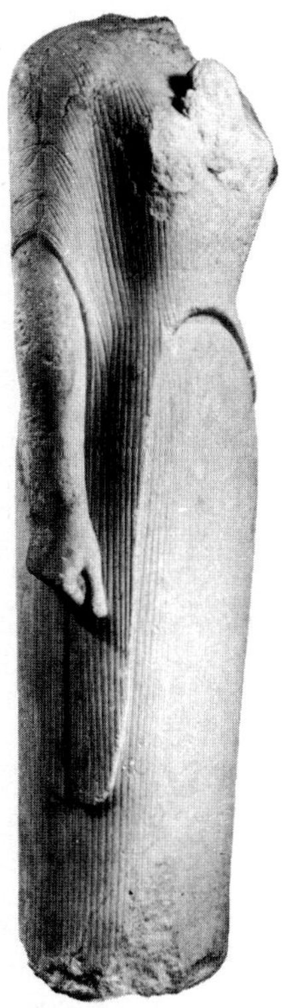

21c

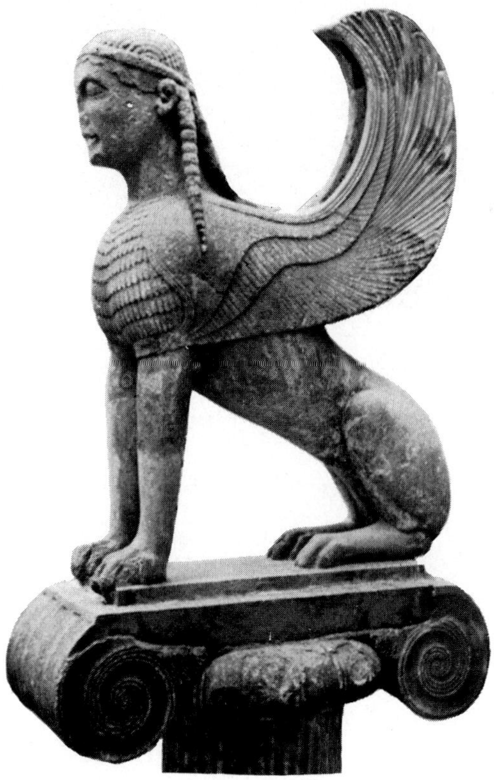

21d

21 **a** Upper part of marble statue from Acropolis. Athens, Acropolis Museum 677. Second quarter of sixth century. H. 0.54. (P. 87) **b** Marble torso from Myus (Asia Minor). Berlin (E) 1664. Mid sixth century. H. 1.02. (P. 76) **c** Marble torso from Acropolis. Athens, Acropolis Museum 619. Second quarter of sixth century. H. 1.43. (Pp. 86–7) **d** Marble sphinx, dedicated in the sanctuary of Apollo at Delphi by the Naxians. Second quarter of sixth century. H. 2.32 (P. 87).

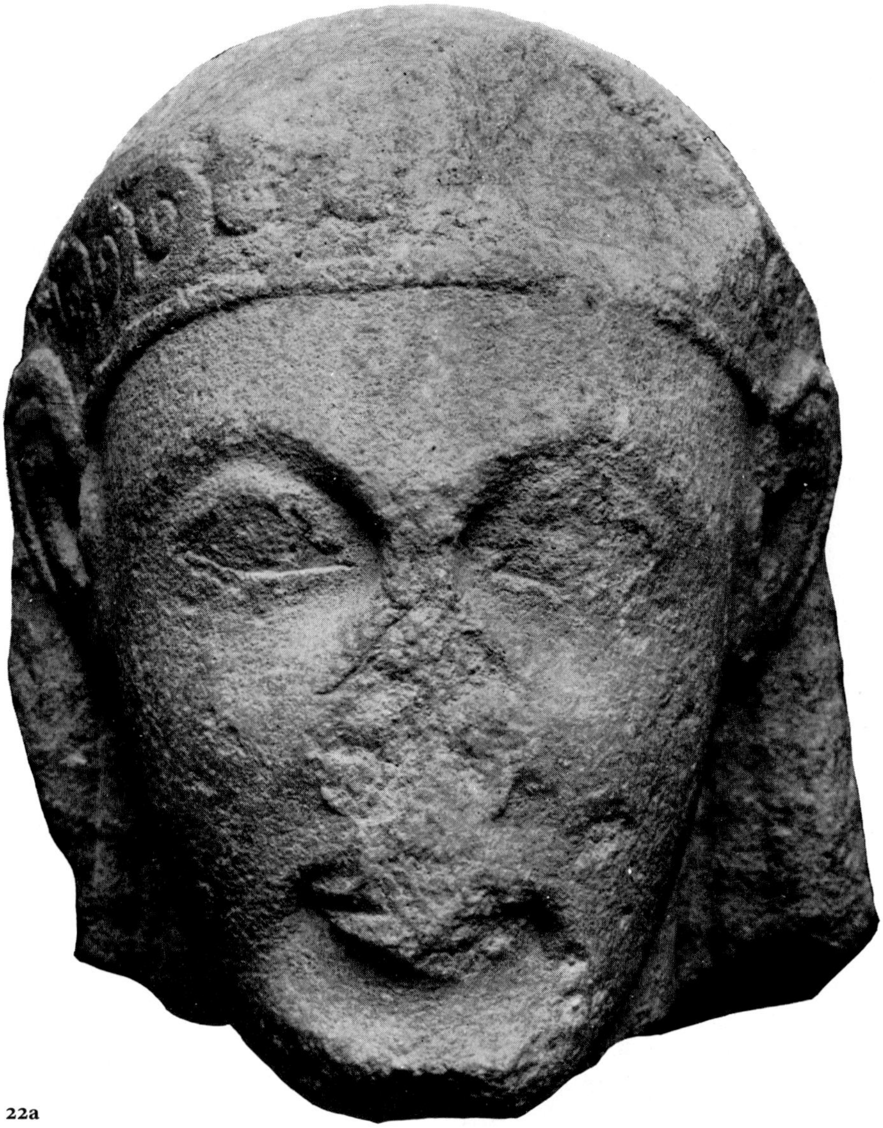

22a

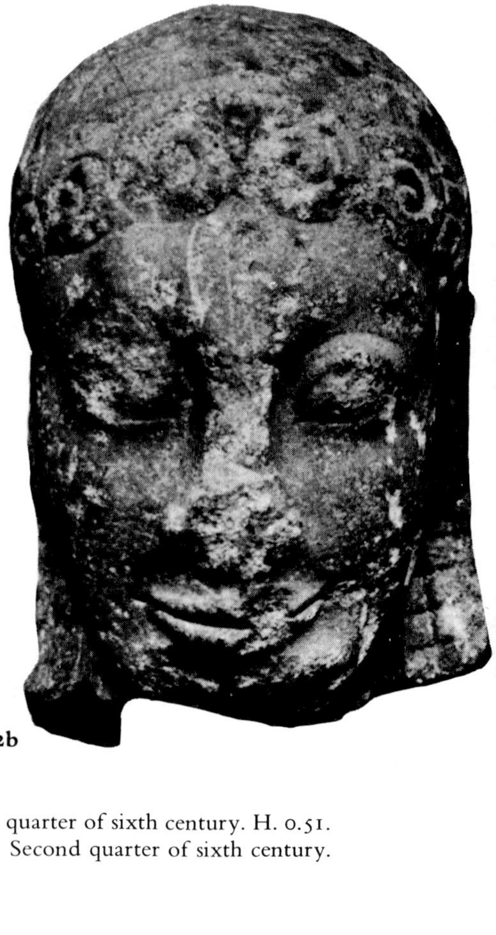

22b

22 **a** Marble head from Naxos. Copenhagen, Ny Carlsberg Glyptotek 2821. First quarter of sixth century. H. 0.51. (Pp. 88, 114) **b** Marble head from Epidaurus. Athens, National Museum 63. Second quarter of sixth century. H. 0.34. (Pp. 89, 113–14).

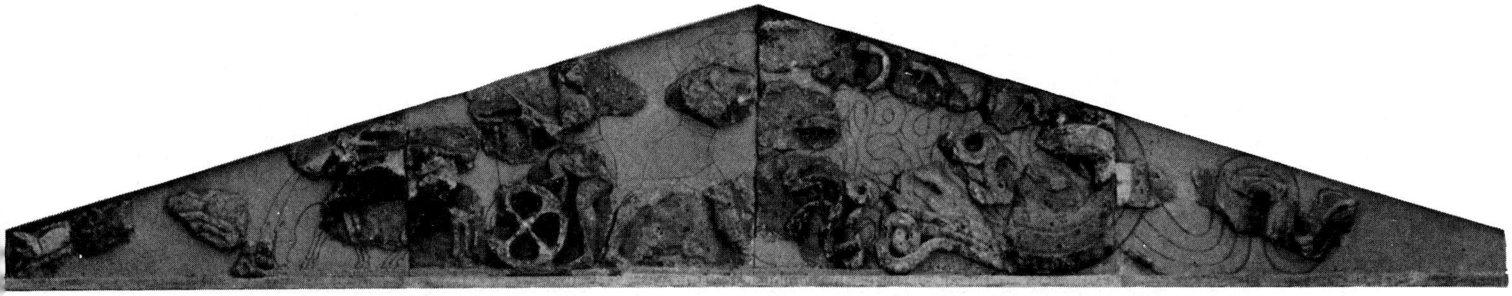

23a

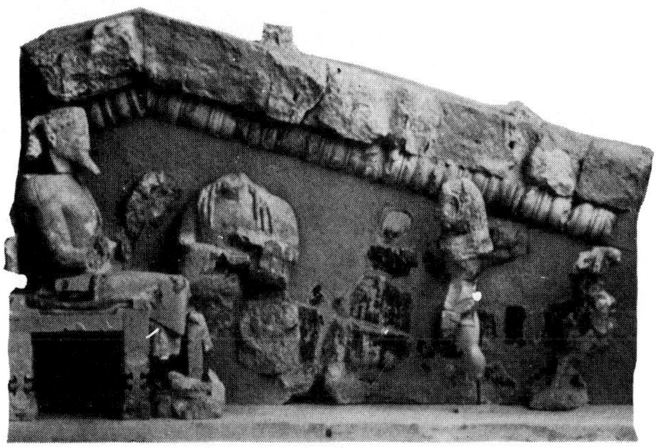

23b

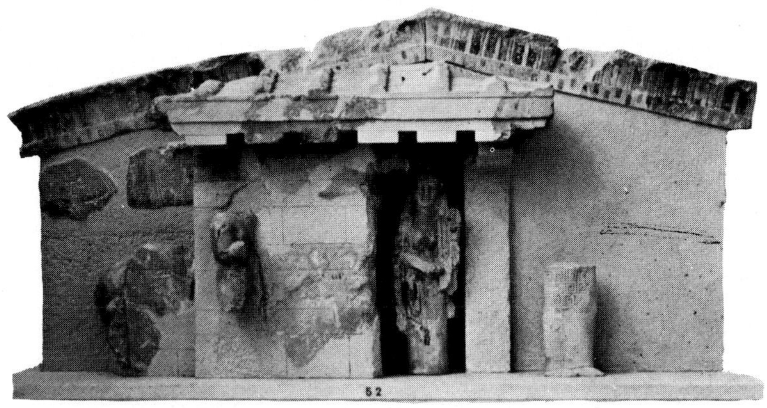

23c

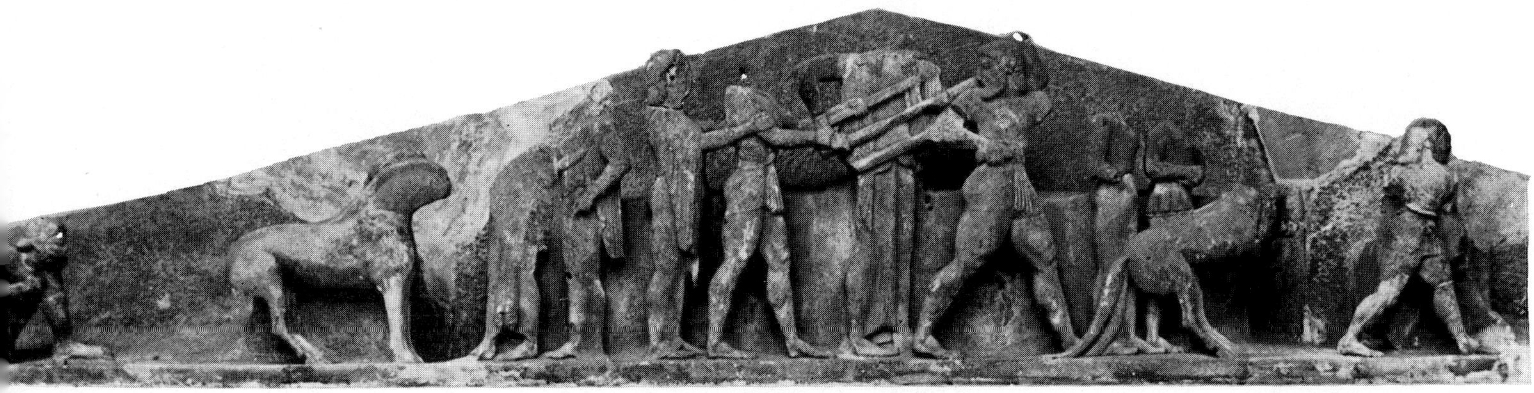

3d

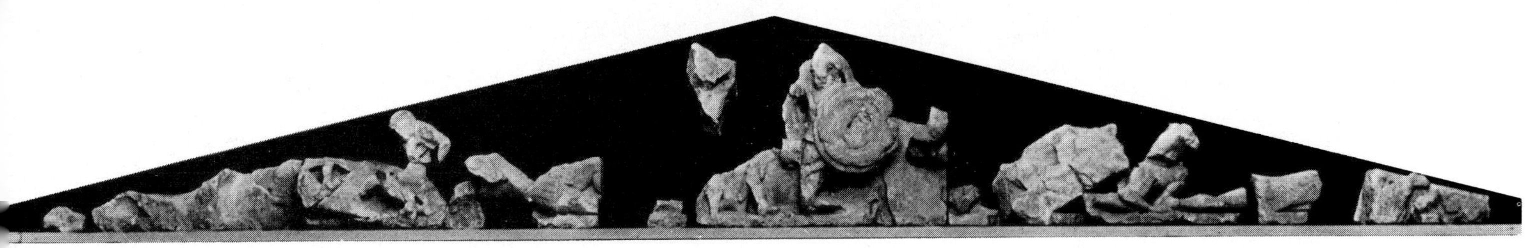

3e

23 **a** Limestone pediment from Acropolis. Athens, Acropolis Museum. Fairly early sixth century. H. 0.79. (P. 91) **b** Limestone pediment from Acropolis. Athens, Acropolis Museum. Second quarter of sixth century. H. 0.94. (Pp. 91–2, 128) **c** Limestone pediment from Acropolis. Athens, Acropolis Museum. Second quarter of sixth century. H. 0.80. (P. 92) **d** Marble pediment from Treasury of the Siphnians, Delphi. Delphi Museum. Shortly before 525 B.C. H. 0.74. Cf. pls. 46–8. (Pp. 157ff.) **e** Limestone pediment from Treasury of Megarians, Olympia. Olympia Museum. End of sixth century. H. 0.74. (P. 162).

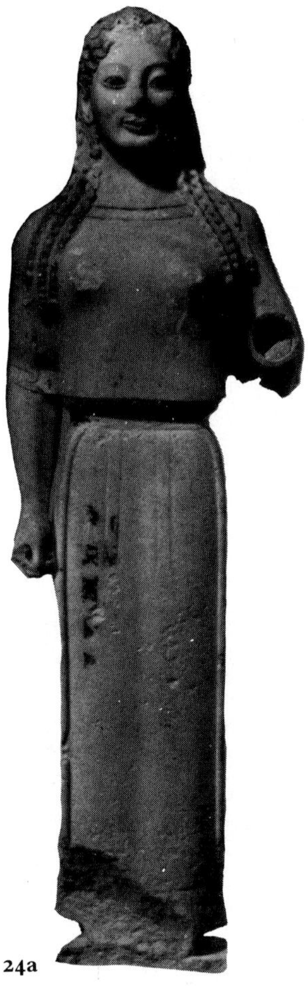

24a

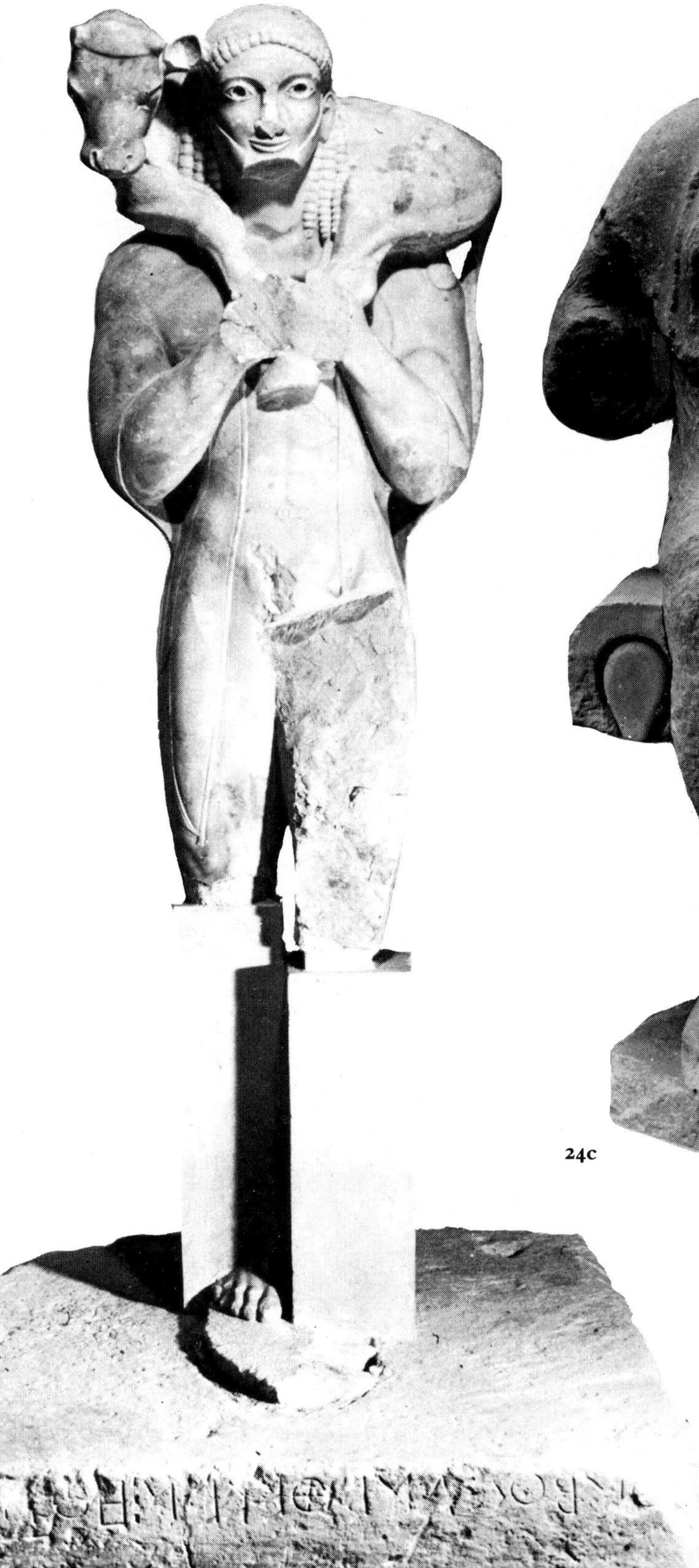

24b

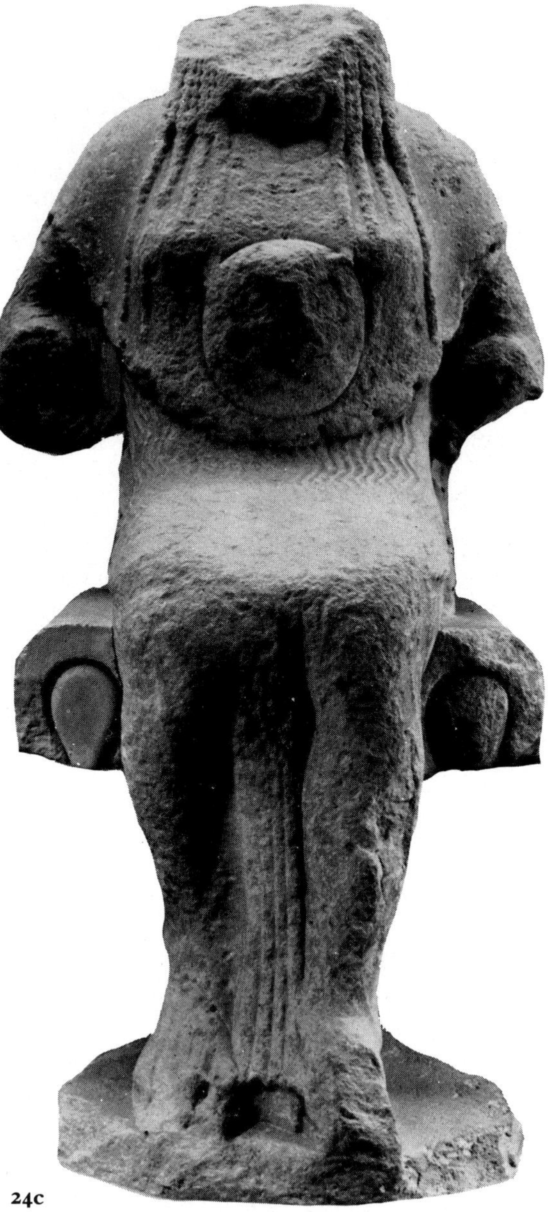

24c

24 **a** Marble statue from Acropolis. Athens, Acropolis Museum 679. Third quarter of sixth century. H. 1.20. (Pp. 101–2, 135) **b** Marble group from Acropolis. Athens, Acropolis Museum 624. Second quarter of sixth century. H. 1.65. (Pp. 94ff., 129, 135) **c** Marble statue from Acropolis. Athens, Acropolis Museum 625. Mid sixth century. H. 1.47. (Pp. 106ff.).

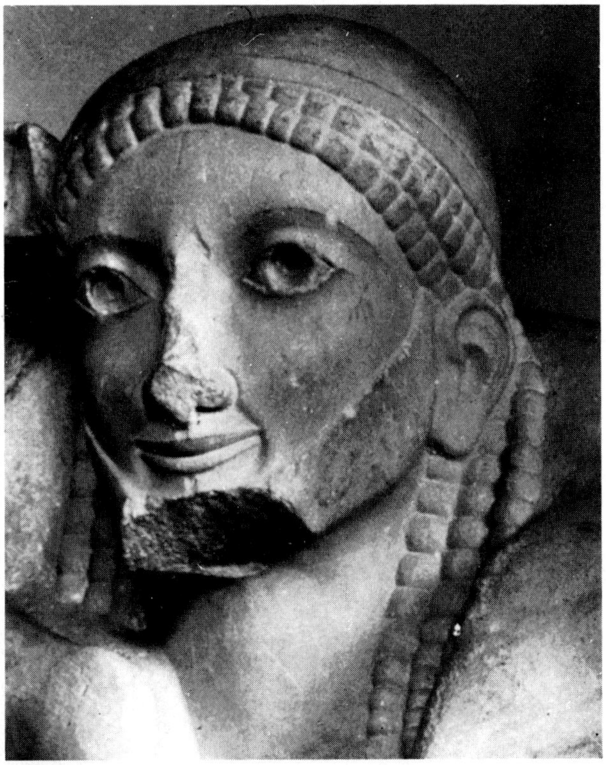

25a

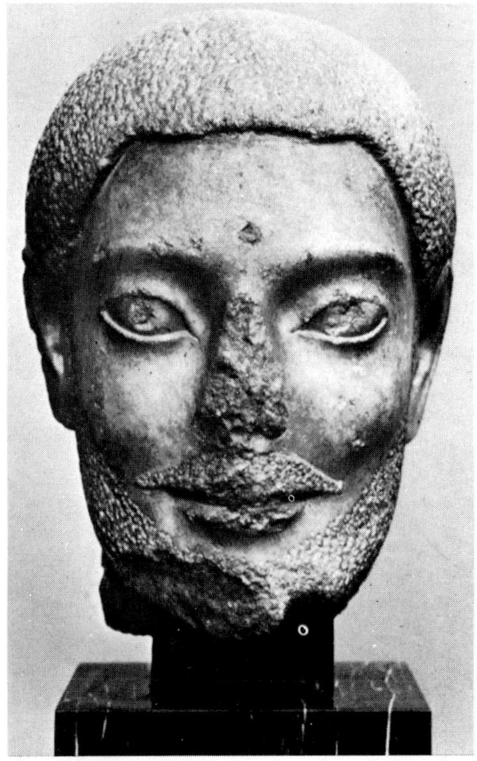

25b

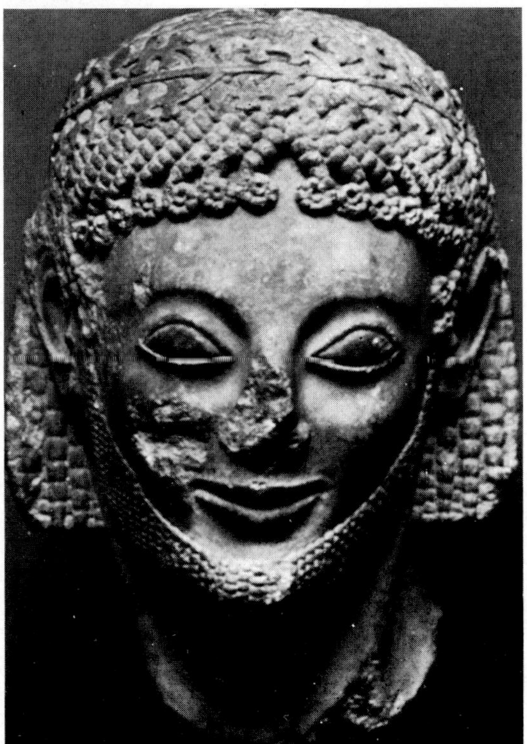

25c

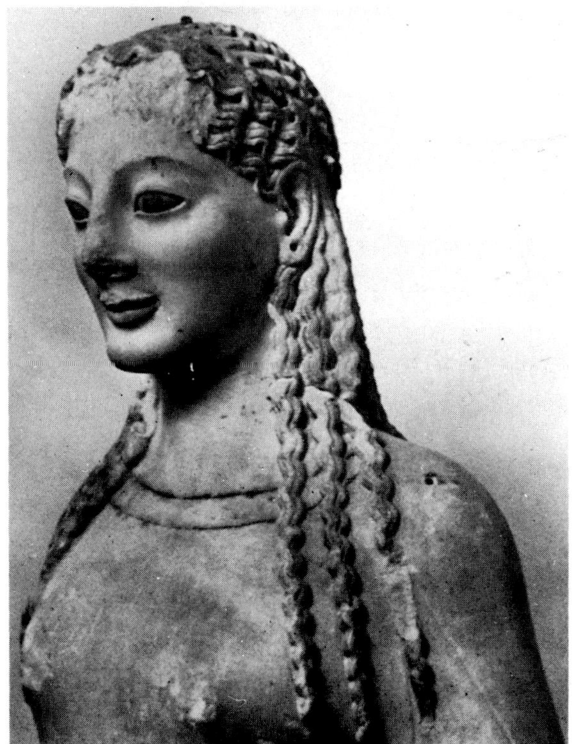

25d

25 **a** Head of statue in pl. 24b. (Pp. 94ff.) **b** Marble head from Athens or Aegina. Berlin (E) 608. Mid sixth century. H. 0.23. (Pp. 98, 111) **c** Marble head of statue from Acropolis of Athens. Louvre 3104. Mid sixth century. H. 0.29. Cf. pl. 27b. (Pp. 96ff.) **d** Upper part of statue in pl. 24a. (Pp. 101–2).

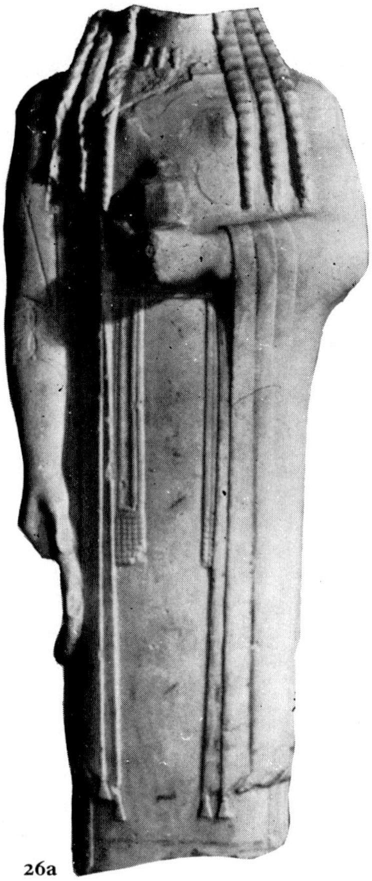

26a

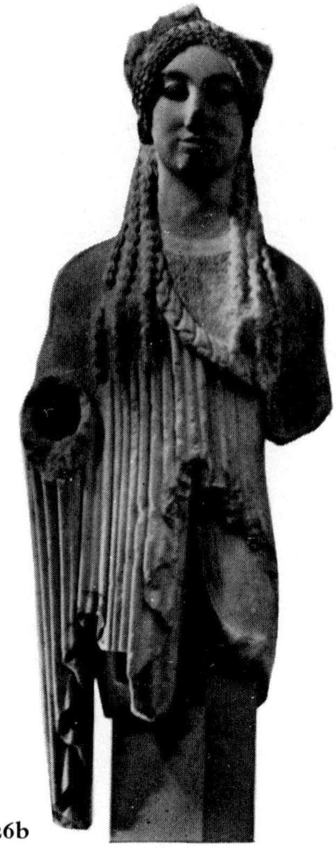

26b

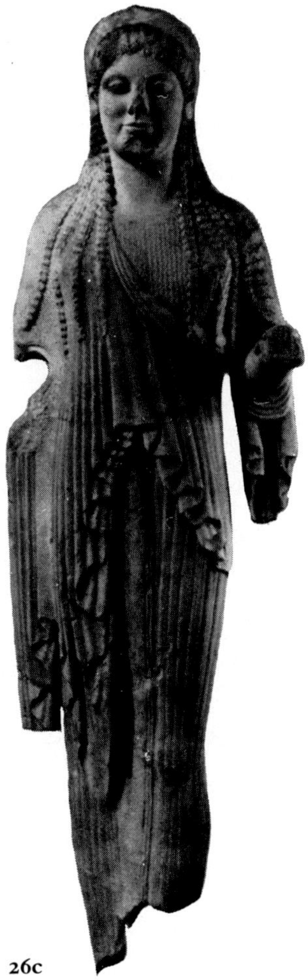

26c

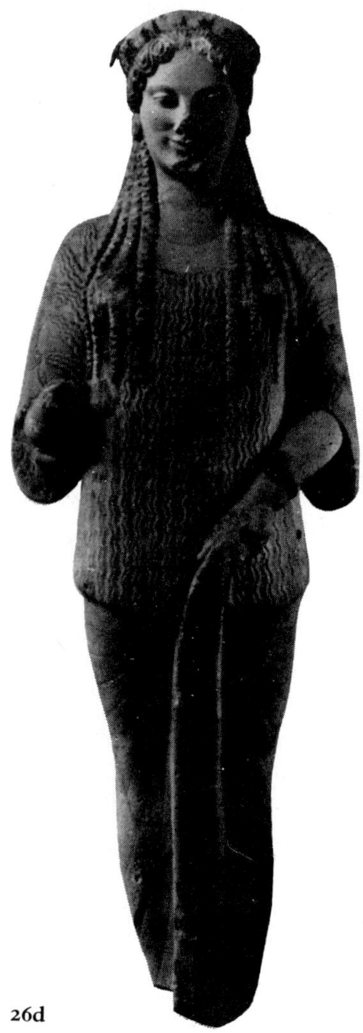

26d

26 **a** Marble torso from Acropolis. Athens, Acropolis Museum 593. First or second quarter of sixth century. H. 1.01. (P. 99) **b** Marble statue from Acropolis. Athens, Acropolis Museum 674. Late sixth century. H. 0.92. (P. 104) **c** Marble statue from Acropolis. Athens, Acropolis Museum 685. Late sixth century. H. 1.25. (P. 104) **d** Marble statue from Acropolis. Athens, Acropolis Museum 670. Last quarter of sixth century. H. 1.15. (Pp. 104–5).

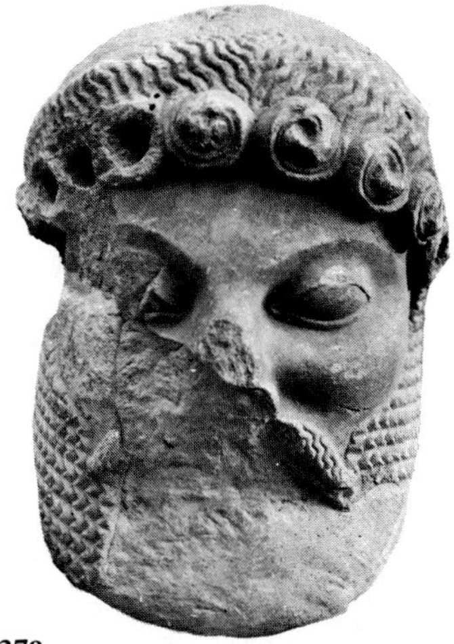

27a

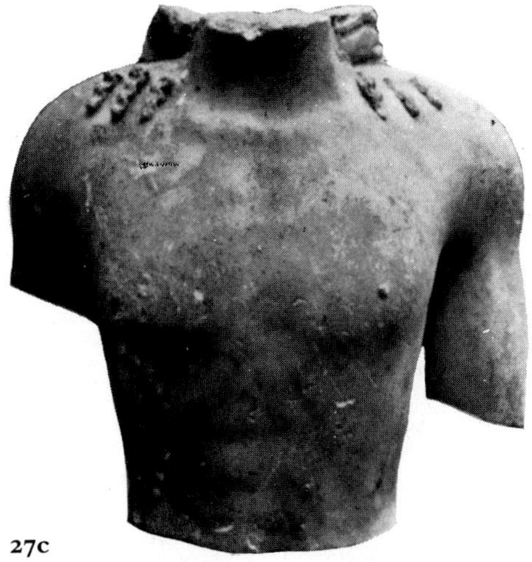

27c

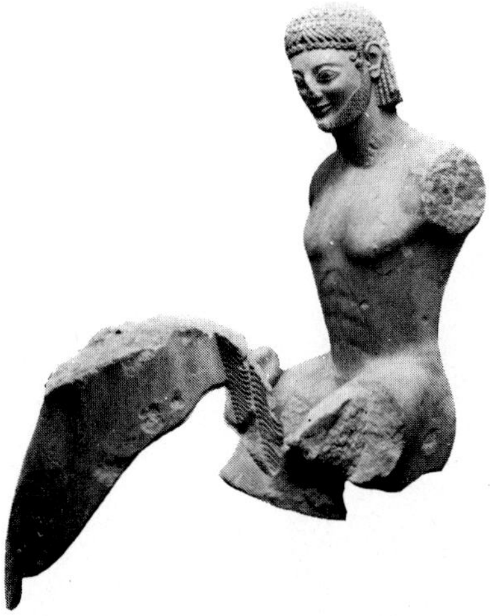

27b

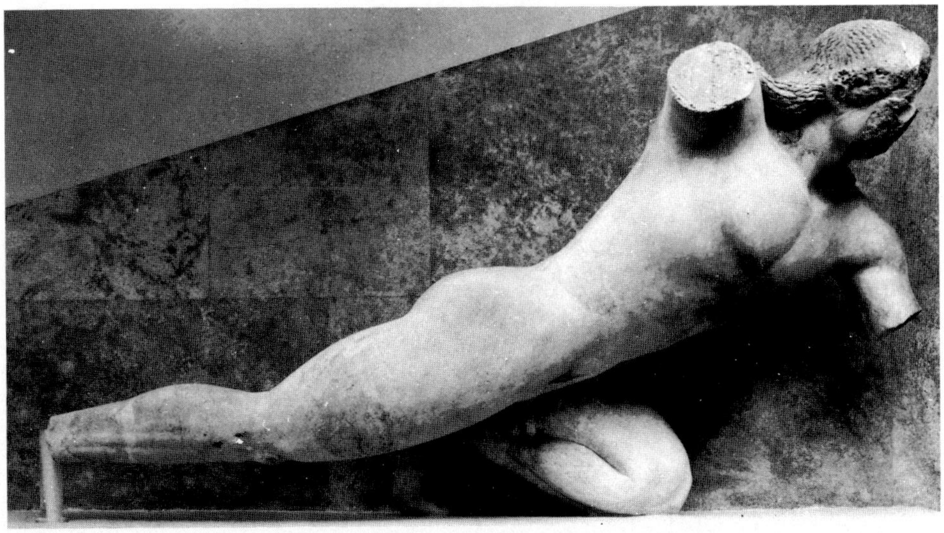

27d

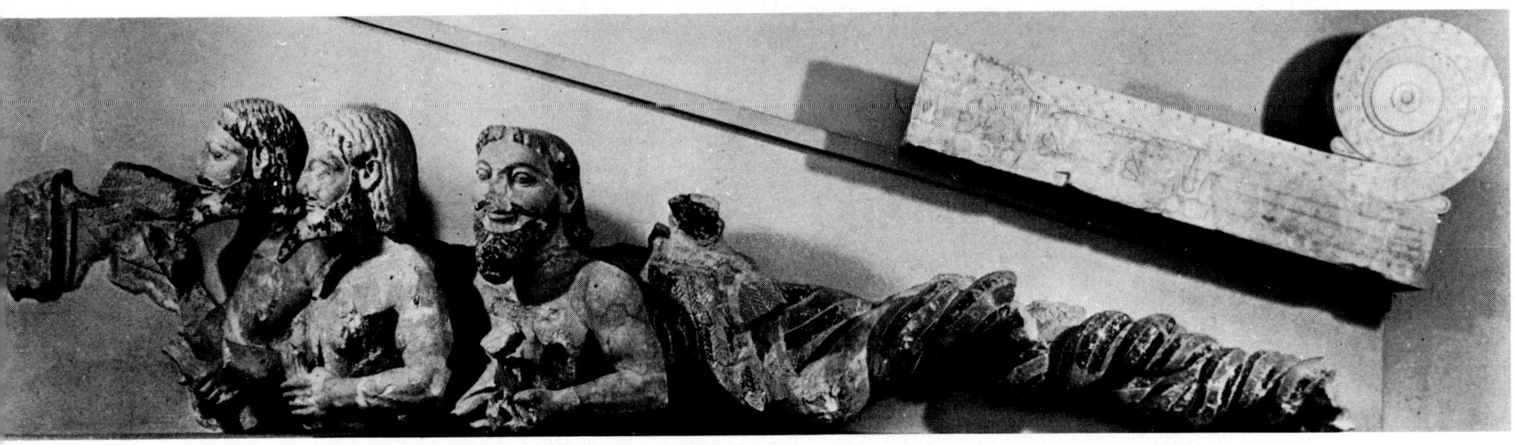

27e

27 **a** Marble mask from Ikaria (Attica). Athens, National Museum 3072. Third or last quarter of sixth century. H. 0.41. (P. 105) **b** Marble statue from Acropolis (with cast of head in pl. 25c). Athens, Acropolis Museum 590. Mid sixth century. H. *c.* 1.00. (Pp. 96ff.) **c** Marble torso from Attica (?). Boston, Museum of Fine Arts 39.552, Archibald Cary Coolidge Fund. Third quarter of sixth century. H. 0.40. (P. 96) **d** Marble pediment-figure from Acropolis. Athens, Acropolis Museum 631c. Third or last quarter of sixth century. H. 1.02. Much modern patching on body and limbs. (P. 160) **e** Limestone pediment-figure from Acropolis. Athens, Acropolis Museum 35. Second quarter of sixth century. H. *c.* 0.90. (Pp. 93–4).

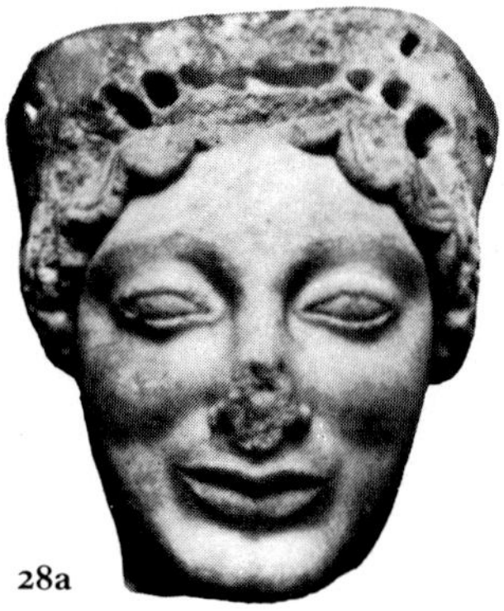

28a

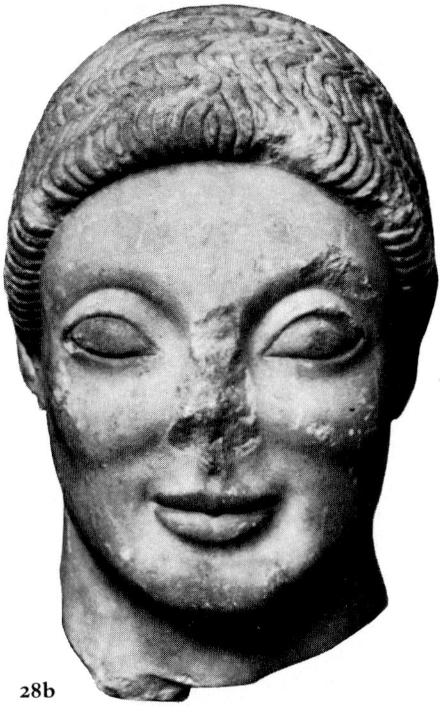

28b

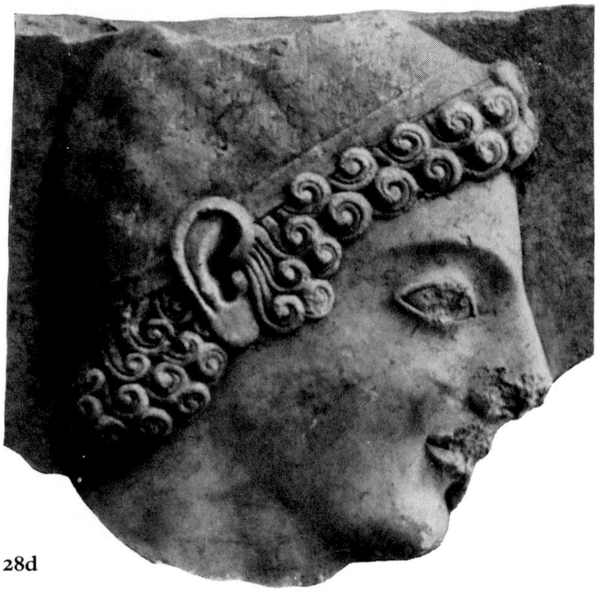

28d

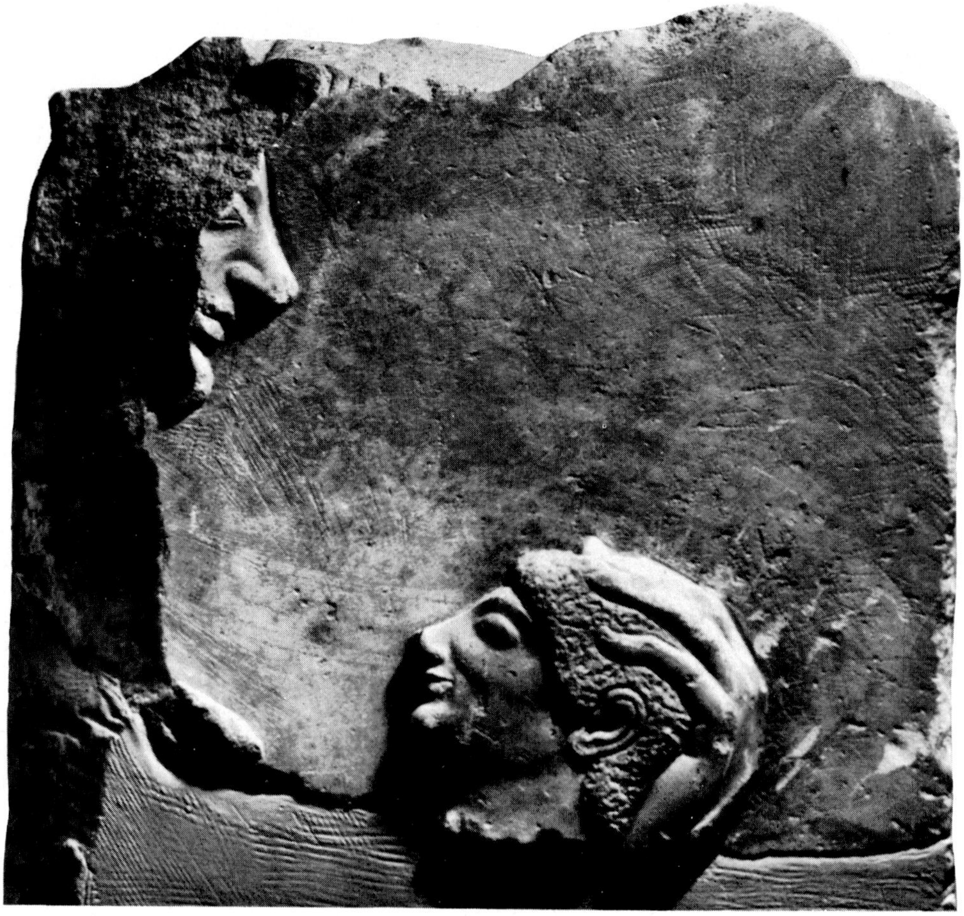

28c

28 **a** Marble head from Acropolis. Athens, Acropolis Museum 643. Late sixth century. H. 0.16. (Pp. 105, 142, 174) **b** Marble head from Athens. Copenhagen, Ny Carlsberg Glyptotek 418. Last quarter of sixth century. H. 0.31. (Pp. 105, 107, 142) **c** Fragment of marble grave-relief from Anavysos (Attica). Athens, National Museum 4472. Third quarter of sixth century. H. 0.38. (Pp. 99, 112) **d** Fragment of marble grave-relief from Attica. New York, Metropolitan Museum of Art 42.11.36, Rogers Fund. Third quarter of sixth century. H. 0.25. (P. 109).

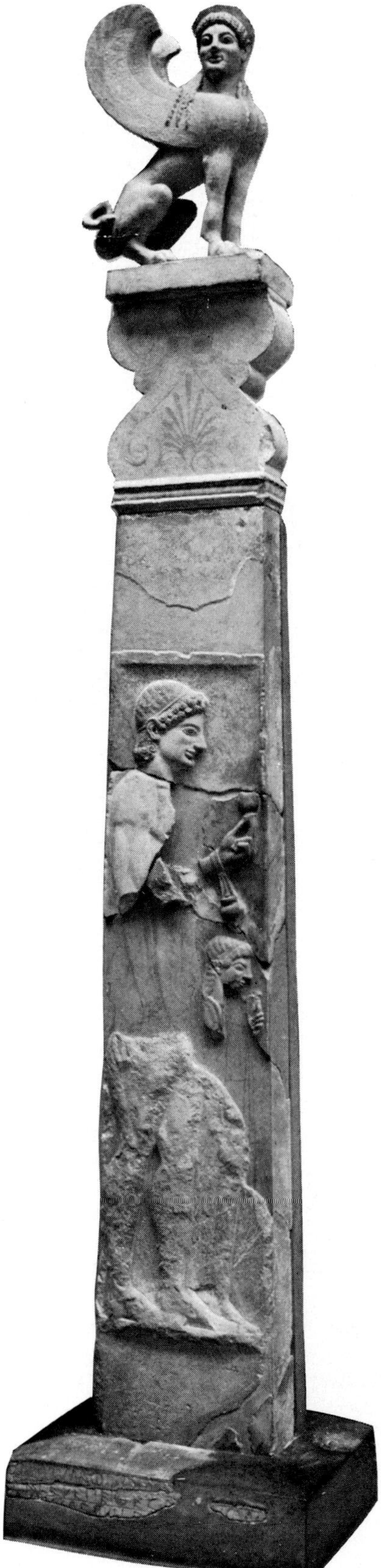

29a

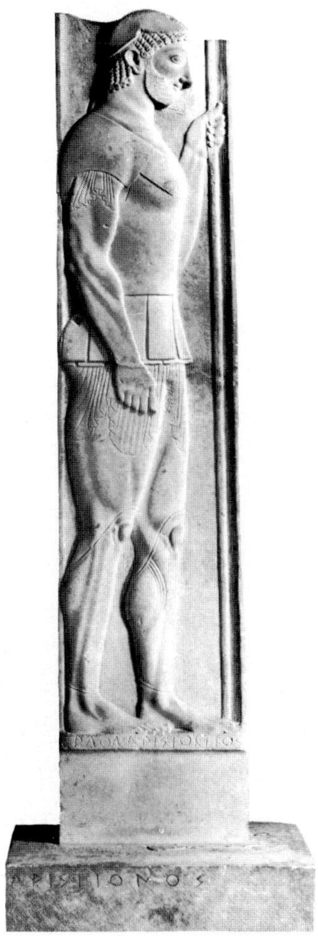

29b

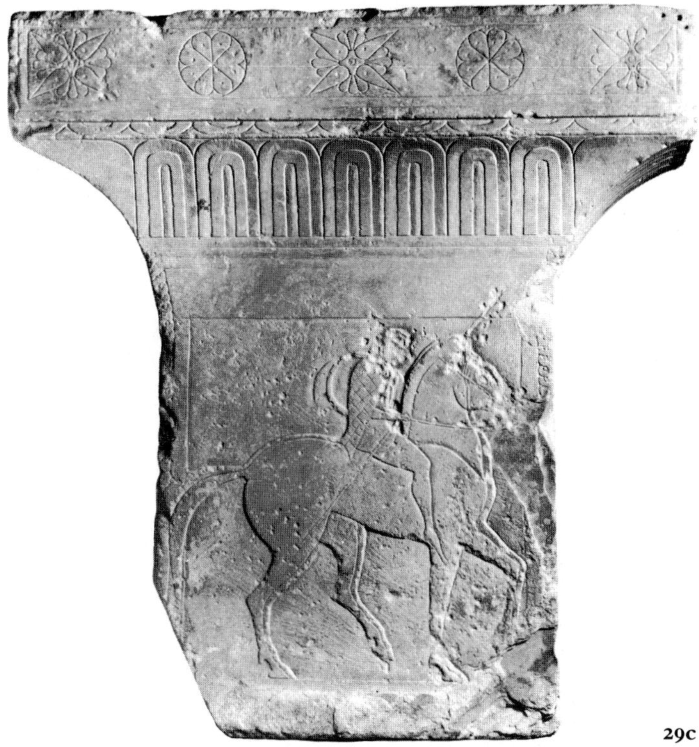

29c

29 a Reconstruction of marble gravestone from Attica. New York, Metropolitan Museum of Art 11.185, Hewitt Fund, Munsey Fund and Anonymous Gift (the girl a cast from Berlin (E) A 7). Third quarter of sixth century. H. 4.24. (Pp. 108ff.) **b** Marble grave-relief of Aristion, by Aristokles, from Velanediza (near Marathon, Attica). Athens, National Museum 29. Last quarter of sixth century. H. 2.40. (P. 110) **c** Marble relief-capital of gravestone from Lamptrai (Attica). Athens, National Museum 41. Mid sixth century. H. 0.73. (P. 110).

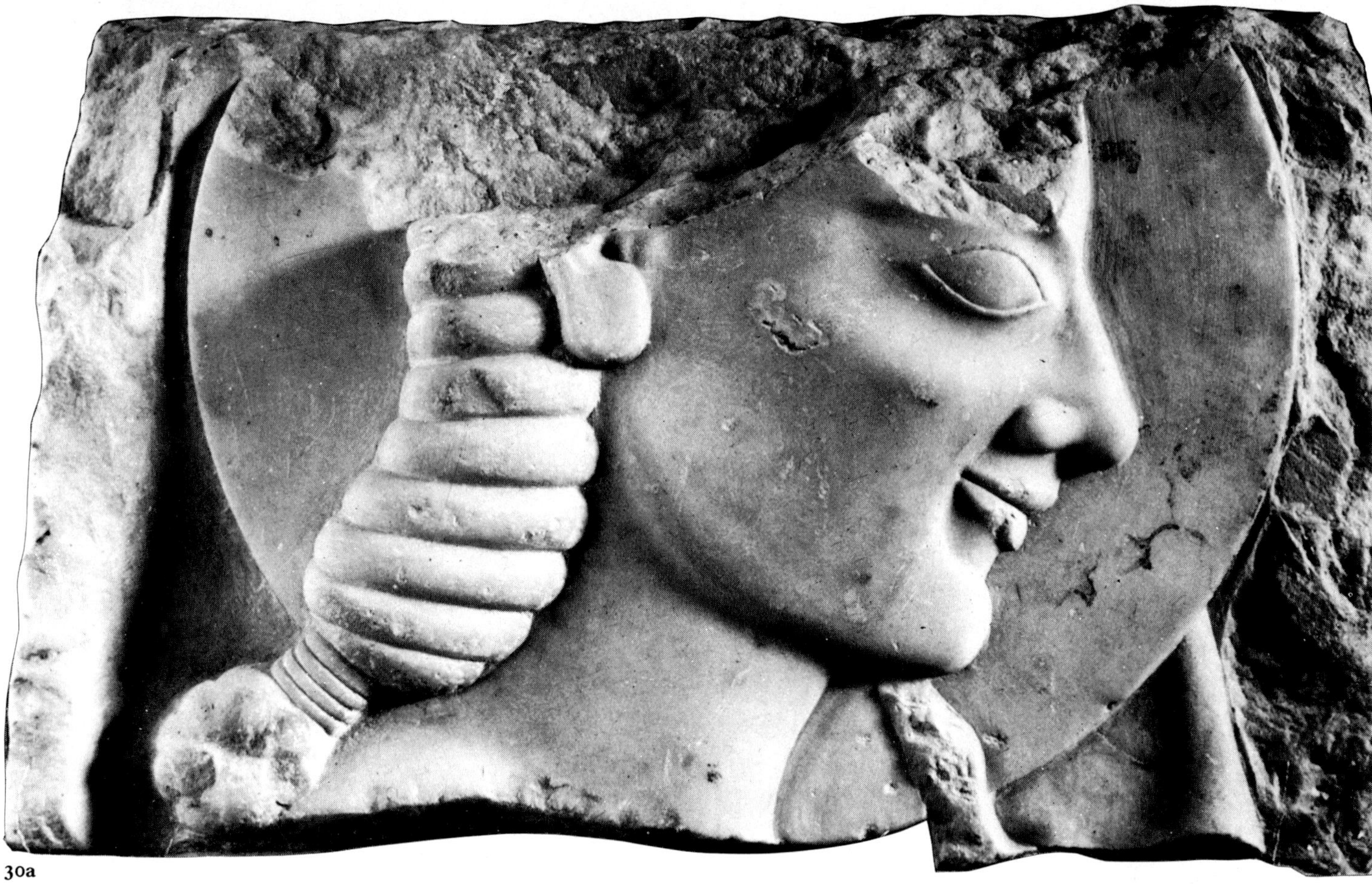

30a

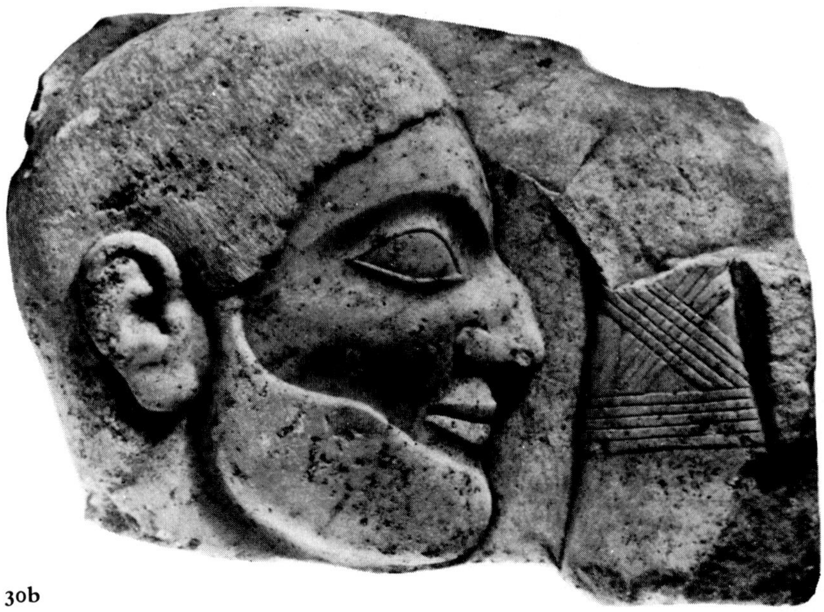

30b

30 **a** Fragment of marble grave-relief from Athens. Athens, National Museum 25. Second quarter of sixth century. H. 0.34. (P. 109) **b** Fragment of marble grave-relief from Athens. Athens, Kerameikos Museum. Mid sixth century. H. 0.23. (P. 109).

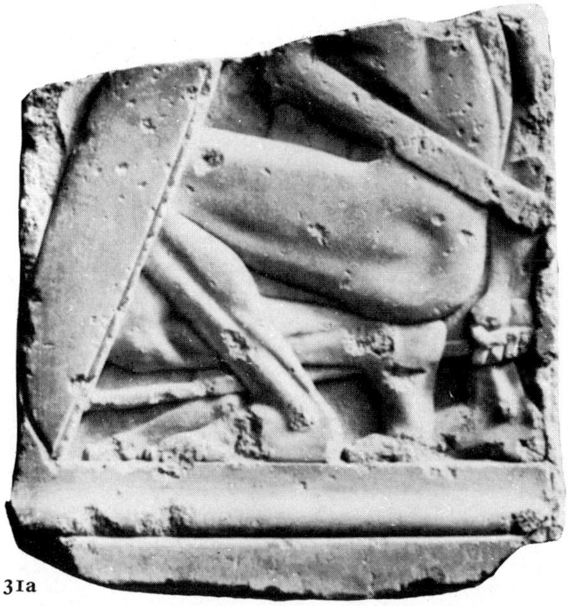
31a

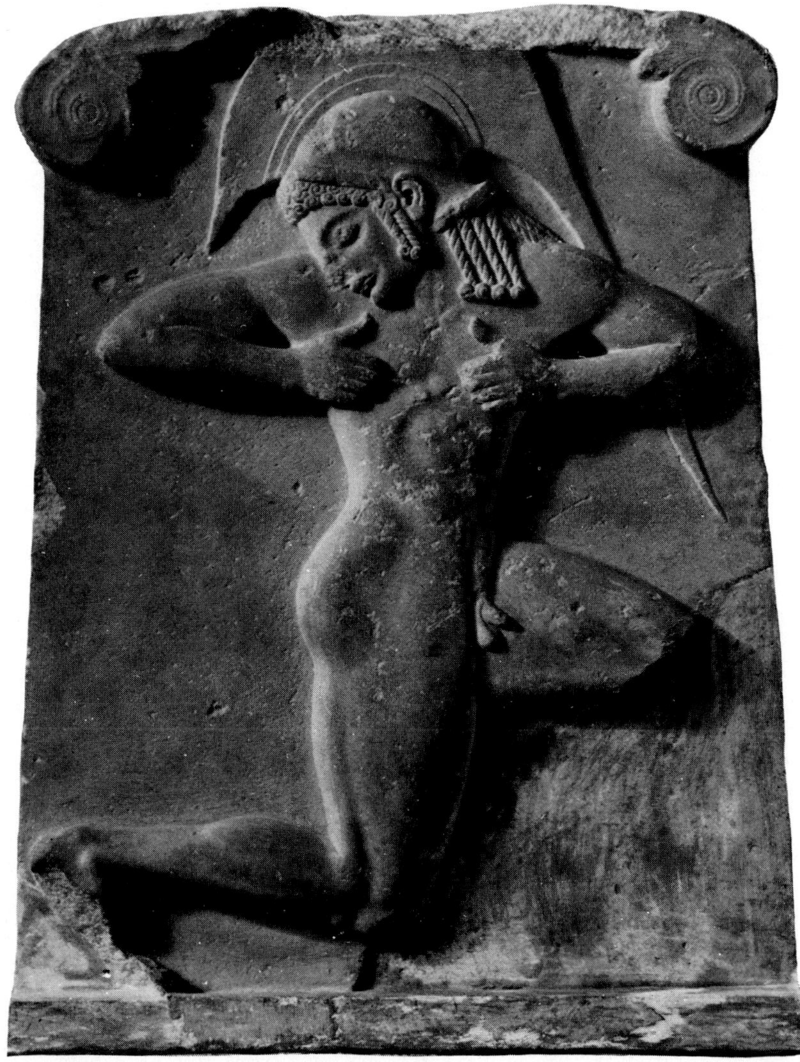
31b

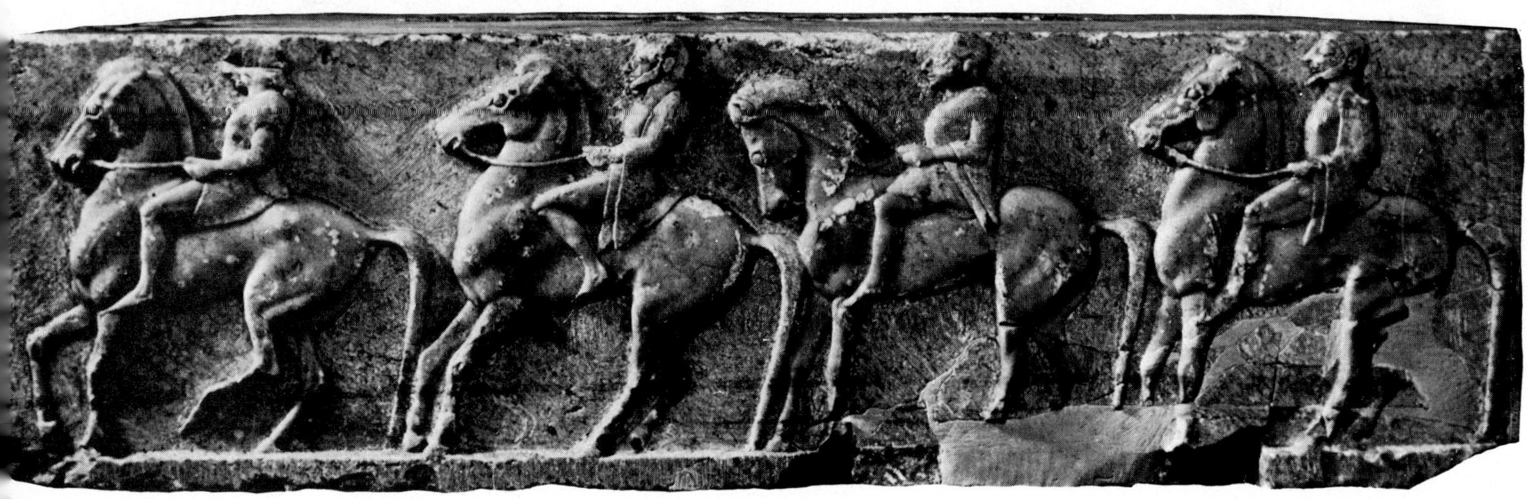
1c

31 **a** Fragment of marble grave-relief from Athens. Copenhagen, Ny Carlsberg Glyptotek IN 2787. End of sixth century. H. 0.57. (P. 111) **b** Marble grave-relief from Athens. Athens, National Museum 1959. Last quarter of sixth century. H. 1.00. (Pp. 111–12, 135) **c** Marble relief-base from Athenian grave. Athens, Kerameikos Museum P 1001. Mid sixth century. L. *c.* 1.00. (P. 109).

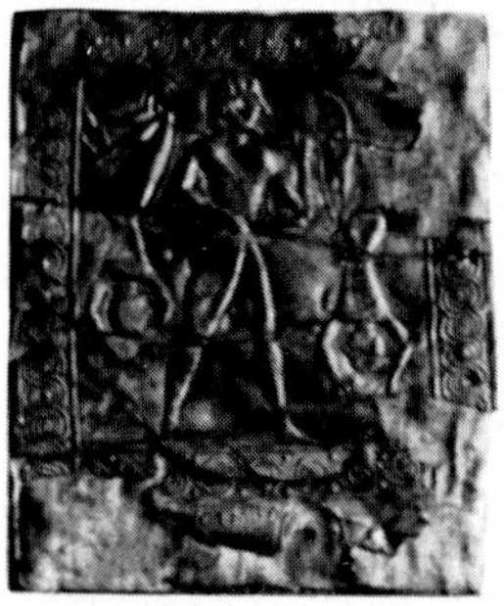

32a

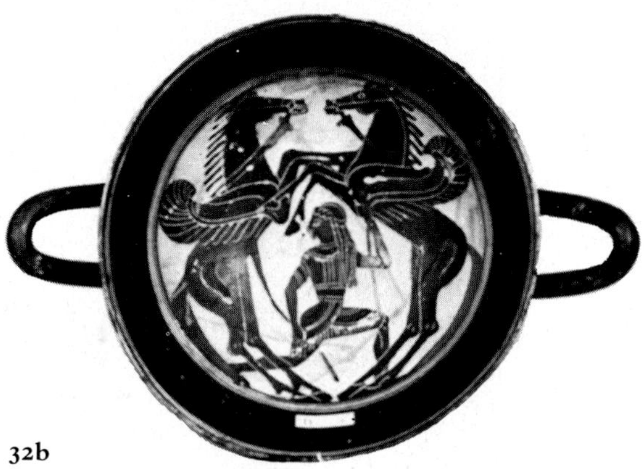

32b

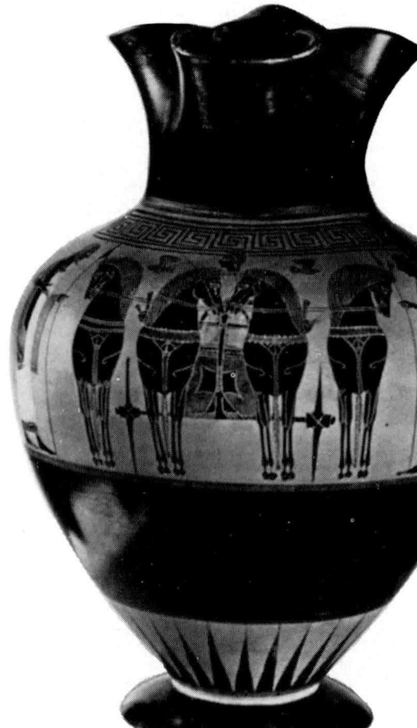

32c

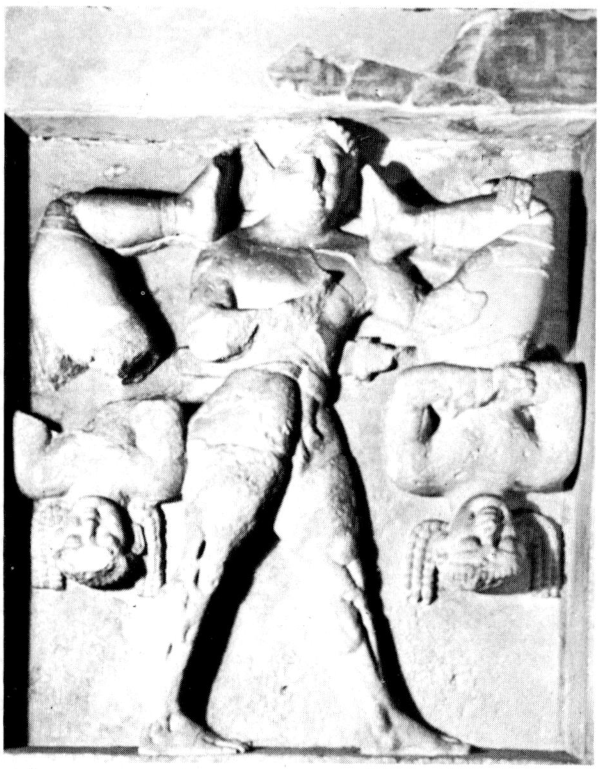

32d

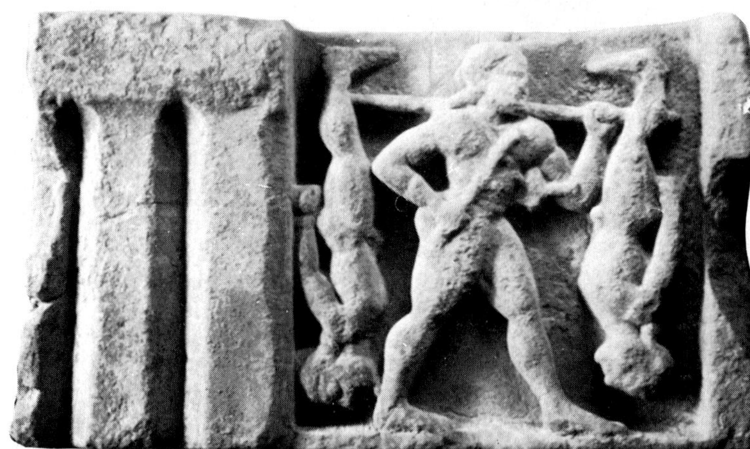

32e

32 **a** Bronze relief from interior of shield, from Olympia. Olympia Museum. First half of sixth century. H. 0.08. (Pp. 116, 119, 141) **b** Laconian black-figure cup from Capua. British Museum B 2. Second quarter of sixth century. D. 0.13. (Pp. 119, 136) **c** Attic black-figure jug from Italy. British Museum B 524. Third quarter of sixth century. H. 0.20. (Pp. 97, 136) **d** Limestone metope from Selinus. Palermo Museum. Mid sixth century. H. 1.47. (P. 119) **e** Sandstone metope from Foce del Sele. Paestum Museum. First half of sixth century. H. 0.77. (Pp. 116, 119).

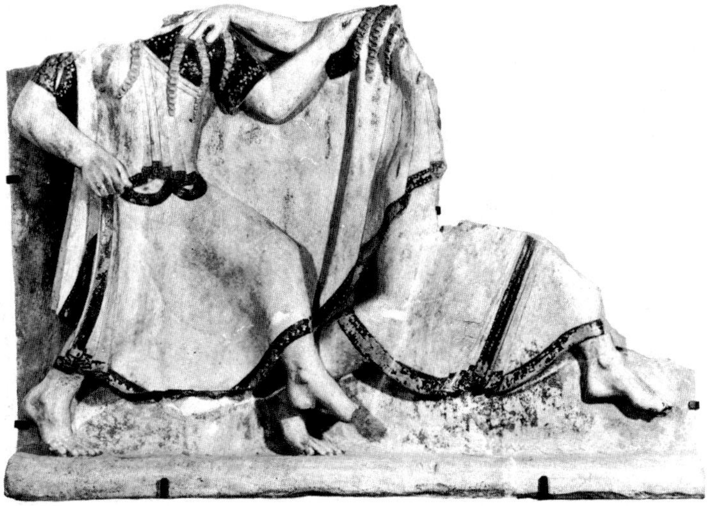

33a

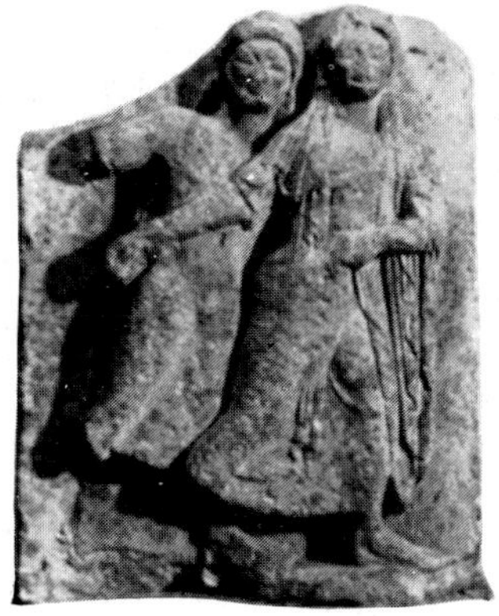

33b

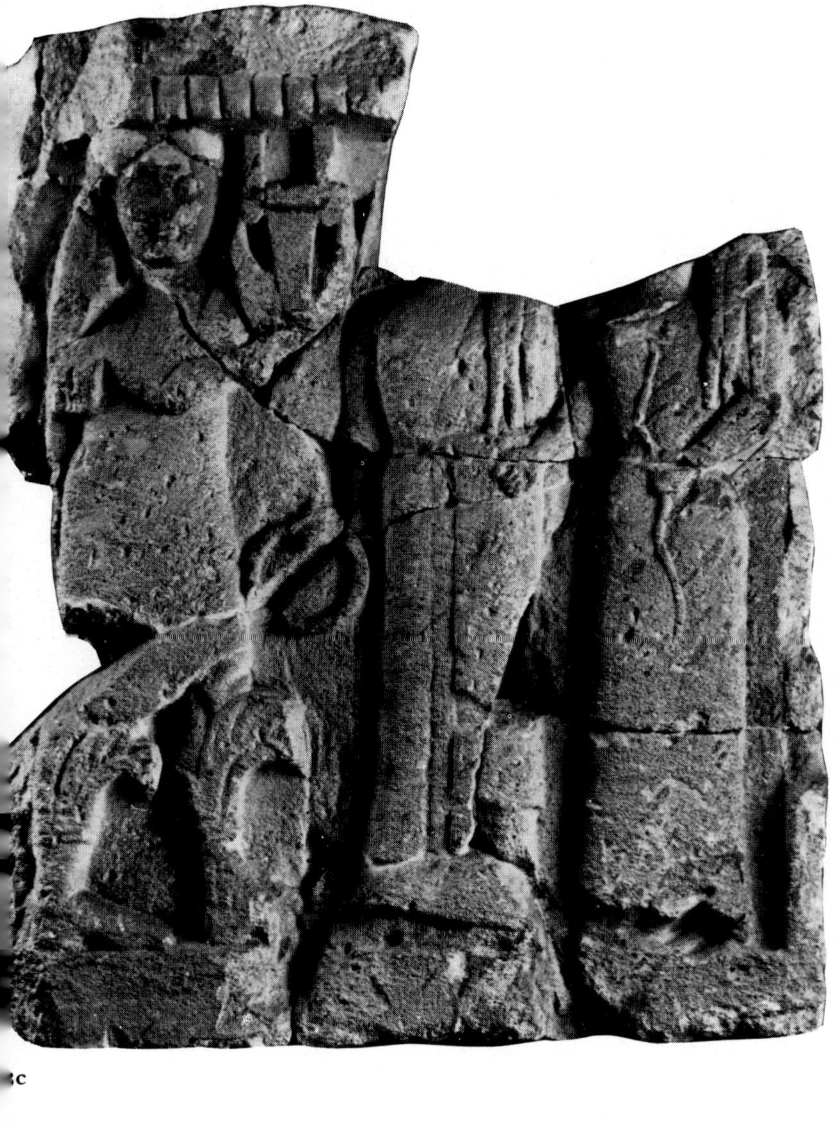

33c

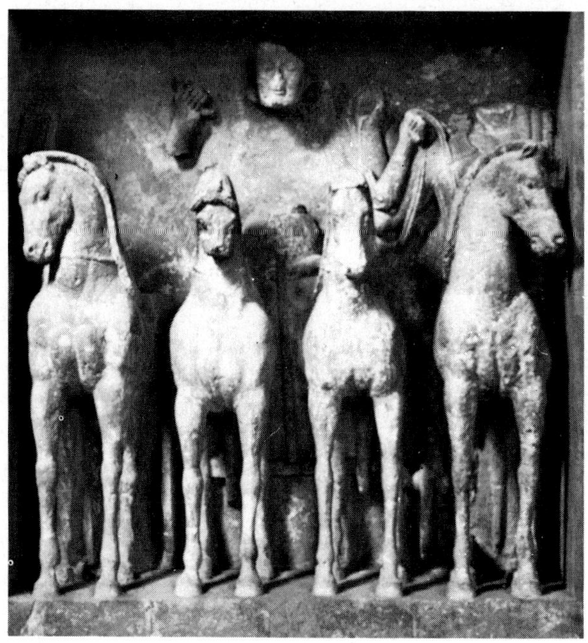

33d

33 **a** Terracotta metope (?) from Reggio. Locri Museum. Third quarter of sixth century. Width 0.96. (Pp. 117, 146) **b** Limestone metope from sanctuary of Demeter Malophoros at Selinus. Palermo Museum. Last quarter of sixth century. H. 0.51. (P. 120) **c** Limestone metope from Selinus. Palermo Museum. Second quarter of sixth century. H. 0.84. (P. 118) **d** Limestone metope from Selinus. Palermo Museum. Mid sixth century. H. 1.47. (Pp. 97, 119).

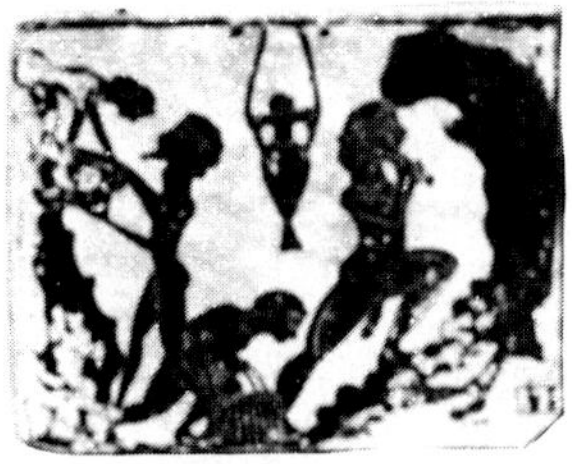

34a

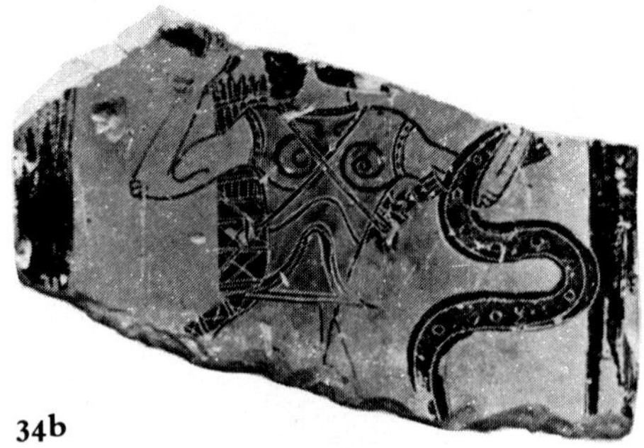

34b

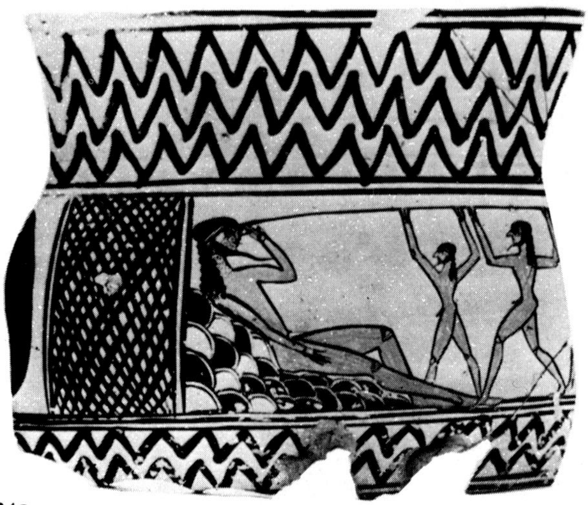

34c

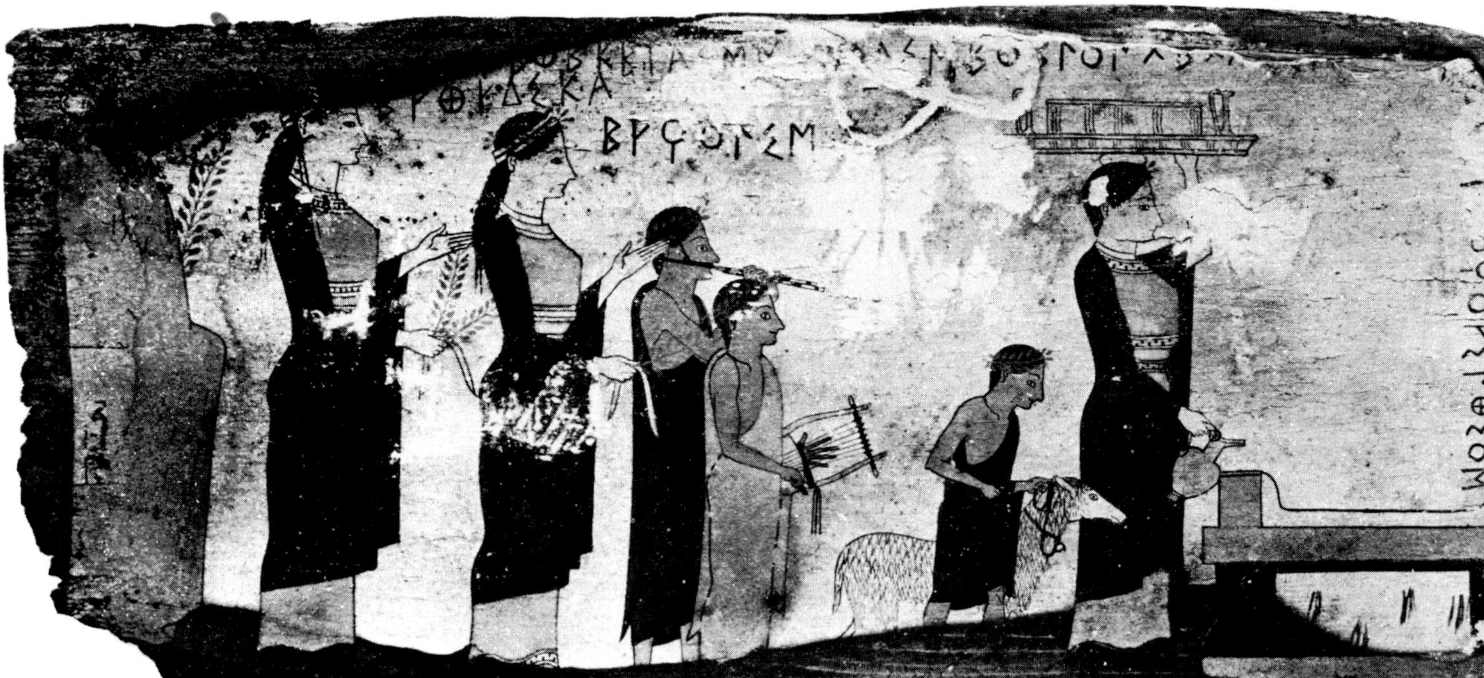

34d

34 **a** Clay plaque from Pente Skouphia (near Corinth). Berlin (E) F871. First quarter of sixth century. H. 0.07. (Pp. 121, 123) **b** Fragment of clay plaque from Corinth. Corinth Museum. First quarter of sixth century. Width 0.10 (P. 123) **c** Fragment of Argive krater from Argos. Argos Museum. Mid seventh century. H. 0.25. (P. 50) **d** Wooden panel dedicated in a cave of the Nymphs at Pitsa (near Sicyon). Third quarter of sixth century. H. 0.15. (Pp. 120–1).

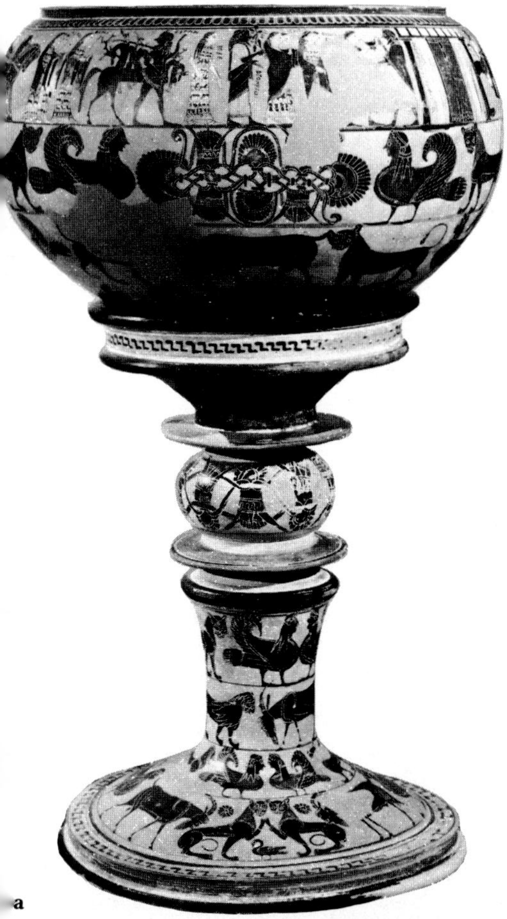

a

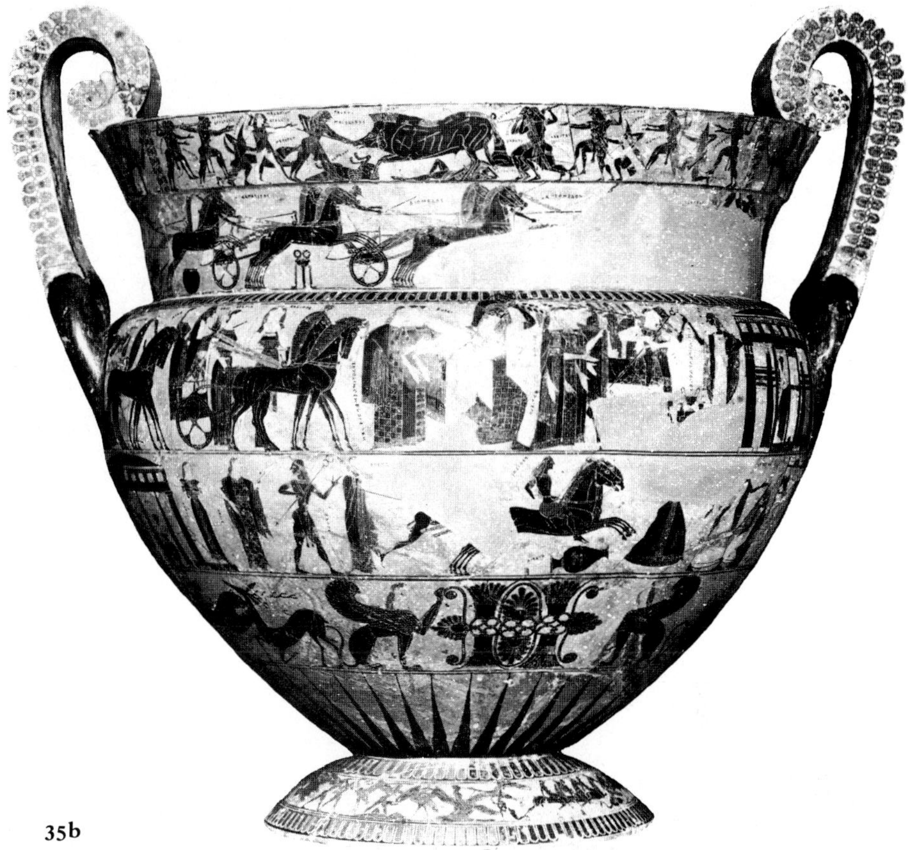

35b

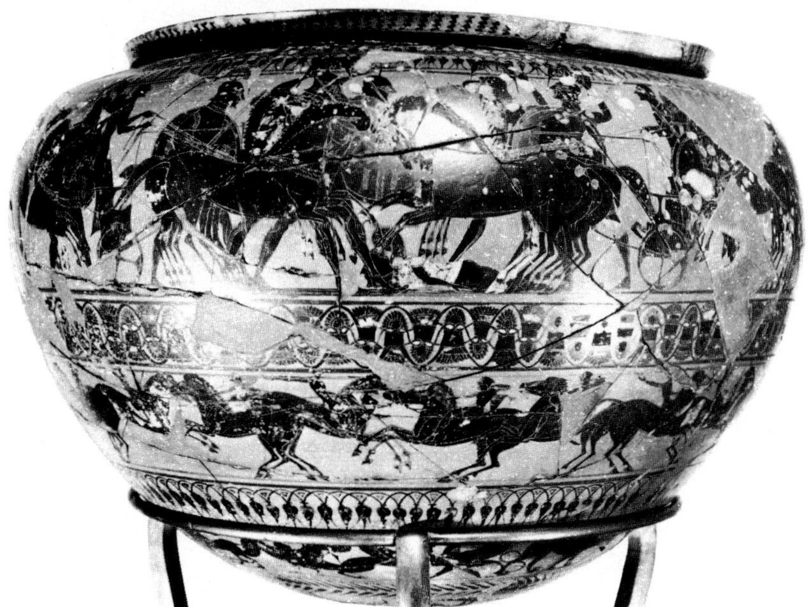

35c

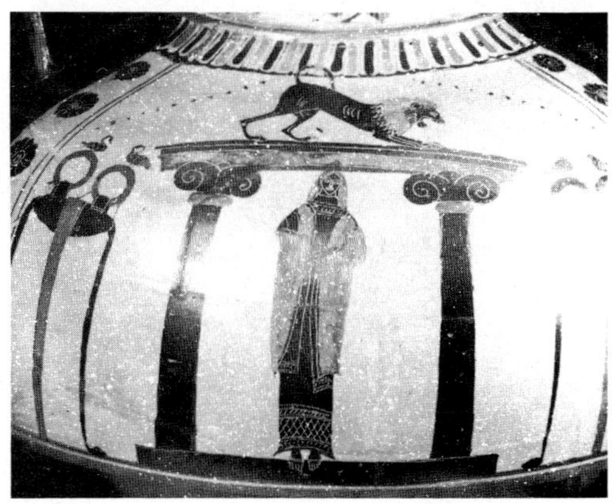

35d

35 **a** Attic black-figure dinos (signed by painter Sophilos). British Museum 1971.11–1.1. First quarter of sixth century. H. 0.71. (P. 127) **b** Attic black-figure volute-krater (signed by potter Ergotimos and painter Kleitias) from Chiusi. Florence, Museo Archeologico 4209. Second quarter of sixth century. H. 0.66. (Pp. 124ff., 238) **c** Attic black-figure dinos from Acropolis. Athens, National Museum Acrop. 606. Second quarter of sixth century. H. 0.46. (P. 128) **d** Attic black-figure neck-amphora. British Museum B49. Mid sixth century. H. 0.31. (P. 128).

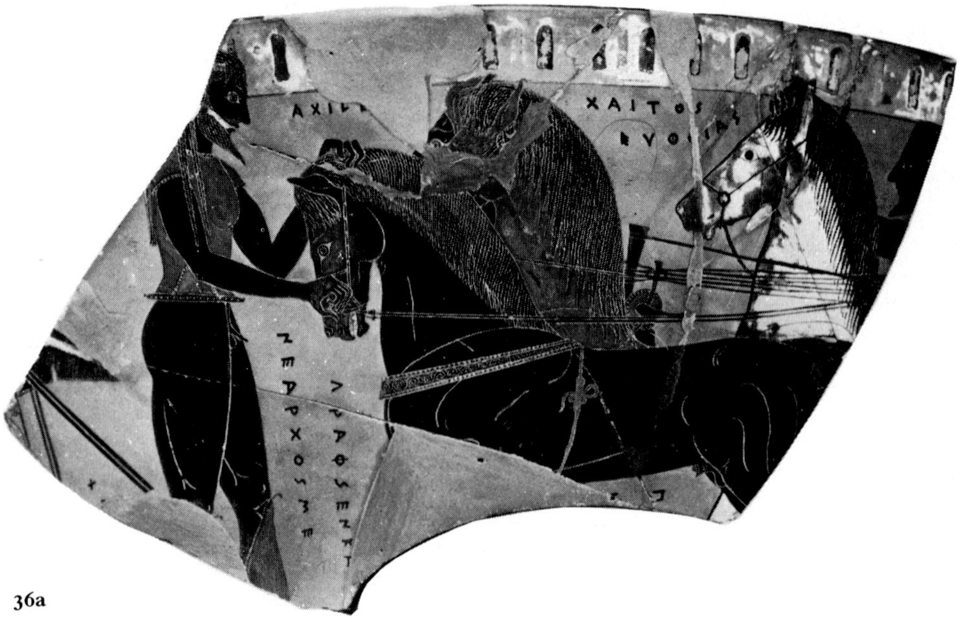

36a

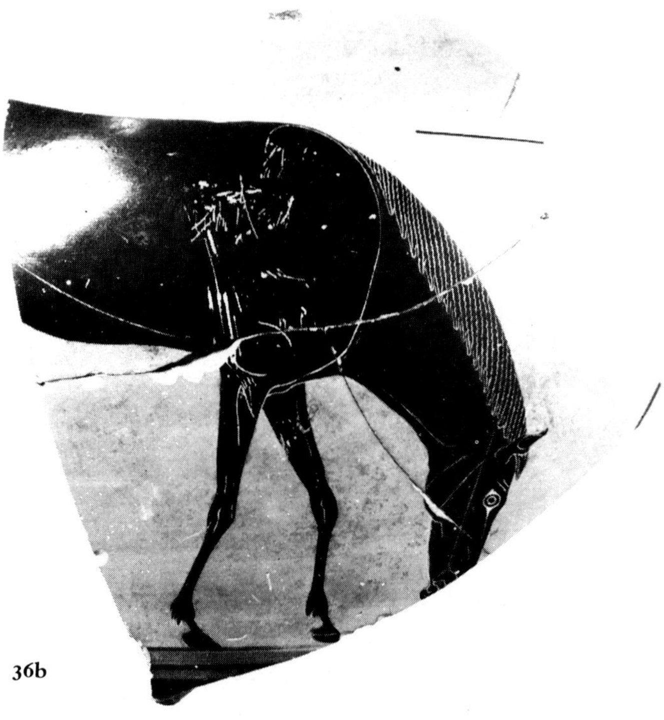

36b

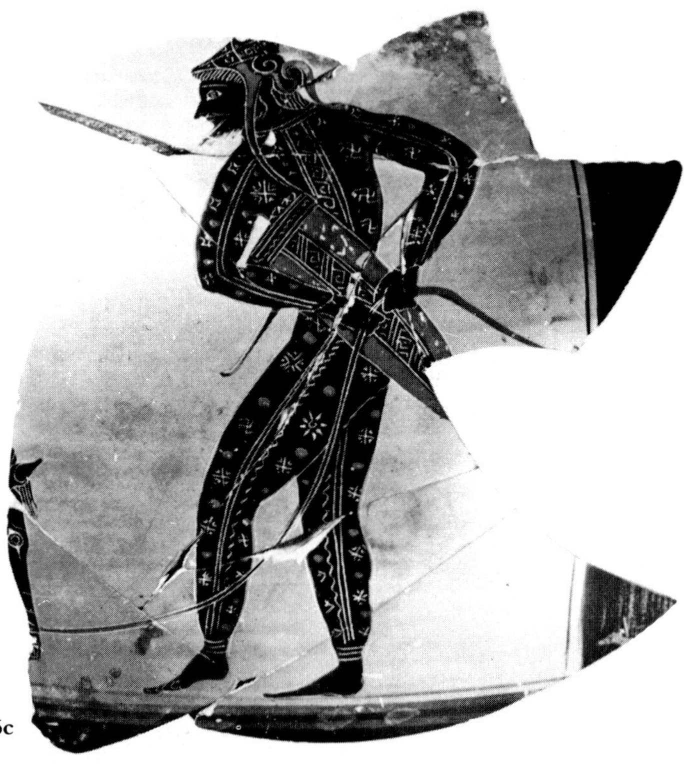

36c

36 **a** Fragment of Attic black-figure kantharos, signed by Nearchos as painter and probably as potter, from Acropolis. Athens, National Museum Acrop. 611. Second quarter of sixth century. H. 0.15. (Pp. 129–30) **b** and **c** Fragments of Attic black-figure amphora from Orvieto. Philadelphia, University Museum 4873. Third quarter of sixth century. H. of **c** *c.* 0.18; **b** is from a similar scene on the other side of the vase. (P. 132).

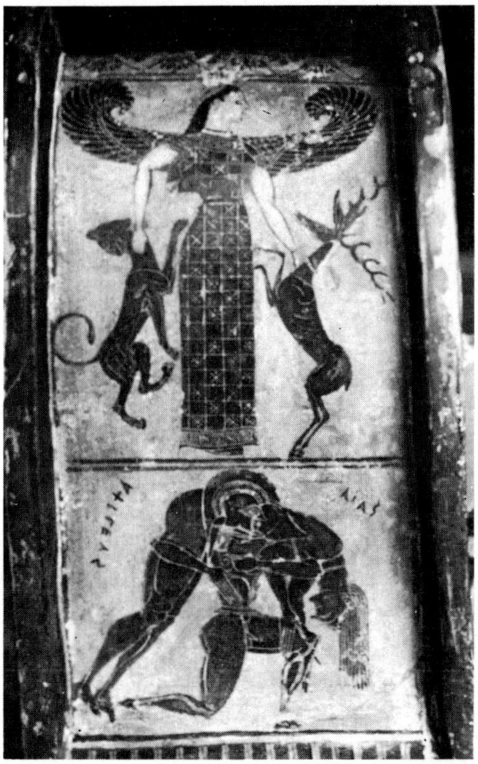

37a

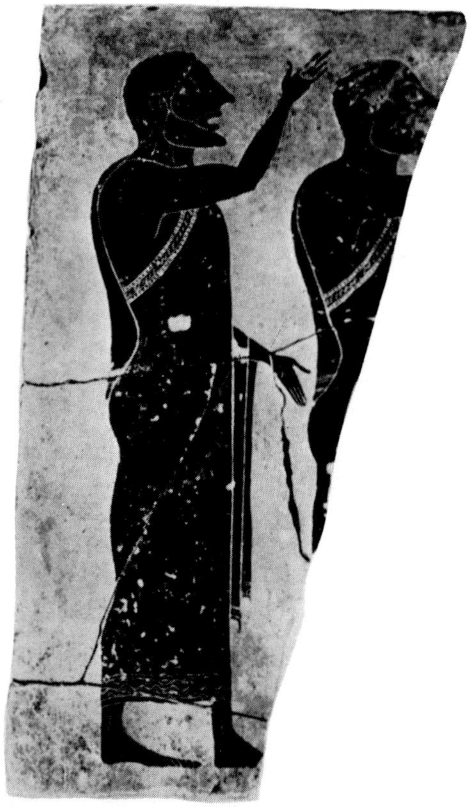

37b

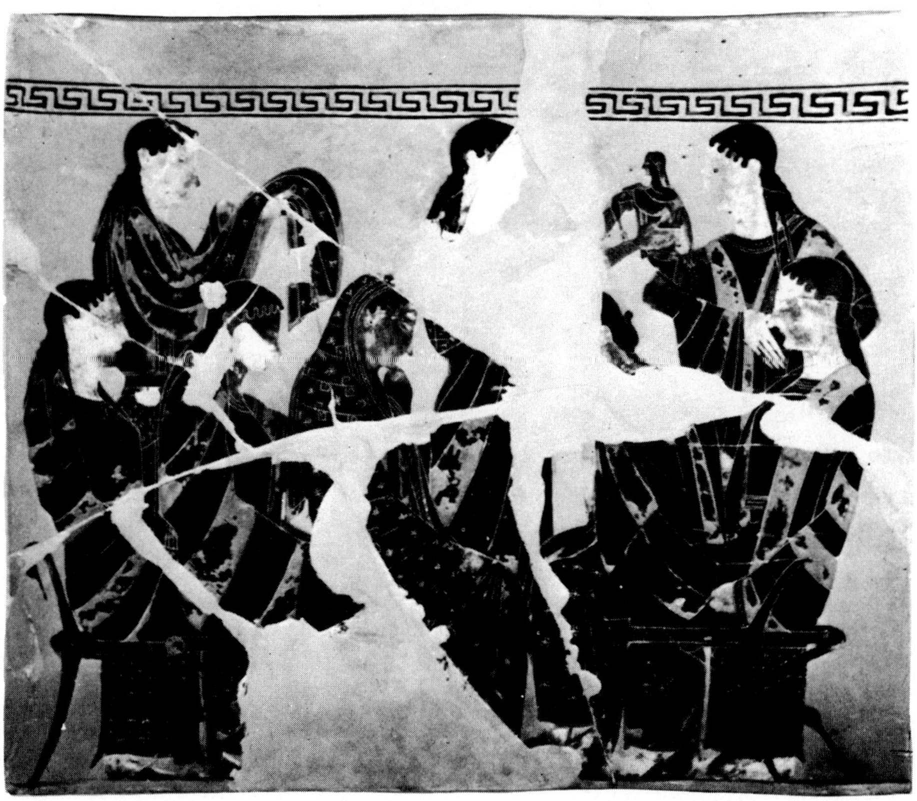

37c

37 **a** Handle of vase in pl. 35b. (Pp. 64, 124, 126) **b** Fragment of Attic black-figure tomb plaque from Spata (Attica). Athens, Vlastos Collection. Mid sixth century. H. 0.37. (P. 131) **c** Attic black-figure tomb-plaque from Athens. Berlin (Charlottenburg) 1813. Third quarter of sixth century. H. 0.37. (Pp. 131–2, 366).

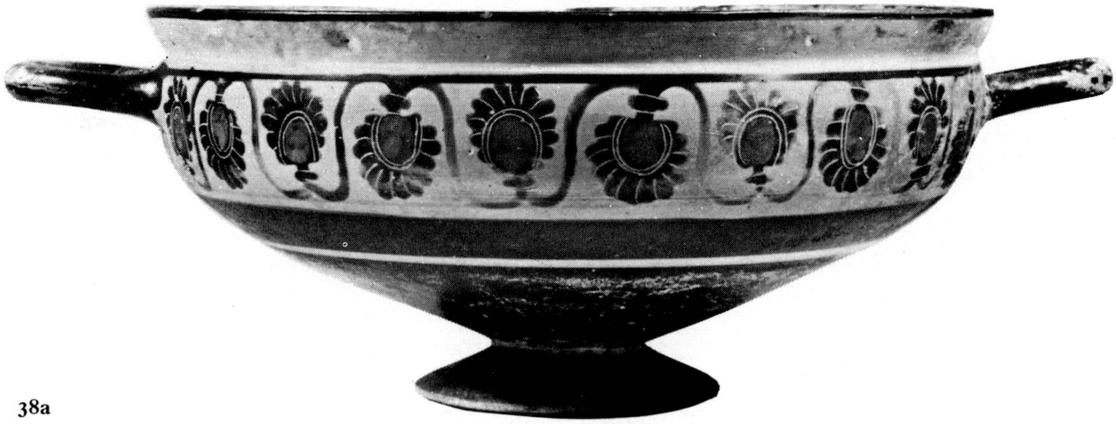

38a

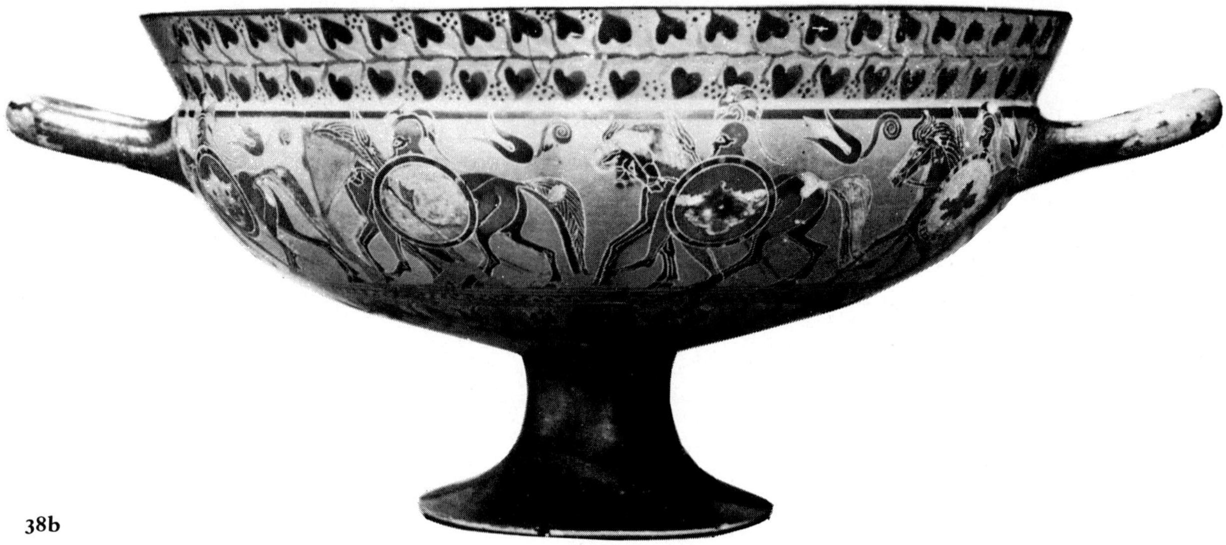

38b

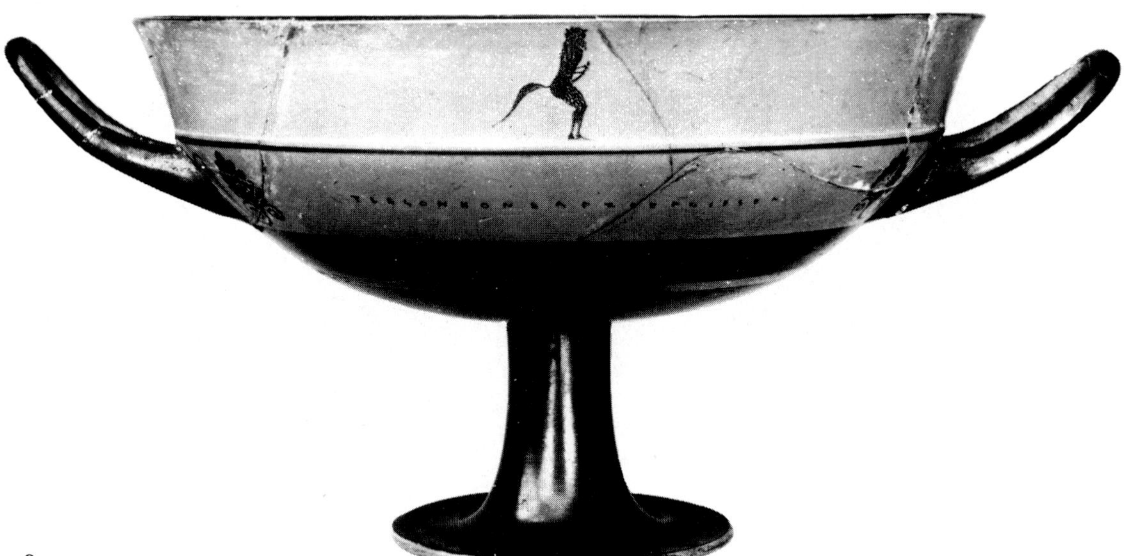

38c

38 **a** Attic black-figure cup. Oxford, Ashmolean Museum 1907.108. First half of sixth century. H. 0.11. (P. 132) **b** Attic black-figure cup from Siana (Rhodes). British Museum B 380. Second quarter of sixth century. H. 0.14. (P. 132) **c** Attic black-figure cup signed by Tleson, from Vulci. British Museum B 410. Third quarter of sixth century. H. 0.15. (Pp. 130, 133).

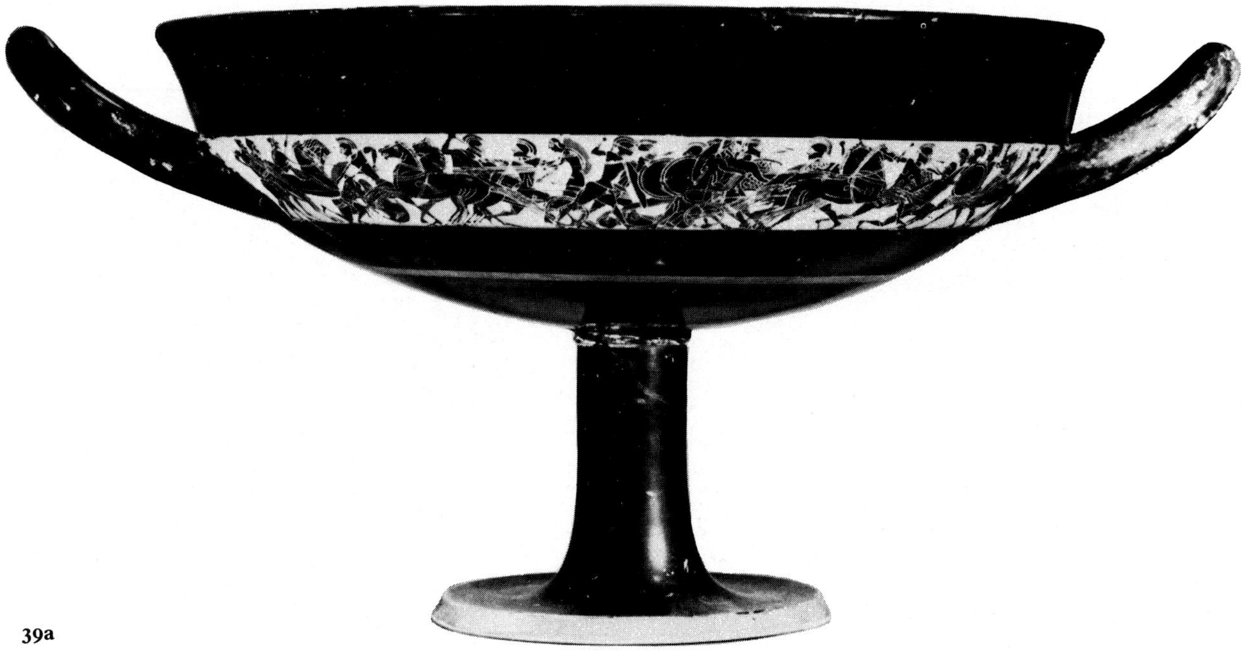

39a

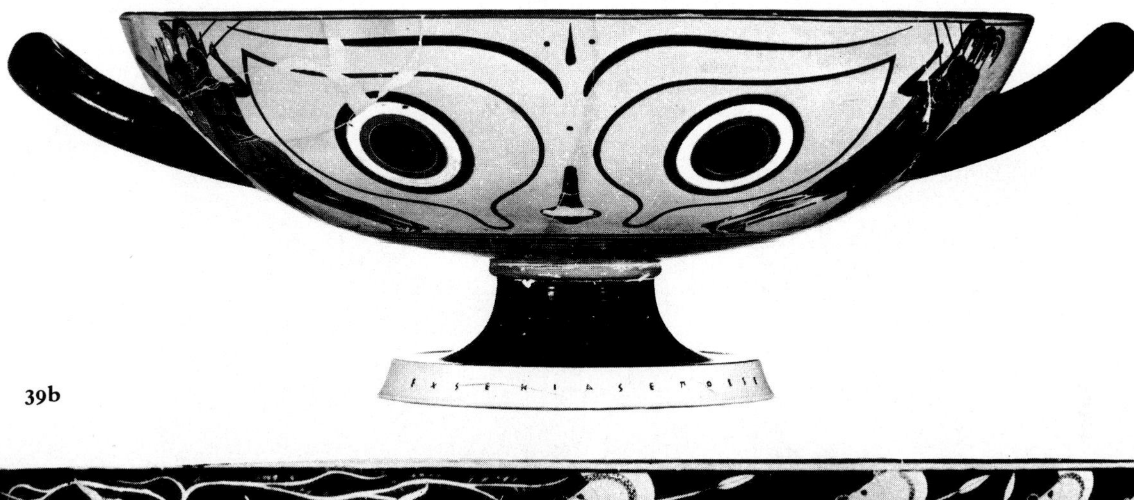

39b

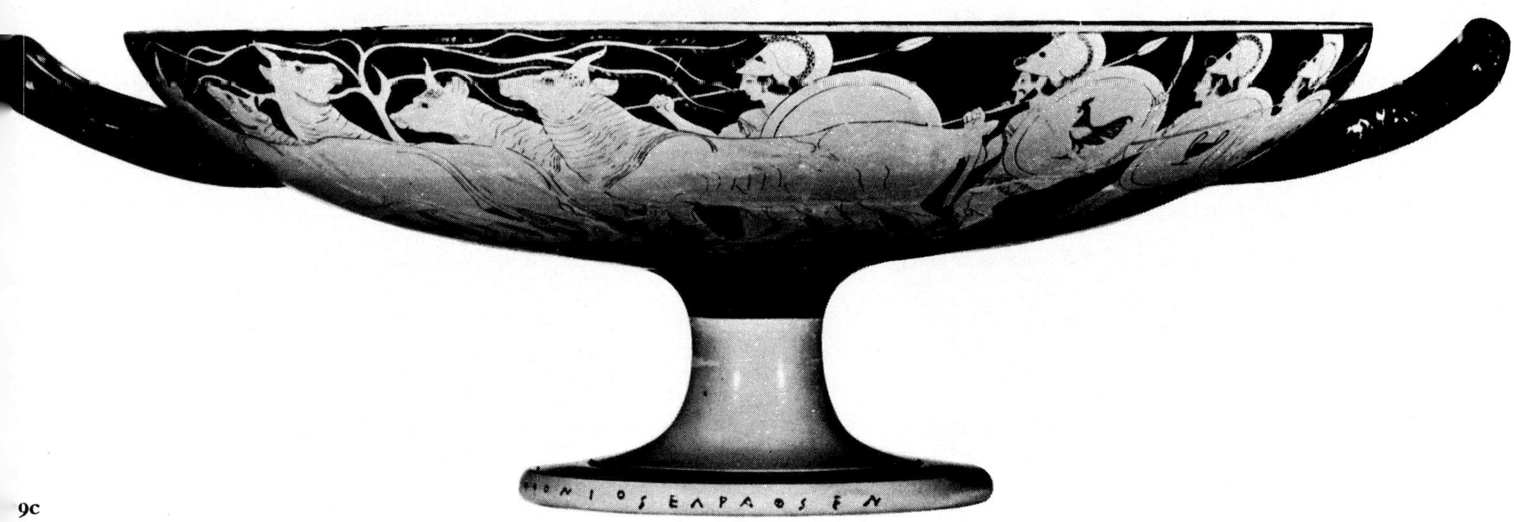

9c

39 **a** Attic black-figure cup from Vulci. British Museum B 400. Third quarter of sixth century. H. 0.22. (Pp. 130, 133) **b** Attic black-figure cup signed by Exekias as potter, from Vulci. Munich 2044. Third quarter of sixth century. H. 0.14. (Pp. 133, 139, 217–18. See also pl. 70a) **c** Attic red-figure cup signed by potter Kachrylion and painter Euphronios, from Vulci. Munich 2620. Late sixth century. H. 0.17. (Pp. 218, 228. See also pl. 75c).

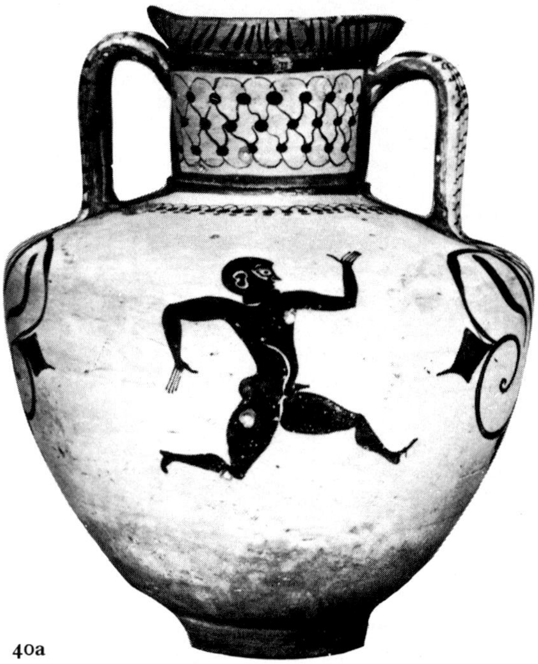

40a

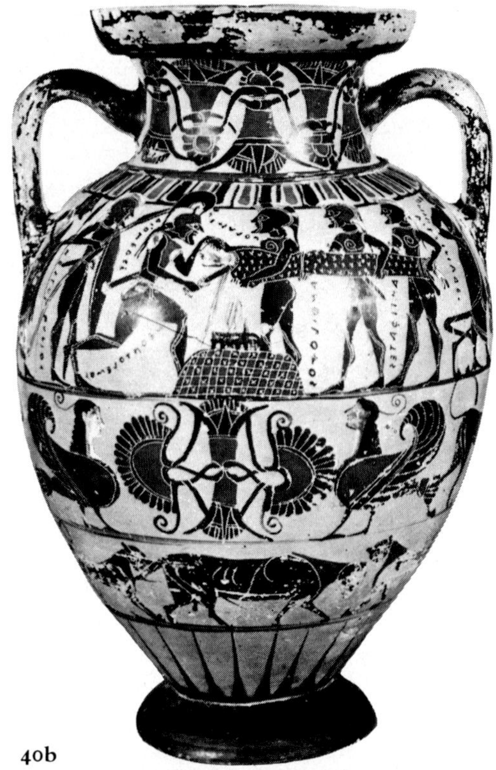

40b

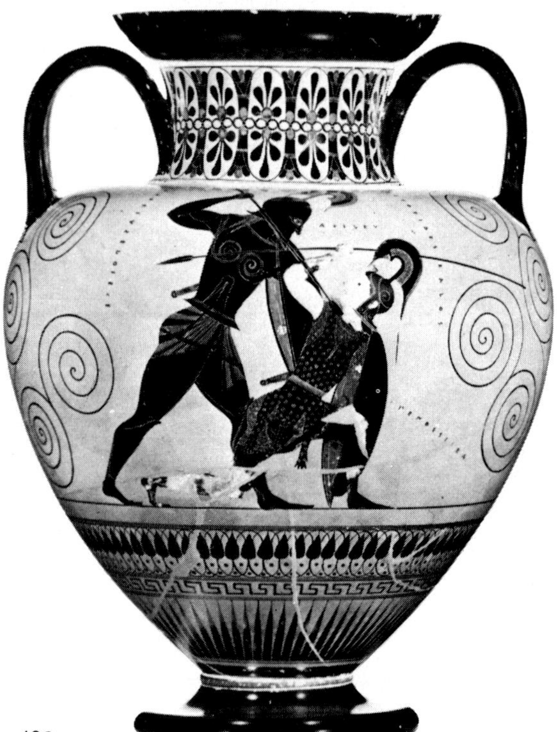

40c

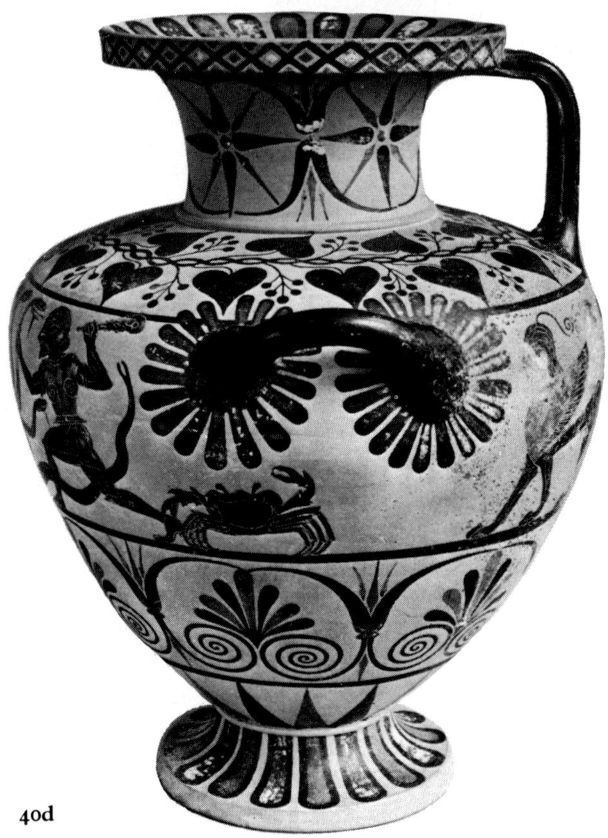

40d

40 **a** East Greek ('Fikellura') neck-amphora from Kameiros (Rhodes). British Museum 64. 10–7.156 Mid sixth century. H. 0.34. (P. 137) **b** Attic black-figure neck-amphora. British Museum 97.7–27.2. Second quarter of sixth century. H. 0.40. (Pp. 93, 134) **c** Attic black-figure neck-amphora signed by Exekias as potter. British Museum B210. Third quarter of sixth century. H. 0.41. (Pp. 134–5) **d** 'Caeretan' black-figure hydria (cf. pl. 42a). London, Count Antoine Seilern. Second half of sixth century. H. 0.44. (P. 139).

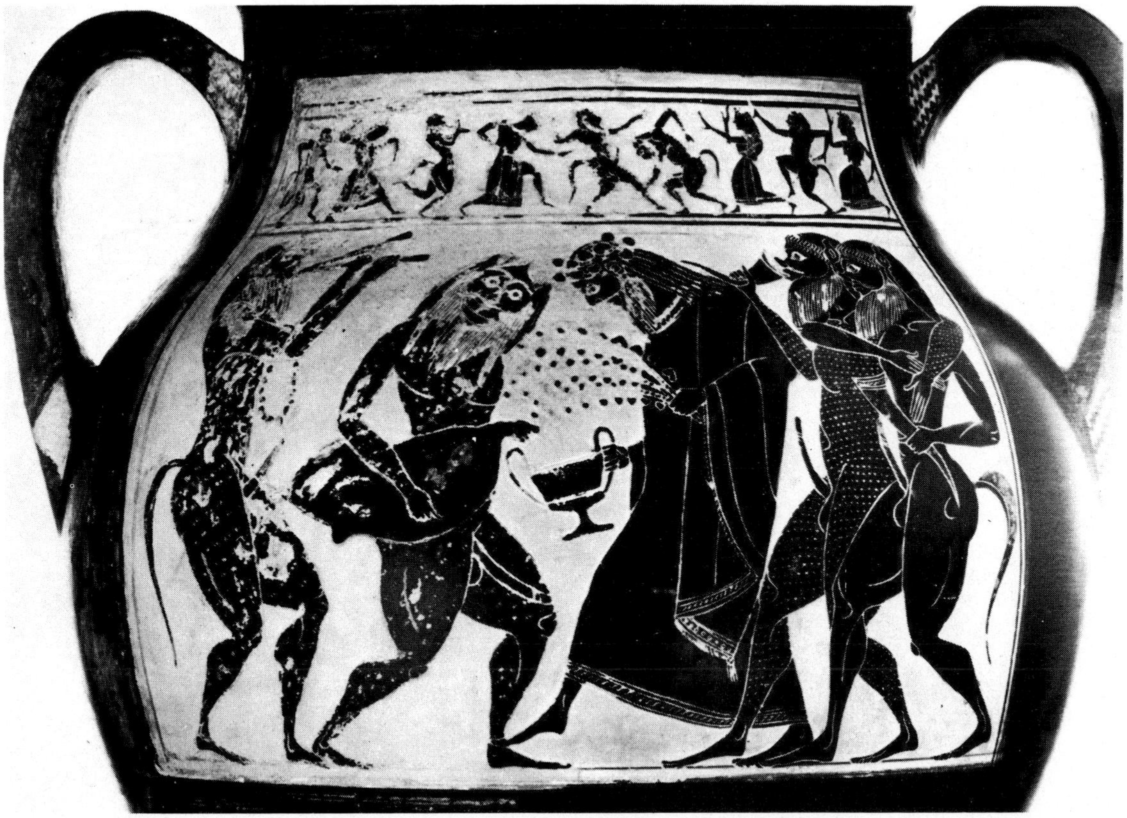

41a

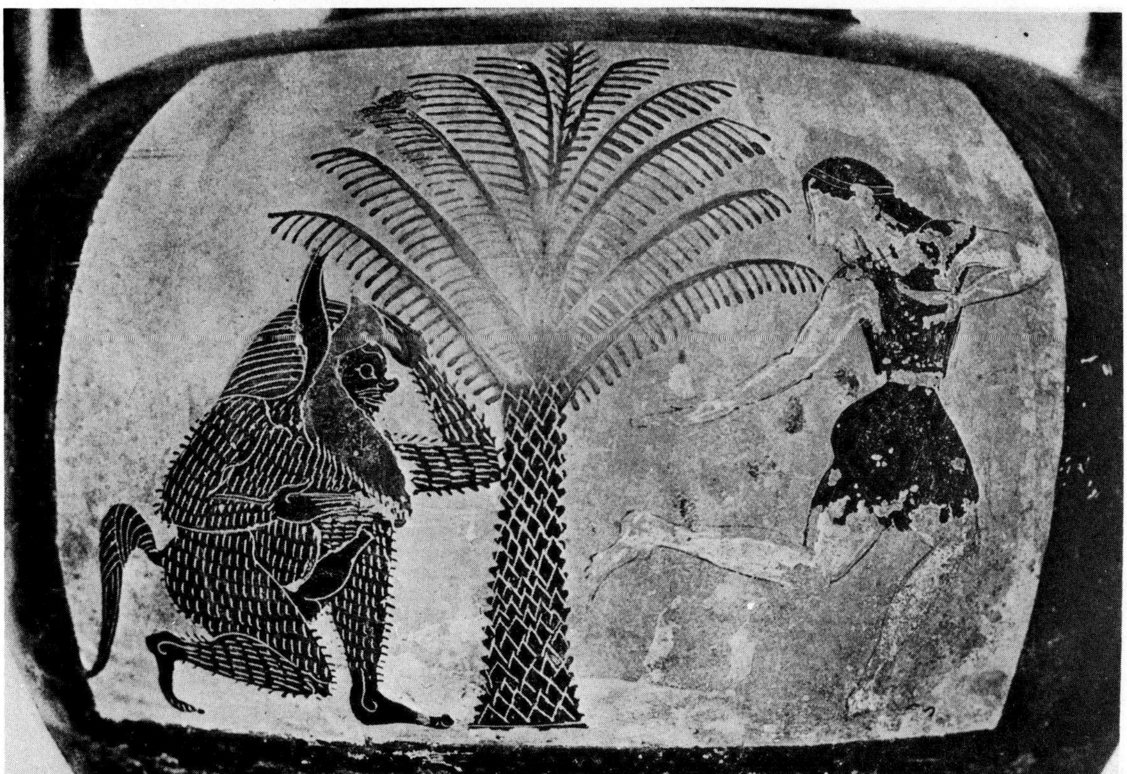

41b

41 **a** Picture on Attic black-figure amphora, probably from Vulci. Würzburg 265. Third quarter of sixth century. H. of picture, *c.* 0.16. (Pp. 130, 135–6) **b** Picture on Chalcidian psykter-neck-amphora, from Caere. Rome, Villa Giulia, Castellani 47. Mid sixth century. H. of picture *c.* 0.16. (P. 138).

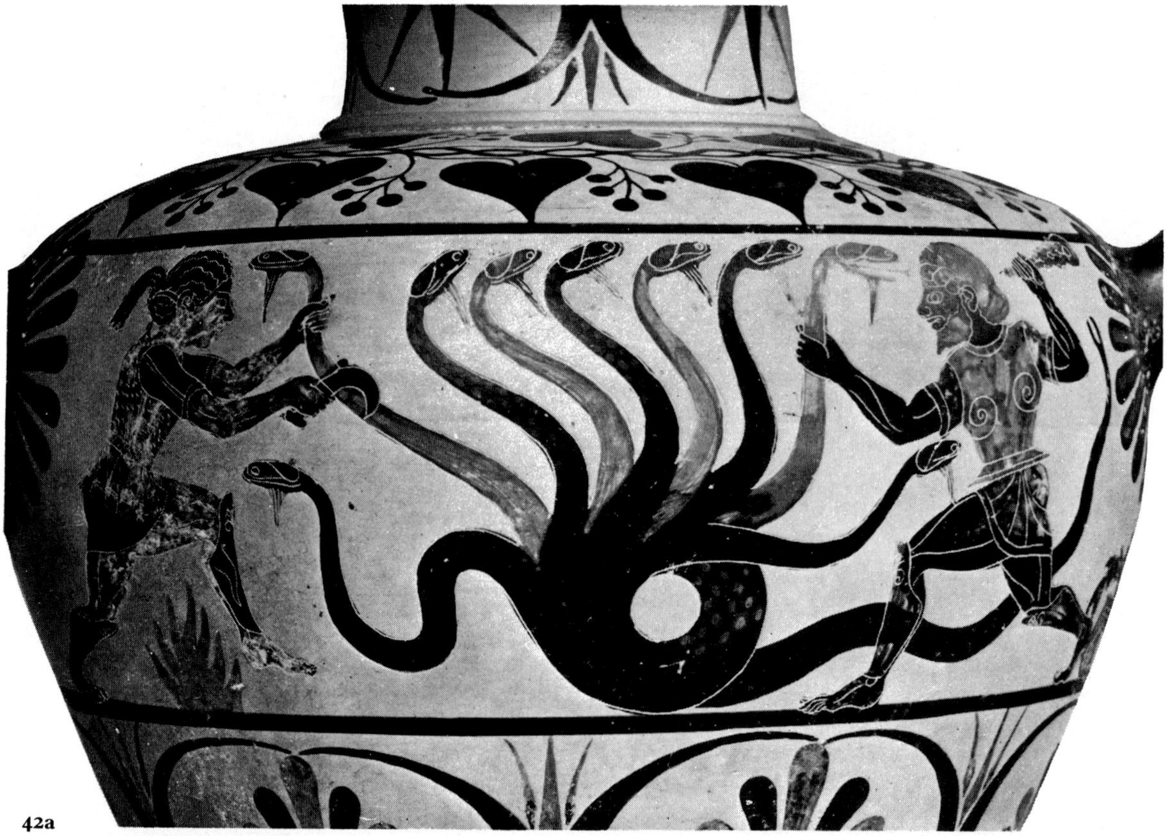

42a

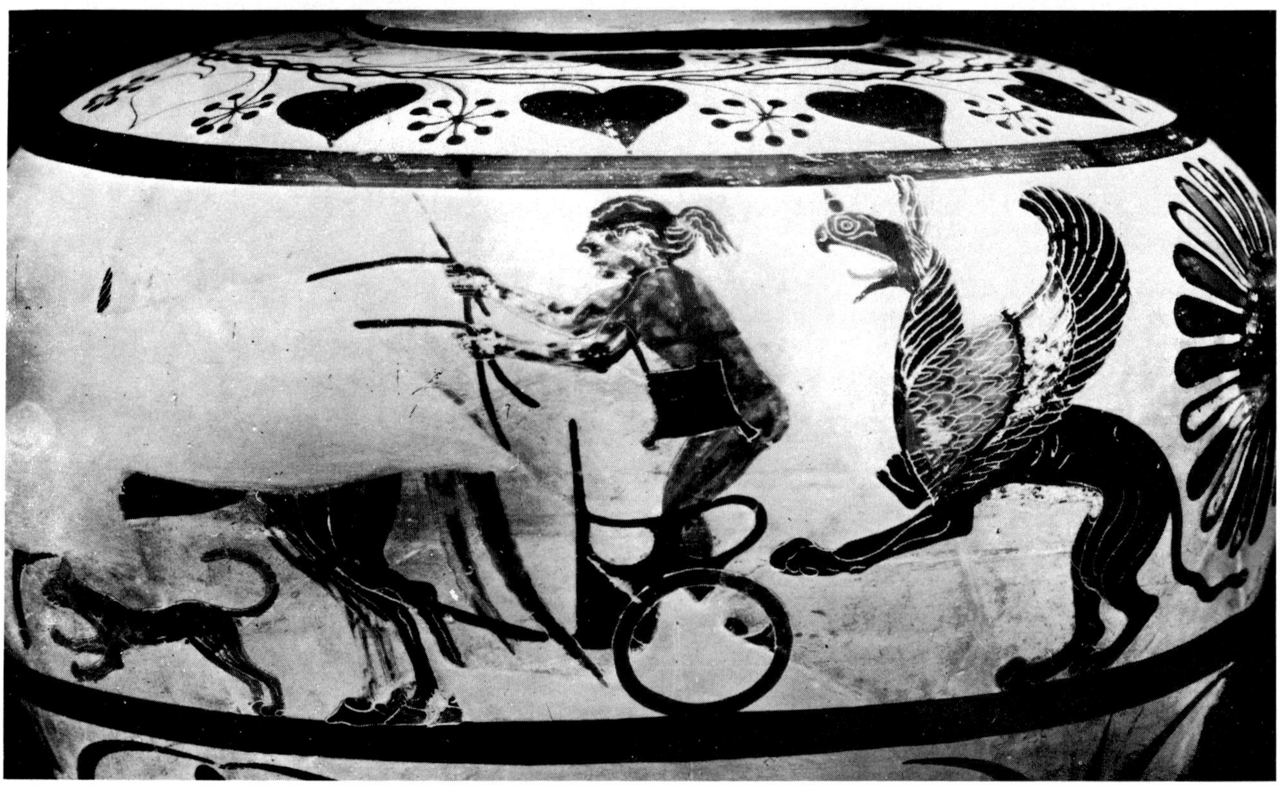

42b

42 **a** Picture on vase in pl. 40d. (P. 139) **b** Picture on fragmentary 'Caeretan' hydria. British Museum 1923.4–19.1. Second half of sixth century. H. of picture *c.* 0.15. (Pp. 139–40).

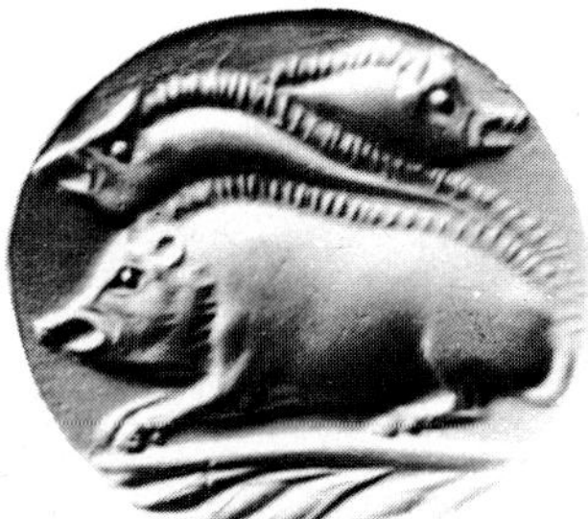

43a

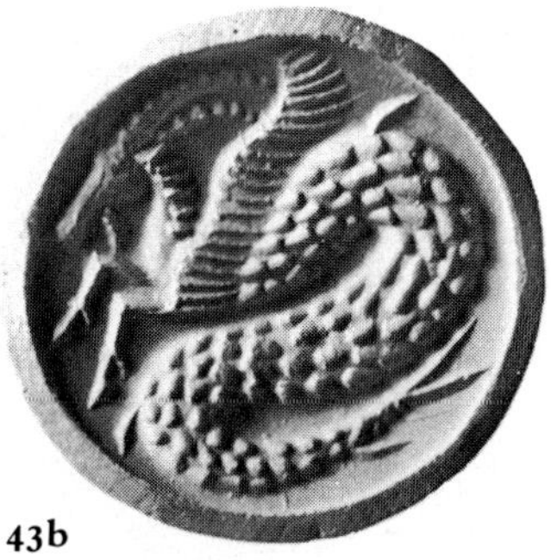

43b

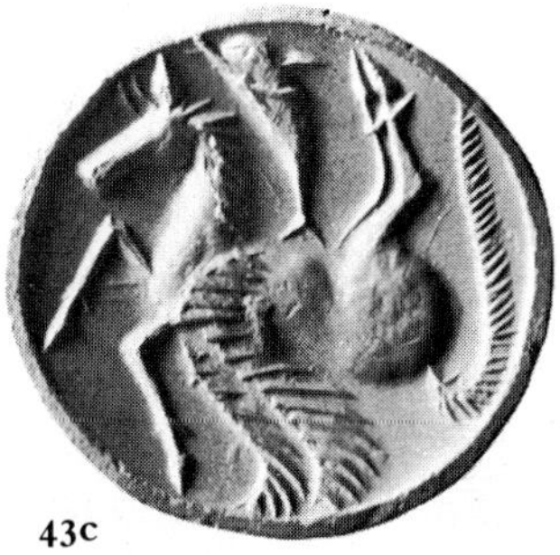

43c

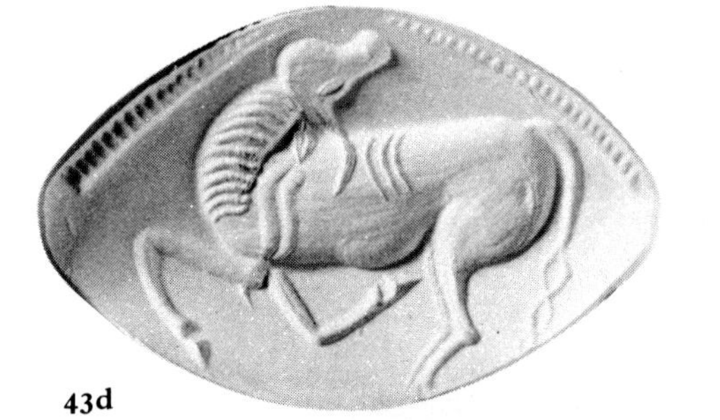

43d

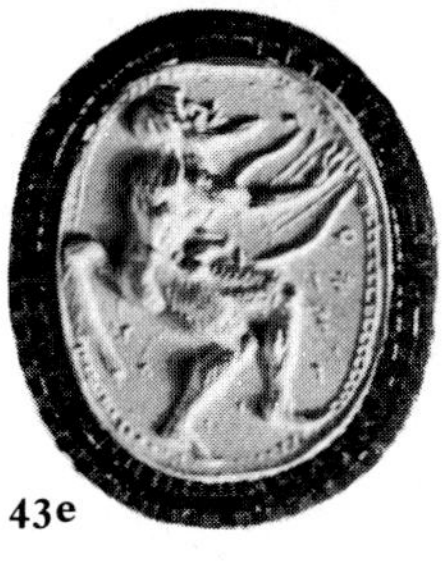

43e

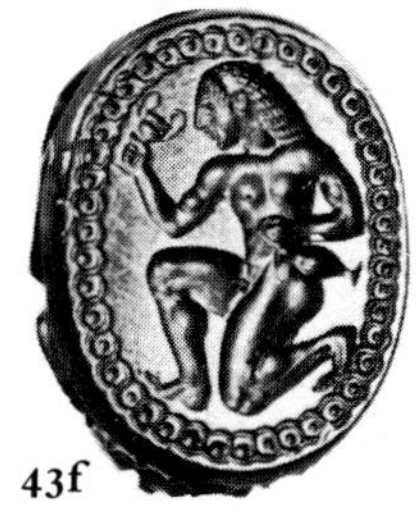

43f

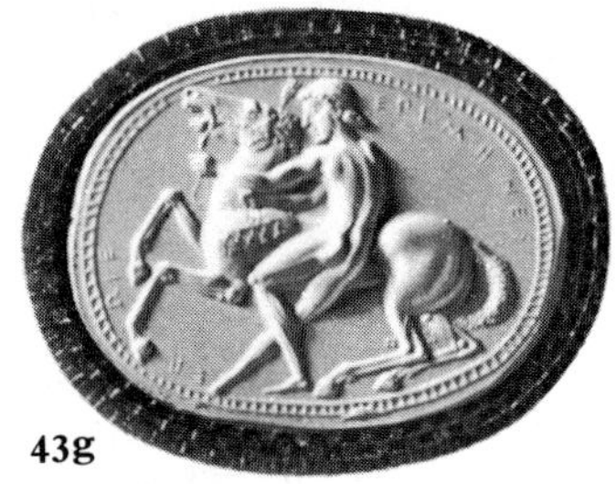

43g

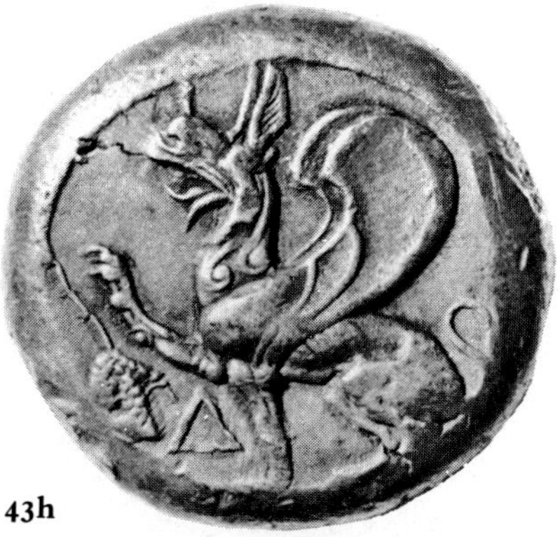

43h

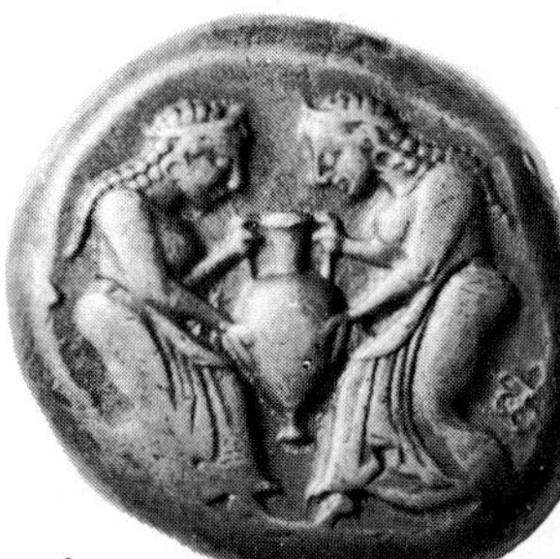

43i

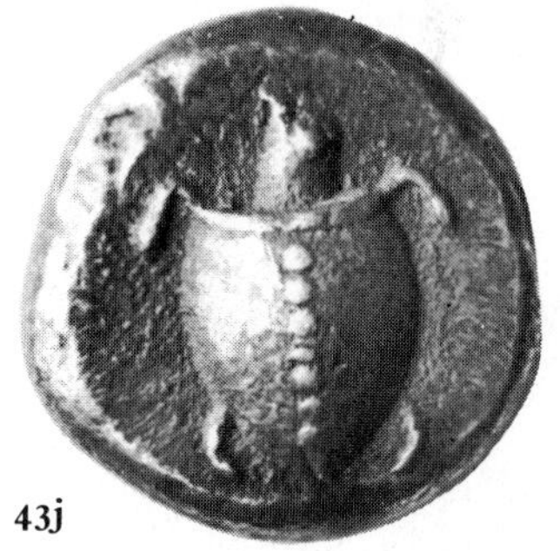

43j

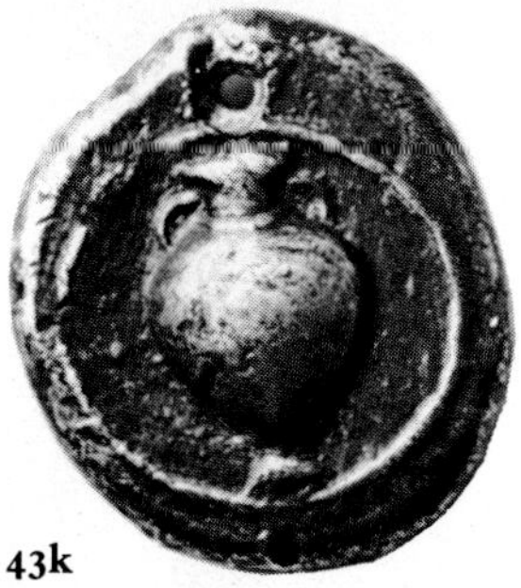

43k

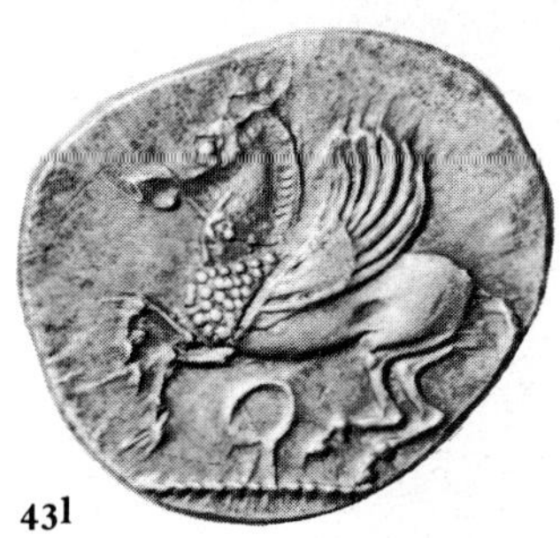

43l

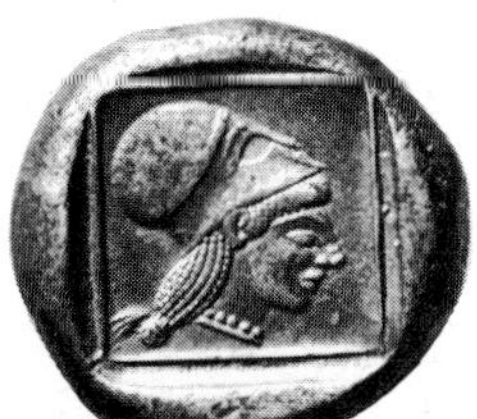

43m

43 **a** Impression from cornelian lentoid, from Greek Islands. Paris, Cabinet des Médailles. 15–14 century. D. 0.02. (Pp. 10, 147) **b** and **c** Impression from 'steatite' lentoid. New York, Metropolitan Museum of Art 42.11.9. Late seventh century. D. 0.02. (P. 147) **d** Impression from white stone amygdaloid. Whereabouts unknown. Impression, Ashmolean Museum, Oxford. Late seventh century. L. 0.03. (P. 147) **e** Impression from 'steatite' scarab, signed by Syries. Boston, Museum of Fine Arts (ex Lewes House). End of sixth century. H. 0.015. (P. 147) **f** Cornelian scarab. Ionides Collection. Second half of sixth century. H. 0.016. (P. 148) **g** Impression from chalcedony scarab, signed by Epimenes. Boston, Museum of Fine Arts (ex Lewes House). *c.* 500 B.C. L. 0.17. (P. 148) **h** Silver octadrachm of Abdera. Berlin (Regling 106). Late sixth or early fifth century. D. 0.025. (P. 149) **i** Silver tetradrachm of Macedonia. British Museum. Late sixth century. D. 0.02. (P. 151) **j** Silver stater of Aegina. Paris (Luynes 2126). First half of sixth century. D. 0.02. (P. 149) **k** Silver tetradrachm of Athens. British Museum. Second quarter of sixth century. D. 0.02. (Pp. 149–50) **l** Silver stater of Corinth. Berlin (Ravel 12). Mid sixth century. D. 0.025. (P. 149) **m** Silver stater of Corinth. British Museum (Ravel 97). Late sixth century. D. 0.015. (P. 150).

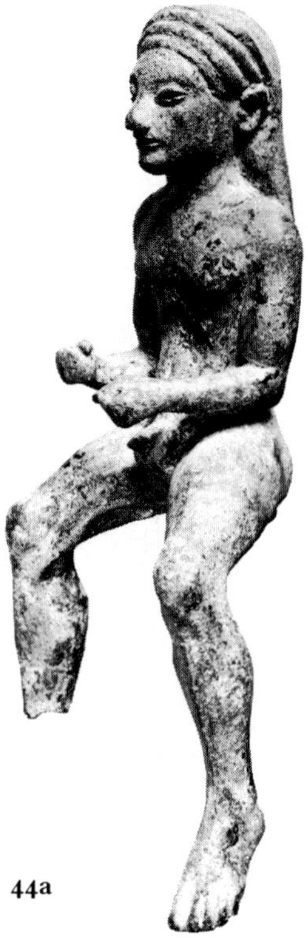

44a

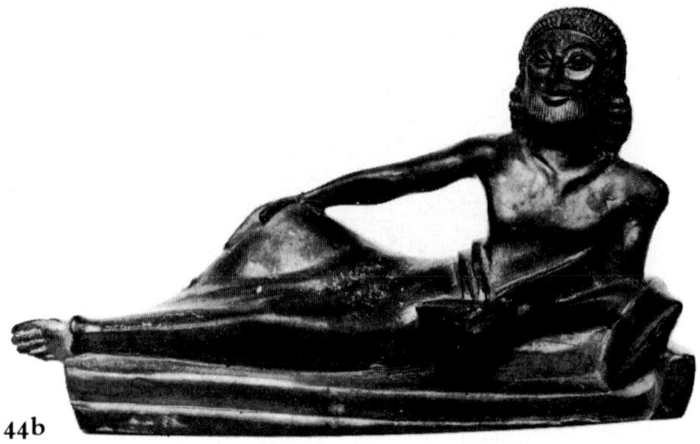

44b

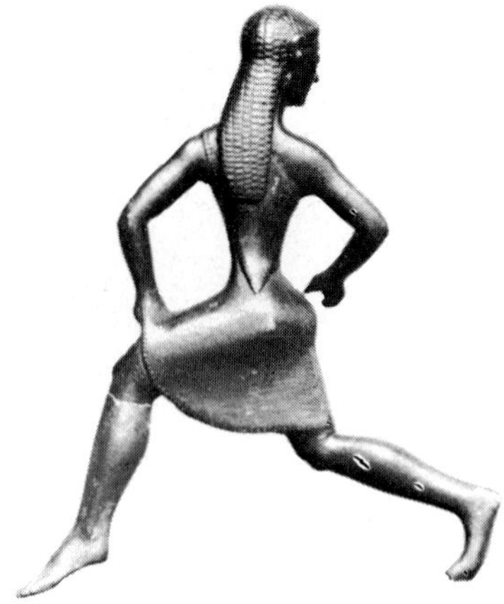

44c

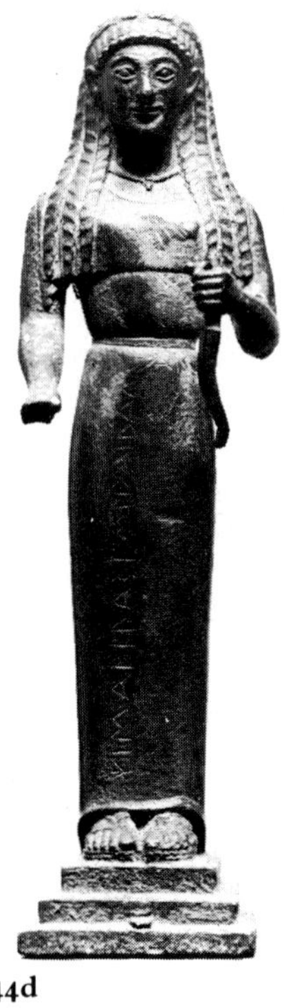

44d

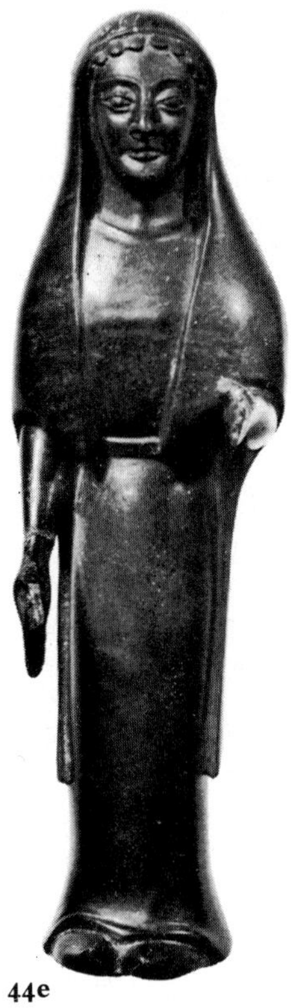

44e

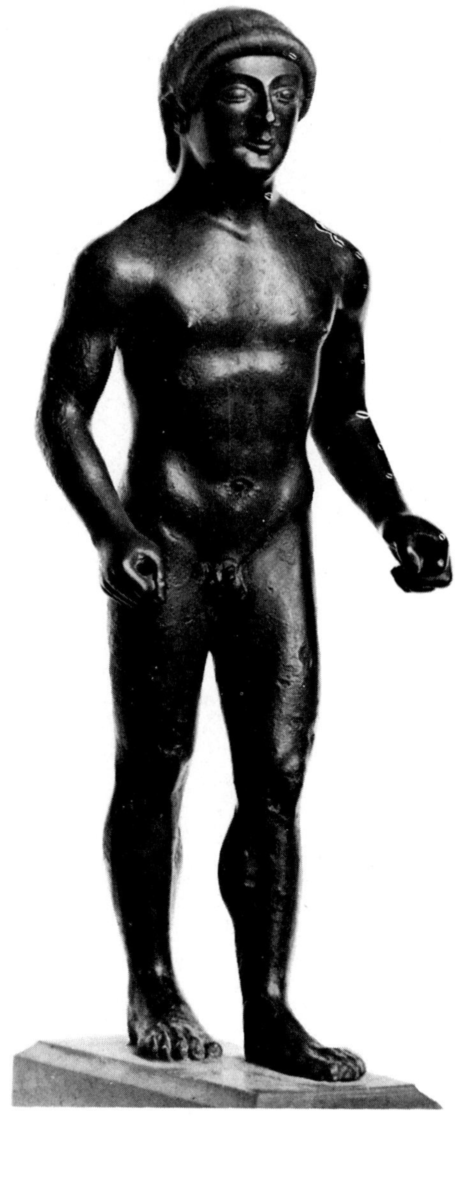

44f

44 **a** Bronze statuette from Samos. Samos Museum. Mid sixth century. H. 0.19. (P. 142) **b** Bronze statuette. British Museum 1954.10–18.1. Second half of sixth century. L. 0.10. (Pp. 143, 146) **c** Bronze statuette, probably from Albania. British Museum 208. Second half of sixth century. H. 0.11. Modern: left lower leg. (Pp. 143, 146) **d** Bronze statuette from Mazi (Elis). Boston Museum of Fine Arts 98.658, H. L. Pierce Fund. Mid sixth century. H. 0.18. (Pp. 101, 142) **e** Bronze statuette from lid of krater, pl. 45. Mid sixth century. H. 0.19. (Pp. 101, 142, 144) **f** Bronze statuette from Acropolis. Athens, National Museum 6445. Last quarter of sixth century. H. 0.27. (P. 142).

45

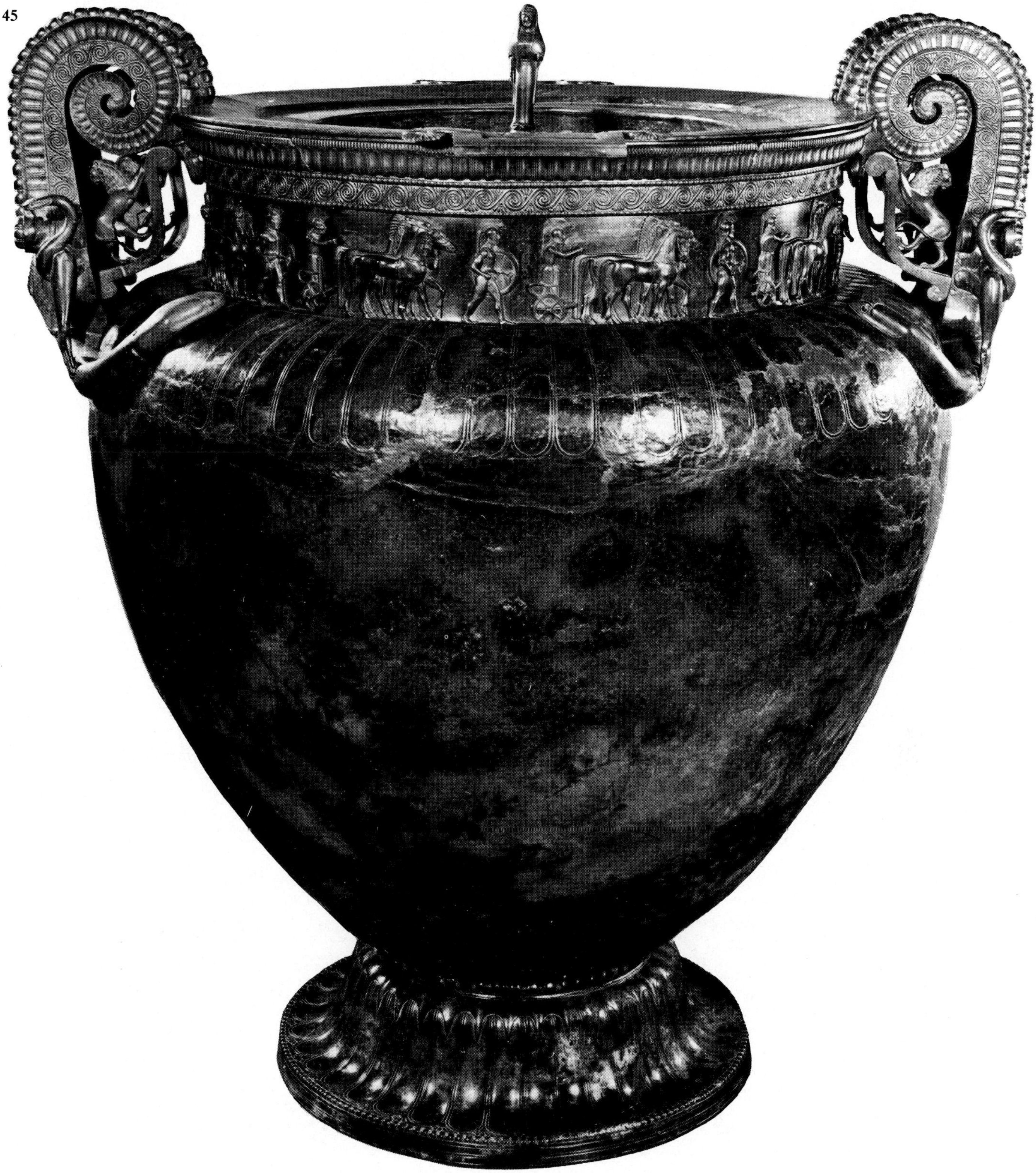

45 Bronze krater from Vix (Upper Seine). Châtillon-sur-Seine. Mid sixth century. H. 1.64. (Pp. 124, 144ff., 238).

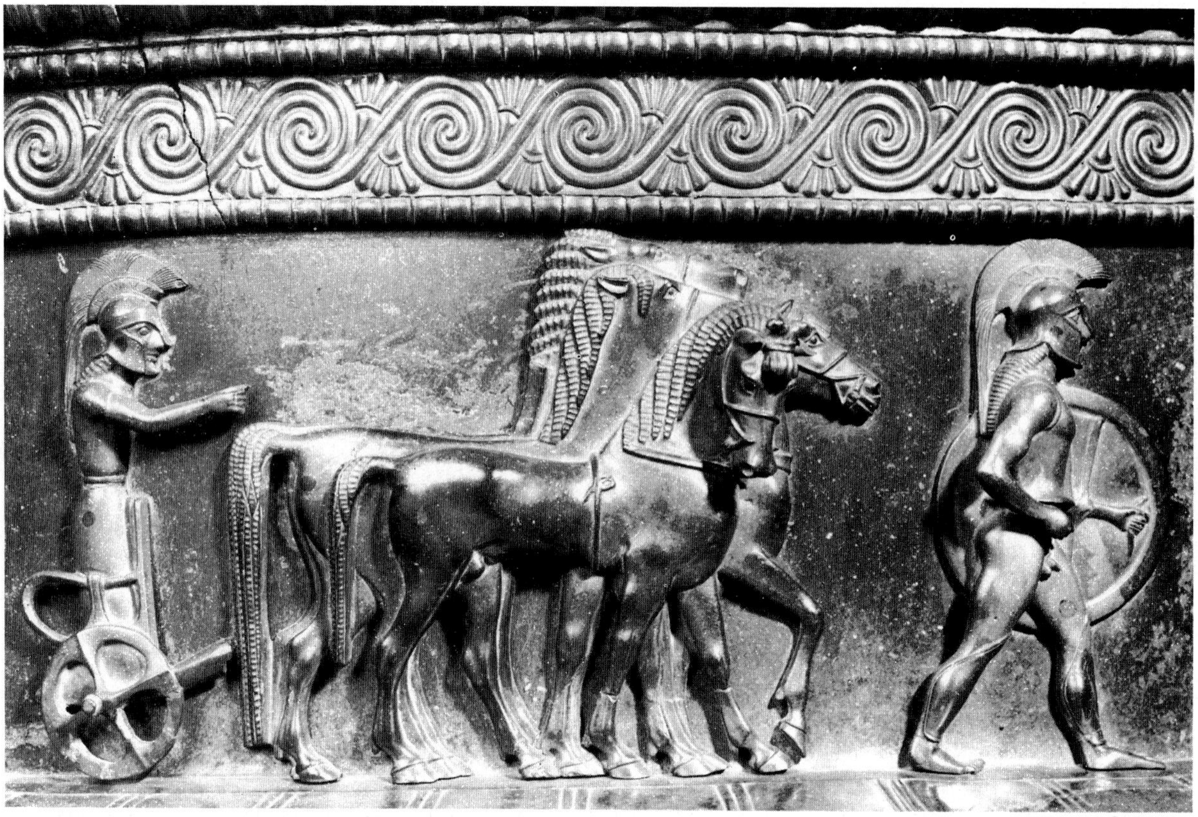

46a

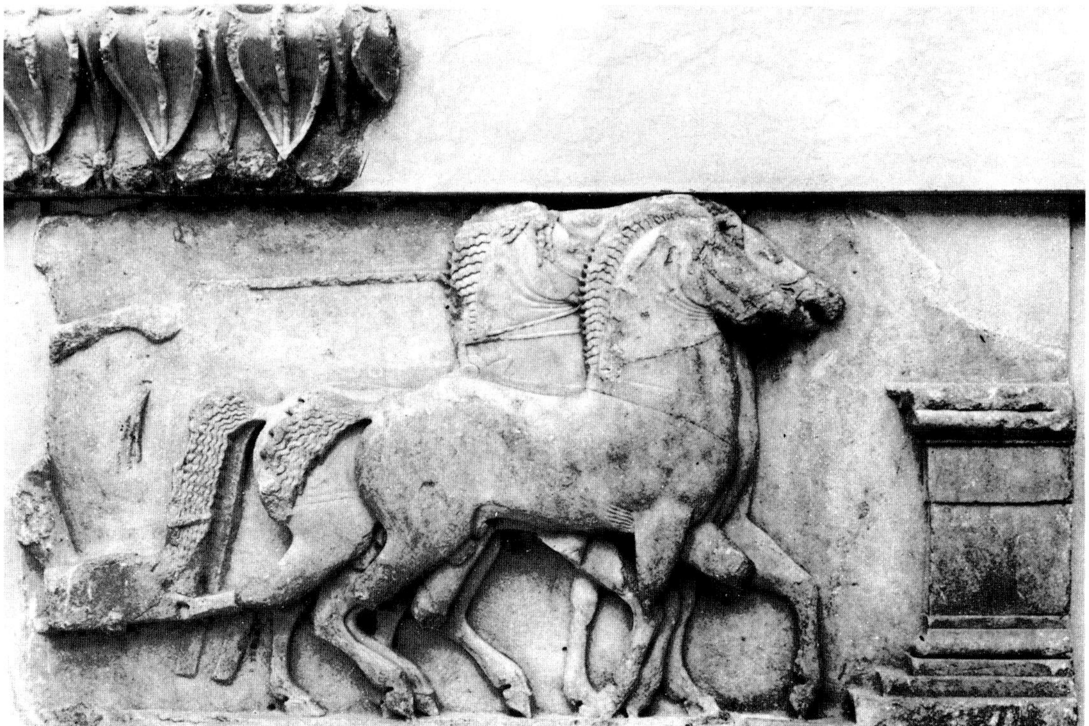

46b

46 **a** Part of neck-frieze from bronze krater, pl. 45. H. of figures 0.14. (Pp. 144–5) **b** Marble slab from south frieze of Siphnian Treasury at Delphi. Delphi Museum. Shortly before 525 B.C. H. 0.64. (Pp. 154, 155).

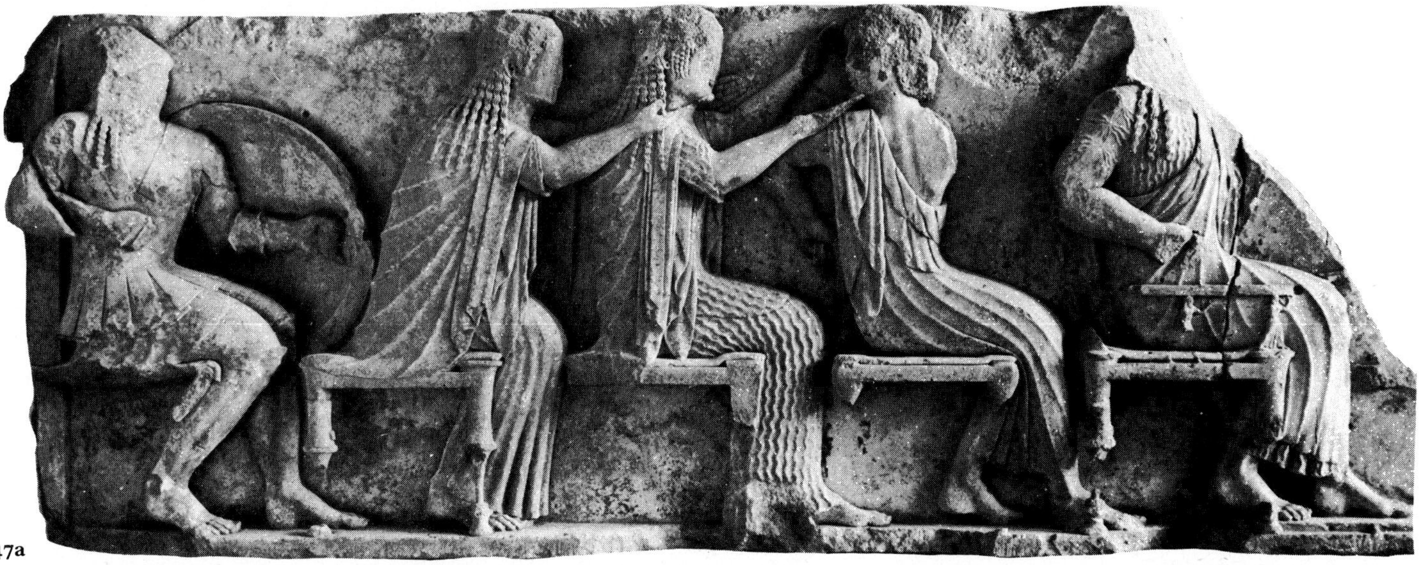

47a

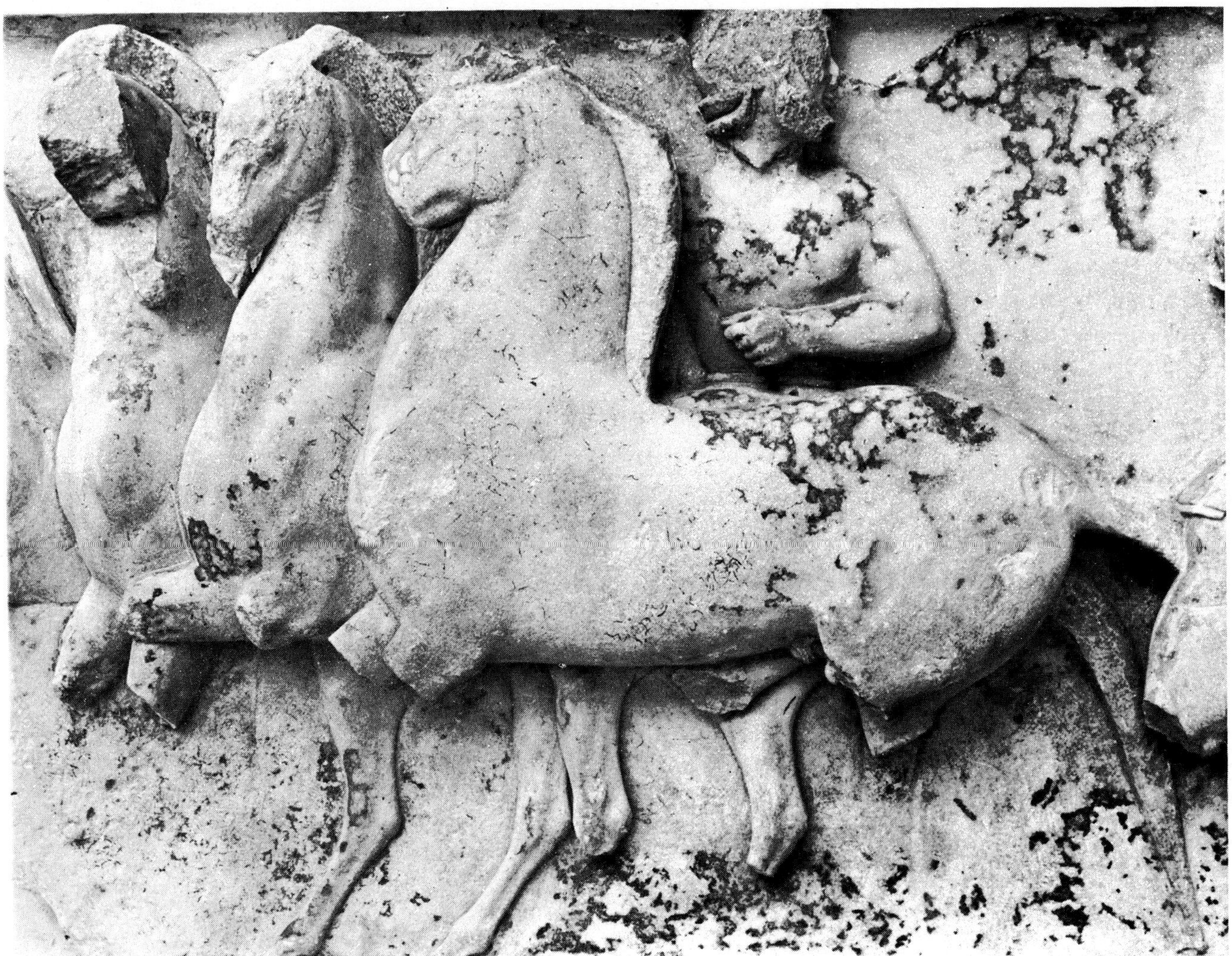

47b

47 **a** and **b** Parts of marble east frieze of Siphnian Treasury at Delphi. Delphi Museum. Shortly before 525 B.C. H. 0.64. (Pp. 153ff.).

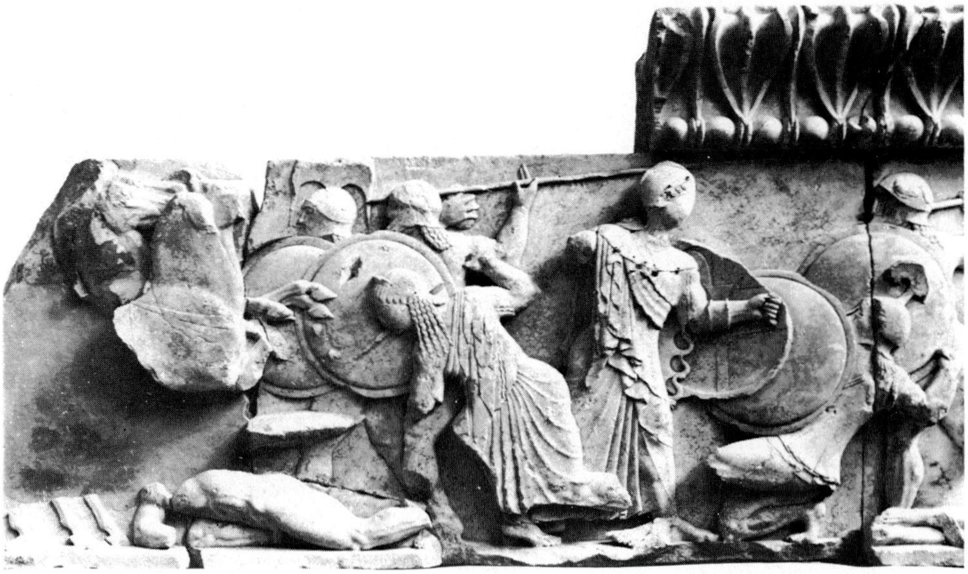

48a

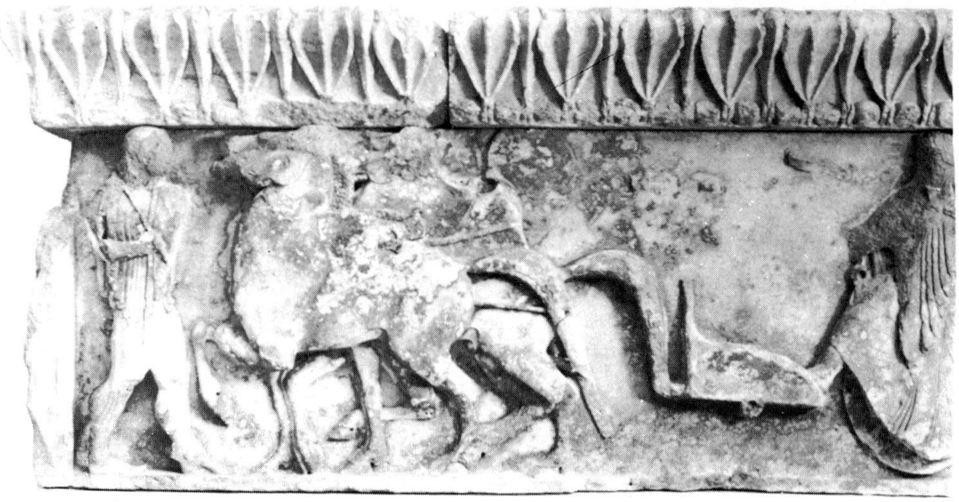

48b

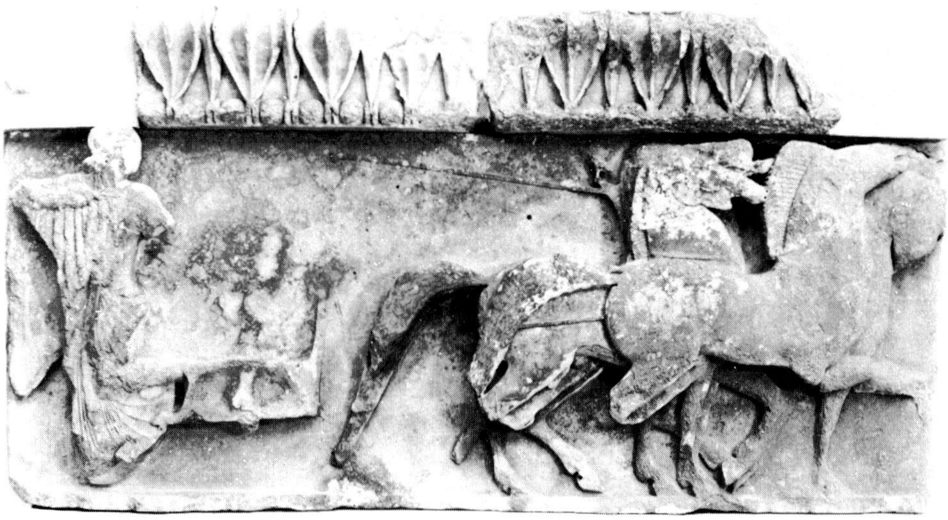

48c

48 **a** Part of marble north frieze of Siphnian Treasury at Delphi. Delphi Museum. Shortly before 525 B.C. H. 0.64. (Pp. 155–6) **b** and **c** Marble slabs from west frieze of Siphnian Treasury at Delphi. Delphi Museum. Shortly before 525 B.C. H. 0.64. (P. 154ff.).

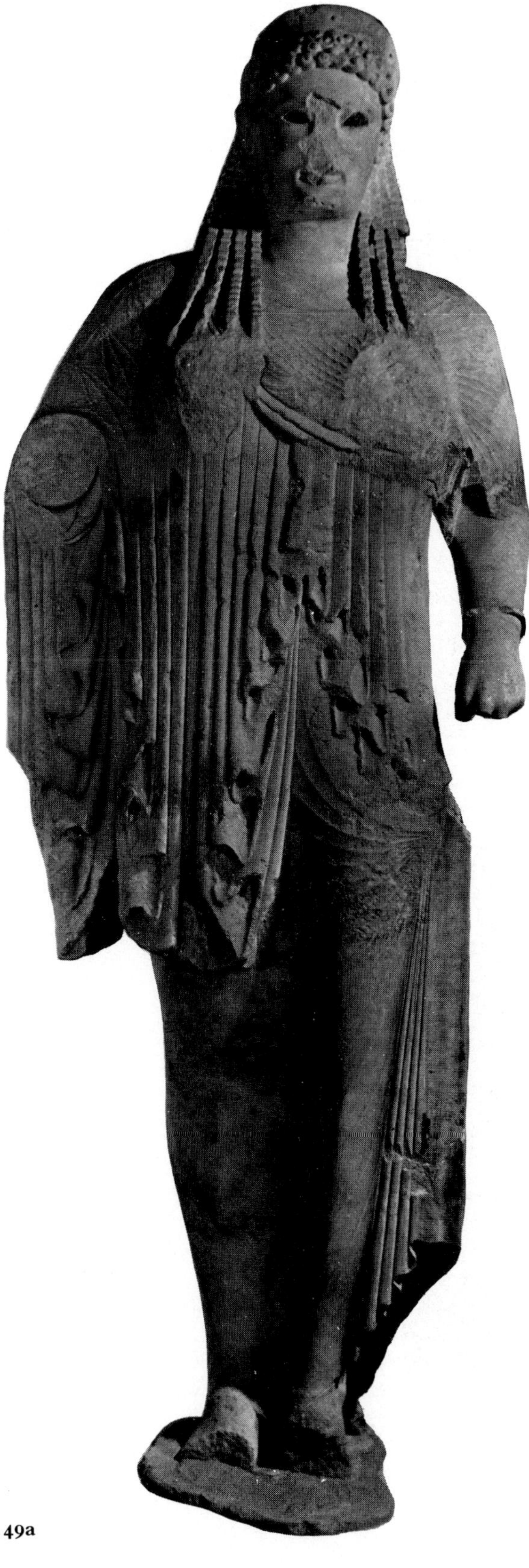

49a

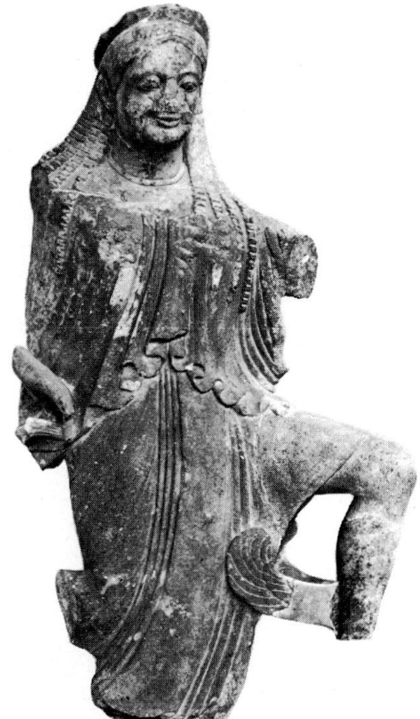

49b

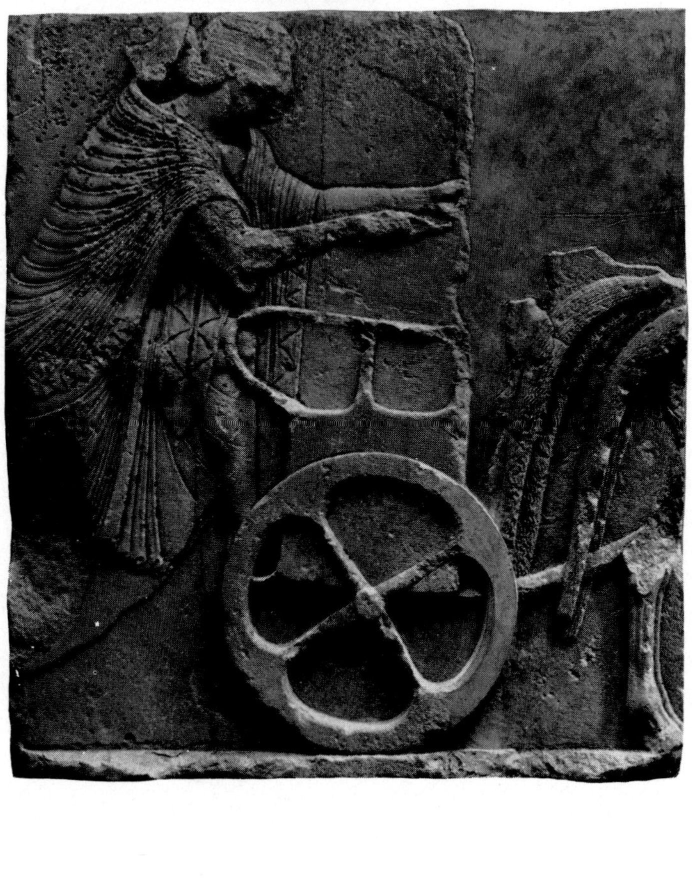

49c

49 **a** Marble statue from Acropolis. Athens, Acropolis Museum 681. Last quarter of sixth century. H. 2.55. (Pp. 103, 130, 162, 186) **b** Marble akroterion from Temple of Apollo at Delphi. Delphi Museum. Last quarter of sixth century. H. 1.13. (P. 162) **c** Marble relief from Acropolis. Athens, Acropolis Museum 1342. Late sixth century. H. 1.20. (P. 160).

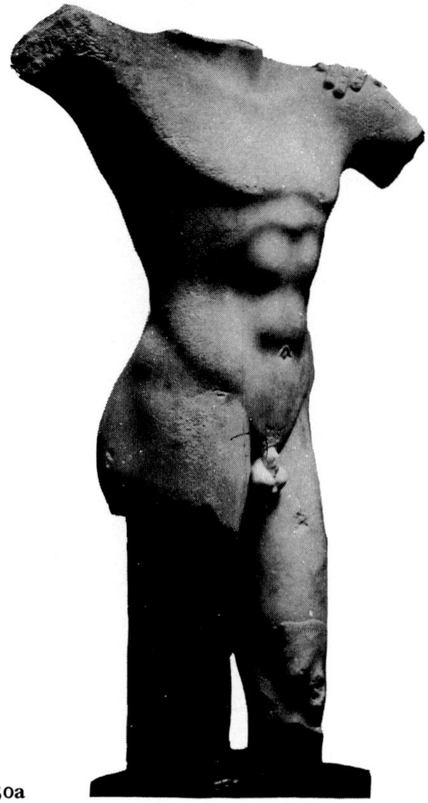

50a

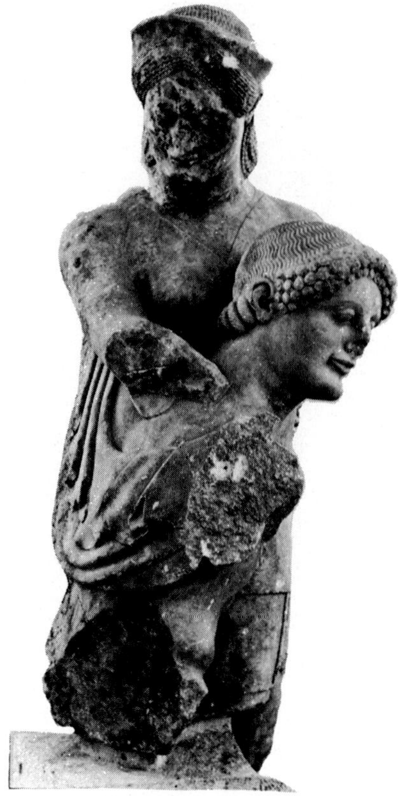

50b

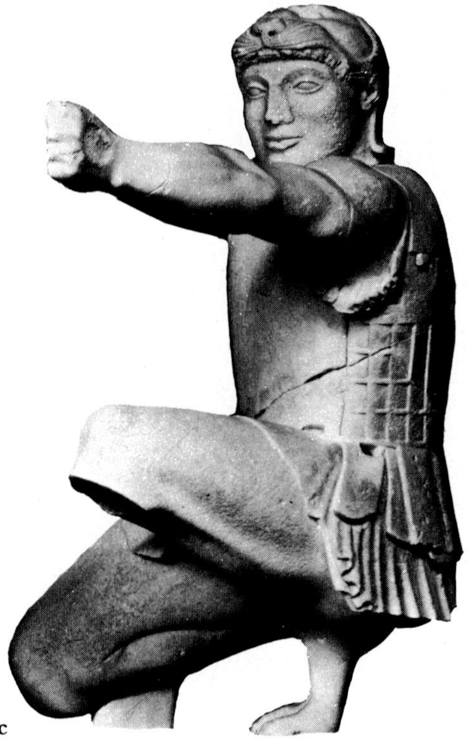

50c

50 **a** Marble statue from Acropolis. Athens, Acropolis Museum 145. Last quarter of sixth century. H. 0.63. (P. 162) **b** Marble group from pediment of Temple of Apollo at Eretria. Chalkis Museum. End of sixth century. H. 1.10. (Pp. 163–4) **c** Marble figure from east pediment of Temple of Aphaia on Aegina. Munich 84. First quarter of fifth century. H. 0.79. (P. 166).

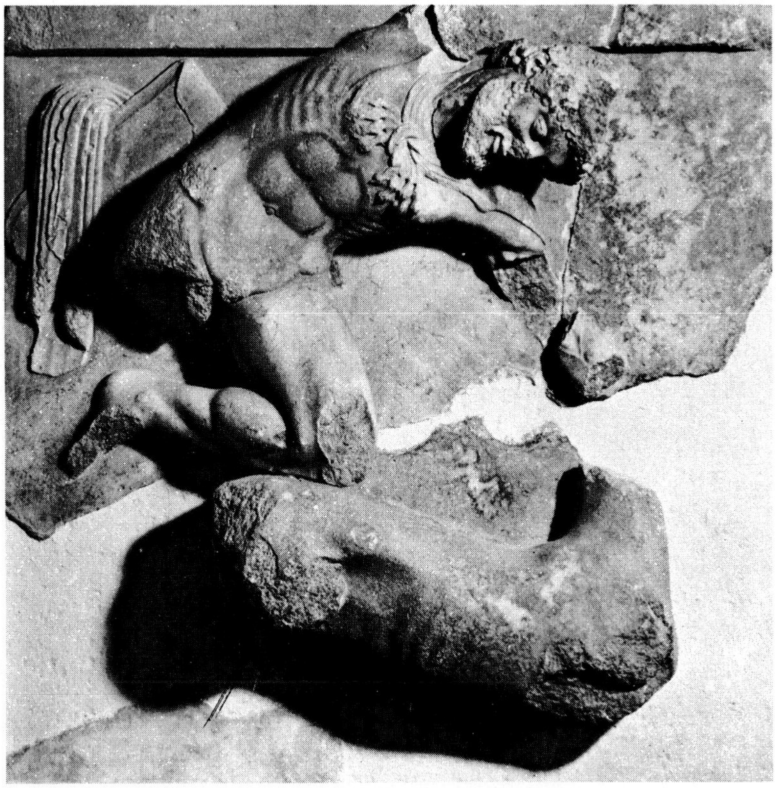

51a

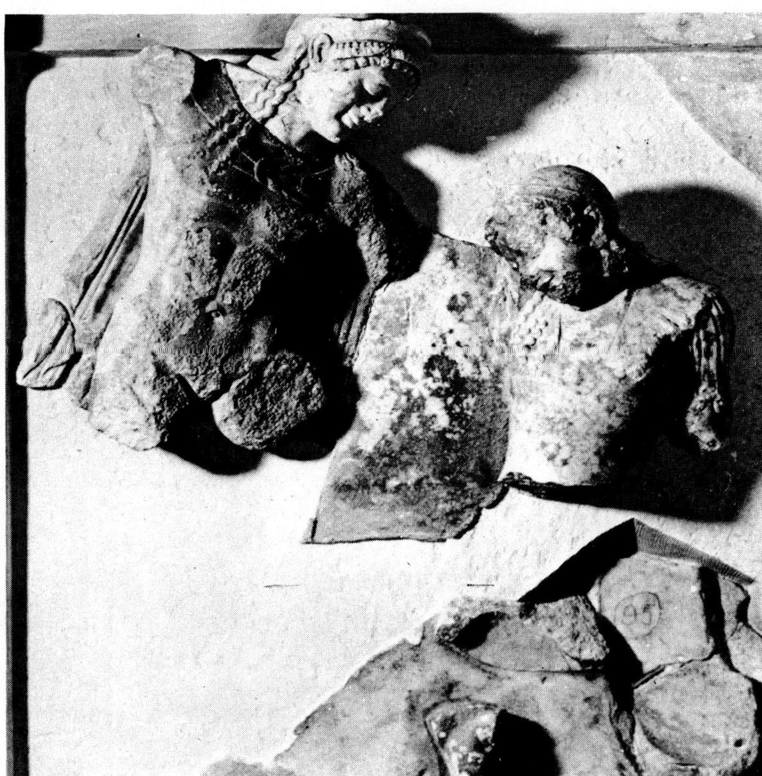

51b

51 a and **b** Marble metopes from Treasury of Athenians at Delphi. Delphi Museum. End of sixth or beginning of fifth century. H. 0.67. (Pp. 168ff.).

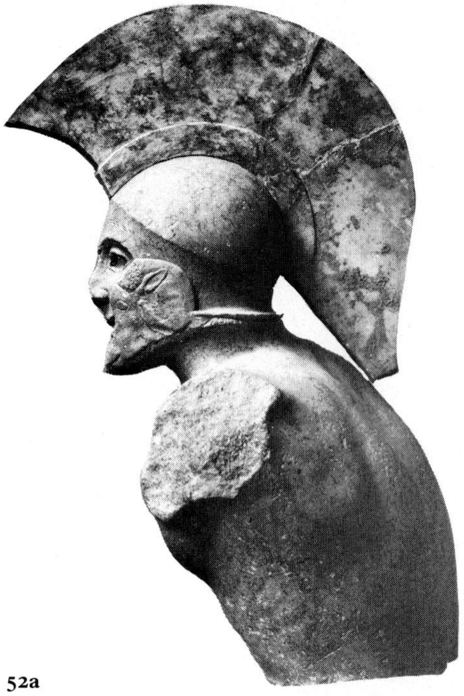
52a

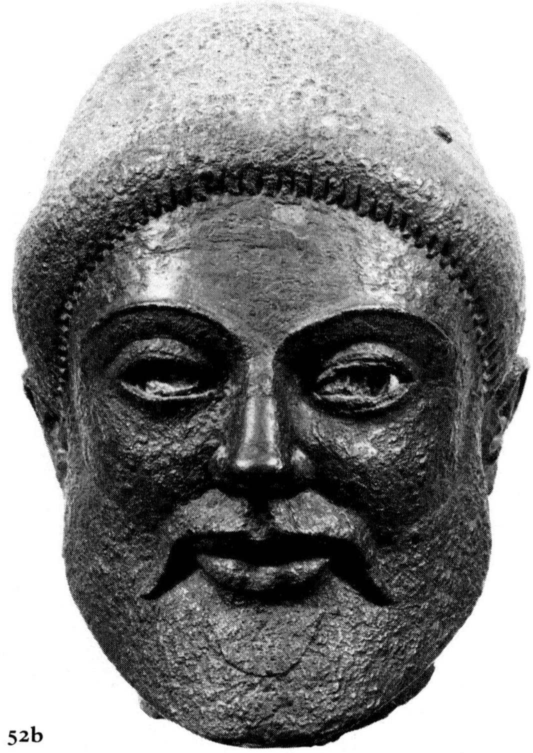
52b

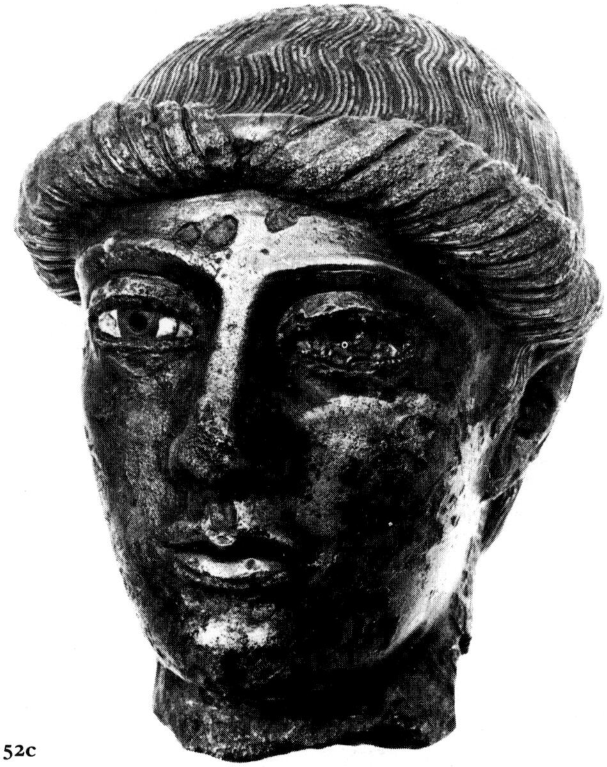
52c

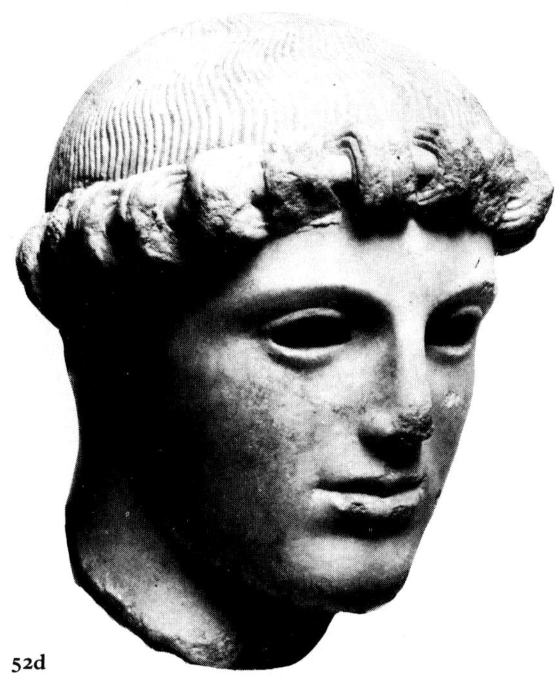
52d

52 **a** Upper part of marble statue from Sparta. Athens, National Museum 3613. First quarter of sixth century. H. 0.85. (P. 184) **b** Bronze head from Acropolis. Athens, National Museum x 6446. First quarter of fifth century. H. 0.27. (Pp. 167, 184) **c** Bronze head from Acropolis. Athens, National Museum 6590. First quarter of fifth century. H. 0.13. (Pp. 180, 183) **d** Head of marble statue, pl. 53d. (P. 176).

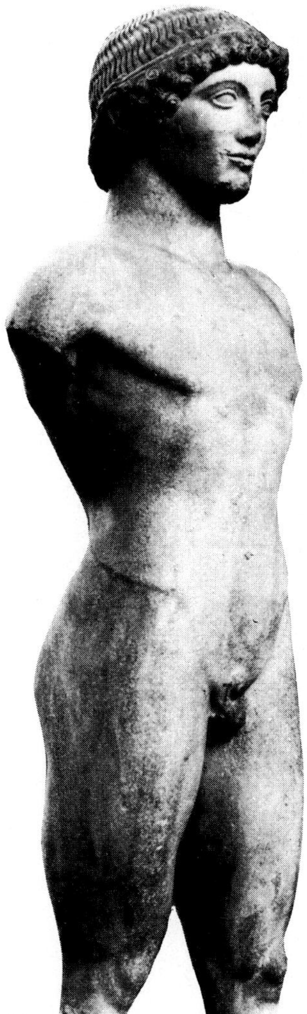

53a

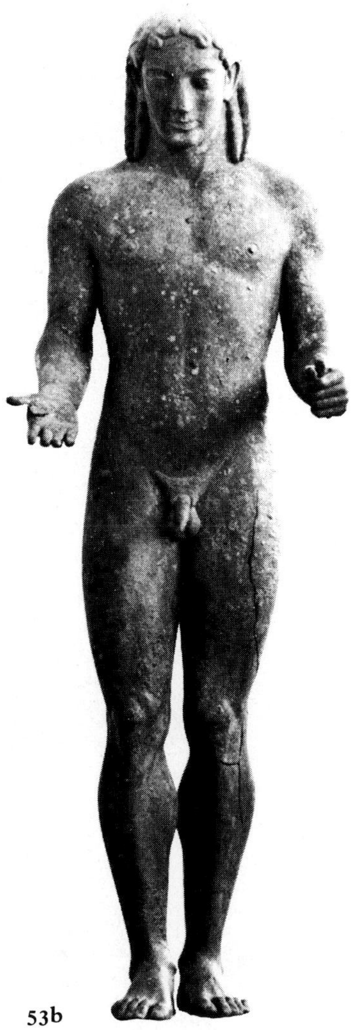

53b

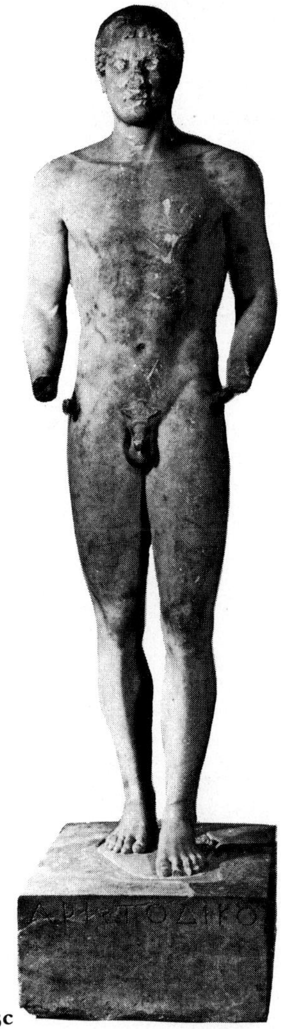

53c

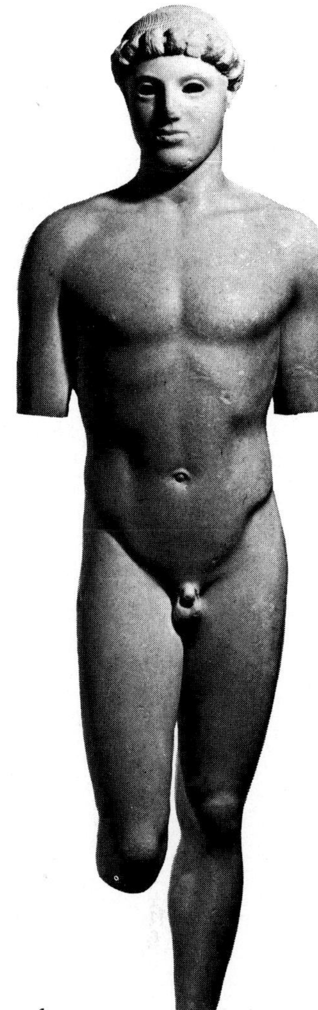

53d

53 **a** Marble statue from Anaphe (Sporades Islands). British Museum B475. End of sixth century. H. 1.01. (P. 175). **b** Bronze statue from Piraeus. Athens, National Museum. Second half of sixth century. H. 1.92. (Pp. 181ff.) **c** Marble grave-statue of Aristodikos, from Attica. Athens, National Museum 3938. End of sixth or beginning of fifth century. H. 1.95. (P. 175) **d** Marble statue from Acropolis. Athens, Acropolis Museum 698. First quarter of fifth century. H. 0.86. Cf. pl. 52d. (Pp. 175ff., 329).

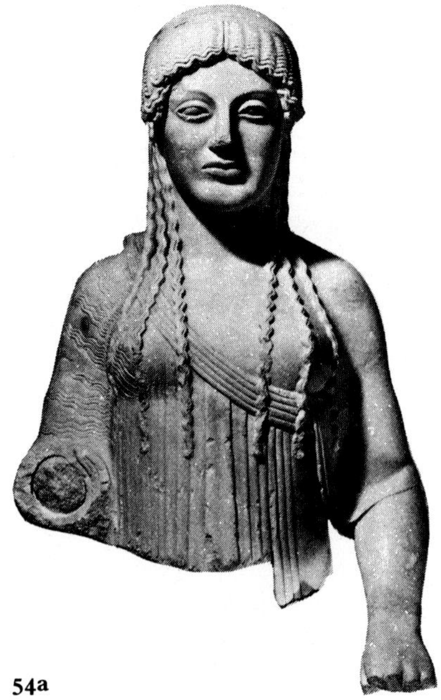

54a

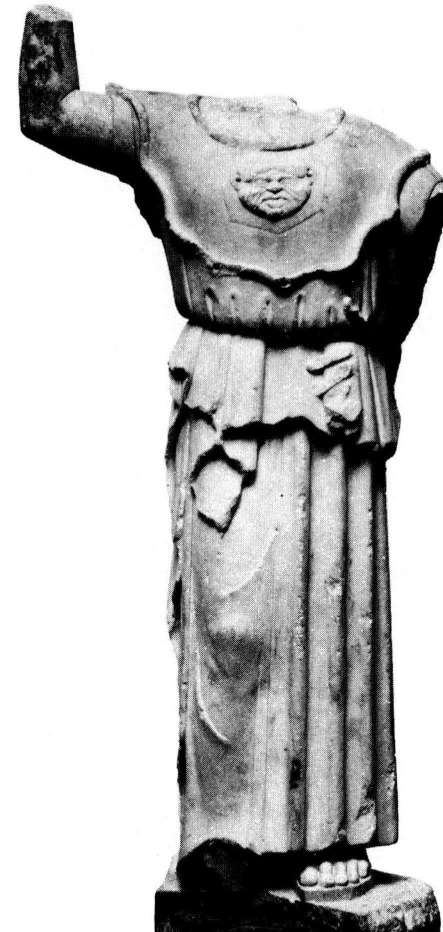

54b

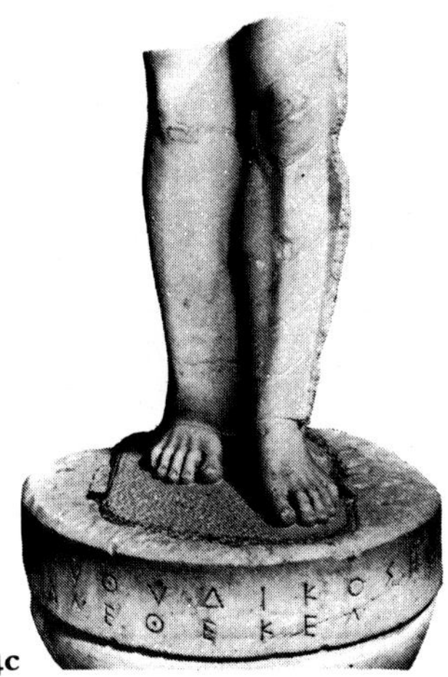

54c

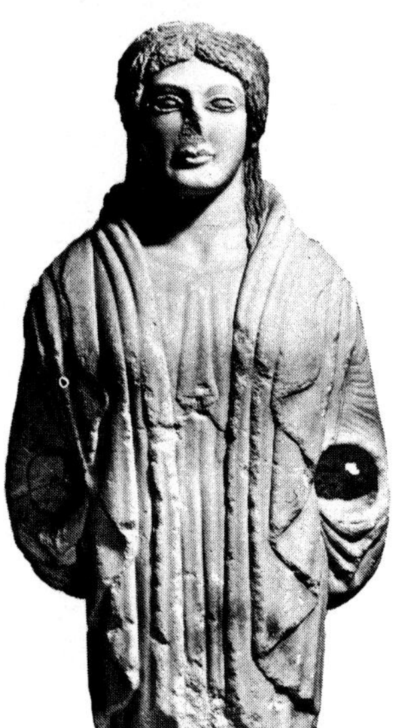

54d

54 **a** and **c** Upper and lower parts of marble statue from Acropolis, dedicated by Euthydikos. Athens, Acropolis Museum 686 and 609. Early fifth century. H. (**a**) 0.58; (**c**) 0.41. (Pp. 173ff.) **b** Marble statue from Acropolis, made by Euenor and dedicated by Angelitos. Athens, Acropolis Museum 140. First quarter of fifth century. H. 0.89. (Pp. 179, 192, 345) **d** Upper part of marble statue from Acropolis. Athens, Acropolis Museum 688. First quarter of fifth century. H. 0.51. (Pp. 179–80).

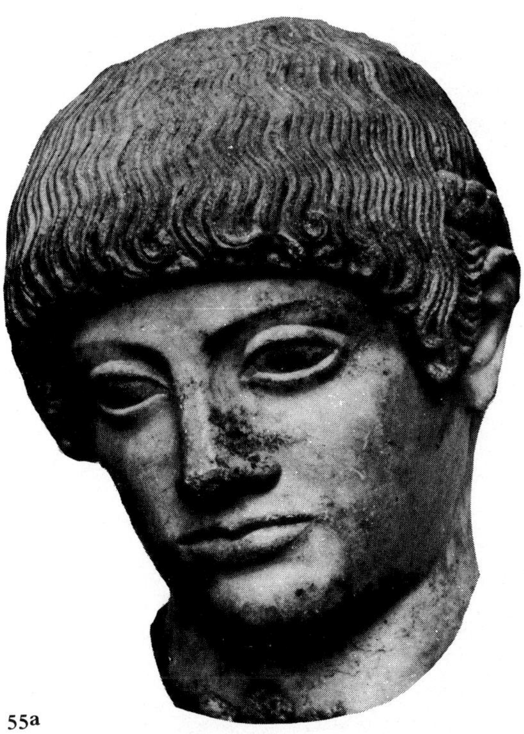

55a

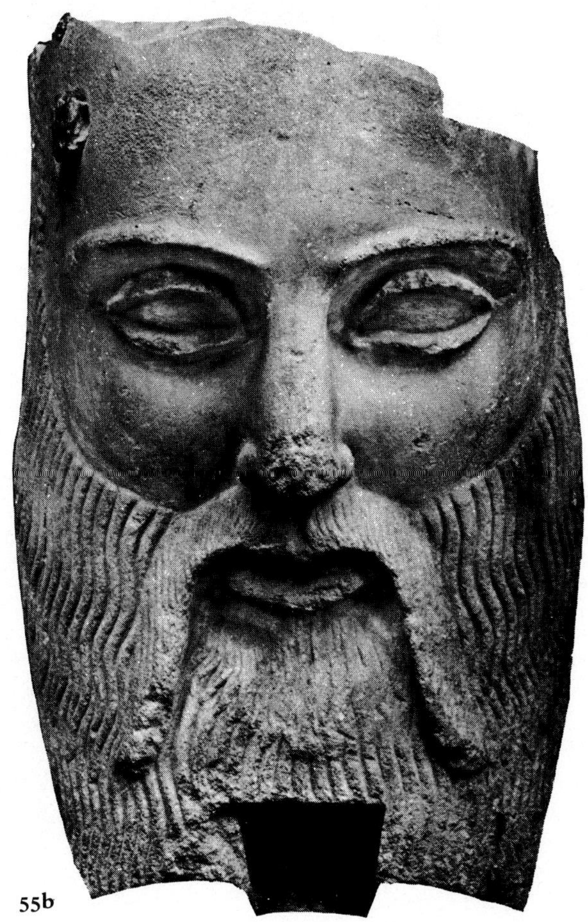

55b

55 **a** Marble head from Acropolis. Athens, Acropolis Museum 689. First quarter of fifth century. H. 0.25. (Pp. 174ff., 290) **b** Marble mask from Marathon. Berlin (E) 100. First quarter of fifth century. H. 0.32. (P. 177).

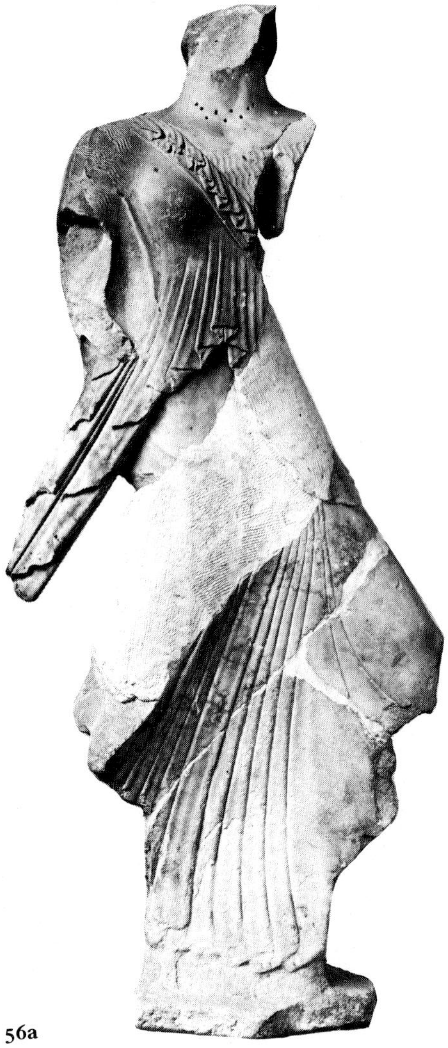

56a

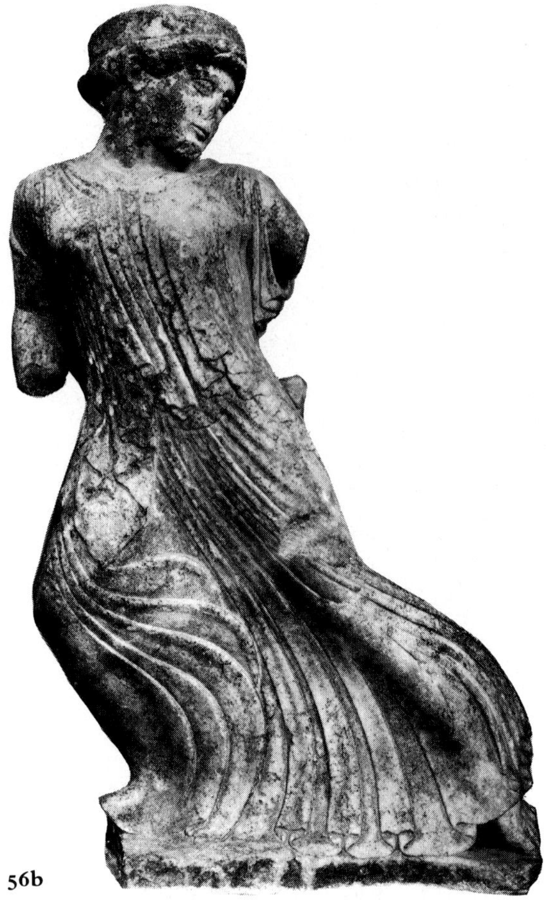

56b

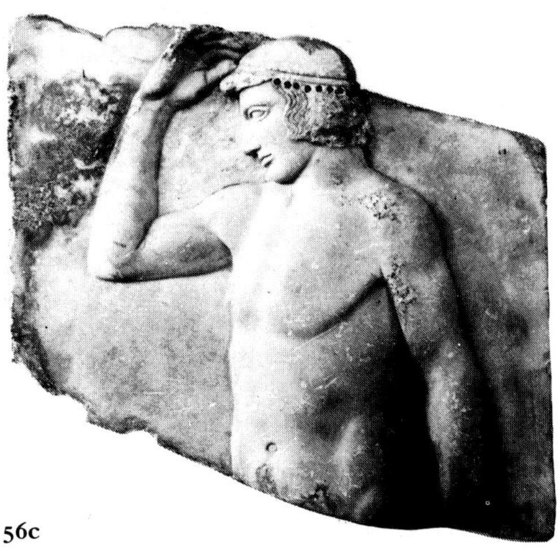

56c

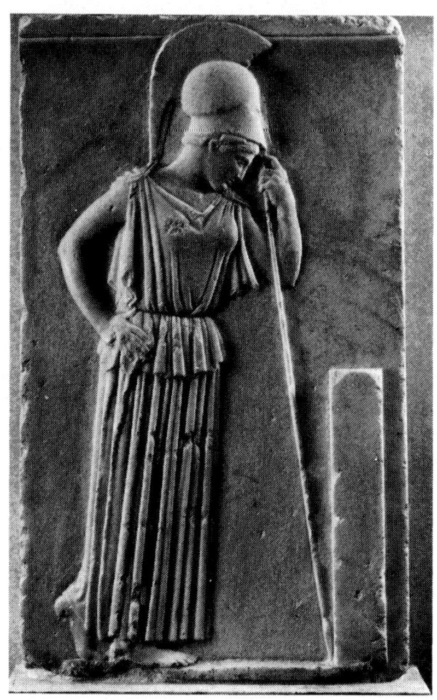

56d

56 **a** Fragmentary marble statue from Acropolis. Athens, Acropolis Museum 690. Probably 490–489 B.C. H. as restored 1.40. (Pp. 176–7) **b** Marble figure from Eleusis. Eleusis Museum. First quarter of fifth century. H. 0.70. (P. 177) **c** Marble relief from Temple of Athena, Sunium. Athens, National Museum 3344. Probably first quarter of fifth century. H. 0.61. (Pp. 177–8) **d** Marble relief from Acropolis. Athens, Acropolis Museum 695. Second quarter of fifth century. H. 0.54. (P. 178).

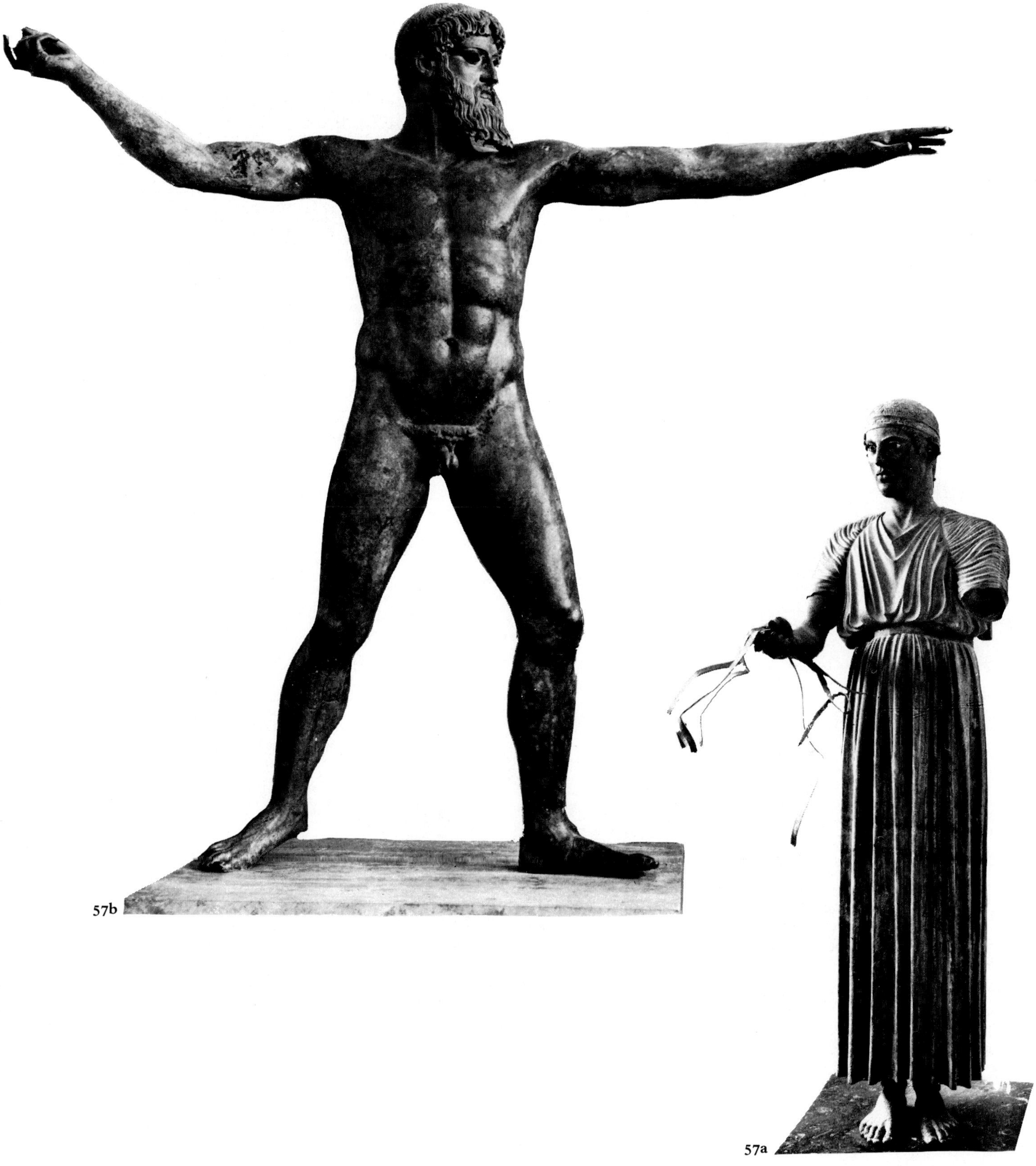

57b

57a

57 **a** Bronze statue from Delphi. Delphi Museum. First or second quarter of fifth century. H. 1.80. (Pp. 188ff.)
b Bronze statue from sea off Cape Artemision (north point of Euboea). Athens, National Museum 15161. Second quarter of fifth century. H. 2.09. (Pp. 196–7). Cf. pl. 62a.

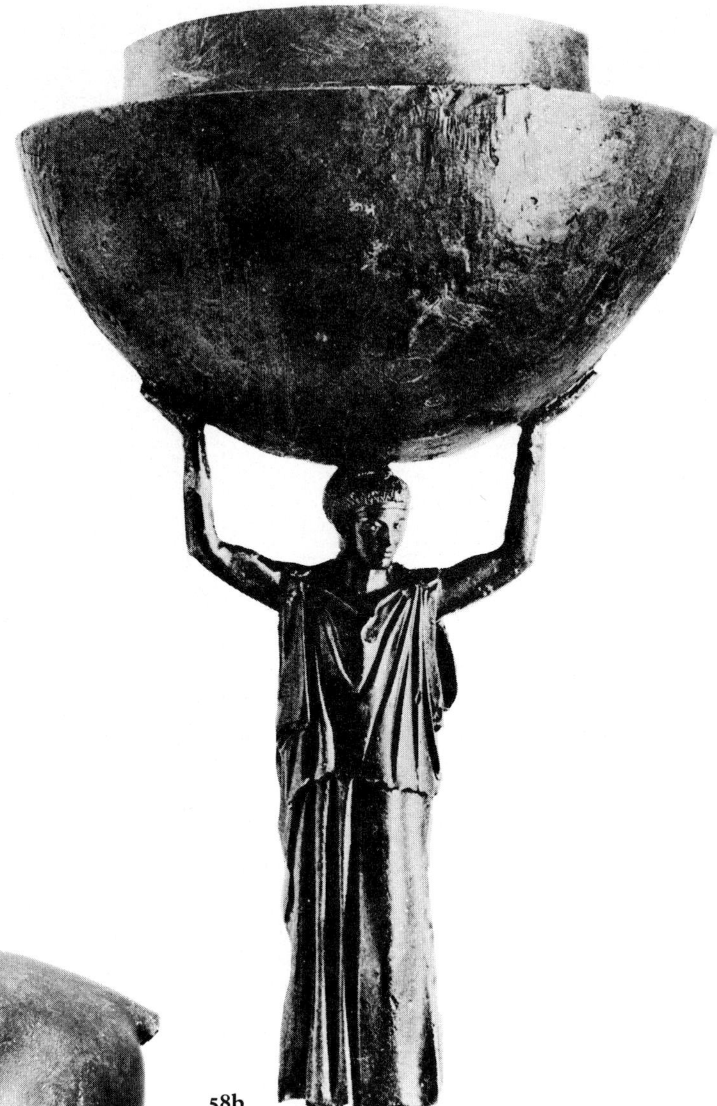

58b

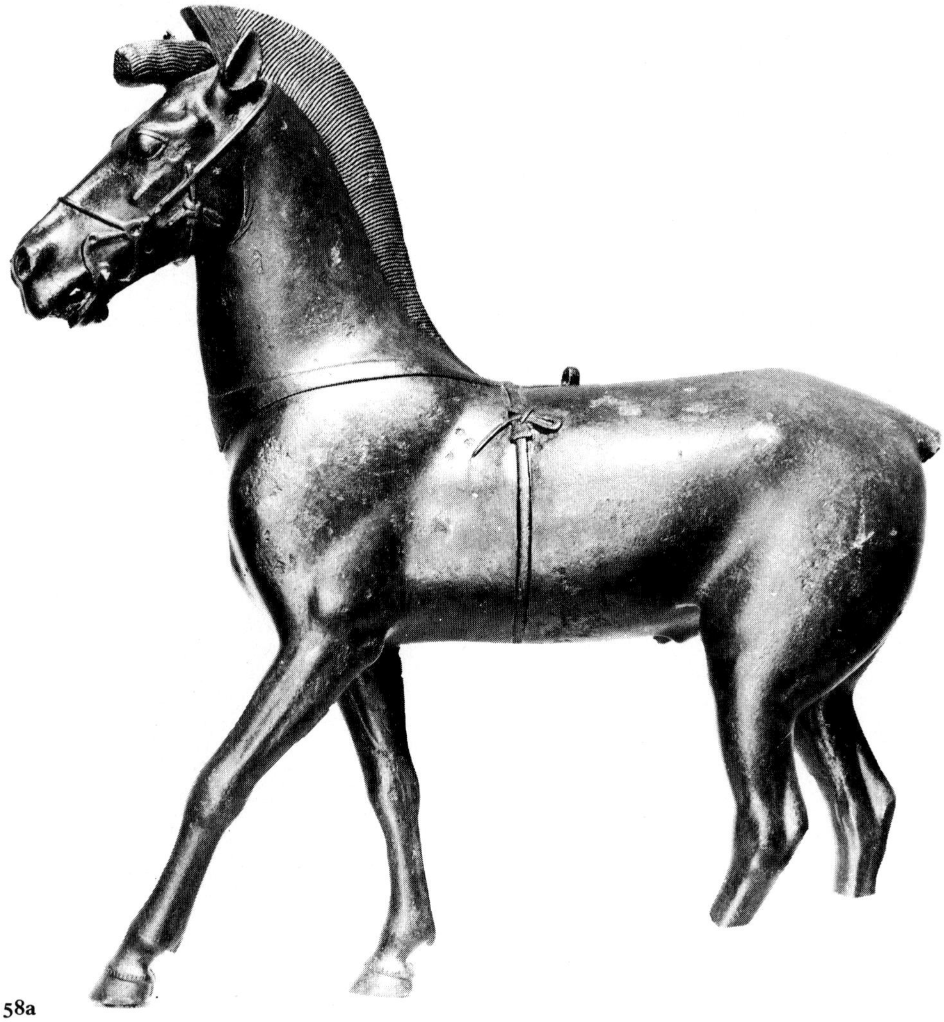

58a

58 **a** Bronze statuette of horse from Olympia. Athens, National Museum. First half of fifth century. H. 0.23. (P. 190)
b Bronze statuette supporting vessel, from Delphi. Delphi Museum. Second quarter of fifth century. H. 0.26. (Pp. 140, 192).

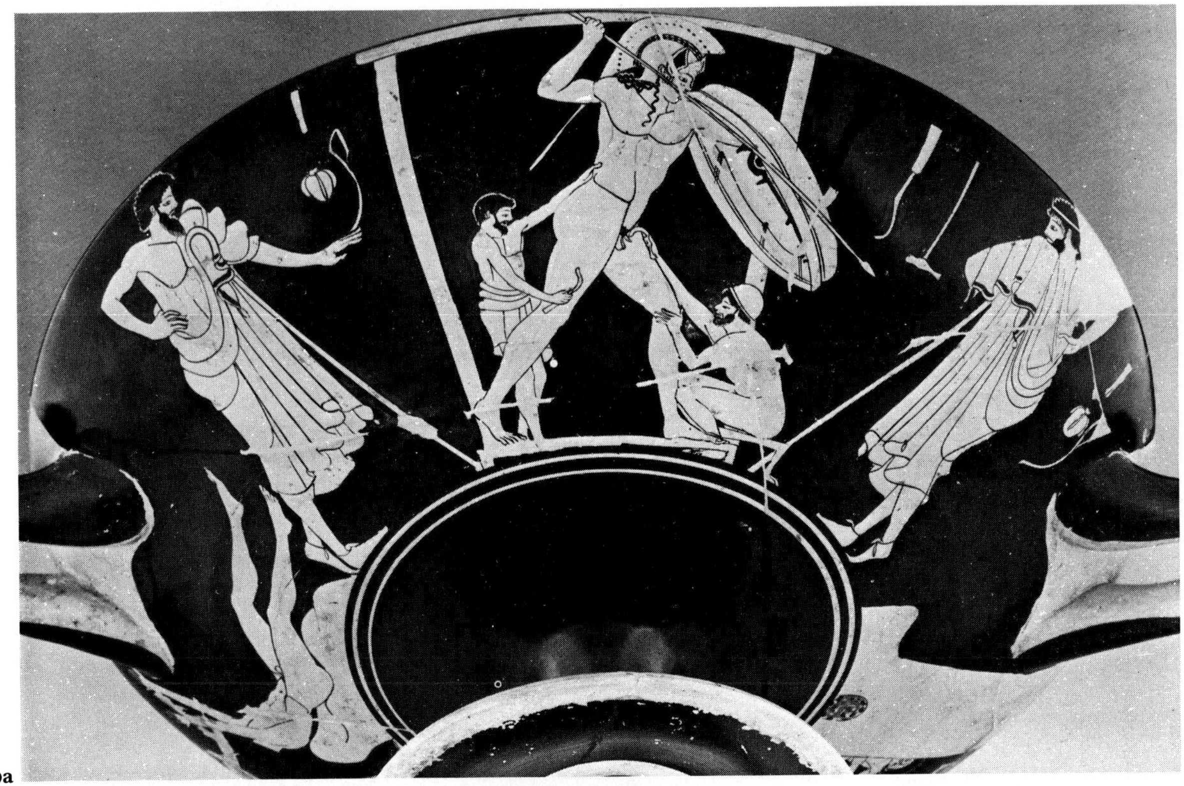

59a

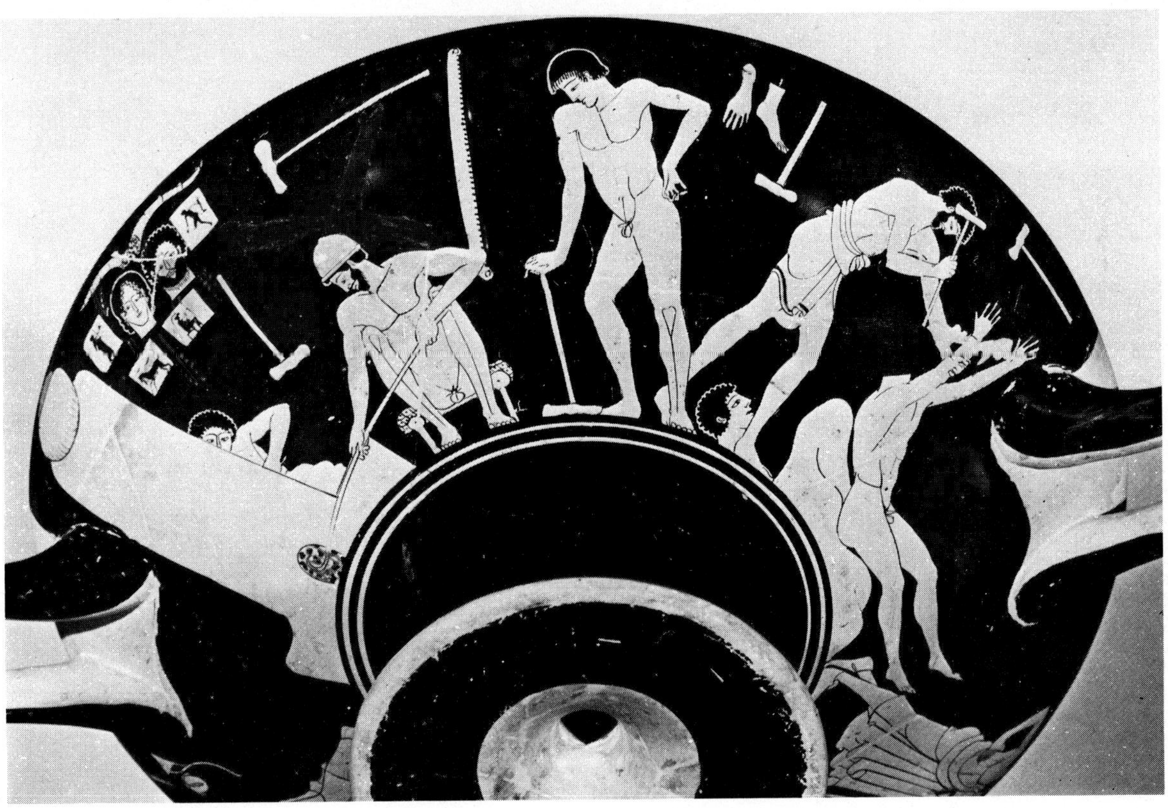

59b

59 **a** and **b** Pictures on outside of Attic red-figure cup from Vulci. Berlin (Charlottenburg) 2294. First quarter of fifth century. D. 0.30. (Pp. 183–4).

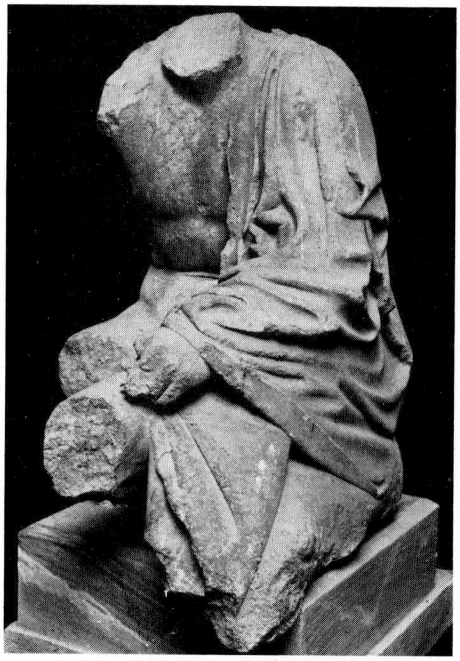

60a

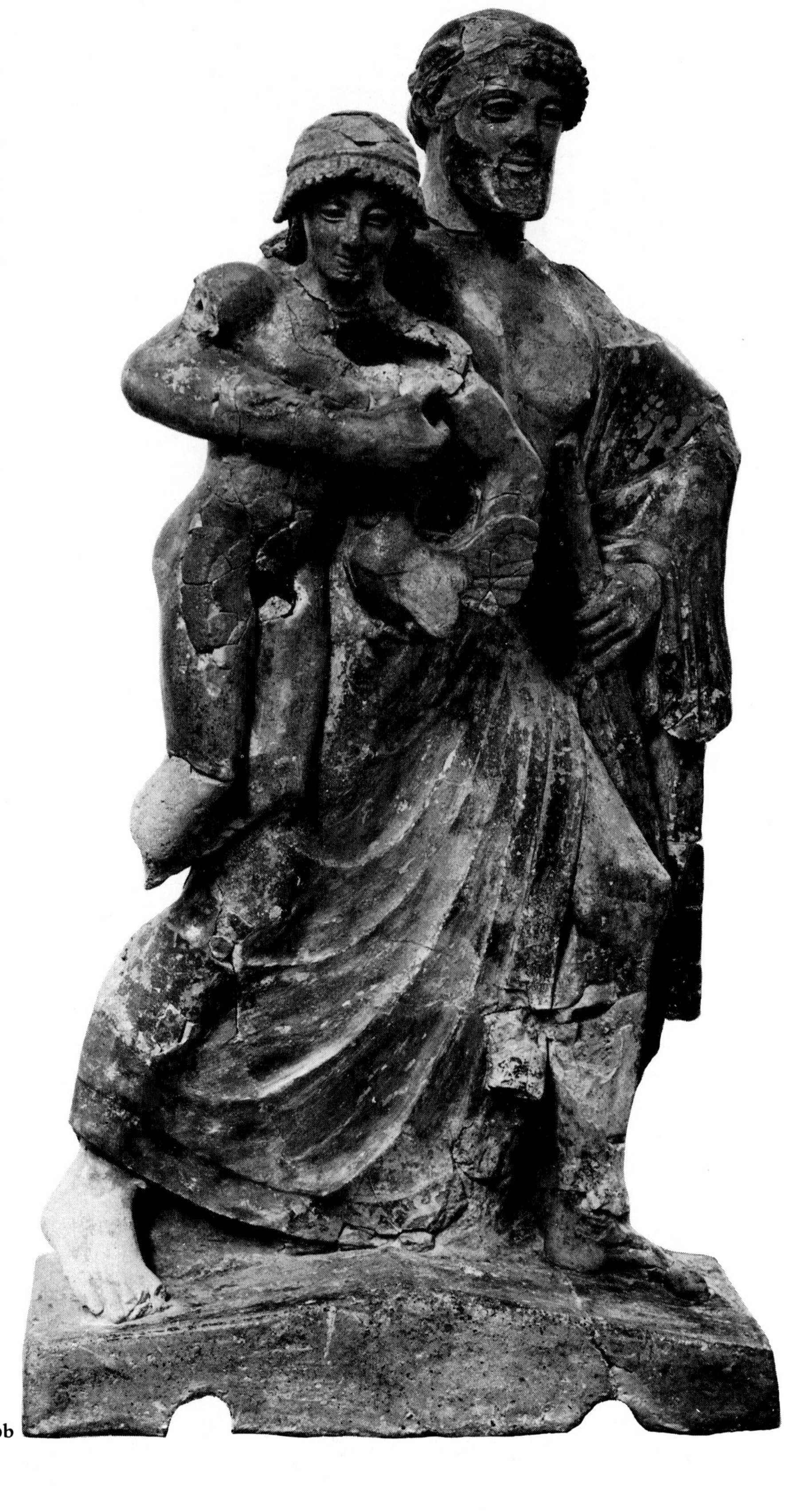

60b

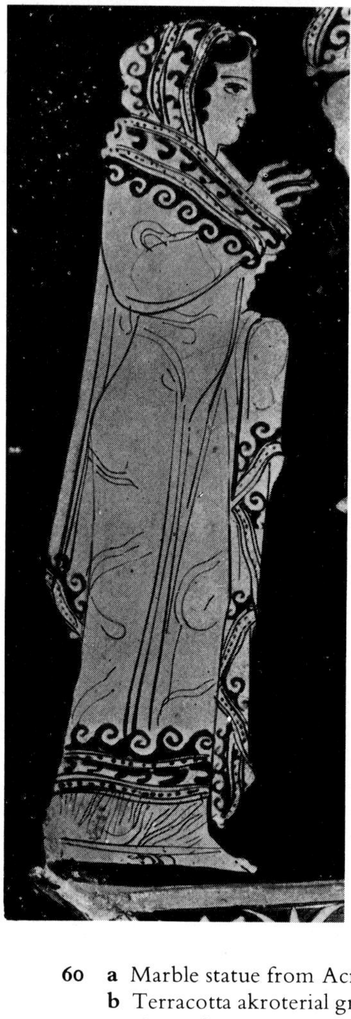

60c

60 **a** Marble statue from Acropolis. Athens, Acropolis Museum 1346. Mid fifth century. H. 0.45. (Pp. 191, 473, 560)
b Terracotta akroterial group from Olympia. Olympia Museum. Second quarter of fifth century. H. 1.10. (P. 277)
c Figure from Attic red-figure calyx-krater. Adolphseck, Landgraf Philipp of Hesse, 77. End of fifth or beginning of fourth century. H. of figure *c.* 0.18. (Pp. 193, 240).

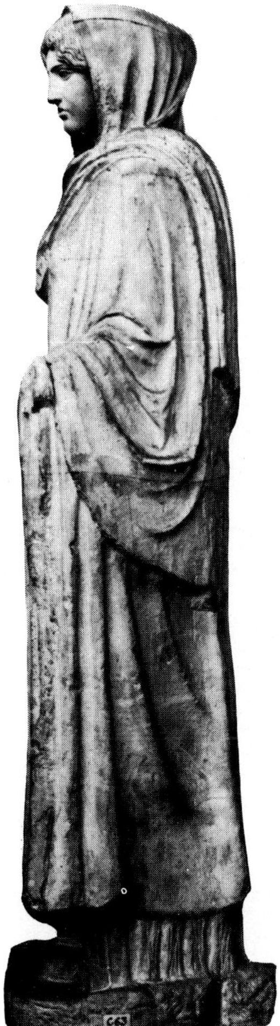

61a

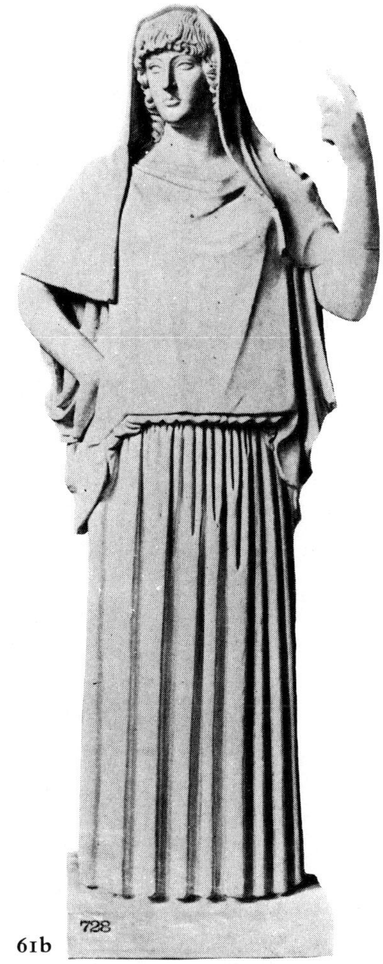

61b

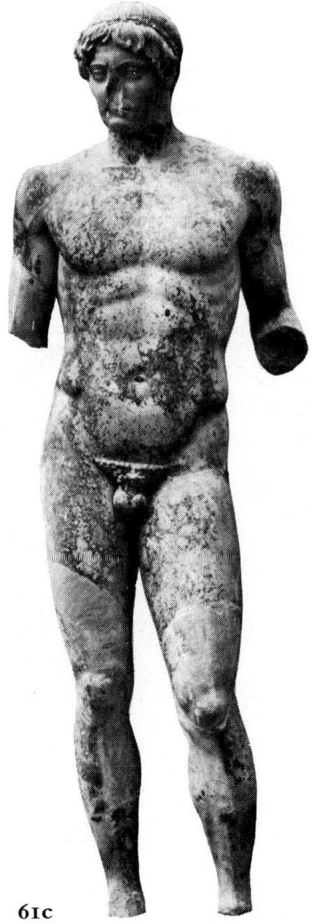

61c

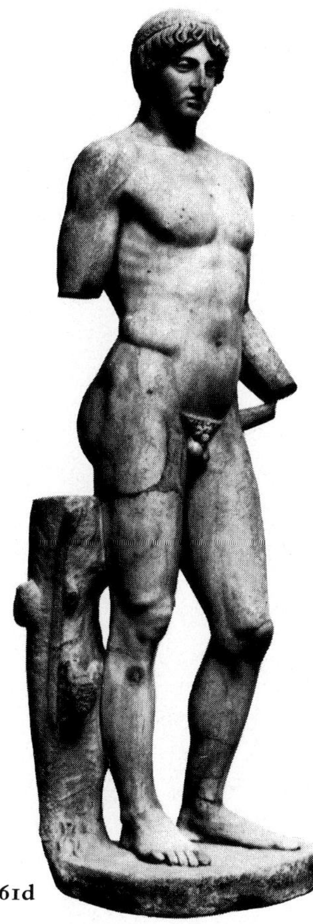

61d

61 **a** Cast of marble figure reconstructed from copies of the imperial age. Oxford, Ashmolean Museum. Date of bronze (?) original, second quarter of fifth century. H. 1.97. (Pp. 192, 420) **b** Marble statue. Rome, Museo Torlonia. Copy of the imperial age after bronze (?) original of second quarter of fifth century. H. 1.93. See also pl. 63d. (Pp. 191ff.) **c** Marble statue from Athens. Athens, National Museum 45. Copy of the imperial age after bronze original of second quarter of fifth century. H. 1.78. (Pp. 194–5) **d** Marble statue. British Museum 209. Copy of the imperial age after same original as **c**. H. 1.76. (Pp. 194–5, 329).

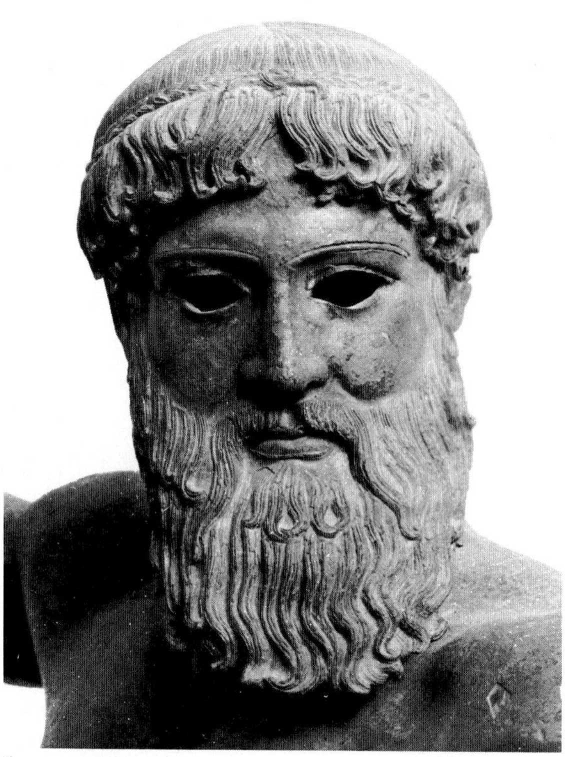

62a

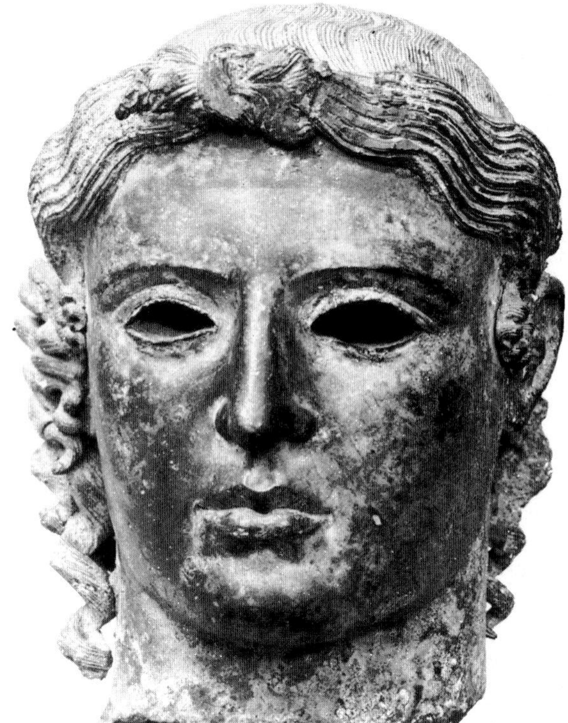

62b

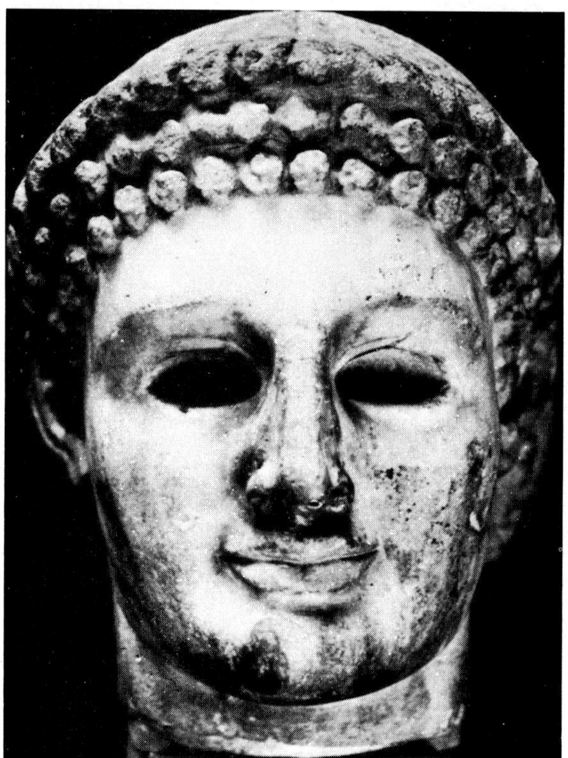

62c

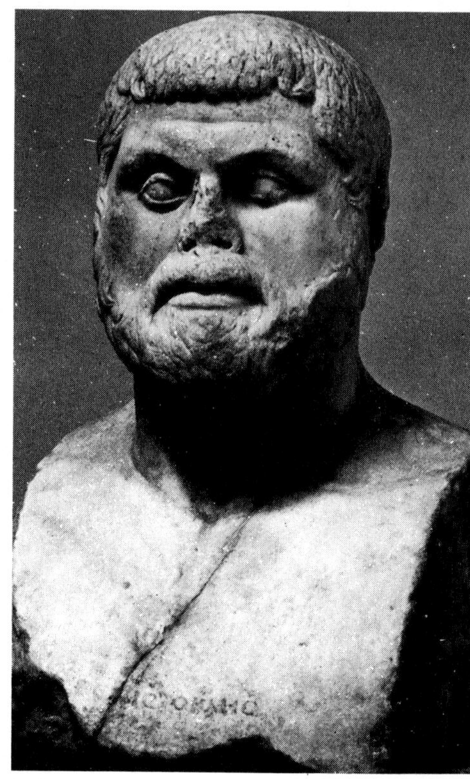

62d

62 **a** Head of bronze statue, pl. 57b. (Pp. 195ff.) **b** Head of bronze statue from Cyprus. British Museum 1958.4–18.1. Second quarter of fifth century. H. 0.20. (Pp. 195–6) **c** Marble head. British Museum 2728. Copy of the imperial age, probably from bronze original of late sixth century. H. 0.29. (P. 186) **d** Marble head from Ostia. Ostia Museum. Copy of the imperial age, probably from bronze original of second quarter of fifth century. H. of head, 0.26. (Pp. 187ff., 263, 504).

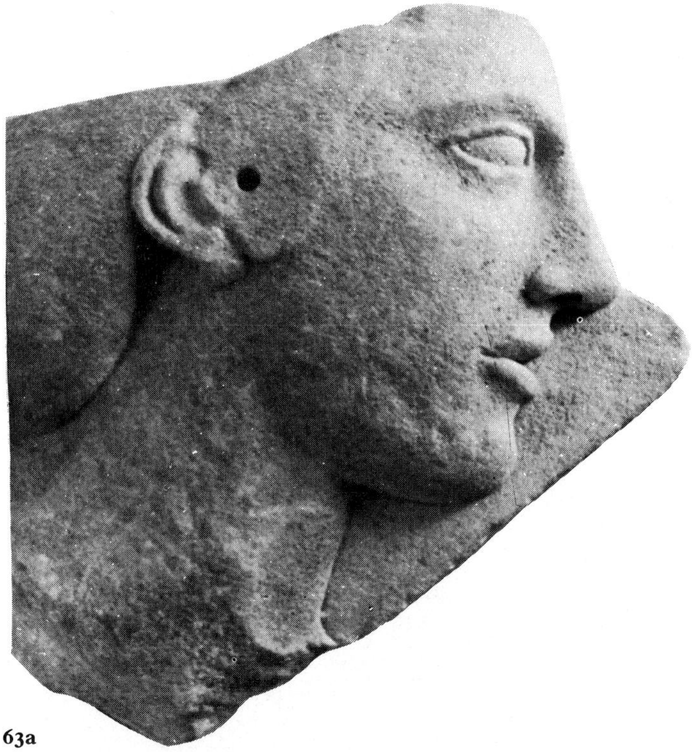

63a

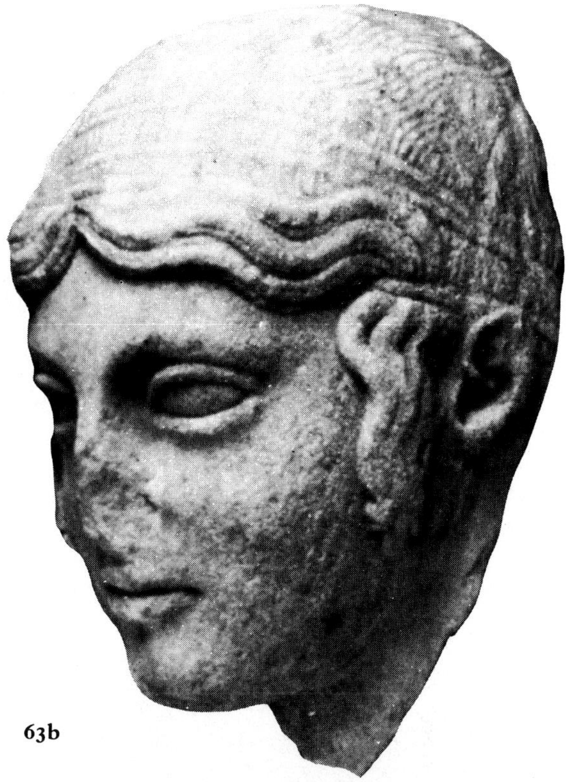

63b

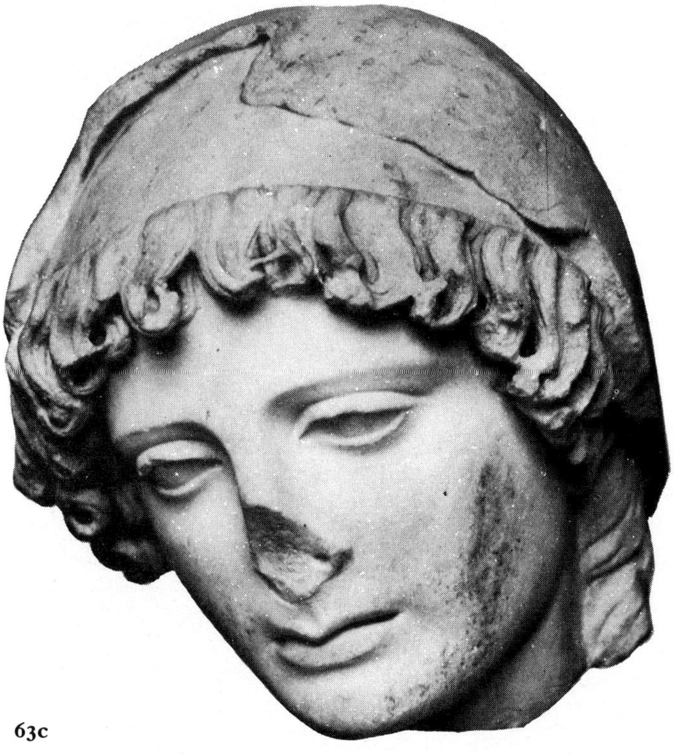

63c

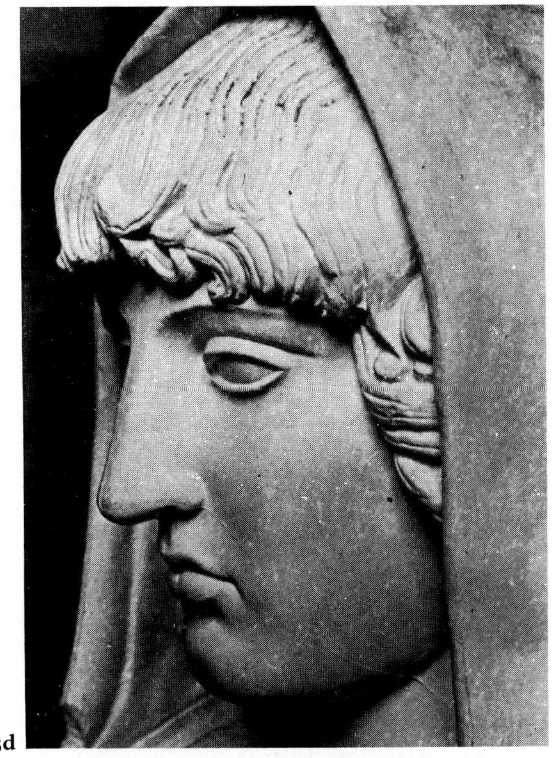

63d

63 **a** Fragment of marble disk from Melos. Athens, National Museum 3990. Second quarter of fifth century. H. 0.32. (P. 199) **b** Marble head in relief from south slope of Acropolis. Athens, National Museum 1949. Second quarter of fifth century. H. 0.14. (Pp. 178, 208) **c** Marble head. Copenhagen, Ny Carlsberg Glyptotek 407. Copy of the imperial age, probably from marble original of second quarter of fifth century. H. 0.26. (P. 210) **d** Head of statue, pl. 61b; from cast, Ashmolean Museum, Oxford. (Pp. 191ff.).

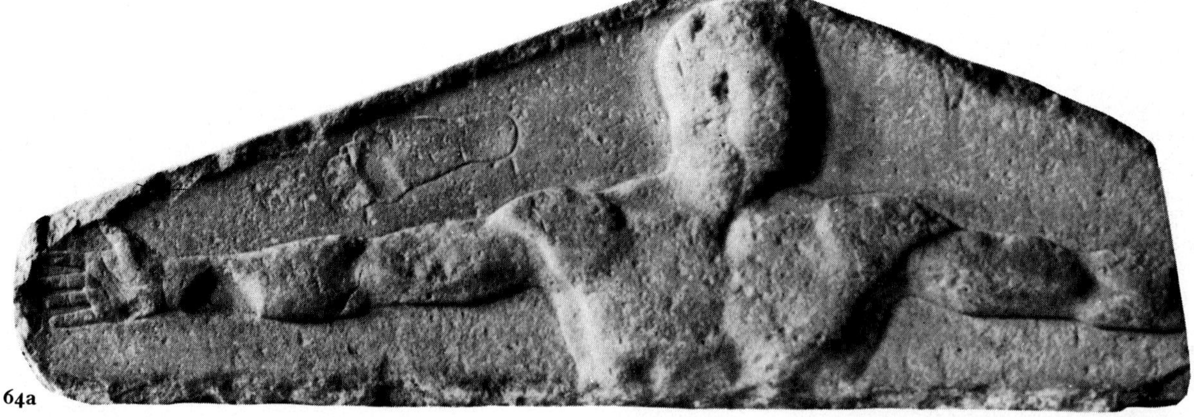

64a

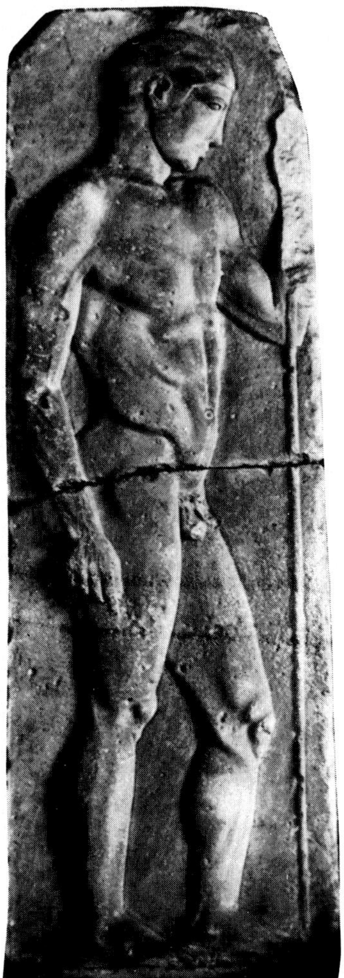

64b

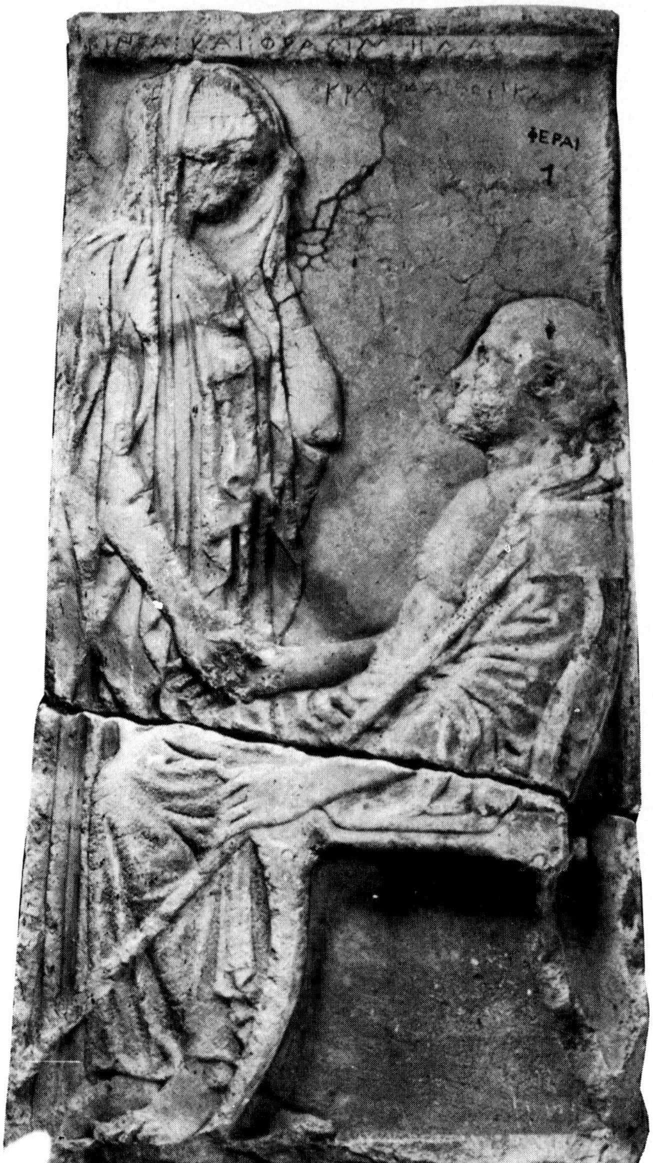

64c

64 **a** Marble relief. Ashmolean Museum, Oxford. Second quarter of fifth century. H. at apex 0.63. (P. 199) **b** Marble grave-relief from Nisyros (Dodecanese). Istanbul, Archaeological Museum. Second quarter of fifth century. H. 1.83. (Pp. 197–8, 290) **c** Marble grave-relief of Kineas and Phrasimeda, from Pherae (Thessaly). Volos Museum. Mid fifth century. H. 1.54. (Pp. 198–9).

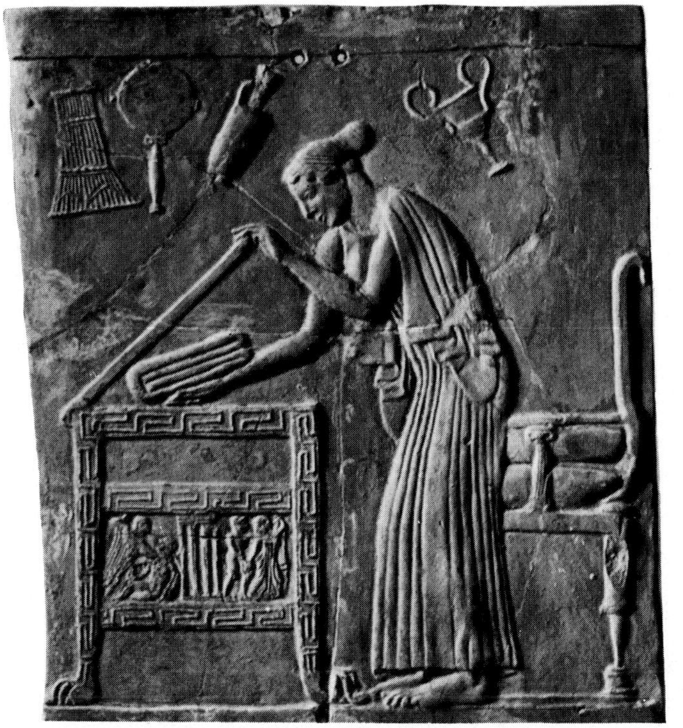

65a

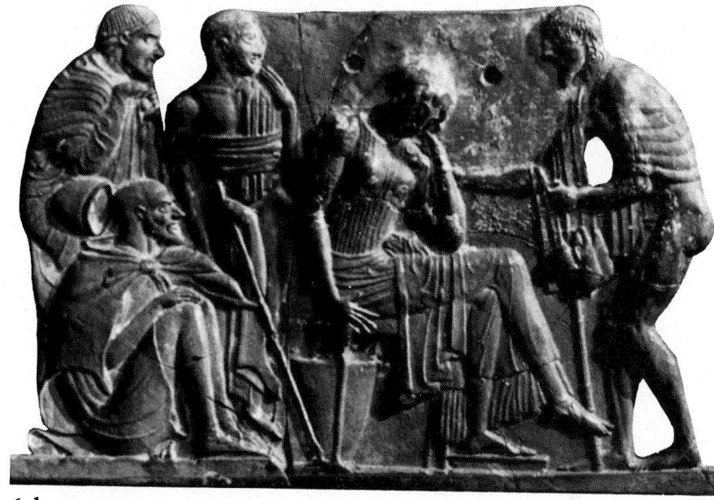

65b

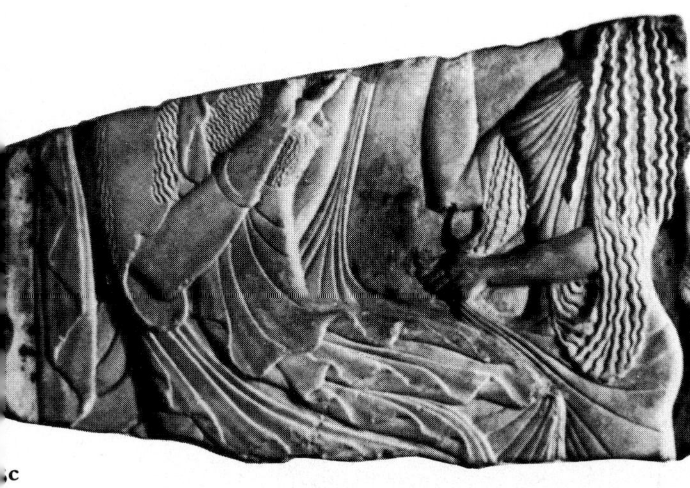

c

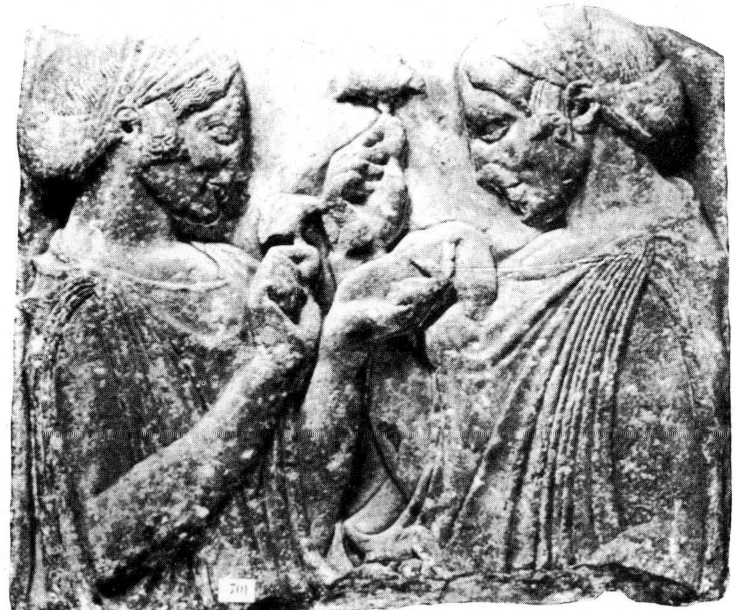

65d

65 **a** Terracotta relief from Locri. Taranto Museum. Second quarter of fifth century. H. 0.26. (Pp. 202, 209, 213) **b** Terracotta relief from Melos. New York, Metropolitan Museum of Art 30.11.9. Second quarter of fifth century. H. 0.18. (Pp. 202, 209, 473) **c** Fragment of marble relief from Athens. Athens, National Museum 36. End of sixth century or beginning of fifth. H. 0.43. (P. 199) **d** Marble grave-relief from Pharsalos (Thessaly). Louvre 701. Second quarter of fifth century. H. 0.57. (Pp. 198–9, 253).

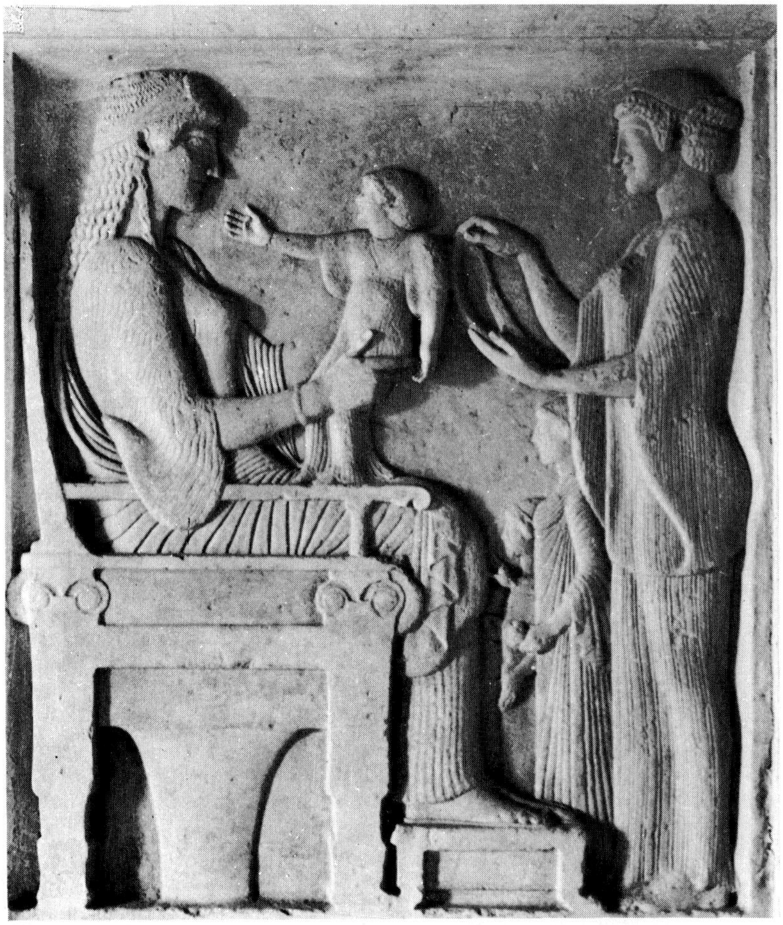

66a

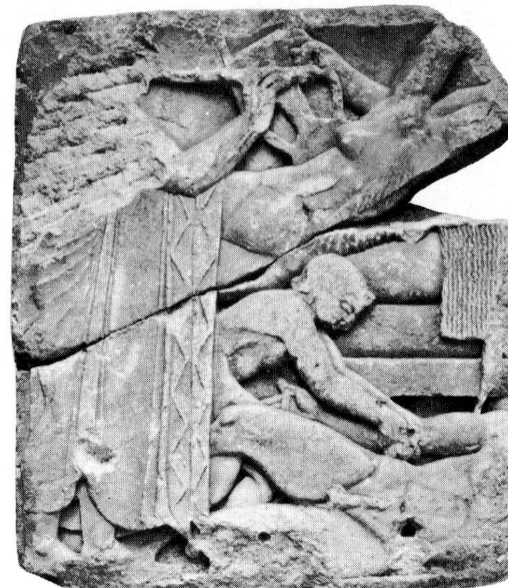

66b

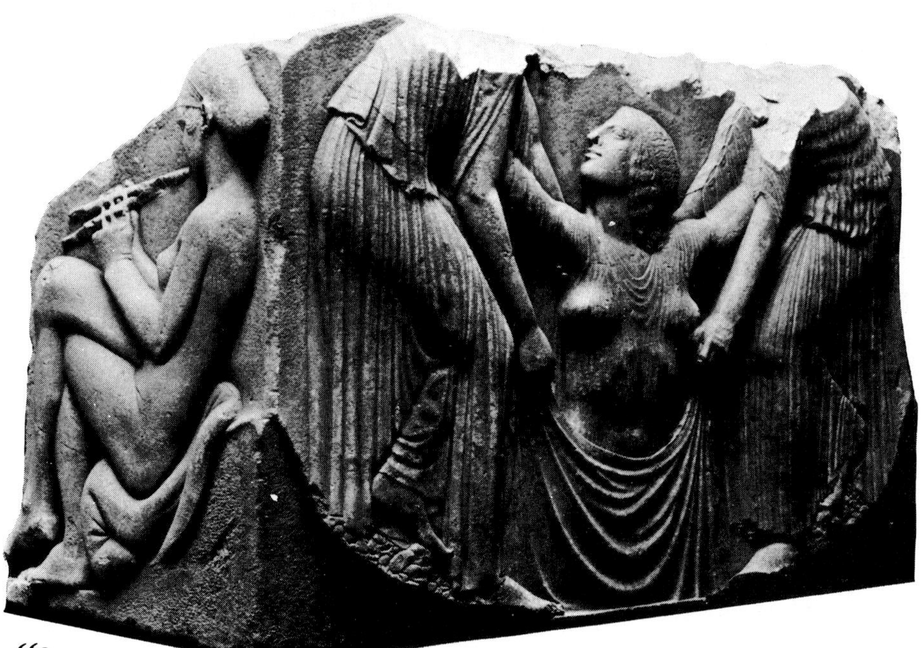

66c

66 **a** Marble relief. Rome, Villa Albani. Early fifth century. H. 1.30. (P. 203) **b** Fragmentary marble relief from Kos. Kos Museum. Beginning of fifth century. H. 0.72. (P. 200) **c** Marble three-sided relief from Rome. Rome, Museo Nazionale 8670 (152). Second quarter of fifth century. H. at corner 0.84. (Pp. 203ff., 391).

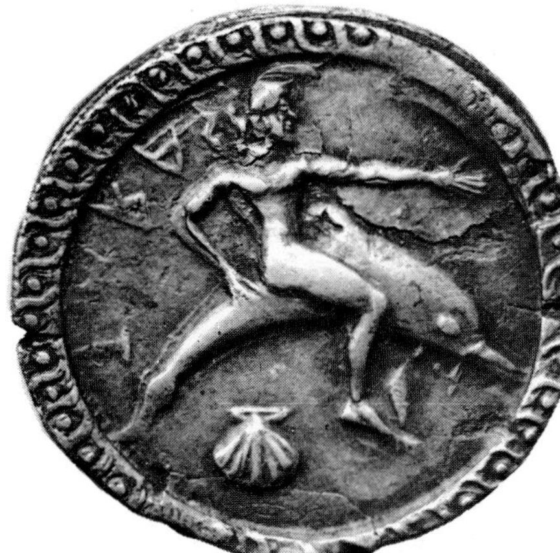

67a

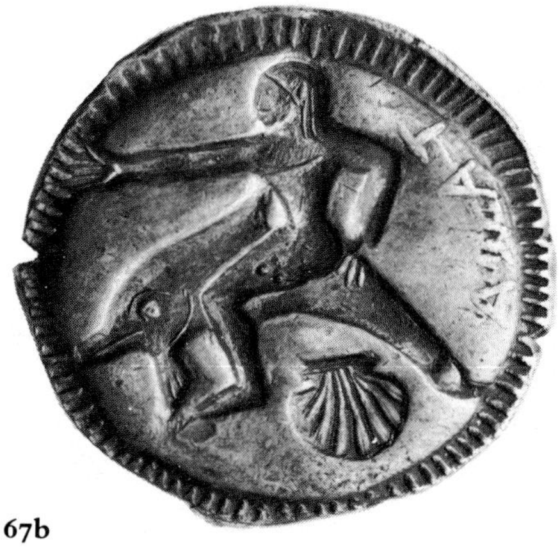

67b

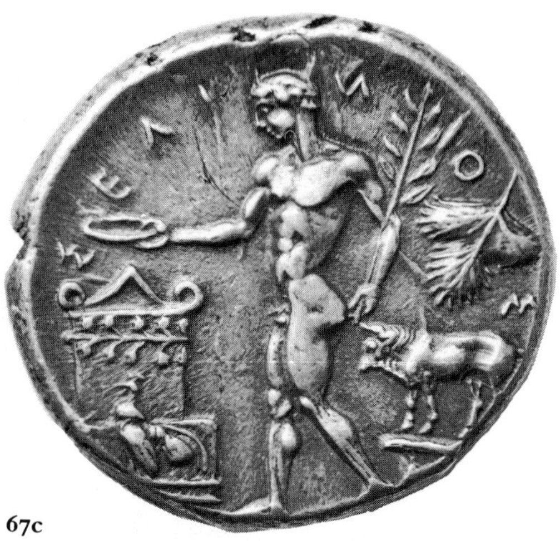

67c

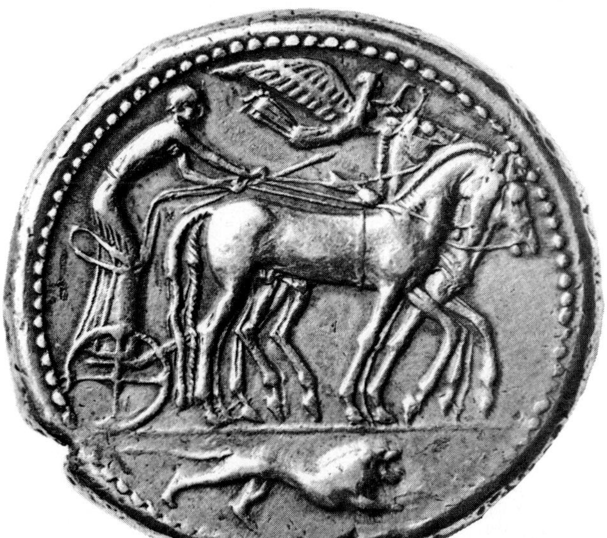

67d

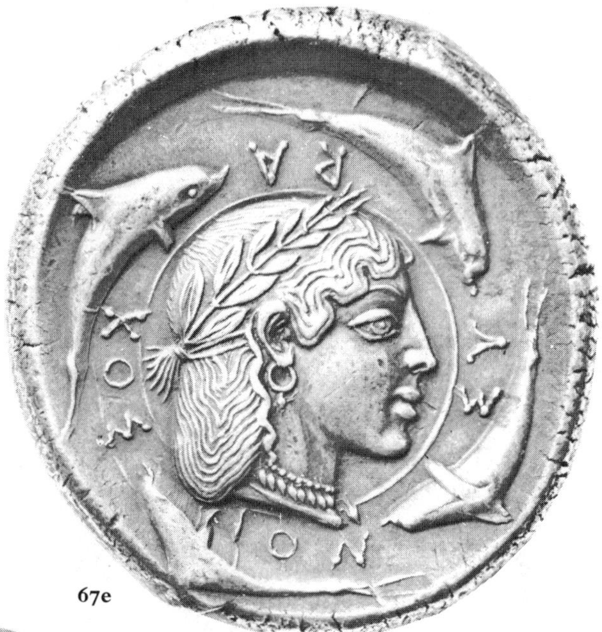

67e

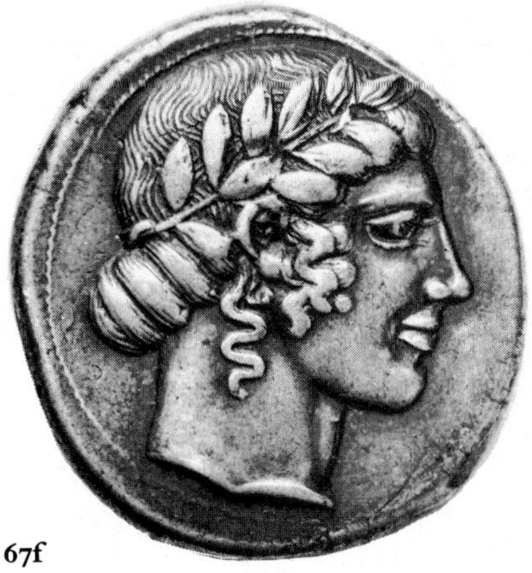

67f

67 **a** and **b** Silver stater of Taras (Tarentum, Taranto). Private Coll. About 500 B.C. D. 0.025. (P. 211) **c** Silver tetradrachm of Selinus. Brussels. Second quarter of fifth century. D. 0.027. (Pp. 211–12) **d** Silver decadrachm of Syracuse. Paris, Cabinet des Médailles. Probably second quarter of fifth century. D. 0.035. (P. 211. See also **e**) **e** Silver decadrachm of Syracuse. British Museum. As last; these two dies are always used together. (P. 211) **f** Silver tetradrachm of Leontini. Brussels. Second quarter of fifth century. D. 0.025. (P. 211).

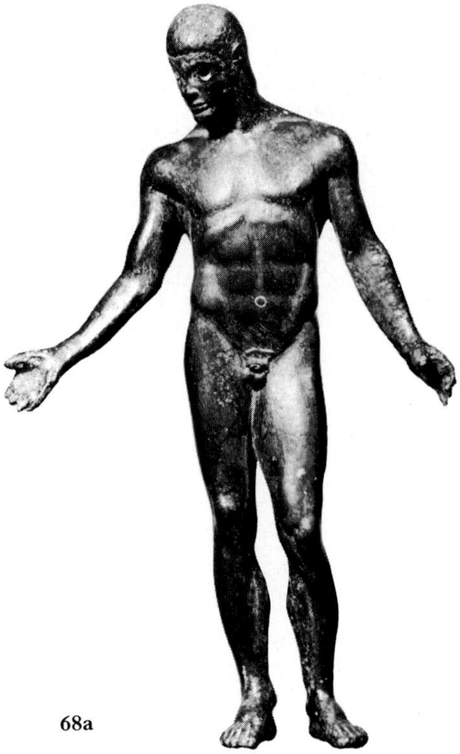

68a

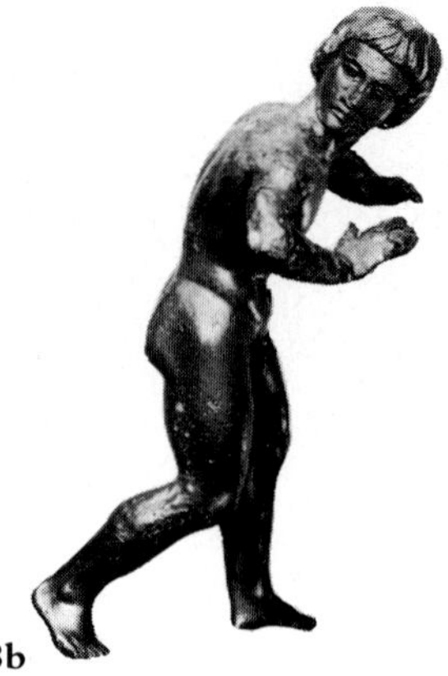

68b

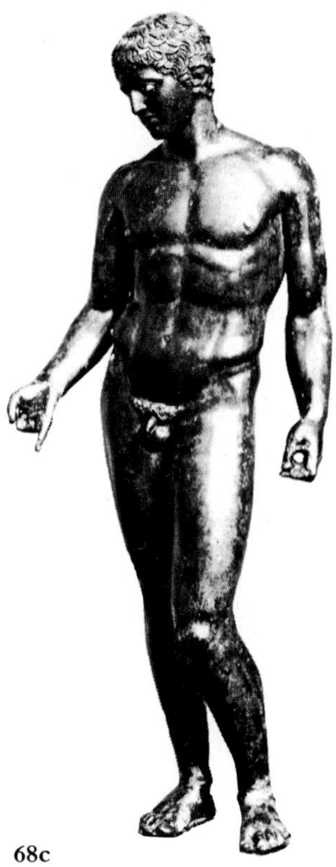

68c

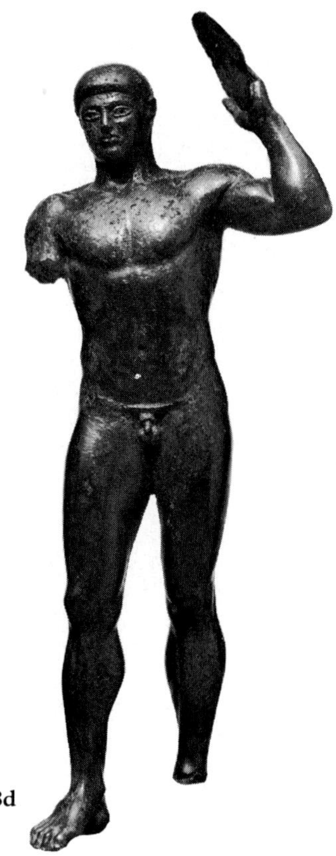

68d

68 **a** Bronze statuette from Adernò (Adrano, Sicily). Syracuse Museum. Second quarter of fifth century. H. 0.20. (P. 212) **b** Bronze statuette. Copenhagen, Thorwaldsen Museum 17. Mid fifth century. H. 0.11. (P. 212) **c** Bronze statuette. Louvre 183. Third quarter of fifth century. H. 0.21. (P. 332) **d** Bronze statuette from Peloponnese. New York, Metropolitan Museum of Art 07.286.87. Second quarter of fifth century. H. 0.23. (P. 291).

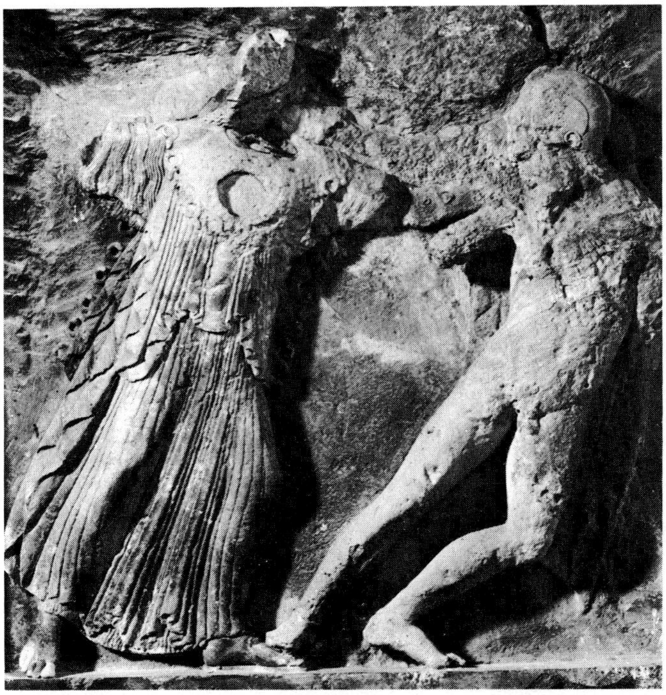

69a

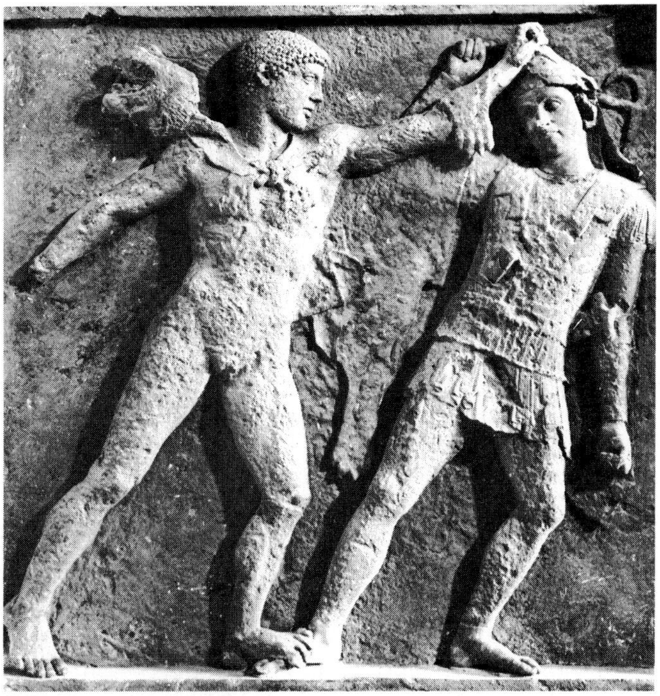

69b

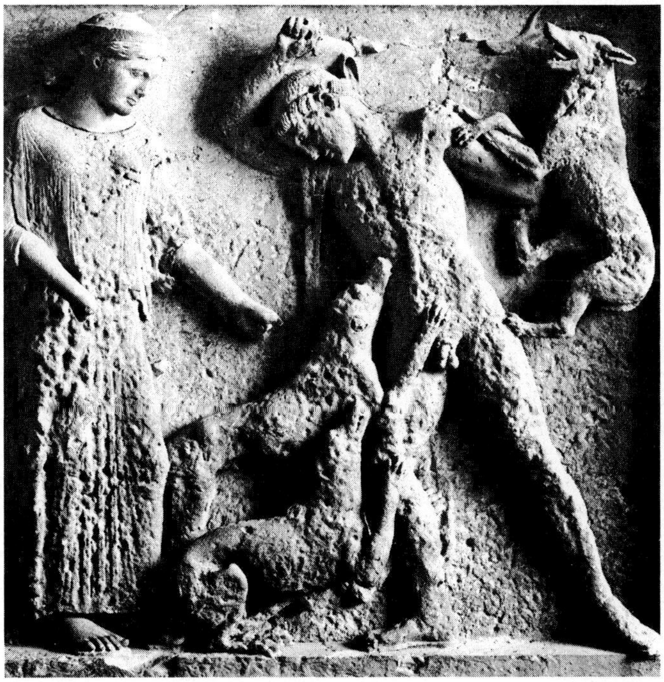

69c

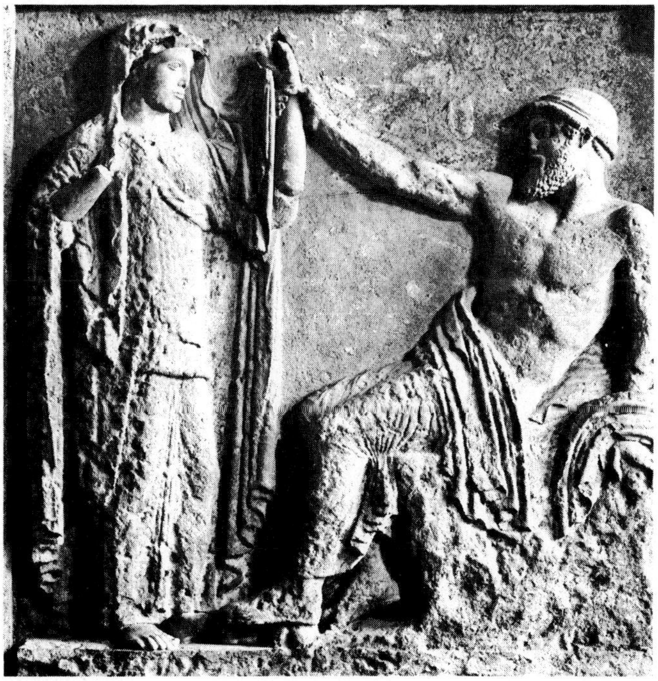

69d

69 **a–d** Limestone metopes with marble additions, from Selinus. Second quarter of fifth century. H. 1.62. (Pp. 212ff., 253, 275).

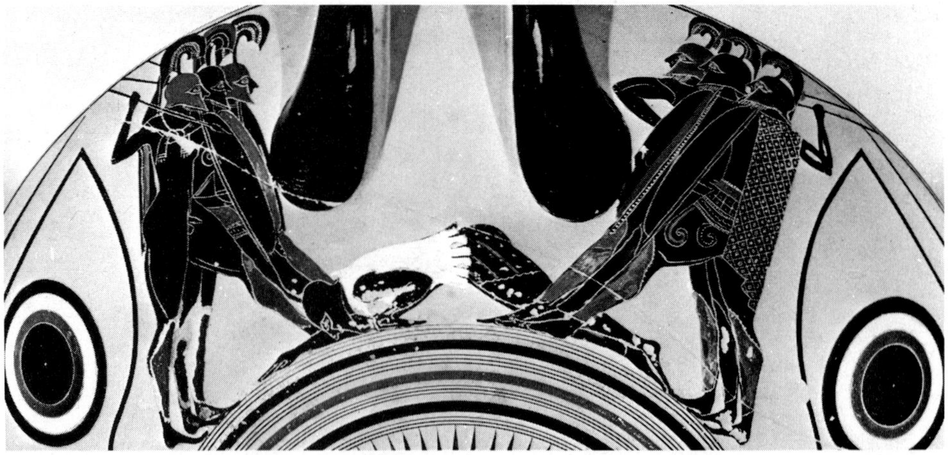

70a

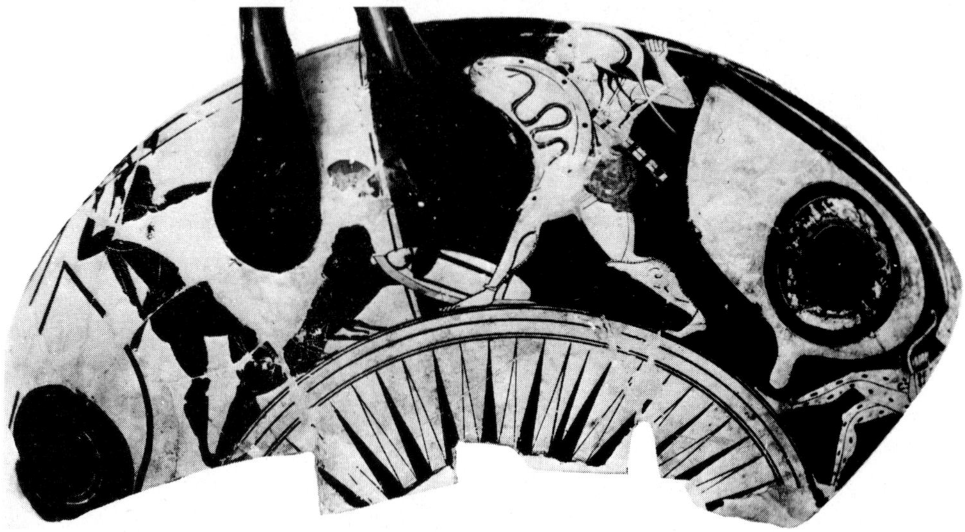

70b

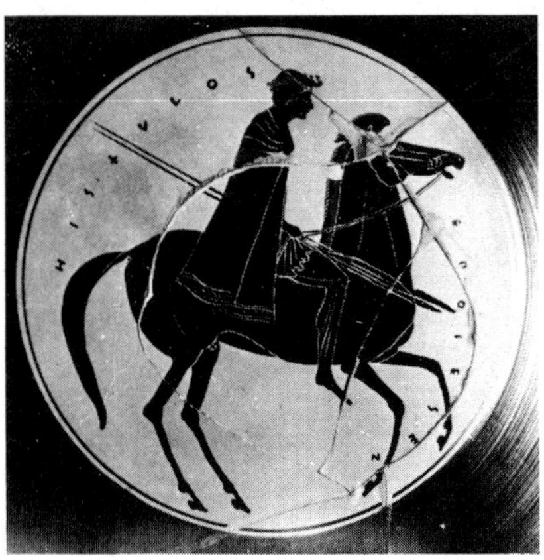

70c

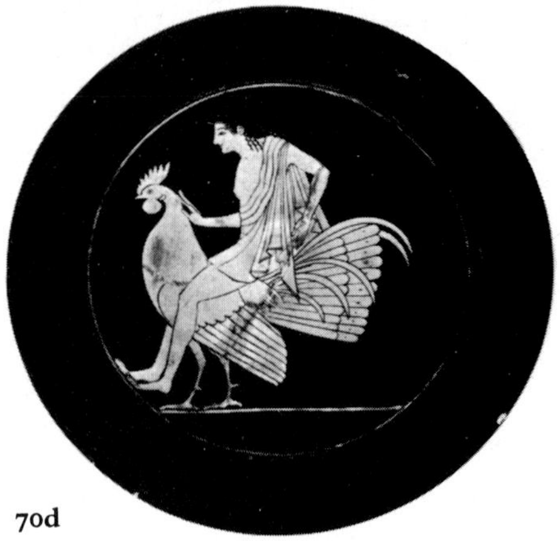

70d

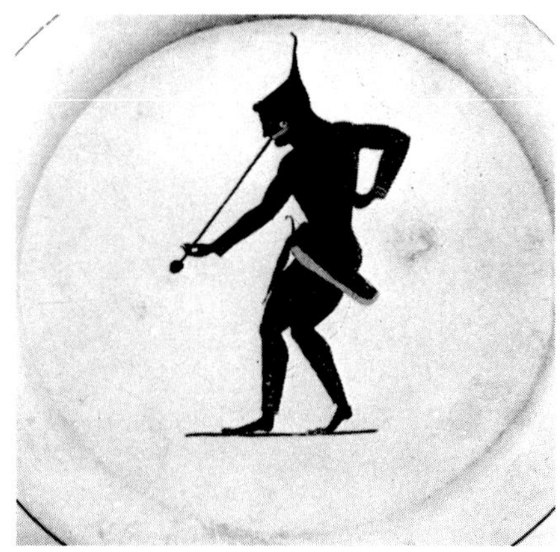

70e

70 **a** Handle-picture from cup, pl. 39b. (P. 217) **b** Handle-picture on Attic black and red-figure cup, signed by potter Andokides, from Chiusi. Palermo Museum V650. Third or last quarter of sixth century. H. of picture *c.* 0.10. (P. 217) **c** Attic black and red-figure cup (black-figure interior) signed by potter Hischylos and painter Epiktetos. British Museum E3. Last quarter of sixth century. D. of picture *c.* 0.11. (Pp. 218–19) **d** Attic red-figure plate from Vulci, signed by painter Epiktetos. Castle Ashby, Marquess of Northampton, 79. Last quarter of sixth century. D. 0.19. (P. 219) **e** Attic black-figure plate from Vulci. British Museum B591. Last quarter of sixth century. D. 0.19. (P. 219).

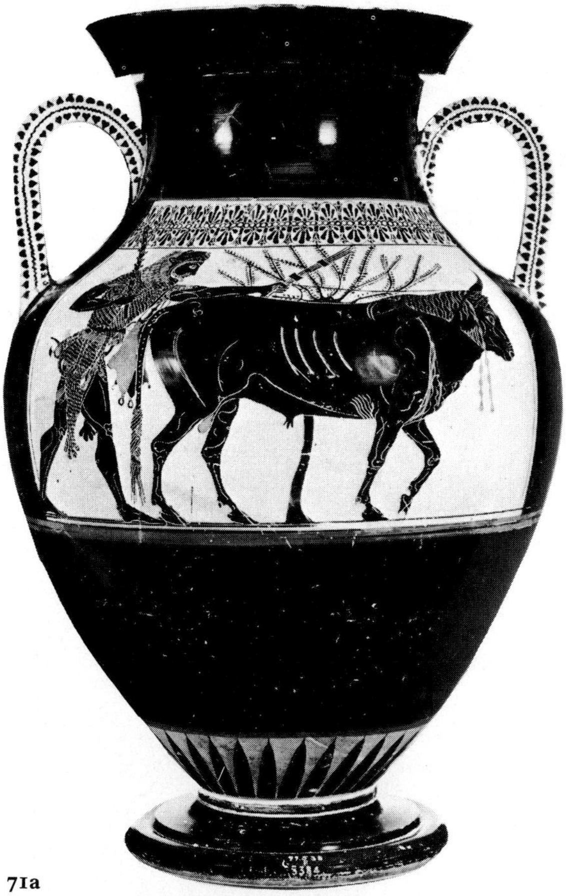

71a

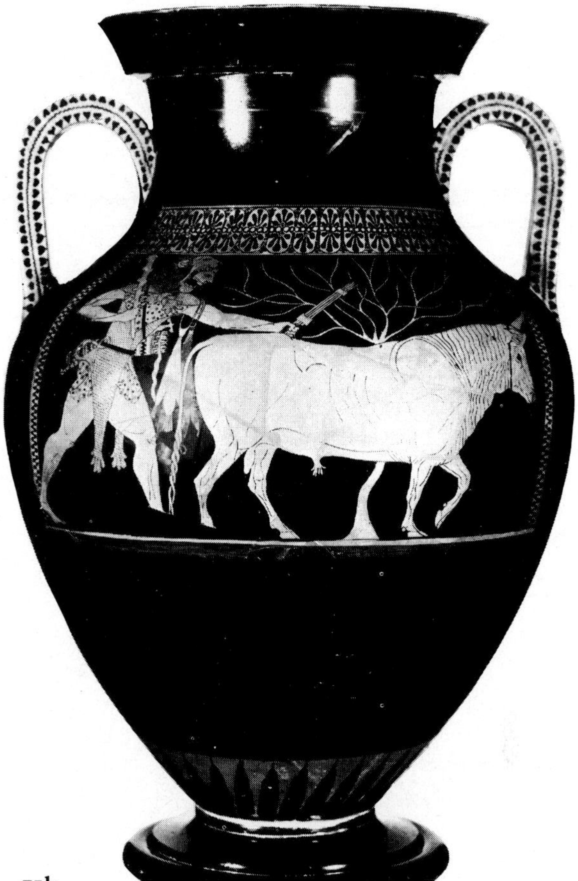

71b

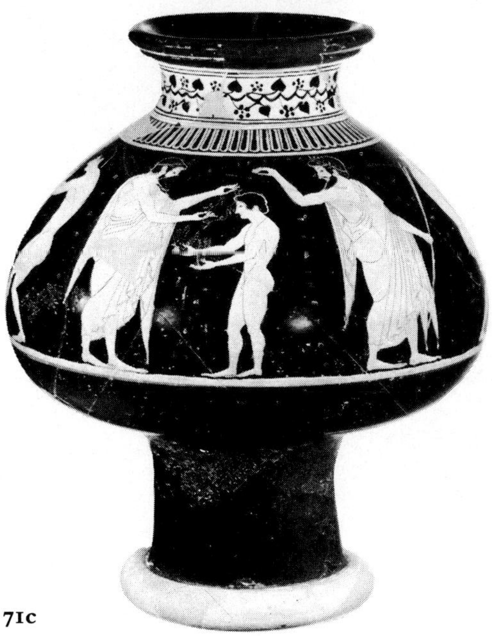

71c

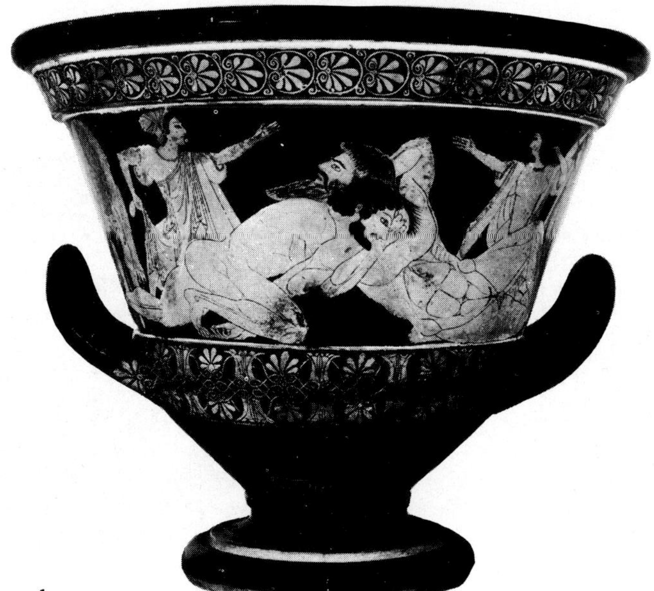

71d

71 **a** and **b** Attic black and red-figure amphora. Boston, Museum of Fine Arts 99.538, H. L. Pierce Fund. Third or last quarter of sixth century. H. 0.53. (Pp. 134, 216) **c** Attic red-figure psykter from Campagnano (north of Rome). New York, Metropolitan Museum of Art 10.210.218, Rogers Fund. Last quarter of sixth century. H. 0.34. (Pp. 218, 221) **d** Attic red-figure calyx-krater from Cervetri, signed by Euphronios as painter. Louvre G 103. Late sixth century. H. 0.46. (Pp. 221–2, 258).

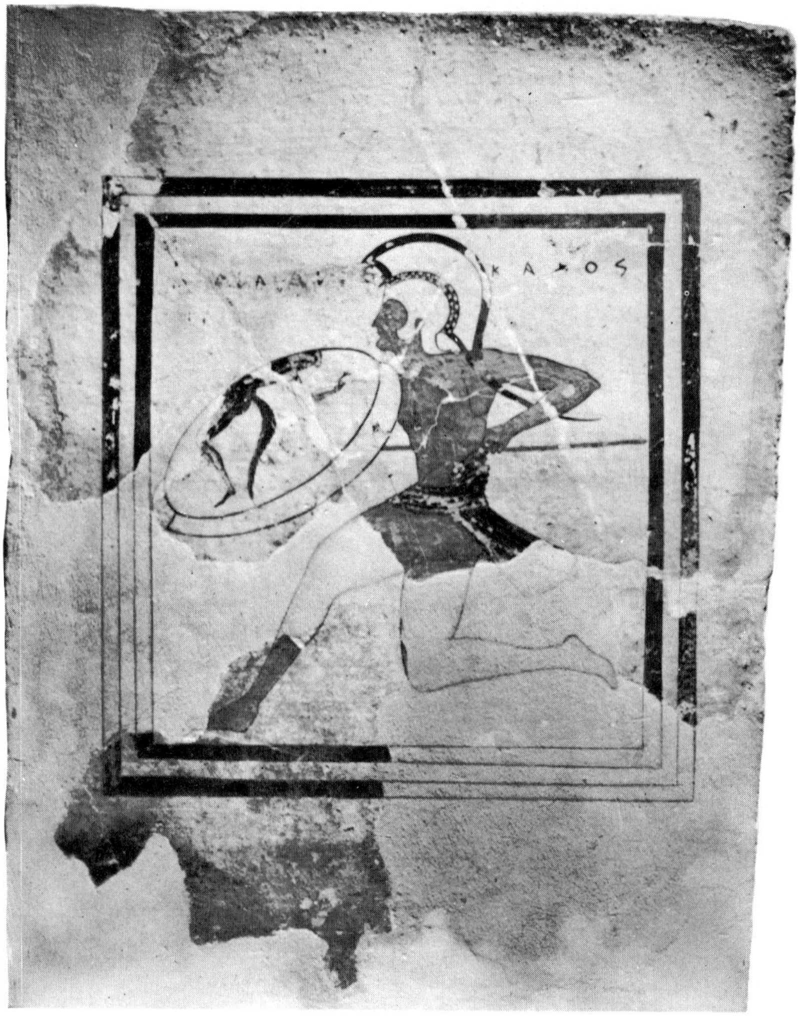

72a

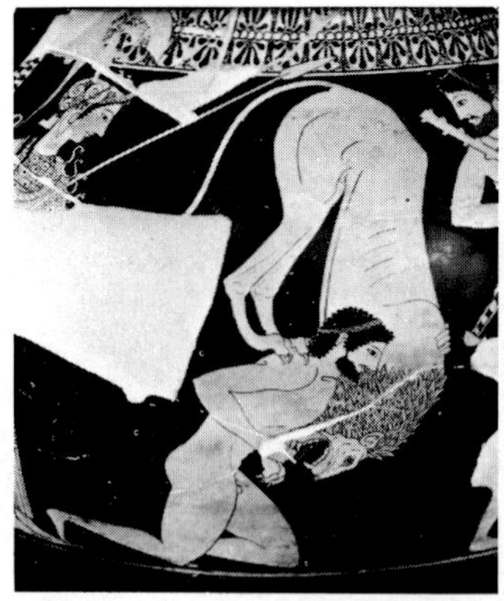

72b

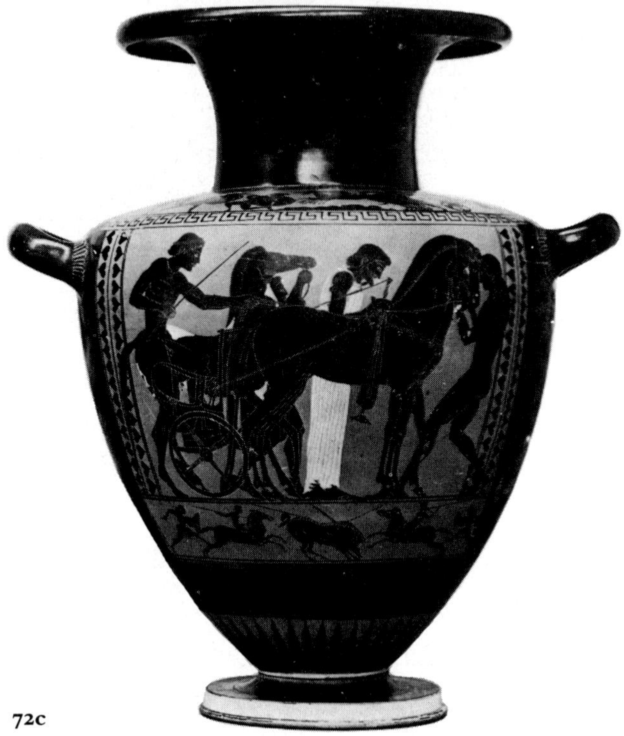

72c

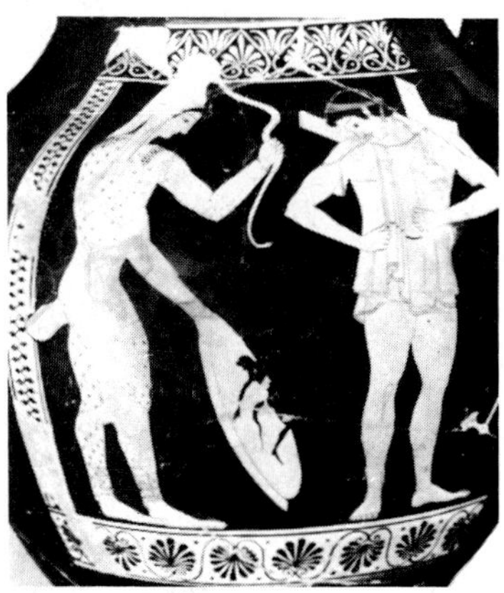

72d

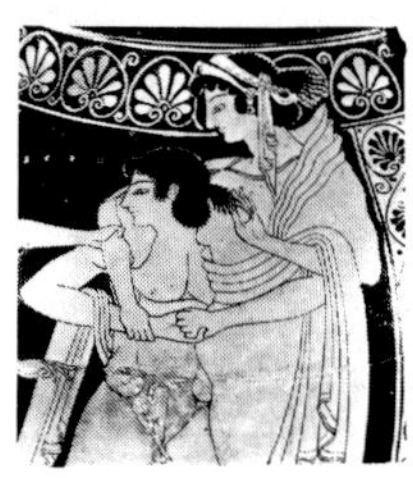

72e

72 **a** Painted clay plaque from Acropolis. Athens, Acropolis Museum 1037. Late sixth century. H. 0.65. (P. 225) **b** Attic black and red-figure amphora (red-figure detail), from Etruria. British Museum B 193. Third or last quarter of sixth century. H. of picture *c.* 0.24. (P. 222) **c** Attic black-figure hydria from Vulci. British Museum B 304. Third or last quarter of sixth century. H. 0.46. (Pp. 217, 220, 364) **d** Detail of Attic red-figure amphora from Vulci, signed by painter Euthymides. Munich 2308. Late sixth century. H. of picture *c.* 0.25. (Pp. 223, 228; cf. pl. 74c) **e** Detail of Attic red-figure amphora from Vulci, signed by painter Euthymides. Munich 2309. Late sixth century. H. of detail *c.* 0.14. (P. 224).

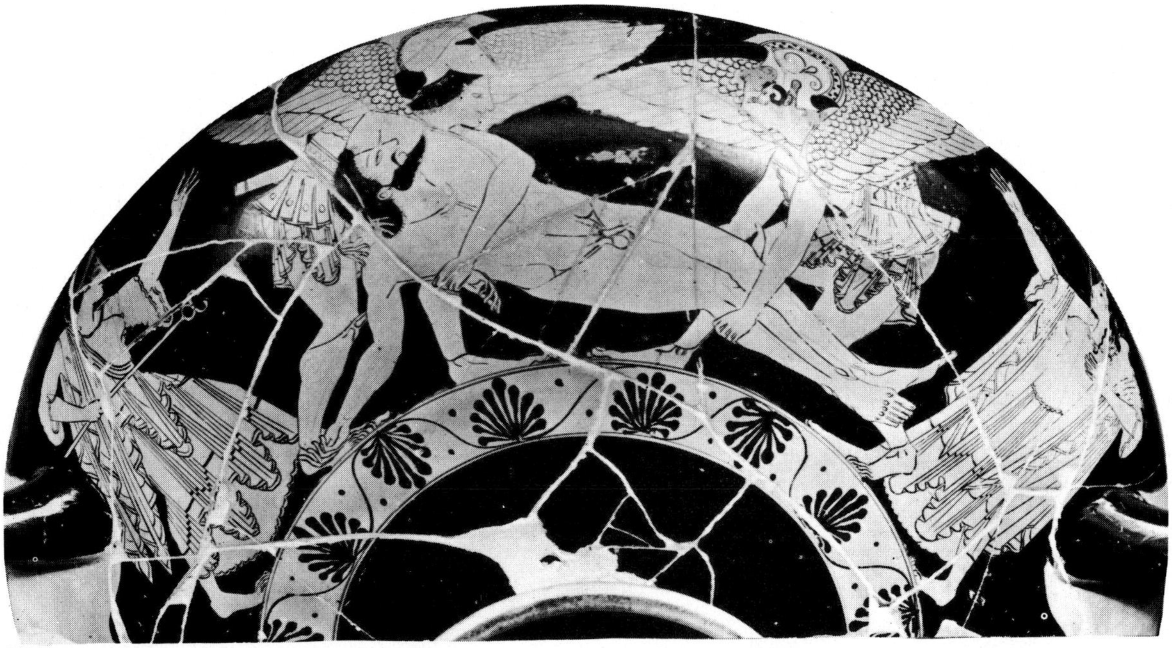

73a

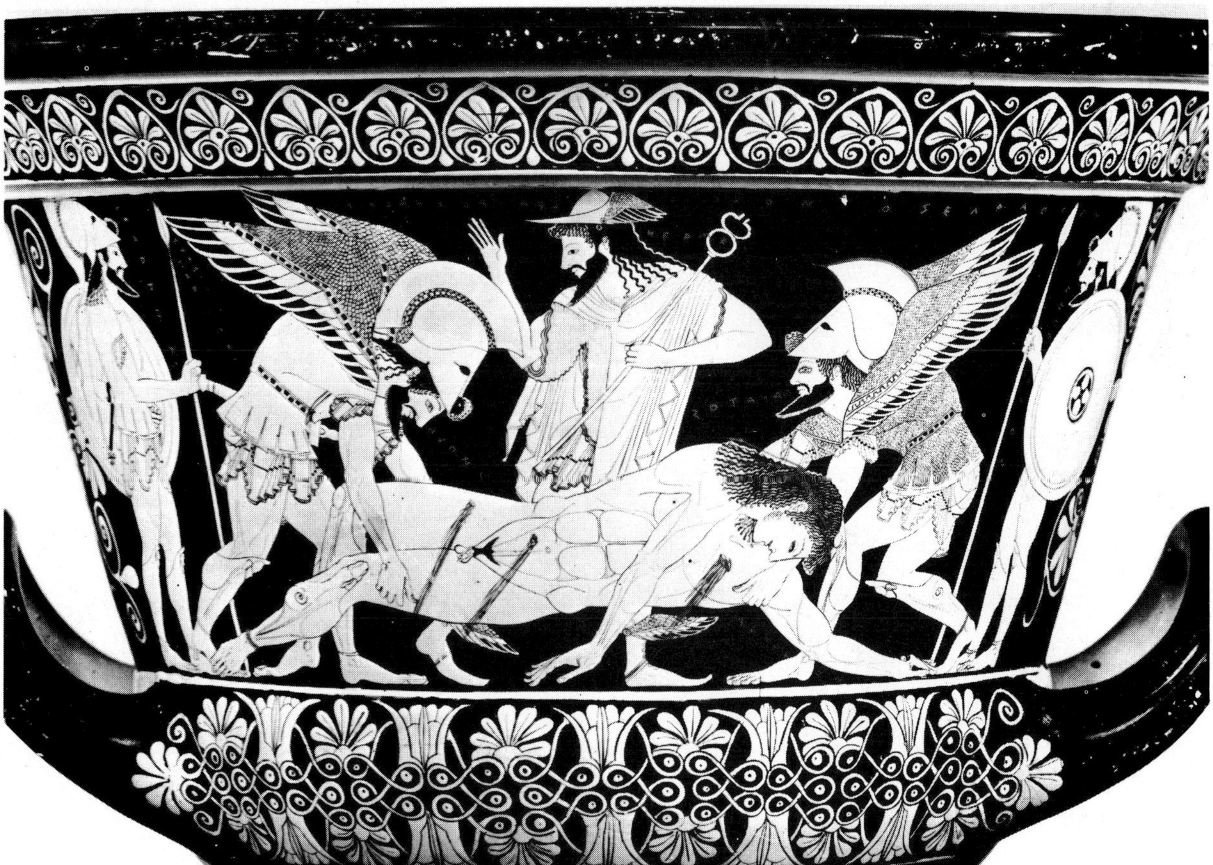

73b

73 **a** Picture on Attic red-figure cup, signed by potter Pamphaios, from Vulci. British Museum E 12. Late sixth century. H. of picture *c.* 0.11. (Pp. 326, 408) **b** Picture on Attic red-figure calyx-krater, signed by potter Euxitheos and painter Euphronios. New York, Metropolitan Museum of Art, Bequest of Joseph V. Durkheim, by exchange. Late sixth century. H. of picture 0.19. (Pp. 222, 326).

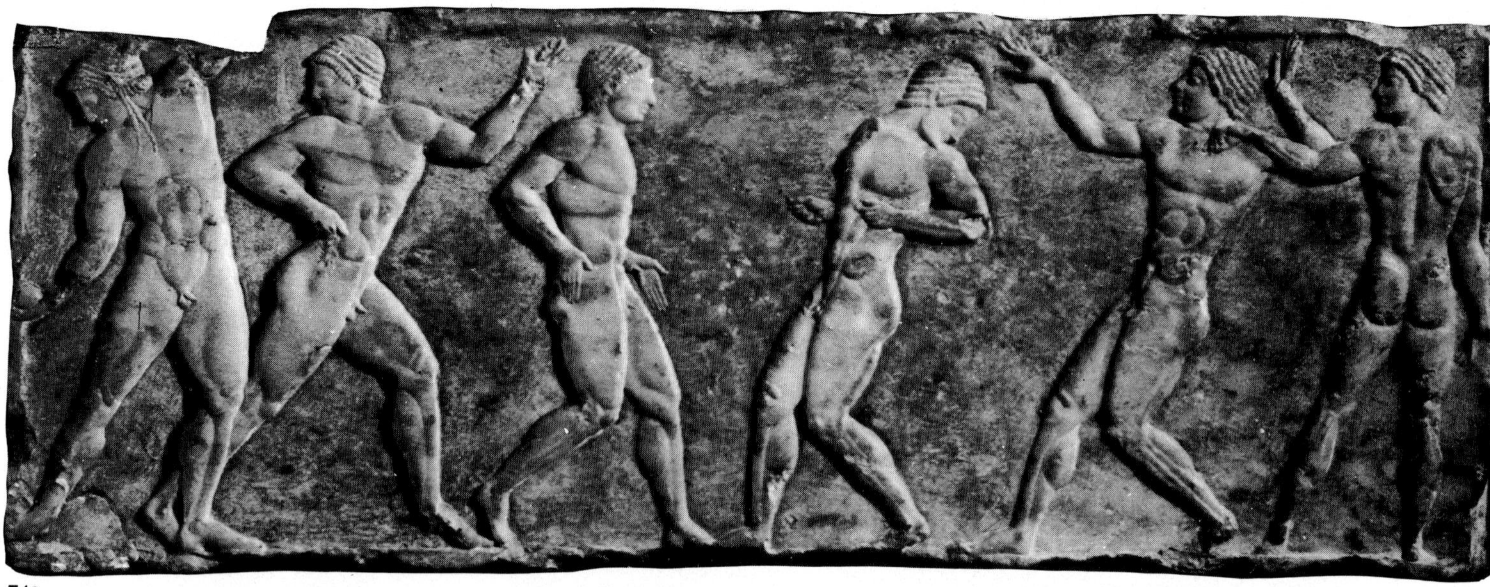

74a

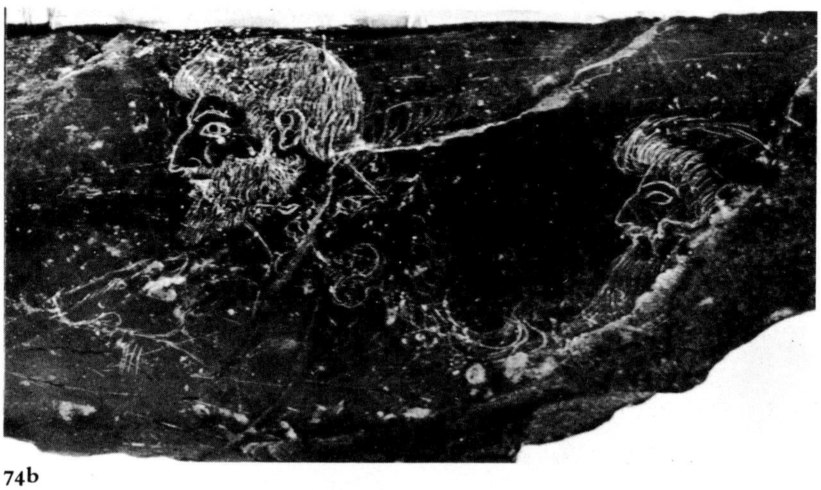

74b

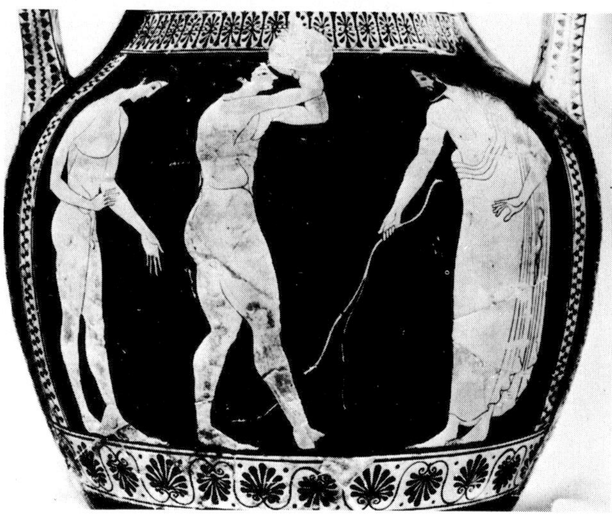

74c

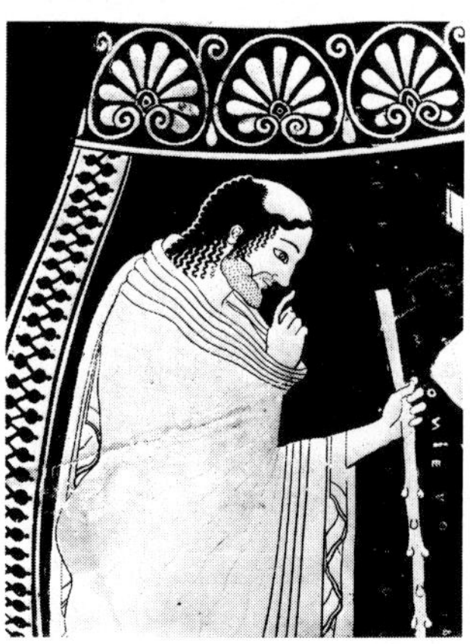

74d

74 **a** Marble relief on statue-base from Athens. Athens, National Museum 3476. Late sixth century. H. 0.29. (Pp. 107, 227) **b** Fragment of stone statue of Darius from Persepolis. New York, Metropolitan Museum of Art 45.11.17, Rogers Fund. Late sixth or early fifth century. L. *c.* 0.15. (P. 201) **c** Picture on back of vase, pl. 72d. H. of picture *c.* 0.25. (P. 223) **d** Detail of Attic red-figure amphora from Vulci. Munich 2307. Late sixth century. H. of detail *c.* 0.10. (Pp. 223, 263; cf. pl. 82a).

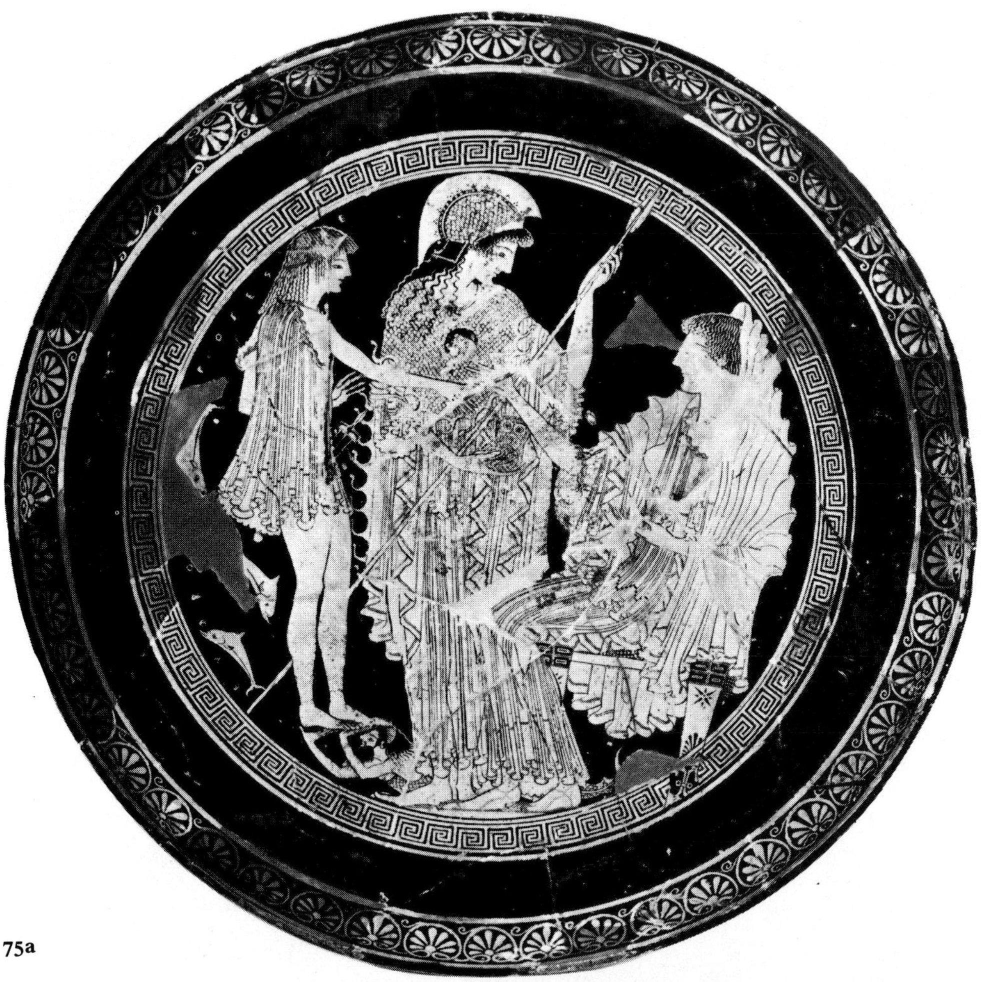

75a

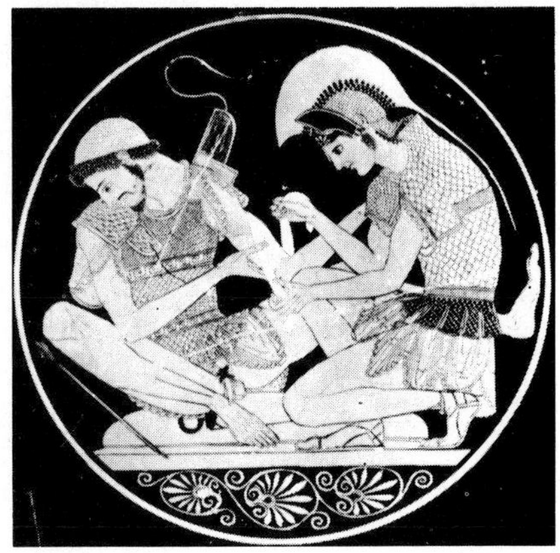

75b

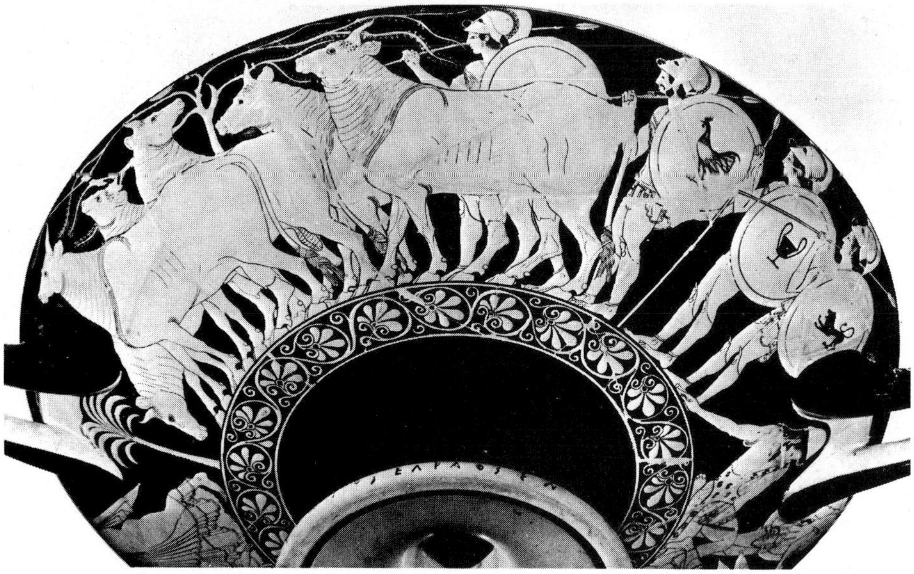

75c

75 **a** Picture in interior of Attic red-figure cup from Cervetri signed by Euphronios as potter. Louvre G 104. Beginning of fifth century. D. 0.39. (Pp. 230, 242) **b** Picture in interior of Attic red-figure cup from Vulci, signed by potter Sosias. Berlin (Charlottenburg) 2278. End of sixth century. D. of picture 0.18. (Pp. 229, 261) **c** Picture from exterior of cup, pl. 39c. H. of picture *c.* 0.13. (P. 228).

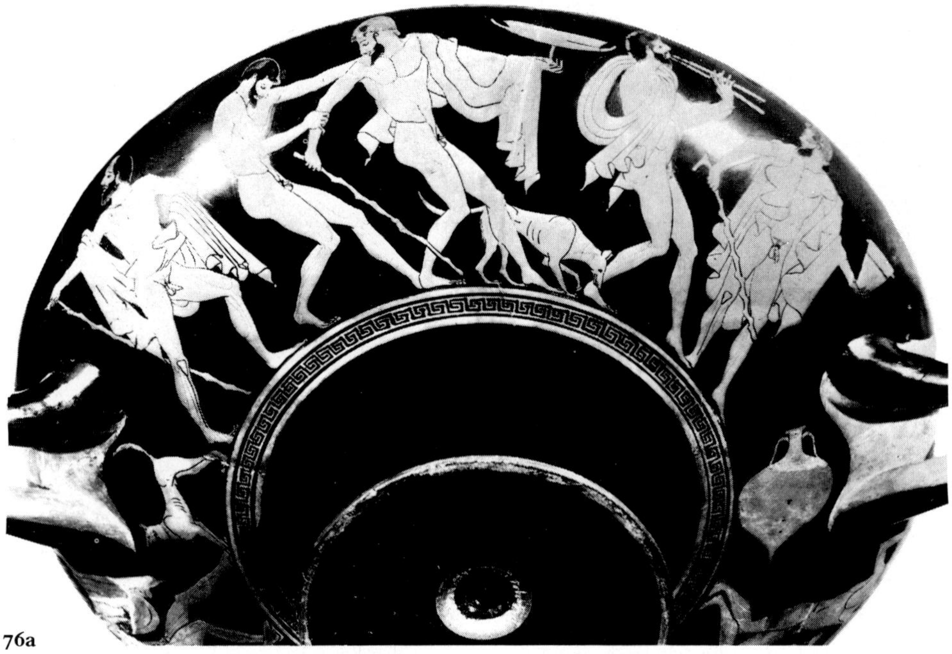

76a

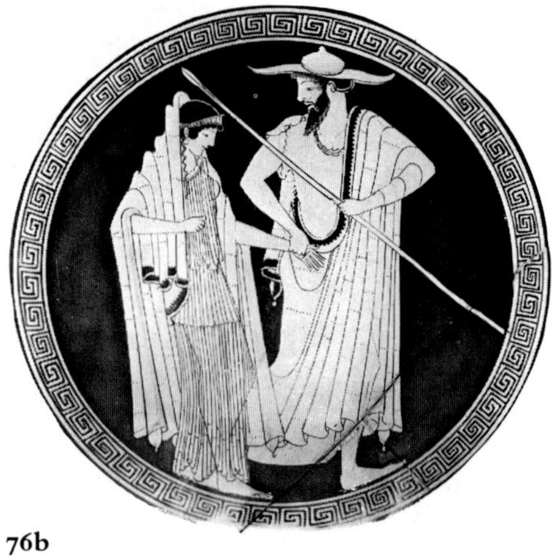

76b

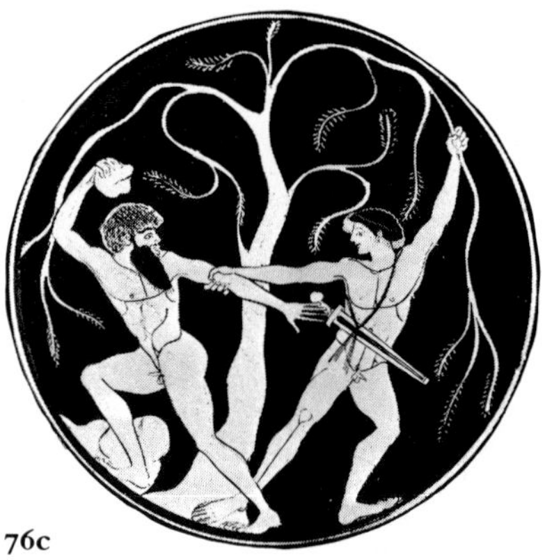

76c

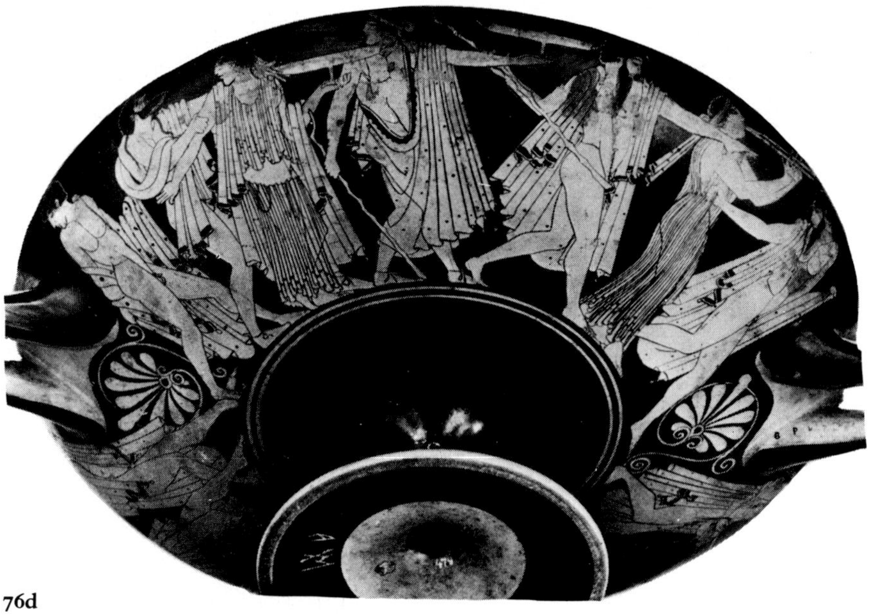

76d

76 **a** Picture on exterior of Attic red-figure cup from near Viterbo, signed by Euphronios as potter. Boston, Museum of Fine Arts 95.27, Catharine Page Perkins Fund. Early fifth century. H. of picture *c.* 0.11. (P. 230) **b** Picture on interior of Attic red-figure cup from Vulci. British Museum E69. First quarter of fifth century. D. of picture *c.* 0.16. (P. 232) **c** Picture on interior of Attic red-figure cup. Munich 8771. Early fifth century. D. of picture *c.* 0.13. (Pp. 229, 276) **d** Picture on exterior of Attic red-figure cup from Vulci, signed by potter Brygos. Würzburg 479. First quarter of fifth century. H. of picture *c.* 0.10. (P. 230).

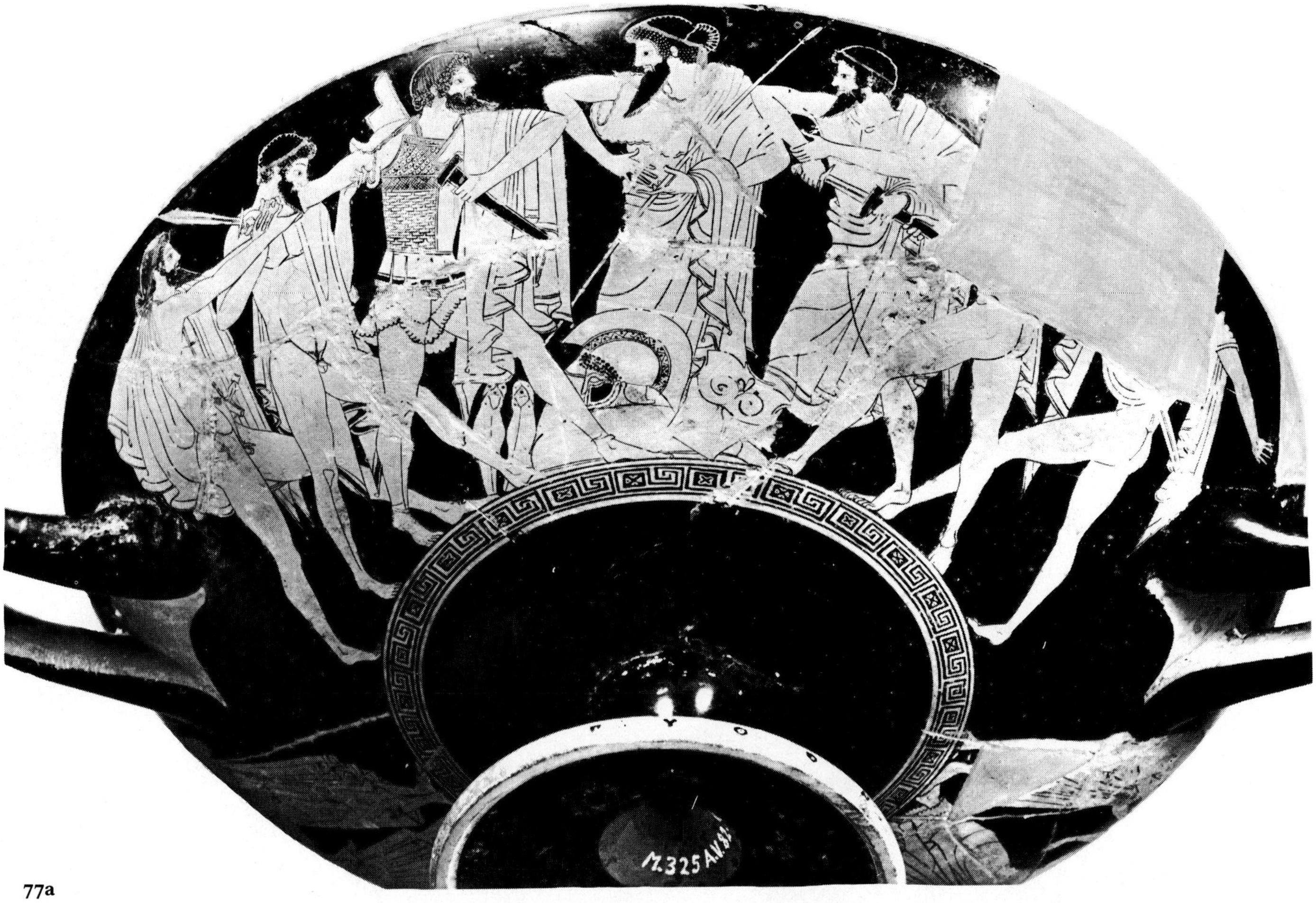

77a

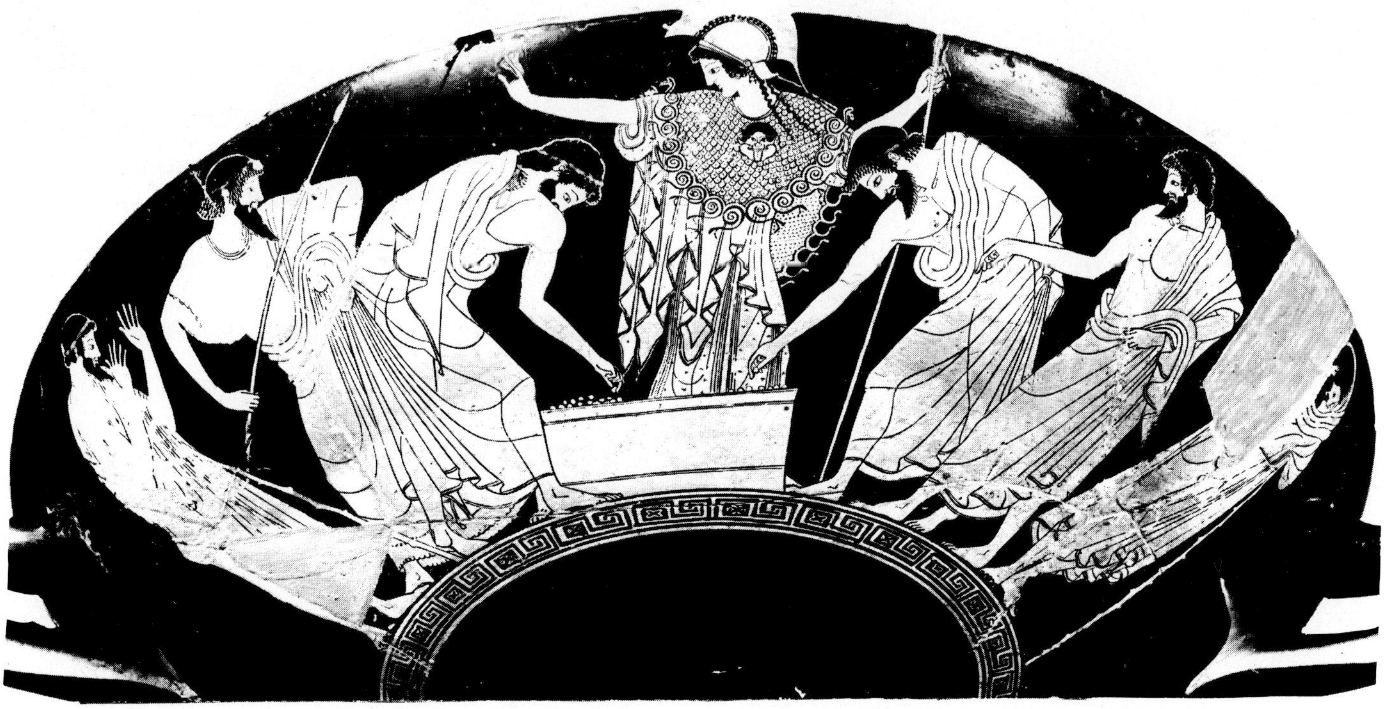

77b

77 **a** and **b** Pictures from exterior of Attic red-figure cup from Cervetri, signed by painter Douris and with name of Python (potter). Vienna 3695. H. of pictures *c.* 0.11 (Pp. 232, 412).

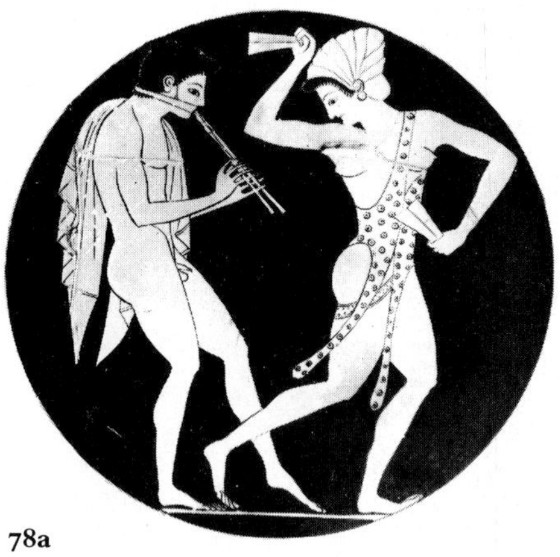

78a

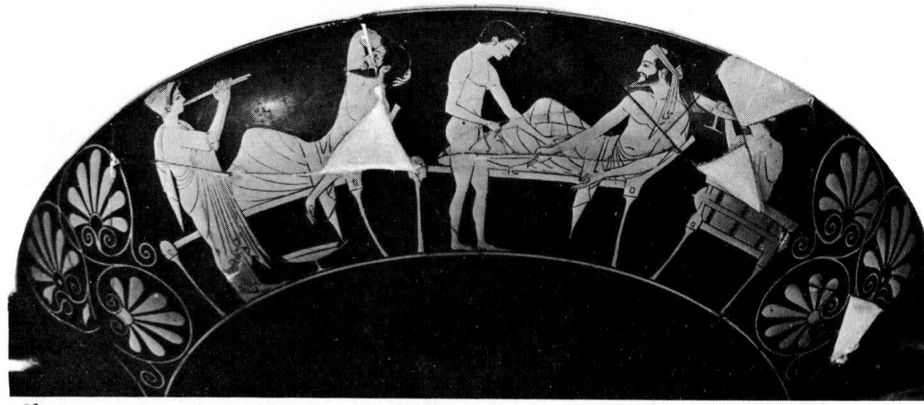

78b

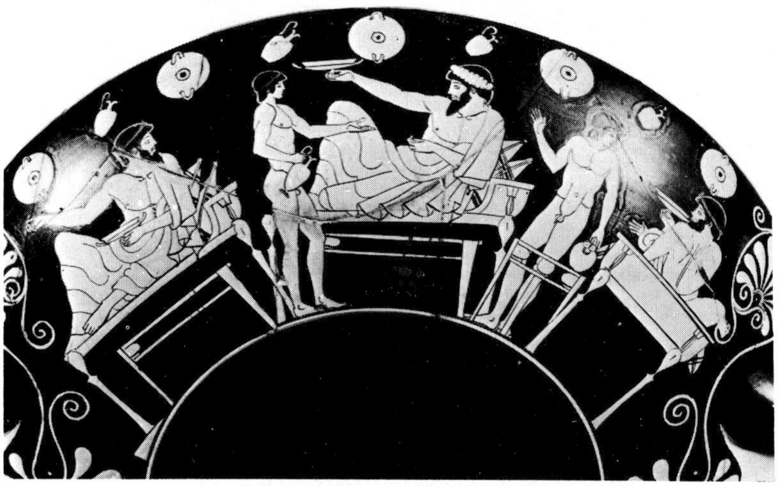

78c

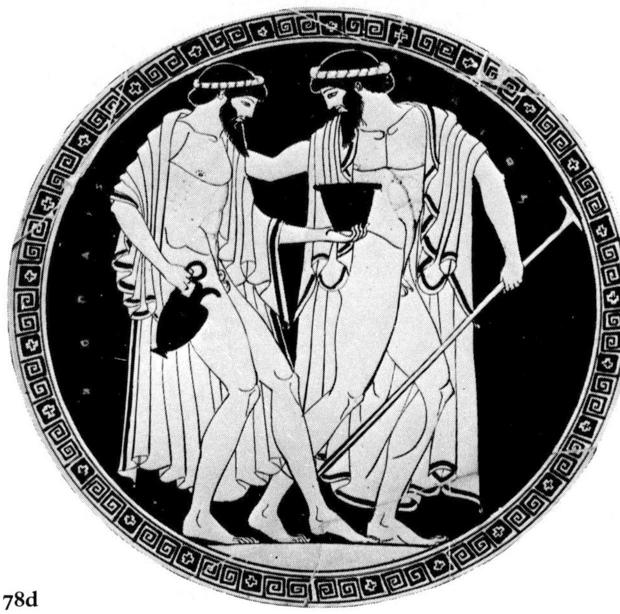

78d

78 **a** Picture on interior of cup from Vulci, signed by potter Python and painter Epiktetos. British Museum E 38. First quarter of fifth century. D. of picture *c.* 0.14. (Pp. 219, 232) **b** Picture on exterior of same cup. H. of picture *c.* 0.08. (Pp. 219, 232) **c** Picture on exterior of Attic red-figure cup from Vulci, signed by painter Douris. British Museum E 49. First quarter of fifth century. H. of picture *c.* 0.10. (P. 232) **d** Picture on interior of Attic red-figure cup from Vulci. British Museum E 54. First quarter of fifth century. D. of picture *c.* 0.20. (Pp. 231–2).

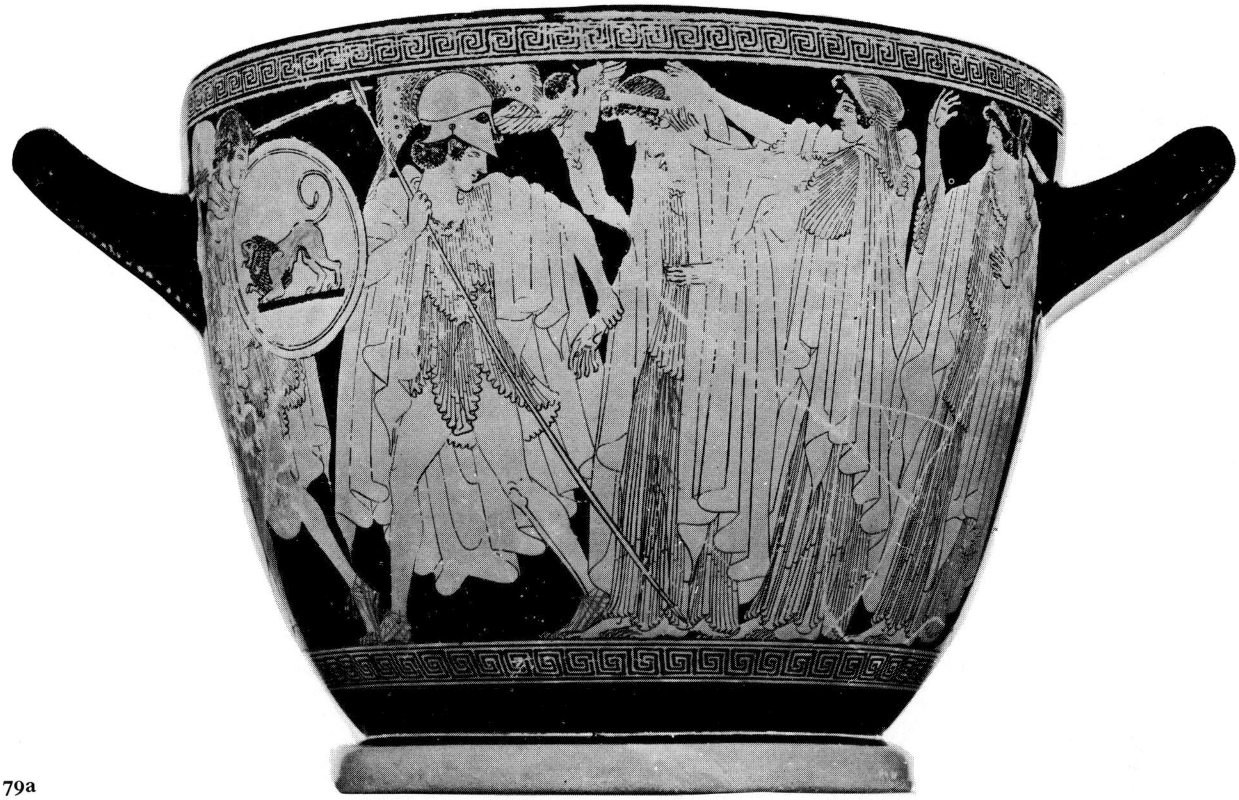

79a

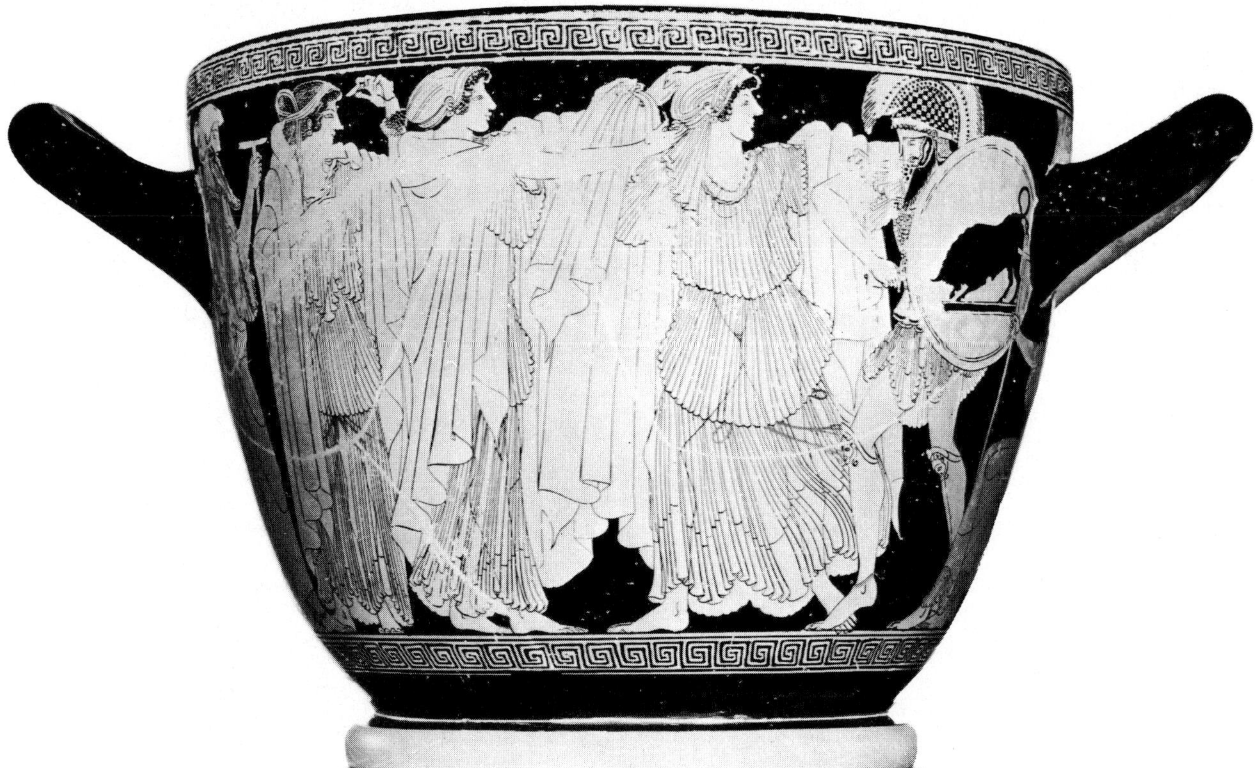

79b

79 **a** and **b** Attic red-figure skyphos from Suessula (province of Naples), signed by potter Hieron and painter Makron. Boston, Museum of Fine Arts 13.186. First quarter of fifth century. H. 0.21. (Pp. 231, 264).

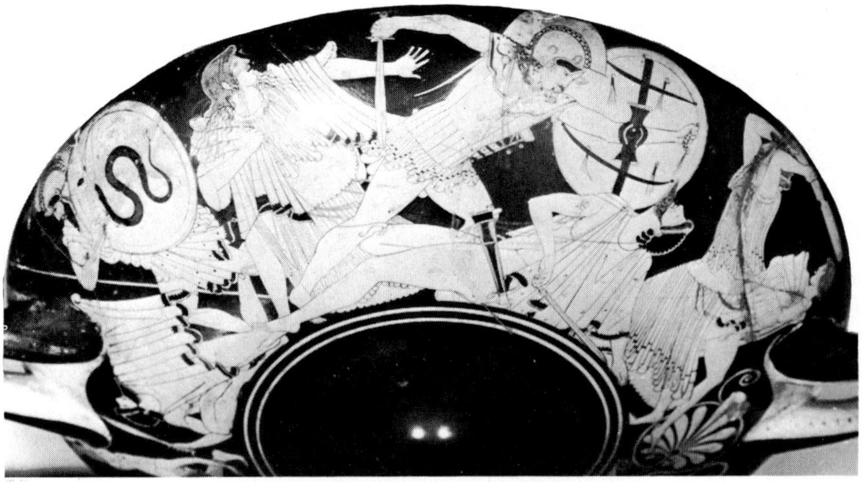

80a

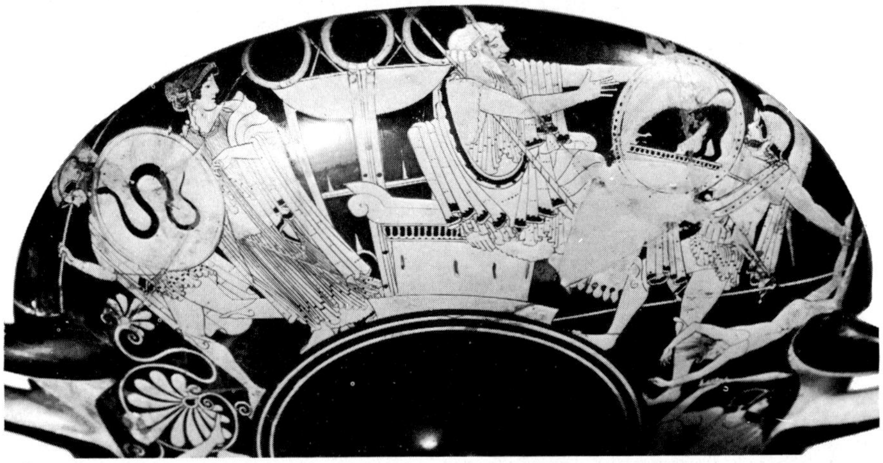

80b

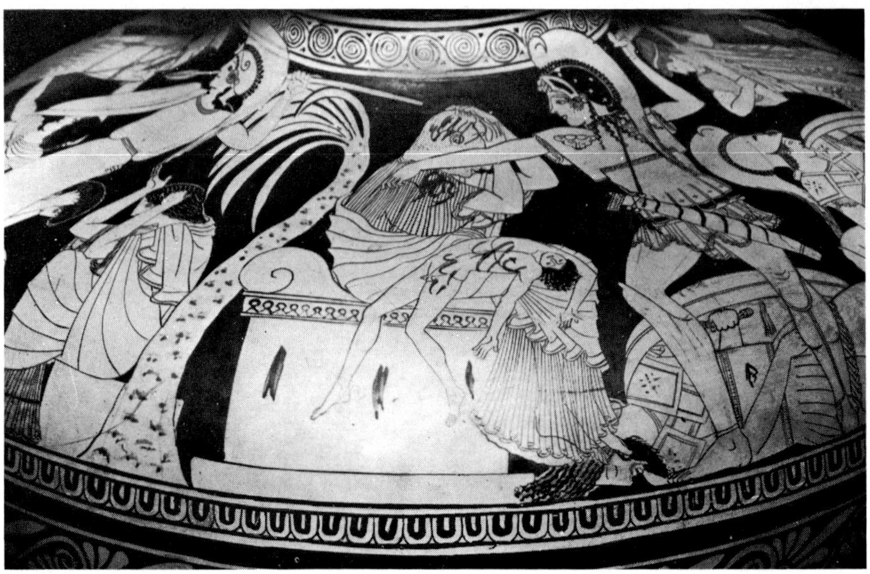

80c

80 **a** and **b** Pictures from exterior of Attic red-figure cup from Vulci, signed by potter Brygos. Louvre G 152. First quarter of fifth century. H. of pictures *c.* 0.12. (Pp. 232–3, 250) **c** Detail from picture on Attic red-figure hydria from Nola. Naples 2422. First quarter of fifth century. H. of picture *c.* 0.17. (Pp. 233ff., 250–1).

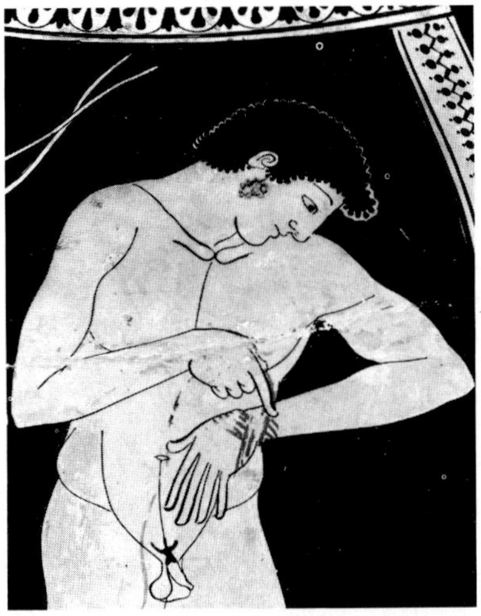

81a

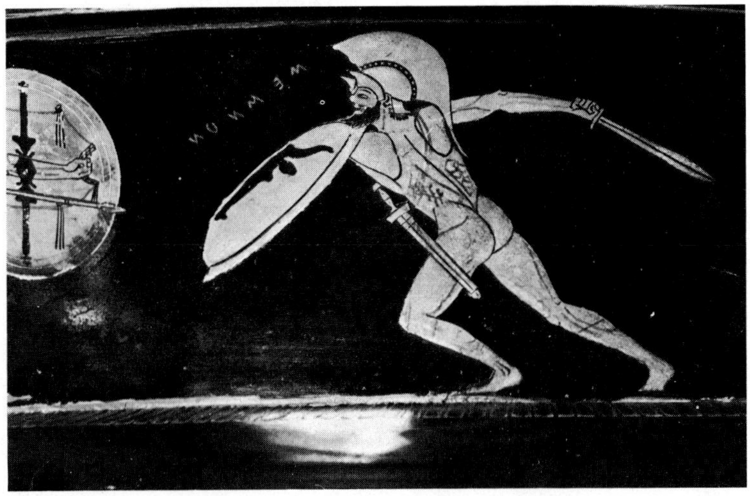

81b

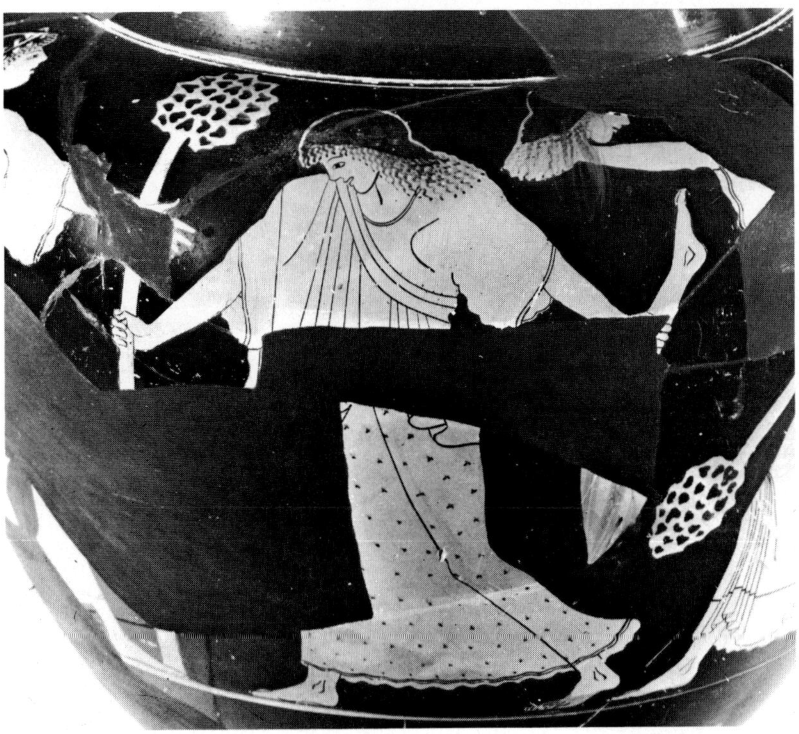

81c

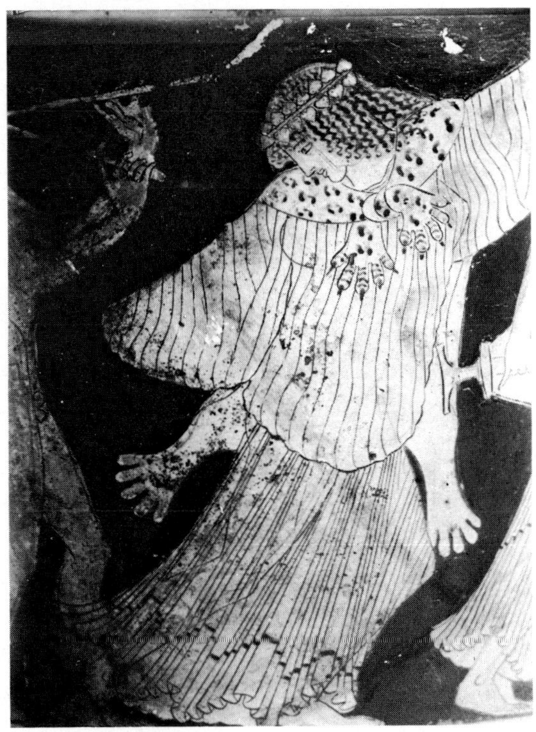

81d

81 **a** Detail from picture on Attic red-figure amphora from Vulci. Munich 2305. End of sixth or beginning of fifth century. H. of detail *c.* 0.12. (P. 235) **b** Detail from picture on back of vase, pl. 83d. H. of picture *c.* 0.10. (Pp. 238–9) **c** Detail from picture on Attic red-figure stamnos from Cervetri. Oxford, Ashmolean Museum 1912.1165. First quarter of fifth century. H. of picture *c.* 0.17. (Pp. 236, 238, 269) **d** Detail from picture on Attic red-figure calyx-krater, probably from Vulci. Louvre G 162. First quarter of fifth century. H. of picture *c.* 0.20. (Pp. 236, 238).

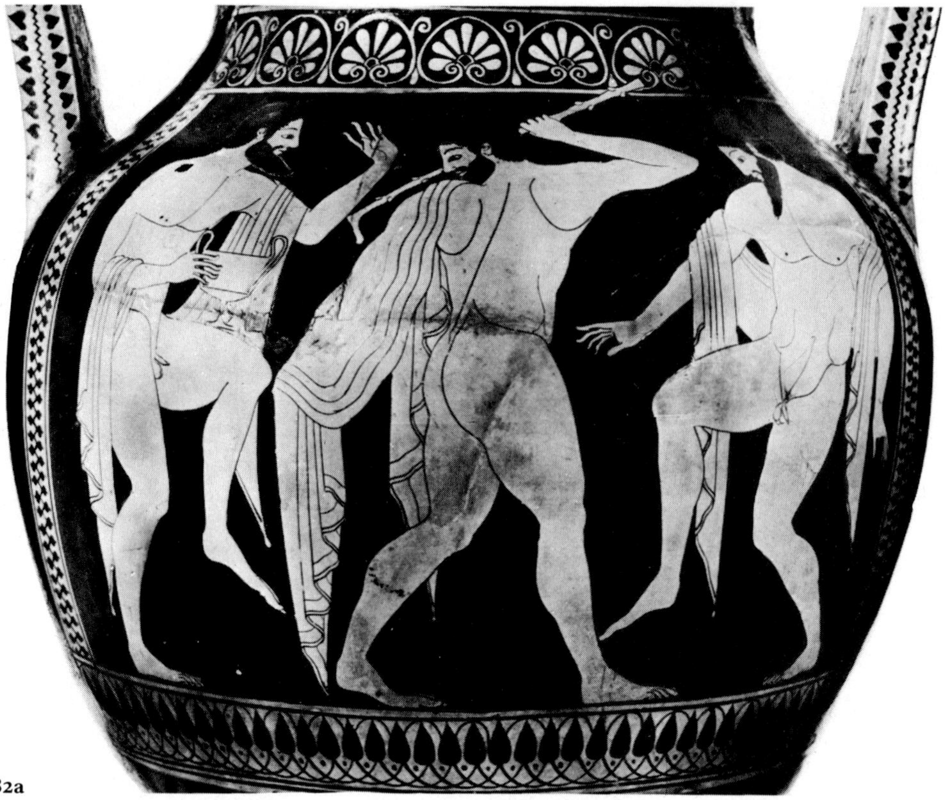

82a

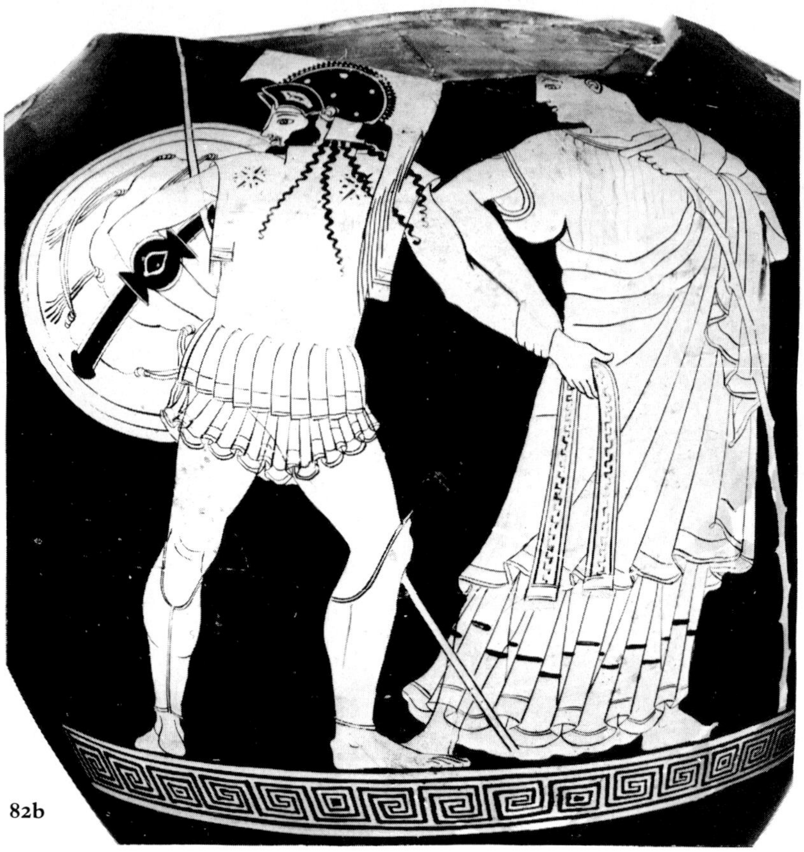

82b

82 a Picture from back of vase, pl. 74d. H. of picture *c.* 0.25. (P. 223) **b** Picture on Attic red-figure amphora from Vulci. Würzburg 508. First quarter of fifth century. H. of picture *c.* 0.29. (P. 236).

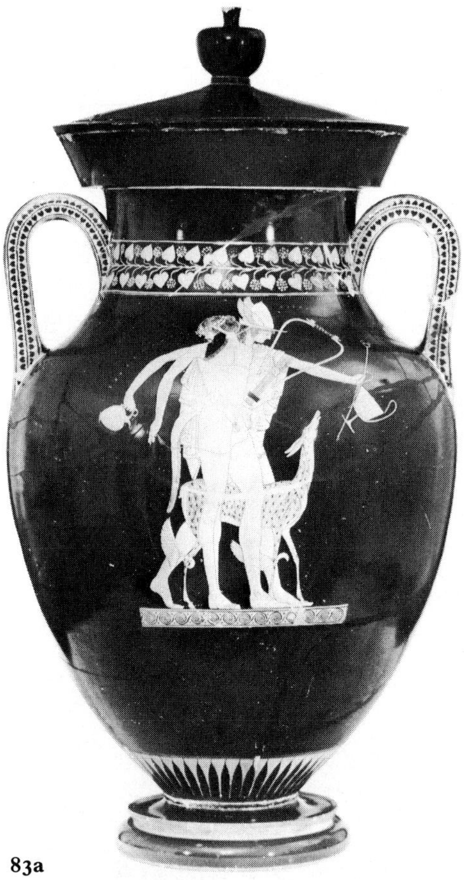

83a

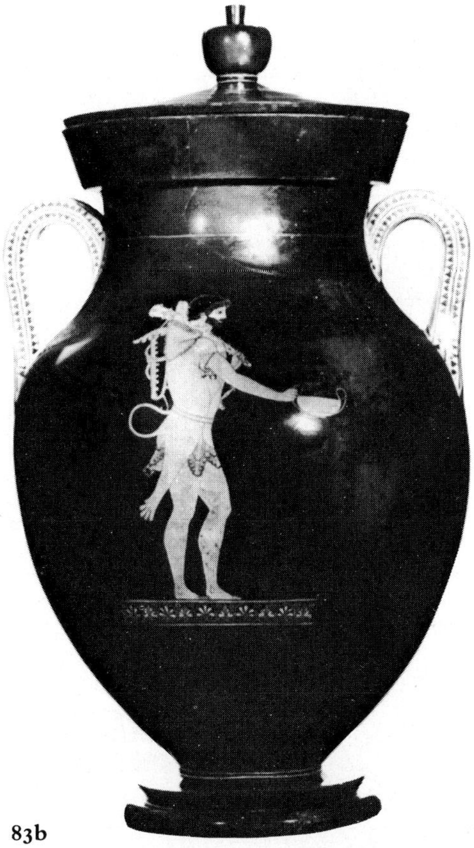

83b

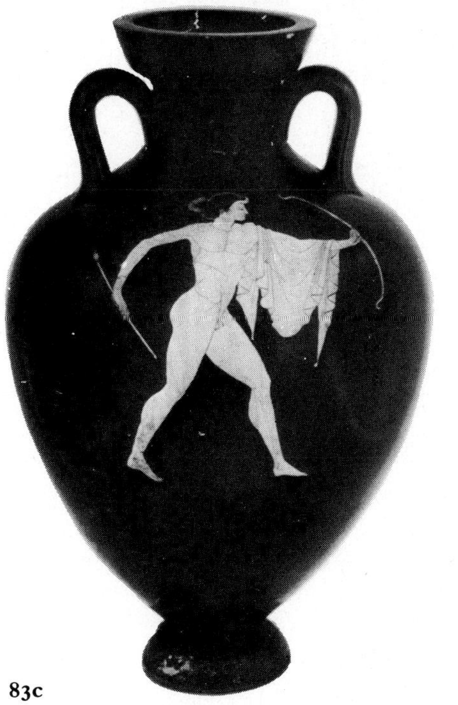

83c

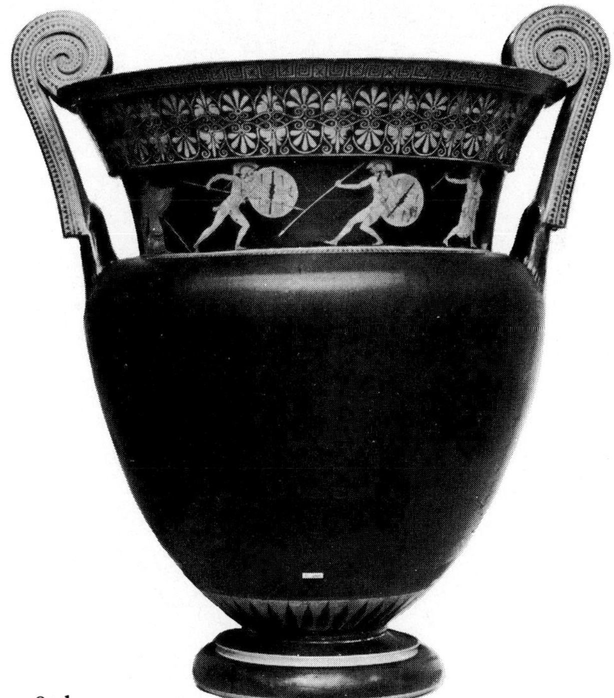

83d

83 **a** Attic red-figure amphora from Vulci. Berlin 2160. First quarter of fifth century. H. with lid 0.81. (Pp. 236–7) **b** Attic red-figure amphora. Basle, Antikenmuseum. First quarter of fifth century. H. with lid 0.79. See also pl. 12d. (P. 236) **c** Attic red-figure amphora (Panathenaic shape) from Vulci. Würzburg 500. First quarter of fifth century. H. 0.52. (P. 238) **d** Attic red-figure volute-krater from Cervetri. British Museum E468. First quarter of fifth century. H. 0.65. See also pl. 81b. (Pp. 124, 238–9).

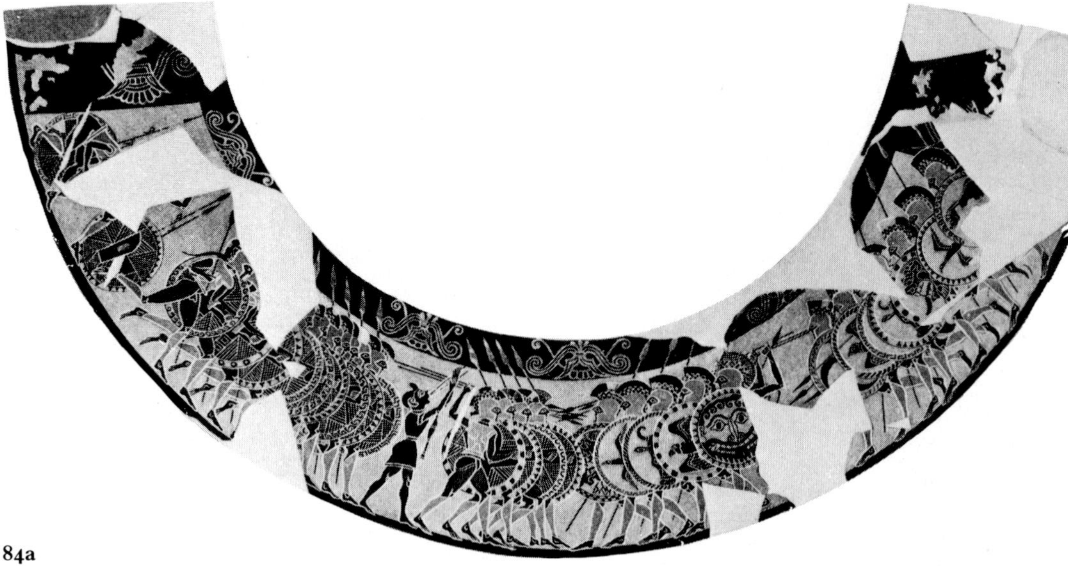

84a

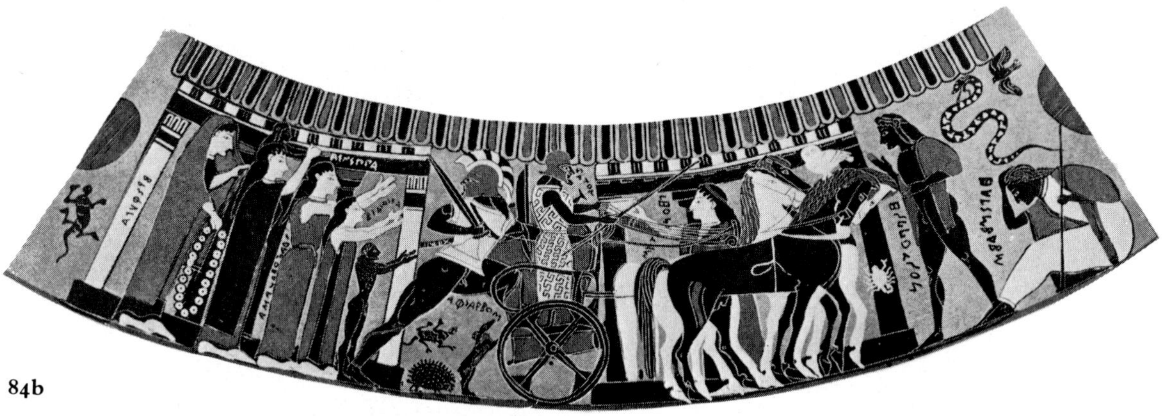

84b

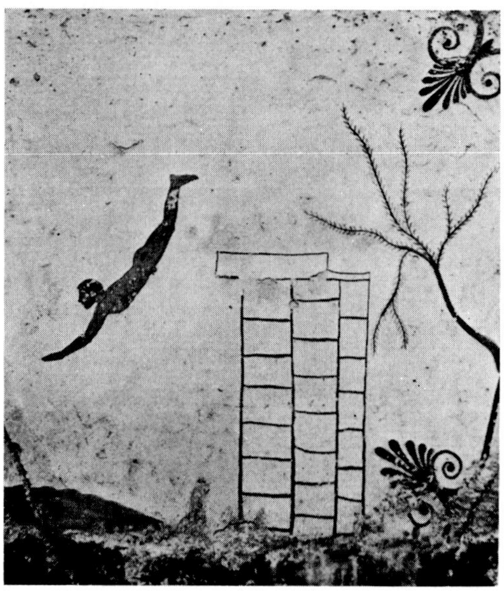

84c

84 **a** Drawing from picture on protocorinthian oenochoe, from Formello (Veii). Rome, Villa Giulia. Third quarter of seventh century. H. of picture *c.* 0.05. (Pp. 52–3, 431) **b** Drawing of picture on Corinthian column-krater from Cervetri. Formerly Berlin 1655 (destroyed). Second quarter of sixth century. H. of picture *c.* 0.15. (Pp. 121ff.) **c** Part of painting in tomb from Paestum. Paestum Museum. First quarter of fifth century. H. 0.98. (Pp. 240–1).

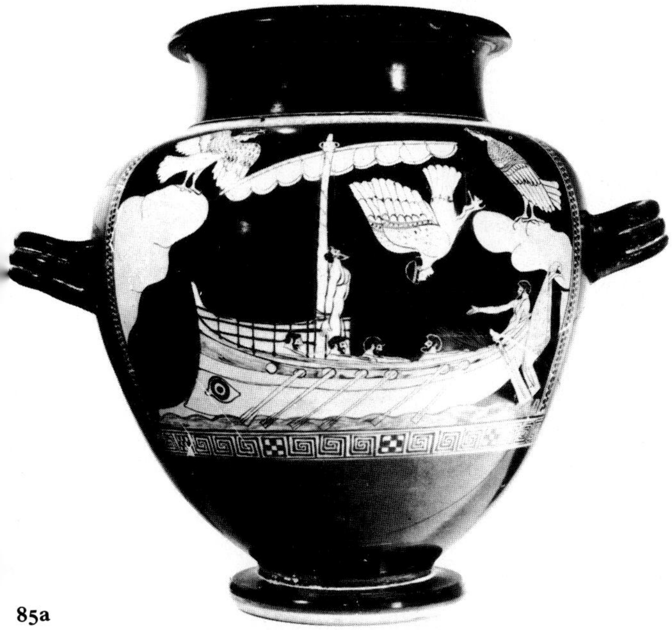

85a

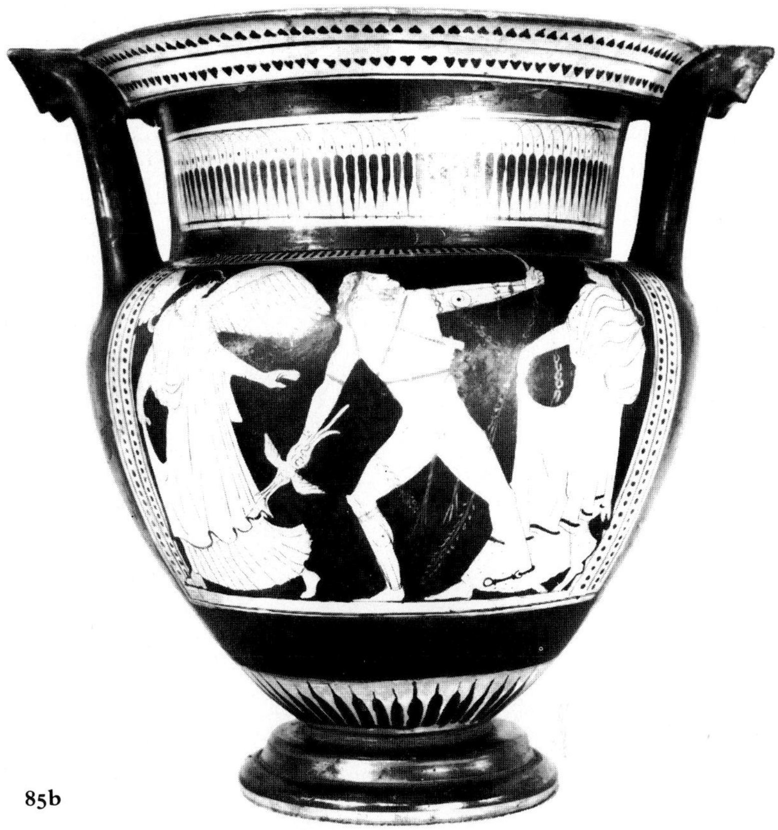

85b

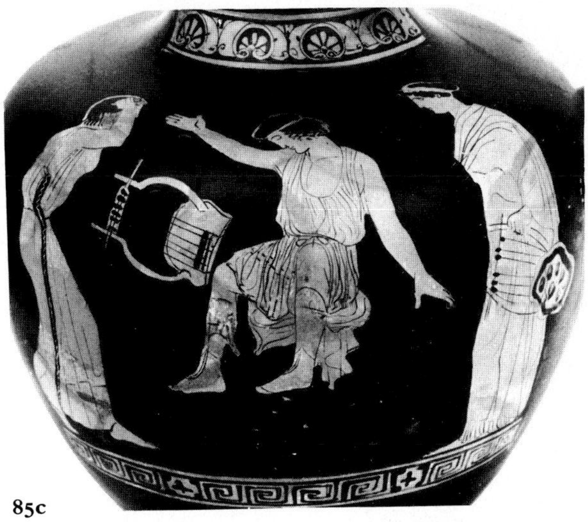

85c

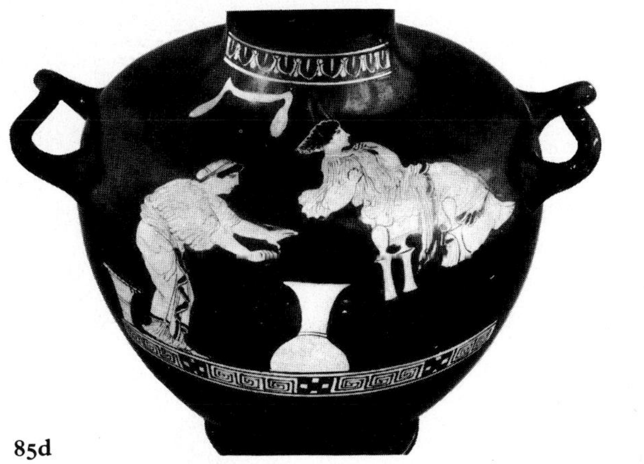

85d

85 **a** Attic red-figure stamnos from Vulci. British Museum E440. First quarter of fifth century. H. 0.35. (Pp. 218, 241) **b** Attic red-figure column-krater. Chicago, Art Institute 89.16, P. D. Armour and C. L. Hutchinson Gift. Second quarter of fifth century. H. 0.46. (P. 246) **c** Attic red-figure hydria from Greece. Oxford, Ashmolean Museum 530. Third quarter of fifth century. H. 0.28. (P. 270) **d** Attic red-figure hydria from Nola. Berlin 2394. Last quarter of fifth century. H. 0.18. (P. 269).

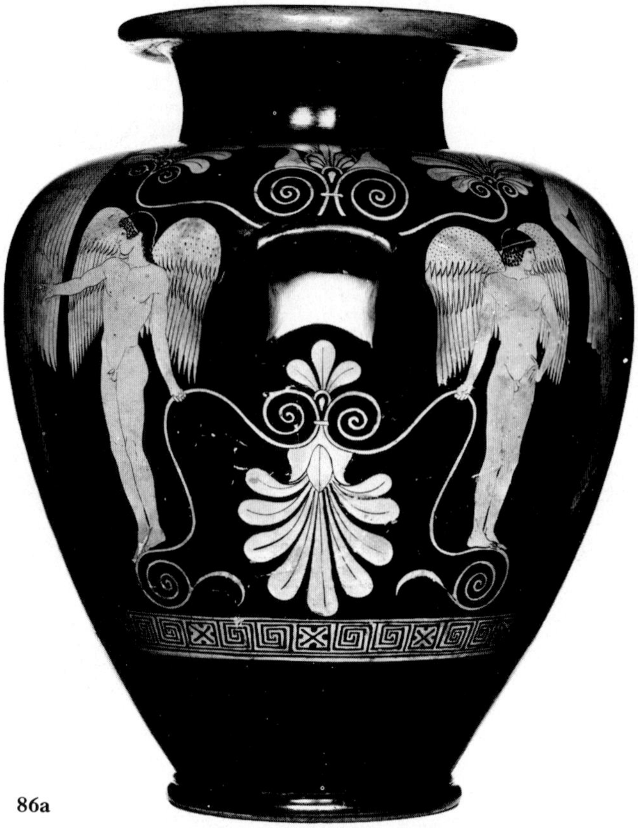

86a

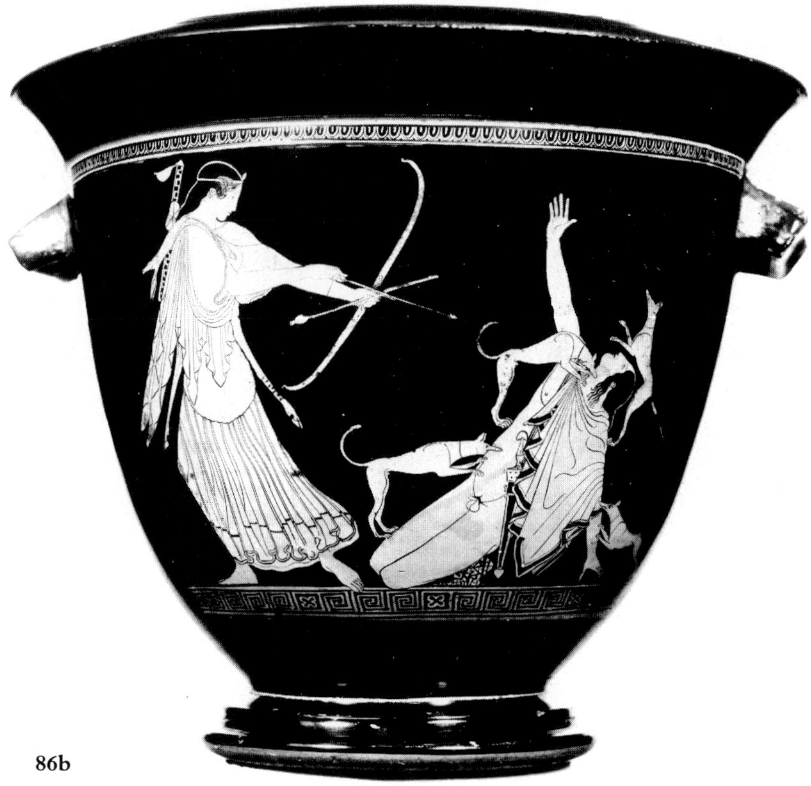

86b

86 **a** Attic red-figure stamnos from Vulci. Munich 2413. Second quarter of fifth century. H. 0.39. (Pp. 218, 253)
b Attic red-figure bell-krater from Cumae. Boston, Museum of Fine Arts 10.185. H. 0.37. (P. 253).

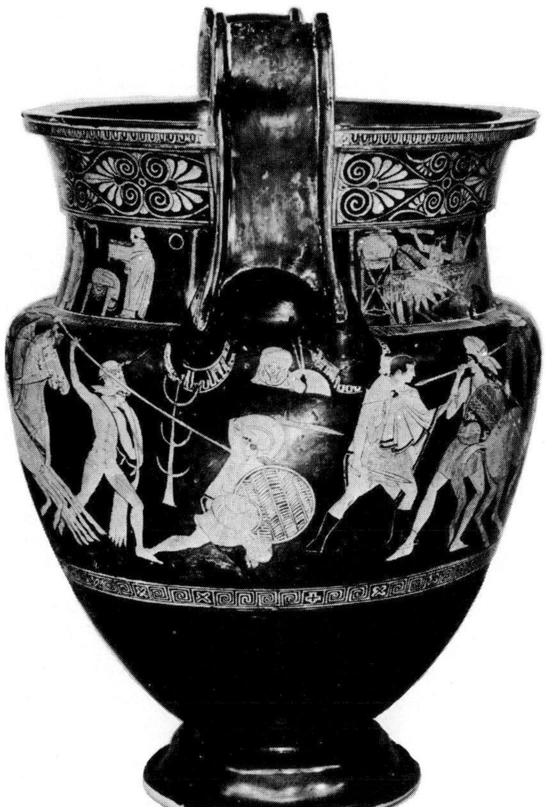

87a

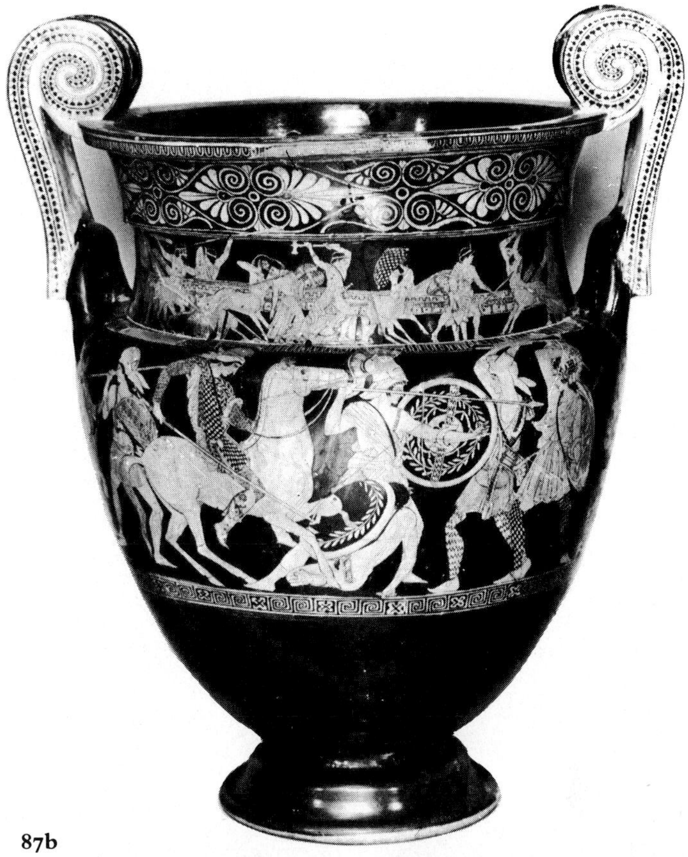

87b

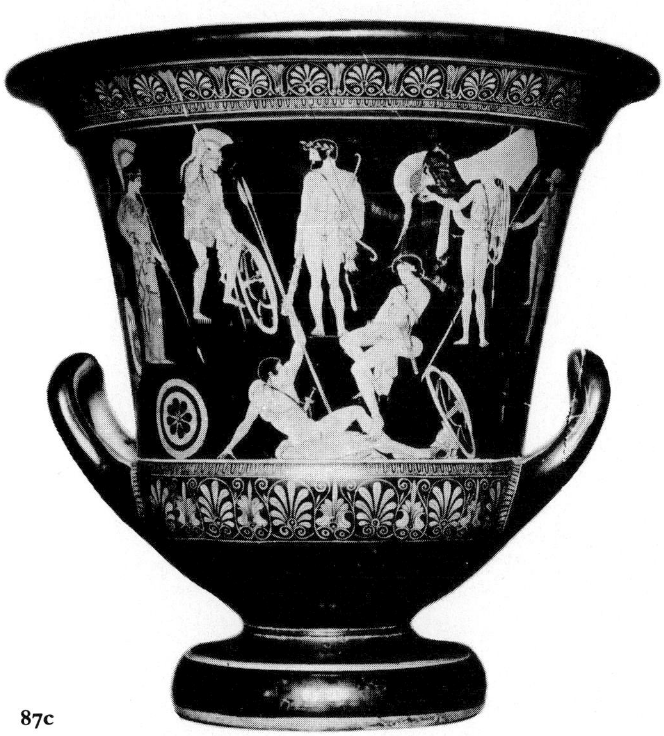

87c

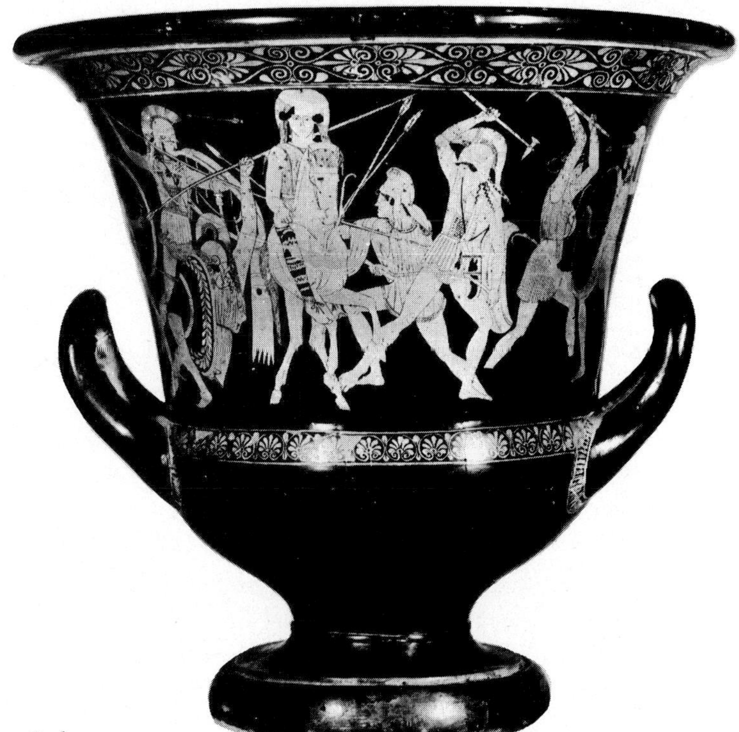

87d

87 **a** and **b** Attic red-figure volute-krater from Numana (south of Ancona). New York, Metropolitan Museum of Art 07.286.84, Rogers Fund. Second quarter of fifth century. H. 0.63. (Pp. 124, 259, 281; cf. pl. 88a) **c** Attic red-figure calyx-krater from Orvieto. Louvre G 341. Second quarter of fifth century. H. 0.53. (Pp. 253ff.; cf. pl. 88b) **d** Attic red-figure calyx-krater from Numana. New York, Metropolitan Museum of Art 07.286.86, Rogers Fund. Second quarter of fifth century. H. 0.56. (Pp. 258–9, 501).

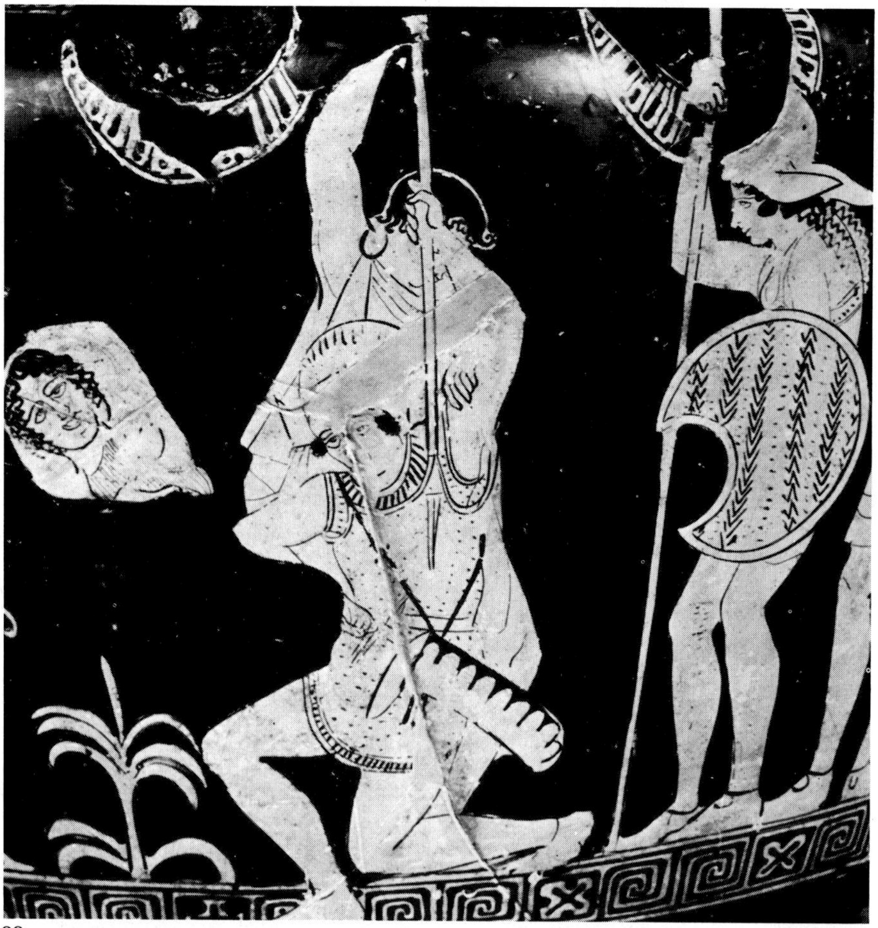

88a

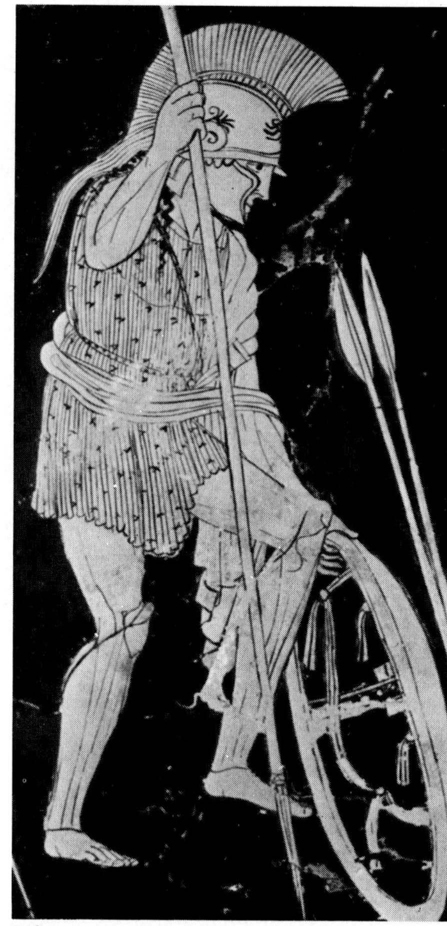

88b

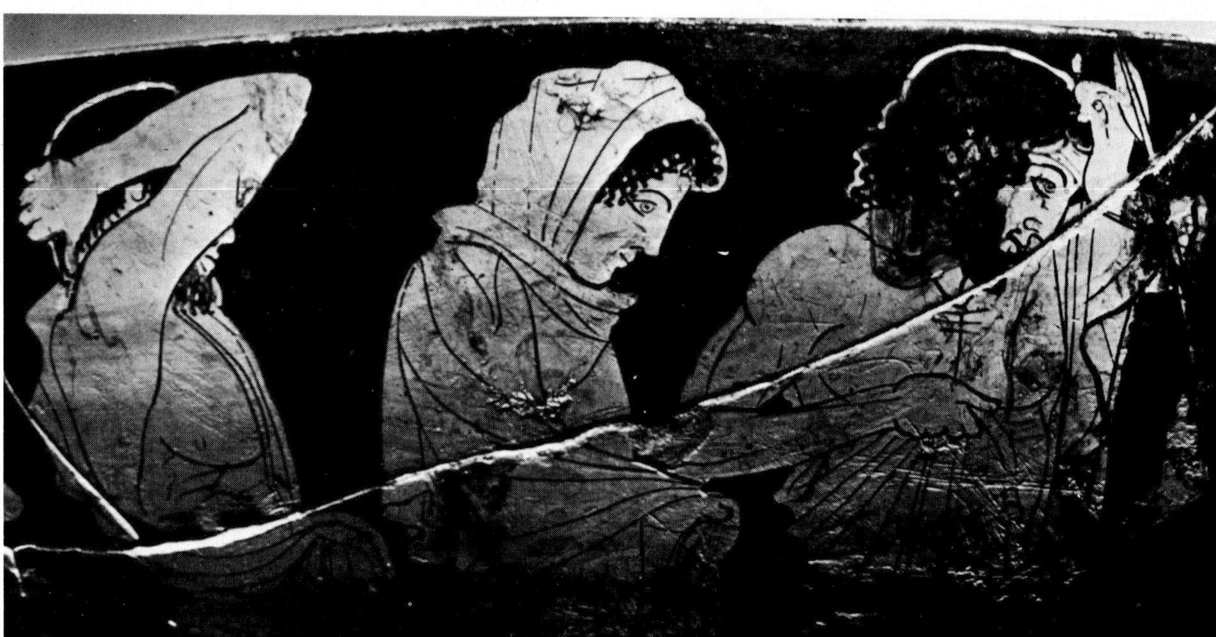

88c

88 **a** Detail from vase, pl. 87a and b. (P. 259) **b** Detail from vase, pl. 87c. (Pp. 253–4) **c** Detail of picture on outside of Attic red-figure cup from Spina. Ferrara T.18cVP. Second quarter of fifth century. H. of detail *c.* 0.10. (P. 263).

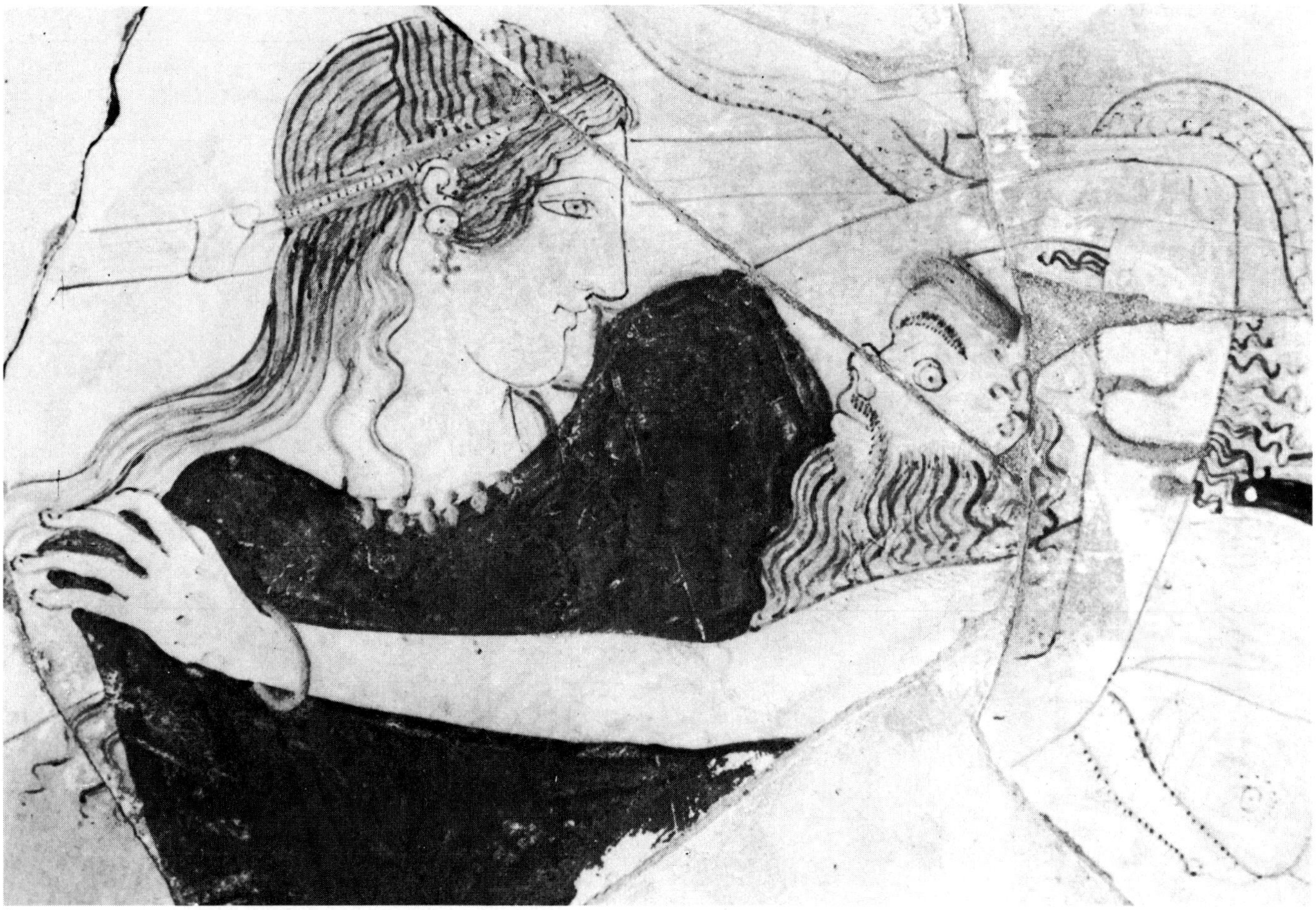

89a

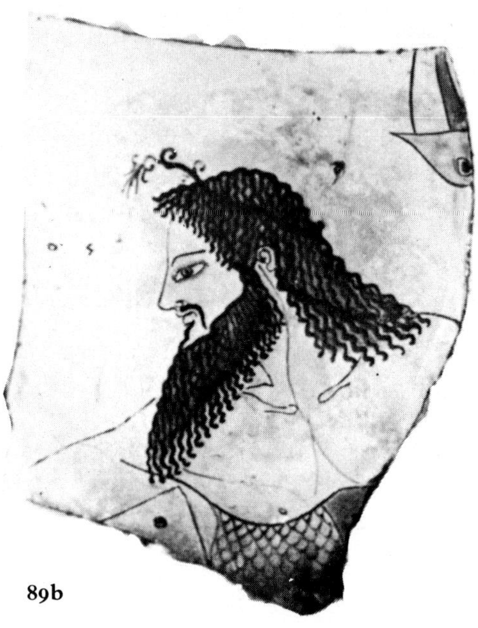

89b

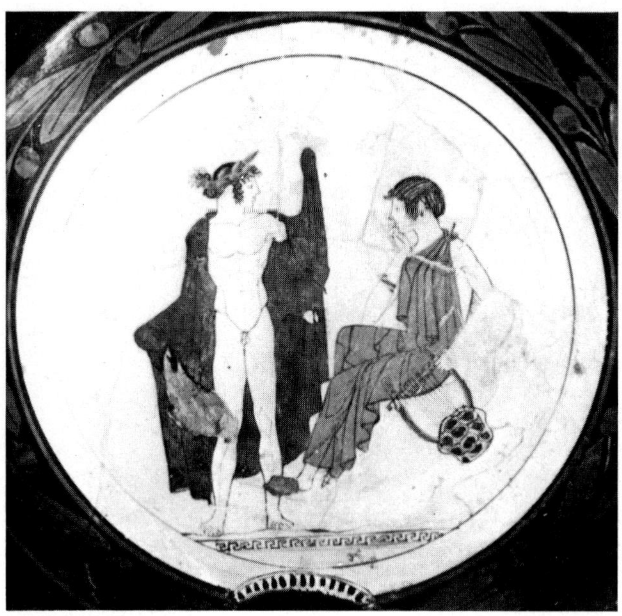

89c

89 **a** Attic white-ground cup-fragment from Locri. Taranto Museum. First or second quarter of fifth century. H. of detail *c.* 0.18. (P. 261) **b** Attic white-ground cup-fragment from Eleusis. Eleusis Museum 618. End of sixth or beginning of fifth century. H. *c.* 0.11. (P. 259) **c** Attic white-ground covered cup from Vari (Attica). Boston, Museum of Fine Arts 00.356. Second quarter of fifth century. D. 0.11. (Pp. 261–2, 275).

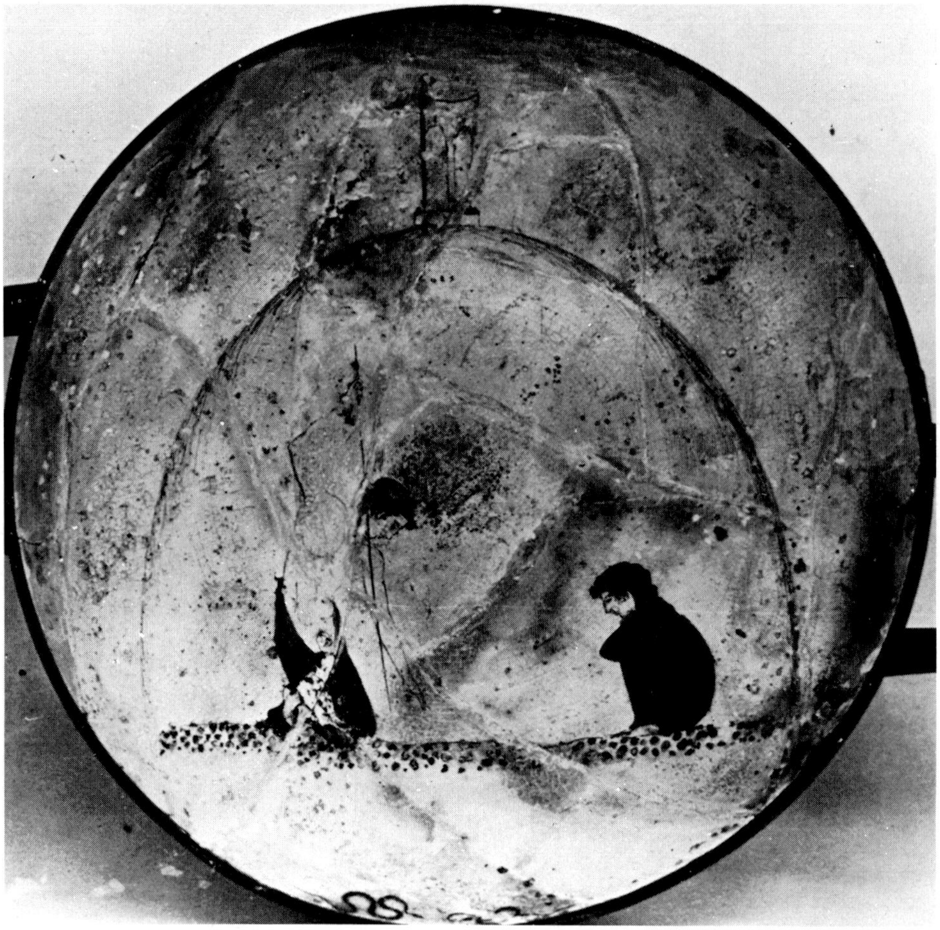

90a

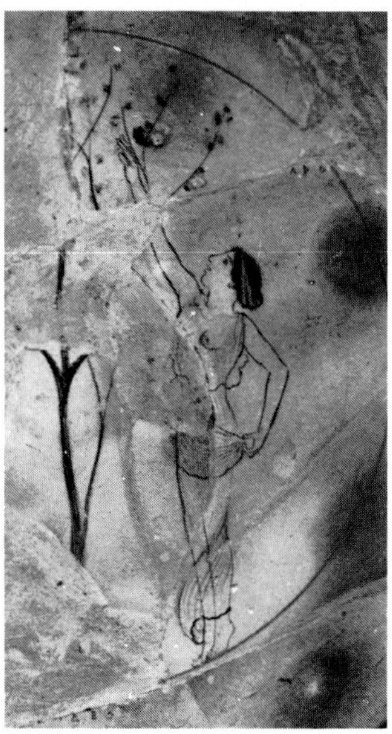

90b

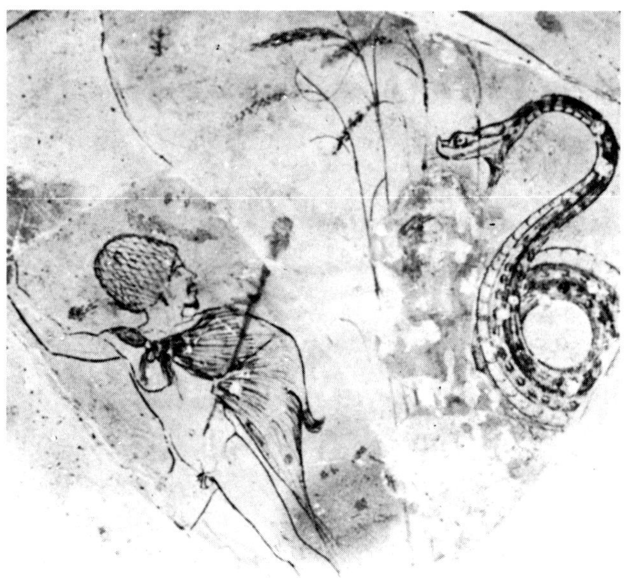

90c

90 **a** Attic white-ground cup from Athens, with name of Sotades (potter). British Museum D 5. Second quarter of fifth century. D. 0.13. (Pp. 265–6) **b** Detail of picture in fragmentary Attic white-ground cup from Athens, signed by potter Sotades. British Museum D 6. Second quarter of fifth century. H. of detail *c.* 0.08. (P. 264) **c** Detail of picture in fragmentary Attic white-ground stemless cup from Athens. British Museum D 7. Second quarter of fifth century. H. of detail *c.* 0.08. (Pp. 264–5).

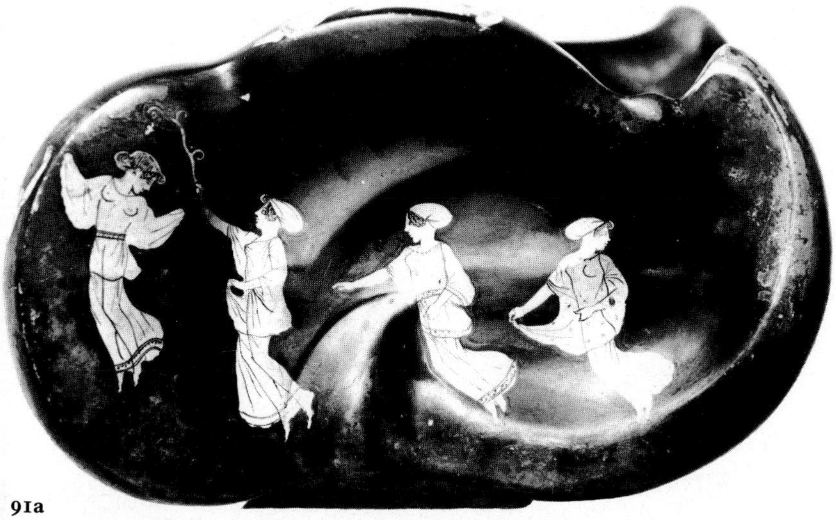
91a

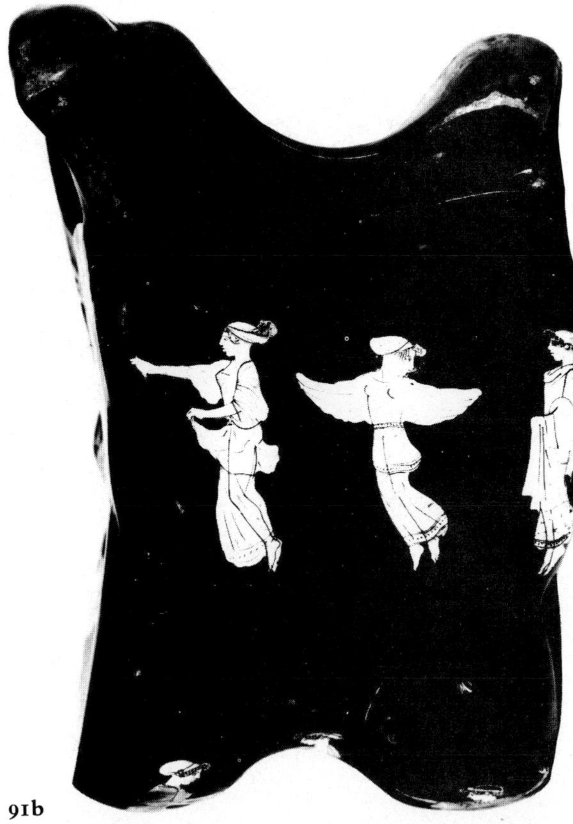
91b

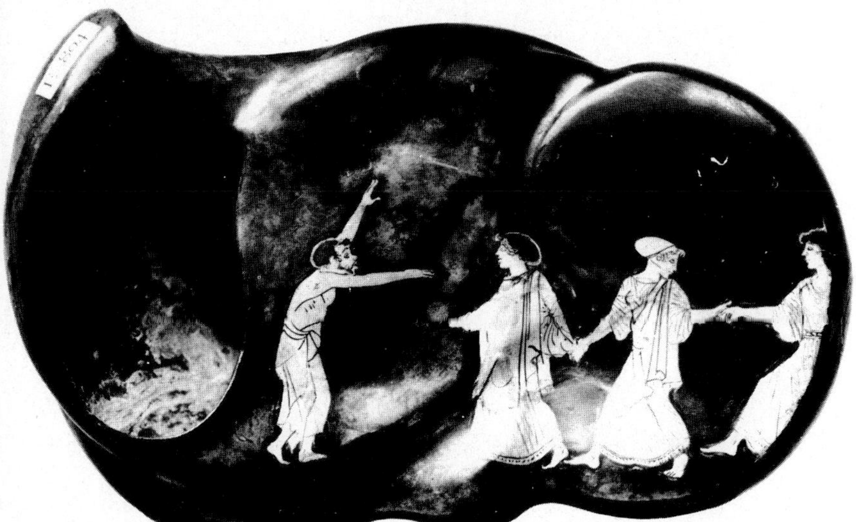
91c

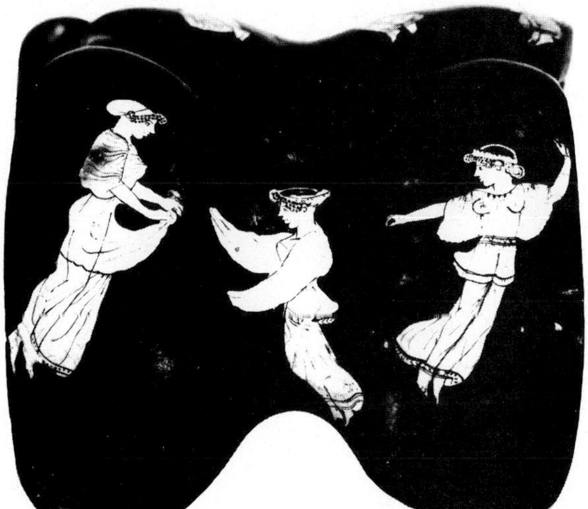
91d

91 a–d Attic red-figure vase in form of astragalos (knucklebone), from Aegina. British Museum E804. Second quarter of fifth century. Greatest length *c.* 0.17. (P. 264).

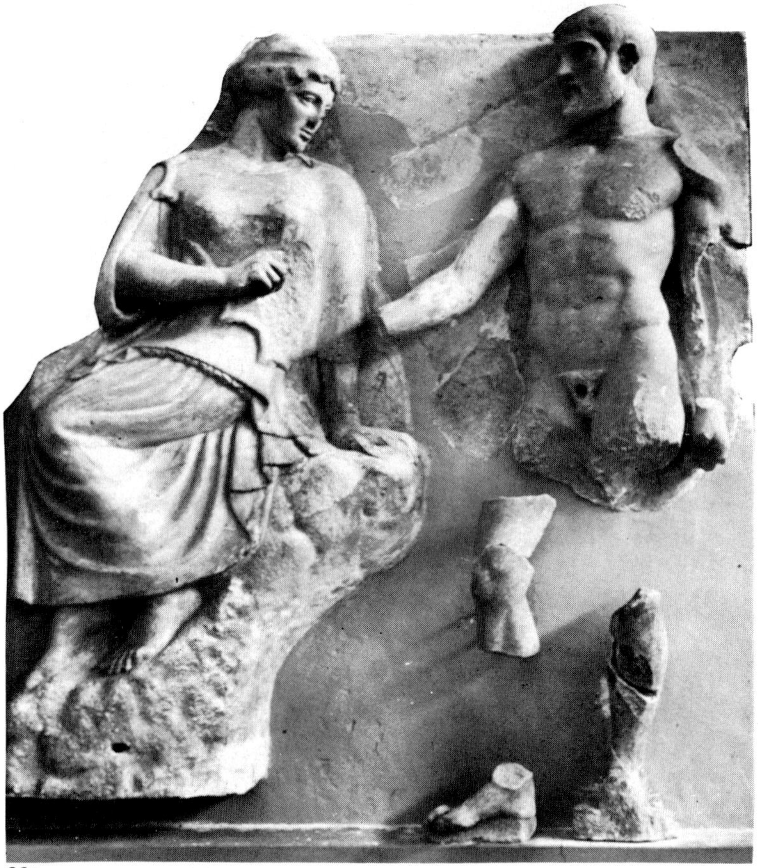

92a

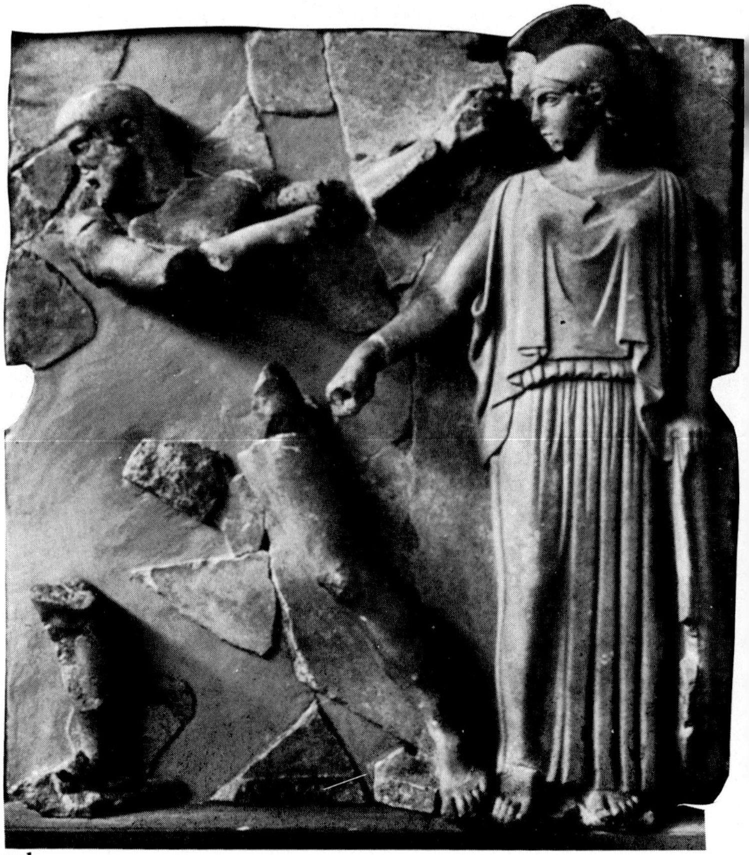

92b

92 **a** Marble metope from west end of Temple of Zeus at Olympia. Olympia Museum; figure of Athena, head and right arm of Herakles, casts from originals in Louvre. Second quarter of fifth century. H. 1.60. (Pp. 274–5)
b Marble metope from east end of Temple of Zeus at Olympia. Olympia Museum. Second quarter of fifth century. H. 1.60. (Pp. 273ff.).

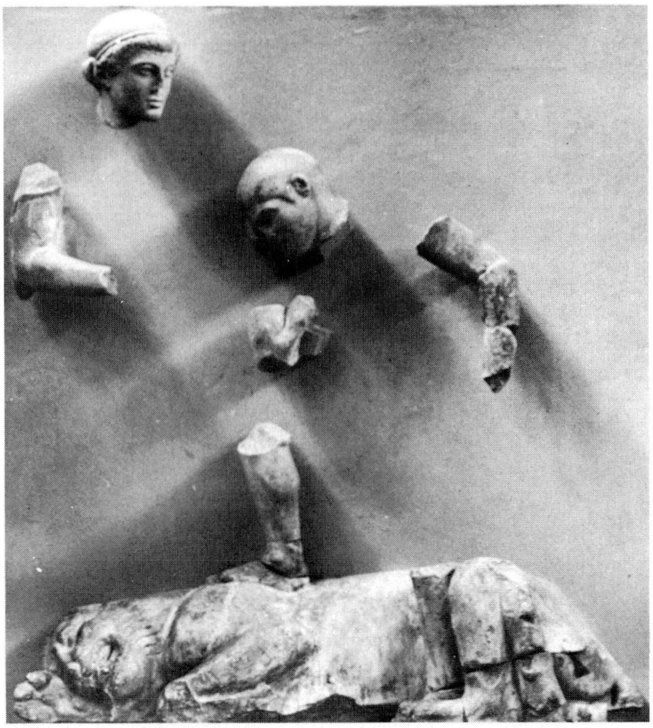

93a

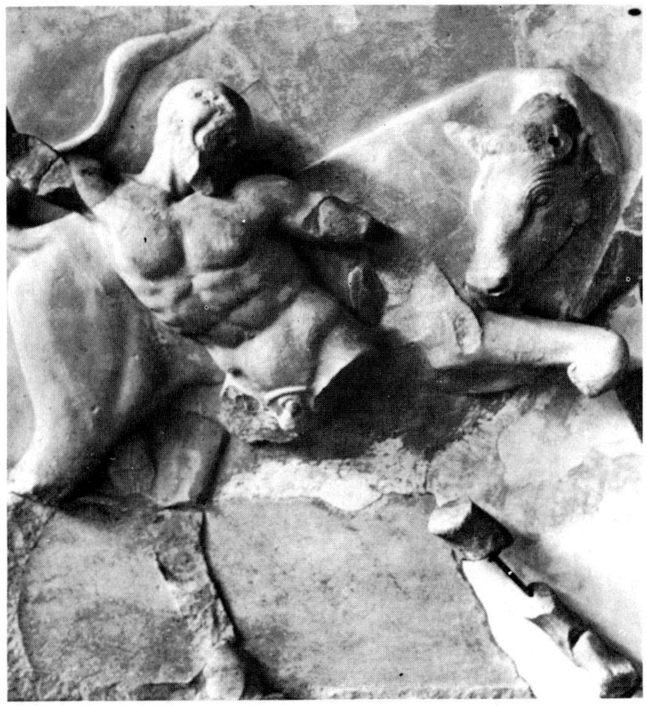

93b

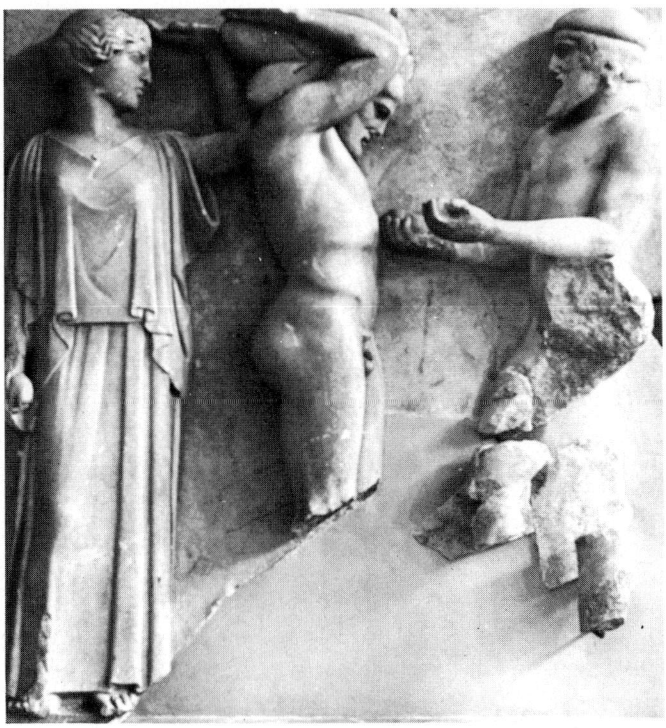

93c

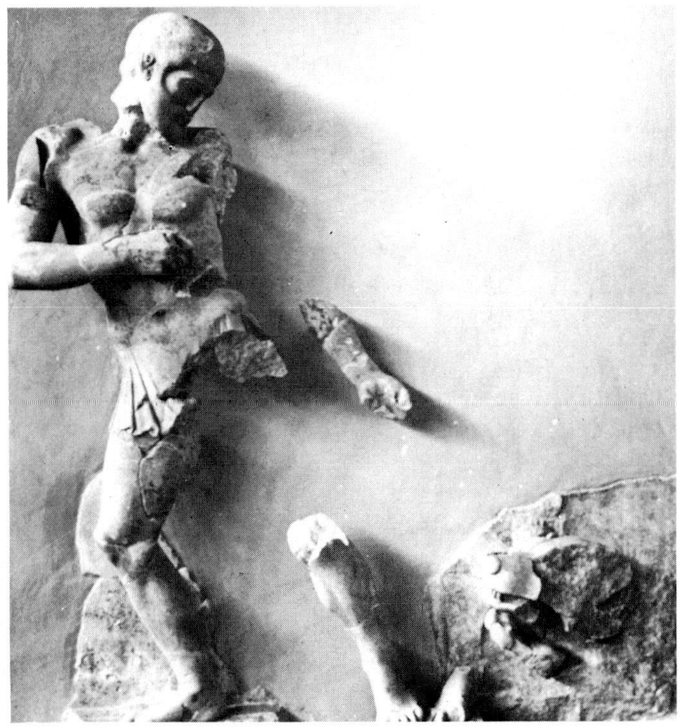

93d

93 **a** Fragments of marble metope from west end of Temple of Zeus at Olympia. Olympia Museum; forepart of lion cast from original in Louvre. Second quarter of fifth century. H. 1.60. (Pp. 273, 276, 291) **b** Marble metope from west end of Temple of Zeus at Olympia. Olympia Museum; upper part, except head of bull, cast from original in Louvre. Second quarter of fifth century. H. 1.60. (Pp. 274, 276) **c** Marble metope from east end of Temple of Zeus at Olympia. Olympia Museum. Second quarter of fifth century. H. 1.60. (P. 274) **d** Fragments of marble metope from east end of Temple of Zeus at Olympia. Olympia Museum. Second quarter of fifth century. H. 1.60. (P. 275).

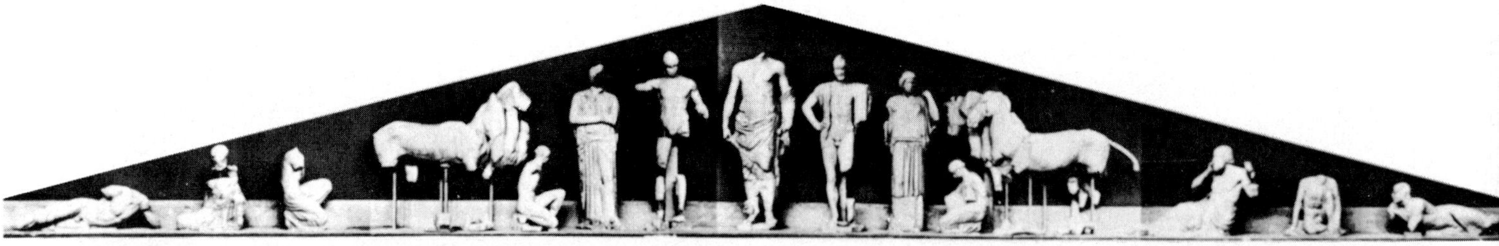

94a

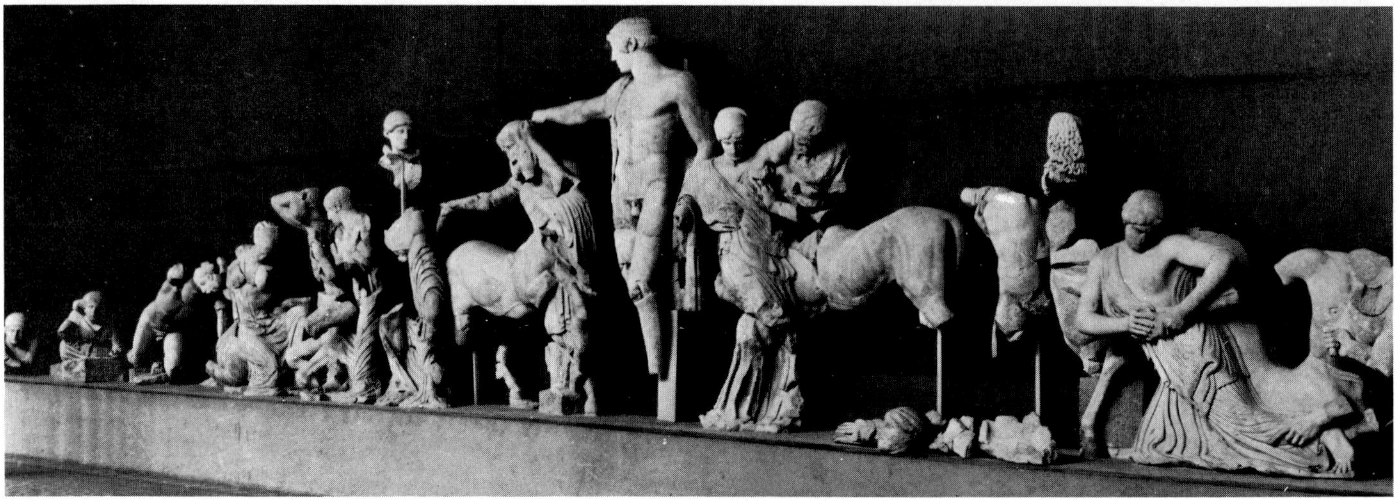

94b

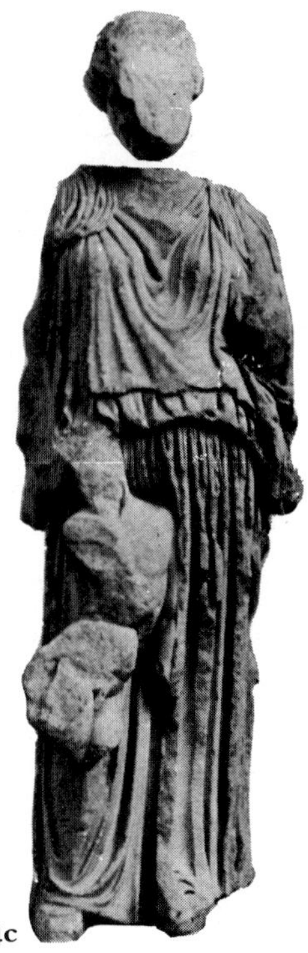

94c

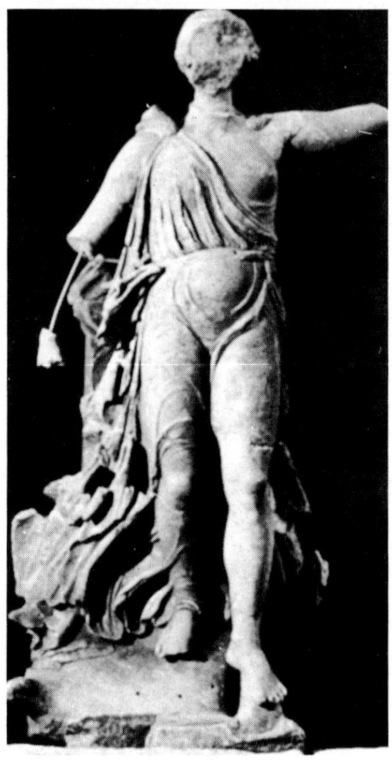

94d

94 **a** Marble figures from east pediment of Temple of Zeus at Olympia. Olympia Museum. Second quarter of fifth century. Original h. at apex 3.15. (Pp. 276ff., 345) **b** Marble figures from west pediment of Temple of Zeus at Olympia. Olympia Museum. Second quarter of fifth century. Original h. at apex 3.15. (Pp. 276, 280ff.) **c** Marble group from Acropolis. Athens, Acropolis Museum 1358 and 2789. Third or last quarter of fifth century. H. *c.* 2.00. (Pp. 286ff., 345–6, 590) **d** Marble figure from base signed by Paionios of Mende, at Olympia. Olympia Museum. Third or last quarter of fifth century. H. 1.95. (Pp. 284, 287–8, 350).

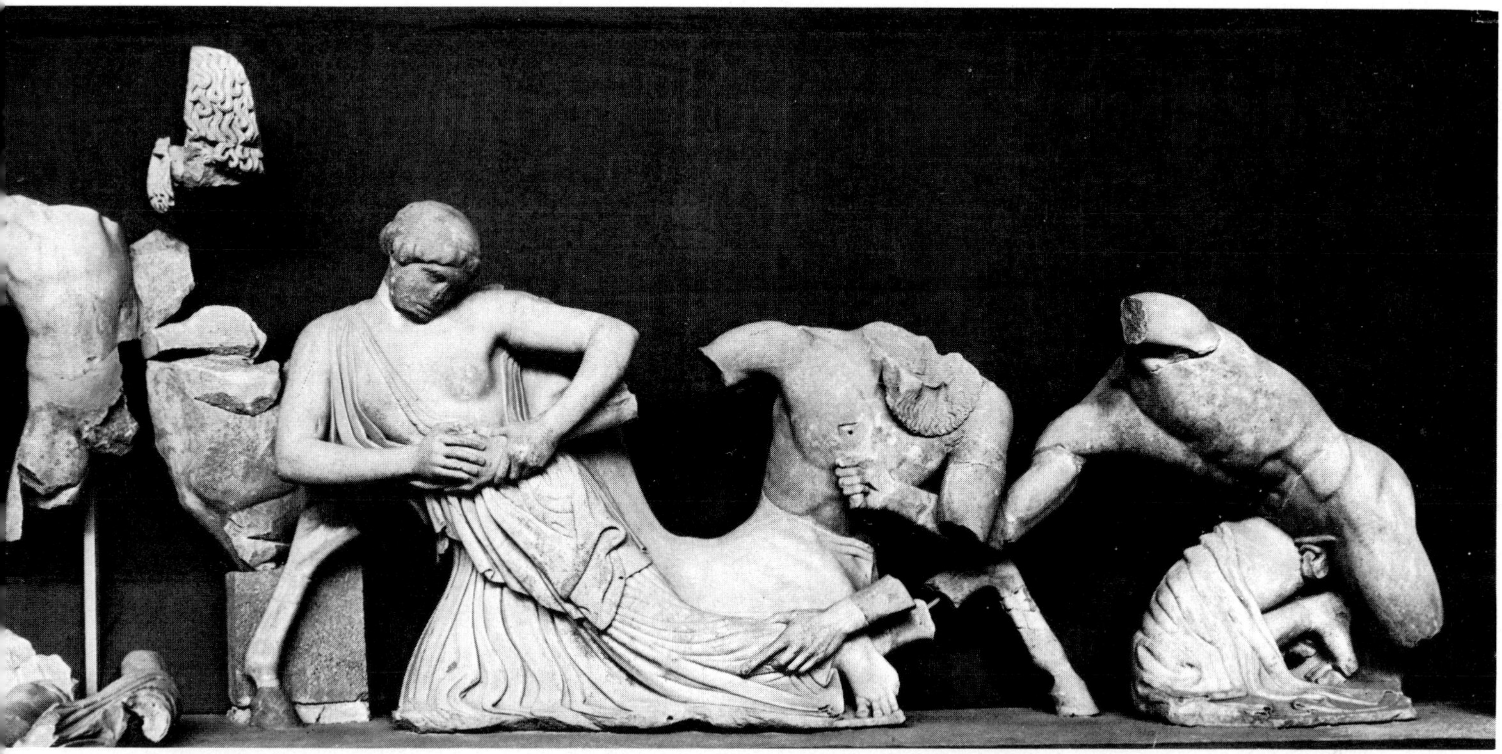

95a

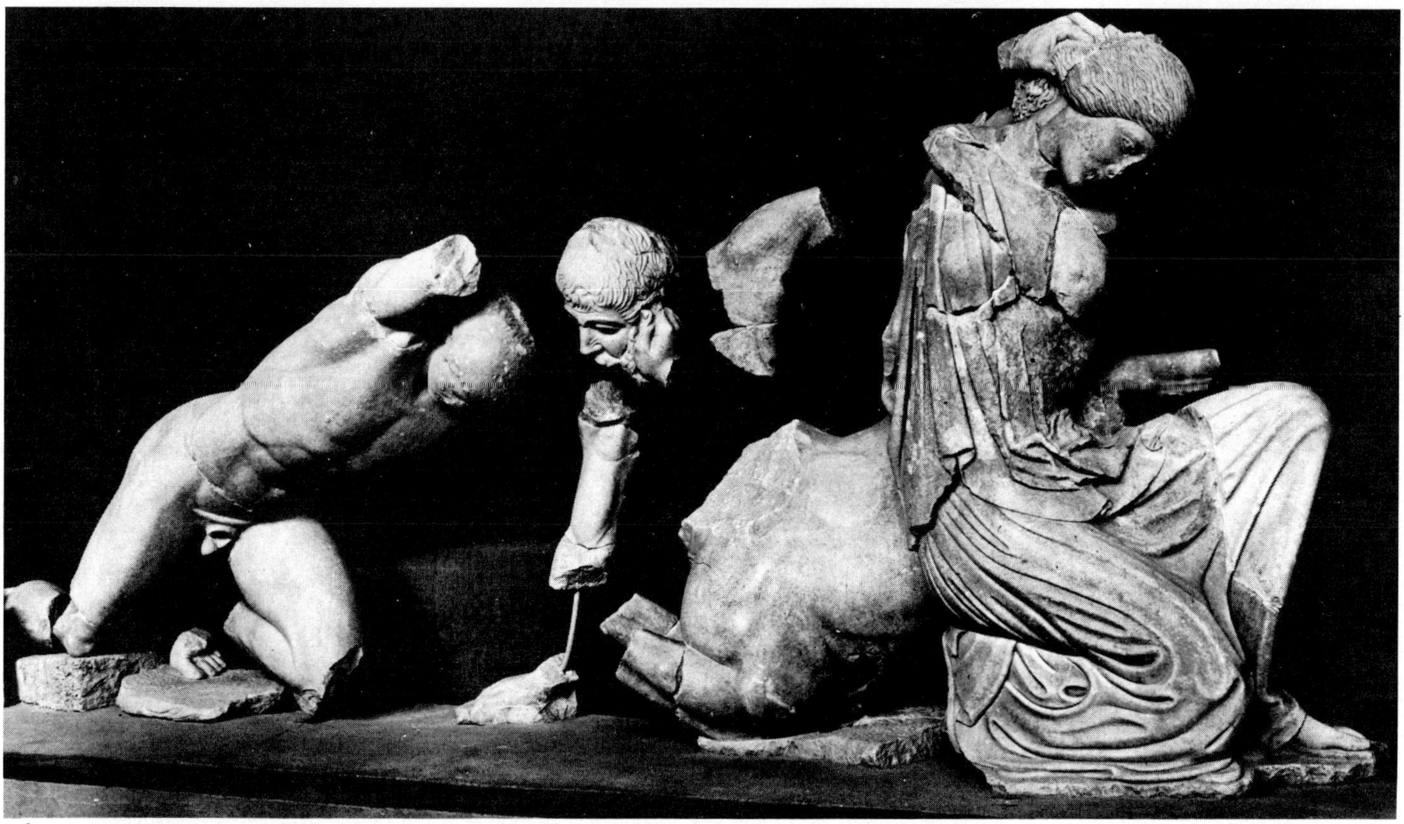

95b

95 a and **b** Marble groups from west pediment of Temple of Zeus at Olympia. Olympia Museum. Second quarter of fifth century. Original lengths *c.* 2.35 and 2.25. (P. 282).

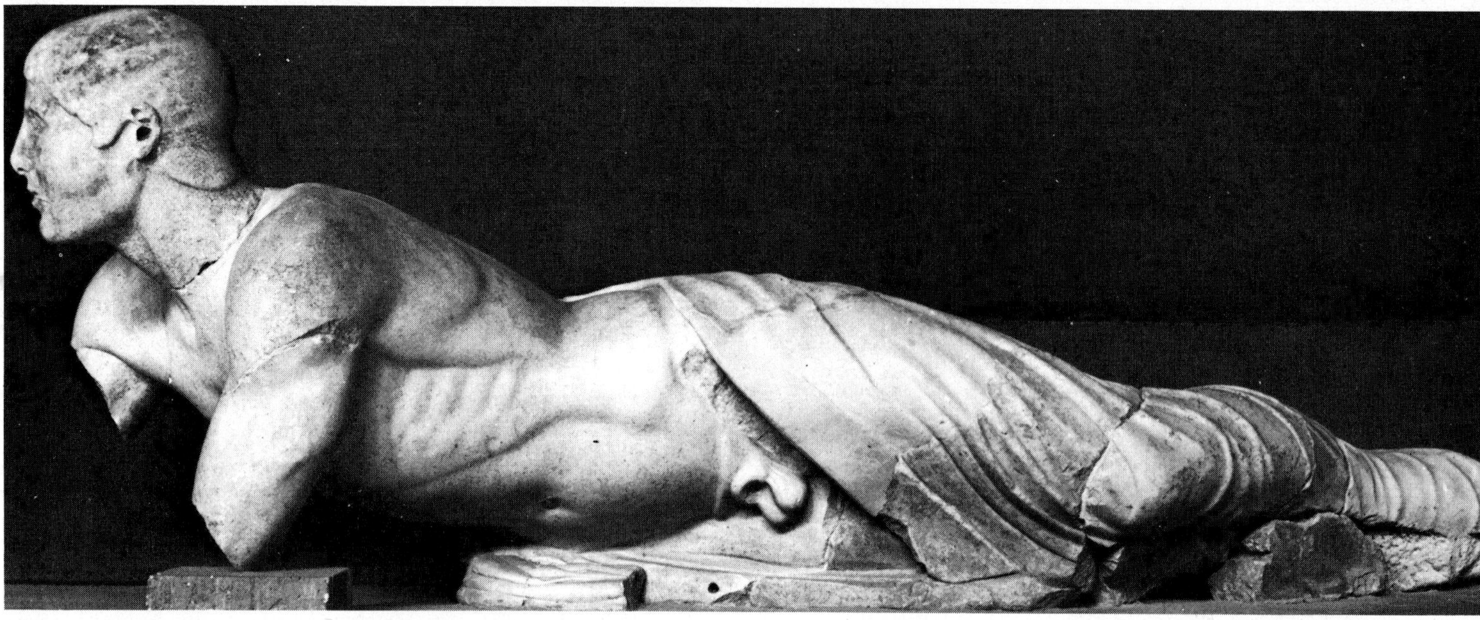

96a

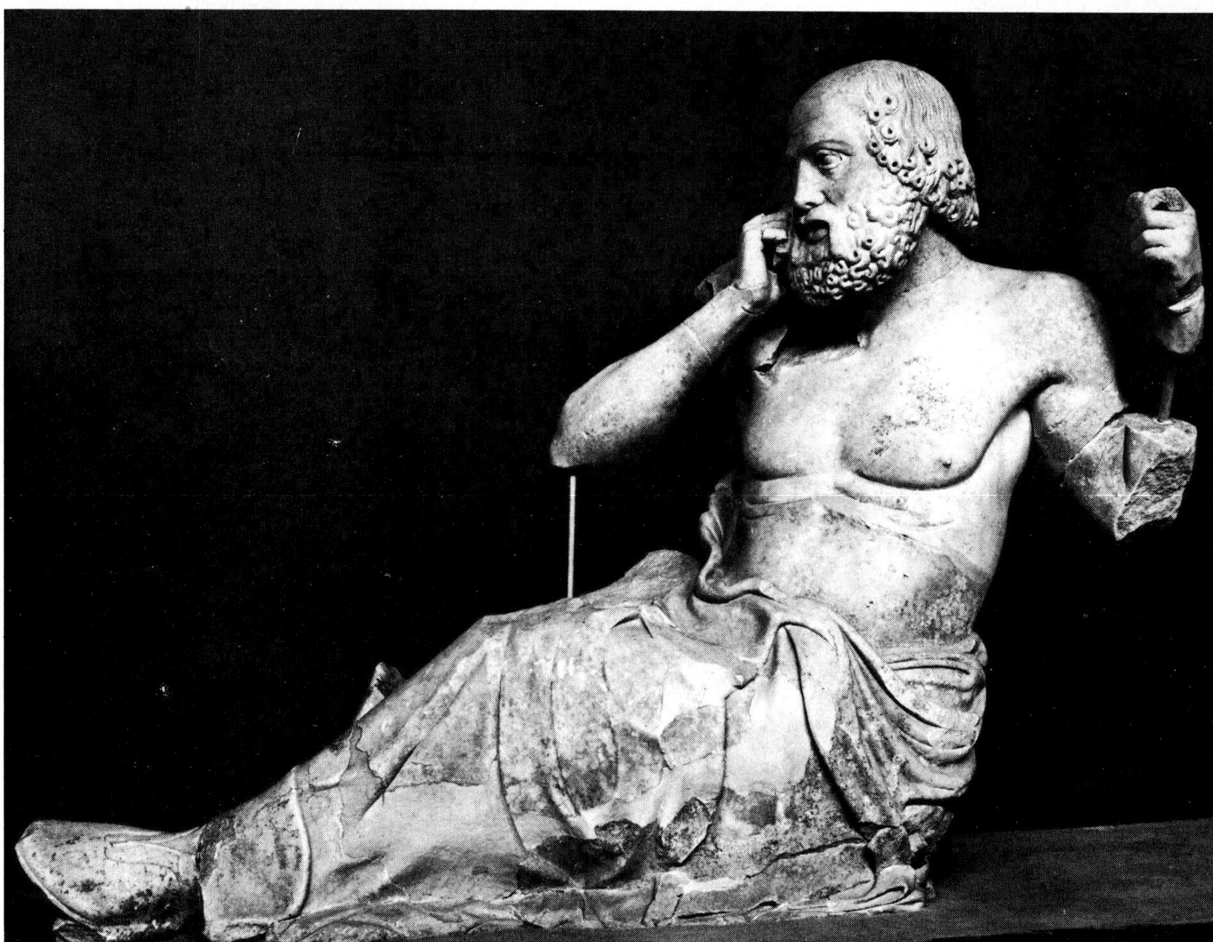

96b

96 **a** and **b** Marble figures from east pediment of Temple of Zeus at Olympia. Second quarter of fifth century. L. of **a** 2.30; h. of **b** 1.38. (Pp. 278ff., 300).

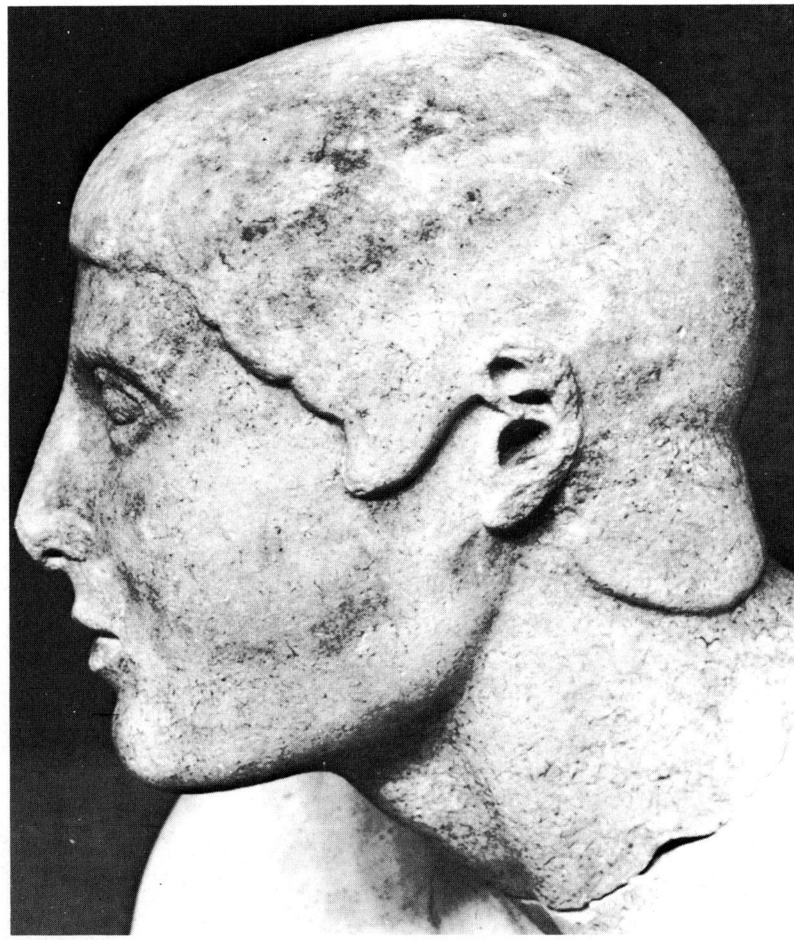

97a

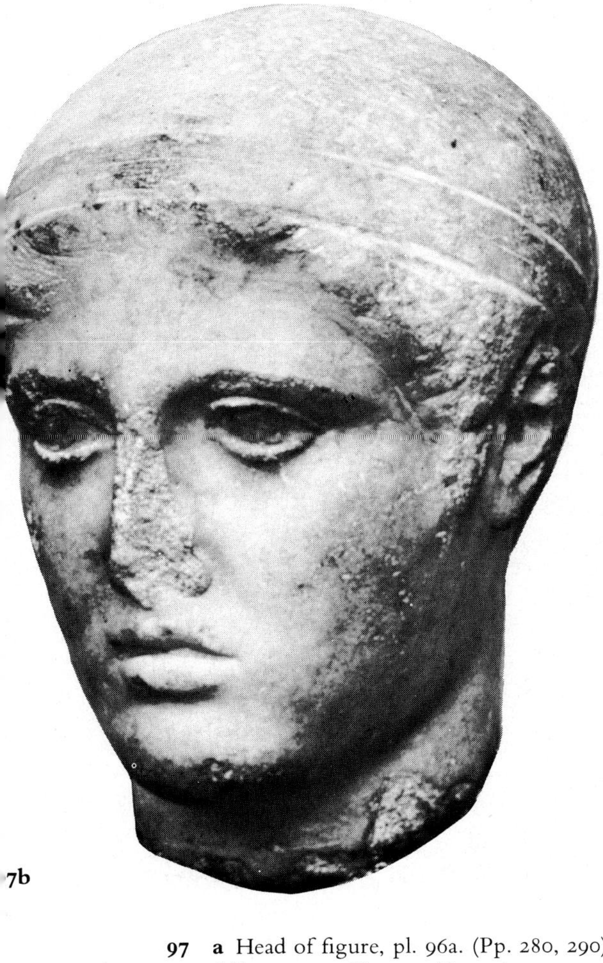

7b

97 **a** Head of figure, pl. 96a. (Pp. 280, 290) **b** Marble head from Acropolis. Athens, Acropolis Museum 699. Mid fifth century. H. 0.23. (P. 344).

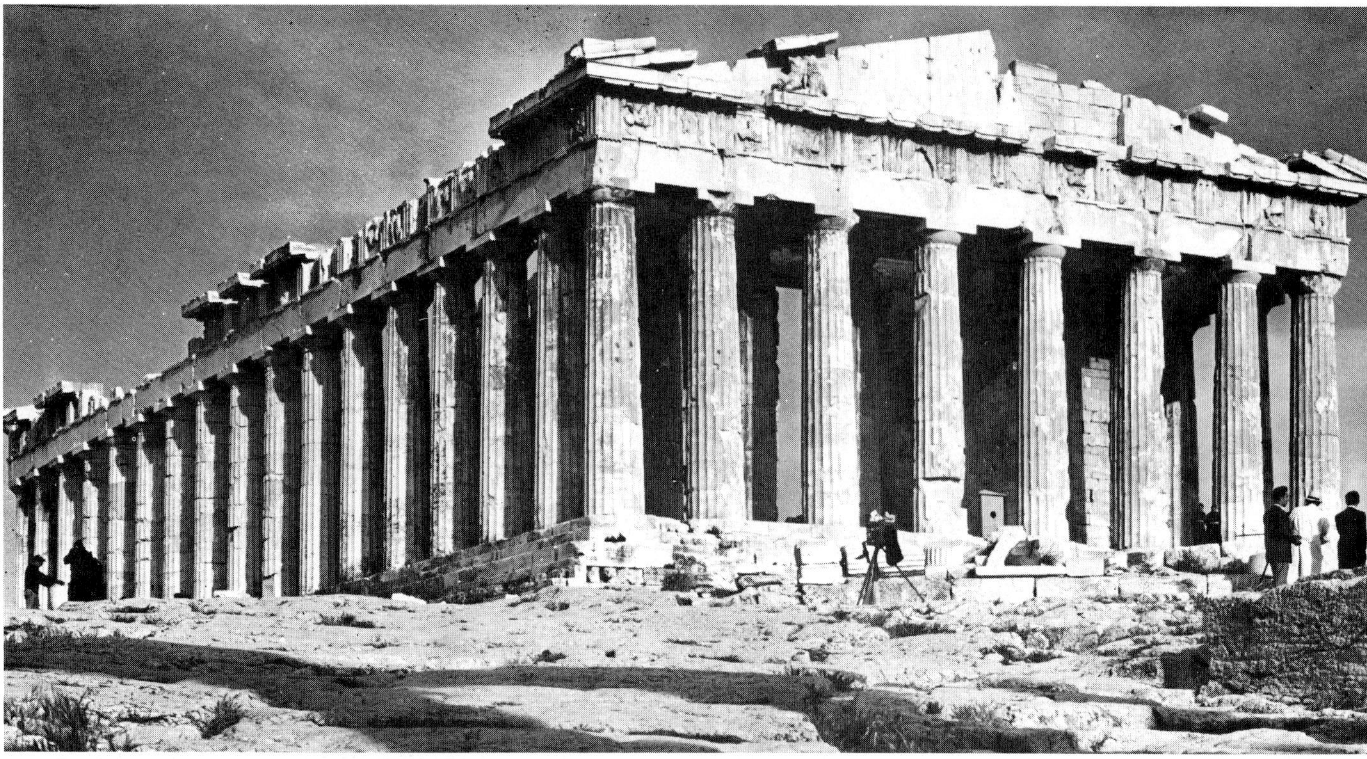

98a

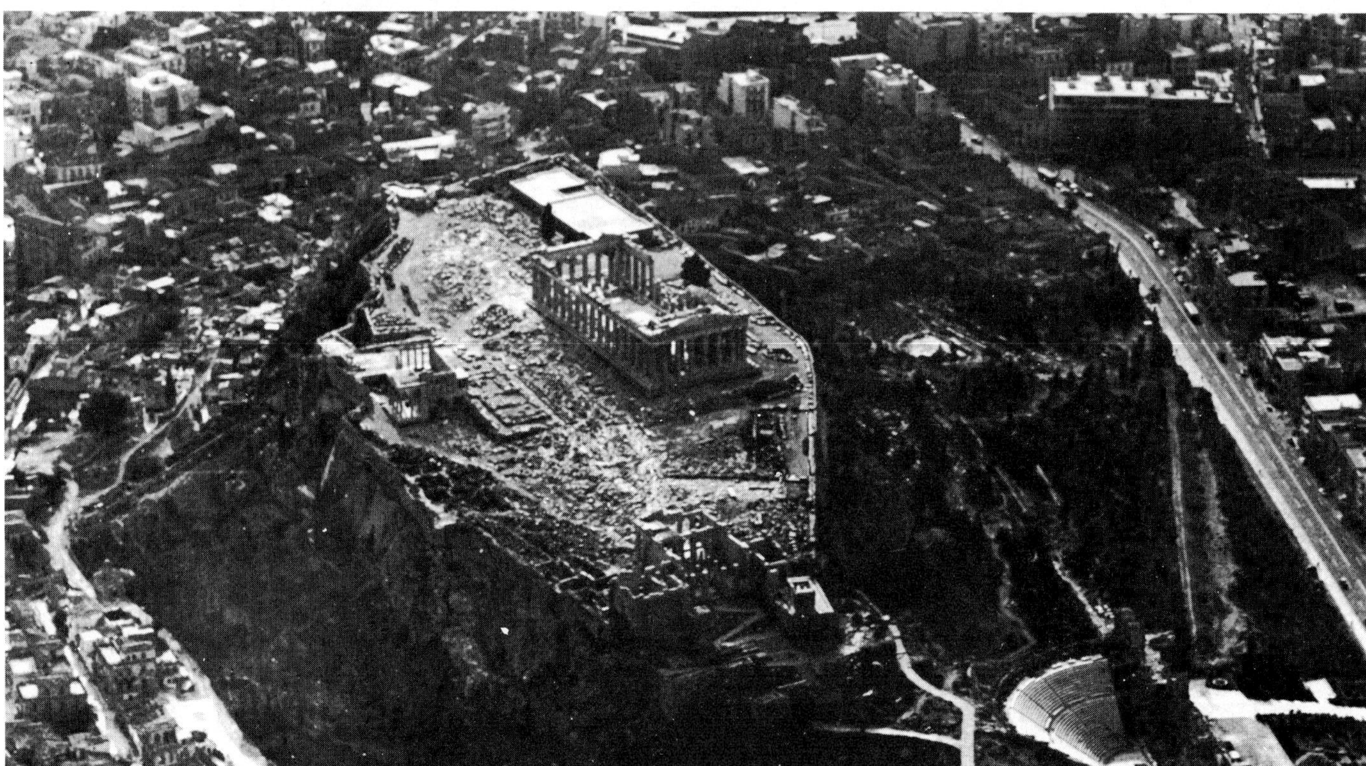

98b

98 **a** The Parthenon from north-west, 448–432 B.C. W. of top step 30.86. (Pp. 61, 292ff.) **b** The Acropolis from the air, from north-west. (Pp. 159, 292–3, 345ff., 368).

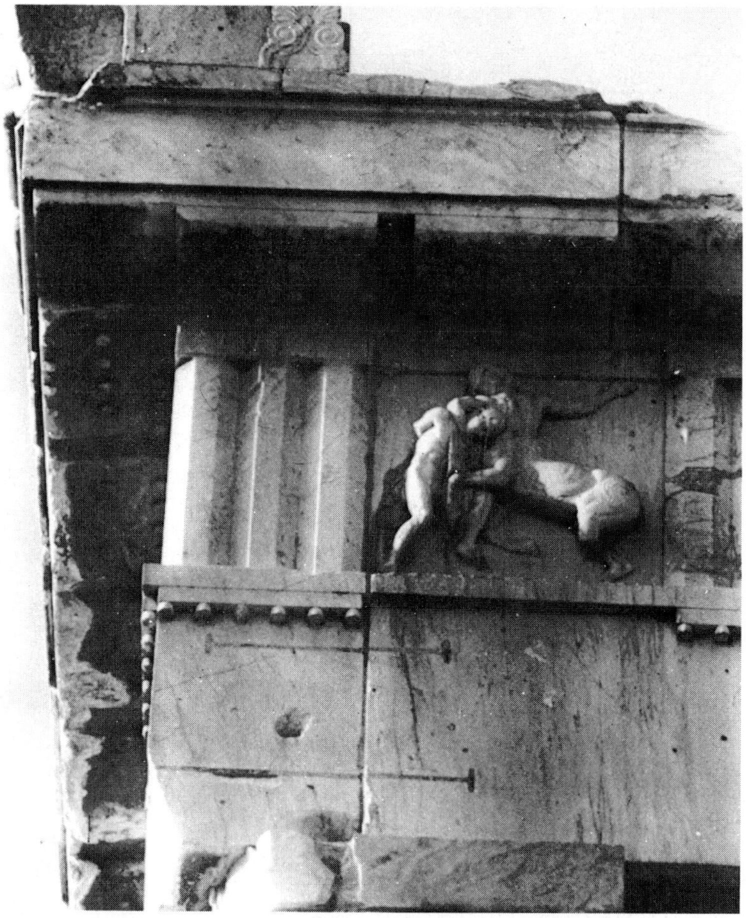

99a

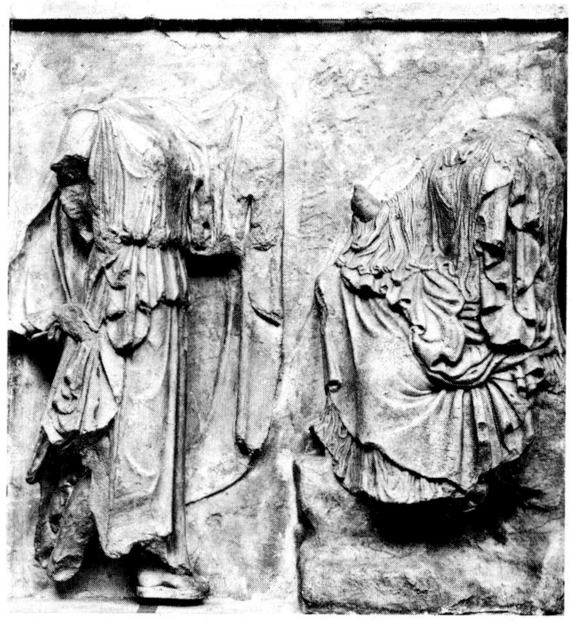

99b

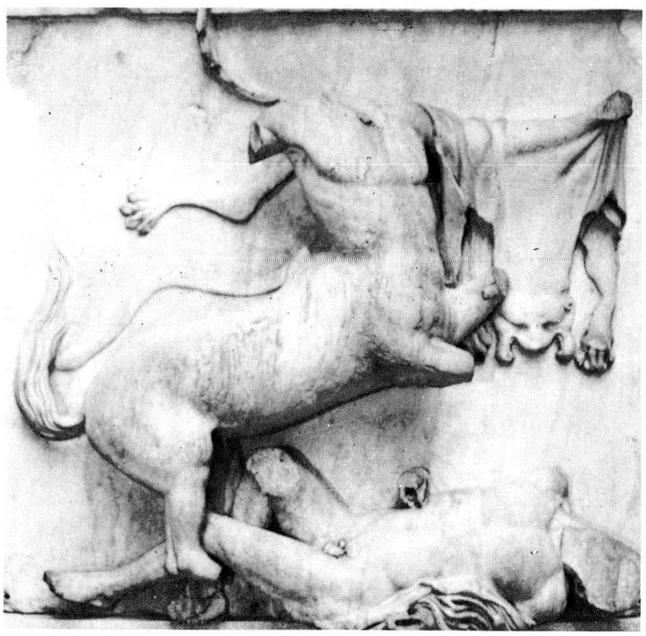

99c

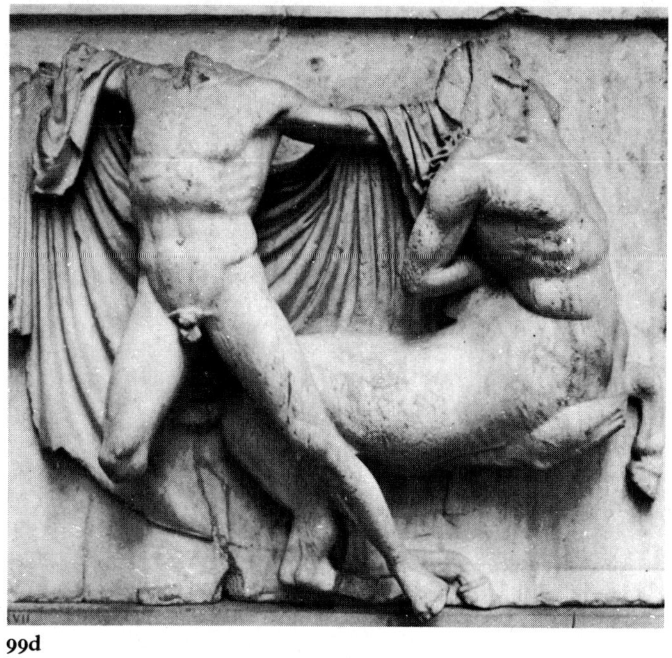

99d

99 **a** Marble metope in position on south side of Parthenon (west corner). Third quarter of fifth century. H. of carved field of metope 1.20. (P. 297) **b** Cast from marble metope on north side of Parthenon (west corner). British Museum 322. Third quarter of fifth century. H. 1.20. (Pp. 275, 298, 304) **c** Marble metope from south side of Parthenon (28). British Museum 317. Third quarter of fifth century. H. 1.20. (P. 297) **d** Marble metope from south side of Parthenon (27). British Museum 316. Third quarter of fifth century. H. 1.20. (Pp. 297–8, 539).

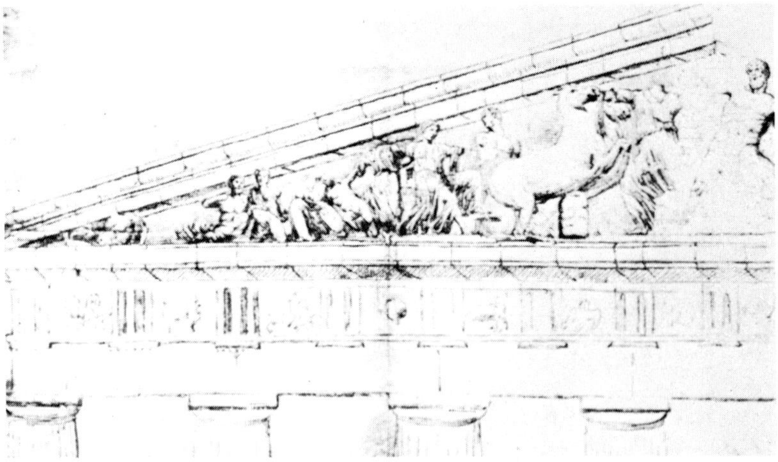

100a

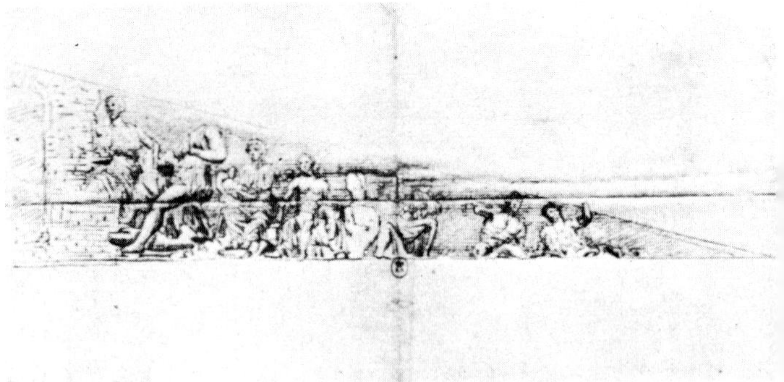

100b

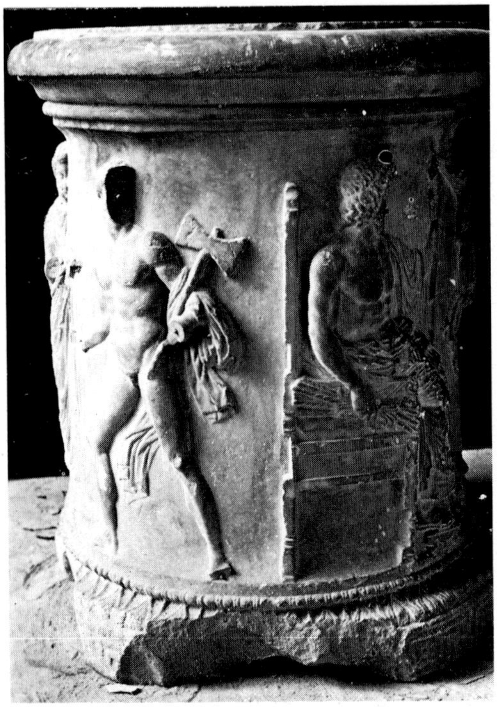

100c

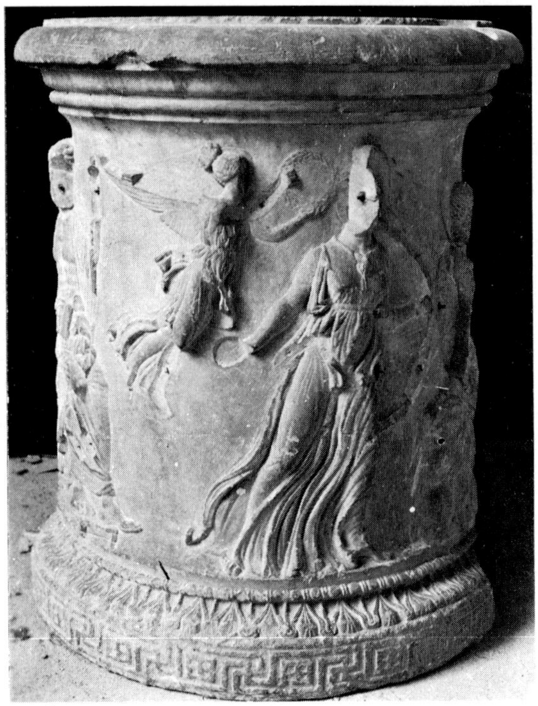

100d

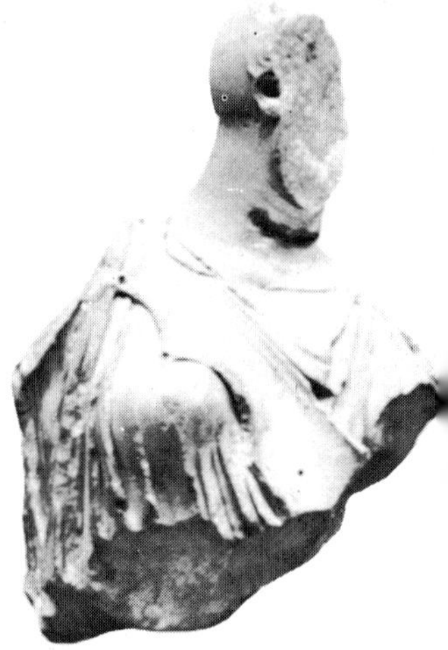

100e

100 **a** and **b** Seventeenth-century drawings of west pediment of Parthenon, probably by Jacques Carrey. Paris, Cabinet des Médailles. Drawings made before A.D. 1687; sculptures, third quarter of fifth century. Original h. of pediment at apex *c.* 3.50. H. of drawing **b** 0.20. (Pp. 229, 276ff., 357, 539) **c** and **d** Marble circular altar. Madrid, Museo Arqueológico 2.691. First or second century A.D., probably copying design of central part of east pediment of Parthenon (third quarter of fifth century). H. 0.99. (Pp. 301ff., 539) **e** Marble torso-fragment from west pediment of Parthenon. British Museum 304L, made up with cast of neck-fragment in Acropolis Museum, Athens. Third quarter of fifth century. H. 0.76. (Pp. 299, 304f.).

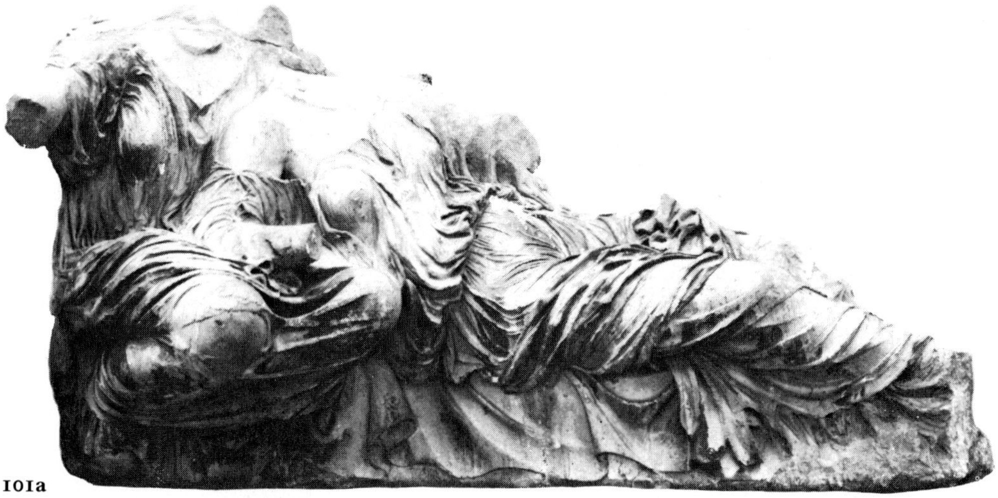

101a

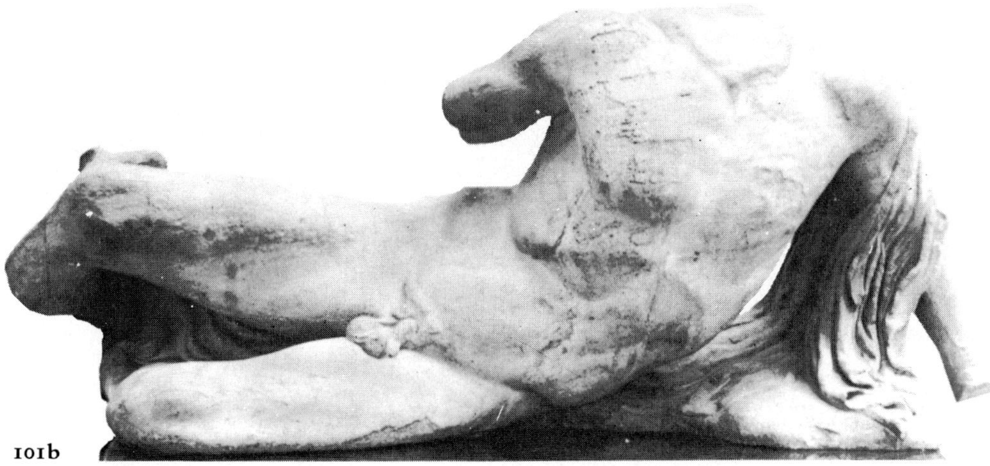

101b

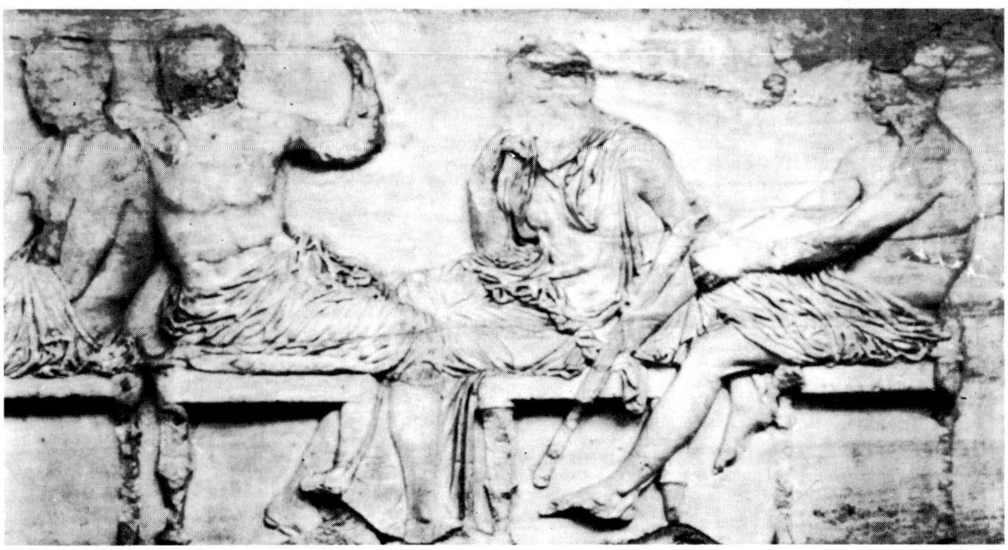

101c

101 **a** Marble group from east pediment of Parthenon. British Museum 303 L and M. Third quarter of fifth century L. 2.33. (Pp. 269, 303) **b** Marble figure from west pediment of Parthenon. British Museum 304 A. Third quarter of fifth century. L. 1.56. (Pp. 300, 357) **c** Marble slab from east frieze of Parthenon. British Museum 324 IV. Third quarter of fifth century. H. 1.05. (P. 308).

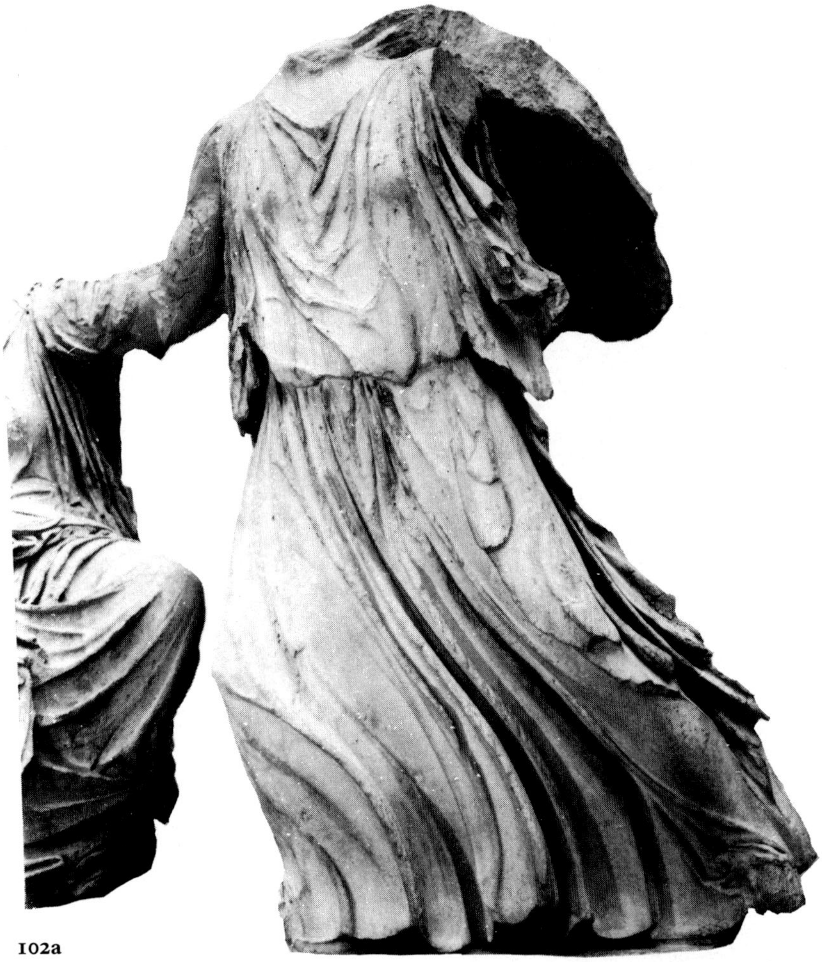

102a

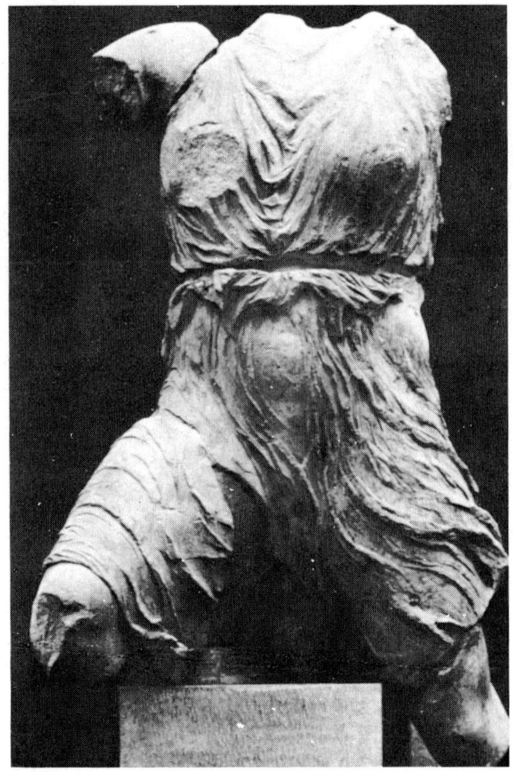

102b

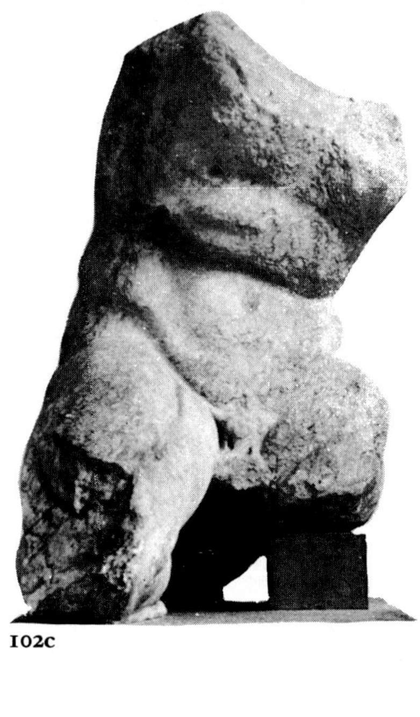

102c

102 **a** Marble figure from east pediment of Parthenon. British Museum 303 G. Third quarter of fifth century. H. 1.73. (P. 302) **b** Marble figure from west pediment of Parthenon. British Museum 303 J. Third quarter of fifth century. H. 1.35. (Pp. 299–300) **c** Marble figure from west pediment of Parthenon. Athens, Acropolis Museum. Third quarter of fifth century. H. 0.94. (Pp. 268, 300).

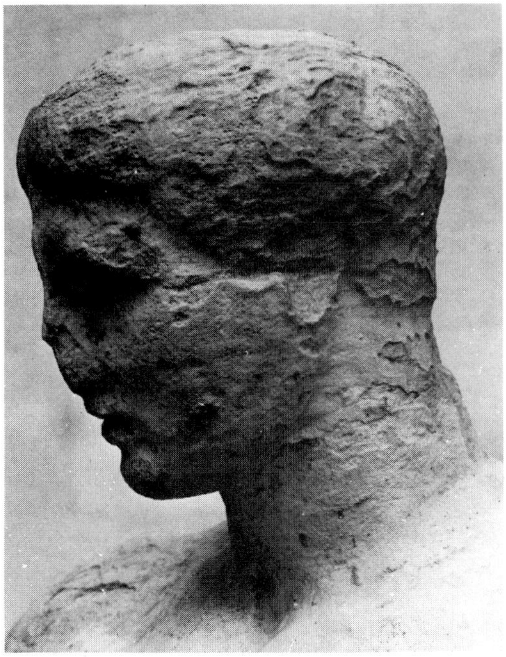

103a

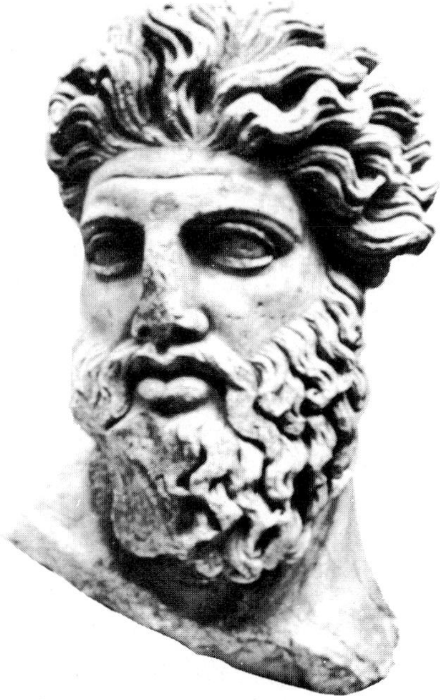

103b

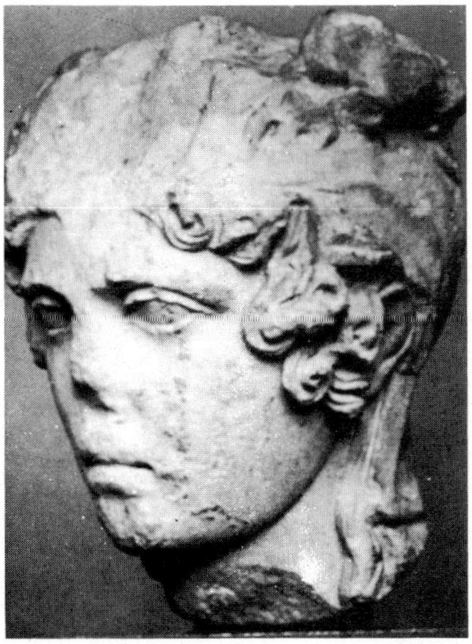

103c

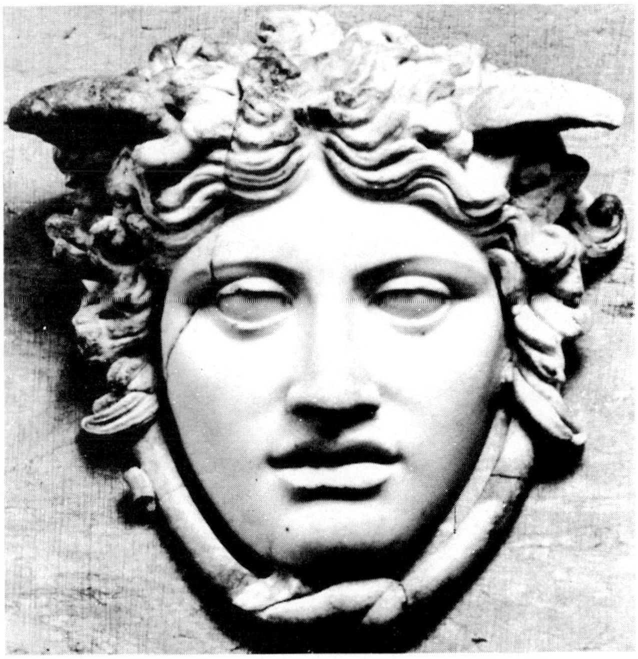

103d

103 **a** Head of marble figure from east pediment of Parthenon. British Museum 303 D. Third quarter of fifth century. H. of head 0.32. (Pp. 302, 304) **b** Head of marble figure from Odeion in the Athenian Agora. Mid second century A.D., apparently copied from Poseidon of west pediment of Parthenon (third quarter of fifth century). H. 0.57. (P. 304) **c** Marble head. Copenhagen, Ny Carlsberg Glyptotek 98 (1791). Copy of the imperial period after Pheidias's Athena Parthenos (third quarter of fifth century). H. 0.34. (Pp. 311ff.) **d** Marble mask. Munich. Copy of the imperial age, probably after original of second half of fifth century. H. 0.40. (P. 313).

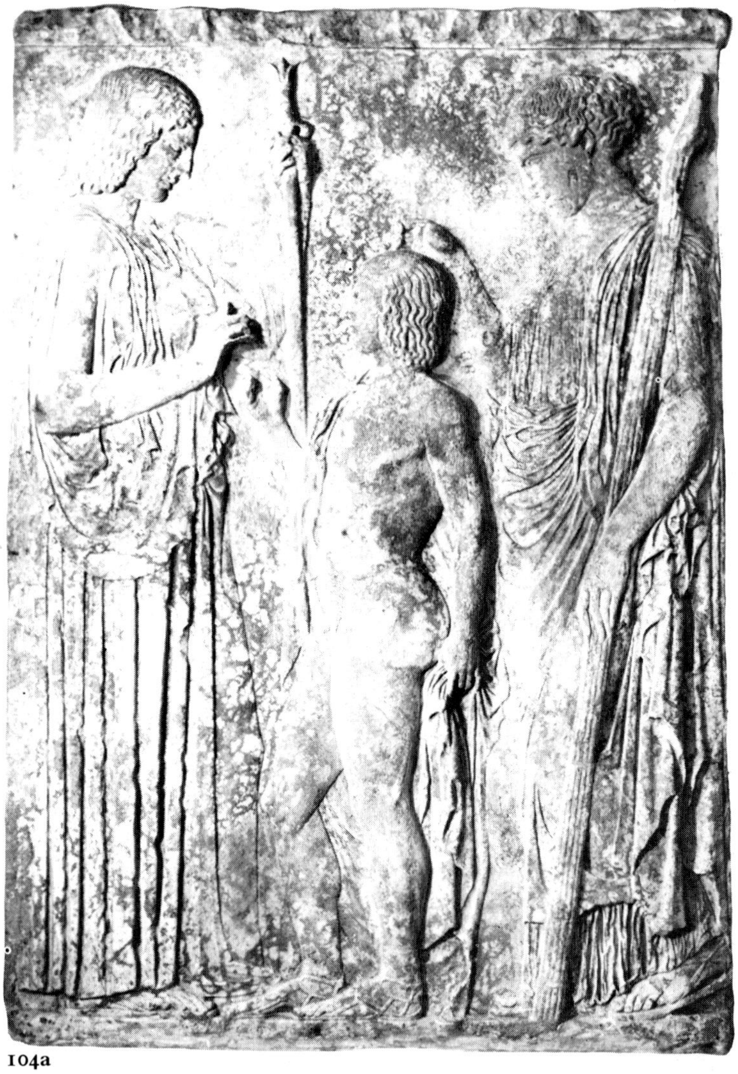

104a

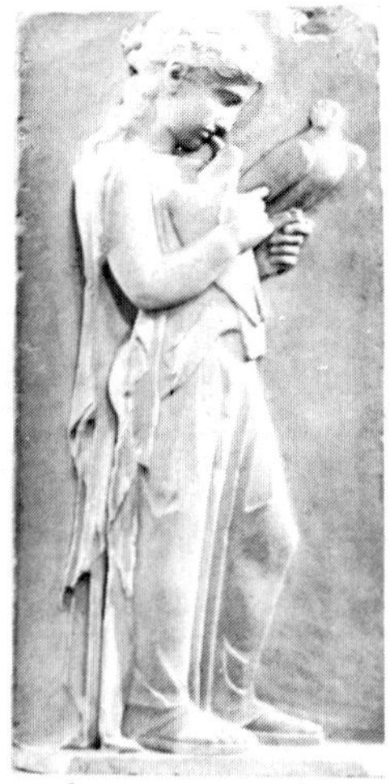

104b

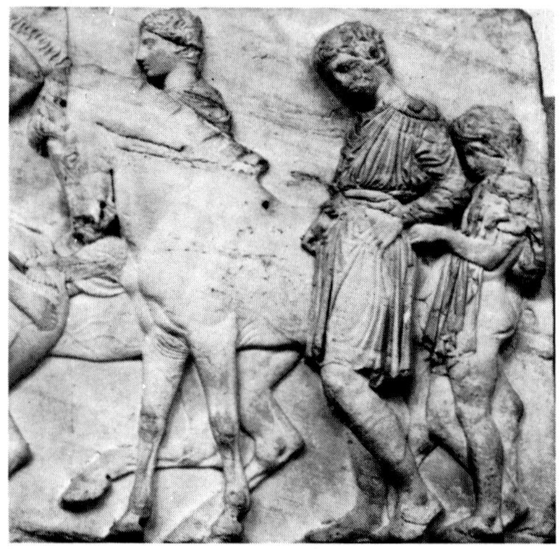

104c

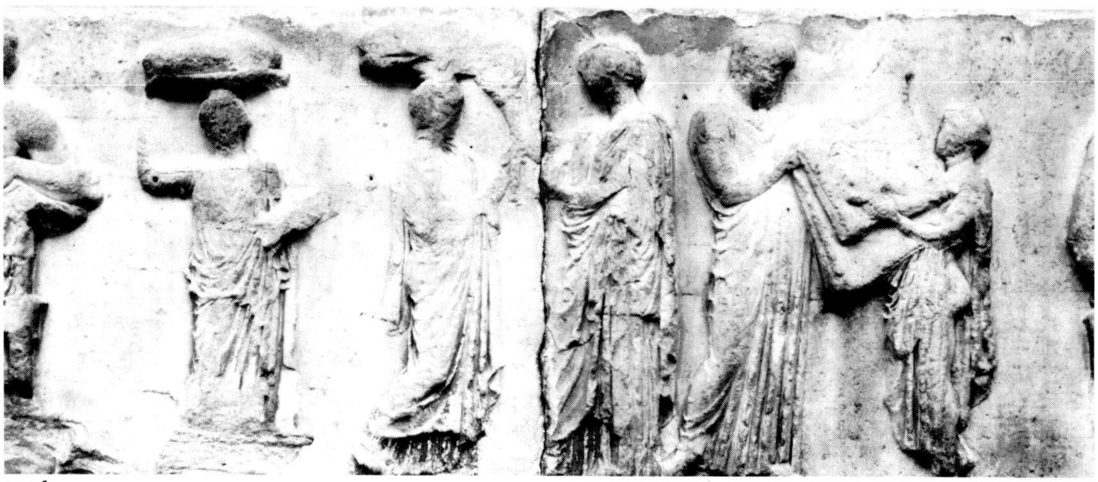

104d

104 **a** Marble relief from Eleusis. Athens, National Museum 126. Second half of fifth century. H. 2.20 (Pp. 309–10) **b** Marble grave-relief from Paros. New York, Metropolitan Museum of Art 27.45, Fletcher Fund. Mid fifth century. H. 0.80. (Pp. 308, 363) **c** Part of marble slab from north frieze of Parthenon. British Museum 325 XLII. Third quarter of fifth century. H. 1.05. (P. 307) **d** Part of marble slab from east frieze of Parthenon. British Museum 324 V. Third quarter of fifth century. H. 1.05. (Pp. 307–8).

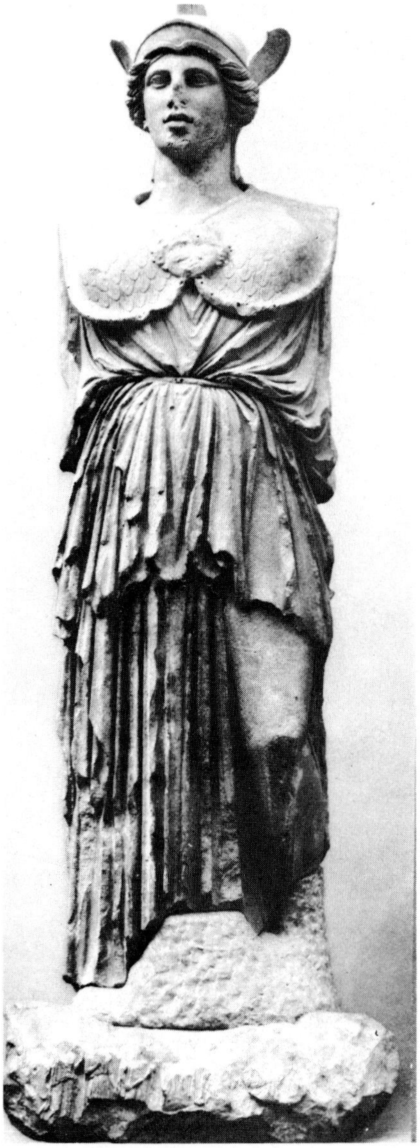

105a

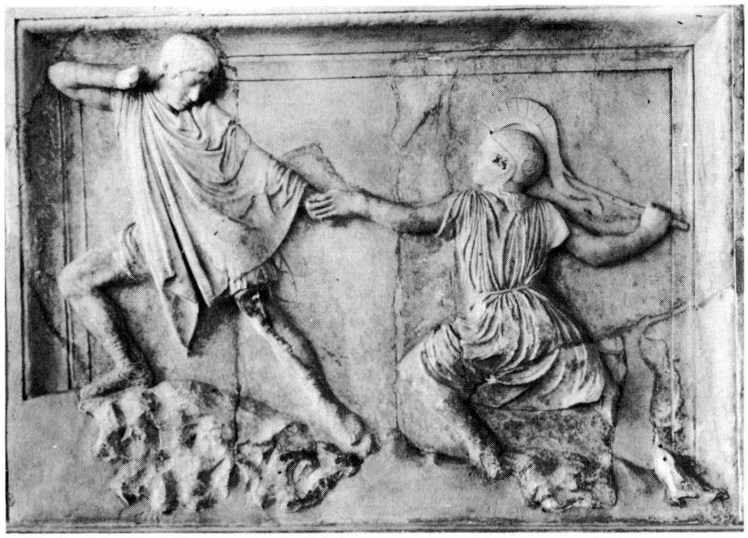

105b

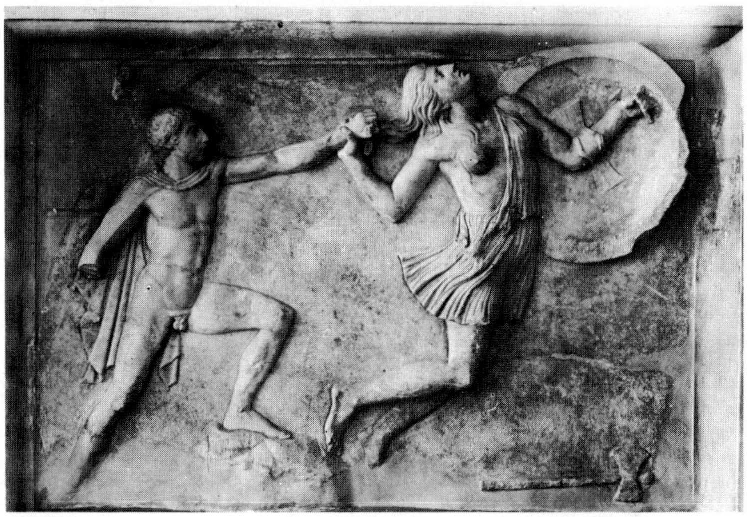

105c

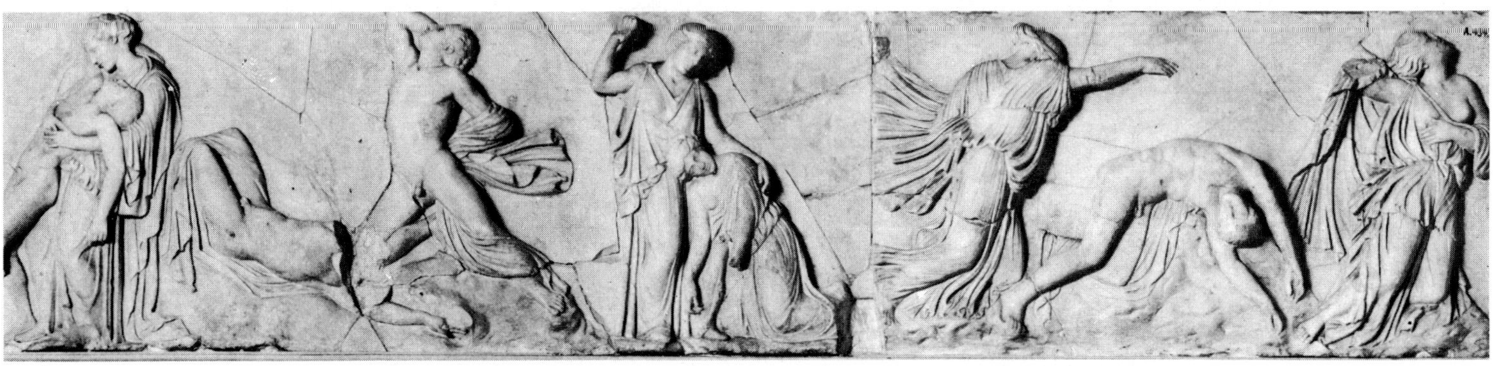

105d

105 **a** Marble statue and base from Pergamon. Berlin (E). Second century, based on Pheidias's Athena Parthenos (third quarter of fifth century). H. with base 3.51. (Pp. 311–12, 354, 546) **b** and **c** Marble reliefs from ship sunk in Piraeus harbour. Piraeus Museum. Copies of the imperial period after groups on shield of Pheidias's Athena Parthenos (third quarter of fifth century). H. 0.90. (Pp. 315–16) **d** Marble relief. Leningrad, Hermitage. Copy of the imperial age after figures on throne of Pheidias's Zeus at Olympia (third to last quarter of fifth century). H. 0.30. (Pp. 319–20, 338).

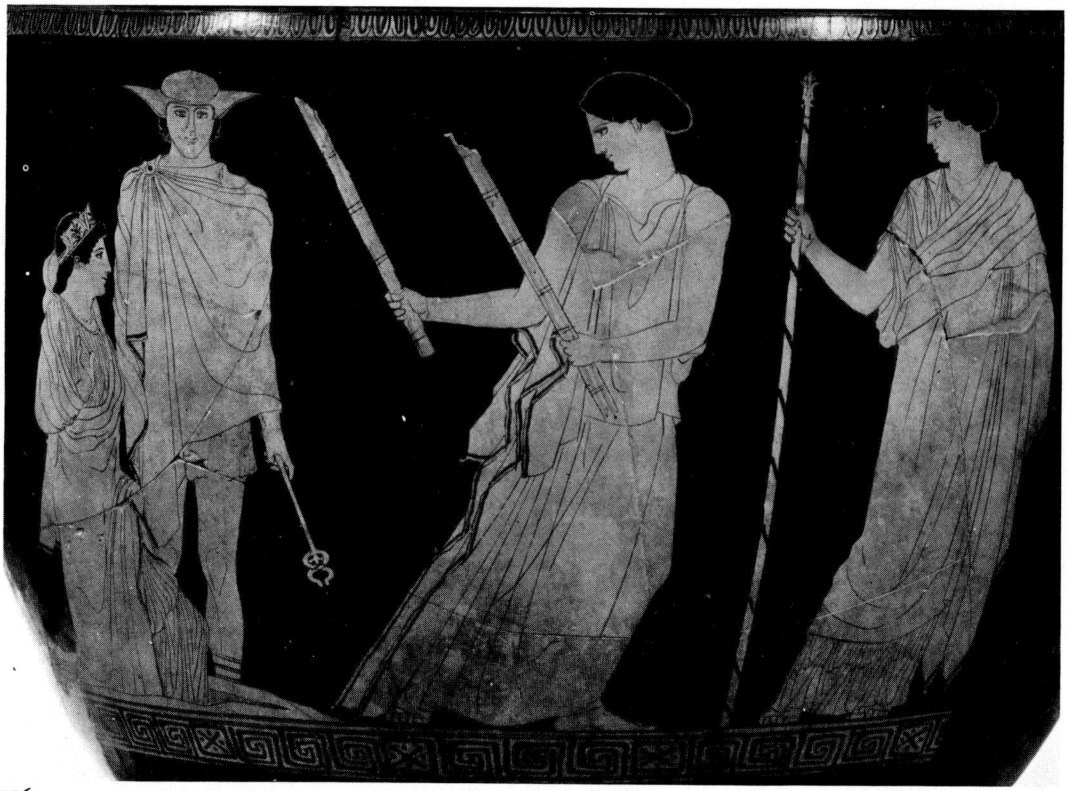

106a

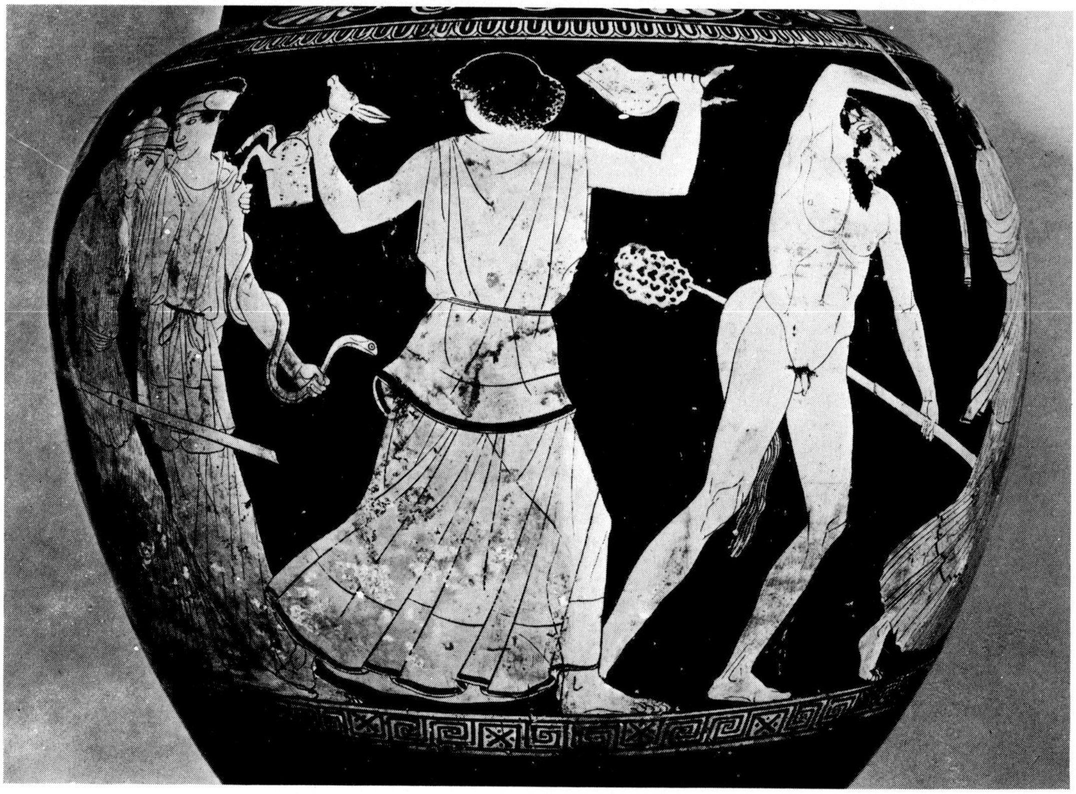

106b

106 **a** Picture from Attic red-figure bell-krater. New York, Metropolitan Museum of Art 28.57.23, Fletcher Fund. Third quarter of fifth century. H. of picture *c.* 0.25. (Pp. 326–7, 408). **b** Details from picture on Attic red-figure pointed amphora. Paris, Cabinet des Médailles 357. Third quarter of fifth century. H. of picture *c.* 0.25. (P. 324).

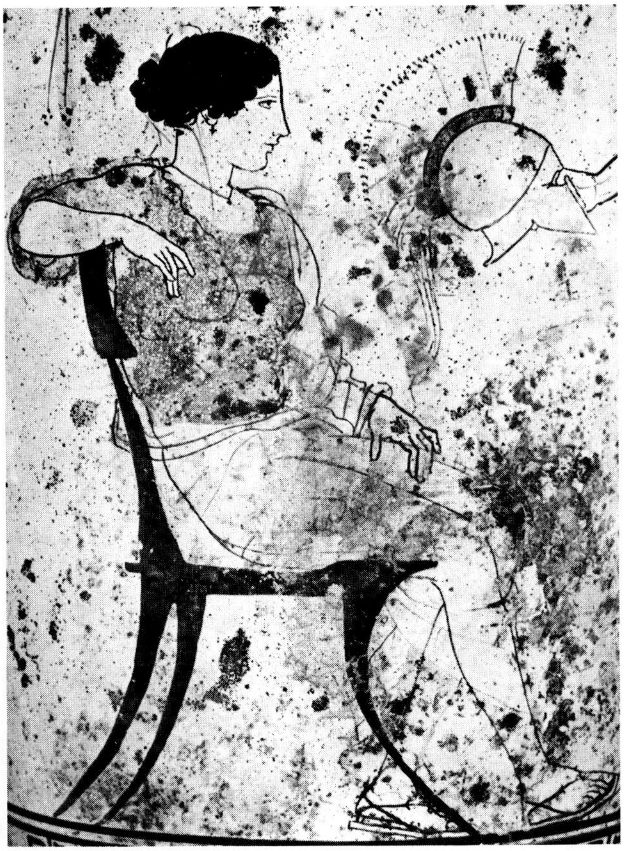

107a

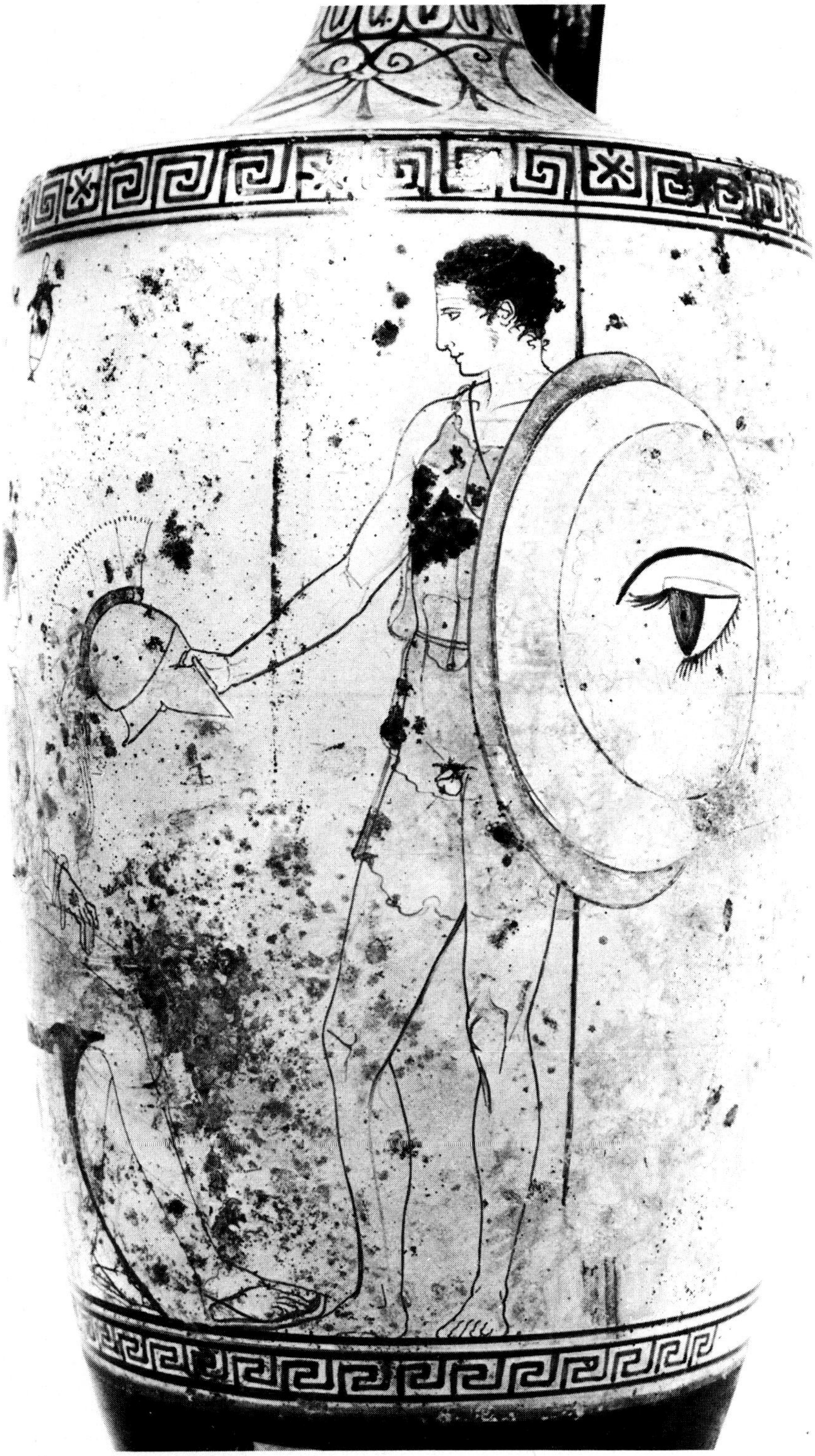

107b

107 **a** and **b** Picture from Attic white funeral lekythos, from Eretria. Athens, National Museum 1818. Third quarter of fifth century. H. of picture 0.21. (Pp. 325, 366).

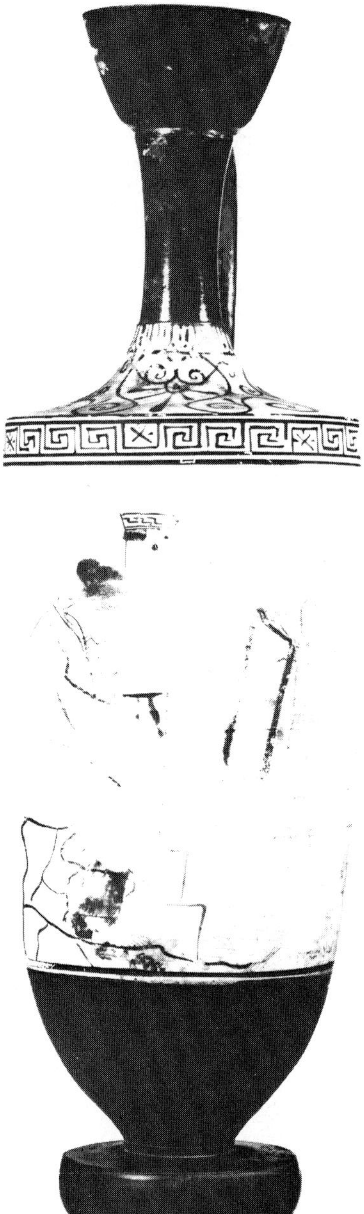

108a

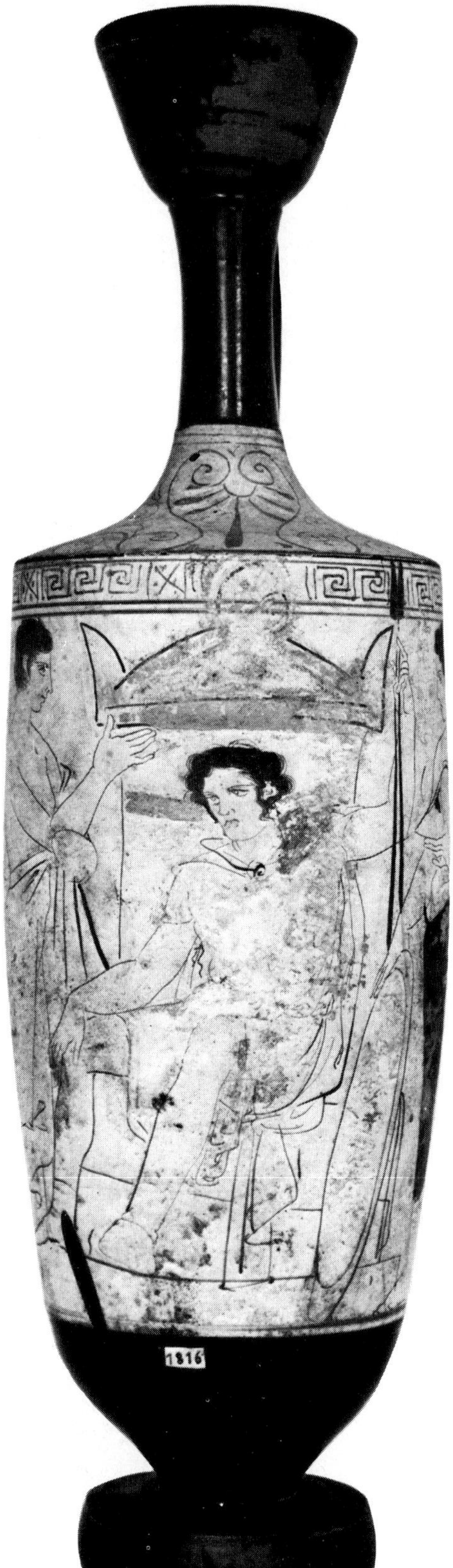

108b

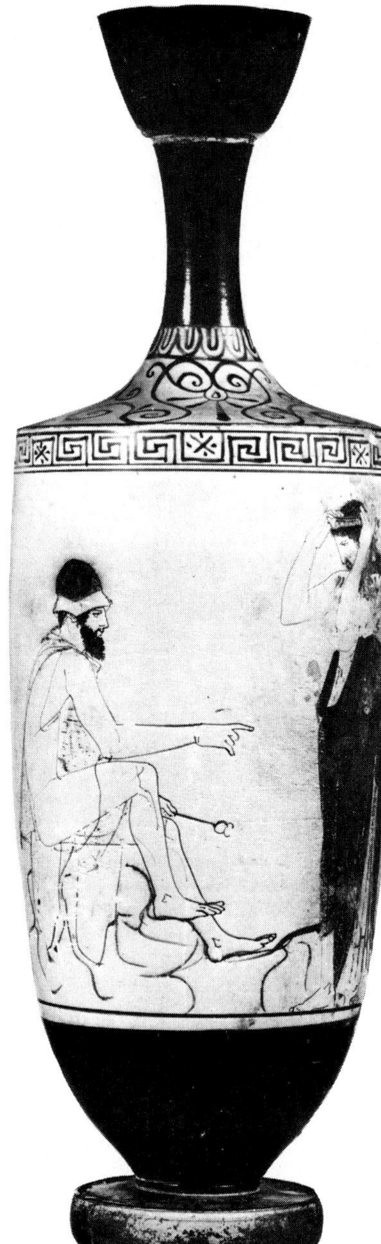

108c

108 **a** Attic white funeral lekythos from Oropos (Attica). Munich 2798. Third or last quarter of fifth century. H. 0.36. (Pp. 326, 421) **b** Attic white funeral lekythos from Eretria. Athens, National Museum 1816. End of fifth century. H. 0.48. (P. 422) **c** Attic white funeral lekythos from Oropos (Attica). Munich 2797. Third or last quarter of fifth century. H. 0.37. (Pp. 326, 421).

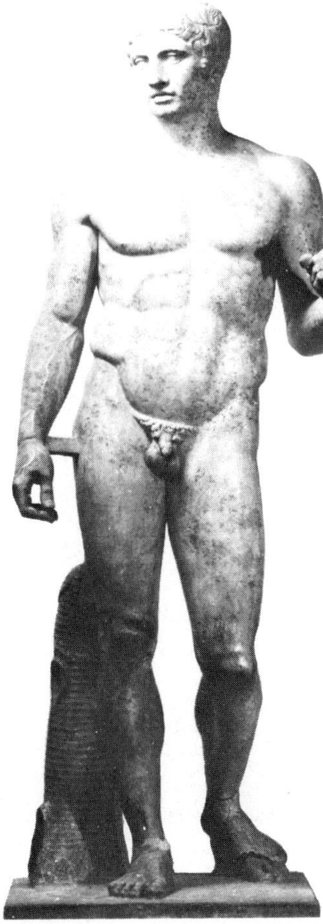

109a

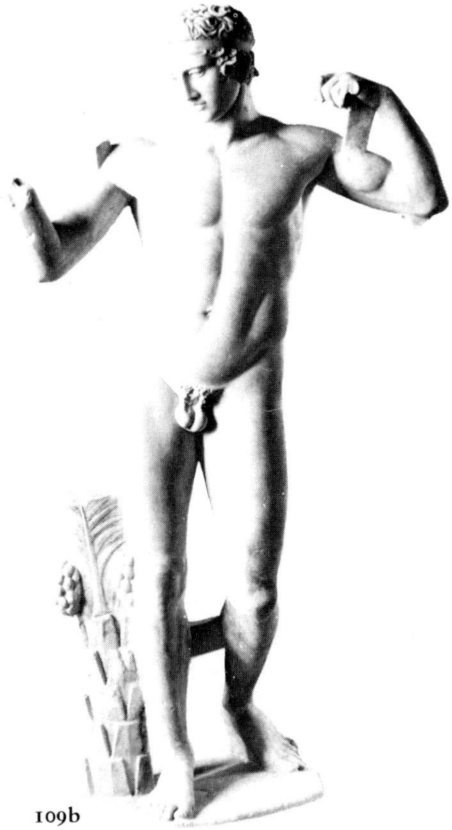

109b

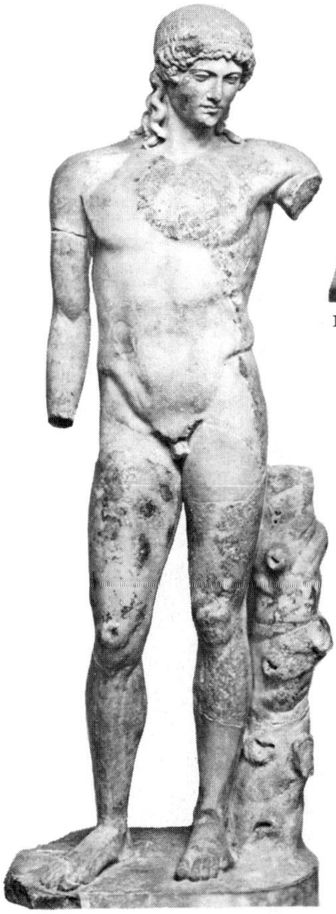

109c

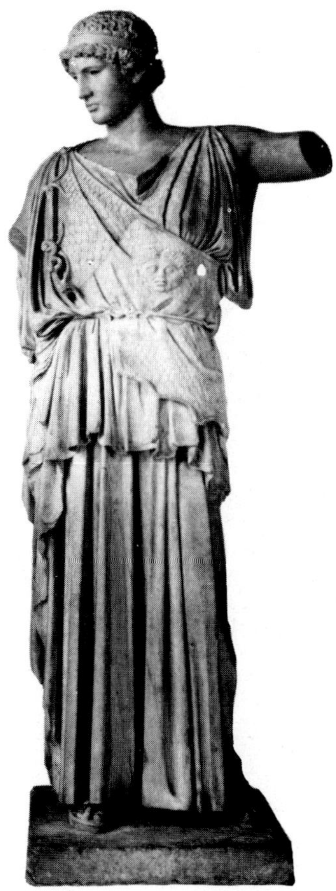

109d

109 **a** Marble statue from Pompeii. Naples Museum. Copy, made before A.D. 79, from a bronze of third quarter of fifth century. Cf. pl. 110a. H. 2.12. (Pp. 329ff., 409, 463–5) **b** Marble fragments (head, arms, hand, lower legs and feet, support) made up with cast of statue from Delos (Athens, National Museum 1826). New York, Metropolitan Museum of Art 25.56.78, Fletcher Fund. Copies of the imperial age after bronze of third or last quarter of fifth century. H. 1.95. (Pp. 331–2, 409) **c** Marble statue from the Tiber in Rome. Rome, Museo Nazionale. Copy of the imperial age after bronze of mid fifth century. H. 2.04. (Pp. 329–30) **d** Marble statue. Dresden 50 (with cast of head in Bologna, pl. 110b). Copies of the imperial age after original, probably in bronze, of third quarter of fifth century. H. *c.* 2.00. (Pp. 320–1, 345).

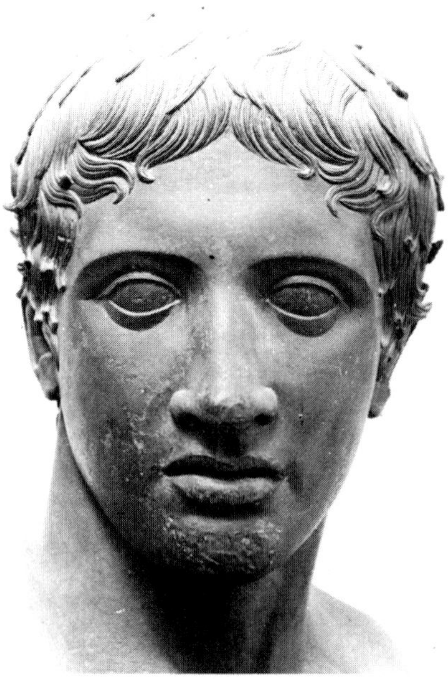

110a

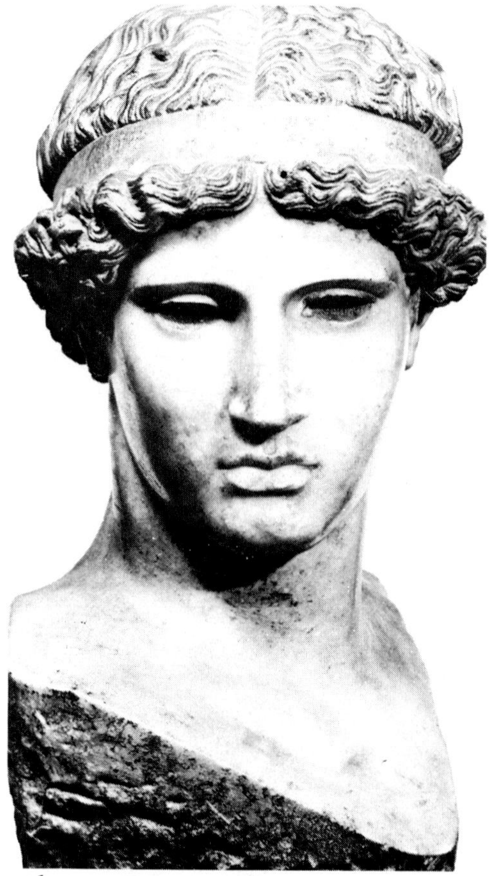

110b

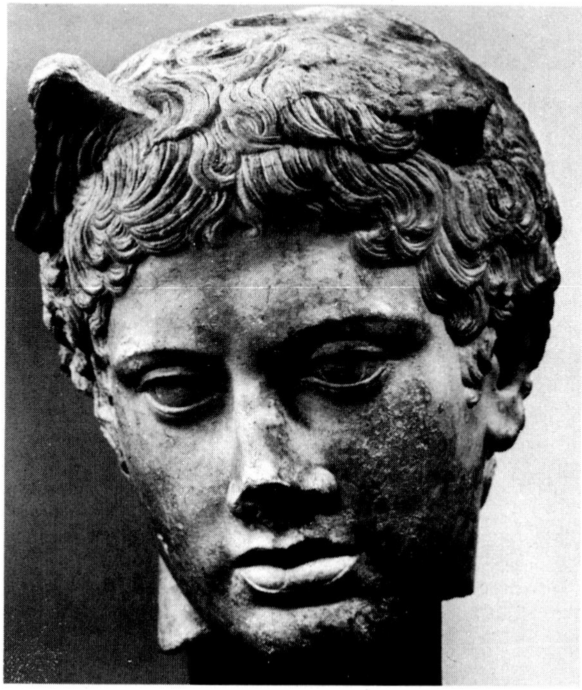

110c

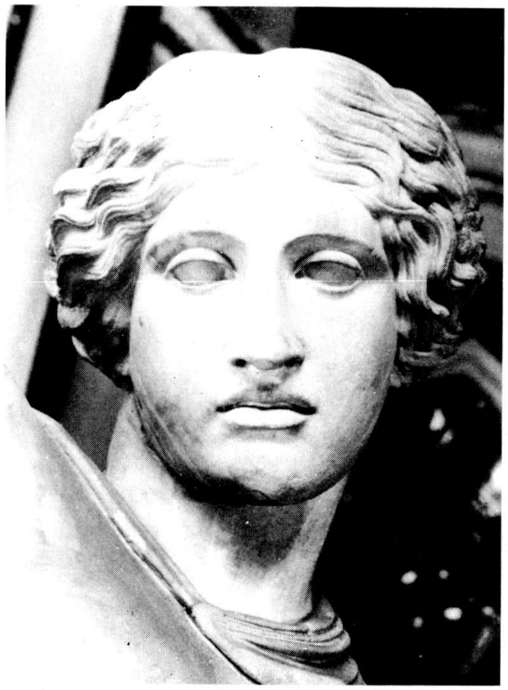

110d

110 **a** Bronze head from Herculaneum. Naples Museum. Copy, made before A.D. 79, from same original as pl. 109a. H. of part shown *c.* 0.30. (Pp. 329–30, 337) **b** Marble head. Bologna Museum. See pl. 109d. H. 0.40. (Pp. 320–1) **c** Marble head. Berlin (E) 1833. Marble copy of the imperial age after original, probably in bronze, of third or last quarter of fifth century. H. 0.25. (Pp. 333, 337) **d** Head of statue, pl. 111c. (Pp. 334, 337).

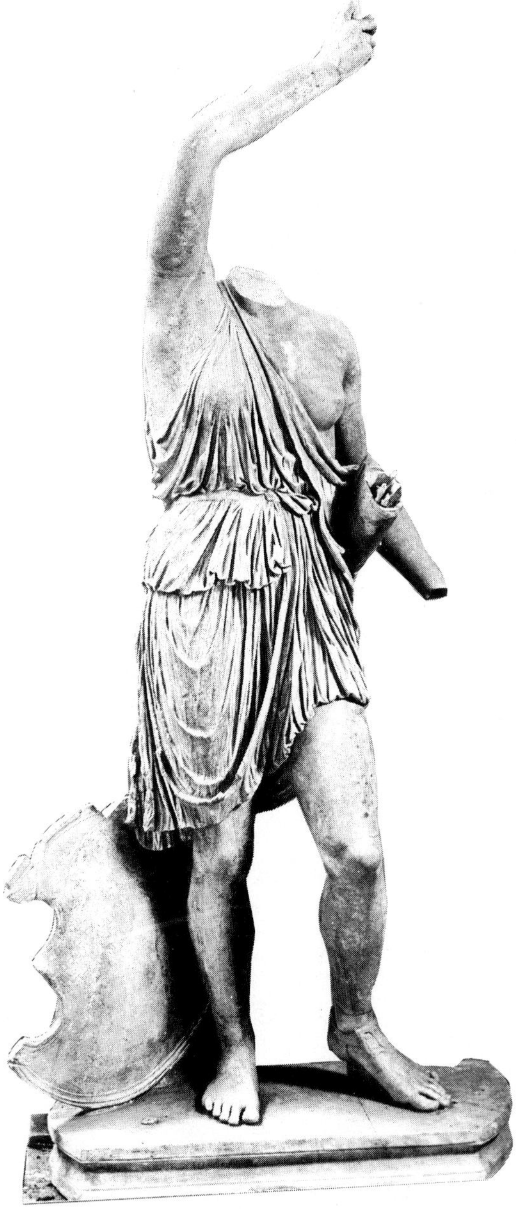

111a

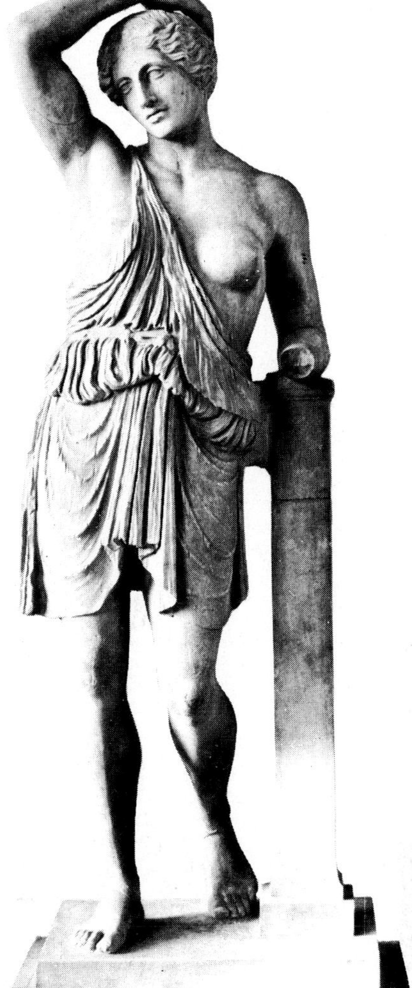

111b

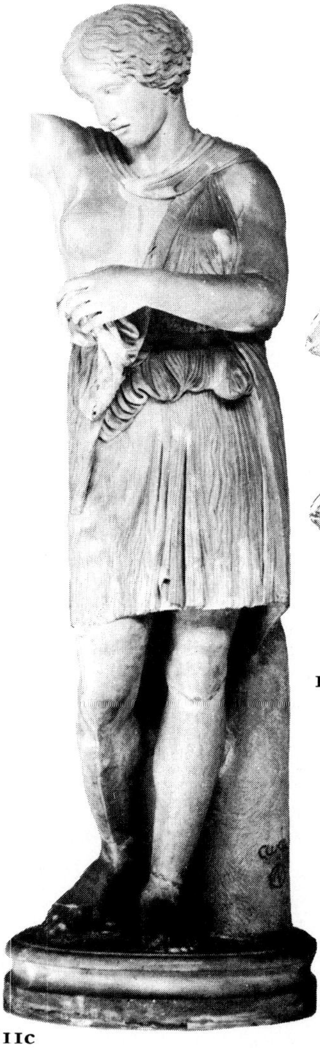

111c

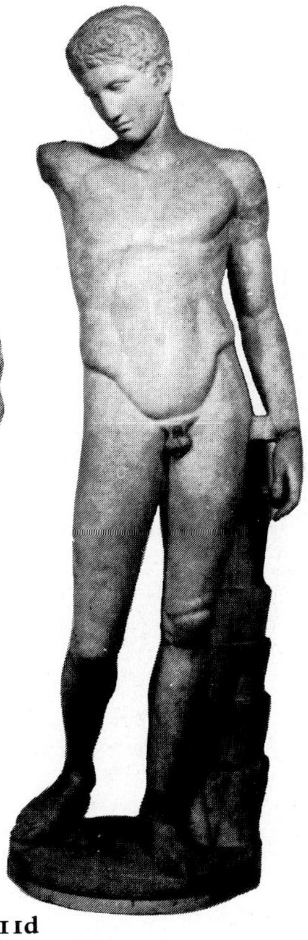

111d

111 **a** Marble statue from Hadrian's Villa, Tivoli. Marble copy (second century A.D.) after bronze original of third quarter of fifth century. Figure on same scale as **b** and **c**. (Pp. 335ff.) **b** Marble statue. New York, Metropolitan Museum of Art 32.11.4. Gift of John D. Rockefeller. Copy of the imperial age after bronze original of third quarter of fifth century. H. 2.03. (Pp. 334ff.) **c** Marble statue, signed by copyist Sosikles. Rome, Museo Capitolino. Copy of the imperial age after bronze original of third quarter of fifth century. H. 1.98. (Pp. 334ff.) **d** Marble statue. British Museum 1754. Copy of the imperial age after bronze original of third quarter of fifth century. H. 1.50. (Pp. 331–2, 337–8).

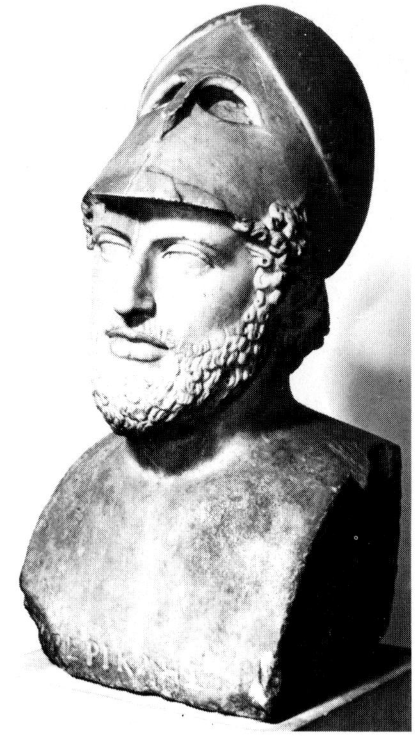

112a

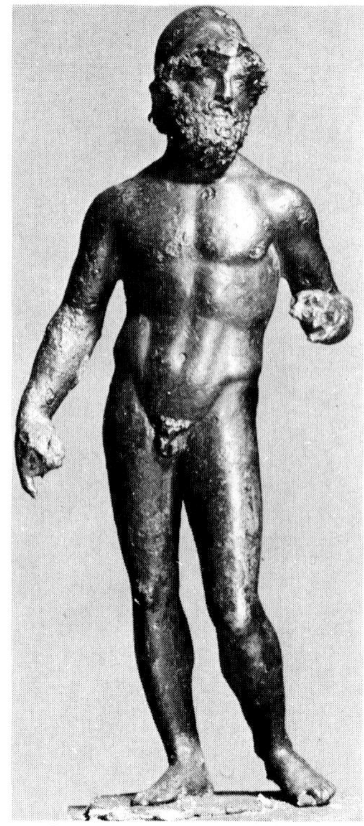

112b

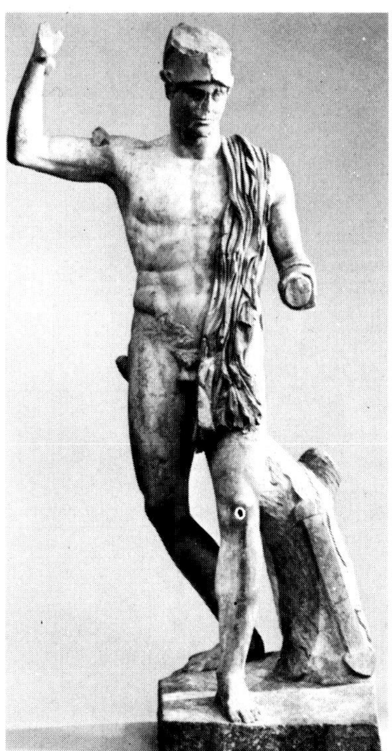

112c

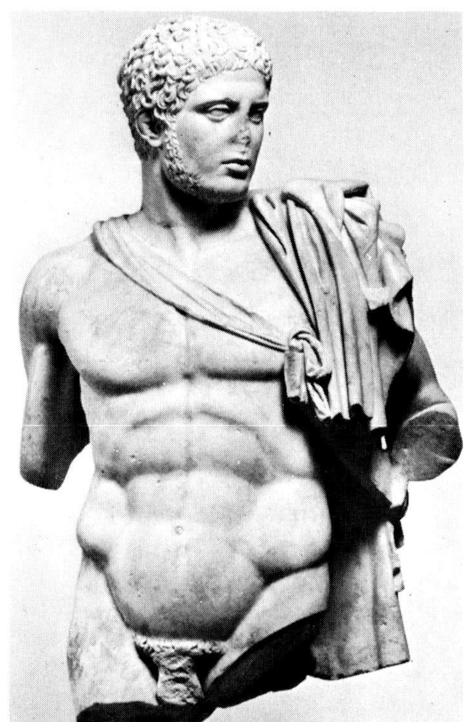

112d

112 **a** Marble bust from Tivoli, inscribed with name of Pericles. British Museum 549. Copy of the imperial age after bronze original of third quarter of fifth century. H. 0.48. (P. 336) **b** Bronze statuette from the Tiber near Rome. Hartford, Conn., Wadsworth Athenaeum, 1917.280. Probably a copy, of the imperial period, after an original statue of the late fifth century. H. 0.29. (P. 336) **c** Marble statue. New York, Metropolitan Museum of Art 25.116, Hewitt Fund. Copy of the imperial age after bronze original of mid fifth century. H. of figure 1.97. (Pp. 338, 343–4) **d** Upper part of marble statue. Munich. Copy of the imperial age after bronze original of third quarter of fifth century. H. 1.02. (P. 336).

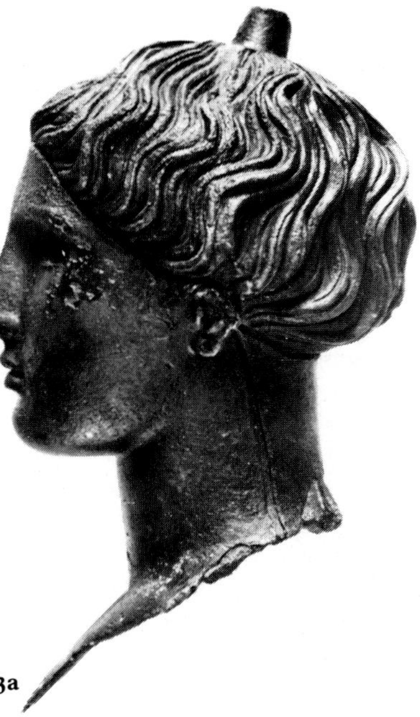

113a

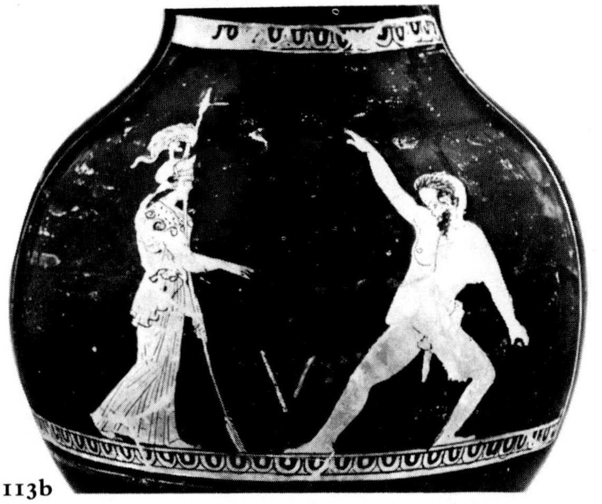

113b

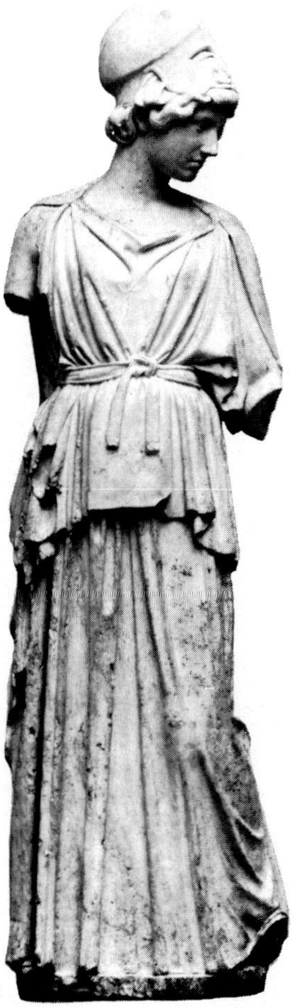

113c

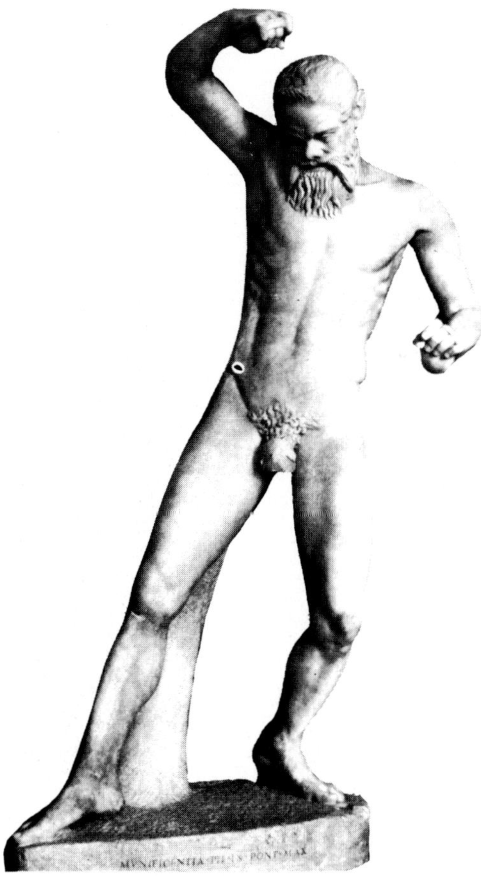

113d

113 **a** Small bronze head, prepared for gold plating, from Agora. Athens, Agora Museum. Third or last quarter of fifth century. H. 0.20. (P. 322) **b** Picture from Attic red-figure oinochoe. Berlin (Charlottenburg) F2415. End of fifth century. H. of picture *c.* 0.14. (Pp. 341ff., 420) **c** Marble statue. Frankfurt/Main 195. Copy of the imperial age after original, probably in bronze, of mid fifth century. H. 1.73. (Pp. 341ff.) **d** Marble statue. Vatican (ex Lateran). Copy of the imperial age after bronze original of mid fifth century. H. 1.59. Modern: hands and much of arms. (Pp. 341ff., 395).

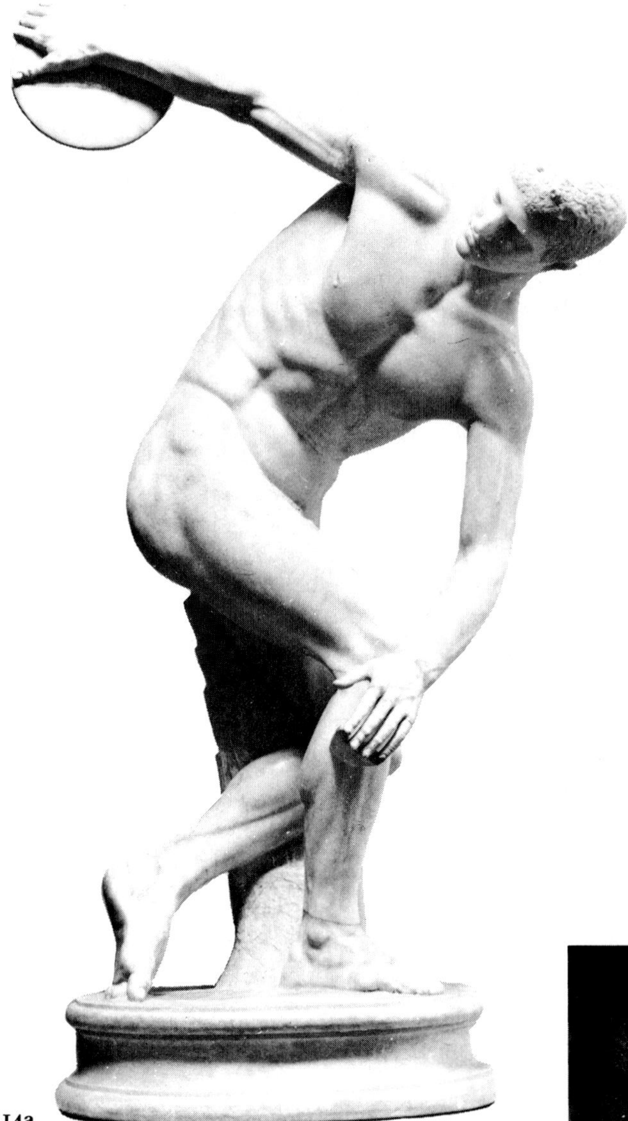

114a

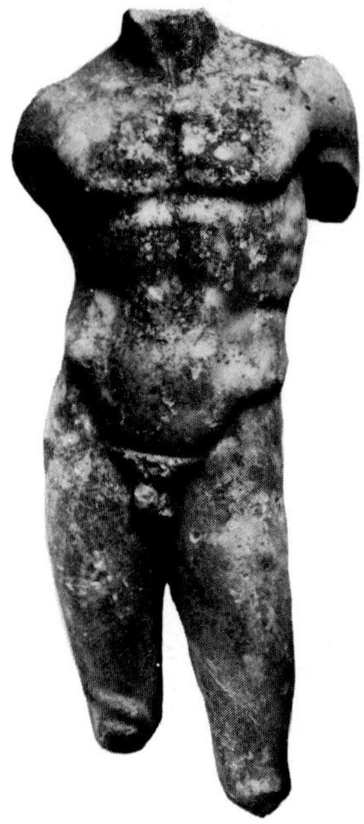

114b

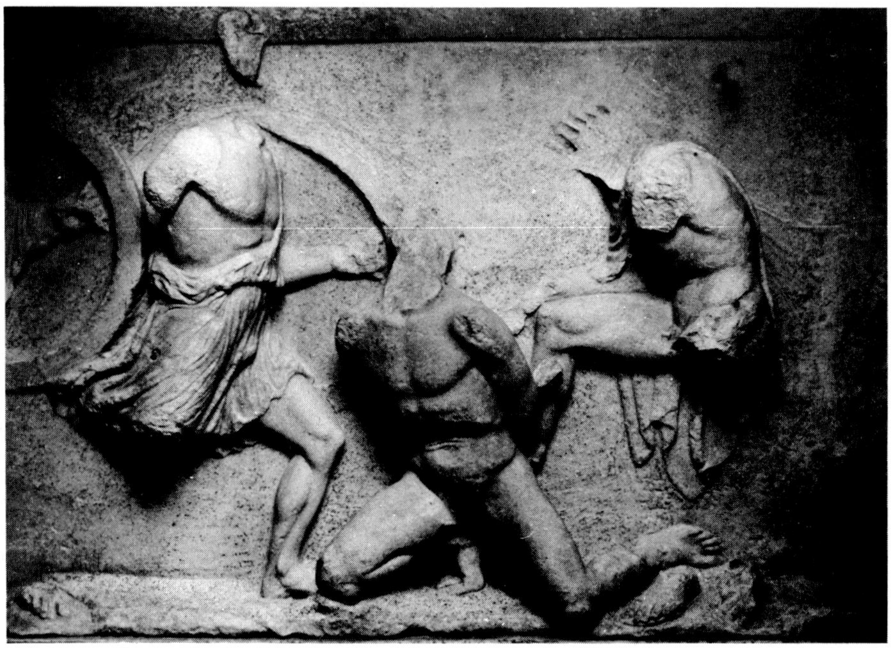

114c

114 **a** Marble statue. Rome, Museo Nazionale 20. Reconstructed copy of the imperial age after bronze original of mid fifth century. H. 1.53. (Pp. 340–1) **b** Marble torso from Agora. Athens, Agora Museum. Third quarter of fifth century. H. 0.83. (P. 345) **c** Marble slab from east frieze of Temple of Hephaestus, Athens. Third quarter of fifth century. H. 0.85. (P. 344).

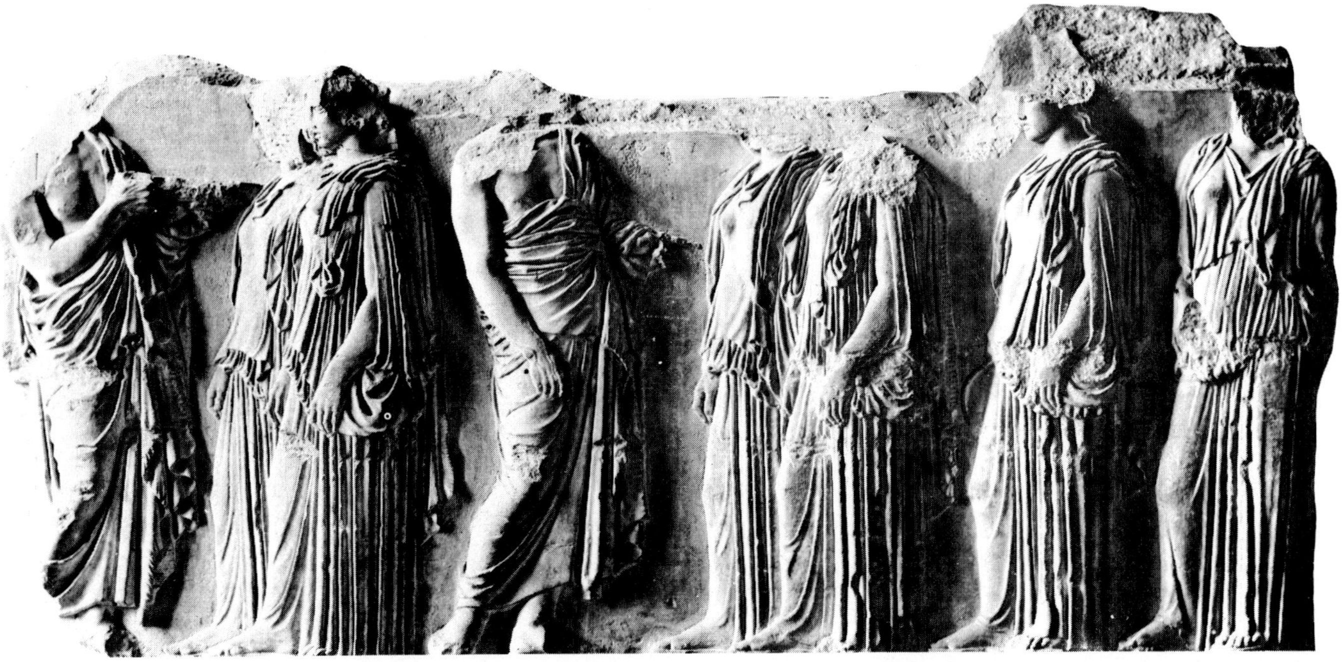

115a

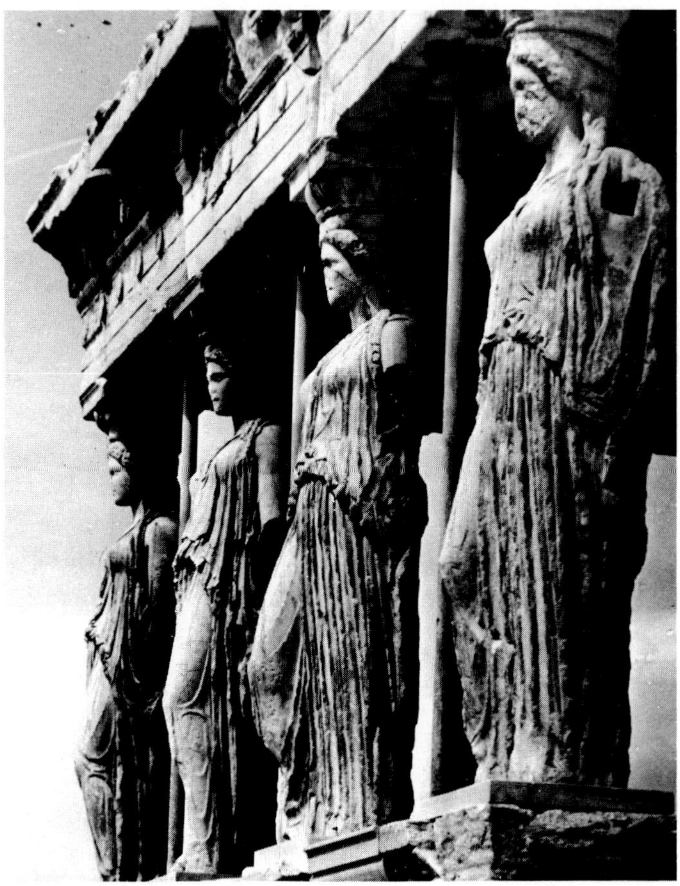

115b

115 **a** Marble slab from east frieze of Parthenon. Louvre 738. Third quarter of fifth century. H. 1.05. (Pp. 308, 346)
b Marble Caryatid porch of Erechtheum. Athens, Acropolis. Last quarter of fifth century. H. of figures, with capitals, 2.30. (Pp. 345–6).

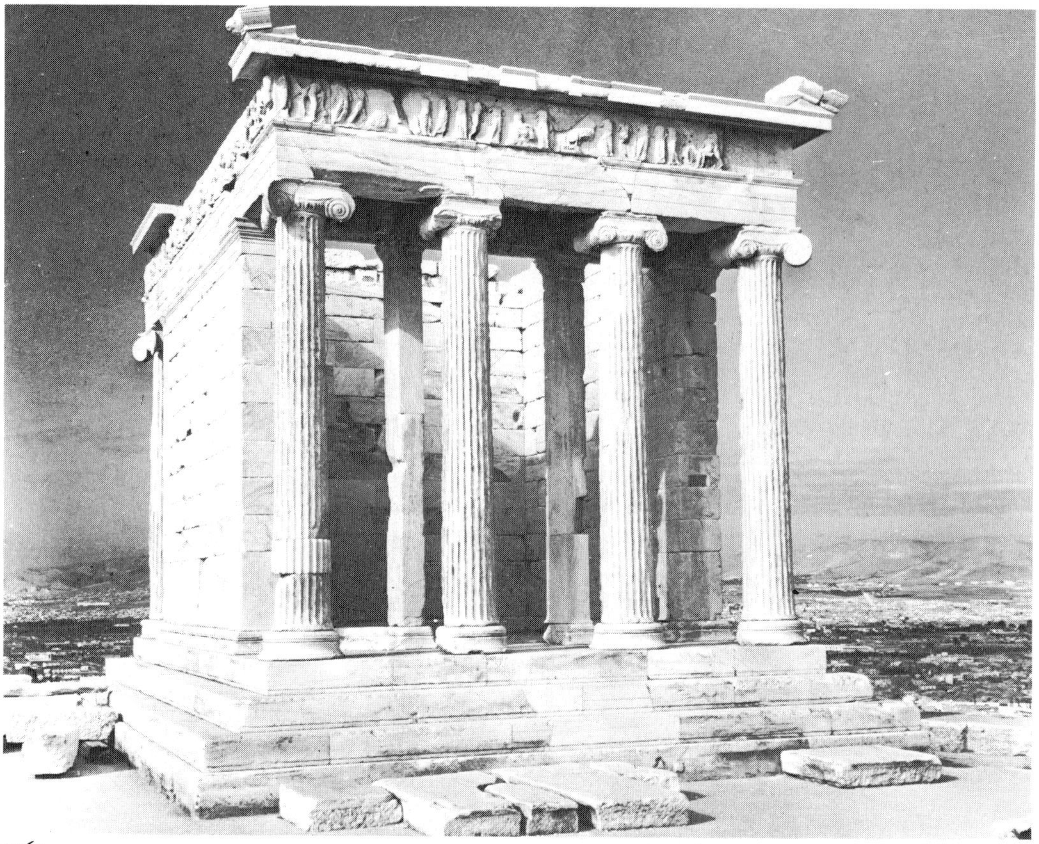

116a

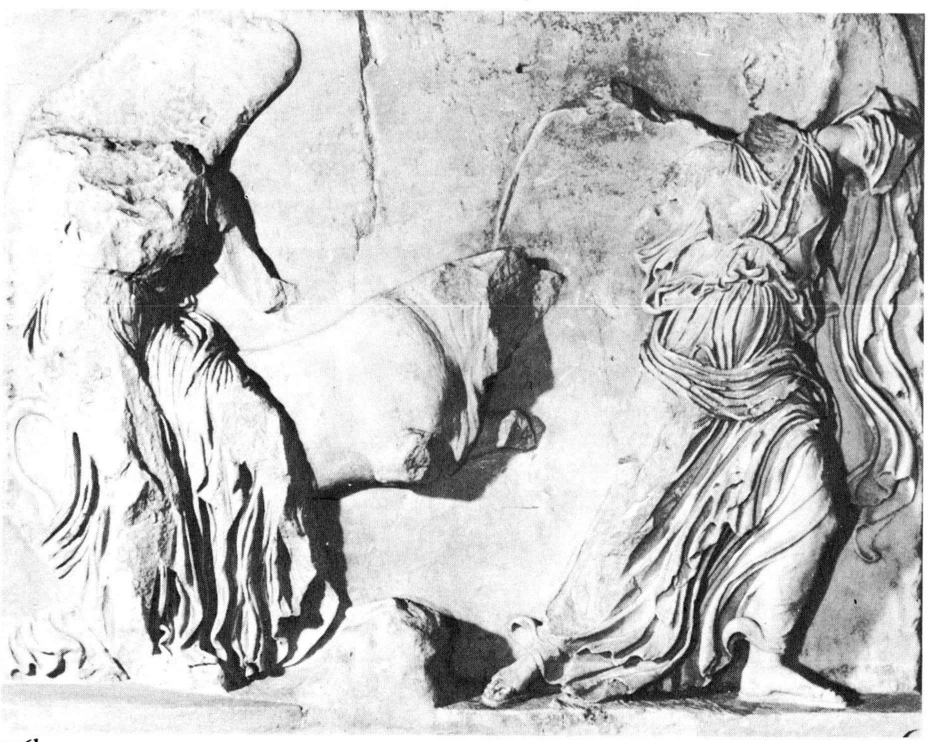

116b

116 **a** Marble Temple of Athena Nike. Athens, Acropolis. Third to last quarter of fifth century. W. of top step *c.* 5.40. (Pp. 83, 347–8) **b** Marble relief-slab from parapet of Temple of Athena Nike. Athens, Acropolis Museum. Last quarter of fifth century. H. 1.40. See also pl. 117a. (Pp. 349–50, 355).

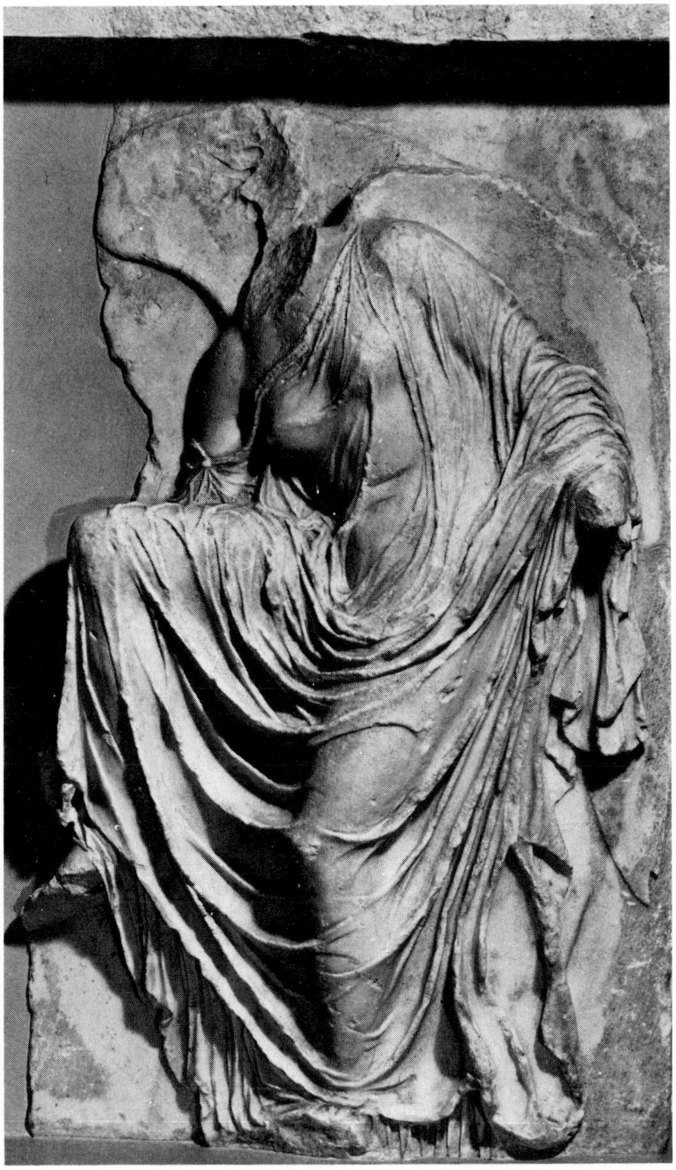

117a

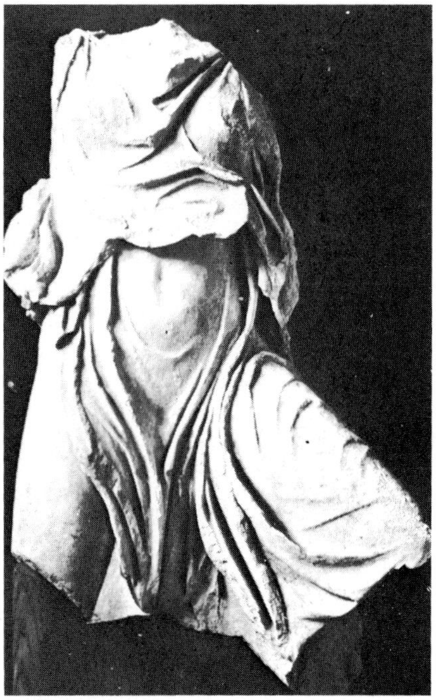

117b

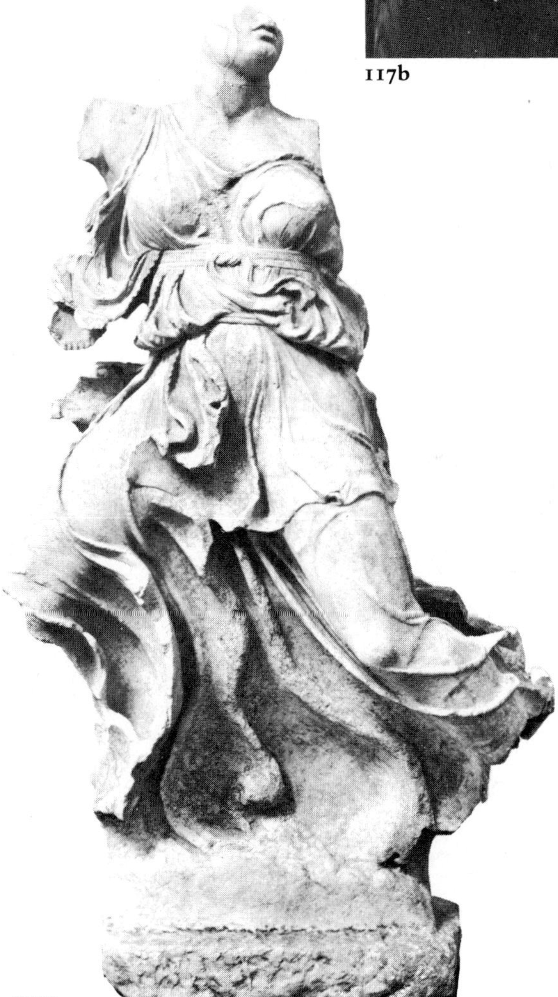

117c

117 **a** Marble relief-slab from parapet of Temple of Athena Nike. Athens, Acropolis Museum. Last quarter of fifth century. H. 1.40. See also pl. 116. (Pp. 349–50, 391) **b** Marble torso from Rome. Rome, Museo Nazionale. Late fifth or early fourth century. H. 0.81. (P. 350) **c** Marble akroterion from Stoa of Zeus, Athens. Athens, Agora Museum. Late fifth century. H. 1.20. (P. 350).

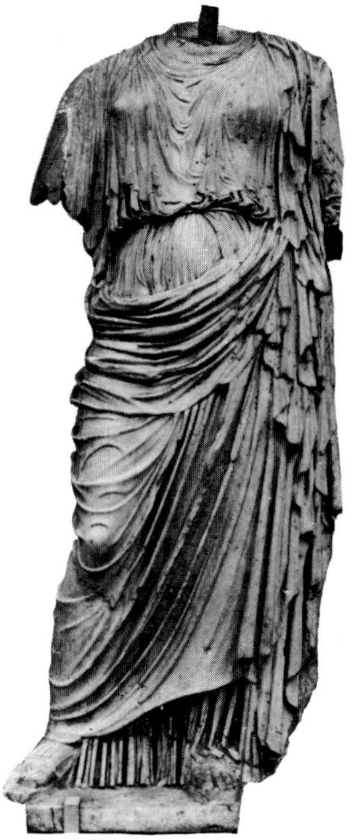

118a

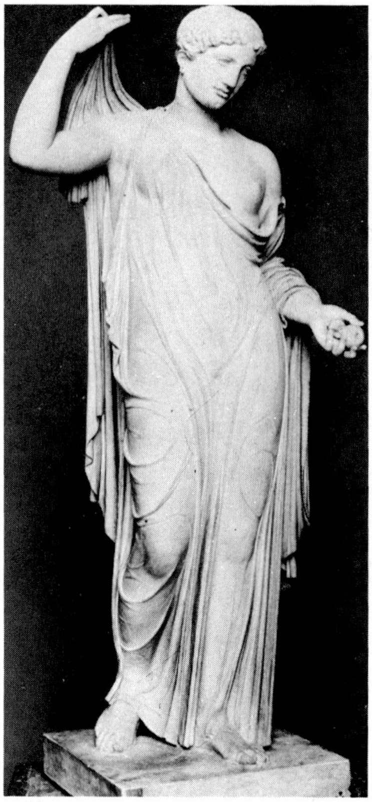

118b

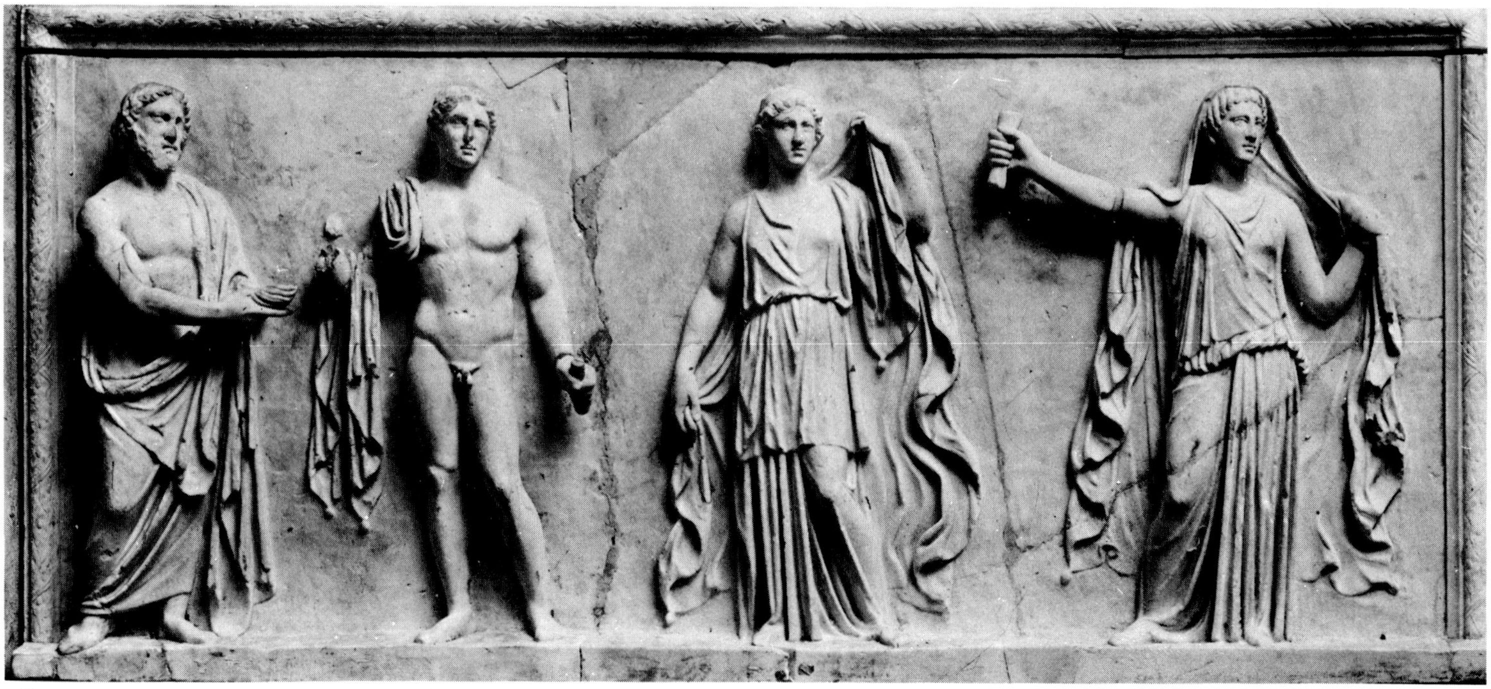

118c

118 **a** Marble statue. Copenhagen, Ny Carlsberg Glyptotek 304a. Reduced copy of the imperial age after marble original of third quarter of fifth century. H. 1.93. (P. 355) **b** Marble statue, probably from south Italy. Louvre. Copy of the imperial age after original of last quarter of fifth century. H. 1.65. The neck is modern, and the head not quite rightly set. (Pp. 350–1, 355, 391, 549, 601) **c** Marble relief, fragmentary and restored. Stockholm, Nationalmuseum 150. Copy of the imperial age after marble original of third quarter of fifth century. H. (with modern frame) 0.51. Modern, besides the frame, are part of the background, the right hand of figure 1, left hand of figure 2, nose and right hand of figure 3, right forearm and hand of figure 4. (P. 353).

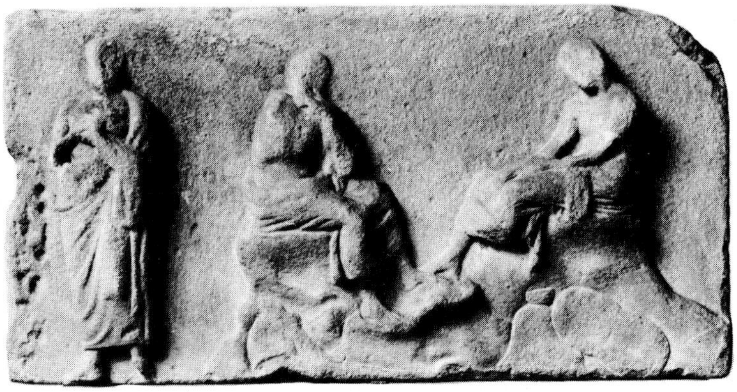

119a

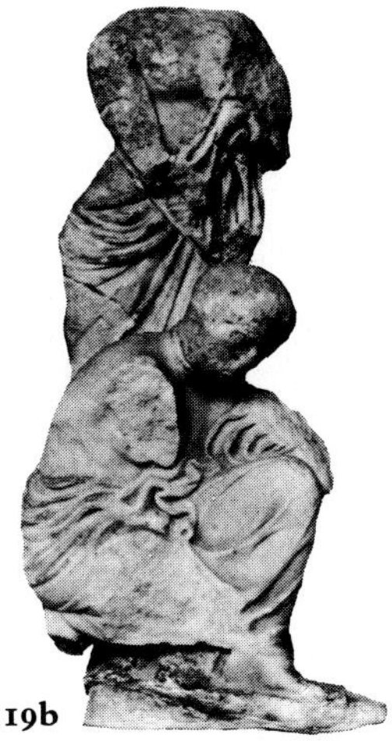

119b

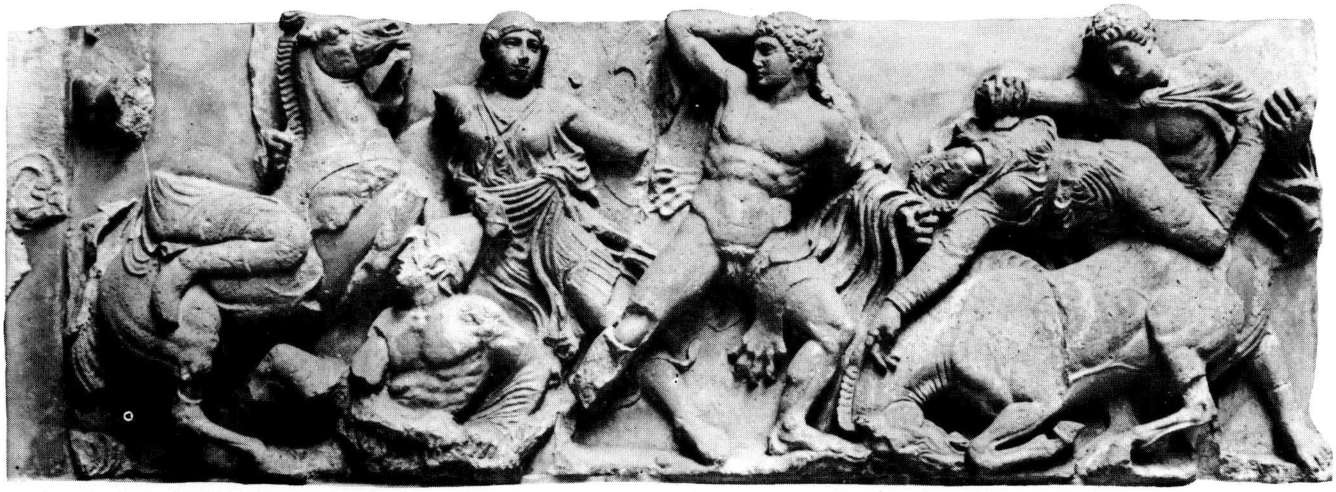

119c

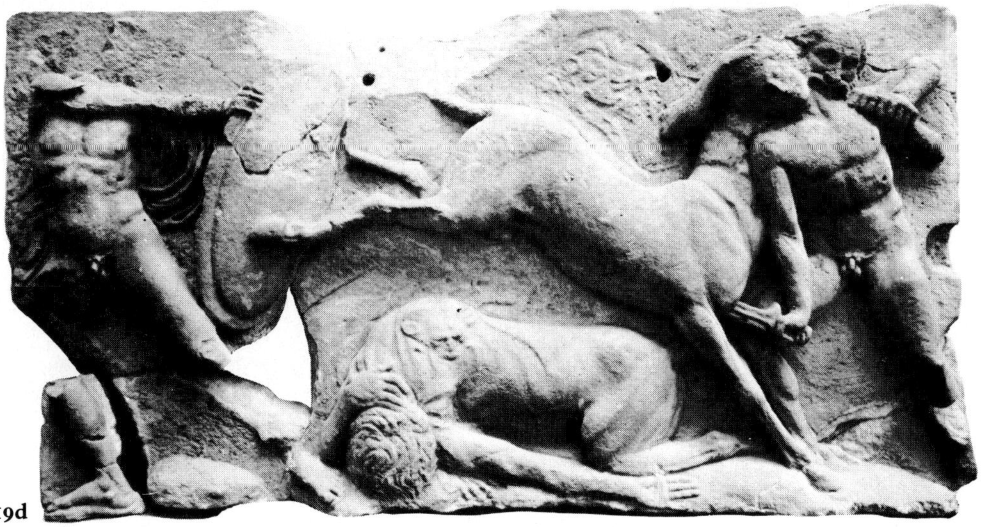

119d

119 **a** Marble relief-slab from frieze of temple by the Ilissos, Athens. Berlin (E) K 14. Third quarter of fifth century. H. 0.47. (P. 348) **b** Marble group carved to be attached to a background, from frieze of Erechtheum. Athens, Acropolis Museum 1073. Late fifth century. H. 0.59. (P. 346) **c** and **d** Marble relief-slabs from interior frieze of Temple of Apollo at Bassae–Phigaleia (Arcadia). British Museum 541 and 527. Probably late fifth century. H. 0.64. (Pp. 357–8).

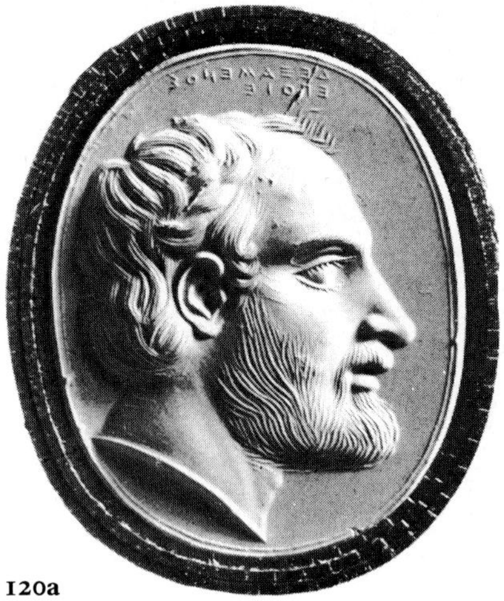

120a

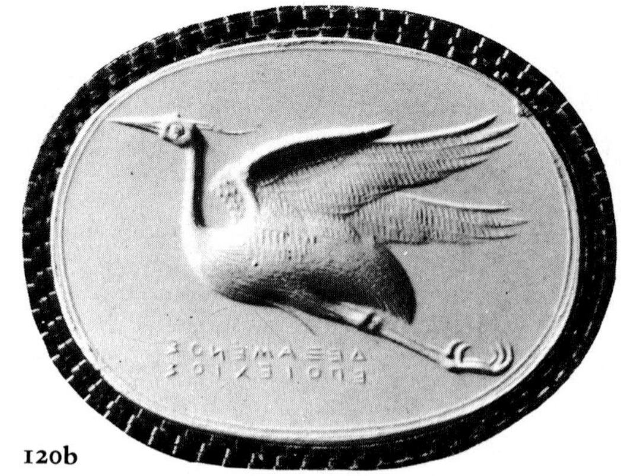

120b

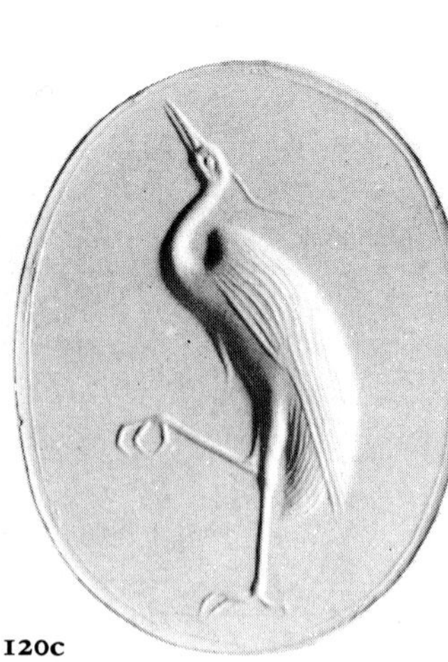

120c

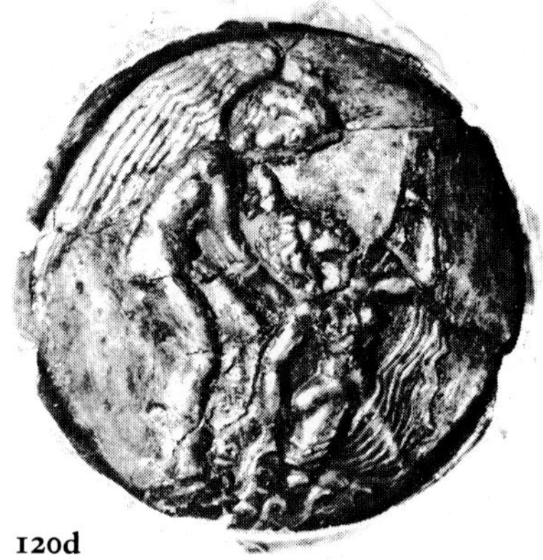

120d

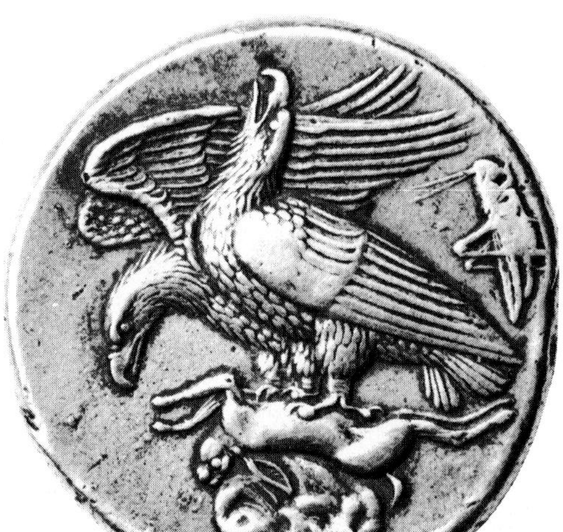

120e

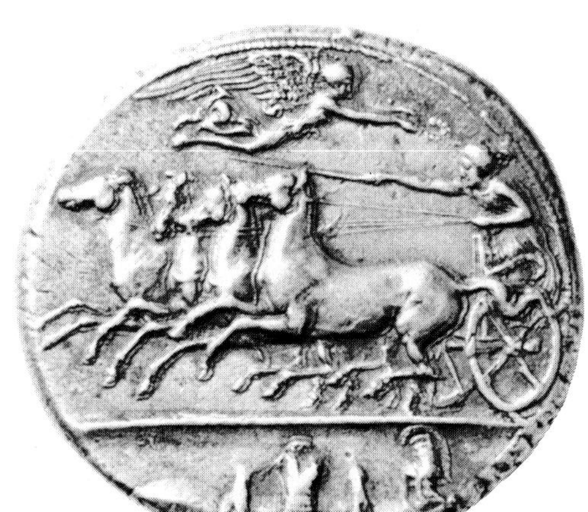

120f

120 **a** Impression from chalcedony scaraboid, signed by Dexamenos of Chios, from Kara (Attica). Boston, Museum of Fine Arts 27.580. Late fifth century. H. 0.02. (P. 362) **b** Impression from chalcedony scaraboid, signed by Dexamenos, from Kerch (South Russia). Leningrad. Late fifth century. L. 0.02. (Pp. 344, 362) **c** Impression from chalcedony scaraboid. Boston, Museum of Fine Arts (ex Lewes House). Late fifth century. H. 0.02. (Pp. 344, 362) **d** Silver-gilt roundel (centre of cup?) from Galaxidi (Locrian Oiantheia), on the Corinthian Gulf. Louvre. Late fifth century. D., within border, *c.* 0.03. (Pp. 205, 318) **e** Silver decadrachm of Akragas. Munich. Late fifth century. D. 0.04. (P. 361) **f** Silver decadrachm of Syracuse. Pennisi (Jongkees A/a). Late fifth century. D. 0.035. (P. 360).

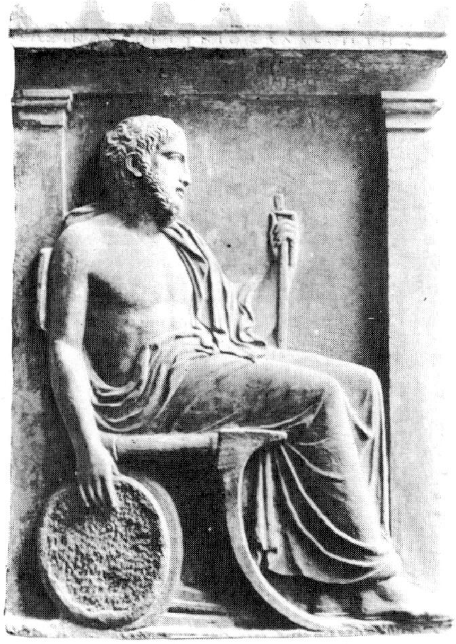

121a

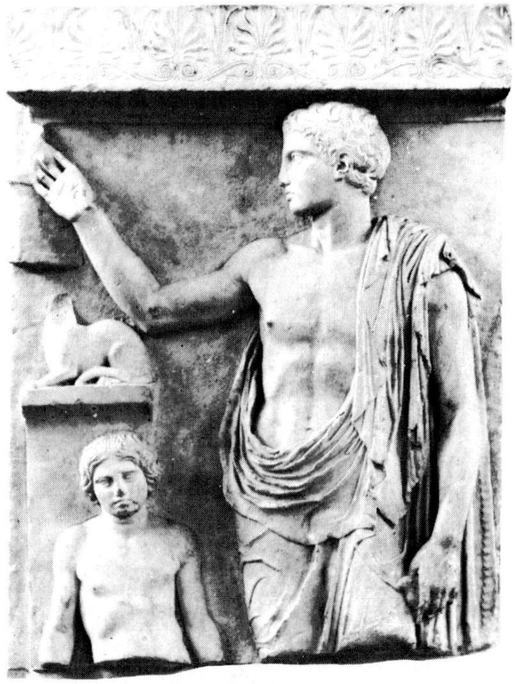

121b

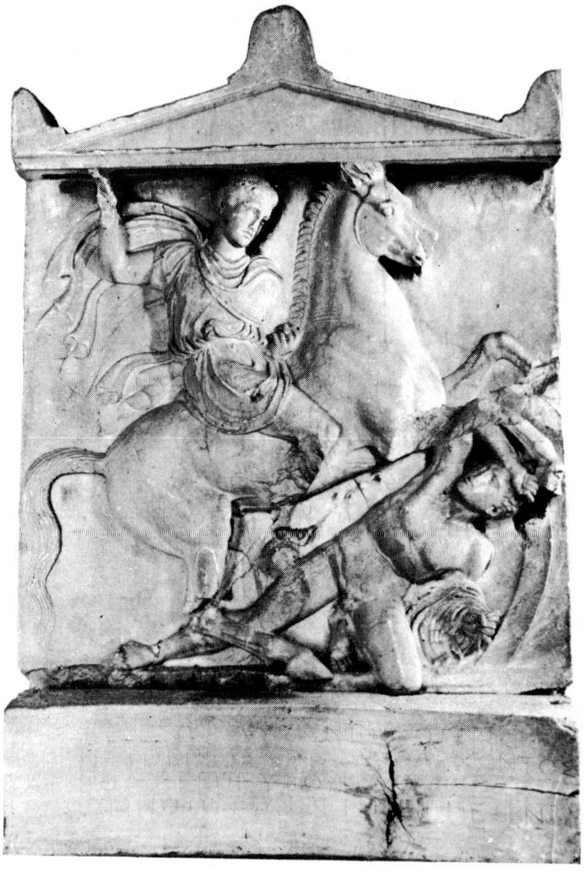

121c

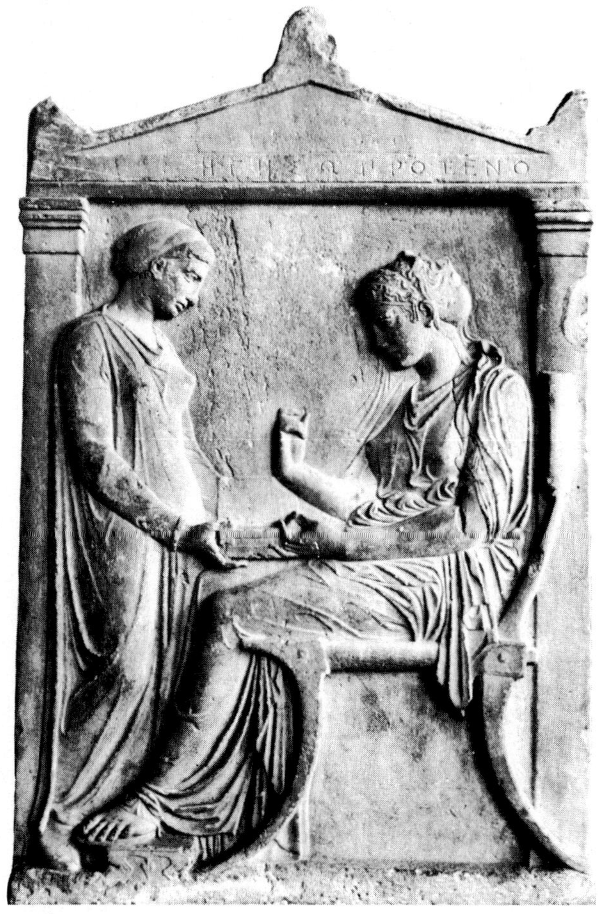

121d

121 **a** Marble grave-relief of Sosinos from Athens. Louvre. Third quarter of fifth century. H. 1.00. (Pp. 363, 365) **b** Marble grave-relief, probably from Aegina. Athens, National Museum 715. Third or last quarter of fifth century. H. 1.10. (P. 367) **c** Marble grave-relief of Dexileos, killed in 394 B.C., from Athens. Athens, Kerameikos Museum. H. 1.40. (Pp. 363, 369) **d** Marble grave-relief of Hegeso. Athens, National Museum 3624. First quarter of fourth century. H. 1.49. (Pp. 363, 367).

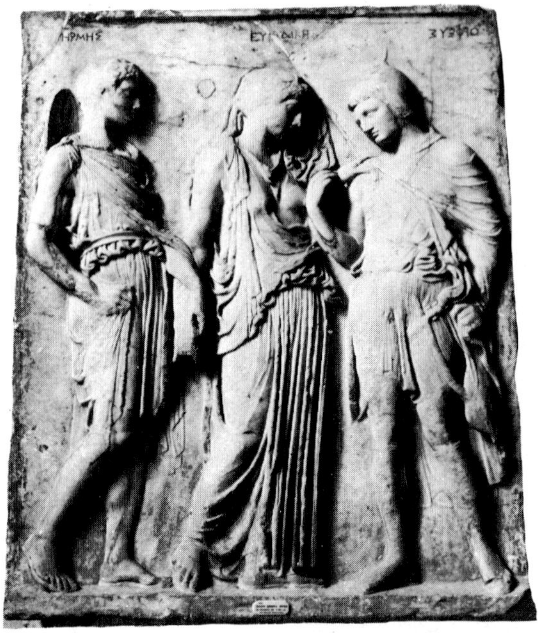

122a

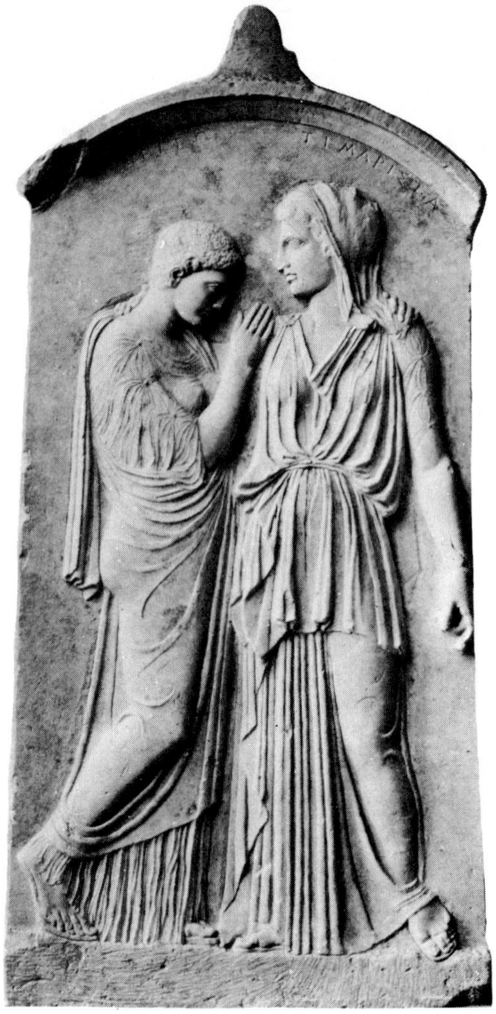

122b

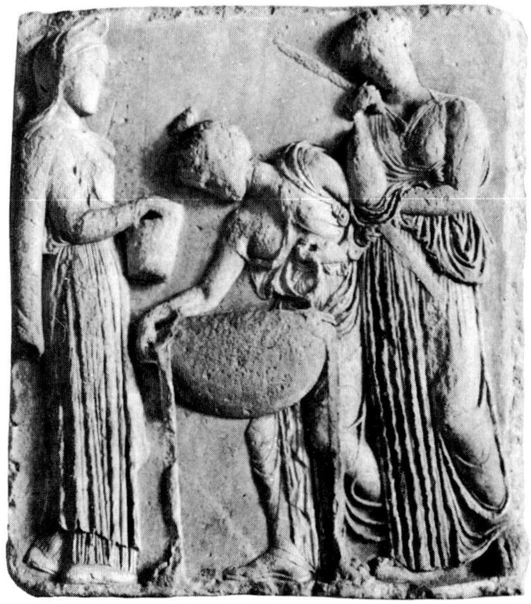

122c

122 **a** Marble relief. Naples Museum 6729. Copy (first or second century A.D.) after original of late fifth century. H. 1.18. (Pp. 374, 408, 414) **b** Marble grave-relief from Rhodes. Rhodes Museum. Probably late fifth or early fourth century B.C. H. 2.00. (Pp. 369, 374, 414) **c** Marble relief. Vatican (ex Lateran). Copy (first or second century A.D.) after original of late fifth century. H. 1.18. (P. 374).

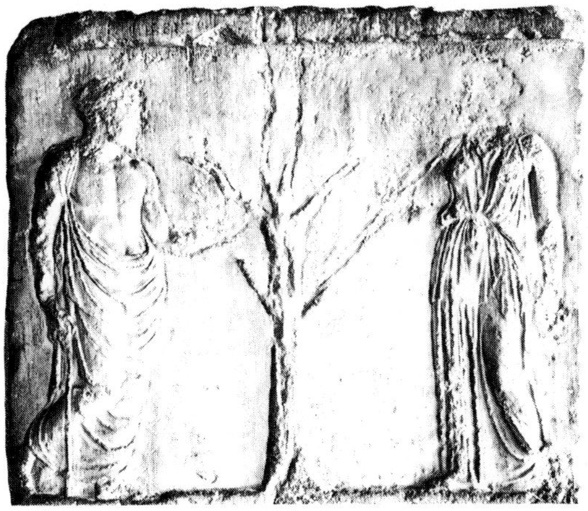

123a

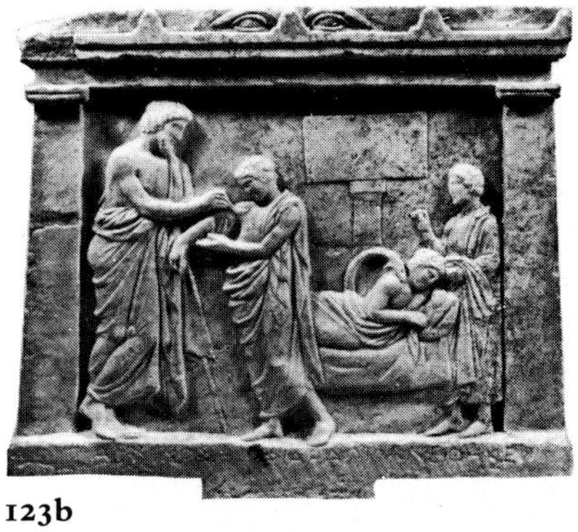

123b

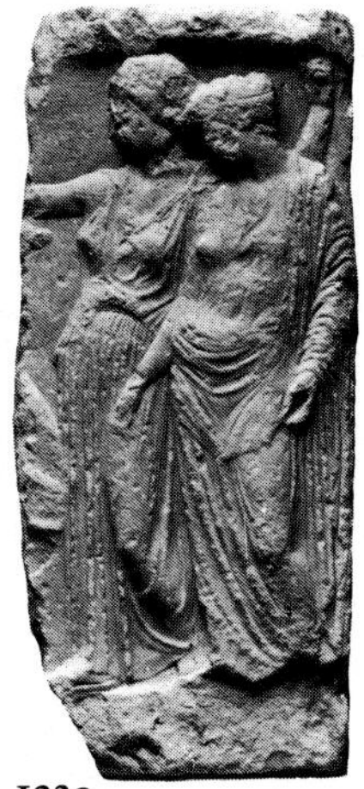

123c

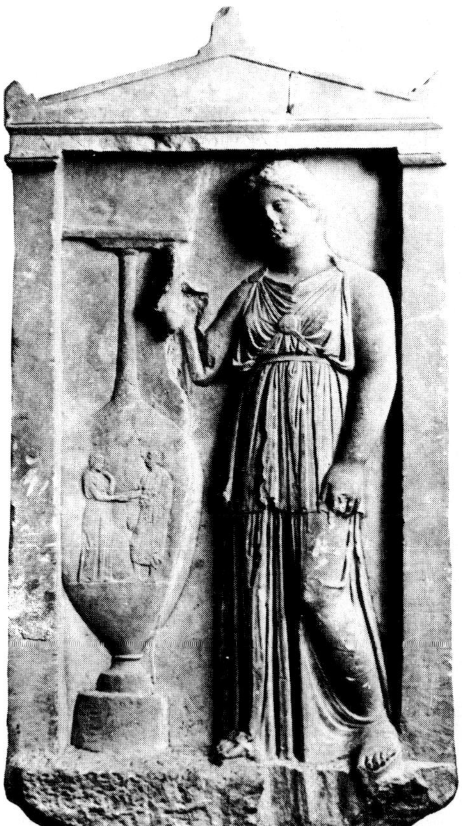

123d

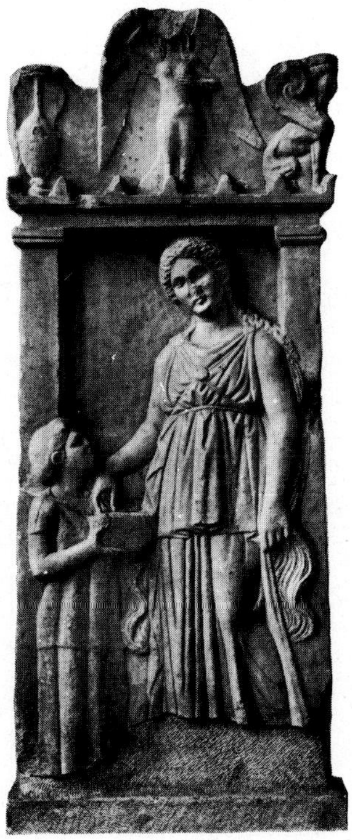

123e

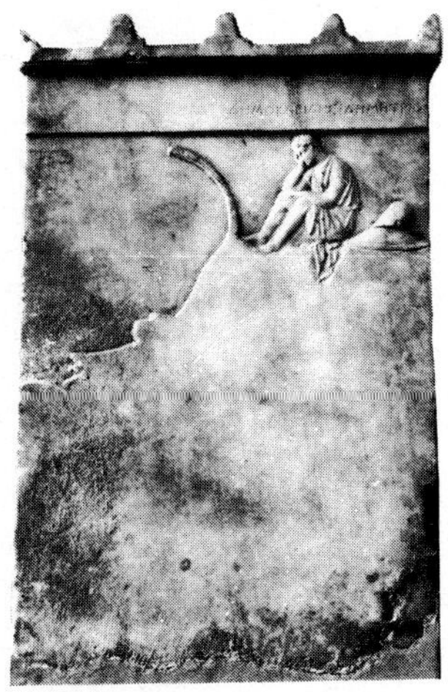

123f

123 **a** Marble relief surmounting inscription of 409/8 B.C., from Athens. Louvre. H. 0.70. (P. 373) **b** Marble relief dedicated by Archinos from Oropos (Attica). Athens, National Museum 3369. First half of fourth century. H. 0.49. (P. 377) **c** Marble relief from Acropolis. Athens, Acropolis Museum 1348. Late fifth century. H. 0.73. (P. 374) **d** Marble grave-relief of Hagnostrate, from Athens. Athens, National Museum 1863. Mid fourth century. H. 1.31. (P. 381) **e** Marble grave-relief of Silenis, from Athens. Berlin (E) 1492 (K 40). Mid fourth century. H. 1.10. (P. 381) **f** Marble grave-relief of Demokleides, from Athens. Athens, National Museum 752. Early fourth century. H. 0.67. (P. 370).

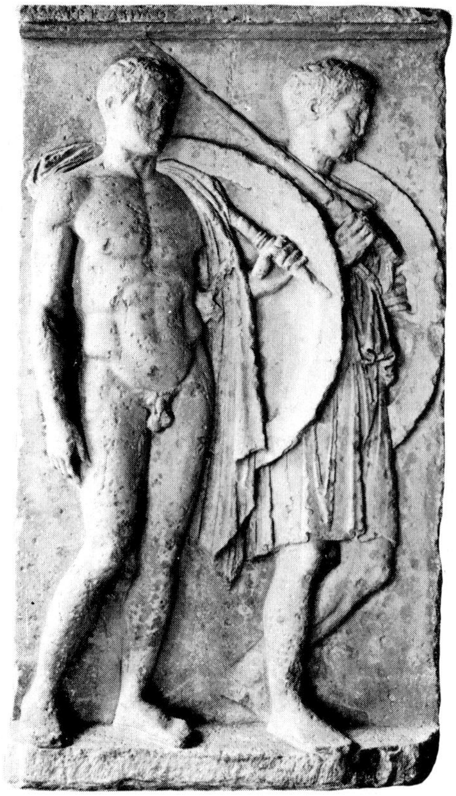
124a

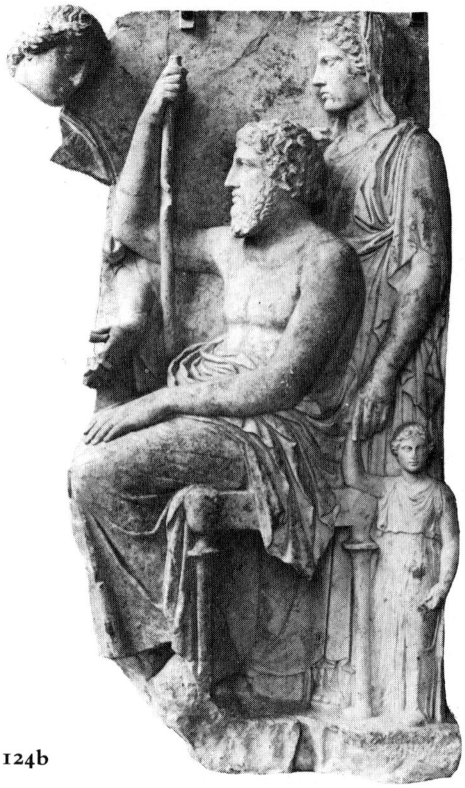
124b

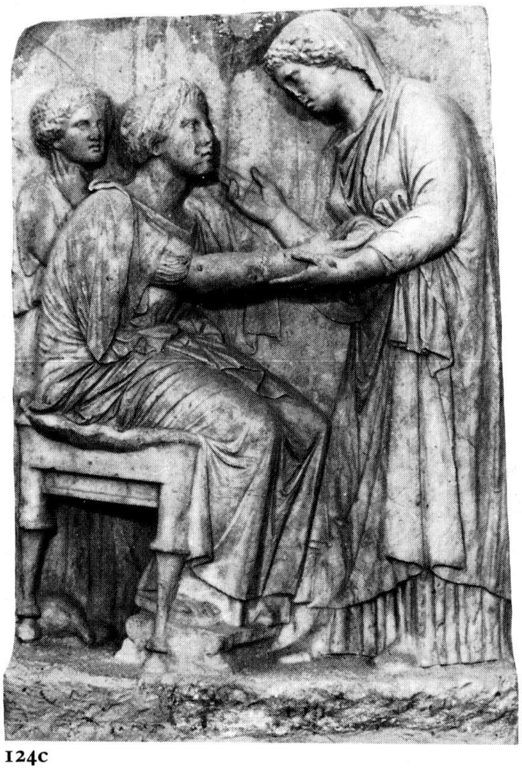
124c

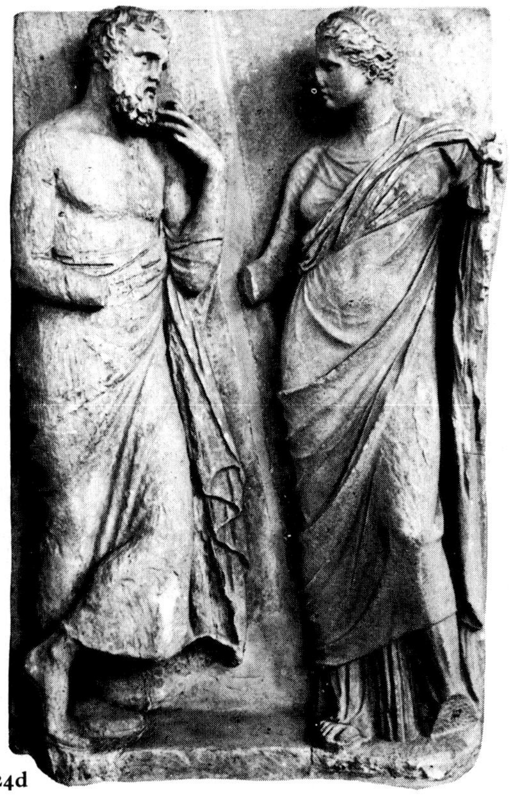
124d

124 **a** Marble grave-relief of Lykeas and Chairedemos from Salamis. Piraeus Museum. Late fifth or early fourth century. H. 1.81. (P. 369) **b** Marble grave-relief from Attica. New York, Metropolitan Museum of Art, 11.100.2, Rogers Fund. First quarter of fourth century. H. 1.71. (Pp. 379, 512, 590) **c** Marble grave-relief from Athens. Athens, National Museum 870. Third quarter of fourth century. H. 1.70. (P. 380) **d** Marble grave-relief from Rhamnus (Attica). Athens, National Museum 833. Third or last quarter of fourth century. H. 1.81. (P. 382).

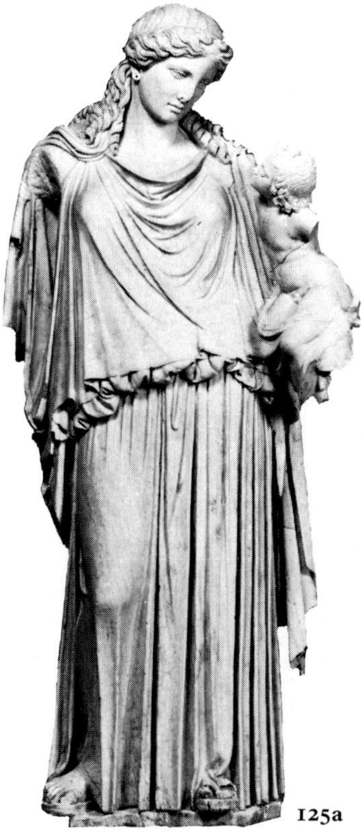

125a

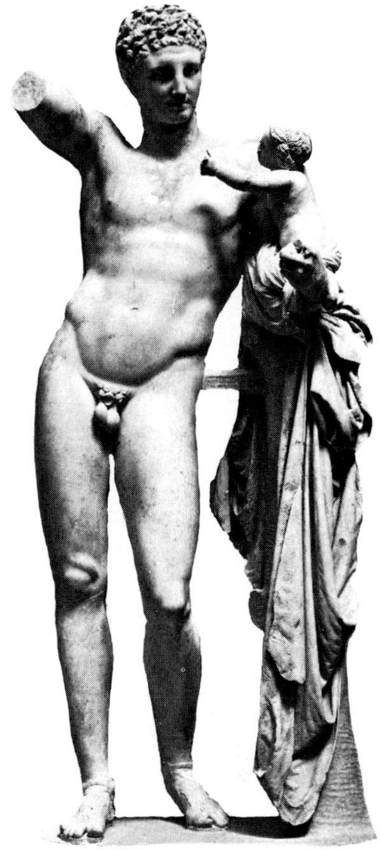

125b

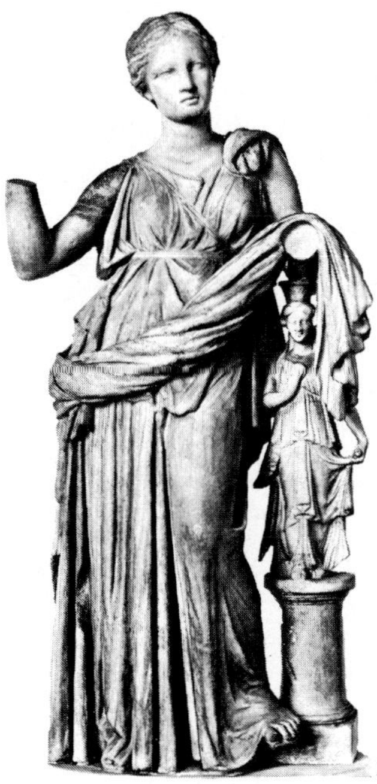

125c

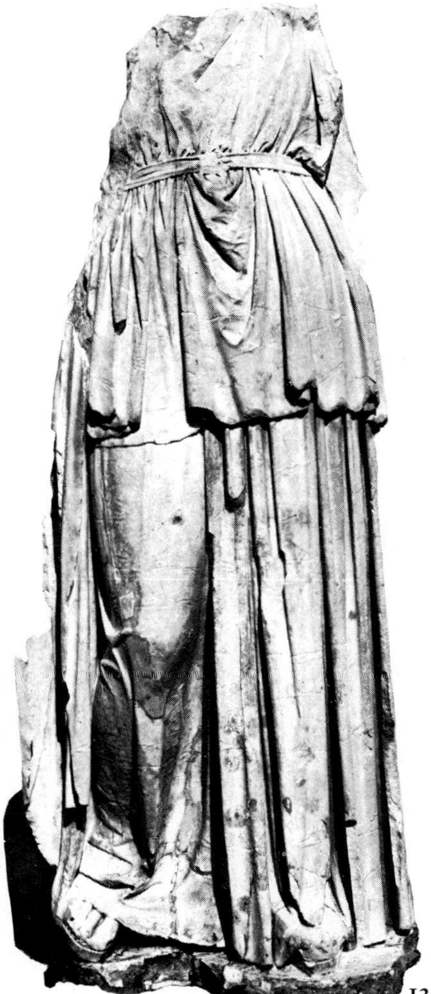

125d

125 **a** Marble group. Munich. Copy of the imperial age after original of first or second quarter of fourth century. The goddess's nose, and the child's head are modern. H. 1.99. (Pp. 384ff., 409) **b** Marble group from Olympia. Olympia Museum. Perhaps copy of first century after original of second half of fourth century. The lower legs and left foot are modern. H. 2.13. (Pp. 386ff.) **c** Marble statuette from Larnaka (Cyprus). Vienna. End of fourth or beginning of third century. H. 0.80. (P. 394) **d** Fragmentary marble statue from Agora. Athens, Agora Museum. Third quarter of fourth century. H. 2.54. (Pp. 386, 410).

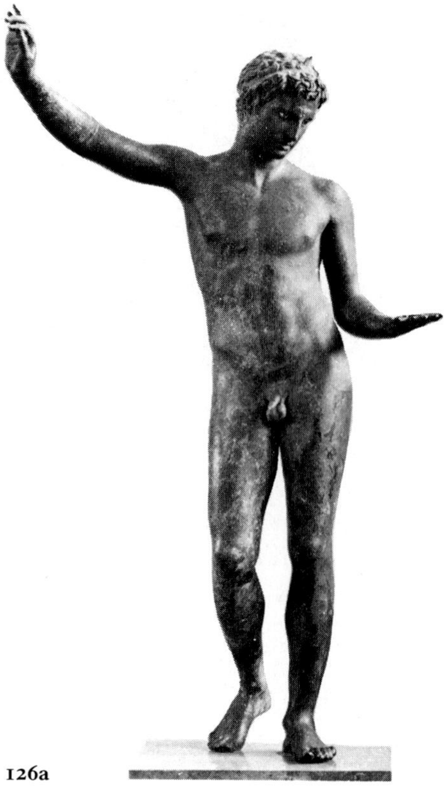

126a

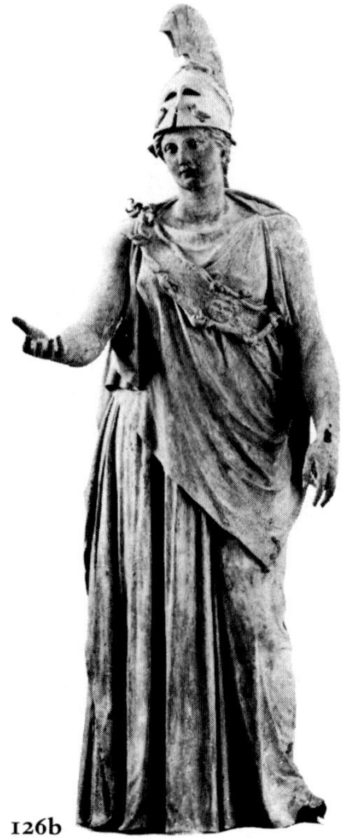

126b

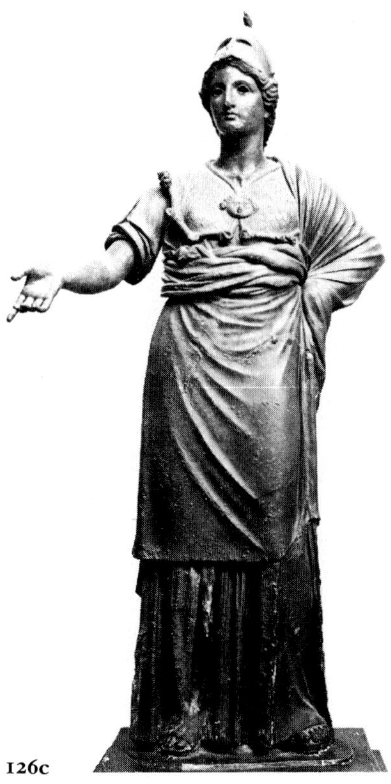

126c

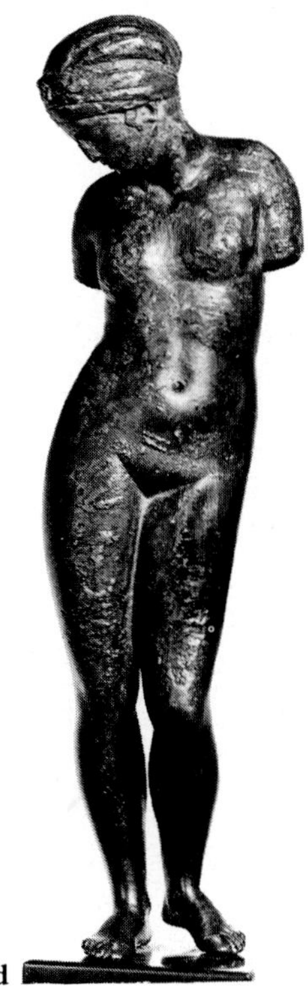

126d

126 **a** Bronze statue from sea off Marathon. Athens, National Museum 15118. Second half of fourth century. H. 1.30. (P. 390) **b** Bronze statue from Piraeus. Athens, National Museum. Probably second quarter of fourth century. H. 2.35. (Pp. 386, 410) **c** Bronze statue from Arezzo. Florence, Museo Archeologico. Probably copy of the imperial age after original of last quarter of fourth century. H. 1.55. (Pp. 396, 480) **d** Bronze statuette from Beroea (Macedonia). Munich 3669. Perhaps second century. H. 0.25. (Pp. 391, 549).

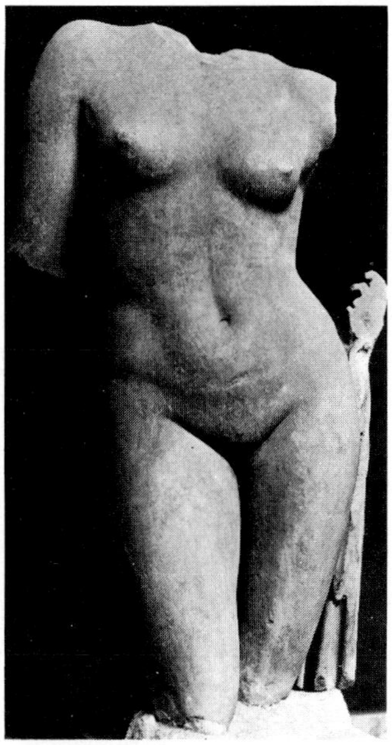

127a

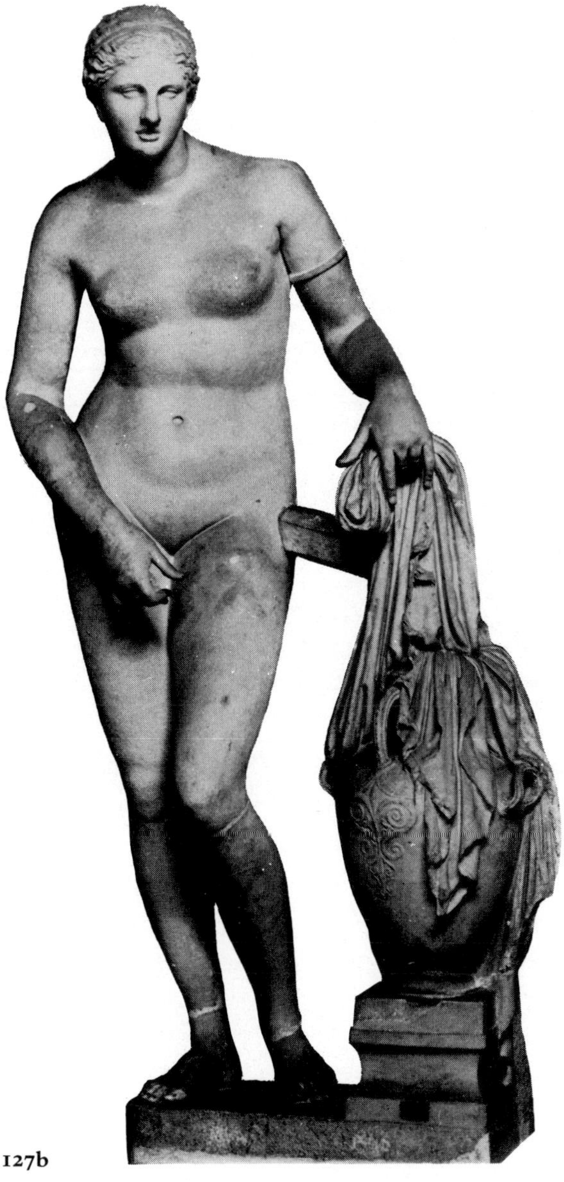

127b

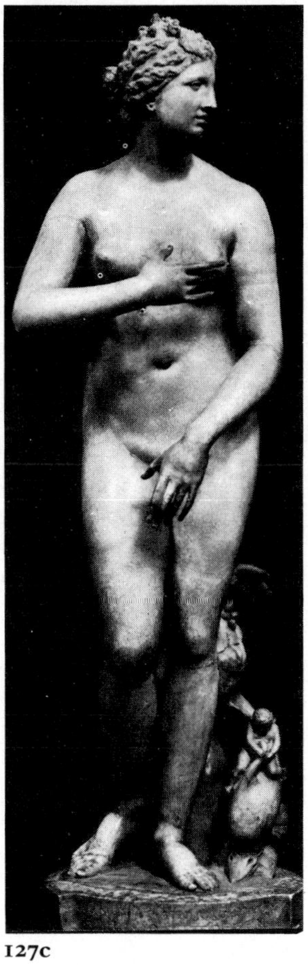

127c

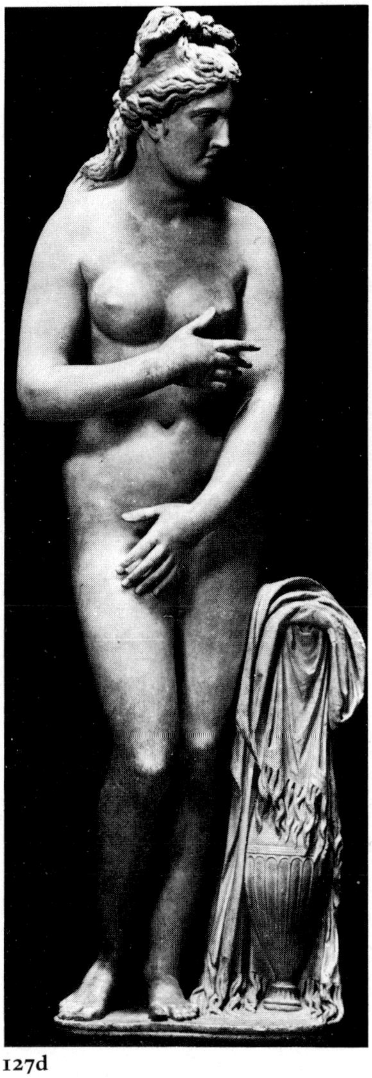

127d

127 **a** Marble torso. Naples 6035. Copy of the imperial age after original probably of early fourth century. H. 1.04. (Pp. 387, 391, 410) **b** Marble statue. Vatican. Copy of the imperial age after original of mid fourth century. H. 2.05. Right forearm and hand are modern, and the neck. The head, which comes from another copy of the same original, should be turned a little to the figure's left. (Pp. 390–3, 548) **c** Marble statue. Florence, Uffizi. Copy of the imperial age after original perhaps of second century. The nose and some patches are modern. H. 1.53. (Pp. 393, 548–9) **d** Marble statue from Rome. Rome, Museo Capitolino. Copy of the imperial age after original perhaps of second century. H., with plinth, 1.87. (Pp. 209, 393, 548–9).

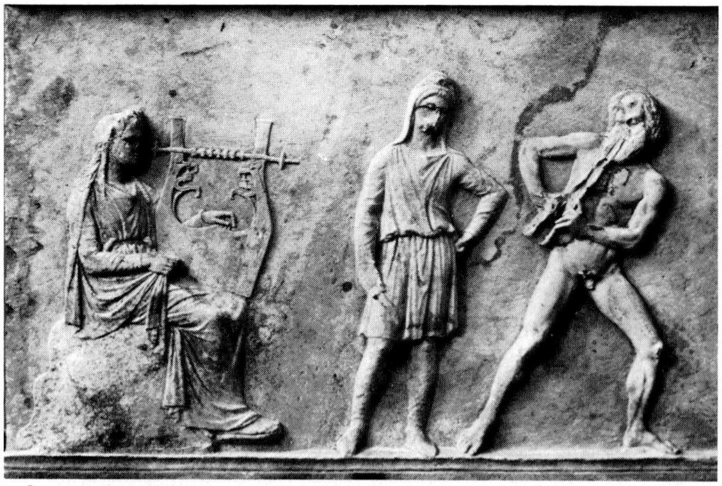

128a

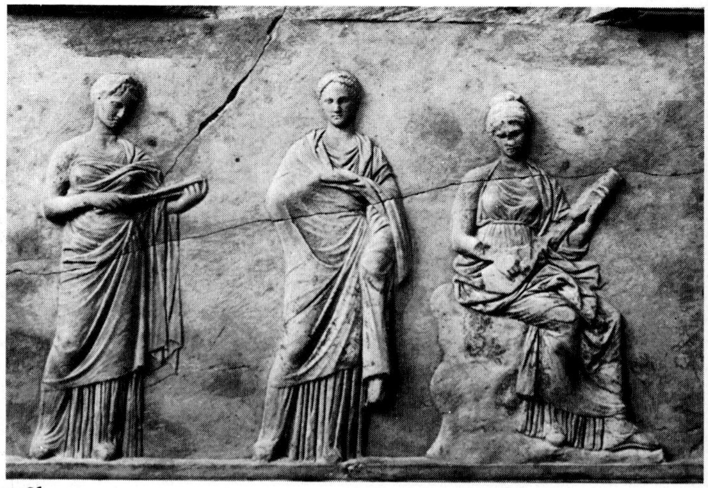

128b

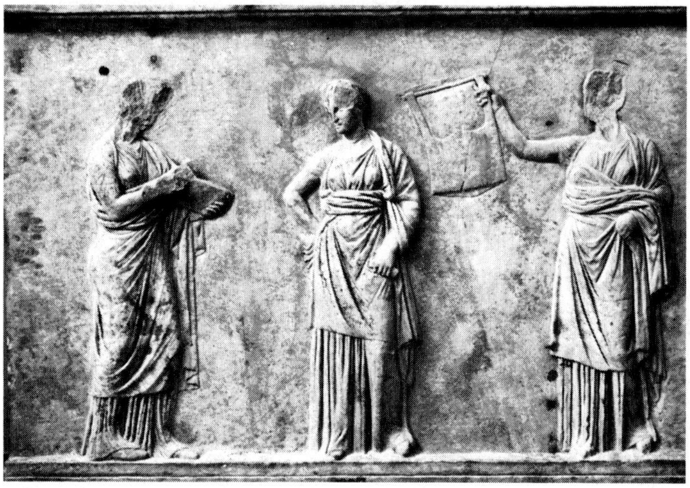

128c

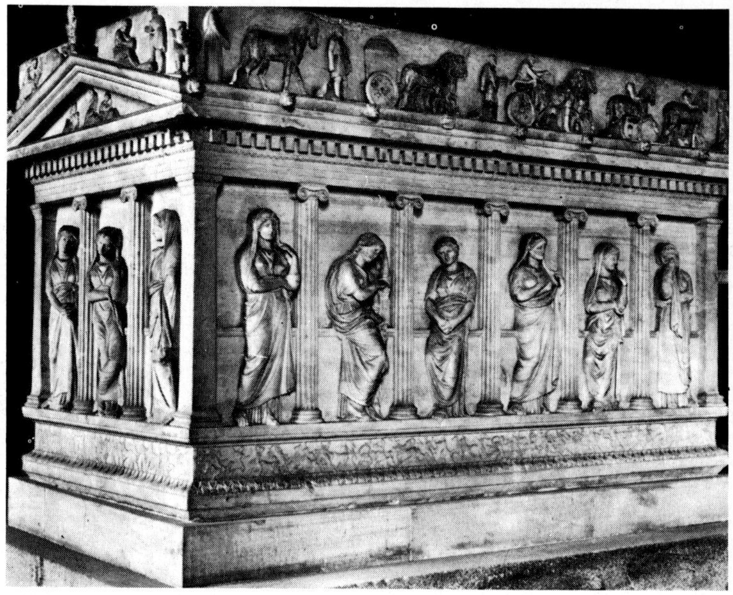

128d

128 **a–c** Three marble relief-slabs from Mantinea. Athens, National Museum 215–217. Last quarter of fourth century. H. 0.96. (Pp. 395, 408, 480, 536) **d** Marble sarcophagus from Sidon. Istanbul Museum. Second half of fourth century. H. 1.80. (Pp. 404, 479–80).

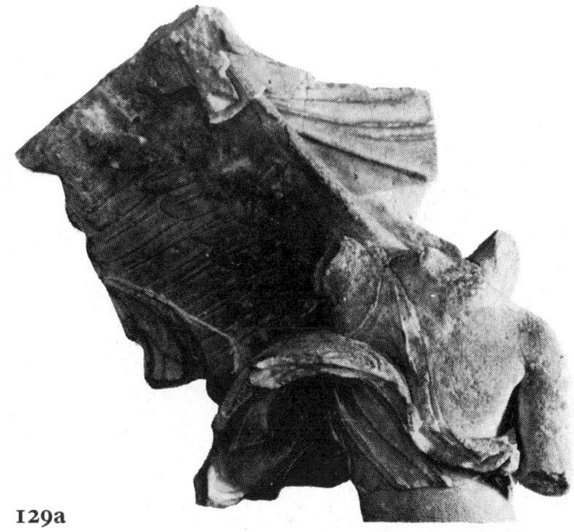

129a

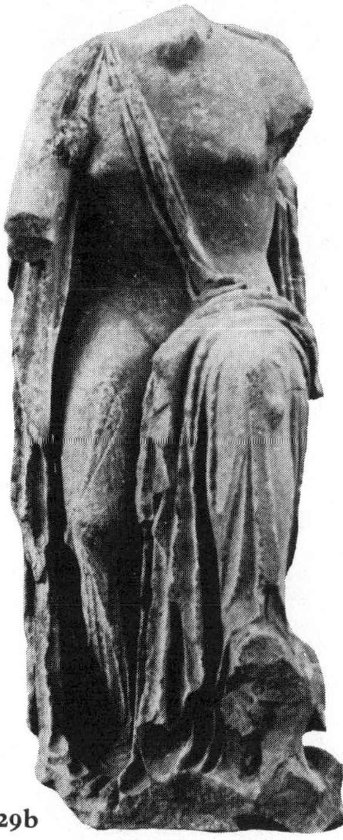

129b

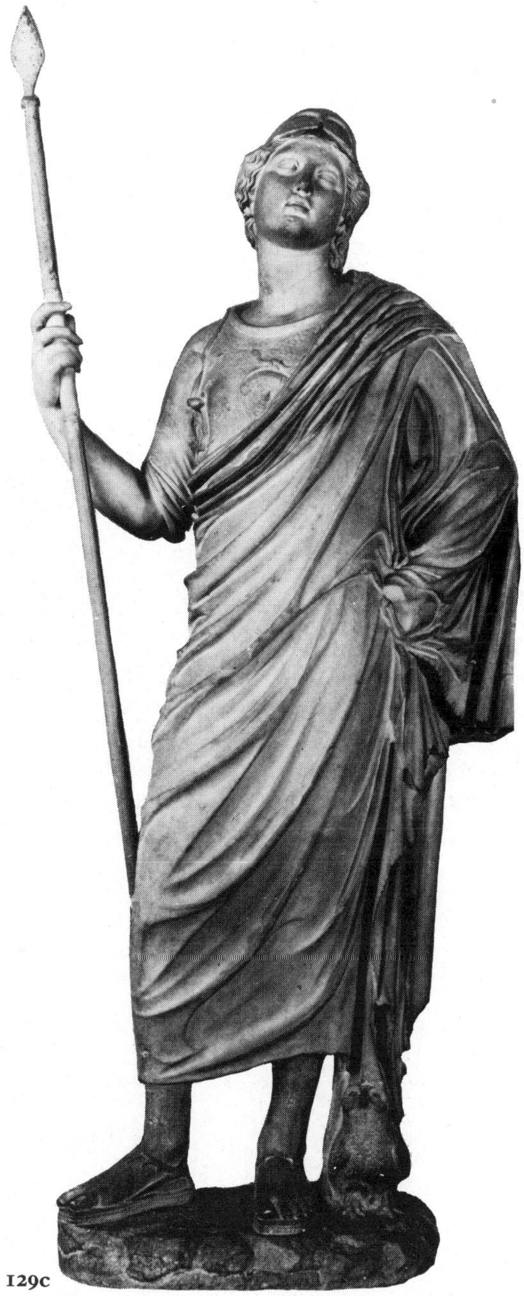

129c

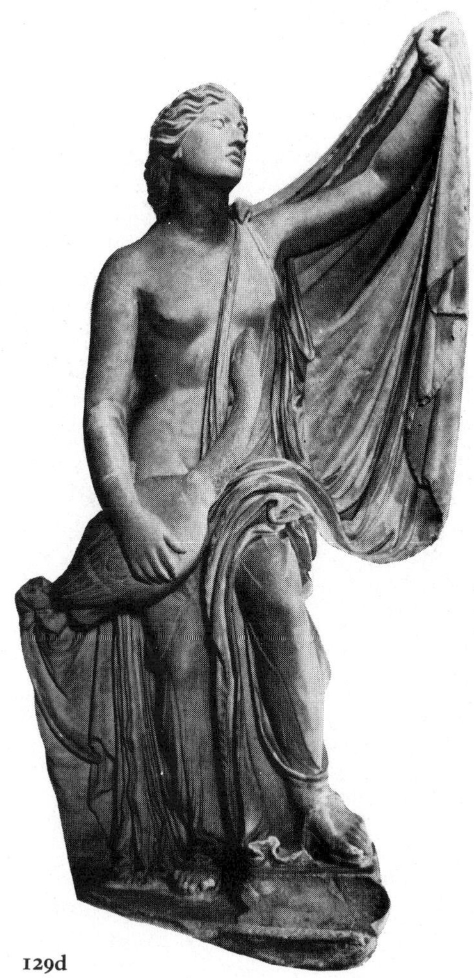

129d

129 **a** Marble akroterion-fragment from Epidaurus. Athens, National Museum 162. First or second quarter of fourth century. H. 0.25. (Pp. 400–1) **b** Marble statue from Epidaurus. Athens, National Museum 299. First half of fourth century. H. 0.87. (P. 402) **c** Marble statue. Florence, Uffizi (ex Rospigliosi Collection). Copy of the imperial age after original of first half of fourth century. H. 1.60. Modern are the nose and the right arm and hand with the spear. (P. 402) **d** Marble statue. Rome, Museo Capitolino. Copy of the imperial age after original of first half of fourth century. H. 1.32. The right upper arm is modern, and the swan's head and neck. (P. 402).

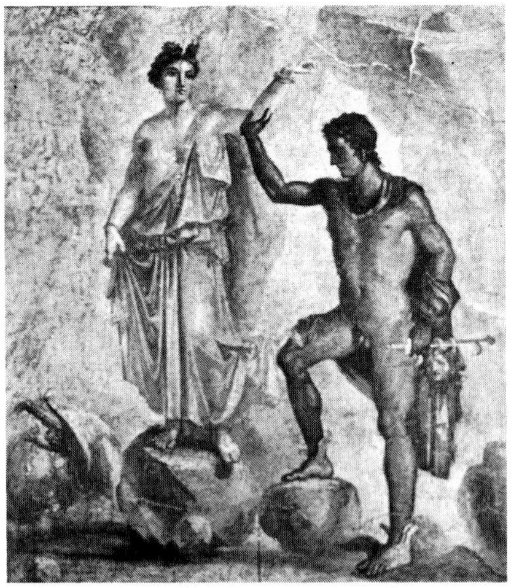

138a

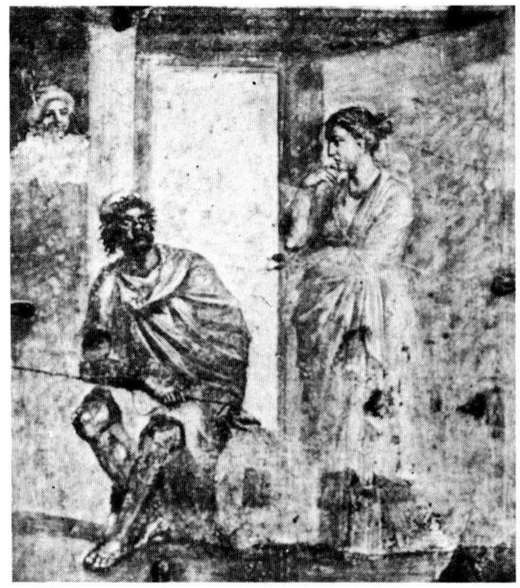

138b

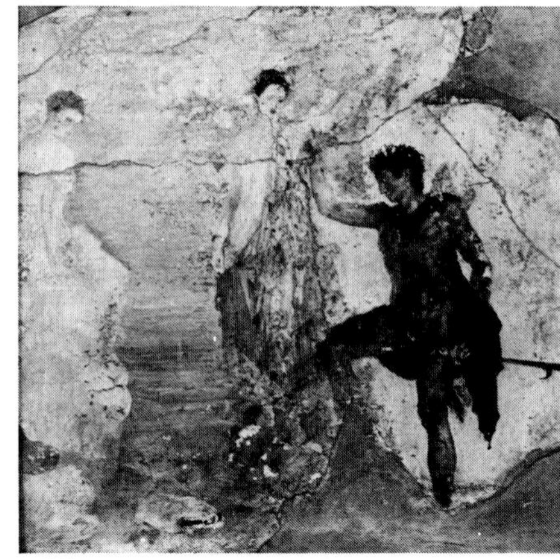

138d

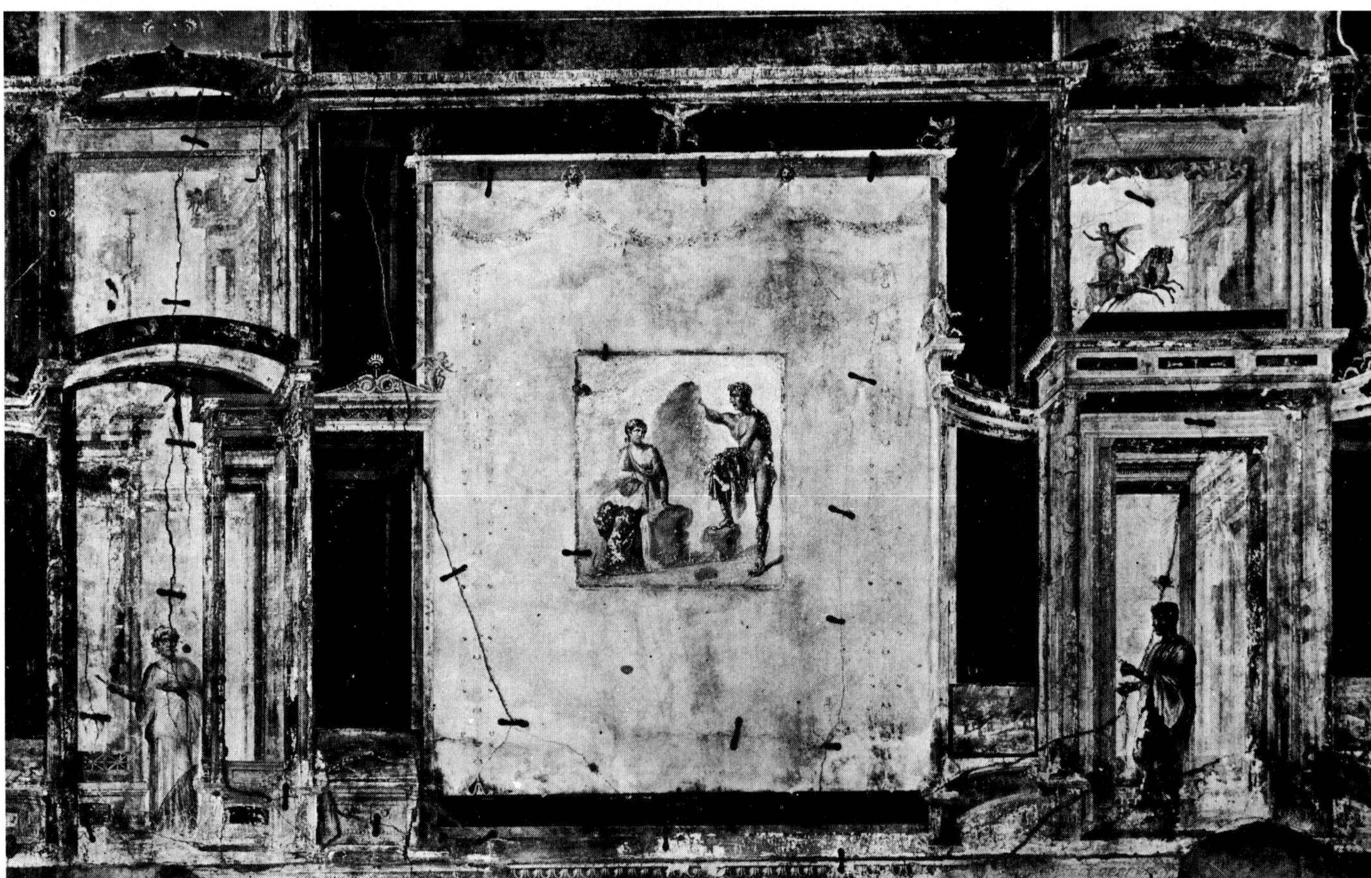

138c

138 **a** Wall-painting from Pompeii. Naples Museum 8998. Early to mid first century A.D., perhaps based on original of fourth century. H. 1.06. (P. 438) **b** Wall-painting from Pompeii. Naples Museum 9107. Early to mid first century A.D., perhaps based on original of fourth century. H. 0.83. (P. 439) **c** Painted wall of *Macellum* (covered market) at Pompeii. Third quarter of first century A.D., the central picture perhaps based on original of fourth century. (P. 438) **d** Wall-painting from Pompeii. Naples Museum 8993. Early first century A.D., based on same original as **a**. H. 0.38. (P. 438).

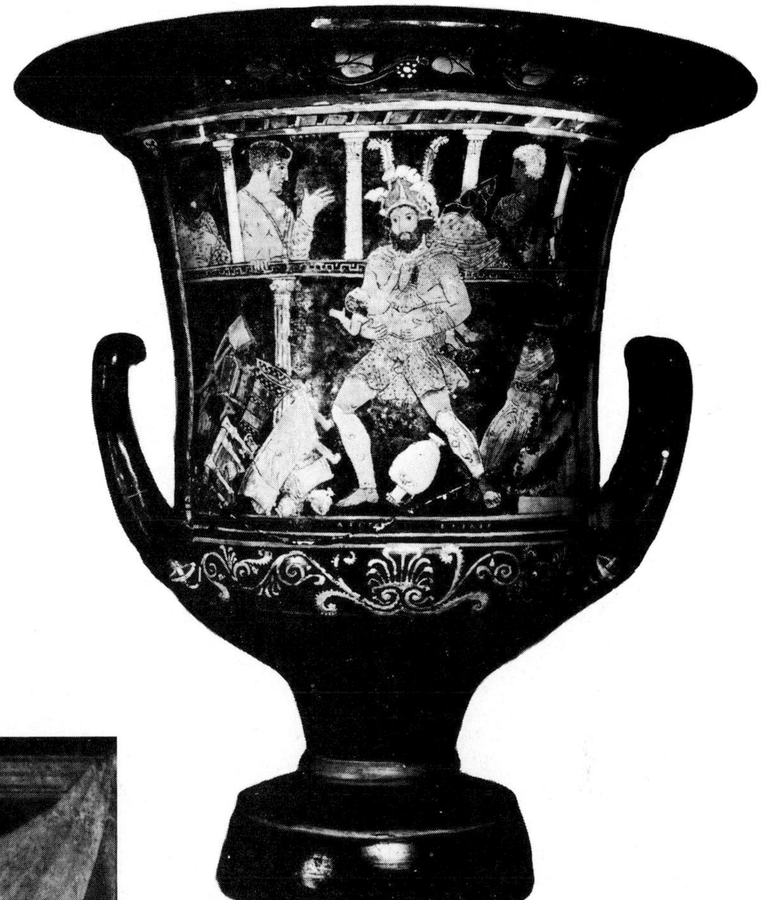

139a

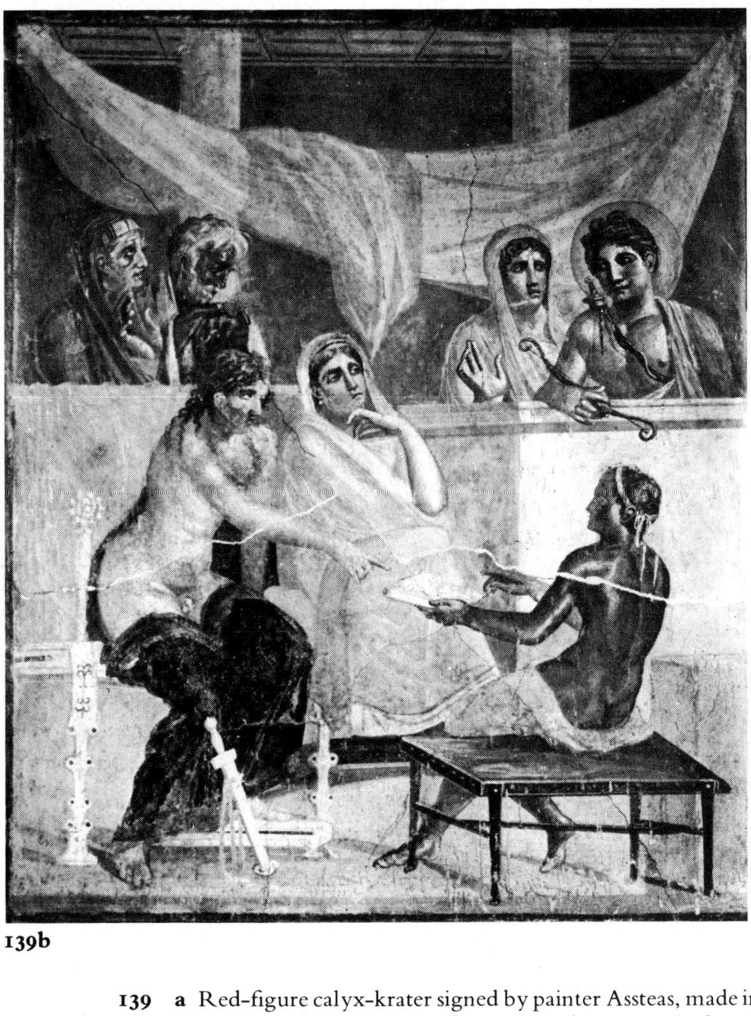

139b

139 **a** Red-figure calyx-krater signed by painter Assteas, made in Paestum. Madrid 11094. Mid fourth century. H. 0.55. (P. 440) **b** Wall-painting from Herculaneum. Naples Museum 9025. First century A.D., perhaps based on original of fourth century. H. 1.45. (P. 440).

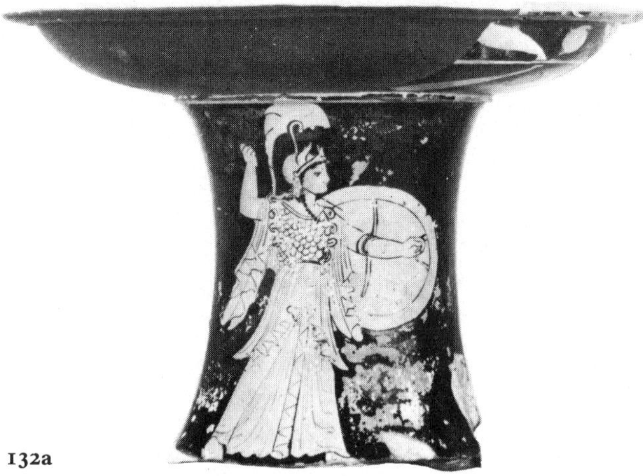

132a

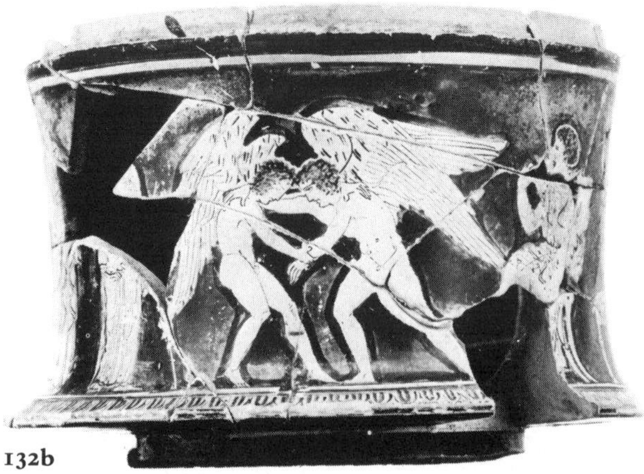

132b

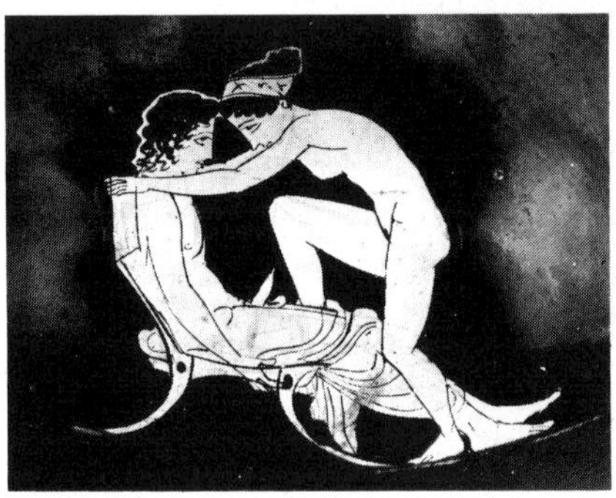

132c

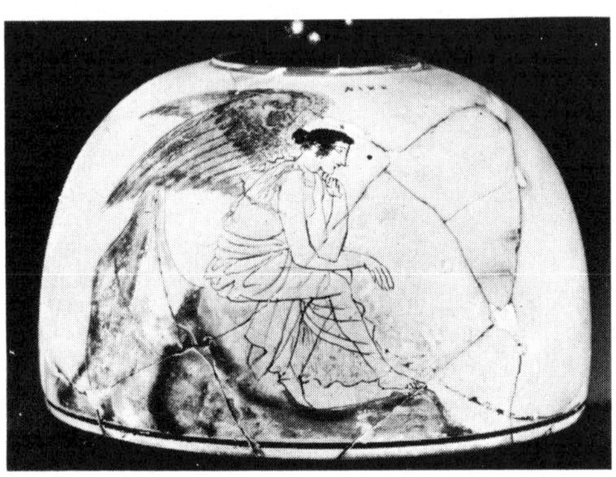

132d

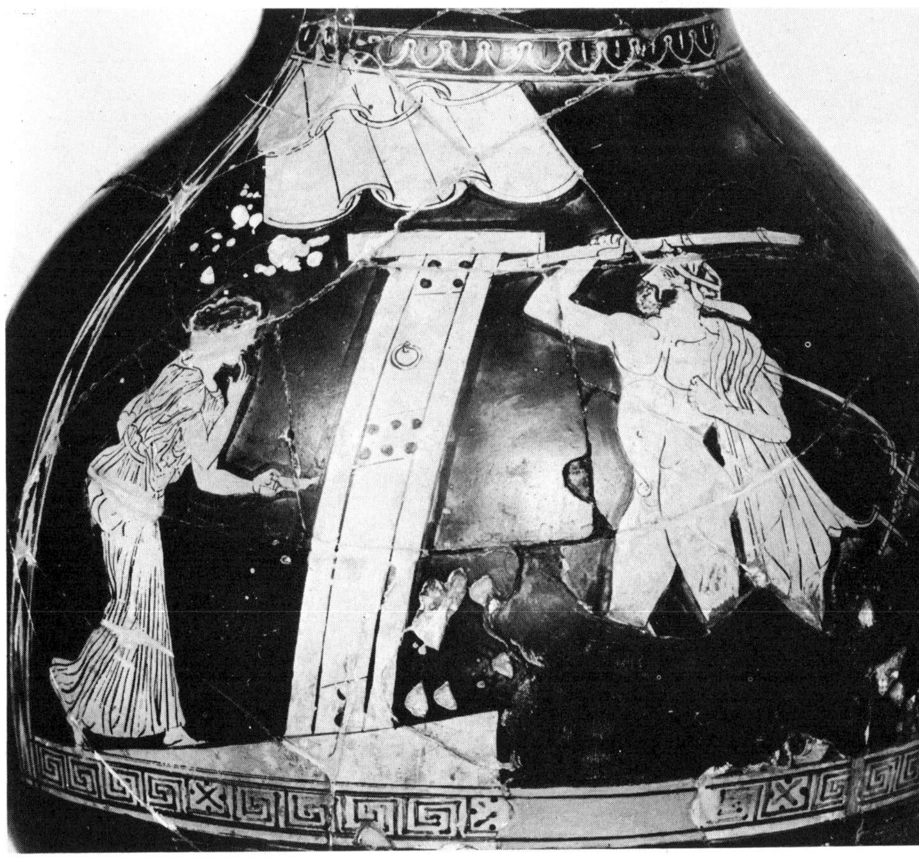

132e

132 **a** Attic red-figure oinochoe-neck from Agora. Athens, Agora Museum P 14793. End of fifth century. H. 0.10. (Pp. 347, 420) **b** Attic red-figure pyxis from Attica. Würzburg 541. Third to last quarter of fifth century. H. 0.09. (P. 418) **c** Picture on Attic red-figure oinochoe from Locri. Berlin (Charlottenburg) 2414. Third to last quarter of fifth century. H. of picture *c.* 0.06. (Pp. 391, 418) **d** Picture on Attic white-ground squat lekythos from Nola. Brussels A 1021. Third to last quarter of fifth century. H. of picture *c.* 0.06. (Pp. 212, 262) **e** Picture on Attic red-figure oinochoe. New York, Metropolitan Museum of Art 37.11.19, Fletcher Fund. Third to last quarter of fifth century. H. of picture *c.* 0.15. (P. 419).

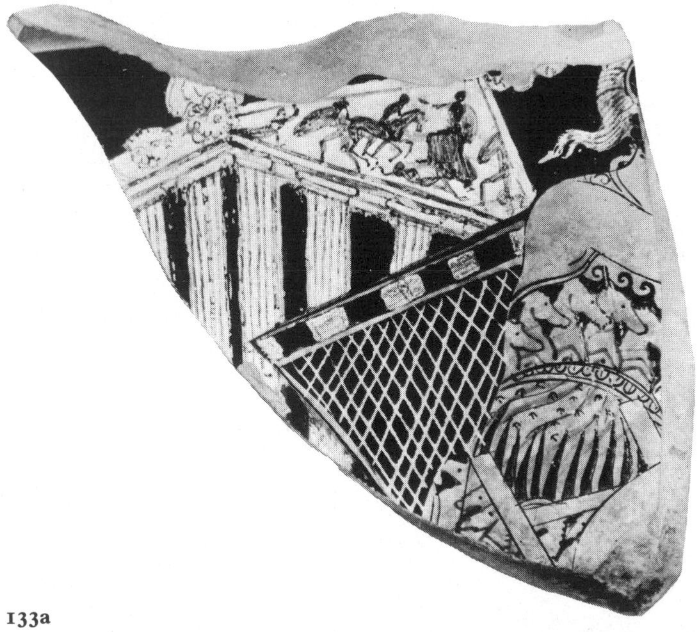

133a

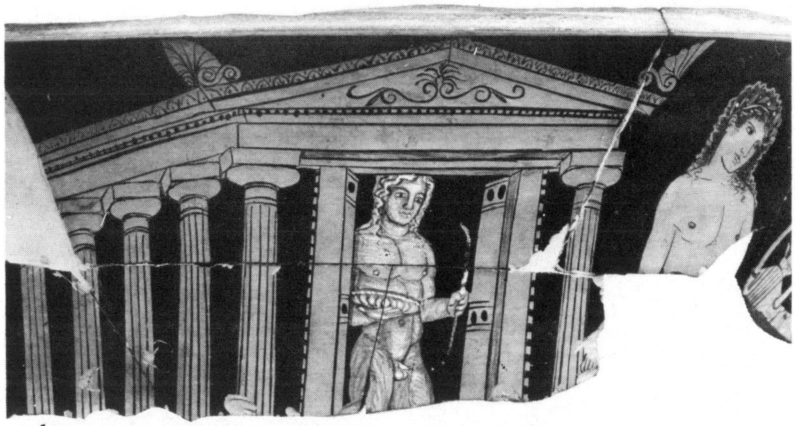

133b

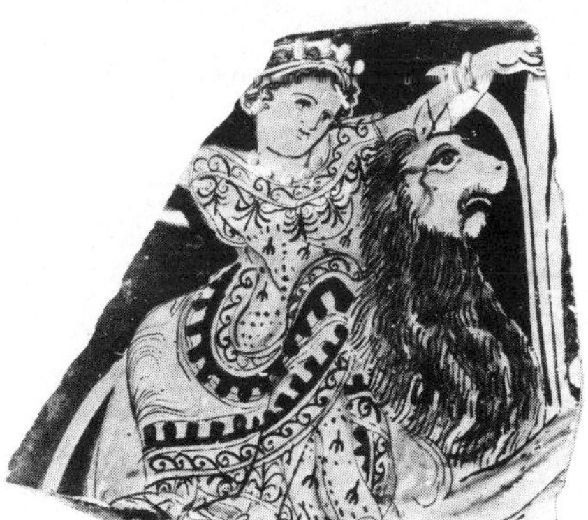

133c

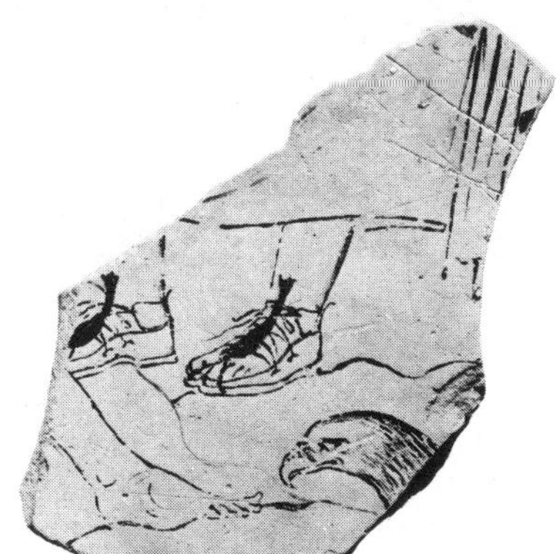

133d

133 **a** Attic red-figure krater-fragment from Taranto. Würzburg. Late fifth or early fourth century. H. 0.13. (Pp. 419–20) **b** Part of fragmentary South Italian red-figure calyx-krater from Taranto. Amsterdam, Allard Pierson Museum 2579. Beginning of fourth century. H. of part of picture shown *c.* 0.09. (Pp. 430, 485) **c** Attic red-figure plate-fragment from Greece. Boston, Museum of Fine Arts 10.187. Late fifth or early fourth century. Same scale as **d**. (Pp. 423, 579) **d** Attic red-figure plate-fragment from Agora. Athens, Agora Museum P14982. Late fifth or early fourth century. H. 0.12. (P. 423).

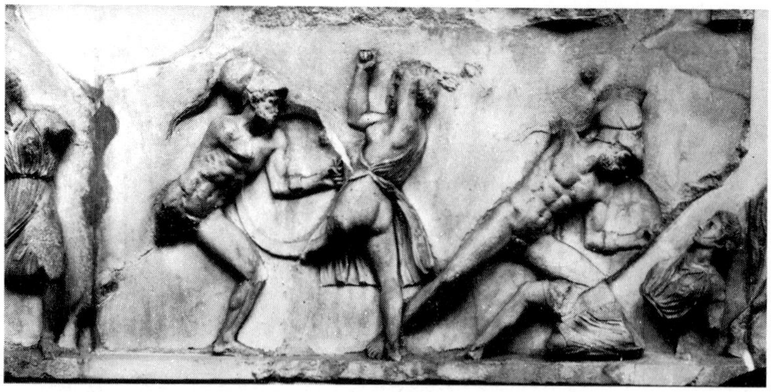

142a

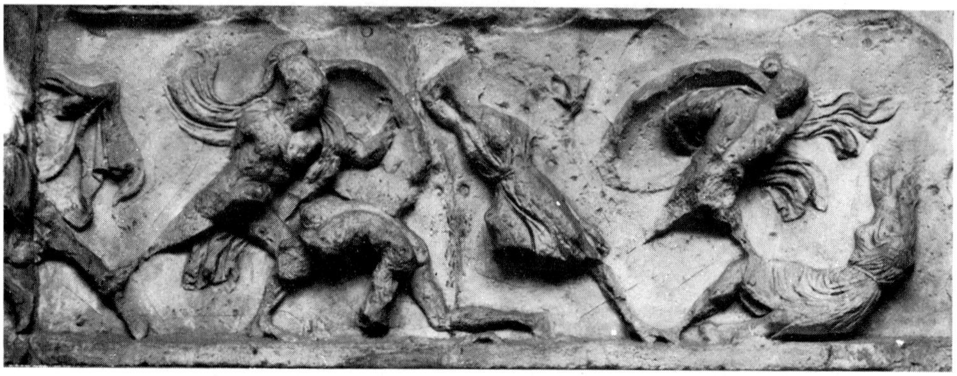

142b

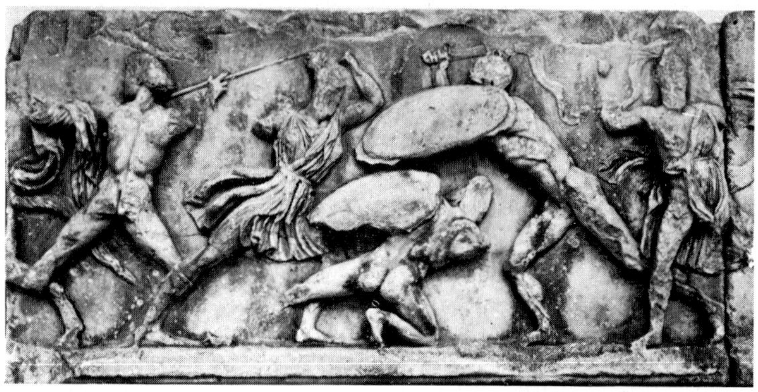

142c

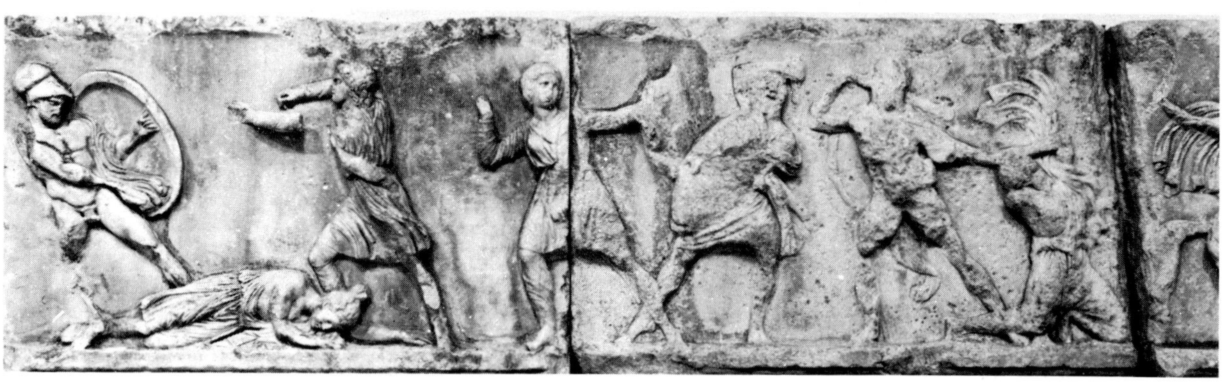

142d

142 a–d Marble frieze-slabs from Mausoleum of Halicarnassus. British Museum 1014, 1021, 1020 and 1007. Third quarter of fourth century. H. 0.89. (Pp. 450ff.).

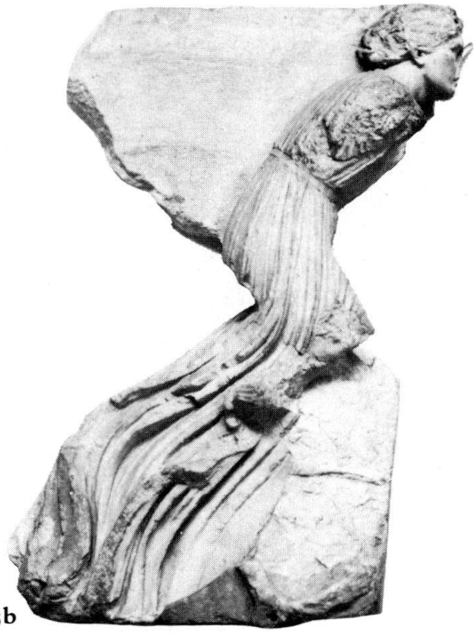

143b

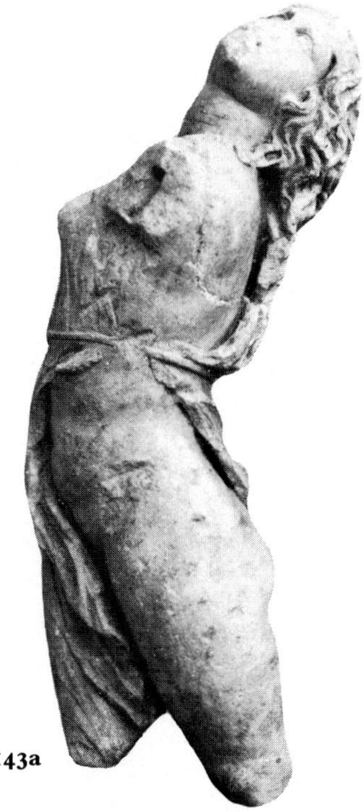

143a

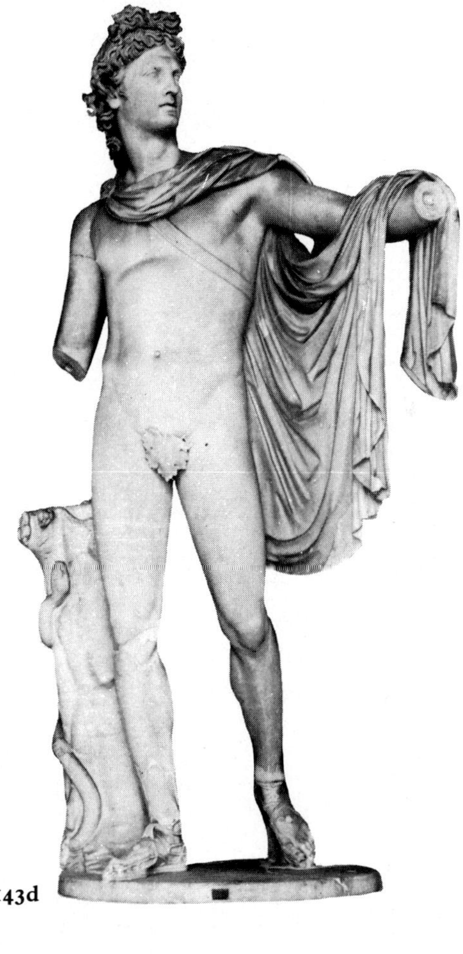

143d

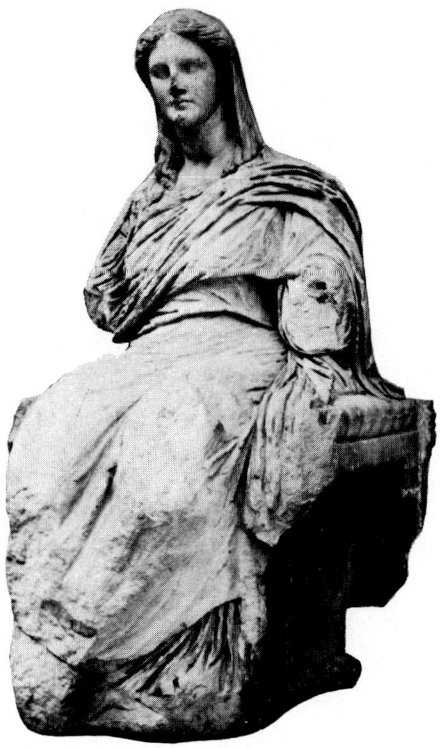

143c

143 **a** Fragmentary marble statuette. Dresden Museum. Copy of the imperial age, probably after statue of mid fourth century. H. 0.45. (Pp. 455, 472) **b** Marble relief-figure from a frieze of Mausoleum of Halicarnassus. British Museum 1037. Third quarter of fourth century. H. 0.40. See also pl. 145a. (P. 452) **c** Marble statue from Knidos. British Museum 1300. Second half of fourth century. H. 1.47. See also pl. 144a. (P. 462) **d** Marble statue. Vatican Copy of the imperial age probably after bronze original of second half of fourth century. H. 2.24. (P. 460).

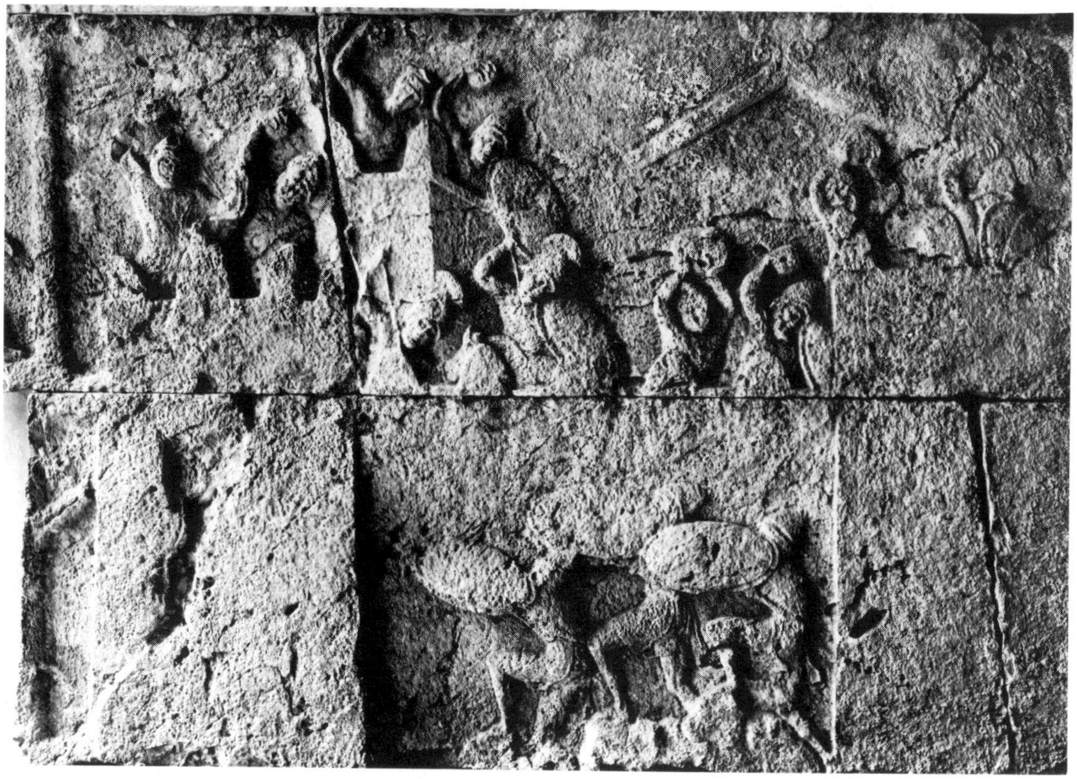
136a

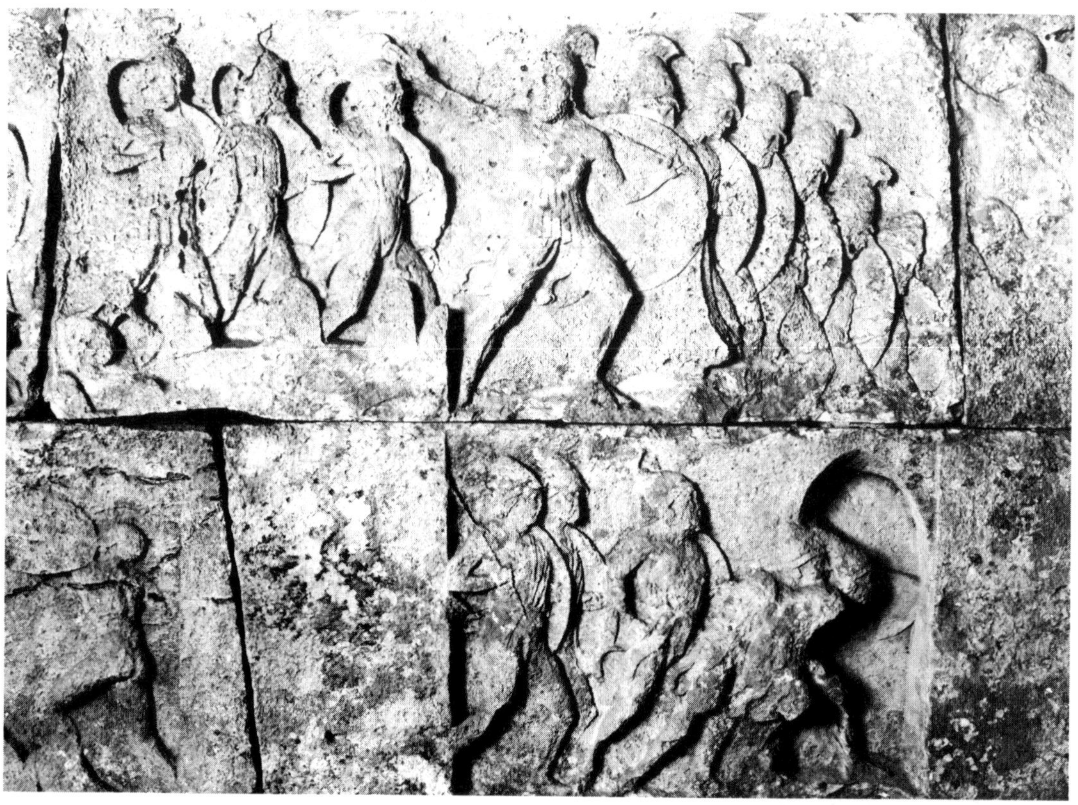
136b

136 **a** and **b** Limestone slabs from relief-frieze of Heroon at Gjölbaschi-Trysa (Lycia). Vienna. Early fourth century. H. 1.20. (Pp. 405, 431).

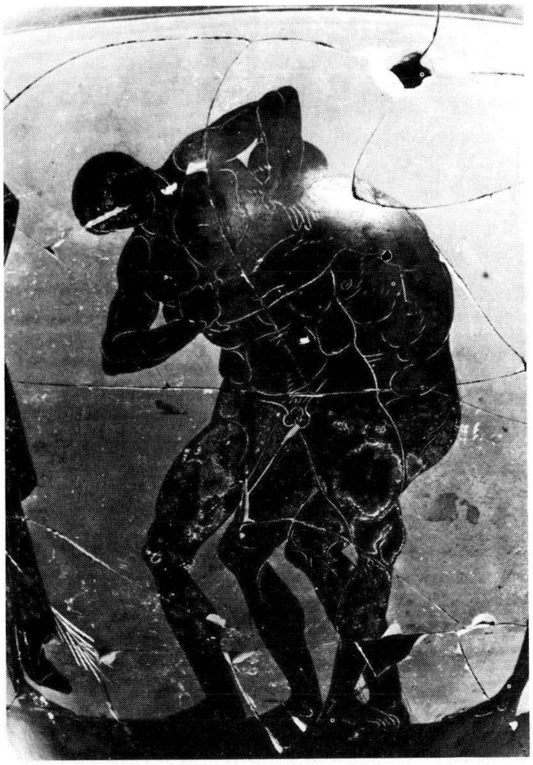

137a

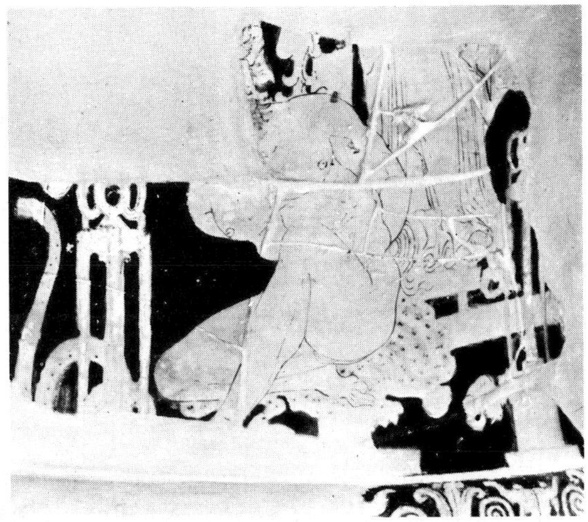

137b

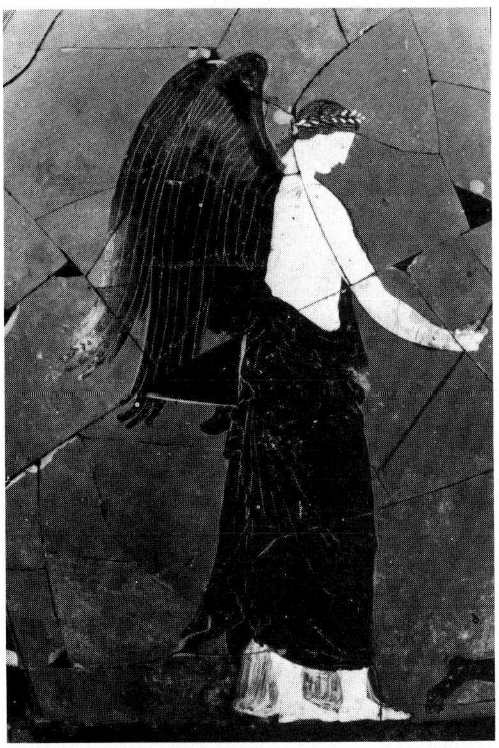

137c

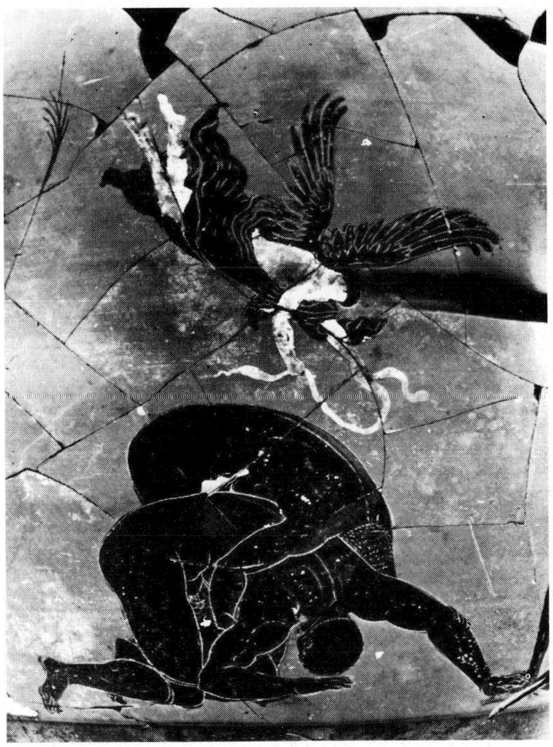

137d

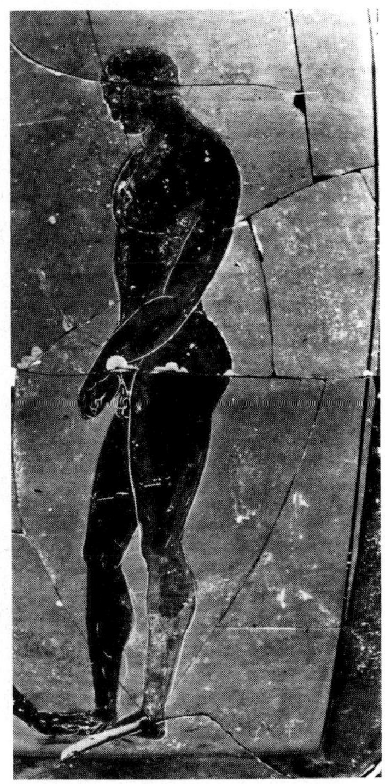

137e

137 **a** Detail of reverse-picture on Attic black-figure Panathenaic prize-amphora with name of Kallimedes, Archon 360/59 B.C., from Eretria. Chalkis Museum. H. of picture *c.* 0.25. (Pp. 384, 436) **b** Figure in picture on fragmentary Attic red-figure calyx-krater from Al Mina (Syria). Oxford, Ashmolean Museum 1939.597. Mid fourth century. H. of figure *c.* 0.12. (Pp. 435, 493) **c–e** Figures from reverse-picture of Attic black-figure Panathenaic prize-amphora with name of Kallimedes, Archon 360/59 B.C., found at Eretria with the one of which a detail is shown in **a** and several others. Chalkis Museum. H. of picture *c.* 0.25. (Pp. 384, 436).

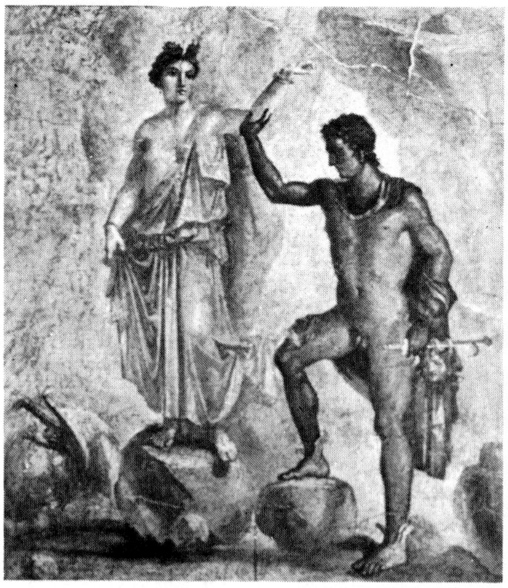

138a

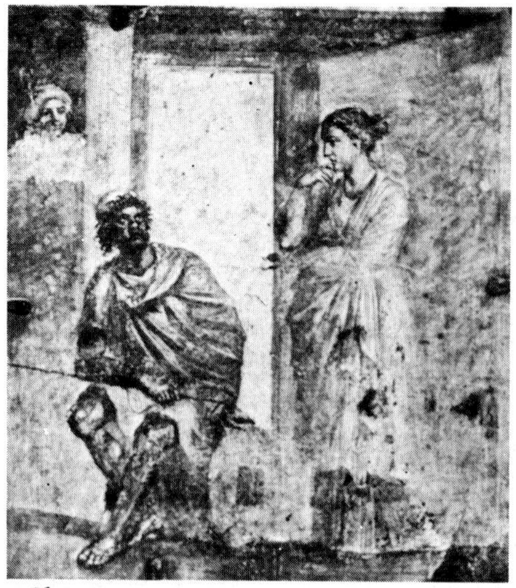

138b

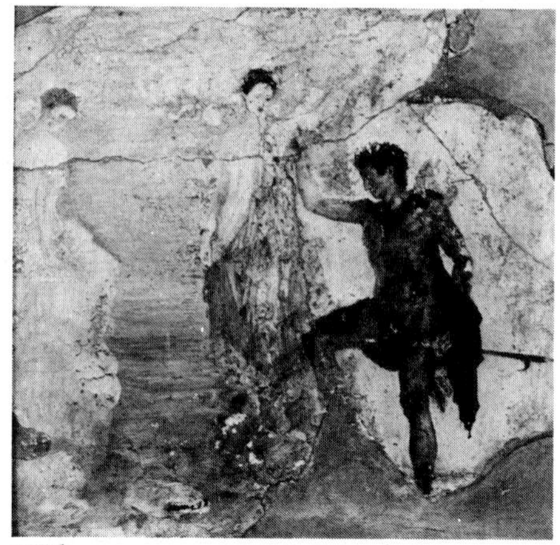

138d

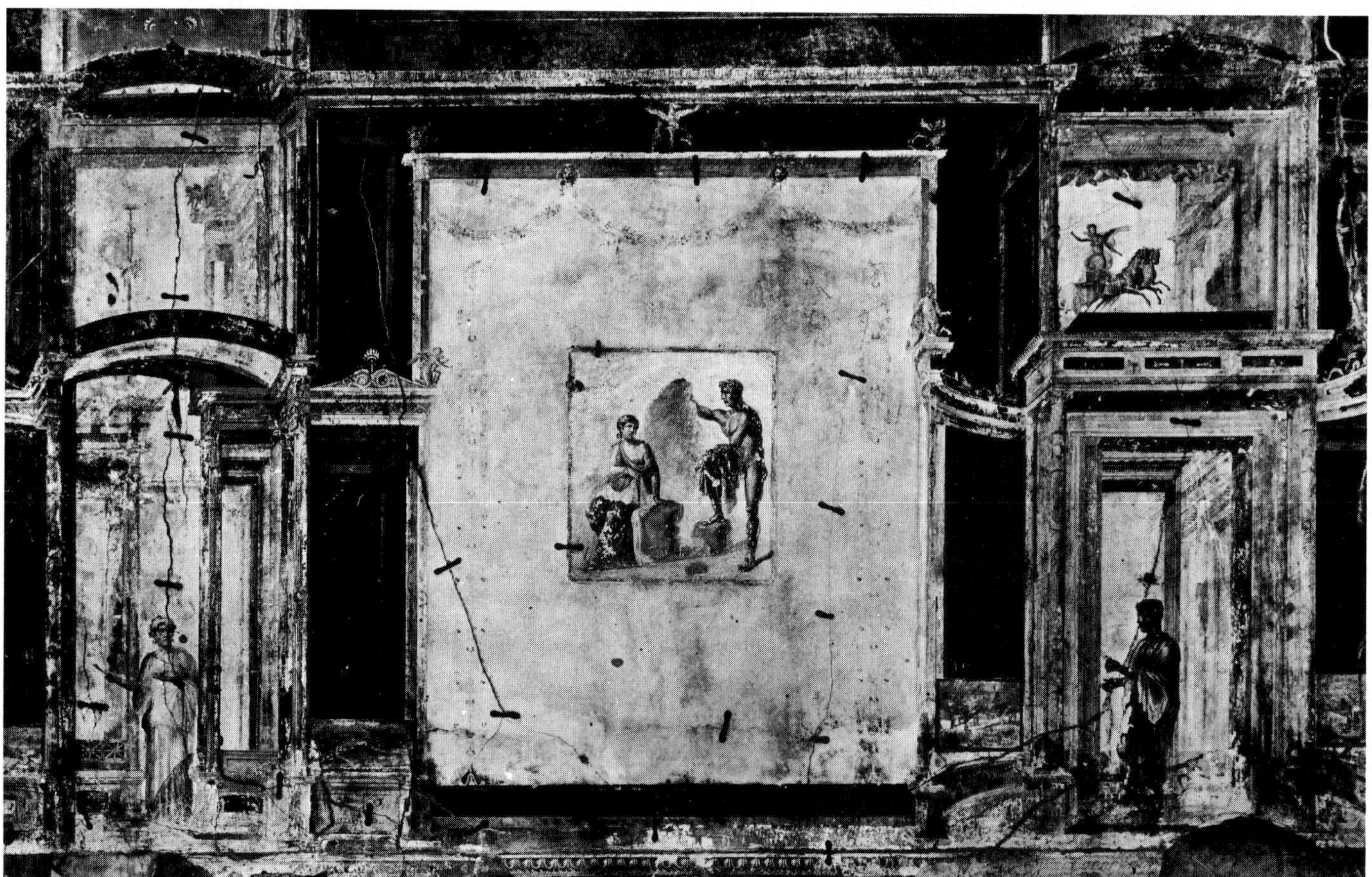

138c

138 **a** Wall-painting from Pompeii. Naples Museum 8998. Early to mid first century A.D., perhaps based on original of fourth century. H. 1.06. (P. 438) **b** Wall-painting from Pompeii. Naples Museum 9107. Early to mid first century A.D., perhaps based on original of fourth century. H. 0.83. (P. 439) **c** Painted wall of *Macellum* (covered market) at Pompeii. Third quarter of first century A.D., the central picture perhaps based on original of fourth century. (P. 438) **d** Wall-painting from Pompeii. Naples Museum 8993. Early first century A.D., based on same original as **a**. H. 0.38. (P. 438).

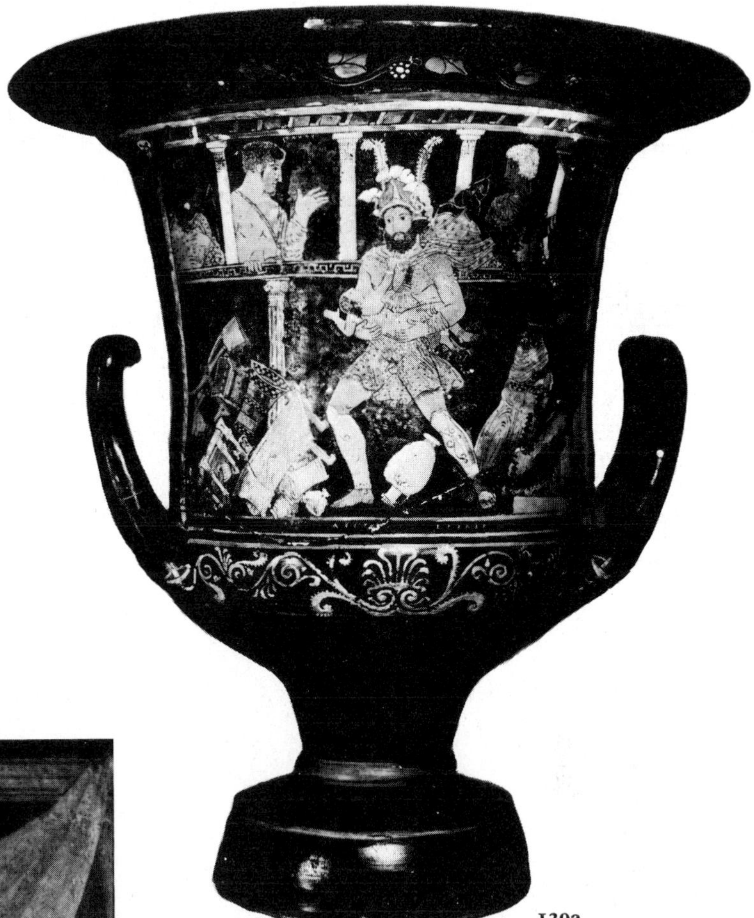

139a

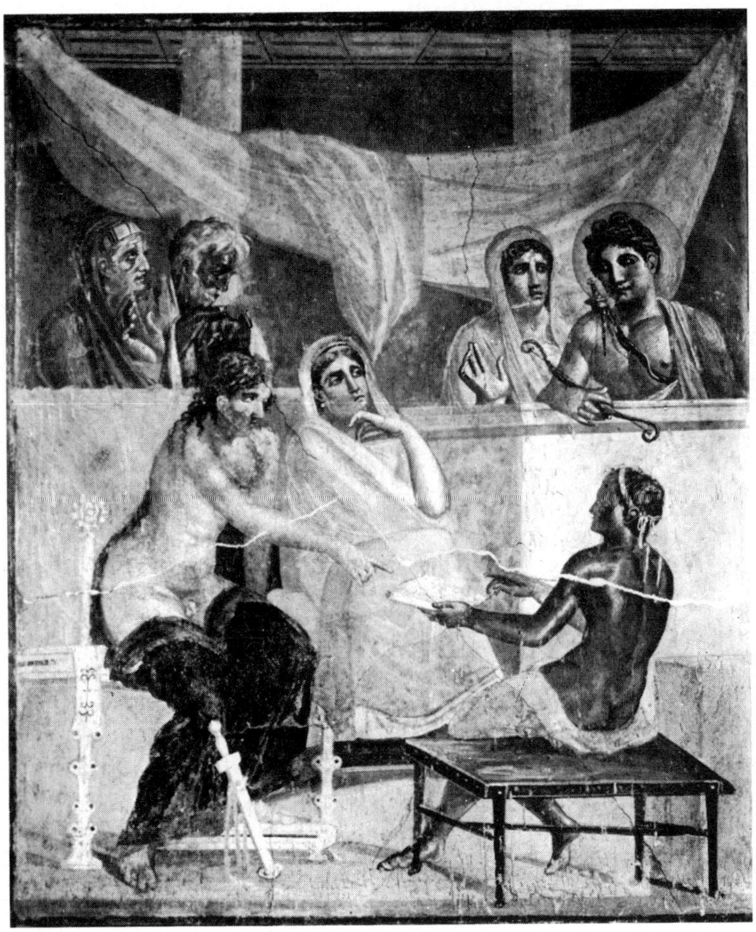

139b

139 **a** Red-figure calyx-krater signed by painter Assteas, made in Paestum. Madrid 11094. Mid fourth century. H. 0.55. (P. 440) **b** Wall-painting from Herculaneum. Naples Museum 9025. First century A.D., perhaps based on original of fourth century. H. 1.45. (P. 440).

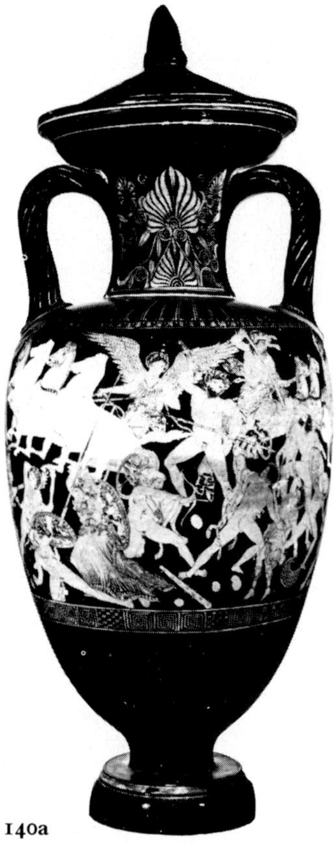

140a

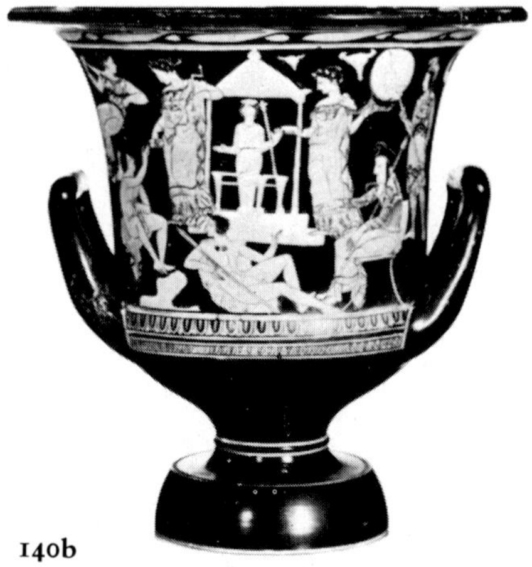

140b

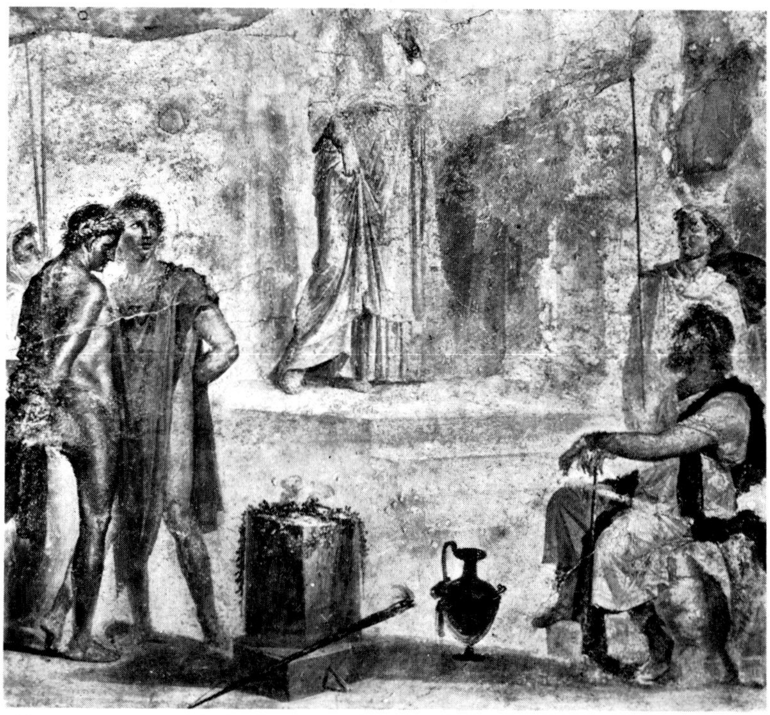

140c

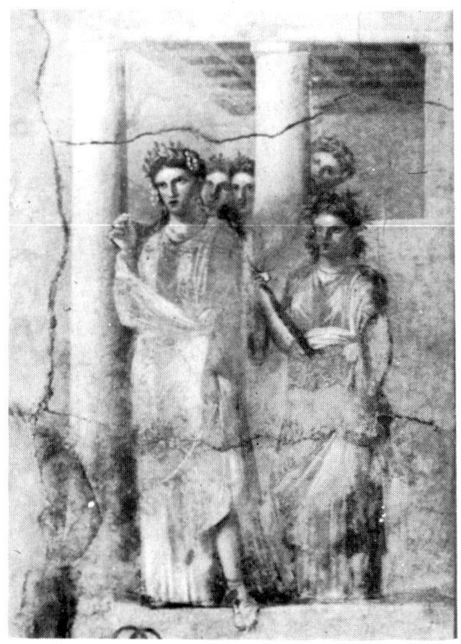

140d

140 **a** Attic red-figure neck-amphora, probably from Italy. Louvre S 1677. End of fifth or early fourth century. H. 0.76. (Pp. 324, 420, 431) **b** Attic red-figure calyx-krater from Spina (near mouth of Po). Ferrara T. 1145. First half of fourth century. H. 0.42. (P. 441) **c** Wall-painting from Pompeii. Naples Museum 9111. First half of first century A.D., perhaps based on original of fourth century or perhaps one of first century B.C. H. 1.14. (P. 442) **d** Wall-painting from Pompeii. Naples Museum 111439. Late first century B.C. or early first century A.D., the composition related to **c**. H. 1.11. (P. 442).

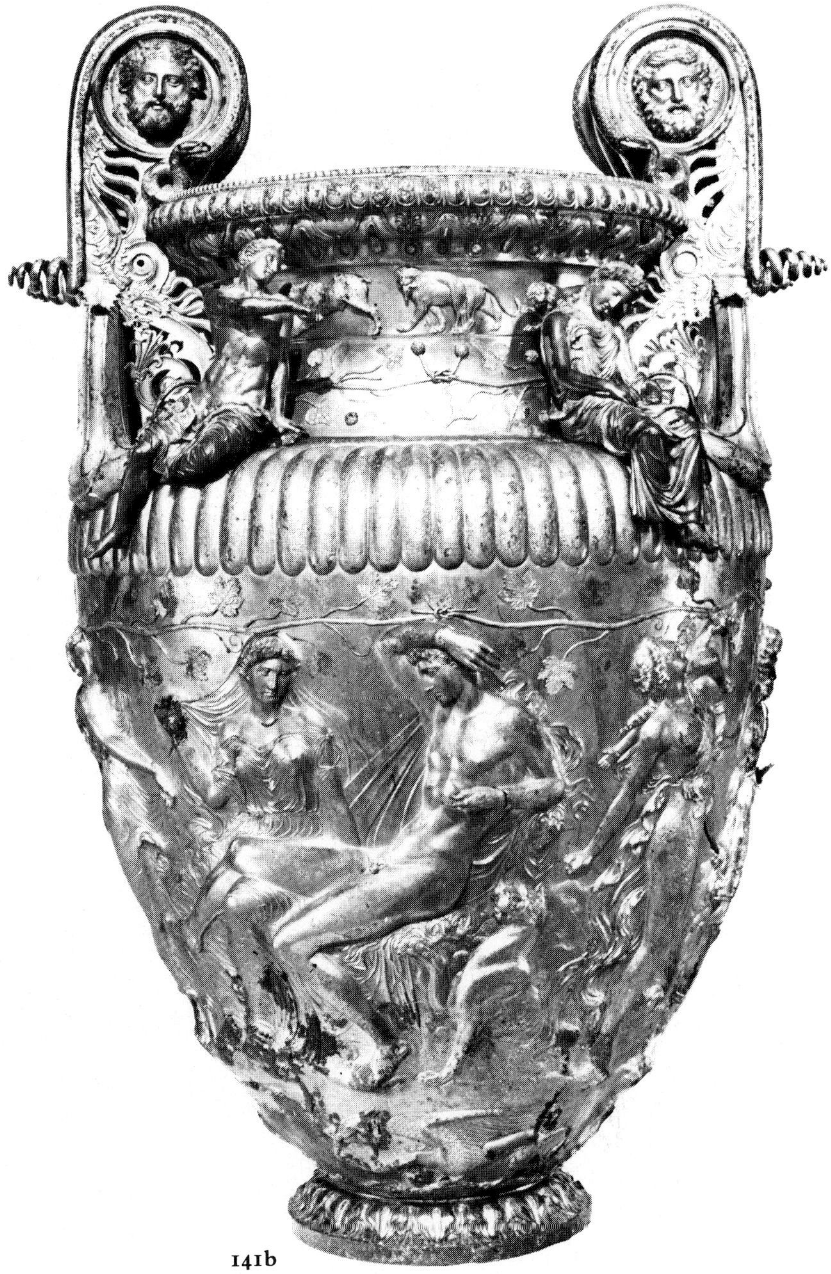

141b

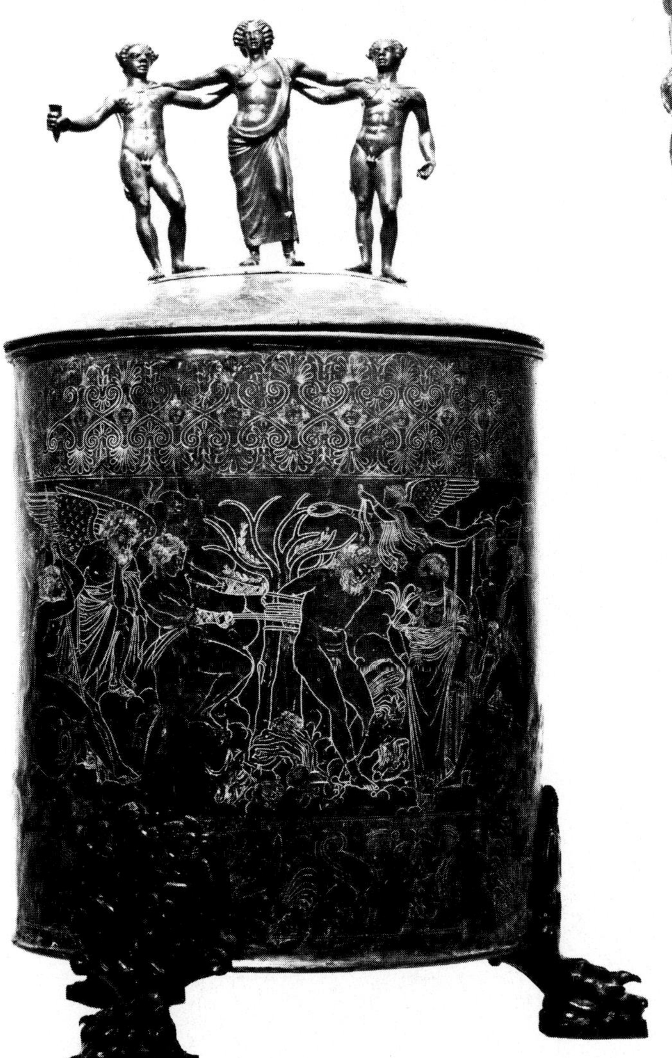

141a

141 **a** Etruscan bronze cista signed by Novios Plautios at Rome, from near Praeneste (Palestrina). Rome, Villa Giulia. Last quarter of fourth century. H., including figures on lid, 0.74. (Pp. 444, 595) **b** Bronze krater from Derveni (Thrace). Salonica Museum. Second half of fourth century. H. *c.* 0.85. (Pp. 482ff., 579).

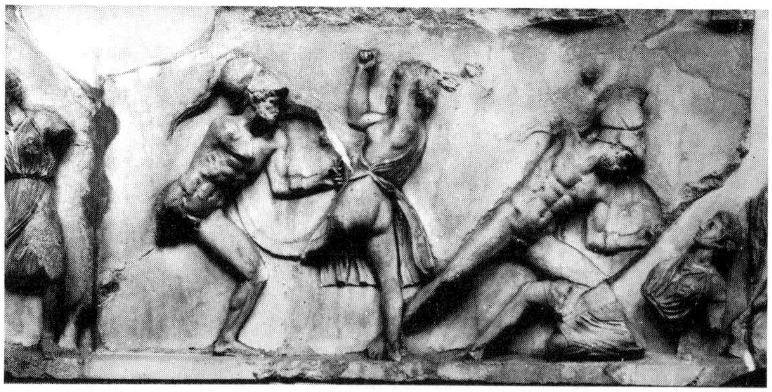

142a

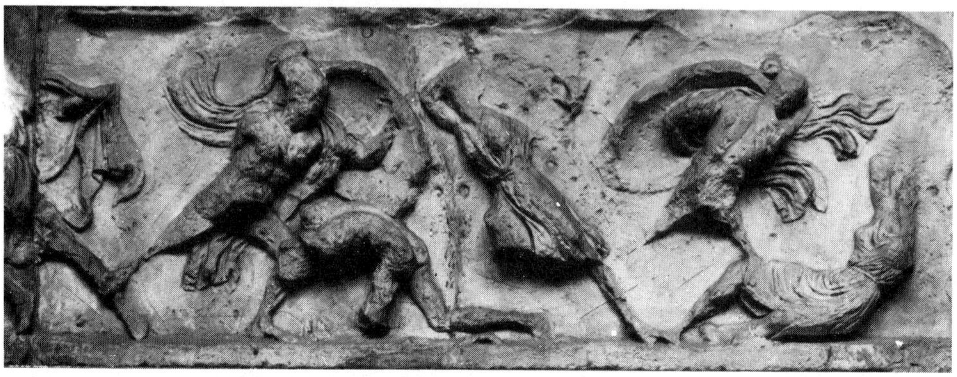

142b

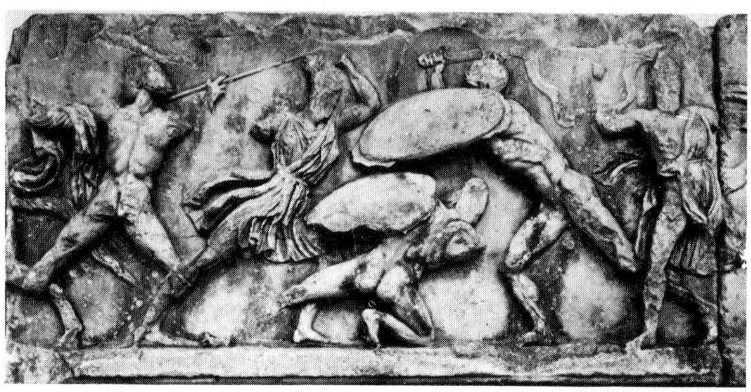

142c

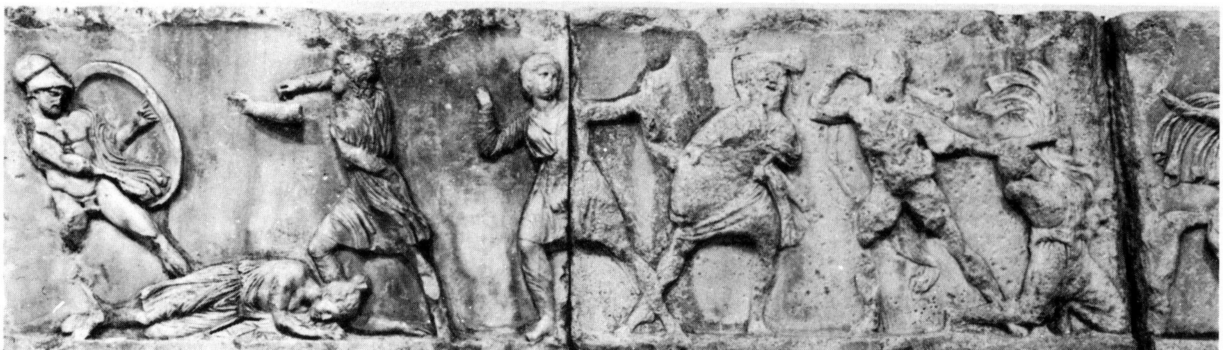

142d

142 a–d Marble frieze-slabs from Mausoleum of Halicarnassus. British Museum 1014, 1021, 1020 and 1007. Third quarter of fourth century. H. 0.89. (Pp. 450ff.).

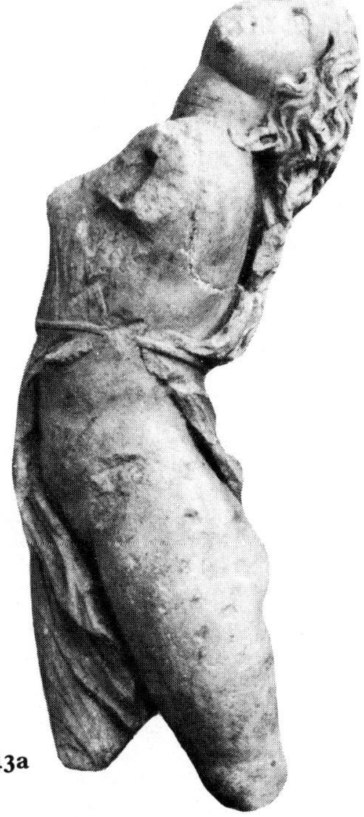

143a

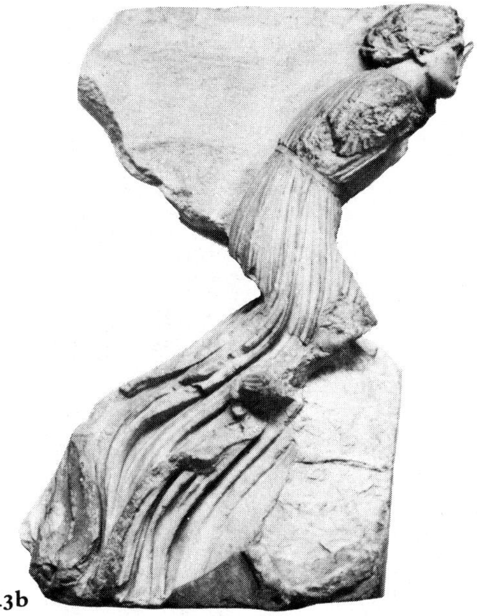

143b

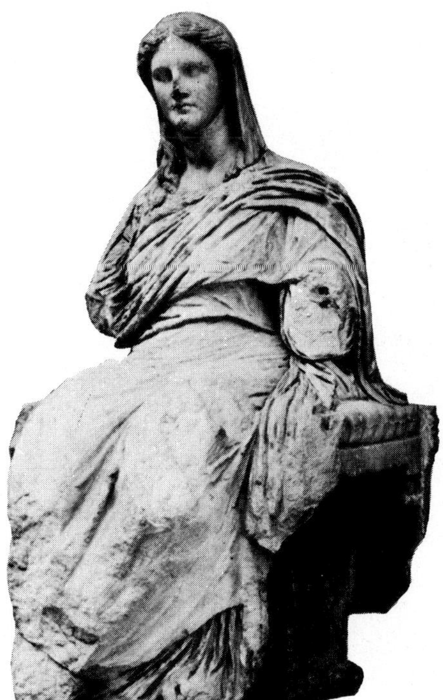

143c

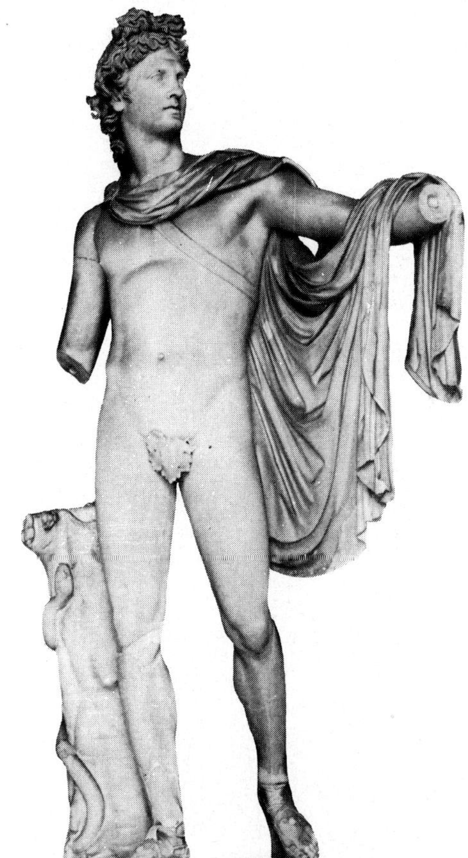

143d

143 **a** Fragmentary marble statuette. Dresden Museum. Copy of the imperial age, probably after statue of mid fourth century. H. 0.45. (Pp. 455, 472) **b** Marble relief-figure from a frieze of Mausoleum of Halicarnassus. British Museum 1037. Third quarter of fourth century. H. 0.40. See also pl. 145a. (P. 452) **c** Marble statue from Knidos. British Museum 1300. Second half of fourth century. H. 1.47. See also pl. 144a. (P. 462) **d** Marble statue. Vatican Copy of the imperial age probably after bronze original of second half of fourth century. H. 2.24. (P. 460).

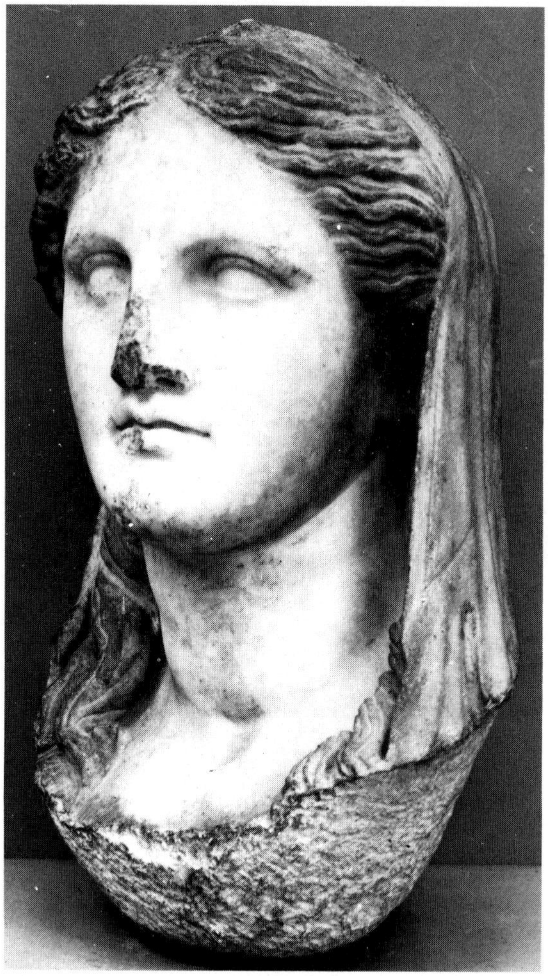

144a

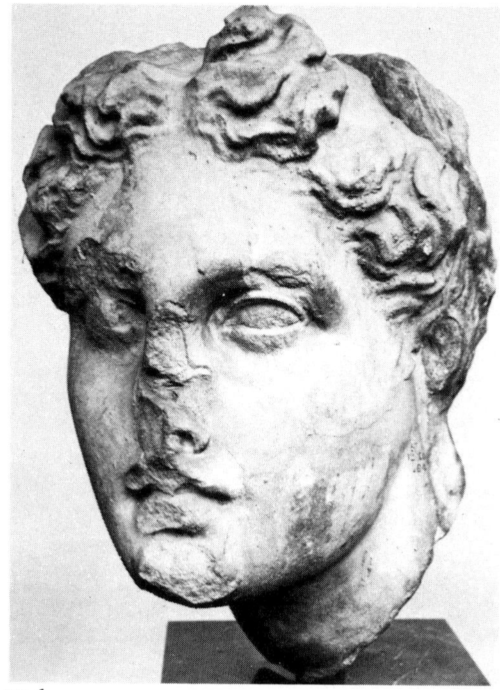

144b

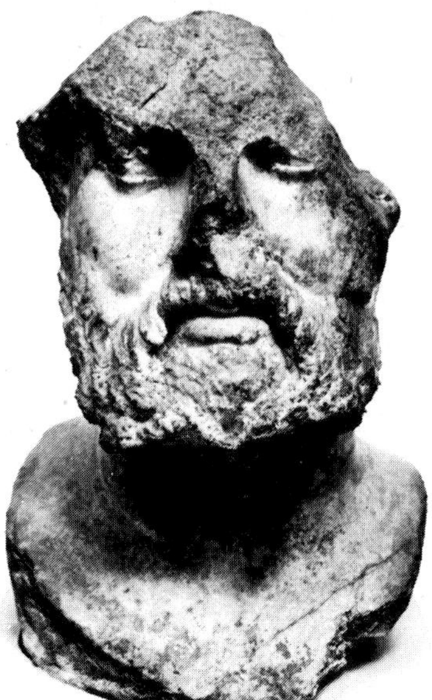

144c

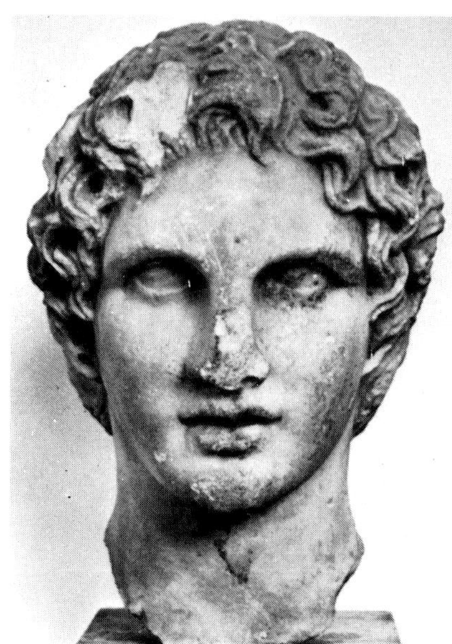

144d

144 **a** Head of statue, pl. 143c. (P. 462) **b** Marble head from Mausoleum of Halicarnassus. British Museum 1058. Third quarter of fourth century. H. 0.40. (P. 457) **c** Marble head from Mausoleum of Halicarnassus. British Museum 1055. Third quarter of fourth century. H. 0.35. (P. 457) **d** Marble head from Acropolis. Athens, Acropolis Museum 1331. Third quarter of fourth century. H. 0.35. (Pp. 462, 513).

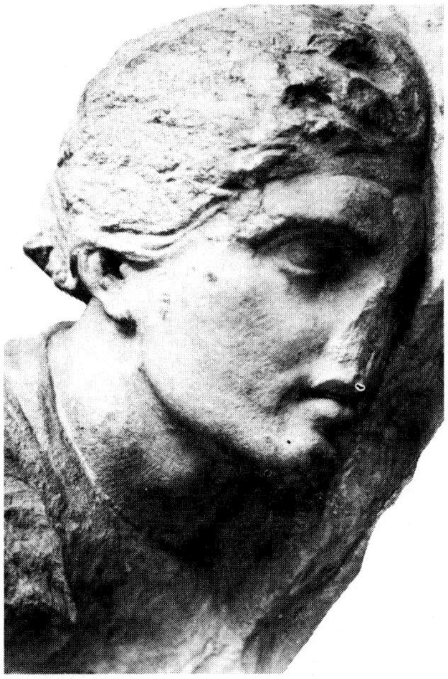

145a

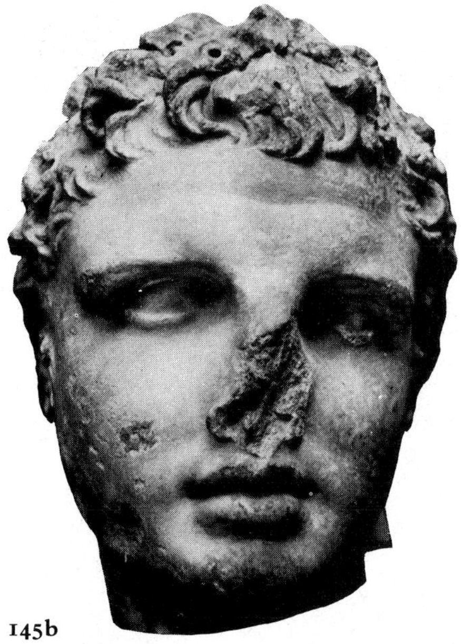

145b

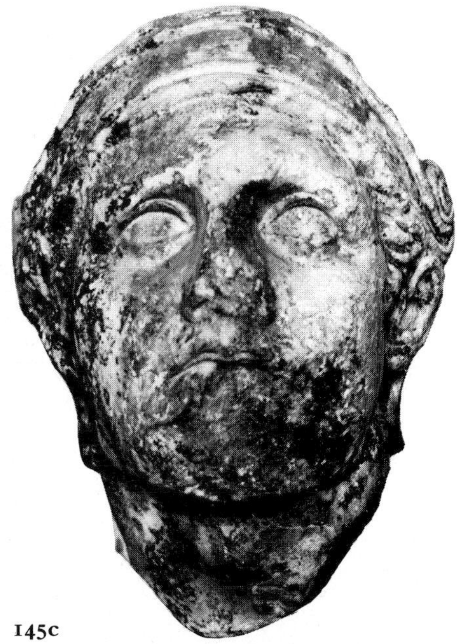

145c

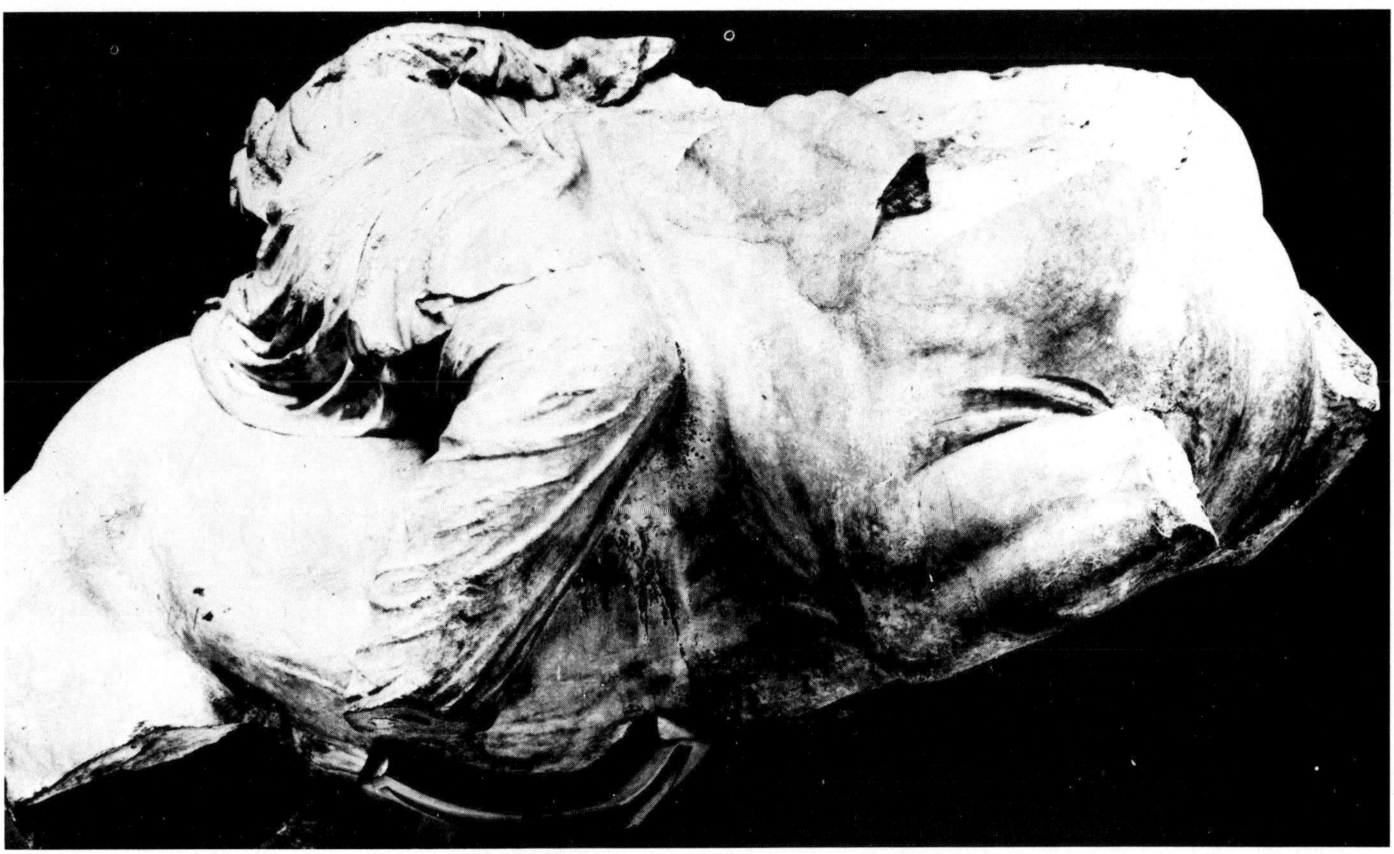

145d

145 **a** Head of relief-figure, pl. 143b. (Pp. 452, 462) **b** Marble head from Greece. British Museum 1600. Middle or second half of fourth century. H. 0.29. (P. 394) **c** Marble head from Temple of Athena Alea at Tegea. Athens, National Museum 180. Second or third quarter of fourth century. H. 0.30. (P. 454) **d** Fragment of marble group from Mausoleum of Halicarnassus. British Museum 1045. Third quarter of fourth century. H. 1.10. (P. 457).

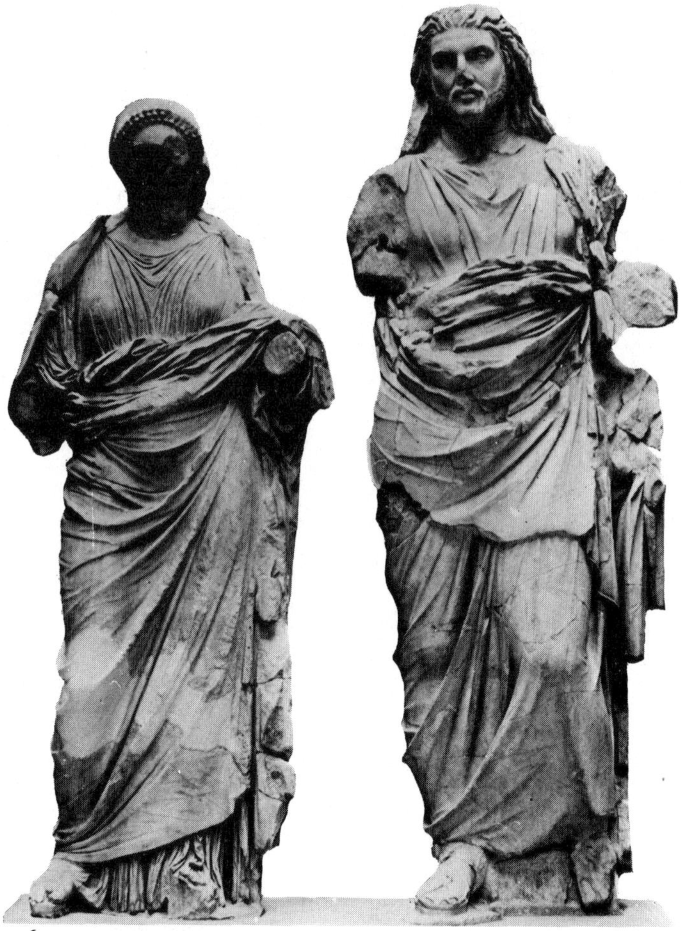

146a

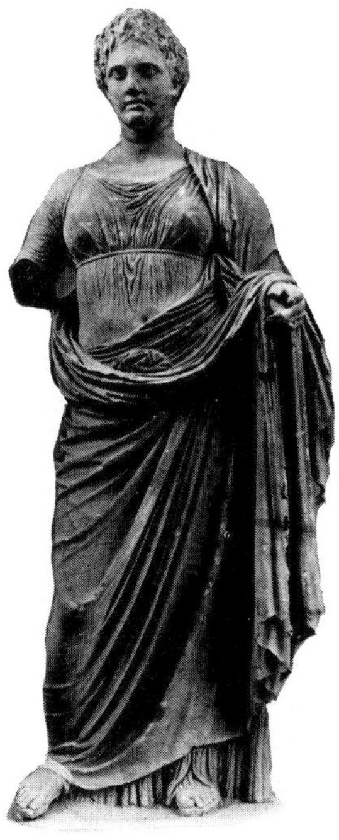

146b

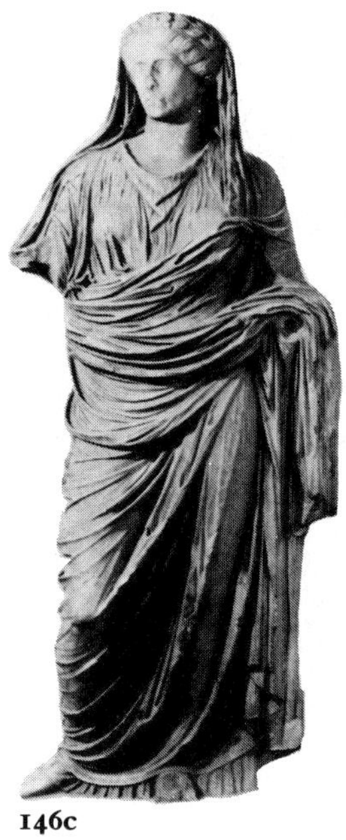

146c

146 **a** Marble statues from Mausoleum of Halicarnassus. British Museum 1000 (see also pl. 157b) and 1001. Third quarter of fourth century. H. 3.00 (1000) and 2.66 (1001). (Pp. 457ff., 504) **b** Marble statue signed by Chairestratos from Rhamnus (Attica). Athens, National Museum 231. Late fourth or early third century. H. 2.22. (P. 459) **c** Marble statue from Atrapalda (near Avellino). British Museum 1988. Portrait of second century A.D. based on statue of mid fourth century. H. 2.03. (Pp. 458, 598, 605).

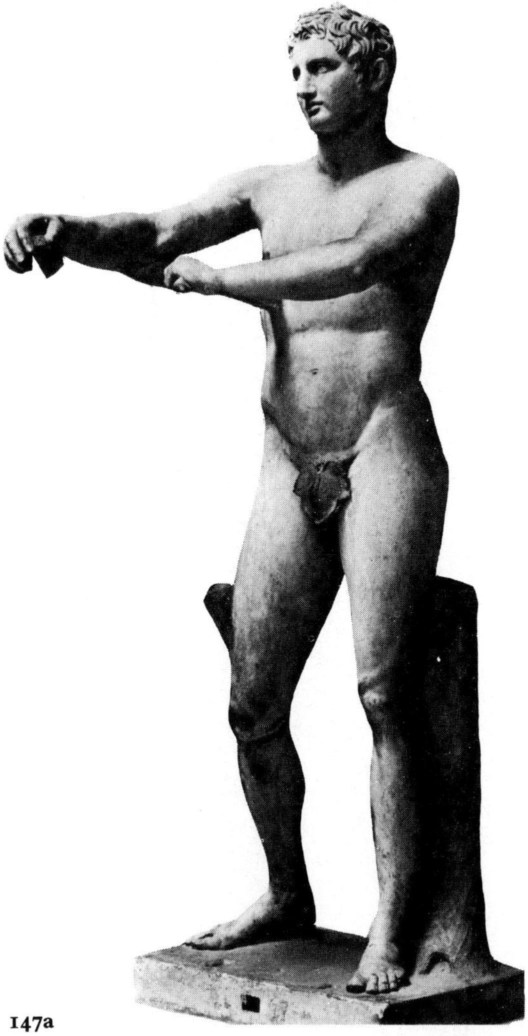

147a

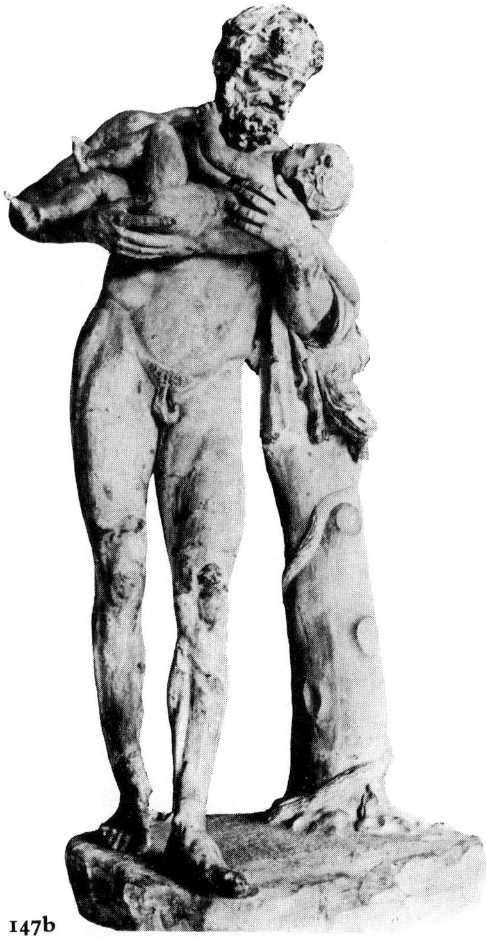

147b

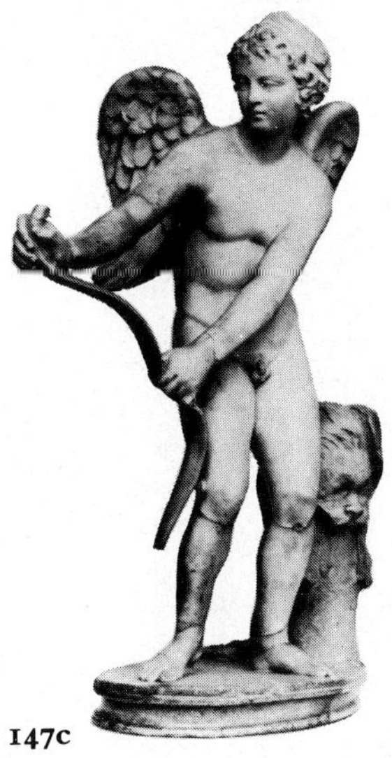

147c

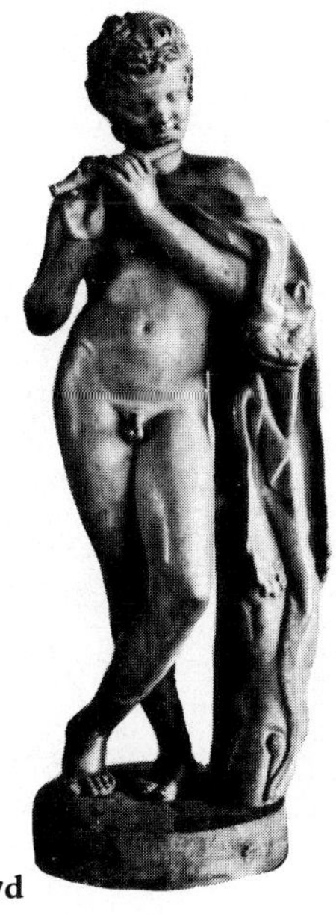

147d

147 **a** Marble statue. Vatican. Copy of the imperial period after bronze original of second half of fourth century. H. 2.05. (Pp. 464ff., 472) **b** Marble group. Louvre. Copy of the imperial age after bronze original of late fourth century. H. 1.90. The silen's hands and the arms and legs of the child are modern. (P. 467) **c** Marble statuette from Castello di Guido (near Rome). British Museum 1673. Copy of the imperial age after bronze statue of second half of fourth century. H. 0.60. (P. 466) **d** Marble statue. Louvre 595. Copy of the imperial age after bronze original of second half of fourth century. H. 1.25. (P. 468).

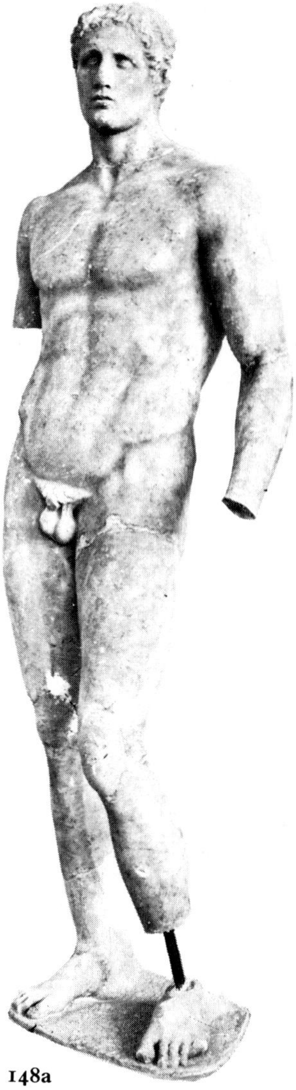

148a

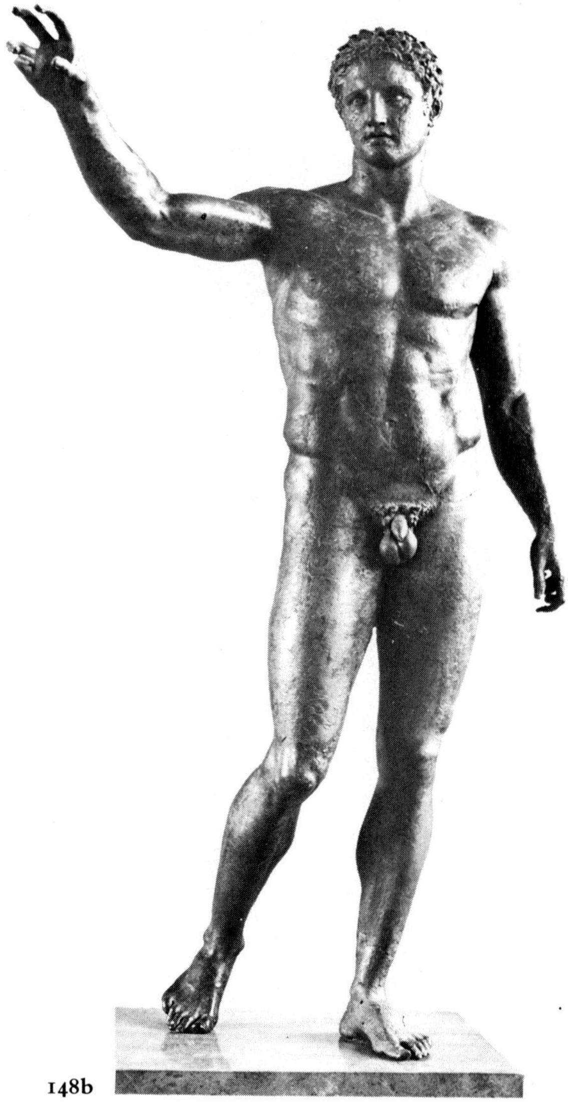

148b

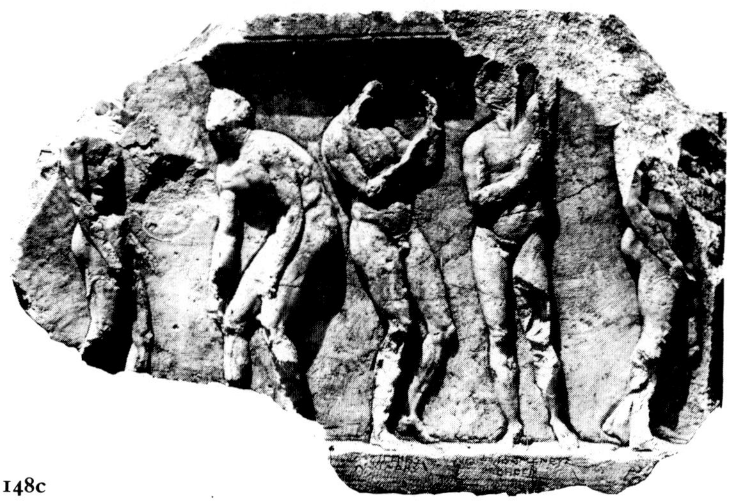

148c

148 **a** Marble statue from Delphi. Delphi Museum. Third quarter of fourth century. H. 1.97. (Pp. 469–70) **b** Bronze statue from sea off Antikythera. Athens, National Museum 13396. Probably mid fourth century. H. 1.94. (Pp. 409, 470) **c** Marble base from Acropolis. Athens, Acropolis Museum. Late fourth century. H. 0.48. (P. 466).

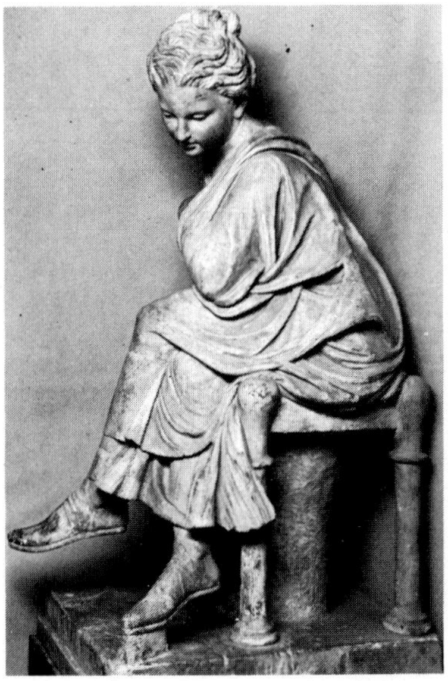

149a

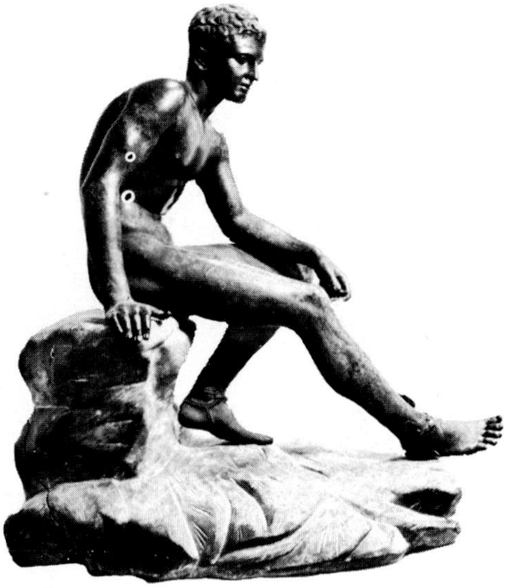

149b

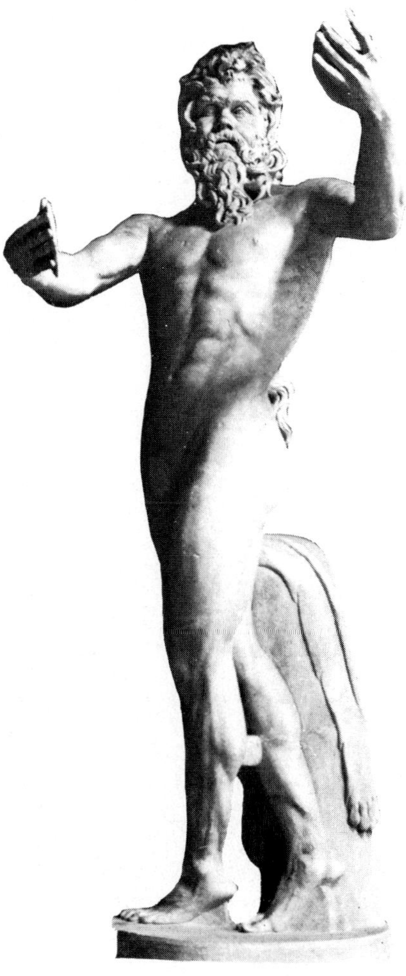

149c

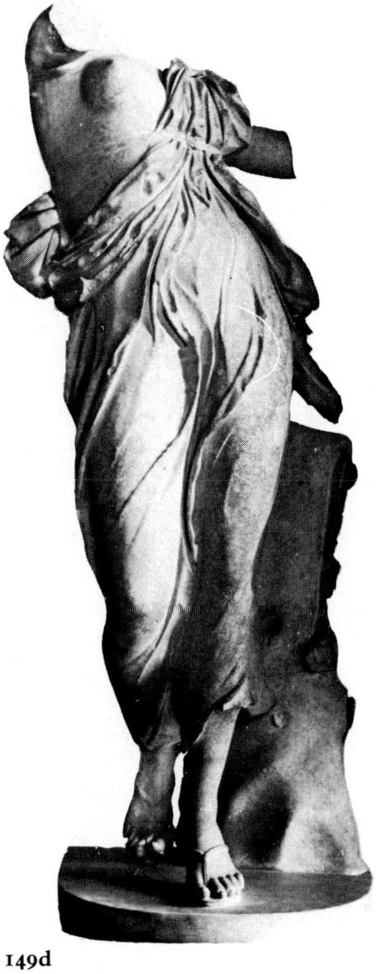

149d

149 **a** Marble statue. Rome, Palazzo dei Conservatori. Copy of the imperial age after bronze original of early third century. H. 1.03. (P. 473) **b** Bronze statue from Herculaneum. Naples Museum. Copy (made before A.D. 79) after original of late fourth or early third century. H. 1.05. (P. 474) **c** Marble statue. Rome, Borghese Gallery. Copy of the imperial age after bronze original of late fourth or early third century. H. 2.06. Arms and hands are modern, and other patches. (Pp. 478, 509) **d** Fragmentary marble statue. Berlin (E) 208. Copy of the imperial age after bronze original of late fourth century. H. 1.18. (Pp. 468, 472).

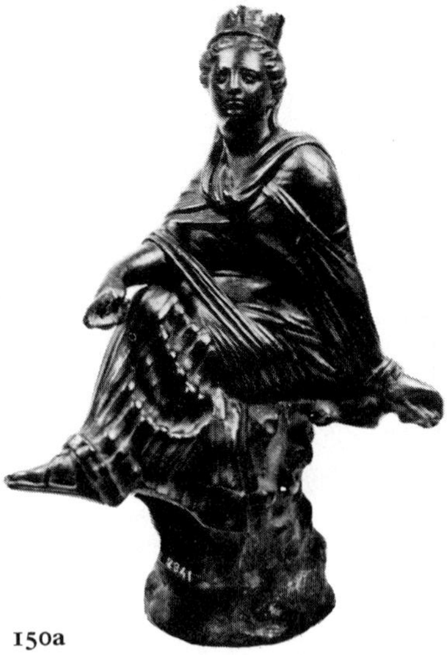

150a

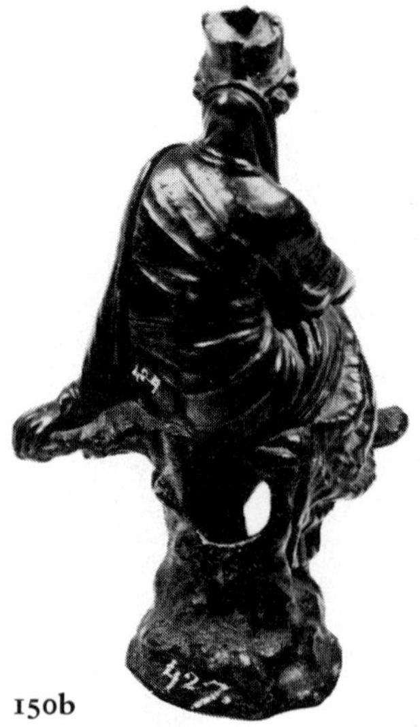

150b

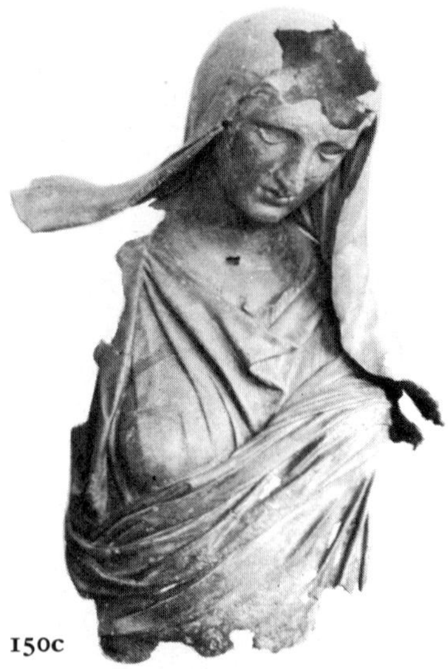

150c

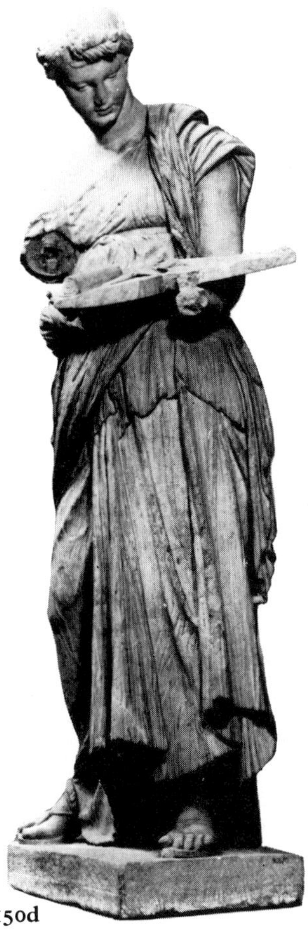

150d

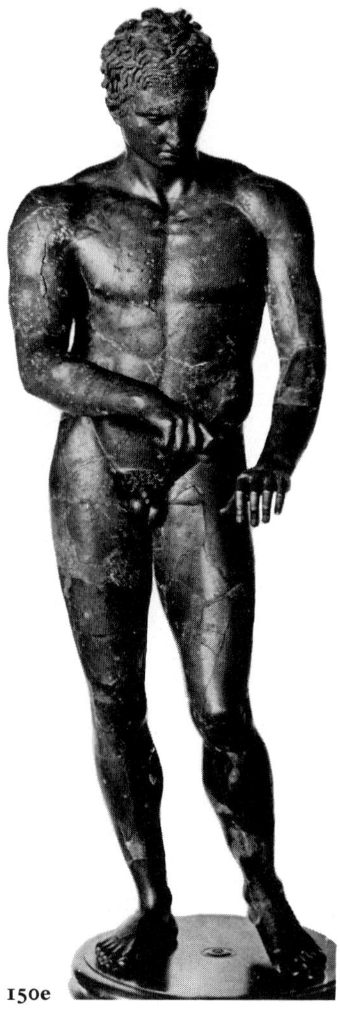

150e

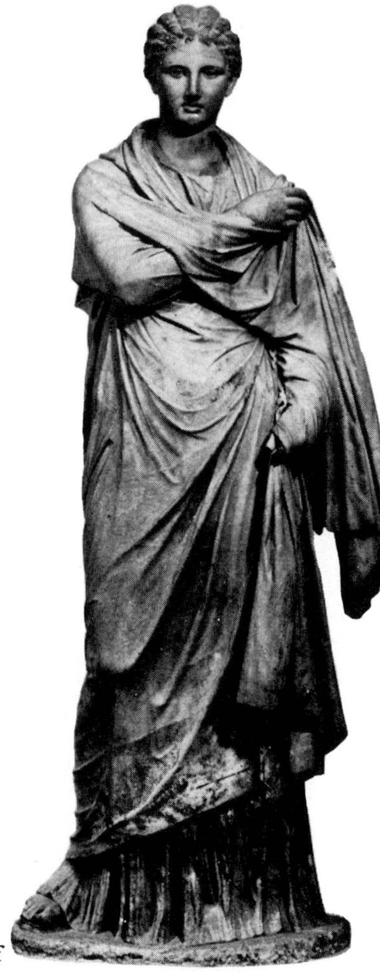

150f

150 **a** and **b** Bronze statuette. Florence, Museo Archeologico 2341. Copy of the imperial age after colossal statue of beginning of third century. H. 0.20. (Pp. 471ff.) **c** Upper part of bronze statue from sea off Smyrna. Smyrna Museum. Late fourth or early third century. H. 0.81. (Pp. 480, 511) **d** Marble statue from Anzio. Rome, Museo Nazionale. Probably copy of the imperial age after bronze original of early third century. H. 1.70. (Pp. 479, 575) **e** Bronze statue from Ephesus. Vienna 3168. Early third century (possibly a copy of the imperial age). H. 1.92. (P. 480) **f** Marble statue from Delos. Athens, National Museum 1827. Copy of the imperial age after original, perhaps in bronze, of late fourth or early third century. H. 1.80. (Pp. 479–80, 511, 546).

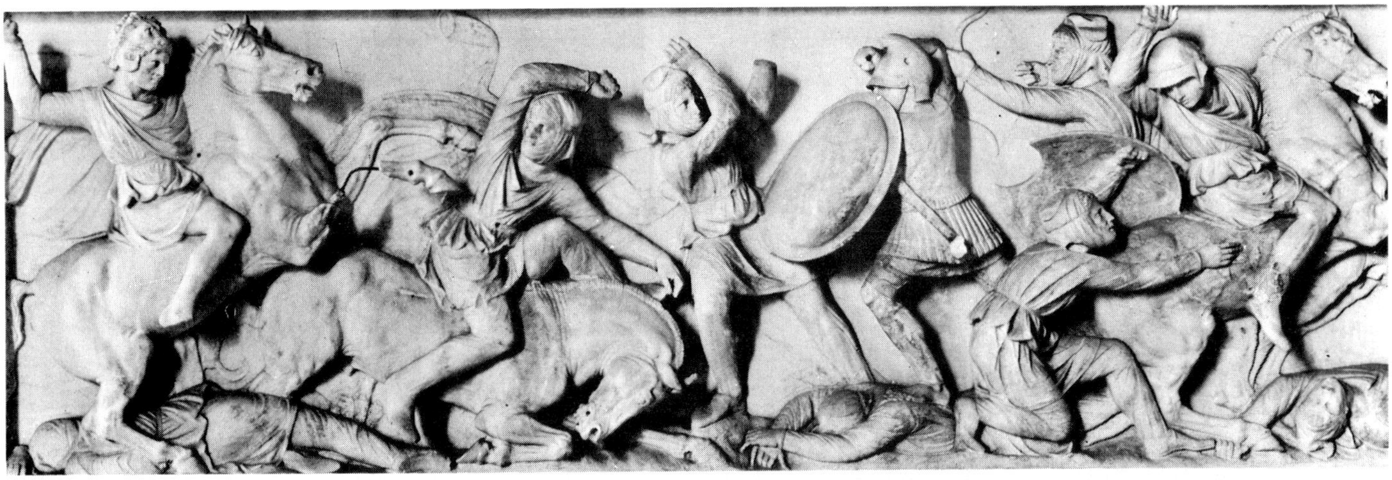

151a

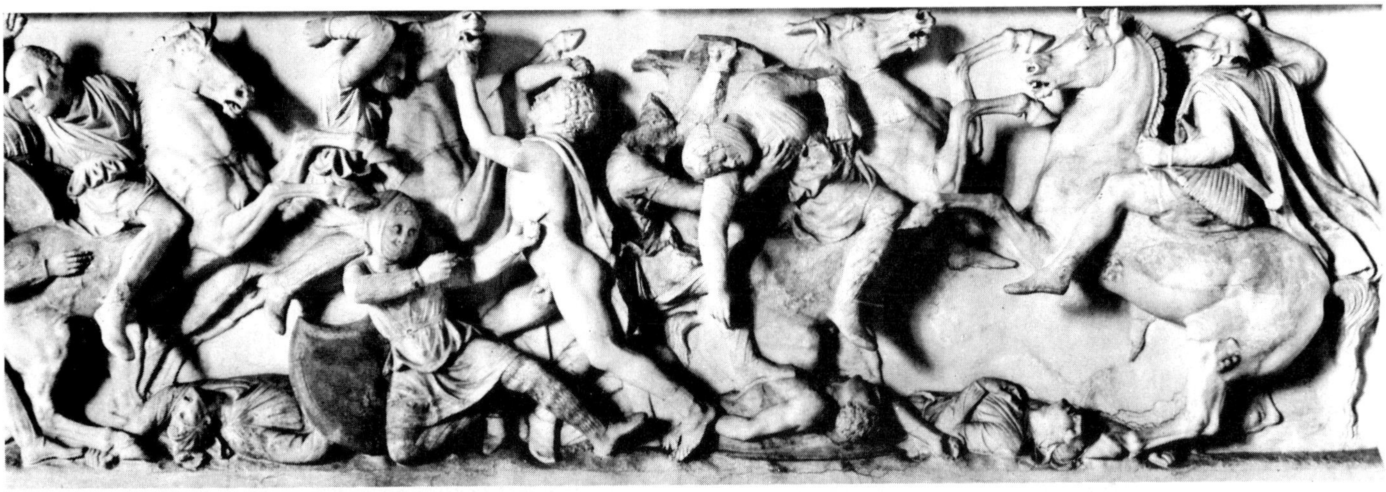

151b

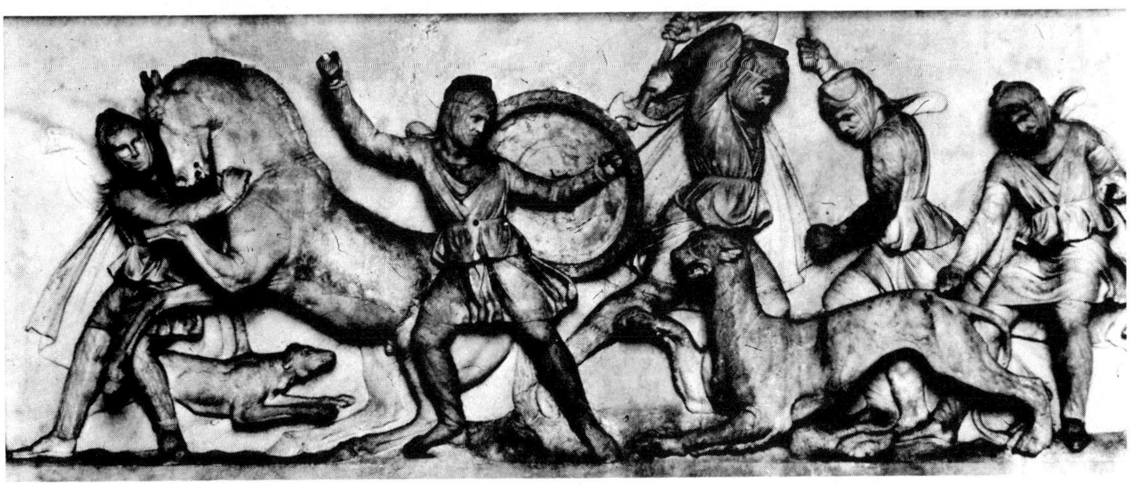

151c

151 **a–c** Marble sarcophagus from Sidon. Istanbul Museum. Last quarter of fourth century. H. of figured friezes 0.69. (Pp. 481–2, 498).

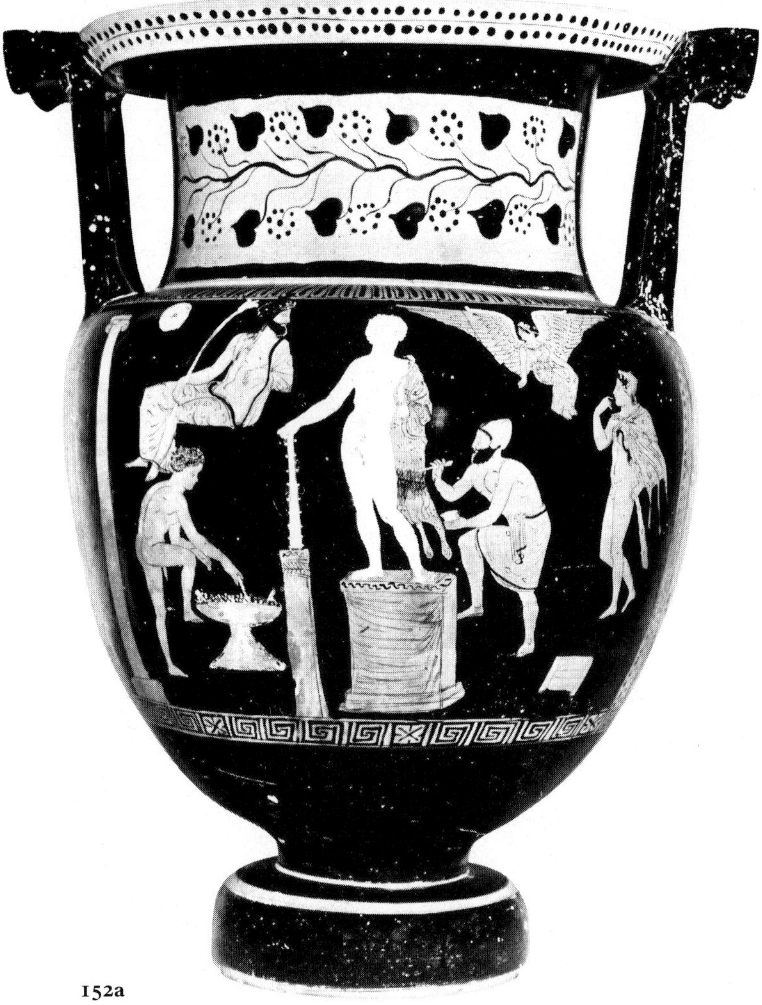

152a

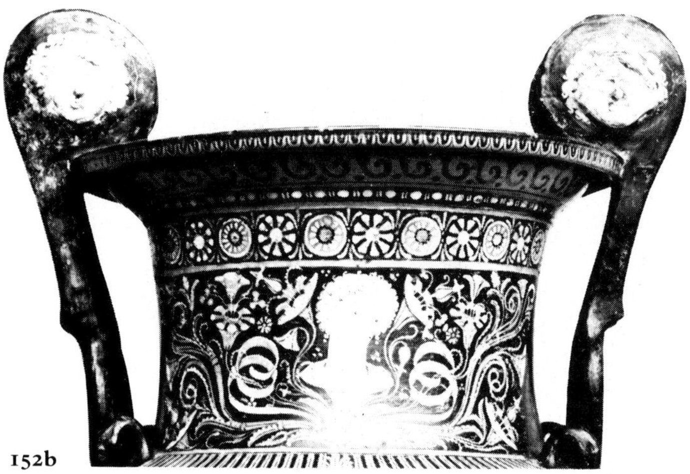

152b

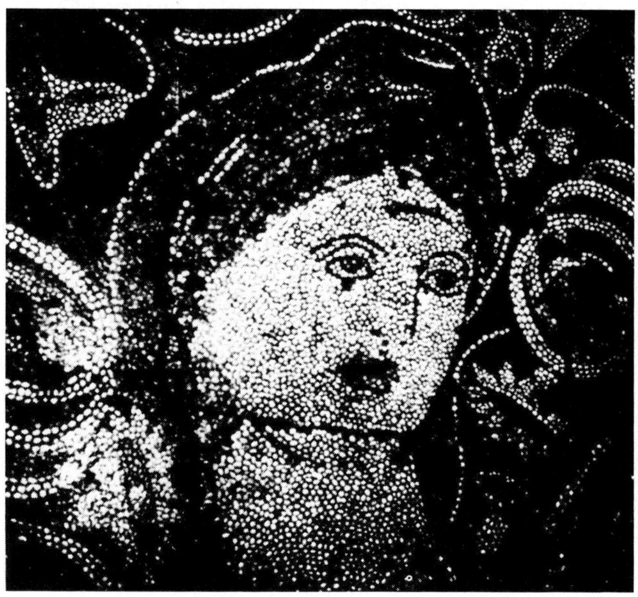

152c

152 **a** South Italian red-figure column-krater. New York, Metropolitan Museum of Art 50.11.4, Rogers Fund. First quarter of fourth century. H. 0.51. (P. 485) **b** Upper part of Apulian krater. British Museum F284. Second half of fourth century. H. of part shown *c.* 0.42. (Pp. 483, 486) **c** Mosiac floor at Dyrracchium Durrës Museum. Late fourth or early third century. H. of head *c.* 1.00. (P. 487).

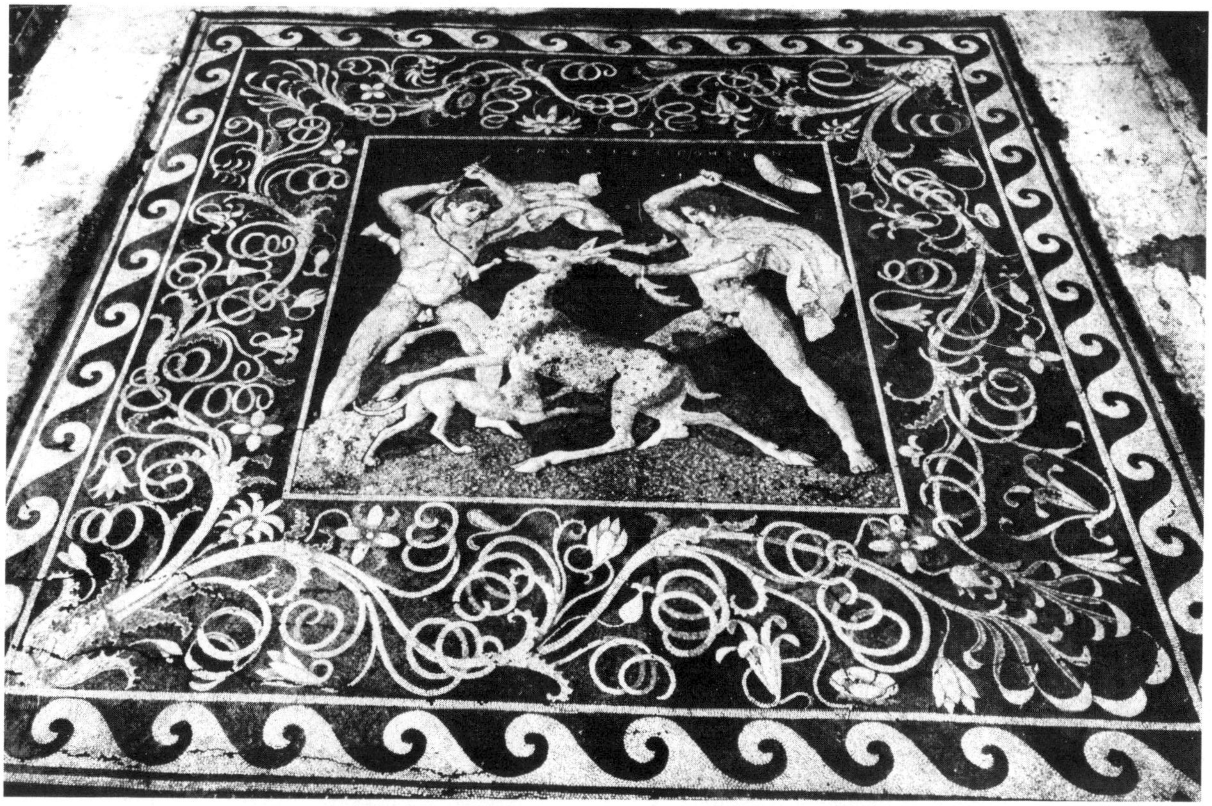

153a

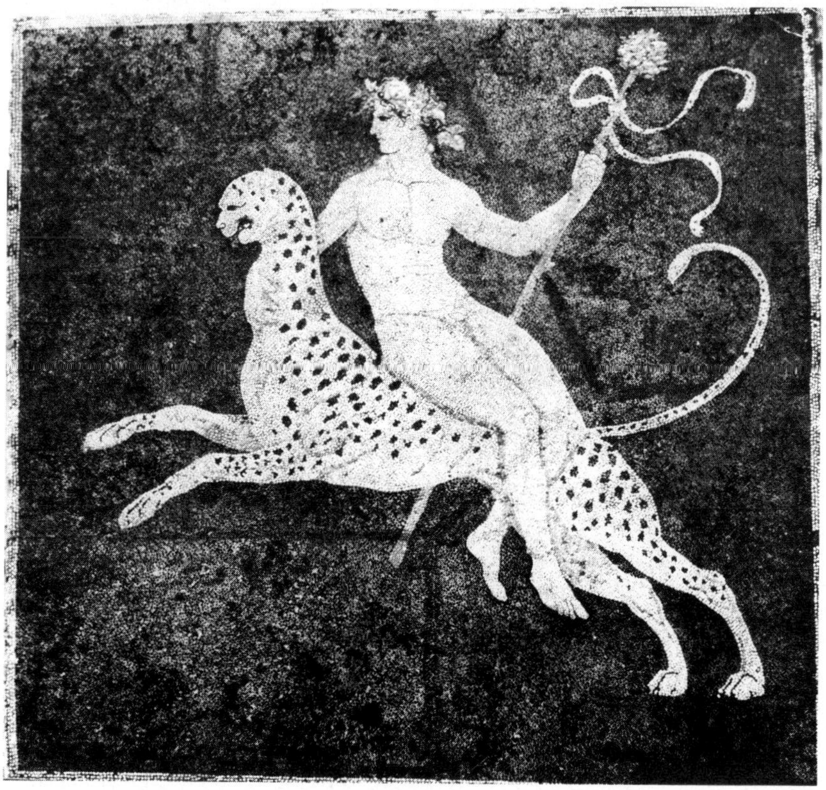

153b

153 **a** Mosaic floor from Pella. Pella Museum. Late fourth or early third century. H. of figured panel 3.10. (Pp. 482, 488) **b** Mosaic floor from Pella. Pella Museum. Late fourth century. H. 2.65. (Pp. 487–8, 579).

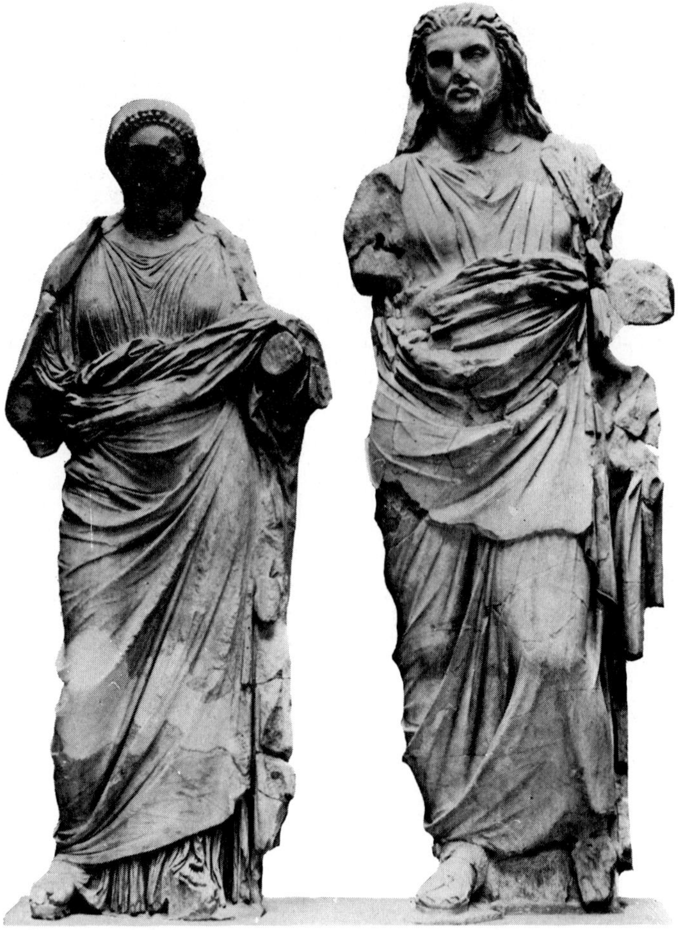

146a

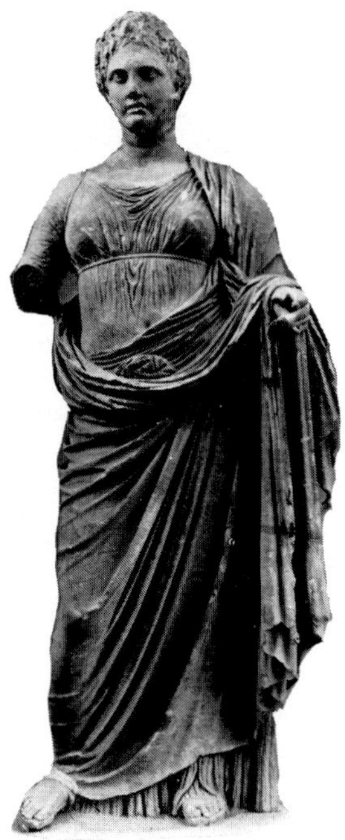

146b

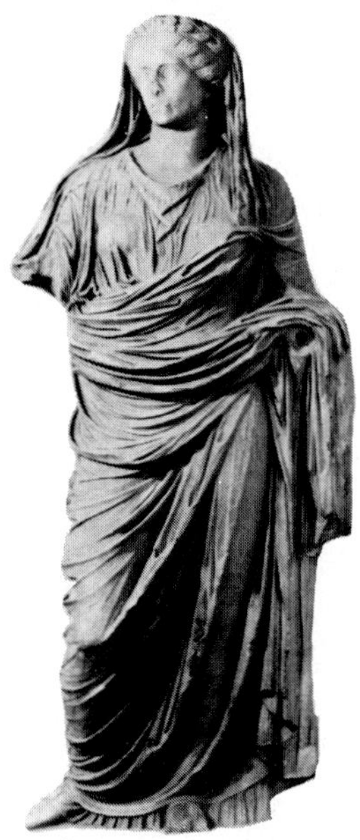

146c

146 **a** Marble statues from Mausoleum of Halicarnassus. British Museum 1000 (see also pl. 157b) and 1001. Third quarter of fourth century. H. 3.00 (1000) and 2.66 (1001). (Pp. 457ff., 504) **b** Marble statue signed by Chairestratos from Rhamnus (Attica). Athens, National Museum 231. Late fourth or early third century. H. 2.22. (P. 459) **c** Marble statue from Atrapalda (near Avellino). British Museum 1988. Portrait of second century A.D. based on statue of mid fourth century. H. 2.03. (Pp. 458, 598, 605).

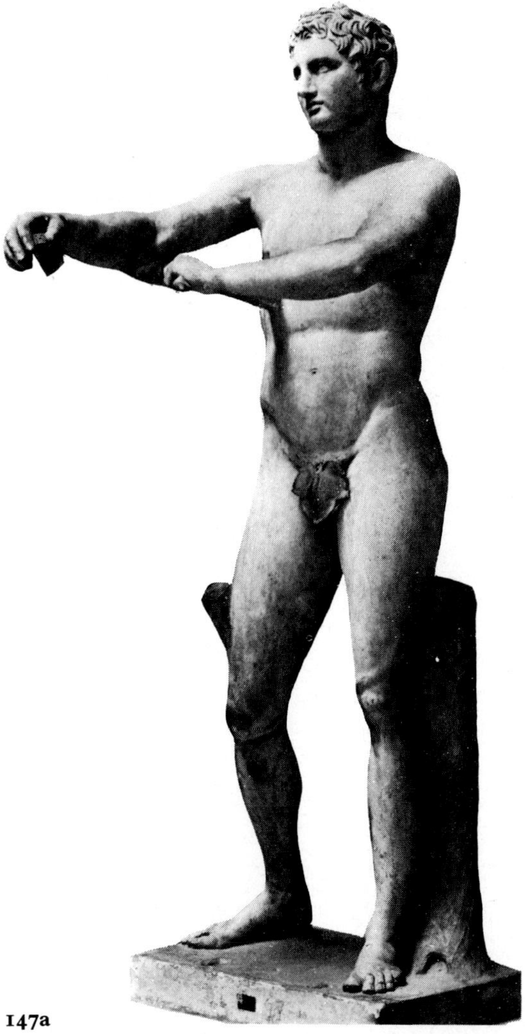

147a

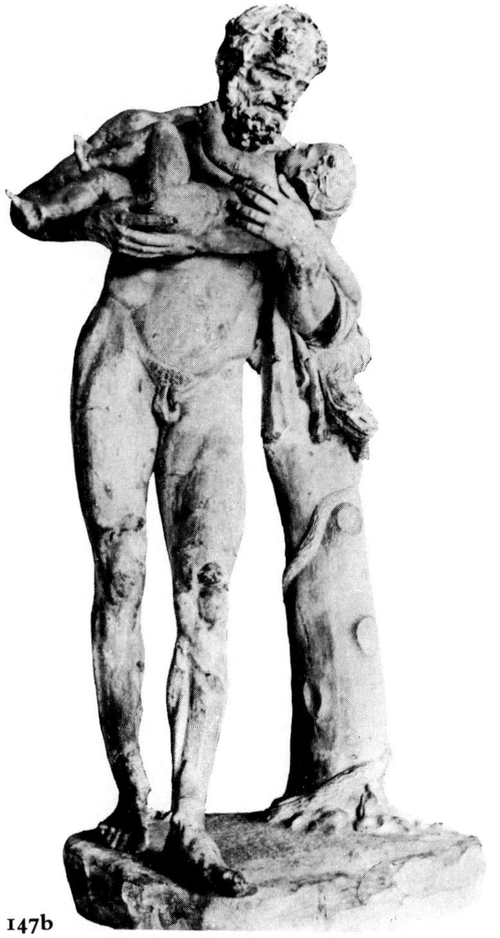

147b

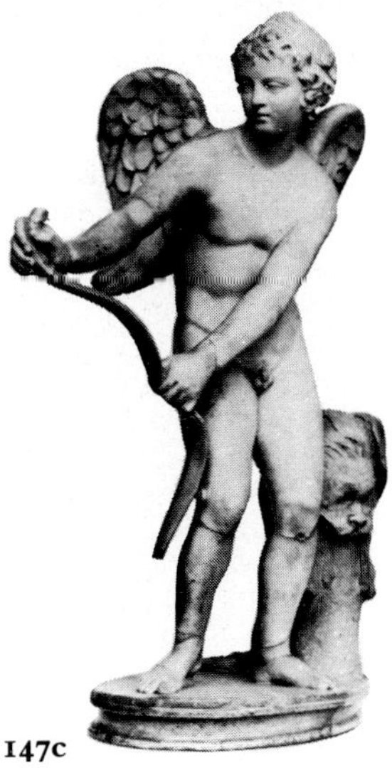

147c

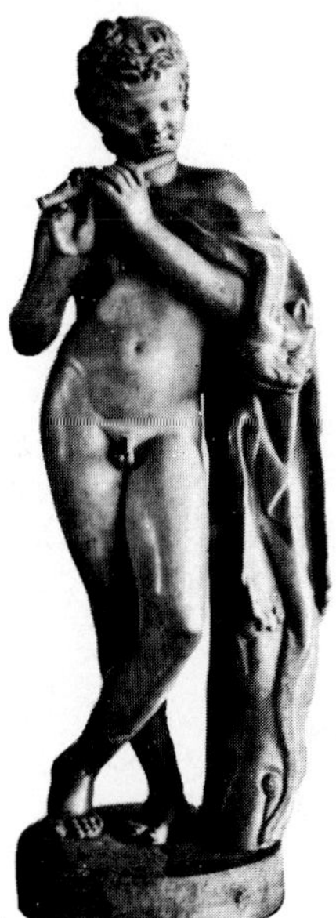

147d

147 **a** Marble statue. Vatican. Copy of the imperial period after bronze original of second half of fourth century. H. 2.05. (Pp. 464ff., 472) **b** Marble group. Louvre. Copy of the imperial age after bronze original of late fourth century. H. 1.90. The silen's hands and the arms and legs of the child are modern. (P. 467) **c** Marble statuette from Castello di Guido (near Rome). British Museum 1673. Copy of the imperial age after bronze statue of second half of fourth century. H. 0.60. (P. 466) **d** Marble statue. Louvre 595. Copy of the imperial age after bronze original of second half of fourth century. H. 1.25. (P. 468).

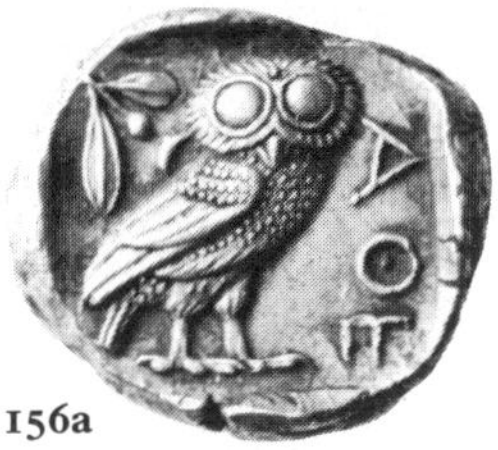
156a

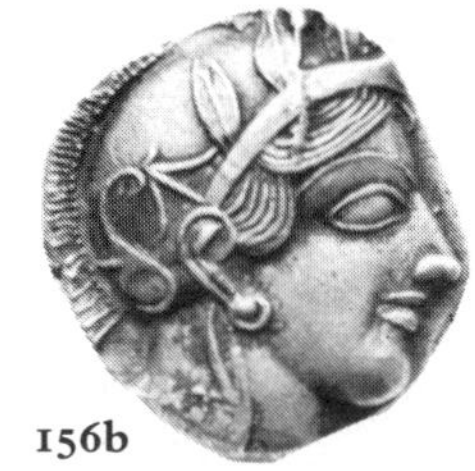
156b

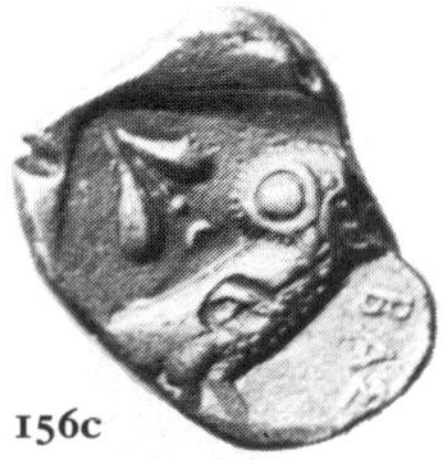
156c

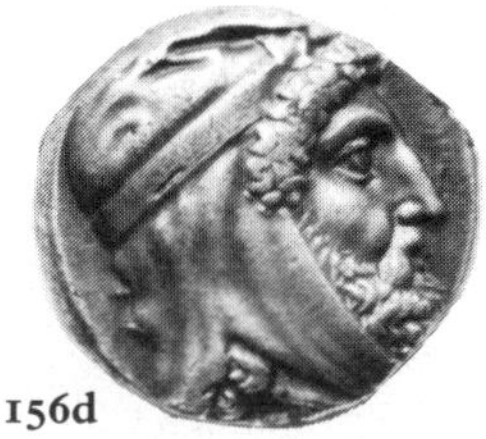
156d

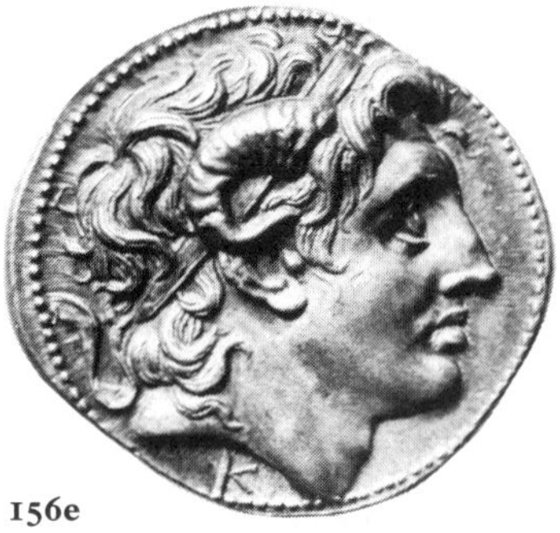
156e

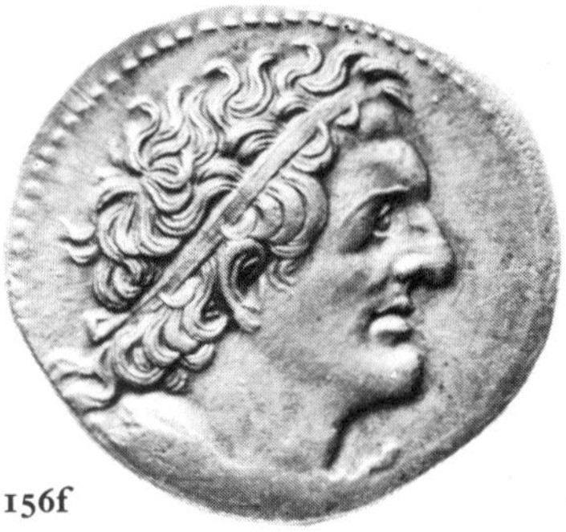
156f

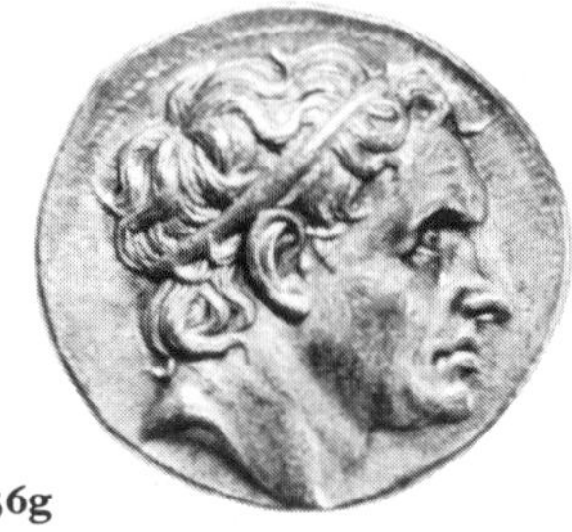
156g

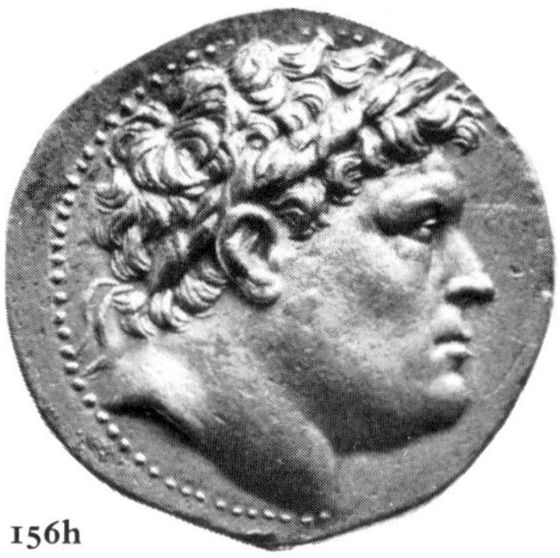
156h

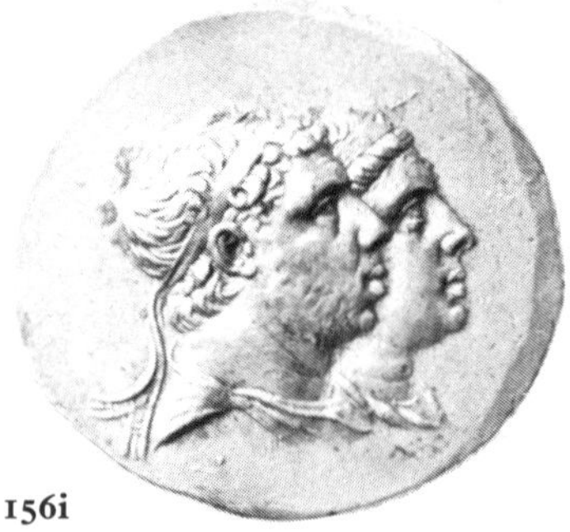
156i

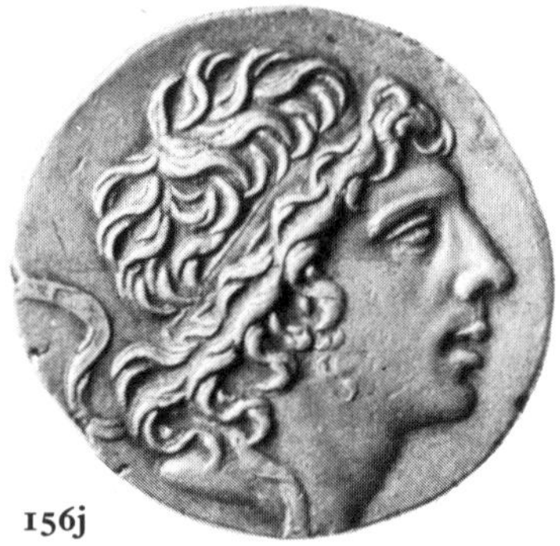
156j

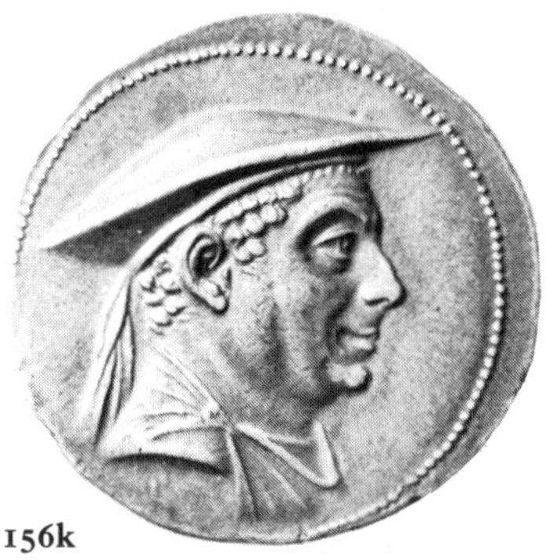
156k

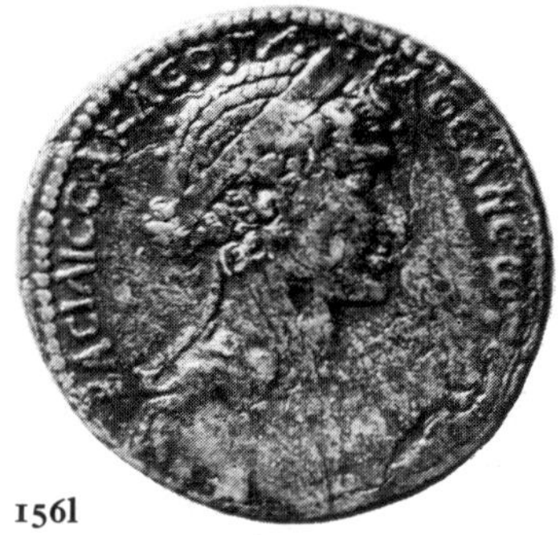
156l

156 **a** and **b** Silver tetradrachm of Athens. Private Coll. Mid fifth century. D. *c.* 0.02. (Pp. 151, 346, 359, 506) **c** Silver tetradrachm of Tissaphernes. British Museum. Last quarter of fifth century. D. *c.* 0.02. (P. 506) **d** Silver tetradrachm of Tissaphernes. British Museum. End of fifth or beginning of fourth century. D. *c.* 0.02. (Pp. 362, 506) **e** Silver tetradrachm of Lysimachus of Thrace (306–281). British Museum. D. *c.* 0.03. (Pp. 507, 514) **f** Silver tetradrachm of Ptolemy I of Egypt (305–283). Private Collection. D. *c.* 0.03. (P. 515) **g** Silver tetradrachm of Philetairos of Pergamon (284–263). Private Collection. *c.* 0.03. (P. 515) **h** Silver tetradrachm of Attalos I of Pergamon (241–197). Von Aulock Collection. D. *c.* 0.03. (P. 529) **i** Silver tetradrachm of Mithradates IV (170–150) of Pontus, and Laodike. Paris, Cabinet des Médailles. D. *c.* 0.03. (P. 522) **j** Silver tetradrachm of Mithradates VI (120–63) of Pontus. Private Collection. D. *c.* 0.03. (P. 522) **k** Silver tetradrachm of Antimachos I of Bactria. British Museum. First quarter of second century. D. *c.* 0.03. (P. 521) **l** Silver tetradrachm of Cleopatra VII (51–30). British Museum. D. *c.* 0.03 (P. 523).

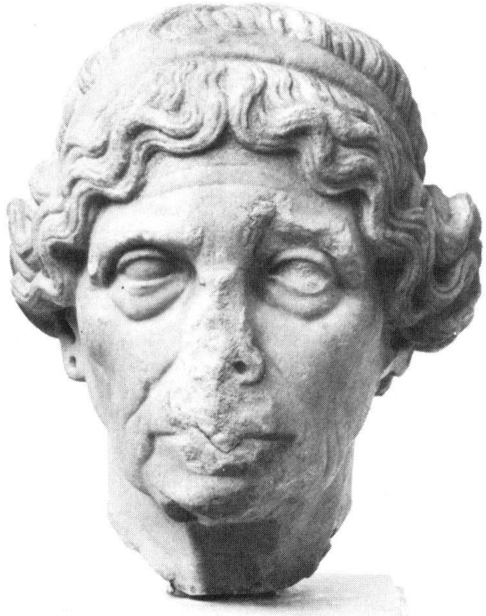

157a

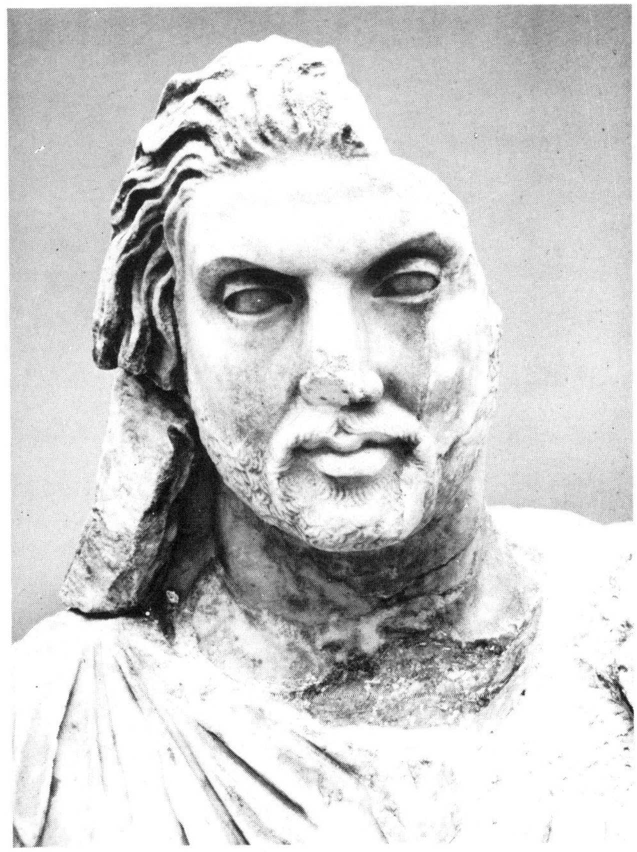

157b

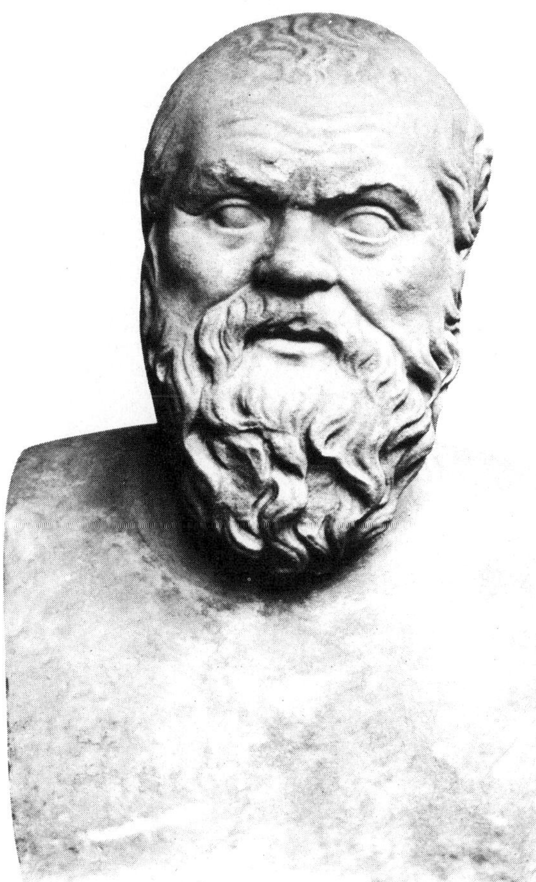

157c

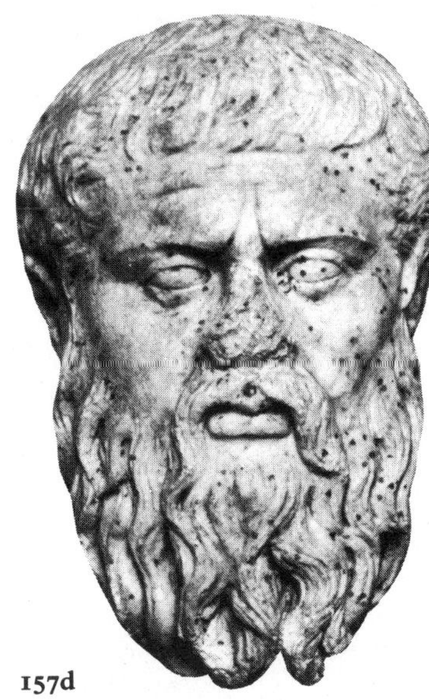

157d

157 **a** Marble head. British Museum 2001. Copy of the imperial age probably after original in bronze of early fourth century. H. 0.16. (P. 505) **b** Head of statue, pl. 146a. British Museum 1000. (Pp. 458, 504, 507, 517) **c** Marble head. Berlin (E) 298 (K 194). Copy of the imperial age probably after original in bronze of second half of fourth century. H. of head and neck *c.* 0.36. (P. 509) **d** Marble head. Copenhagen, Ny Carlsberg Glyptotek 2553. Copy of the imperial age probably after original in bronze of second half of fourth century. H. 0.35. (P. 509).

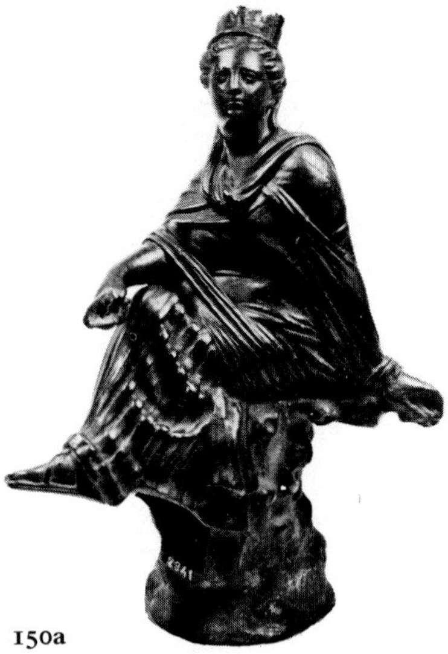

150a

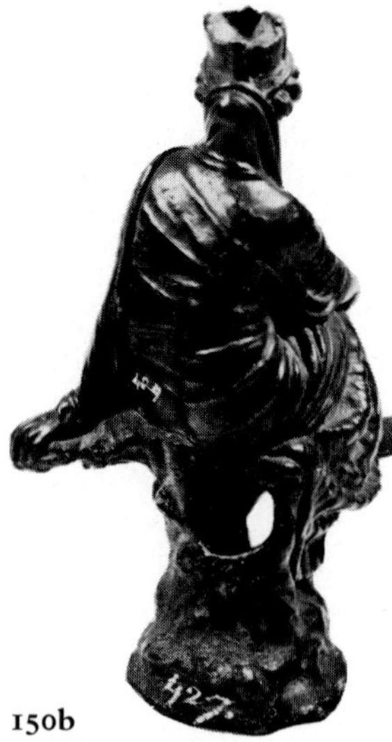

150b

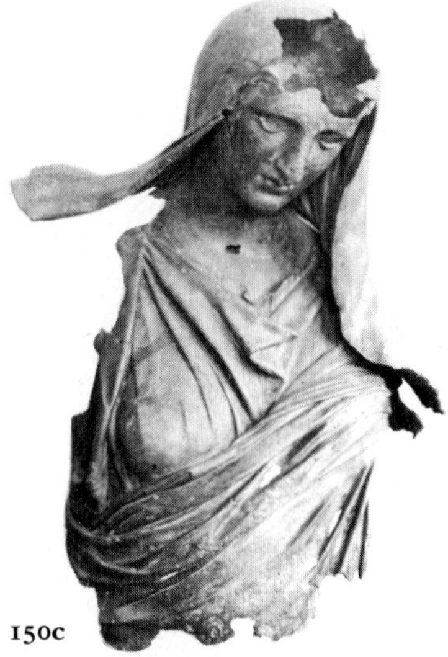

150c

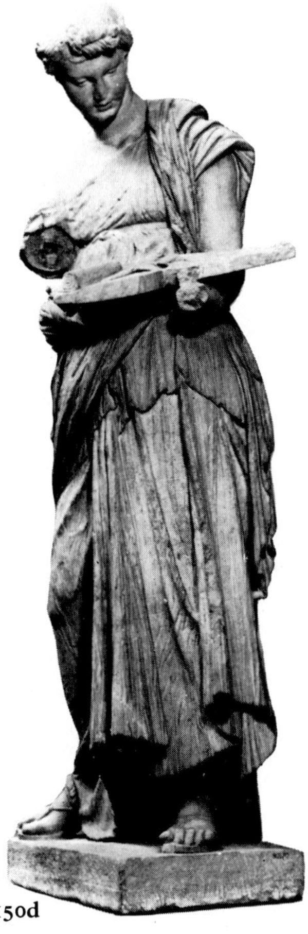

150d

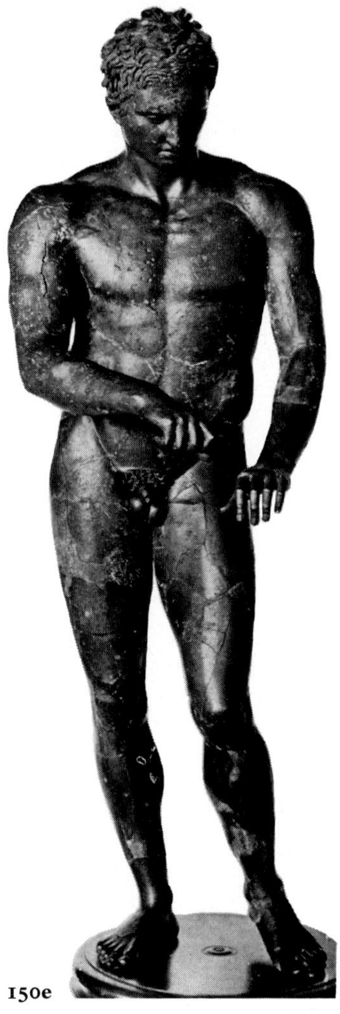

150e

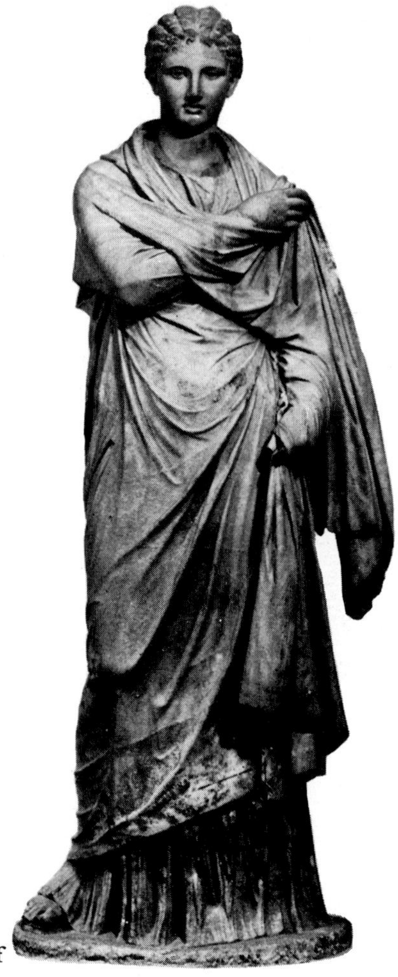

150f

150 **a** and **b** Bronze statuette. Florence, Museo Archeologico 2341. Copy of the imperial age after colossal statue of beginning of third century. H. 0.20. (Pp. 471ff.) **c** Upper part of bronze statue from sea off Smyrna. Smyrna Museum. Late fourth or early third century. H. 0.81. (Pp. 480, 511) **d** Marble statue from Anzio. Rome, Museo Nazionale. Probably copy of the imperial age after bronze original of early third century. H. 1.70. (Pp. 479, 575) **e** Bronze statue from Ephesus. Vienna 3168. Early third century (possibly a copy of the imperial age). H. 1.92. (P. 480) **f** Marble statue from Delos. Athens, National Museum 1827. Copy of the imperial age after original, perhaps in bronze, of late fourth or early third century. H. 1.80. (Pp. 479–80, 511, 546).

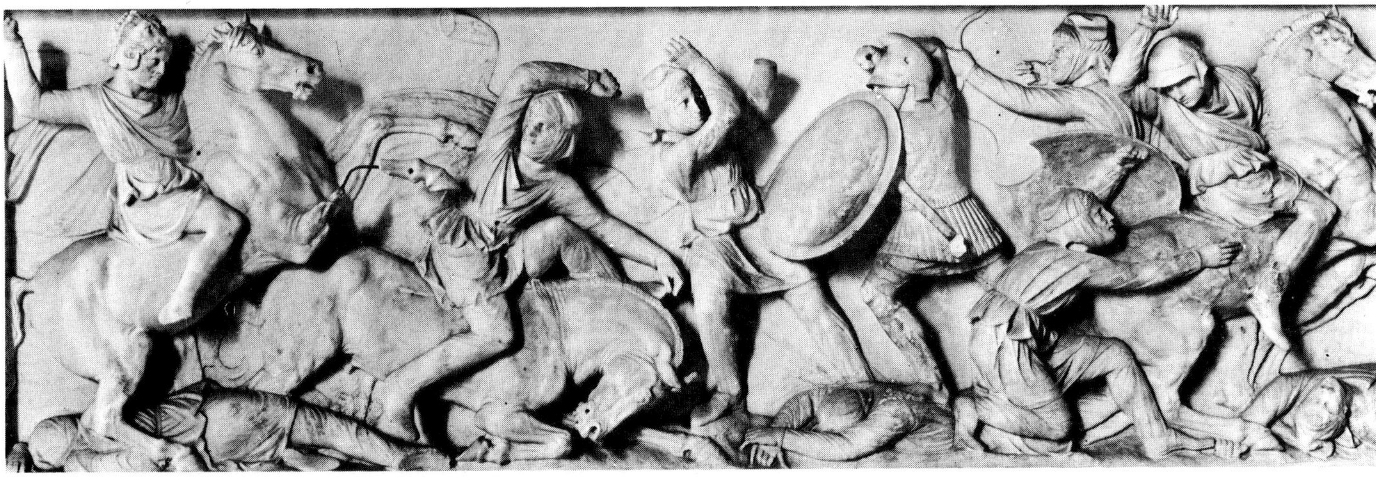
151a

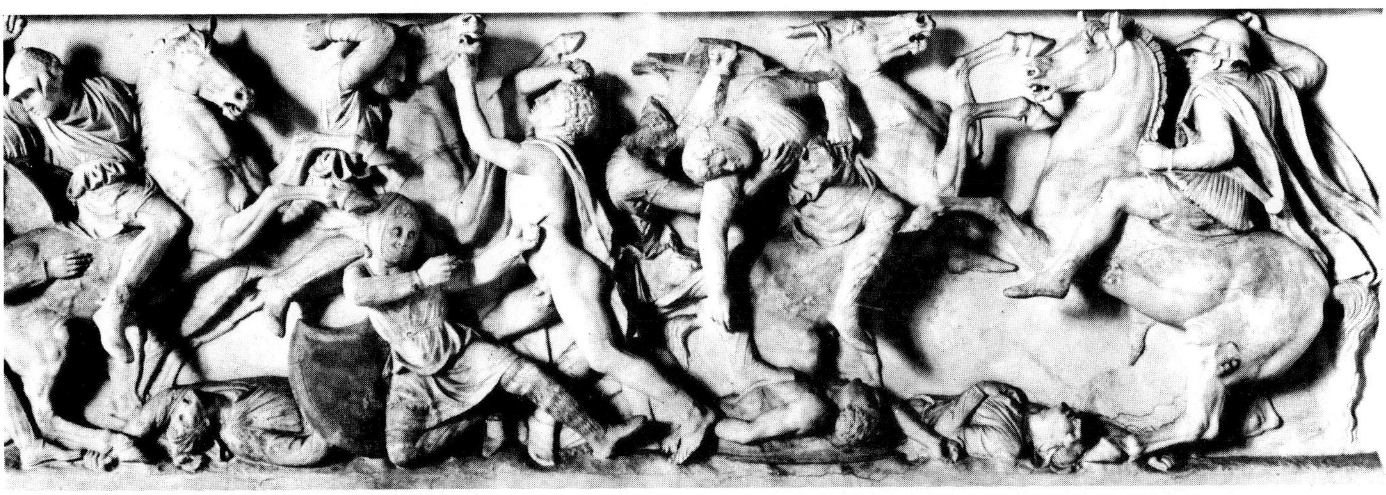
151b

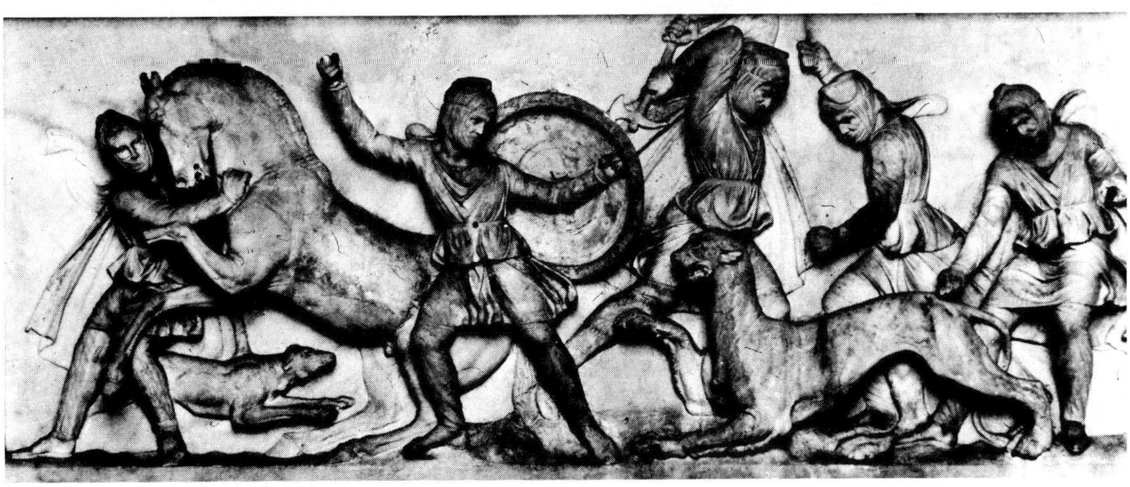
151c

151 a–c Marble sarcophagus from Sidon. Istanbul Museum. Last quarter of fourth century. H. of figured friezes 0.69. (Pp. 481–2, 498).

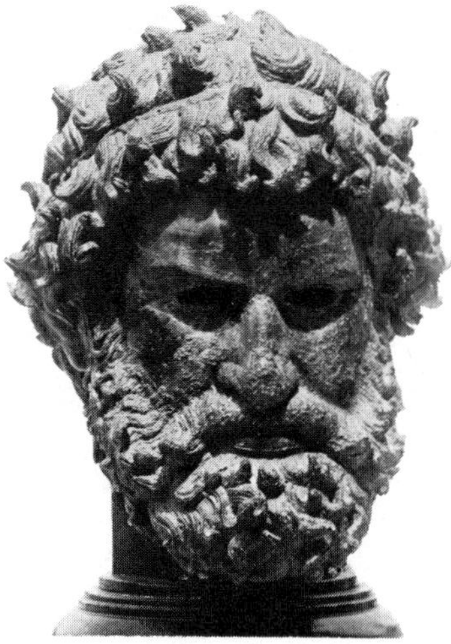

160a

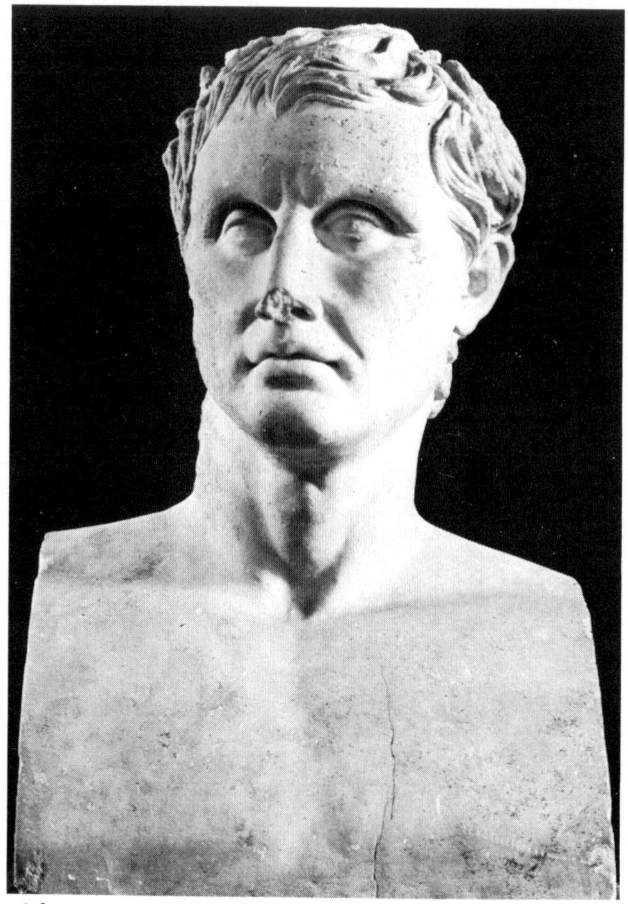

160b

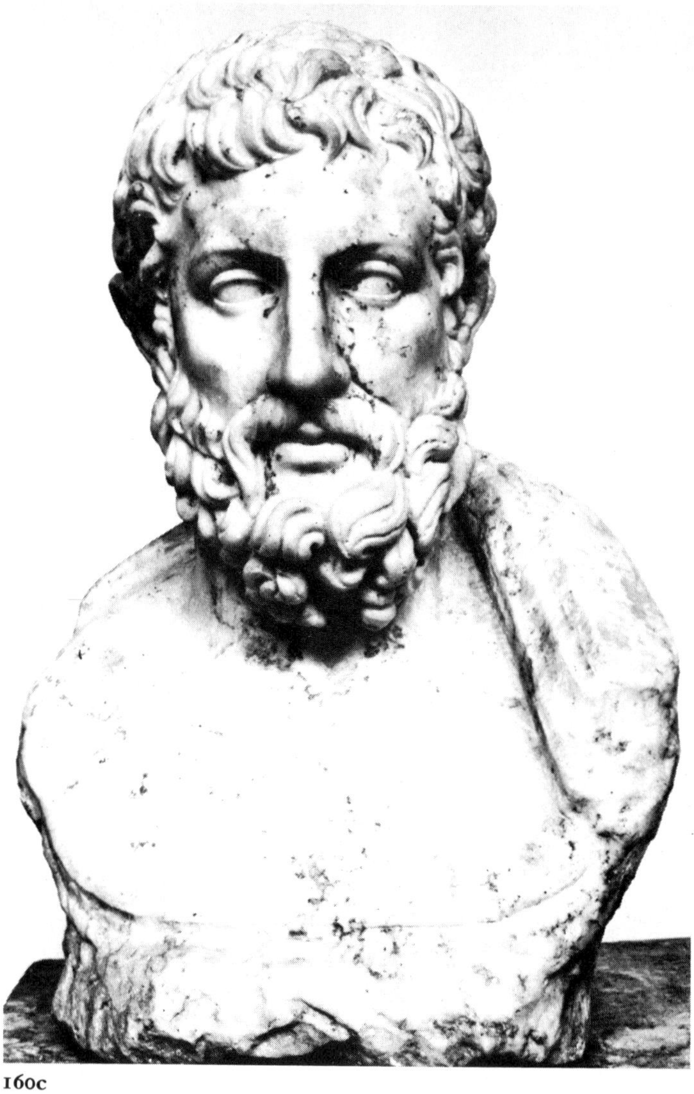

160c

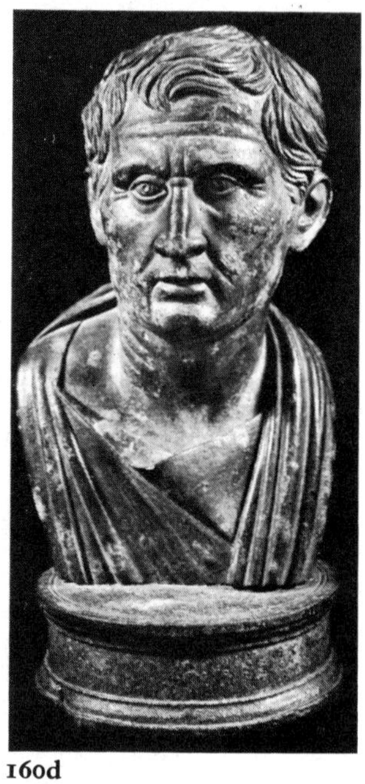

160d

160 **a** Bronze head from Olympia. Athens, National Museum 6439. Probably late fourth century. H. 0.28. (P. 517) **b** Marble bust. Boston, Museum of Fine Arts 97.288, Catharine Page Perkins Fund. Copy of the imperial age probably after bronze original of early third century. H. 0.51. (P. 518) **c** Marble bust. Athens, National Museum 368. Copy of the imperial age probably after original in bronze of second quarter of third century. H. 0.59. (P. 525) **d** Small bronze bust. Malibu (California), J. Paul Getty Museum. Copy of the imperial age after same original as **b**. (P. 519).

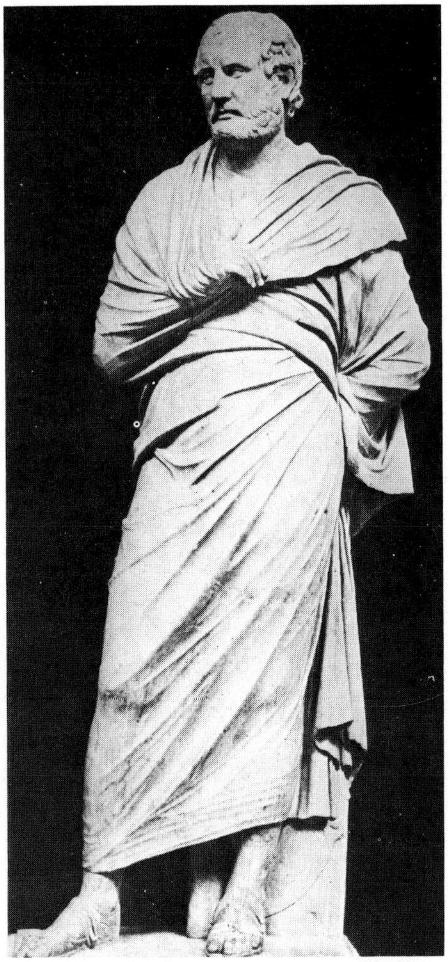

161a

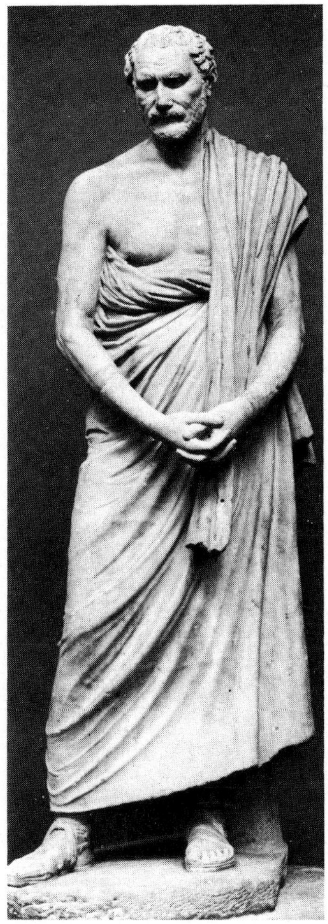

161b

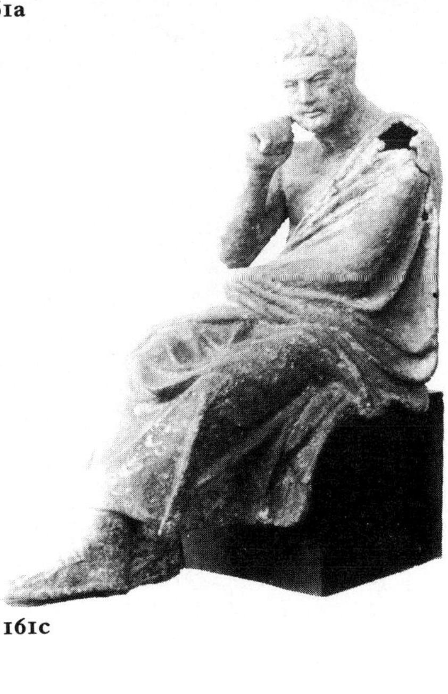

161c

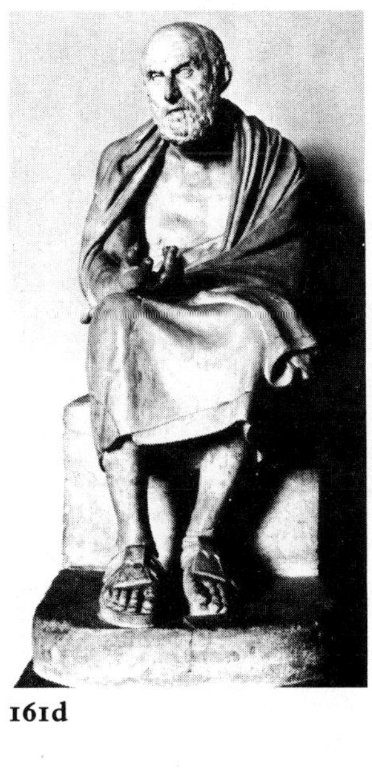

161d

161 **a** Marble statue from Herculaneum. Naples Museum 6018. Copy (before A.D. 79) after bronze original of second half of fourth century. H. 2.10. The nose, and other patches on the face, are modern. (P. 511) **b** Marble statue. Copenhagen, Ny Carlsberg Glyptotek 2782. Copy of the imperial age probably after bronze original set up in 280/79. H. 2.02. (Pp. 511–12, 610) **c** Large bronze statuette. British Museum 348. Probably copy of the imperial age after original statue of third or second century. H. 0.57. (P. 525) **d** Marble torso (restored with cast of head, British Museum 1836). Louvre 80. Copies of the imperial age probably after bronze original of late third or early second century. H. as restored *c.* 1.20. Modern restorations include nose, parts of feet, and most of right hand, but its attitude is certain. (Pp. 526, 555).

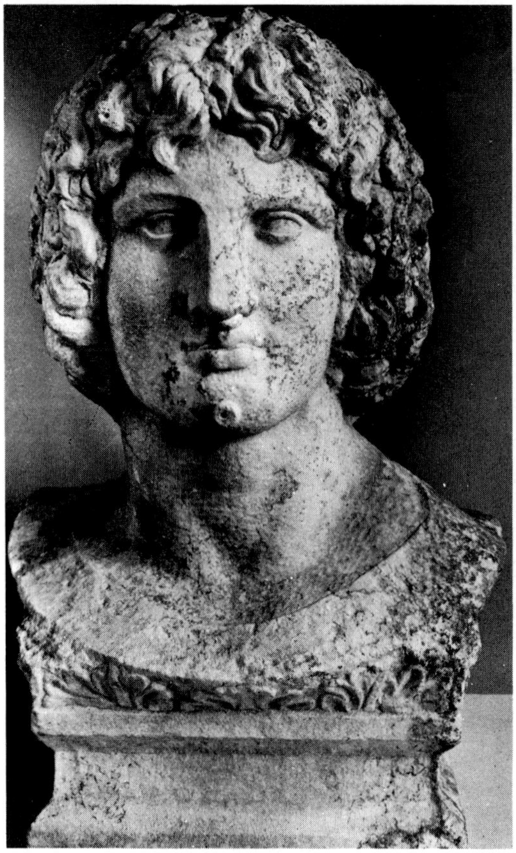

162a

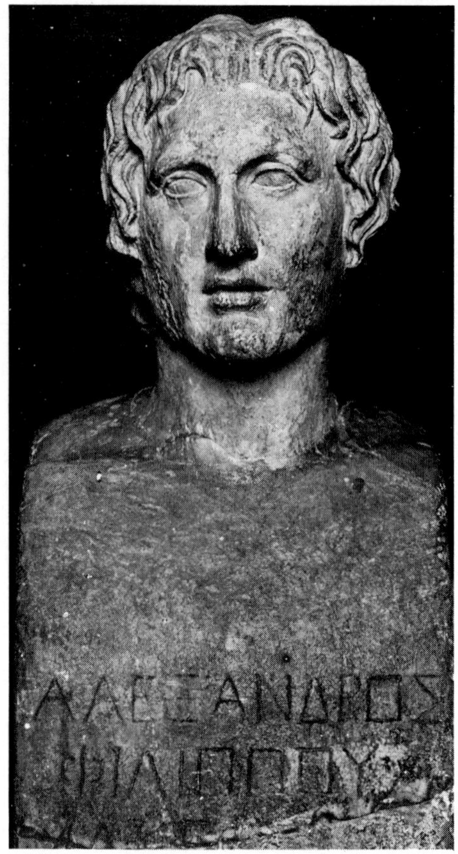

162b

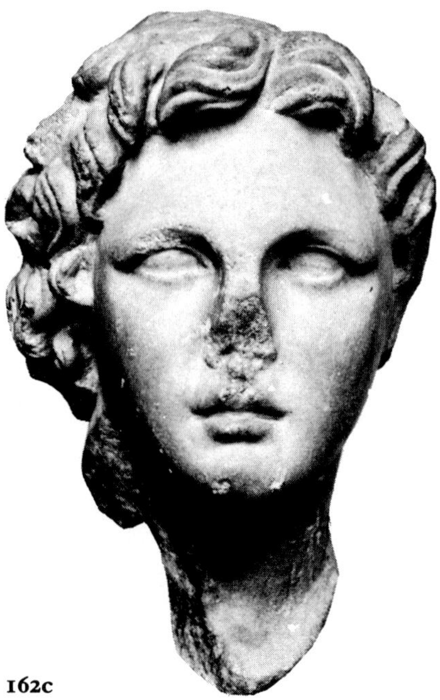

162c

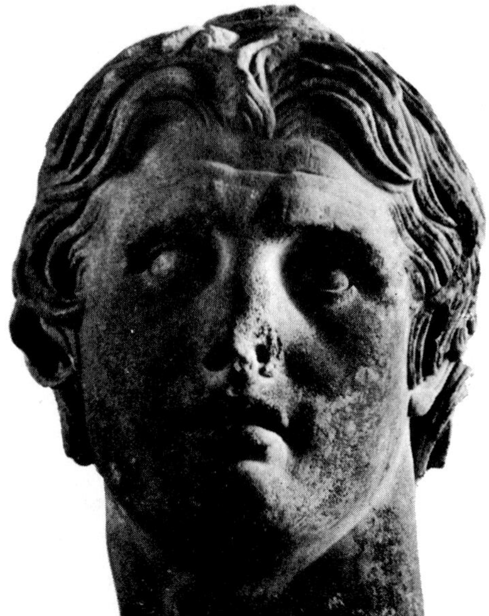

162d

162 **a** Unfinished marble bust from Agora. Athens, Agora Museum. Copy of the imperial age probably after original of third quarter of fourth century. H. 0.61. (P. 514) **b** Inscribed marble portrait-herm from Tivoli. Louvre 436. Copy of the imperial age after original, probably in bronze, of second half of fourth century. H. of head 0.25. (P. 514) **c** Marble head. Louvre 3499 (ex Musée Guimet). Copy of the imperial age after original of perhaps late fourth century. H. 0.21. (P. 514) **d** Marble head from Pergamon. Istanbul Museum. Late third or early second century. H. 0.42. (Pp. 514, 526).

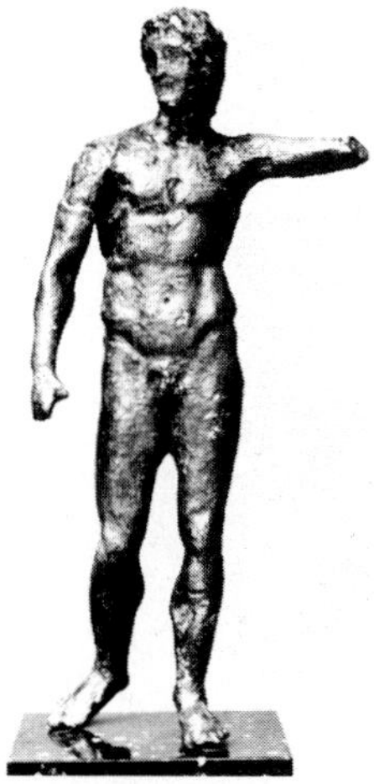

163a

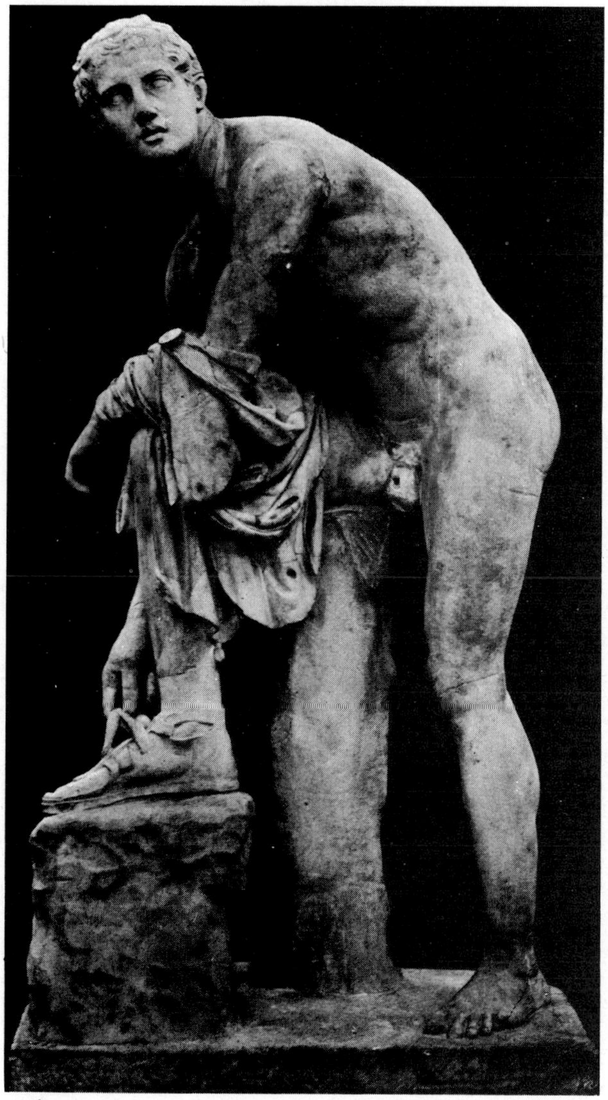

163b

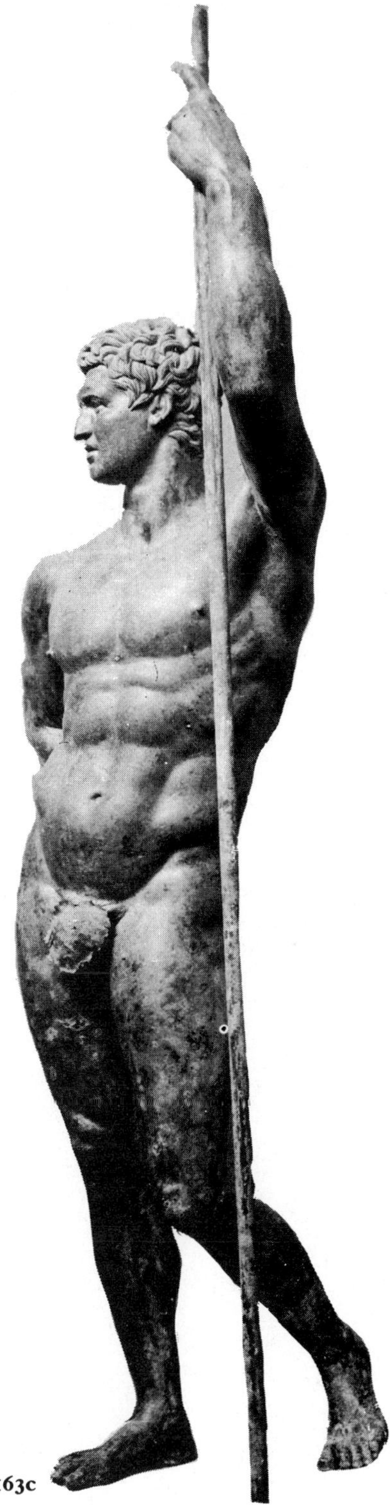

163c

163 **a** Bronze statuette from Lower Egypt. Louvre 370. Copy of the imperial period probably after original statue of second half of fourth century. H. 0.16. (P. 514) **b** Marble statue, from Hadrian's Villa at Tivoli. Copenhagen, Ny Carlsberg Glyptotek 2798. Copy of the imperial age after original bronze of early third century. H. 1.54. (P. 516) **c** Bronze statue from Rome. Rome, Museo Nazionale. Perhaps early third century. H. 2.22. (Pp. 477, 520–1, 554; cf. pl. 164a).

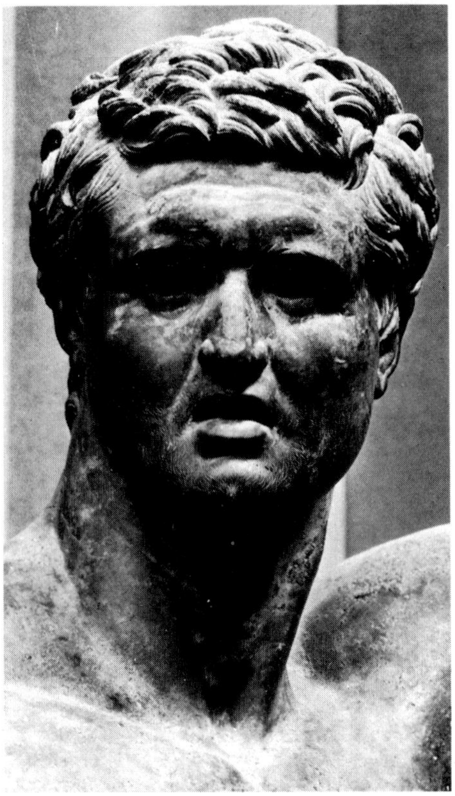

164a

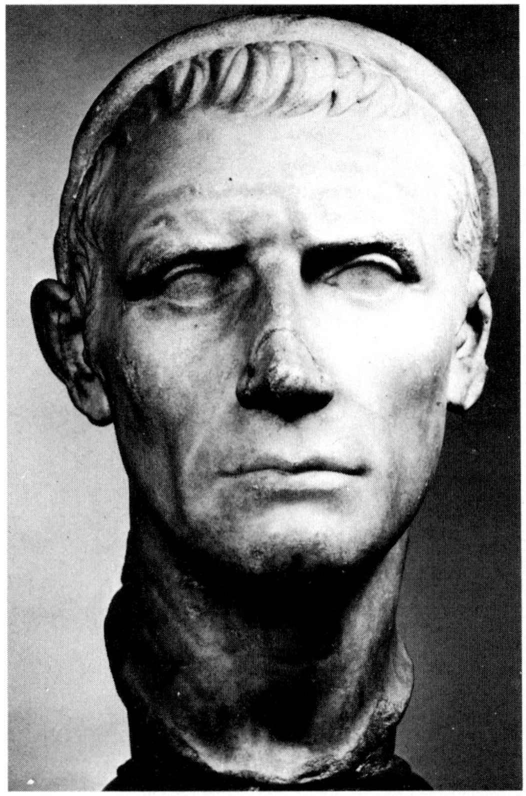

164b

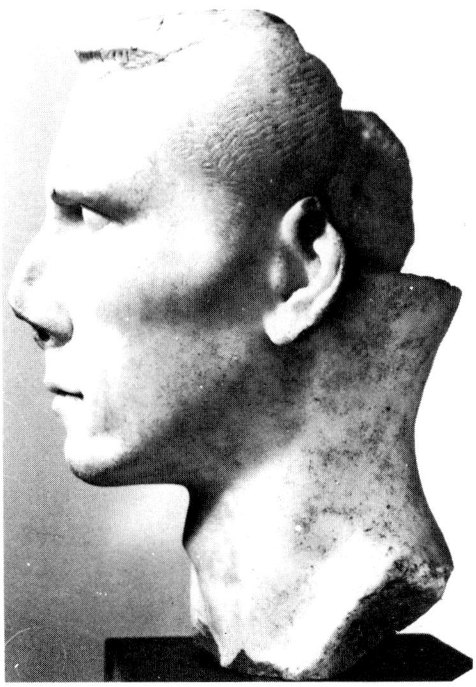

164c

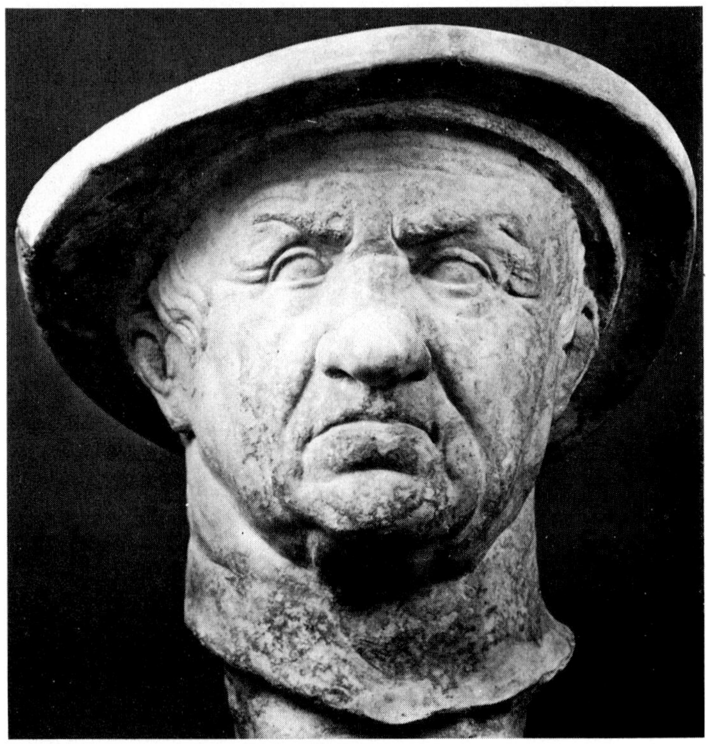

164d

164 **a** Head of statue, pl. 163c. (Pp. 520–1) **b** Marble head. Louvre 1204. Copy of the imperial age after original of late third or early second century. H. 0.35. Part of the nose is modern. (P. 521) **c** Marble head from Cyprus. British Museum 1879.* Perhaps late third or early second century. H. 0.31. (P. 521) **d** Marble head. Rome, Villa Albani (ex Torlonia Collection). Copy of the imperial age after original of late third century. H. 0.33. The front of the hat-brim is modern. (P. 521).

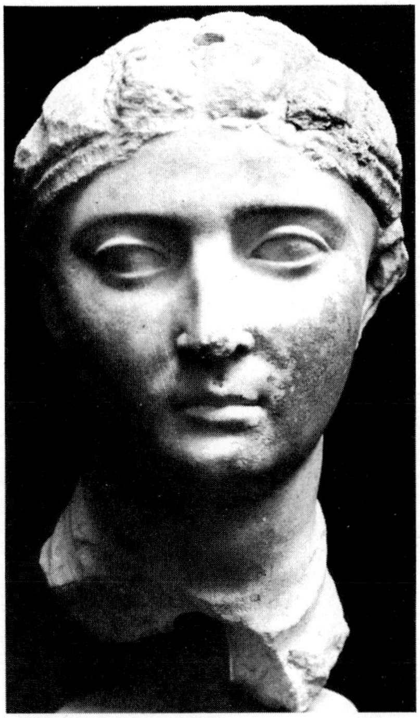

165a

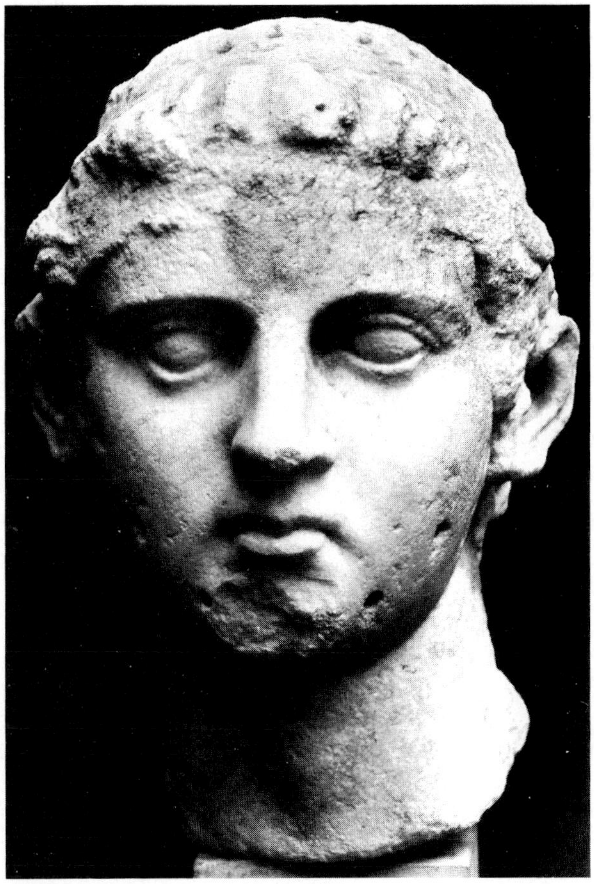

165b

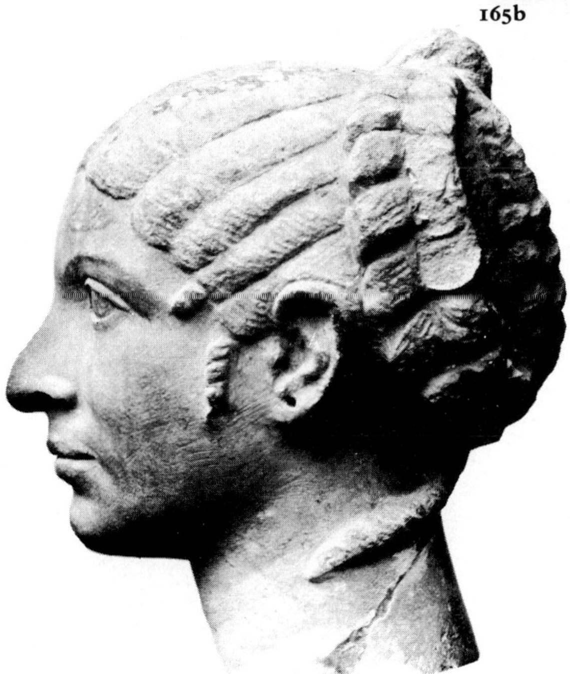

165c

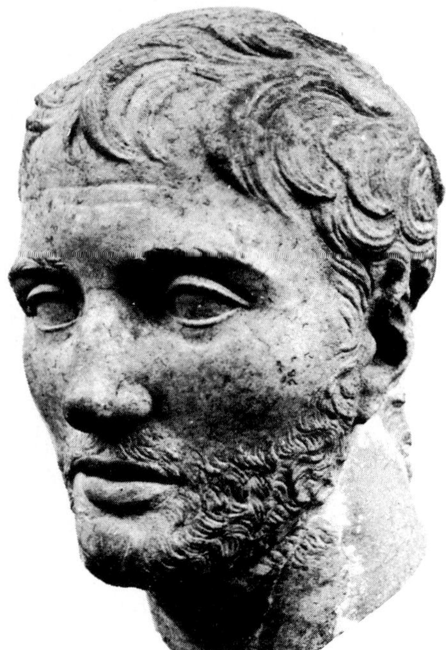

165d

165 **a** and **b** Marble heads. Boston Museum of Fine Arts, 01.8207 and 8208, H. L. Pierce Fund. Late third century. H. 0.28 (**a**) and 0.35 (**b**). (P. 523) **c** Limestone head. British Museum 1873. Middle or second half of first century. H. 0.28 (P. 523) **d** Marble head from Delphi. Delphi Museum. Probably an original of second half of fourth century. H. 0.27. (P. 517).

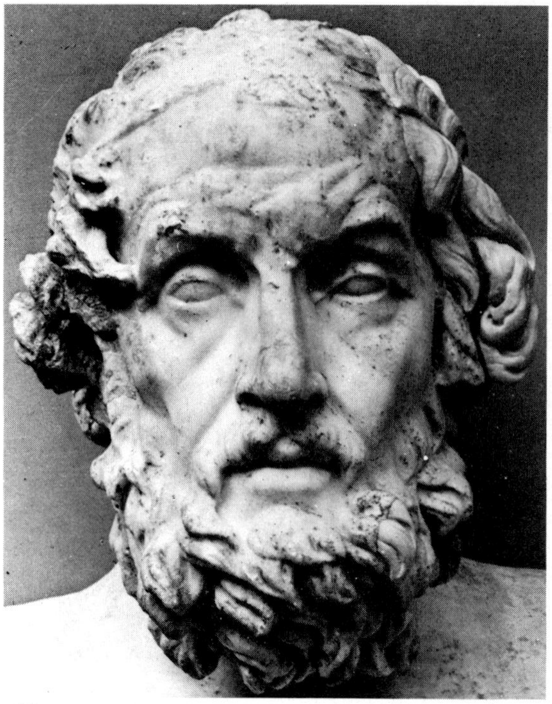

166a

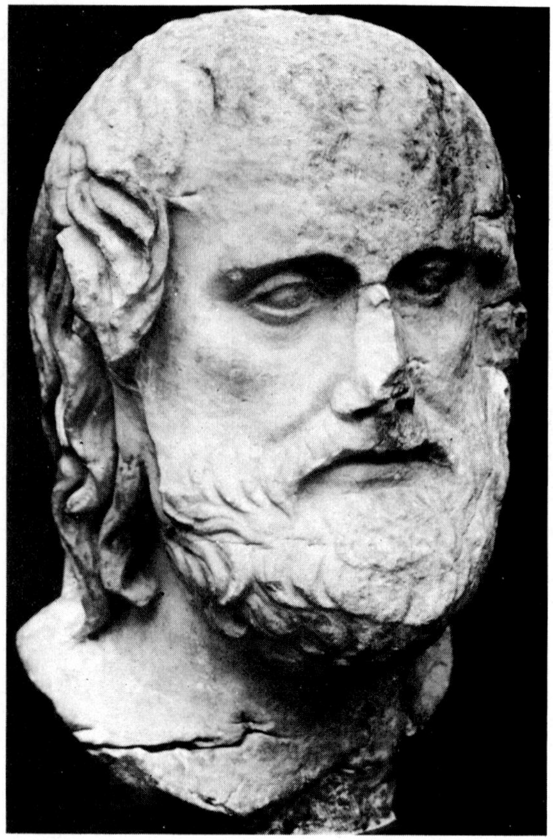

166b

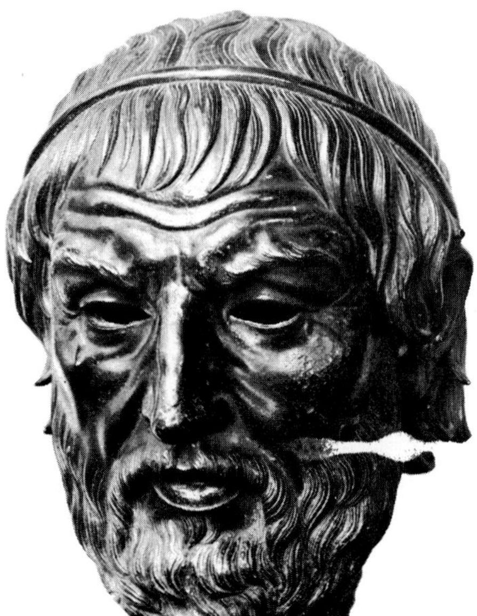

166c

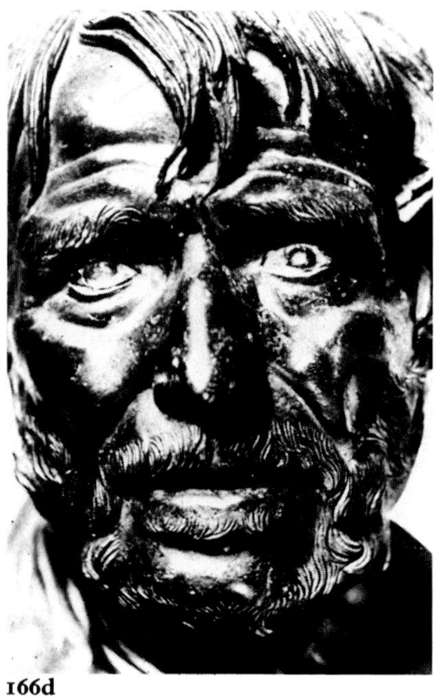

166d

166 **a** Marble head from Rome. Louvre 440. Copy of the imperial age after original of probably second century. H. of head 0.33. (P. 526) **b** Marble head. Copenhagen, Ny Carlsberg Glyptotek 2031. Copy of the imperial age probably after original bronze of third quarter of fourth century. H. 0.40. (P. 511) **c** Bronze head from Asia Minor. British Museum 847. Probably second century. H. 0.29. (P. 526) **d** Bronze head from Herculaneum. Naples Museum. Copy (before A.D. 79) after original of second century. H. of detail *c.* 0.30. (Pp. 526–7).

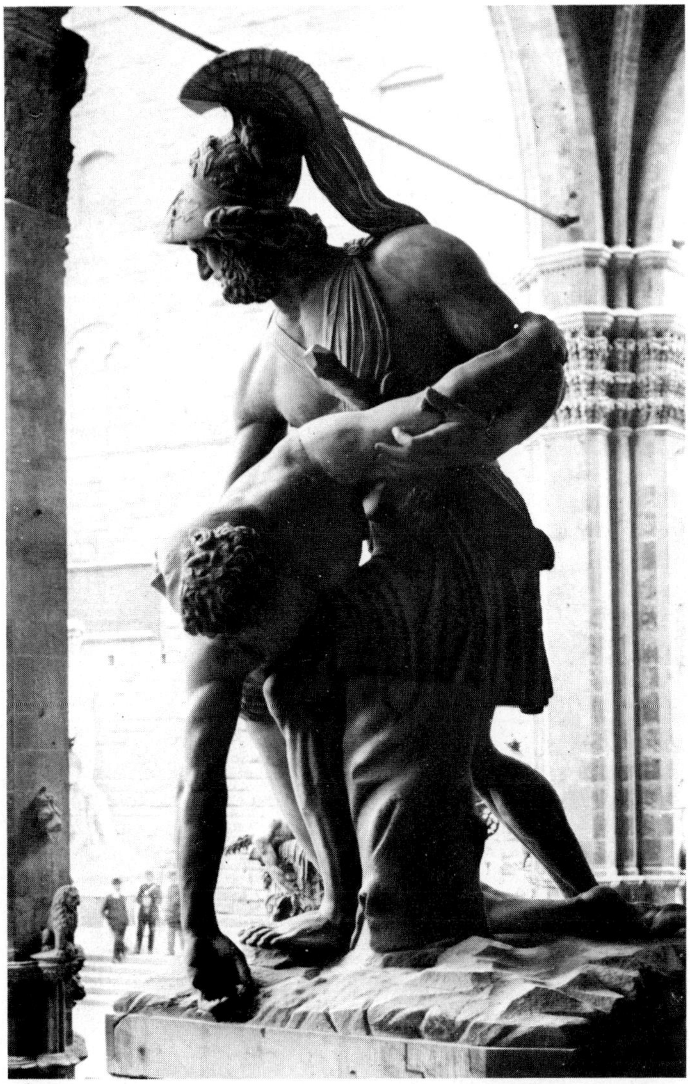

167a

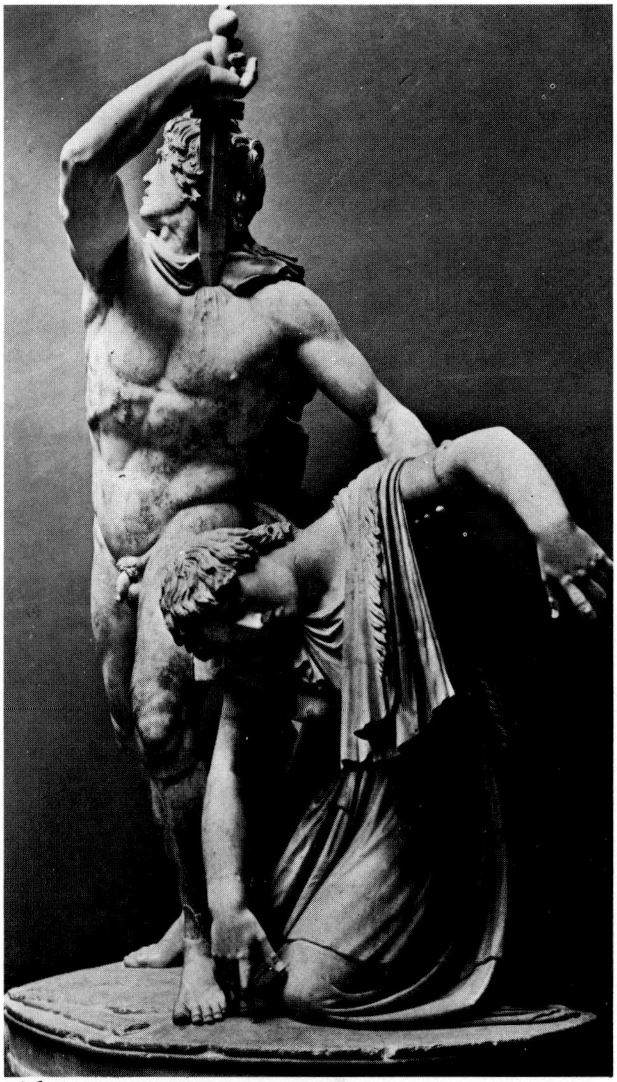

167b

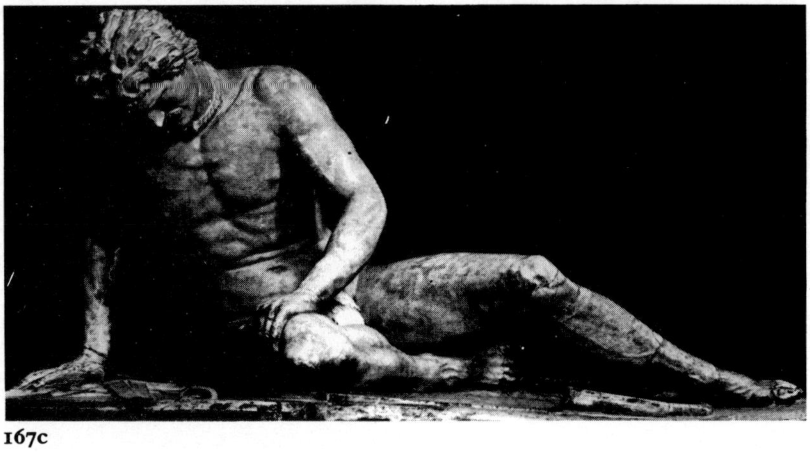

167c

167 **a** Marble group. Florence, Loggia dei Lanzi. Copy of the imperial age after bronze original of probably late third century. Similar scale to **b**. Heavily restored, including all upper part of Menelaus. (P. 534) **b** Marble group. Rome, Museo Nazionale. Marble copy (perhaps first century B.C.) after bronze original of third to second quarter of third century. H. 2.11. Restorations include noses, the man's arms and cloak, the woman's left arm and right hand. (Pp. 531, 534) **c** Marble statue. Rome, Museo Capitolino. Copy (perhaps first century B.C.) after bronze original of third to second quarter of third century. H. 0.93. (Pp. 531, 533; cf. pl. 168b).

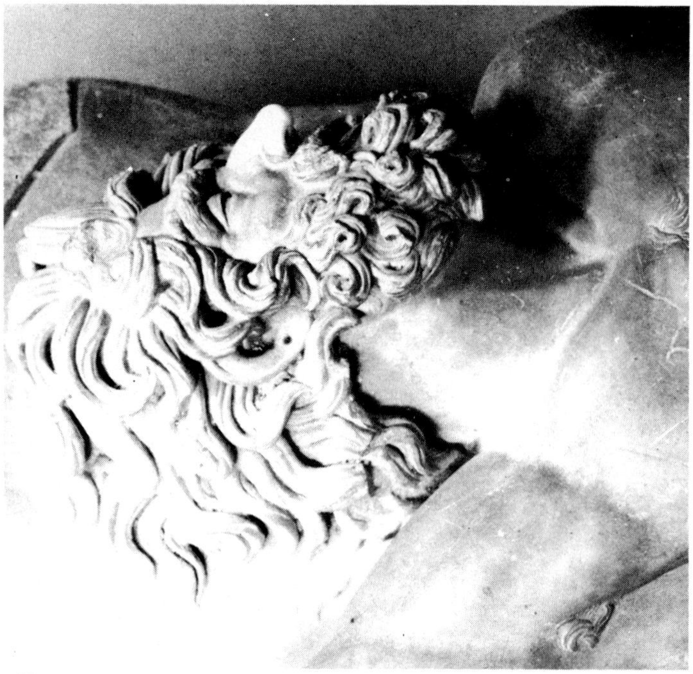

168a

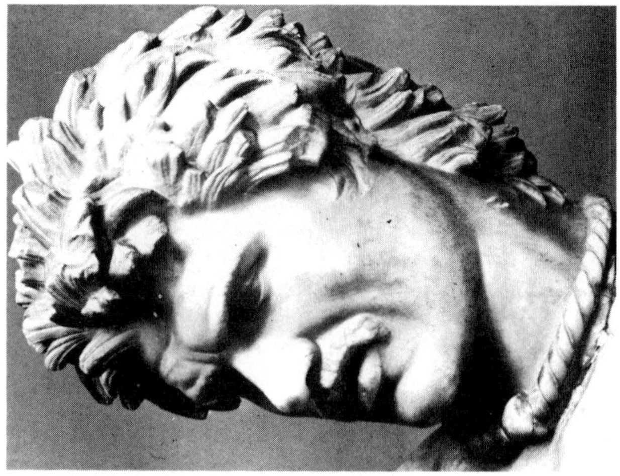

168b

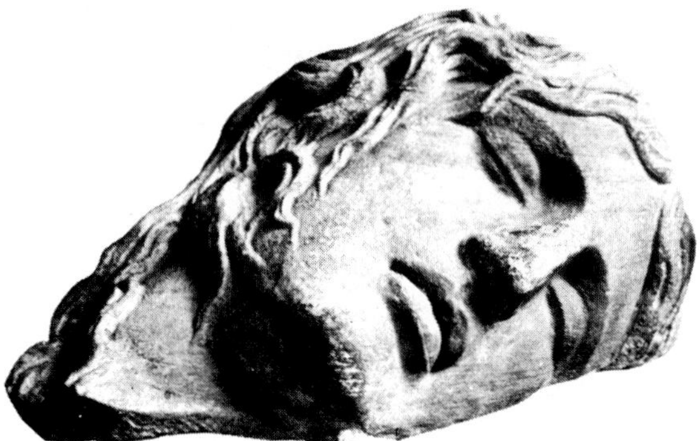

168c

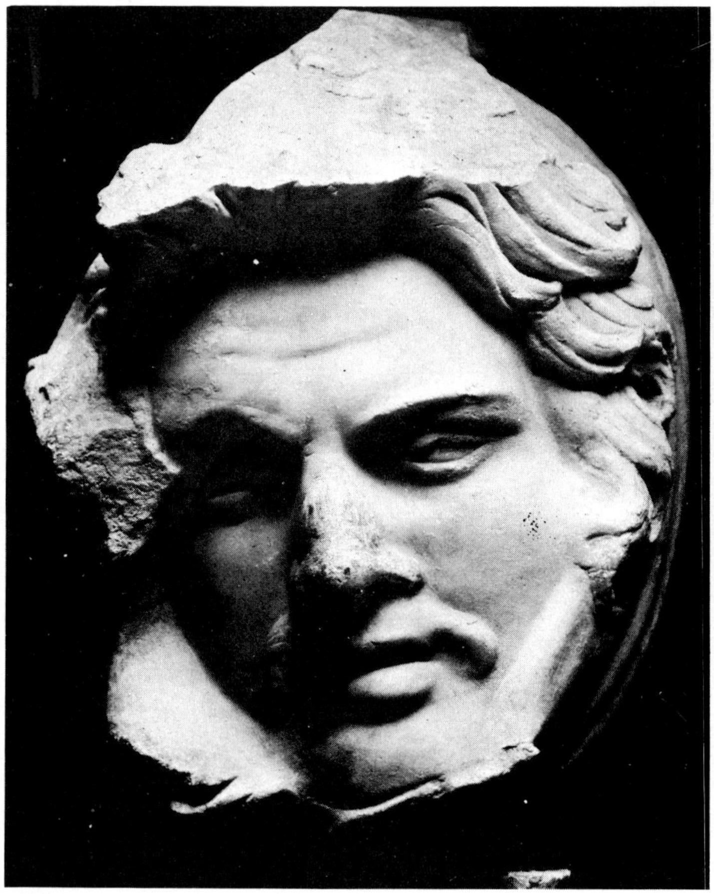

168d

168 **a** Upper part of marble statue. Naples Museum. Copy of the imperial period after bronze original probably of end of third century. H. 0.59. (P. 530) **b** Head of statue, pl. 167c. (P. 531) **c** Marble head. Rome, Museo Nazionale. Copy of the imperial age after bronze original of third to second quarter of third century. L. 0.54. (P. 533) **d** Marble head. Rome, Museo Nazionale. Copy (perhaps first century B.C.) after bronze original of third to second quarter of third century. L. 0.34. (P. 531).

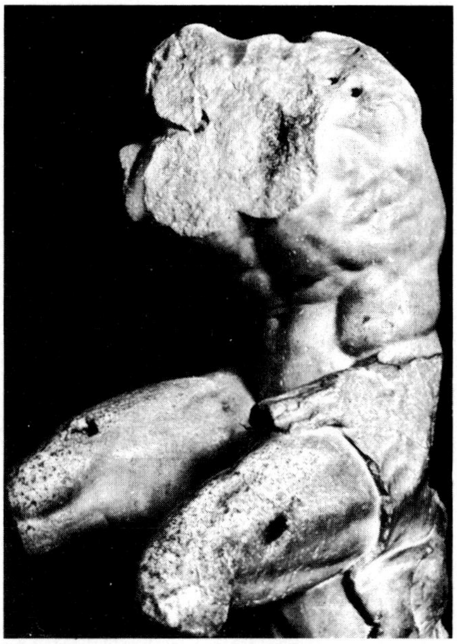

169a

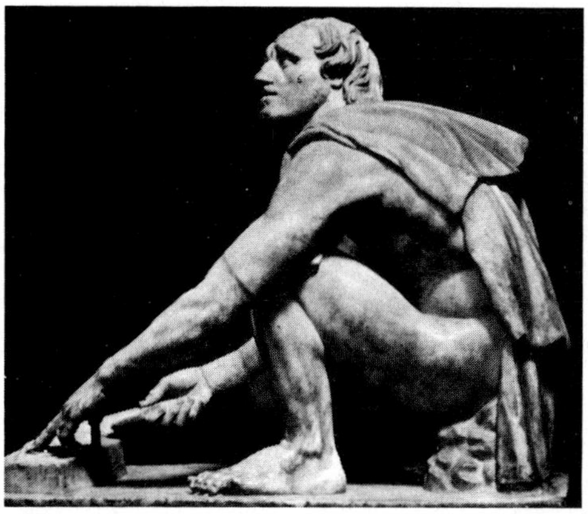

169b

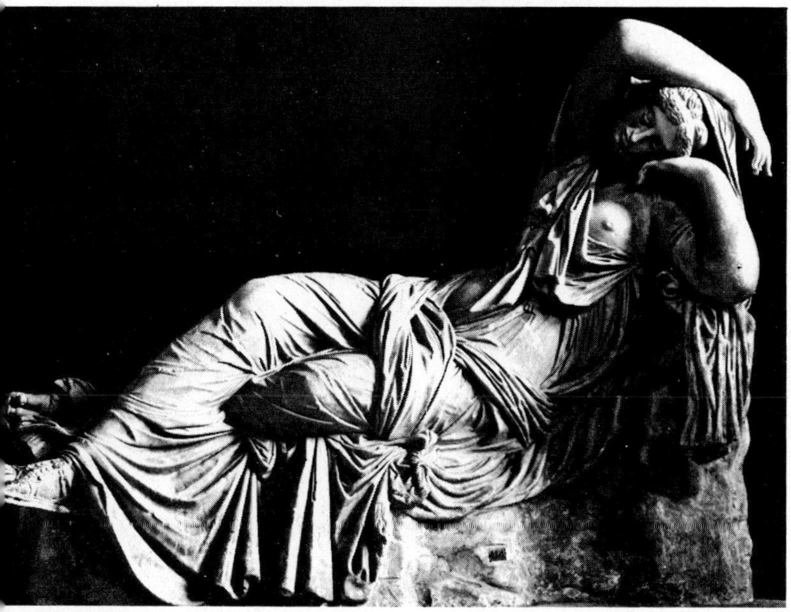

:69c

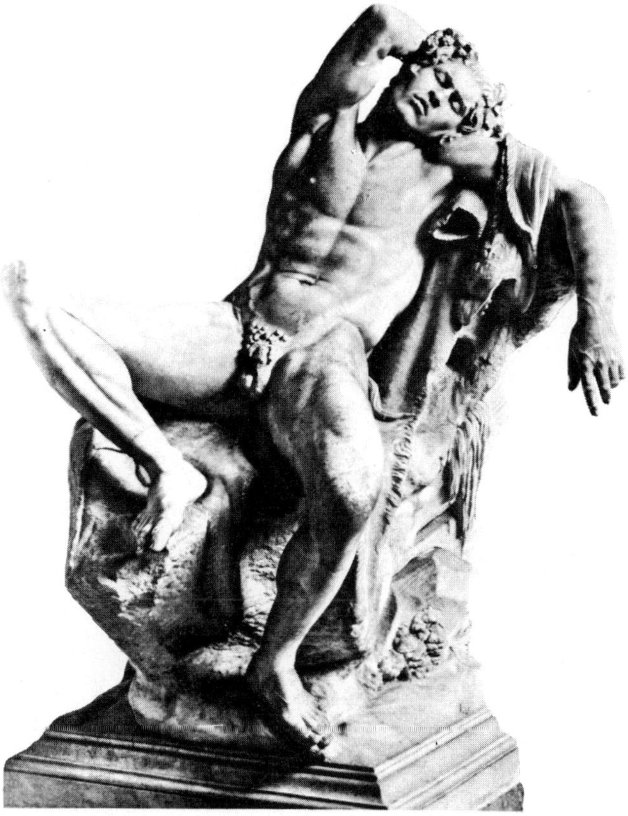

169d

169 **a** Marble torso from Rome, signed by Apollonios son of Nestor of Athens. Vatican. Copy (first century B.C.) probably after original of late third or early second century. H. 1.59. (Pp. 520, 543) **b** Marble statue. Florence, Uffizi 346. Copy (perhaps first century B.C.) probably after original of late third or early second century. H. 1.06. (P. 536) **c** Marble statue. Vatican. Copy of the imperial age probably after original of late third or early second century. H. 1.62. Modern are the nose and other patches on face and body, and the rock. (Pp. 484, 535) **d** Marble statue. Munich. Probably copy (perhaps first century B.C.) after original perhaps in bronze of late third or early second century. H. 2.15. Substantial seventeenth-century restorations include the whole right leg and the pendant left forearm. (Pp. 484, 534–5).

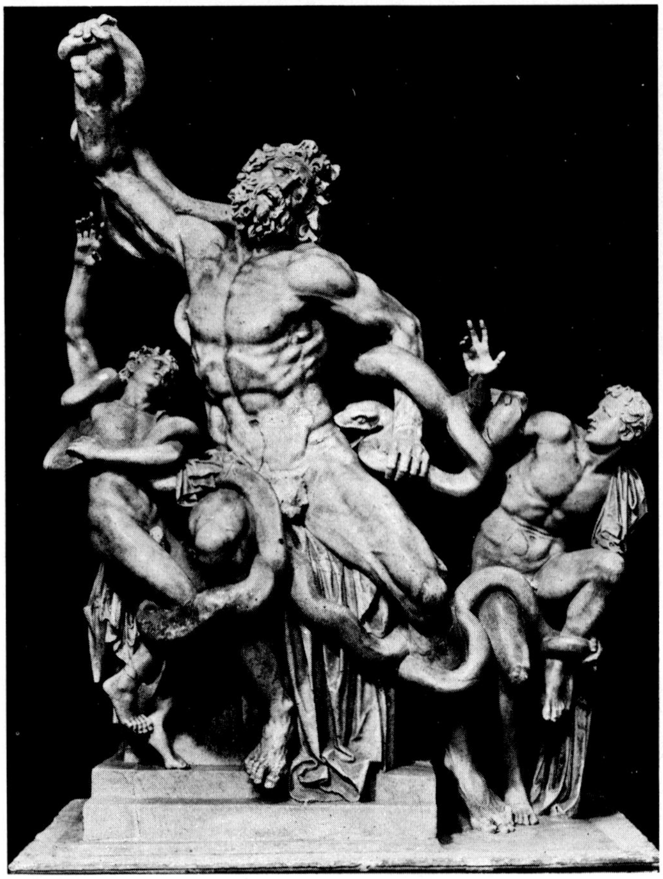

170a

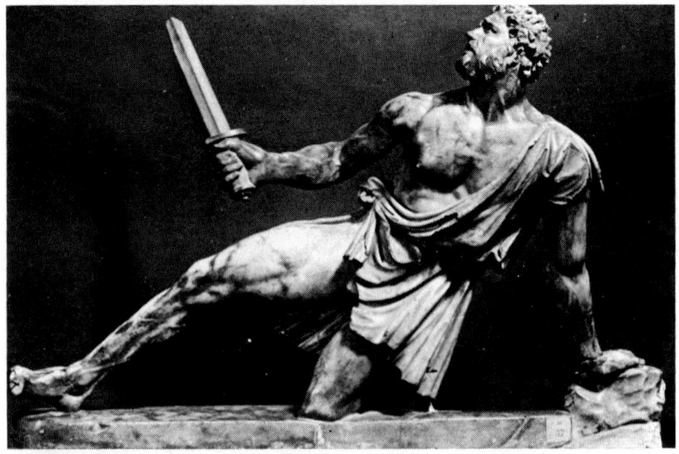

170b

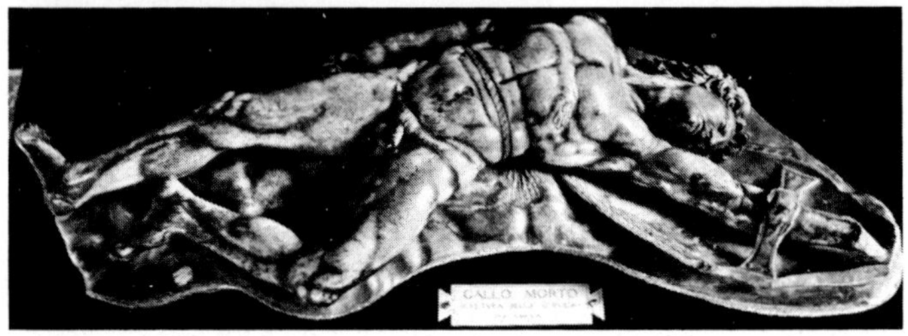

170c

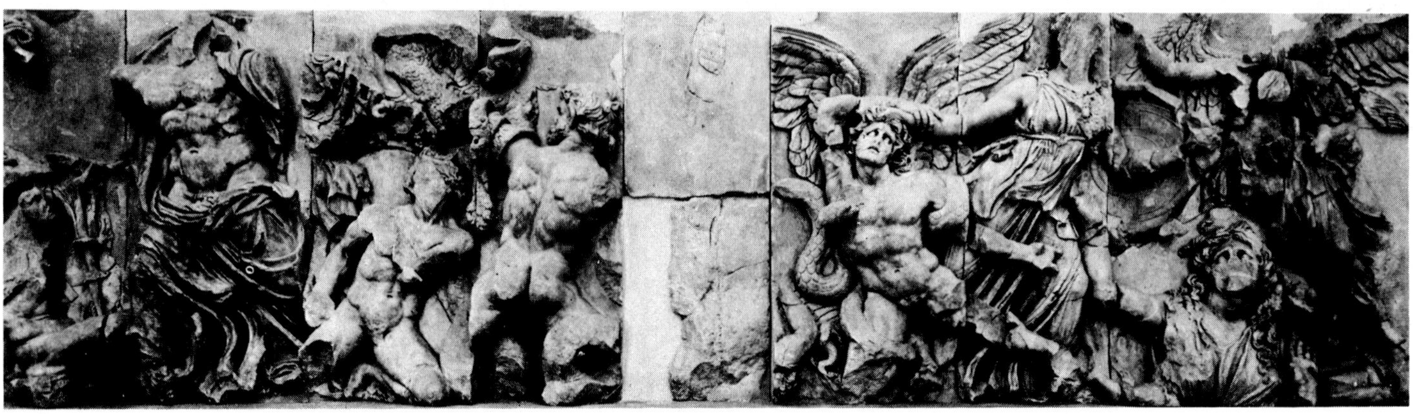

170d

170 **a** Marble group from Rome. Vatican. First century A.D., perhaps adapted from a two-figure bronze group of late third or early second century. (Pp. 541ff., 608) **b** and **c** Marble statues. Venice. Copies of the imperial age after bronze originals probably of end of third century. About half life-size. (P. 530) **d** Marble relief-slabs from Altar of Zeus, Pergamon. Berlin (E). First or second quarter of second century. H. 2.30. (P. 539).

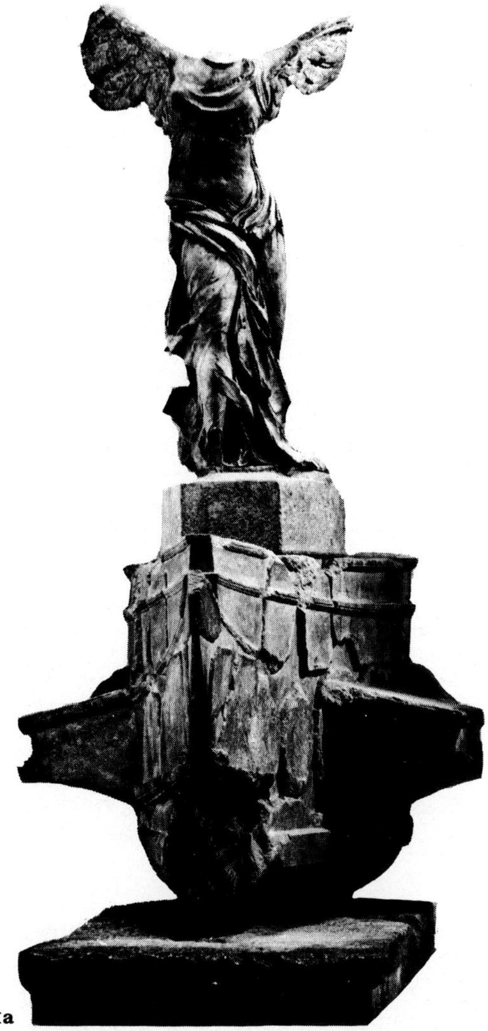

171a

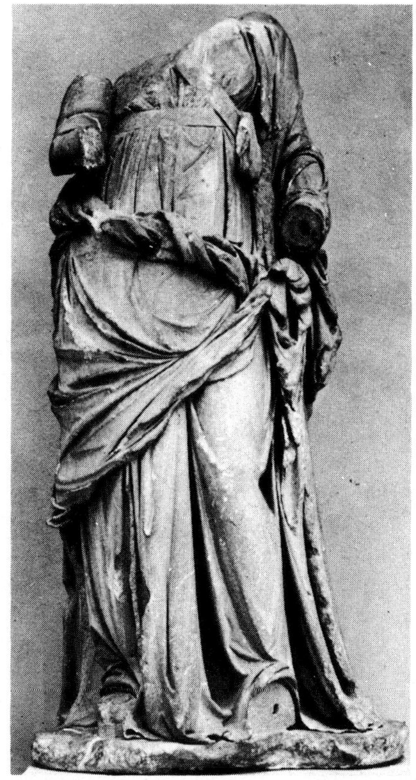

171b

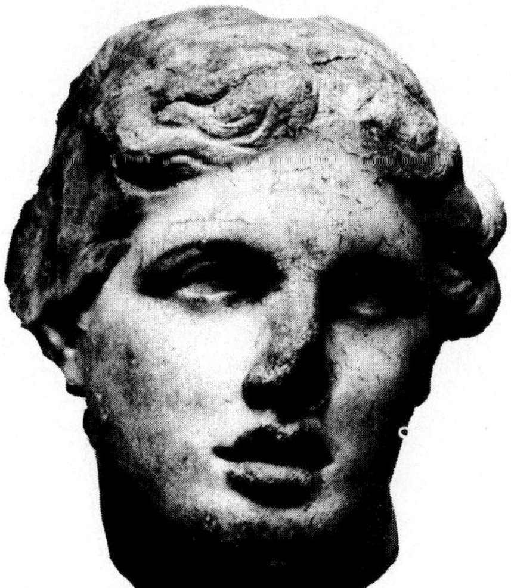

171c

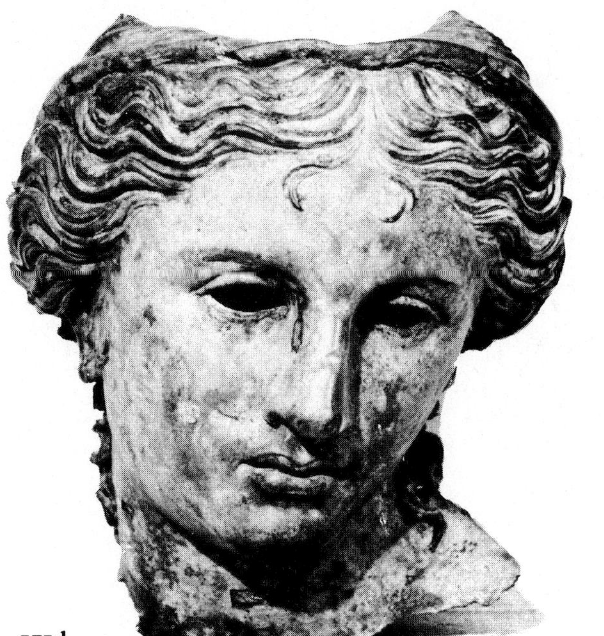

171d

171 **a** Marble statue from Samothrace. Louvre 2369. Late third or early second century. H. of figure *c.* 2.00. (P. 535) **b** Marble statue from Pergamon. Berlin (E). Late third or early second century. H. 1.80. (P. 536) **c** Marble head from Pergamon, probably from the main frieze of the Altar of Zeus. Berlin (E) 90. First or second quarter of second century. H. 0.30. (P. 540) **d** Bronze head from Satala near Erzincan (Armenia). British Museum 266. Probably late second century. H. 0.38. (P. 554).

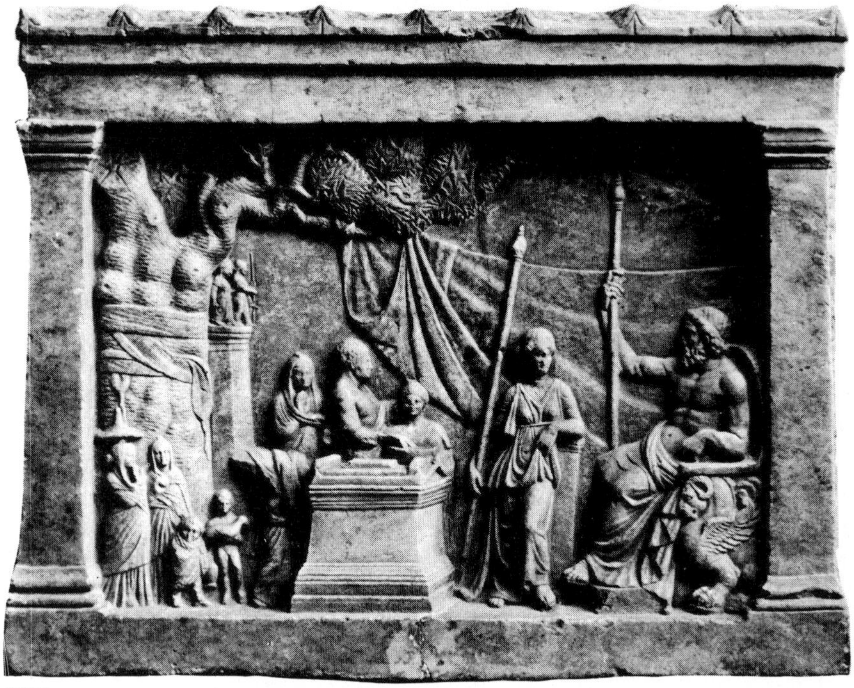

172a

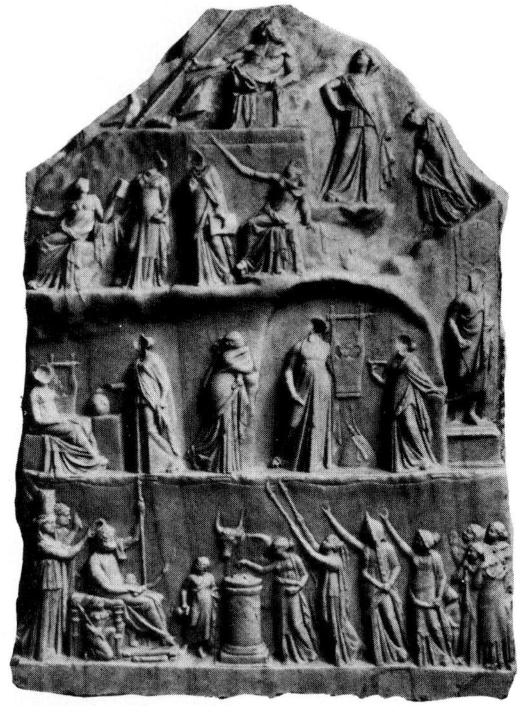

172c

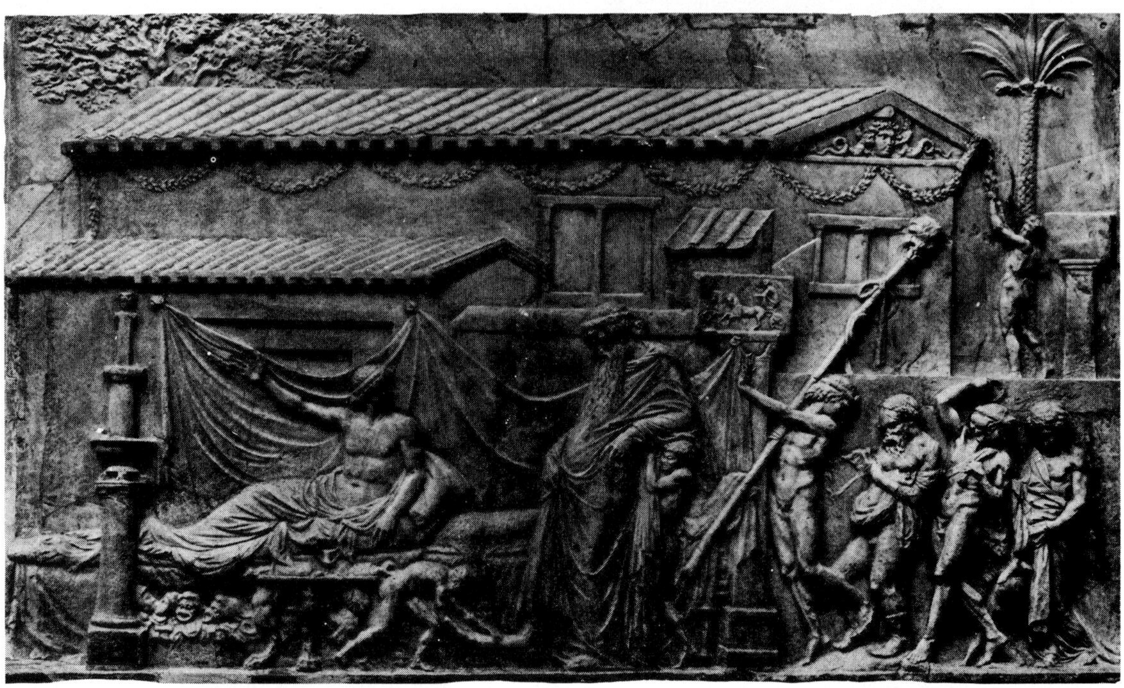

172b

172 **a** Marble relief from Corinth. Munich. Probably late third century. H. 0.61. (Pp. 521, 545–6) **b** Marble relief. British Museum 2190. Copy of the imperial period perhaps from relief or painting of late second or early first century. H. 0.91. Considerable retouching and restoration of details. (P. 545) **c** Marble relief from Bovillae (near Rome), signed by Archelaos of Priene. British Museum 2191. Perhaps second century, perhaps copying a work of the third. H. 1.17. (Pp. 562ff.).

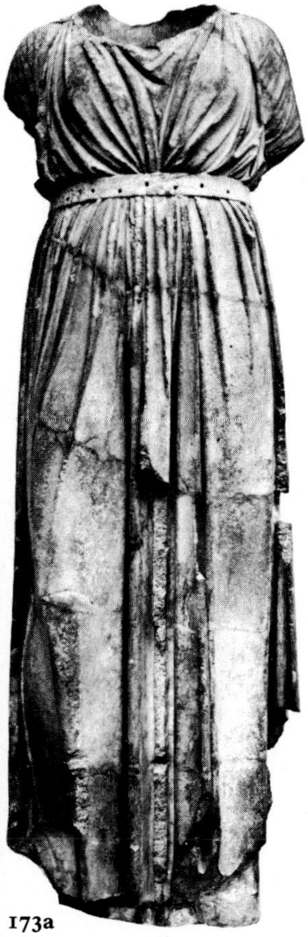

173a

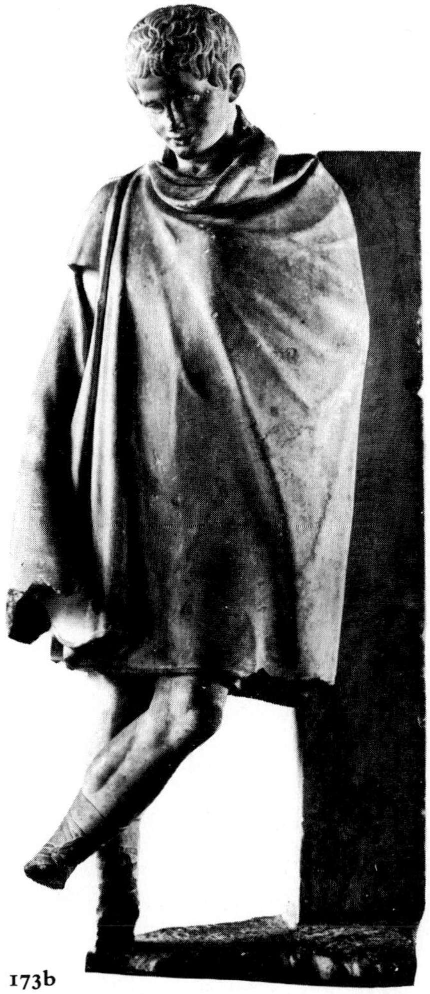

173b

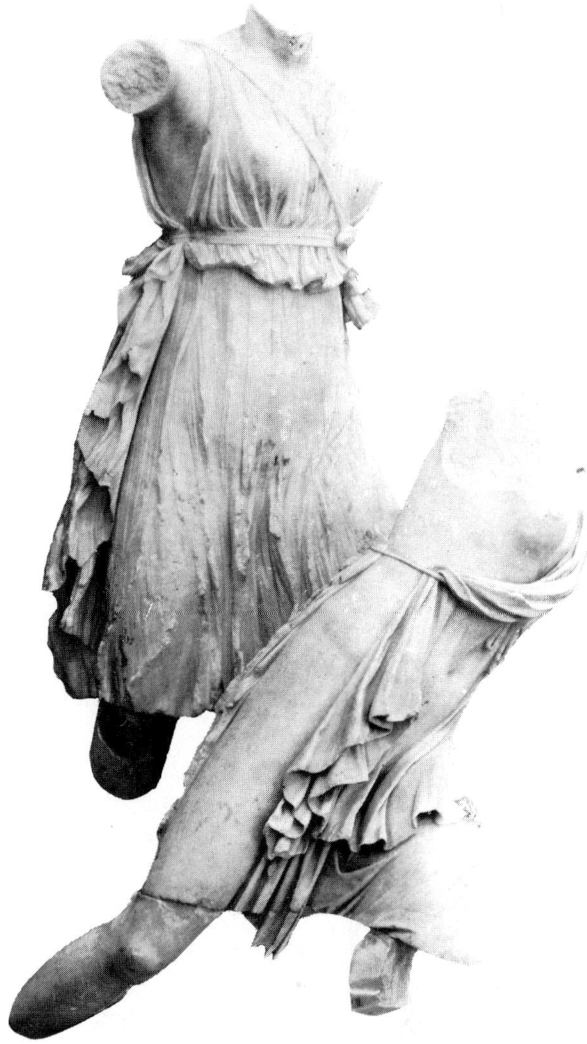

173c

173 **a** Marble torso from Priene. British Museum 1154. Perhaps second or first century. H. 1.30. (P. 546) **b** Marble statue from Tralles. Istanbul Museum. Perhaps second or first century, or even later. H. 1.47. (Pp. 524, 546) **c** Fragments of marble group from Rome. Copenhagen, Ny Carlsberg Glyptotek 481–2. Copy of the imperial age after bronze original, perhaps of early third century, perhaps rather of second or first. H. 1.70. (Pp. 476, 534).

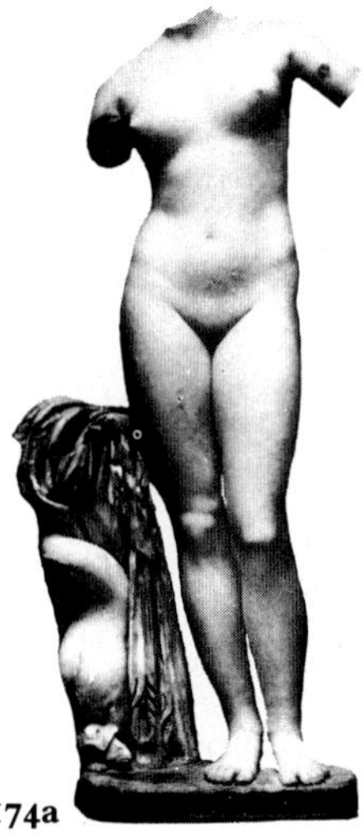

174a

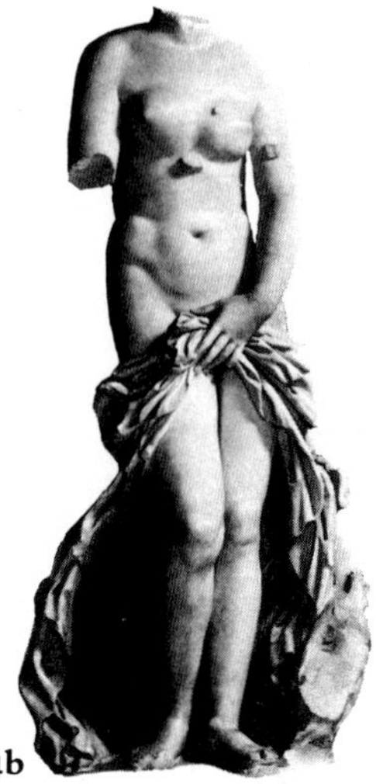

174b

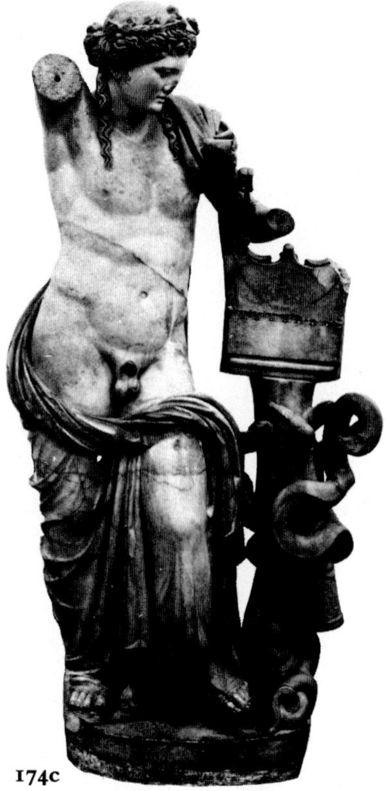

174c

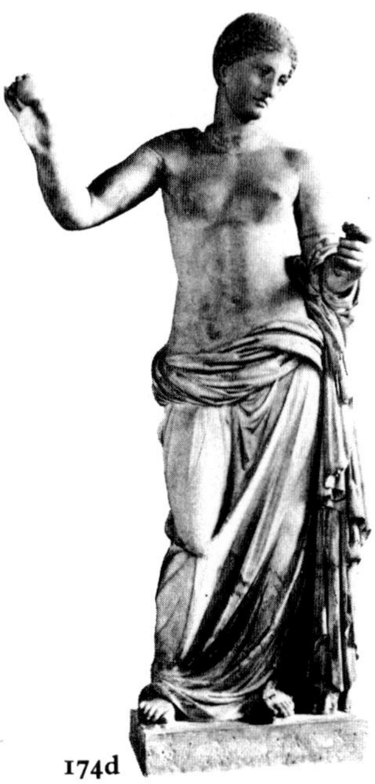

174d

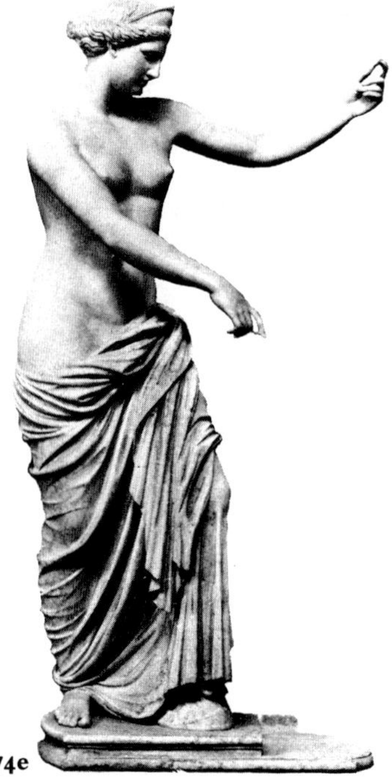

174e

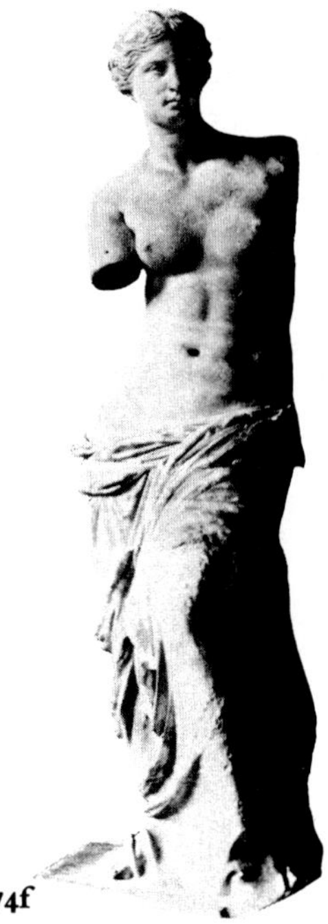

174f

174 **a** Marble statue from Cyrene. Rome, Museo Nazionale. Probably second century. H. 1.49. (P. 549) **b** Marble statue from Syracuse. Syracuse Museum. Copy or adaptation of the imperial age from original perhaps of second century. (P. 549) **c** Marble statue from Cyrene. British Museum 1380. Copy of the imperial period probably from a bronze original of second century. H. 2.29. (Pp. 550, 600) **d** Marble statue from Arles. Louvre 439. Copy of the imperial age after original probably of second half of fourth century. H. 1.94. Right arm, left forearm and both hands are modern. (P. 553) **e** Marble statue from Capua. Naples 6017. Copy of the imperial age perhaps from original of early third century. H. 2.10. The arms are modern. (Pp. 553, 607) **f** Marble statue from Melos, signed by . . . andros of Antioch on the Maeander. Louvre 399. Probably late second century. H. 2.04. (Pp. 515, 553).

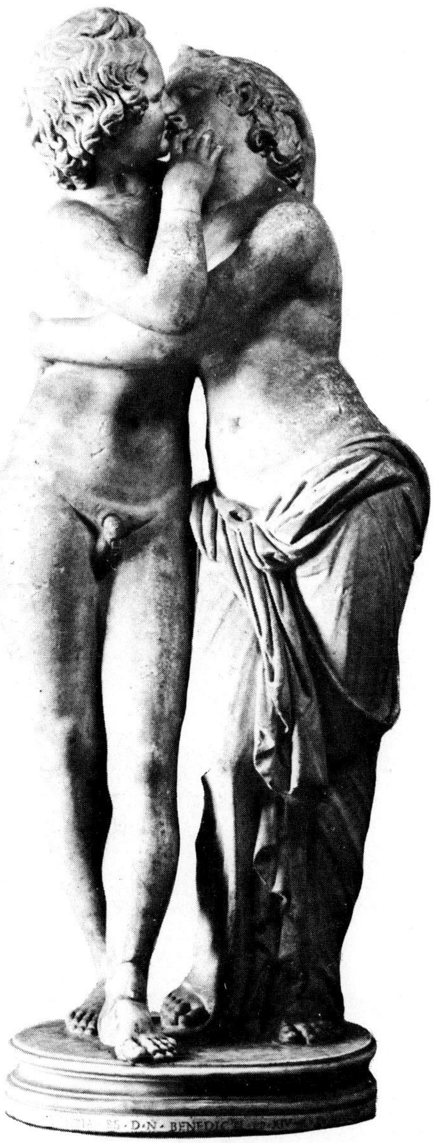

175a

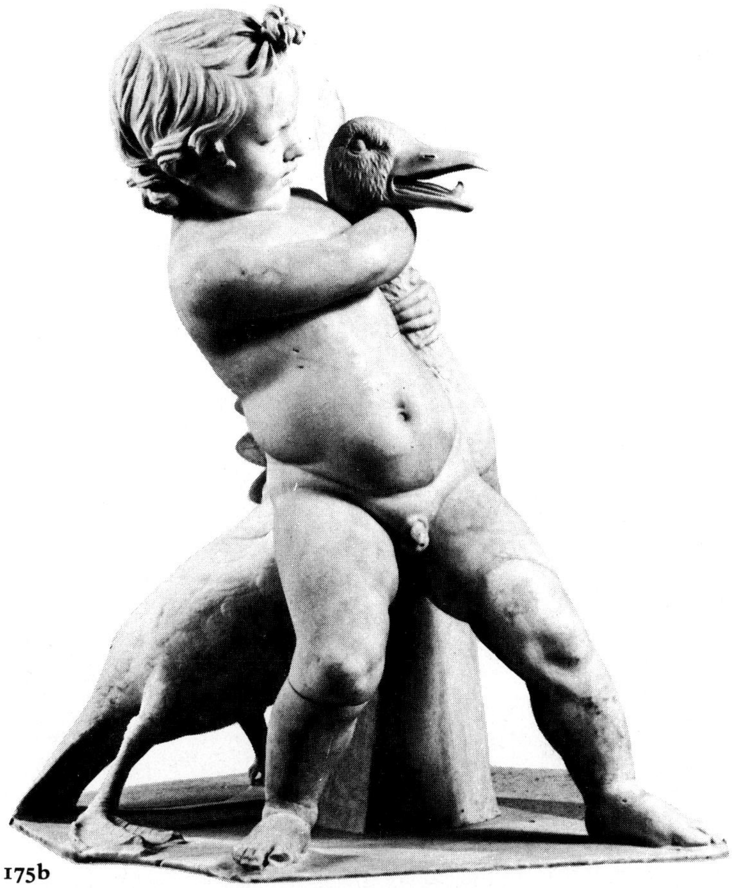

175b

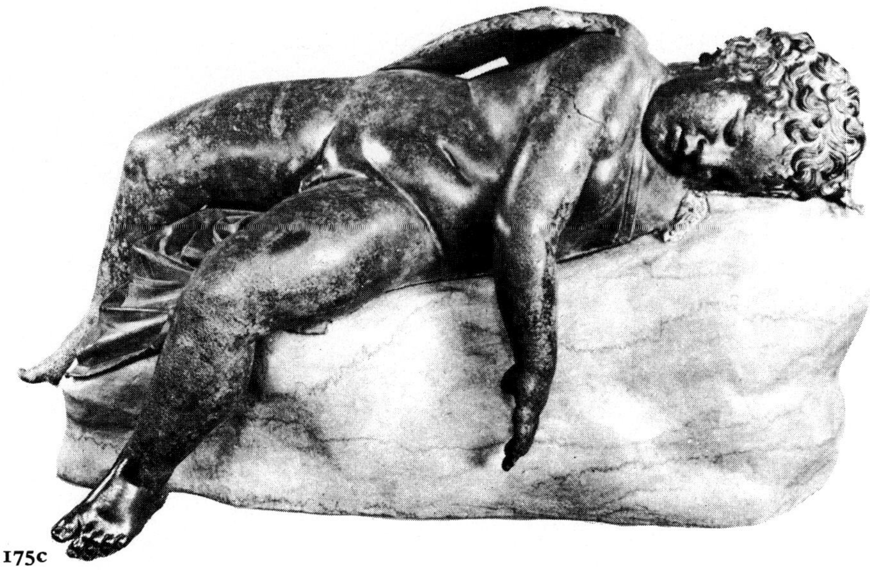

175c

175 **a** Marble group. Rome, Museo Capitolino. Copy of the imperial age after original probably of middle or later second century. H. 1.25. Modern are the boy's hands and feet, his nose and the back of his head with the girl's hand; the girl's nose, and other details. (Pp. 555–6) **b** Marble group. Munich. Copy of the imperial age probably from bronze original of middle or later second century. H. 0.84. The head of the goose and other details are modern. (P. 561) **c** Bronze statue. New York, Metropolitan Museum of Art 43.11.4, Rogers Fund. Probably an original of middle or later second century. L. 0.78. (P. 553).

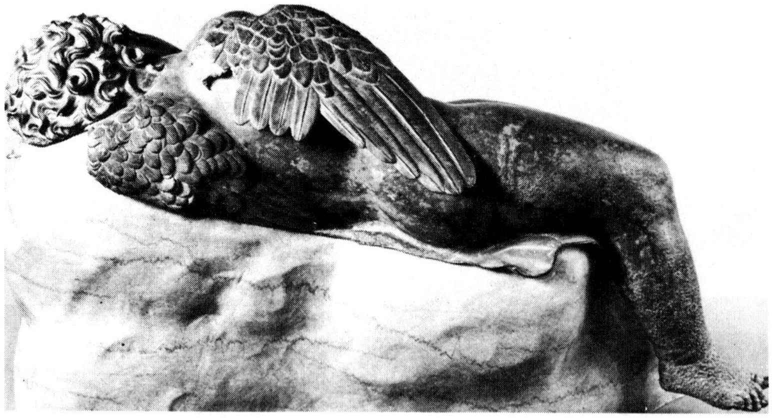

176a

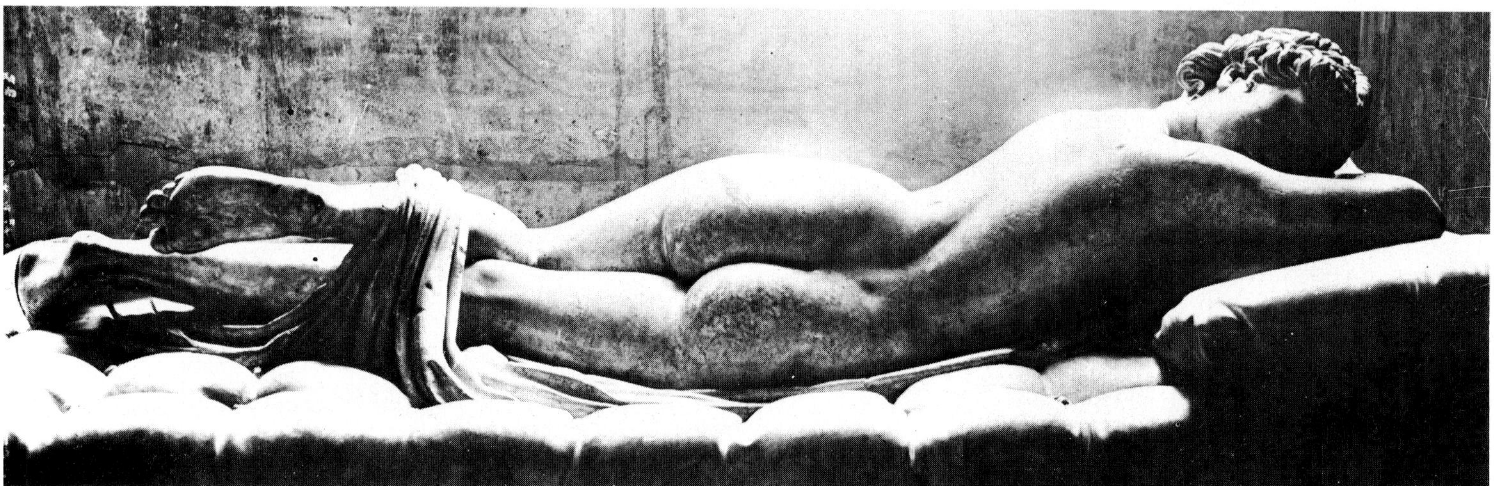

176b

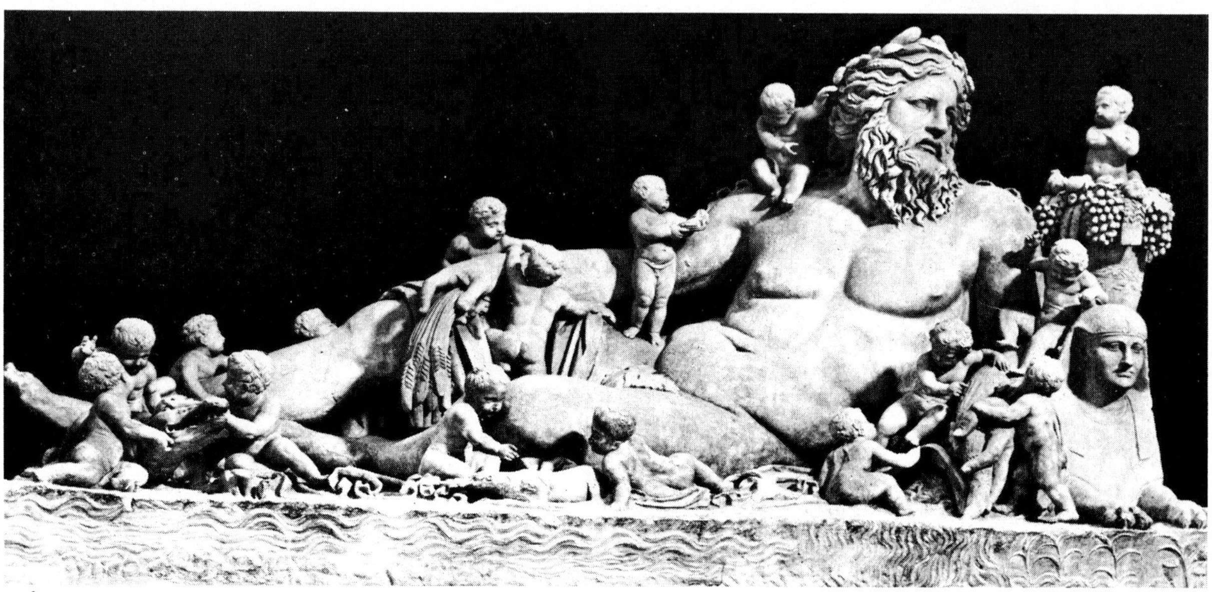

176c

176 Back view of statue, pl. 175c. (P. 553) **b** Marble statue. Louvre 231. Copy of the imperial age probably after original of mid second century. L. 1.47. The mattress is seventeenth century. (Pp. 551ff.) **c** Marble statue. Vatican. Copy of the imperial age probably after bronze original of second century. The upper parts of most of the children are modern. (Pp. 547–8).

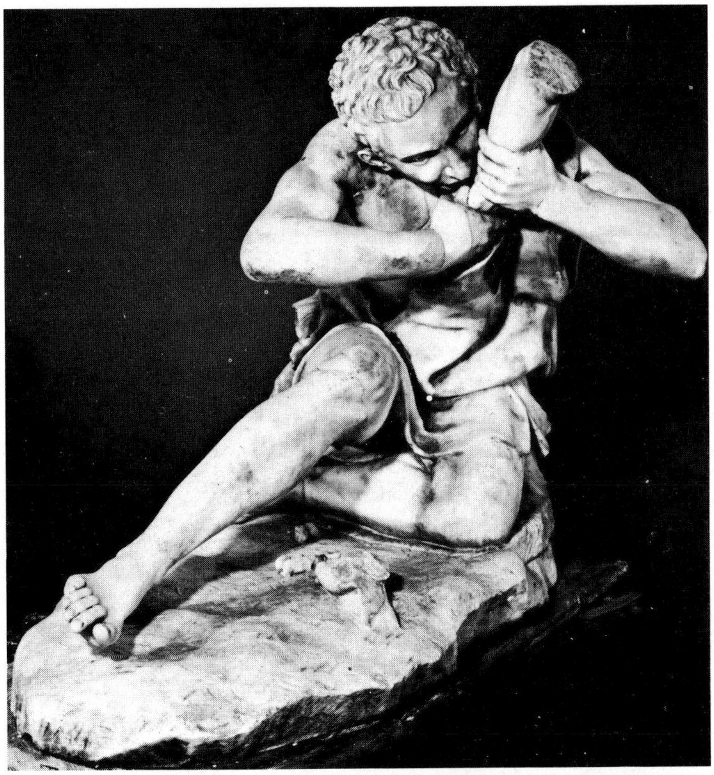

177a

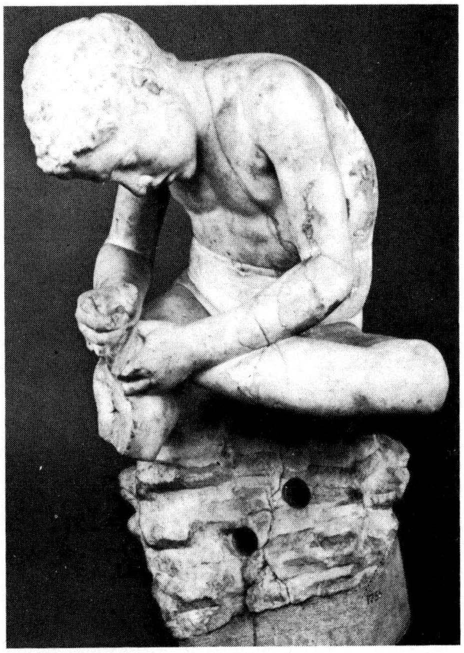

177b

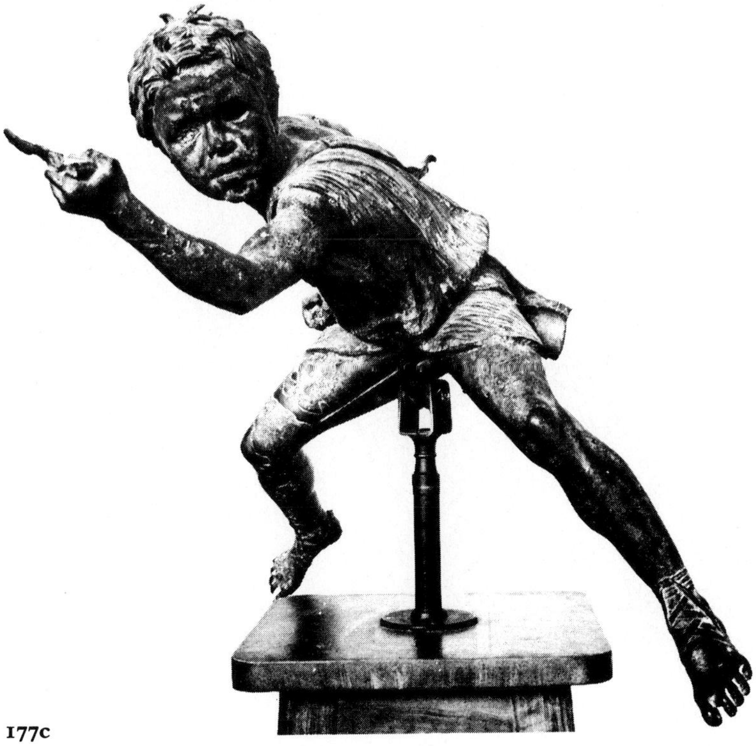

177c

177 **a** Marble statue (fragment of group) from Rome. British Museum 1756. Copy of the imperial age probably after bronze original of late second or early first century. H. 0.69. Parts of all three arms are modern. (P. 559) **b** Marble statue from Rome. British Museum 1755. Copy of the imperial period probably after bronze original of later second century. H. 0.73. (P. 559) **c** Bronze statue from sea off Cape Artemision. Athens, National Museum. Probably late second or early first century. H. 0.84. (Pp. 558–9).

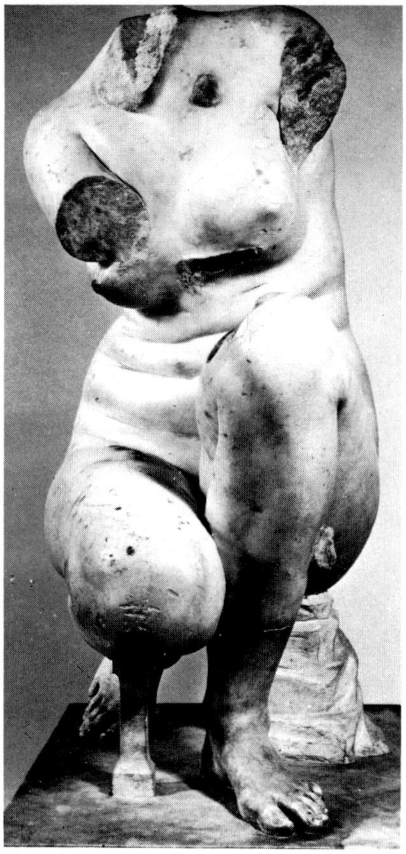

178a

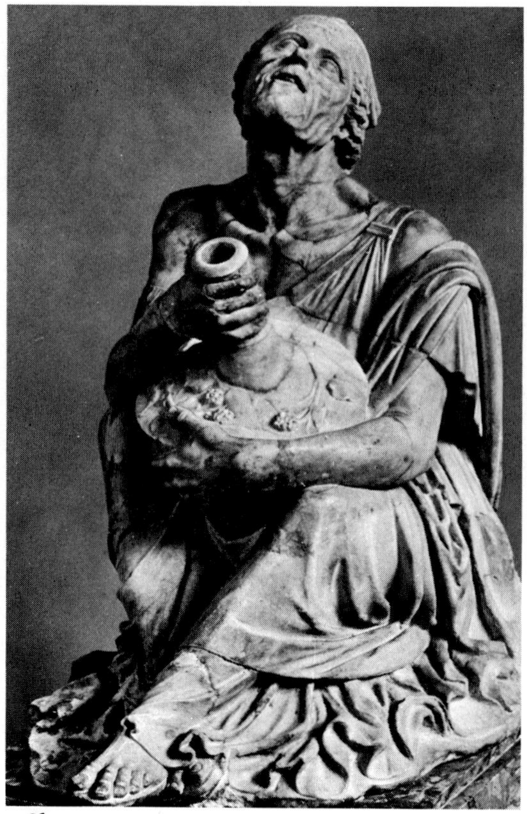

178b

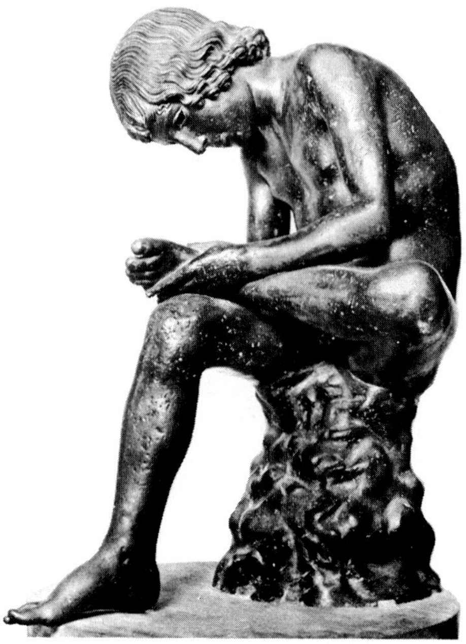

178c

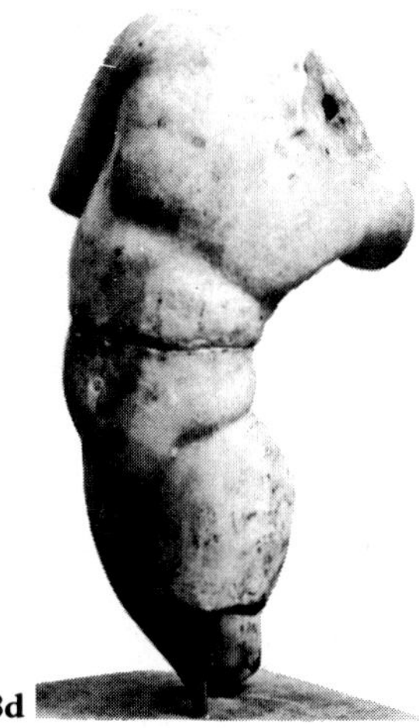

178d

178 **a** Marble statue. Louvre 2240. Copy of the imperial period after original of probably the later third century. H. 0.97. (Pp. 556–7) **b** Marble statue. Munich. Copy of the imperial period after an original in bronze, probably of the late third or early second century. H. 0.92. Modern are the nose, most of the right arm, an area round the left shoulder, the left foot, part of the vessel and other patches. (Pp. 561–2) **c** Bronze statue from Rome. Rome, Museo Capitolino. Probably a pastiche of the first century B.C., based on the type of the statue pl. 177b, with a head of early fifth-century character. H., without plinth, 0.70. (Pp. 559–60, 601) **d** Marble statuette-torso. New York, Metropolitan Museum of Art 19.192.82, Rogers Fund. Copy of the imperial period after a bronze original, probably of late third or early second century. H. 0.34. (Pp. 553, 607).

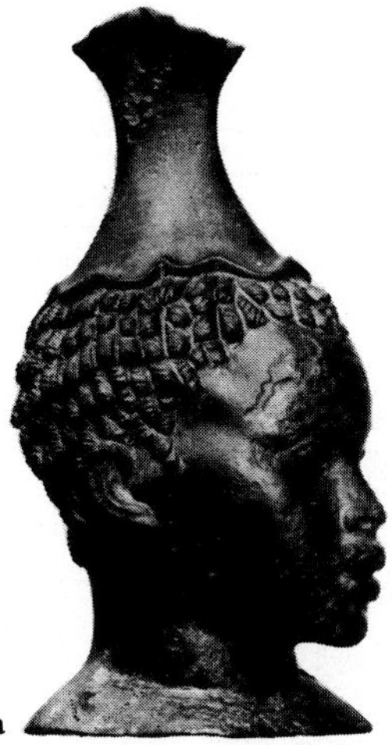

179a

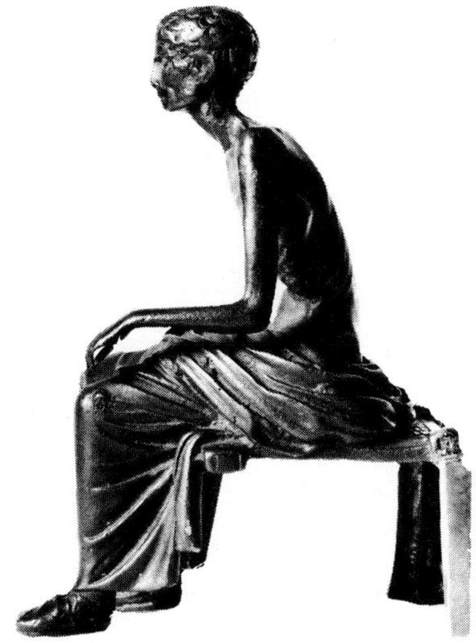

179b

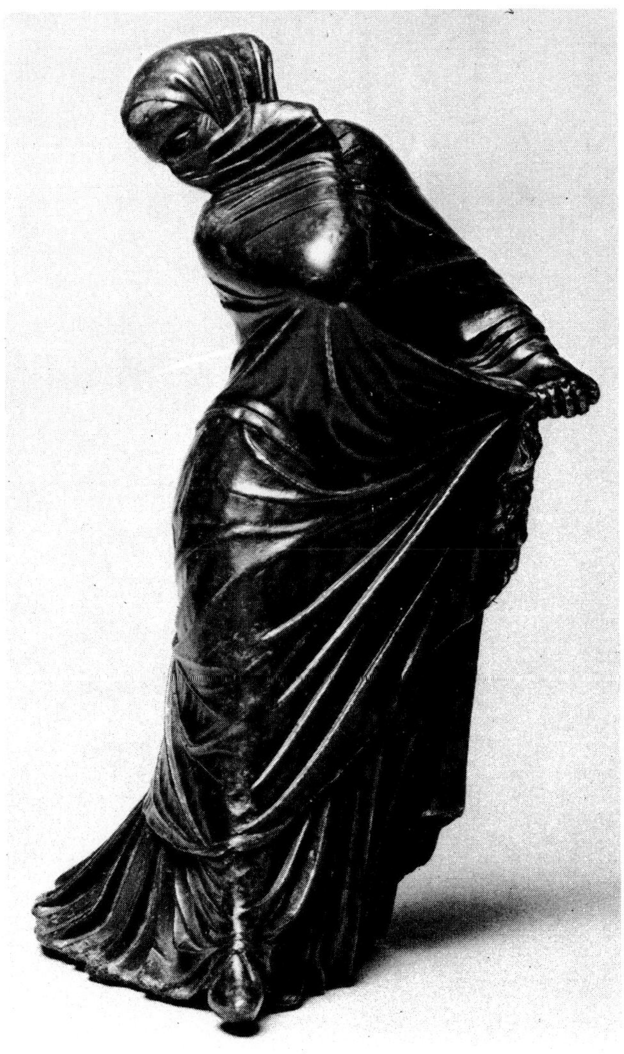

179c

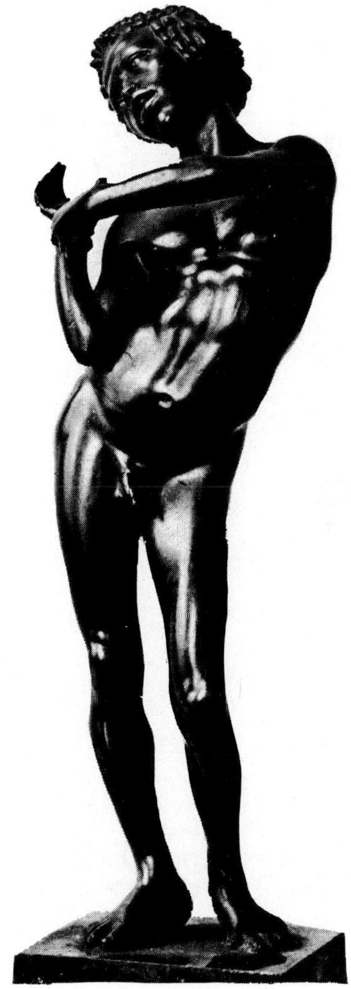

179d

179 **a** Bronze head-jug. British Museum 1955.10–18.1. Probably second century. H. 0.10. (P. 558) **b** Bronze statuette from Soissons. Dumbarton Oaks 47.22. Probably second century rather than an imperial copy. H. 0.11. (P. 558) **c** Bronze statuette. New York, Metropolitan Museum of Art 72.118.95, bequest of Walter C. Baker. Probably late third or early second century. H. 0.21. (P. 564) **d** Bronze statuette from Châlon-sur-Saône. Paris, Cabinet des Médailles 1009. Probably second century. H. 0.20. (Pp. 557–8).

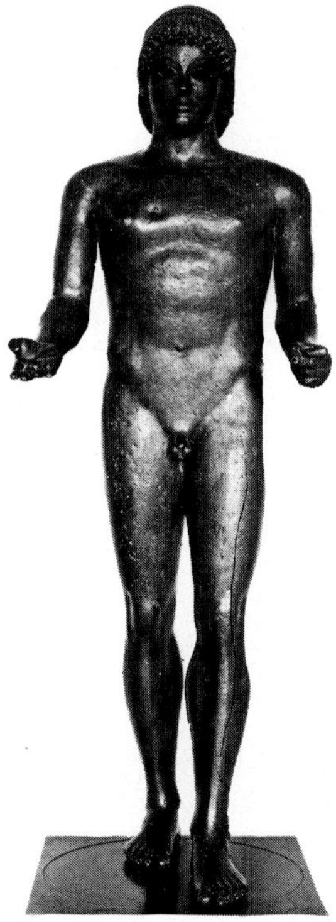

180a

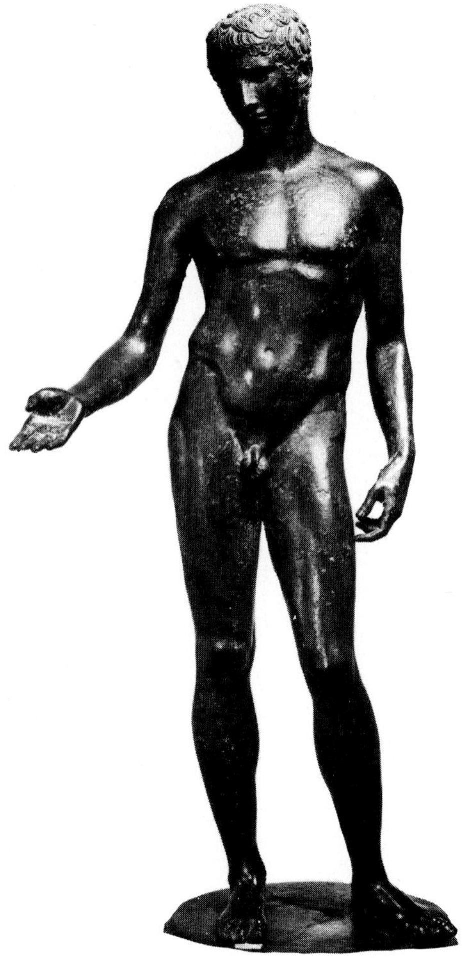

180b

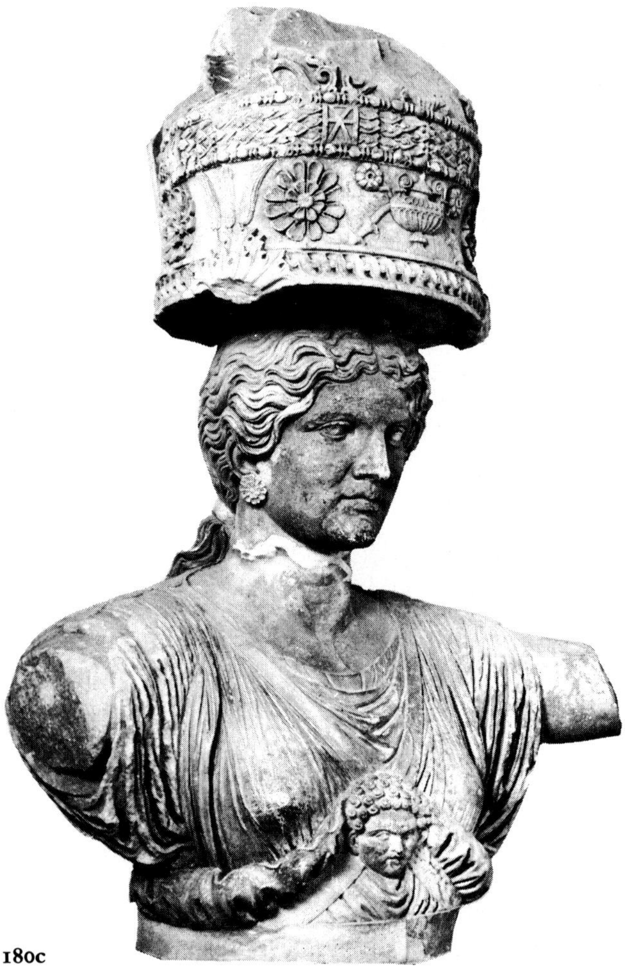

180c

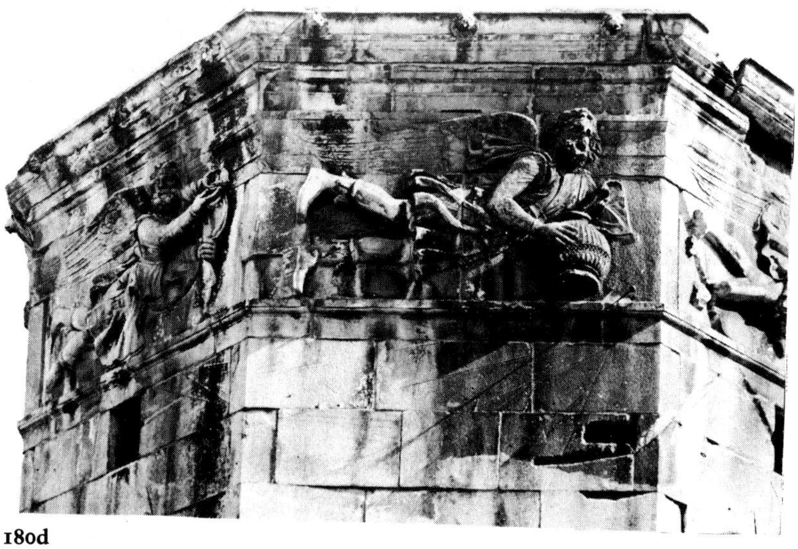

180d

180 **a** Bronze statue from the sea off Cape Piombino (Tuscany, opposite Elba). Louvre 2. Probably first-century work intended to pass for late archaic. H. 1.15. (Pp. 183, 560, 601) **b** Bronze statue from Pesaro. Florence, Archaeological Museum. Probably first century B.C. or A.D., based on fifth-century types. H., without plinth, 1.50. (Pp. 332, 601) **c** Marble Caryatid from Eleusis, Eleusis Museum. Mid first century. H. *c.* 2.00. (P. 565) **d** Marble relief on Tower of the Winds, Athens. Mid first century. H. of frieze 1.77. (P. 565).

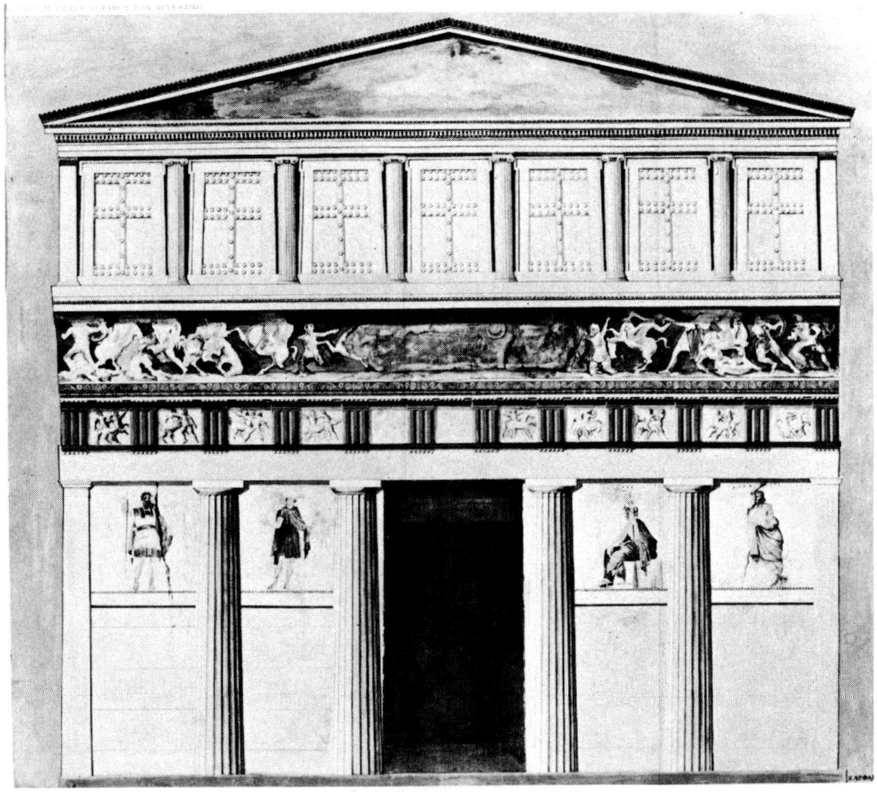

181a

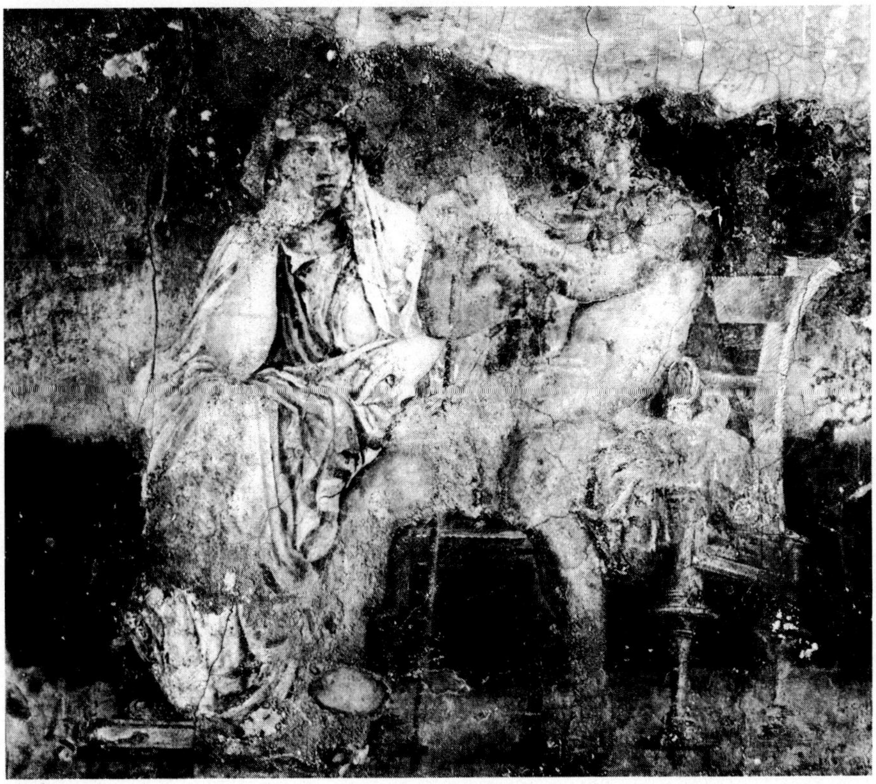

181b

181 **a** Reconstruction of painted tomb-façade. Leucadia (Macedonia). Early third century. H. *c.* 8.20. See also p. 182a and b. (Pp. 568ff.) **b** Wall-painting from Boscoreale (near Pompeii). New York, Metropolitan Museum of Art 03.14.6, Rogers Fund. Mid first century, copied from paintings of third century. H. 1.76. See also pl. 182c. (Pp. 572ff., 577–8).

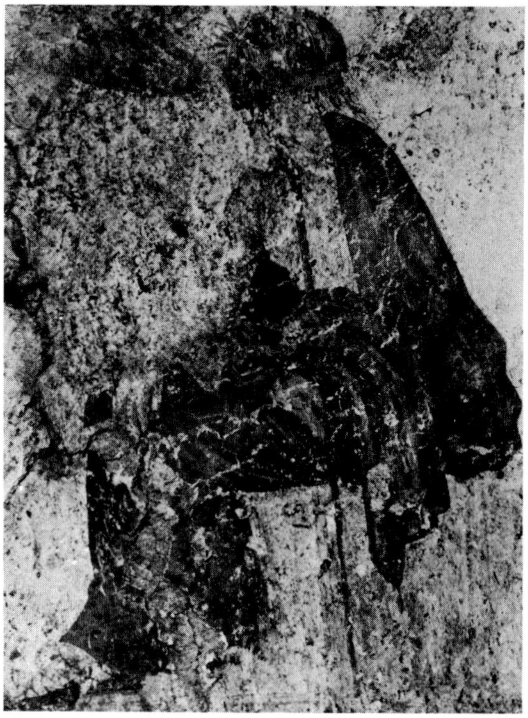

182a

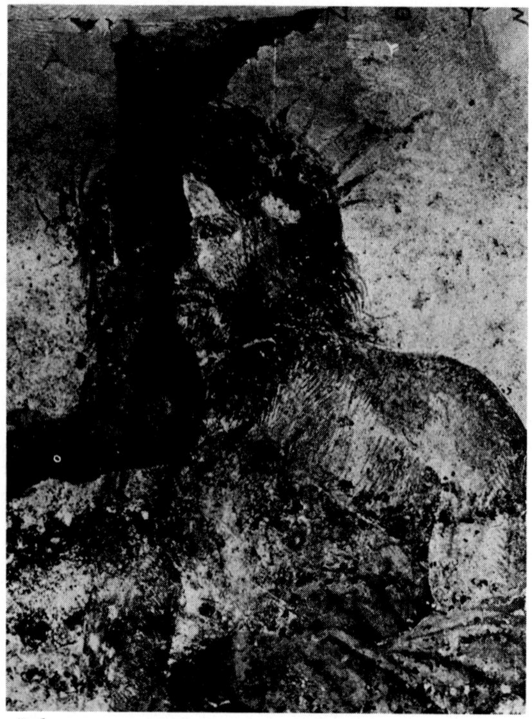

182b

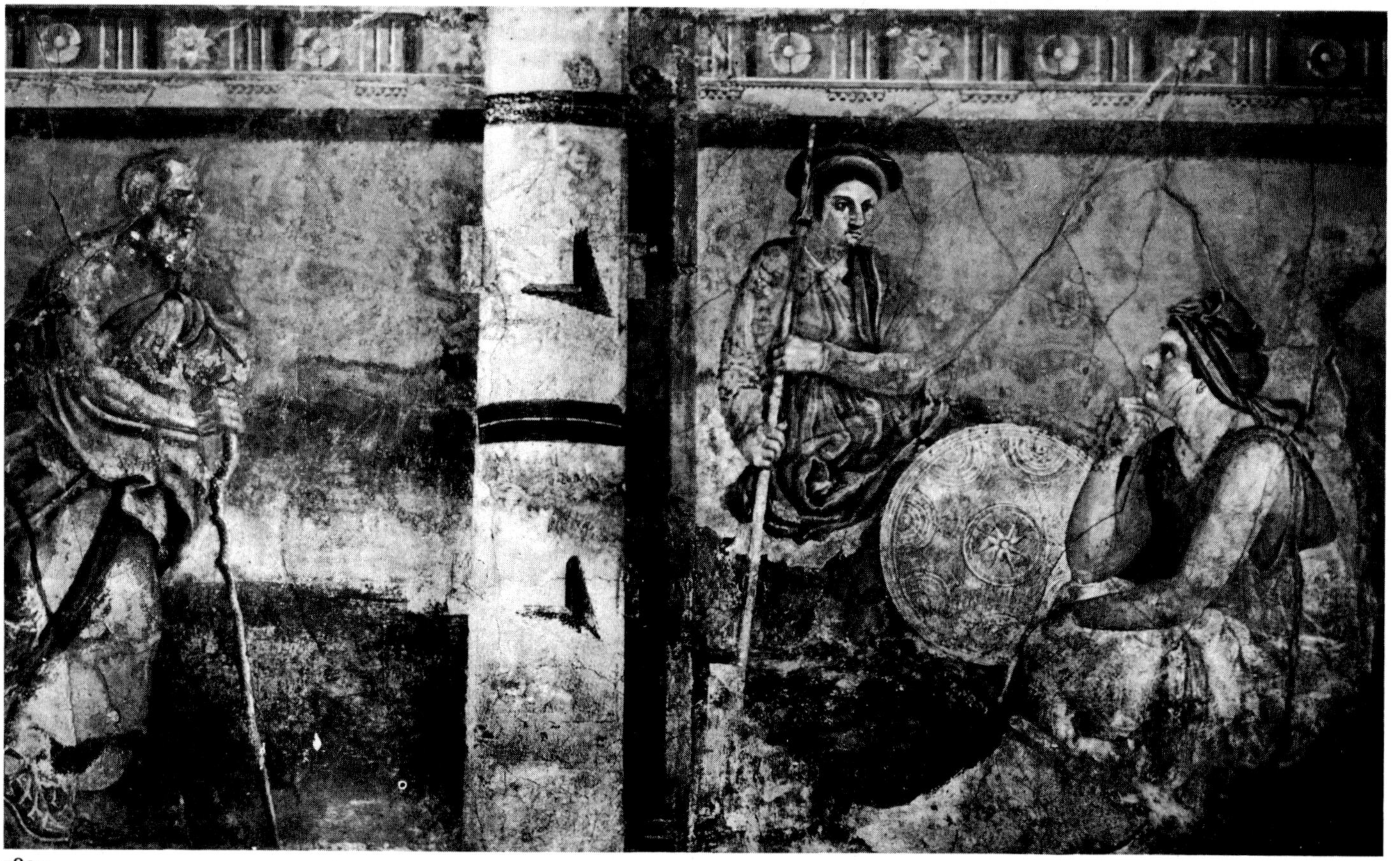

182c

182 **a** and **b** Paintings from tomb-façade. pl. 181a. H. *c.* 1.15 (**a**) and 0.42 (**b**). (Pp. 570–1, 573) **c** Wall-painting from same set as pl. 181b. Naples Museum. H. 2.37. (Pp. 257, 571ff., 577–8, 594, 599).

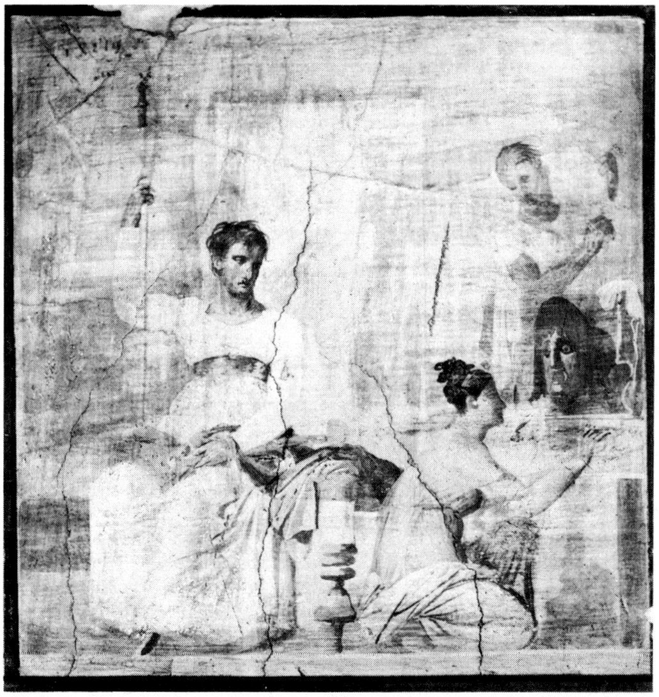

183a

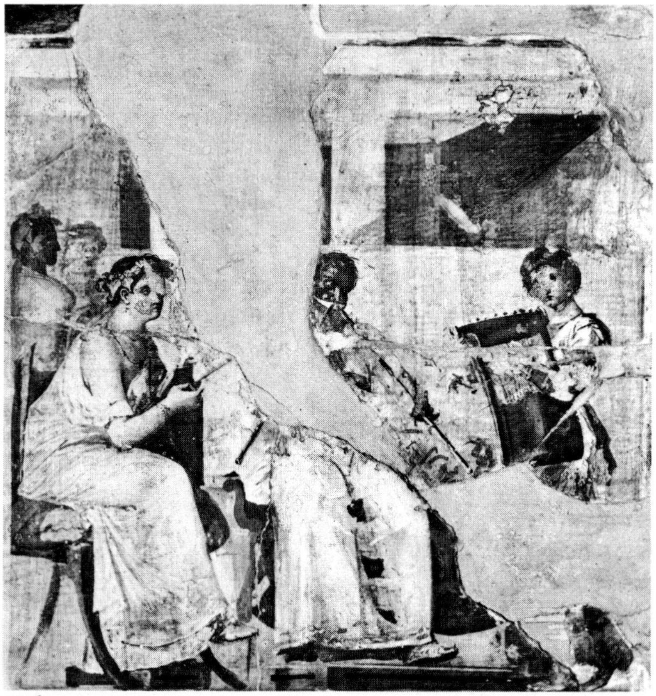

183b

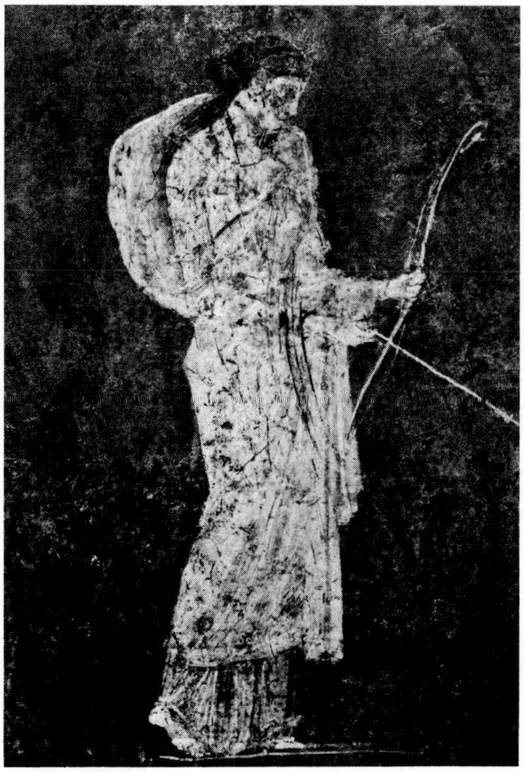

183c

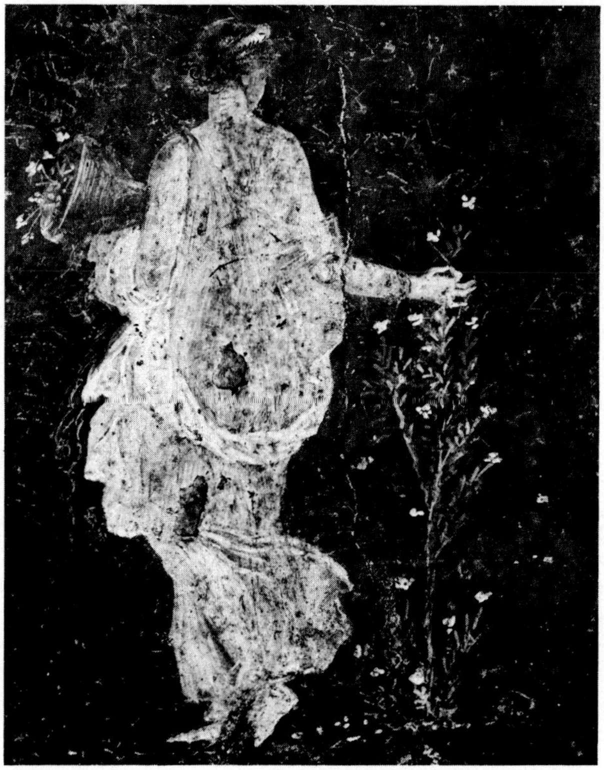

183d

183 **a** and **b** Small paintings once inset into walls of room at Herculaneum. Naples Museum 9019, 9021. Late first century B.C. or early first century A.D., probably copied from originals of late fourth or early third century (**a**) and late third or early second (**b**). H. of each 0.39. (Pp. 575, 582) **c** and **d** Two small decorations from walls of room at Stabiae. Naples Museum 9243 and 8824. Late first century B.C. or early first century A.D., the figures probably derived from originals of fourth century (**a**) and third (**b**). H. of each 0.39. (P. 575).

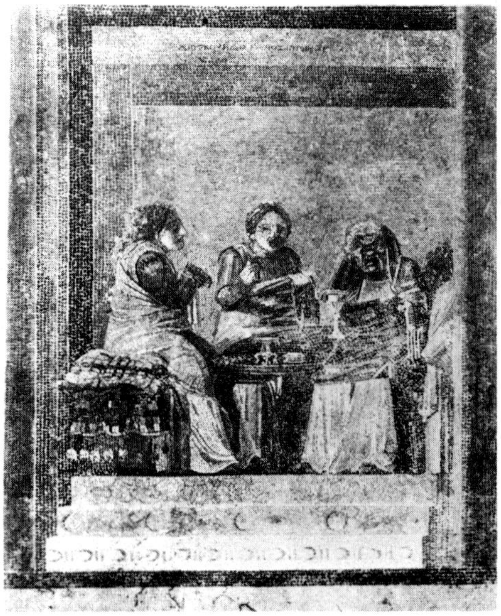

184a

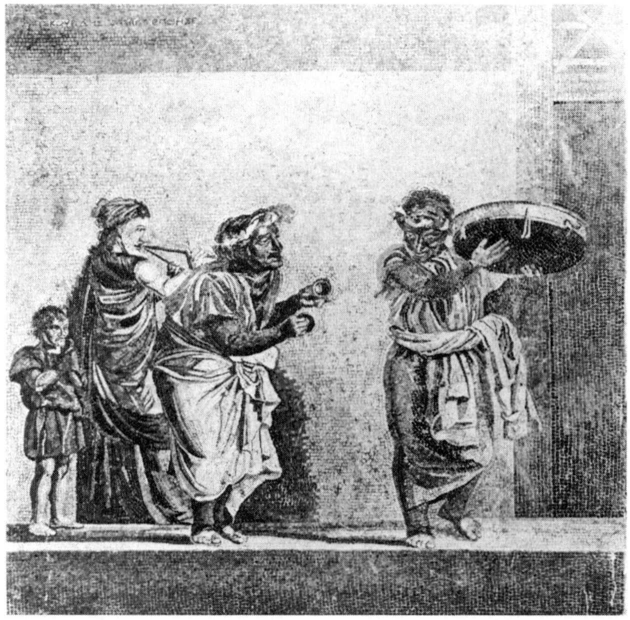

184b

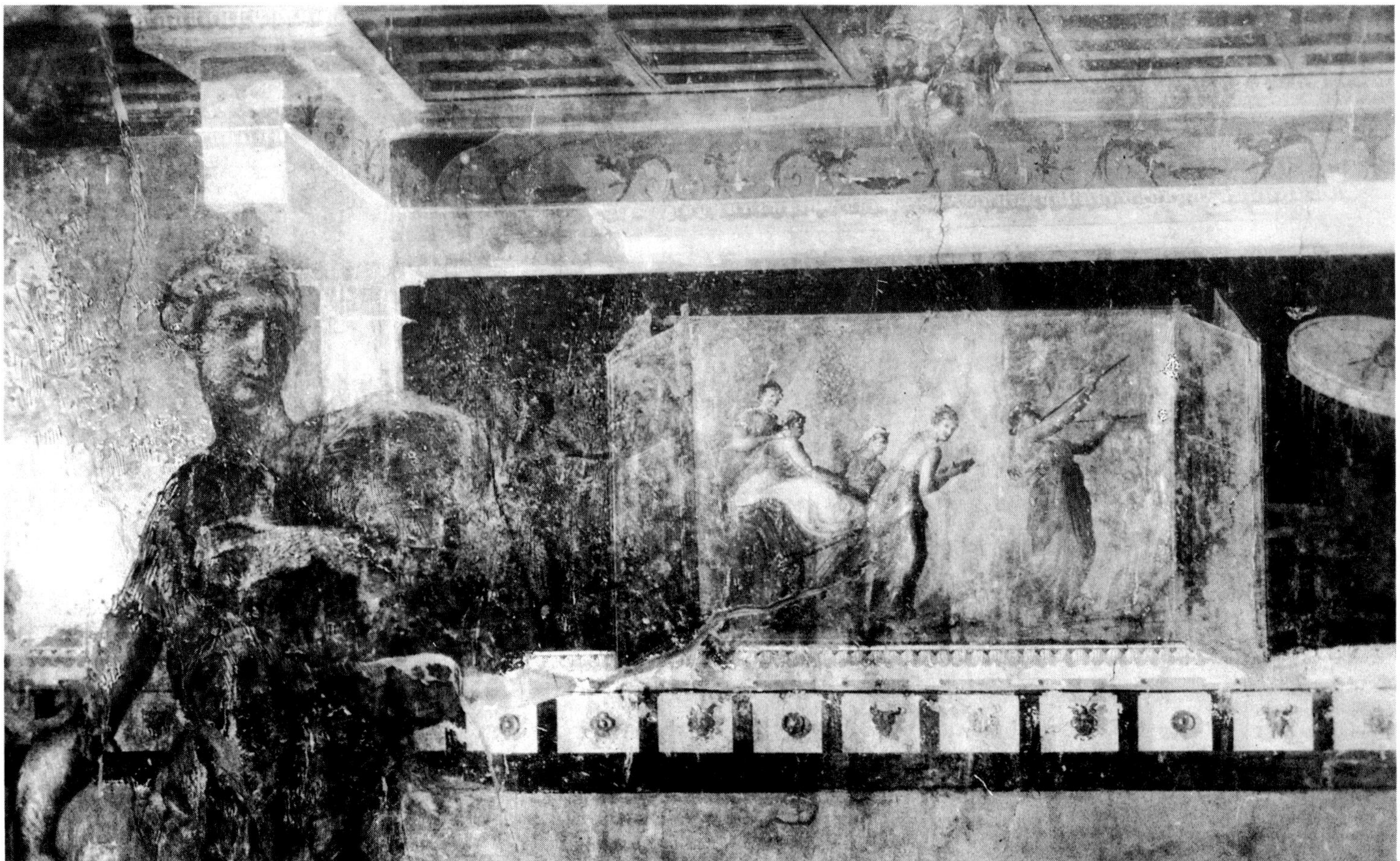

184c

184 **a** and **b** Miniature mosaics from Pompeii, signed by Dioskourides of Samos. Naples Museum 9987 and 9985. Perhaps second century, copied from paintings of end of fourth or early third. H. 0.45 (**a**) and 0.48 (**b**). (P. 581)
c Detail of wall-painting from House of Cryptoporticus, Pompeii. Second half of first century, the little picture perhaps copied from original of third century. L. of little picture *c.* 0.40. (Pp. 575, 599).

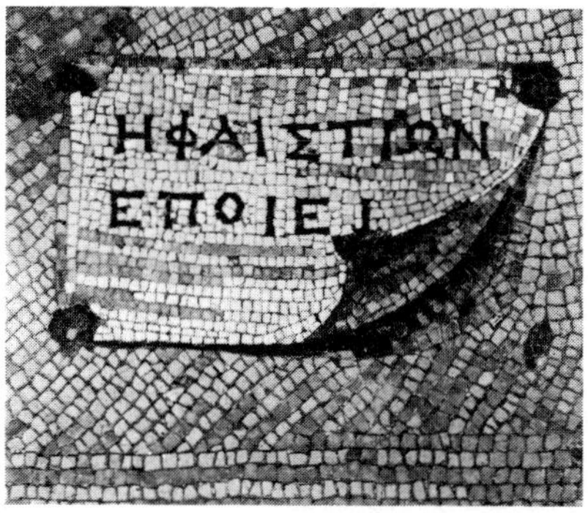

185a

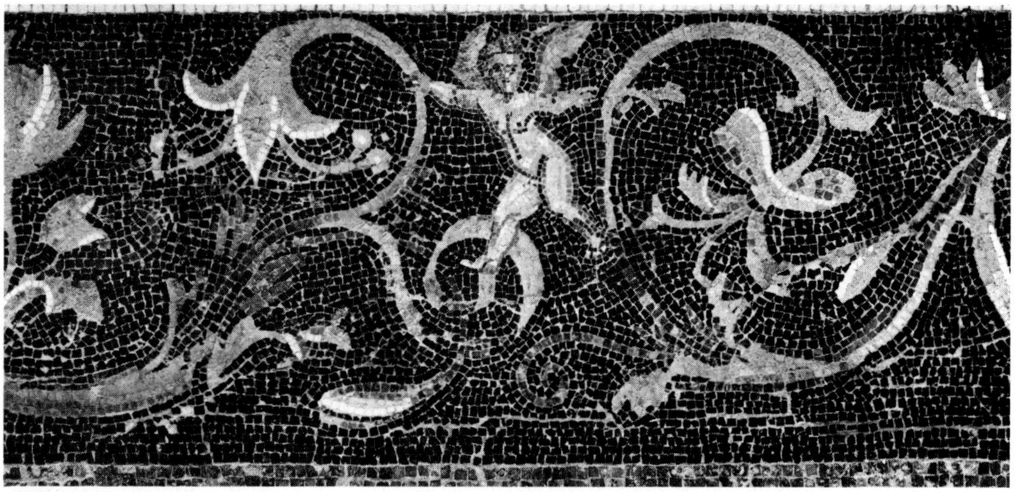

185b

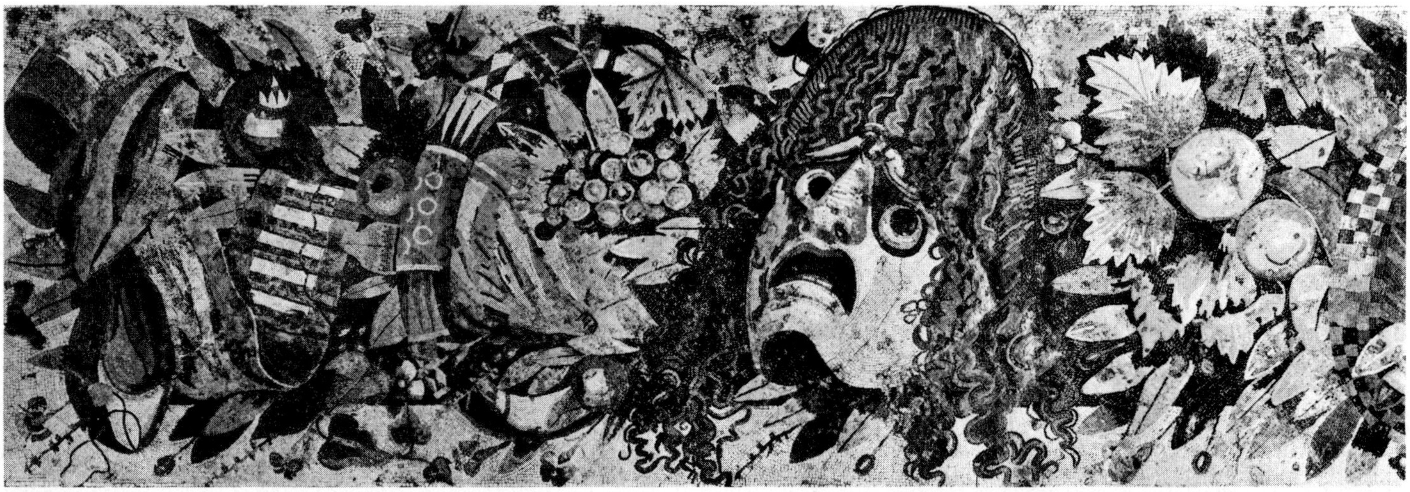

185c

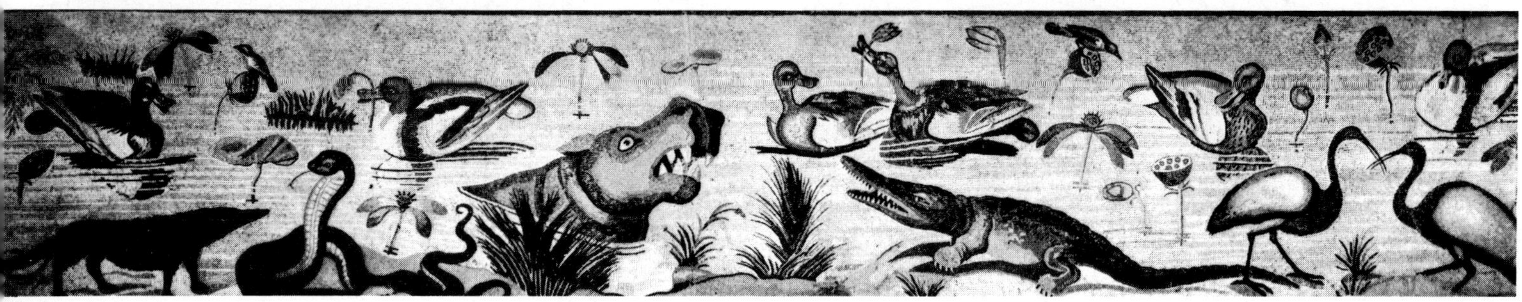

185d

185 **a** Fragment of mosaic from Pergamon, signed by Hephaistion. Berlin (E). Second century. (P. 581) **b** Detail of mosaic from Pergamon (border of floor in which **a** was part of central emblema). Berlin (E). Second century. H. of scroll-frieze *c.* 0.45. (P. 581) **c** Mosaic border from House of Faun, Pompeii. Naples Museum. Second century. H. 0.49. (P. 579) **d** Mosaic from House of Faun, Pompeii (same room as pl. 155). Naples Museum. Second century. (Pp. 502, 589).

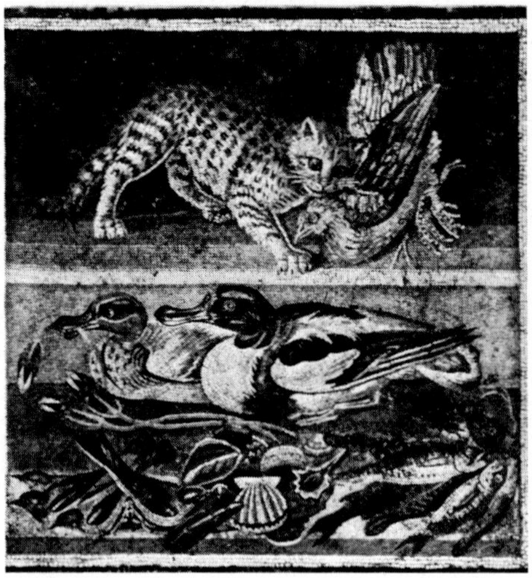

186a

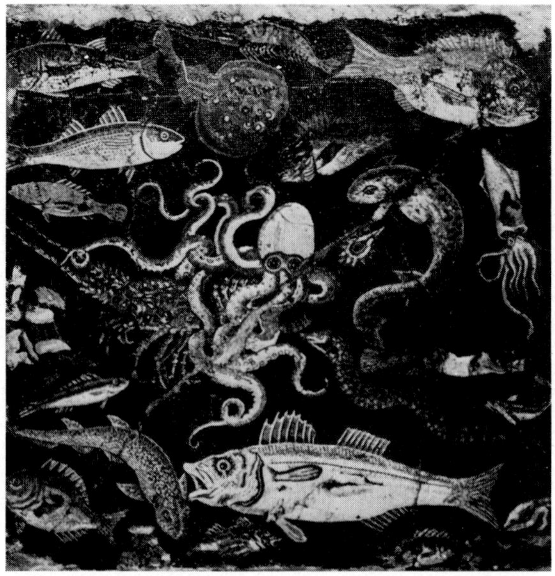

186b

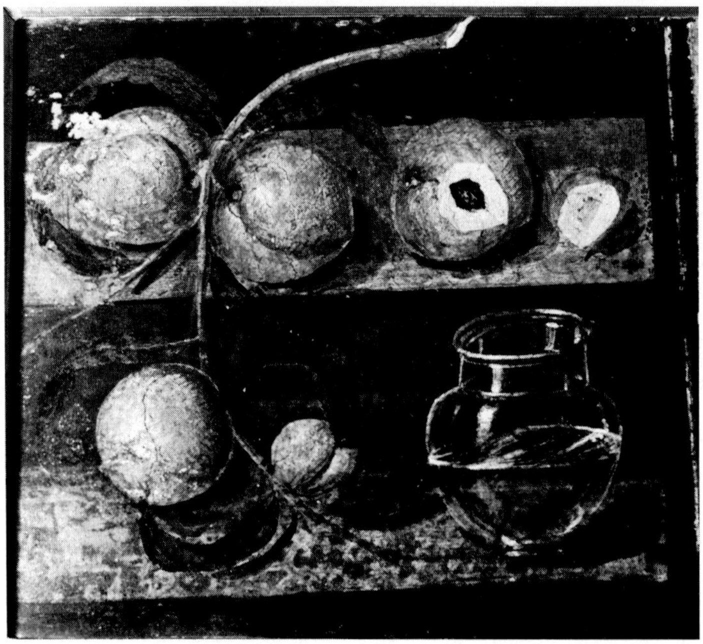

186c

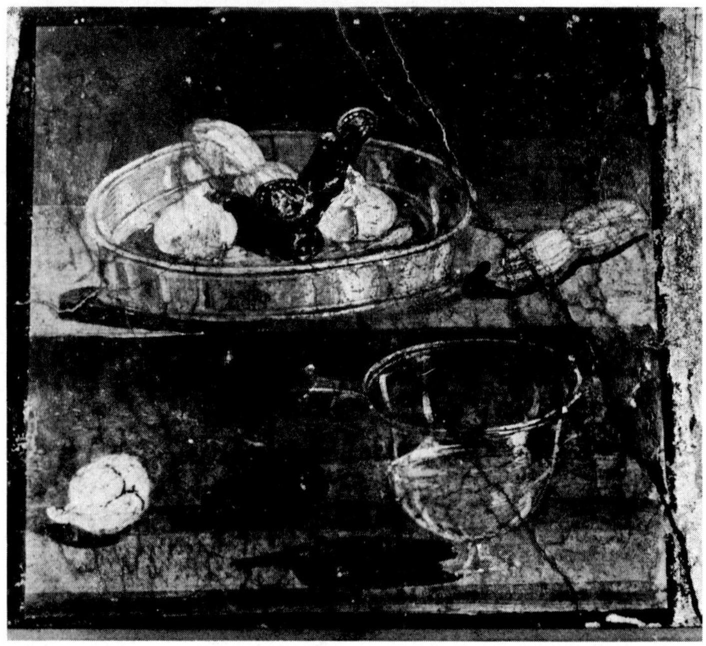

186d

186 **a** Mosaic from House of Faun, Pompeii. Naples Museum 9993. Second century, probably copied from painting of third or second. H. 0.53. (P. 580) **b** Mosaic from House of Faun, Pompeii. Naples Museum 9997. Second century, probably copied from painting of third or second. H. 0.62. (Pp. 437, 580) **c** and **d** Parts of wall-painting from Pompeii. Naples Museum 8645. First century A.D., perhaps derived from a tradition of third and second centuries. H. 0.70. (Pp. 486, 580).

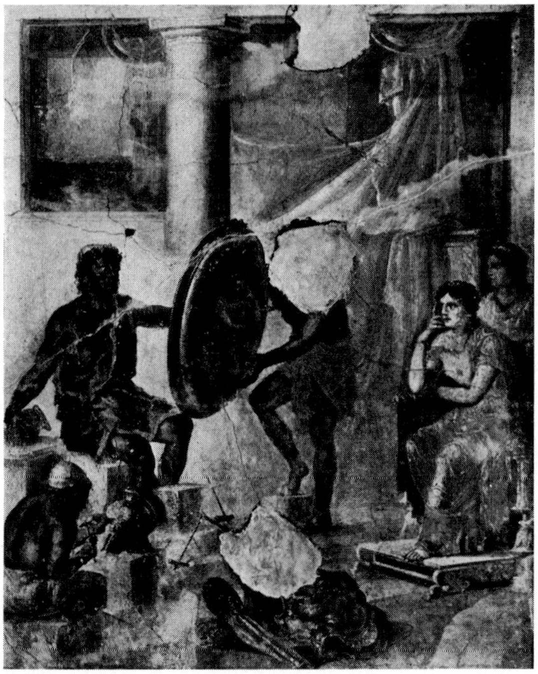

187a

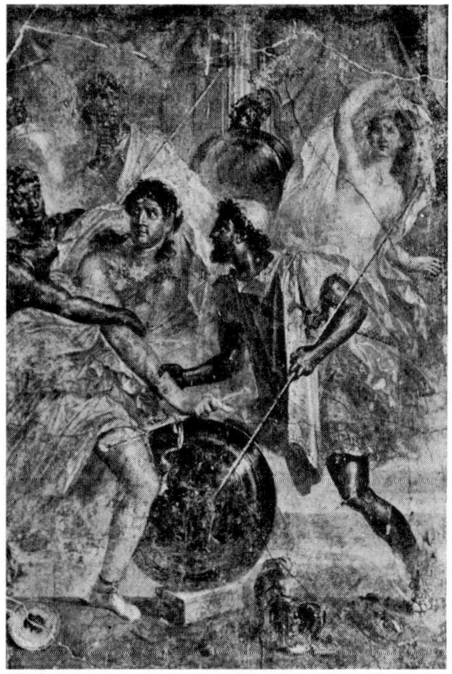

187b

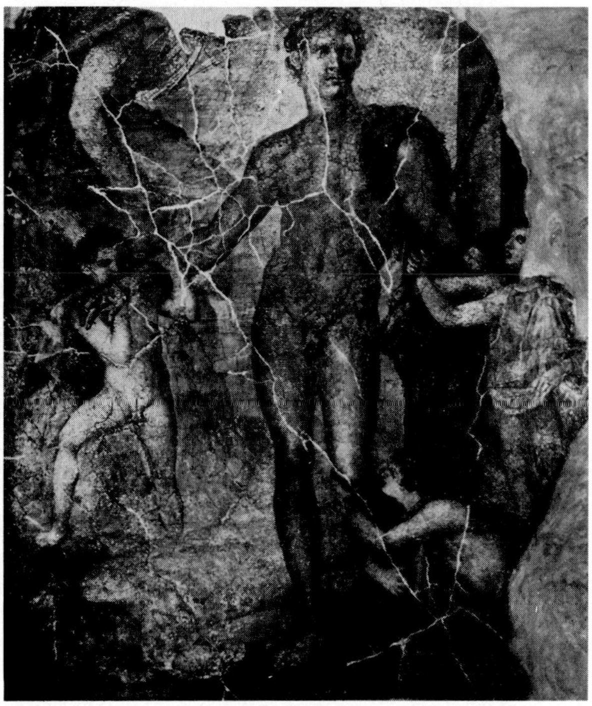

187c

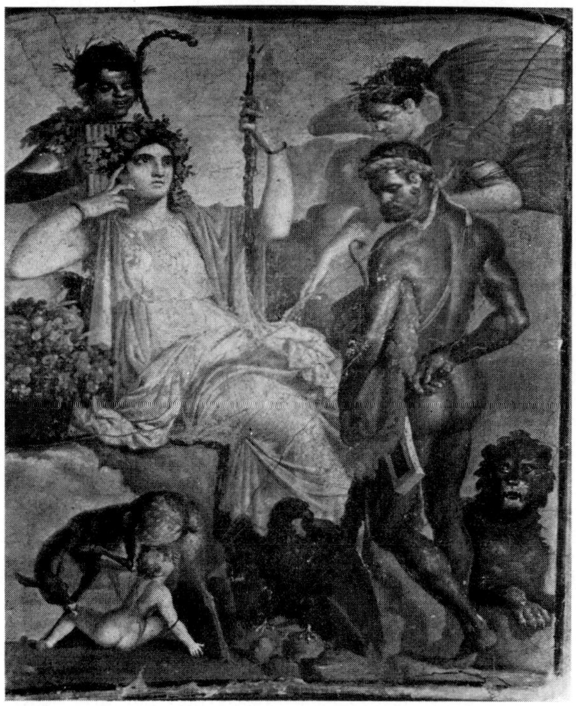

187d

187 **a** Wall-painting from Pompeii. Naples Museum 9528. Before A.D. 79, copied from painting probably of third century. H. 1.30. (Pp. 584ff.) **b** Wall-painting from Pompeii. Naples Museum 9110. Before A.D. 79, copied from painting perhaps of end of fourth or beginning of third century. H. 1.11. (Pp. 583–4) **c** Wall-painting from Basilica, Herculaneum. Naples Museum 9049. Before A.D. 79, copied from painting of second half of fourth century. H. 1.90. (Pp. 443, 577) **d** Wall-painting from Basilica, Herculaneum. Naples Museum 9008. Before A.D. 79, copied from painting of late third or early second century. H. 2.02. (Pp. 443, 544, 577–8).

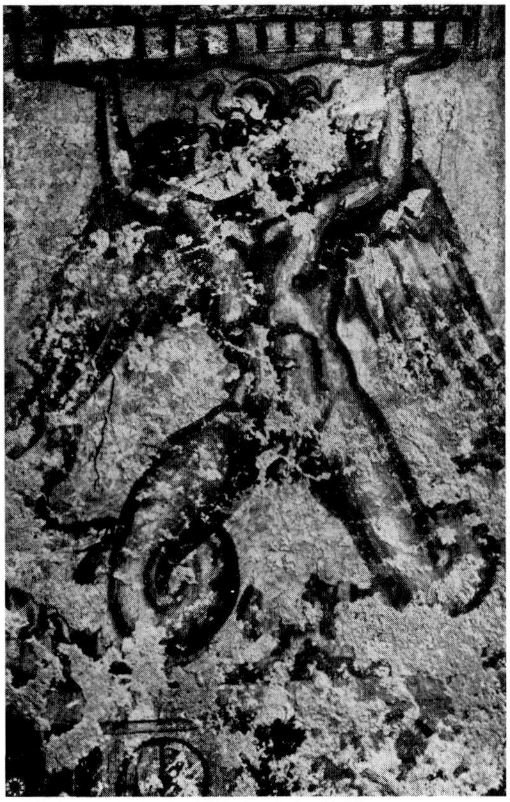

188a

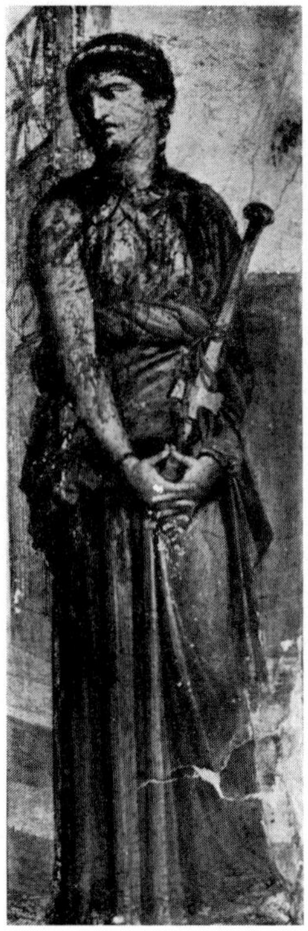

188b

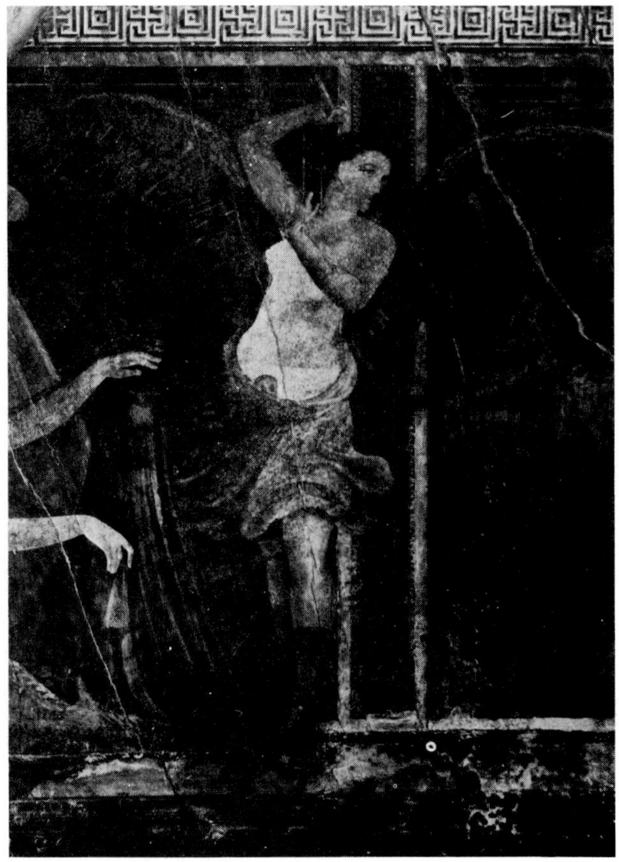

188c

188 **a** Etruscan wall-painting in Tomb of Typhon, Tarquinia. Second century. H. *c.* 1.50. (P. 597) **b** Fragment of wall-painting from Herculaneum. Naples Museum 8976. Before A.D. 79, copied from painting perhaps of first century. H. 1.37. (P. 590) **c** Detail of wall-painting in figured hall in Villa of Mysteries, Pompeii. Mid first century. H. of area with figure-paintings 1.62. (P. 599).

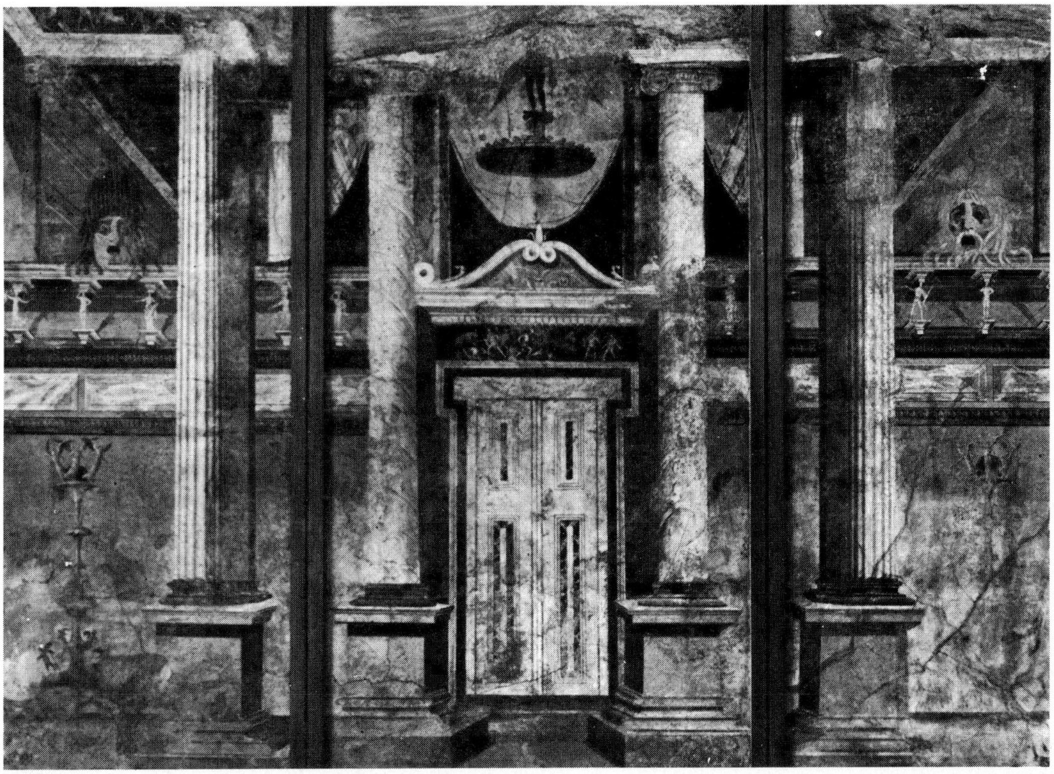

189a

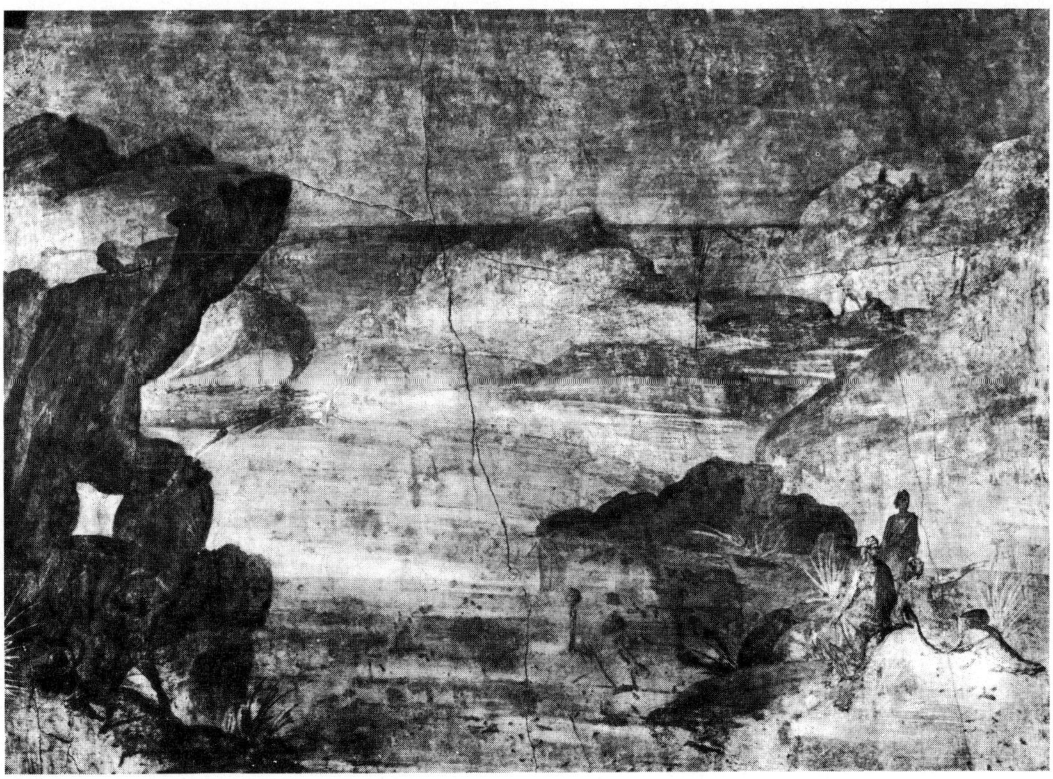

189b

189 **a** Wall-painting from Boscoreale (near Pompeii; see also pl. 181b and 182c). Naples Museum. Mid first century, copied from stage-set of probably later second or earlier first century. H. *c.* 3.40. (P. 587) **b** Wall-painting from Rome. Vatican. Mid first century, probably copied from original of second century. H. 1.16. (Pp. 588–9).

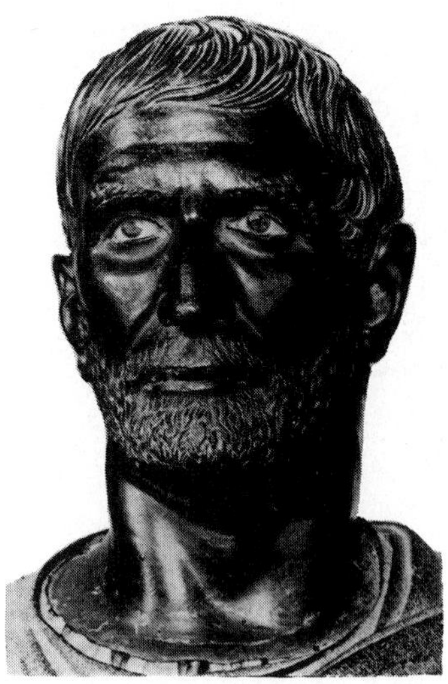

190a

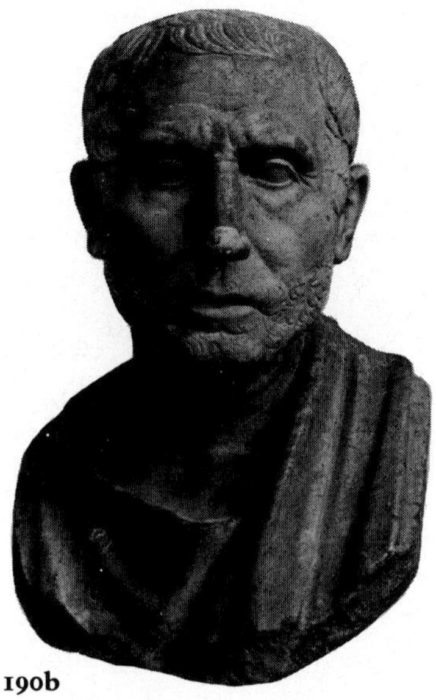

190b

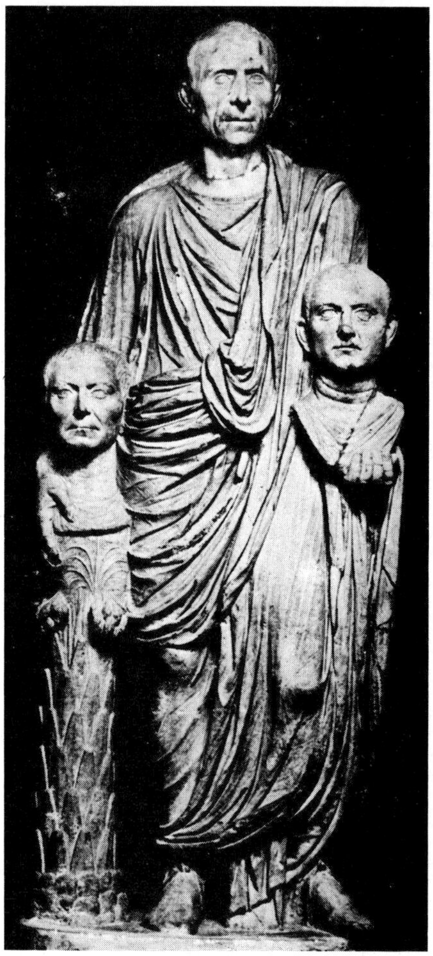

190c

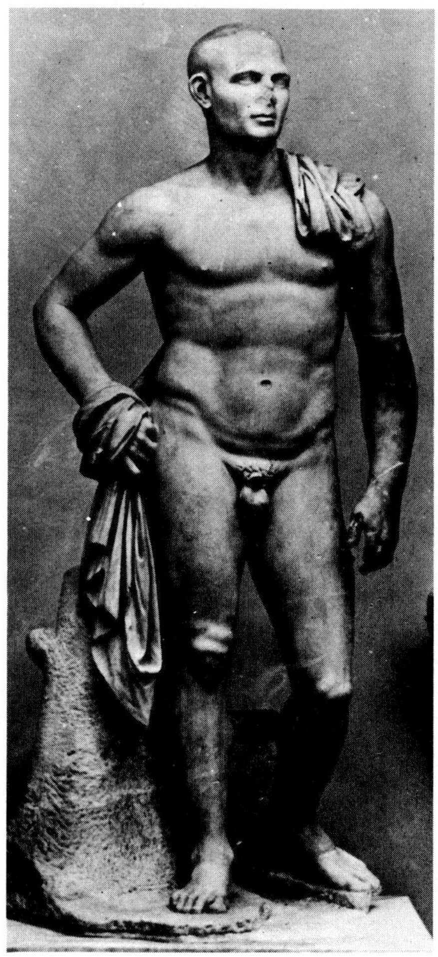

190d

190 **a** Bronze head. Rome, Museo Capitolino. Probably early first century. H. 0.32. (P. 597) **b** Marble bust. Naples Museum 6142. Copy of the imperial period after original of earlier first century. H. 0.44. (Pp. 527, 597) **c** Marble statue. Rome, Palazzo dei Conservatori (ex Palazzo Barberini). First half of first century. H. 1.65. The head is ancient but does not belong; modern are the left hand and foot and the noses of both busts. (P. 597) **d** Marble statue from Delos. Athens, National Museum 1828. Later second or earlier first century. H. 2.55. (P. 598).

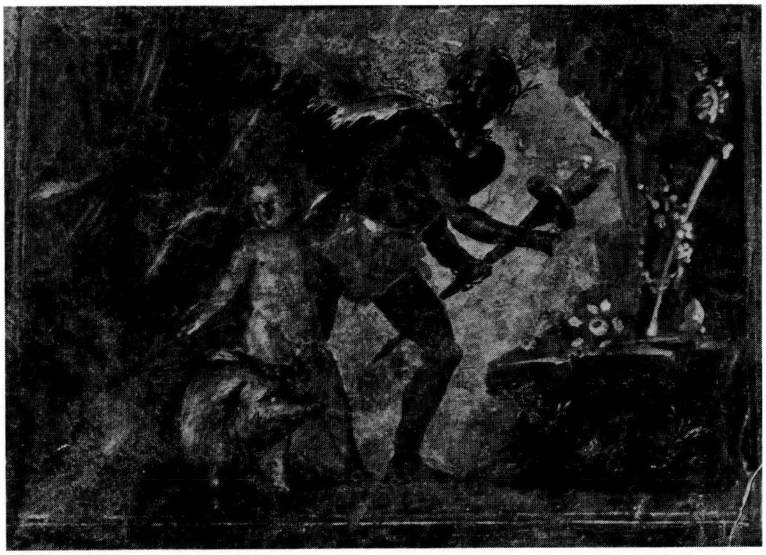

191a

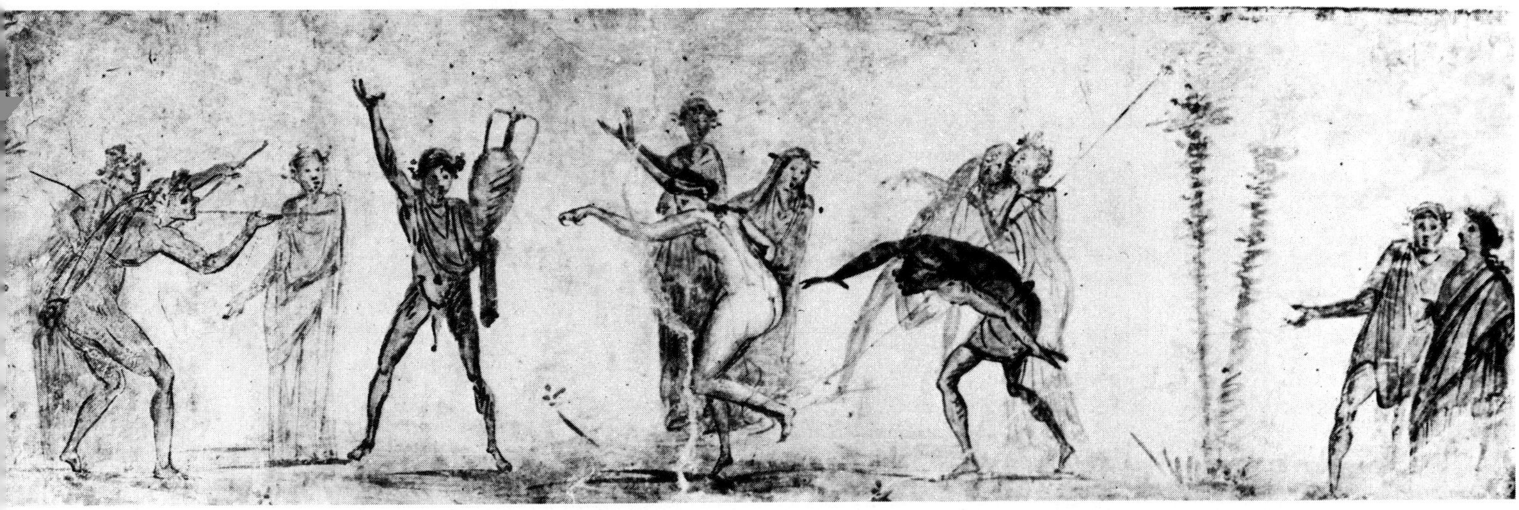

191b

191 **a** Small wall-painting in Villa of Mysteries, Pompeii. Mid first century, perhaps copied from earlier picture. H. 0.23. (P. 599) **b** Tomb-painting from Rome. British Museum 24. Mid first century. H. 0.21. (P. 599).

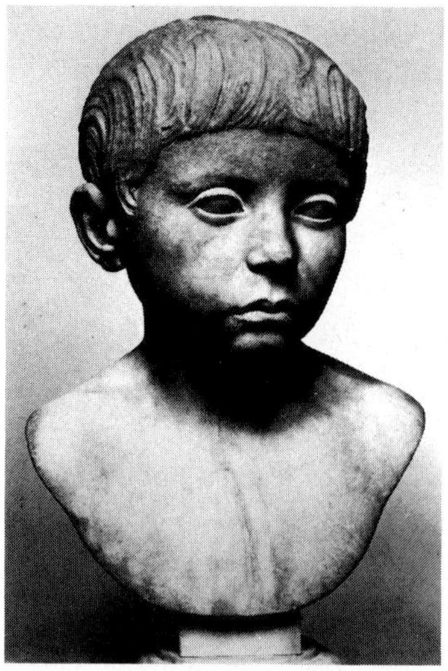

192a

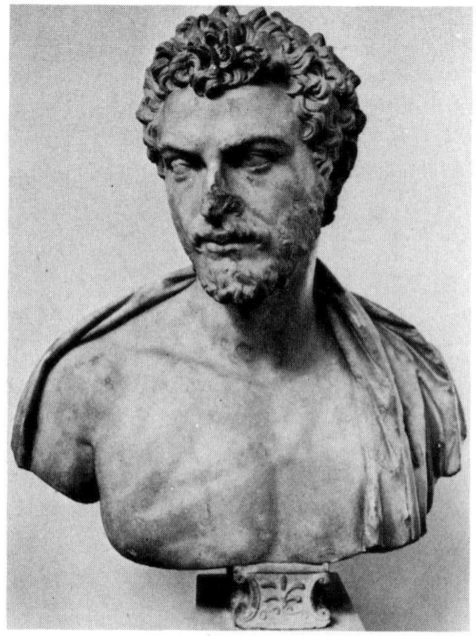

192b

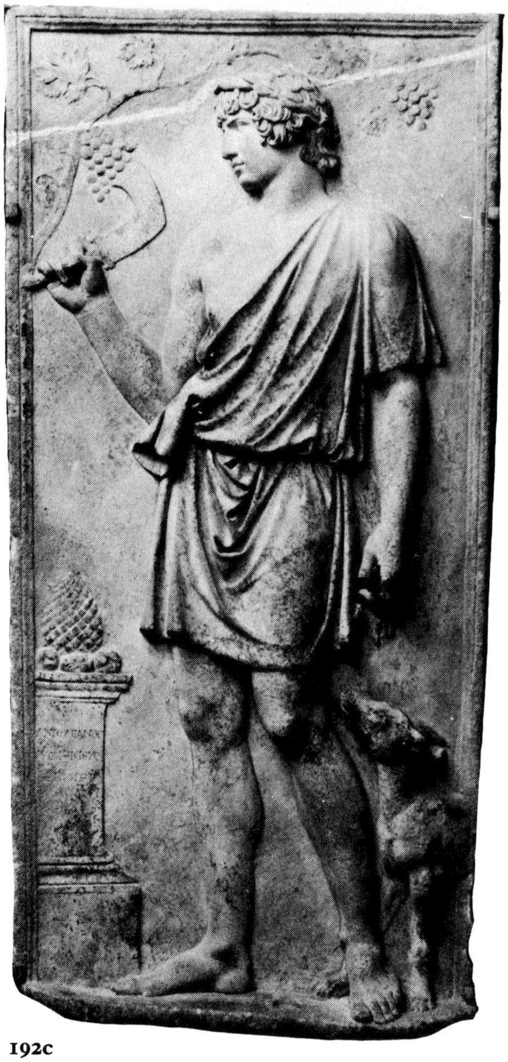

192c

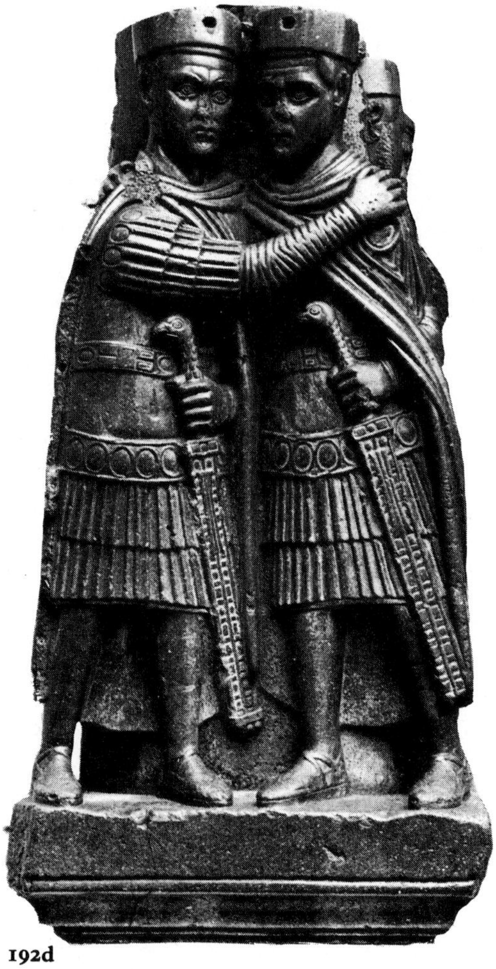

192d

192 **a** Marble bust. Berlin (E) 1467 (R 48). Late first century A.D. H. 0.33. (P. 606) **b** Marble bust. British Museum 1949. Second half of second century A.D. H. 0.66. (P. 610) **c** Marble relief from Torre del Padiglione (between Lanuvium and Anzio). Rome Banca Nazionale (ex Istituto dei Fondi Rustici). Mid second century A.D. H. 1.43. (P. 608) **d** Porphyry group. Venice, St Mark's. End of third or beginning of fourth century A.D. H. *c.* 1.30. (P. 611).

INDEXES

I. GENERAL

I have attempted no consistency in the spelling of Greek names (the Latin form, or a more direct transliteration) following in each case the usage which comes more naturally to me; but other forms are given in the Index in brackets, and where alphabetically distant, there also with a cross-reference.

References to notes are given only when something is mentioned there which does not appear in the text. Modern scholars are indexed, with a few exceptions, only if their names appear in the introduction or text. The same is true of ancient writers, citations of whom in the notes are mainly from Overbeck's old but still invaluable collection (see Bibliography).

2. MUSEUMS AND COLLECTIONS

References are to the text; to the notes only if the object is not mentioned in the text, or if something further is said about it in a note. Plate-references are given for objects illustrated.